Street by Street

SUSSEX

Enlarged areas BOGNOR REGIS, BRIGHTON, CHICHESTER, CRAWLEY, EASTBOURNE, HASTINGS, HORSHAM, LEWES, NEWHAVEN, WORTHING

Plus Haslemere, Havant, Horley, Petersfield, Royal Tunbridge Wells

3rd edition March 2007
© Automobile Association Developments Limited 2007

Original edition printed May 2001

 This product includes map data licensed from Ordnance Survey® with the permission of the Controller of Her Majesty's Stationery Office. © Crown copyright 2007. All rights reserved. Licence number 100021153.

The copyright in all PAF is owned by Royal Mail Group plc.

Published by AA Publishing (a trading name of Automobile Association Developments Limited, whose registered office is Fanum House, Basing View, Basingstoke, Hampshire RG21 4EA. Registered number 1878835).

Produced by the Mapping Services Department of The Automobile Association. (A03123)

A CIP Catalogue record for this book is available from the British Library.

Printed by Leo, China

Key to map pages	ii-iii
Key to map symbols	iv-1
Map pages - 1:10,000	2-21
Map pages - 1:17,500	22-177
Map pages - 1:25,000	178-303
Index – towns & villages	304-305
Index – streets	306-341
Index – featured places	342-348
Acknowledgements	348

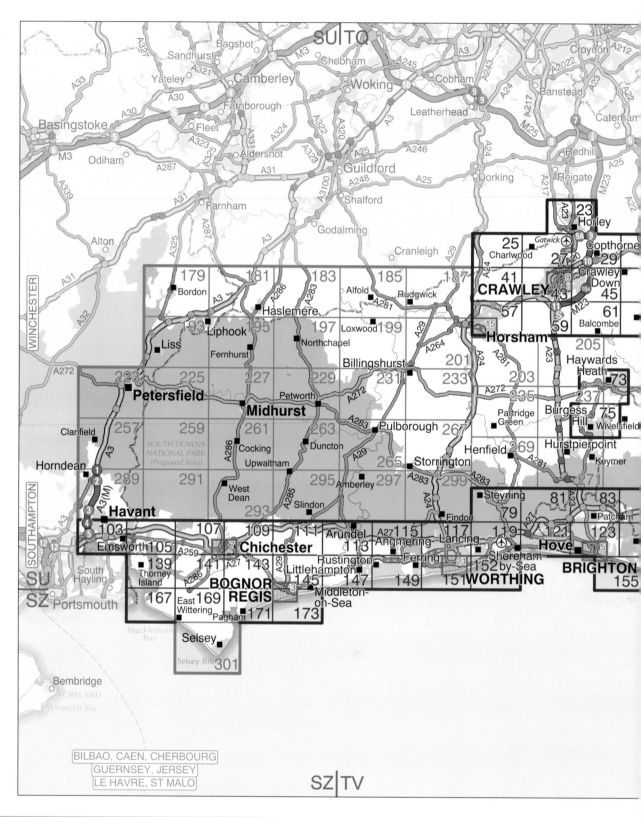

Scale of enlarged map pages 1:10,000 6.3 inches to 1 mile

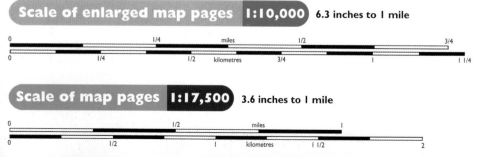

Scale of map pages 1:17,500 3.6 inches to 1 mile

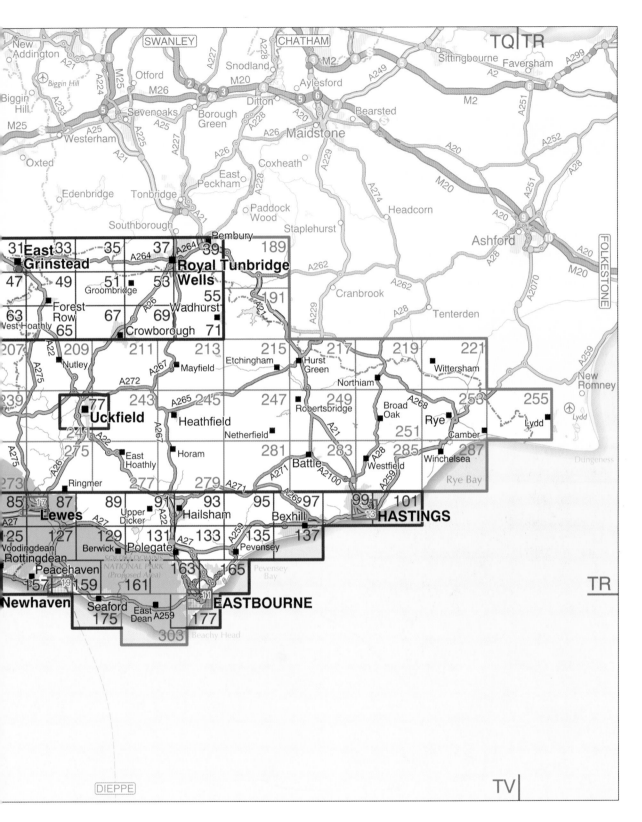

National Grid references are shown on the map frame of each page.
Red figures denote the 100 km square and the blue figures the 1km square.

Example, page 4 : Brighton Station 531 105

The reference can also be written using the National Grid two-letter prefix
shown on this page, where 5 and 1 are replaced by TQ to give TQ3105

2.5 inches to 1 mile   Scale of map pages   1:25,000

0   1/2   miles   1   1 1/2

0   1/2   1   kilometres   1 1/2   2

Junction 9	Motorway & junction	*LC*	Level crossing
Services	Motorway service area	•—•—•—•	Tramway
	Primary road single/dual carriageway	- - - - - - - -	Ferry route
Services	Primary road service area	....	Airport runway
	A road single/dual carriageway	– · – · – · –	County, administrative boundary
	B road single/dual carriageway	ᐱᐱᐱᐱᐱᐱᐱ	Mounds
	Other road single/dual carriageway	**151**	Page continuation 1:25,000
	Minor/private road, access may be restricted	**93**	Page continuation 1:17,500
← ←	One-way street	**7**	Page continuation to enlarged scale 1:10,000
	Pedestrian area		River/canal, lake
= = = = = =	Track or footpath		Aqueduct, lock, weir
▮▮▮▮▮▮▮	Road under construction	465 ▲ Winter Hill	Peak (with height in metres)
[– – – –]	Road tunnel		Beach
P	Parking		Woodland
P+🚌	Park & Ride		Park
🚌	Bus/coach station	✝✝✝	Cemetery
	Railway & main railway station		Built-up area
	Railway & minor railway station		Industrial/business building
⊖	Underground station		Leisure building
⊖	Light railway & station		Retail building
+++++++++	Preserved private railway		Other building

⊓⊔⊓⊔⊓⊔⊓	City wall	♟	Castle
A&E	Hospital with 24-hour A&E department		Historic house or building
PO	Post Office	Wakehurst Place NT	National Trust property
📖	Public library	🏛	Museum or art gallery
i	Tourist Information Centre		Roman antiquity
i	Seasonal Tourist Information Centre		Ancient site, battlefield or monument
▮▮	Petrol station, 24 hour Major suppliers only		Industrial interest
†	Church/chapel	✳	Garden
🚻	Public toilets	◉	Garden Centre Garden Centre Association Member
♿	Toilet with disabled facilities		Garden Centre Wyevale Garden Centre
PH	Public house AA recommended		Arboretum
◑	Restaurant AA inspected		Farm or animal centre
Madeira Hotel	Hotel AA inspected		Zoological or wildlife collection
🎭	Theatre or performing arts centre		Bird collection
👥	Cinema		Nature reserve
⚑	Golf course		Aquarium
▲	Camping AA inspected	**V**	Visitor or heritage centre
⊟	Caravan site AA inspected		Country park
▲⊟	Camping & caravan site AA inspected	⌒	Cave
	Theme park	✗	Windmill
	Abbey, cathedral or priory		Distillery, brewery or vineyard

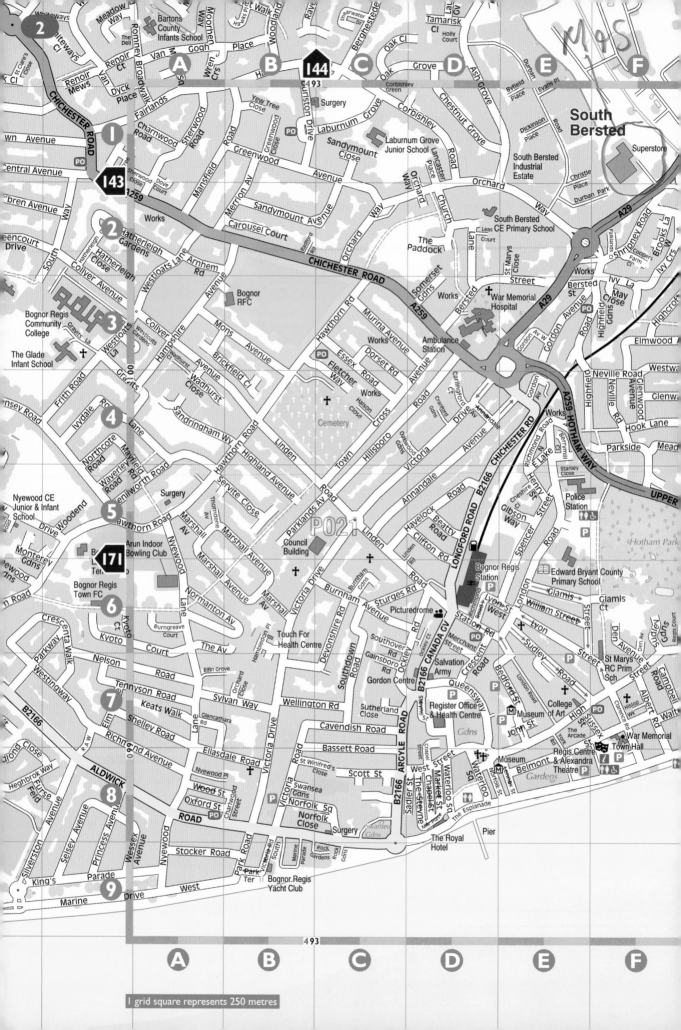

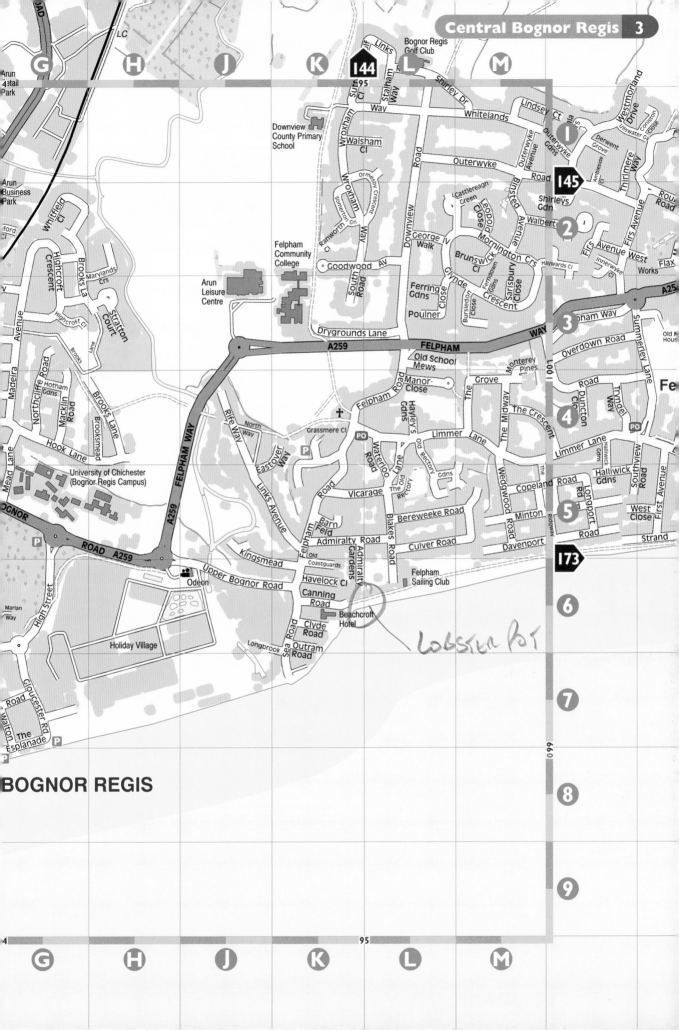

BOGNOR REGIS

LOBSTER POT

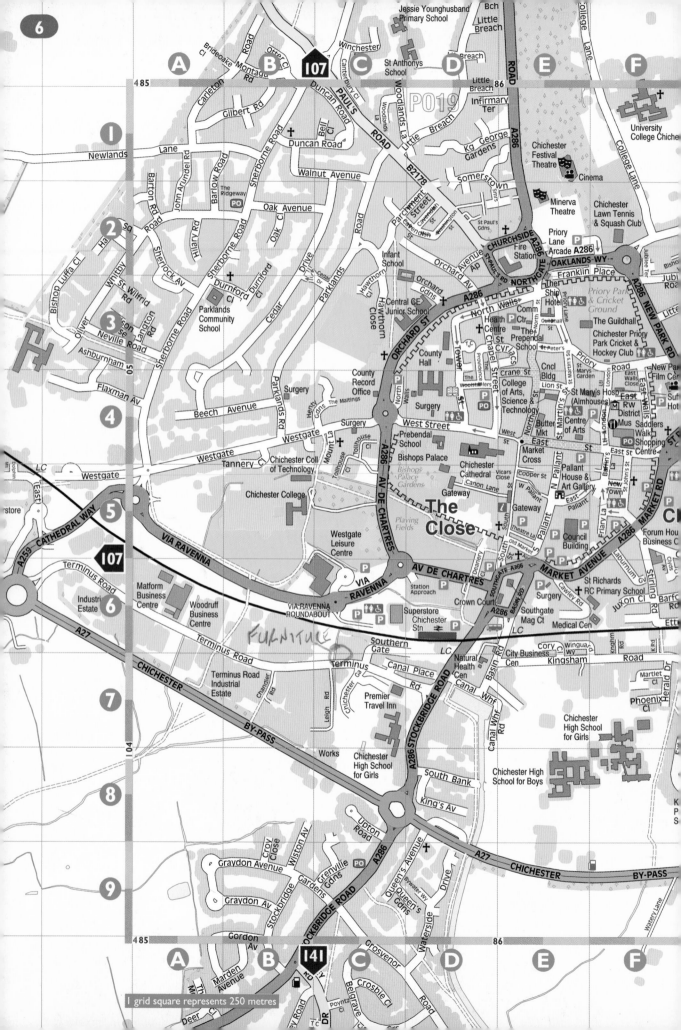

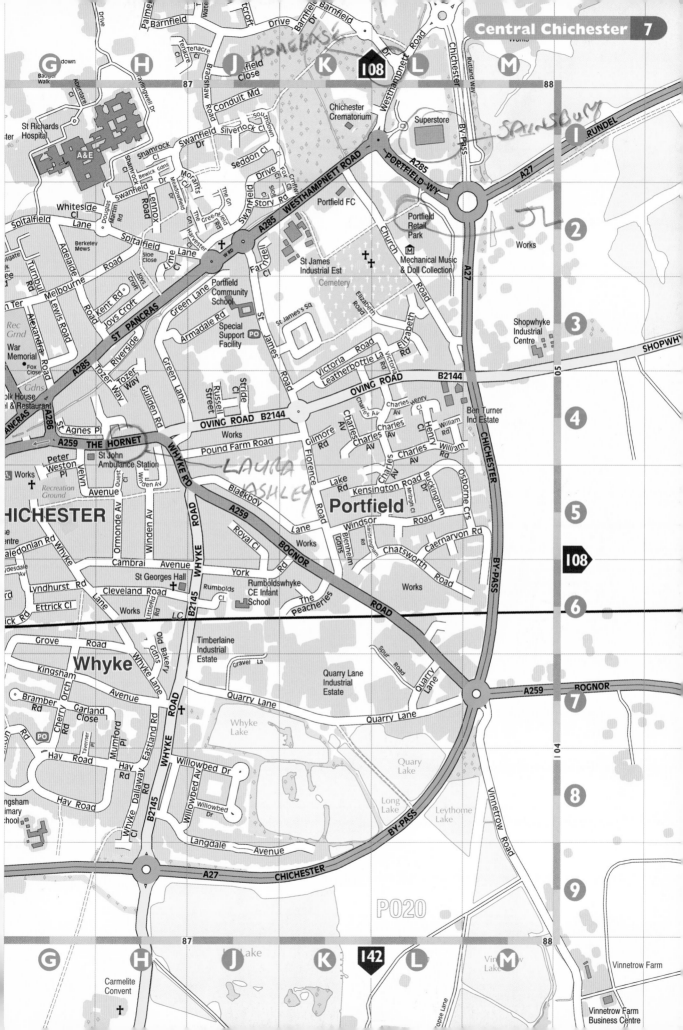

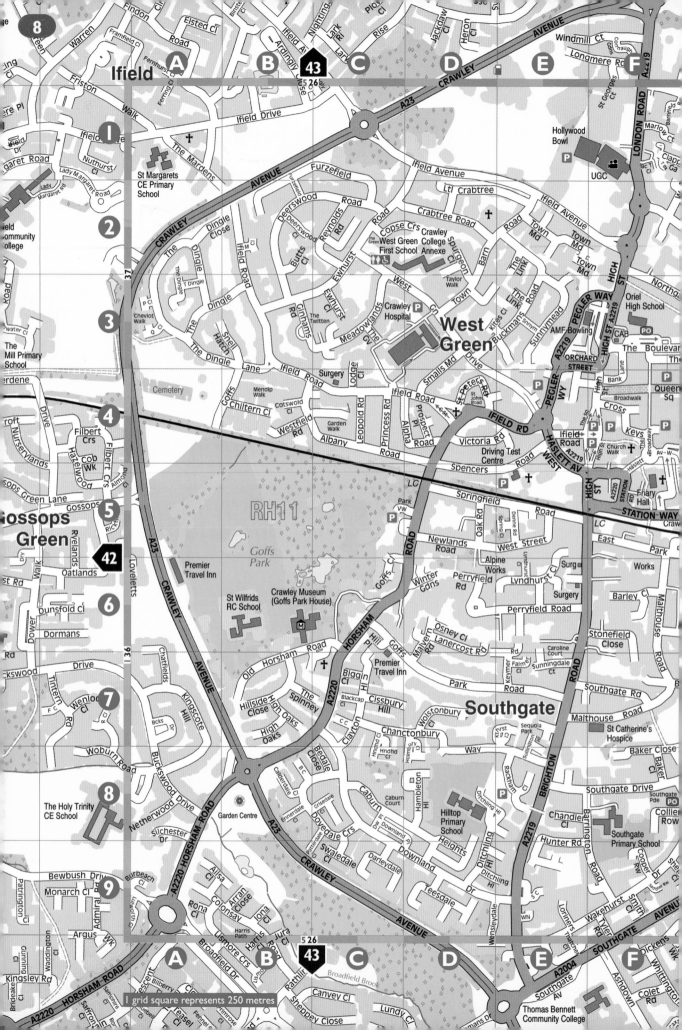

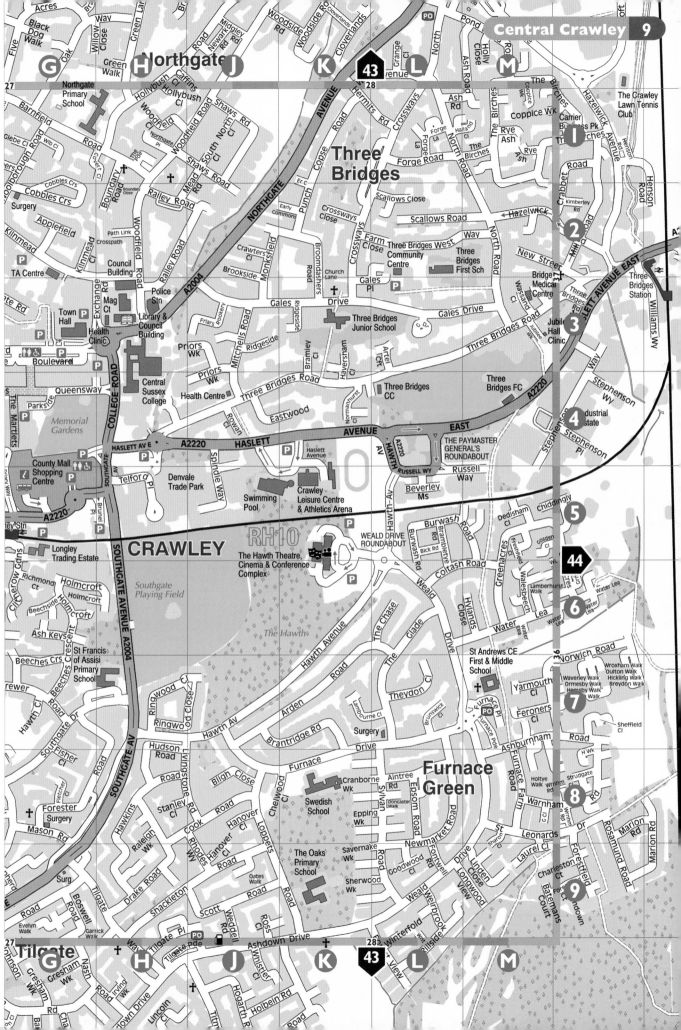

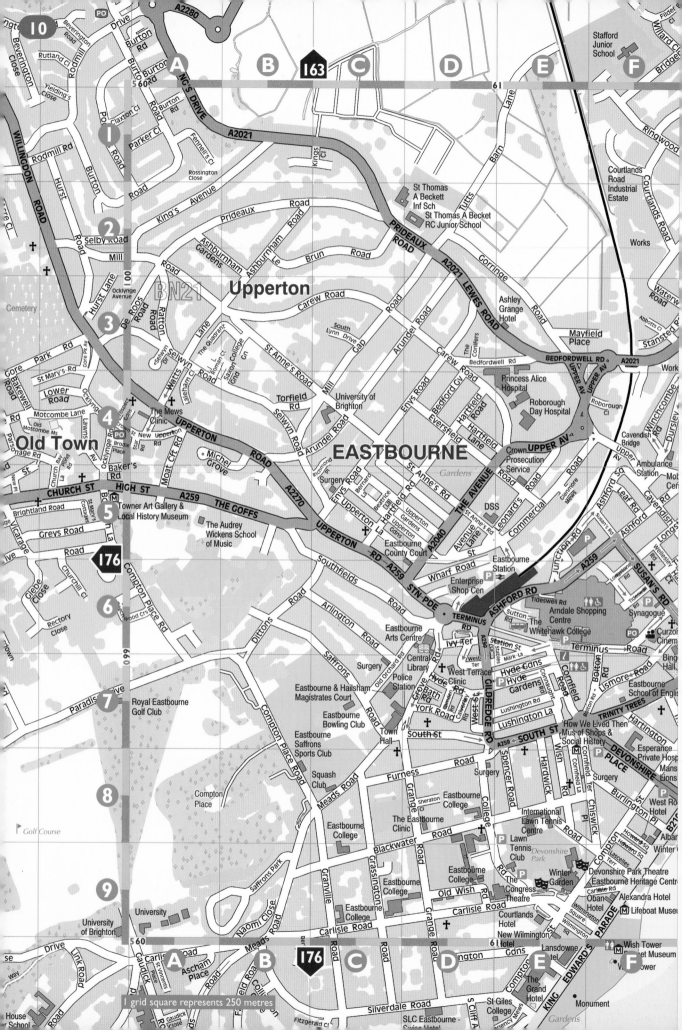

Roselands

Astaire Avenue
Brookmead Close
Harding Avenue
Marlow Avenue
Willoughby Crs
Driving Test

G H J K **164** L M

Hunloke Avenue
St Philip's Avenue
Recycling Centre
Brydges Cl
Archery Youth Centre
A259
St Andrews CE Infants School
Winchelsea Road
Martell
Wartling Rd
Sovereign Leisure C

Ringwood Cl
Ringwood Road
Fitzmaurice Avenue
Baillie Av
Roselands Close
Avenue
Windermere Crescent
Roselands
Rye St
Wartling
Winifred Lee Health Centre
Fort Fun & Rocky's Adventure Land

MOY
St Philip's Avenue
Woodgate
Belle Vue Rd
Roselands Infant School
Seabeach
Romney st
Seaford Road
Channel View
Eastbourne United FC
Crumbles Pond
Prince's Park
Royal Parade
P

Avenue
Annington Road
Ringwood Road
Fairlight Road
Latimer Road
Bexhill Road
Sidley Road
Wannock Road
Desmond Road
Penhale Road
Guestling Road

ROAD A2021
SEASIDE BEACH RD
St Josephs RC School
Glennys Estate
Eshton Rd
B2106
Beach Road
P
Lifeboat Station

WHITLEY
Fire Station
Dudley Road
Kerrara Ter
Mona Road
Kilda Rd
Stanley
Carlton Road
B2106
SIDLEY ROAD
Royal Parade
P
Fishermen's Club

Chawbrook
Albion
Clarence Road
Western Rd
Avondale
Beamsley Rd
Bardenton Rd
Latimer Rd
Latimer Road
Eastbourne Sovereign Sailing Club

Fire Road
Havelock Rd
Neville Rd
Works
Belfring Rd
Oxford Rd
Taddington Rd
Addingham Road
P
Treasure Island Play Centre

Firle
Works
Manifold Rd
St George's Rd
Springfield Road
Hanover Rd
Redoubt Road
Krystone Rd

Cavendish Avenue
Belmore Road
Sydney Rd
Sheen Rd
Seaside Medical Centre
St James Rd
Warrior square
Halton Rd
PARADE

New Rd
Melbourne Road
Willowfield Road
Willowfield Sq
Cambridge Rd
Latimer Road
ROYAL
Pavilion
Gardens

Bourne
Salvation Army
Bourne County Prim Sch
St Aubyn's Rd
TA Centre
Baynam Rd
Langham Hotel

Tilaeswell Rd
Langney Road
Burfld Rd
B2106
Leaf Hall Rd
York House Hotel

Langney
Place
Ceylon Place
Pevensey Road
PO
B2106
MARINE PDE

Royal Hippodrome Theatre
Queen's Gdns
Colonnade Gdns
Lion La
MARINE PDE RD
COLONNADE RD

A259
Bus Depot
SEASIDE ROAD
MARINE
PDE
Queens Hotel

Terminus Rd
Afton Hotel
Elms Av
Burlington
P
Queens Hotel

P
GRAND PARADE
Eastbourne Pier

Chatsworth Hotel
B2106

Bandstand

Lions Hotel
Garden

I 2 3 4 5 **177** 6 7 8 9

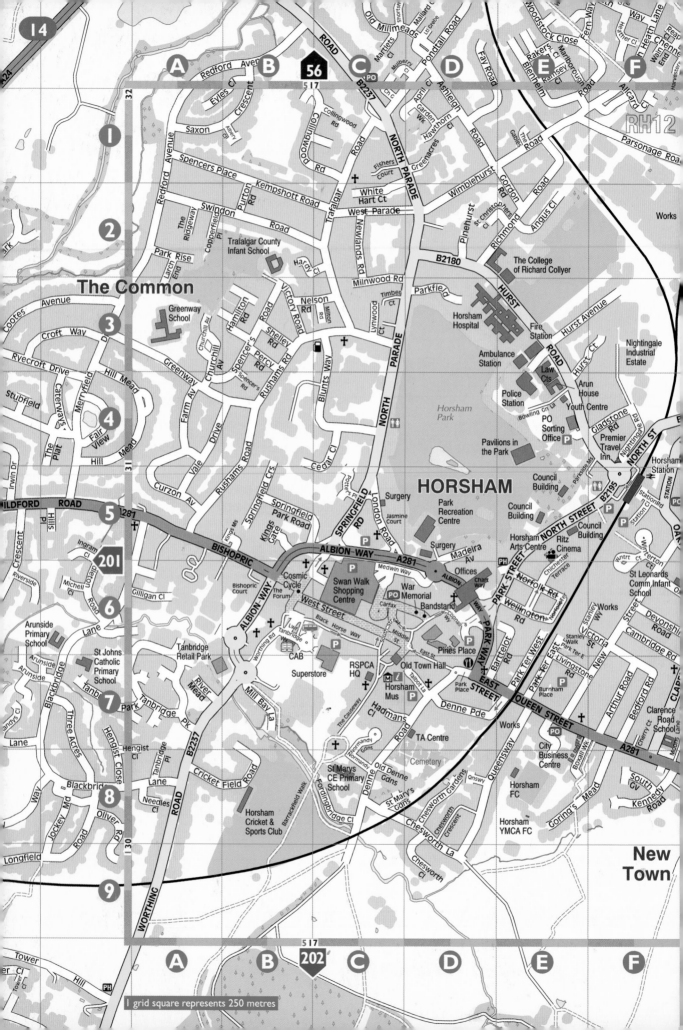

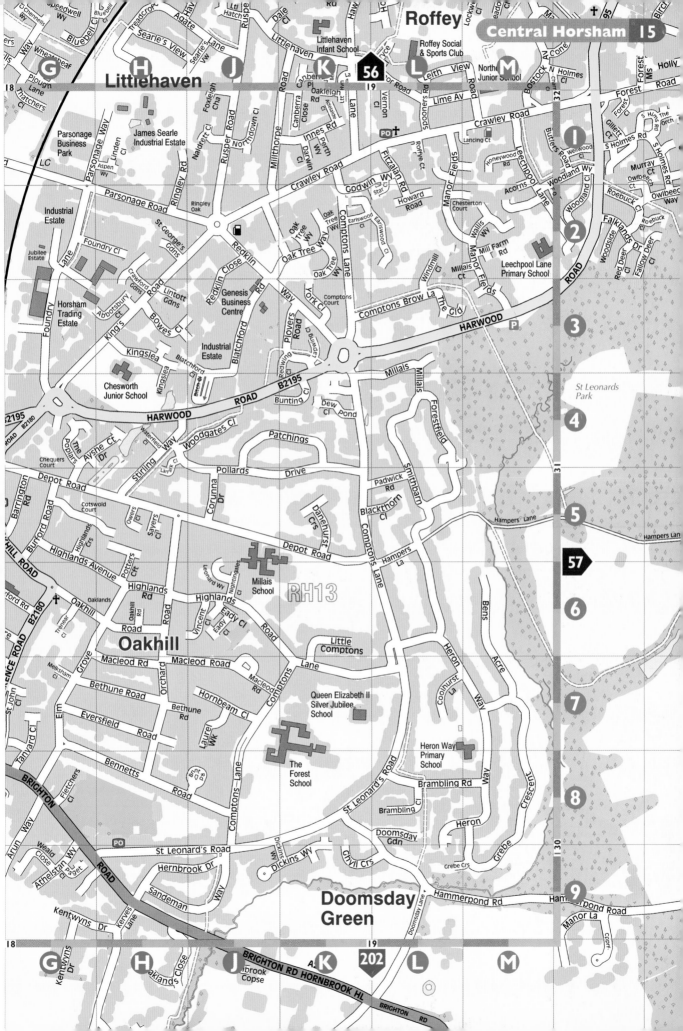

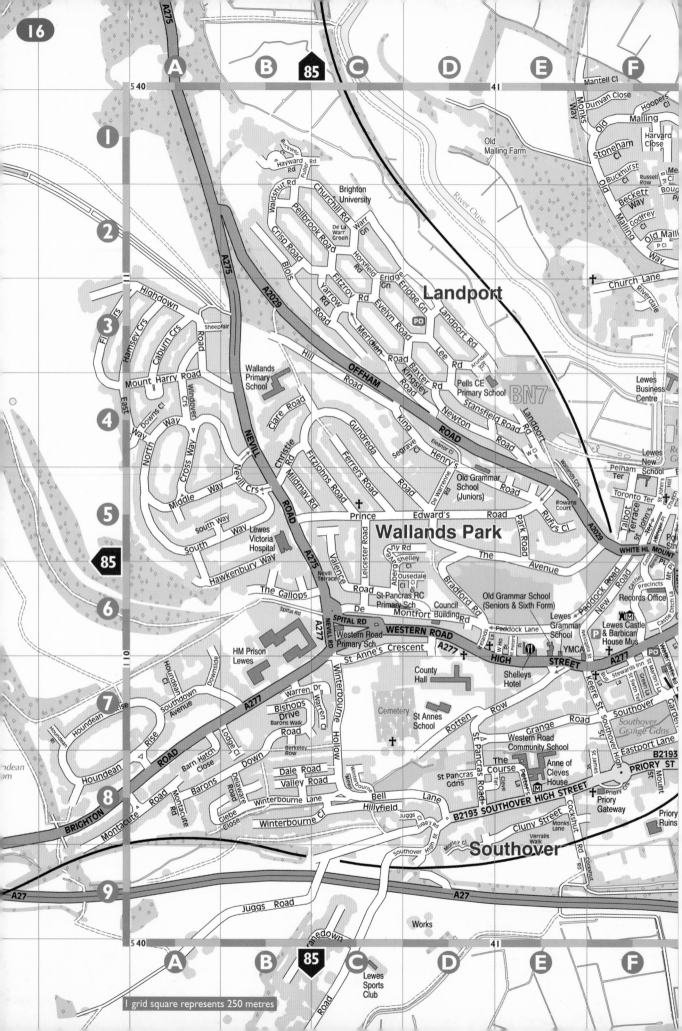

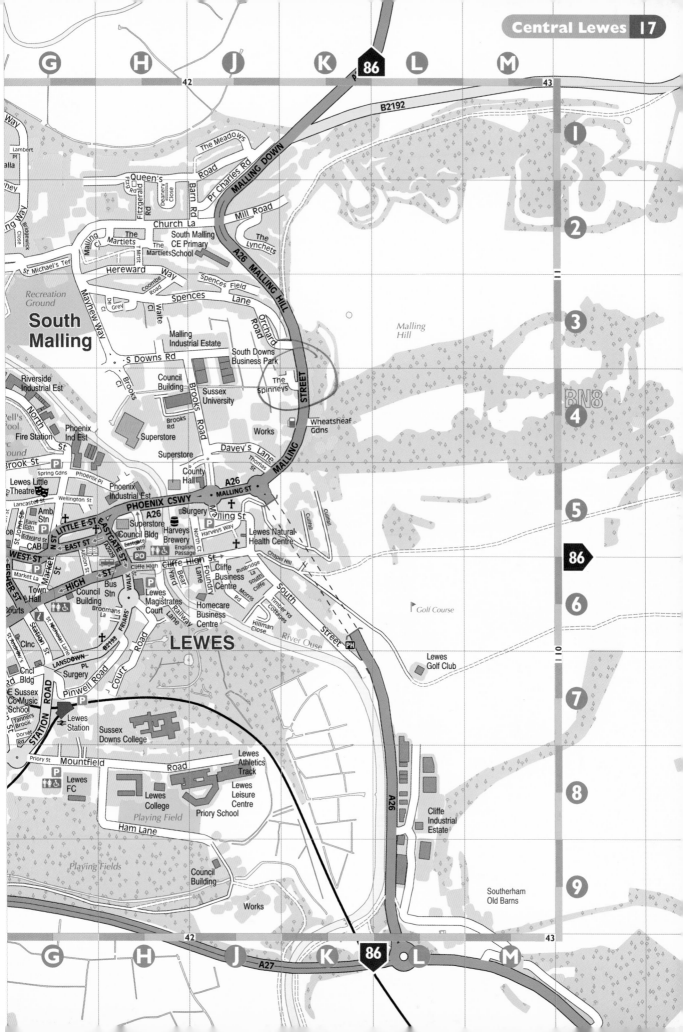

G H J K 86 L M

42 43

B2192

I

The Meadows

Road

Pr Charles Rd

MALLING DOWN

2

Queen's

Fitzgerald Rd

Deanery Close

Barn Rd

Church La

Mill Road

South Malling CE Primary School

A26 MALLING HILL

The Lynchets

St Michael's Ter

Malling

The Martlets

The Martlets

Hereward Way

Coombe Road

De Grey

Waite Cl

Spences Field

Spences Lane

Malling Hill

3

Recreation Ground

South Malling

Mayhew Way

Spences Lane

Orchard Road

Malling Industrial Estate

S Downs Rd

Council Building

Brooks Cl

Sussex University

South Downs Business Park

The Spinneys

STREET

BN8

4

Riverside Industrial Est

Brooks Road

Brooks Rd

Superstore

MALLING

Works

Wheatsheaf Gdns

North

Fire Station

Phoenix Ind Est

Superstore

Davey's Lane

Thomas St

Pell's Pool

Spring Gdns

Phoenix Pl

County Hall

A26

MALLING ST

5

Lewes Little Theatre

Lancaster St

Wellington St

Phoenix Industrial Est

PHOENIX CSWY

Surgery

Cliffhall

Cliffhall

Lancaster St

Amb Stn

Earls Gdn

A26

Superstore

Council Bldg

Harveys Brewery

Malling St

Lewes Natural Health Centre

Chapel Hill

86

St John's

Edward St

CAB

LITTLE E ST

EASTGATE ST

East St

N ST

Albion St

PO

Eastgate Wharf

Cliffe High St

English Passage

Cliffe High St

Bear Yard

North St

Cliffe Business Centre

Rusbridge South

Morris Rd

Cliffe

South

Golf Course

6

WEST ST

FISHER ST

Market La

HIGH

Town Hall

Council Building

Bus Stn

Broomans La

WALK

Railway Lane

Foundry

Cliffe

Lewes Magistrates Court

Homecare Business Centre

Timber Yd Cottages

Hillman Close

STREET

River Ouse

PH

LEWES

Lewes Golf Club

Clnc

St Andrew's

LANSDOWN PL

FRIARS

Court Road

Pinwell Road

Surgery

Council Building

B2193

River Ouse

7

Cncl Bldg

E Sussex Co Music School

Tanners Brook

Dorset Rd

Priory St

STATION ROAD

Lewes Station

Mountfield

Road

Sussex Downs College

Lewes Athletics Track

A26

8

Lewes FC

Lewes College

Priory School

Lewes Leisure Centre

Cliffe Industrial Estate

Playing Field

Ham Lane

9

Playing Fields

Council Building

Works

Southerham Old Barns

42 43

G H J K 86 L M

A27 A26

42 43

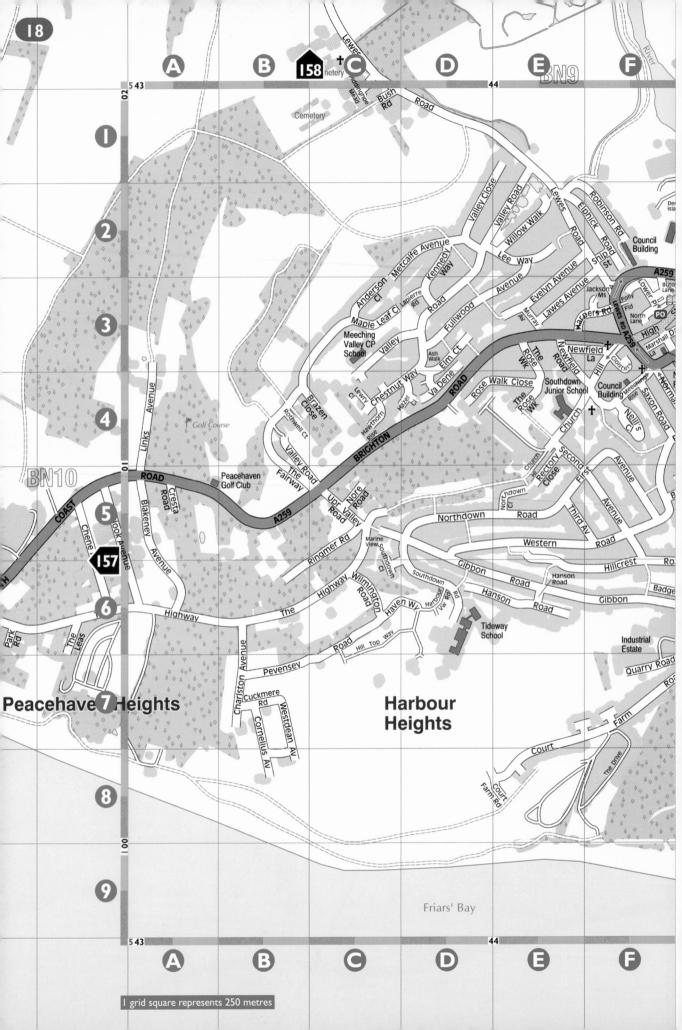

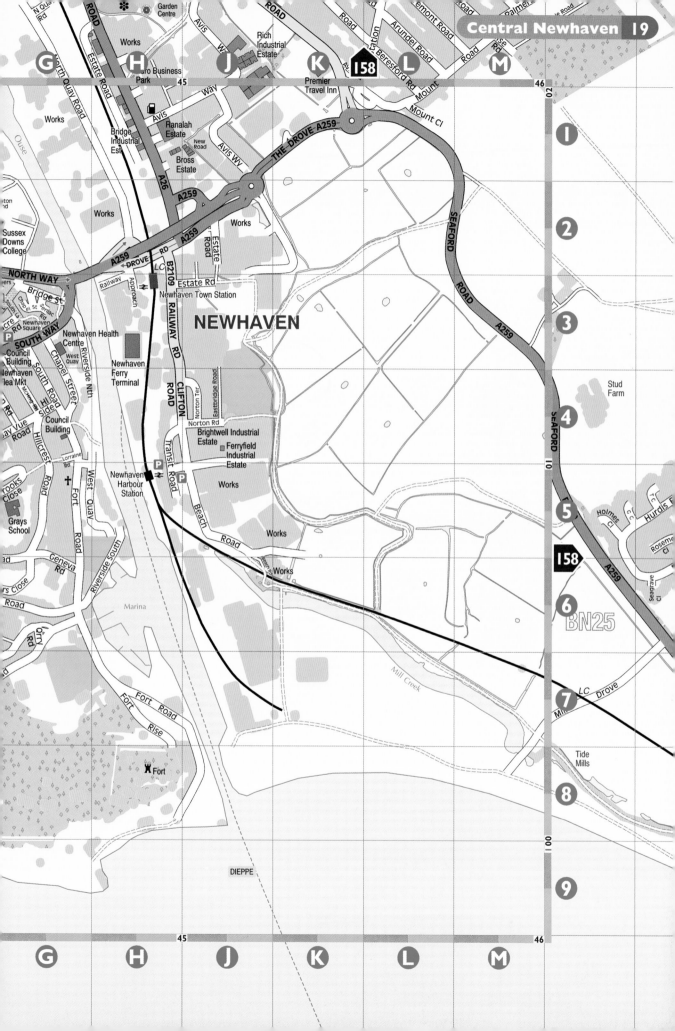

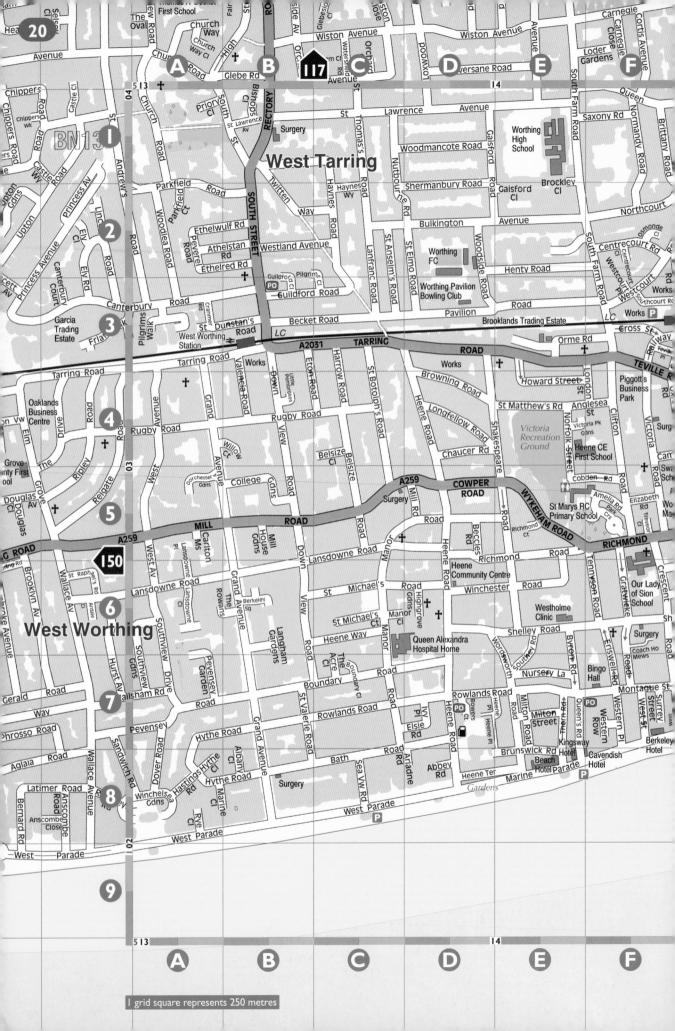

WORTHING

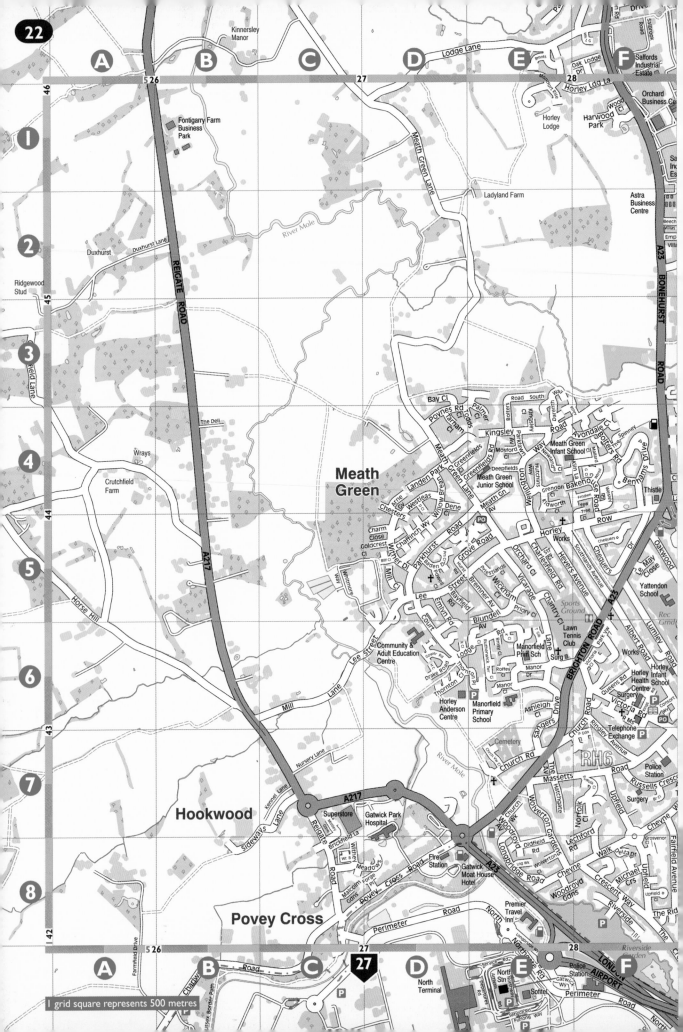

Newdiga

Capel

Clark's Green

1 grid square represents 500 metres

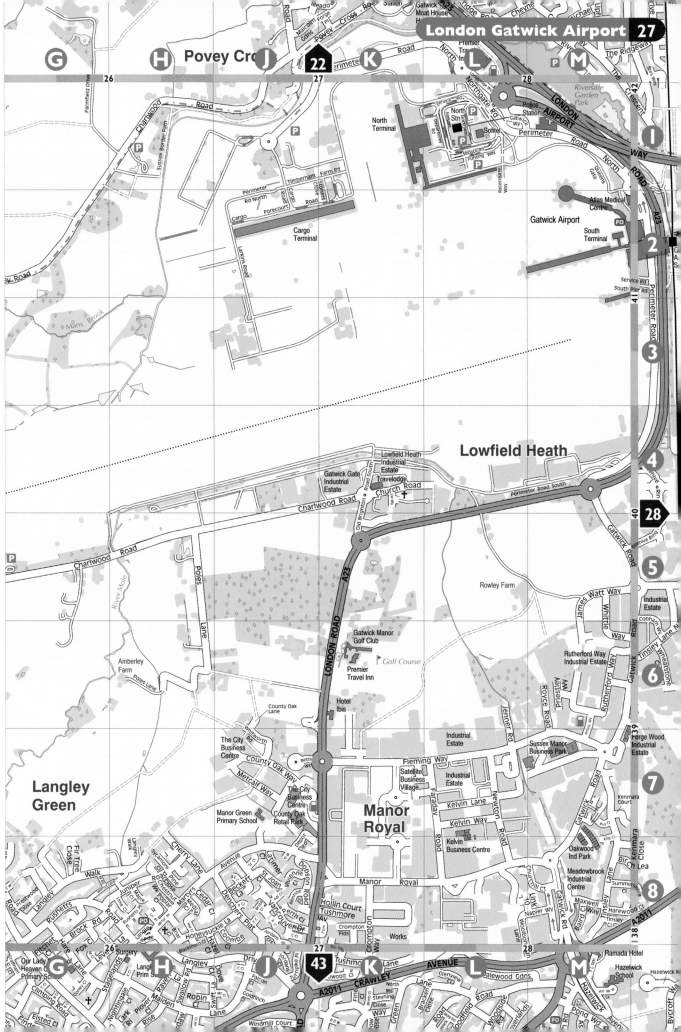

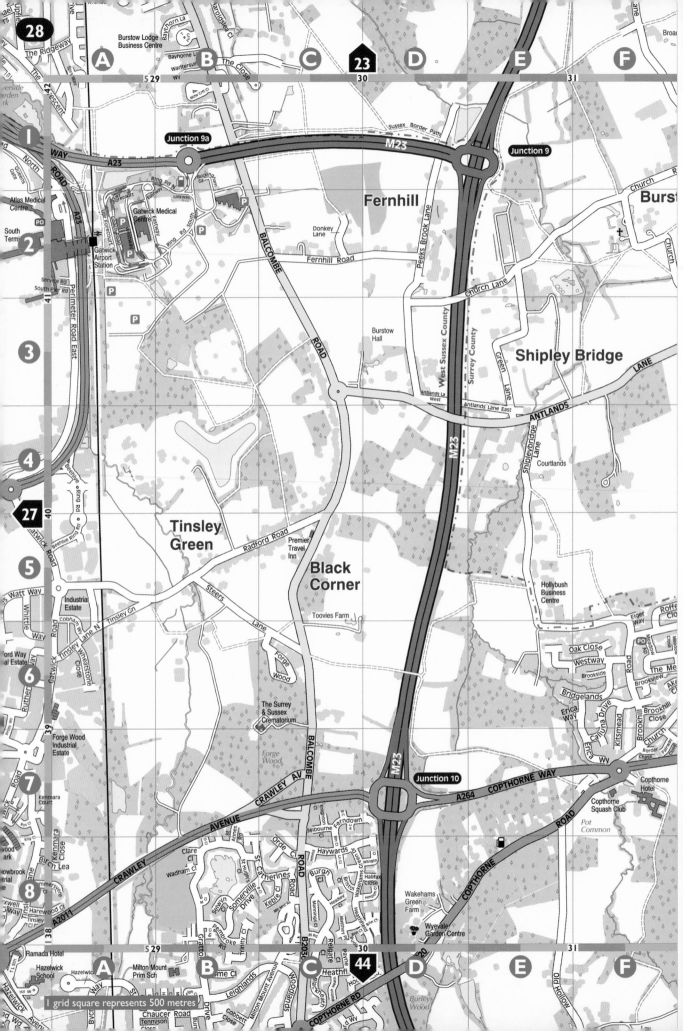

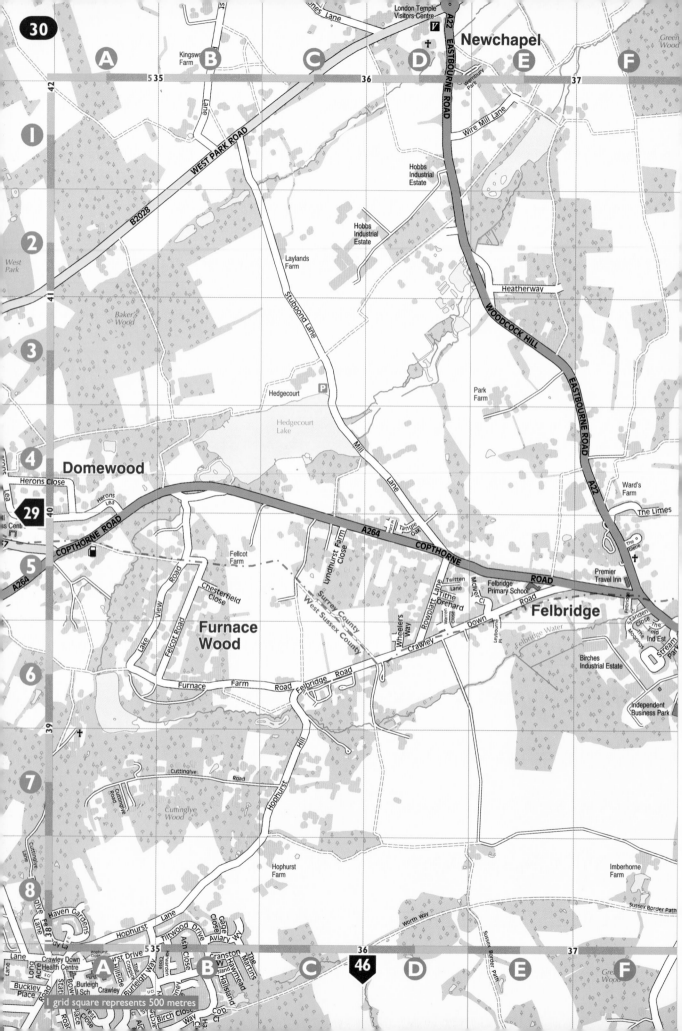

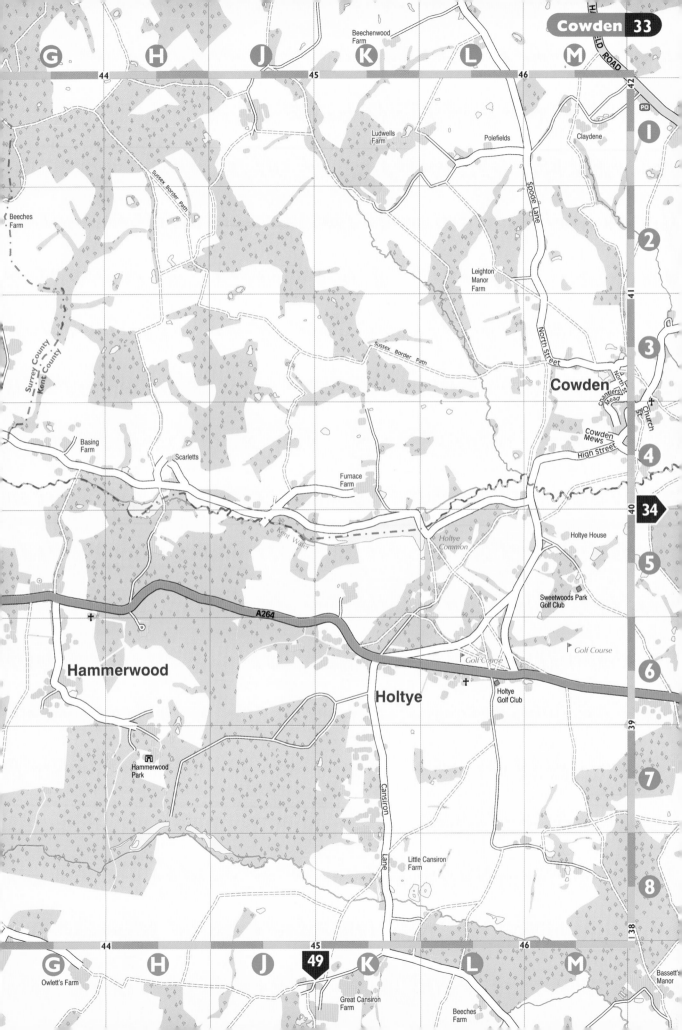

G **H** **J** **K** **L** **M**

44 45 46

Beechenwood
Farm

Ludwells
Farm

Polefields

Claydene

I

Beeches
Farm

Sussex Border Path

Leighton
Manor
Farm

2

Spode Lane

North Street

Sussex Border Path

Surrey County
Kent County

3

North St
Mead

chantlers

North St

Church St

Cowden

Basing
Farm

Scarletts

Cowden
Mews

High Street

4

Furnace
Farm

34

Holtye House

Kent Water

Holtye
Common

5

Sweetwoods Park
Golf Club

A264

Hammerwood

Golf Course

Golf Course

6

Holtye

Holtye
Golf Club

Hammerwood
Park

Cansiron Lane

7

Little Cansiron
Farm

8

44 45 46

G **H** **J** **49** **K** **L** **M**

Owlett's Farm

Great Cansiron
Farm

Beeches
Farm

Bassett's
Manor

PO

42

41

40

39

38

HI
LD ROAD

Horseshoe
Green

34

A   B   Edells   C   D   E   F

5 47   48   49

PO

1   Clayde

Pyle Gate
Farm

Wickens

Cowden
Station

Blowers Hill

2   The
Paddocks

Moat Lane

Saxbys

41

Glover's
Hawes

The
Moat

Moat Lane

3   North St.
Chantlers
Mead

Kent County
East Sussex County

Sussex Border Path

Church St.

HARTFIELD ROAD

4   Cowden
Mews

High

Holywych
House

Tollhurst
Farm

Holywych
Farm

33   40   Sussex House
Farm

Salehurst

oltye House

5   Hethe

Blac

Cullinghurst
Farm

HARTFIELD ROAD

Golf Course

6   A264

39   B2026

Edenbridge
Road

7   Goodtrees Lane

Chantlers
Farm

EDENBRIDGE ROAD

Tye Farm

Highfields

8   Beech Green
Park

B2026

Beech Green Lane

1 38

5 47   48   49

A   B   C   50   D   E   F

Bassetts
Manor

1 grid square represents 500 metres

Henry VIII
Experience M

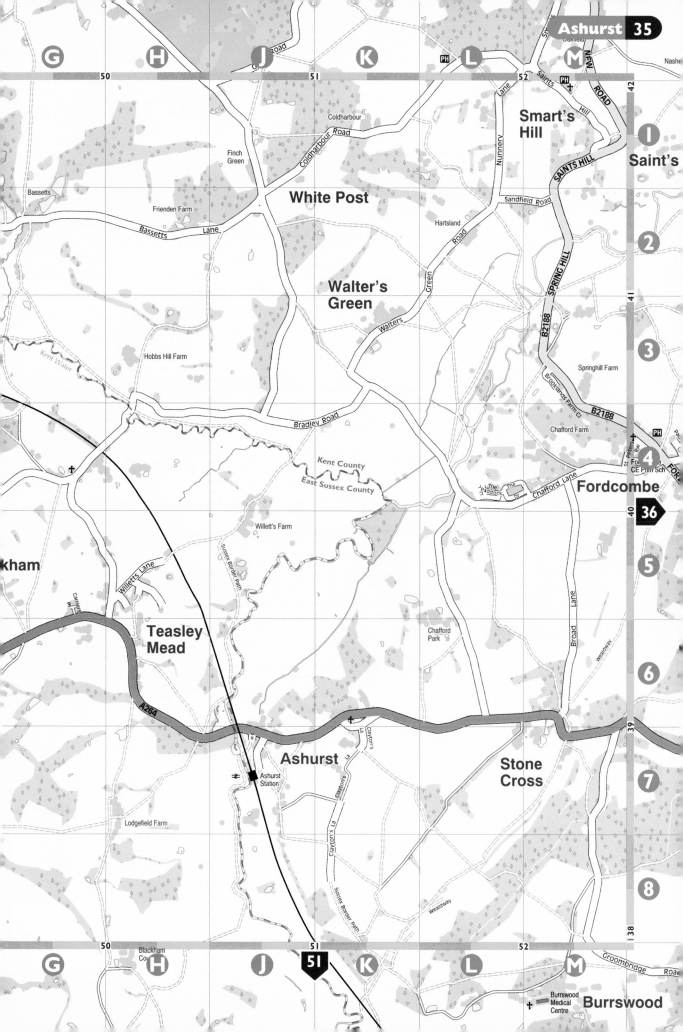

G   H   J   K   L   M   NEW

50   51   52   42

Oakfield

PH

Saints

Hill

**Smart's
Hill**

1

Saint's

Coldharbour

Coldharbour   Road

Finch
Green

Nunnery

Lane

SAINTS HILL

Sandfield Road

2

White Post

Bassetts

Frienden Farm

Bassetts   Lane

Hartsland

Green

Road

SPRING HILL

B2188

**Walter's
Green**

Walters

Springhill Farm

3

Kent Water

Hobbs Hill Farm

Brooklands Farm Cl

B2188

Chafford Farm

†

Bradley Road

Chafford Farm

St Peter's
CE Prim Sch   PH

4

Fordcombe

FOR

Kent County

East Sussex County

†

The
Paddock   The
Dr   Chafford Lane

Fordcombe

40   36

Willett's Farm

5

kham

Willetts Lane

Sussex Border Path

Carriers
Pl   †

Chafford
Park

Broad

Lane

Wealdway

6

**Teasley
Mead**

A264

39

7

Ashurst

Clayton's

La

†

Clayton's

Stone
Cross

Ashurst
Station

8

Clayton La

Lodgefield Farm

Sussex Border Path

Wealdway

50   51   52

G   H   J   K   L   M   Groombridge   Road

51

Blackham
Co

Burrswood
Medical
Centre   †   **Burrswood**

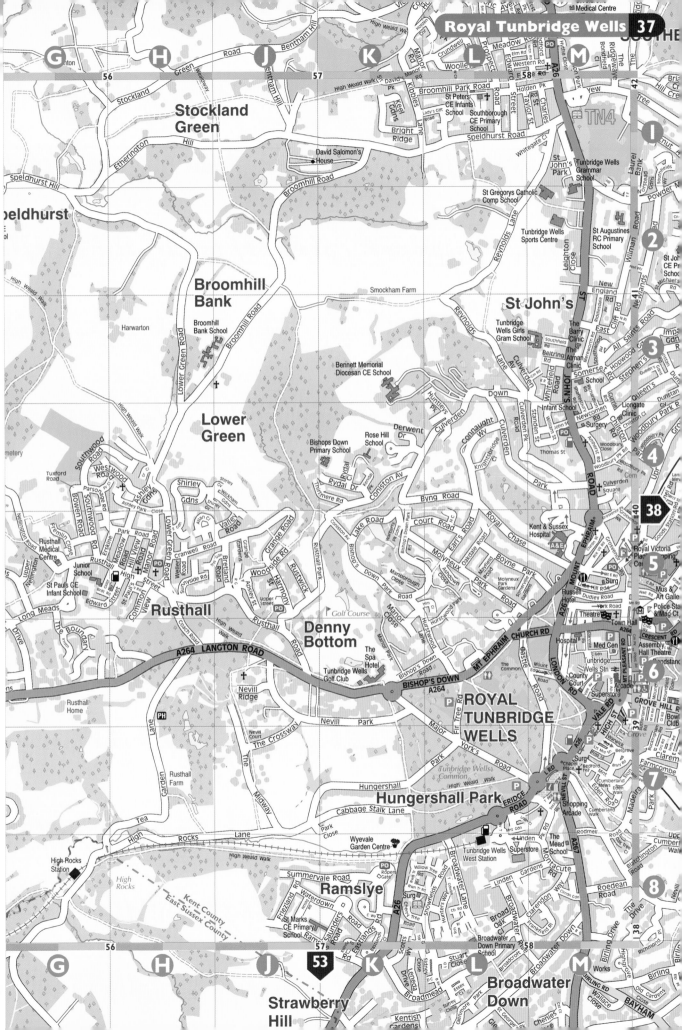

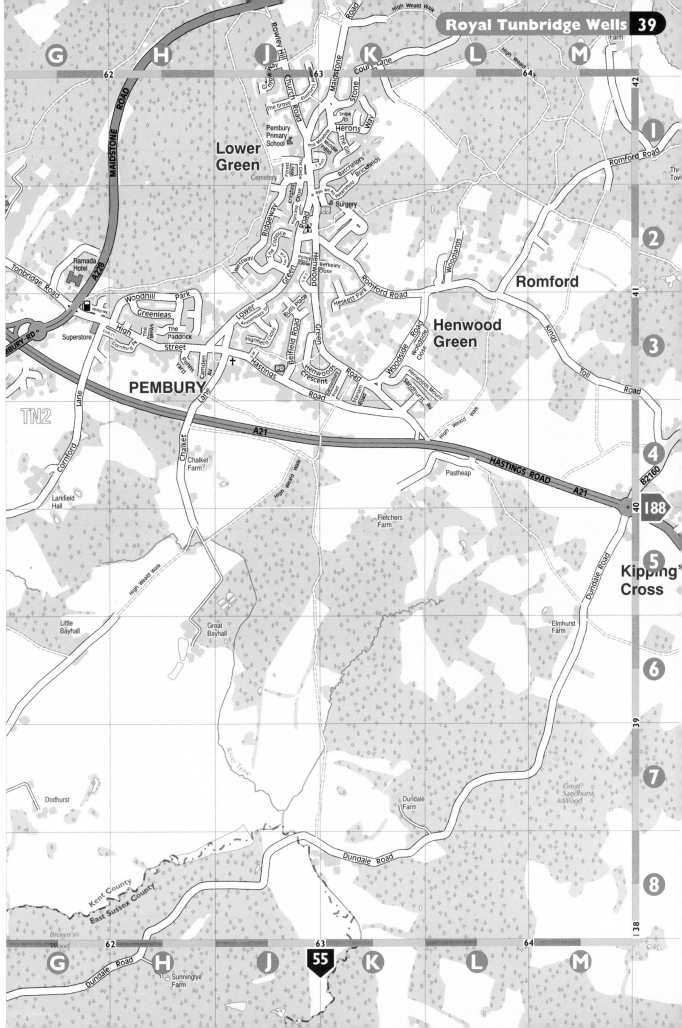

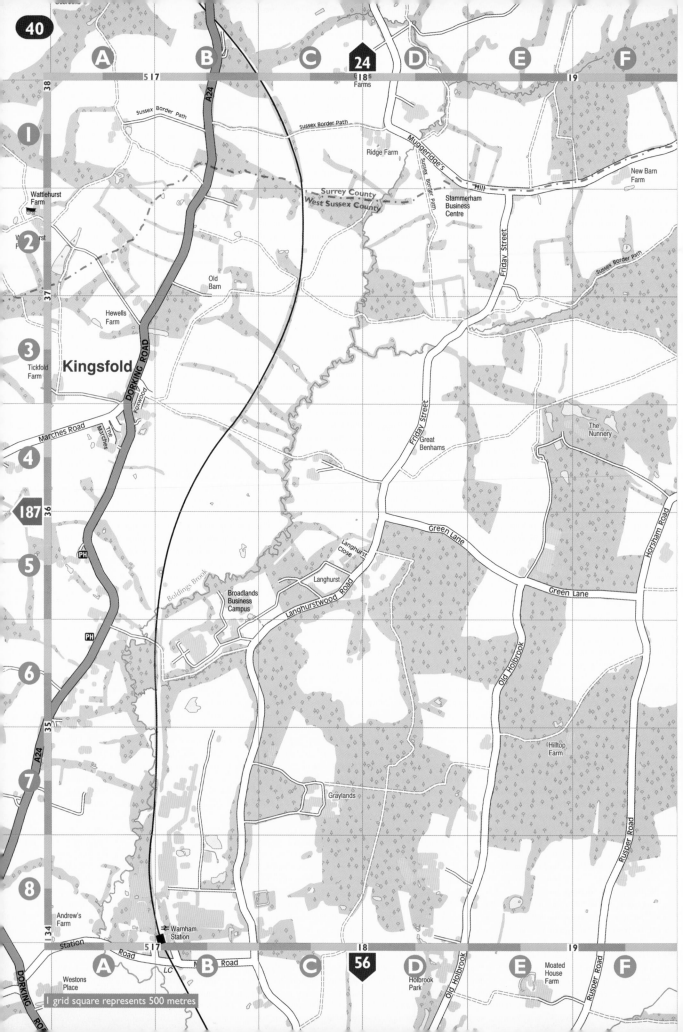

A B C **24** D E F

517

18
Farms

I

Sussex Border Path

Sussex Border Path

Ridge Farm

New Barn
Farm

Wattlehurst
Farm

Surrey County
West Sussex County

Stammerham
Business
Centre

Sussex Border Path

2

Old
Barn

Friday Street

Hewells
Farm

3 **Kingsfold**

Tickfold
Farm

DORKING ROAD

Foxwood

Marches Road

The Nunnery

The Marches

4

Great
Benhams

Friday Street

187 36

PH

Green Lane

Langhurst
Close

Horsham Road

5

Boldings Brook

Broadlands
Business
Campus

Langhurst

Green Lane

Langhurstwood Road

Old Holbrook

PH

6

Hilltop
Farm

35

A24

7

Graylands

Rusper Road

8

Andrew's
Farm

134

Westons
Place

Warnham
Station

Station

517

Road

LC

Road

DORKING ROAD

A B C **56** D E F

18   19

Holbrook
Park

Old Holbrook

Moated
House
Farm

Rusper Road

I grid square represents 500 metres

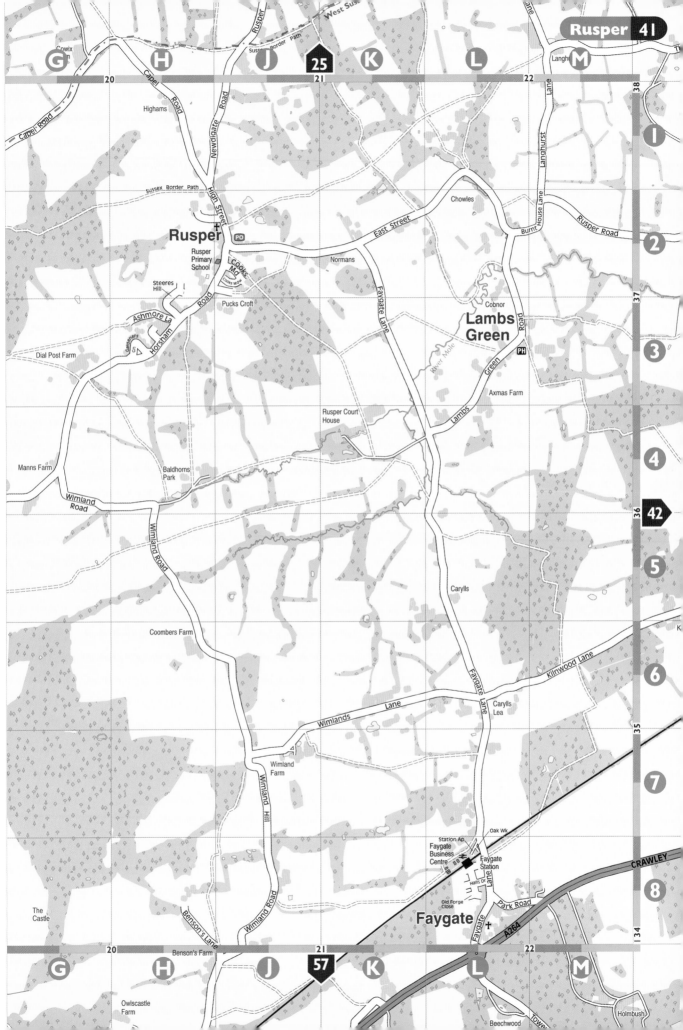

Cowix

West Sus

Sussex Border Path

G 20 **H** **J** **25** 21 **K** **L** 22 **M** 38

Capel Road

Highams

Capel Road

Newgate Road

Rusper

Langh

Sussex Border Path

High Street

I

Chowles

East Street

Langhurst Lane

Burnt House Lane

Rusper Road

2 37

Rusper
PO

Rusper
Primary
School

Cooks
Mq

Normans

Cobnor

**Lambs
Green**

PH

3

Steeres
Hill

Ashmore La

Horsham Road

Pucks Croft

Faygate Lane

River Mole

Axmas Farm

Dial Post Farm

Gardeners

Rusper Court
House

Lambs Green Road

4

Manns Farm

Baldhorns
Park

42 36

Wimland
Road

Carylls

5

Coombers Farm

Wimland Road

Kilnwood Lane

6 35

Wimlands Lane

Carylls
Lea

Faygate Lane

7

Wimland
Farm

Wimland Hill

Oak Wk

Station Ap

CRAWLEY

The
Castle

Faygate
Business
Centre

Faygate
Station

Halls D

8 34

Old Forge
Close

Faygate

Park Road

A264

Benson's Lane

Wimland Road

G 20 **H** **J** **57** 21 **K** **L** 22 **M**

Benson's Farm

Owlscastle
Farm

Beechwood

Tower

Holmbush

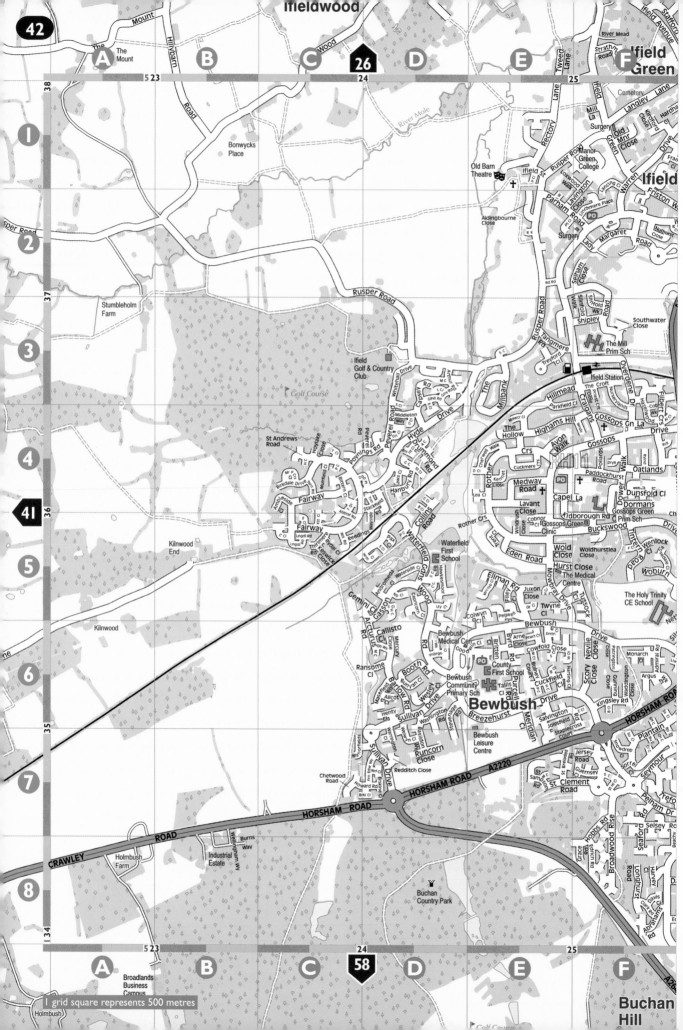

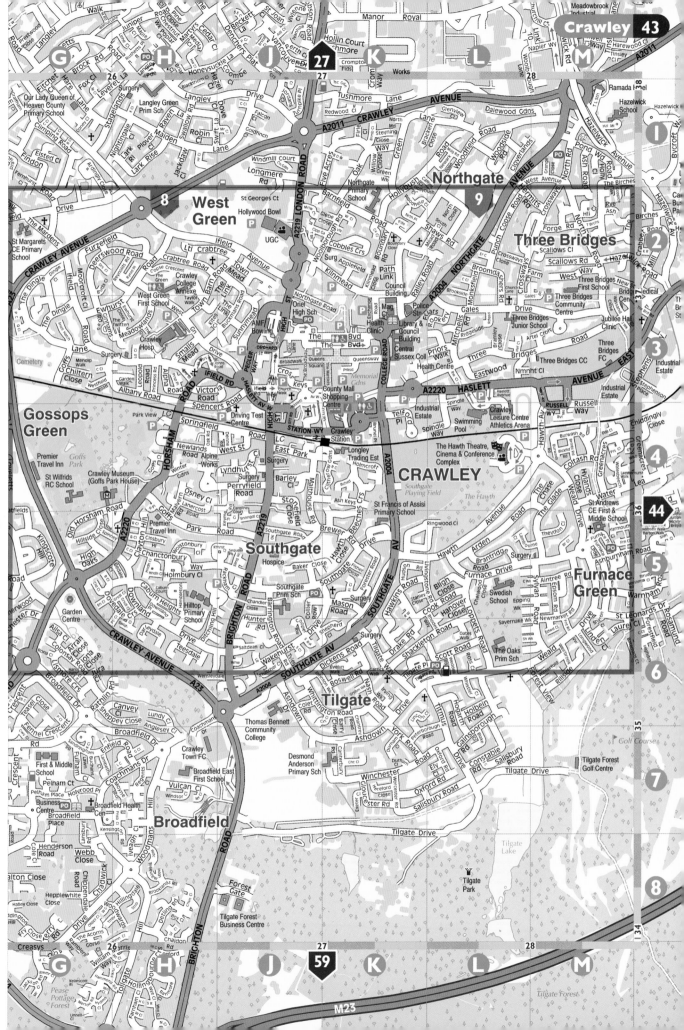

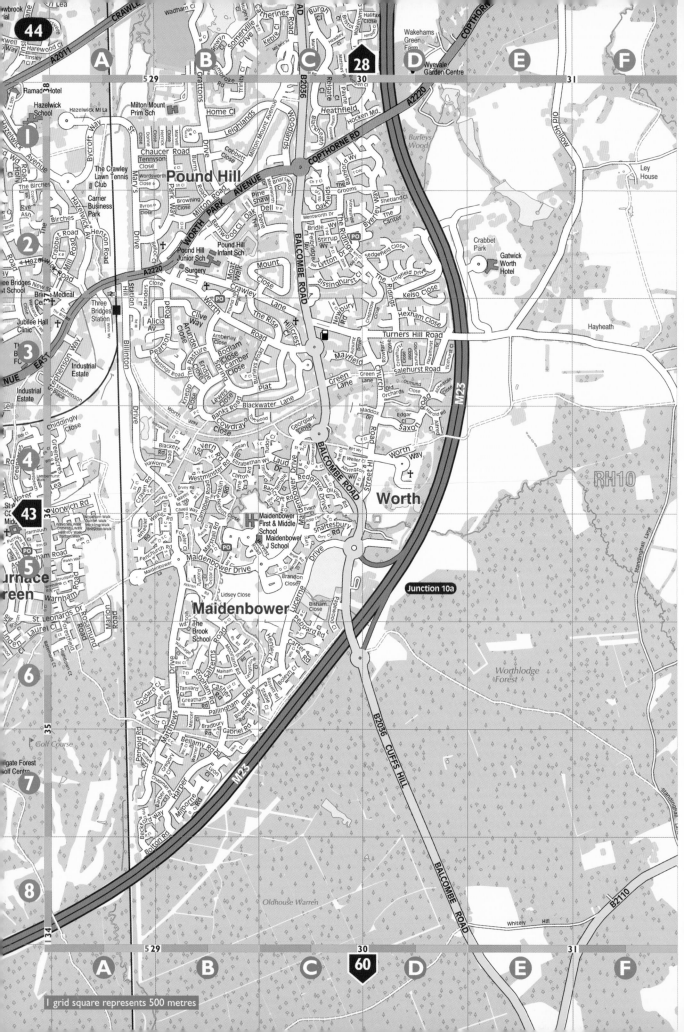

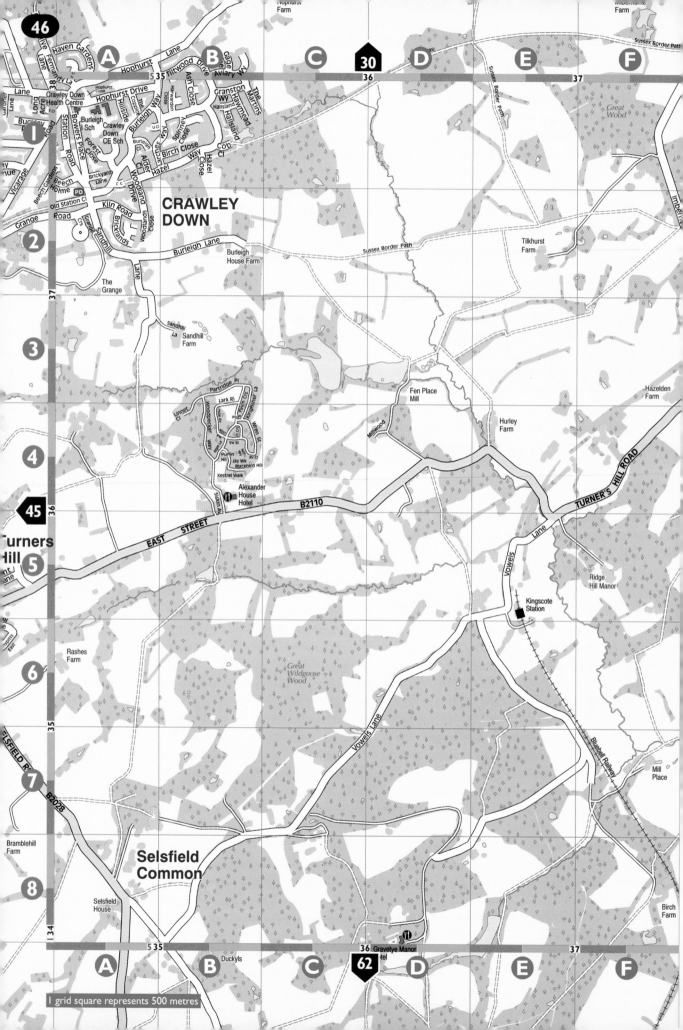

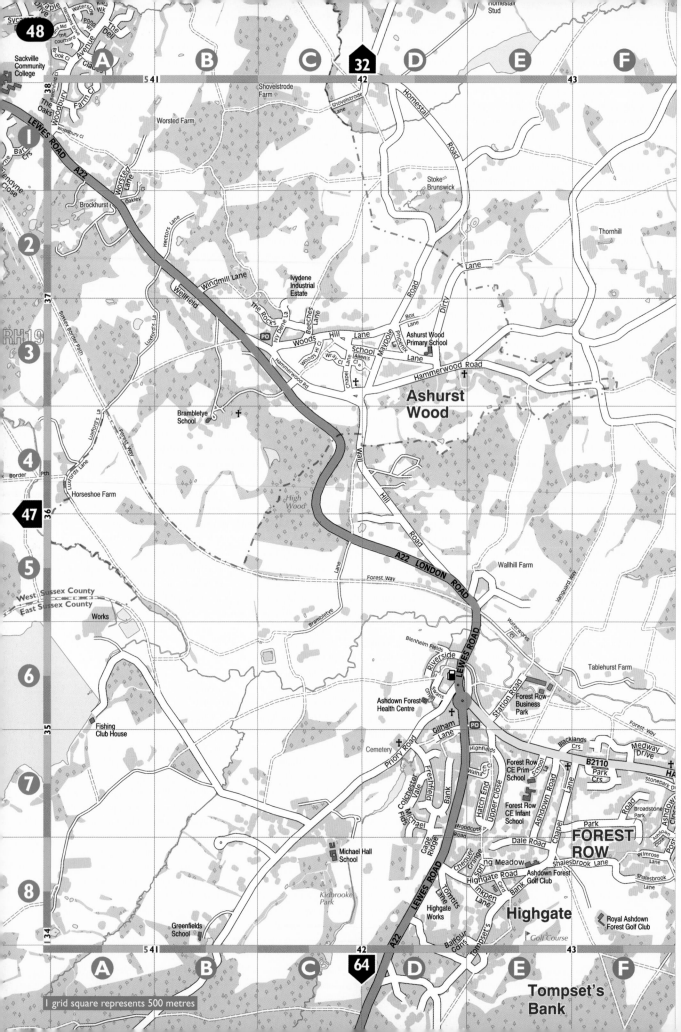

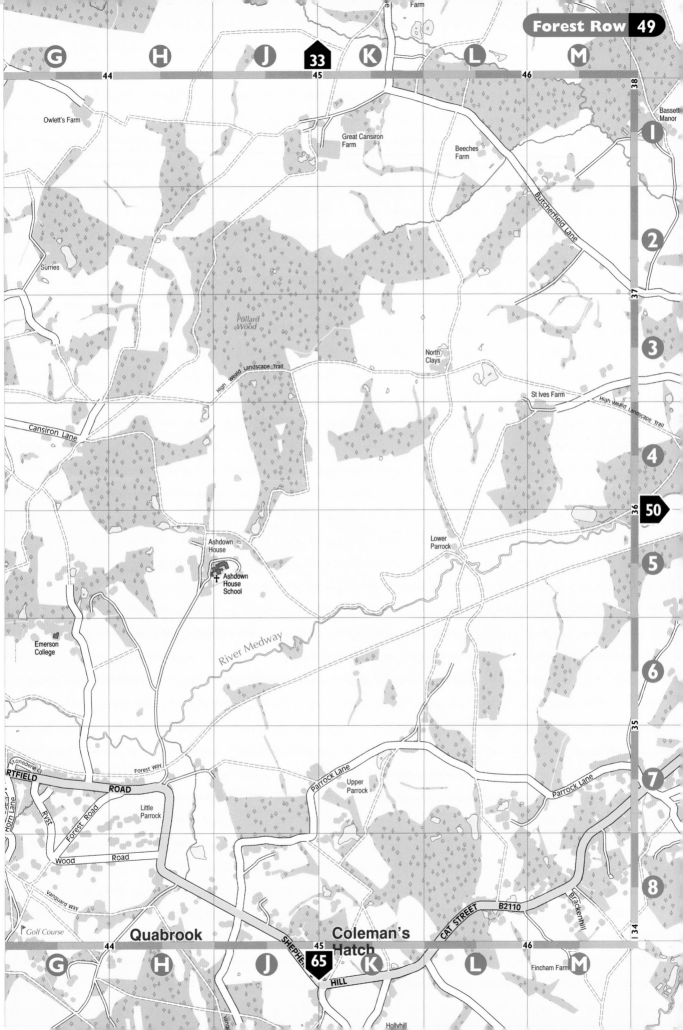

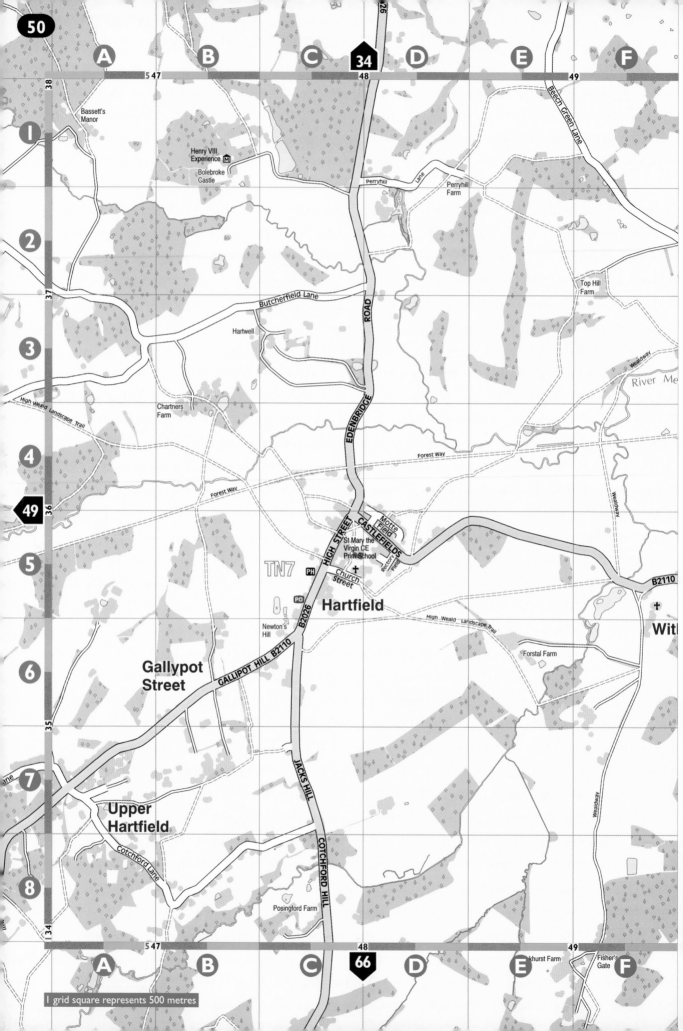

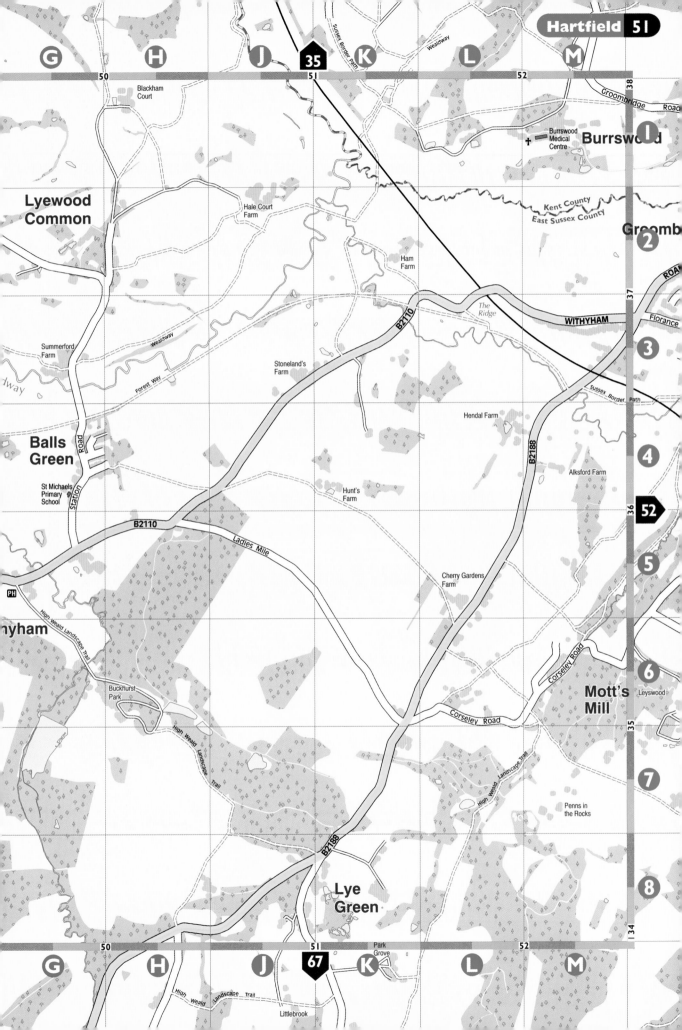

A   B   C   36   D   E   F

5 53   GROOMBRIDGE HILL   54   55

Top Hill
Farm

Pokehill

River Grom

Butlswood

Groombridge Place Gardens
& Enchanted Forest

Spa Valley Railway

Lodge

Works

Broadwater Forest Lane

2 Groombridge

PO

Newton
Willows

Lealands

Meadow
Road

Surgery

Orchard   Rise
Oaklands   Road   Broad
Oak

Groombridge
Station

Lynwood

Broadwater Forest Lane

WTHYHAM

Florance Lane

Groombridge
St Thomas CE
Aided Prim Sch

Birchden

3

Sussex Border Path

Eridge   Road

4

ksford Farm

Cem

Park Corner

51

Harrison's
Rocks

Warren
Farm

5

Glen Andred

High Weald Walk

Forge
Farm

Forge Road

LC

The
Forstal

6

Mott's
Mill

Leyswood

Hamsell Wood
Farm

A26

7

Mott's Farm

ns in
Rocks

Eridge
Station

8

A   B   C   68   D   E   F   Hamsell
Manor

5 53   54   55

I grid square represents 500 metres

Renby Farm

Copyhold
Farm

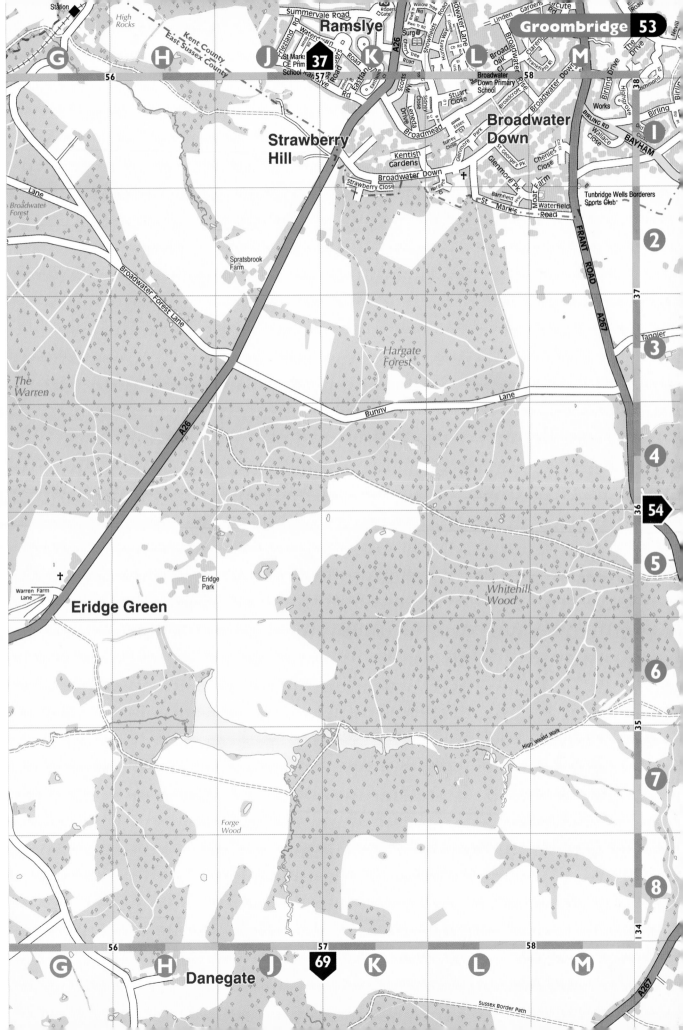

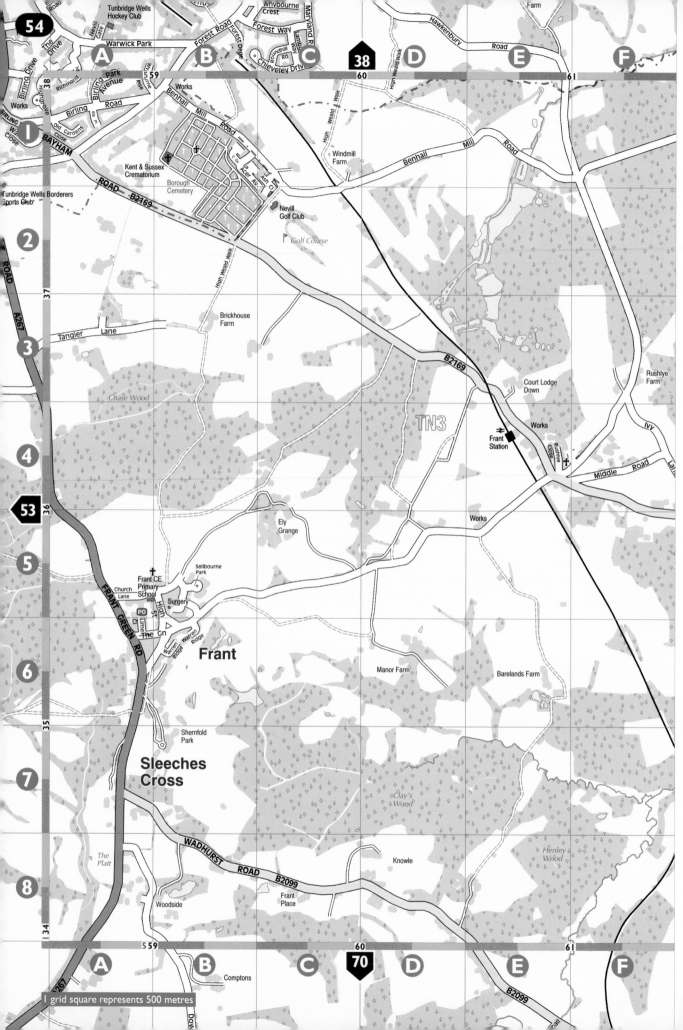

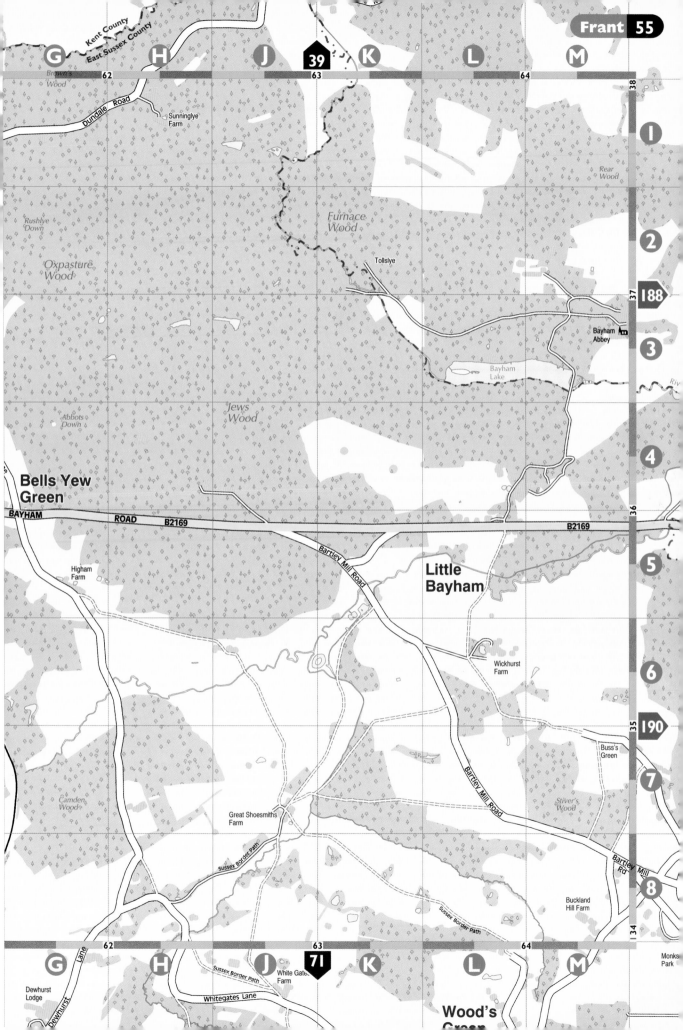

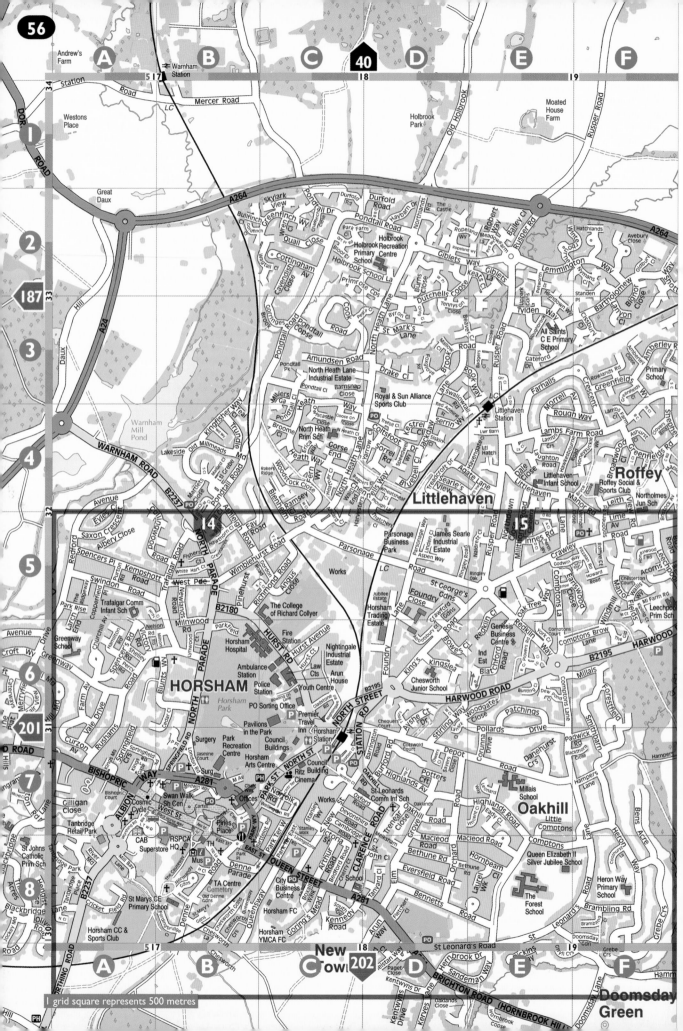

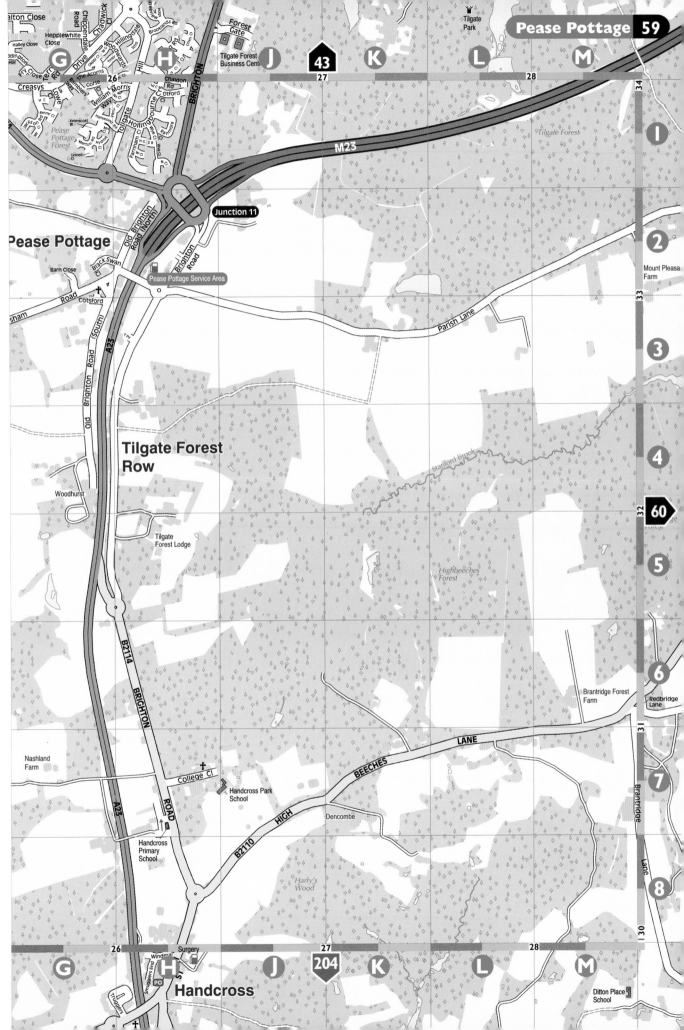

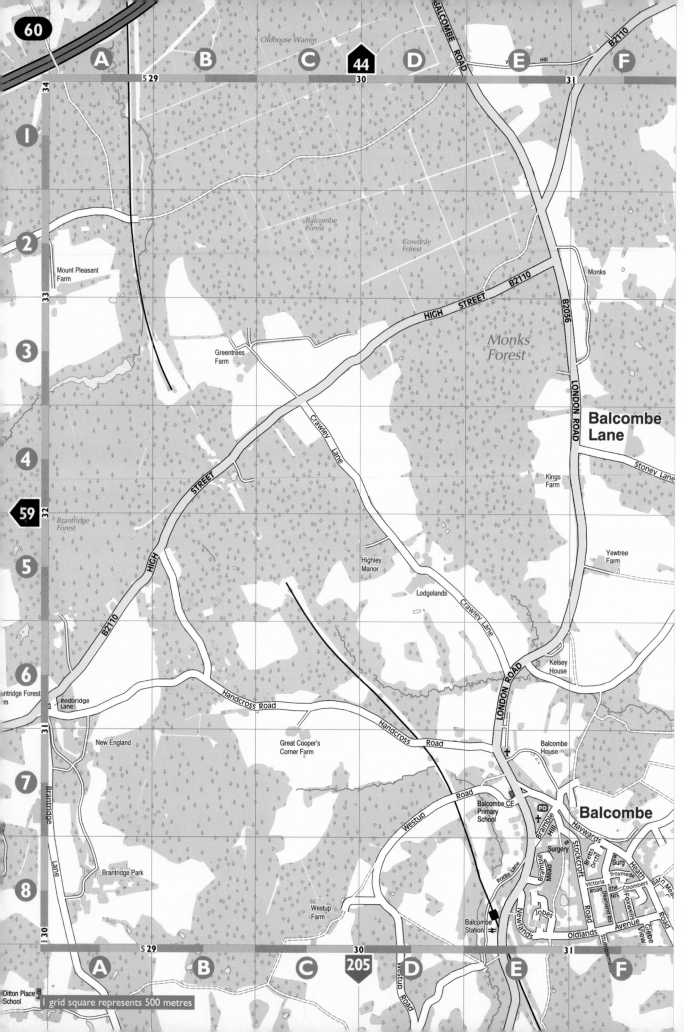

A   **B**   **C**   **D**   **E**   **F**

5 29   30   31

B2110

Oldhouse Warren

BALCOMBE ROAD

B2110

Hill

34

I

Balcombe
Forest

Cowdray
Forest

Monks

33

2

Mount Pleasant
Farm

HIGH STREET

B2110

B2056

3

Greentrees
Farm

Monks
Forest

LONDON ROAD

**Balcombe
Lane**

Crawley Lane

Stoney Lane

HIGH STREET

4

Kings
Farm

32

Brantridge
Forest

Highley
Manor

Yewtree
Farm

5

HIGH STREET

B2110

Lodgelands

Crawley Lane

Kelsey
House

Brantridge Forest
m

Redbridge
Lane

6

Handcross Road

LONDON ROAD

31

New England

Handcross Road

Balcombe
House

7

Brantridge Lane

Great Cooper's
Corner Farm

Westup Road

Balcombe CE
Primary
School

PO

Balcombe

Bramble Hill

Haywards Heath

Surgery

Stockcroft

Betts Orch

Surg

Troymede

Victoria Road

the Coombers

Nrs

Bar Mead

Brantridge Park

8

Westup
Farm

Rocks Lane

Balcombe
Station

Newlands

Jobes

Oldlands

Deanland Rd

Avenue

Glebe View

Stumblemead

Foxwells

Road

30

Ditton Place
School

A   **B**   **C**   **D**   **E**   **F**

5 29   30   31

1 grid square represents 500 metres

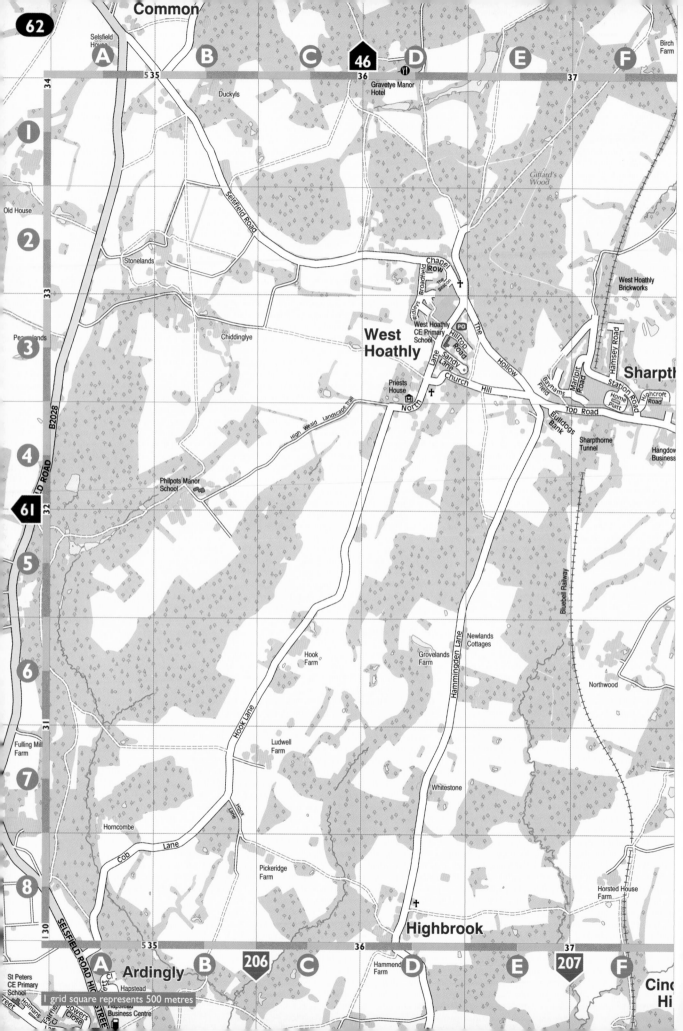

G H J **47** K L M

38 39 40 34

Neylands Farm

I

Mayes

Blackland Farm

Grinstead Lane

East Sussex County
West Sussex County

Plaw Wood

Legsheath Farm

2

New Coombe Farm

Legsheath Lane

33

3

horne

Plawhatch Hall

Coldharbour Manor

Priory Road

Tyes Cross

P

P

Top Road

Plaw Hatch Lane

Hindleap Lane

4

Courtlands

Horsted Lane

n Mead Park

64

32

Chilling Street

Horncastle Wood

Cripps Manor

5

Deanlands Farm

Wickenden Farm

Hillsdow

6

31

Twyford Lodge

Restlands

Balcombe Lane

Stumblewood Common

7

Horsted Lane

Westlands

Birchgrove Lane

Hurstwood Lane

Birchgrove Lane

8

Cinder Hill

Tanyard

Ravenswood

Broadhurst Manor

Birchgrove

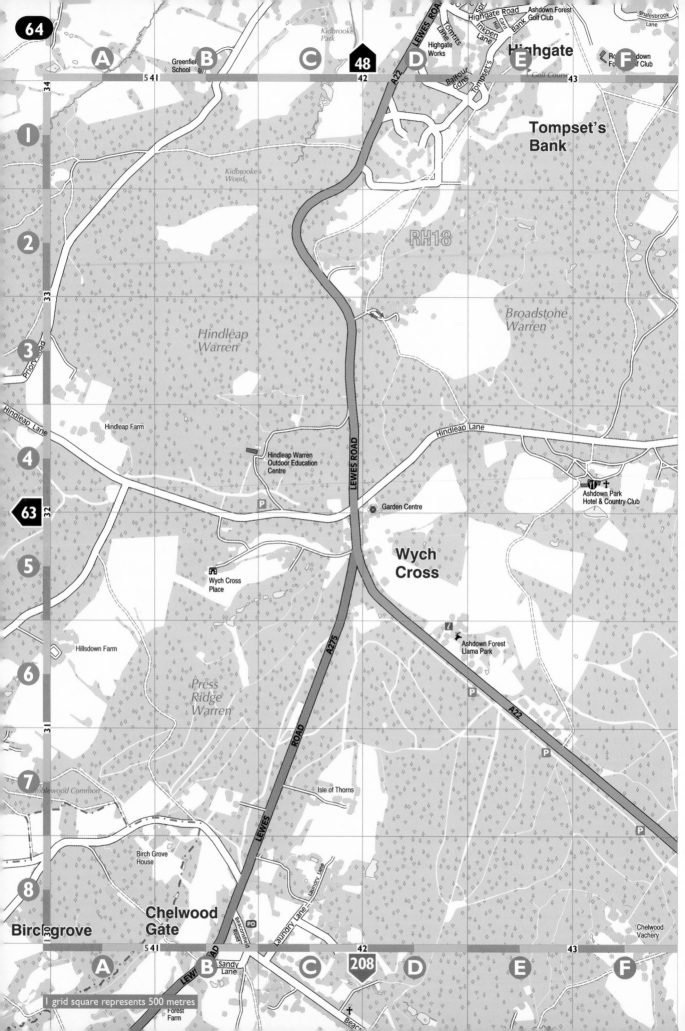

G
Golf Course
Quabrook
H
J
49
K
Coleman's Hatch
CAT STREET
B2110
L
M
Fincham Farm

1

Vanguard way

SHEPHERD'S HILL

Vanguard Way

Hollyhill

2

Broadstone Farm

The Ridge

3

PH

P   P

Sandy Lane

Vanguard Way

Newbridge

Colemans Hatch Road

Kidd's Hill

New Lodge Farm

4

Vanguard Way

66

5

P

6

Ashdown Forest

31

7

Pippingford Park

Raven Wood

8

130

G   P   208
H
J
K   209
L
M

44
45
46

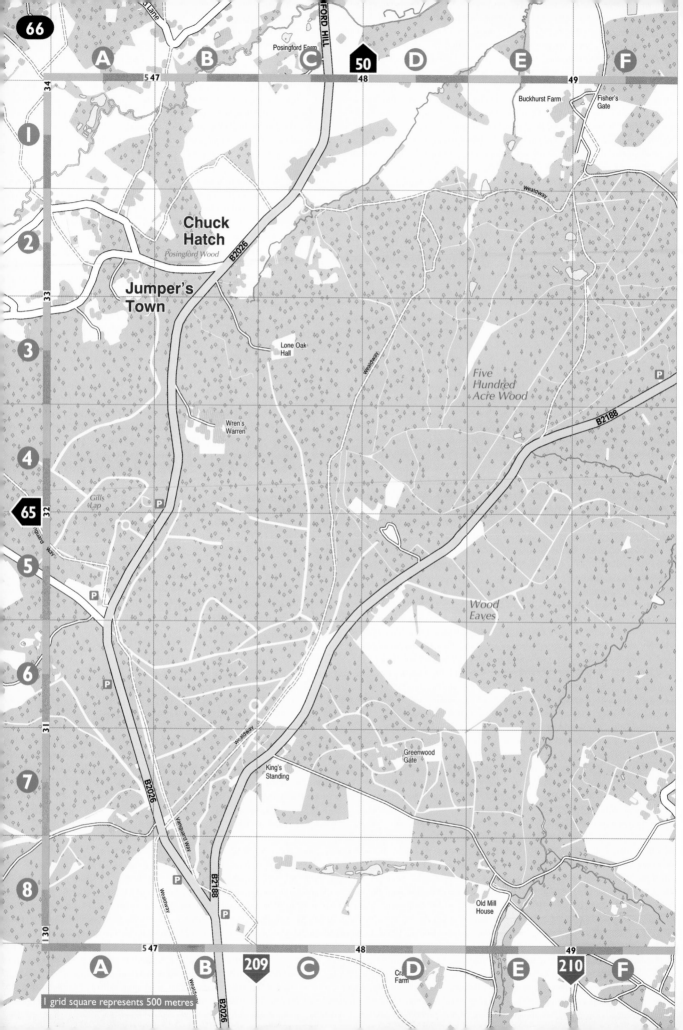

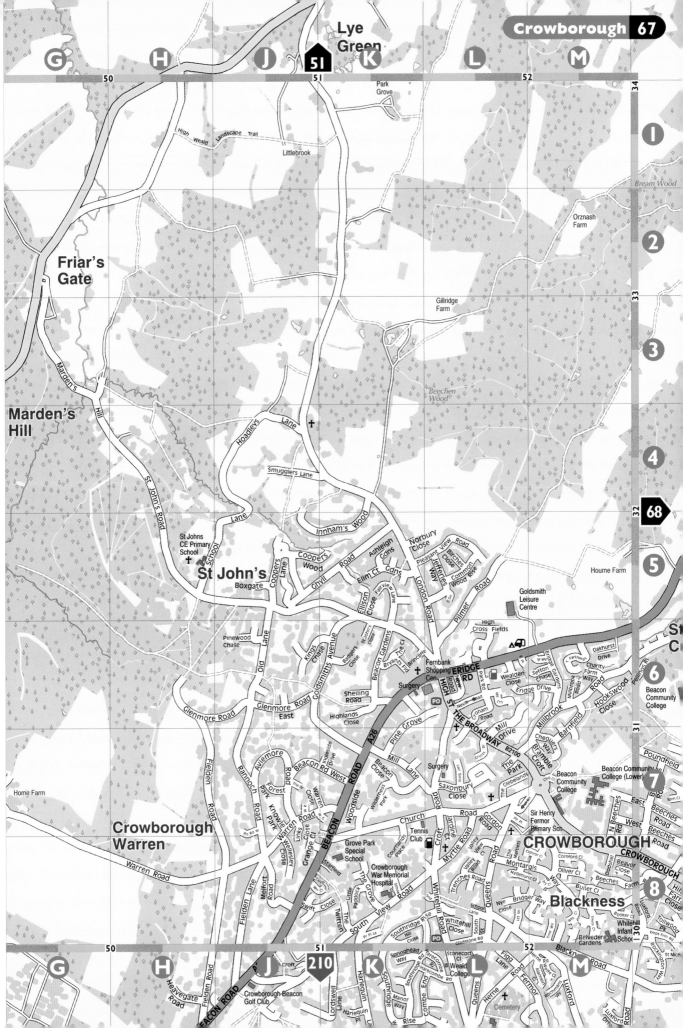

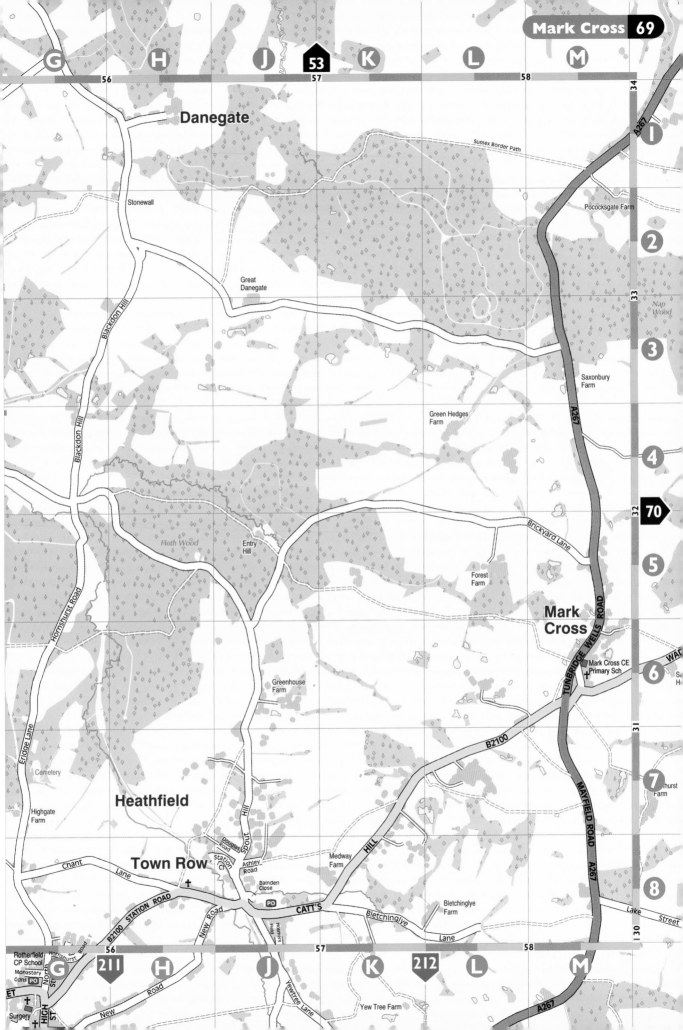

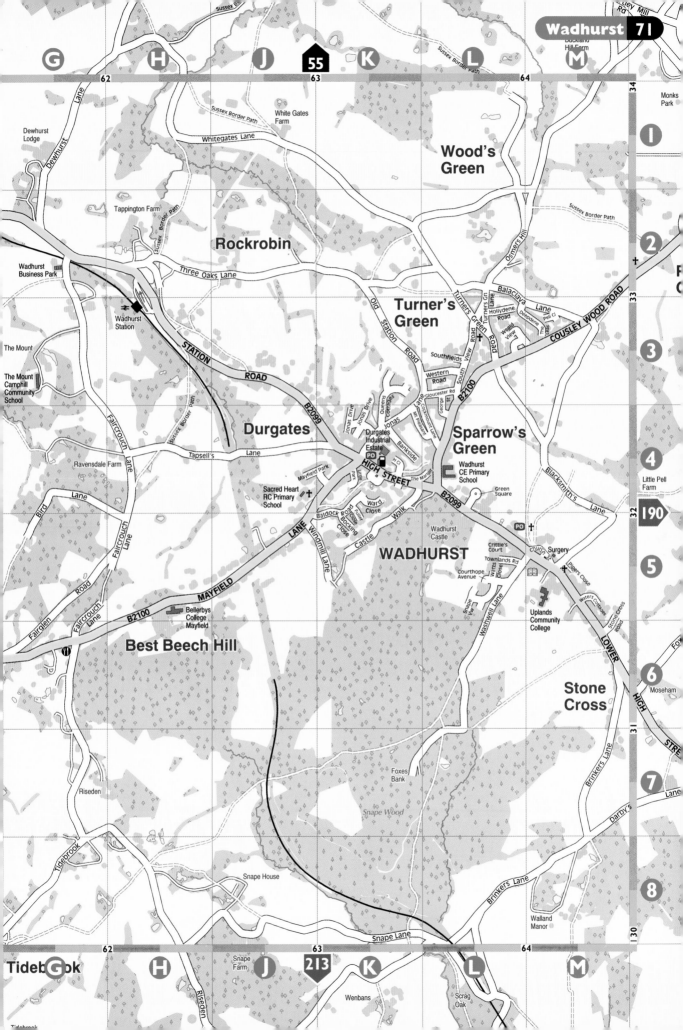

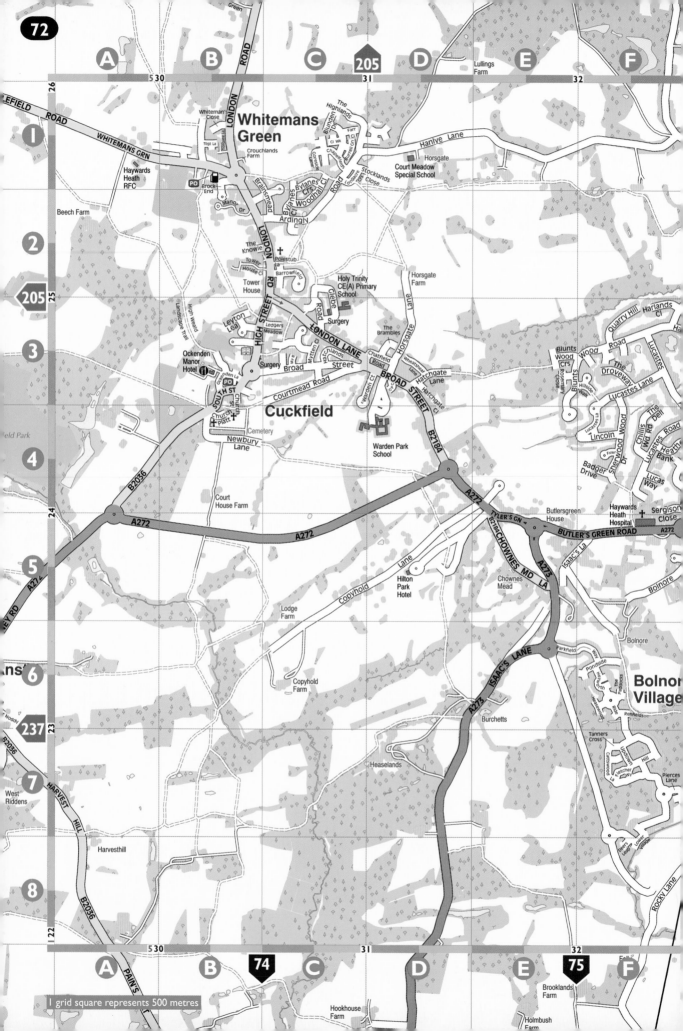

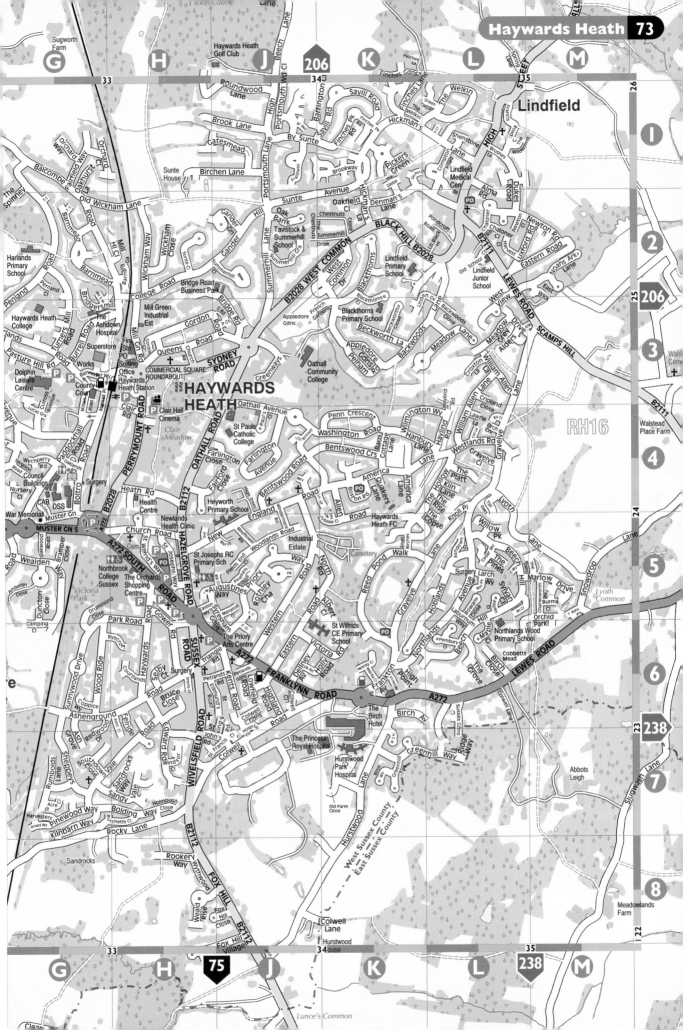

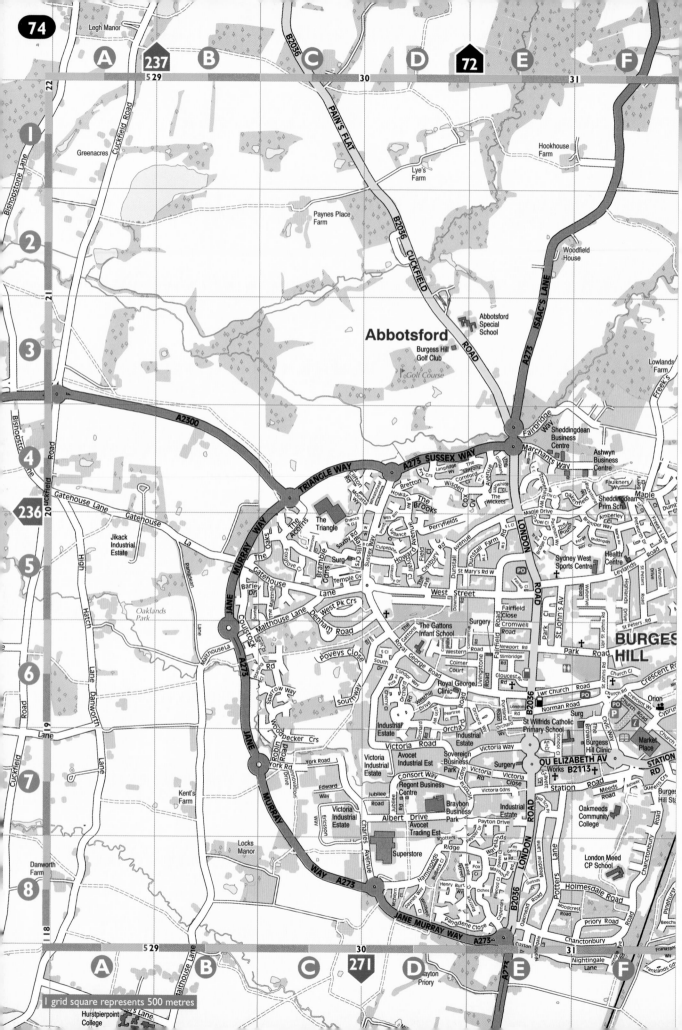

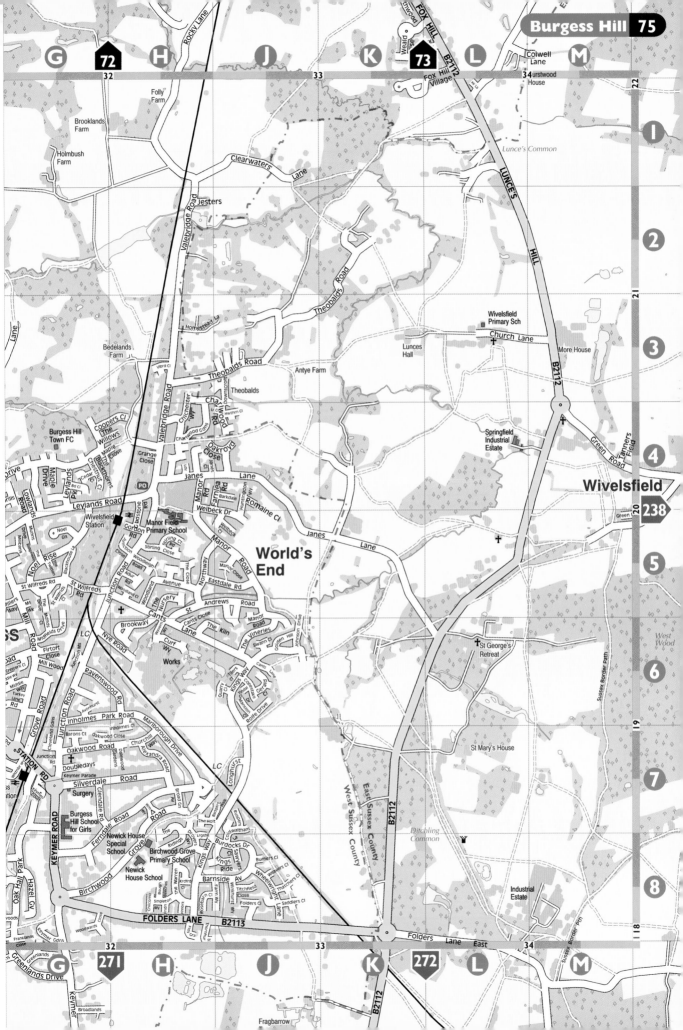

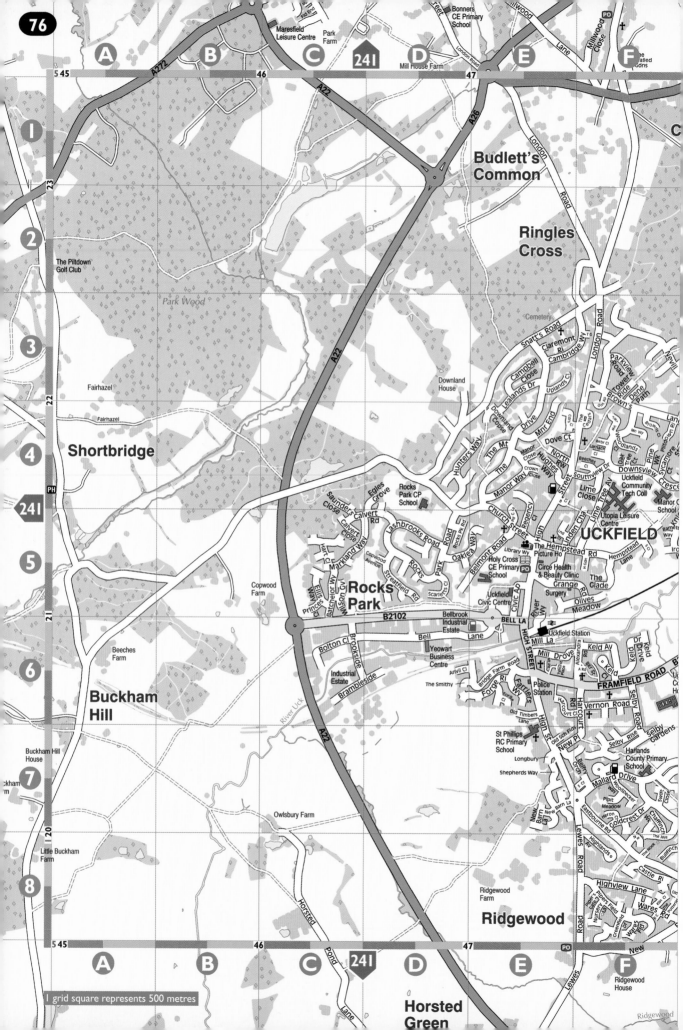

A A272 B 241 D E F

5 45 46 47

23

I

2

The Piltdown
Golf Club

Budlett's
Common

Ringles
Cross

Park Wood

Cemetery

Snatt's Road

3

22

Fairhazel

Downland
House

Claremont
Rd

Campbell
Close

Cambridge Wy

London Road

Parkview
Road

Tower
Ride

Dene

Brown's

Lealands Dr

Uplands

The Cedars

Woodlands

Nevill

4

Shortbridge

Fairhazel

Hunters Way

The Mt

Downland
Copse

Manor
Close

North
RW

Manor Way

Crown
Close

Dove Ct

Hughes
Way

Larch

Oak
Tree

Beeches

Pine

Sycamore

Downsview
Cresce

Uckfield
Community
Tech Coll

Manor

School

PH

241

Rocks Park CP
School

Egles
Grove

Saunders
Close

Calvert
Rd

Lashbrooks Road

Rocks Pk Rd

Church Street

Regency

High Street

Lime
Close

Lime Tree Av

Linden Cnr

UCKFIELD

Utopia Leisure
Centre

5

21

Copwood
Farm

Hart La

Markland Wy

Wilson Dr

Batchelor Wy

Ellis
Way

Princes

Copwood
Avenue

Streatfield
Rd

Rocks

Park
Road

Oaklea Wy

Scarletts Cl

Belmont Road

Holy Cross
CE Primary
School

Library Wy

The Hempstead
Picture Ho

Circe Health
& Beauty Clinic
Surgery

Grange

Olives
Meadow

Hempstead
Rd

Hempstead
Lane

The
Clade

6

Beeches
Farm

Rocks
Park

B2102

Uckfield
Civic Centre

CIVIC A D

River
Wy

Bellbrook
Industrial
Estate

BELL LA

Mill La

Uckfield Station

Mill Drive

Alexandra

Keld
Dr

Keld
Drive

Keld
Av

FRAMFIELD ROAD

Selby
Road

Buckham
Hill

Bolton Cl

Brookside

Brambleside

Bell
Lane

Yeowart Business
Centre

Industrial
Estate

Anvil Cl

The Smithy

Bridge
Farm Rd

Forge
Rd

Police
Station

Farmers

Vernon Road

Selby
Gardens

Buckham Hill
House

7

20

Little Buckham
Farm

ckham

Old Timbers
Lane

St Phillips
RC Primary
School

Longbury

Shepherds Way

New Pl

Old Sch Flds

High St

New Pl

Selby Rise

Harlands
County Primary
School

Mallard Drive

Woodpecker
Way

Pipit
Meadow

Highlands

Goldcrest Dr

Channich

Swift

8

Owlsbury Farm

Horsted
Lane

Ridgewood
Farm

Lewes
Road

New
Barn

Earlbourne Rd

Greenfields

New

Highview Lane

Pipers Field

Highview

Castle Ri

Wares Rd

Ridgewood

5 45 46 241 47 New

A B C 241 D E F

Horsted
Green

Ridgewood
House

Ridgewoo

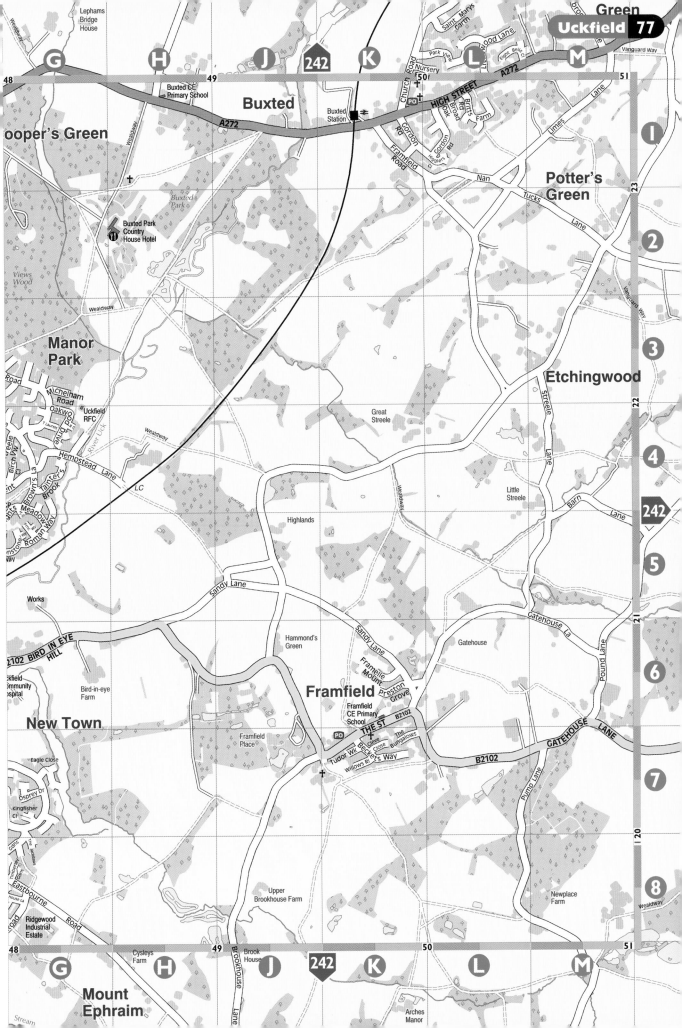

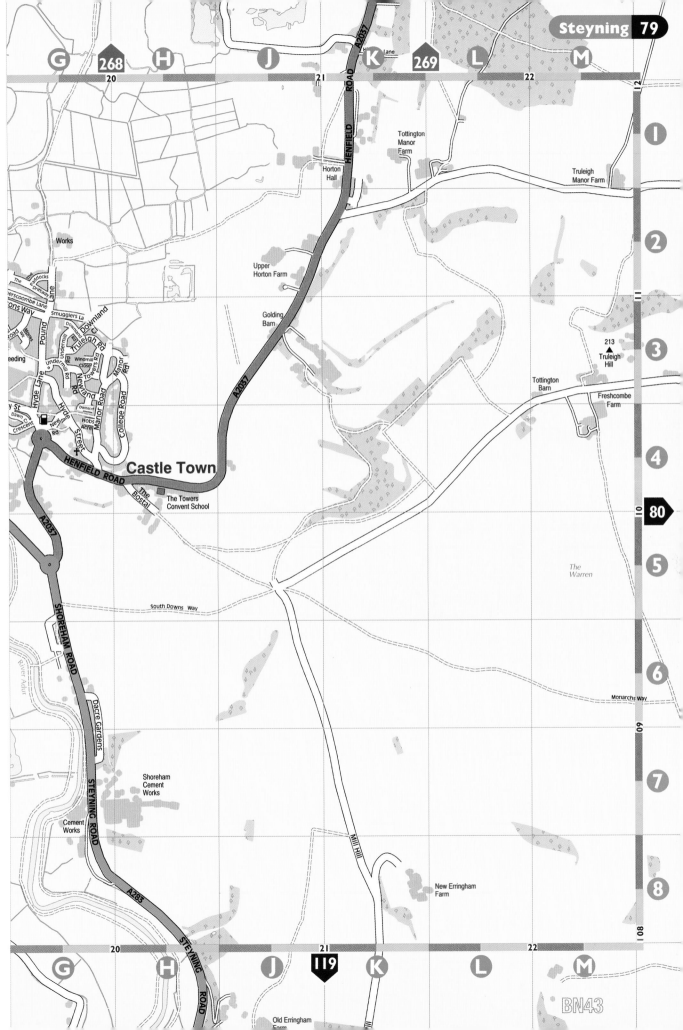

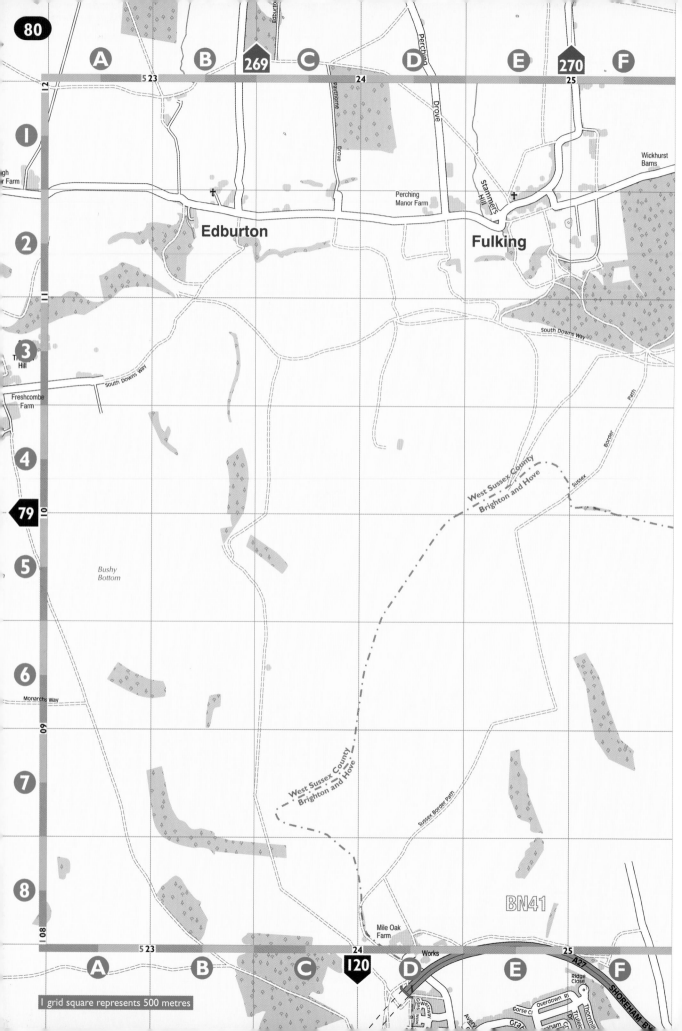

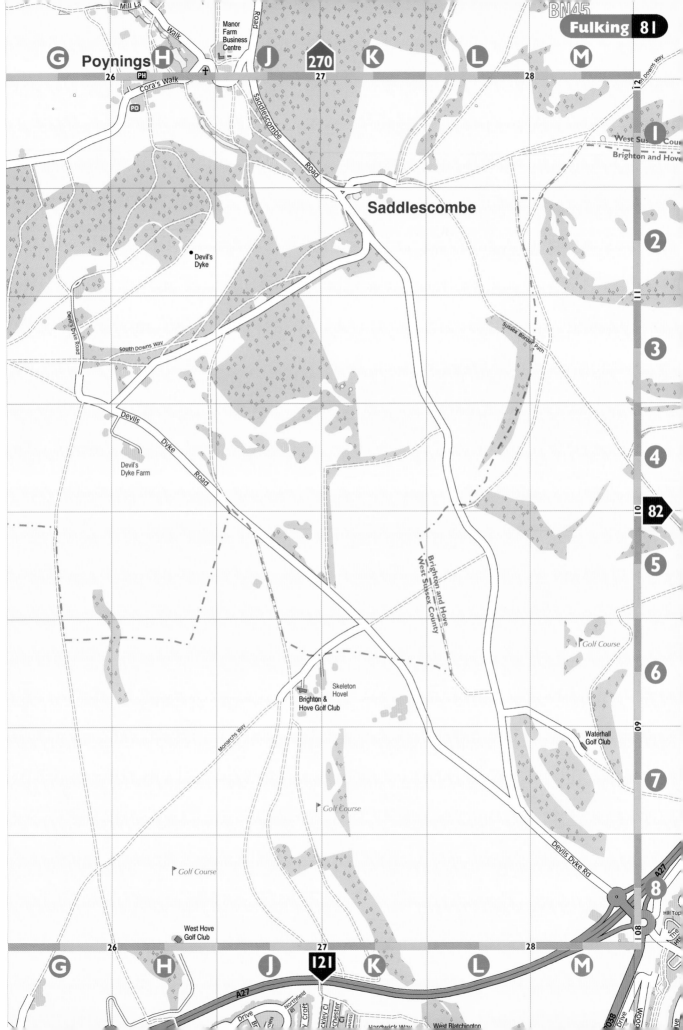

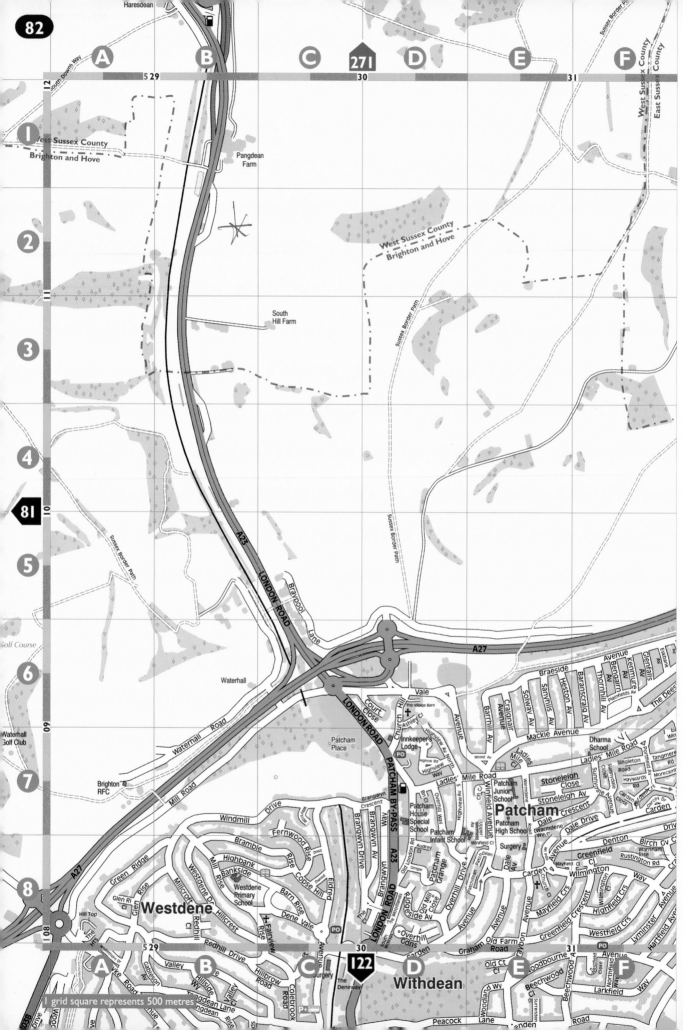

G 271 H J K 272 L M
32 33 34 12

1

2

Stanmer Down

3

East Sussex County
Brighton and Hove

4

84

East Sussex County
Brighton & Hove

Stanmer Park

Stanmer

5

University of Sussex

6

Gardner Arts Centre Cinema

University of Sussex Sports Centre

University of Sussex

7

LEWES R

8

University of Brighton

University of Brighton

Lower Standean

Heathy Brow

High Park Farm

New Barn

Hollingbury Industrial Estate

Superstore

Crowhurst Road

Hollingbury Industrial Estate

Ditchling Road

Coldean Lane

Mackie Avenue

Carden Avenue

BN1

Eastwick Cl

Saunders Hill

Beatty Av

Kenwards

Coldean Primary School

A27

Great Wood

Crawley Road

Haig Av

Beatty Av

Hawkhurst Av

Walton Road

Coldean Lane

Selham Drive

Surgery

PO

Framfield Close

Chalkton Bdge

Knepp Cl

Jersey Cl

Nanson Rd

Wyford Rd

Ingham Dr

Rushlake Road

Coldean Lane

Monk Cl

Forest Rd

A27

Wolseley Road

Ashburnham Dr

The Byway

Reeves Hill

Walton Bank

Middleton

Arl Cl

Ardingly Vw

Park Road

Coldean

The Meads

Roundway

Highfields

Park Close

Park Road

Council Building

Avenue

County Oak Av

Carden Hill

Clovers End

Buttercup Wk

Petworth Road

Midhurst Rd

Cruelwood Cl

Orchid Vw

Cuckmere Way

Elsted

Bramble Way

Crescent

Ditchling Crescent

Fernhurst Crs

Keymer Rd

Hurst Hl

Rotherfield Crescent

Cuckmere

Way

Hollingbury

LEWES ROAD

A270

University of Brighton

Falmer High School

Eggington Close

Lucraft Road

Eggington Road

Ashurst Road

Barcombe Rd

Newick Road

Ringmer Rd

PO

Chailey Road

Newick Road

Stonecross Rd

Bolney Rd

Hall

Frister Way

Fairway Trading Estate Superstore

Hollingbury Castle

Hollingbury Park Golf Club

G 32 H J 33 123 Moulsecoomb K Newick L M 34

East

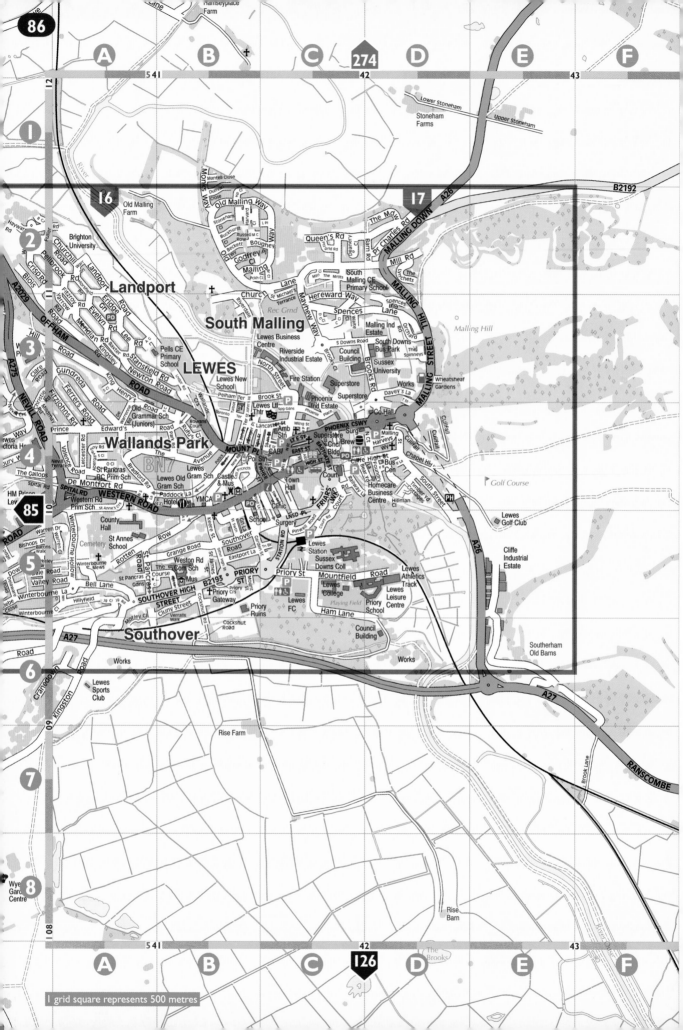

Rushy Green

Ashton Green

Ringmer CP School

Ringmer FC

Gote Farm

Oldhouse Farm

Wakelands

Little Heaven

New Road

Week Lane

Glyndebourne

Glyndebourne Opera House

Saxon Down

Glyndebourne Farm

Lacys

88

Lacys Hill

Glynde Place

Glynde

Mount Caburn

National Nature Reserve

Ranscombe Farm

HILL

Ranscombe Lane

PO

Glynde Reach

Glynde Station

LC

A27

127

Preston Home

Beddingham

Middleham

274

275

44 Middleham

Greenacres Dr

Middleham Cl

Sadlers

Harvard Rd

Gote Lane

Mill Gdns

Mill Md

Mill Road

Shepherd

Harris

Neaves Lane

Moor Lane

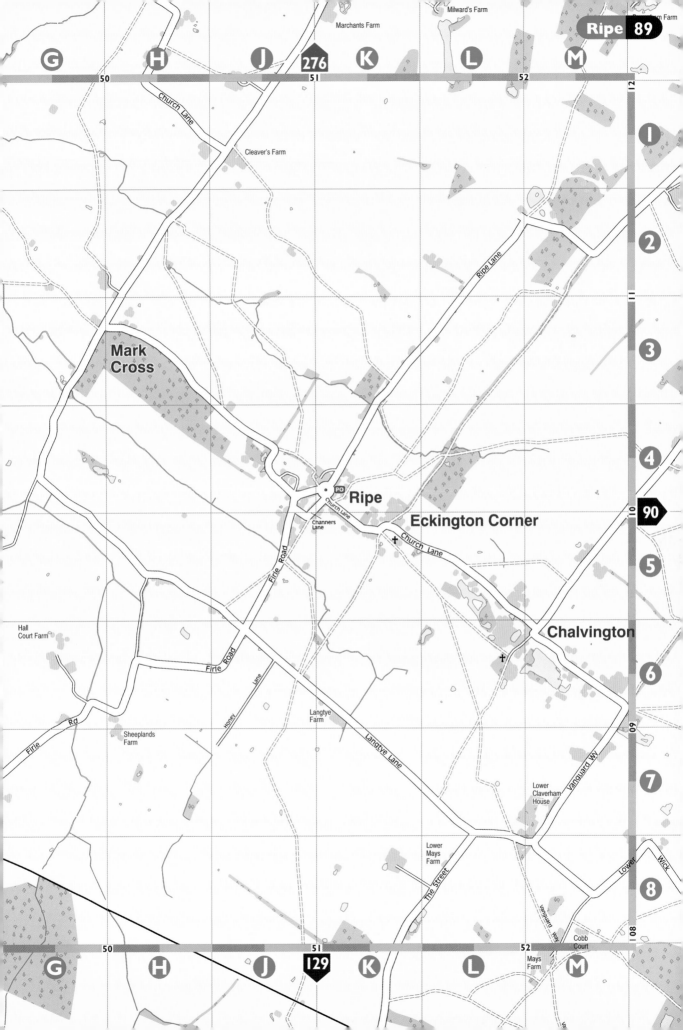

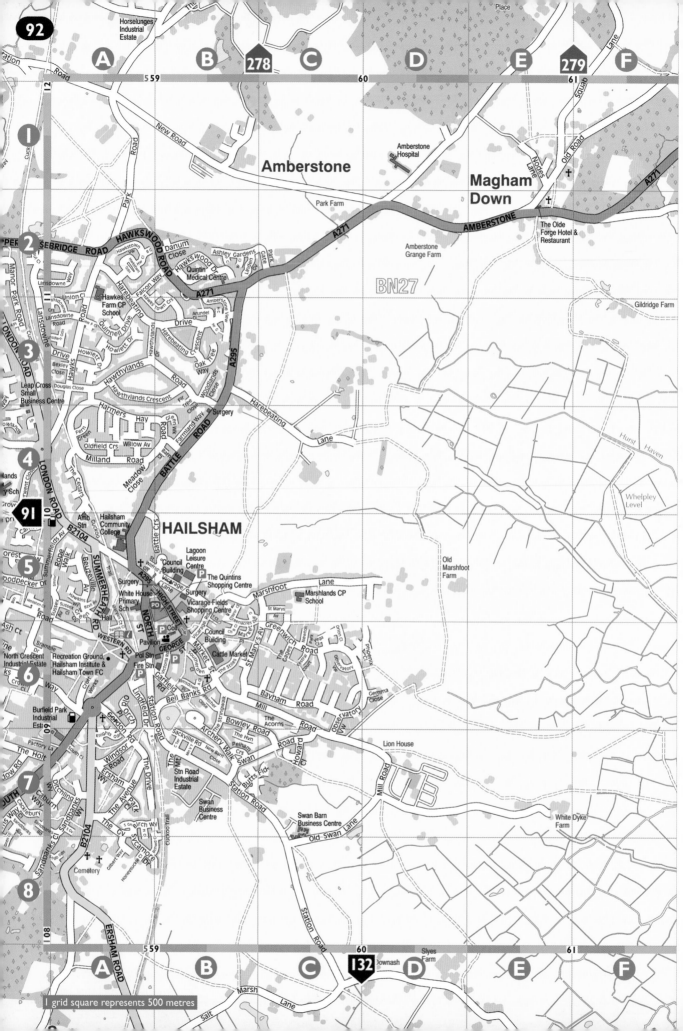

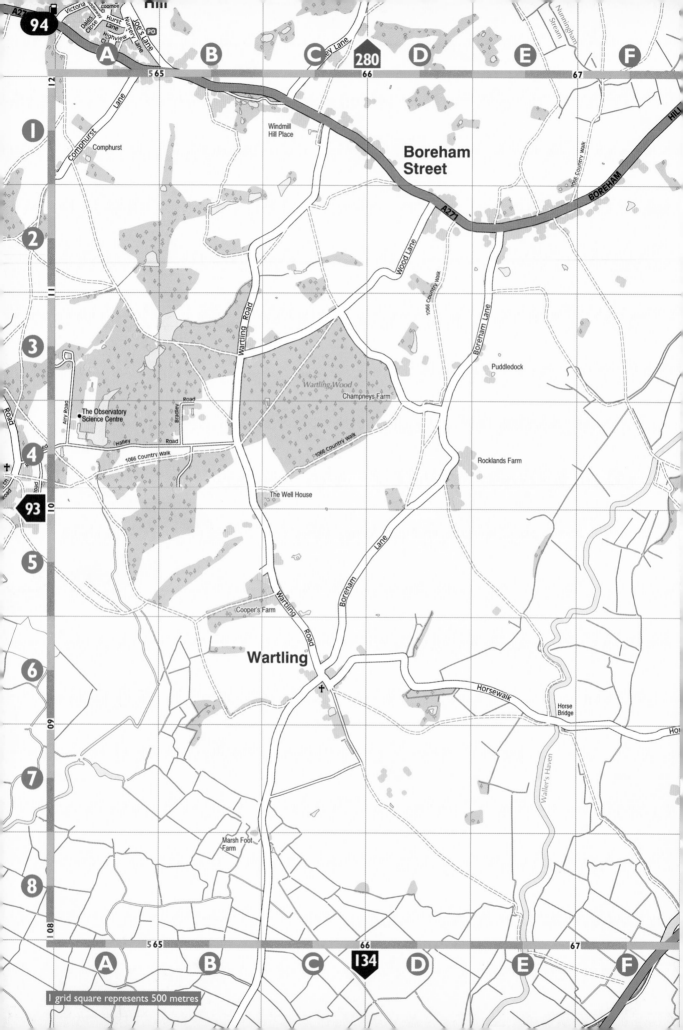

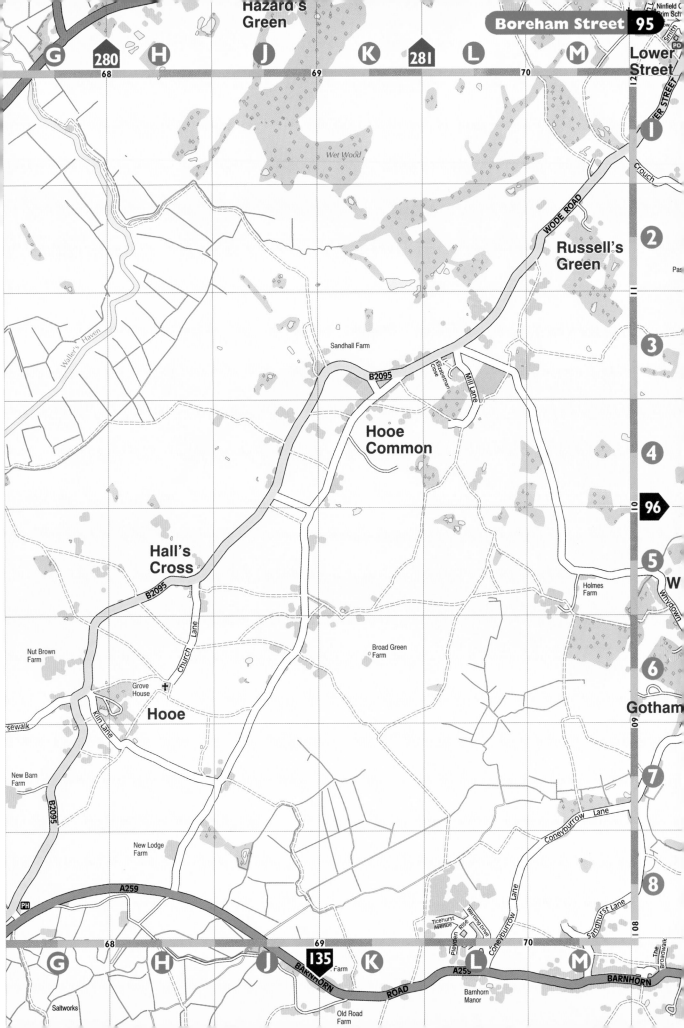

Lower Street

Ninfield CE Prim Sch
Stocks Meadow

281

Sprays Wood

282

New Barn Farm

Ingram's House

Potmans Place

Potman's Lane

Hollis Street Farm

Messens Farm

ROAD

Pashley Farm

BEXHILL

Thorne Farm

Lunsford's Cross

Crouch Lane

LOWER STREET

A269

95

The Thorne

NINFIELD ROAD

Thorne Crs

Freezeland Lane

Freezeland Farm

A269

High Woods

Bexhill Cemetery

The Highlands

Beacon Hill

Paton Road

Mount Idol View

Clinch Green Avenue

The Highlands

Jubilee Road

Whydown

Holmes Farm

Whydown Road

The Ridings

Jubilee Road

Works

Turkey Road

Greenways

Bexhill College

Glenleigh Park

Gotham

Sandhurst Lane

Highwoods Golf Club

Highwoods Avenue

Pembury

Holly Close

Peartree Lane

TN39

Golf Course

Ellerslie Lane

Gunter's

Bidwell Avenue

Hillcrest Av

Pevensey

Wealden Way

Woodstock Road

Cowdray Park Road

Frayatts Way

Kingswood Avenue

The Fairway

Glenleigh Avenue

Glenleigh Park Road

Charters Ancaster College

Oakfield Way

Lavant Close

Berwick Close

Cowdray Close

Eastergate

Broad View

Ward Way

Beatrice Walk

Magpie Cl

Fontwell Avenue

Frant Close

The Byeway

Summer Hill

Piemont

Broadoak Lane

Kenton Close

Gorseway

Lane

Lovebird Close

Knebworth Road

Warwick Road

Little Common

Chestnut Walk

Green Lane

Foxhill

Deerswood Close

Squirrel Cl

Byfields Croft

Bushy Croft

Courthope Drive

Riders Bolt

Sussex Close

Bexhill Down

Sandhurst Lane

Willow Drive

Sycamore Close

Oaklands Road

LITTLE COMMON ROAD

A259

A259

LITTLE COMMON R

136

Barnhorn Road

The Broadway

Prowting Mead

Barnhorne Manor

Hillborough

Little Common Primary School

Grenada Close

Collington Grove

Sutherland Crs

White Hill Drive

Alexander Drive

Winston Drive

Cranston Avenue

Sutherland Avenue

SUTHERLAND AV

Birk Dale

Drayton Rise

The Mead

Copse Road

Westaway Drive

1 grid square represents 500 metres

Mallydams
Wood

86   Battery   Road   87   88

Fairlight Cove

PO

Farley Way

Wates

Broad

Primrose Hill

Briar Close

Lane

Coastguard   Hill

Fairlight

Warren

The Close

Lane

New

Road

Road

Meadow Way

Knole Road

Woodland Way

Commanders Walk

Corsethorn Way

Fyrsway

Channel

Fire Hills

Saxon Shore Way

Lane

Lower

The Avenue

Blackthorn Way

Smugglers Way

Shepherds Way

Bramble Way

Stock Dale

heather Way

Rockmead Road

Cliff Way

Wates

Hastings
Country
Park

Covehurst
Bay

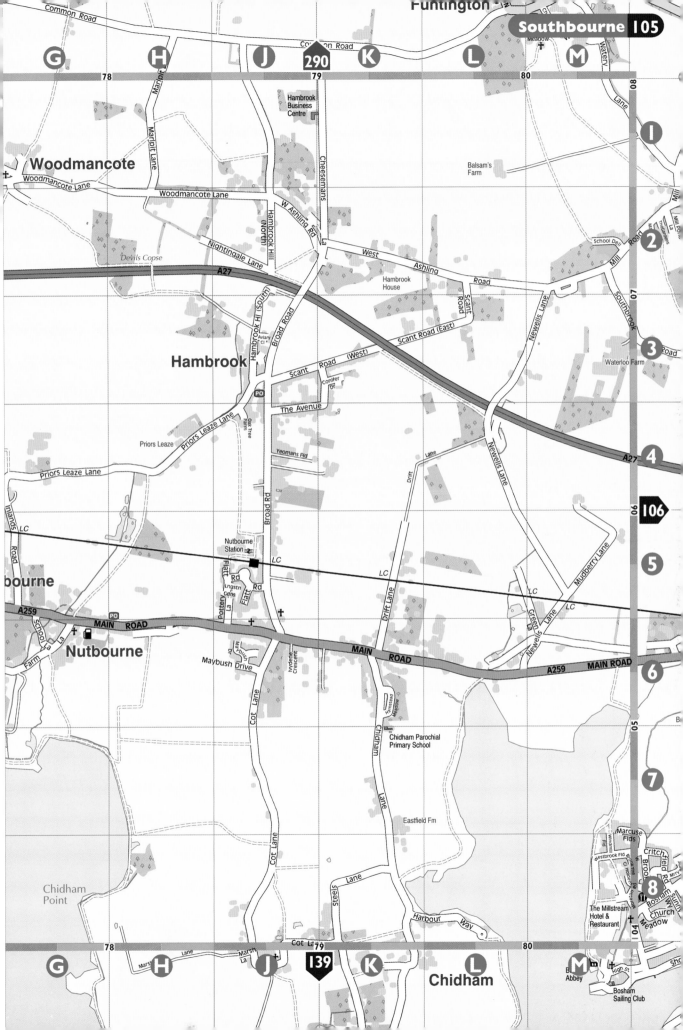

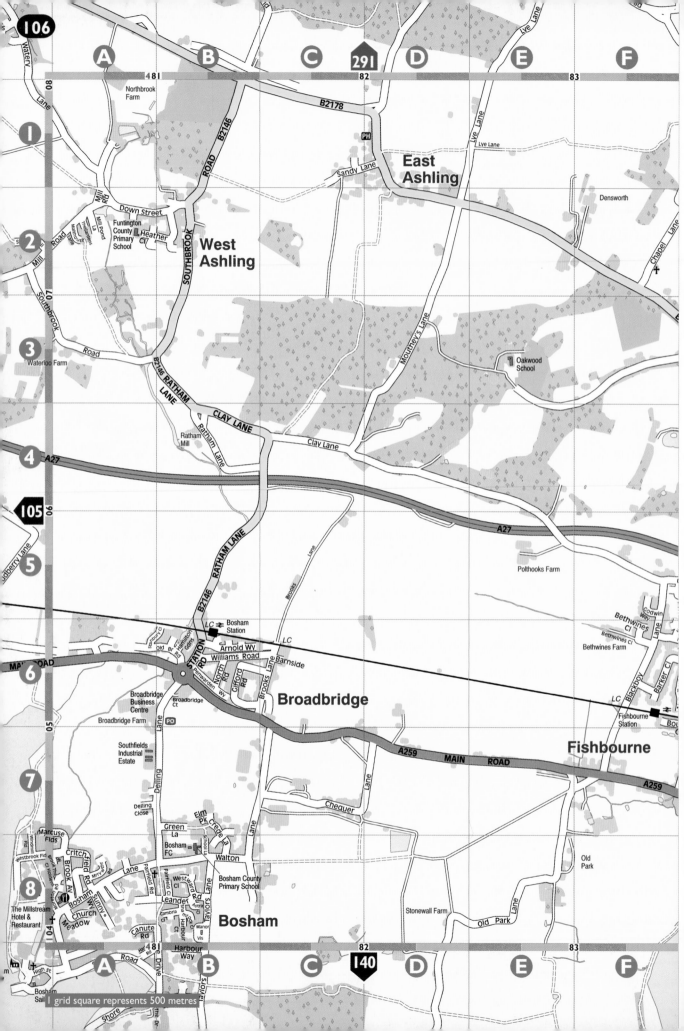

106

Watery Lane

481 80

A

B2146 ROAD

B

B2178

C

291
82

PH

Sandy Lane

East Ashling

D

Lye Lane

Lye Lane

E

83

F

Densworth

Chapel Lane

1

Northbrook Farm

2

Mill RD
La Manhouse
Thatchers
Mill Pond

Road
Marsh Dale

Down Street

SOUTHBROOK

Heather Cl

Funtington County Primary School

West Ashling

3

Waterloo Farm

Southbrook Road

07

Road

B2146 RATHAM LANE

Mouthey's Lane

Oakwood School

4

A27

Ratham Mill

Ratham Lane

CLAY LANE

Clay Lane

Clay Lane

A27

105
06

Mudberry Lane

5

RATHAM LANE

B2146

Brooks Lane

Lane

Polthooks Farm

6

MAIN ROAD

Saxbury Cl
Old Br Rd

Hamilton Gdns

STATION RD

LC

Arnold Wy

Williams Road

Barnside

North Rd

Clifford Rd

Penwarden Wy

Brooks Lane

LC

Bosham Station

Broadbridge

Bethwines Cl
Godwin Way

Bethwines Cl

Bethwines Farm

Blackboy Lane

Barker Cl

LC

Fishbourne Station

Bou

05

Broadbridge Business Centre

Broadbridge Ct

Broadbridge Farm

PO

Delling Lane

Delling Close

Southfields Industrial Estate

A259 MAIN ROAD

Fishbourne

A259

7

Marcuse Flds

Windmill Fld

Westbrook Fld

Critchfield Rd

Brook Av

Bosham Wy

Sunny Wy

Green La

Bosham FC

Elm Pk

Creda La

Lane

Chequer

Lane

Old Park

8

The Millstream Hotel & Restaurant

Church Meadow

Canute Rd

Fairfield Rd
Westward Cl
Leander Cl
Cambria Cl
Harbour Vis
Manor Vis

Walton

Bosham County Primary School

Bosham

Stonewall Farm

Old Park Lane

Old Park

Bosham Sail

A

481

Shore Road

High St

Harbour Way

Harbour Drive

B

140
82

C

D

E

83

F

1 grid square represents 500 metres

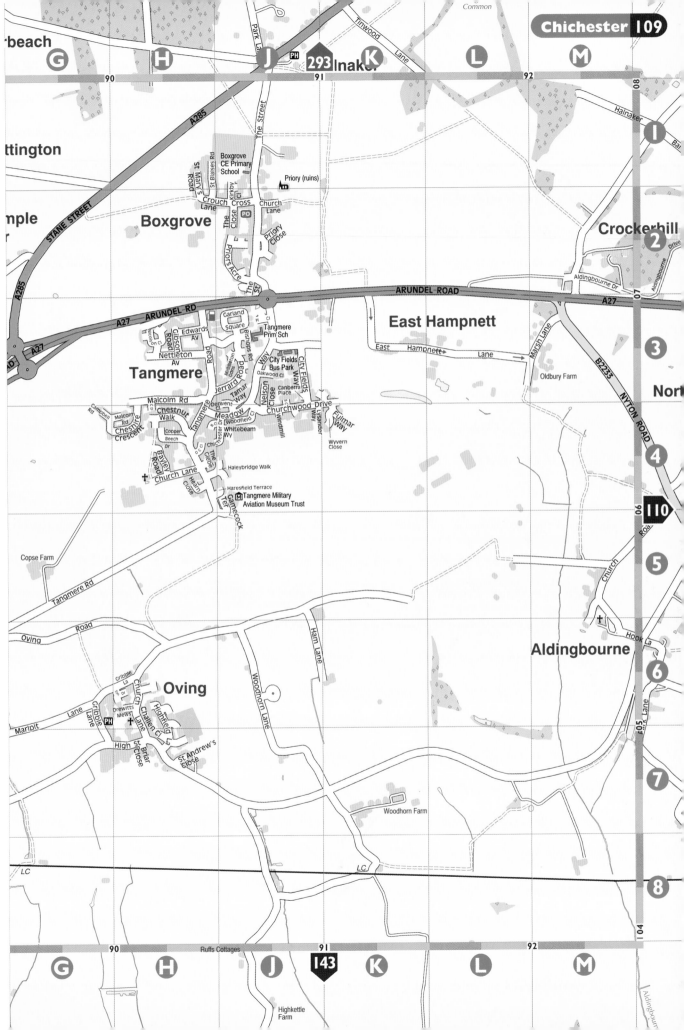

G H J **293** Jnaker K L M I

Common

Tinwood Lane

Park La

The Street

PH

A285

STANE STREET

A285

ttington

mple

St Mary's Road

St Blaises Rd

The Kirkby

Boxgrove CE Primary School

Priory (ruins)

Boxgrove

Crouch Cross Lane

The Close

PO

Church Lane

Priory Close

Priors Acre

The St

Crockerhill

2

Aldingbourne Dr

Aldingbourne Drive

A27

ARUNDEL RD

ARUNDEL ROAD

A27

Nicholson C

Gibson Road

Edwards Av

Nettleton Av

Garland Square

Bishops Rd

Tangmere Prim Sch

Tangmere

Middleton Gdns

Gerrard Rd

Tamar Way

Road

Nelson Way

City Fields Way

Jason

City Fields Bus Park

Oakwood Cl

Canberra Place

East Hampnett

East   Hampnett   Lane

Marsh Lane

Oldbury Farm

NYTON ROAD

B2233

Nort

3

Malcolm Rd

Campbell Rd

Malcolm Rd

Chesnut Crescent

Chestnut Walk

Copper Beech Dr

Tangmere

Derwent

Meadow

Whitebeam Wy

Woodfield

Churchwood Drive

Windmill

Lysander Way

Fulmar Way

Wyvern Close

4

90

110

Bayley Road

Church Lane

Hearn Close

The Glebe

Haleybridge Walk

Haresfield Terrace

Ter

Gamecock

Tangmere Military Aviation Museum Trust

Copse Farm

Tangmere Road

Church Road

5

Church Road

Hook La

Aldingbourne

6

Oving Road

Gribble La

Dr

Church Lane

Gribble Lane

Marlpit Lane

Oving

Drewitts Mews

PH

Challen Cl

Highfield La

High St

Briar Close

St Andrew's Close

Woodhorn Lane

Ham Lane

Fox Lane

7

Woodhorn Farm

LC

LC

8

104

G 90 H Ruffs Cottages J **143** 91 K L M 92

Highkettle Farm

Aldingbourne

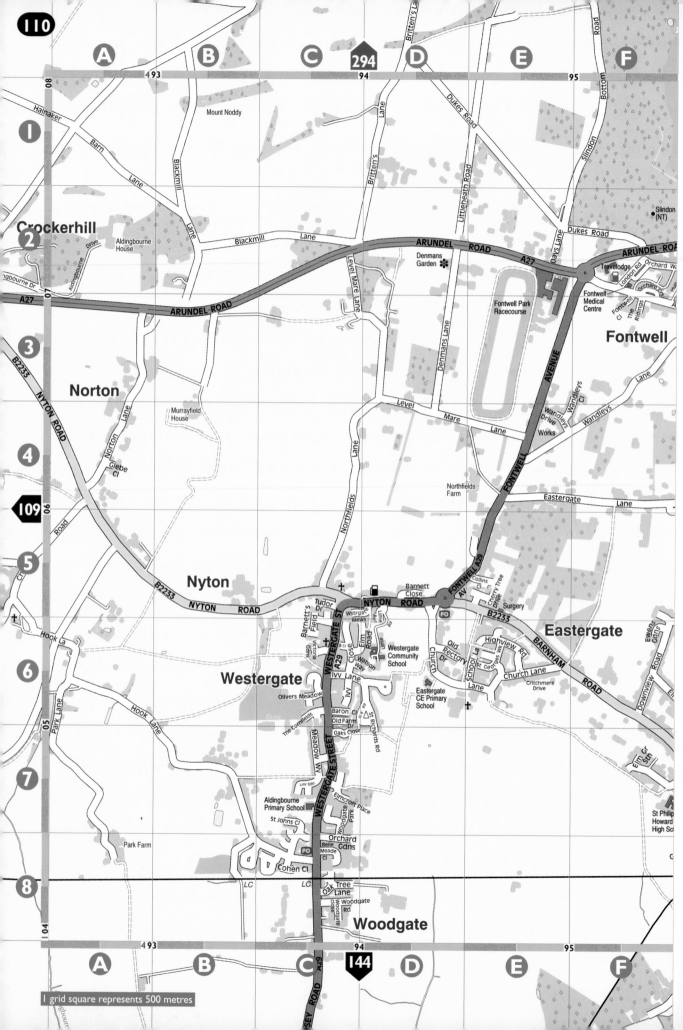

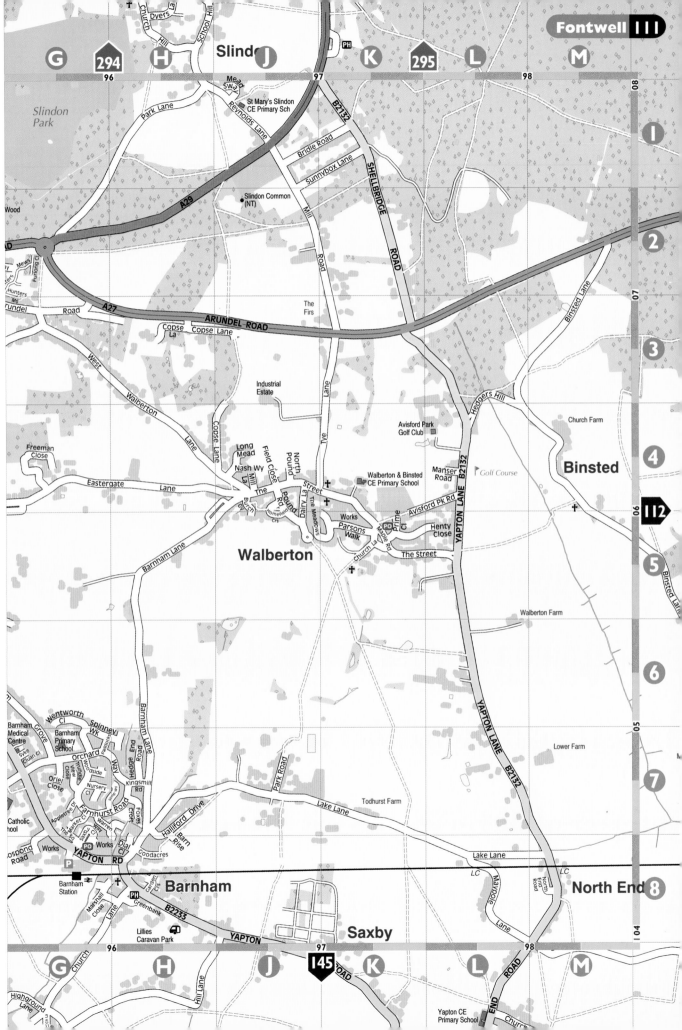

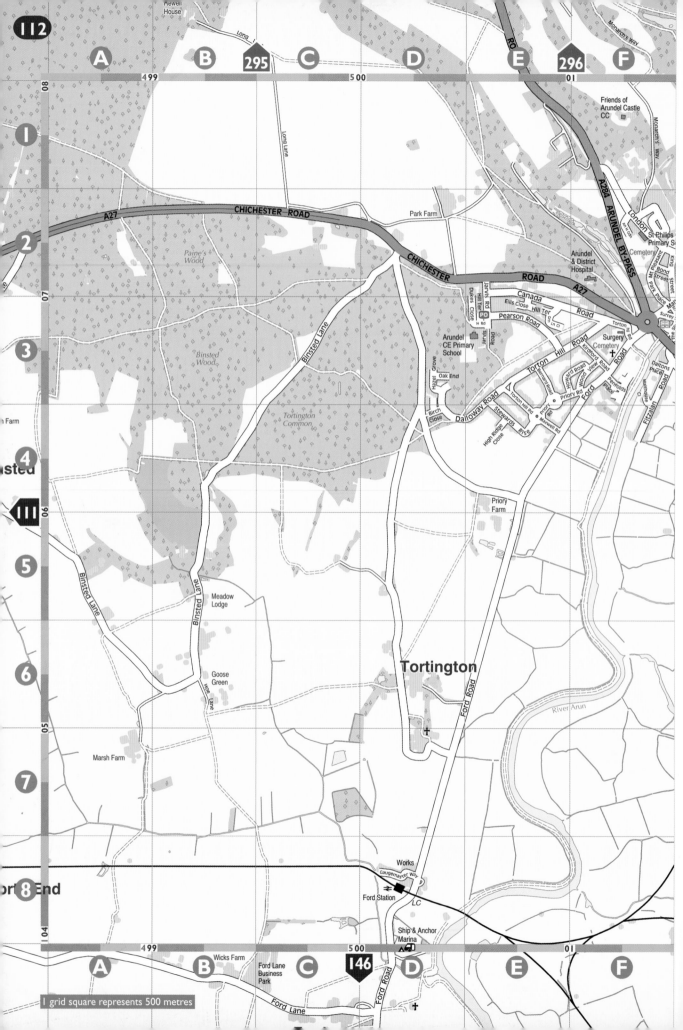

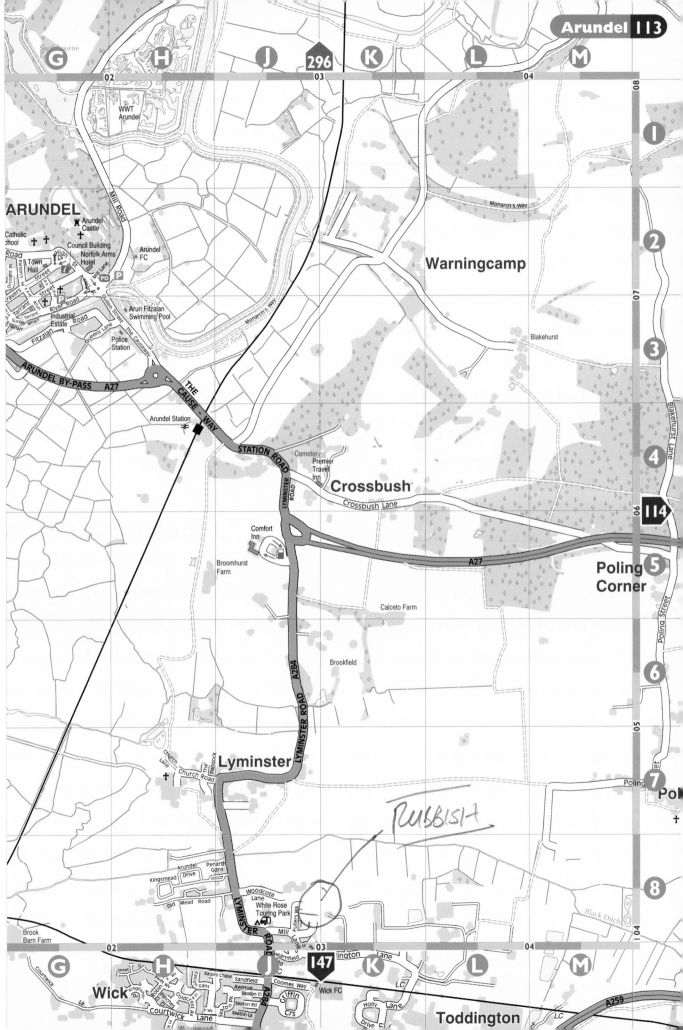

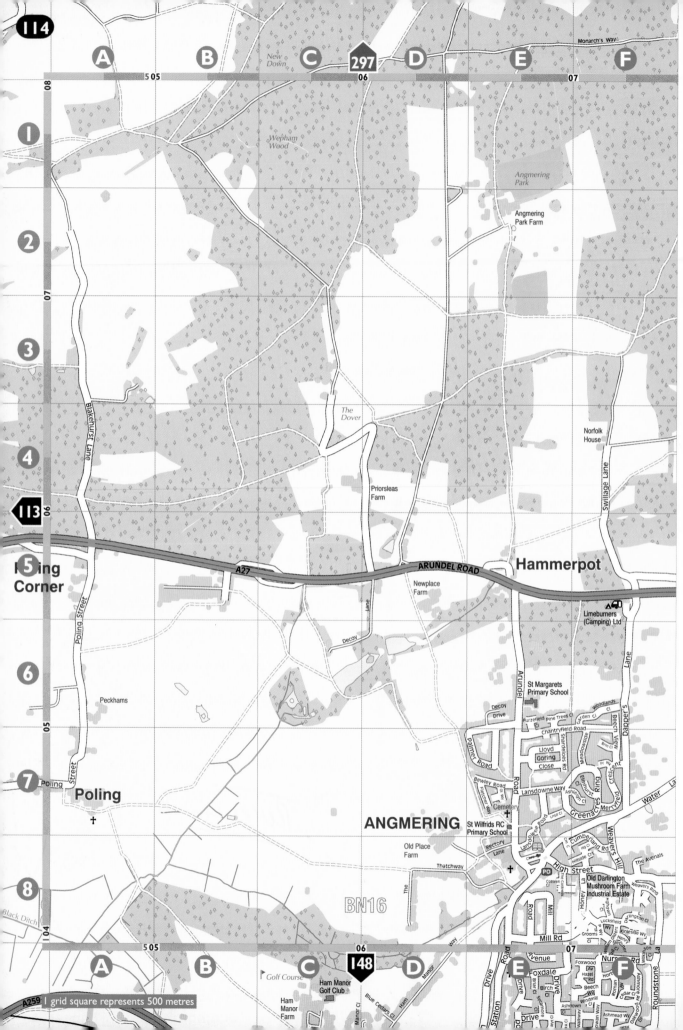

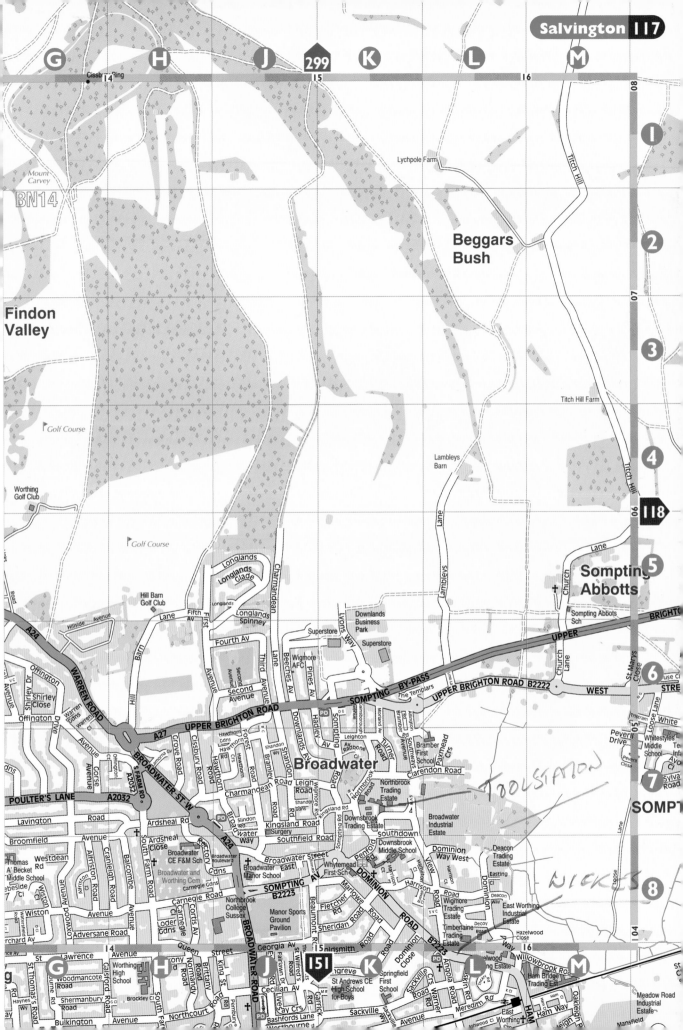

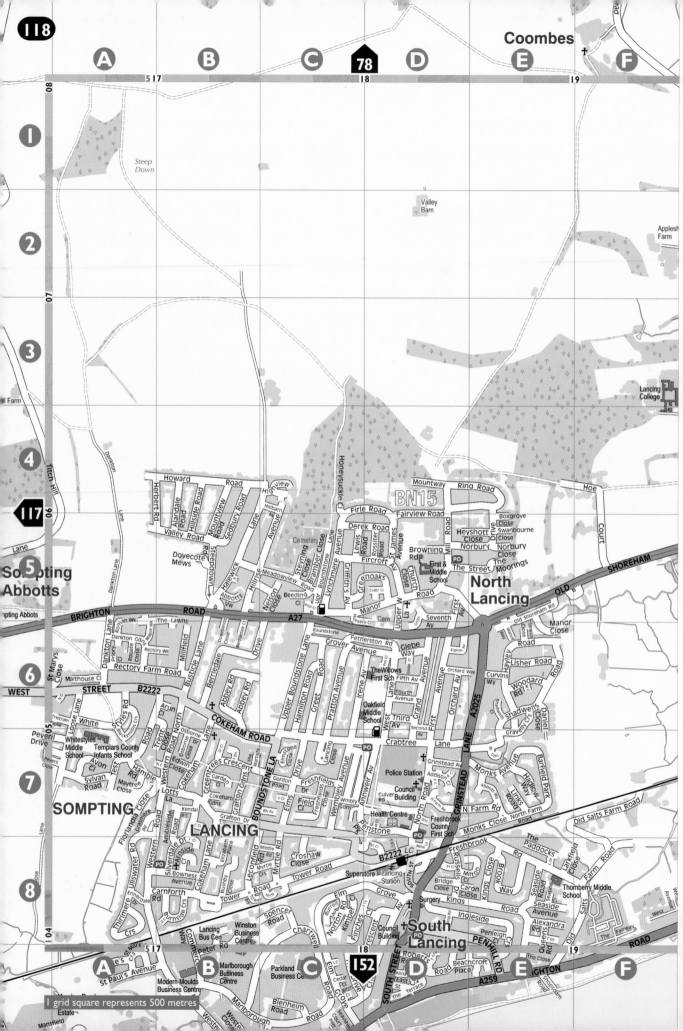

BN43

Old Shoreham

SHOREHAM-BY-PASS

Lancing College Chapel

College Farm

River Adur

A283

STEYNING ROAD

A27

Old Shoreham Road

ROAD

Coombes Road

The Drive

Almond Avenue

Cecil Pashley Way

D-Day Museum

Shoreham Airport

Nature Reserve

New Salts Farm Road

BRIGHTON ROAD

OLD SHOREHAM ROAD

A283

Shoreham First School

Riverbank Business Centre

Marlipins Museum

HIGH STREET

A259

Shoreham-by-Sea Station

Buckingham Middle School

Northbourne Medical Centre

St Nicholas & St Mary CE First & Middle Sch

St Peter's Catholic Prim Sch

Southlands Hospital

120

Kingston Buci First School

Rosslyn Road

Gordon Road

Eastern Avenue

Park Avenue

Crown Road

Superstore

Cyril Richings Business Centre

Council Building

Ham Business Centre

Riverside Business Centre

Shoreham Beach First School

The Marlinspike

Emerald Quay

Anchor Cl

Harbour Way

SHOREHAM-BY-SEA

DCWELM

Shore Beach

Old Fort Road

West Beach Road

A259

Kings Crs

Kings Walk

Woodards View

Mardyke

Beach Green

Beach Road

Havenside

Ferry Rd

River Rd

Riverside Road

Cheal Cl

The Meadway

E Meadway

Lower Beach Road

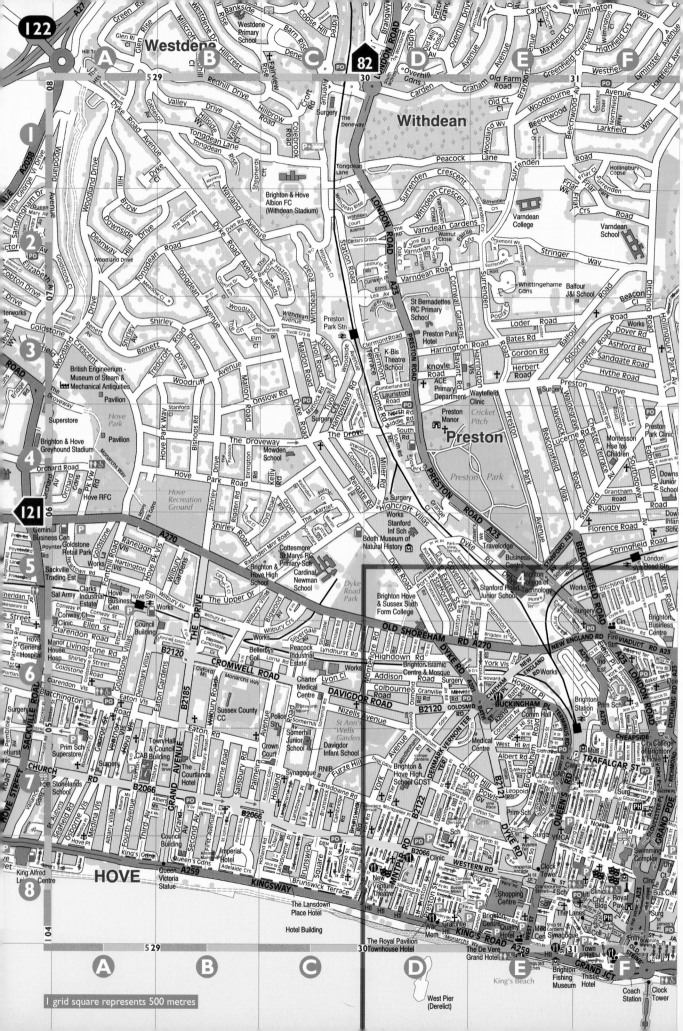

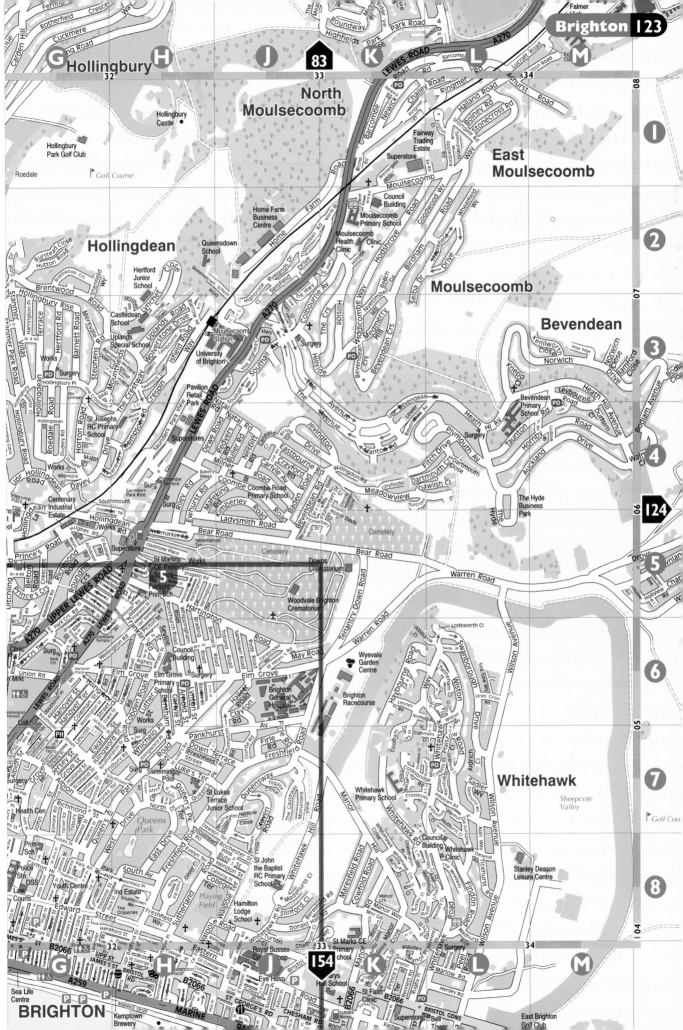

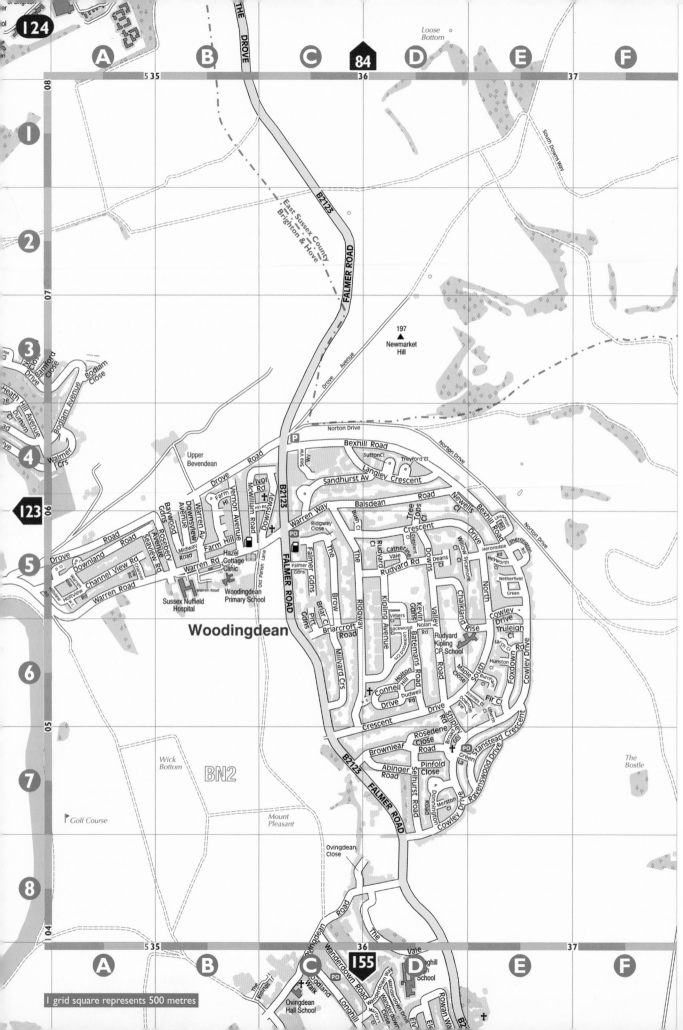

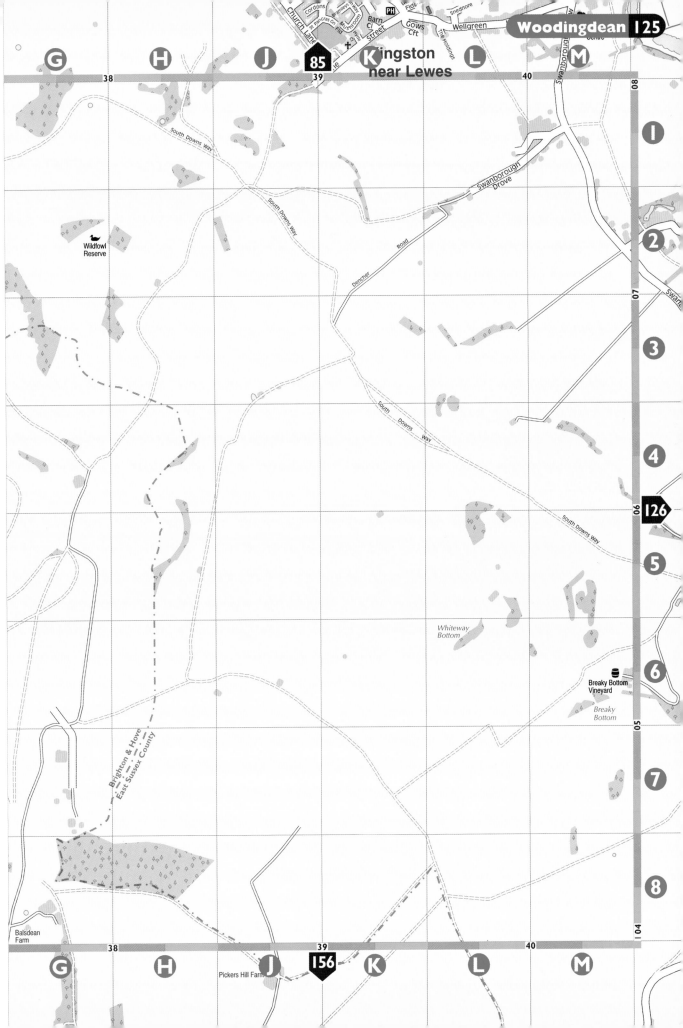

Kingston
near Lewes

Wildfowl
Reserve

South Downs Way

Dencher Road

Swanborough Drive

South Downs Way

126

Whiteway
Bottom

South Downs Way

Breaky Bottom
Vineyard

Breaky
Bottom

Brighton & Hove
East Sussex County

Balsdean
Farm

Pickers Hill Farm

156

G   H   J   85   K   L   M   I

G   H   J   156   K   L   M

85

38   39   40   08

07

06

05

04

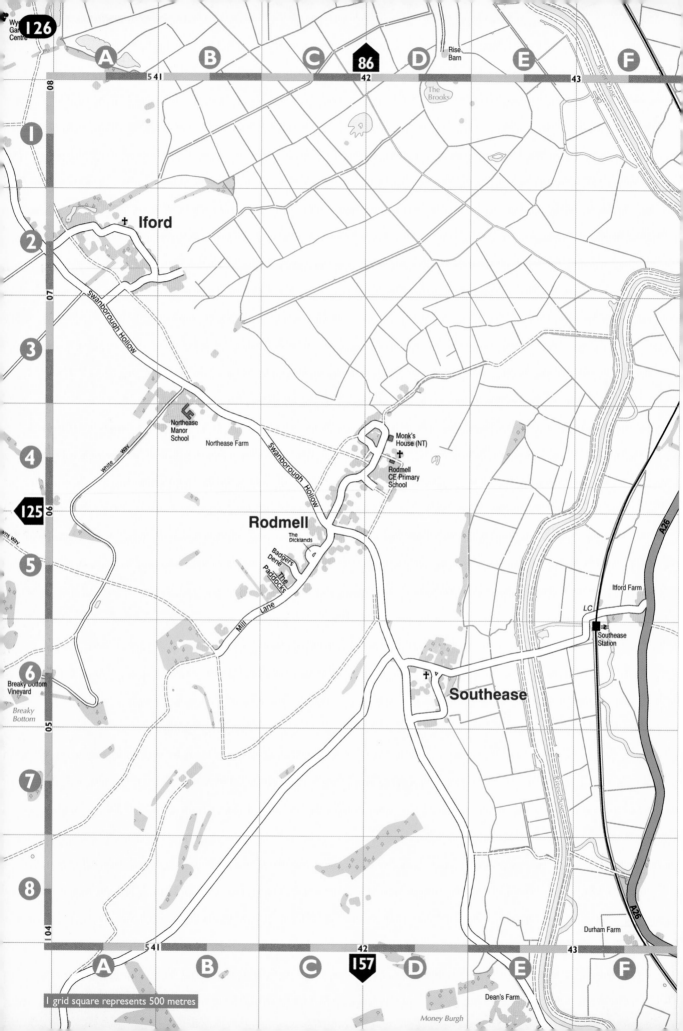

86

42

A   B   C   D   E   F

541   42   43

The Brooks

Rise Barn

1 2 3 4 5 6 7 8

Iford

Swanborough Hollow

White Way

Northease Manor School

Northease Farm

Swanborough Hollow

Monk's House (NT)

Rodmell CE Primary School

125

Rodmell

The Dicklands

Badgers Dene

The Paddocks

Mill Lane

Itford Farm

LC

Southease Station

Breaky Bottom Vineyard

Breaky Bottom

Southease

River Ouse

A26

River Ouse

07 06 05 04

08

541

42

43

A   B   C   D   E   F

157

Durham Farm

Dean's Farm

Money Burgh

1 grid square represents 500 metres

G H J 87 K L M

44 45 A27 46

Preston nume

A27

+

Beddingham

Cobbe
Place

Little
Dene

Preston Court

Firle
Prim
Sch

Bost
Rd

1

2

Newelm

A26

The Furlongs

Firle Bostal

The
Lay

3

4

128

White
Lion
Pond

Males Burgh

5

Red Lion
Pond

South Downs Way

Blackcap
F

6

05

Well
Bottom

7

04

8

44 45 158 46

G H J K L M

+

**Tarring
Neville**

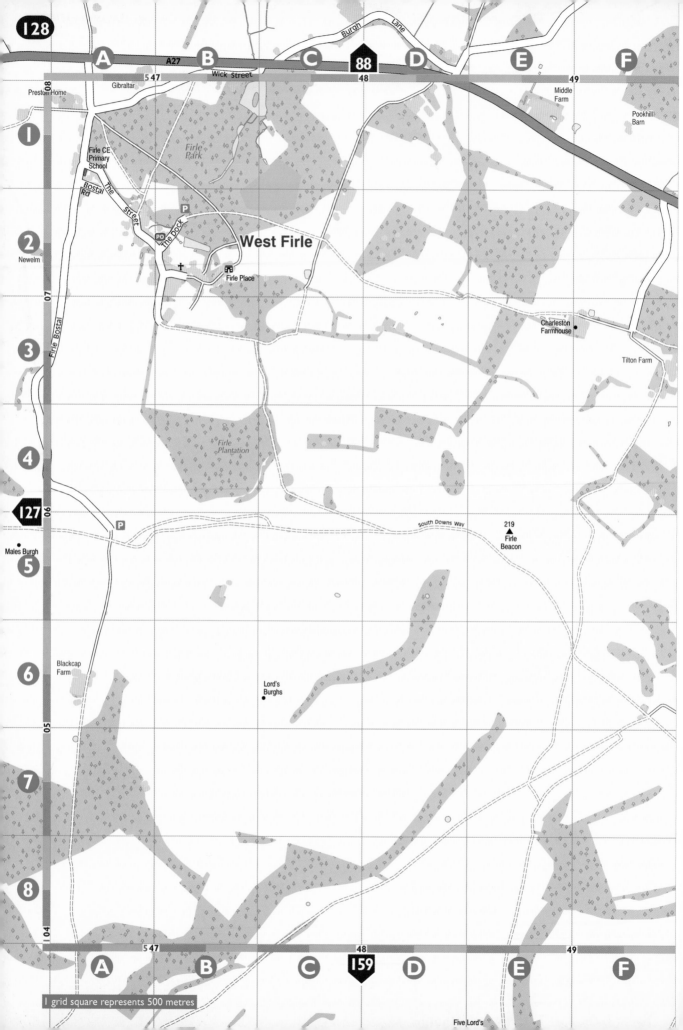

A A27 **B** Wick Street **C** 88 **D** 48 **E** F

Burgh Lane

5 47

Gibraltar

Middle
Farm

Pookhill
Barn

Preston Home

I

Firle CE
Primary
School

Firle
Park

2

Newelm

PO
The Dock
P

West Firle

Firle Place

Charleston
Farmhouse

3

Tilton Farm

Firle Bostal

4

Firle
Plantation

P

South Downs Way

219
▲
Firle
Beacon

Males Burgh

5

Blackcap
Farm

6

Lord's
Burghs

7

8

5 47

48

49

A **B** **C** 159 **D** **E** **F**

1 grid square represents 500 metres

Five Lord's

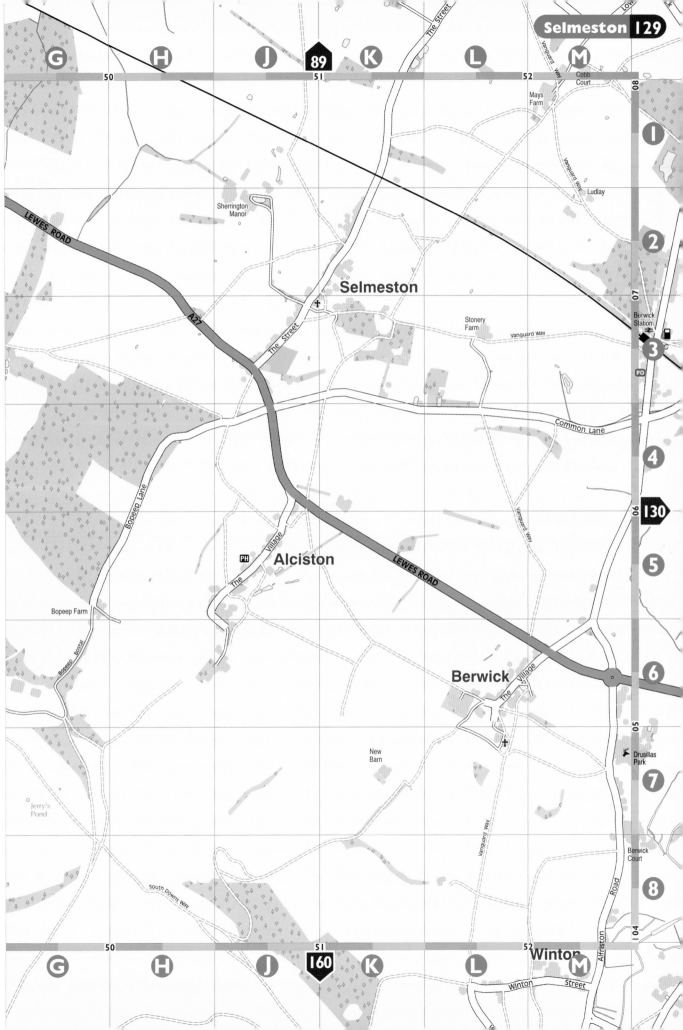

G   H   J   **89**   K   L   M

50   51   52   Cobb Court

Mays Farm

I

Ludlay

2

LEWES ROAD

A27

Sherrington Manor

Selmeston

Stonery Farm

Vanguard Way

Berwick Station

3

PO

Common Lane

4

130

The Street

Bopeep Lane

5

PH   The Village   **Alciston**

The

LEWES ROAD

Vanguard Way

6

Bopeep Farm

Bopeep Bostal

Berwick

The Village

Jerry's Pond

New Barn

Vanguard Way

Drusillas Park

7

Berwick Court

8

south Downs Way

Winton

Alfriston Road

50   51   52   **Winton**

Winton   Street

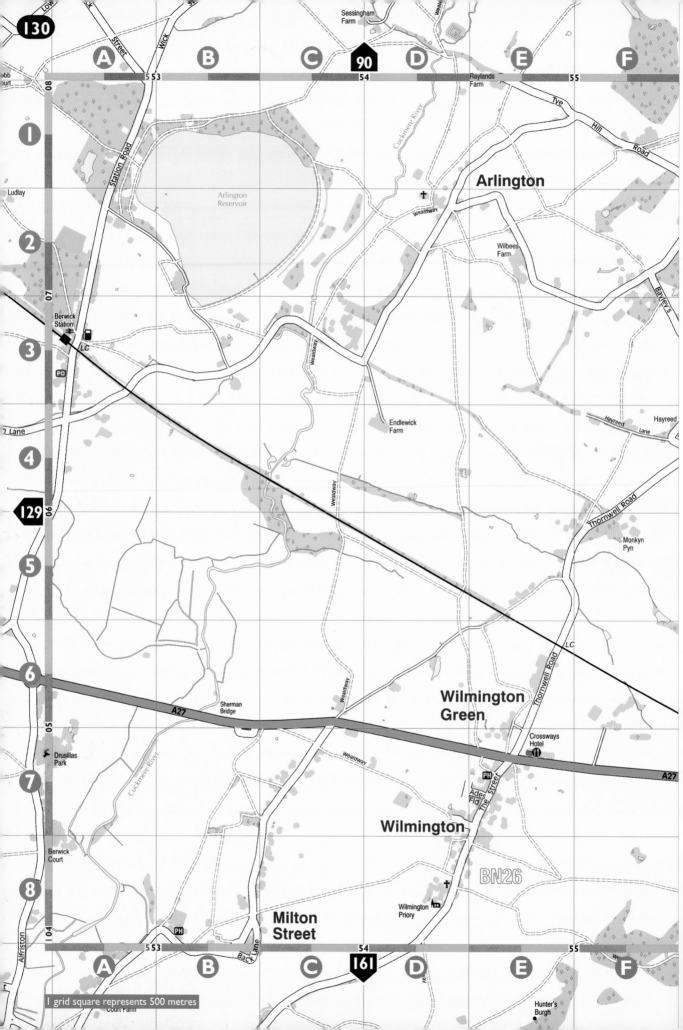

I

2

3

4

129

5

6

7

8

A 5 53 Wick B 54 **90** D Raylands Farm 55 F

Sessingham Farm

Cuckmere River

Tye Hill Road

Arlington

Wealdway

Wilbees Farm

Bayley's

Ludlay

Station Road

Berwick Station

LC

PO

Endlewick Farm

Hayreed Lane

Hayreed

Lane

Thornwell Road

Monkyn Pyn

Wealdway

Wealdway

Arlington Reservoir

LC

Wilmington Green

A27

Sherman Bridge

Cuckmere River

Wealdway

Thornwell Road

Crossways Hotel

A27

Drusillas Park

PH

The Street

Ades Fld

Wilmington

Berwick Court

BN26

Wilmington Priory

Afriston

Court Farm

PH

Back Lane

Milton Street

A 5 53 B 54 **161** D E 55 F

Hunter's Burgh

1 grid square represents 500 metres

G   H   J   **91**   K   L   M

56   57   58   08

I

Summer
Hill

2

3

4

132

5

6

7

8

POLEGA

G   H   J   **162**   K   L   M

56   57   58

Folkington

ARLINGTON EAGLES
ROUNDABOUT

Cemetery

Wilmington
Wood

Abbot's
Wood

Caneheath

Nature Reserve

Nate
Wood

Mulbrooks
Farm

Coppards

Woodside
Way

Woodside
Hall

Coldthorn Lane

Cuckoo Trail

Nightingale
Farm

Sayerland
House

A22

Otham Court Lane

Otteham
Court

Bay Tree Lane

Saverland La

A27

Premier
Travel Inn

POLEGATE BY-PASS A27

Mp G

Saverland Road

Greenleaf Gardens

Malcolm
Gdns

Polegate
CP School

B2247

Palma Windsor Wy

Honeycrag Close

Oakfield Drive

Old School Close

Crest

Northern
Av

Western Av

West Cl

East

Brookside Av

HAILSHAM ROAD

St Le Ter

School

Westfield

Albert
Rd

Victoria Rd

PO

Downland Medical
Centre

Gilda Crs

Polegate
Porters
Stn

STATION ROAD

Junction St

Black

Eas

Het

Otte
Cl

Brook Street

Cosford Wy

Council
Building

Polegate
Porters
Wy

LC

Council
Building

LEWES ROAD

Old Drive

Manor Park
Medical Centre

High

St John's Rd

Walnut
Wk

Chestnut
Dr

Manor Wa

Windmill Road

Spurway
Park

Hyperion Avenue

Bahram Rd

Golden Miller
Lane

Sunstar Lane

Gainsborough La

Church Rd

Brightling

A2270

Hilary Cl

Barons Way

Bernard Gdns

Council
Building

Northfield

Wannock Road

Wannock Drive

Willow
Dr

Courtland Rd

EASTBOURNE

ROAD

Southfield

Clement Cl

The
Millrace

Grosvenor
Cl

Watermill Close

Windmill Pl

Polegate
Windmill

PO

Polegate
Park

Surgery

Folkington
Manor

Mortimer
Gdns

Lancing Gdns

Mill Gdns

Paddock Gdns

MayFair

Farmlands Wy

Willingdon
Community
School

Glen Cl

Farmlands Close

Farmlands
Road

Downsvalley Rd

Oldfield Rd

Church

Coppi

Cornmill
Gardens

Wealdway

Wootton
Manor

Folkington Road

Robin

Post

Lane

Lane

Hayreed
La

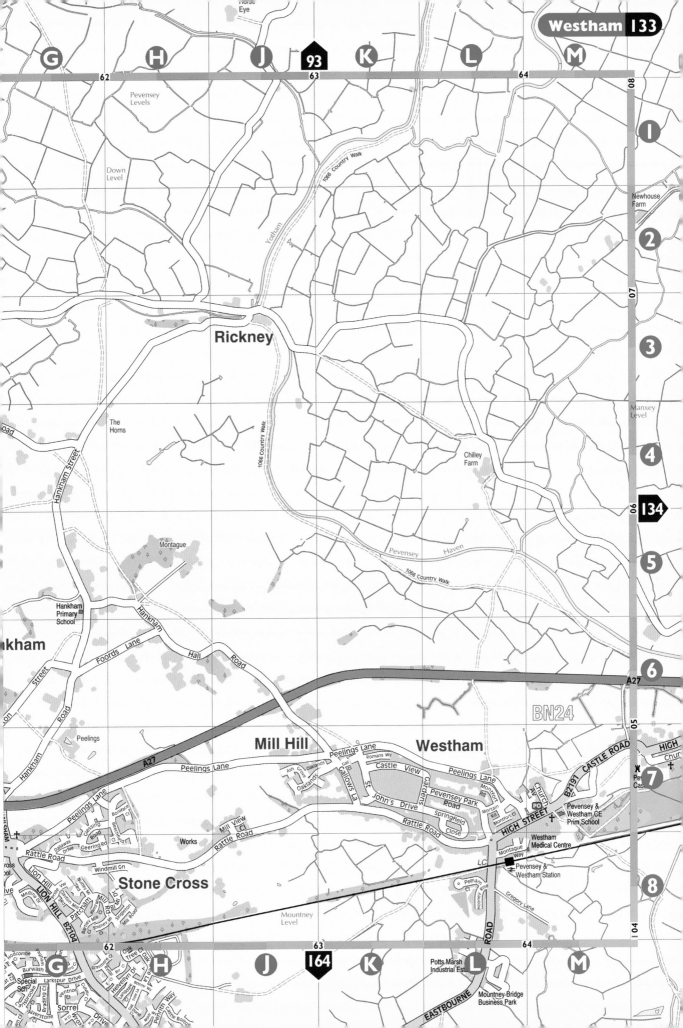

I

Newhouse
Farm

2

07

Pevensey
Levels

Down
Level

3

Manxey
Level

The
Horns

Rickney

Chilley
Farm

4

134

06

5

1066 Country Walk

Yotham

1066 Country Walk

Hankham Street

Montague

Pevensey   Haven

1066 country Walk

Hankham
Primary
School

6   A27

05

A27

Foords Lane   Hall   Road

Peelings

BN24

Street

Hankham

Mill Hill

Westham

Peelings Lane

Peelings Lane

Romans Wy

Castle View

Peelings Lane

HIGH
Chur

7

B2191 CASTLE ROAD

Per
Cast

kham

Road

Ash Grove Oaklands

Oaklands

Callows La

St John's Drive

Gardens

Pevensey Park
Road

Montfort
Rd

Church
Av

PO

Pevensey &
Westham CE
Prim School

Peelings Lane

Mill View
Cl

Works

Rattle Road

Rattle Road

Springfield
Close

Montfort
Rd

Montain
Rd

HIGH STREET

Westham
Medical Centre

Dallaway
Drive

Geering Rd

Beeching Cl

Bontface
Cl

Gessing
Road

Hankham

Montague
Way

LC

Pevensey &
Westham Station

Rattle Road

Windmill Gn

Pelham
Cl

Honey Rise

8

Stone Cross

LION HILL B2104

Mill Rd

Parchate

Singleton Cl

Gregory Lane

04

Mountney
Level

Special
Sch

Larkspur Drive

Helvellyn Dr

Burwash

Oak Tree Cl

Potts Marsh
Industrial Est.

EASTBOURNE

Mountney Bridge
Business Park

Sorrel

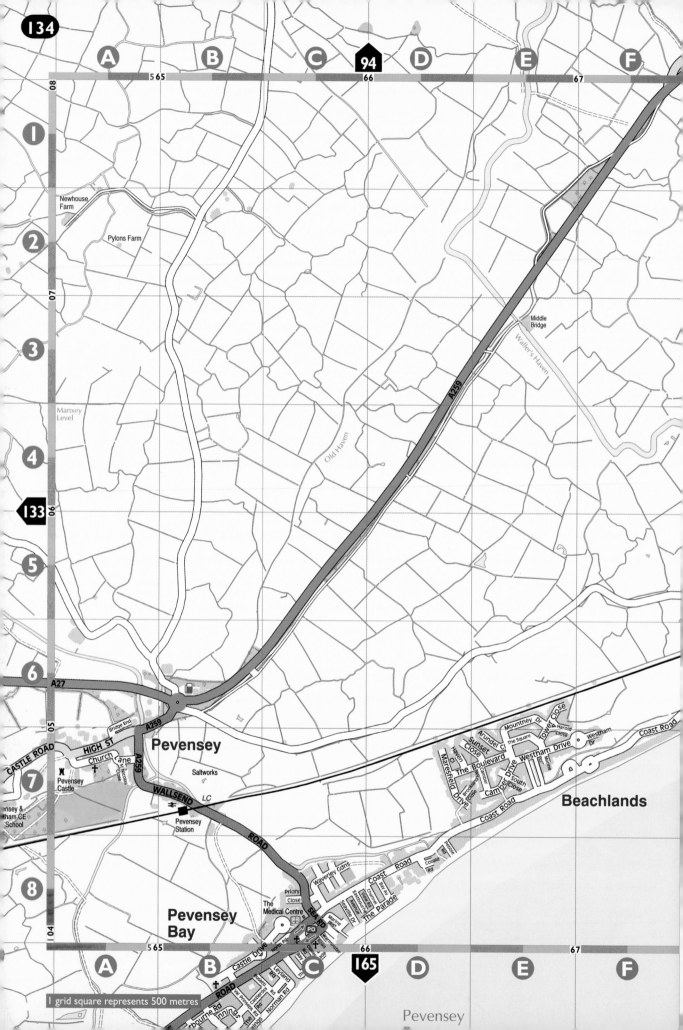

G   H   J   **95**   K   L   M

PH

A259

68   69   70   08

Ticehurst
Avenue

Pleyden Rise
Drive
Coneyburrow Lane
Sandhurst Lane

The Broadwalk

BARNHORN ROAD

Hill Farm

A259

BARNHORN

Old Road
Farm

Barnhorn
Manor

I

Saltworks

2

07

Clay

Hooe
Level

3

Gol

Cooden B

4

LC
Herbrand Walk

06 **136**

5

Rockhouse
Bank

Norman's Bay
Station

LC

6

Norman's
Bay

Coast Road

05

7

8

04

68   A259   69   70

G   H   J   K   L   M

Nature
Reserve

A B C 104 D E F
76

Wicko...
Point
475 77

Great D...

Prinsted
P...

Sussex Border Path

Thorn...

Emsworth Road

1

Hampshire County,
West Sussex County

Stanbury
Point

Hunter
Rd
Swift Road
Spartan Cl
N Bay
S Bay
Meteor
Road
Javelin
Road
Canberra Rd
Hornet Road
Emsworth Rd

2

Thorney Island

3

Thorney Island
Primary School

†

Barracks

West Thorney

Thorney Island
Airfield

Smith
Lane

Thorney
Old Pk
†

Thorney
Channel

Church
Road

4

Marker
Point

Emsworth Rd

Victor Rd
Pleasant Lane
Vulcan
Road
Valiant
Road
Valetta Road
Varsity Road

5

6

Sussex
Border
Path

Longmere
Point

7

Pilsey
Island

01

8

Pilsey
Sand

Chichester Harbour

1.00

475 76 77

A B C 166 D E F

Stocker's Lake

I grid square represents 500 metres

West Sussex Cou...
Hamp...
Co...

G H J **105** K Harbour L M The Millstream Hotel & Restaurant

Steels Lane

78 Cot Lane 79 80 04

Marsh Lane Marsh La

Chidham

Bosham Abbey

High St

Bosham Sailing Club

I

Shore Road 2

03

New Barn

Cobnor Farm

Bosham Channel

Lower Hone Lane

Lowerhone Farm

3

Gerald Daniel Sailing Club

Cobnor House

Smuggler's Lane 4

02 **140**

Cobnor Point

5 B

Chichester Channel

West Itchenor

Itchenor Sailing Club

The Street

Orchard Lane WC

6

01

Spinney Lane 7

Itchenor House

Itchenor Road

Oldhouse Farm

Chalkdock Lane

The Spinney

Glebe Field Road

8

00

78 79 80

G **167** K L M

Rookwood Lane

Sheepwash Lane

Redlands Fm

Itchenor Road

Shipton Green

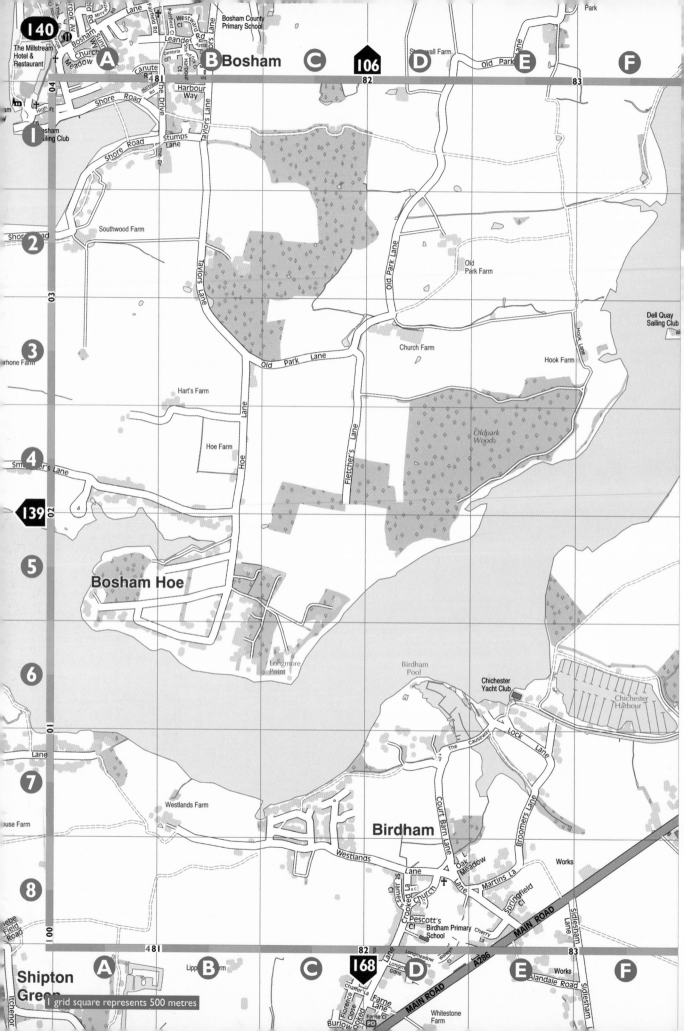

140 The Millstream Hotel & Restaurant

A

B Bosham

C

106 82 83

D Stonewall Farm   Old Park Lane

E

F

Bosham County Primary School

Leander

Fairfield Rd

Brook Av

Bosham Meadow

Church Rd

Lane

Canute R 481

Cambria Cl

Harbour Way

I Bosham Sailing Club

High St

Shore Road

The Drive

Stumps Lane

Taylors Lane

Harbour Way

2 Shore Road

Southwood Farm

Old Park Lane

Old Park Farm

3 Thorne Farm

Church Farm

Hook Farm

Hook Lane

Dell Quay Sailing Club

Park

Old Park Lane

Hart's Farm

Hoe Lane

Lane

4 Smugglers Lane

Hoe Farm

Fletcher's Lane

Oldpark Wood

139 02

5

Bosham Hoe

6

Longmore Point

Birdham Pool

Chichester Yacht Club

Chichester Harbour

Lock Lane

01

7 Lane

Westlands Farm

The Causeway

House Farm

Court Barn Lane

Broomers Lane

Birdham

Works

8

Shipton Green
Itchenor

Glebe Field Road

1 grid square represents 500 metres

A

B Lipp

St James's Cl

Crooked La

Church Lane

Oak Meadow

Martins La

Springfield Cl

Works

C

168 82

Westlands Lane

Longmeadows

Longm Gdns

Pescott's Cl

Birdham Primary School

Cherry Lane

Walwin

D

A286

MAIN ROAD

Chaffer La

Farne Lane

Florence Close

Farne Cl

Burlow

PO

Whitestone Farm

E

MAIN ROAD

Alandale Road

Sidlesham Lane

Works

F

83

481

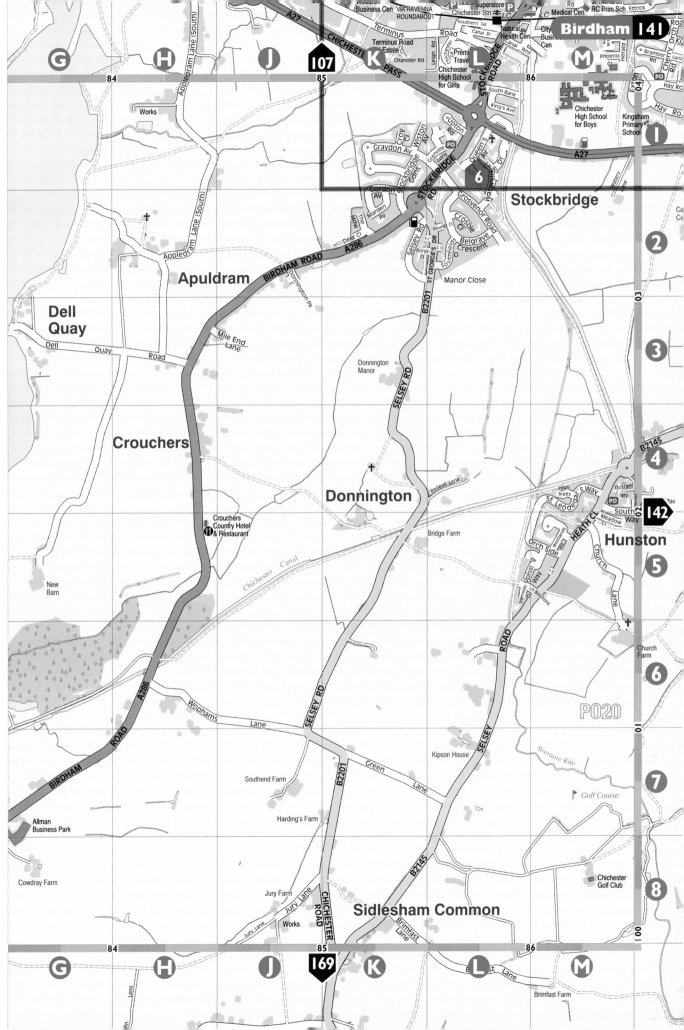

G   H   J   107   K   L   M   I

Works

Apuldram

Dell
Quay

Dell   Quay   Road

Crouchers

New
Barn

Cowdray Farm

Appledram Lane (South)

BIRDHAM ROAD   A286

Mile End
Lane

Donnington Pk

Crouchers
Country Hotel
& Restaurant

Chichester Canal

BIRDHAM   ROAD   A286

Wophams   Lane

Allman
Business Park

Southend Farm

Harding's Farm

Jury Farm

Jury Lane   Jury Lane

Jury Lane

Works

Woodruff
Business Cen   P   Superstore   St Richards
VIA RAVENNA   Chichester Stn   P   RC Prim Sch   Ettrick
ROUNDABOUT   Southern Ga   Medical Cen   LC
Terminus   Road   Natural   City   Phoenix
Terminus Road   Leigh Rd   Canal Pl   Health Cen   Business   Herald
Estate   Chandler Rd   Chichester   Cen   Bramber   Cherry   Orch
Chichester   Premii   Rd   Rd   Garli
High School   Travel   Chichester   Hay Rd
for Girls   South Bank   High School   Kingsham   PO
King's Ave   for Boys   Primary   Hay Ro
School
84   86
Croy   Wiston   Upton   ✠
Graydon Av   Rd   South Ga   Watery
A27   Lane
Stockbridge   PO   Greville   Queen's   King's
Gdns   Gdns   Av   Dr   03
Gordon   Grenville   A27
Av   The   RD   Grosvenor Road   Stockbridge
Marden   STOCKBRIDGE   Crosbie   6   Waterside
Av   Cl   Belgrave
Deer Cl   Selsey Rd   Forge   Crescent   Manor Close
St   Poyntz   Dr   Southfield
GEORGES   Southchu

B2201   SELSEY   RD

Donnington
Manor

✠

Belley's Lane

Donnington

Bridge Farm

SELSEY   RD

B2201

Green
Lane

Kipson House

SELSEY
ROAD

B2145

Golf Course ▶

CHICHESTER
ROAD

Sidlesham Common

Brimfast
Lane

84   85   86
G   H   J   169   K   L   M

High   St Leodegar's Way   Outram
Trees   WV   B2145   4
St Leodeg   PO
Westgate   Meadow   WV   142
Orch Side   Heath Cl   South   Way   Hunston
Church   Way   Hunston   5
Church
Lane   ✠
Church
Farm   6

P020   01   02   03

2

3

4

5

6

7

8

Bremere Rife

Chichester
Golf Club

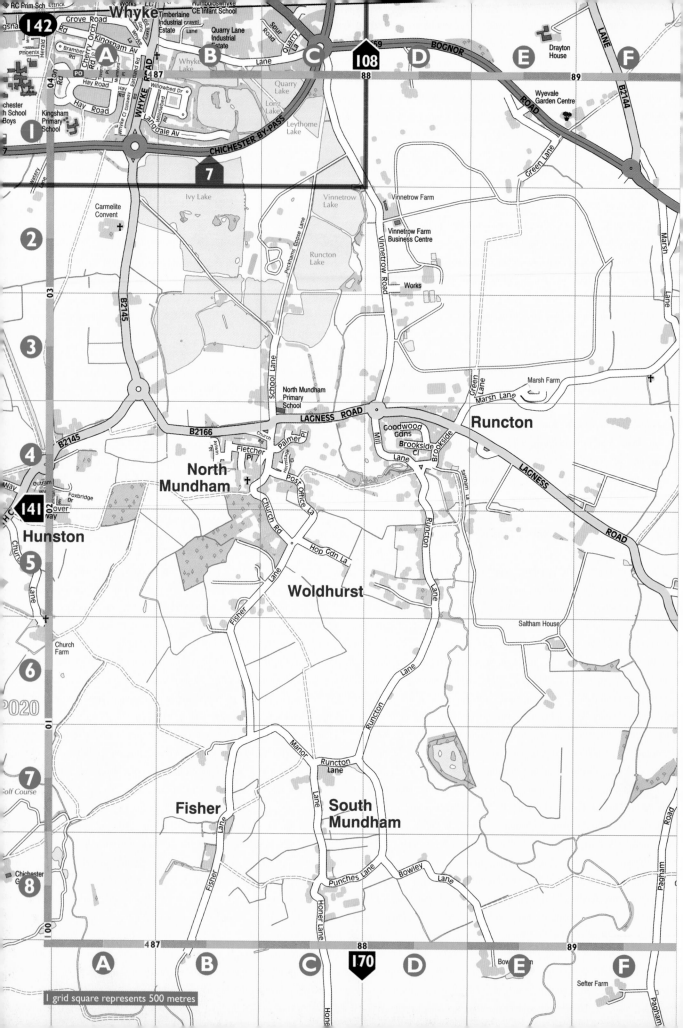

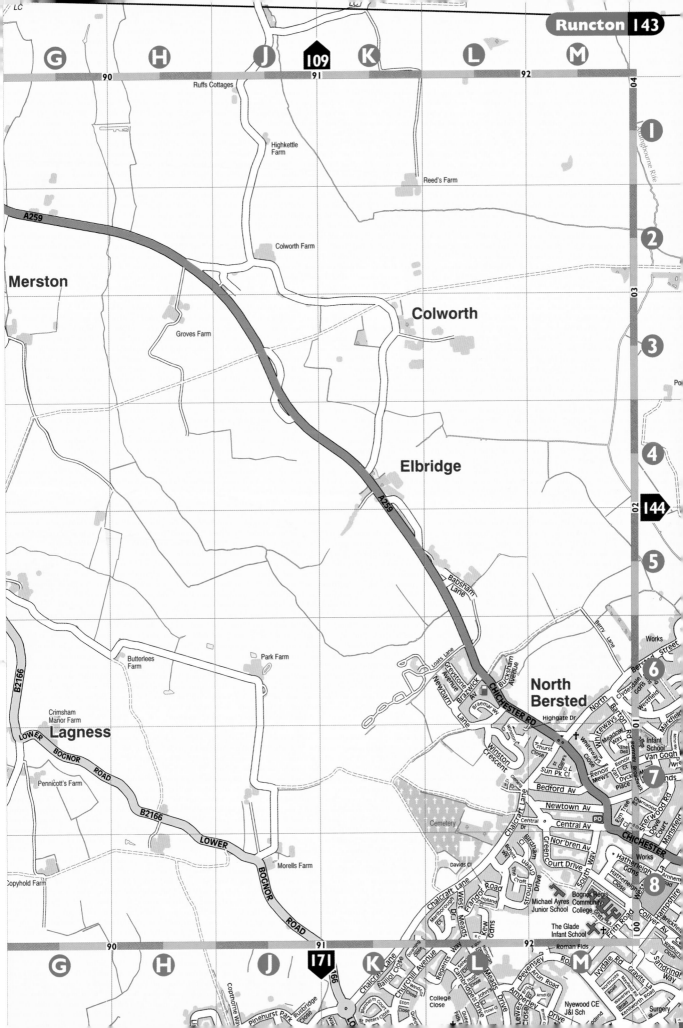

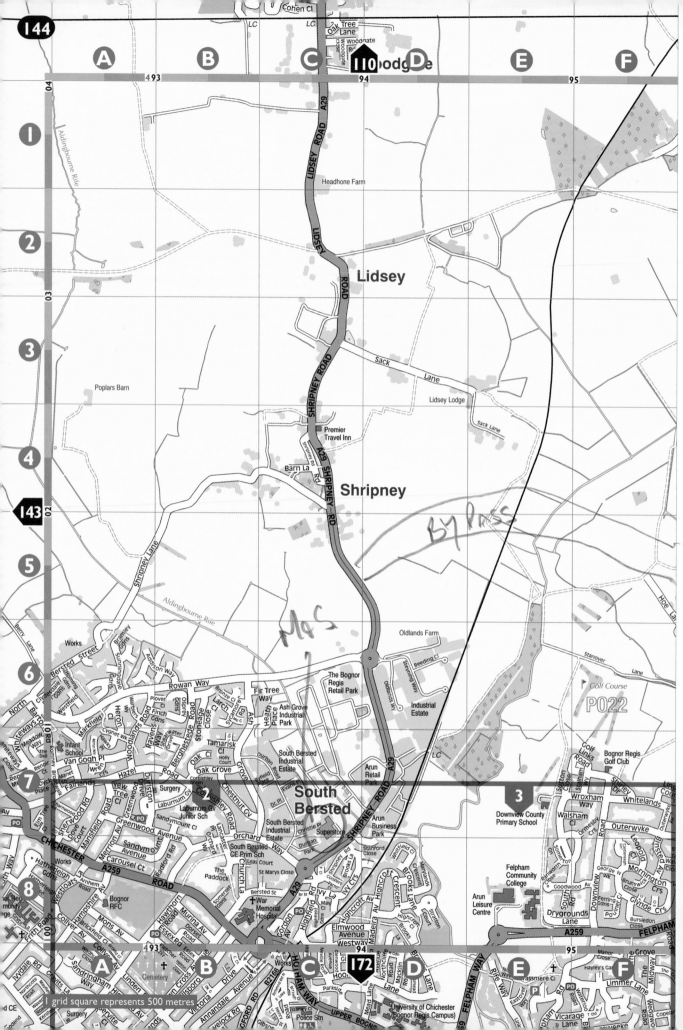

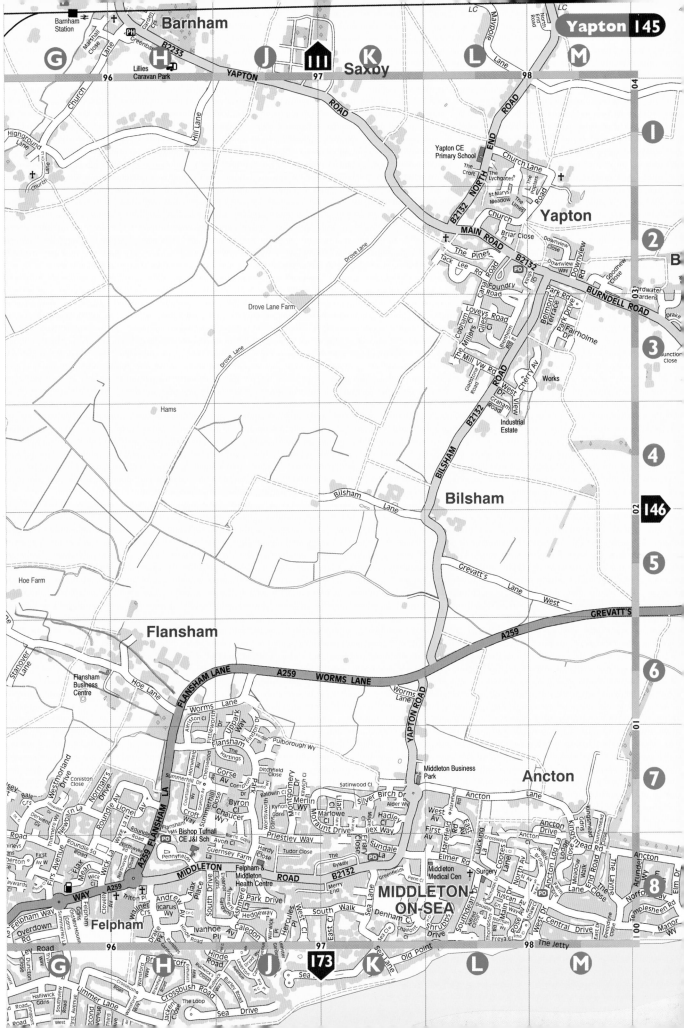

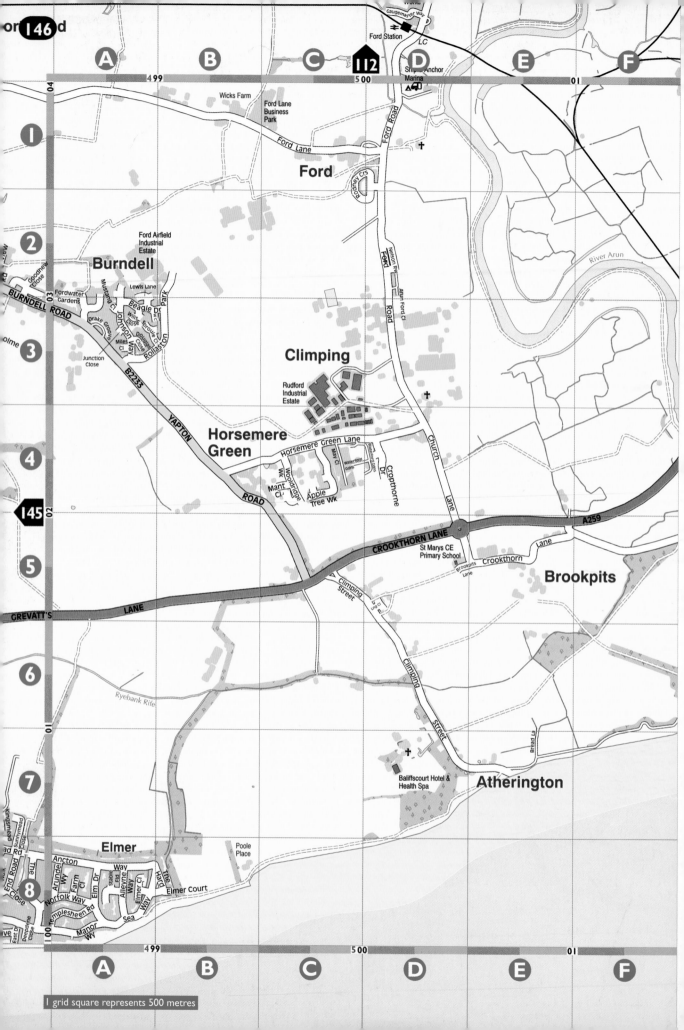

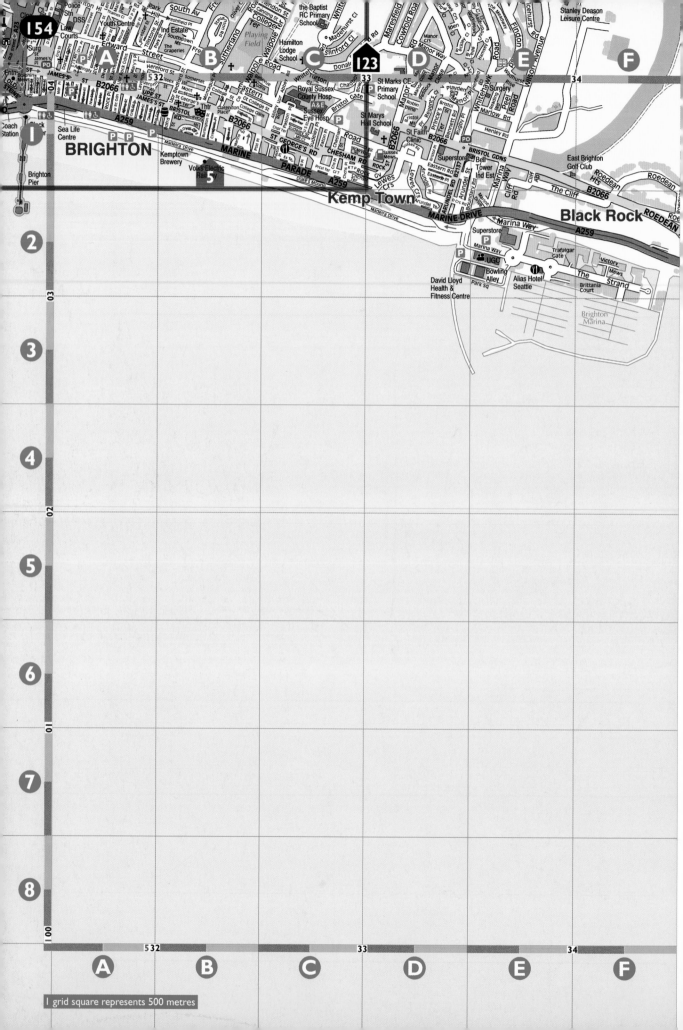

124

Balsdean Farm

G **H** **J** **K** **L** **M**

35 36 37 04

I

Longhill High School

The Ridings

Woodland Walk

PO

Ovingdean Hall School

Longhill

Longhill Road

Greenways

Ainsworth Close

Ainsworth Avenue

Wanderdown Way

Wanderdown Road

Wanderdown Drive

Martyns Way

DeMor Close

Vale

Rowan Way

Eley

Rowan Wy

Eley Crescent

Eley Drive

Eley Crs

New Barn Road

Court Farm Rd

B2123

Court Ord Rd

Meadow Pde

FALMER ROAD

Surgery

2

Crescent

Roedean Way

Roedean Vale

Roedean School

Path

Beacon Hill

Ovingdean

Wilkinson Close

Rottingdean FC

Bazehill Road

Gorham Avenue

Welesmere Rd

Court Road

Listrells

Whiteway Lane

Road

03

Roedean

MARINE

DRIVE

A259

Greenways

The Rootyns

Challoners Ms

The Burwash

Challoners

Northgate Close

Northcliffe

Dean Court Road

Royles Close

Gorham Close

Dean

3

ROTTINGDEAN

Westmeston Aven

Our Lady of Lourdes RC Prim School

THE GREEN

THE GREEN

St Olde Pl

MS

Nevill Road

Steyning Road

Whiteway Lane

Chailey Av

Knole Rd

Grand Crs

Crescent

Cranleigh

Founthill Road

Rd E

Nevill Rd

Park Rd

West St

West St

High Street

PO

St Aubyn's Md

Newlands Road

Romney Rd

Lenham Rd W

Lenham Rd

Little Avenue

Eileen Av

Mart

4

St Aubyns School

MARINE DRIVE

High St

Marine Clinic

02

156

5

10

6

7

01

8

00

G **H** **J** **K** **L** **M**

35 36 37

G 41 H J 126 K L M 43 A26 A26 04

Durham Farm

I

Dean's Farm

Money Burgh

Telscombe

2

Piddinghoe

Bullock Down

03 Burt Farm Close

Brookside

The Lookout

Valley Road

Halcombe Farm

3

Greenacres

Telscombe Road

Nore Down

4

Hoddern Farm

Cemetery

158 02

Cemetery

BN10

PEACEHAVEN

5

Anderson Close

Maple Close

6

Meeching Valley CP

Brighton

Golf Course

Links Avenue

Peacehaven Golf Club

18 Cresta Road

The Fairway

BRIGHTON

7

Outlook Avenue

Chene Road

A259

The Leas

Highway

Pevensey Road

Hill Top

8

Peacehaven Heights

Friars' Bay

Westdean Rd

Cornelius Avenue

G 41 H J 42 K L M 43 00

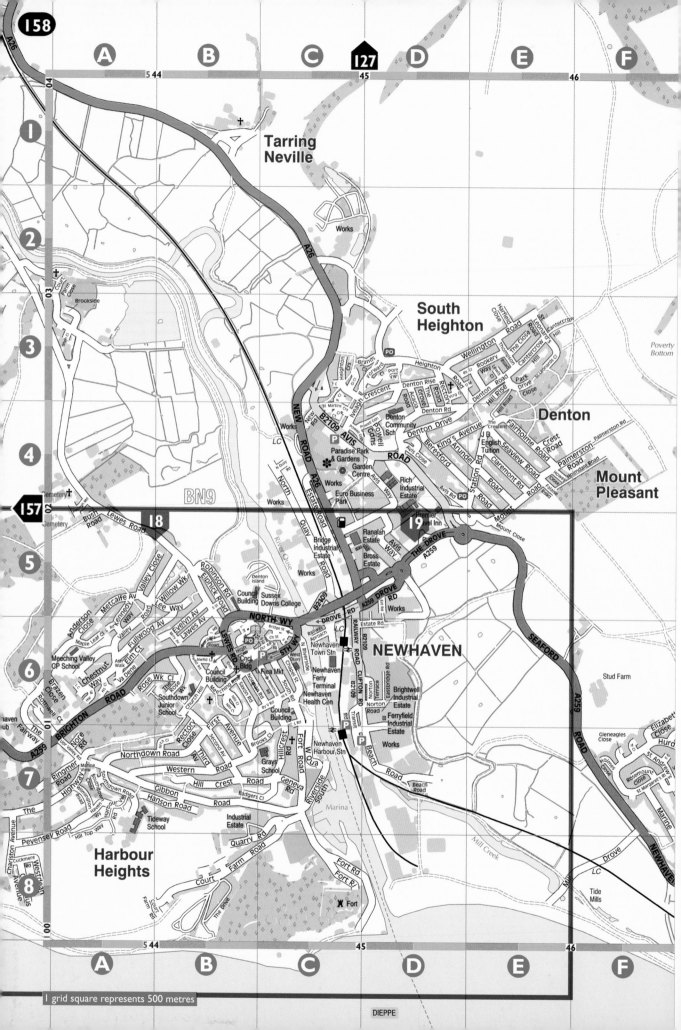

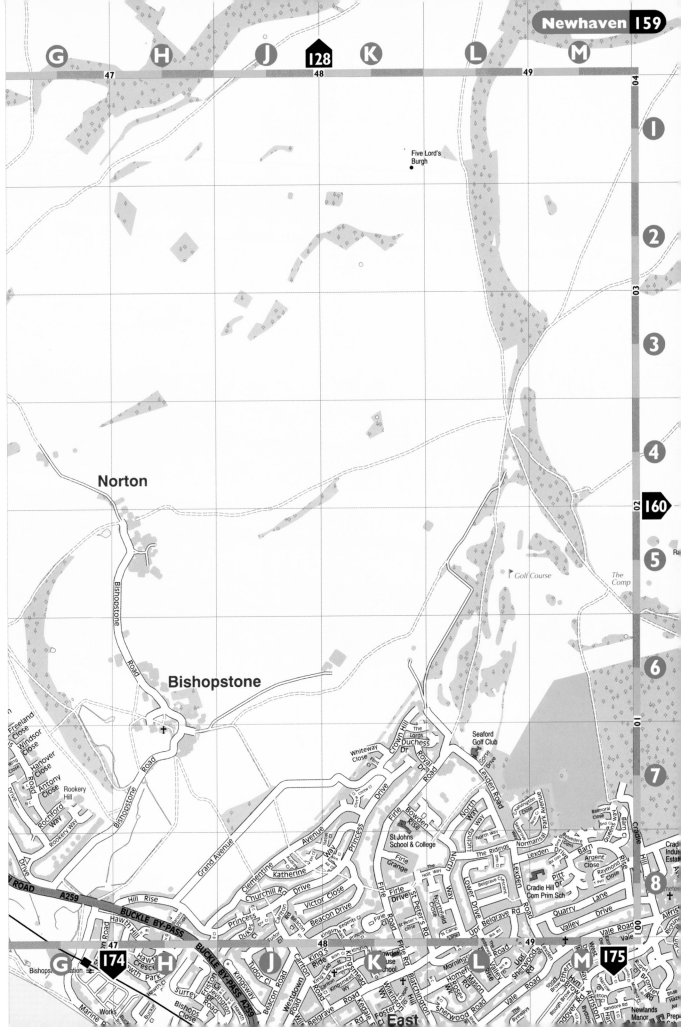

Norton

Bishopstone

Five Lord's Burgh

Golf Course

The Comp

Seaford Golf Club

St Johns School & College

Cradle Hill Com Prim Sch

BUCKLE BY-PASS

A259

East

128

160

174

175

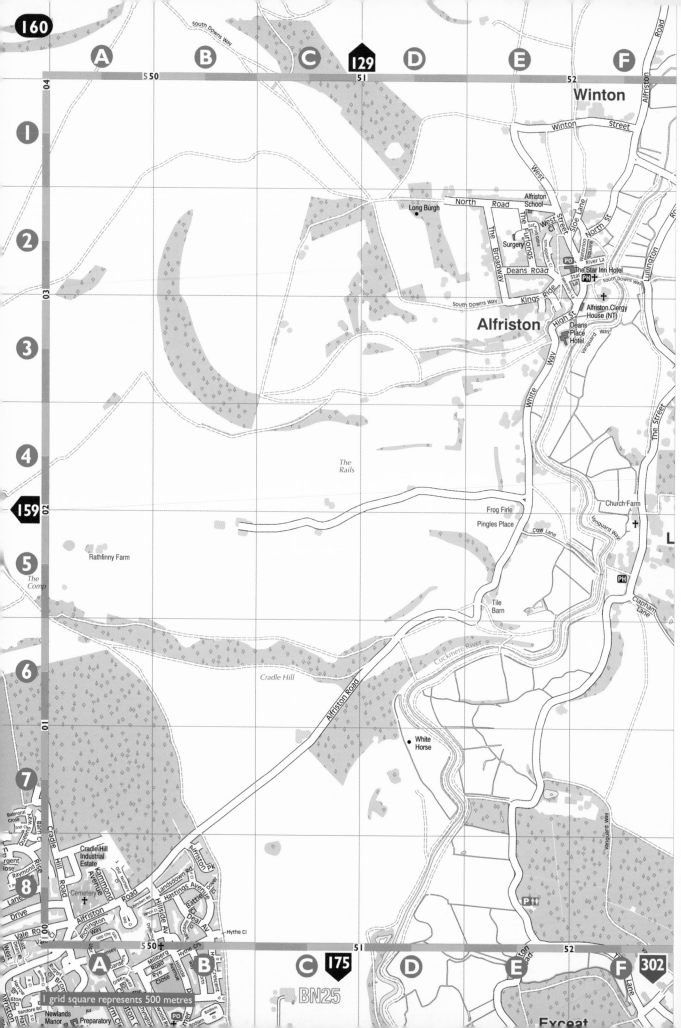

A B C **129** D E F

04 550 51 52

Winton

159

160

I

2

3

4

5

6

7

8

South Downs Way

Long Burgh

Winton Street

West Lane

Alfriston School

North Road

The Furlongs

Surgery

The Broadway

Deans Road

South Downs Way

Kings Ride

PO

River Lane

The Star Inn Hotel
PH

Alfriston Clergy House (NT)

Deans Place Hotel

Alfriston

High St

White Way

Vanguard Way

The Street

The Rails

Frog Firle

Pingles Place

Cow Lane

Church Farm

Vanguard Way

PH

Rathfinny Farm

The Comp

Tile Barn

Clapham Lane

Cuckmere River

Cradle Hill

Alfriston Road

White Horse

Balmoral Close

Cradle Hill Industrial Estate

Kammond Avenue

Alfriston Road

Hastings Avenue

Landsdown Rd

Battle Av

Deal Av

Cemetery

Vale Rd

Hythe Cl

PO

A B C **175** D E F **302**

550 51 52

BN25

Exceat

1 grid square represents 500 metres

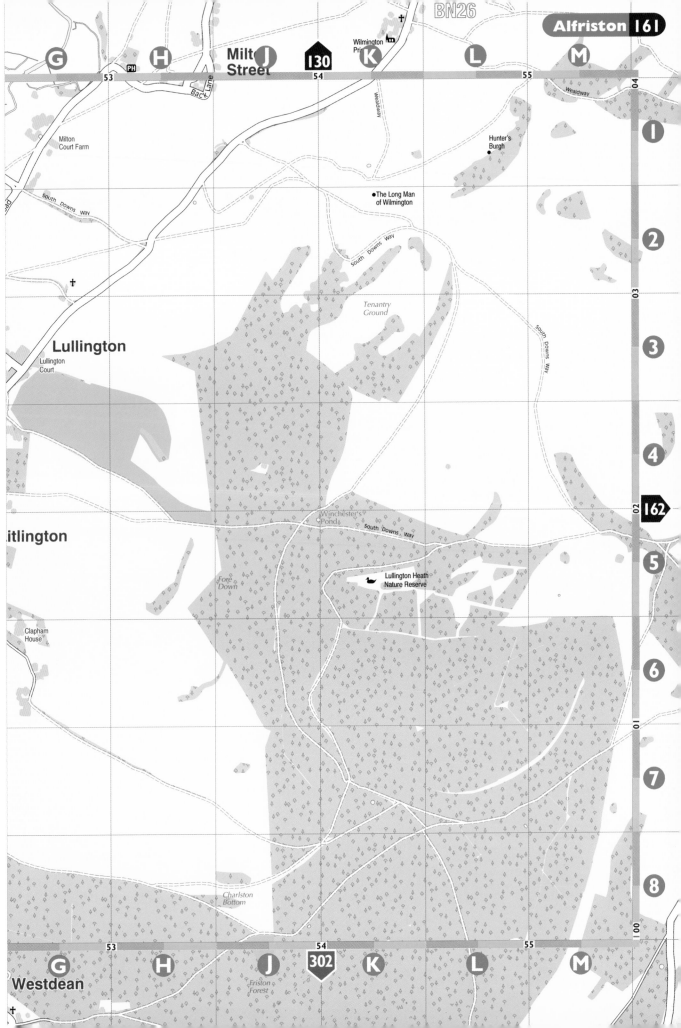

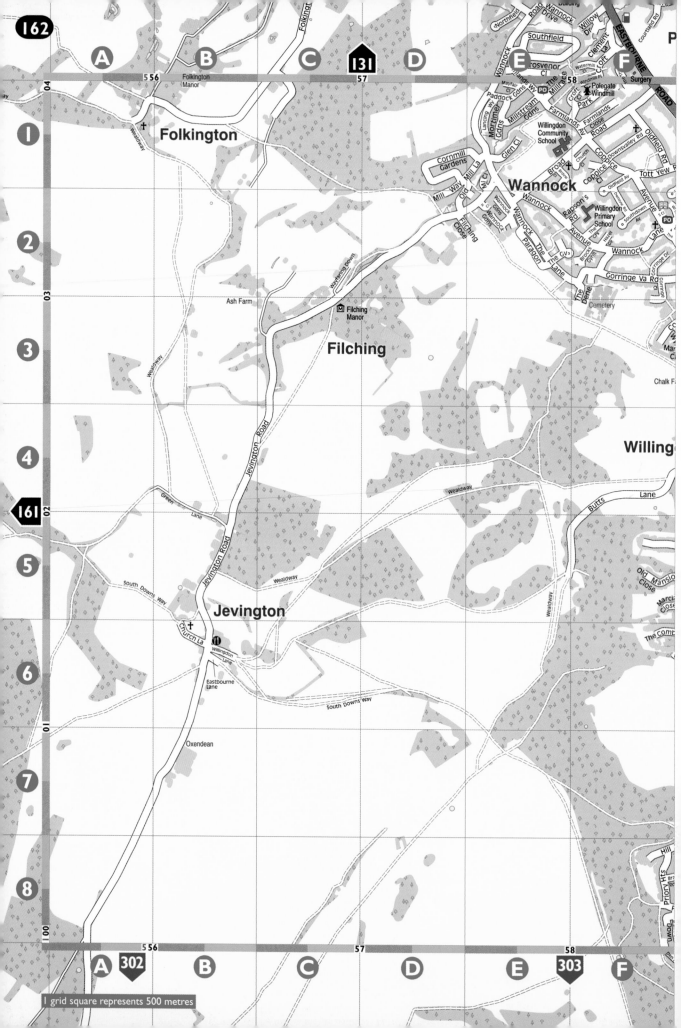

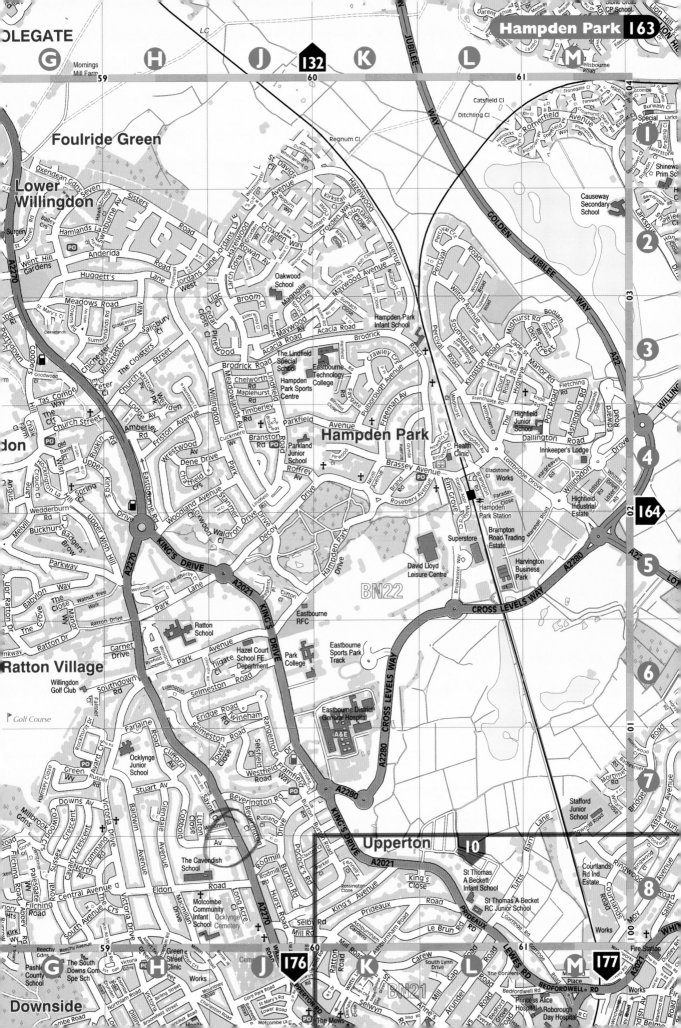

G **Peve** **Hey**
H **Bay**

Priory
Close

The
Medical Centre

J **134**

K L M

65 66 67 04

I

Waverley Gdns
Coast
Parade

Pevensey
Bay

Castle Drive

EASTBOURNE ROAD

Eastbourne Rd

Grenville Rd

Innings Dr

Timberlaine Road

Millward Rd

2

A259

03

Pevensey Bay
Sailing Club

3

Bay View Park

Samoa Wy

Vancouver Rd

PACIFIC DRIVE

Anchorage Wy

Admiralty Wy

Chatham Cl

4

02

Beach Vw

Long Beach Vw

Eugene Wy

Caroline Wy

5

Quay

01

6

7

00

8

65 66 67

G H J K L M

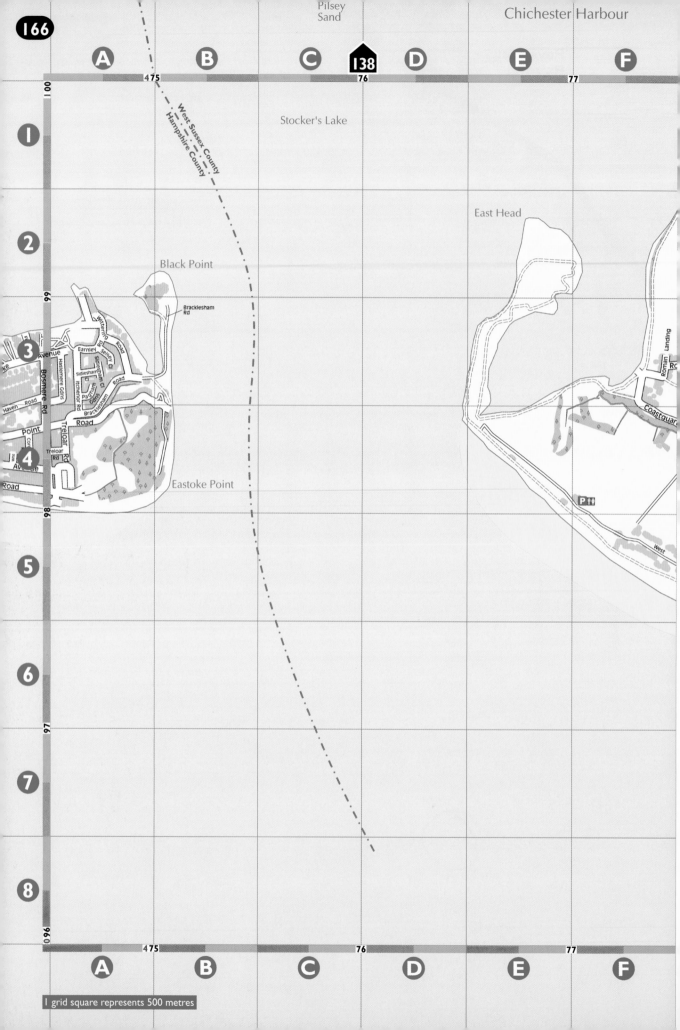

Pilsey
Sand

Chichester Harbour

Stocker's Lake

West Sussex County
Hampshire County

East Head

Black Point

Bracklesham
Rd

Avenue

Earnley

Witterina Rd

Selsey Road

Sidlesham Cl

Haslemere Gdns

Bosmere Rd

Itchenor Rd

Pagham Gdns

Bracklesham

Haven ──── Road

Road

Point

Treloar Rd

Road

Roman Landing Rd

Coastguard

Treloar
Rd

Avenue

Road

Eastoke Point

P ⛉

West

1 grid square represents 500 metres

G · H · J · K · L · M

78 · 79 · 139 · 80 · 100

Shipton Green 1

Rookwood Lane

Sheepwash Lane

Redlands Fm

Rookwood Lane

Redlands Lane

Itchenor Road

2

B2179

Sheepwash Lane

99

Chapel Lane

Acre Street

3

Hall Lane

Holmes Fm

Hale Farm

Ellanore Lane

Summerfield Rd

Roman Landing

Summerfield Road

PO

Locksash

Elmstead Gdns

Elmstead Pk Rd

Meadow La

Nunnington Farm

Elms Lane

Elms Lane

Piggery Road

Furzefield

4

98

168 5

ROOKWOOD RD

Rookwood Road

West Wittering Parochial Prim Sch

B2179

Pound Rd

Royce Way

Elms Ride

Royce Close

The Byeway

Middlefield

Seaward Dr.

Wellsfield

West Wittering

Church Farm

Briar Av

Hilton Pk

East Wittering Business Centre

Stubcroft

The Wad

CAKEHAM

Strand

Berrydown Lane

East Strand

ROAD

Watersedge Gardens

Howard Avenue

B2179

Jolliffe Road

Southcote Av

Owers Way

Marine Dr West

Marine Dr

Cullimore Rd

The Crs

The Crs

Russell Road

Cambridge Av

Oxford

Harrow Dr

Windsor Dr

Forwarren Cl

Drive

Chichester

Bennetts

Witterings Health Cen

NORTHERN CRS

PO

Cakeham Road

Windmill Court

Oakfield

Oakfield Av

Coney Rd

Barn Rd

Mill Gdns

East Wittering County Primary School

Church Road

Meadows Rd

Wessex Av

Downview Rd

B2179

STOCKS LA

East Wittering

Stubcroft La

97

6

Marine Close

Marine Dr

Shore Road

Shoreside Walk

Longlands Road

Solent Rd

Barn Wk

Nab Wk

Tamarisk Wk

Coney Six

Shingle Wk

Coney Six

Charlmead

Seafield Way

Coney Rd

Charlmead

Peerley Rd

Magpie Cl

Kimbridge Rd

Peerley Road

Seafield Cl

West Bracklesham Drive

Legion Way

Cormorant Way

Westfield Cl

Picker Cl

Middleton Close

Beech

STOCKS LANE

Bracklesham Close

Sandtrin

PO

First Av

East Farm

7

96

8

G · H · J · K · L · M

78 · 79 · 80

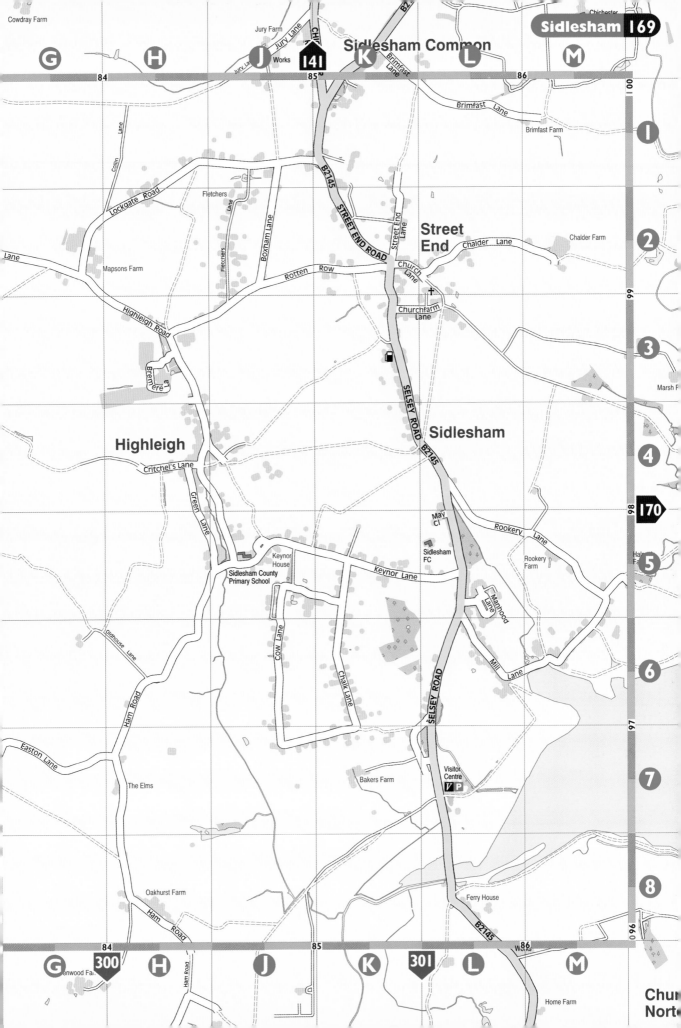

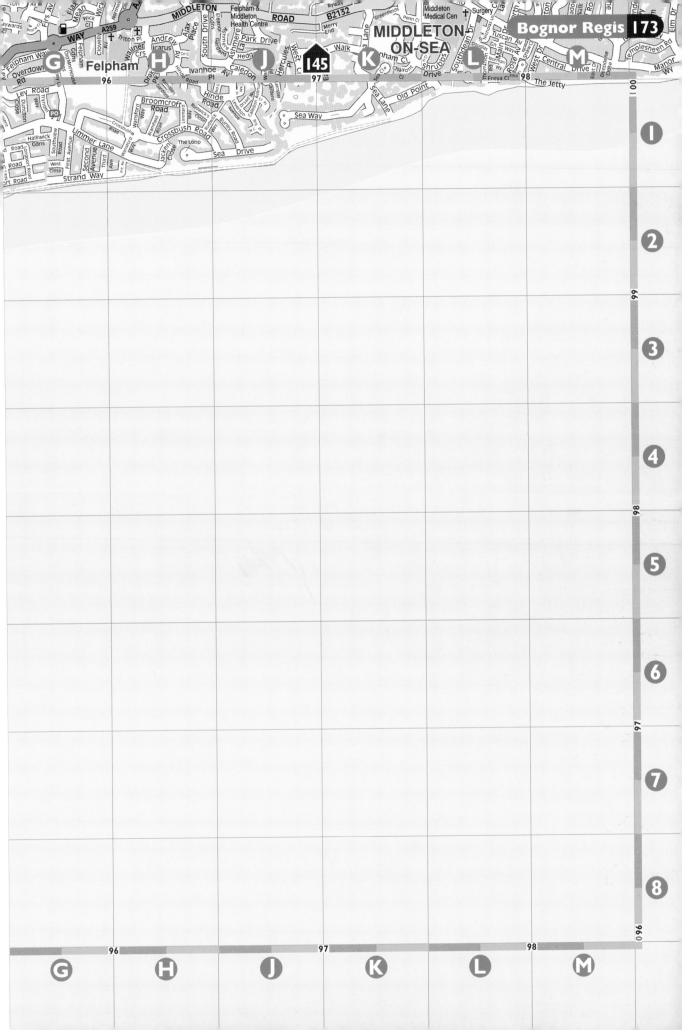

Tide Mills

158

A259

AVEN ROAD

HILL RISE

BUCKLE BY-PASS

A259

Hawth Hill

Station Road

Hawth Crescent

Hawth Park Road

Bishopstone Station

Works

Marine Parade

Surrey Road

Bishops Close

Kingsway

Beacon Road

Tudor Road

Westdown Road

Salisbury Road

Grosvenor Rd

Belgrave Road

King's Ride

Princess Drive

Dukes Drive

Churchill Rd

Clementine

Katherine

Grange

Firle Drive

St Peter's Rd

Belgrave Rd

Upr Belgrave Rd

Lexden Rd

Claremont Road

Albany Road

Edinburgh Rd

Connaught Rd

Park

CLAREMONT RD

St Crisplans

STATION AP

Seaford Primary Sch

East
Blatchington

Sports &
Leisure Cen

Blatchington Rd Ind. Est

Bowden
House School

Morningside Rd

Homefield
Rd

Mason
Rd

Sherwood Rd

Upr
Sutton

Seaford
Day
Hospital

Sutton
Mead

Cornfield

159

Seaford Station

Seaford RFC

Richmond Rd

Health
Cen

Dane Rd

CLINTON
PL

SUTTON
PARK
ROAD

SUTTON

SEAFORD

Little
Theatre

Police
Stn

High
Street

Barn
Theatre

Seaford
Head Lower
School

Community
College

Corsica Hall
Education
Training Centre

Esplanade

College

Marine
Crs

The Covers

Martello Tower &
Seaford Museum

Cliff Gdns

Cliff Rd

Corsica Rd

Esplanade

Seaford
Bay

100

5 46

99

98

97

096

I

2

3

4

5

6

7

8

A   158   B   C   D   159   E   F

5 46   47   48

A   B   C   D   E   F

1 grid square represents 500 metres

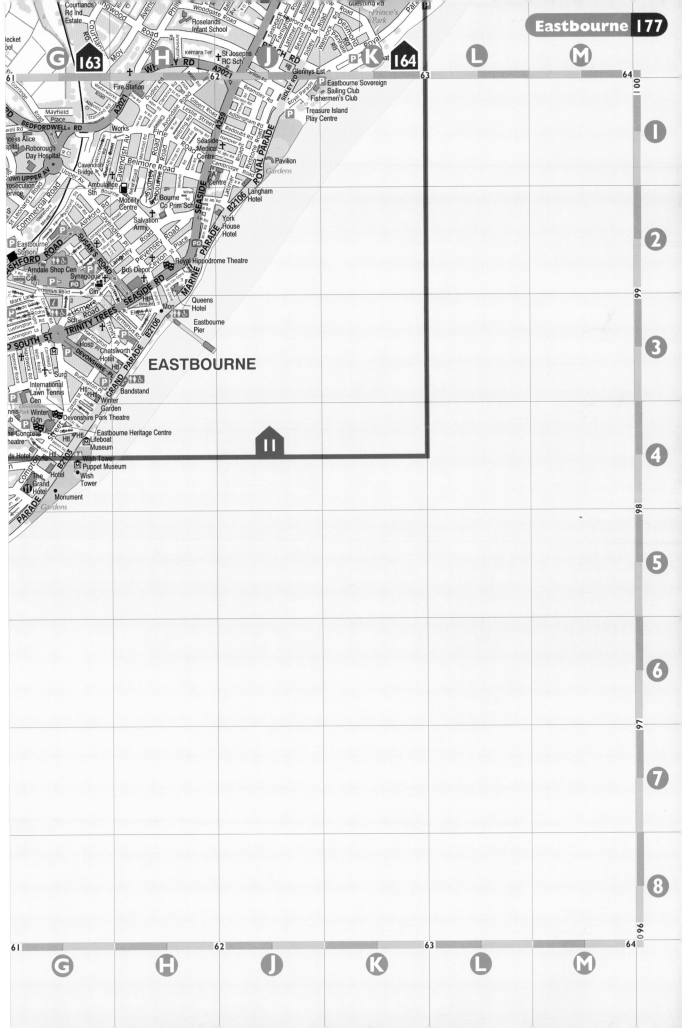

EASTBOURNE

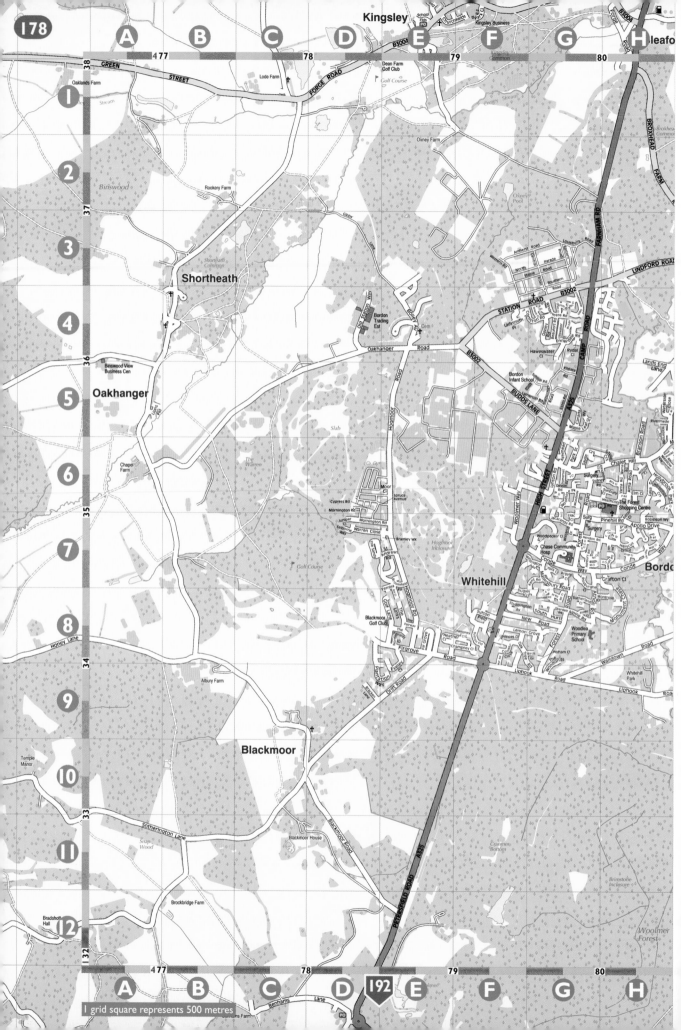

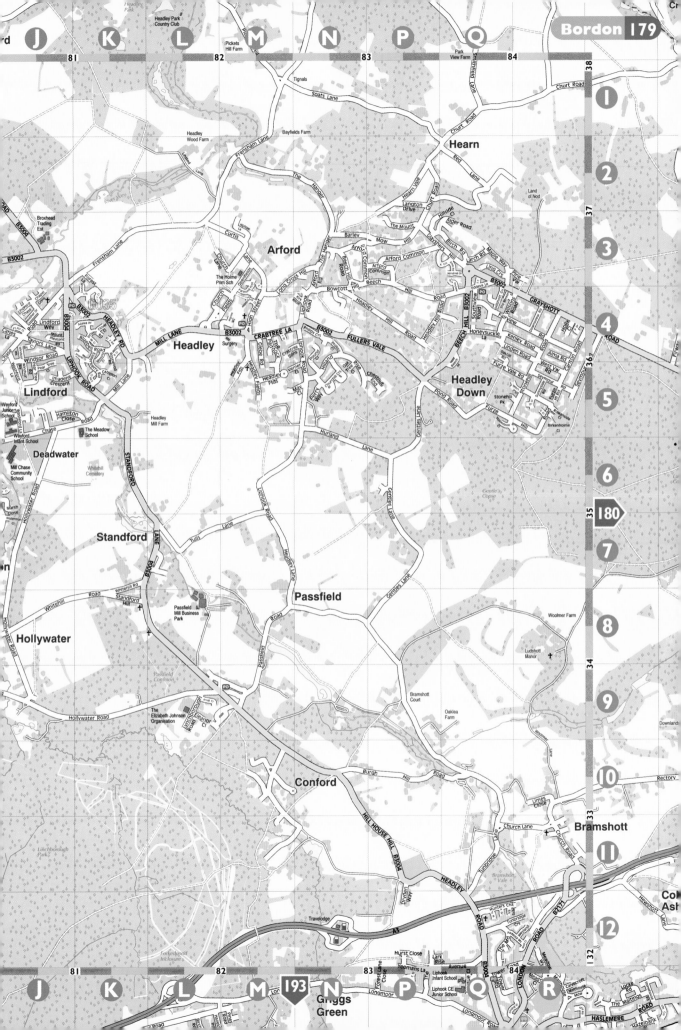

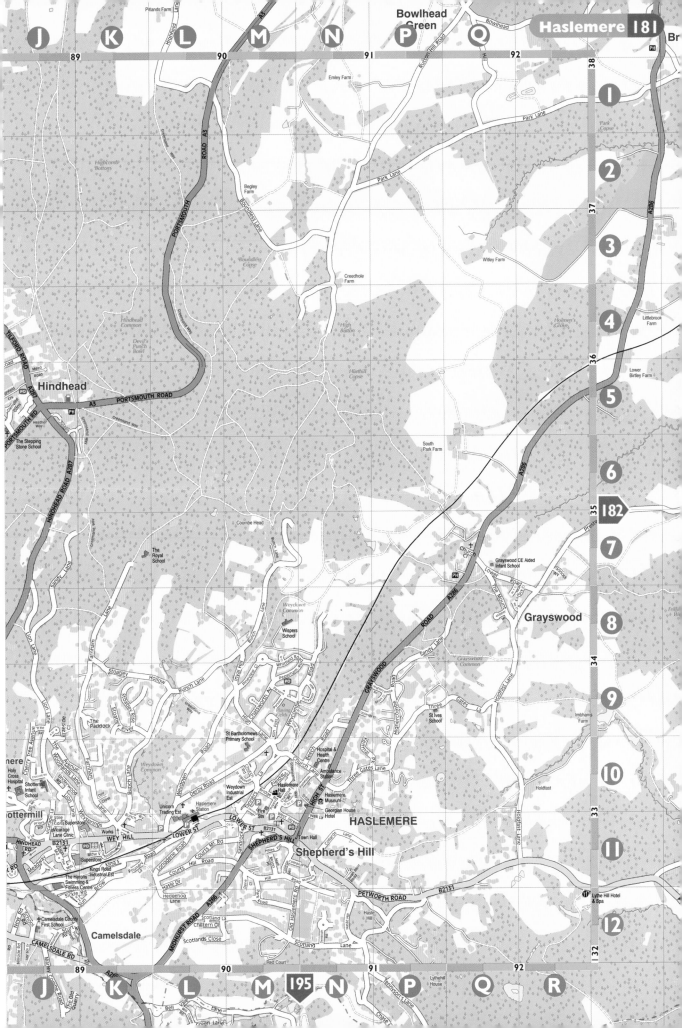

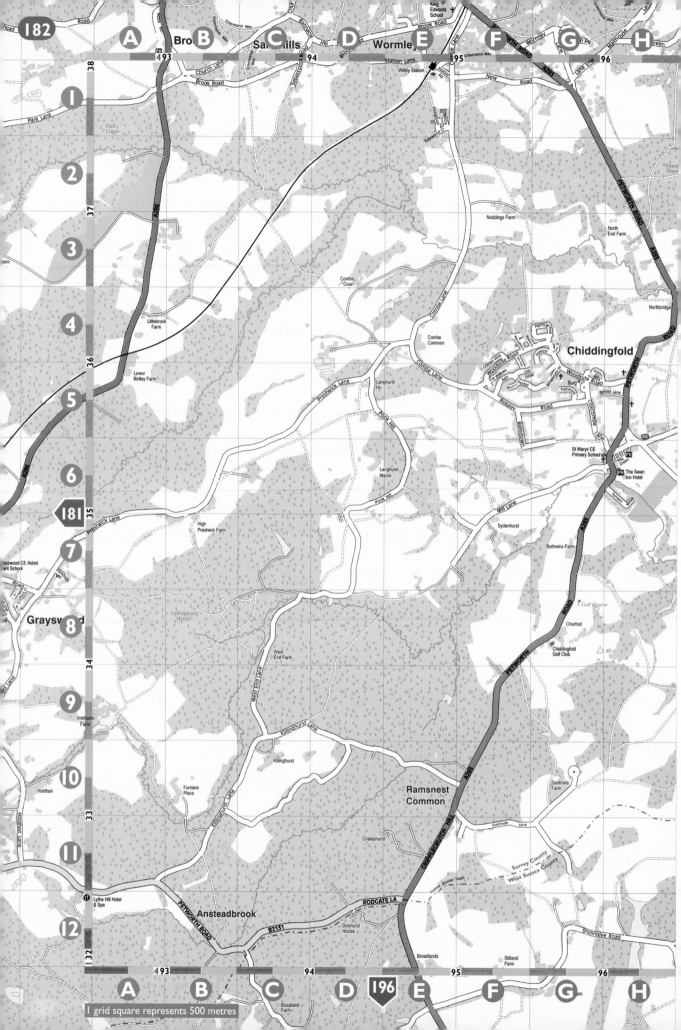

A Bro B Sandhills C Wormle D E Firth F G H
Green

38 493 94 95 96

King
Edwards
School
Brook Road Wormley
Station Lane Firth Road Lane
Witley Station New Road

Lane End
Park Lane

1

Park
Copse

2

Noddings Farm

North
End Farm

3

Combe
Court

Northbridge

4

Littlebrook
Farm

Combe Common

Combe Lane

Chiddingfold

5

Lower
Birtley Farm

Prestwick Lane

Langhurst
Ho

Woodside Road

St Marys CE
Primary School

6

Pook Hill

Langhurst
Manor

Mill Lane

Sydenhurst

The Swan
Inn Hotel

35

Prestwick Lane

High
Prestwick Farm

Bethwins Farm

7

Grayswood CE Aided
School

Golf Course

Grayswood 8

Fullinghurst
Wood

West
End Farm

West End Lane

Cherfold

Chiddingfold
Golf Club

34

9

Imbhams
Farm

Killinghurst Lane

10

Holdfast

Furnace
Place

Killinghurst

Gostrode
Farm

33

Ramsnest
Common

Gostrode Lane

11

Chaleshurst

CRIPPLECRUTCH HILL

Surrey County
West Sussex County

Lythe Hill Hotel
& Spa

PETWORTH ROAD

Ansteadbrook

RODGATE LA

Dickhurst
House

Shillinglee Road

12

B2131

Broadlands

Stilland
Farm

32

493 94 95 96

A B C D   E F G H

Boxalland
Farm

I grid square represents 500 metres

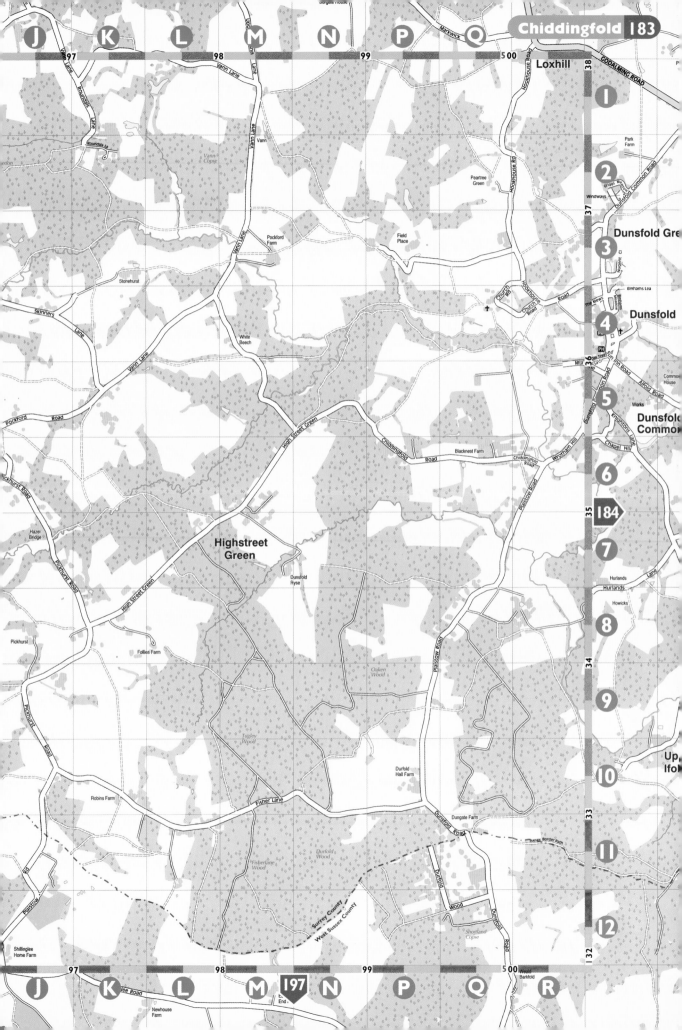

Loxhill

GODALMING ROAD

Dunsfold Gre

Dunsfold

Dunsfold
Common

184

Up.
Ifo

Vann Copse

Peartree
Green

Park
Farm

Windways

Nupent Cl

The Mews

Binhams Lea

Stonehurst

Pockford
Farm

Field
Place

Church Rd

Church
Road

Hookhouse
Road

Hookhouse Rd

Vann Lane

Vann Lane

Vann

Skinners
Lane

White
Beech

Vann Lane

Pockford   Road

High Street Green

Chiddingfold
Road

Blacknest Farm

Chiddingfold
Road

Wrotham Hill

Chapel Hill

Common
House

Works

Knightons Lane

Arfold Road

Hazel
Bridge

Highstreet
Green

Dunsfold
Ryse

Hurlands

Hurlands

Howicks

Pickhurst Road

Pickhurst

Follies Farm

Oaken
Wood

Plaistow Road

Pickhurst Road

High Street Green

Tugley
Wood

Durfold
Hall Farm

Robins Farm

Fisher Lane

Dungate Farm

Dunsfold Road

Plaistow Rd

Fisherlane
Wood

Durfold
Wood

Durfold
Wood

Shotland
Copse

Sussex Border Path

Surrey County
West Sussex County

Shillinglee
Home Farm

Lee Road

End

Weald
Barkfold

Newhouse
Farm

197

J K L M N P Q

J K L M N P Q R

97   98   99   500

97   98   99   500

1 grid square represents 500 metres

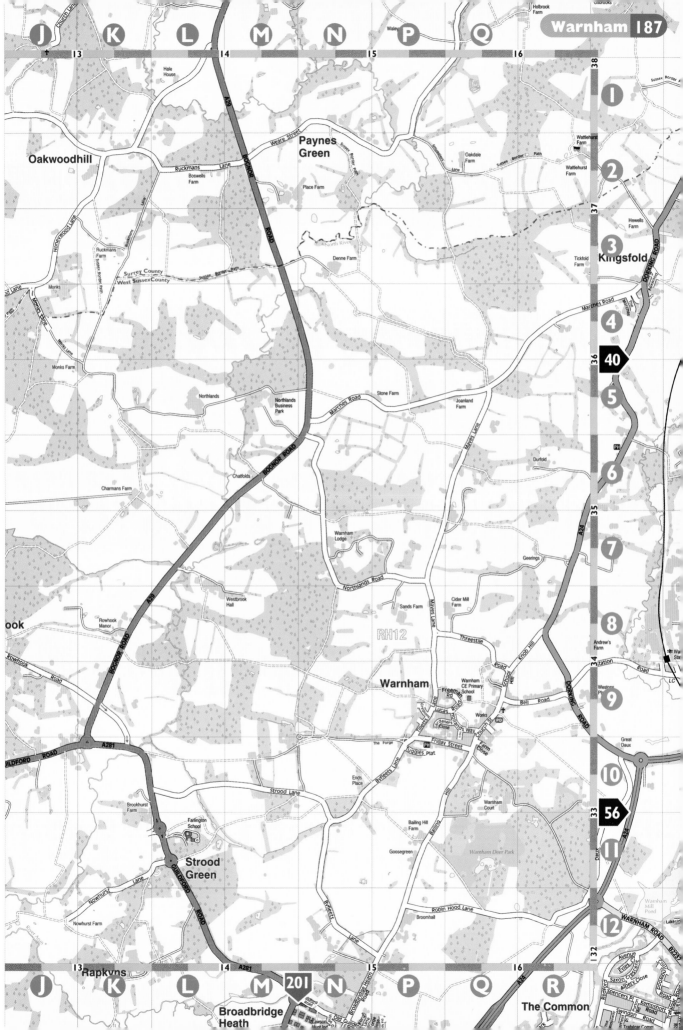

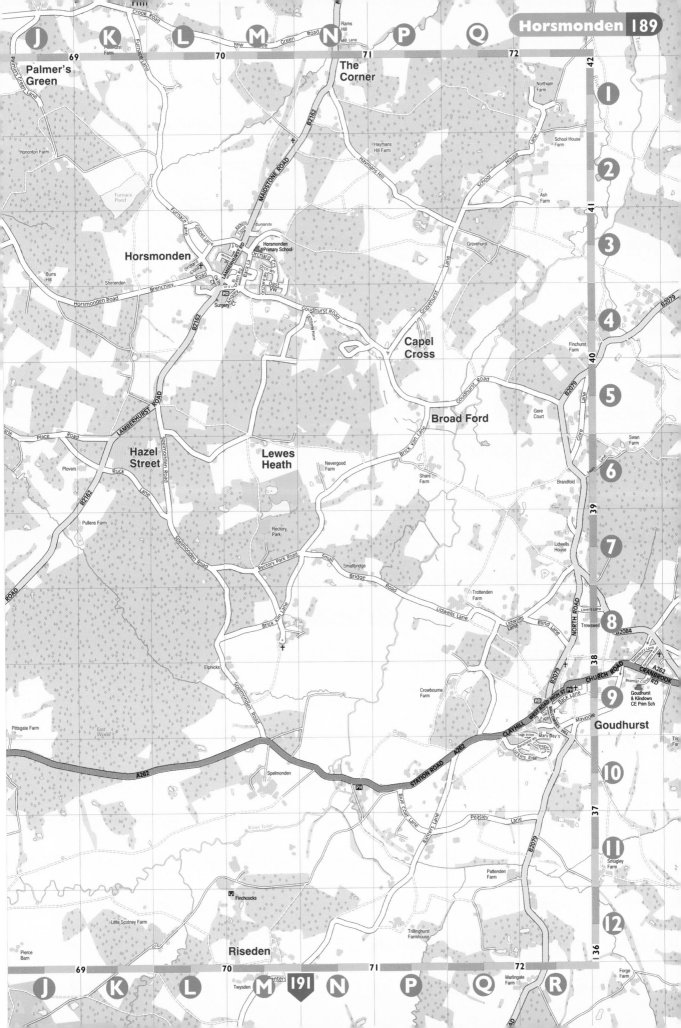

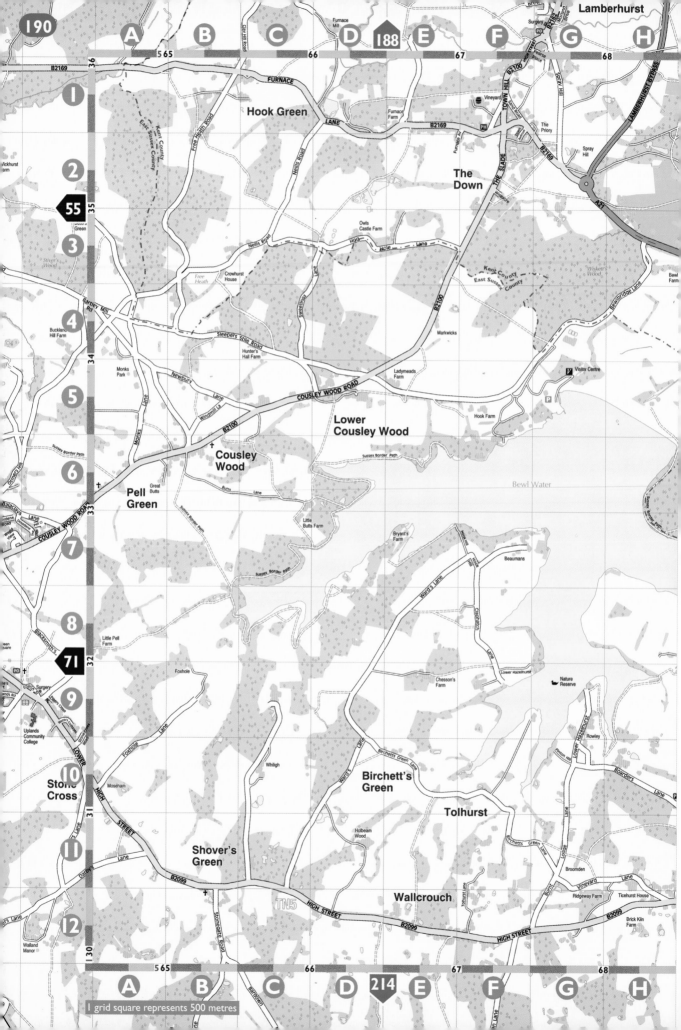

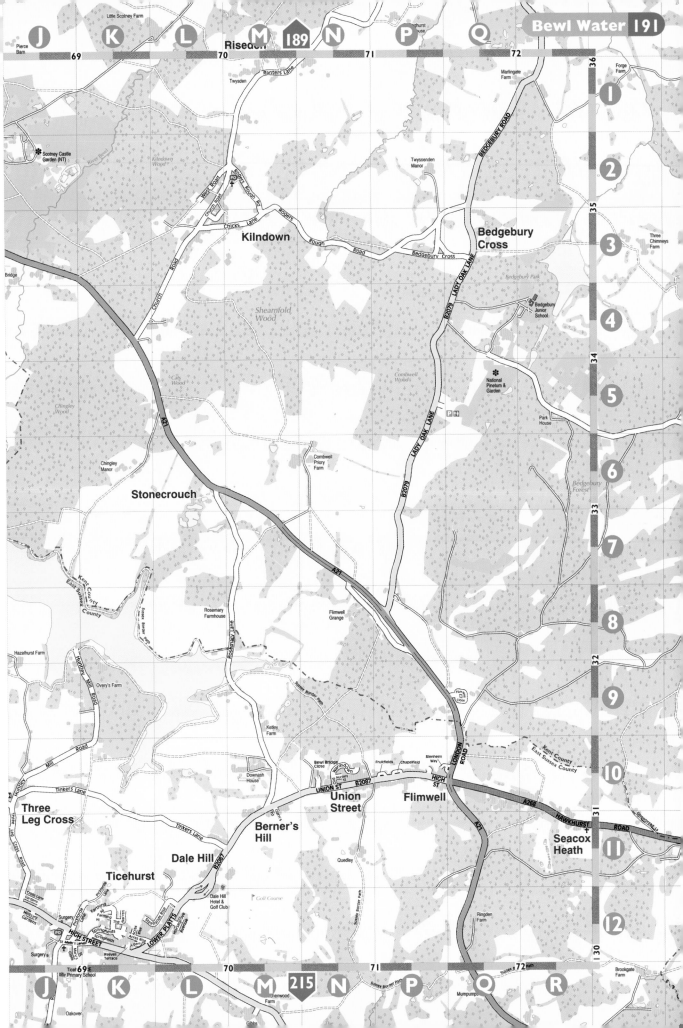

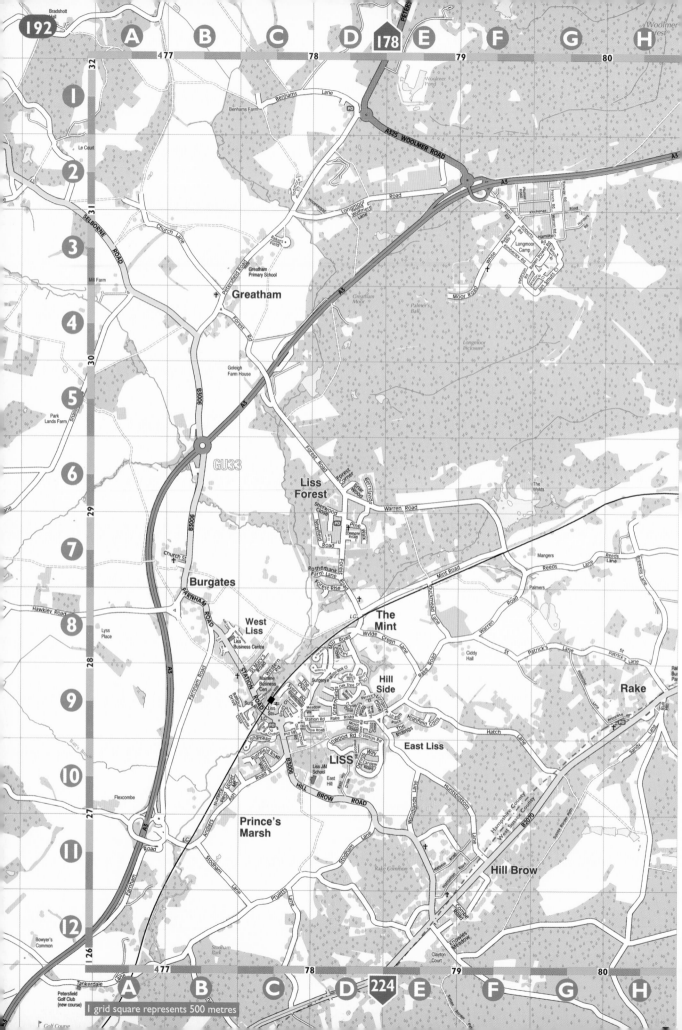

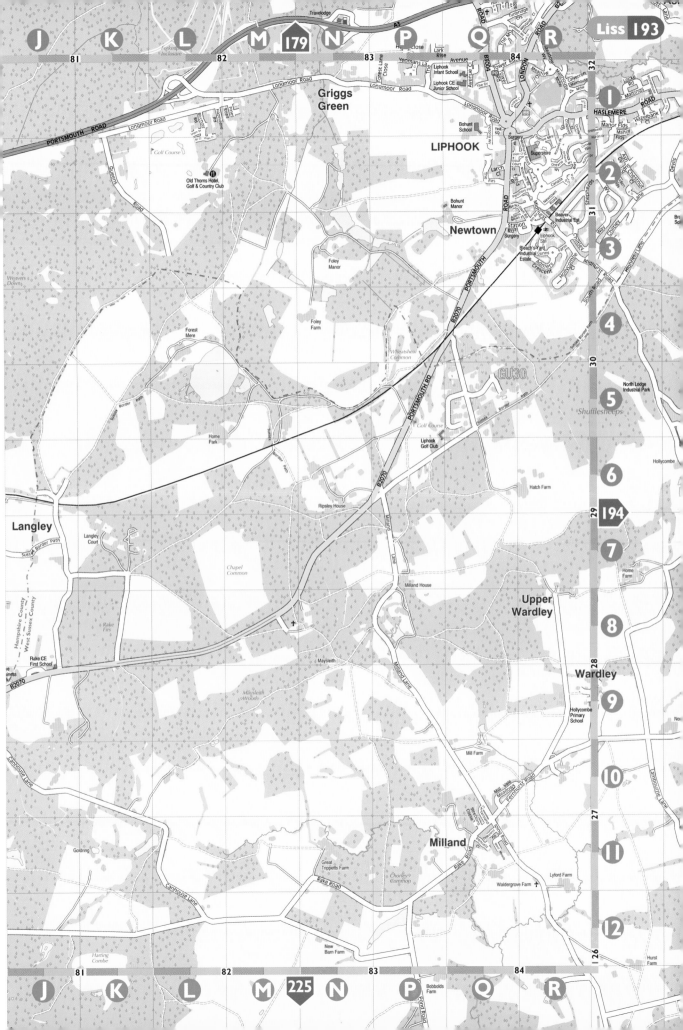

J K L M **179** N P Q R

81 82 83 84 32

1

Griggs Green

HASLEMERE

LIPHOOK

2

31

3

Newtown

4

30

GU30

5

Shufflesheeps

6

29 **194**

7

Langley

Upper Wardley

8

28

Wardley

9

Milland

10

27

11

12

26

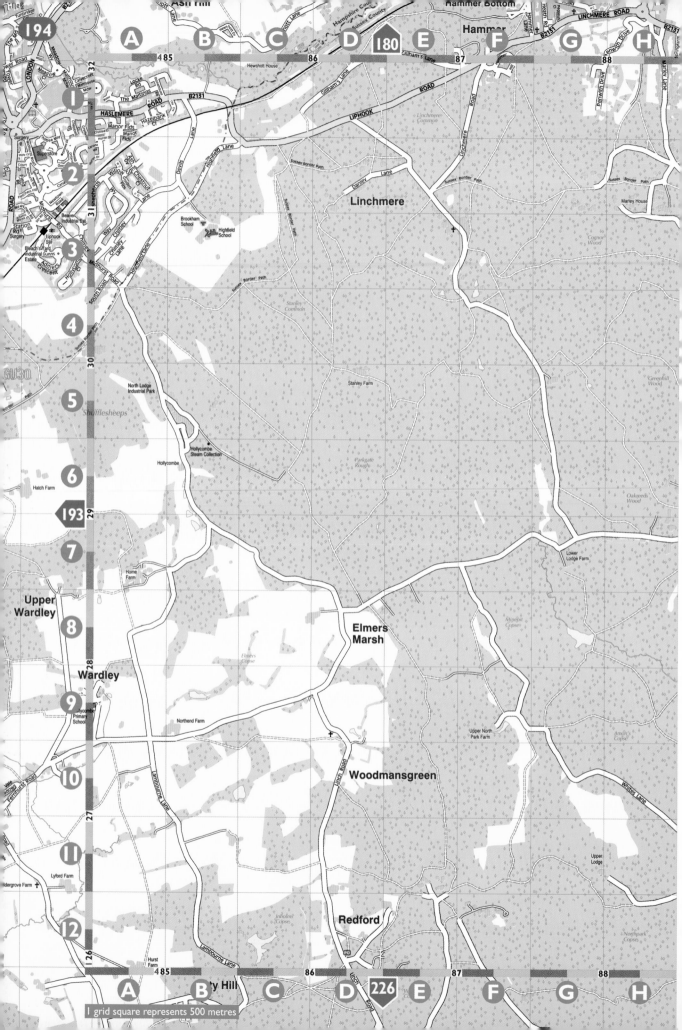

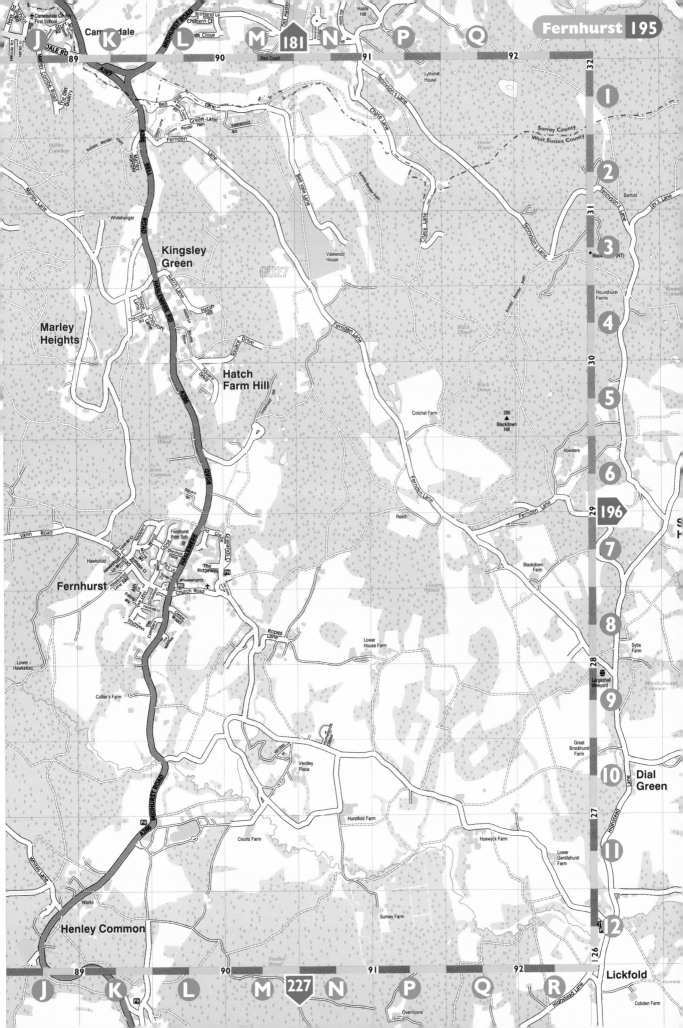

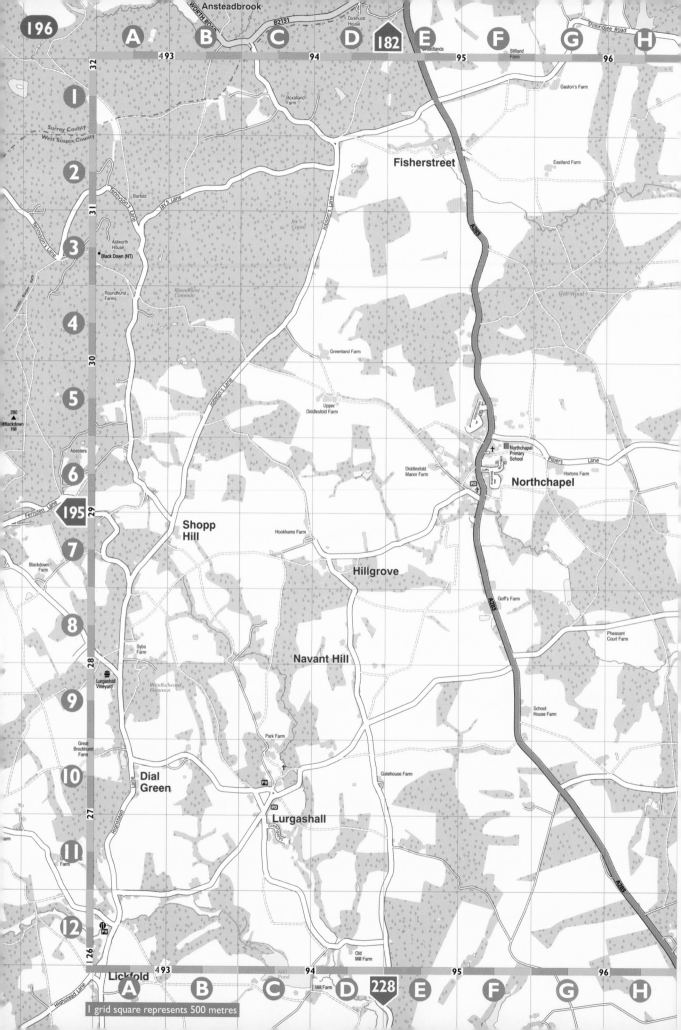

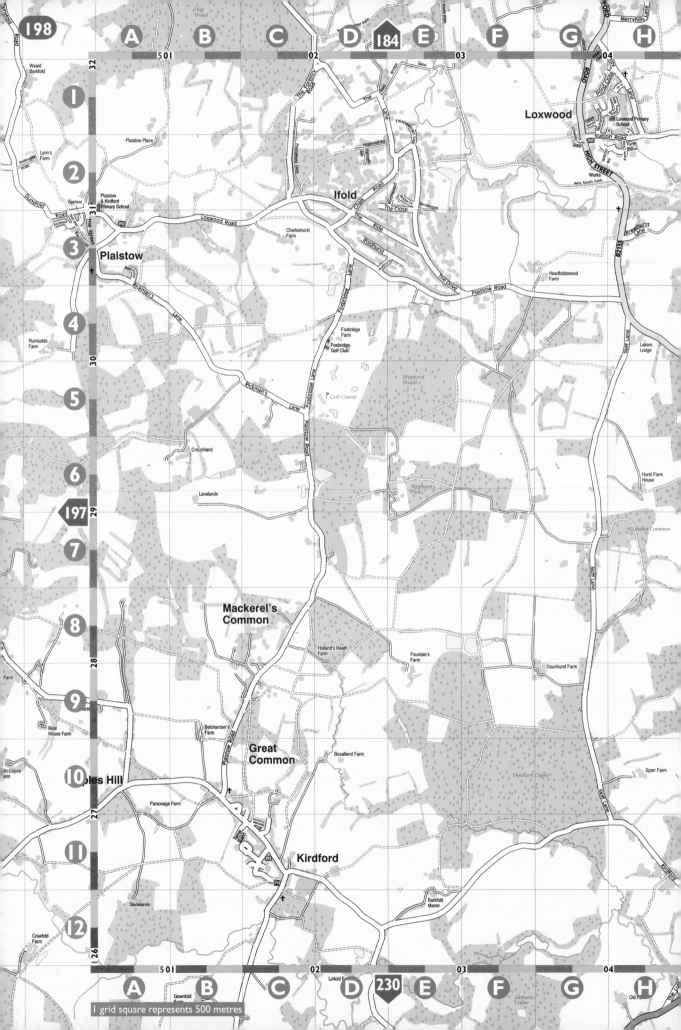

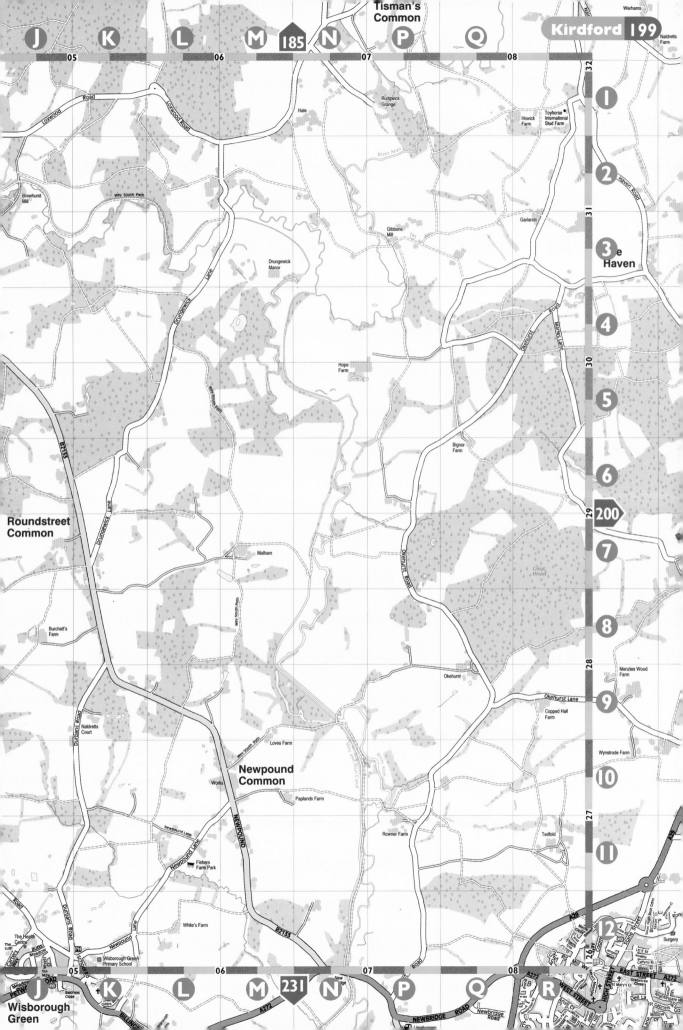

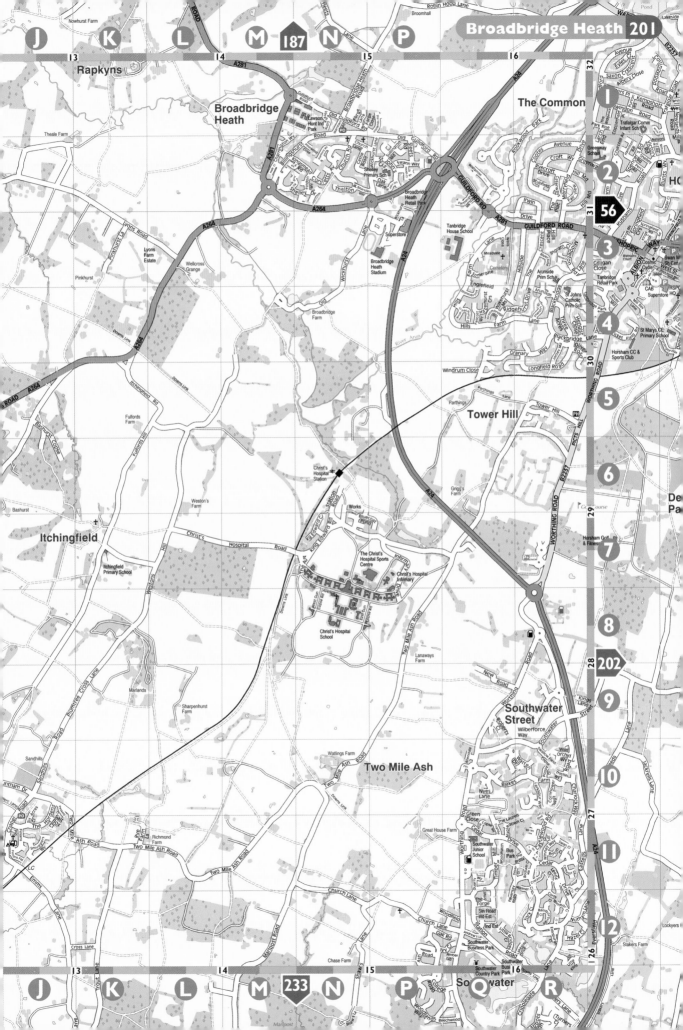

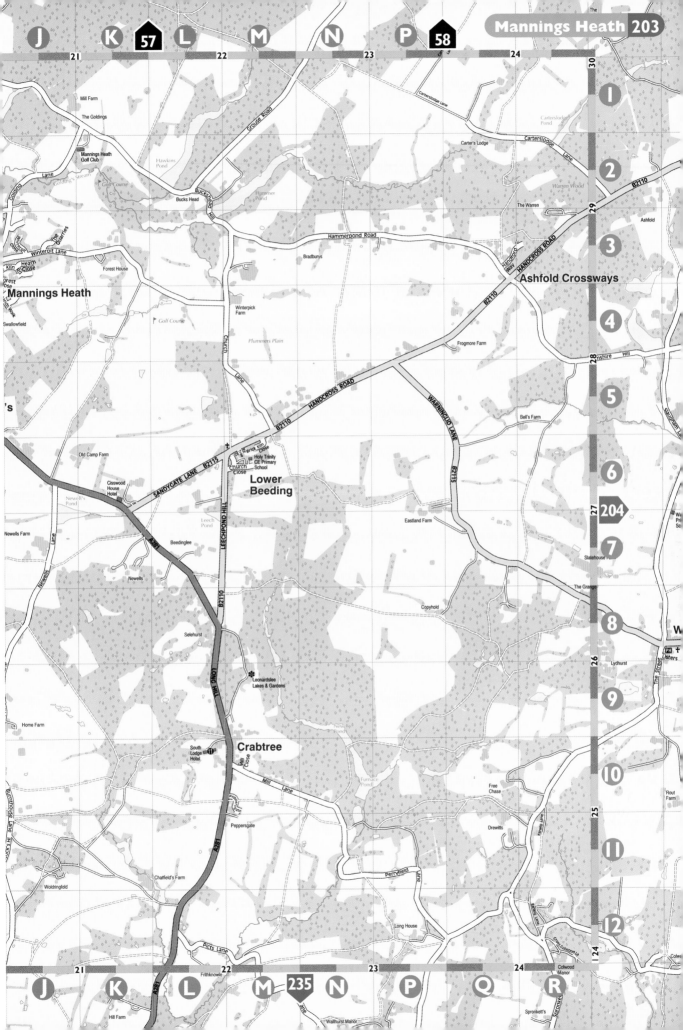

J K 57 L M N P 58

21 22 23 24

30 1

Mill Farm

The Goldings

Mannings Heath Golf Club

Golding's Stream Golf Course Hawkins Pond

Lane Golding's Lane Bucks Head Hammer Pond

29 2 BZ110

Warren Wood

Carterslodge Lane

Carter's Lodge Carterslodge Pond

Carterslodge Lane

The Warren

Ashfold

Bucks Head Hill Hammerpond Road

Bradburys Handcross Way Handcross Road 3

Winterpit Lane The Quarries Heath Close Kiln Forest House

Forest Close Swallowfield

Mannings Heath

Winterpick Farm

Plummers Plain

Golf Course

Frogmore Farm

28 nshire Hill

B2110 Handcross Road

Ashfold Crossways

4

Salisbury

Church Lane

B2110 Handcross Road

Warninglid Lane

Bell's Farm

5

Old Camp Farm

Sandygate Lane B2115 Church Close

Brick Kiln Close Holy Trinity CE Primary School

Lower Beeding

B2115

6

27 204

Cisswood House Hotel

Newell's Pond Leechpond Hill B2110

Leech Pond

Newells Farm Newells Lane A281

Beedinglee

Newells

Eastland Farm

Slatehouse

7

The Grange

8

Copyhold

26 Lydhurst

9

Home Farm

A281 Leechpond Hill

Selehurst

Leonardslee Lakes & Gardens

New Pond

10

Free Chase

Rout Farm

South Lodge Hotel Crabtree

Mill Close Mill Lane

Furnace Pond

Drewitts

25 11

Burnthouse Lane A281

Peppersgate

Perryfield Lane

Chatfield's Farm

Woldringfold

Long House

24 12

Picts Lane

Frithknowle

J K L M 235 N P Q R

21 22 23 24

Hill Farm Wallhurst Manor Spronkett's

Colwood Manor

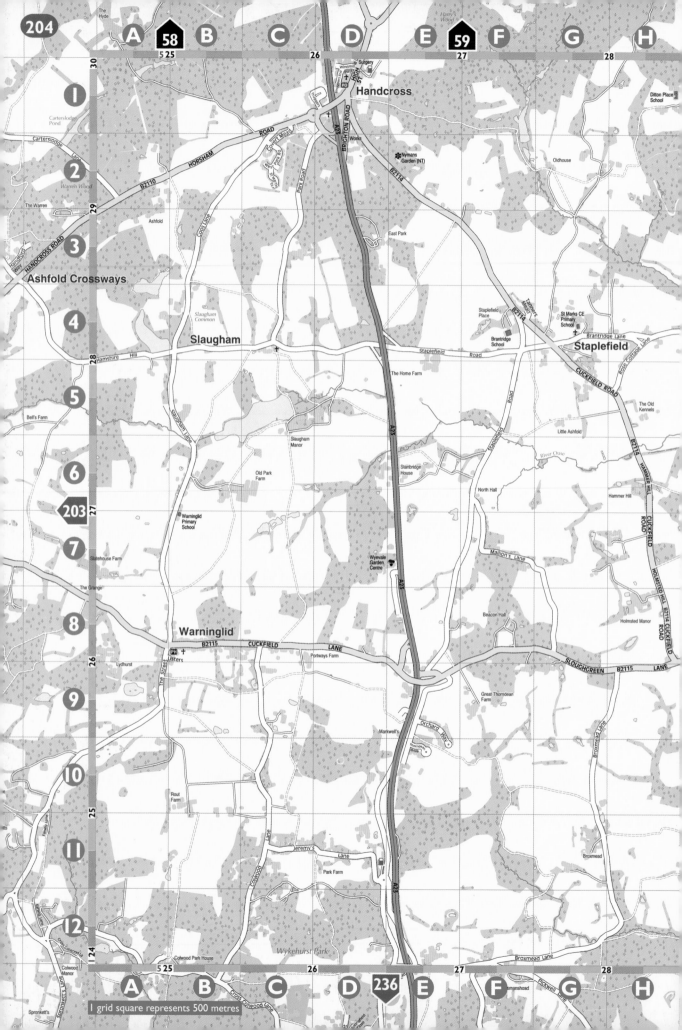

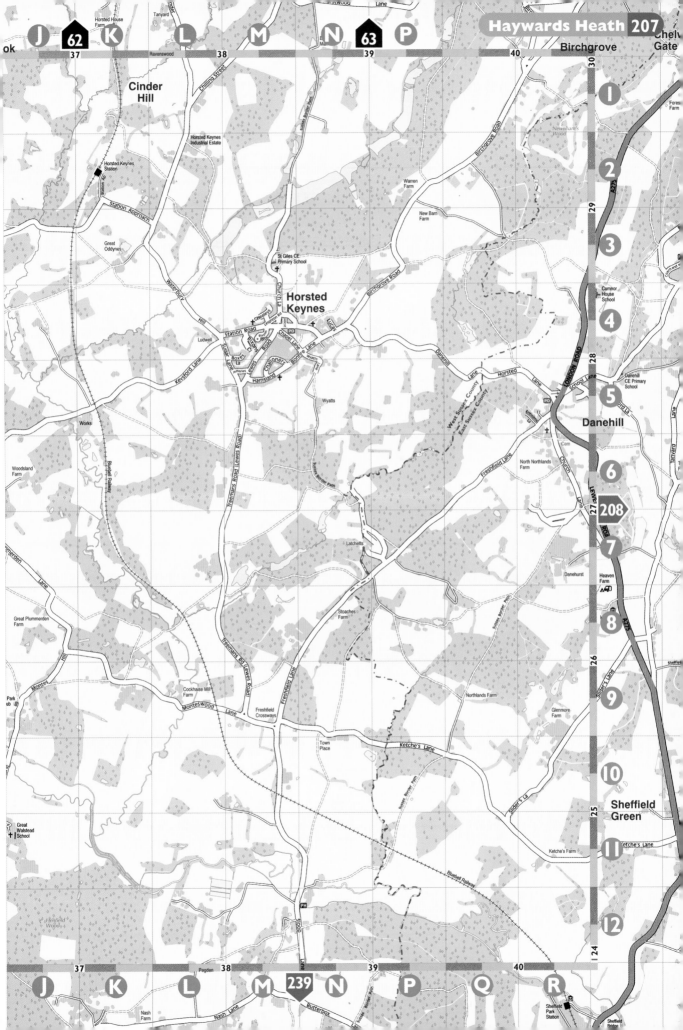

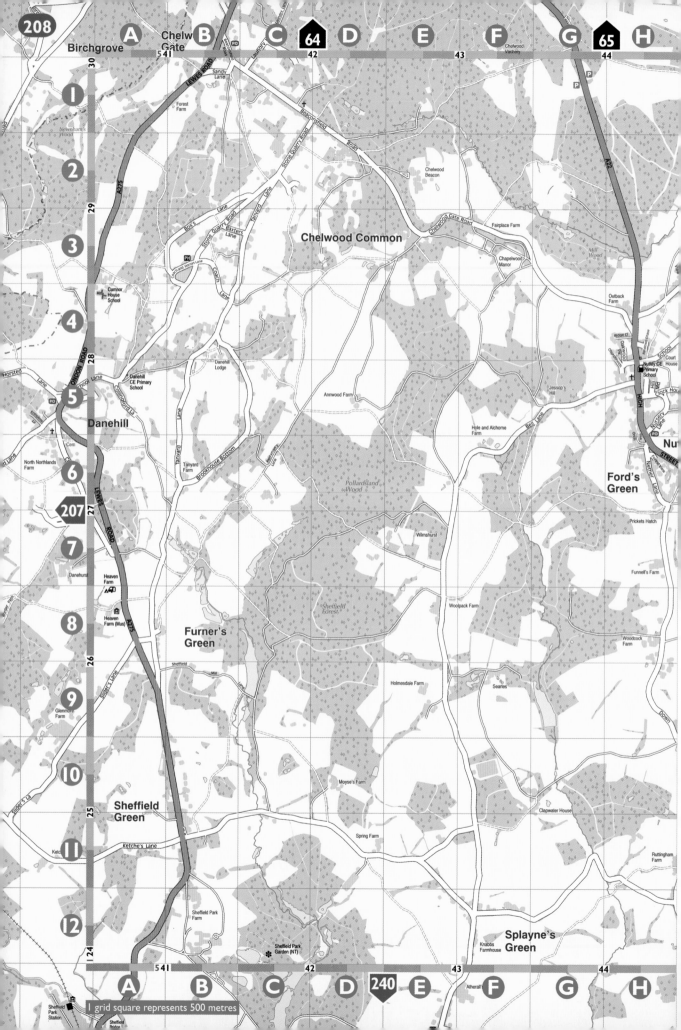

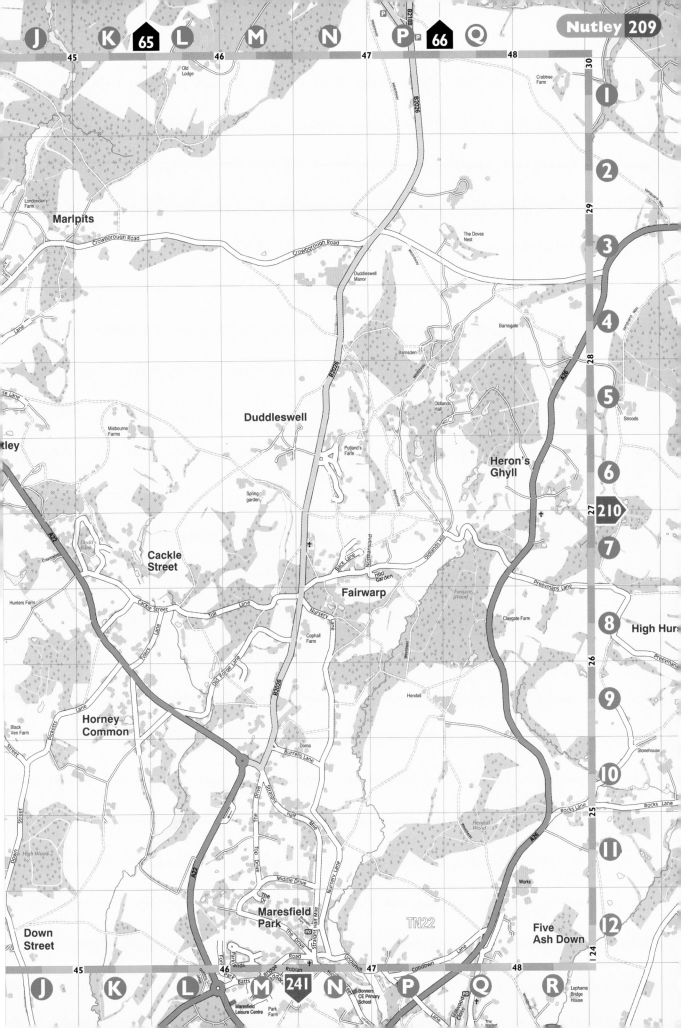

J K **65** L M N P **66** Q

45 46 47 48

30

1

2

29

3

4

28

5

6

27 **210**

7

8 High Hur

26

9

10

25

11

12

24

Londonderry Farm

Marlpits

Old Lodge

Crowborough Road

Crowborough Road

Duddleswell Manor

The Doves Nest

Barnsgate

Barnsden

Duddleswell

Oldlands Hall

Stroods

Misbourne Farms

utley

Heron's Ghyll

Spring garden

Putland's Farm

Cackle Street

Dodd's Bank

Back Lane

Normansland

Hop Garden

Fairwarp

Furnace Wood

Claygate Farm

Hunters Farm

Cackle Street

Toll Lane

Nursery Lane

Cophall Farm

Preemans Lane

Preyman

Black Ven Farm

Tylers Lane

Old Forge Lane

Hendall

Stonehouse

Horney Common

Picketts Lane

B2026

Doma

Burrells Lane

Rocks Lane

Rocks Lane

Hendall Wood

High Wood

Down Street

The Drive

Straight Half Mile

Top Drive

Middle Drive

The Dr

Maresfield Park

Nursery Lane

Works

TN22

Five Ash Down

Down Street

J K L M **241** N P Q R

45 46 47 48

Fort

Park Lands

Batts

Bridge

Roblan Road

Underhill

Cobdown Lane

Bonners CE Primary School

Lephams Bridge House

Maresfield Leisure Centre

Park Farm

Milwood Close

The Wallett

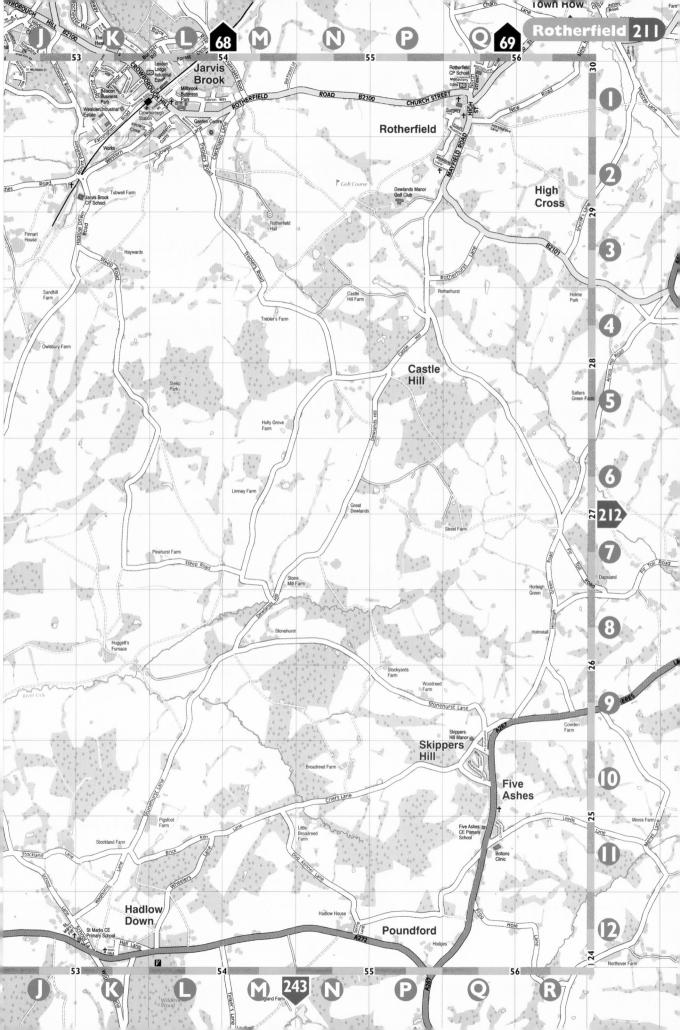

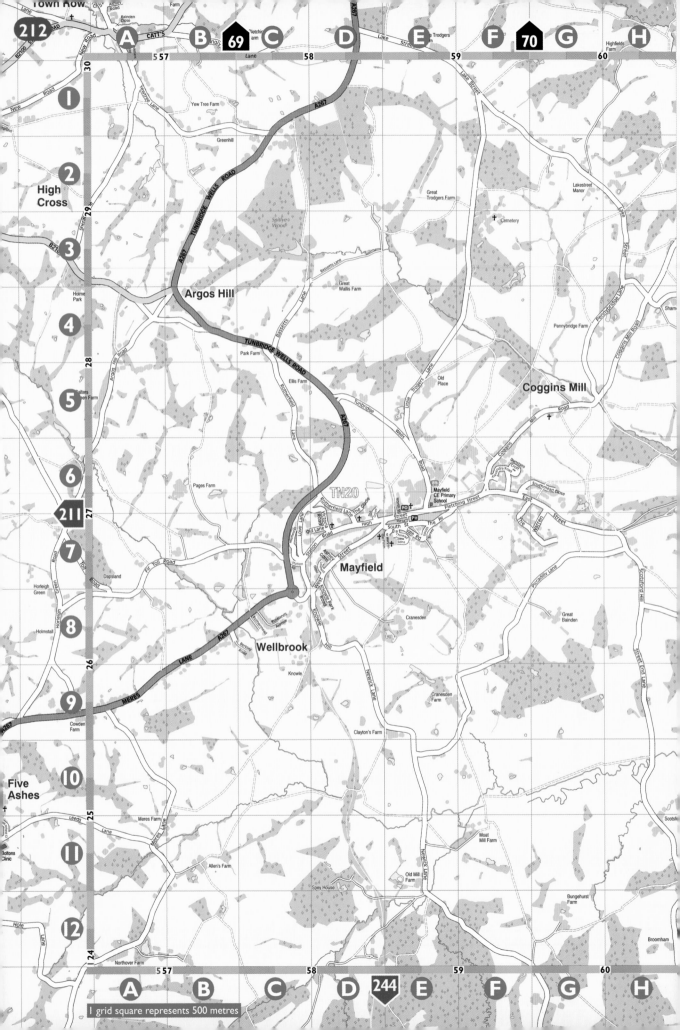

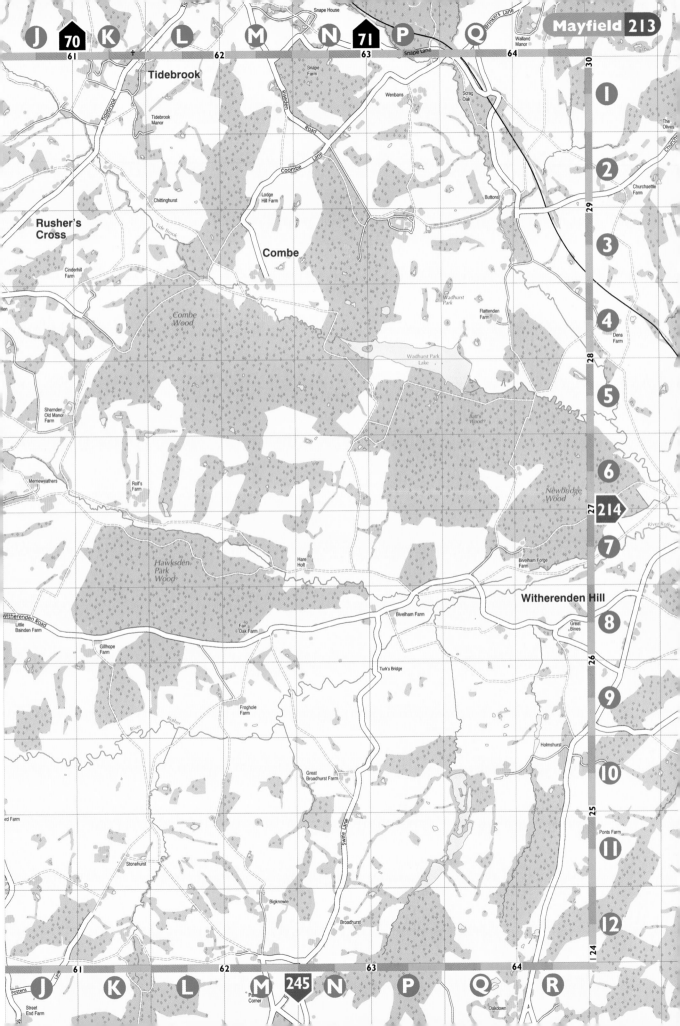

J 70 K L M N 71 P Q

61 62 63 64

30

1
2
3
4
5
6
214
7
8
9
10
11
12

29

28

27

26

25

24

Tidebrook

Rusher's
Cross

Combe

Snape House

Snape Lane

Brinker's Lane

Walland
Manor

The
Olives

Churchsettle
Farm

Wenbans

Scrag
Oak

Buttons

Snape
Farm

Chittinghurst

Lodge
Hill Farm

Tidebrook
Manor

Tide Brook

Coombe Lane

Riseden Road

Cinderhill
Farm

Combe
Wood

Wadhurst
Park

Flattenden
Farm

Dens
Farm

Wadhurst Park
Lake

Sharnden
Old Manor
Farm

Batt's
Wood

Merneweathers

Rolf's
Farm

Newbridge
Wood

River Rother

Hawksden
Park
Wood

Hare
Holt

Bivelham Forge
Farm

Witherenden Hill

Witherenden Road

Little
Bainden
Farm

Gillhope
Farm

Fair
Oak Farm

Bivelham Farm

Great
Bines

Turk's Bridge

Holmshurst

Froghole
Farm

River
Rother

Great
Broadhurst Farm

Ponts Farm

Stonehurst

Swift Lane

Bigknowle

Broadhurst

Oakdown

Potters

Street
End Farm

J 61 K L M 245 N P Q R

62 63 64

Corner

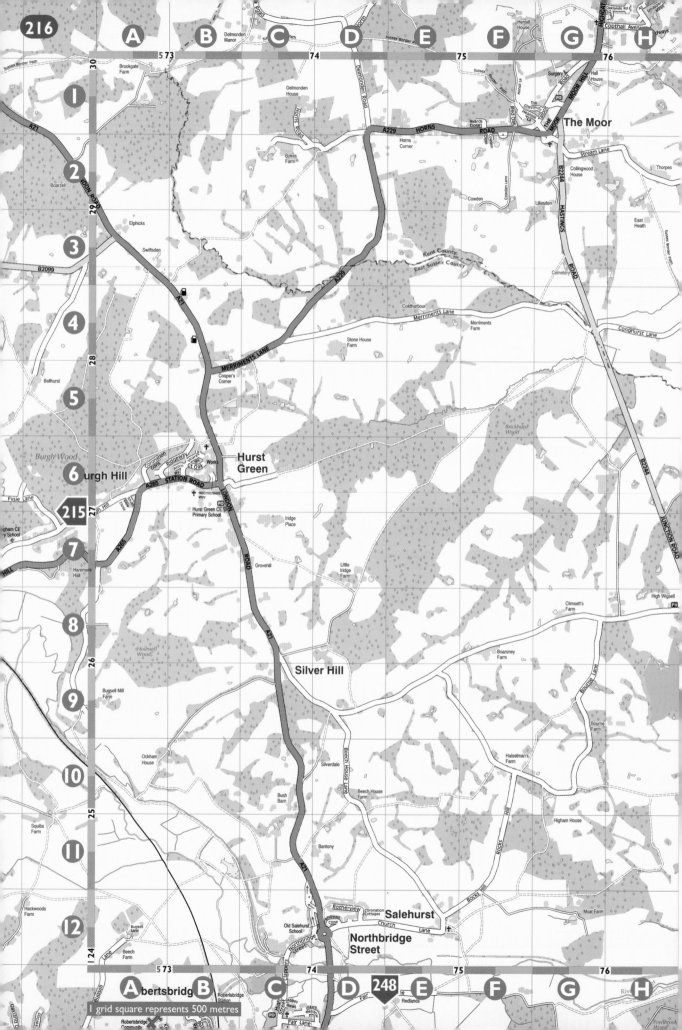

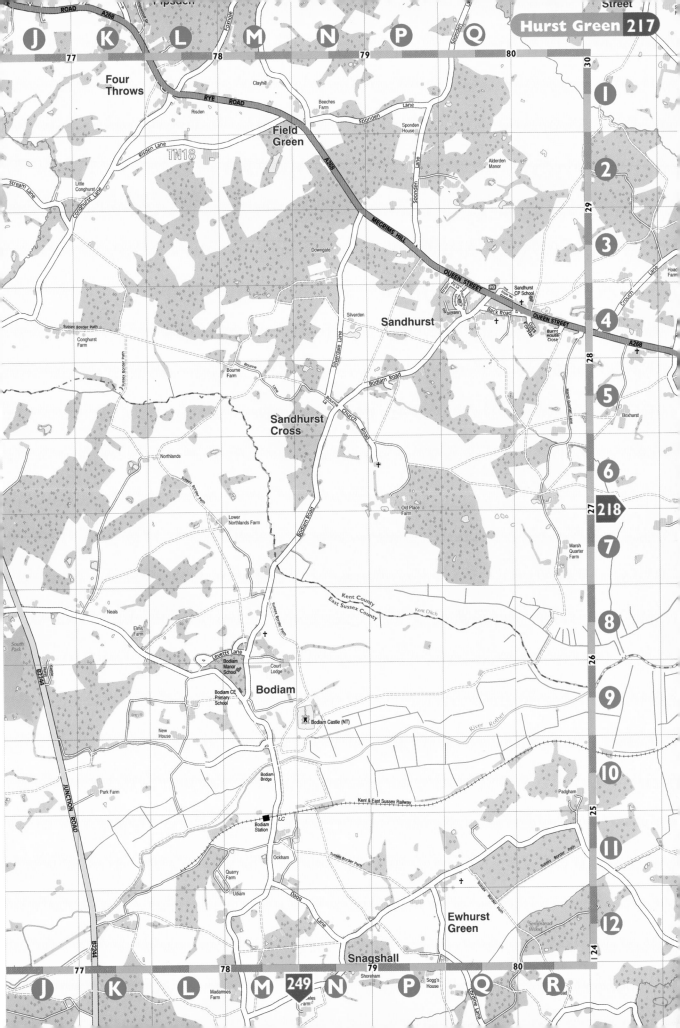

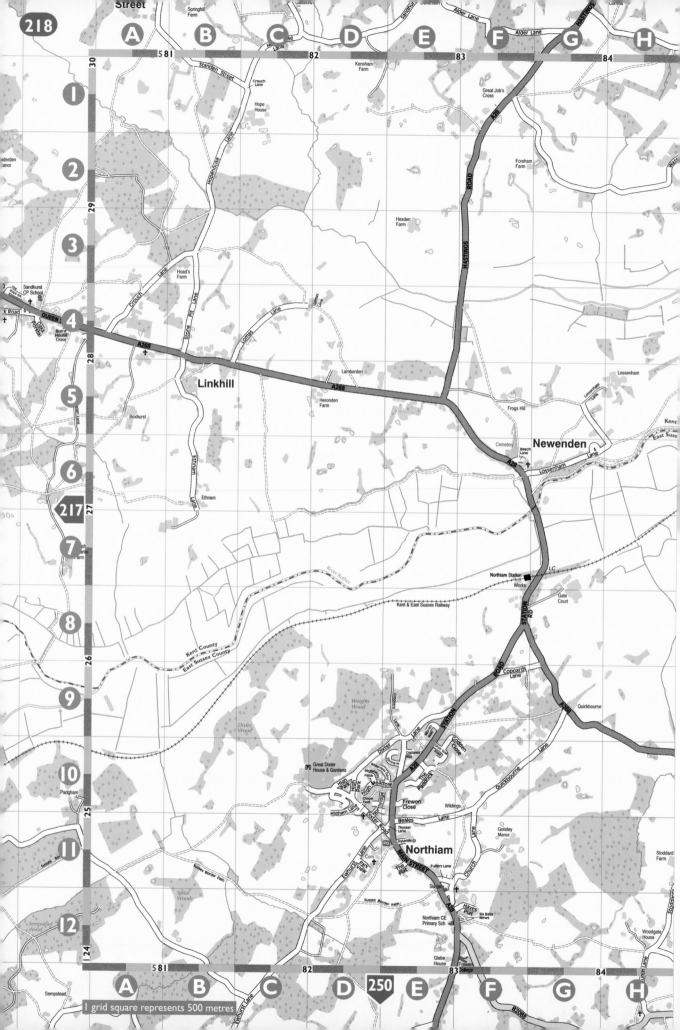

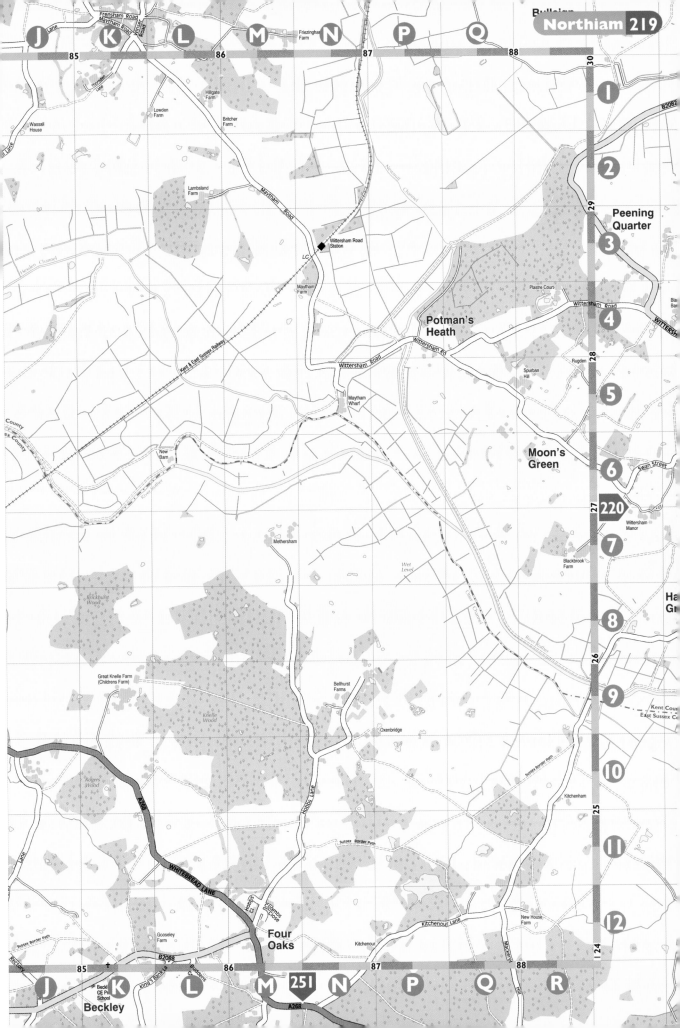

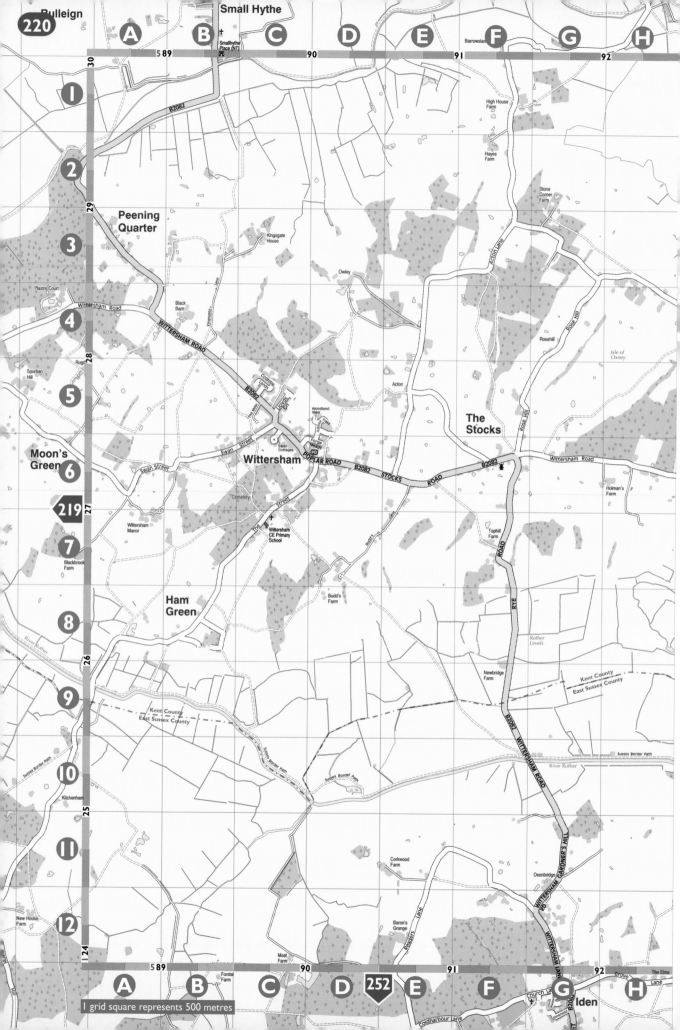

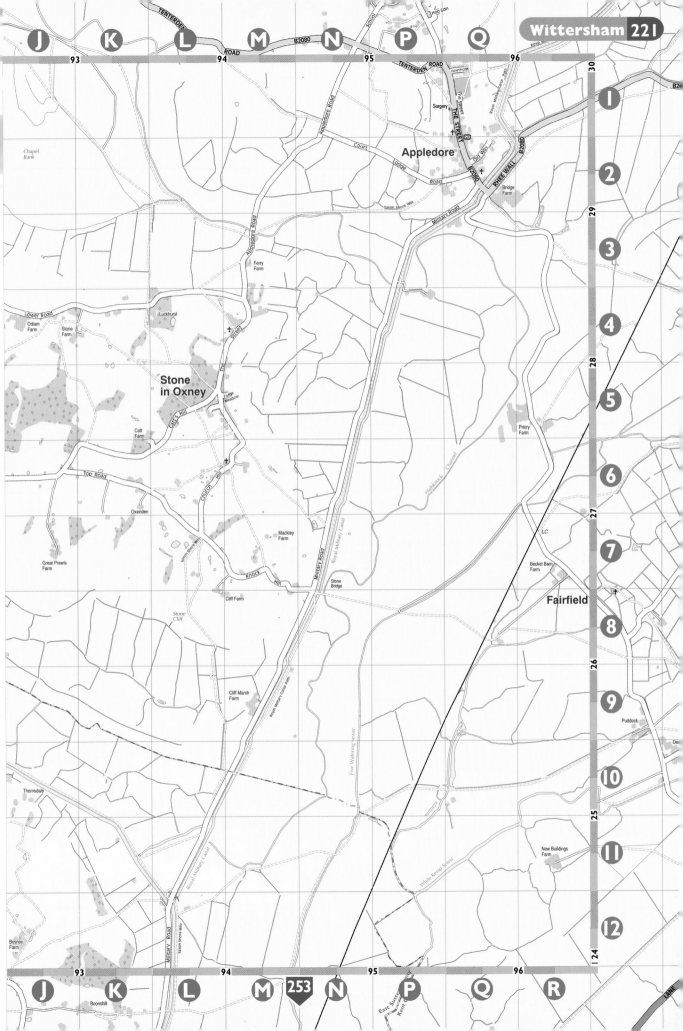

J K L M N P Q

TENTERDEN ROAD
B2080
ROAD
93 94 95 96
30

School
Hop Gdn

TENTERDEN ROAD
Hawthorn
1

Surgery
THE STREET
2

Appledore
PO
Court
Lodge
Old Wall
RHEE WALL
B2080
Road
Bridge Farm

Chapel Bank

Military Road
29

Saxon Shore Way

3

Ferry Farm
4

Lower Road
Luckhurst
The Street
28

Odiam Farm
Stone Farm

Stone in Oxney
Forge Meadow
Catt's Hill

5

Priory Farm

Catt Farm
Top Road

Church Hill
6

Oxenden

Mackley Farm
Highknock Channel
27

Great Prawls Farm

Saxon Shore Way
Royal Military Canal
LC
7

Knock Hill
Military Road
Becket Barn Farm
Cliff Farm
Stone Bridge
Fairfield
8

Stone Cliff
26

Cliff Marsh Farm
9

Royal Military Canal Path
Puddock

Thornsdale
Five Watering Sewer
10

25

New Buildings Farm
11

Royal Military Canal
White Kemp Sewer
Bosney Farm

Military Road
Saxon Shore Way
12
24

J K L M 253 N P Q R
Boonshill
93 94 95 96

East Sussex
Kent
LANE

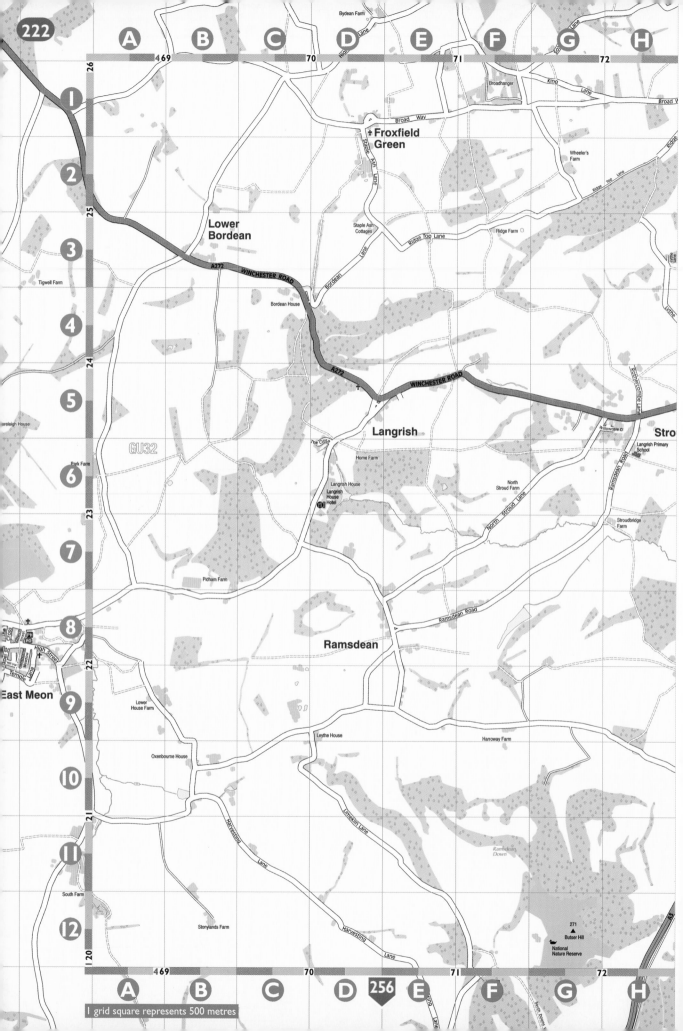

A 469 B C 70 D High E 71 F G Soke 72 H

Bydean Farm

1

26

2

25

Lower
Bordean

3

Tigwell Farm

4

24

5

ereleigh House

GU32

Park Farm

6

23

7

8

East Meon

9

22

10

21

11

South Farm

12

20

Stonylands Farm

Froxfield
Green

Broad Way

Staple Ash
Cottages

Ridge Top Lane

Ridge Farm

Bordean House

Bordean Lane

A272 WINCHESTER ROAD

A272

WINCHESTER ROAD

Langrish

The Cross

Home Farm

Langrish House

Langrish
House
Hotel

Pidham Farm

Ramsdean

Ramsdean Road

North Stroud Lane

North
Stroud Farm

Lower
House Farm

Leythe House

Oxenbourne House

Harroway Farm

Harvesting Lane

Limekiln Lane

Ramsdean
Down

Butser Hill

271

National
Nature Reserve

Broadhanger

King Lane

Wheeler's
Farm

Ridge Top Lane

Rothercombe Lane

Willowdale Cl

Langrish Primary
School

Ramsdean Road

Stroudbridge
Farm

Stro

1 grid square represents 500 metres

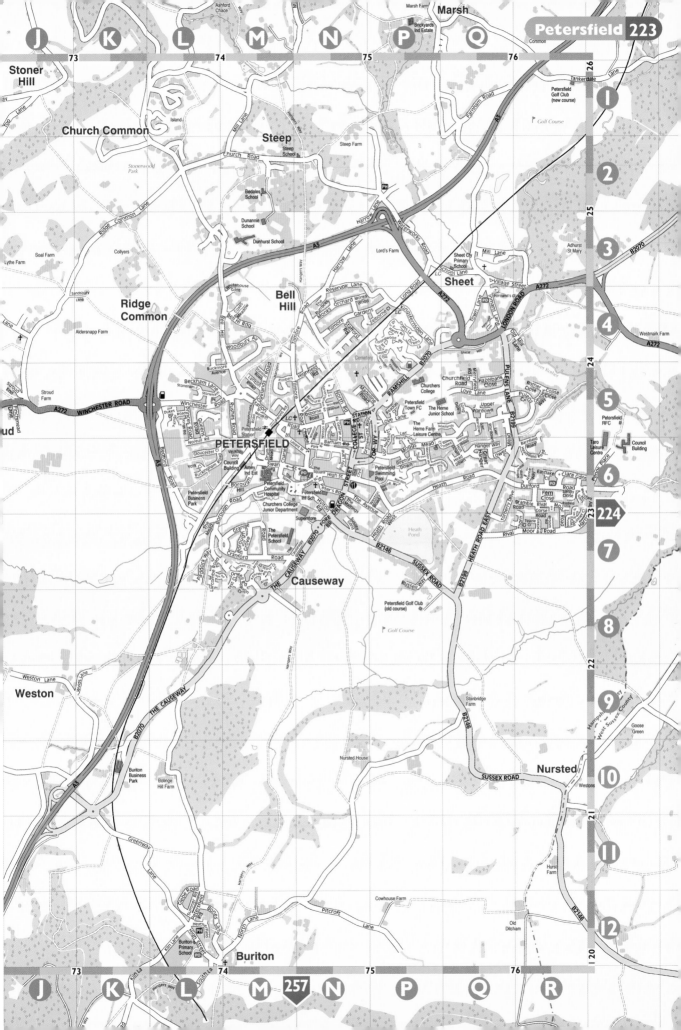

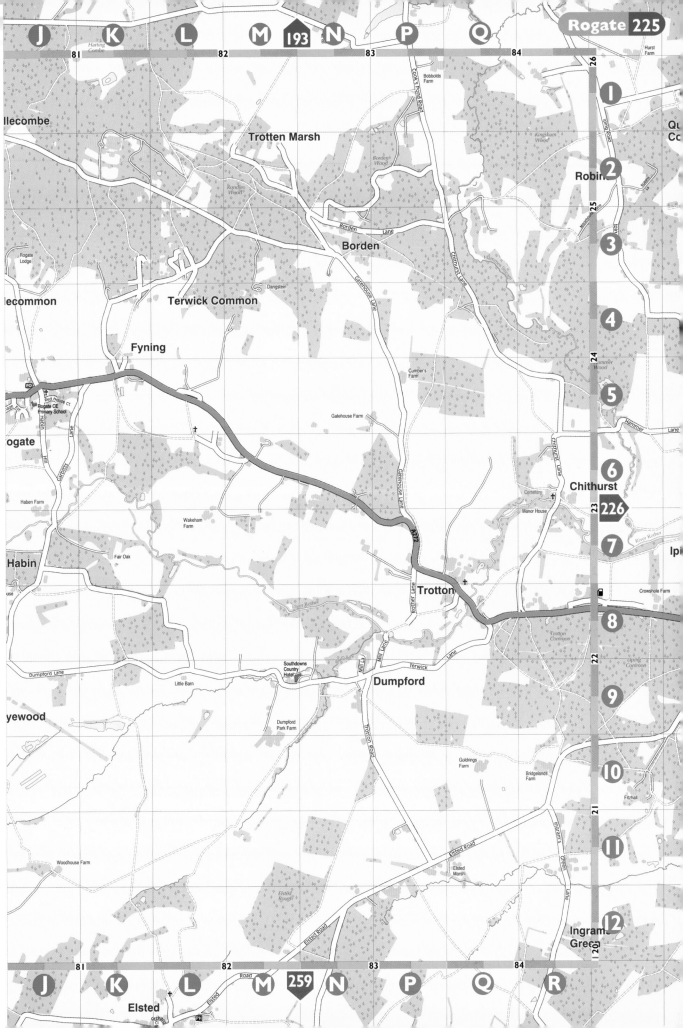

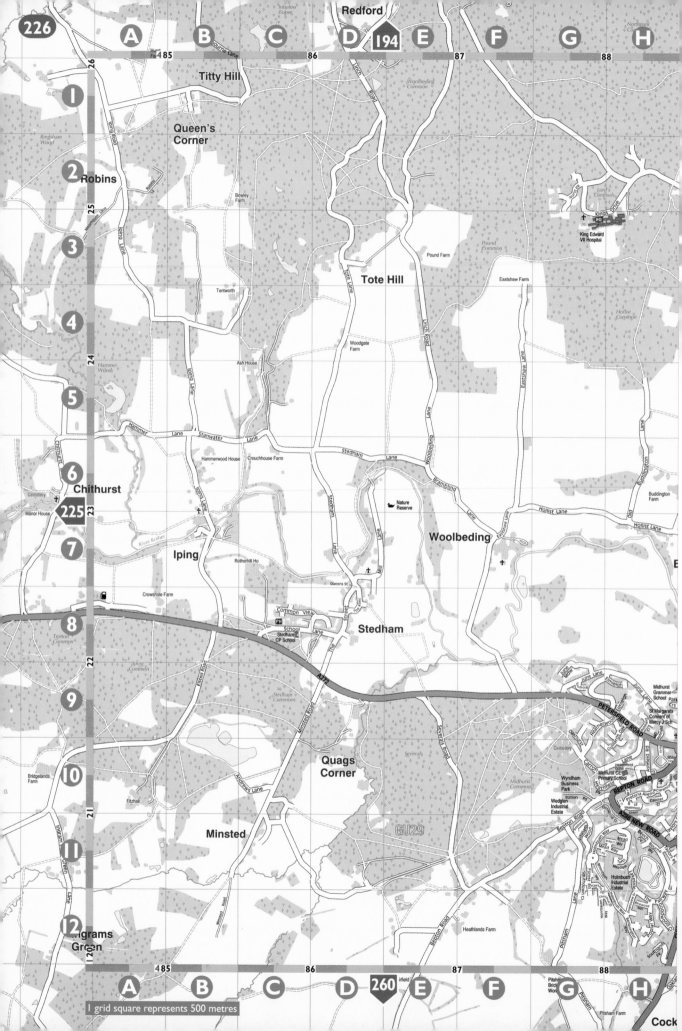

Redford

A B C D 194 E F G H

Titty Hill

1

Queen's Corner

2 Robins

3

4

5

Chithurst **6**

225 23

7

Iping

8

9

Quags Corner

10

Minsted

11

12 Ingrams Green

Woolbeding Common

Tote Hill

Woodgate Farm

Nature Reserve

Woolbeding

Stedham

Pound Farm

Pound Common

Eastshaw Farm

Hollist Common

Buddington Farm

Hollist Lane

King Edward VII Hospital

Kings Drive

Lord's Common

Northpark

Peterfield Road

Bepton Road

Midhurst

GU29

Heathlands Farm

A 4 85 B C D 260 E F G 88 H

Cock

1 grid square represents 500 metres

Hammerwood House

Crouchhouse Farm

Stedham Lane

Bowley Farm

Tentworth

Ash House

Hammer Wood

River Rother

Crowshole Farm

Rotherhill Ho

Queens St

Common View

Stedham CP School

Stedham Commons

Iping Common

Tepton Common

Bridgelands Farm

Fitzhall

Andrew's Lane

Severals Road

Quags Corner

Wyndham Business Park

Midhurst Common

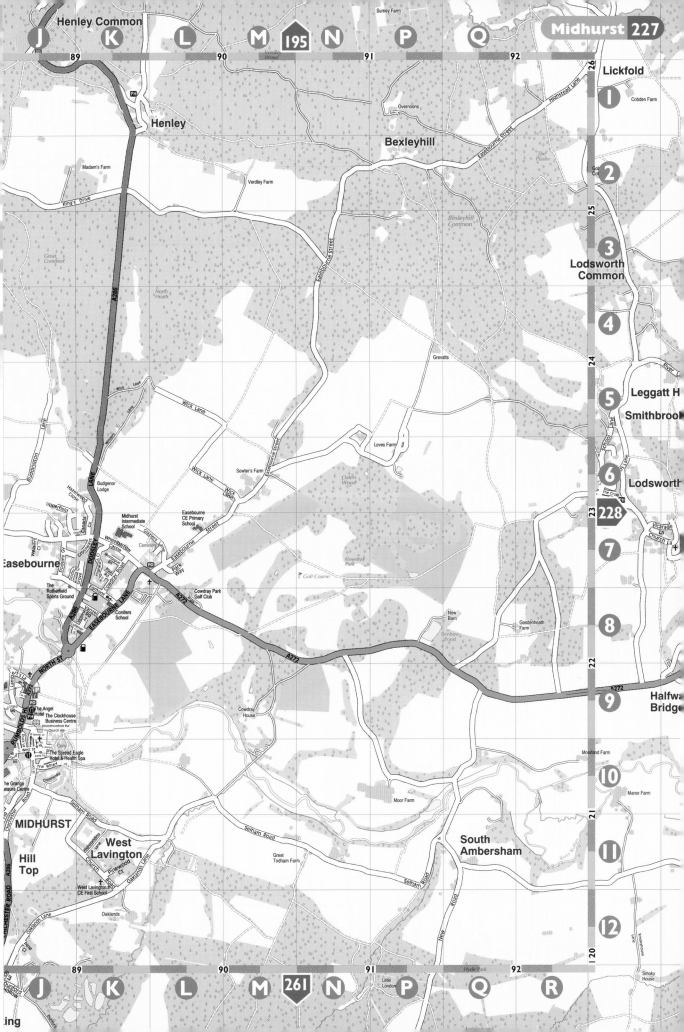

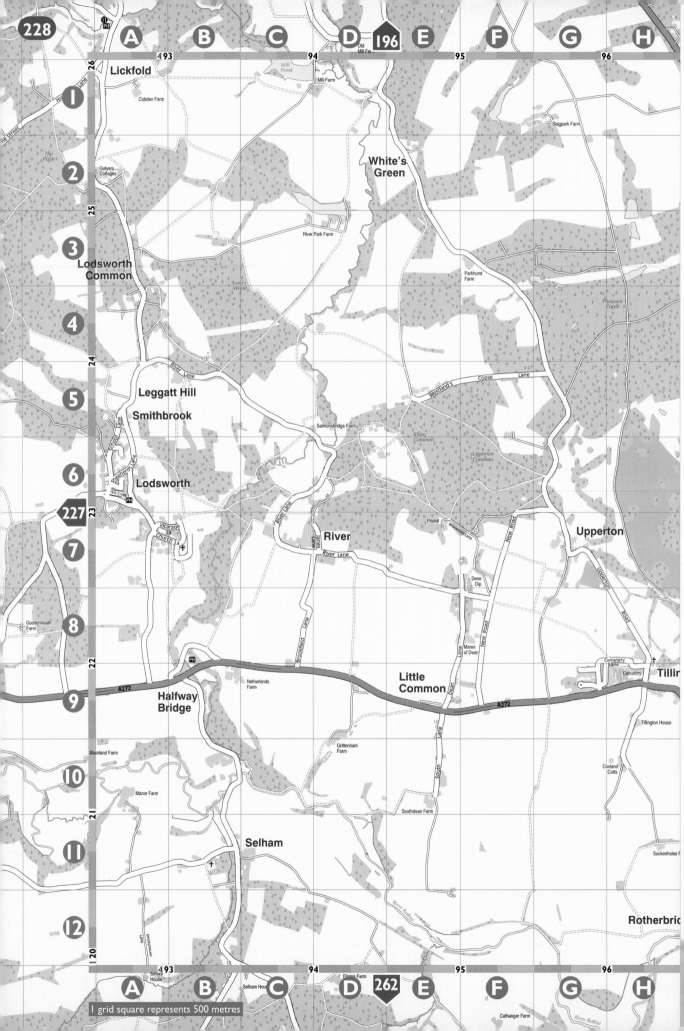

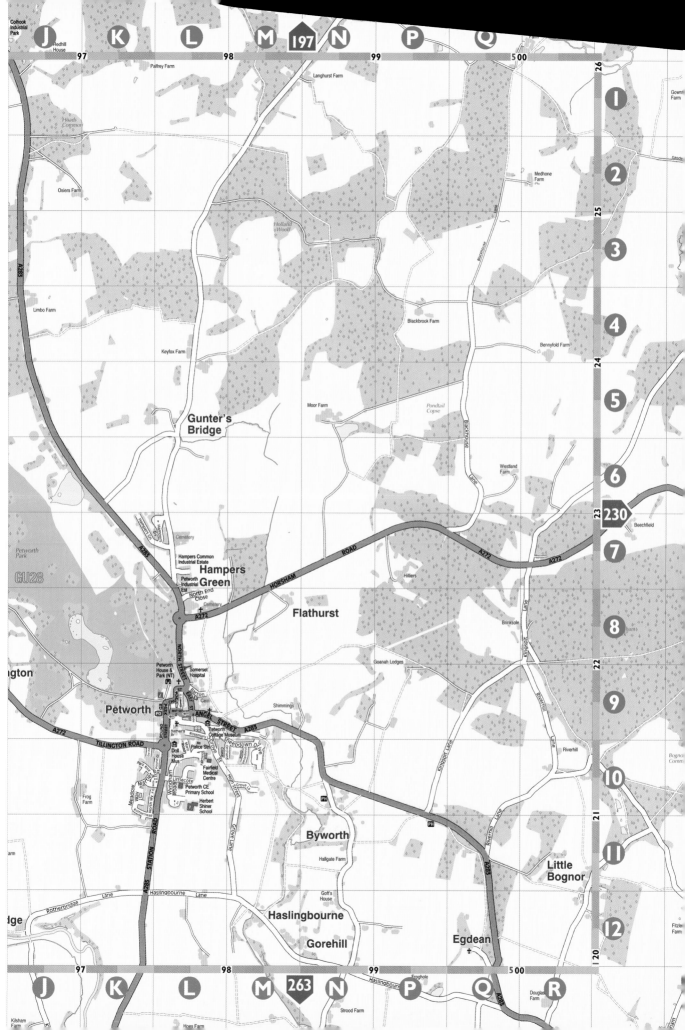

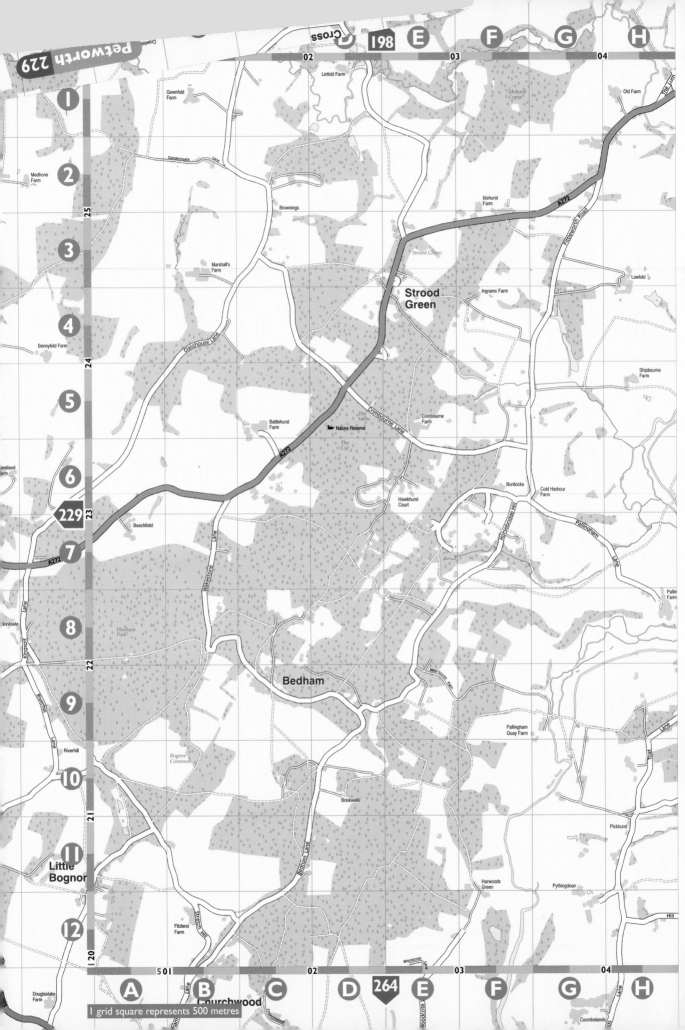

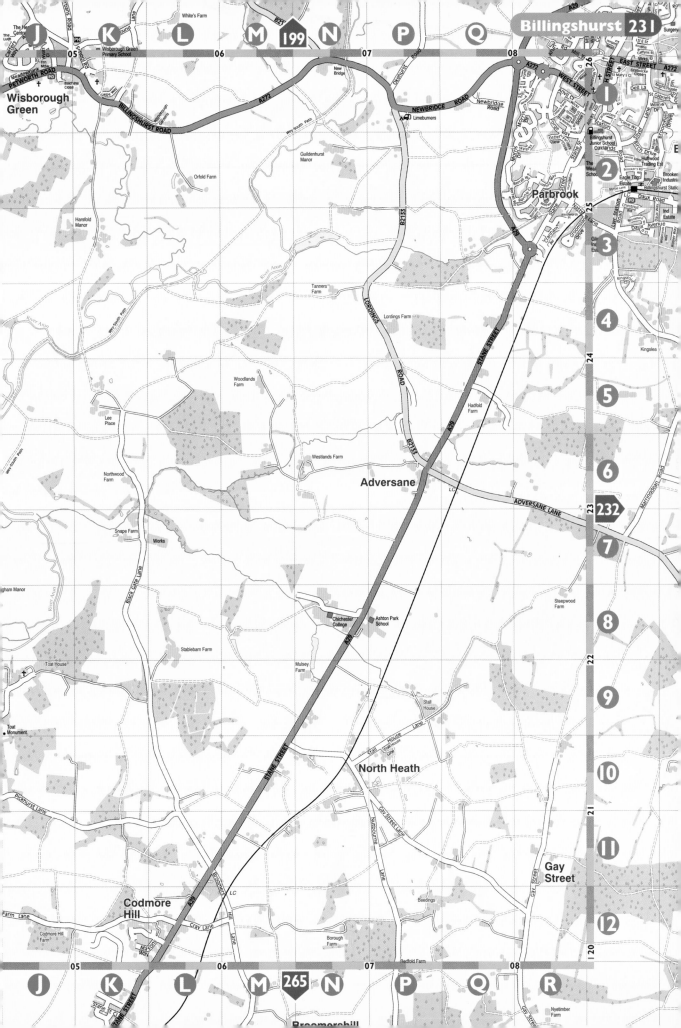

1 grid square represents 500 metres

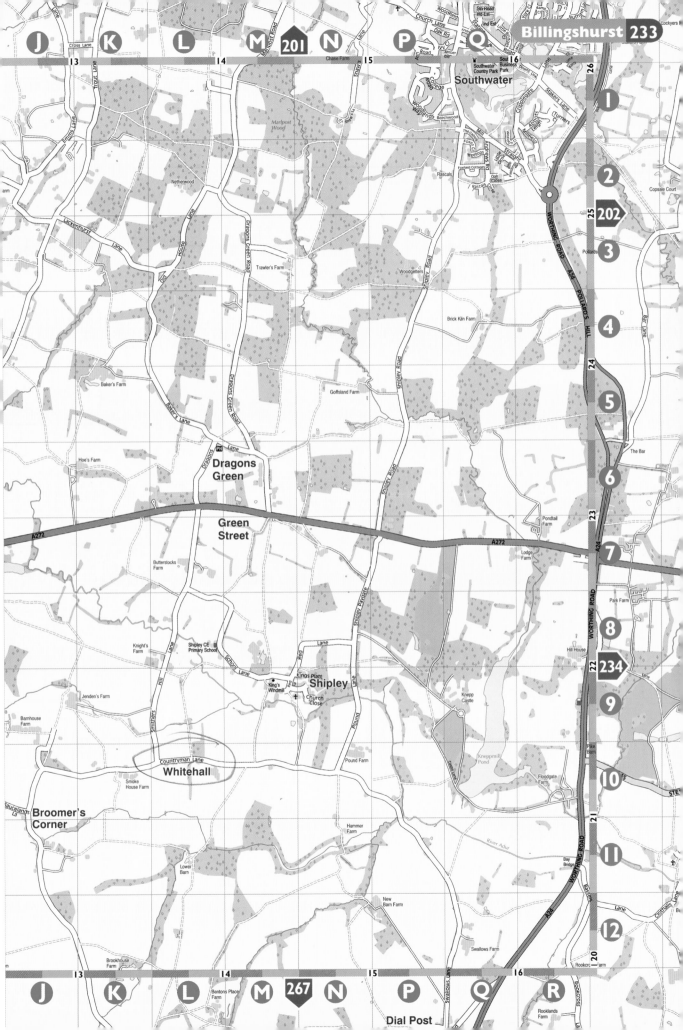

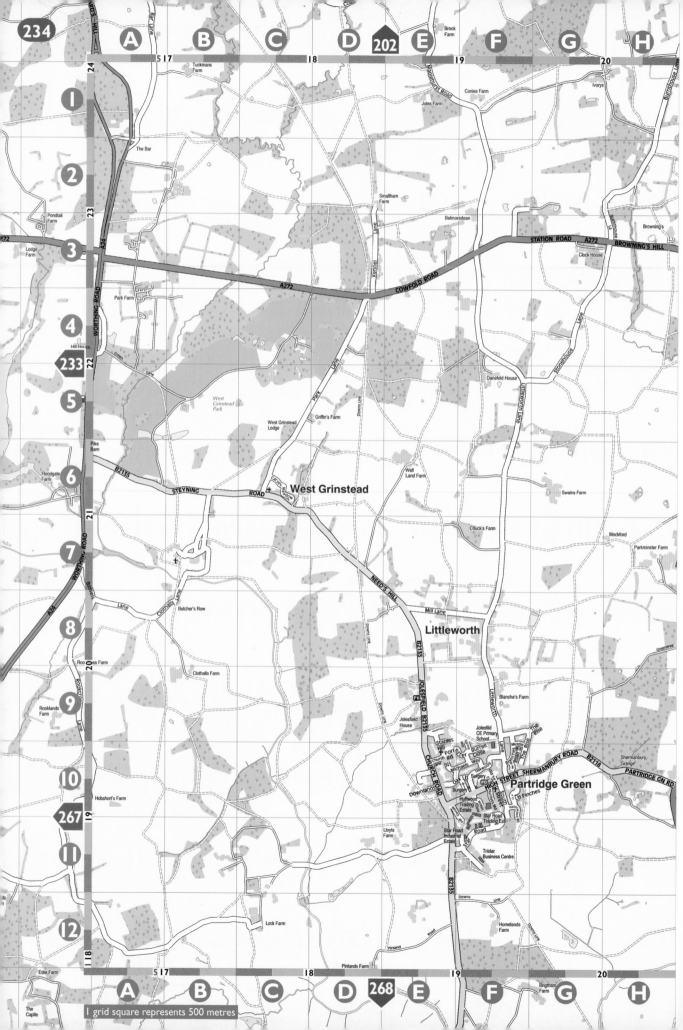

A B C D E F G H

517 18 19 20

I
2
23
3
4
22
5
6
21
7
8
20
9
10
19
11
12
118
517 18 19 20

A B C D E F G H

Tuckmans Farm
The Bar
Pondtail Farm
Lodge Farm
A272
A24
WORTHING ROAD
Park Farm
Hill House
Green Lane
West Grinstead Park
Pike Barn
B2135
Floodgate Farm
STEYNING ROAD
West Grinstead Lodge
West Grinstead
Griffin's Farm
Park Lane
Downs Lane
Ross Farm
Bassels Lane
Clothalls Lane
Butcher's Row
Clothalls Farm
Rooklands Farm
Brookbarn Lane
Hobshort's Farm
Lock Farm
Eden Farm
The Capite

Brook Farm
Conies Farm
Joles Farm
Smallham Farm
Belmoredean
STATION ROAD A272 BROWNING'S HILL
Browning's
Clock House
Burntbouse La
Ivorys
Maplehurst Road
Kennel Lane
COWFOLD ROAD
Danefold House
Littleworth Lane
Storehouse Lane
Well Land Farm
Swains Farm
Chuck's Farm
Mockford
Parkminster Farm
NEED'S HILL
Mill Lane
Littleworth
B2135
Jolesfield House
Blanche's Farm
Jolesfield CE Primary School
Jolesfield B2135
CHURCH ROAD
Staples Hill
Church Lane
Burrell House
HIGH STREET
Partridge Green
SHERMANBURY ROAD
B2116
PARTRIDGE GN RD
Shermanbury Grange
Finches
Downlands
Star Road Trading Est
Huffwood Trading Estate
Lloyts Farm
Star Road Industrial Estate
Tristar Business Centre
Pinland
Pinlands Farm
Homelands Farm
Brigtham Farm
B2135
Downs
Adur

1 grid square represents 500 metres

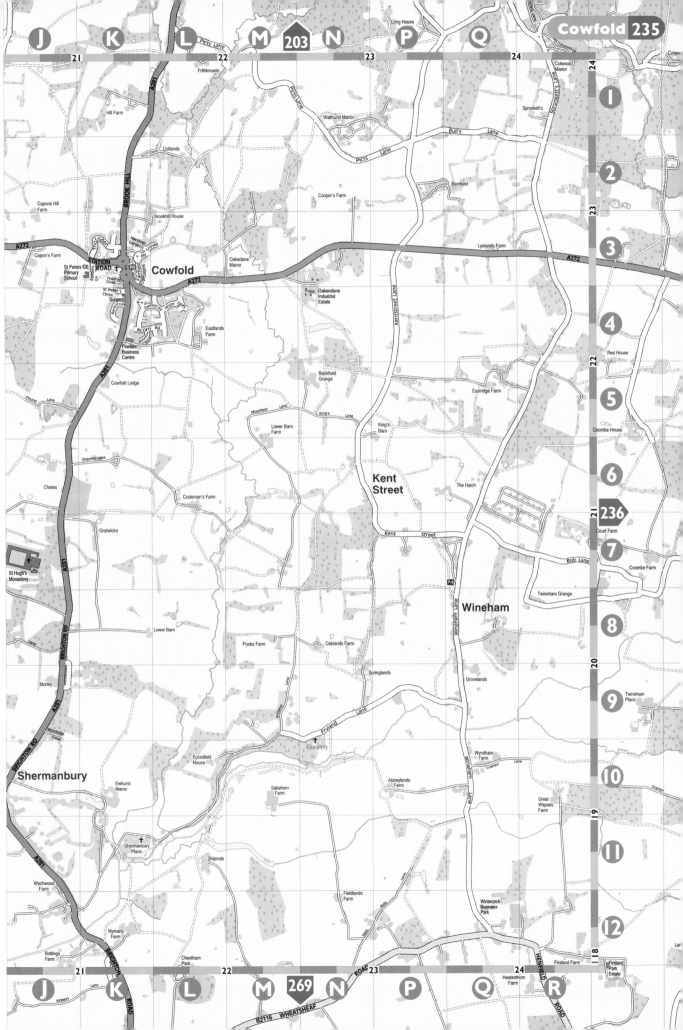

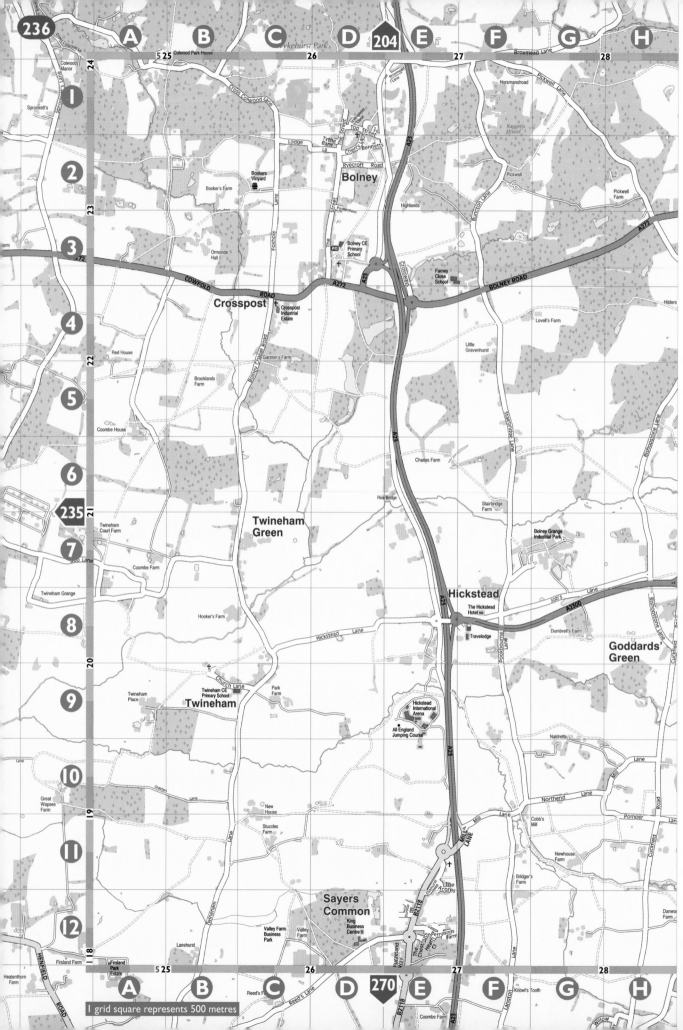

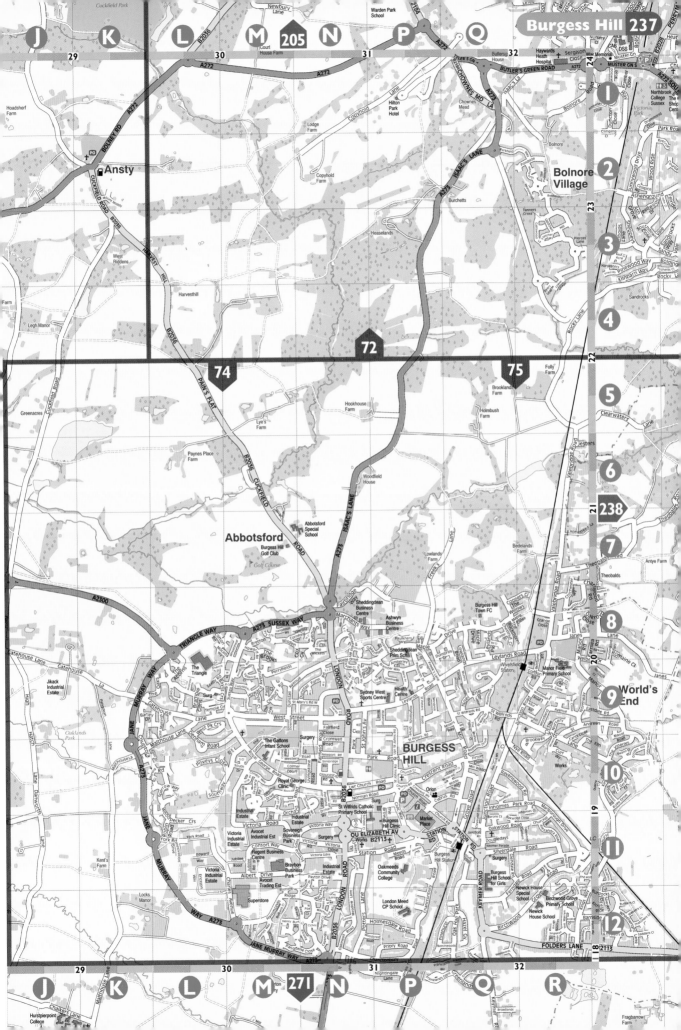

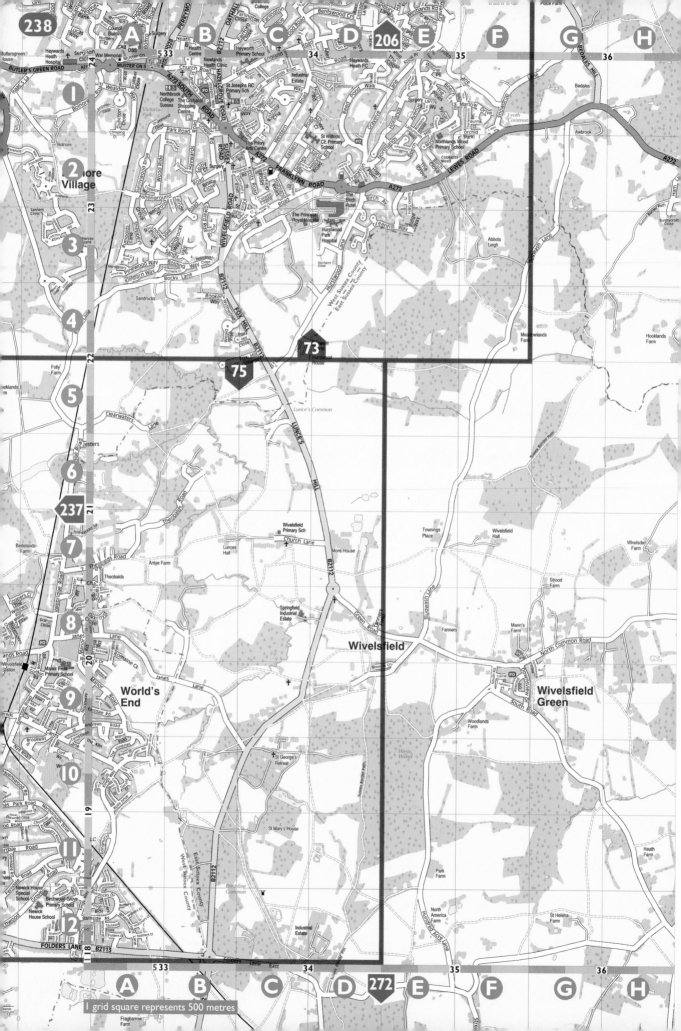

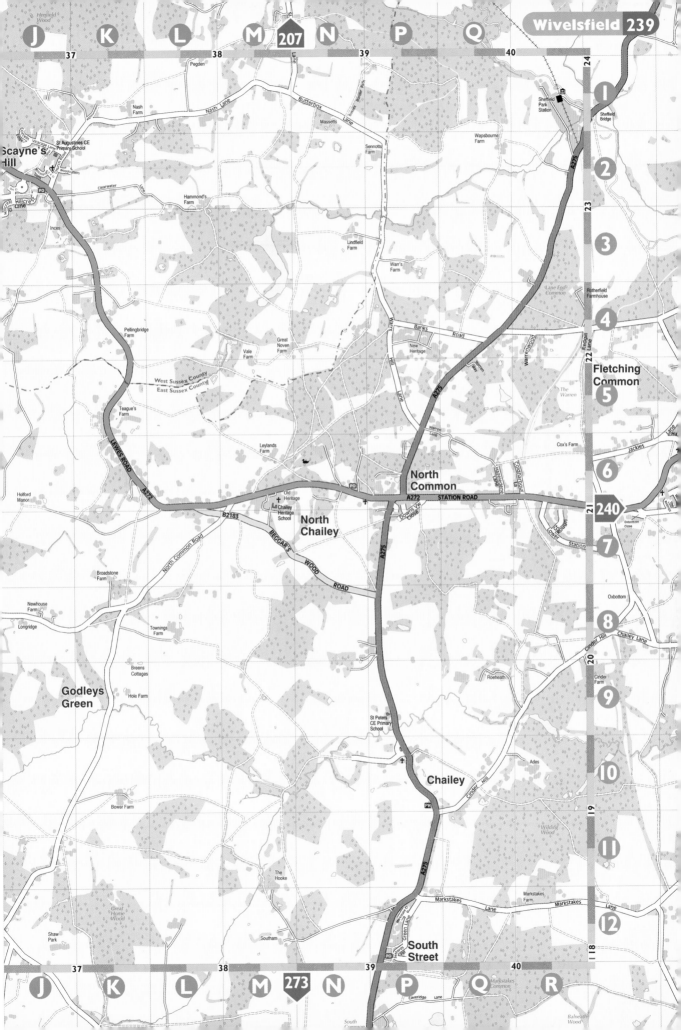

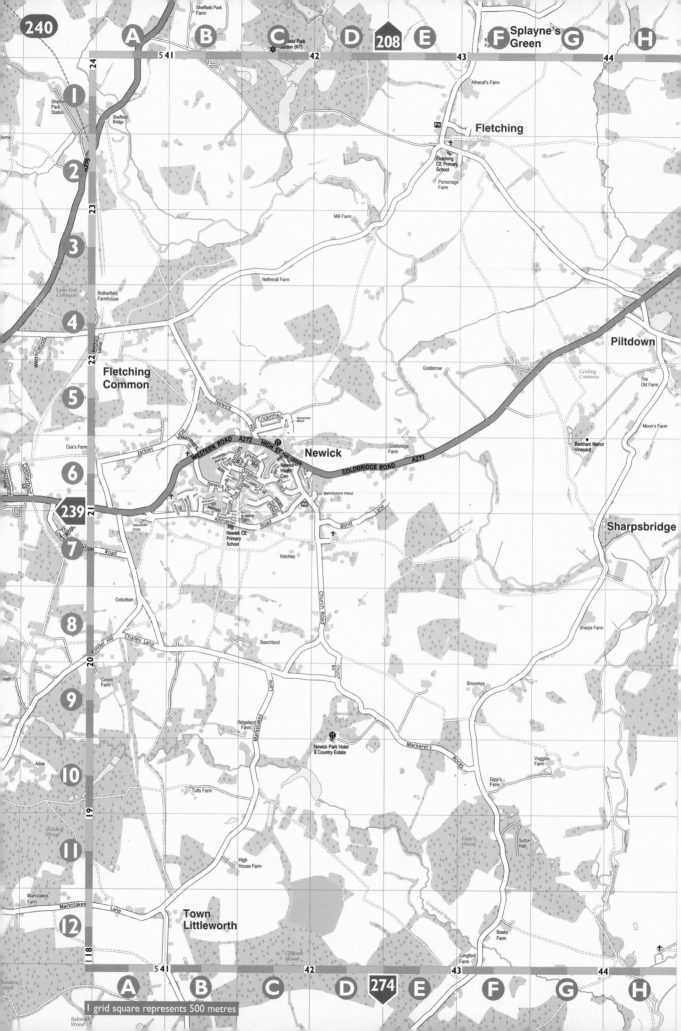

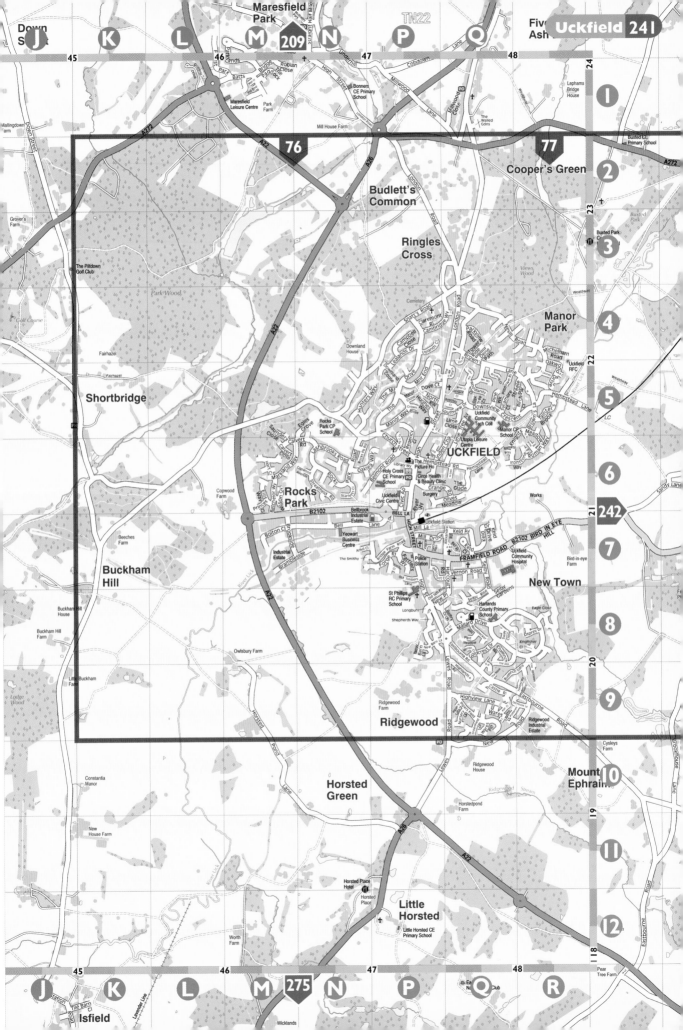

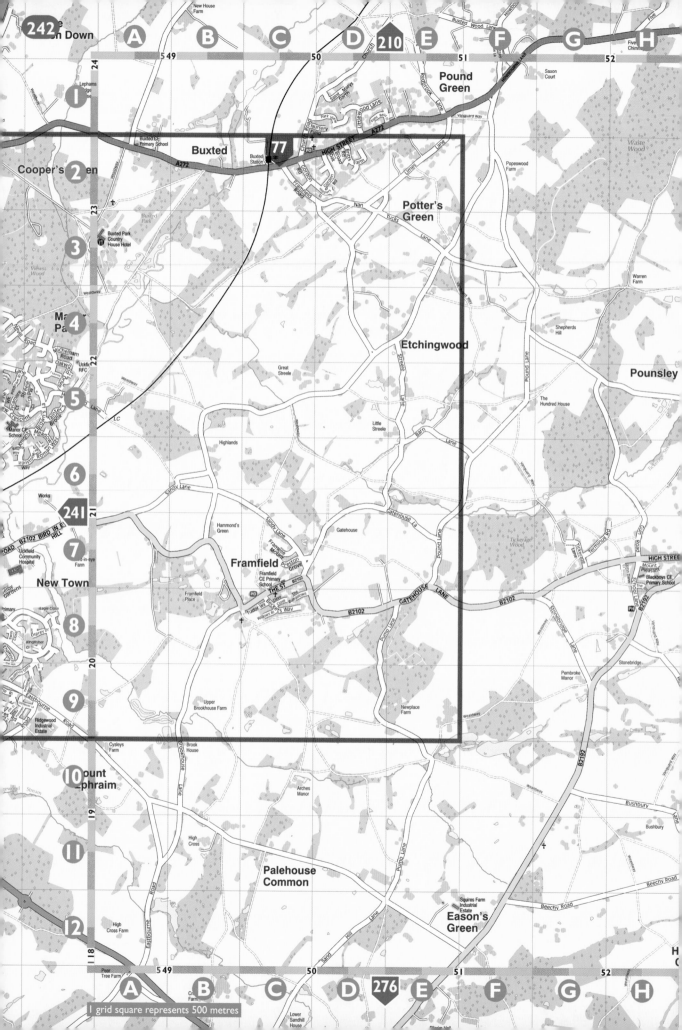

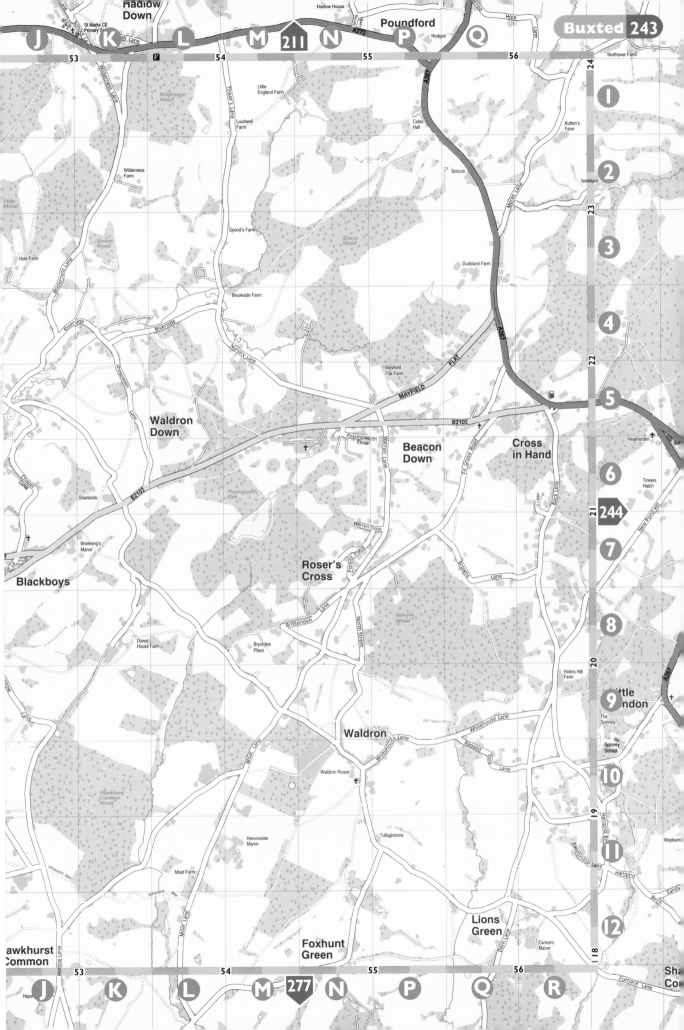

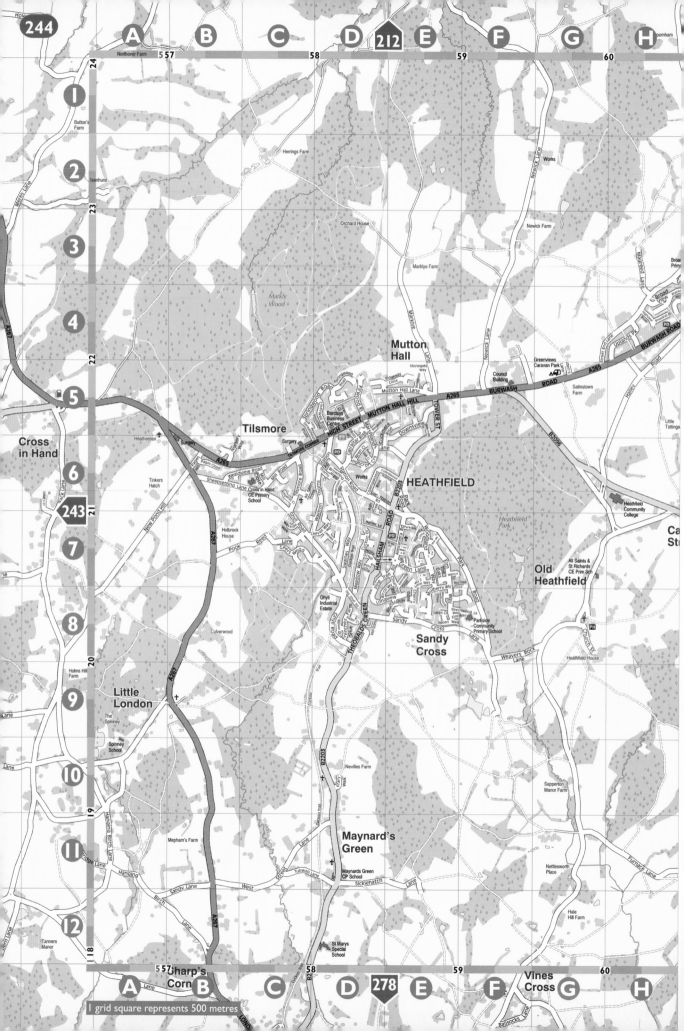

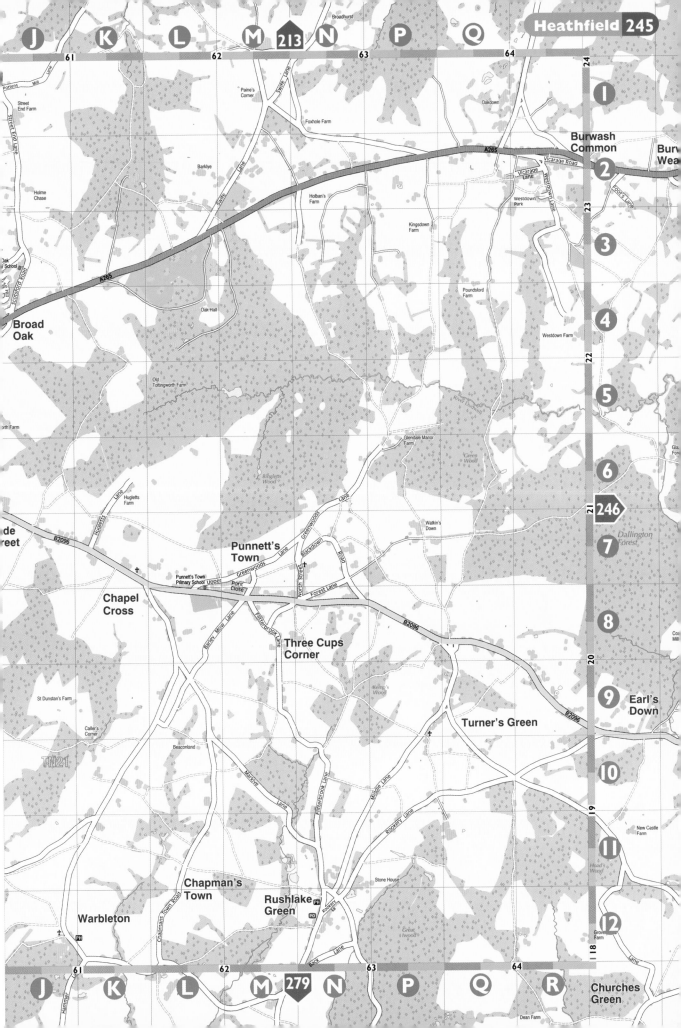

J K L M 213 N P Q
61 62 63 64

Broadhurst

Pottens Mill Lane

Street End Farm

Paine's Corner

Swife Lane

Oakdown

I

Burwash Common

Burw Wea

Foxhole Farm

A265

Holme Chase

Barklye

Swife Lane

Vicarage Road

Vicarage Lane

Westdown Lane

Poots Lane

2

3

Holban's Farm

Kingsdown Farm

Westdown Park

Oak School

Scotsford Road

A265

Poundsford Farm

4

22

Oak Hall

Westdown Farm

Broad Oak

5

Old Toftingworth Farm

River Dudwell

Binglett's Wood

Glendale Manor Farm

Green Wood

6

246

21

Hugletts Lane

Hugletts Farm

Greenwoods Lane

Lane

Watkin's Down

Dallington Forest

7

de reet

B2096

Punnett's Town

Blackdown

Greenwoods

North Street

Forest Lane

8

Punnett's Town Primary School Upper

Pont Close

Flitterbrook Lane

B2096

Chapel Cross

Barley Mow Lane

Three Cups Corner

20

9

Earl's Down

St Dunstan's Farm

Icleny's Wood

TN21

Turner's Green

Caller's Corner

Markove Lane

Flitterbrook Lane

Middle Lane

10

Beaconland

19

New Castle Farm

Rookery Lane

11

Chapman's Town

Stone House

Hoad's Wood

Warbleton

Chapmans Town Road

Rushlake Green

PH

PO

Rookery La

Back Lane

Great Iwoods

12

18

Grove Farm

Dean Farm

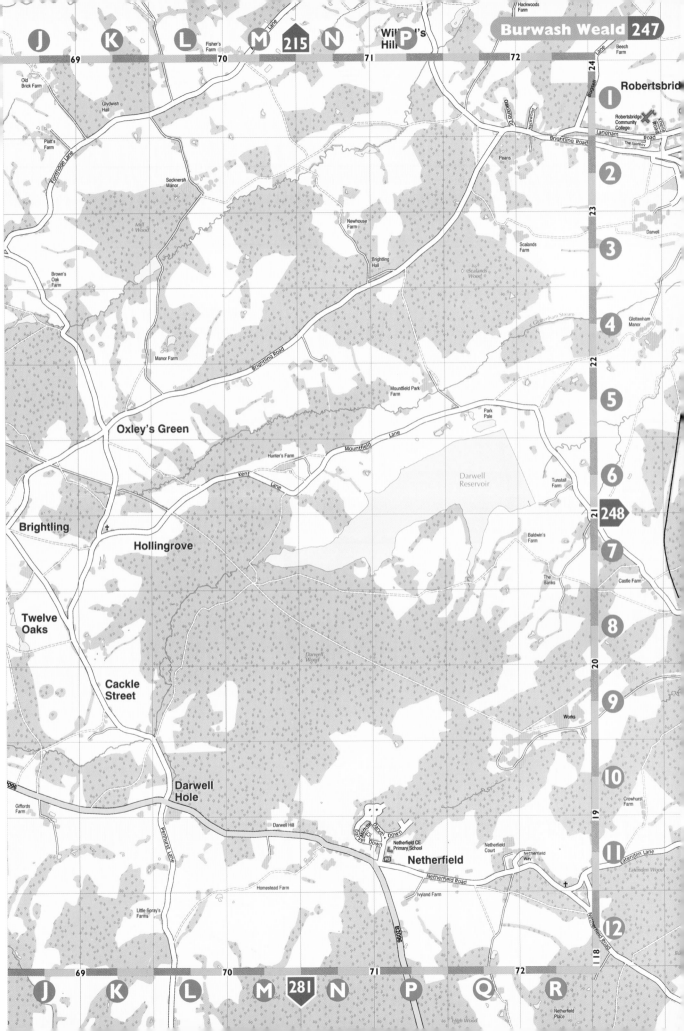

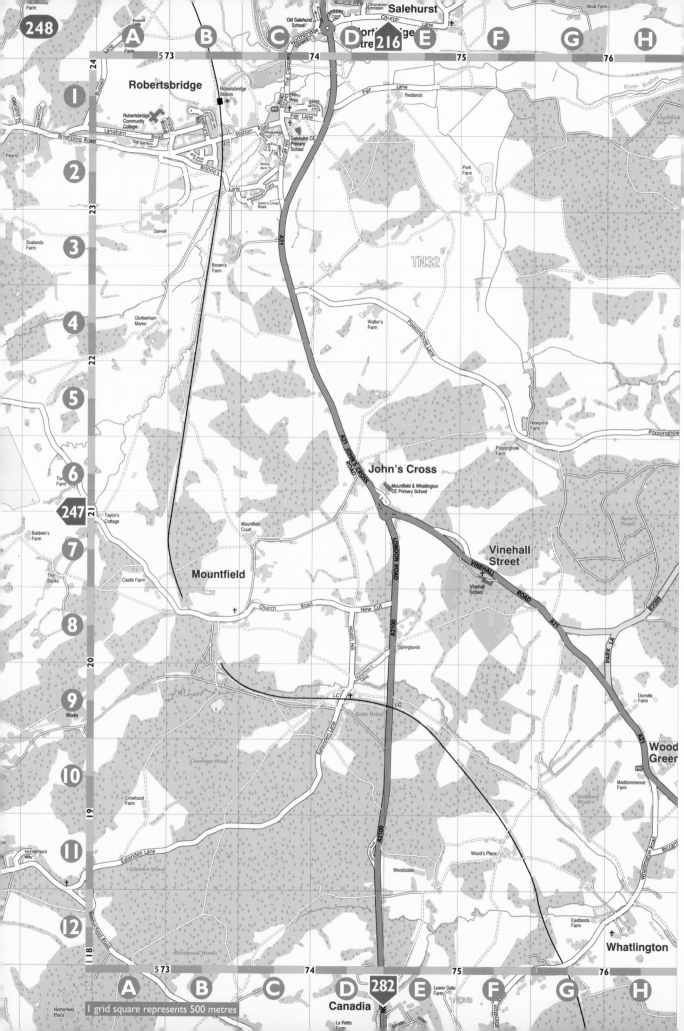

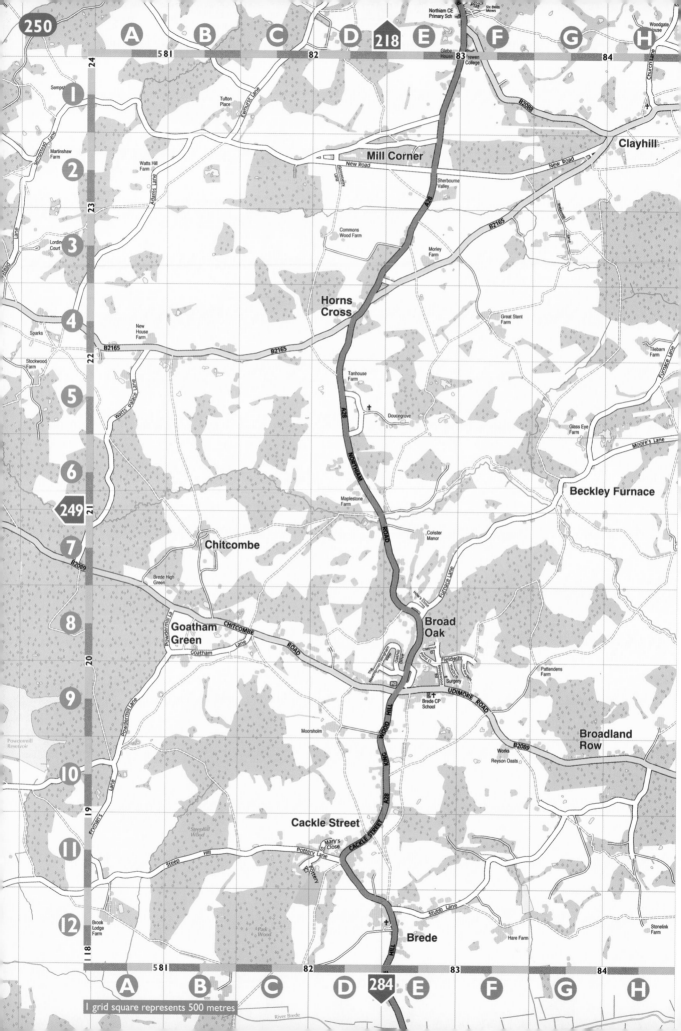

A   B   C   D   218   E   F   G   H

581   82   83   84

1
Sempstead Lane
Tufton Place
Exmurst Lane

Northiam CE Primary Sch
Six Bells Mews
Plot
Brewen College
Glebe House

2
Martinshaw Farm
Watts Hill Farm
Adams Lane
New Road
Mill Corner
Sherbourne Valley
New Road
Clayhill
B2088

3
Lording Court
A28
Commons Wood Farm
Morley Farm
B2165

4
Sparks
New House Farm
B2165
B2165
Horns Cross
Great Stent Farm
Tilebarn Farm
Furnace Lane

5
Stockwood Farm
Watts Palace Lane
Tanhouse Farm
A28
Doucegrove
Glass Eye Farm
Moore's Lane

6
249
A28
NORTHIAM ROAD
Maplestone Farm
Conster Manor
Beckley Furnace

7
B2089
Chitcombe
Brede High Green
Furnace Lane

8
Goatham Green
CHITCOMBE ROAD
Goatham Lane
Powdermill La
Broad Oak
Pattendens Farm

9
Powdermill Lane
Moorsholm
WOOD HILL
Brede CP School
UDIMORE ROAD
Broadland Row
B2089
Works
Reyson Oasts

10
Powdermill Reservoir

11
Ewhurst Lane
Steephill Wood
Steep Hill
Pottery Lane
Cackle Street
Mary's Close
CACKLE STREET
KING
A28

12
Brook Lodge Farm
Park Wood
Pottery Lane
HILL
Brede
Stubb Lane
Hare Farm
Stonelink Farm

581   82   83   84

A   B   C   D   284   E   F   G   H

24 23 22 21 20 19 18

1 grid square represents 500 metres

River Brede

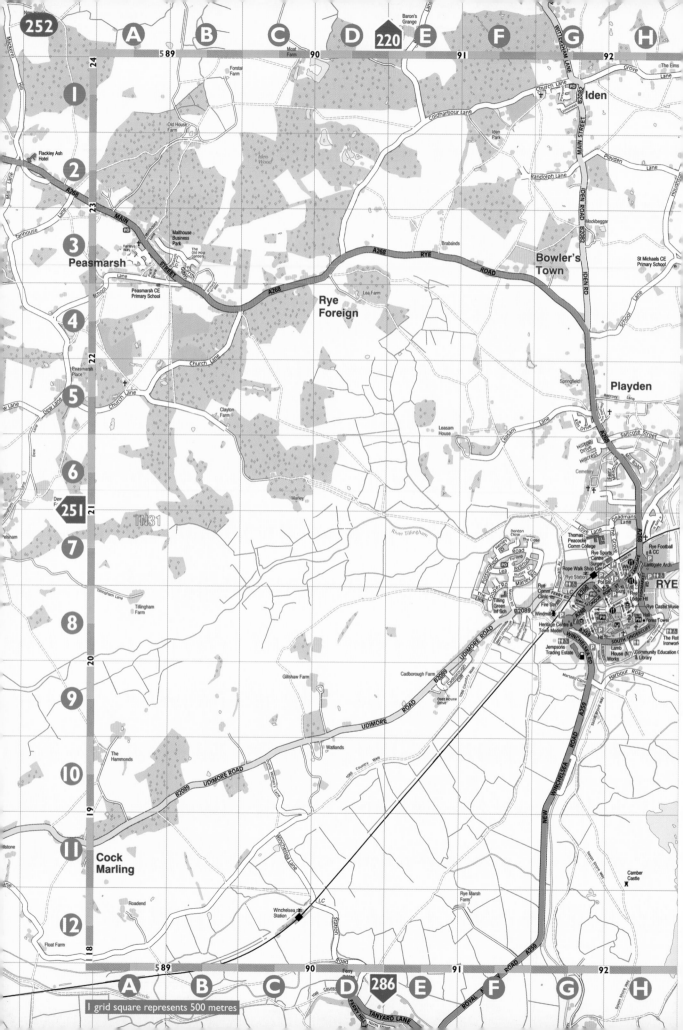

A   B   C   D   E   F   G   H

5 97   98   99   6 00

Whitehouse Farm

Walland Marsh

Hook Wall

Blue House Farm

Baynham Farm

Old Cheyne Court

Walland Marsh

Lower Agney

Little Cheyne Court

Barn Farm

Kent Ditch

Red House

Kent County
East Sussex County

Broomhill Level

Jury's

Camber

Holiday Village

Camber Sands Holiday Park

New   Lydd   Road

Old   Lydd   Road

First Avenue
Second Avenue

The Suttons

Lydd Road

Broomhill Farm

Jury's Gap Road

Jury's Gap

Midrips

Lydd Road

Broomhill Sands

A   B   C   D   E   F   G   H

5 97   98   99   6 00

1 grid square represents 500 metres

1   2   23   3   4   22   5   6   21   7   8   20   9   10   19   11   12   18

GUILDEFORD   LANE   A259

24

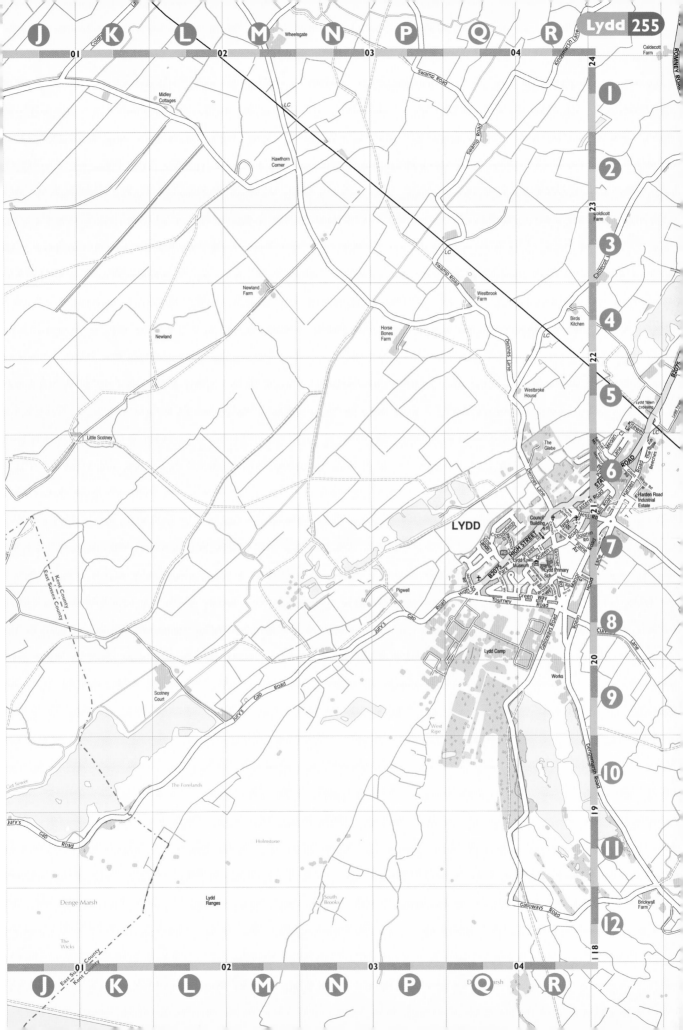

LYDD

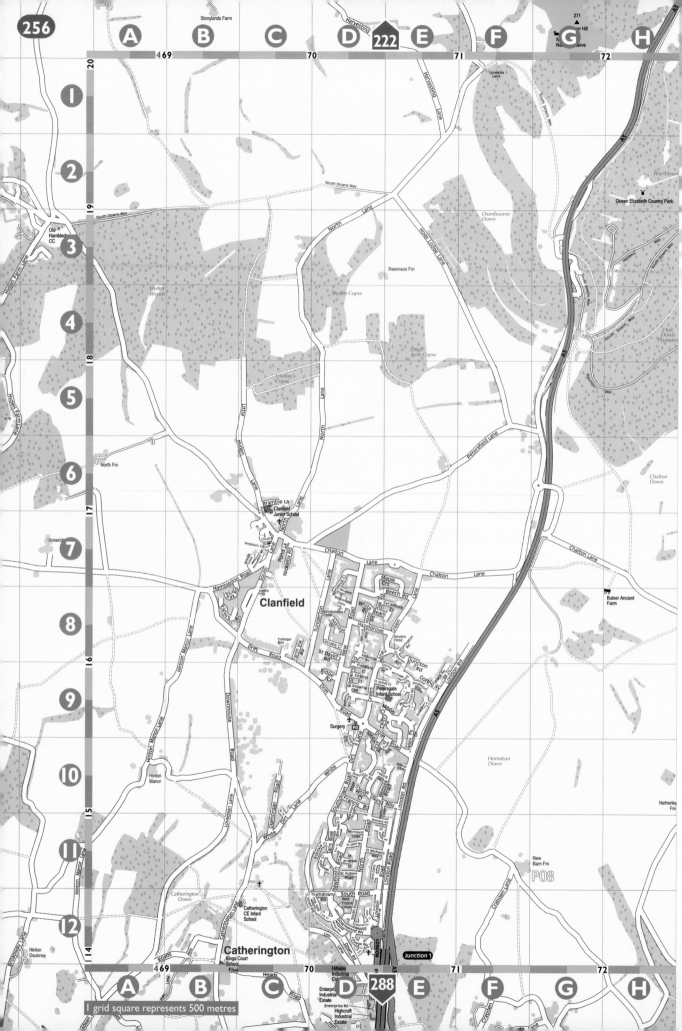

J K L M 223 N P Q

73 74 75 76

Buriton

I
2
3
4
5
6
258
7
8
9
10
11
12

20
19
18
17
16
15
14

Leith Copse

South Downs Way

Coulters Dean Fm

South Downs Way

Forty Acre Lane

Sunwood Fm

South Downs Way

Hampshire County
West Sussex County

Sussex Border Path

West Harting Down

Downley

Ditcham Park Sch

Head Down Plantation

Newbarn Road

Queen Elizabeth Forest

Stantion Way

Glass Braw

Sussex Border Path

Ladyholt

Eckensfield

le Wood

Chalton Lane

Old Farm

Chalton

PH

South Lane

Sussex Border Path

Harris La

Woodcroft Fm

Staunton Way

Cowdown Lane

Cowdown Fm

Huc

Idsworth Down

Old Idsworth Fm

Hampshire County
West Sussex County

Herdens

Old Idsworth

Markwells Wood

Horsley Farm

J K L M 289 N P Q R

73 74 75 76

J K L M 225 N P Q

81 82 83 84

1

Elsted

Piper's Farm

2

New
House Farm

Redlands

Treyford

Didling

Manor Farm

3

Linch Farm

Bugshill Lane

4

Manor Farm

Buriton Farm

5
Linch
Down

Telegraph House

Devil's
Jumps

Monkton House

6

260

Phillsswood
Down

Linchball
Wood

7

Monkton Farm

Winden
Wood

8

Hooksway

North
Marden

Hill Lands Farm

Phyllis
Wood

9

Brooms Farm

Staple
Ash Farm

10

Manor
Place

East
Marden

B2141

Chilgrove
PH

11

Cobworth
Down

Hillbarn

12

20
19
18
17
16
15
114

J   K   L   M   227   N   P   Q

89   90   91   92

1
2
3
4
5
6
262
7
8
9
10
11
12

Selham Common
Smoky House
Hyde Park
Little London
Amersham Common
Graffham Court
Shrublands
Wiblings Farm
Nonnington
Graffham
Callo
Graffham First School

Topleigh
Hoyle Farm
Hoyle
Polecats
New Road
Hoyle Lane

Heyshott Green
Heyshott
Down Close
Hoyle Lane
Manor Farm
Woodcote Farm
Hayland Farm
Tagents Farm

Dunford House
Oatscroft
Oaklands
Mill Lane
Peace Rd
Mill Ln

Hoe Copse
Heyshott Down

Manorfarm Down
South Downs Way
Broad Walk

Charlton Forest
Herringdean Wood
Forest Hanger
Eastdean Wood
Lamb Lea
North Side

Broadham House
Wood Tease
Yorkhurst Hill
North Lane
North Down
Newhouse Farm
New Road
Malecomb

Nature Reserve

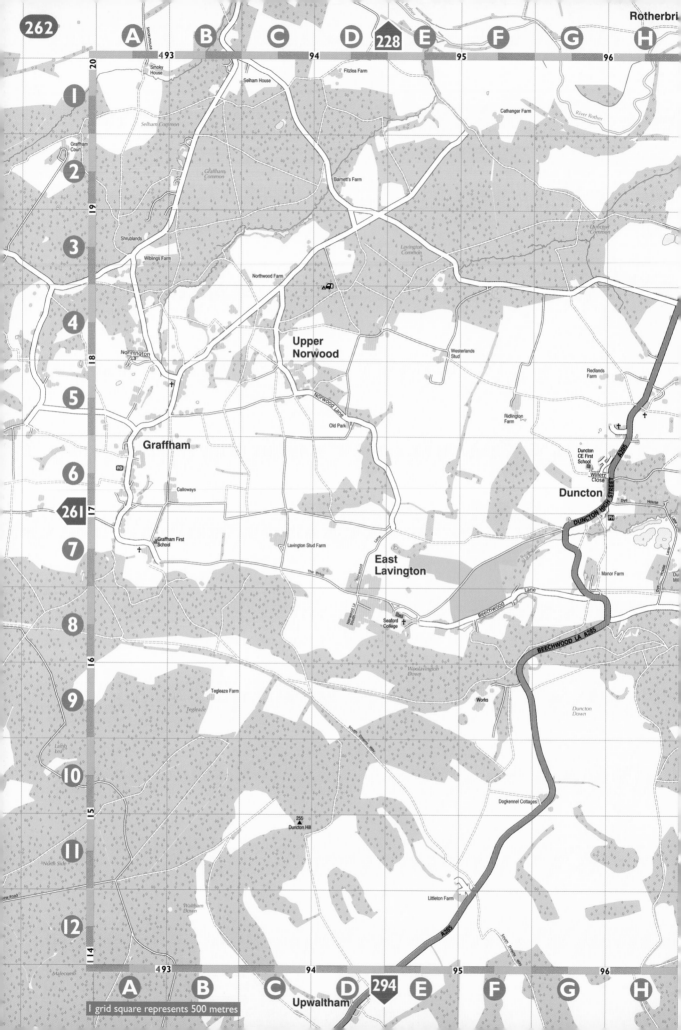

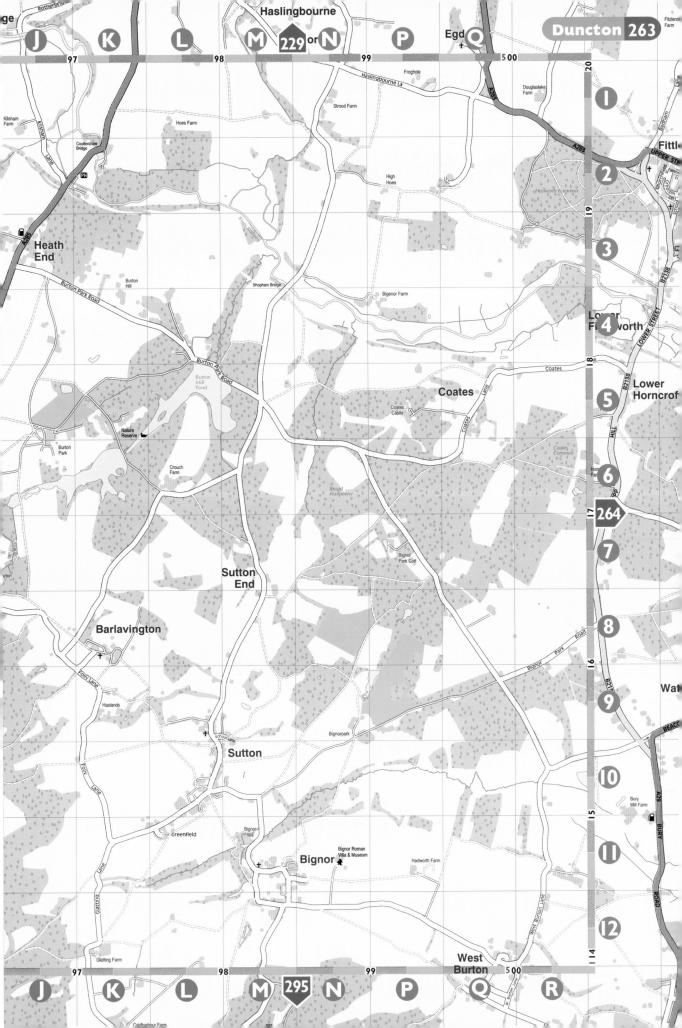

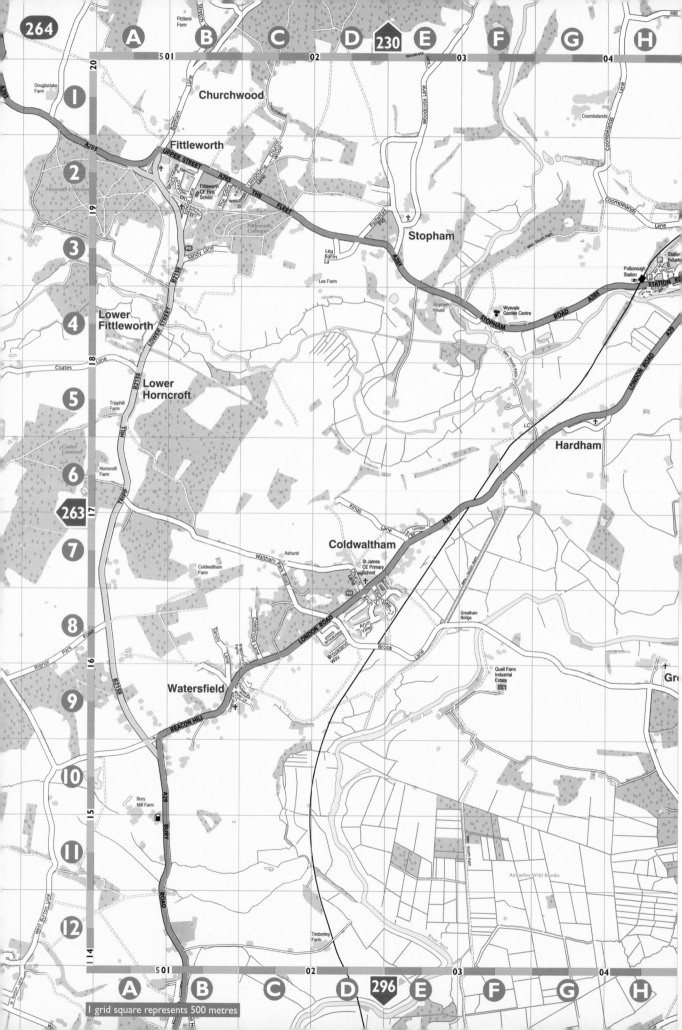

A B C D 230 E F G H

501 02 Woodcote 03 04

20

19

18

17

16

15

114

1 Douglaslake Farm

Churchwood

Fitzleroi Farm

2 Hesworth Common

Fittleworth
UPPER STREET
Fittleworth CE First School

3 Sandy Lane
B2138
Lea Farm La
Lee Farm

Stopham
Stopham House
Wyevale Garden Centre

Pulborough Station
STATION
Station Industrial

4 Lower Fittleworth
LOWER STREET

Coates Lane

STOPHAM
STOPHAM ROAD
A283
A29
LONDON ROAD

5 Tripphill Farm
Lower Horncroft

Hardham

6 Coates Common
Horncroft Farm

TRIPP HILL

7 Waltham Park Road
Ashurst
Coldwaltham
Coldwaltham Farm
St James CE Primary School
Kings Lane
A29

8 Sandy Lane
Colebrook Lane
Blackhurst Farm
LONDON ROAD
Brookdene
Brookland Way
Arun Vale
Brook
Greatham Bridge
Brook Lane
Quell Farm Industrial Estate
Gr

9 Bignor Park Road
Watersfield
BEACON HILL

10 Bury Mill Farm
A29 BURY ROAD

11 West Burton Lane

12 Timberley Farm
River Arun
Amberley Wild Brooks

A B C 296 D E F G H

501 02 03 04

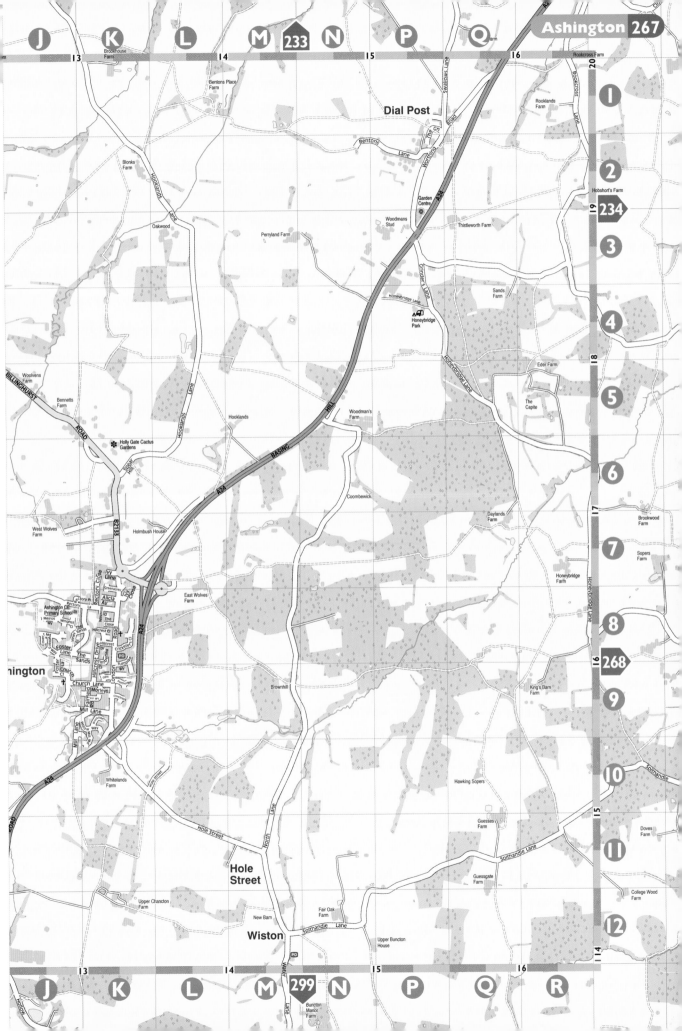

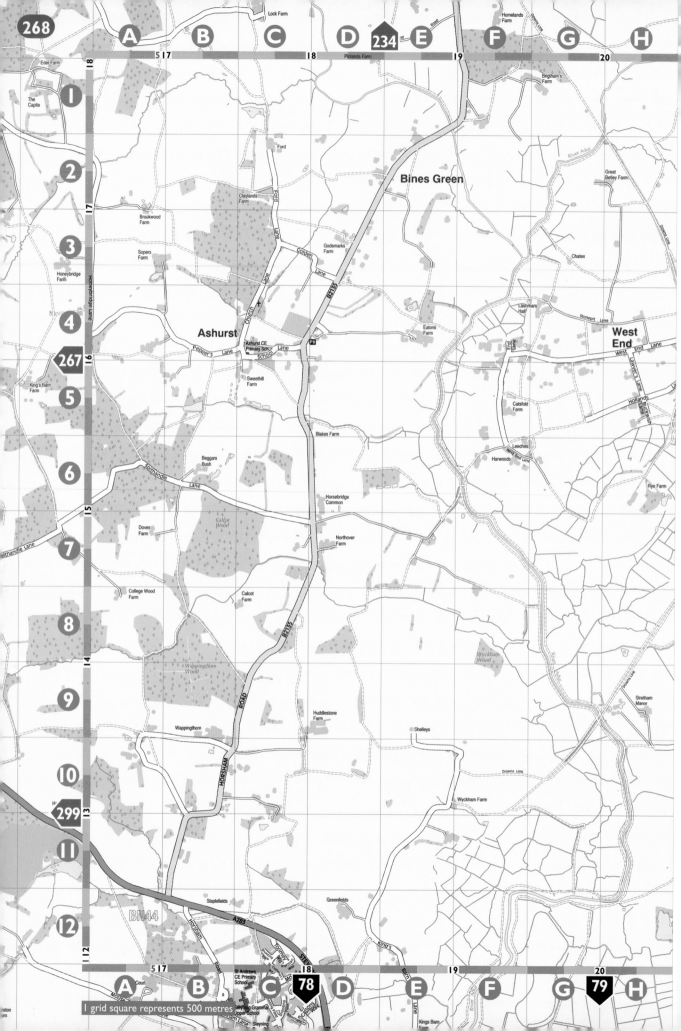

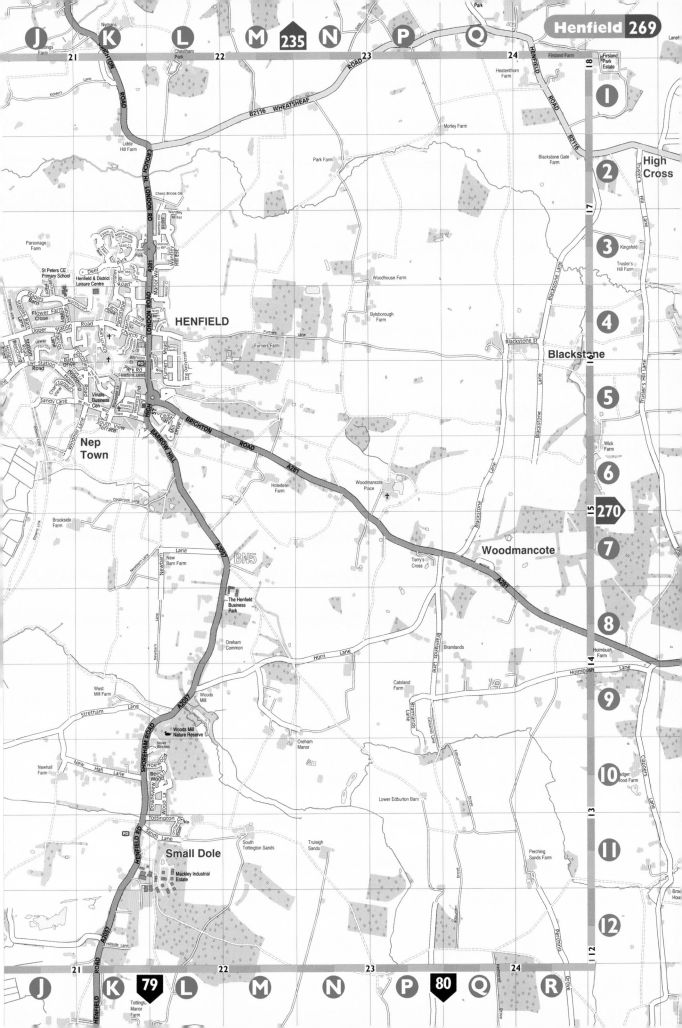

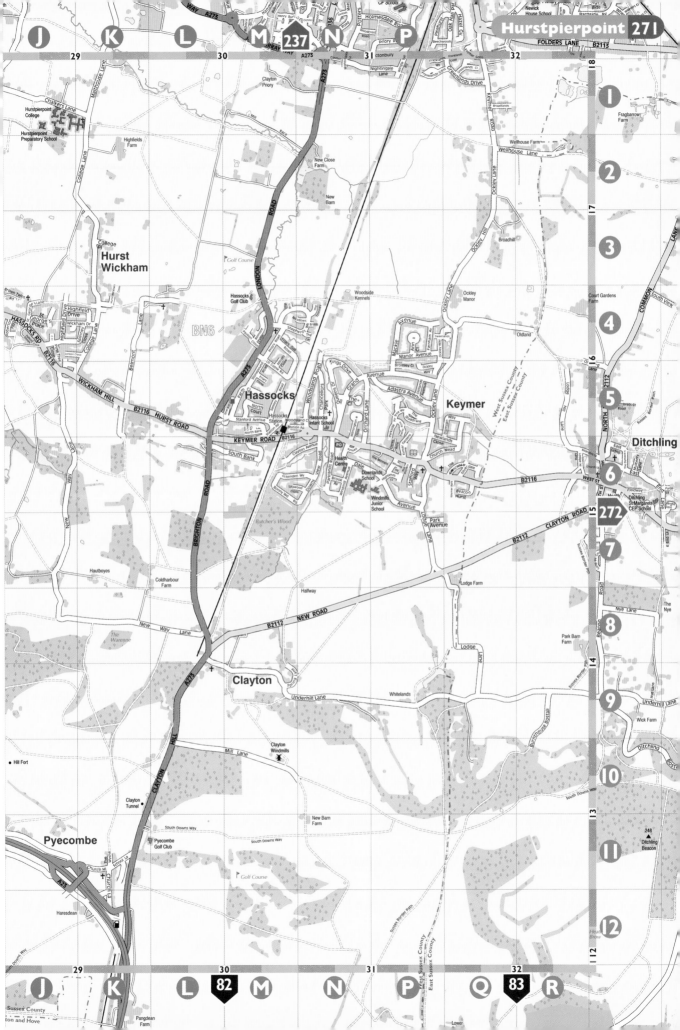

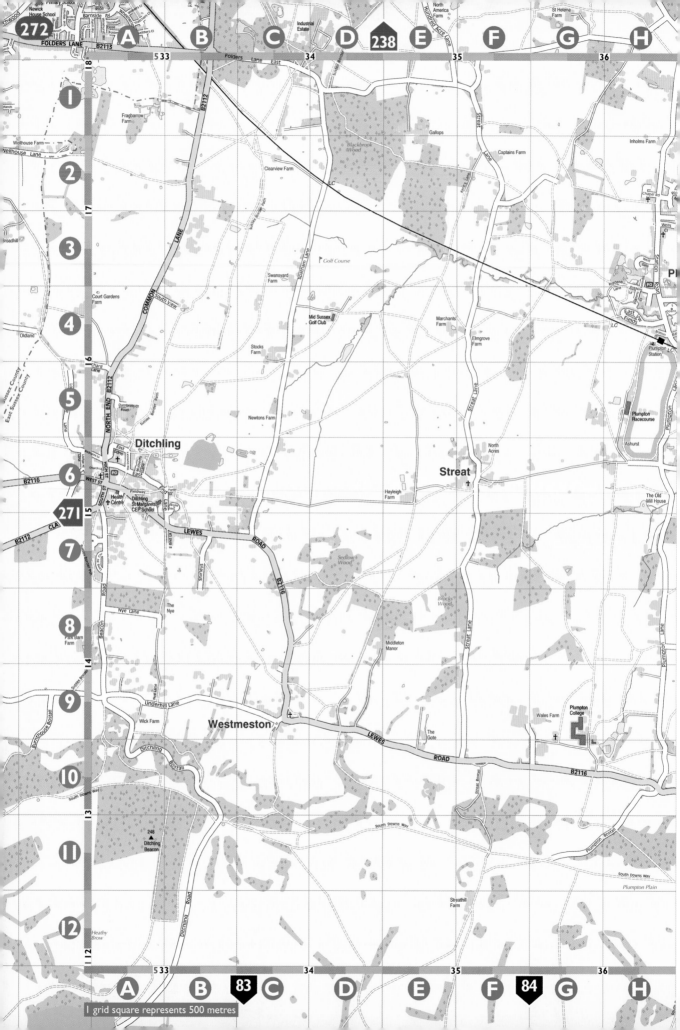

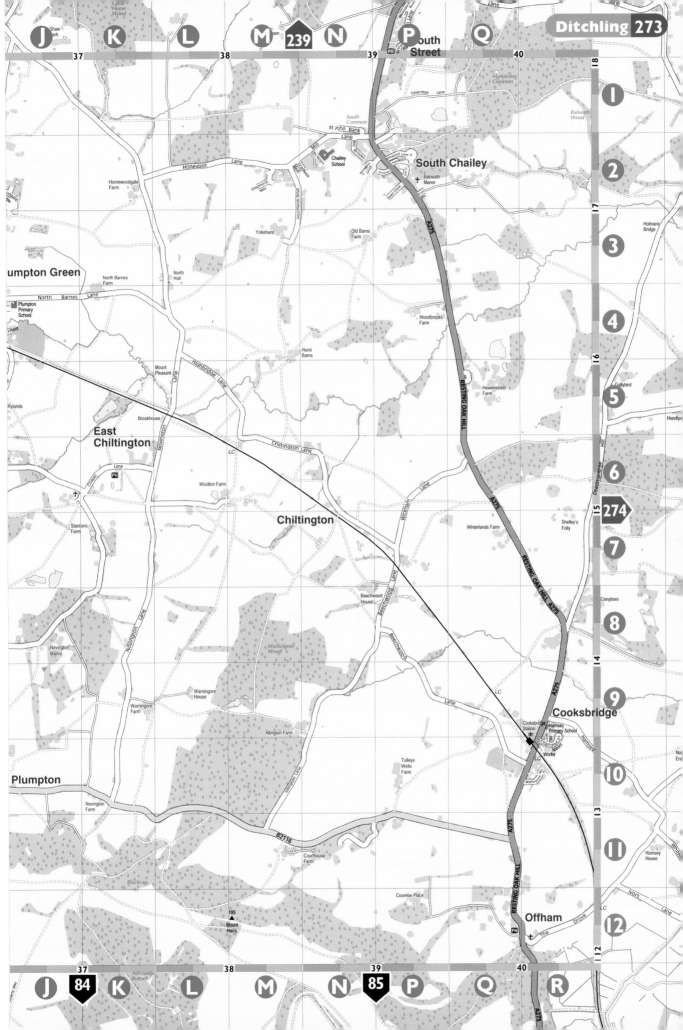

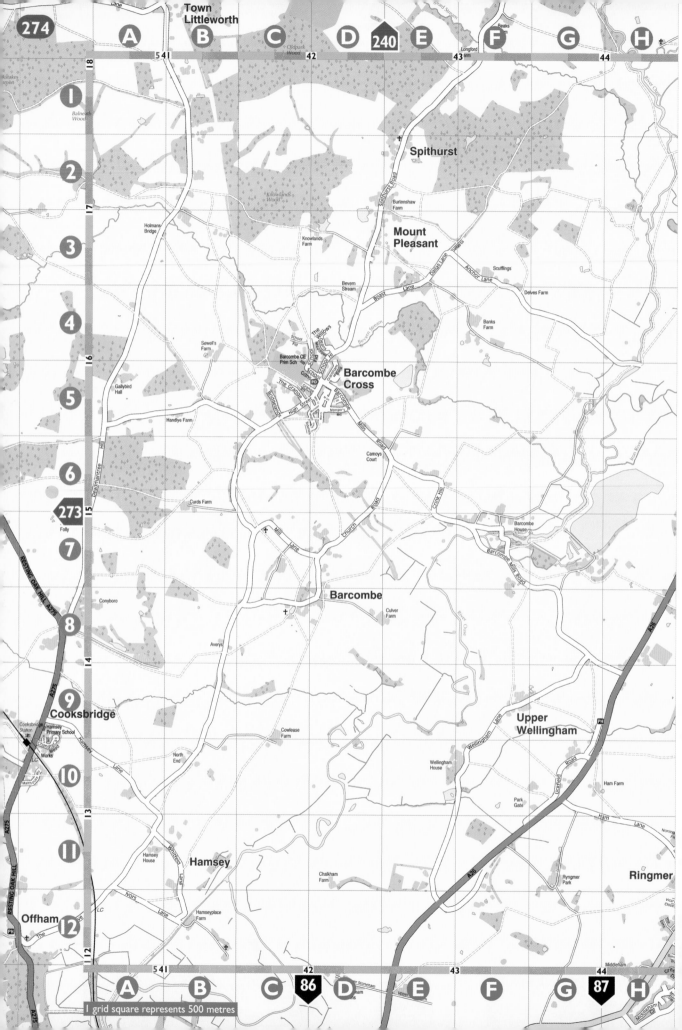

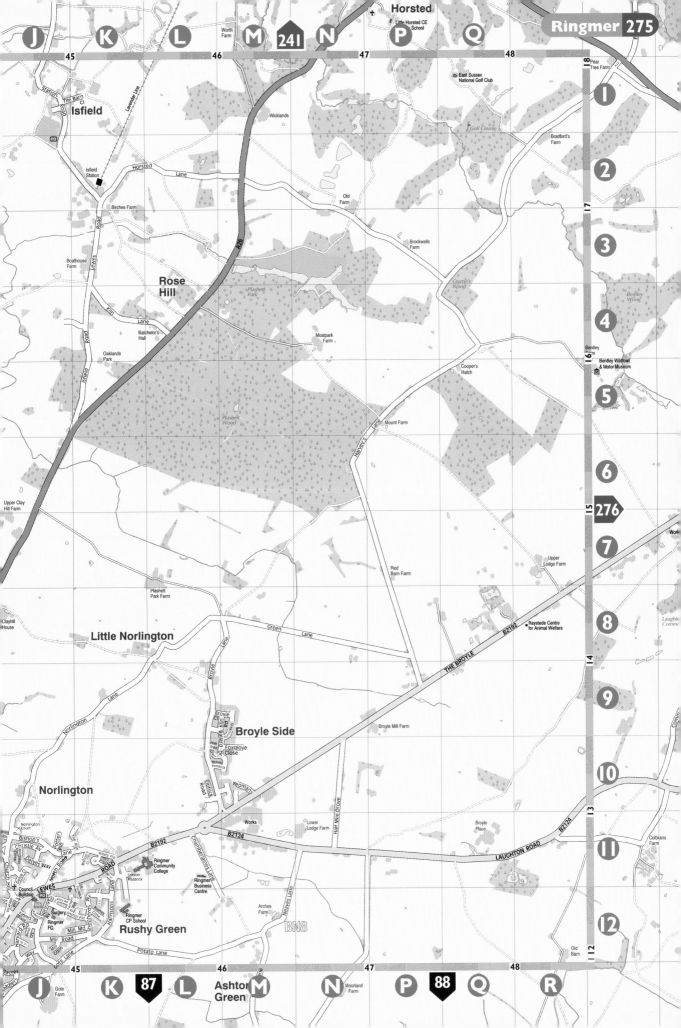

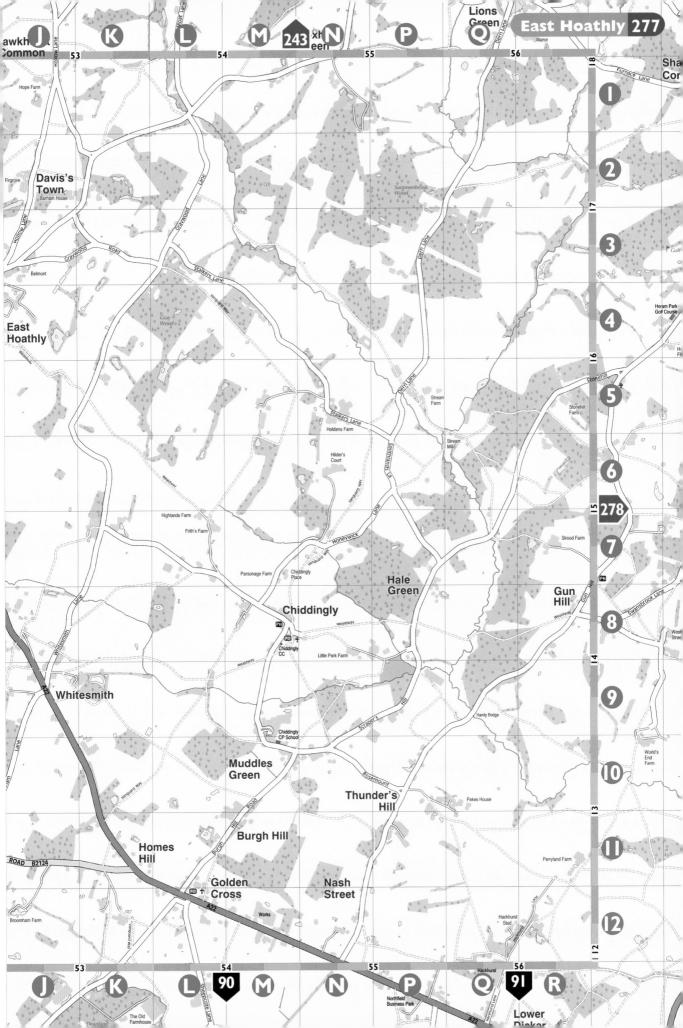

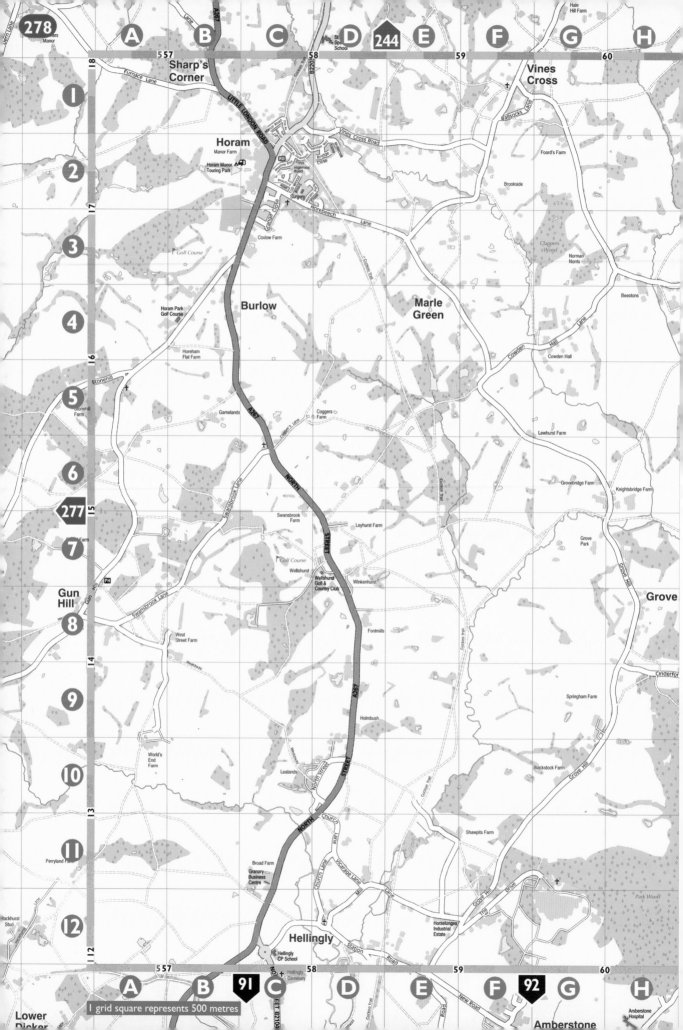

A B C D E F G H

244

557 58 59 60

18

Sharp's Corner

Vines Cross

Furnace Lane

LITTLE LONDON ROAD

1

Manors Manor

Horam

Ballsocks Lane

Foord's Farm

Manor Farm

Vines Cross Road

2

Horam Manor Touring Park

PO

Brookside

17

Surgery

Horebeech Lane

Clappers Wood

Norman Norris

3

Golf Course

Coxlow Farm

Grange Close

Burlow

Marle Green

Beestons

4

Horam Park Golf Course

Horeham Flat Farm

16

Cowden Hall Lane

Stonehill

Cowden Hall

5

Stonehill Farm

A267

Gamelands

Coggers Lane

Coggers Farm

Lewhurst Farm

Swanbrook Lane

NORTH

6

Grovebridge Farm

Knightsbridge Farm

277

15

Swansbrook Farm

Leyhurst Farm

Grove Park

7

Farm

STREET

Wellshurst

Winkenhurst

Grove Hill

PH

Wellshurst Golf & Country Club

Gun Hill

Swanbrook Lane

8

West Street Farm

Weavers Way

14

Fontmills

Springham Farm

Cinderford

9

Holmbush

World's End Farm

Grove Hill

10

Lealands

North Street

STREET

Blackstock Farm

13

Church Lane

NORTH

11

Perryland Farm

Broad Farm

Vicarage Lane

Mill Lane

Shawpits Farm

Park Wood

Granary Business Centre

12

Blackhurst Stud

Horselunges Industrial Estate

Amberstone Hospital

112

Hellingly

Hellingly CP School

Station Road

557 58 59 60

A B C D E F G H

91 92

Lower Dicker

Amberstone

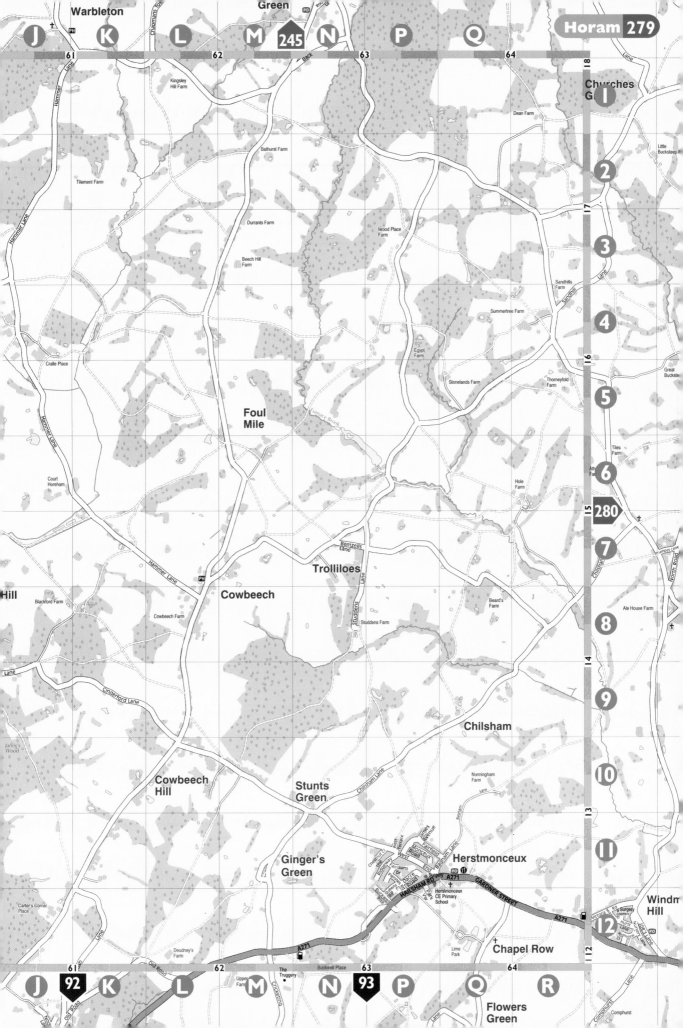

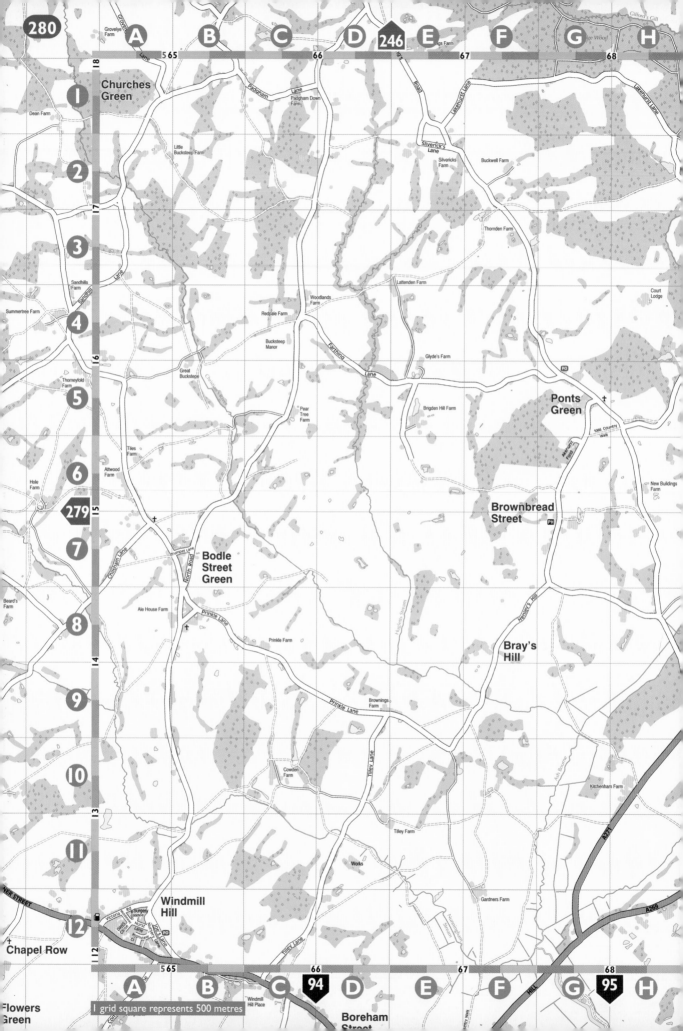

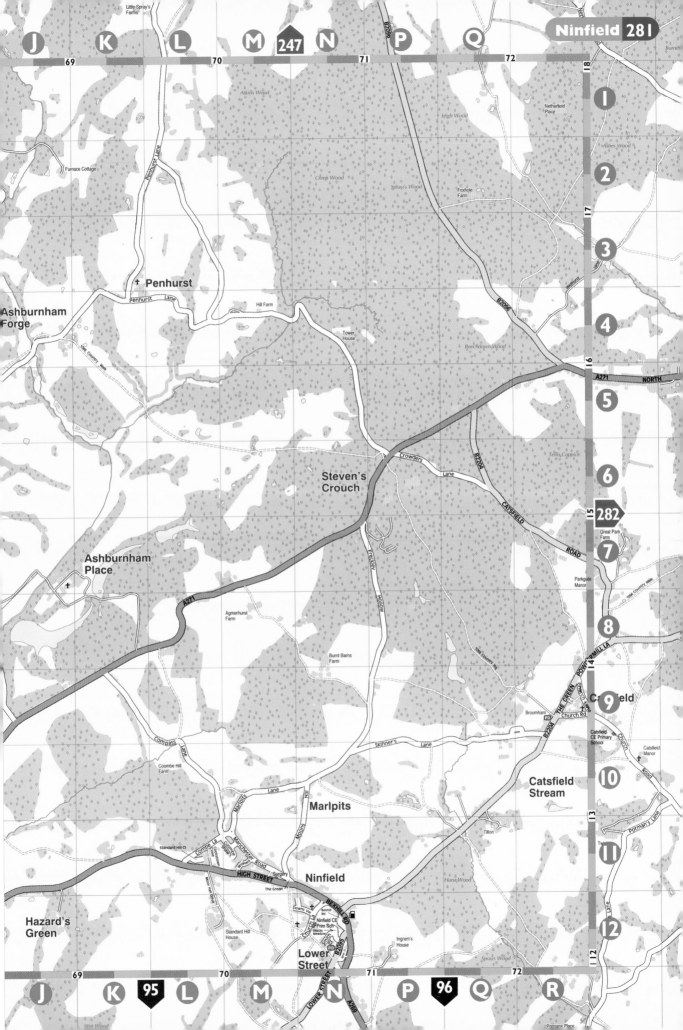

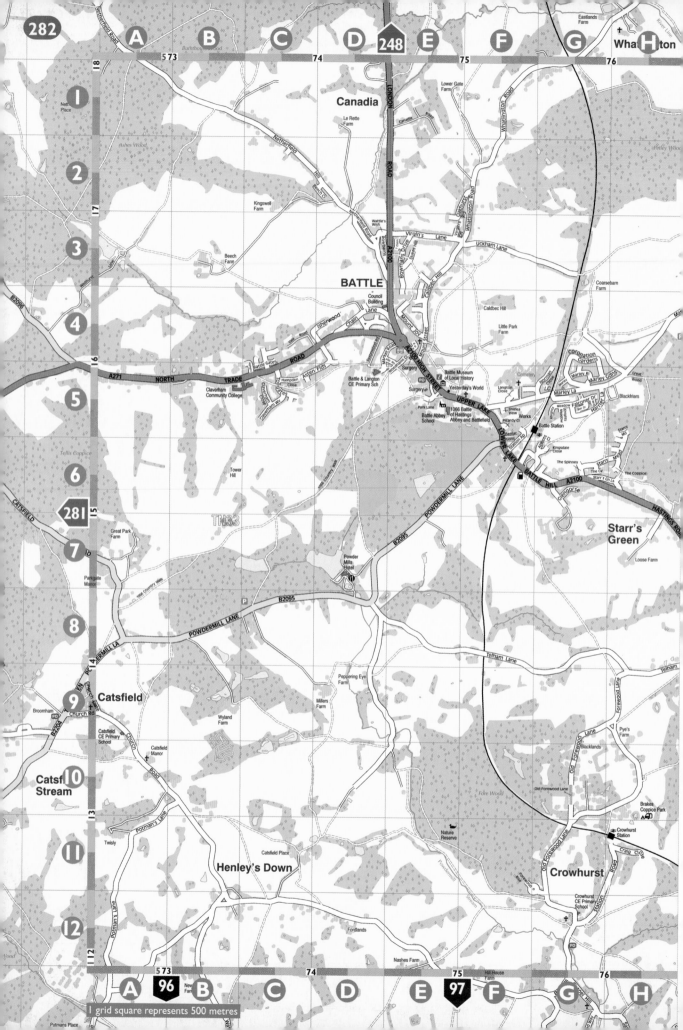

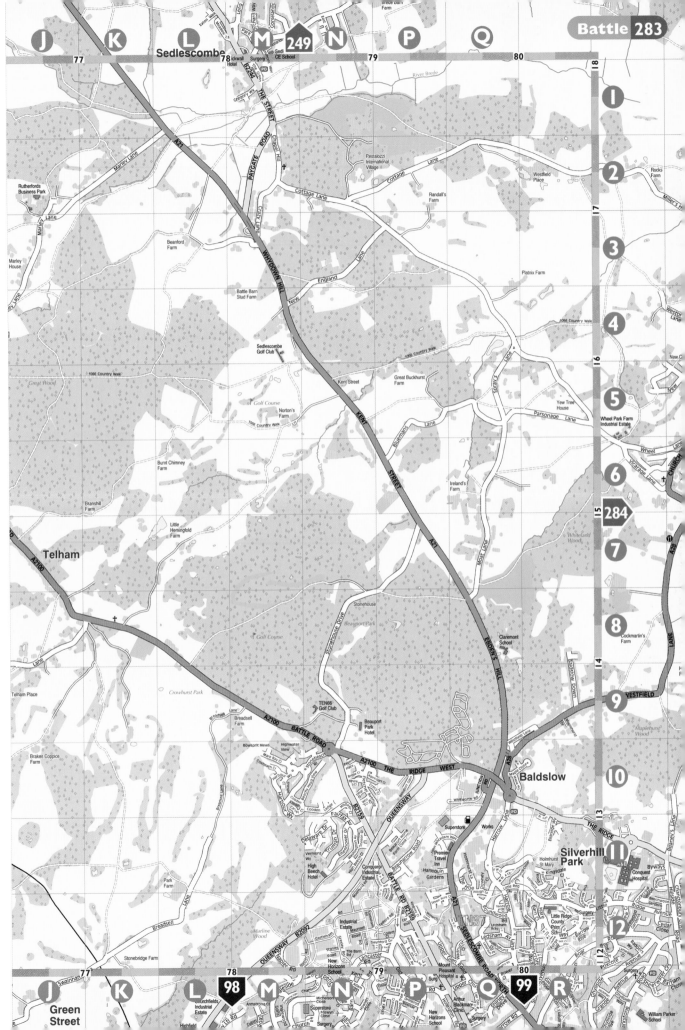

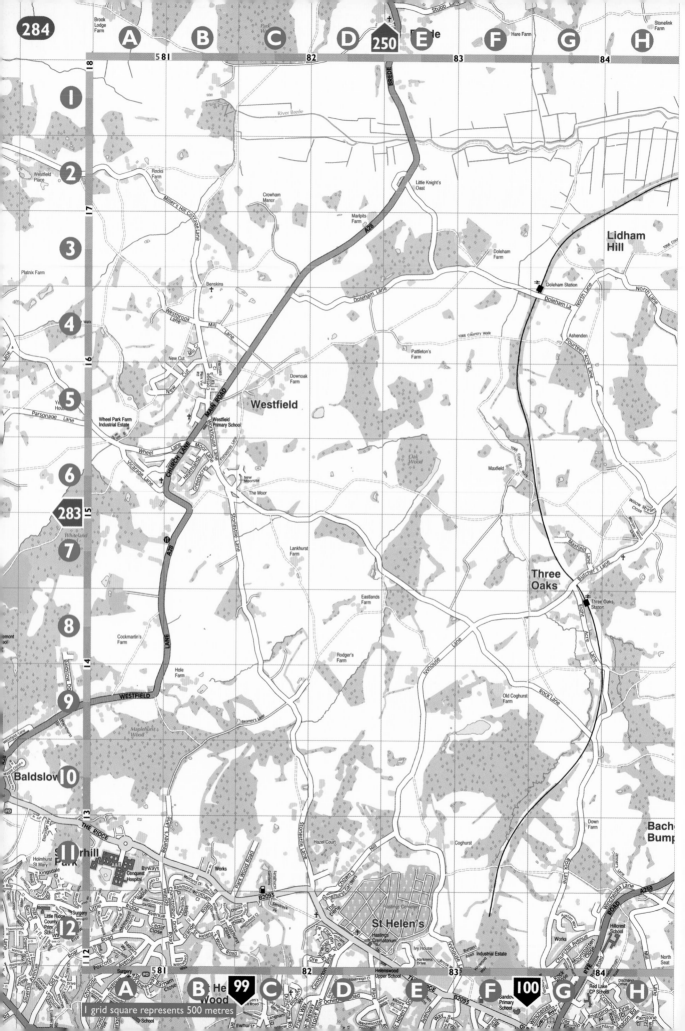

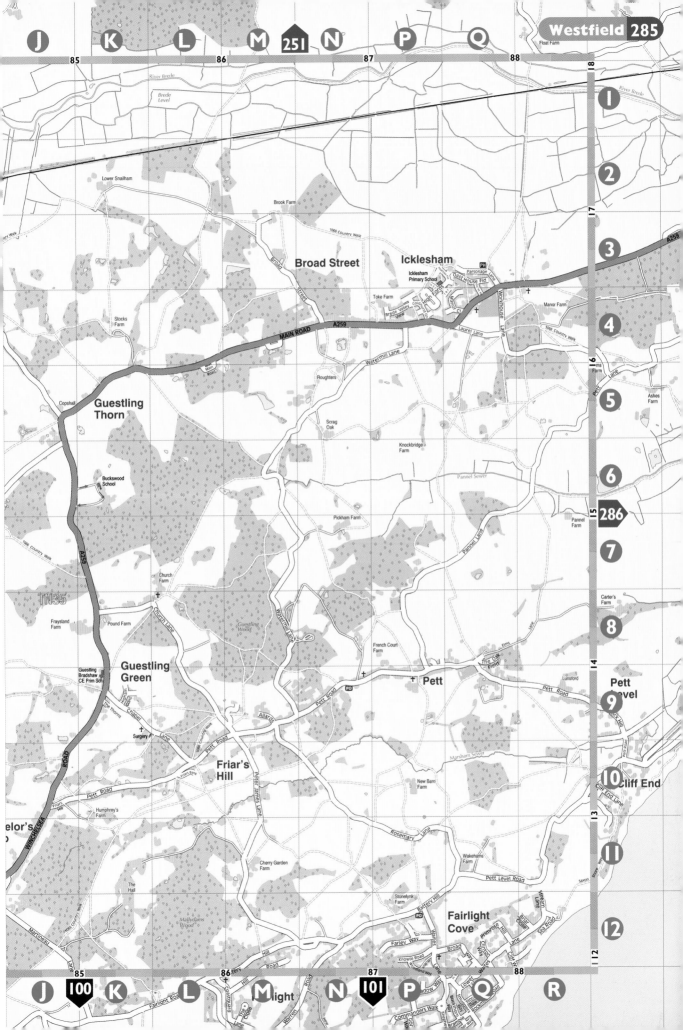

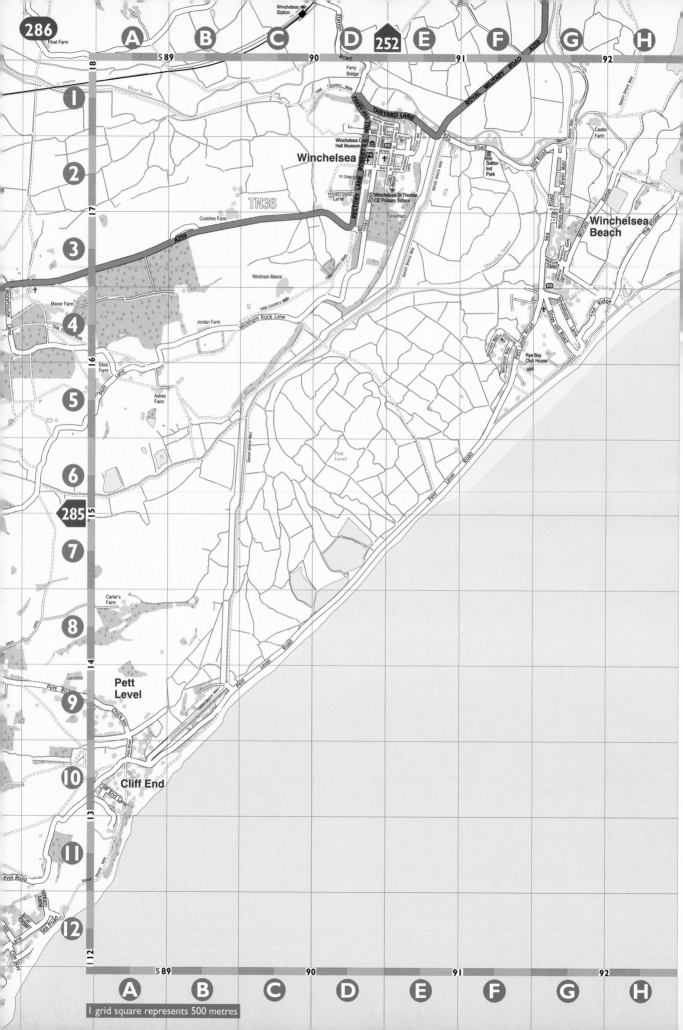

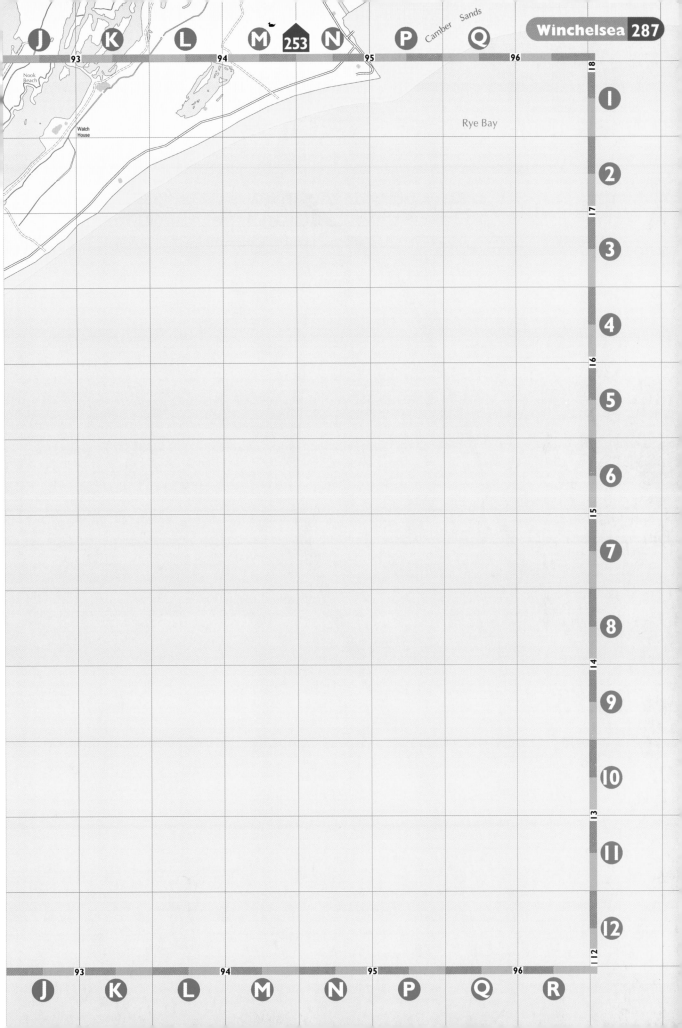

Nook Beach

Watch House

Rye Bay

Camber Sands

93   94   95   96

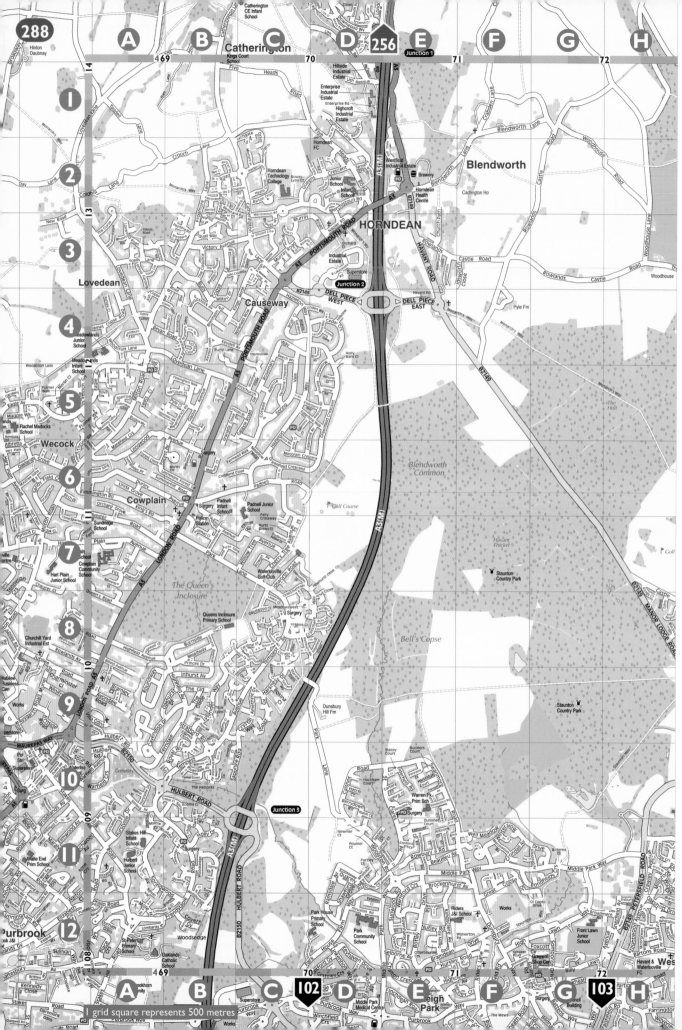

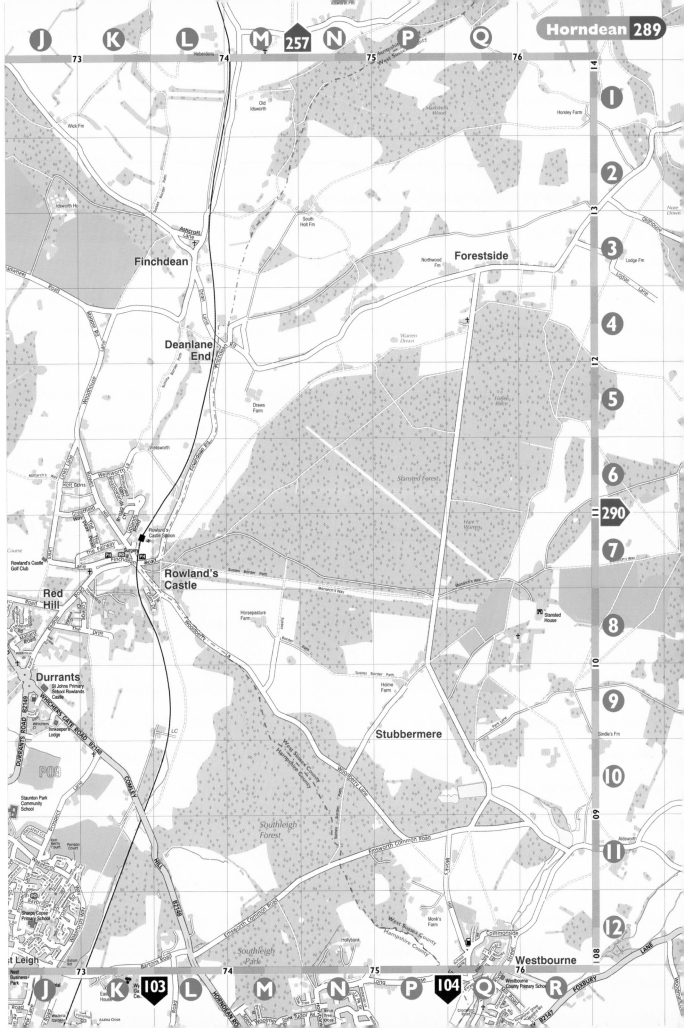

J K L M **257** N P Q

73 74 75 76

1
2
3
4
5
6
290
7
8
9
10
11
12

Finchdean

Forestside

Deanlane End

Stansted Forest

Rowland's Castle

Red Hill

Durrants

Stubbermere

Southleigh Forest

Southleigh Park

Westbourne

J K **103** L M N P **104** Q R

73 74 75 76

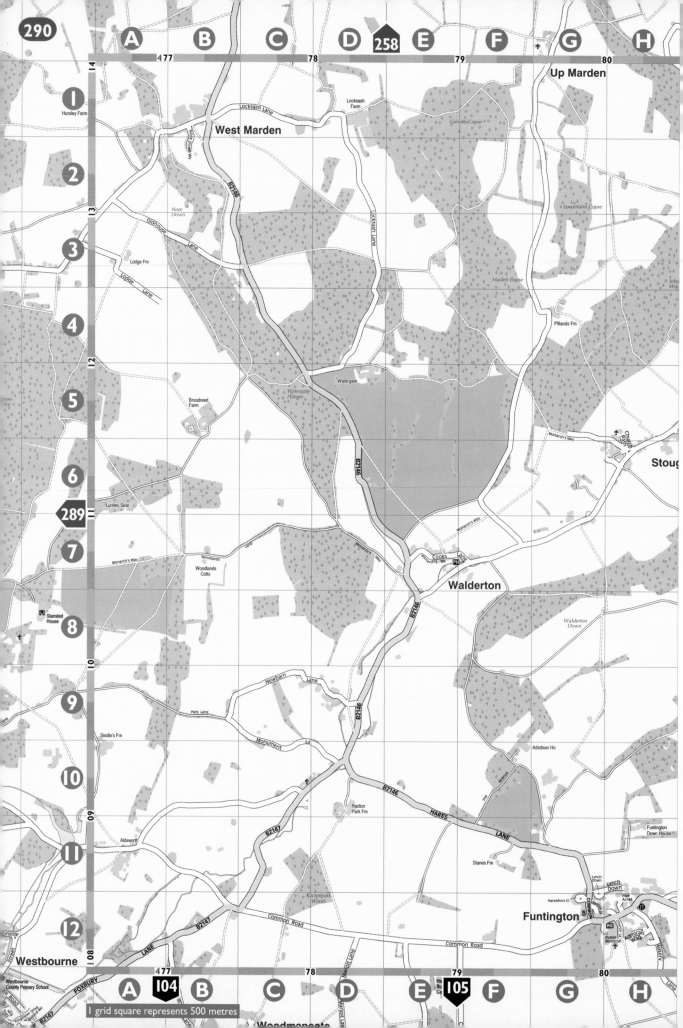

A   B   C   D   E   F   G   H

477   78   79   80

Up Marden

1 Horsley Farm

Locksash Lane

Locksash Farm

Grevatts Copse

2

West Marden

Nore Down W

B2146

Nore Down

Lowerfarm Copse

3

Oldhouse Lane

Lodge Fm

Lodge Lane

Locksash Lane

Haslett Copse

Inholms Fm

4

Watergate

Pitlands Fm

5

Broadreed Farm

Watergate Hanger

B2146

6

Lumley Seat

Monarch's Way

Church Path

Stoug

7

Monarch's Way

Woodlands Lane

Woodlands Cotts

Monarch's Way

Monarch's Way

Cooks Lane

PH

Walderton

8

Stansted House

B2146

Walderton Down

9

Newbarn Lane

Park Lane

B2146

Monument La

Adsdean Ho

10

Sindle's Fm

11

Aldsworth

B2147

Racton Park Fm

B2146

HARES LANE

Avenue

Funtington Down House

Haresfoot Cl

Lynch Down

Five Acres

12

Ractonpark Wood

Stanes Fm

COMMON RD

Funtington

Dukes Meadow

Admirals Walk

Westbourne

Foxbury Lane

B2147

Common Road

Marlpit Lane

Common Road

Church La

Waterly

Westbourne County Primary School

B2147

477   78   79   80

A   **104**   B   C   D   E   **105**   F   G   H

1 grid square represents 500 metres

Woodmancote

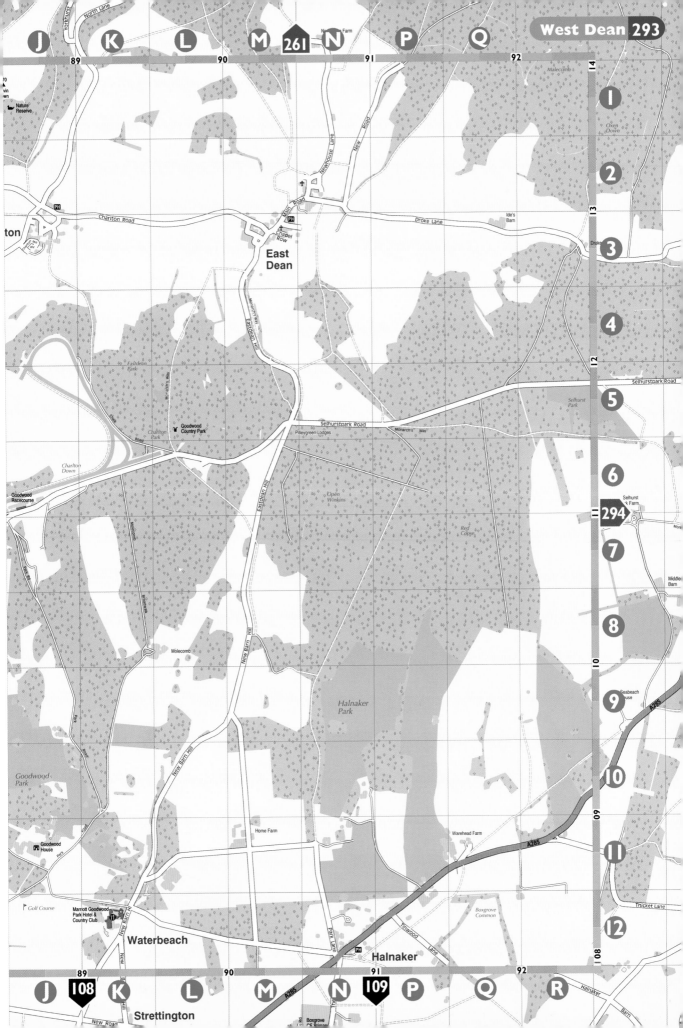

J K L M 263 N P Q
West Burton

Glatting Farm
Coldharbour Farm

225
Bignor Hill

Clatting Lane

South Downs Way

South Downs Way
Monarch's Way

Great Bottom

The Denture

Stammers

Houghton Forest

Monarch's Way

South Downs Way

South Downs Way

Great Down

B2139
296
Whiteways Lodge

Parletts Farm

New Barn Farm
Madehurst

Cemetery

Little Down

Dale Park

FAIRMILE BOTTOM
Fairmile Bottom

Punchbowl

Sherwood Rough

Rewell Wood

BN18

Baycombe Lane

Rewell House

Long Lane

Slindon

Bridle Road

J K III L M N P II2 Q R

Bury CE First School

Coombe Wood

LONDON ROAD

A29

A284

LONDON ROAD

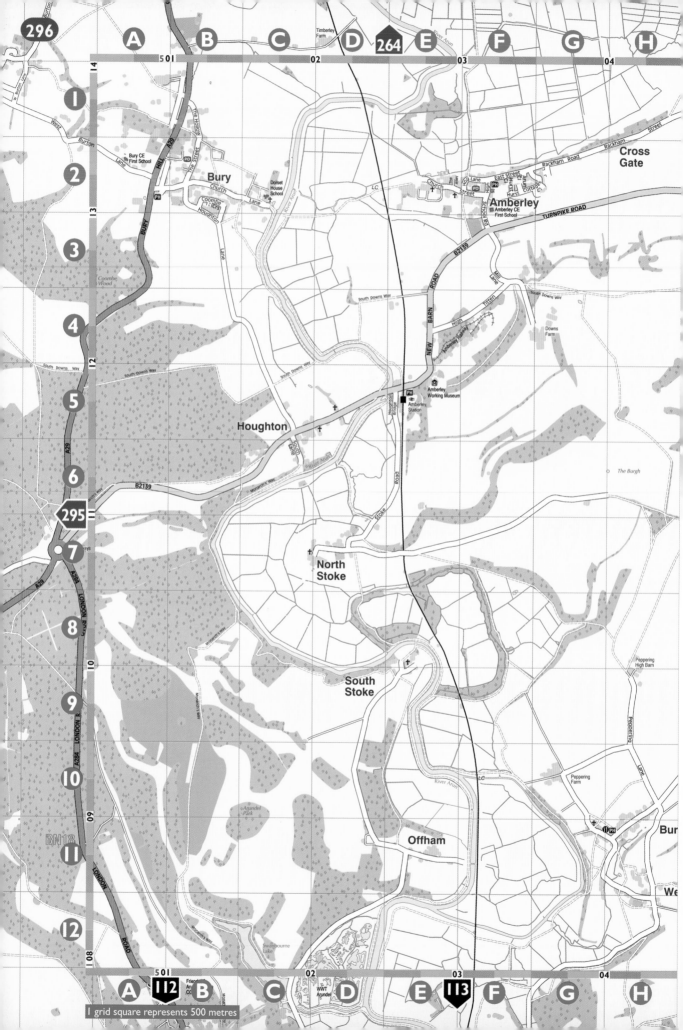

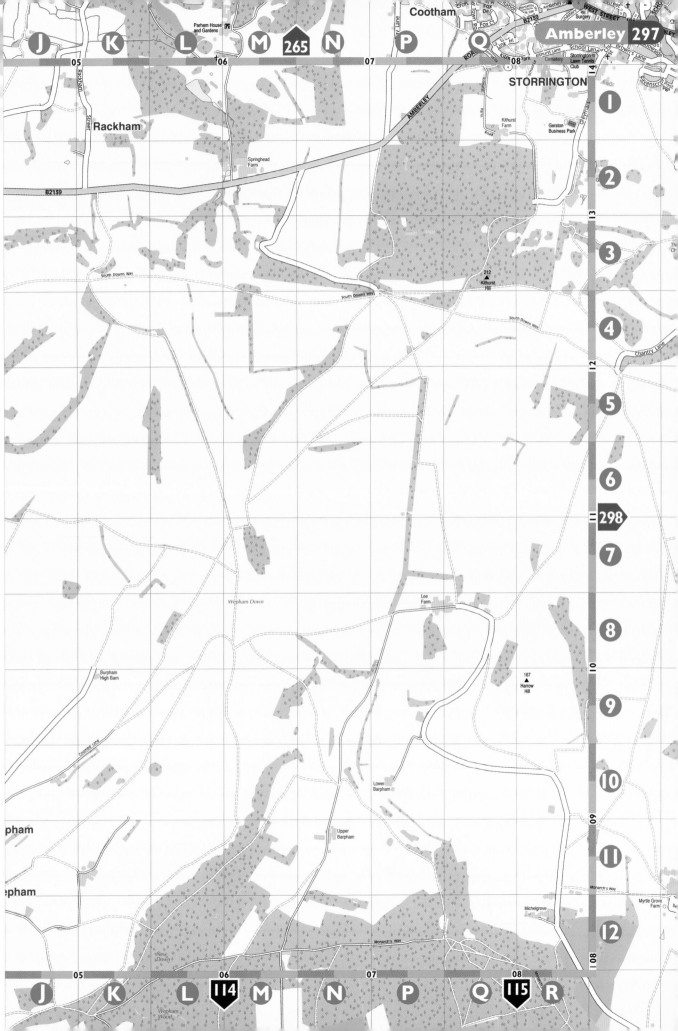

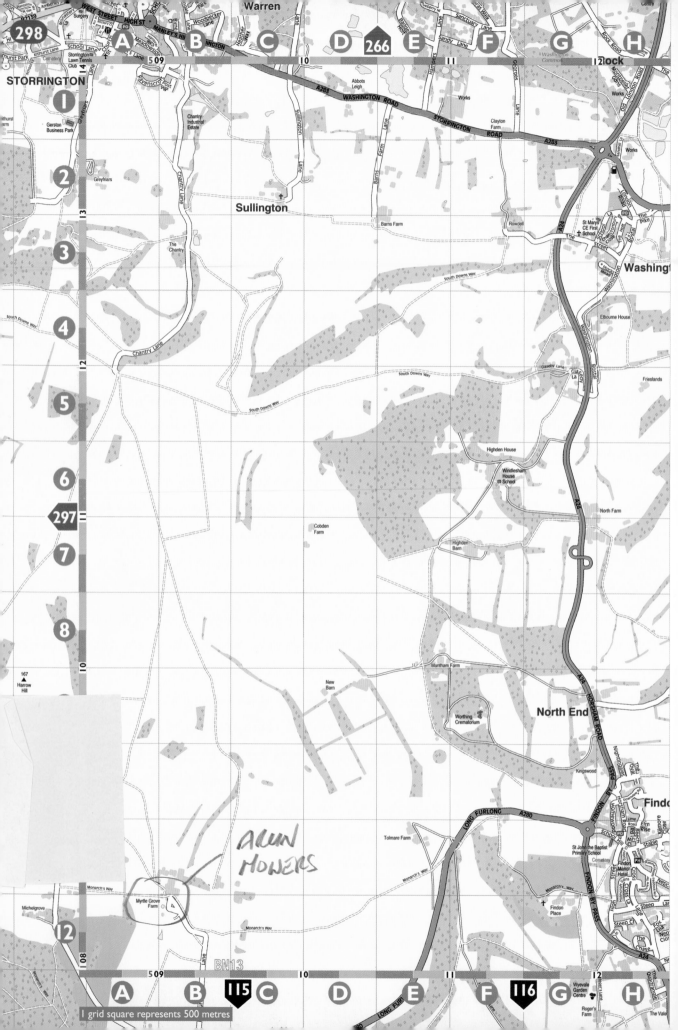

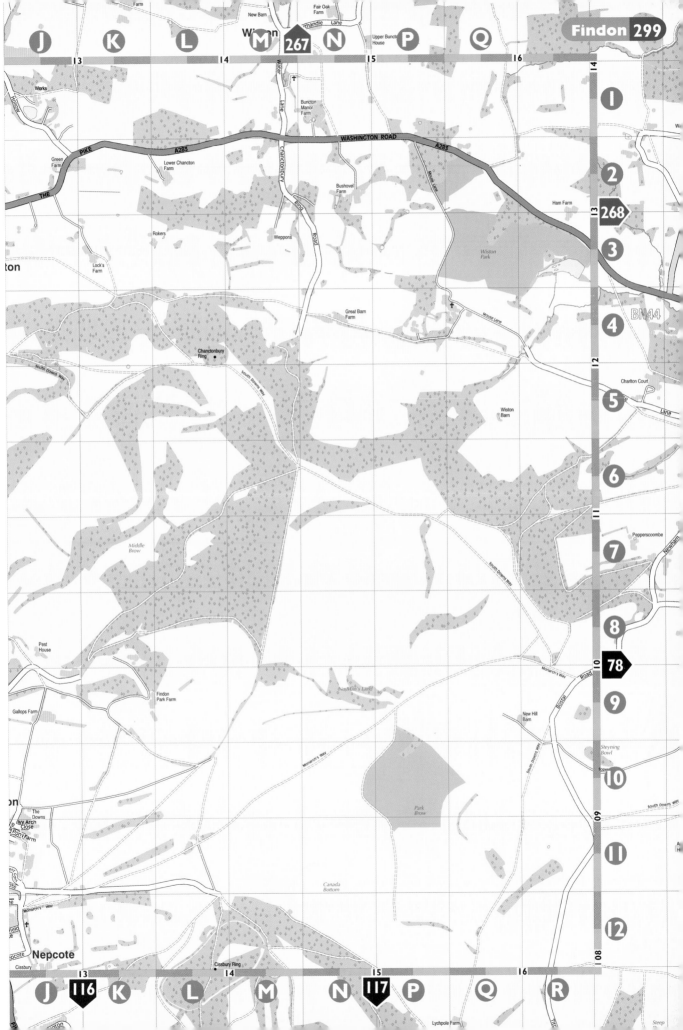

267   268   78

Works

Green Farm

THE PIKE

A283   WASHINGTON ROAD   A283

Lower Chancton Farm

Buncton Manor Farm

Bushovel Farm

Rokers

Weppons

Ham Farm

Wiston Park

BN44

Lock's Farm

Great Barn Farm

Charlton Court

Chanctonbury Ring

South Downs Way

Wiston Barn

South Downs Way

Pepperscoombe

Middle Brow

Newham Lane

Pest House

South Downs Way

Findon Park Farm

No Man's Land

Monarch's Way

Gallops Farm

New Hill Barn

Boston Road

Steyning Bowl

The Downs

Ivy Arch Close

Monarch's Way

Park Brow

South Downs Way

Canada Bottom

Nepcote

Cissbury

Cissbury Ring

New Barn

Fair Oak Farm

Upper Buncton House

Wiston

Chanctonbury Ring Road

Water Lane

1   2   3   4   5   6   7   8   9   10   11   12

14   13   12   11   10   09   08

116   117

Lychpole Farm

Steep

Bracklesham

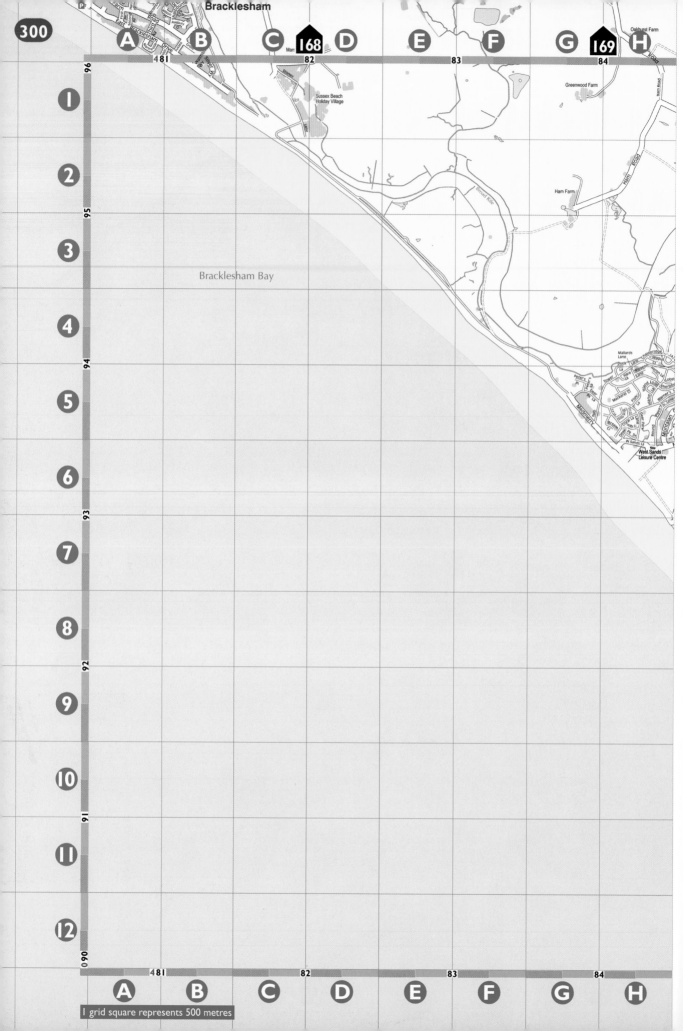

A B C 168 D E F G 169 H

481 82 83 84

1

2

Bracklesham Bay

3

Sussex Beach
Holiday Village

Broad Rife

Ham Farm

Greenwood Farm

Oakhurst Farm

Ham Road

4

5

Mallards
Lane

West Sands
Leisure Centre

6

7

8

9

10

11

12

A B C D E F G H

481 82 83 84

1 grid square represents 500 metres

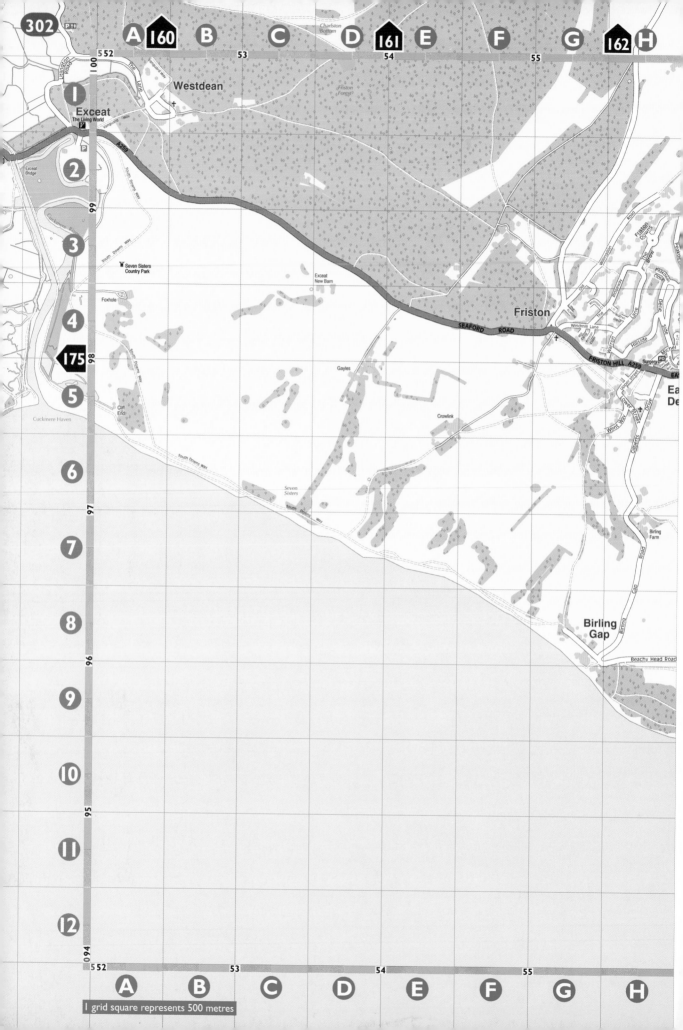

A 160   B   C   D 161   E   F   G   H 162

5 52   53   54   55
100

Westdean

I
Exceat
The Living World

99

2
Exceat
Bridge

Cuckmere River

South Downs Way

A259

3

Seven Sisters
Country Park

Foxhole

Exceat
New Barn

4

98

175

Gayles

5
Cliff End

Cuckmere Haven

97

6

South Downs Way

Seven
Sisters

7

96

8

9

95

10

11

12

94
5 52   53   54   55

A   B   C   D   E   F   G   H

Charlston
Bottom

Friston
Forest

Friston

Seaford Road

FRISTON HILL A259

Windmill Lane

Crowlink

Birling
Farm

Birling
Gap

Beachy Head Road

Ea
De

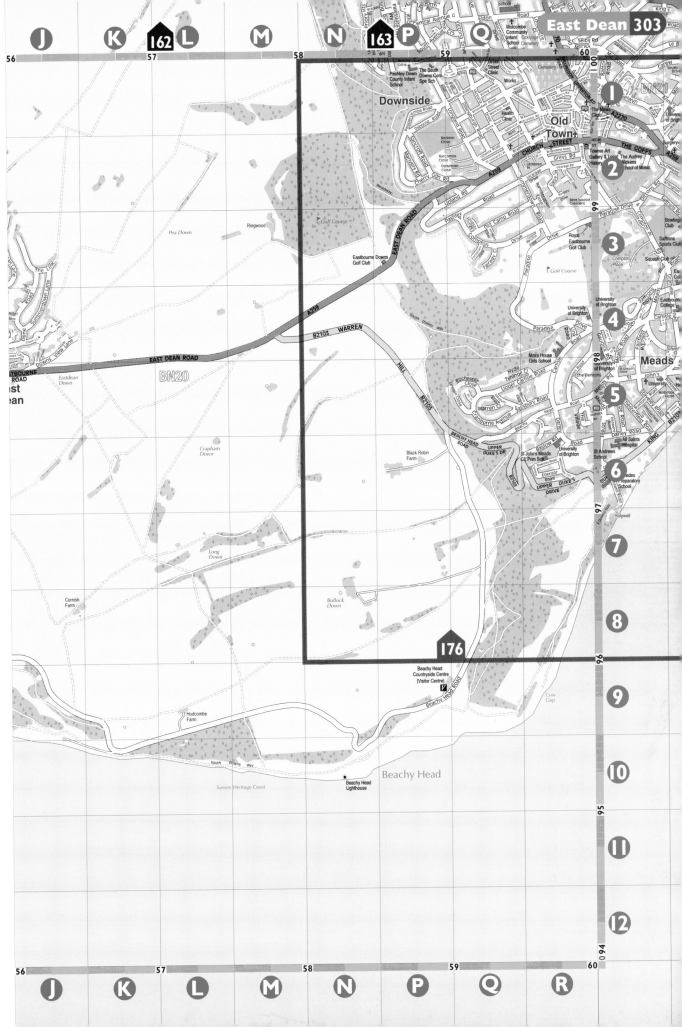

Abbotsford....74 D3
Abingworth....266 D7
Adversane....231 N6
Albourne....270 D4
Albourne Green....270 D3
Alciston....129 J5
Alderbrook....210 G2
Aldingbourne....109 H4
Aldington....121 K6
Aldwick....171 K3
Alfold....184 C8
Alfold Bars....184 G10
Alfold Crossways....184 H6
Alfriston....160 E3
Almodington....168 E5
Amberley....296 F2
Amberstone....92 C1
Ancton....145 L7
Angmering....114 D7
Ansteadbrook....182 B12
Ansty....237 K2
Appledore....221 P2
Apuldram....141 H2
Ardingly....206 M4
Arford....179 M3
Argos Hill....212 B4
Arlington....130 E1
Arundel....113 C2
Ashburnham Forge....281 J4
Ashburnham Place....281 K4
Ashfold Crossways....203 R3
Ashington....266 H9
Ashton Green....87 L1
Ashurst....35 J7
Ashurst....268 B4
Ashurst Wood....48 B3
Atherington....146 E7
Bachelor's Bump....284 H11
Balcombe....60 F7
Balcombe Lane....60 F4
Baldslow....283 Q10
Baldwins Hill....31 H6
Balls Cross....197 N12
Balls Green....51 L4
Balls Green....232 D6
Barcombe....274 D8
Barcombe Cross....274 D5
Bardown....214 D2
Barford....180 B1
Barlavington....263 K8
Barnham....111 H8
Barns Green....200 H11
Battle....282 D3
Beachlands....134 E7
Beacon Down....243 P6
Beacon Hill....180 G2
Beckley....251 K1
Beckley Furnace....250 G6
Beddingham....127 J1
Bedgebury Cross....191 Q3
Bedham....230 C9
Bedhampton....102 D4
Bedlam Street....270 G5
Beggars Bush....117 L2
Bell Hill....223 M4
Bells Yew Green....55 G4
Belmont....100 B4
Bepton....260 D4
Berner's Hill....191 M11
Berwick....129 L6
Best Beech Hill....71 H6
Bevendean....123 M3
Bewbush....42 E6
Bexhill....136 F1
Bexleyhill....227 P2
Bignor....263 N11
Billingshurst....232 B2
Bilsham....145 L4
Bines Green....268 E2
Binsted....111 M4
Birchden....52 C3
Birchett's Green....190 D10
Birchgrove....63 M8
Birdham....140 D7
Birling Gap....302 G8
Bishopstone....159 H6
Blackboys....243 J7
Black Corner....28 C5
Blackham....34 F5
Blacklands....12 D2
Blackmoor....178 C10
Blackness....67 M8
Black Rock....154 E2
Blackstone....269 R4
Blackwell....31 K7
Blendworth....288 C2
Boarshead....68 A3
Bodiam....217 M9
Bodle Street Green....280 B7
Bognor Regis....3 G8
Bohemia....12 B5
Bolney....236 D2
Bolnore Village....72 F6
Borden....225 N3
Bordon....178 H7
Boreham Street....94 D1
Bosham....106 B8
Bosham Hoe....140 A5
Botolphs....78 E6
Bowler's Town....252 G3
Boxgrove....109 H2
Bracklesham....168 B8
Bramber....78 E3
Bramshott....179 R11
Bray's Hill....280 F8
Breach....104 E4
Brede....250 E12
Brenchley....188 H1
Brightling....247 J7
Brighton....4 D8
Broadbridge....106 C6
Broadbridge Heath....201 L1
Broadfield....43 H7
Broad Ford....189 P5
Broadford Bridge....232 C9
Broadham Row....250 D9
Broad Oak....245 J4
Broad Oak....250 E8
Broad Street....285 M3
Broadwater....117 J7
Broadwater Down....53 L1
Brockhampton....102 F5
Brookpits....146 E5
Brooks Green....232 H2
Brook Street....205 N7
Broomer's Corner....233 J10

Broomershill....265 M1
Broomgrove....13 K1
Broomham....276 G11
Broomhill Bank....37 H2
Brownbread Street....280 F6
Broyle Side....275 M9
Buchan Hill....58 F1
Buckham Hill....76 A6
Bucks Green....185 Q11
Budlett's Common....76 E1
Bulverhythe....98 B7
Burgates....192 B3
Burgess Hill....74 F6
Burgh Hill....215 R6
Burgh Hill....277 M11
Buriton....223 M12
Burlow....278 C4
Burndell....146 A2
Burnt Oak....210 G6
Burpham....296 H11
Burrswood....51 M1
Burstow....28 F2
Burwash....214 F11
Burwash Common....245 R2
Burwash Weald....246 B2
Bury....296 B2
Buxted....77 J1
Byworth....229 N11
Cackle Street....209 K7
Cackle Street....247 K9
Cackle Street....250 C11
Cade Street....244 H7
Camber....254 A10
Camden Park....38 B7
Camelsdale....181 K12
Canadia....282 D1
Capel....24 C3
Capel Cross....189 P4
Castle Hill....211 P5
Castle Town....79 H4
Catherington....256 B12
Catsfield....282 A9
Catsfield Stream....281 R10
Causeway....223 M7
Causeway....288 C4
Chailey....239 P10
Chalton....257 J8
Chalvington....89 M6
Chapel Cross....245 K8
Chapel Row....279 Q12
Chapman's Town....245 L11
Charlton....292 H3
Charlwood....26 E2
Charlwood....47 K8
Chelwood Common....208 C3
Chelwood Gate....64 A8
Chichester....6 F5
Chiddingfold....182 C4
Chiddingly....277 M8
Chidham....139 L1
Chilgrove....259 N11
Chilsham....188 F3
Chiltington....273 M7
Chitcombe....250 B7
Chithurst....225 R6
Chuck Hatch....66 B2
Church Common....223 J1
Churches Green....280 A1
Church Norton....301 N1
Churchwood....264 B1
Cinder Hill....207 K1
Clanfield....256 C8
Clapham....115 L4
Clark's Green....24 B5
Clayhill....250 H2
Clayton....271 M9
Cliff End....286 A10
Climping....146 C3
Clive Vale....100 C3
The Close....6 D5
Coates....263 P5
Cocking....260 H5
Cocking Causeway....260 H1
Cock Marling....252 A11
Codmore Hill....231 K12
Coggins Mill....212 F5
Cold Ash Hill....180 B12
Coldean....83 J8
Coldwaltham....264 D7
Coleman's Hatch....49 K8
Colgate....58 B3
Collier's Green....249 P4
Colworth....143 K3
Combe....213 M3
The Common....201 N1
Compton....258 B11
Coneyhurst....232 E5
Conford....179 N10
Cooden....136 C2
Cooksbridge....273 R9
Coolham....232 G7
Coombes....78 E8
Cooper's Green....76 F1
Cootham....265 P12
Copsale....202 B11
Copthorne....29 G6
The Corner....189 N1
Cote....116 B5
Cousley Wood....190 B6
Cowbeech....279 M8
Cowbeech Hill....279 L10
Cowden....33 M3
Cowfold....235 L3
Cowplain....288 A6
Cox Green....186 B7
Crabtree....203 M10
Crawley....9 H5
Crawley Down....46 B2
Cripp's Corner....249 L6
Critchmere....180 H10
Crockerhill....109 M2
Crossbush....113 K4
Cross Gate....296 H2
Cross in Hand....243 Q6
Crosspost....236 B4
Crouchers....141 G4
Crowborough....67 L8
Crowborough Warren....67 H7
Crowhurst....282 G11
Cuckfield....72 C4
Cudworth....25 K1
Dale Hill....191 L11
Dallington....246 C10
Danegate....69 H1
Danehill....207 R5

Darwell Hole....247 L10
Davis's Town....277 J2
Deadwater....179 J6
Deanlane End....289 L4
Dell Quay....141 G3
Denne Park....202 B2
Denny Bottom....37 J6
Denton....158 E4
Denvilles....103 K3
Dial Green....196 A10
Dial Post....267 P1
Didling....259 Q3
Ditchling....272 A6
Dittons....132 D7
Domewood....30 A4
Donnington....141 K4
Doomsday Green....15 K9
Doomsday Green....202 F1
Dormans Park....31 K2
Down Park....29 M8
Downside....176 B1
Down Street....209 J12
Dragons Green....233 L6
Duddleswell....209 M5
Dumpford....225 P9
Duncton....262 G6
Dunsfold....184 A4
Dunsfold Common....184 A5
Dunsfold Green....184 A3
Durgates....71 J4
Durleighmarsh....224 D6
Durrants....289 J9
Durrington....116 C6
Earl's Down....246 A9
Earnley....168 B7
Easebourne....226 H7
Eason's Green....242 E12
East Ashling....106 D1
East Beach....301 N4
East Blatchington....174 E1
Eastbourne....10 C4
East Chiltington....273 K5
East Dean....293 M3
East Dean....302 H5
Eastergate....110 E6
East Grinstead....31 K7
East Guldeford....253 L6
East Hampnett....109 K3
East Harting....258 G2
East Hoathly....277 J4
East Kingston....149 H4
East Lavant....292 D12
East Lavington....262 D7
East Liss....192 E10
East Marden....259 J11
East Moulsecoomb....123 L1
East Preston....149 G5
East Wittering....167 M7
East Worthing....152 A2
Ebernoe....197 L9
Eckington Corner....89 K5
Edburton....80 B2
Egdean....229 Q12
Elbridge....143 K4
Ellen's Green....186 B5
Elmer....146 A8
Elmers Marsh....194 D8
Elsted....259 K1
Emsworth....103 M6
Eridge Green....53 G5
Etchingham....215 N8
Etchingwood....77 M3
Ewhurst Green....217 Q12
Exceat....175 M1
Fairfield....221 R8
Fairlight....101 H1
Fairlight Cove....285 Q12
Fairwarp....209 N8
Falmer....84 C7
Faygate....41 K8
Felbridge....30 E5
Felcourt....31 H1
Felpham....145 G8
Ferndale....38 C4
Fernhill....28 D2
Fernhurst....195 J7
Ferring....149 L3
Field Green....217 M1
Filching....162 C3
Finchdean....289 K3
Findon....298 H10
Findon Valley....117 G3
Fishbourne....106 E7
Fisher....142 B7
Fishersgate....120 E6
Fisherstreet....196 E2
Fittleworth....264 B2
Five Ash Down....209 R12
Five Ashes....211 Q10
Five Oaks....200 B8
Flackley Ash....251 Q2
Flansham....145 H6
Flathurst....229 M8
Fletching....240 F1
Fletching Common....240 A5
Flimwell....191 P10
Flowers Green....93 L1
Folkington....162 B1
Fontwell....110 F3
Ford....146 C1
Fordcombe....35 M4
Ford's Green....208 H2
Forest Row....48 B8
Forestside....289 Q3
Foul Mile....279 M5
Foulride Green....163 G1
Four Oaks....219 M12
Four Throws....217 K1
Foxhunt Green....243 N12
Framfield....77 J6
Frant....54 B6
Friar's Gate....67 G2
Friar's Hill....285 L10
Friston....302 F4
Froxfield Green....222 D1
Fulking....80 D2
Funtington....290 F12
Furnace Green....9 L8
Furnace Wood....30 B6
Furner's Green....208 B2
Fyning....225 K4
Gallypot Street....50 A6
Gay Street....231 R11
Ginger's Green....279 M11

Glenleigh Park....96 E6
Glynde....87 K6
Glyndebourne....87 K3
Glyne Gap....98 B8
Goatham Green....250 B8
Goddards' Green....236 H8
Godleys Green....239 J3
Golden Cross....93 K3
Golden Cross....277 L11
Goose Green....266 G3
Gorehill....229 N12
Goring-by-Sea....150 C2
Gossops Green....43 G4
Gotham....95 M6
Graffham....262 A6
Grayshott....180 E6
Grayswood....181 R8
Great Common....198 C10
Greatham....192 B4
Greatham....264 H9
Green Street....98 A1
Green Street....233 L7
Griggs Green....193 N1
Groombridge....51 M2
Grove Hill....278 H8
Guestling Green....285 K9
Guestling Thorn....285 K5
Gun Hill....277 R8
Gunter's Bridge....229 L5
Habin....225 J7
Hadlow Down....211 K12
Hailsham....92 B5
Halecommon....224 H4
Hale Green....277 P7
Halfway Bridge....228 A9
Halland....276 D3
Hall's Cross....95 H5
Halnaker....293 N12
Hambrook....105 H3
Ham Green....220 B8
Hammer....180 F12
Hammer Bottom....180 E12
Hammerpot....114 E5
Hammerwood....33 G6
Hampden Park....163 K4
Hampers Green....229 L7
Hamsey....274 B11
Handcross....204 D1
Hangleton....121 K2
Hangleton....149 H1
Hankham....132 F6
Hardham....264 G6
Harley Shute....98 E5
Hartfield....50 C5
Haslemere....181 N11
Haslingbourne....229 M12
Hassocks....271 L5
Hastings....12 E5
Hatch Farm Hill....195 M5
Havant....102 F2
The Haven....200 A3
Hawkenbury....38 C7
Hawkhurst Common....242 H12
Haywards Heath....73 H3
Hazard's Green....281 J12
Hazel Street....189 K6
Headley....179 L4
Headley Down....179 Q5
Hearn....179 Q2
Heath Common....266 F11
Heath End....263 J3
Heathfield....69 H7
Heathfield....244 E6
Hellingly....278 C12
Henfield....269 L4
Henley....227 L1
Henley Common....195 J12
Henley's Down....282 B11
Henwood Green....39 L3
Hermitage....104 B4
Heron's Ghyll....209 Q6
Herstmonceux....279 Q11
Heyshott....261 K4
Heyshott Green....261 K3
Hickstead....236 B8
Highbrook....62 D8
High Brooms....38 B1
High Cross....211 R2
High Cross....270 A2
Highgate....48 B8
High Hurstwood....210 A8
The Highlands....96 E5
Highleigh....169 H4
High Salvington....116 B4
Highstreet Green....183 L7
Hill Brow....192 F11
Hillgrove....196 D7
Hill Side....192 D9
Hill Top....227 J11
Hindhead....181 J5
Hole Street....267 M11
Hollingbury....83 G8
Hollingdean....123 G2
Hollingrove....247 K7
Hollington....98 C2
Hollywater....179 J8
Holtye....33 K6
Homes Hill....277 K11
Hooe....95 H6
Hooe Common....95 K4
Hook Green....190 C1
Hooksway....259 K8
Hookwood....22 B7
Horam....278 B2
Horley....23 G4
Horndean....288 D3
Horney Common....209 K9
Horns Cross....250 D4
Horsemere Green....146 B4
Horsham....14 D5
Horsmonden....189 K3
Horsted Green....244 N10
Horsted Keynes....207 M4
Houghton....296 B5
Houghton Green....253 J4
Hove....24 A8
Hoyle....261 N3
Hungershall Park....37 K7
Hunston....141 M5
Hunt's Green....216 B6
Hurstpierpoint....270 F4
Hurst Wickham....271 G6
Icklesham....285 P3
Iden....252 G1
Ifield....42 F1

Ifield Green....26 F8
Ifieldwood....26 C8
Ifold....198 D2
Iford....126 A2
Ingrams Green....225 R12
Iping....226 K1
Isfield....275 K1
Itchingfield....201 L1
Jarvis Brook....211 L1
Jevington....162 B5
John's Cross....248 D6
Jumper's Town....66 A2
Jury's Gap....254 F12
Kemp Town....154 C2
Kent Street....235 P6
Keymer....271 Q5
Key's Green....188 B5
Kilndown....191 M3
Kingsfold....40 A3
Kingsley Green....195 L3
Kingston by Sea....120 B6
Kingston Gorse....148 F6
Kingston near Lewes....85 K8
Kipping's Cross....39 M5
Kirdford....198 C11
Lagness....143 H7
Laker's Green....184 G5
Lamberhurst....188 G12
Lamberhurst Quarter....188 C7
Lambs Green....41 L3
Lancing....118 B7
Landport....16 D3
Langley....193 J7
Langley Green....27 G7
Langney....164 C3
Langrish....222 F9
Langstone....102 F7
Langton Green....36 A3
Laughton....276 D10
Leggatt Hill....228 A3
Leigh Park....102 E1
Lewes....17 H6
Lewes Heath....189 M6
Lickfold....228 A1
Lidham Hill....284 H3
Lidsey....144 C3
Linchmere....194 D2
Lindfield....73 L1
Lindford....179 J5
Linkhill....218 B5
Lions Green....243 Q12
Liphook....193 C6
Liss....192 D10
Liss Forest....192 C10
Litlington....160 F5
Little Bayham....55 L5
Little Bognor....229 R11
Little Common....96 A8
Little Common....228 E9
Littlehampton....147 K4
Littlehaven....56 D4
Little Horsted....241 P12
Little London....244 A9
Little Norlington....275 K8
Littleworth....234 E8
Lodsworth....228 A6
Lodsworth Common....227 R3
Lower Beeding....203 M6
Lower Bordean....222 B3
Lower Cousley Wood....190 D5
Lower Dicker....91 G1
Lower Fittleworth....264 A4
Lower Green....37 H4
Lower Green....39 J1
Lower Horncroft....264 A5
Lower Horsebridge....91 K1
Lower Street....281 N12
Lower Willingdon....163 G2
Lowfield Heath....27 L4
Loxhill....183 R1
Loxwood....198 F1
Lullington....161 G3
Lumley....104 B4
Lunsford's Cross....96 D3
Lurgashall....196 C11
Lydd....255 Q7
Lye Green....51 K8
Lyewood Common....51 G2
Lyminster....113 J2
Mackerel's Common....198 B8
Madehurst....295 N8
Magham Down....92 E1
Maidenbower....44 B5
Mannings Heath....203 J4
Manor Park....77 G3
Manor Royal....27 K7
Maplehurst....202 E11
Marden's Hill....67 G4
Marehill....265 M3
Maresfield Park....209 M12
Mark Cross....69 M5
Mark Cross....89 H3
Marle Green....278 C6
Marley Heights....195 J4
Marlpits....209 J3
Marlpits....281 N10
Matfield....188 D3
Maudlin....108 D3
Mayfield....212 D7
Maynard's Green....244 D11
Meads....176 B5
Meath Green....22 C4
Merston....143 G2
Middleton-on-Sea....145 K8
Midhurst....227 J11
Mid Lavant....292 B11
Mile Oak....120 E3
Milland....193 P11
Mill Corner....250 D2
Mill Hill....133 J7
Milton Street....130 C8
Minsted....226 B11
The Mint....192 D8
Monk's Gate....202 H5
Moon's Green....219 R6
The Moor....216 G1
Mott's Mill....51 M6
Moulsecoomb....123 L2
Mount Ephraim....241 R10
Mountfield....248 B7
Mount Pleasant....158 F4
Mount Pleasant....274 E3
Muddles Green....277 M10
Mutton Hall....244 E4
Nash Street....277 N11
Navant Hill....196 C8

Nepcote 299 J12
Nep Town 269 K6
Netherfield 247 P11
Newbridge 65 K3
New Brighton 104 B2
Newenden 218 G6
Newhaven 19 J3
Newick 240 C6
Newpound Common 199 M10
New Town 14 F9
New Town 77 G6
Newtown 193 Q3
Ninfield 281 N11
Norlington 275 J10
Norman's Bay 135 J5
North Bersted 143 M6
Northbridge Street 216 D12
North Chailey 239 N7
Northchapel 196 F6
North Common 239 P6
North End 31 G5
North End 111 M8
North End 298 G9
Northgate 43 L1
North Heath 231 N10
Northiam 218 E11
North Lancing 118 E5
North Marden 259 J8
North Moulsecoomb 123 J1
North Mundham 142 B4
North Stoke 296 D7
Norton 110 A3
Norton 159 G4
Norton 301 M2
Nursted 223 R10
Nutbourne 105 G6
Nutbourne 265 P3
Nutbourne Common 265 Q3
Nutcombe 180 G7
Nuthurst 202 E8
Nutley 208 H6
Nyetimber 170 F3
Nyewood 224 H9
Nyton 110 B5
Oakhanger 178 A5
Oakhill 15 H6
Oakwoodhill 187 J2
Offham 273 R12
Offham 296 E11
Old Cryals 188 C4
Old Heathfield 244 G7
Old Shoreham 119 K4
Old Town 13 M6
Old Town 97 H7
Old Town 176 D1
Ore 100 B2
Oving 109 H6
Ovingdean 155 K2
Oxley's Green 247 K5
Pagham 170 D5
Palehouse Common 242 C11
Palmer's Green 189 J1
Parbrook 231 R2
Park Corner 52 D4
Park Corner 276 G7
Park Street 200 F2
Partridge Green 234 F10
Passfield 179 N8
Patcham 82 E7
Patching 115 J3
Paynes Green 187 N2
Peacehaven 157 H5
Peacehaven Heights 157 K8
Pease Pottage 58 F2
Peasmarsh 251 R3
Pebsham 97 L7
Peening Quarter 220 A3
Pell Green 190 A6
Pembury 39 H3
Penhurst 281 L3
Petersfield 223 L6
Pett 285 P9
Petteridge 188 E3
Pett Level 286 A9
Petworth 229 K9
Pevensey 134 A7
Pevensey Bay 134 B8
Piddinghoe 157 M3
Piltdown 240 H4
Plaistow 198 A3
Playden 252 H5
Plumpton 273 J10
Plumpton Green 272 H3
Polegate 131 M8
Poling 114 A7
Poling Corner 113 M5
Ponts Green 280 G5
Portfield 7 K5
Portslade-by-Sea 121 G2
Portslade Village 120 F3
Potman's Heath 219 P4
Potter's Green 77 M1
Poundfield 68 A7
Poundford 211 P12
Poundgate 210 B2
Pound Green 242 E1
Pound Hill 44 B1
Poundsbridge 36 B1
Pounsley 242 H5
Povey Cross 22 B8
Poynings 270 C12
Preston 122 D4
Prince's Marsh 192 C11
Prinsted 104 D6
Pulborough 265 J4
Punnett's Town 245 M7
Pyecombe 271 J11
Quabrook 49 H8
Quags Corner 226 D10
Queen's Corner 226 B1
Rackham 297 L11
Rake 192 H9
Ramsdean 222 D8
Ramslye 37 J8
Ramsnest Common 182 E10
Rapkyns 201 K1
Ratton Village 163 G6
Redford 194 D12
Red Hill 289 J8
Rickney 133 J3
Ridge Common 223 K4
Ridgewood 76 E8
Ringles Cross 76 E2
Ringmer 274 H11
Ripe 89 K4
Riseden 189 M12
River 228 D7
Robertsbridge 248 A1
Robins 225 R2
Rock 266 G12
Rockrobin 71 J2
Rocks Park 76 C5
Rodmell 126 B5
Roedean 155 H2
Roffey 56 F4
Rogate 224 H6
Romford 39 L2
Rose Green 171 H2
Rose Hill 275 L3
Roselands 164 B6
Roser's Cross 243 N7
Rotherbridge 228 H12
Rotherfield 211 P1
Rottingdean 155 M3
Roundstreet Common .. 199 J7
Rowhook 186 H8
Rowland's Castle 289 L7
Royal Tunbridge Wells . 37 L6
Rudgwick 185 R10
Runcton 142 E4
Rusher's Cross 213 J3
Rushlake Green 245 M12
Rusky Green 275 K12
Rusper 41 H2
Russell's Green 95 M2
Russ Hill 26 B4
Rusthall 37 H5
Rustington 148 C4
Rye 252 H7
Rye Foreign 252 D4
Rye Harbour 253 L11
Saddlescombe 81 K2
St Anthony's Hill 164 C5
St Helen's 284 D12
St Helen's Wood 99 K1
Saint Hill 47 J5
St John's 37 L3
St John's 67 H5
St Leonards 98 F6
Saint's Hill 36 A1
Salehurst 216 D12
Saltdean 156 C3
Salvington 116 F6
Sandhurst 217 P4
Sandhurst Cross 217 M5
Sandown Park 38 E3
Sandy Cross 244 E8
Saxby 111 K8
Sayers Common 236 D12
Scayne's Hill 239 J2
Seacox Heath 191 R11
Seaford 174 D3
Sedlescombe 249 L12
Selham 228 C11
Selmeston 129 K2
Selsey 301 M7
Selsfield Common 46 A8
Sharpsbridge 240 H7
Sharp's Corner 278 B1
Sharpthorne 62 F3
Sheet 223 Q3
Sheffield Green 208 A10
Shepherd's Hill 181 M11
Shermanbury 235 J10
Sherwood Park 38 D3
Shipley 233 N9
Shipley Bridge 28 E3
Shipton Green 167 M1
Shopp Hill 196 B7
Shopwyke 108 E6
Shoreham Beach 120 A8
Shoreham-by-Sea 119 L8
Shortbridge 76 A4
Shortgate 276 C6
Shortheath 178 B3
Shottermill 180 H11
Shover's Green 190 B11
Shripney 144 C4
Sidlesham 169 L4
Sidlesham Common 141 K8
Sidley 97 G7
Silverhill 99 H2
Silver Hill 216 C9
Silverhill Park 283 R11
Singleton 292 F2
Skippers Hill 211 P10
Slaugham 204 B4
Sleeches Cross 54 A7
Slindon 295 J12
Slinfold 200 G2
Slough Green 205 J8
Small Dole 269 L11
Smallfield 23 M7
Smart's Hill 35 L1
Smithbrook 228 A5
Smock Alley 266 A6
Snagshall 217 N12
Somerley 168 B3
Sompting 118 A7
Sompting Abbotts 117 M5
South Ambersham 227 Q11
South Bersted 2 E1
Southbourne 104 F5
South Chailey 273 P2
Southease 126 D6
Southern Cross 120 F5
Southgate 8 D7
South Harting 258 D1
South Heighton 158 D3
South Lancing 118 D8
South Malling 17 G3
South Mundham 142 C7
Southover 16 D9
Southover 214 B9
South Stoke 296 D9
South Street 239 P12
Southwater 233 Q1
Southwater Street 201 Q9
Southwick 120 D5
Sparrow's Green 71 L4
Speldhurst 36 F2
Spithurst 274 E2
Splayne's Green 208 F12
Standford 179 K7
Stanmer 83 K5
Staplecross 249 M4
Staplefield 204 G4
Staples Hill 197 R10
Starr's Green 282 H7
Stedham 226 D8
Steel Cross 68 A6
Steep 223 M2
Steven's Crouch 281 N6
Steyning 78 C3
Stockbridge 141 L2
Stockheath 102 F2
Stockland Green 37 H1
The Stocks 220 F5
Stone Cross 35 L7
Stone Cross 71 M6
Stone Cross 133 M8
Stone Cross 210 G3
Stonecrouch 191 K6
Stonegate 214 D3
Stone in Oxney 221 L5
Stonequarry 31 M6
Stoner Hill 223 J1
Stopham 264 E3
Storrington 297 Q1
Stoughton 290 H6
Strawberry Hill 53 J1
Streat 272 E6
Street End 169 L2
Strettington 108 F1
Strood Green 187 L11
Strood Green 230 E4
Stroud 222 H5
Stubbermere 289 P9
Stunts Green 279 N10
Sullington 298 C2
Sullington Warren 266 C12
Summer Hill 131 M1
Summersdale 107 M3
Sunnyside 47 K3
Sutton 175 G1
Sutton 263 M10
Sutton End 263 L7
Swaile's Green 249 K6
Sweethaws 210 D3
Tangmere 109 H3
Tarring Neville 158 C1
Teasley Mead 35 H6
Telham 283 J7
Telscombe 157 G2
Telscombe Cliffs 156 F5
Temple Bar 108 F2
Terwick Common 225 L4
Thakeham 266 E6
Thorney Island 138 D2
Three Bridges 9 K1
Three Cups Corner 245 M8
Three Leg Cross 191 J10
Three Oaks 284 G7
Thunder's Hill 277 N10
Ticehurst 191 K11
Tidebrook 213 L1
Tilgate 43 J8
Tilgate Forest Row 59 H4
Tillington 228 H9
Tilsmore 244 C5
Tinsley Green 28 B5
Tisman's Common 185 P12
Titty Hill 226 B1
Toddington 147 L1
Tolhurst 190 E11
Tompset's Bank 64 E1
Topleigh 261 Q3
Tortington 112 D6
Tote Hill 226 D3
Tower Hill 201 Q5
Town Littleworth 240 B12
Town Row 69 H8
Treyford 259 M3
Trolliloes 279 N7
Trotten Marsh 225 M2
Trotton 225 P8
Tullecombe 224 H1
Turner's Green 71 K3
Turner's Green 245 Q9
Turners Hill 45 M5
Twelve Oaks 247 J8
Twineham 236 B9
Twineham Green 236 C7
Two Mile Ash 201 N10
Uckfield 76 F5
Udimore 251 N11
Union Street 191 N10
Up Marden 290 G1
Upwaltham 294 C1
Upper Beeding 78 E4
Upper Dicker 90 F5
Upper Hartfield 50 A7
Upper Horsebridge 91 K2
Upper Ifold 184 B10
Upper Norwood 262 C4
Upperton 10 B3
Upperton 228 G7
Upper Wardley 193 R8
Upper Wellingham 274 F9
Vinehall Street 248 F7
Vines Cross 278 F1
Wadhurst 71 K5
Walberton 111 J5
Walderton 290 E7
Waldron 243 N9
Waldron Down 243 L5
Wallands Park 16 C5
Wallcrouch 190 E12
Walter's Green 35 K2
Wannock 162 E1
Warbleton 245 K12
Warblington 103 J5
Wardley 193 R9
Warminghurst 266 F7
Warnham 187 P9
Warningcamp 113 L2
Warninglid 204 B8
Wartling 94 B6
Washington 298 H3
Waterbeach 293 K12
Watermill 97 G1
Watersfield 264 B9
Weatherhill 23 M5
Wellbrook 212 C8
Wepham 296 H11
West Ashling 106 B2
West Blatchington 121 L4
Westbourne 289 Q12
West Burton 263 Q12
West Chiltington 266 B3
West Chiltington Common 265 Q12
West Dean 292 D3
Westdean 302 B1
Westdene 82 A8
West End 268 H4
Westergate 110 B6
Westerton 108 G2
Westfield 284 C5
West Firle 128 B2
West Green 8 D3
West Grinstead 234 C6
Westham 133 K7
Westhampnett 108 D4
West Harting 224 D10
West Hill 13 K4
West Hill 61 H8
West Hoathly 62 D3
West Itchenor 139 K6
West Kingston 149 H4
West Lavington 227 K11
West Leigh 288 H12
West Liss 192 C8
West Marden 290 B1
West Marina 98 E7
Westmeston 272 B9
Weston 223 J9
West Stoke 291 P11
West Tarring 20 B1
West Thorney 138 C3
West Town 270 F3
West Wittering 167 H4
West Worthing 150 E3
Whatlington 248 H12
Whitehall 233 L10
Whitehawk 123 L7
Whitehill 178 F7
Whitehill 210 F1
Whitemans Green 72 B1
White Post 35 J2
White's Green 228 D2
Whitesmith 277 J9
Whydown 96 A5
Whyke 7 G7
Wick 147 G1
Wickstreet 90 D7
Wiggonholt 265 L2
Willard's Hill 215 P12
Willingdon 162 F4
Wilmington 130 D7
Wilmington Green 130 D6
Winchelsea 286 C2
Winchelsea Beach 286 G3
Windmill Hill 280 A12
Wineham 235 Q8
Winton 160 F1
Wisborough Green 231 J1
Wiston 267 M12
Withdean 122 D1
Witherenden Hill 213 B8
Withyham 50 F6
Wittersham 220 C6
Wivelsfield 75 M4
Wivelsfield Green 238 G9
Woldhurst 142 C5
Woodgate 110 C8
Woodingdean 124 B6
Woodmancote 105 G1
Woodmancote 269 Q7
Woodmansgreen 194 D10
Woodmans Green 248 H10
Wood's Corner 246 E10
Wood's Corner 71 L1
Wood's Green 226 E2
Woolbeding 180 F10
Woolmer Hill 75 J5
World's End 35 K2
Worth 44 D4
Worth Abbey 45 G8
Worthing 21 G8
Wych Cross 64 D5
Yapton 145 M2

USING THE STREET INDEX

Street names are listed alphabetically. Each street name is followed by its postal town or area locality, the Postcode District, the page number, and the reference to the square in which the name is found.

Standard index entries are shown as follows:

Abberton Fld *HPPT/KEY* BN6...... **271** J4

Street names and selected addresses not shown on the map due to scale restrictions are shown in the index with an asterisk:

Aberdeen Ter *GSHT* GU26 *........ **180** G6

GENERAL ABBREVIATIONS

ACC	ACCESS	CEN	CENTRE	CP	CAPE	DRY	DRIVEWAY	FTS	FLATS
ALY	ALLEY	CFT	CROFT	CPS	COPSE	DWGS	DWELLINGS	FWY	FREEWAY
AP	APPROACH	CH	CHURCH	CR	CREEK	E	EAST	FY	FERRY
AR	ARCADE	CHA	CHASE	CREM	CREMATORIUM	EMB	EMBANKMENT	GA	GATE
ASS	ASSOCIATION	CHYD	CHURCHYARD	CRS	CRESCENT	EMBY	EMBASSY	GAL	GALLERY
AV	AVENUE	CIR	CIRCLE	CSWY	CAUSEWAY	ESP	ESPLANADE	GDN	GARDEN
BCH	BEACH	CIRC	CIRCUS	CT	COURT	EST	ESTATE	GDNS	GARDENS
BLDS	BUILDINGS	CL	CLOSE	CTRL	CENTRAL	EX	EXCHANGE	GLD	GLADE
BND	BEND	CLFS	CLIFFS	CTS	COURTS	EXPY	EXPRESSWAY	GLN	GLEN
BNK	BANK	CMP	CAMP	CTYD	COURTYARD	EXT	EXTENSION	GN	GREEN
BR	BRIDGE	CNR	CORNER	CUTT	CUTTINGS	F/O	FLYOVER	GND	GROUND
BRK	BROOK	CO	COUNTY	CV	COVE	FC	FOOTBALL CLUB	GRA	GRANGE
BTM	BOTTOM	COLL	COLLEGE	CYN	CANYON	FK	FORK	GRG	GARAGE
BUS	BUSINESS	COM	COMMON	DEPT	DEPARTMENT	FLD	FIELD	GT	GREAT
BVD	BOULEVARD	COMM	COMMISSION	DL	DALE	FLDS	FIELDS	GTWY	GATEWAY
BY	BYPASS	CON	CONVENT	DM	DAM	FLS	FALLS	GV	GROVE
CATH	CATHEDRAL	COT	COTTAGE	DR	DRIVE	FM	FARM	HGR	HIGHER
CEM	CEMETERY	COTS	COTTAGES	DRO	DROVE	FT	FORT	HL	HILL

306

HLS HILLS
HO HOUSE
HOL HOLLOW
HOSP HOSPITAL
HRB HARBOUR
HTH HEATH
HTS HEIGHTS
HVN HAVEN
HWY HIGHWAY
IMP IMPERIAL
IN INLET
IND EST INDUSTRIAL ESTATE
INF INFIRMARY
INFO INFORMATION
INT INTERCHANGE
IS ISLAND
JCT JUNCTION
JTY JETTY
KG KING
KNL KNOLL
L LAKE
LA LANE
LDG LODGE
LGT LIGHT
LK LOCK
LKS LAKES
LNDG LANDING
LTL LITTLE
LWR LOWER
MAG MAGISTRATE
MAN MANSIONS
MD MEAD
MDW MEADOWS
MEM MEMORIAL
MI MILL
MKT MARKET
MKTS MARKETS
ML MALL
MNR MANOR
MS MEWS
MSN MISSION
MT MOUNT
MTN MOUNTAIN
MTS MOUNTAINS
MUS MUSEUM
MWY MOTORWAY
N NORTH
NE NORTH EAST
NW NORTH WEST
O/P OVERPASS
OFF OFFICE
ORCH ORCHARD
OV OVAL
PAL PALACE
PAS PASSAGE
PAV PAVILION
PDE PARADE
PH PUBLIC HOUSE
PK PARK
PKWY PARKWAY
PL PLACE
PLN PLAIN
PLNS PLAINS
PLZ PLAZA
POL POLICE STATION
PR PRINCE
PREC PRECINCT
PREP PREPARATORY
PRIM PRIMARY
PROM PROMENADE
PRS PRINCESS
PRT PORT
PT POINT
PTH PATH
PZ PIAZZA
QD QUADRANT
QU QUEEN
QY QUAY
R RIVER
RBT ROUNDABOUT
RD ROAD
RDG RIDGE
REP REPUBLIC
RES RESERVOIR
RFC RUGBY FOOTBALL CLUB
RI RISE
RP RAMP
RW ROW
S SOUTH
SCH SCHOOL
SE SOUTH EAST
SER SERVICE AREA
SH SHORE
SHOP SHOPPING
SKWY SKYWAY
SMT SUMMIT
SOC SOCIETY
SP SPUR
SPR SPRING
SQ SQUARE
ST STREET
STN STATION
STR STREAM
STRD STRAND
SW SOUTH WEST
TDG TRADING
TER TERRACE
THWY THROUGHWAY
TNL TUNNEL
TOLL TOLLWAY
TPK TURNPIKE
TR TRACK
TRL TRAIL
TWR TOWER
U/P UNDERPASS
UNI UNIVERSITY
UPR UPPER
V VALE
VA VALLEY
VIAD VIADUCT
VIL VILLA
VIS VISTA
VLG VILLAGE
VLS VILLAS
VW VIEW
W WEST
WD WOOD
WHF WHARF
WK WALK
WKS WALKS
WLS WELLS
WY WAY
YD YARD
YHA YOUTH HOSTEL

POSTCODE TOWNS AND AREA ABBREVIATIONS

ALTN Alton
ANG/EP Angmering/East Preston
ARUN Arundel
BAT Battle
BEX Bexhill
BEXW Bexhill west
BIL Billingshurst
BOGR Bognor Regis
BOR Bordon
BRI Brighton
BRIE/ROTT Brighton east/Rottingdean
BUR/ETCH Burwash/Etchingham
BURH Burgess Hill
CCH Chichester
CHAM Cosham
CRAN Cranleigh
CRAWE Crawley east
CRAWW Crawley west
CRBK Cranbrook
CROW Crowborough
EAST Eastbourne
EDEN Edenbridge
EDN/EASTW East Dean/Eastbourne west
EGRIN East Grinstead
EMRTH Emsworth/Southbourne
EPSF Petersfield east
FERR Ferring
FROW Forest Row
GSHT Grayshott
HAIL Hailsham
HAS Hastings
HASM Haslemere
HAV Havant
HAWK Hawkhurst
HFD Henfield
HISD Hayling Island
HORL Horley
HORN Horndean
HORS Horsham
HOVE Hove
HPPT/KEY Hurstpierpoint/Keymer
HRTF Hartfield
HTHF Heathfield
HWH Haywards Heath
LAN/SOMP Lancing/Sompting
LEWES Lewes
LGNY Langney
LHPTN Littlehampton
LING Lingfield
LIPH Liphook
LISS Liss
LW/ROSE Lower Willingdon/Roselands
LYDD Lydd
MAYF Mayfield
MFD/CHID Milford/Chiddingfold
MIDH Midhurst
MSEA/BNM Middleton-on-Sea/Barnham
NEWHV Newhaven
PEAHV Peacehaven
PETW Petworth
PEV Pevensey
POLE Polegate
POY/PYE Poynings/Pyecombe
PSF Petersfield
PTSD Portslade
PUL/STOR Pulborough/Storrington
RASHW Rural Ashford west
RBTBR Robertsbridge
RCCH Rural Chichester
RDKG Rural Dorking
REDH Redhill
REIG Reigate
RFNM Rural Farnham
RHAS Rural Hastings
RHWH Rural Haywards Heath
RING/NEW Ringmer/Newick
RRTW Rural Royal Tunbridge Wells
RTON Rural Tonbridge
RTW Royal Tunbridge Wells
RTWE/PEM Royal Tunbridge Wells east/Pembury
RYE Rye
SALV Salvington
SBGH/RUST Southborough/Rusthall
SEAF Seaford
SELS Selsey
SHOR Shoreham
SLVH Silverhill
STEY/UB Steyning/Upper Beeding
STHW Southwick
STLEO St Leonards
STPH/PW Staplehurst/Paddock Wood
SWTR Southwater
TENT Tenterden
UCK Uckfield
WADH Wadhurst
WSEA Winchelsea
WTHG Worthing
WVILLE Waterlooville/Denmead

Index - streets

1066 - Amb

1

1066 Country Wk BAT TN33 283 K5
HAIL BN27 93 K7
RHAS TN35 100 B5
WSEA TN36 285 N3

A

Abberton Fld HPPT/KEY BN6 271 J4
Abbey Cl LAN/SOMP BN15 119 G7
PEAHV BN10 157 H4
Abbeydore Cl BOR GU35 179 M4
Abbey Dr STLEO TN38 98 A8
Abbey Ms RBTBR TN32 248 C1
Abbey Rd BRIE/ROTT BN2 5 L8
EDN/EASTW BN20 163 G8
LAN/SOMP BN15 118 B6
STEY/UB BN44 78 D1
WTHG BN11 20 D8
Abbey Vw BEX TN40 97 J7
Abbey Wy BAT TN33 282 D4
Abbotsbury Cl BRIE/ROTT BN2 156 A4
Abbotsbury Ct SWTR RH13 15 H3
Abbots Cl BAT TN33 282 G6
HPPT/KEY BN6 271 M5
Abbotsfield Cl HAS TN34 99 L2
Abbotsfield Rd CRAWW RH11 42 C4
Abbots Leigh SWTR RH13 233 R1
Abbotstone Av HAV PO9 103 H1
Abbots Wy LAN/SOMP BN15 118 E7
Abbotswood Wk
ANG/EP BN16 148 B5
Abbottsbury BOGR PO21 170 F5
Abbotts Cl LW/ROSE BN22 10 F3
WTHG BN11 20 F5
Abbotts Vw LAN/SOMP BN15 118 B5
A'Becket Gdns SALV BN13 116 E7
A'Becket's Av BOGR PO21 171 G4
Aberdale Rd POLE BN26 132 B7
Aberdare Cl CCH PO19 108 A5
Aberdeen Rd BRIE/ROTT BN2 5 H1
Aberdeen Ter GSHT GU26 * 180 G6
Abergavenny Rd LEWES BN7 16 C6
Abingdon Ldg ANG/EP BN16 * 148 C4
Abinger Pl LEWES BN7 16 F5
Abinger Rd BRIE/ROTT BN2 124 D7
PTSD BN41 121 G5
Abrahams Rd CRAWW RH11 42 F8
Acacia Av HOVE BN3 121 L4
SALV BN13 116 E6
Acacia Gdns HORN PO8 288 C4
Acacia Rd LW/ROSE BN22 163 K3
NEWHV BN9 158 D3
Acer Av RTWE/PEM TN2 54 B1
Acer Wy HAV PO9 103 J1
Acorn Av SWTR RH13 235 K4
Acorn Cl ANG/EP BN16 148 E1
EGRIN RH19 47 K1
HORL RH6 23 H5
SELS PO20 301 K6
SLVH TN37 99 H1
Acorn End BOGR PO21 171 J3
Acorns SWTR RH13 15 M2
The Acorns BURH RH15 74 C5
CRAWW RH11 43 G8
HAIL BN27 92 C6
HPPT/KEY BN6 236 E11
WADH TN5 214 E3
Acorn Wy BUR/ETCH TN19 216 B6
Acre Cl ANG/EP BN16 148 A3
HWH RH16 73 G7
The Acre Cl WTHG BN11 20 C6
Acre La WVILLE PO7 288 D8
Acres Ri WADH TN5 191 K12
Acre St SELS PO20 167 L3
Acton La TENT TN30 220 F3
Adam Cl CROW TN6 210 H3
STLEO TN38 98 E1
Adams Cl BRI BN1 123 G4
Adams La RYE TN31 250 A3
Adams Ms LIPH GU30 193 Q3
Adastra Av HPPT/KEY BN6 271 P5
Adderbury Av EMRTH PO10 104 A2
Addingham Rd LW/ROSE BN22 11 J3
Addington Cl STLEO TN38 98 E6
Addison Cl LAN/SOMP BN15 118 D7
Addison Rd HOVE BN3 4 A3
Addison Wy MSEA/BNM PO22 144 A6
Adelaide Cl CRAWW RH11 27 J8
HORS RH12 15 K1
SALV BN13 116 B7
SEAF BN25 159 K8
Adelaide Crs HOVE BN3 122 B8
Adelaide Man HOVE BN3 122 B8
Adelaide Rd CCH PO19 7 G2
STLEO TN38 99 G2
Adelaide Sq SHOR BN43 120 A6
Adelphi Cl CRAWE RH10 44 C5
Ades Fld POLE BN26 130 E7
Adhurst Rd HAV PO9 103 H1
Admers Crs LIPH GU30 193 R3
Admiral Rd CRAWW RH11 42 F6
Admiral's Bridge La
EGRIN RH19 47 H7
Admirals Wk LHPTN BN17 147 M3
RCCH PO18 290 H12
Admiralty Ct MSEA/BNM PO22 * 3 K6
Admiralty Gdns
MSEA/BNM PO22 3 K5
Admiralty Rd MSEA/BNM PO22 3 K5
Admiralty Wy LGNY BN23 165 G4
Adsdean Cl HAV PO9 102 F1
Adur Av SALV BN13 116 B5
SHOR BN43 119 K4
Adur Cl LAN/SOMP BN15 119 H8
Adur Dr PEV BN24 132 F8
SHOR BN43 119 M6
Adur Rd BURH RH15 75 H5
SHOR BN43 119 K5
Adur Valley Ct STEY/UB BN44 * 79 G3
Adur Vw STEY/UB BN44 * 78 F3
Adversane La BIL RH14 231 Q6
Adversane Rd SALV BN13 117 G8
Agate La HORS RH12 56 D4
Agincourt Cl SLVH TN37 283 N10
Aglaia Rd WTHG BN11 150 E4
Agnes St BRIE/ROTT BN2 5 J2
Aigburth Av BOGR PO21 171 J2
Ailsa Cl CRAWW RH11 8 A9
Ailsworth La RYE TN31 * 252 H7
Ainsdale Cl SALV BN13 116 C7
Ainsdale Rd SALV BN13 116 C7
Ainsworth Av BRIE/ROTT BN2 155 J2
Ainsworth Cl BRIE/ROTT BN2 155 J1
Aintree Dr WVILLE PO7 288 C8
Aintree Rd CRAWE RH10 9 L8
Airport Wy HORL RH6 27 M1
Air St BRI BN1 * 4 D6
Airy Rd HAIL BN27 94 A4
Ajax Pl MSEA/BNM PO22 145 H8
Akehurst Cl CRAWE RH10 28 F6
Akehurst Fld BAT TN33 280 G6
Alamein Cl CROW TN6 210 H1
Alandale Rd LAN/SOMP BN15 118 B5
SELS PO20 168 E1
Alan Wy BRIE/ROTT BN2 123 L8
Albany Cl WTHG BN11 20 B7
Albany Hl RTWE/PEM TN2 38 B4
Albany Man BEX TN40 * 137 H2
Albany Ms HOVE BN3 122 A7
Albany Rd BEX TN40 137 H2
CRAWW RH11 8 C4
SEAF BN25 174 C2
STLEO TN38 99 G5
Albany Vls HOVE BN3 122 A8
The Albemarle BRIE/ROTT BN2 * 4 F8
Alberta Dr HORL RH6 23 M6
Alberta Rd SALV BN13 116 C7
Albert Cl HWH RH16 73 K5
Albert Cottages RTW TN1 * 38 A5
Albert Dr BURH RH15 74 D7
Albert Man HOVE BN3 * 122 B7
Albert Ms HOVE BN3 122 A7
Albert Rd ANG/EP BN16 148 B3
BEX TN40 137 H2
BOGR PO21 2 F7
BRI BN1 4 C4
CCH PO19 107 H7
HAS TN34 13 H7
HORL RH6 22 F6
LHPTN BN17 147 J4
POLE BN26 131 L6
STHW BN42 120 C6
UCK TN22 76 F6
Albert Ter EAST BN21 163 H8
Albery Cl HORS RH12 14 B1
Albion Cl CRAWE RH10 44 C4
Albion Ct BURH RH15 74 E7
Albion Hl BRIE/ROTT BN2 5 H5
Albion La HAS TN34 * 13 J7
Albion Rd LW/ROSE BN22 11 G3
RTW TN1 38 A4
SELS PO20 301 M7
Albion St BRIE/ROTT BN2 5 G4
LEWES BN7 17 G5
PTSD BN41 121 G6
STHW BN42 120 C7
Albion Wy HORS RH12 14 C5
Alborough Wy BOGR PO21 171 J3
Albourne Cl BRIE/ROTT BN2 123 K6
STLEO TN38 98 E5
Albourne Rd HPPT/KEY BN6 270 F3
Albury Keep HORL RH6 23 G5
Aldborough Rd SLVH TN37 12 B4
Aldbourne Dr BOGR PO21 171 J3
Alderbrook Cl CROW TN6 210 H3
Alderbrook Wy CROW TN6 210 H3
Alder Cl CRAWE RH10 46 A1
HTHF TN21 244 D8
LGNY BN23 164 B5
SALV BN13 116 B8
SLVH TN37 283 R12
Alderfield PSF GU32 223 M6
Alderman's Wk CCH PO19 * 6 E3
Aldermoor Av PUL/STOR RH20 266 B11
Alderney Rd FERR BN12 149 L5
Alder Rd BOR GU35 179 Q3
Alders Av EGRIN RH19 31 J6
Alders View Dr EGRIN RH19 31 K6
Aldervale Cottages CROW TN6 210 H2
Alder Wy MSEA/BNM PO22 145 K7
Alderwood Cl HAV PO9 102 C2
Aldingbourne Cl CRAWW RH11 42 E2
Aldingbourne Dr RCCH PO18 109 M2
Aldingbourne Pk SELS PO20 * 110 C8
Aldrich Cl BRIE/ROTT BN2 123 L7
Aldridge Cl HORN PO8 256 D8
Aldrington Av HOVE BN3 121 M5
Aldrington Cl HOVE BN3 121 J6
Aldsworth Av FERR BN12 150 A3
Aldsworth Ct FERR BN12 150 A3
Aldsworth Pde FERR BN12 150 A3
Aldwick Av BOGR PO21 171 L4
Aldwick Cl ANG/EP BN16 148 A6
Aldwick Crs SALV BN13 116 F4
Aldwick Felds BOGR PO21 171 L3
Aldwick Gdns BOGR PO21 171 L2
Aldwick Hundred
BOGR PO21 * 171 K4
Aldwick Pl BOGR PO21 171 L3
Aldwick Rd BOGR PO21 171 L2
Aldwick St BOGR PO21 171 K3
Alexander Cl BOGR PO21 171 K3
Alexander Dr BEXW TN39 136 E1
Alexander Md RING/NEW BN8 240 C5
Alexander Ter WTHG BN11 * 21 H6
Alexandra Cl SEAF BN25 159 K8
Alexandra Ct BOR GU35 178 G6
CRAWE RH10 * 8 F6
FERR BN12 150 B2
Alexandra Pde HAS TN34 99 J2
Alexandra Rd BURH RH15 75 H7
CCH PO19 7 G3
HTHF TN21 244 E7
LAN/SOMP BN15 118 E8
LW/ROSE BN22 164 C7
MAYF TN20 212 F6
SLVH TN37 12 A6
UCK TN22 76 F6
WTHG BN11 21 M5
Alexandra Ter BOGR PO21 * 2 F7
Alexandra Vls BRI BN1 4 C4
CROW TN6 * 67 L8
Alfold By-Pass CRAN GU6 184 G3
Alfold Rd MFD/CHID GU8 184 A5
Alford Cl SALV BN13 116 F6
Alford Wy BEX TN40 97 K7
Alfray Rd BEX TN40 97 M8
Alfred Cl CRAWE RH10 44 D4
MSEA/BNM PO22 145 L8
Alfred Pl WTHG BN11 21 K6
Alfred Rd BRI BN1 4 C4
LGNY BN23 164 E5
RHAS TN35 100 B2
Alfred St STLEO TN38 12 A8
Alfrey Cl EMRTH PO10 104 D5
Alfriston Cl BEXW TN39 96 B7
BRIE/ROTT BN2 123 L7
EDN/EASTW BN20 176 C3
MSEA/BNM PO22 145 H7
SALV BN13 117 G8
Alfriston Pk SEAF BN25 160 B8
Alfriston Rd POLE BN26 160 F1
SALV BN13 117 G8
SEAF BN25 175 G1
Alice Bright La CROW TN6 210 G2
Alice Cl HOVE BN3 * 122 C8
Alice St HOVE BN3 122 C8
Alicia Av CRAWE RH10 44 A3
PUL/STOR RH20 267 K8
Alicks Hl BIL RH14 232 A1
Alinora Av FERR BN12 150 C3
Alinora Cl FERR BN12 150 C3
Alinora Crs FERR BN12 150 C4
Alinora Dr FERR BN12 150 B4
Allan Cl SBGH/RUST TN4 37 H5
Allandale Cl SELS PO20 301 L5
Allandale Rd RTWE/PEM TN2 38 C3
Allangate Dr ANG/EP BN16 148 C3
Allards RHAS TN35 285 M9
Allbrook Ct HAV PO9 288 E11
Allcard Cl HORS RH12 56 C4
Allcot Cl CRAWW RH11 42 D6
Allee Dr LIPH GU30 179 Q12
Allendale SWTR RH13 201 Q10
Allendale Av EMRTH PO10 103 M2
SALV BN13 116 F4
Allen Rd HWH RH16 73 K4
Allen's Cl EGRIN RH19 48 C3
Allen Wy BEX TN40 97 L7
Alley Groves SWTR RH13 235 K3
Alleyne Wy MSEA/BNM PO22 146 A8
The Alley ARUN BN18 296 E2
MIDH GU29 226 D8
Allfrey Rd LW/ROSE BN22 164 C7
Allfreys La CROW TN6 210 E3
Allfreys Whf PUL/STOR RH20 265 J3
Allington Crs RING/NEW BN8 240 B6
Allington La LEWES BN7 273 M10
Allington Rd RING/NEW BN8 240 B7
SALV BN13 117 K6
All Saints Crs RHAS TN35 13 M5
All Saints Gdns HTHF TN21 244 C6
All Saints La BEXW TN39 97 G6
All Saints Ri SBGH/RUST TN4 * 37 M3
All Saints Rd SBGH/RUST TN4 37 M3
All Saints' St HAS TN34 13 L6
Allwood Crs RHWH RH17 238 F9
Allyington Wy CRAWE RH10 44 C4
Alma Ct SLVH TN37 * 12 A1
Alma Rd BOR GU35 178 H6
BOR GU35 179 R4
HWH RH16 73 L1
Alma St LAN/SOMP BN15 152 D1
Alma Ter SLVH TN37 12 A1
Alma Vls SLVH TN37 12 A1
Almodington La SELS PO20 168 C6
Almond Av SHOR BN43 119 H5
Almond Cl CRAWW RH11 42 F4
HAV PO9 102 A5
HORN PO8 288 D5
Almonry Flds BAT TN33 * 282 C5
Alpha Cottages
PUL/STOR RH20 * 265 L3
Alpha Rd CRAWW RH11 8 C4
Alpine Rd BOR GU35 178 G8
HAS TN34 13 K5
HOVE BN3 121 L5
Alresford Rd HAV PO9 102 F1
Alverstone Cl LGNY BN23 164 A1
Alverstone Rd WTHG BN11 21 L3
Amanda Cl BEX TN40 97 L6
Amber Cl BOR GU35 178 H7
Amber Gld SWTR RH13 201 Q12
Amberleaze Dr RTWE/PEM TN2 39 J3
Amberley Cl BURH RH15 74 F5
CRAWE RH10 44 B3
HORS RH12 56 F3
HWH RH16 73 G5
LHPTN BN17 147 K3
PUL/STOR RH20 265 R12
SHOR BN43 119 L4
Amberley Ct CRAWW RH11 * 27 J6
Amberley Dr BOGR PO21 171 L1
FERR BN12 150 A4
HOVE BN3 121 K2
Amberley Ga PUL/STOR RH20 265 Q12
Amberley Rd ANG/EP BN16 148 B5
HORN PO8 256 E8
HORS RH12 56 F3

LW/ROSE BN22 ......163 H4
PUL/STOR RH20 ......297 P1
Ambersham Crs ANG/EP BN16 ..148 E2
Amberstone HAIL BN27 ......92 D2
Amberstone Cl HAS TN34 ......99 M1
Amberstone Vw HAIL BN27 ......92 B3
Ambleside Cl CRAWW RH11 ......156 F6
MSEA/BNM PO22 * 145 G7
Ambleside Rd
LAN/SOMP BN15 ......118 D3
Ambrose Pl WTHG BN11 ......21 G5
Amelia Rd WTHG BN11 ......20 F5
America La HWH RH16 ......73 K4
Amesbury Crs HOVE BN3 ......121 K6
Amethyst Gv WVILLE PO7 ......288 C9
Amherst Cl HAS TN34 ......12 C3
Amherst Crs HOVE BN3 ......121 L5
Amherst Gdns HAS TN34 ......12 D4
Amherst Rd BEX TN40 ......137 H1
BOR GU35 ......178 D3
HAS TN34 ......12 B4
SBGH/RUST TN4 ......37 M4
Amhurst Rd PEAHV BN10 ......156 E6
Ampfield Pl HAV PO9 ......102 C1
Amport Ct HAV PO9 ......288 E11
Amundsen Rd HORS RH12 ......56 C3
Anchorage Wy LGNY BN23 ......165 C3
Anchor Cl SHOR BN43 ......119 M7
Anchor Ct FERR BN12 * 150 D4
HORS RH12 * 14 D7
RCCH PO18 ......105 G6
Anchor Fld RING/NEW BN8 ......275 J12
Anchor La RING/NEW BN8 ......274 F3
Anchor Springs LHPTN BN17 ......147 J4
Ancren Cl FERR BN12 ......149 L1
Ancton Cl MSEA/BNM PO22 ......145 L8
Ancton Dr MSEA/BNM PO22 ......145 M7
Ancton La MSEA/BNM PO22 ......145 L7
Ancton Lodge La
MSEA/BNM PO22 ......145 M8
Ancton Wy MSEA/BNM PO22 ......146 A8
Anderida Cl BEXW TN39 * 136 E3
Anderida Rd LW/ROSE BN22 ......163 G2
Anderson Cl HAV PO9 ......103 H2
NEWHV BN9 ......18 C3
Andlers Ash Rd LISS GU33 ......192 B11
Andrew Av MSEA/BNM PO22 ......145 H8
Andrew Cl ANG/EP BN16 ......148 A3
STEY/UB BN44 ......78 C1
Andrew Rd SBGH/RUST TN4 ......38 B1
Andrews La MIDH GU29 ......226 B10
SWTR RH13 ......201 L12
Andrews Rd SWTR RH13 ......233 Q2
Andromeda Cl CRAWW RH11 ......42 E6
Angela Cl BEX TN40 ......97 L6
Angell Est CCH PO19 * 7 L7
Angelo Cl WVILLE PO7 ......288 B9
Angel St PETW GU28 ......229 L9
Anglesea Ter STLEO TN38 ......12 A6
Anglesea Av HAIL BN27 ......91 M3
Anglesey Cl CRAWW RH11 ......43 H6
Angley Ct STPH/PW TN12 ......189 M4
Angmering La ANG/EP BN16 ......148 D5
Angmering Wy ANG/EP BN16 ......148 C5
Angola Rd SALV BN13 ......21 L1
Angus Cl EDN/EASTW BN20 ......163 G4
HORS RH12 ......14 E2
Angus Rd FERR BN12 ......102 E1
Annandale Av BOGR PO21 ......2 B3
Ann Cl HPPT/KEY BN6 ......271 P4
Anne Howard Gdns
ARUN BN18 ......112 F2
Annington Gdns SHOR BN43 ......119 L4
Annington Rd LW/ROSE BN22 ......11 H2
STEY/UB BN44 ......78 C1
STEY/UB BN44 ......78 F7
Ann St BRI BN1 ......4 E3
HAS TN34 ......13 M1
WTHG BN11 ......21 H6
Annweir Av LAN/SOMP BN15 ......118 D7
Anscombe Cl WTHG BN11 ......150 M4
Anscombe Rd WTHG BN11 ......150 M4
Ansisters Rd FERR BN12 ......149 K4
Anson Cl LGNY BN23 ......164 D6
Anson Ct FERR BN12 * 150 E1
Anson Rd BOGR PO21 ......171 G5
FERR BN12 ......150 B1
Anstead MFD/CHID GU8 * 182 H6
Ansty Cl BRIE/ROTT BN2 ......123 K8
Anthony Pl CSHT GU26 * 181 J8
Antioch St LEWES BN7 * 16 E7
Antlands La HORL RH6 ......28 C4
Antlands La East HORL RH6 ......28 D4
Antlands La West HORL RH6 ......28 D3
Antony Cl SEAF BN25 ......159 G7
Antrona Cl STLEO TN39 ......136 D2
Anvil Cl BIL RH14 ......231 R1
PTSD BN41 ......121 G3
SWTR RH13 ......201 Q12
UCK TN22 ......76 D6
WVILLE PO7 ......288 D8
Anvil Ct SLVH TN37 ......283 R12
Anzac Cl PEAHV BN10 ......157 H4
Apex Pk HAIL BN27 * 91 M6
Apollo Dr BOGR PO21 ......178 C4
WVILLE PO7 ......102 A2
Appledene Cnr
RING/NEW BN8 ......273 P7
Appledore Cl LGNY BN23 ......164 C3
Appledore Ct HWH RH16 ......73 K5
Appledore Gdns HWH RH16 ......73 K5
Appledore Rd BRIE/ROTT BN2 ......123 L1
TENT TN30 ......221 M3
Appledram La (North)
CCH PO19 ......107 H7
Appledram La (South)
SELS PO20 ......141 G2
Applefield CRAWE RH10 ......9 G2
Applegate Pl HORN PO8 * 288 D4
Apple Gv BOGR PO21 ......171 G4
EMRTH PO10 ......104 C4
Applesham Av HOVE BN3 ......121 K3
Applesham Wy PTSD BN41 ......120 D1
Appleshaw Gn HAV PO9 ......102 D1
Appletree Dr MSEA/BNM PO22 ......111 G7
Apple Tree La RTWE/PEM TN2 ......38 D7
Appletrees ANG/EP BN16 ......148 C4
Apple Tree Wk LHPTN BN17 ......146 C4
Applewalk BURH RH15 * 74 F6
Applewood Cl SLVH TN37 ......99 Q7
Applewood Rd HAV PO9 ......102 D2

The Approach BRI BN1 ......122 D2
EGRIN RH19 ......31 M3
April Cl FERR BN12 ......149 K5
HORS RH12 ......14 D1
April Pl BEX TN40 * 137 H1
Apsley St SBGH/RUST TN4 ......37 J5
Apsley Wy SALV BN13 ......115 M8
Aquarius Cl PEAHV BN10 ......157 H7
Aquila Pk SEAF BN25 ......175 G2
Arbourvale STLEO TN38 ......98 F4
Arcade Buildings WTHG BN11 * ..21 H7
Arcade Rd LHPTN BN17 ......147 J4
The Arcade BOGR PO21 ......2 B8
LISS GU33 ......192 B8
Archery Rd STLEO TN38 ......99 G8
Archery Wk HAIL BN27 ......92 B7
Archibald Rd WTHG BN11 ......151 M2
Archie Ct STLEO TN38 * 99 G7
Arcturus Rd CRAWW RH11 ......42 D5
Ardale Rd WTHG BN11 ......150 E3
Arden Rd CRAWE RH10 ......43 K7
Ardingly Cl CRAWW RH11 ......43 H1
Ardingly Ct BRIE/ROTT BN2 * 5 G7
Ardingly Dr FERR BN12 ......150 A2
Ardingly Rd BRIE/ROTT BN2 ......156 C5
HWH RH16 ......206 A12
RHWH RH17 ......72 C2
Ardingly St BRIE/ROTT BN2 ......5 G7
Ardings Cl RHWH RH17 ......206 A12
Ardsheal Cl SALV BN13 ......117 H8
Ardsheal Rd SALV BN13 ......117 H7
Arford Common BOR GU35 ......179 N3
Arford Rd BOR GU35 ......179 N5
Argent Cl SEAF BN25 ......159 M8
Argos Hill Rd MAYF TN20 ......212 A5
Argus Wk CRAWW RH11 ......42 F6
Argyle Circ BOGR PO21 * 2 D7
Argyle Cl BOR GU35 ......178 C2
Argyle Rd BOGR PO21 ......2 C8
BRI BN1 ......4 D2
Arle Cl HORN PO8 ......256 D9
Arlington Av FERR BN12 ......150 A5
Arlington Cl FERR BN12 ......150 A4
Arlington Crs ANG/EP BN16 ......148 A4
BRI BN1 ......83 K8
Arlington Eagles Rbt
HAIL BN27 ......91 L8
Arlington Gdns
BRIE/ROTT BN2 ......156 C3
Arlington Rd EAST BN21 ......10 C6
Arlington Rd East HAIL BN27 ......91 M7
Arlington Rd West HAIL BN27 ......91 L7
Armadale Rd CCH PO19 ......7 H3
Armada Wy LHPTN BN17 ......147 M3
Armstrong Cl CRAWW RH11 ......42 E6
Arnbury Ms STLEO TN38 ......98 F4
Arndale Rd LHPTN BN17 ......147 G3
Arne Cl CRAWW RH11 ......42 E6
Arne Gv HORL RH6 ......22 D4
Arnell Av SELS PO20 ......301 L7
Arnfield Cl CRAWW RH11 ......42 D4
Arnhem Rd BOGR PO21 ......2 A2
Arnold Cl BRIE/ROTT BN2 ......5 K3
Arnold Wy RCCH PO18 ......106 B6
Arnside Cl LAN/SOMP BN15 ......118 D8
Arnside Rd STLEO TN38 ......98 D2
Aron Cl EPSF GU31 ......223 M7
Arragon Ct WVILLE PO7 ......288 D8
Arran Cl CRAWE RH10 ......8 B9
HAIL BN27 ......91 M1
Arrivals Rd HORL RH6 ......27 L1
Artel Cft CRAWE RH10 ......9 L3
Artex Av ANG/EP BN16 ......148 B2
Arthur Rd BEXW TN39 ......137 G1
CRAWW RH11 ......42 D3
SWTR RH13 ......14 F7
Arthur St BRI BN1 ......4 F3
HOVE BN3 ......121 M5
Artisans Dwellings EAST BN21 * ..10 D7
Arun Cl ANG/EP BN16 ......148 B3
ARUN BN18 ......296 F2
EPSF GU31 ......223 M7
LAN/SOMP BN15 ......116 C6
SALV BN13 ......116 C6
Arun Ct ANG/EP BN16 * 148 F4
PUL/STOR RH20 ......265 K3
Arun Crs SALV BN13 ......116 B6
Arundel By-Pass ARUN BN18 ......112 F2
Arundel Cl BOGR PO21 ......171 M1
CRAWE RH10 ......44 B3
HAIL BN27 ......92 B3
LIPH GU30 ......179 L4
PEV BN24 ......134 E7
SHOR BN43 ......120 B5
SWTR RH13 ......201 R12
Arundel Dr ANG/EP BN16 ......113 H8
Arundel Dr East
BRIE/ROTT BN2 ......156 B4
Arundel Dr West
BRIE/ROTT BN2 ......156 B4
Arundel Gn LEWES BN7 ......16 D3
Arundel Ms BRIE/ROTT BN2 * 154 D1
Arundel Pl BRIE/ROTT BN2 ......154 D1
Arundel Rd ANG/EP BN16 ......114 D5
ARUN BN18 ......110 D3
BRIE/ROTT BN2 ......154 D2
EAST BN21 ......147 J4
LHPTN BN17 ......147 J4
NEWHV BN9 ......158 C4
PEAHV BN10 ......157 H6
RCCH PO18 ......108 F3
RTW TN1 ......38 A7
SALV BN13 ......115 H6
SEAF BN25 ......175 G2
SELS PO20 ......109 H5
Arundel Rd Central
PEAHV BN10 ......157 G6
Arundel Rd West BRIE/ROTT BN10..156 F5
Arundel St BRIE/ROTT BN2 ......154 D2
Arundel Ter BRIE/ROTT BN2 ......154 D2
Arundel Wy MSEA/BNM PO22 ......146 A8
Arun Ford Cl ARUN BN18 ......146 D2
Arun Pde LHPTN BN17 ......147 J6
Arun Prospect
PUL/STOR RH20 * 264 D1
Arun Rd BIL RH14 ......199 R12
BOGR PO21 ......171 M1
Arunside HORS RH12 ......201 R4
Arun St ARUN BN18 ......113 G3
Arun Ter ARUN BN18 ......112 F3
Arun V PUL/STOR RH20 ......264 D8
Arun Wy BOGR PO21 ......171 G5
PEV BN24 ......132 F4
SWTR RH13 ......15 G9
Ascham Pl EDN/EASTW BN20 ......176 A3
Ascot Cl EDN/EASTW BN20 ......176 F5

SELS PO20 ......167 L5
Ascot Ms STLEO TN38 ......98 F5
Ascot Wy ANG/EP BN16 ......148 D3
Ashacre La SALV BN13 ......116 E6
Ashacre Ms SALV BN13 ......116 E6
Ashacre Wy SALV BN13 ......116 E6
Ashampstead Pl EAST BN21 * 10 C5
Ashbrook Rd SLVH TN37 ......99 G1
CCH PO19 ......107 A8
SALV BN13 ......298 H11
Ashburnham Cl BRI BN1 ......83 K8
CCH PO19 ......107 A8
SALV BN13 ......298 H11
Ashburnham Dr BRI BN1 ......83 J7
Ashburnham Gdns EAST BN21 ......10 A2
Ashburnham Pl HAIL BN27 ......91 M8
Ashburnham Rd CRAWE RH10 ......10 B3
EAST BN21 ......10 A2
RHAS TN35 ......100 B4
Ashbury Rd BOR GU35 ......178 D2
Ashby Cl BEXW TN39 ......96 F6
Ash Cl CRAWE RH10 ......30 B6
HOVE BN3 ......123 A2
LW/ROSE BN22 ......163 K2
RTWE/PEM TN2 ......54 C1
SALV BN13 ......298 H11
Ash Combe MFD/CHID GU8 ......182 F5
Ashcombe Dr BEXW TN39 ......136 C2
Ashcombe Hollow LEWES BN7 ......85 J6
Ashcombe La LEWES BN7 ......85 A4
Ash Copse HORN PO8 ......91 M6
Ash Ct HAIL BN27 ......91 M6
Ashcroft Cl RING/NEW BN8 ......275 J12
SHOR BN43 ......120 C6
Ashcroft La HORN PO8 ......289 L7
Ashcroft Wy BOGR PO21 ......170 F6
Ashdene Gdns
PUL/STOR RH20 ......267 K9
Ashdown Ar CROW TN6 * 67 L6
Ashdown Av BRIE/ROTT BN2 ......156 A4
Ashdown Cha UCK TN22 ......208 H4
Ashdown Cl ANG/EP BN16 ......148 L1
FROW RH18 ......48 F7
HWH RH16 ......73 L5
SBGH/RUST TN4 ......37 M4
STLEO TN38 ......98 D3
Ashdown Cottages
CROW TN6 * 67 L6
Ashdown Ct CRAWE RH10 * 43 L6
Ashdown Dr CRAWE RH10 * 43 K7
Ashdown Pl HTHF TN21 ......244 E7
Ashdown Rd BEX TN40 ......137 K1
BRIE/ROTT BN2 ......123 G5
FROW RH18 ......48 F7
WTHG BN11 ......21 H3
Ashdown Vw EGRIN RH19 ......47 K2
Ash Dr SEAF BN25 ......175 J2
Ashenden Av RYE TN31 ......252 F1
Ashenden Wk RTWE/PEM TN2 ......38 D1
Ashenground Cl HWH RH16 ......73 H6
Ashenground Rd HWH RH16 ......73 G6
Ashfield BIL RH14 ......197 R3
Ashfield Cl MIDH GU29 ......226 H9
Ashfield Rd MIDH GU29 ......226 H10
Ashfold Av SALV BN13 ......116 F4
Ashford Cl HAIL BN27 ......92 B6
Ashford Rd BRI BN1 ......122 F3
EAST BN21 ......10 D6
HAS TN34 ......12 E2
Ashford Sq EAST BN21 ......10 F5
Ashford Wy HAS TN34 ......12 E1
Ashgate Rd LGNY BN23 ......164 D3
Ash Gv HASM GU27 ......195 K8
HWH RH16 ......73 G1
LIPH GU30 ......194 A2
MSEA/BNM PO22 ......144 A4
PEV BN24 ......133 J7
WTHG BN11 ......21 J5
Ashington Cl HORN PO8 ......288 B6
Ashington Gdns PEAHV BN10 ......157 H4
Ashington Rd LW/ROSE BN22 ......163 H4
Ash Keys CRAWE RH10 ......9 L8
Ash La ANG/EP BN16 ......148 B4
Ashleigh Cl ANG/EP BN16 ......114 E7
HORL RH6 ......22 E6
Ashleigh Gdns CROW TN6 ......67 K5
Ashleigh Rd HORS RH12 ......56 B6
Ashley Cl BRI BN1 ......82 D6
HAV PO9 ......102 E1
HORN PO8 ......288 A4
Ashley Gdns HAIL BN27 ......92 B2
MAYF TN20 ......212 D4
SBGH/RUST TN4 ......37 H4
Ashley Park Cl SBGH/RUST TN4 ......37 H4
Ashley Rd CROW TN6 ......69 J8
Ashlings Wy HOVE BN3 ......121 K3
SHOR BN43 ......120 A4
Ashmead BOR GU35 ......178 C6
Ashmead Wy ANG/EP BN16 ......148 G6
Ashmere Gdns
MSEA/BNM PO22 ......145 J8
Ashmere La
MSEA/BNM PO22 ......145 J8
Ashmore Av ANG/EP BN16 ......148 F1
Ashmore Cl HWH RH16 ......157 J3
Ashmore Cl HORS RH12 ......41 H3
Ash Rd CRAWE RH10 ......9 L1
SWTR RH13 ......201 P12
Ashton Gdns ANG/EP BN16 ......148 B5
Ashton Ri BRIE/ROTT BN2 ......5 G5
Ashtonville Cl RING/NEW BN8 ......275 K12
Ash Tree Cl HASM GU27 ......181 Q8
HTHF TN21 ......244 D5
Ashurst Av BRIE/ROTT BN2 ......156 D5
Ashurst Cl BOGR PO21 ......143 M7
FERR BN12 ......150 A4
HORS RH12 ......56 F2
Ashurst Dr CRAWE RH10 ......44 C3
EAST BN21 ......150 A4
Ashurst Rd BRIE/ROTT BN2 ......83 L8
RRTW TN3 ......36 A7
SEAF BN25 ......174 F3
Ashurst Wy ANG/EP BN16 ......148 F2
EAST BN21 ......
Ash V MFD/CHID GU8 ......182 F4
Ash Wk MSEA/BNM PO22 ......18 G3
Ashway BURH RH15 ......74 F3
Ashwood Cl HAV PO9 ......102 C2
WTHG BN11 ......21 M2
Ashwood Dr ANG/EP BN16 ......148 A4
Aspen Cl BOR GU35 ......178 G8
EBR RH19 ......73 H5
Aspen Ct LAN/SOMP BN15 * 152 B1
Aspen Rd LW/ROSE BN22 ......163 K3
Aspen Wk HTHF TN21 ......244 D5
Aspen Wy BEXW TN39 ......136 G4

HORN PO8 ......288 B4
HORS RH12 ......15 H1
MSEA/BNM PO22 ......145 K7
Astaire Av LW/ROSE BN22 ......11 J1
Asten Cl STLEO TN38 ......98 D6
Asten Flds BAT TN33 ......282 C5
Aston Ri PUL/STOR RH20 ......265 K2
Astra Cl RCCH PO18 ......106 B3
Athelstan Cl CRAWE RH10 ......44 D3
LGNY BN23 ......164 E5
Athelstan Rd RHAS TN35 ......100 C3
SALV BN13 ......21 L1
Athelstan Wy SWTR RH13 ......15 C9
Athena Av WVILLE PO7 ......102 A2
Atholl Rd BOR GU35 ......178 C8
Atkinson Cl HORL RH6 * 23 C7
Atkinson Rd CRAWE RH10 ......44 B5
Atlantic Dr LGNY BN23 ......164 F6
Atlantis Av WVILLE PO7 ......102 A3
Atlingworth St BRIE/ROTT BN2 ......5 J8
Attree Dr BRIE/ROTT BN2 ......5 J5
Auchinleck Cl CRAWE RH10 * 46 A2
Auckland Cl CRAWW RH11 ......27 J8
Auckland Dr BRIE/ROTT BN2 ......123 L4
Auckland Quay LGNY BN23 ......164 F4
Auckland Rd RTW TN1 ......38 B3
Audrey Cl BRI BN1 ......82 D8
SEAF BN25 ......159 J8
Augusta Pl WTHG BN11 ......21 G7
Augustines Wy HWH RH16 ......73 G5
Augustus Wy SLVH TN37 ......283 N11
Auriol Dr HAV PO9 ......102 E1
Aurum Cl HORL RH6 ......23 C7
Austen Cl EGRIN RH19 ......31 G8
Austen Wy RHAS TN35 ......284 C12
Avalon Dr SALV BN13 ......116 C3
Avard Crs BRIE/ROTT BN20 ......163 G3
Avards Cl HAWK TN18 ......216 F1
Avebury Cl HORS RH12 ......56 F2
SELS PO20 ......168 B8
Aveling Cl HORL RH6 ......44 B5
The Avenals ANG/EP BN16 ......114 D5
Avenue Ap CCH PO19 * 6 D2
Avenue De Chartres CCH PO19 ......6 B6
Avenue Gdns HORL RH6 * 23 H7
Avenue La EAST BN21 ......10 D5
Avenue Ms EAST BN21 * 10 D5
Avenue Pl EAST BN21 * 10 D5
Avenue Rd CSHT GU26 ......180 G6
The Avenue BOGR PO21 ......2 D5
BRIE/ROTT BN2 ......123 J3
CCH PO19 ......107 J3
EAST BN21 ......10 D5
EGRIN RH19 ......31 M3
EGRIN RH19 ......32 A3
EPSF GU31 ......223 N6
FERR BN12 ......150 B1
GSHT GU26 ......180 G6
HAIL BN27 ......92 A7
HASM GU27 ......181 J10
HORL RH6 ......22 A7
HTHF TN21 ......244 E7
HTHF TN21 ......278 C1
LEWES BN7 ......16 D5
LEWES BN7 ......85 J8
LIPH GU30 ......193 P1
MAYF TN20 ......212 A4
RCCH PO18 ......105 J4
RCCH PO18 ......290 F10
RHAS TN35 ......101 L1
SHOR BN43 ......119 K4
WSEA TN36 ......201 N7
Avery Cl PTSD BN41 ......120 E1
Avian Gdns BOGR PO21 ......171 G3
Aviary Cl RCCH PO18 ......105 J3
Aviary Wy CRAWE RH10 ......30 B8
Aviemore Rd CROW TN6 ......67 J7
Avis Cl NEWHV BN9 ......158 D4
Avisford Park Rd ARUN BN18 ......111 K5
Avisford Ter BOGR PO21 * 171 J2
Avis Rd NEWHV BN9 ......158 C4
Avis Wy NEWHV BN9 ......19 J1
Avocet Quay EMRTH PO10 ......104 B6
Avocet Wy HORN PO8 ......288 D2
Avon Cl EPSF GU31 ......223 M7
LAN/SOMP BN15 ......118 A7
MSEA/BNM PO22 ......145 H8
Avondale Cl FERR BN12 ......150 C2
HORL RH6 ......22 E4
Avondale Rd HOVE BN3 ......4 A4
LW/ROSE BN22 ......11 H3
SEAF BN25 ......174 F2
STLEO TN38 ......98 F3
WVILLE PO7 ......288 A9
Avonhurst BURH RH15 ......75 G4
Avon Rd LHPTN BN17 ......147 J4
Avon St RTW TN1 ......38 B3
Avon Wk CRAWW RH11 ......42 E4
Awbridge Rd HAV PO9 ......102 D1
Aylesbury Av LGNY BN23 ......164 D5
Aylwin Pl SELS PO20 ......142 B4
Aymer Rd HOVE BN3 ......121 M7
Ayshe Court Dr SWTR RH13 ......15 G9
Azalea Av BOR GU35 ......179 K4
Azalea Cl HAV PO9 ......103 K1
Azalea Dr HASM GU27 ......181 J9

B

Babsham La BOGR PO21 ......143 L5
Babylon Wy EDN/EASTW BN20 ......163 G5
Back La BIL RH14 ......197 R3
CRAWE RH10 ......45 J8
CRBK TN17 ......189 R9
HTHF TN21 ......243 R6
HTHF TN21 ......279 N1
POLE BN26 ......161 H1
STPH/PW TN12 ......189 M3
UCK TN22 ......209 N7
WSEA TN36 ......286 D2
Back Rd HAWK TN18 ......217 Q4
Backwoods Cl HWH RH16 ......73 H5
Backwoods La HWH RH16 ......73 H5
Baden Dr HORL RH6 ......22 A5
Baden Powell Pl LISS GU33 ......192 B11
Baden Rd BRIE/ROTT BN2 ......123 J5
Badens Cl RING/NEW BN8 ......240 B7
Badger Brow WVILLE PO7 ......288 B11
Badger Cl PTSD BN41 ......121 G2
Badger Dr HWH RH16 ......72 F4

Badgers Brow
EDN/EASTW BN20 ......163 G5
Badgers Cl CROW TN6 ......67 K6
HORS RH12 ......56 E3
NEWHV BN9 ......18 F6
Badgers Copse SEAF BN25 ......175 J2
Badgers Dene LEWES BN7 ......126 C5
Badgers Fld PEAHV BN10 ......157 H4
Badgers Holt PUL/STOR RH20 ......266 E12
RTWE/PEM TN2 ......38 D4
Badgers Mt BEXW TN39 ......96 D8
Badgers Wk BURH RH15 ......75 J7
HAIL BN27 ......90 B2
Badgers Wy BIL RH14 ......198 H1
EGRIN RH19 ......31 K6
SLVH TN37 ......284 A12
Badgers Wd PUL/STOR RH20 ......266 A7
Badger Wk CCH PO19 ......108 A5
Badger Wy BRI BN1 ......83 K7
Badlesmere Rd
LW/ROSE BN22 ......163 M7
Baffin's La CCH PO19 ......6 F5
Bagham La HAIL BN27 ......279 Q11
Bahram Rd POLE BN26 ......131 K7
Bailey Cl HORS RH12 ......56 E2
LHPTN BN17 ......147 M2
Bailing Hl HORS RH12 ......187 P11
Baillie Av LW/ROSE BN22 ......11 J1
Bainbridge Cl SEAF BN25 ......174 F3
Bainden Cl CROW TN6 ......69 J8
Baird Cl CRAWE RH10 ......27 M8
Baird Dr HAS TN34 ......99 K2
Bakehouse Barn Cl
HORS RH12 ......56 D2
Bakehouse Rd HORL RH6 ......22 E4
Baker Cl CRAWE RH10 ......8 F8
Bakers Arms Hl ARUN BN18 ......113 G2
Bakers Farm Pk HAIL BN27 ......91 M2
Bakers Farm Pk Homes HAIL
BN27 ......91 M2
Bakers Fld LISS GU33 ......192 C3
Baker's La SWTR RH13 ......233 L5
Baker's Rd EAST BN21 ......176 D2
Baker St BRI BN1 ......4 F3
NEWHV BN9 ......76 F6
Bakers Wy RDKG RH5 ......204 B4
Bakery La BOGR PO21 ......2 C8
Bakery Ms BRIE/ROTT BN2 ......123 H4
Bakewell Rd EAST BN21 ......176 D1
Bala Crs MSEA/BNM PO22 ......145 G7
Balchins Cl BIL RH14 ......231 J1
Balcombe Av SALV BN13 ......117 H8
Balcombe Gdns HORL RH6 ......23 H7
Balcombe La EGRIN RH19 ......63 K7
RHWH RH17 ......206 C13
Balcombe Rd CRAWE RH10 ......44 C2
CRAWE RH10 ......23 G5
HORL RH6 ......23 G5
HWH RH16 ......73 J5
PEAHV BN10 ......157 H5
Balcombes HI CRBK TN17 ......189 R9
Baldock Rd WADH TN5 ......71 L3
Baldslow Down SLVH TN37 ......283 R8
Baldslow Rd HAS TN34 ......13 G2
Baldwin Av EAST BN21 ......163 H7
Baldwin Cl CRAWE RH10 * 44 B6
MSEA/BNM PO22 ......145 J2
Baldwins Fld EGRIN RH19 ......31 H5
Bale Cl BEXW TN39 ......96 D8
Bal Edmund SLVH TN37 ......99 G3
Balfour Dr LISS GU33 ......192 B9
Balfour Gdns FROW RH18 ......64 D1
Balfour Rd BRI BN1 ......122 E3
Ballard Dr RING/NEW BN8 ......275 J12
Ballards HI BAT TN33 ......282 C4
Balliol Cl BOGR PO21 ......171 K1
CRAWE RH10 ......8 B9
Ballsdown MFD/CHID GU8 ......182 F5
Ballsocks La HTHF TN21 ......278 F1
Balmoral Cl ANG/EP BN16 ......148 A2
BOGR PO21 ......171 K3
CCH PO19 ......7 K5
SEAF BN25 ......159 M7
Balmoral Wy PSF GU32 ......223 N5
Balsdean Rd BRIE/ROTT BN2 ......124 A4
Bamborough Cl SWTR RH13 ......201 R12
Bamford Cl BRIE/ROTT BN2 ......123 M3
Bampfield St PTSD BN41 ......121 G5
Bancroft Rd BEXW TN39 ......97 G8
CRAWE RH10 ......44 C4
Banjo Rd LHPTN BN17 ......147 K6
Bank Buildings HAS TN34 * 13 G4
Bankfield Wy CRBK TN17 ......189 Q10
Bank La CRAWE RH10 ......8 F7
Bank Pas STEY/UB BN44 ......78 C2
Bank Prec CRAWE RH10 * 27 M8
Bank Rd BEXW TN39 ......97 G8
Banks Cft PUL/STOR RH20 ......266 B11
Bankside BRI BN1 ......82 B6
HPPT/KEY BN6 ......271 N4
WADH TN5 ......71 K4
Bankside Ct BRI BN1 * 82 B6
Banks Rd CRAWE RH10 ......44 B4
RING/NEW BN8 ......239 P4
Bank Ter CRAWE RH10 * 45 M5
The Bank CRAWE RH10 * 45 M5
Bankview Ct MSEA/BNM PO22 * ..2 E4
Banner Farm Rd
RTWE/PEM TN2 ......38 A7
Bannerman Rd PSF GU32 ......223 N5
Bannings V BRIE/ROTT BN2 ......156 C5
Bannister Gdns
PUL/STOR RH20 ......266 B10
Bannisters Fld RING/NEW BN8 ......240 B7
Bannister Wy HWH RH16 ......73 G3
Banstead Cl FERR BN12 ......150 B4
Baranscraig Av BRI BN1 ......82 F6
Barbary La FERR BN12 ......149 L4
Barber Cl CRAWE RH10 ......44 B7
Barbuda Quay LGNY BN23 ......164 F6
Barcombe Av SEAF BN25 ......175 J3
Barcombe Cl
EDN/EASTW BN20 ......176 B2
SEAF BN25 ......175 J3
Barcombe Mills Rd
RING/NEW BN8 ......274 D5
Barcombe Rd BRI BN1 ......83 J8
Bardown Rd WADH TN5 ......71 J4
Barfield Pk LAN/SOMP BN15 ......118 C4
Barford Rd CCH PO19 ......6 F6
Bargate Cl BEXW TN39 ......97 G8
Barham Cl HAS TN34 ......99 K1

Barham Rd PSF GU32 223 N6
Barkdale BURH RH15 75 J4
Barker Cl RCCH PO18 106 F6
Barkworth Wy
PUL/STOR RH20 265 R6
Bar La SWTR RH13 202 A12
Barlavington Wy MIDH GU29 226 H12
Barley Av RHAS TN35 100 B4
Barley Cl BOGR PO21 170 E3
CRAWE RH10 8 F6
PEAHV BN10 157 G3
Barleycroft SWTR RH13 235 K4
Barley Dr BURH RH15 74 B5
Barley La RHAS TN35 100 B4
Barley Mow Hl BOR GU35 179 N3
Barley Mow La HTHF TN21 245 L8
Barlow Rd CCH PO19 6 A2
CRAWW RH11 42 D6
Barming Cl LGNY BN23 164 C3
Barnard Ga HWH RH16 73 H2
Barn Cl CRAWW RH11 59 G2
EMRTH PO10 103 L5
HAIL BN27 92 B4
HPPT/KEY BN6 270 D3
LEWES BN7 85 K8
LHPTN BN17 147 K1
PEV BN24 132 F7
SALV BN13 116 E6
SEAF BN25 159 M8
SLVH TN37 283 R12
Barn Cottage La HWH RH16 73 K4
Barn Ct CRAWE RH10 29 K7
Barncroft Cl SELS PO20 109 H4
Barncroft Wy HAV PO9 102 E2
Barn End HFD BN5 269 L4
Barnes Cl SELS PO20 301 L8
Barnes Rd PTSD BN41 120 F5
Barnes Wy HAV PO9 102 D2
Barnett Cl SELS PO20 110 D5
Barnett Rd BRI BN1 123 G3
Barnett's Fld SELS PO20 110 C6
Barnett Wy UCK TN22 76 F5
Barnet Wy HOVE BN3 121 K2
Barn Feld MSEA/BNM PO22 3 K5
Barnfield CROW TN6 67 M7
LEWES BN7 272 H4
RTWE/PEM TN2 53 L2
Barnfield Cl EMRTH PO10 104 F3
HAS TN34 12 D4
Barnfield Dr CCH PO19 108 B5
Barn Field Gdns BRIE/ROTT BN2 5 K5
Barnfield Gdns HPPT/KEY BN6 272 B6
Barnfield Rd CRAWE RH10 8 F1
CRAWE RH10 9 G1
EPSF GU31 223 R6
Barn Fold WVILLE PO7 * 288 C8
Barnham La ARUN BN18 111 H6
Barnham Rd SELS PO20 110 E6
The Barnhams BEXW TN39 136 D2
Barn Hatch Cl LEWES BN7 16 A8
Barnhorn Cl BEXW TN39 136 B1
Barnhorn Rd BEXW TN39 135 J1
Barnhouse Cl PUL/STOR RH20 265 K3
Barn House La
PUL/STOR RH20 265 K3
Barn La MSEA/BNM PO22 144 C4
UCK TN22 77 M4
Barnmead HWH RH16 73 G2
Barn Meadow RHWH RH17 60 F8
Barn Ri BRI BN1 82 C8
MSEA/BNM PO22 111 H7
SEAF BN25 159 M8
Barn Rd LEWES BN7 17 J2
SELS PO20 167 L6
Barns Farm La
PUL/STOR RH20 298 E2
Barnsfold La HORS RH12 185 M11
Barnside RCCH PO18 106 C6
Barnside Av BURH RH15 75 H8
Barnside Wy LISS GU33 192 C10
Barnsite Gdns ANG/EP BN16 148 A3
Barnsnap Cl HORS RH12 56 C3
Barn Wk SELS PO20 167 L7
Barnwood Cl CRAWE RH10 44 B2
Baron Cl SELS PO20 110 C6
Barons Cl SEAF BN25 159 H8
Barons Ct BURH RH15 75 G7
Barons Down Rd LEWES BN7 16 B8
Barons Md BOGR PO21 170 F5
Barons Wk LEWES BN7 16 B7
Barons Wy POLE BN26 131 L8
Barque Cl LHPTN BN17 147 M3
Barrackfield Wk HORS RH12 14 B8
Barrack La BOGR PO21 171 J4
Barrack Rd BEX TN40 97 H8
Barrack Rw ARUN BN18 * 111 J4
Barrack Sq WSEA TN36 286 E2
Barrhill Av BRI BN1 82 E6
Barrie Cl LGNY BN23 164 D3
Barrier Reef Wy LGNY BN23 164 F3
Barrington Cl FERR BN12 150 B3
HWH RH16 73 K1
Barrington Rd CRAWE RH10 8 E8
FERR BN12 150 C3
SWTR RH13 15 G5
Barrington Wd HWH RH16 73 J1
Barrow Cl BIL RH14 231 R2
BRI BN1 123 H3
Barrowfield RHWH RH17 72 C2
Barrowfield Cl HOVE BN3 122 B2
Barrowfield Dr HOVE BN3 122 C3
Barrow Hl BRI BN1 123 H3
HFD BN5 269 L5
Barrow La RRTW TN3 36 E8
Barrow Ri SLVH TN37 283 R12
Barry Cl CRAWE RH10 43 K6
Barry Wk BRIE/ROTT BN2 5 K5
Bartholomew Cl HASM GU27 181 M9
Bartholomews BRI BN1 4 E7
Bartholomew Sq BRI BN1 * 4 D7
Bartholomew Wy HORS RH12 56 F3
Bartley Mill Cl PEV BN24 133 G8
Bartley Mill Rd RRTW TN3 55 K5
Barton Cl BOGR PO21 170 F4
SALV BN13 116 F8
Barton Crs EGRIN RH19 47 M1
Barton Cross HORN PO8 288 C2
Barton La PETW GU28 229 L9
Barton Rd CCH PO19 6 A1
MSEA/BNM PO22 143 M6
Bartons Rd HAV PO9 103 K1
Barton Wk CRAWE RH10 44 A5
Barton Wy SELS PO20 168 A7
Barttelot Rd HORS RH12 14 D7
Barwell Gv EMRTH PO10 103 M2
Barwick Cl ANG/EP BN16 148 A2
Bashfords La SALV BN13 21 H2
Bashford Wy CRAWE RH10 44 C1
Bashurst Copse SWTR RH13 201 J5
Bashurst Hl SWTR RH13 200 G10
Basildon Wy CRAWW RH11 42 D6
Basing Hl PUL/STOR RH20 267 M6
Basing Rd HAV PO9 288 F12
Basin Rd CCH PO19 6 E6
Basin Rd North PTSD BN41 121 G7
Basin Rd South PTSD BN41 120 E7
Baslow Rd EDN/EASTW BN20 176 D6
Bassels La SWTR RH13 233 R11
Bassenthwaite Gdns
BOR GU35 178 G4
Bassett Rd BOGR PO21 2 C8
CRAWE RH10 44 C6
Bassetts La CROW TN6 70 D6
EDEN TN8 35 H2
MAYF TN20 212 D3
Batchelors RTWE/PEM TN2 39 K1
Batchelor Wy UCK TN22 76 C5
Batchmere Rd SELS PO20 168 E3
Bateman Ct CRAWE RH10 * 9 M9
Batemans Cl SALV BN13 116 A8
Batemans Ct CRAWE RH10 9 M9
Bateman's La BUR/ETCH TN19 246 F1
Batemans Rd BRIE/ROTT BN2 124 D6
Bates Rd BRI BN1 122 E3
Bathford Cl LGNY BN23 164 C3
Bath Pl WTHG BN11 21 H7
Bath Rd EAST BN21 10 D7
EMRTH PO10 104 A5
WTHG BN11 20 C8
Bath St BRI BN1 4 C3
Battenhurst Rd WADH TN5 214 G4
Battens Wy HAV PO9 103 G1
Battery Hl RHAS TN35 101 G1
Battle Cl SEAF BN25 160 B8
Battle Crs HAIL BN27 92 B5
SLVH TN37 99 G1
Battle Gates BAT TN33 282 C5
Battle Hl BAT TN33 282 F6
Battle Rd HAIL BN27 92 B4
SLVH TN37 283 N9
Batts Bridge Rd UCK TN22 241 M1
Batts Dr HFD BN5 269 J5
Batts La PUL/STOR RH20 265 N4
Bavant Rd BRI BN1 122 D3
Baxter Cl CRAWE RH10 44 A5
Baxter Rd LEWES BN7 16 D3
Baxters La RHWH RH17 208 B3
Baxter St BRIE/ROTT BN2 5 K3
Bay Av PEV BN24 134 D8
Bay Br SWTR RH13 233 R11
Baybridge Rd HAV PO9 289 J12
Bay Cl HORL RH6 22 D3
Baycombe La ARUN BN18 295 J11
Bayencourt North BEXW TN39 97 G8
Bayfield Rd HORL RH6 22 D5
Bayford Rd LHPTN BN17 147 J5
Bayhall Rd RTWE/PEM TN2 38 C6
Bayham Rd HAIL BN27 92 C6
LW/ROSE BN22 11 J5
RRTW TN3 55 G5
RTWE/PEM TN2 53 M1
Bayhams Fld EGRIN RH19 62 E3
Bayhorne La HORL RH6 23 H8
Bayley Rd SELS PO20 109 H4
Bayley's La POLE BN26 130 F2
Baylis Crs BURH RH15 74 C5
Baylis Cresent BURH RH15 74 C5
Baylis Wk CRAWW RH11 * 43 G8
Baynards Rd HORS RH12 185 P7
Bay Pond Rd EAST BN21 * 176 D1
Bay Rd PEV BN24 165 J1
Baythorn La HORL RH6 23 H8
Baytree Cl CCH PO19 107 L3
Bay Tree Cl HTHF TN21 244 F7
SHOR BN43 120 B4
Bay Tree Gdn ANG/EP BN16 * 148 E4
Bay Tree La POLE BN26 131 L5
Bayview Rd PEAHV BN10 157 K8
Bay Vue Rd NEWHV BN9 19 G4
Bay Wk BOGR PO21 171 H5
Baywood Gdns
BRIE/ROTT BN2 124 B4
Bazehill Rd BRIE/ROTT BN2 155 M2
Beach Cl BOGR PO21 171 H4
SEAF BN25 174 D2
Beach Crs LHPTN BN17 147 K6
Beachcroft Pl
LAN/SOMP BN15 152 D1
The Beaches LHPTN BN17 * 146 C4
Beach Gdns SELS PO20 301 K8
Beach Gn SHOR BN43 119 J7
The Beachings PEV BN24 165 H1
Beach Ms LW/ROSE BN22 * 11 K2
Beach Pde WTHG BN11 21 K6
Beach Rd BOGR PO21 170 F6
EMRTH PO10 103 M5
LHPTN BN17 147 K5
LW/ROSE BN22 11 K2
NEWHV BN9 19 J6
SELS PO20 301 M5
SHOR BN43 119 K8
Beachside Cl FERR BN12 150 D4
Beachy Head Rd
EDN/EASTW BN20 176 D5
Beachy Head Vw STLEO TN38 283 M10
Beachy Rd CRAWW RH11 42 F8
Beacon Cl BRI BN1 122 F3
CROW TN6 67 K7
SEAF BN25 159 J8
Beacon Ct SWTR RH13 * 15 M2
Beacon Dr SEAF BN25 159 J8
SELS PO20 301 L7
Beacon Gdns CROW TN6 67 K6
Beacon Hl BEXW TN39 96 E5
BRIE/ROTT BN2 155 K2
LING RH7 32 A1
PUL/STOR RH20 264 B9
Beacon Hill Ct GSHT GU26 180 G3
Beacon Hill Pk GSHT GU26 * 180 E4
Beacon Hill Rd GSHT GU26 180 F3
Beacon Hurst HPPT/KEY BN6 271 Q6
Beacon La RBTBR TN32 249 M5
Beacon Rd CROW TN6 67 K8
HPPT/KEY BN6 272 A8
RHAS TN35 100 D1
SEAF BN25 174 D1
Beacon Rd West CROW TN6 67 J7
Beaconsfield Cl
MSEA/BNM PO22 * 145 K8
Beaconsfield Pde BRI BN1 * 122 F5
Beaconsfield Rd BEX TN40 97 H7
BRI BN1 * 4 E2
HAS TN34 13 H2
LHPTN BN17 147 J2
PTSD BN41 121 G5
RHWH RH17 64 B8
Beaconsfield Vls BRI BN1 122 E4
Beacon Sq EMRTH PO10 103 M6
The Beacon EGRIN RH19 62 D2
Beacon Wy LHPTN BN17 147 M3
Beagle Dr ARUN BN18 146 A3
Beagles Wood Rd
RTWE/PEM TN2 39 K2
Beal Crs BRI BN1 123 G3
Beales La RYE TN31 218 E11
Beale St BURH RH15 74 D8
Beamsley Rd LW/ROSE BN22 11 J3
Beaney's La HAS TN34 284 B11
Bear Rd BRIE/ROTT BN2 123 H5
Bearsden Wy HORS RH12 201 N2
Bear Yd LEWES BN7 17 H6
Beatrice La EAST BN21 10 C5
Beatrice Wk BEXW TN39 96 F7
Beatty Av BRI BN1 83 J7
Beatty Rd BOGR PO21 2 D5
LGNY BN23 164 D7
Beauchamp Rd STLEO TN38 98 F2
Beaufield Cl SELS PO20 301 K8
Beauford Rd HTHF TN21 278 C2
Beaufort Ct SLVH TN37 12 A2
Beaufort Crs SLVH TN37 12 A2
Beaufort Rd BOR GU35 178 G4
HAV PO9 102 E3
SLVH TN37 12 A2
Beaufort Ter BRIE/ROTT BN2 5 J4
Beauharrow Rd SLVH TN37 283 P11
Beaulieu Av HAV PO9 288 E11
Beaulieu Dr PEV BN24 132 F8
Beaulieu Gdns SLVH TN37 283 R11
Beaulieu Rd BEXW TN39 136 B3
Beaumont Cl CRAWW RH11 42 D4
Beaumont Pk LHPTN BN17 147 M5
Beaumont Rd SALV BN13 117 J8
Beauport Gdns SLVH TN37 283 P10
Beauport Home Farm Cl
SLVH TN37 283 P11
Beaver Cl CCH PO19 107 G7
CROW TN6 67 M8
HORS RH12 56 D3
Beavers Ms BOR GU35 178 H5
Beccles Rd WTHG BN11 20 D5
Beckenham Cl HAIL BN27 92 A2
Becket Cl HAS TN34 13 J4
Becket Rd SALV BN13 20 B3
Beckets Wy UCK TN22 77 K7
Beckett La CRAWW RH11 27 J8
Beckett Wy EGRIN RH19 47 L1
LEWES BN7 16 F2
Beckford Wy CRAWE RH10 44 A8
Beckham La PSF GU32 223 L5
Beckley Cl BRIE/ROTT BN2 123 K8
STLEO TN38 98 C3
Beckworth Cl HWH RH16 73 K3
SALV BN13 116 A8
Beckworth La HWH RH16 73 K3
Bedale Cl CRAWW RH11 8 C8
Bedales Hl HWH RH16 206 G12
Bedelands Cl BURH RH15 75 G4
Bedenscroft BOGR PO21 171 M2
Bedford Av BEX TN40 137 J1
BOGR PO21 143 M7
Bedford Cl BOR GU35 178 G8
HAV PO9 103 J5
Bedford Ct UCK TN22 76 E4
Bedford Gv EAST BN21 10 D4
Bedford Pl BRI BN1 4 A6
Bedford Rd PSF GU32 223 L6
RHAS TN35 100 B3
SWTR RH13 14 F7
Bedford Rw WTHG BN11 21 J6
Bedford Sq BRI BN1 4 A7
Bedford St BOGR PO21 2 D7
BRIE/ROTT BN2 5 J8
Bedford Ter RTW TN1 37 M7
Bedfordwell Rd EAST BN21 10 E3
Bedgebury Cl STLEO TN38 98 D3
Bedgebury Cross CRBK TN17 191 P3
Bedgebury Rd CRBK TN17 191 Q2
Bedham La PUL/STOR RH20 230 C11
Bedhampton Hl HAV PO9 102 B4
Bedhampton Hill Rd HAV PO9 102 C4
Bedhampton Rd HAV PO9 102 D3
Bedhampton Wy HAV PO9 103 G1
Bedlam Gn HAIL BN27 * 279 P11
Beecham Pl STLEO TN38 98 E1
Beech Av CCH PO19 6 A4
HAIL BN27 * 90 A2
SELS PO20 168 A7
Beech Cl BAT TN33 282 C2
BEXW TN39 96 B7
BOGR PO21 170 E3
EGRIN RH19 * 31 J7
HORN PO8 * 288 A7
MFD/CHID GU8 182 F5
PTSD BN41 120 E2
SALV BN13 * 298 H10
SELS PO20 110 C6
Beechcroft Cl LIPH GU30 193 L2
Beechers Rd PTSD BN41 120 E2
Beeches Av SALV BN13 117 J6
Beeches Cl HTHF TN21 244 E5
UCK TN22 76 F4
Beeches Crs CRAWE RH10 9 G7
Beeches Farm Rd CROW TN6 67 M8
Beeches La EGRIN RH19 48 C3
Beeches Rd CROW TN6 68 A7
The Beeches BRI BN1 122 C2
CROW TN6 * 68 A8
RTWE/PEM TN2 38 C4
Beechey Cl CRAWE RH10 29 G6
Beechey Wy CRAWE RH10 29 G6
Beech Farm Rd BAT TN33 249 L9
Beechfield Cl PEV BN24 133 H8
Beechfield Pk SELS PO20 * 110 C8
Beech Flds EGRIN RH19 31 L6
Beech Gdns CRAWE RH10 45 M2
Beech Green La HRTF TN7 50 E1
Beech Gv BRIE/ROTT BN2 123 K2
LAN/SOMP BN15 * 118 E8
MIDH GU29 226 H11
PUL/STOR RH20 266 C10
Beech Hanger End GSHT GU26 180 E6
Beech Hl BOR GU35 179 Q5
HWH RH16 73 L6
Beech Hill Rd BOR GU35 179 N3
Beech Holme CRAWE RH10 45 M1
Beech House La
BUR/ETCH TN19 216 D10
Beech Hurst RTWE/PEM TN2 39 J2
Beech Hurst Cl HWH RH16 * 72 F5
Beeching Cl BEXW TN39 137 G1
Beeching Rd BEXW TN39 137 G1
Beechings HFD BN5 269 J4
Beeching Wy EGRIN RH19 31 J8
Beechlands Cl ANG/EP BN16 148 F4
Beech La GSHT GU26 180 E5
HAWK TN18 218 F6
STPH/PW TN12 188 B6
Beech Rd HASM GU27 181 N10
HORN PO8 256 E8
HORS RH12 57 G4
SALV BN13 298 H11
Beechside CRAWE RH10 9 G6
Beech St RTW TN1 38 A4
Beech Tree Cl CRAWE RH10 8 F1
Beech Vw ANG/EP BN16 114 F6
Beech Wy ANG/EP BN16 148 F1
HORN PO8 288 C4
Beech Wd HFD BN5 269 L10
Beechwood SWTR RH13 233 P1
Beechwood Av BRI BN1 122 E1
SALV BN13 116 E6
Beechwood Cl BRI BN1 122 E1
BUR/ETCH TN19 214 G10
HAIL BN27 92 A8
Beechwood Ct LISS GU33 192 D7
Beechwood Crs
EDN/EASTW BN20 176 D2
Beechwood Gdns SLVH TN37 284 A12
Beechwood La HTHF TN21 244 E8
LEWES BN7 273 P7
PETW GU28 262 G8
Beechwood Ms
RTWE/PEM TN2 38 D5
Beechwoods BURH RH15 74 F8
Beechwood Vls REDH RH1 22 F2
Beechworth Rd HAV PO9 103 H4
Beechy Av EDN/EASTW BN20 176 B1
Beechy Gdns
EDN/EASTW BN20 176 B1
Beechy Rd UCK TN22 242 G12
Beeding Av HOVE BN3 121 L2
Beeding Cl HORS RH12 56 F4
LAN/SOMP BN15 118 C5
MSEA/BNM PO22 144 D6
Beedingwood Dr HORS RH12 57 K3
Beehive Cl FERR BN12 149 L4
Beehive La FERR BN12 149 K4
Beehive Ring Rd HORL RH6 28 A5
Bee Rd PEAHV BN10 157 H5
Beggarshouse La HORL RH6 26 B1
Beggar's La POY/PYE BN45 270 E11
Beggar's Wood Rd
RING/NEW BN8 239 M7
Behenna Cl CRAWW RH11 42 D4
Belfast St HOVE BN3 122 A6
Belfield Rd RTWE/PEM TN2 39 J3
Belfry Orch UCK TN22 76 F7
The Belfry HAIL BN27 91 M6
Belgrave Ct BEX TN40 * 137 J2
Belgrave Crs CCH PO19 141 L2
SEAF BN25 159 L8
Belgrave Pl BRIE/ROTT BN2 5 L9
Belgrave Rd RTW TN1 38 A5
SEAF BN25 174 D1
Belgrave St BRIE/ROTT BN2 5 G4
Belgrove RTW TN1 37 M7
Belinus Dr BIL RH14 231 R1
Bellair Rd HAV PO9 103 H4
Bell Alley Rd BUR/ETCH TN19 214 G11
Bellamy Rd CRAWE RH10 44 B7
Bell Banks Rd HAIL BN27 92 B6
Bell Cl CCH PO19 6 C1
PUL/STOR RH20 265 J3
Bell Ct BOGR PO21 171 H3
RCCH PO18 * 105 G6
Bell Davies Rd LHPTN BN17 147 L3
Belle Hl BEX TN40 97 H8
Belle Meade Cl SELS PO20 110 C8
Belle Vue WTHG BN11 * 21 G5
Bellevue Gdns BRIE/ROTT BN2 5 L8
Bellevue La EMRTH PO10 104 A3
Belle Vue Rd LW/ROSE BN22 11 J1
Bell Hammer EGRIN RH19 47 K1
Bell Hl PSF GU32 223 M4
Bell Hill Rdg PSF GU32 223 M4
Bellhurst Rd RBTBR TN32 248 B1
Bellingham Cl SLVH TN37 99 G1
Bellingham Crs HOVE BN3 121 J5
Bell La LEWES BN7 16 C8
MIDH GU29 260 E5
SELS PO20 168 C3
UCK TN22 76 E6
UCK TN22 208 F5
Bell Md HOVE BN3 * 122 C6
Belloc Cl CRAWE RH10 44 A2
Belloc Ct SWTR RH13 * 15 M3
Belloc Rd LHPTN BN17 147 H2
Bell Rd HASM GU27 195 K2
HORS RH12 187 R9
Bellscroft Cl LHPTN BN17 147 L3
Bell Vale La HASM GU27 195 L1
Bellview Rd SALV BN13 116 F8
Belmont BRI BN1 4 B2
Belmont Cl HORN PO8 256 D11
HPPT/KEY BN6 271 M4
Belmont Ct BRI BN1 * 4 B2
Belmont Gv HAV PO9 102 D3
Belmont La HPPT/KEY BN6 271 K5
Belmont Rd RHAS TN35 13 M4
UCK TN22 76 E5
Belmont St BOGR PO21 2 E8
BRI BN1 4 F3
Belmont Ter ARUN BN18 145 M3
Belmore Rd LW/ROSE BN22 11 G4
Belsize Cl WTHG BN11 20 C4
Belsize Rd WTHG BN11 20 C4
Belton Rd BRIE/ROTT BN2 5 G1
Beltring Rd LW/ROSE BN22 11 H4
SBGH/RUST TN4 37 M3
Beltring Ter LW/ROSE BN22 11 H3
Belvedere Av LAN/SOMP BN15 118 C7
Belvedere Gdns CROW TN6 67 M8
SEAF BN25 159 M8
Belvedere Pk STLEO TN38 98 F5
Belvedere Ter HOVE BN3 4 A5
Belverdere Cl PSF GU32 223 N5
Belyngham Crs LHPTN BN17 147 J3
Bembridge Rd LGNY BN23 164 A2
Bembridge St BRIE/ROTT BN2 5 K1
Bembrook Rd HAS TN34 13 L4
Bemzells La HAIL BN27 279 N7
Benbow Av LGNY BN23 164 D7
Benbow Cl HORN PO8 288 D2
SHOR BN43 119 L7
Benbow La MFD/CHID GU8 184 D5
Benchfield Cl EGRIN RH19 48 A1
Benedict Cl WTHG BN11 152 A2
Benedict Dr WTHG BN11 151 M2
Benenden Cl SEAF BN25 175 G1
Benenden Ri HAS TN34 99 K2
Benett Av HOVE BN3 122 A3
Benett Dr HOVE BN3 122 A3
Benfield Cl PTSD BN41 121 H5
Benfield Crs PTSD BN41 121 H4
Benfield Wy PTSD BN41 121 H5
Bengairn Av BRI BN1 82 F6
Benhall Mill Rd RTWE/PEM TN2 54 B1
Benhams Dr HORL RH6 22 F4
Benhams La LISS GU33 192 C1
Benjamin Cl LW/ROSE BN22 163 L3
Benjamin Rd CRAWE RH10 44 C5
Bennett Cl CRAWE RH10 44 A7
Bennett Rd BRIE/ROTT BN2 154 D1
Bennetts RHWH RH17 236 D2
Bennetts Cl SELS PO20 167 L6
Bennetts Rd SWTR RH13 15 J8
Bennetts Ter MIDH GU29 * 226 H10
Bennetts Wd RDKG RH5 24 B4
Bens Acre SWTR RH13 15 M6
Benson Rd HFD BN5 269 L4
Benson's La HORS RH12 41 H8
Bentham Rd BRIE/ROTT BN2 5 J3
Bentley Cl HORN PO8 288 D1
Bentley Ct HAV PO9 289 J12
Bentons La SWTR RH13 267 N2
Bentswood Crs HWH RH16 73 K4
Bentswood Rd HWH RH16 73 J4
Bentworth Cl HAV PO9 102 E1
Bepton Cl MIDH GU29 226 G11
Bepton Down EPSF GU31 223 P6
Bepton Rd MIDH GU29 260 D4
Beresford Ct SHOR BN43 120 A4
Beresford Rd BRIE/ROTT BN2 5 M7
NEWHV BN9 158 D4
Bereweeke Rd MSEA/BNM PO22 3 L5
Bergamot Crs SHOR BN43 120 B4
Berghestede Rd
MSEA/BNM PO22 144 B7
Beristede Cl EDN/EASTW BN20 10 B9
Berkeley Cl CRAWW RH11 42 C7
RTWE/PEM TN2 39 K2
Berkeley Ms CCH PO19 7 G2
Berkeley Pl RTW TN1 * 37 M7
Berkeley Rd RTW TN1 37 M7
Berkeley Rw LEWES BN7 16 B7
Berkeley Sq HAV PO9 103 J4
WTHG BN11 20 B6
Berkley Rd MAYF TN20 212 C8
Berkshire Ct FERR BN12 * 150 A2
Berlin Rd RHAS TN35 100 B3
Bermuda Pl LGNY BN23 164 F6
Bernard La EAST BN21 10 C5
Bernard Pl BRIE/ROTT BN2 5 K2
Bernard Rd ARUN BN18 112 E3
BRIE/ROTT BN2 5 K2
WTHG BN11 150 E4
Bernhard Gdns POLE BN26 131 L8
Berrall Wy BIL RH14 231 R3
Berriedale Av HOVE BN3 121 K7
Berriedale Cl LAN/SOMP BN15 118 B6
Berriedale Dr LAN/SOMP BN15 118 B6
Berrybarn La SELS PO20 167 G5
Berry Cl BURH RH15 74 F4
PEAHV BN10 156 F4
Berry Ct CCH PO19 * 107 G5
Berrydown Rd HAV PO9 288 D10
Berrylands LISS GU33 192 D6
Berrylands Farm
HPPT/KEY BN6 236 E12
Berry La LHPTN BN17 147 L5
MSEA/BNM PO22 143 M6
RHWH RH17 206 F2
Berrymill Cl BOGR PO21 2 E4
Bersted Ms MSEA/BNM PO22 * 2 E2
Bersted St MSEA/BNM PO22 2 E3
Berwick Cl BEXW TN39 96 B7
LW/ROSE BN22 163 H2
SEAF BN25 174 D1
Berwick Rd BRIE/ROTT BN2 156 C2
Bessborough Ter
LAN/SOMP BN15 152 C1
Betchley Cl EGRIN RH19 31 K6
Bethune Cl CRAWE RH10 44 C4
Bethune Rd BEX TN40 137 K2
SWTR RH13 15 H7
Bethune Wy HAS TN34 13 H4
Bethwines Cl RCCH PO18 106 F6
Betts Wy CRAWE RH10 27 J7
Betula Cl WVILLE PO7 288 B11
Beulah Rd RTW TN1 38 B5
Beuzeville Av HAIL BN27 92 A5
Bevan Rd HORN PO8 288 A4
Bevendean Av
BRIE/ROTT BN2 156 C4
Bevendean Crs
BRIE/ROTT BN2 123 K3
Bevendean Rd
BRIE/ROTT BN2 123 J5
Beverington Cl EAST BN21 163 J7
Beverington Rd EAST BN21 163 J7
Beverley Cl SELS PO20 301 M6
Beverley Gdns ANG/EP BN16 148 A3
Beverley Ms CRAWE RH10 9 L5
Beverley Wk HAS TN34 13 H1
Bewbush Dr CRAWW RH11 42 E6
Bewick Gdns CCH PO19 7 H1
Bewl Bridge Cl WADH TN5 191 N10
Bewlbridge La RRTW TN3 190 H4
Bewley Rd ANG/EP BN16 114 E7
Bexhill Rd BAT TN33 96 A1
BRIE/ROTT BN2 124 C4
LW/ROSE BN22 11 K2
STLEO TN38 98 B8
Bex La MIDH GU29 260 H3
Bexleigh Av STLEO TN38 98 A8
Bexley Cl HAIL BN27 92 A3
The Bex BEX TN40 * 137 J2
Bicton Gdns BEXW TN39 136 D1
Bidbury La HAV PO9 102 D4
Biddenden Cl LGNY BN23 164 C3
Bidwell Av BEXW TN39 96 F7
Biggin Cl CRAWW RH11 8 C7
Bignor Cl ANG/EP BN16 148 C3
HORS RH12 56 F3
Bignor Park Rd
PUL/STOR RH20 263 R9
Bigwood Av HOVE BN3 122 C6
Bilberry Cl CRAWW RH11 43 G6
Bilbury Ms EAST BN21 * 10 D3

Billam Ter *BRIE/ROTT* BN2 * 5 G4
Billett Av *WVILLE* PO7 .... 288 A8
Billingham La *RYE* TN31 .... 251 M10
Billinghurst Rd
PUL/STOR RH20 .... 266 H5
Billingshurst Rd *BIL* RH14 .... K1
HORS RH12 .... 201 M2
Billinton Dr *CRAWE* RH10 .... 44 A3
Billy Lawn Av *HAV* PO9 .... 288 H10
Bilsham La *ARUN* BN18 .... 145 K4
Bilsham Rd *ARUN* BN18 .... 145 L4
Binderton La *RCCH* PO18 .... 292 A7
Binhams Lea *MFD/CHID* GU8.. 184 A4
Binhams Meadow
MFD/CHID GU8 .... 184 A4
Binney Ct *CRAWE* RH10 .... 28 D8
Binstead Cl *CRAWW* RH11 .... 43 G1
Binsted Av *MSEA/BNM* PO22 ...... 3 M1
Binsted Cl *ANG/EP* BN16.......... 148 A5
LW/ROSE BN22 .... 163 K3
Binsted La *ARUN* BN18 .... 111 M3
Birch Av *RHWH* RH17 .... 73 K6
Birch Cl *ANG/EP* BN16 .... 148 E1
ARUN BN18 .... 112 D4
BOGR PO21 .... 171 J2
BOR GU35 .... 178 H7
CRAWE RH10 .... 46 B1
LAN/SOMP BN15 .... 152 C1
LISS GU33 .... 192 D9
RHWH RH17 .... 73 L6
RTWE/PEM TN2 .... 38 C2
UCK TN22 .... 77 G4
Birch Dr *BIL* RH14 .... 232 A2
Birch End *PUL/STOR* RH20 ...... 266 A6
Birchen La *HWH* RH16 .... 73 H1
Birches Cl *CROW* TN6 .... 67 L5
SALV BN13 .... 116 B8
SELS PO20 .... 301 J6
Birches Rd *HORS* RH12 .... 57 G4
The Birches *CRAWE* RH10 .... 9 M1
SWTR RH13 .... 202 H2
Birchetts Av *RRTW* TN3 .... 36 D6
Birchetts Green La *WADH* TN5.. 190 D10
Birchfield Est *HORL* RH6 * 26 C5
Birch Gv *BOR* GU35 .... 178 G8
PUL/STOR RH20 .... 266 A8
Birch Grove Crs *BRI* BN1 .... 82 F8
Birchgrove La *RHWH* RH17 .... 63 M8
Birchgrove Rd *RHWH* RH17 ...... 207 N4
Birchington Cl *BEXW* BN39 ...... 136 C1
Birch Lea *CRAWE* RH10 .... 27 M8
Bircholt Rd *LIPH* GU30 .... 193 L1
Birch Rd *BOR* GU35 .... 179 J2
LGNY BN23 .... 164 B6
Birch Tree Cl *EMRTH* PO10 ...... 104 A1
Birch Tree Dr *EMRTH* PO10 ...... 104 A2
Birch Tree Gdns *EMRTH* PO10.. 31 G6
Birch Tree La *PUL/STOR* RH20.. 266 A7
Birchview *RHWH* BN39 .... 97 H7
Birch Wy *HAIL* BN27 .... 92 A1
HAS TN34 .... 99 K2
HTHF TN21 .... 244 D8
PUL/STOR RH20 .... 266 E11
RHWH RH17 .... 73 K7
RTWE/PEM TN2 .... 38 C2
Birchwood Cl *BIL* RH14 .... 198 C2
CRAWE RH10 .... 44 B6
HORL RH6 .... 23 G5
Birchwood Grove Rd
BURH RH15 .... 75 H8
Birdham Cl *BOGR* PO21 .... 143 L8
BRIE/ROTT BN2 * 123 K2
Birdham Pl *BRIE/ROTT* BN2 * .. 123 K2
Birdham Rd *BRIE/ROTT* BN2 ... 123 K2
SELS PO20 .... 141 G7
Bird in Eye HI *UCK* TN22 .... 77 G6
Bird in Hand St *RRTW* TN3 .... 52 A1
Bird La *WADH* TN5 .... 71 G5
Birdlip Cl *HORN* PO8 .... 288 B5
Birk Dl *BEXW* BN39 .... 136 C1
Birkdale Cl *SALV* BN13 .... 116 C7
Birkdale Dr *CRAWW* RH11 .... 42 C4
Birkdale Rd *SALV* BN13 .... 116 C7
Birkenholme Cl *BOR* GU35...... 179 R5
Birken Rd *RTWE/PEM* TN2 .... 38 C3
Birk Hall *BEX* TN40 .... 137 H2
Birling Cl *BRIE/ROTT* BN2 .... 123 J4
SEAF BN25 .... 174 D1
Birling Dr *RTWE/PEM* TN2 .... 53 M1
Birling Gap Rd
EDN/EASTW BN20 .... 302 G10
Birling Park Av *RTWE/PEM* TN2 . 54 A1
Birling Rd *RTWE/PEM* TN2 .... 53 M1
Birling St *EDN/EASTW* BN20 ... 176 C1
Biscay Cl *ANG/EP* BN16 .... 148 A3
Bisham Cl *CRAWE* RH10 .... 44 C5
Bishearne Gdns *LISS* GU33 ..... 192 D8
Bishop Luffa Cl *CCH* PO19 .... 107 J6
Bishopric *HORS* RH12 .... 14 A5
Bishopric Ct *HORS* RH12 .... 14 C4
Bishops Cl *BOGR* PO21 .... 170 F7
HASM GU27 .... 195 K7
HFD BN5 .... 269 K4
RING/NEW BN8 .... 275 K11
SALV BN13 .... 20 D7
SEAF BN25 .... 174 C1
Bishops Ctyd *CCH* PO19 * 7 F2
Bishop's Down *SBGH/RUST* TN4.. 37 K6
Bishop's Down Park Rd
SBGH/RUST TN4 .... 37 K5
Bishop's Down Rd
SBGH/RUST TN4 .... 37 G4
Bishops Dr *LEWES* BN7 .... 16 C7
Bishopsgate Wk *CCH* PO19 * 6 F2
Bishop's La *RBTBR* TN32 .... 248 B2
RING/NEW BN8 .... 275 J11
Bishops Rd *HOVE* BN3 .... 122 A4
SELS PO20 .... 109 J3
Bishopstoke Rd *HAV* PO9 .... 288 F12
Bishopstone Dr
BRIE/ROTT BN2 .... 156 A9
Bishopstone La *RHWH* RH17 .... 236 H3
Bishopstone Rd *SEAF* BN25 .... 159 H7
Bishop's Wk *BEX* TN40 .... 97 L7
Bisky Bar *RYE* TN31 * 252 A3
Bitmead Cl *CRAWW* RH11 * 42 D4
Bittern Cl *EMRTH* PO10 .... 288 G11
Bitterne Cl *HAV* PO9 .... 288 G11
Bixlea Pde *BEXW* BN39 * 136 C1
Bixley La *RYE* TN31 .... 251 K4
Black Berry Cl *HORN* PO8 .... 256 H9
Blackberry La *SELS* PO20 .... 301 J5
Blackberry Rd *EGRIN* RH19 .... 31 H1
Blackbird Cl *HORN* PO8 .... 288 A5
Blackbird HI *CRAWE* RH10 .... 46 B4
Black Boy Ct *RCCH* PO18 * 106 F7

Blackboy La *CCH* PO19 .... 7 J5
RCCH PO18 .... 106 F6
Blackbridge La *HORS* RH12 ...... 201 N4
Blackcap Cl *CRAWW* RH11 .... 8 C7
HAV PO9 .... 288 H8
Black Dog Wk *CRAWE* RH10 .... 43 K1
Blackdown Crs *HAV* PO9 .... 102 C1
Blackdown Rd *HTHF* TN21 .... 245 N7
SALV BN13 .... 116 C6
Blacketts Rd *CRAWE* RH10 .... 44 B4
Blackfields Crs *FROW* RH18 .... 48 C7
Blackfold Rd *CRAWE* RH10 .... 9 L5
Blackgate La *PUL/STOR* RH20.. 231 G8
Black Gate La *PUL/STOR* RH20.. 231 K8
Blackheath *CRAWE* RH10 .... 44 C1
Black HI *HWH* RH16 .... 73 K2
Black Horse La *HORS* RH12 .... 14 C6
Blackhouse La *BURH* RH15 .... 75 G5
PETW GU28 .... 229 Q3
Blackman Av *SWTR* RH13 .... 58 B3
Black Lion St *BRI* BN1 .... 4 E8
Blackman Av *STLEO* TN38 .... 98 F2
Blackman St *BRI* BN1 .... 4 E4
Blackman Wy *SELS* PO20 .... 142 A4
Blackmill Cl *BEXW* BN39 .... 96 F5
Blackmill La *RCCH* PO18 .... 110 B2
Blackmoor Rd *LISS* GU33 .... 178 D11
Blackness Rd *CROW* TN6 .... 210 H1
Blackness Vls *CROW* TN6 * 210 H1
Black Pth *POLE* BN26 .... 131 M7
Blacksmiths Cl
PUL/STOR RH20 * 267 K9
Blacksmiths Copse *HAIL* BN27.. 91 M7
Blacksmiths Cl
LAN/SOMP BN15 .... 118 A7
WADH TN5 .... 71 M1
Blackstone St *HFD* BN5 .... 269 N4
Blackstone Wy *BURH* RH15 .... 74 F4
Blackthorn Cl *BRI* BN1 .... 122 C2
CRAWW RH11 .... 43 H1
LW/ROSE BN22 .... 163 K3
PTSD BN41 .... 121 G3
SLVH TN37 .... 99 H1
SWTR RH13 .... 15 K5
Blackthorne Cl *BOR* GU35 .... 178 H6
Blackthorns *HPPT/KEY* BN6 ..... 270 F1
Blackthorns Cl *HWH* RH16 .... 73 K2
Blackthorn Wy *RHAS* TN35 .... 101 L1
Blackwater La *CRAWE* RH10 ...... 44 A1
Blackwater Rd
EDN/EASTW BN20 .... 10 C9
EDN/EASTW BN20 * 10 C9
Blackwell Farm Rd *EGRIN* RH19.. 31 L6
Blackwell Hollow *EGRIN* RH19.. 31 L7
Blackwell Rd *EGRIN* RH19 .... 31 L7
Bladon Cl *HAV* PO9 .... 103 K2
Blake Cl *CRAWE* RH10 .... 43 H1
Blakehurst La *ARUN* BN18 .... 114 A4
Blakehurst Wy *LHPTN* BN17 .... 147 J3
Blakemore Cl *BRI* BN1 .... 82 C7
Blakeney Av *NEWHV* BN9 .... 18 A5
Blaker St *BRIE/ROTT* BN2 * 5 G7
Blakes Farm Rd *SWTR* RH13 ... 201 Q10
Blakes Wy *LGNY* BN23 .... 164 E7
Blake Wy *RTWE/PEM* TN2 .... 38 C2
Blanches La *SWTR* RH13 .... 234 F10
Blanches Wk *SWTR* RH13 .... 234 F10
The Blatchen *LHPTN* BN17 ...... 147 L5
Blatchford Cl *SWTR* RH13 .... 15 J3
Blatchford Rd *SWTR* RH13 .... 15 J3
Blatchington Cl *SEAF* BN25 .... 174 F1
Blatchington HI *SEAF* BN25 .... 174 E1
Blatchington Mill Dr
PEV BN24 .... 133 H8
Blatchington Rd *HOVE* BN3 ..... 121 M6
RTWE/PEM TN2 .... 37 M8
SEAF BN25 .... 174 E2
Bleak Rd *LYDD* TN29 .... 255 R7
Blendworth Crs *HAV* PO9 .... 102 F2
Blendworth La *HORN* PO8 .... 288 F1
Blenheim Av *SALV* BN13 .... 116 D7
Blenheim Cl *ANG/EP* BN16 ...... 148 A5
CRAWE RH10 .... 28 C7
EGRIN RH19 .... 31 M6
Blenheim Ct *BOGR* PO21 .... 171 K1
Blenheim Dr *ANG/EP* BN16...... 148 A5
Blenheim Flds *FROW* RH18 .... 48 C6
Blenheim Gdns *CCH* PO19 .... 7 K5
HAV PO9 .... 103 J3
Blenheim Pl *BRI* BN1 .... 4 F5
Blenheim Rd *ARUN* BN18 .... 145 L3
HORN PO8 .... 288 B4
HORS RH12 .... 56 C4
LAN/SOMP BN15 .... 152 C1
Blenheim Wy *POLE* BN26 .... 132 C7
WADH TN5 .... 191 P10
Bletchinglye La *CROW* TN6 .... 69 K8
Bligh Cl *CRAWE* RH10 .... 9 L5
Blind La *CRBK* TN17 .... 189 R8
RING/NEW BN8 .... 240 D7
Blindley Rd *CRAWE* RH10 .... 28 C3
Blissford Cl *HAV* PO9 .... 289 J11
Blois Rd *LEWES* BN7 .... 16 D2
Blomfield Dr *CCH* PO19 .... 107 M4
Blomfield Rd *SLVH* TN37 .... 12 D1
Blondell Dr *BOGR* PO21 .... 171 J2
Bloomsbury Pl *BRIE/ROTT* BN2... 5 K9
Bloomsbury St *BRIE/ROTT* BN2.. 5 K8
Bloor Cl *HWH* RH16 .... 56 C2
Blount Av *EGRIN* RH19 .... 31 H8
Blowers HI *EDEN* TN8 .... 34 C1
Bluebell Cl *CRAWW* RH11 * 43 G6
EGRIN RH19 .... 31 G8
HORS RH12 .... 56 D4
HWH RH16 .... 73 K2
WVILLE PO7 .... 288 A11
Bluebell Gld *HAIL* BN27 * 90 A2
Bluebell Rd *BOR* GU35 .... 179 K4
Blueberry HI *PUL/STOR* RH20.. 266 E12
Blue Cedars Cl *ANG/EP* BN16.. 148 D3
Blue Coat La *CRBK* TN17 .... 189 P10
Blue Haze Av *SEAF* BN25 .... 175 H1
Bluemans La *BAT* TN33 .... 283 P6
Bluestone Cl *STLEO* TN38 .... 98 E3

Blundell Av *HORL* RH6 .... 22 E6
Blunden Dr *RHWH* RH17 .... 72 C1
Blunts Wy *HORS* RH12 .... 14 C4
Blunts Wood Crs *HWH* RH16 ...... 72 E3
Blunts Wood Rd *HWH* RH16 .... 72 E3
The Blytons *EGRIN* RH19 .... 31 G8
Boarders La *WADH* TN5 .... 190 H10
Boardwalk *CCH* PO19 * 6 E3
Boast La *RING/NEW* BN8 .... 274 D4
Bob La *RHWH* RH17 .... 235 R7
Bocking Cl *WADH* TN5 .... 71 K5
Bocks HI *RBTBR* TN32 .... 216 F12
Boddingtons La
HPPT/KEY BN6 .... 271 R6
Boderton Ms *PETW* GU28 * 263 J5
Bodiam Av *BEX* TN40 .... 97 J7
BRIE/ROTT BN2 .... 124 A4
FERR BN12 .... 149 M3
Bodiam Br *RBTBR* TN32 .... 217 M10
Bodiam Crs *LW/ROSE* BN22 ..... 163 M3
Bodiam Dr *STLEO* TN38 .... 98 C3
Bodiam Rd *RBTBR* TN32 .... 217 N7
Bodle Crs *BEXW* BN39 .... 97 G6
Bodmin Cl *EDN/EASTW* BN20.. 176 B2
SALV BN13 .... 116 C5
Bodmin Rd *SALV* BN13 .... 116 C5
Bognor Rd *CCH* PO19 * 7 J5
HORS RH12 .... 187 K9
RDKG RH5 .... 187 M2
SELS PO20 .... 108 D8
Bohemia Rd *SLVH* TN37 .... 12 A4
STLEO TN38 .... 99 G4
Bolding Wy *HWH* RH16 .... 73 G7
Boldre Cl *HAV* PO9 .... 102 D1
Bolebrooke Rd *BEX* TN40 .... 137 J2
Boley Rd *HAIL* BN27 .... 92 B6
Bolney Av *PEAHV* BN10 .... 157 H7
Bolney Chapel Rd *RHWH* RH17.. 236 C5
Bolney Ct *CRAWW* RH11 .... 42 C6
Bolney Rd *BRIE/ROTT* BN2 .... 123 L1
RHWH RH17 .... 236 F4
Bolnore Rd *HWH* RH16 .... 72 F5
Bolsover Rd *EDN/EASTW* BN20.. 176 F1
HOVE BN3 .... 121 K6
SALV BN13 .... 150 D2
Bolters Rd *HORL* RH6 .... 22 F4
Bolters Rd South *HORL* RH6 ...... 22 F4
Bolton Cl *UCK* TN22 .... 76 C5
Bolton Rd *CRAWE* RH10 .... 44 A8
EAST BN21 .... 10 F7
Boltro Rd *HWH* RH16 .... 73 G4
Bonchurch Rd *BRIE/ROTT* BN2... 5 K1
Bondfields Crs *HAV* PO9 .... 288 G11
Bond St *ARUN* BN18 .... 112 F2
BRI BN1 .... 4 E6
Bonehurst Rd *HORL* RH6 .... 22 F2
Bones La *EPSF* GU31 .... 223 L12
Bonfire La *RHWH* RH17 .... 207 M5
Boniface Cl *PEV* BN24 .... 133 H7
Bonnar Cl *SELS* PO20 .... 301 J7
Bonnar Rd *SELS* PO20 .... 301 K7
Bonnetts La *CRAWW* RH11 .... 26 C3
Bonny Wood Rd
HPPT/KEY BN6 .... 271 M6
Booker Cl *CROW* TN6 .... 67 M8
Bookers La *SELS* PO20 .... 168 B5
Bookers Yd *CRAWW* RH11 .... 42 D6
Booth Rd *CRAWW* RH11 .... 42 D6
Bopeep Bostal *POLE* BN26 ...... 129 H5
Bopeep La *POLE* BN26 .... 129 H5
Borage Cl *CRAWW* RH11 .... 42 D4
Bordean La *PSF* GU32 .... 222 D4
Bordehill La *HWH* RH16 .... 206 A5
Borden La *LIPH* GU30 .... 225 N5
Border Cha *CRAWE* RH10 .... 28 F7
Border Ct *EGRIN* RH19 .... 31 L5
Border End *HASM* GU27 .... 180 G11
Border La *HASM* GU27 .... 180 G11
Borders La *BUR/ETCH* TN19 .... 215 M9
Bordon Rd *HAV* PO9 .... 103 G1
The Boreen *BOR* GU35 .... 179 Q4
Boreham La *HAIL* BN27 .... 94 D1
Boreham La *HAIL* BN27 .... 94 C5
Borers Arms Rd *CRAWE* RH10.. 29 G5
Borers Cl *CRAWE* RH10 * 29 H6
The Borodales *BEXW* TN39 * 136 D1
Borough Gv *PSF* GU32 .... 223 M6
Borough HI *PSF* GU32 .... 223 M6
Borough La *EDN/EASTW* BN20.. 176 D2
Borough Rd *PSF* GU32 .... 223 L7
Borough St *BRI* BN1 .... 4 B8
Borrowdale Cl *CRAWW* RH11 ...... 8 B8
LGNY BN23 .... 164 A1
Borrow King Cl
BRIE/ROTT BN2 .... 123 J5
Boscawen Cl *LGNY* BN23 .... 164 A6
Boscobel Rd *STLEO* TN38 .... 98 F6
Boscobel Rd North
STLEO TN38 .... 98 F6
Bosham La *RCCH* PO18 .... 106 A8
Bosham Rd *CRAWE* RH10 .... 44 B6
Boship Cl *LGNY* BN23 .... 163 M4
Bosmere Gdns *EMRTH* PO10 ... 103 M4
Bostal Rd *RING/NEW* BN8 .... 128 A1
STEY/UB BN44 .... 78 E4
The Bostal *STEY/UB* BN44 .... 79 H4
Bost HI *SALV* BN13 .... 116 D3
Bostock Av *HORS* RH12 .... 15 M1
Boston Cl *LGNY* BN23 .... 164 B6
Boston Rd *HWH* RH16 .... 73 K4
Boswell Rd *CRAWE* RH10 .... 9 G5
CRAWE RH10 .... 43 K6
Botany Cl *ANG/EP* BN16 .... 288 E12
Botley Dr *HAV* PO9 .... 102 C1
Bottings HI *SWTR* RH13 * 233 R1
Bough Beeches *BURH* RH15 ...... 75 H8
Boughey Pl *LEWES* BN7 .... 16 F2
The Boulevard *CRAWE* RH10 ...... 8 C3
PEV BN24 .... 134 D7
SALV BN15 .... 150 D1
Boundary Cl *CRAWE* RH10 .... 9 H2
Boundary Rd *BRIE/ROTT* BN2 ... 154 D2
CRAWE RH10 .... 9 H2
CSHT GU26 .... 180 G6
LAN/SOMP BN15 .... 119 G8
RHWH RH17 .... 61 G5
RTWE/PEM TN2 .... 38 C2
WTHG BN11 .... 20 B7

Boundary & Station Roads
HOVE BN3 .... 121 H7
The Boundary *RRTW* TN3 .... 37 H1
SEAF BN25 .... 174 G3
Boundary Wy *ANG/EP* BN16 ..... 148 C3
HAV PO9 .... 102 F4
Boundless La *MFD/CHID* GU8.. 181 M2
Boundstone Cl
LAN/SOMP BN15 .... 118 C6
Boundstone La
LAN/SOMP BN15 .... 118 B7
Bourg-de-peage Av
EGRIN RH19 .... 31 M8
Bourne Cl *CCH* PO19 .... 106 F7
HORN PO8 .... 288 C2
SALV BN13 .... 116 A7
Bourne La *EAST* BN21 .... 11 G5
RBTBR TN32 .... 216 C2
Bourne St *EAST* BN21 .... 11 G5
HPPT/KEY BN6 .... 271 N6
Bourne View Cl *EMRTH* PO10 .. 104 A1
Bourne Wy *MIDH* GU29 .... 226 H11
Bowater Rd *CRAWE* RH10 .... 44 B6
Bowcott HI *BOR* GU35 .... 179 N4
Bowden Ri *SEAF* BN25 .... 159 G4
Bowen Rd *SBGH/RUST* TN4 ...... 37 L5
Bower Cl *SLVH* TN37 .... 99 G1
Bower La *PUL/STOR* RH20 .... 266 A7
Bowers Cl *HORN* PO8 .... 288 B5
Bowers Cl *WTHG* BN11 .... 20 D7
Bowers Pl *CRAWE* RH10 .... 46 A1
The Bower *RHWH* RH16 * 75 G4
Bowes Cl *SWTR* RH13 .... 15 H3
Bowes HI *HAV* PO9 .... 289 G10
Bowes-Lyon Ct *HORN* PO8 ...... 288 C2
Bowhill La *RCCH* PO18 .... 291 L10
Bowley La *SELS* PO20 .... 142 D8
Bowley Rd *HAIL* BN27 .... 92 B6
Bowling Green La *HORS* RH12 .... 14 C4
Bowman Ct *CRAWE* RH10 * 8 F1
Bowmans St *STEY/UB* BN44 ...... 78 C1
Bowmans Dr *BAT* TN33 .... 282 D12
Bowness Av *LAN/SOMP* BN15... 118 D3
Bowood Av *LW/ROSE* BN22 ..... 164 A1
Bowrey Pl *BEX* TN40 .... 97 H3
Bowring Wy *BRIE/ROTT* BN2 * 5 M8
Bowsprit Ms *STLEO* TN58 .... 283 M10
Boxall Wk *SWTR* RH13 .... 14 E8
Boxes La *RHWH* RH17 .... 207 M5
Boxgate *CROW* TN6 .... 67 J5
Boxgrove Cl *BEX* TN40 .... 150 A1
Boxgrove Cl *BEX* TN40 .... 137 L1
Boxgrove Gdns *BOGR* PO21 .... 171 H3
Boxham La *SELS* PO20 .... 169 J2
Box La *EGRIN* RH19 .... 48 D3
Box's La *RHWH* RH17 .... 207 N8
Box Tree Av *ANG/EP* BN16 ...... 148 A4
Boyce's St *BRI* BN1 * 4 D7
Boyne Pk *SBGH/RUST* TN4 .... 37 L5
Boyne Rd *RHAS* TN35 .... 100 E3
Brackenbury Cl *PTSD* BN41 ..... 121 G3
Bracken Cl *EDN/EASTW* BN20.. 29 G7
CRAWE RH10 .... 43 K1
CROW TN6 .... 68 B8
PUL/STOR RH20 .... 266 E11
RTWE/PEM TN2 .... 38 C2
Brackendale *RHAS* TN35 .... 100 C3
Bracken Gv *HORS* RH12 .... 57 G4
Bracken Heath *WVILLE* PO7 .... 288 C8
Brackenhill *HRTF* TN7 .... 49 M8
Bracken La *BOR* GU35 .... 178 D9
PUL/STOR RH20 .... 266 D11
Bracken Rd *EDN/EASTW* BN20.. 162 F8
EPSF GU31 .... 223 R7
RTWE/PEM TN2 .... 38 C2
SEAF BN25 .... 175 J3
Brackenside *HORL* RH6 .... 23 G5
Bracken Wy *HTHF* TN21 .... 244 H3
Bracken Wy *BEXW* BN39 .... 136 B3
Bracklesham Cl *SELS* PO20 .... 168 A2
Bracklesham La *SELS* PO20 .... 168 A7
Bracklyn Av *RING/NEW* BN8 * 31 M3
Bradbury Rd *CRAWE* RH10 .... 44 B6
Bradford Rd *LEWES* BN7 .... 16 C6
Bradford St *EAST* BN21 .... 176 C2
Brading Cl *HAS* TN34 .... 12 F1
LGNY BN23 .... 164 C1
Brading Rd *BRIE/ROTT* BN2 * 5 K2
Bradley Ct *HAV* PO9 .... 289 J12
Bradley Rd *HAIL* BN27 .... 94 B4
RRTW TN3 .... 35 H3
Bradlord Cl *BOGR* PO21 .... 171 H3
Bradshaw Rd *CCH* PO19 .... 7 J5
Braemar Wy *BOGR* PO21 .... 143 L6
Braemore Rd *HOVE* BN3 .... 121 M4
Braeside Av *BRI* BN1 .... 82 E6
Braeside Cl *HASM* GU27 .... 181 G4
Brainsmead *RHWH* RH17 .... 72 C1
Brainsmead Cl *RHWH* RH17 * 72 C1
Braishfield Rd *HAV* PO9 .... 103 H1
Bramber Av *HOVE* BN3 .... 121 K6
PEAHV BN10 .... 157 H7
PUL/STOR RH20 .... 265 R11
Bramber Av North
PEAHV BN10 .... 157 H7
Bramber Cl *BOGR* PO21 .... 171 H3
CRAWE RH10 .... 29 G6
HAV PO9 .... 103 H2
LGNY BN23 .... 164 C2
SEAF BN25 .... 174 B1
Bramber Crs *SALV* BN13 .... 116 C5
Bramber Ct *CROW* TN6 * 67 M7
Brambledean Rd *PTSD* BN41 .. 121 J6
Bramble Dr *HAIL* BN27 .... 91 M6
Bramble Gdns *BURH* RH15 .... 74 D5
Bramble HI *HWH* RH16 .... 77 H6
Bramble La *HORN* PO8 .... 256 C5
PUL/STOR RH20 .... 266 C5
SALV BN13 .... 116 C5
Bramble Md *RHWH* RH17 .... 60 H3

Bramble Reed La
STPH/PW TN12 .... 188 B3
Bramble Ri *BRI* BN1 .... 82 B8
Bramble Rd *EPSF* GU31 .... 223 R6
Brambles *HPPT/KEY* BN6 .... 271 N4
Brambleside *SALV* BN13 .... 116 C5
The Brambles *RHWH* RH17 .... 72 D3
Brambletye La *FROW* RH18 .... 48 C6
Brambletye Rd *CRAWE* RH10 ...... 9 L5
Brambletyne Av
BRIE/ROTT BN2 .... 156 C4
Brambletyne Cl *ANG/EP* BN16.. 114 F7
Bramble Wk *RTWE/PEM* TN2 * ... 38 C2
Bramble Wy *BRI* BN1 .... 83 H7
RHAS TN35 .... 101 L1
Brambling Cl *SWTR* RH13 .... 15 L8
Brambling La *MIDH* GU29 .... 226 E6
Brambling Rd *HAV* PO9 .... 289 J8
SWTR RH13 .... 15 L8
The Bramblings *ANG/EP* BN16 . 148 C4
Bramdean Dr *HAV* PO9 .... 288 E12
Bramfield Rd
MSEA/BNM PO22 .... 173 H1
Bramlands La *HFD* BN5 .... 269 P9
Bramley Cl *CRAWE* RH10 .... 9 K3
SALV BN13 .... 117 J6
WVILLE PO7 .... 288 A9
Bramley Gdns *EMRTH* PO10 .... 104 C5
MSEA/BNM PO22 .... 144 A6
Bramley Rd *POLE* BN26 .... 132 B7
SALV BN13 .... 117 J7
Bramleys *LEWES* BN7 .... 85 K8
Bramley Wk *BOR* GU35 .... 178 E7
HAIL BN27 .... 280 A12
HORL RH6 .... 23 H6
Bramley Wy *ANG/EP* BN16 .... 148 C1
Brampton Av *BEXW* BN39 .... 136 E1
Brampton Cl *SELS* PO20 .... 301 K6
Brampton Rd *LW/ROSE* BN22 .. 163 L4
Brampton Vls *EAST* BN21 * 10 A4
Bramshaw Cl *HAV* PO9 .... 289 J12
Bramshott Ct *LIPH* GU30 * 179 P9
Brandon Cl *CRAWE* RH10 .... 44 C5
Brand Rd *LW/ROSE* BN22 .... 163 K4
Brandy Hole La *CCH* PO19 ...... 107 L3
Brangwyn Av *BRI* BN1 .... 82 D7
Brangwyn Crs *BRI* BN1 .... 82 C7
Brangwyn Dr *BRI* BN1 .... 82 C7
Brangwyn Wy *BRI* BN1 .... 82 D7
Branksome Rd *STLEO* TN38 ...... 98 F5
Bransgore Av *HAV* PO9 .... 102 D1
Branston Rd *LW/ROSE* BN22 ... 163 J4
Brantridge La *RHWH* RH17 .... 59 M7
Brassey Av *LW/ROSE* BN22 ..... 163 L4
Brassey Pde *LW/ROSE* BN22 *. 163 L4
Brassey Rd *BEX* TN40 .... 137 J2
Brasslands Dr *PTSD* BN41 .... 120 F4
Braybon Av *BRI* BN1 .... 122 E1
Braybrooke Cl *HAS* TN34 .... 12 F6
Braybrooke Rd *HAS* TN34 .... 13 G5
Braybrooke Ter *HAS* TN34 .... 12 E6
Bray Cl *CRAWE* RH10 .... 44 C5
Braypool La *BRI* BN1 .... 82 C5
Brazen Cl *NEWHV* BN9 .... 18 B4
Brazwick Av *BOGR* PO21 .... 143 L6
Breach Av *EMRTH* PO10 .... 104 C3
Breach Cl *STEY/UB* BN44 .... 78 C2
Bread La *LHPTN* BN17 .... 146 F2
Breadsell La *STLEO* TN38 .... 283 K12
Bread St *BRI* BN1 .... 4 E6
Bream Cl *SELS* PO20 .... 300 H5
Brecon Cl *SALV* BN13 .... 116 C6
Brede Cl *BRIE/ROTT* BN2 .... 123 K8
LW/ROSE BN22 .... 164 C2
SLVH TN37 .... 283 N10
Brede HI *RYE* TN31 .... 250 E11
Brede La *BAT* TN33 .... 249 N12
Brede Valley Vw *WSEA* TN36 ... 285 P14
Breezehurst Dr *CRAWW* RH11... 42 E6
Bremere La *SELS* PO20 .... 169 H3
Bremner Av *HORL* RH6 .... 22 E5
Brenchley Rd *STPH/PW* TN12 .. 189 L4
Brendon Cl *LGNY* BN23 .... 164 D1
RTWE/PEM TN2 .... 38 C4
Brendon Ri *HAS* TN34 .... 100 A2
Brendon Rd *SALV* BN13 .... 116 D5
Brendon Wy *ANG/EP* BN16 ..... 148 A3
Brent Ct *EMRTH* PO10 .... 103 M6
Brent Rd *BOGR* PO21 .... 171 H1
Brentwood Crs *BRI* BN1 .... 123 G2
Brentwood Rd *BRI* BN1 .... 123 G2
Bretland Rd *SBGH/RUST* TN4 ... 37 J5
Brett Dr *BEX* TN40 .... 97 L8
Brettingham Cl *CRAWW* RH11 *.. 42 D6
Bretton Burh* RH15 .... 74 D4
Bretts Fld *PEAHV* BN10 .... 157 H3
Bretts Orch *RHWH* RH17 .... 60 F8
Brewells La *LISS* GU33 .... 192 H5
Brewer Rd *CRAWE* RH10 .... 8 F7
Brewers Gv *MAYF* TN20 * 212 G1
Brewer St *BRIE/ROTT* BN2 * 5 M2
RRTW TN3 .... 188 F12
Brewery Yd *PUL/STOR* RH20 ... 266 A12
Brewery HI *ARUN* BN18 .... 113 G3
Brewhurst La *BIL* RH14 .... 198 H3
Brewster Ct *HORN* PO8 .... 288 B6
Breydon Wk *CRAWE* RH10 .... 44 A1
Brian Crs *SBGH/RUST* TN4 .... 38 A1
Brian Rd *SELS* PO20 .... 167 L4
Briar Av *SELS* PO20 .... 167 L4
Briar Cl *ANG/EP* BN16 .... 148 E1
ARUN BN18 .... 145 L2
BOGR PO21 .... 170 E2
BRIE/ROTT BN2 .... 124 C5
CRAWW RH11 .... 27 H8
HORN PO8 .... 288 C4
RHAS TN35 .... 285 R12
SELS PO20 .... 109 H7
Briarcroft Rd *BRIE/ROTT* BN2.. 124 C4
Briarfield Gdns *HORN* PO8 ..... 288 C3
Briar Pl *LGNY* BN23 .... 164 A2
Briars Wd *HORL* RH6 .... 23 H5
Briarswood Cl *CRAWE* RH10 ..... 44 C1
Briar Wd *LISS* GU33 .... 192 H6
The Briary *BEX* TN40 .... 97 J8
Brickfield Cl *BOGR* PO21 * 2 A3
Brickfield La *HORL* RH6 .... 22 C4
Brickfields *RTWE/PEM* TN2 .... 53 M8
Brickhurst La *RING/NEW* BN8 .. 276 D9
Brick Kiln La *STPH/PW* TN12 ... 189 M8
UCK TN22 .... 211 L11
Bricklands *CRAWE* RH10 .... 46 A4
Brickyard La *CRAWE* RH10 .... 46 A1

CROW TN6 ....69 L5
The Bricky PEAHV BN10 ....157 J5
Brideake Cl CRAWW RH11 .....42 F6
Brideoake Cl CCH PO19 ....107 K5
Bridge Cl BURH RH15 ....74 E5
  FERR BN12 ....150 D3
  HTHF TN21 ....278 D2
  LAN/SOMP BN15 ....118 D8
Bridge End PEV BN24 ....134 A7
Bridge Farm UCK TN22 ....76 B3
Bridgefield Cl MIDH GU29 .....226 H11
Bridgelands CRAWE RH10 ....28 C6
Bridgefoot Pth EMRTH PO10 .....104 A3
Bridgelands CRAWE RH10 ....28 C6
  RING/NEW BN8 ....274 C5
Bridge Mdw LISS GU33 ....192 C9
Bridgemere Rd
  LW/ROSE BN22 ....164 C3
Bridge Rd EMRTH PO10 ....104 A4
  HASM GU27 ....181 M10
  HORS RH12 ....186 A10
  HWH RH16 ....73 J2
  LHPTN BN17 ....147 J3
  SALV BN13 ....21 G3
Bridgersmill HWH RH16 ....73 G3
Bridger Wy CROW TN6 ....67 L8
Bridges Cl HORL RH6 ....23 J6
Bridge St NEWHV BN9 ....19 G3
Bridget Cl HORN PO8 ....288 C2
Bridge Wy STLEO TN38 ....98 B7
The Bridgeway SELS PO20 ....301 M7
Bridgewick Cl LEWES BN7 ....17 G2
Bridgnorth Cl SALV BN13 ....116 H8
Bridle Cl GSHT GU26 ....180 D6
Bridle Rd ARUN BN18 ....111 J1
Bridle Wy CRAWE RH10 ....44 C2
  PEAHV BN10 ....156 F4
The Bridle Wy SELS PO20 ....301 K6
Bridorley Cl BOGR PO21 ....171 J6
Brierley Gdns LAN/SOMP BN15 ..118 C4
Briers Av SLVH TN37 ....99 H3
Briers Gdns HAS TN34 ....99 H2
The Briers SLVH TN37 ....99 H1
Brigden St BRI BN1 ....4 C2
Brigham Pl MSEA/BNM PO22 .....173 J1
Brightland Rd
  EDN/EASTW BN20 ....176 D2
Brightling Av RHAS TN35 ......100 C1
Brightling Rd POLE BN26 ......131 M8
  RBTBR TN32 ....247 M5
Brighton Pl BRI BN1 ....4 E4
Brighton Rd CRAWE RH10 ....8 E2
  CRAWW RH11 ....59 J3
  HFD BN5 ....235 K12
  HFD BN5 ....269 U5
  HORL RH6 ....22 E6
  HPPT/KEY BN6 ....270 D1
  HPPT/KEY BN6 ....270 G6
  LAN/SOMP BN15 ....152 A1
  LEWES BN7 ....85 K6
  NEWHV BN9 ....18 C4
  RHWH RH17 ....59 H6
  SHOR BN43 ....119 J7
  SWTR RH13 ....15 C8
  SWTR RH13 ....202 H4
  SWTR RH13 ....235 J10
  WTHG BN11 ....21 L6
Brighton Rd (Hornbrook HI)
  SWTR RH13 ....202 E1
Brighton Sq BRI BN1 ....4 E2
Bright Rdg SBGH/RUST TN4 ......37 K1
Brills La BRI BN1 ....4 E4
Brimfast La SELS PO20 ....141 K8
Brincliffe CROW TN6 ....67 K6
Brisbane Cl CRAWW RH11 ....27 J3
  SALV BN13 ....116 A7
Bristol Av LAN/SOMP BN15 .....119 E8
Bristol Cl CRAWE RH10 ....28 C8
  CCH PO19 ....107 L3
Bristol Ga BRIE/ROTT BN2 ....5 M8
Bristol Ms BRIE/ROTT BN2 .....154 D1
Bristol Pl BRIE/ROTT BN2 ....5 J8
Bristol Rd BRIE/ROTT BN2 ....5 J8
  STLEO TN38 ....98 F2
Bristol St BRIE/ROTT BN2 .....154 D1
Britannia Cl BURH GU35 ....178 H6
Britannia St EPSF GU31 ....223 P4
Britland Est LW/ROSE BN22 * ..164 B7
Brittania Rd BRIE/ROTT BN2 ...154 C1
Brittany Ms STLEO TN38 ....99 G6
Brittany Rd HOVE BN3 ....121 J7
  SALV BN13 ....20 F1
  STLEO TN38 ....99 G6
Britten Cl CRAWW RH11 ....42 E6
  LGNY BN23 ....164 C2
Brittenden La HTHF TN21 ......243 M8
Britten's La ARUN BN18 ....110 D1
Britts Farm Rd UCK TN22 ....77 L1
Broadbridge Ct RCCH PO18 .....106 B6
Broadbridge Heath Rd
  HORS RH12 ....201 N1
Broadbridge MI RCCH PO18 * ...106 B6
Broad Cft HAV PO9 ....289 K7
Broadcroft RTWE/PEM TN2 ....53 L1
Broadfield EGRIN RH19 ....31 K2
Broadfield Dr CRAWW RH11 ....43 H7
Broadfield Pk CRAWW RH11 * 43 G7
Broadfield Pl CRAWW RH11 ......43 G7
Broadfields BRIE/ROTT BN2 ....154 D1
Broadfields Rd
  BRIE/ROTT BN2 ....123 K2
Broadford Bridge Rd
  PUL/STOR RH20 ....232 C11
Broad Gn BRIE/ROTT BN2 ....124 D7
Broad Green Av BURH RH15 ......75 H7
Broad Gv RTWE/PEM TN2 ....37 M8
Broadhill Cl HTHF TN21 ....244 H4
Broadlands BURH RH15 ....271 Q1
  HORL RH6 ....23 H6
  RHAS TN35 ....100 C1
Broad La RRTW TN3 ....36 E8
Broadmark Av ANG/EP BN16 .....148 B5
Broadmark La ANG/EP BN16 .....148 B5
Broadmark Pde
  ANG/EP BN16 * 148 B4
Broadmark Wy ANG/EP BN16 .....148 B5
Broadmead HORL RH6 ....23 H5
  RTWE/PEM TN2 ....53 K1
Broadmead Av RTWE/PEM TN2 .....53 H1
Broadmeadows La
  WVILLE PO7 ....288 B10
Broadmere Av HAV PO9 ....288 G12
Broad Oak RRTW TN3 ....52 A3
  STPH/PW TN12 ....188 H1

UCK TN22 ....77 L1
Broad Oak Cl LGNY BN23 ....163 M1
  RTWE/PEM TN2 ....37 L8
  STPH/PW TN12 ....188 H1
Broad Oak Coppice
  BEXW TN39 ....96 C8
Broadoak La BEXW TN39 ....96 B8
Broad Piece LHPTN BN17 ....147 G3
Broad Rdg RRTW TN3 ....121 J2
Broad Rd EDN/EASTW BN20 .....162 E1
  RCCH PO18 ....105 J5
Broadstone Pk FROW RH18 ....48 F7
Broad Strd ANG/EP BN16 ......148 C6
Broad St BRIE/ROTT BN2 ....4 B2
  RHWH RH17 ....72 D3
  SEAF BN25 ....174 E2
  WSEA TN36 ....285 M3
Broad Vw BEXW TN39 ....96 E7
  HTHF TN21 ....244 H4
  SELS PO20 ....301 M6
Broadview Cl
  EDN/EASTW BN20 ....162 E1
Broadview Gdns SALV BN13 .....116 D5
Broadwalk CRAWE RH10 ....8 F4
The Broadwalk BEXW TN39 .....136 A1
The Broad Wk PO18 ....291 K11
Broadwater Bvd SALV BN13 ....117 H8
Broadwater Down
  RTWE/PEM TN2 ....53 M1
Broadwater Forest La
  RRTW TN3 ....52 D3
Broadwater Hall SALV BN13 * ...20 E2
Broadwater La RTWE/PEM TN2 ....37 L8
  SWTR RH13 ....202 C8
Broadwater Ms SALV BN13 * 117 J8
Broadwater Ri RTWE/PEM TN2 ....37 L8
Broadwater Rd SALV BN13 ....21 G3
  SALV BN13 ....117 J8
Broadwater St East
  SALV BN13 ....117 J8
Broadwater St West
  SALV BN13 ....117 H7
Broadwater Wy
  LW/ROSE BN22 ....163 L5
  SALV BN13 ....117 J8
Broad Wy PSF GU32 ....222 E1
  RHAS TN35 ....285 Q12
Broadway SELS PO20 ....301 J5
Broadway Pk EPSF GU31 ....223 N8
The Broadway CCH PO19 ....107 M5
  CRAWE RH10 ....8 F4
  CROW TN6 ....67 L6
  LAN/SOMP BN15 ....119 G8
  LW/ROSE BN22 ....160 B3
  POLE BN26 ....160 G2
  RHAS TN35 ....100 C1
Broadwood Cl HORS RH12 ....56 C4
Broadwood Rd CRAWW RH11 ....42 F8
  PTSD BN41 ....120 F2
Brock Ct SEAF BN25 * 175 J2
Brock End RHWH RH17 ....72 B1
Brockenhurst Av HAV PO9 .....288 E11
Brockhampton La HAV PO9 .....102 F4
Brockhampton Rd HAV PO9 .....102 F4
Brockhurst St HORS RH12 .....201 Q4
Brockhurst Farm
  PUL/STOR RH20 ....264 D8
Brocklands HAV PO9 ....102 E4
Brockley Cl SALV BN13 ....20 E2
Brockley Rd BEXW TN39 ....136 F2
Brock Rd CRAWW RH11 ....27 C8
Brocks Gyhll
  EDN/EASTW BN20 ....162 F2
Brodie Pl EAST BN21 ....176 D1
Brodrick Cl LW/ROSE BN22 ....163 L4
Brodrick Rd LW/ROSE BN22 ....163 K3
Bromley Cl HPPT/KEY BN6 .....271 P5
  LGNY BN23 ....164 C3
Bromley Rd BRIE/ROTT BN2 ......5 G1
  SEAF BN25 ....175 H1
Brompton Cl BRI BN1 ....82 D7
The Brontes EGRIN RH19 * 31 H1
Bronze Cl MSEA/BNM PO22 .....144 B6
Brook Av HPPT/KEY BN6 ....271 N6
  RCCH PO18 ....106 A8
Brook Barn Wy FERR BN12 .....150 D4
Brook Cha PUL/STOR RH20 * 265 R7
Brook Cl BOGR PO21 ....171 M1
  CROW TN6 ....68 C8
  EGRIN RH19 ....32 A8
  PUL/STOR RH20 ....266 C10
  WTHG BN11 ....151 M3
Brook Cottages HAS TN34 * 13 H5
Brookdale Cl WVILLE PO7 .....288 A9
Brookdean Rd WTHG BN11 ......152 A2
Brooke Gdns RING/NEW BN8 ....240 C7
Brookenbee Cl ANG/EP BN16 ...148 A2
Brooker Pl HOVE BN3 ....121 M6
Brooker's Rd BIL RH14 ....232 A2
Brooker St HOVE BN3 ....121 M6
Brookfield Cl HAV PO9 ....102 F3
Brookfield La PETW GU28 .....228 C9
Brookfield Rd BEX TN40 ......137 K1
Brookfield Wy HAIL RH14 ......82 G4
Brook Gdns EMRTH PO10 ....103 L5
Brook HI SWTR RH13 ....235 K2
Brookhill Cl CRAWE RH10 ....28 F6
Brookhill Rd CRAWE RH10 ......28 F7
Brookhouse Bottom
  UCK TN22 ....208 B10
Brookhouse La UCK TN22 ......242 E10
Brookhurst Fld HORS RH12 * ...186 A9
Brookland Cl HAS TN34 ....13 H2
  PEV BN24 ....134 D7
Brooklands BOGR PO21 ....170 F4
  RTWE/PEM TN2 ....38 C2
Brooklands Av CROW TN6 ......210 G2
Brooklands Farm CI RRTW TN3 ...35 M3
Brooklands Rd CRAWW RH11 .....43 H8
  HAV PO9 ....102 C3
Brooklands Wy EGRIN RH19 .....47 J1
Brookland Wy
  PUL/STOR RH20 ....264 D8
Brook La ANG/EP BN16 ....148 B2
  FERR BN12 ....149 G2
  HORS RH12 ....73 J2
  HWH RH16 ....73 J2
  PUL/STOR RH20 ....264 D8
  RING/NEW BN8 ....86 D7
Brooklyn Av WTHG BN11 ....150 E3
Brooklyn Chambers
  WTHG BN11 * 150 E3
Brooklyn Dr WVILLE PO7 ......288 A9
Brooklyn Rd SEAF BN25 ......174 E2
Brookmead Cl LW/ROSE BN22 ....11 G1

Brookmead Wy HAV PO9 ....103 G6
Brookpits La LHPTN BN17 .....146 D5
Brook Rd HORS RH12 ....56 D3
  MFD/CHID GU8 ....182 B1
  RTWE/PEM TN2 ....38 B2
Brooks Cl HAST 17 H4
  NEWHV BN9 ....19 G5
Brookside CRAWE RH10 ....9 J2
  CRAWE RH10 ....28 F6
  HPPT/KEY BN6 * 271 N6
  MSEA/BNM PO22 ....158 A3
  PUL/STOR RH20 ....267 K9
  SELS PO20 ....142 D4
  UCK TN22 ....76 C6
Brookside Av ANG/EP BN16 ....148 B2
  POLE BN26 ....131 L6
Brookside Cl FERR BN12 ......149 K2
  SELS PO20 ....142 D4
Brookside Rd ANG/EP BN16 ....149 J5
  HAV PO9 ....102 D3
Brooks La MSEA/BNM PO22 ....3 H1
  RCCH PO18 ....106 C6
Brooks La West
  MSEA/BNM PO22 ....2 F2
Brooksmead MSEA/BNM PO22 * 3 H4
Brooks Rd LEWES BN7 ....17 J4
The Brooks BURH RH15 ....74 D4
  LEWES BN7 ....16 F5
  POLE BN26 ....131 L7
  RHWH RH17 ....205 M8
Brooks Wy LYDD TN29 ....255 R8
  PUL/STOR RH20 ....265 K3
The Brook CRAWE RH10 ....8 F1
  SWTR RH13 ....201 R11
Brookview CRAWE RH10 ....28 F5
  PUL/STOR RH20 ....264 D8
Brookway BURH RH15 ....75 H6
  HWH RH16 ....73 K1
Brook Wy LAN/SOMP BN15 ......118 E8
  RHAS TN35 ....284 E12
Brookwood HORL RH6 ....23 C5
Brookwood Pk HORL RH6 ....23 C7
Broomans La LEWES BN7 ....17 H4
Broom Cl LW/ROSE BN22 ....163 J3
  WVILLE PO7 ....288 B12
Broomcroft Rd
  MSEA/BNM PO22 ....173 H1
Broomdashers Rd CRAWE RH10 * ..9 K2
Broome Cl HORS RH12 ....56 C4
Broomers Hill La
  PUL/STOR RH20 ....231 L11
Broomers Hill Pk
  PUL/STOR RH20 ....231 L12
Broomers La SELS PO20 ....140 E8
Broomfield Av PEAHV BN10 ....156 E8
  SALV BN13 ....117 G8
Broomfield Dr BIL RH14 ......232 B2
  PTSD BN41 ....120 F2
Broomfield Rd BOR GU35 .....178 E7
  HFD BN5 ....269 J4
  SELS PO20 ....301 M5
Broomfield St
  EDN/EASTW BN20 ....176 D1
Broomgrove Rd HAS TN34 ....13 H1
Broomham La RING/NEW BN8 ...276 H10
Broomhill Park Rd
  SBGH/RUST TN4 ....37 K1
Broomhill Rd RRTW TN3 ....37 J3
Broom La RRTW TN3 ....36 E8
Broom Pk RRTW TN3 ....36 D6
Broom Rd EPSF GU31 ....223 R7
Brou Cl ANG/EP BN16 ....149 G4
Brougham Rd WTHG BN11 ....151 M2
Browning Cl CRAWE RH10 ....44 B3
Browning Rd HTHF TN21 ....244 D6
  LAN/SOMP BN15 ....118 D7
Browning's HI SWTR RH13 ....234 H3
The Brownings EGRIN RH19 .....31 H8
Brown Jack Av POLE BN26 ....131 L7
Brownleaf Rd BRIE/ROTT BN2 ..124 D7
Browns Cl UCK TN22 ....76 F4
Browns La HTHF TN21 ....243 Q7
  PUL/STOR RH20 ....266 A12
  UCK TN22 ....76 F3
Browns Wd EGRIN RH19 ....31 K5
Brown Twins Rd
  HPPT/KEY BN6 ....271 J4
The Brow BRIE/ROTT BN2 ......124 C5
  BURH RH15 ....74 F6
Broxhead Farm Rd BOR GU35 ...178 H11
Broxmead La RHWH RH17 ....204 F12
Broyle Cl CCH PO19 ....107 L4
  RING/NEW BN8 ....275 L9
Broyle La RING/NEW BN8 .....275 L9
Broyle Paddock
  RING/NEW BN8 ....275 L10
Broyle Rd CCH PO19 ....107 L4
The Broyle RING/NEW BN8 ....275 Q9
Bruce Av WTHG BN11 ....150 E3
Bruce Cl HWH RH16 ....73 H6
Bruce Vls WTHG BN11 ....150 E3
  SALV BN13 ....150 E3
Bruce Wy WTHG BN11 ....150 E3
Brunel Pl CRAWE RH10 ....9 J4
Brunel Rd STLEO TN38 ....98 D2
Brunswick Cl CRAWE RH10 ....9 J4
  MSEA/BNM PO22 ....3 M2
Brunswick Gdns HAV PO9 .....102 E3
Brunswick Ms HOVE BN3 * 122 C8
Brunswick Pl HOVE BN3 ......122 C7
Brunswick Rd HOVE BN3 ......122 C7
  SHOR BN43 ....119 L6
  WTHG BN11 ....20 E8
Brunswick Sq HOVE BN3 ......122 C8
Brunswick St East HOVE BN3 ..122 C8
Brunswick St West HOVE BN3 ..122 C8
Brunswick Ter HOVE BN3 .....122 C8
  RTW TN1 * 37 M7
Brushes La HWH RH16 ....73 L1
Brushwood Rd HORS RH12 ....57 G3
Bryants Fld CROW TN6 ....67 K6
Bryce Cl HORS RH12 ....56 F4
Brydges La HORS RH12 ....164 B7
Bryony Wy WVILLE PO7 ....288 B11
Buchans Lawn CRAWW RH11 ......43 G7
Buci Crs SHOR BN43 ....120 B5
Buckholt Av SELS PO20 ....56 D2
Buckholt La BEXW TN39 ....97 H4
Buckhurst Cl
  EDN/EASTW BN20 ....163 G5
  EGRIN RH19 ....31 H6
  LEWES BN7 ....16 F1

Buckhurst La WADH TN5 ....70 E5
Buckhurst Rd BEX TN40 ....137 H1
  PEAHV BN10 ....157 H6
Buckhurst Wy EGRIN RH19 ......31 H6
Buckingham Cl BRI BN1 * 4 C3
  SEAF BN25 ....174 C1
  SHOR BN43 ....119 M5
Buckingham Dr CCH PO19 ....7 L3
  EGRIN RH19 ....47 M2
Buckingham Ga RDKG RH6 ....28 B1
Buckingham Ms SHOR BN43 ....119 M5
Buckingham Pl ANG/EP BN16 ...148 A2
  BRI BN1 ....4 C3
Buckingham Rd BRI BN1 ....4 D4
  PSF GU32 ....223 L5
  RTW TN1 ....38 A7
  SHOR BN43 ....119 L6
  STLEO TN38 ....98 F1
  WTHG BN11 ....21 G7
Buckingham St BRIE/ROTT BN2 ..119 K6
  HAV PO9 ....289 H7
Buckland Dr BOGR PO21 ......171 G3
Buckland Rd SEAF BN25 ......159 L8
Buckle By-Pass SEAF BN25 ...159 H8
Buckle Cl SEAF BN25 ....174 C1
Buckle Dr SEAF BN25 ....174 C1
Buckle Ri SEAF BN25 ....174 C1
Bucklers Cl RTWE/PEM TN2 .....38 B6
Bucklers Ct HAV PO9 ....288 E10
Buckler St PTSD BN41 ....121 G2
Buckley Cl HOVE BN3 ....121 G2
Buckley Pl CRAWE RH10 ....45 M1
Buckmans Rd CRAWW RH11 ....8 D2
Buckmore Av PSF GU32 ....223 L5
Bucknor Cl BOGR PO21 ....171 H3
Bucksham Av BOGR PO21 ......143 G6
Buckshead HI SWTR RH13 .....203 L2
Buckswood Dr CRAWW RH11 * 8 A8
Buckthorn Cl SEAF BN25 .....175 J2
Buckwell Ct LEWES BN7 ....16 B1
Buckwell Ri HAIL BN27 ......279 P12
Buckwish La HFD BN5 ....268 H5
Buddens Gn RYE TN31 ....251 L1
Buddington La MIDH GU29 ....227 J6
Budds La BOR GU35 ....178 F5
  TENT TN30 ....220 D7
Budgen Cl CRAWE RH10 ....28 C8
Buffbeards La HASM GU27 ....180 H10
Bugsell La RBTBR TN32 ......216 A12
Bugshill La MIDH GU29 ......259 R4
Bulbeck Cl BURH RH15 ....74 D8
Bulbeck Rd HAV PO9 ....103 G4
Bulkington Av SALV BN13 ......20 D2
Bulldogs Bank EGRIN RH19 .....62 D4
Buller Cl CROW TN6 ....67 M8
Buller Rd BRIE/ROTT BN2 ....123 J4
Bullfinch Cl HORL RH6 ....22 F7
  HORS RH12 ....56 B2
Bullfinch Gdns UCK TN22 ......76 F8
Bull HI LISS GU33 ....192 H9
Bullingstone La RRTW TN3 .....36 E2
Bull La LEWES BN7 ....16 F7
Bulls Cape La HORN PO8 .....288 B4
Bull's La SWTR RH13 ....235 Q1
Bulrush Pl STLEO TN38 ....98 D4
Bulverhythe Rd STLEO TN38 ...98 F7
Bunbury Cl PUL/STOR RH20 ...266 E11
Bunch La HASM GU27 ....181 K10
Bunch Wy HASM GU27 ....181 K11
Buncton La RHWH RH17 ....236 F5
The Bungalows UCK TN22 ....77 K7
Bunny La RRTW TN3 ....53 K4
Bunting Cl STLEO TN38 ....98 D5
  SWTR RH13 ....15 J4
Bunting Gdns HORN PO8 ......288 A5
Bunyan Cl CRAWW RH11 ....42 D6
The Burchens SALV BN13 * 117 H7
Burchetts Cl HWH RH16 ....73 G7
Burchett Wk BOGR PO21 ......143 L8
Burch Gv ARUN BN18 ....111 J4
Burden Pl STLEO TN38 ....98 F2
Burdett Cl CRAWE RH10 ....44 C4
Burdett Pl HAS TN34 ....13 K6
Burdett Rd CROW TN6 ....68 B8
  SBGH/RUST TN4 ....37 G5
Burdock Cl CRAWW RH11 ....42 F7
Burdocks Dr BURH RH15 ....75 H8
Burfield Rd LW/ROSE BN22 ....11 H2
Burford Cl SALV BN13 ....116 F6
Burford Rd SWTR RH13 ....15 G5
Burgate Cl HAV PO9 ....102 E2
Burgess Rd RHAS TN35 ......284 F12
Burghclere Rd HAV PO9 ......289 J11
Burgh Cl CRAWE RH10 ....28 C8
Burgh HI BUR/ETCH TN19 .....215 R7
Burgh HI Rd LIPH GU30 ......179 N10
  RING/NEW BN8 ....277 M11
Burgh La RING/NEW BN8 ....88 C8
Burhill STLEO TN38 ....98 E6
Burlands CRAWW RH11 ....26 F8
Burleigh Cl CRAWE RH10 ....46 A1
Burleigh La CRAWE RH10 ....46 B2
Burleigh Pl LW/ROSE BN22 ...164 B7
Burley Cl BIL RH14 ....198 H1
  HAV PO9 ....289 J11
  LAN/SOMP BN15 * 118 D7
Burley Rd MSEA/BNM PO22 ....173 J1
Burlow Cl CRAWE RH10 ....44 C3
Burlington Gdns PTSD BN41 ..121 H4
  SELS PO20 ....301 M7
Burlington Pl EAST BN21 ......10 F8
Burlington Rd EAST BN21 ......11 G7
  FERR BN12 ....149 K2
Burlington St BRIE/ROTT BN2 ...5 J9
Burma Cl HWH RH16 ....73 M5
Burnaby Ct SEAF BN25 ......148 D2
Burndell Rd ARUN BN18 ......145 M2
Burnes V BRIE/ROTT BN2 .....155 L3
Burngreave Ct BOGR PO21 ......2 A6
Burnham Av BOGR PO21 ....2 C6
Burnham Gdns BOGR PO21 ....2 C6
Burnham Rd SALV BN13 ......116 D7
Burn Cl SALV BN13 ....56 D2
Burns Gdns MSEA/BNM PO22 ...145 J8
Burnside POLE BN26 ....131 M7
  WVILLE PO7 ....288 D1
Burnside Crs
  LAN/SOMP BN15 ....118 B8

Burnside Ms BEXW TN39 ....137 H1
Burns Rd CRAWE RH10 ....44 B1
Burns Wy EGRIN RH19 ....31 H8
  HORS RH12 ....42 B8
Burnt Barn Cottages
  BAT TN33 ....281 P9
Burnthouse Bostall
  HPPT/KEY BN6 ....271 R10
Burnt House Cl HAWK TN18 ....217 R4
Burnt House La HORS RH12 .....41 L2
  RRTW TN3 ....36 E4
Burnthouse La SWTR RH13 ....203 J10
  SWTR RH13 ....234 H2
Burnt Lodge La WADH TN5 ....190 G12
Burnt Oak La RDKG RH5 ....25 K1
Burnt Oak Rd UCK TN22 ......210 D7
Burrell Av LAN/SOMP BN15 ....118 C8
Burrell Buildings
  LAN/SOMP BN15 * 118 C8
Burrell Cl SWTR RH13 ....234 F10
Burrell Gn RHWH RH17 ....72 C1
Burrell Rd HWH RH16 ....73 G3
Burrells La UCK TN22 ....209 M10
The Burrells SHOR BN43 .....120 A7
Burrow Down
  EDN/EASTW BN20 ....162 F8
Burrows Cl HAV PO9 ....103 H2
Burrswood Vls RRTW TN3 * 52 B2
Burry Rd SLVH TN37 ....99 H2
Bursiedon Cl MSEA/BNM PO22 ...3 M3
Burslem Rd RTWE/PEM TN2 .....38 D3
Burstead Cl BRI BN1 ....123 G2
Burston Gdns EGRIN RH19 ......31 J5
Burstowhill La RHWH RH17 ...206 C6
Burton Cl HORL RH6 ....22 F7
Burton Park Rd PETW GU28 ...263 L5
Burton Rd EAST BN21 ....10 A1
Burtons Ct HORS RH12 * 14 D6
Burton Vls HOVE BN3 ....122 C5
Burton Wy STLEO TN38 * 99 G6
Burwash Cl ANG/EP BN16 .....149 G2
  HAS TN34 ....284 D12
  LGNY BN23 ....164 A1
Burwash Rd CRAWE RH10 ....9 L5
  HOVE BN3 ....121 L2
  HTHF TN21 ....244 F5
Bury Dr FERR BN12 ....150 A3
Bury HI PUL/STOR RH20 ......296 A3
Bury Rd PUL/STOR RH20 ......264 A11
Bushbury La UCK TN22 ....242 H10
Bushby Av LAN/SOMP BN15 ....148 C4
Bushby Cl LAN/SOMP BN15 ....118 B8
Bush Cl BRIE/ROTT BN2 ......124 C4
  PEAHV BN10 ....
Bush Cottage Cl PTSD BN41 ..121 H3
Busheyfields HAIL BN27 ....91 H3
Bush Farm Dr PTSD BN41 .....121 H3
Bushfield BIL RH14 ....198 A3
Bush Rd NEWHV BN9 ....18 C1
Bushy Cft BEXW TN39 ....96 C8
Bushy Gill RRTW TN3 ....36 F6
Busticle La LAN/SOMP BN15 ...118 B6
Butcherfield La HRTF TN7 .....49 M2
Butchers La NEWHV BN9 ....18 F3
  RHAS TN35 ....284 C1
Bute St BRIE/ROTT BN2 ....5 L8
Butler Ct SALV BN13 ....116 E7
Butler's Green Rd HWH RH16 ...72 B5
Butler's La HAIL BN27 ....93 K2
Butlers Rd SWTR RH13 ....15 M1
Butlers Wy RING/NEW BN8 ....274 H12
Butterbox La RHWH RH17 .....239 N1
Buttercup Cl BOGR PO21 .....179 K4
Buttercup Wk BRI BN1 ....83 C7
Buttercup Wy SWTR RH13 .....201 R11
Butterfield EGRIN RH19 ....31 K6
Buttermere Cl BOR GU35 ......178 G4
  HORS RH12 ....57 G3
Buttermere Wy LGNY BN23 ....164 B1
  LHPTN BN17 ....147 H3
Butt La ARUN BN18 ....294 H11
Button Ct BRIE/ROTT BN2 ......5 G2
Butts Cl CRAWW RH11 ....8 B2
Butts Fld HAIL BN27 ....92 B7
Buttsfield La RING/NEW BN8 ..276 H4
Butts La EDN/EASTW BN20 ....162 F4
  WADH TN5 ....190 B6
Butts Meadow BIL RH14 ......199 J12
Butts Rd STHW BN42 ....120 B3
Buxshalls HI HWH RH16 ......206 F8
Buxted Ri BRI BN1 ....83 G8
Buxted Wood La UCK TN22 ....210 E12
Buxton Dr BEXW TN39 ....97 C7
Buxton Rd BRI BN1 ....4 B2
  EDN/EASTW BN20 ....176 B5
Bycroft Wy CRAWE RH10 ....44 A4
Bydown SEAF BN25 ....175 G1
Byerley Cl EMRTH PO10 ......289 Q12
Byerley Wy CRAWE RH10 ....44 D2
The Byeways SEAF BN25 .....174 F1
The Bye Wy BOGR PO21 ....171 H5
The Byeway BEXW TN39 ....96 C8
  HAS TN34 ....99 M1
  SELS PO20 ....167 K4
Byfield Pl MSEA/BNM PO22 ......2 E1
Byfields Cft BEXW TN39 ......96 E8
Byfleets La HORS RH12 ......187 N12
Byland Cl LW/ROSE BN22 .....163 K2
Bylanes Cl RHWH RH17 ....72 C2
Bylanes Crs RHWH RH17 ....72 C2
Byne Cl PUL/STOR RH20 ......266 B12
Byng Rd SBGH/RUST TN4 ....37 K4
Byrd Rd CRAWW RH11 ....42 E6
Byron Cl CRAWE RH10 ....44 A2
  HORS RH12 ....56 D3
  MSEA/BNM PO22 ....145 J7
Byron Gv EGRIN RH19 ....47 H1
Byron Rd ANG/EP BN16 ....147 M4
  WTHG BN11 ....20 E6
Byron St HOVE BN3 ....121 M6
By Sunte HWH RH16 ....73 J1
Bywater Wy CCH PO19 ....6 C7
Bywaves SELS PO20 ....300 D1
Byways SELS PO20 ....301 K8
  SLVH TN37 ....284 A11
The Byway BRI BN1 ....83 G8
  MSEA/BNM PO22 ....145 J7
Byworth Cl BEXW TN39 ....96 B5
  BRIE/ROTT BN2 ....123 L7

Cabbage Stalk La
  SBGH/RUST TN4 ....37 K7

Cabot Cl *LGNY* BN23 .... 164 F7
Caburn Cl *LGNY* BN23 .... 163 M1
Caburn Ct *CRAWW* RH11 .... 8 C8
Caburn Crs *LEWES* BN7 .... 16 A3
Caburn Hts *CRAWW* RH11 .... 8 B8
Caburn Wy *HAIL* BN27 .... 91 M7
Cacklebury *HAIL* BN27 * 91 M7
Cacklebury Cl *HAIL* BN27 .... 91 M7
Cackle St *RYE* TN31 .... 250 D11
UCK TN22 .... 209 K8
The Cackstones *CRAWE* RH10 * 44 C2
Cadborough Cliff *RYE* TN31 .... 252 F9
Cade St *LW/ROSE* BN22 .... 163 L3
Caedwalla Dr *SELS* PO20 .... 109 H3
Caerleon Cl *GSHT* GU26 .... 180 F3
Caernarvon Rd *CCH* PO19 .... 7 L5
Caffins Cl *CRAWW* RH11 .... 43 K1
Caffyns Ri *BIL* RH14 .... 200 A12
Cagefoot La *HFD* BN5 .... 269 K5
Cairngorm Cl *LGNY* BN23 .... 164 C2
Cairo Av *PEAHV* BN10 .... 156 F6
Cairo Av South *PEAHV* BN10 .... 156 F6
Caister's Cl *HOVE* BN3 .... 122 B5
Cakeham Rd *SELS* PO20 .... 167 H5
Cakeham Wy *SELS* PO20 .... 167 K6
Calbourne *HRH* RH16 .... 73 G4
Caldbec Hl *BAT* TN33 .... 282 E4
Calderdale Cl *CRAWW* RH11 .... 8 B8
Caldicotts La *HAIL* BN27 .... 91 H2
Caledon Av *MSEA/BNM* PO22 .... 145 J8
MSEA/BNM PO22 .... 173 J1
Caledonian Pl *WTHG* BN11 * 21 G7
Caledonian Rd *BRIE/ROTT* BN2 ... 5 H1
CCH PO19 .... 7 G6
Caledonian Wy *HORL* RH6 * 28 A1
Caley Ri *RTWE/PEM* TN2 .... 38 C1
Callao Quay *LGNY* BN23 .... 165 G5
Calgary *BEXW* TN39 .... 97 G6
Callender Wk *RHWH* RH17 .... 72 C5
Callisto Cl *CRAWW* RH11 .... 42 D6
Callon Cl *SALV* BN13 * 116 A7
Callums Wk *BEX* TN40 .... 97 K8
Calshot Rd *HAV* PO9 .... 288 D10
Calvecroft *LIPH* GU30 .... 193 Q1
Calverley Ct *RTW* TN1 .... 38 C6
Calverley Pk *RTW* TN1 .... 38 A6
Calverley Park Crs *RTW* TN1 ... 38 A6
Calverley Park Gdns *RTW* TN1 ... 38 A5
Calverley Rd *EAST* BN21 .... 10 D7
RTW TN1 .... 38 A6
Calverley St *RTW* TN1 .... 38 A6
Calverley Wk *EAST* BN21 * 10 D7
Calvert Cl *UCK* TN22 .... 76 C5
Calvert Rd *HAS* TN34 .... 13 K2
UCK TN22 .... 76 C5
Camber Cl *BEX* TN40 .... 97 K7
CRAWE RH10 .... 44 B3
Camber Dr *PEV* BN24 .... 134 E7
Camberlot Rd *HAIL* BN27 .... 90 F2
Camber Rd *RYE* TN31 .... 253 L6
Camber Wy *PEV* BN24 .... 134 C7
Cambrai Av *CCH* PO19 .... 7 H6
Cambria Cl *RCCH* PO18 .... 106 D8
Cambrian Rd *SBGH/RUST* TN4 ... 38 B2
Cambridge Av *SELS* PO20 .... 167 G5
Cambridge Dr *BOGR* PO21 .... 171 L1
Cambridge Gdns *HAS* TN34 .... 12 F7
RTWE/PEM TN2 * 38 A7
Cambridge Gv *HOVE* BN3 .... 122 B6
Cambridge La *HTHF* TN21 .... 243 R11
Cambridge Lodge Pk
HORL RH6 * 22 F3
Cambridge Ms *HOVE* BN3 * 122 B6
Cambridge Pde
LW/ROSE BN22 * 11 H4
Cambridge Rd *BEX* TN40 .... 97 J7
HAS TN34 .... 12 F7
HOVE BN3 .... 122 C7
LW/ROSE BN22 .... 11 H4
SWTR RH13 .... 14 F6
WTHG BN11 .... 21 G4
Cambridge St *RTWE/PEM* TN2 ... 38 B6
Cambridge Wy *UCK* TN22 .... 76 C5
Camden Av *RTWE/PEM* TN2 .... 39 H3
Camden Hl *RTWE/PEM* TN2 .... 38 A6
Camden Pk *RTW* TN1 .... 38 A6
RTWE/PEM TN2 .... 38 A6
Camden Rd *EAST* BN21 .... 10 D7
RTW TN1 .... 38 A6
Camden St *PTSD* BN41 .... 121 H7
Camelford St *BRIE/ROTT* BN2 ... 5 L8
Camelia Cl *HAV* PO9 .... 103 K2
LHPTN BN17 .... 147 M2
Camelot Cl *SWTR* RH13 .... 201 R11
Camelsdale Rd *HASM* GU27 .... 181 J12
Cameron Cl *HAIL* BN27 .... 91 M5
Campbell Cl *UCK* TN22 .... 76 C3
Campbell Ct *FERR* BN12 * 149 M2
Campbell Crs *EGRIN* RH19 .... 31 G2
Campbell Dr *ANG/EP* BN16 .... 148 A3
Campbell Rd *BOGR* PO21 .... 171 J7
BRI BN1 .... 4 D1
CRAWE RH10 .... 44 B1
SBGH/RUST TN4 .... 37 M3
SELS PO20 .... 109 G4
Camperdown St *BEXW* TN39 .... 96 F6
Campion Cl *BOR* GU35 .... 179 K5
WVILLE PO7 .... 288 B11
Camp Rd *BOR* GU35 .... 178 C4
Canada Av *PEAHV* BN10 .... 157 G4
Canada Gv *BOGR* PO21 .... 2 D7
MIDH GU29 .... 227 J10
Canada Rd *ARUN* BN18 .... 112 C2
Canada Wy *BEXW* TN39 .... 97 G6
BOR GU35 .... 178 C5
LIPH GU30 .... 193 R2
Canadian Crs *SELS* PO20 .... 301 L8
Canadia Rd *BAT* TN33 .... 282 D3
Canal Pl *CCH* PO19 .... 6 C7
Canal *ARUN* BN18 .... 145 J3
Canal Whf *CCH* PO19 .... 6 D7
Canal Wharf Rd *CCH* PO19 .... 6 C7
Canary Quay *LGNY* BN23 .... 164 C5
Canberra Cl *SELS* PO20 .... 301 L8
Canberra Dr *CRAWW* RH11 .... 27 J8
HORS RH12 .... 15 K1
Canberra Pl *HORS* RH12 * 56 C1
Canberra Rd *EMRTH* PO10 .... 138 A3
SALV BN13 .... 116 B7
Candleford Ga *LIPH* GU30 * 193 Q1
Canfield Cl *LGNY* BN23 .... 164 C2
Canfield Cl *BRIE/ROTT* BN2 .... 123 J4
Canfield Rd *BRIE/ROTT* BN2 ... 123 J4
Canhouse La *LISS* GU33 .... 193 J10

Canning Rd *MSEA/BNM* PO22 ...... 3 K6
Canning St *BRIE/ROTT* BN2 .... 5 K6
Cannon Pl *BRI* BN1 .... 4 C7
Cannon St *LYDD* TN29 .... 255 P4
Canon La *CCH* PO19 .... 6 D5
Canons Cl *BOGR* PO21 .... 171 J4
Canons Wy *STEY/UB* BN44 .... 78 D1
Cansiron La *EDEN* TN8 .... 33 K7
EGRIN RH19 .... 49 G4
Cantelupe Cl *BEX* TN40 .... 137 J2
Cantelupe Ms *EGRIN* RH19 * 31 K8
Cantelupe Rd *BEX* TN40 .... 137 J2
EGRIN RH19 .... 31 L8
Canterbury Cl *BOGR* PO21 .... 170 F4
CCH PO19 .... 107 L5
LW/ROSE BN22 .... 163 H3
Canterbury Ct *SALV* BN13 .... 150 E2
Canterbury Dr *BRIE/ROTT* BN2 ... 5 L5
Canterbury Ri *HAS* TN34 .... 99 K2
Canterbury Rd *ANG/EP* BN16 ... 148 C5
CRAWE RH10 .... 43 K7
RTWE/PEM TN2 .... 39 K3
SALV BN13 .... 150 E2
Cantercrow Hl *NEWHV* BN9 .... 158 A5
The Canter *CRAWE* RH10 .... 44 D2
Cants Cl *BURH* RH15 .... 75 J6
Cants La *BURH* RH15 .... 75 J6
Canute Cl *LGNY* BN23 .... 164 E5
Canute Rd *RCCH* PO18 .... 106 A8
RHAS TN35 .... 100 C2
Canvey Cl *CRAWW* RH11 .... 43 H6
Cape Copse *HORS* RH12 .... 186 A10
Capel Av *PEAHV* BN10 .... 157 H7
Capel La *CRAWW* RH11 .... 42 E4
Capel Rd *HORS* RH12 .... 25 H8
Capenors *BURH* RH15 .... 74 E9
The Cape *LHPTN* BN17 .... 147 M4
Caple Gdns *STLEO* TN38 .... 99 G3
Capricorn Cl *CRAWW* RH11 .... 42 D5
Capsey Rd *CRAWW* RH11 .... 42 E6
Capstan Dr *LHPTN* BN17 .... 147 M5
Caraway Cl *CRAWW* RH11 .... 43 G5
Carbery Cl *HAV* PO9 .... 288 E10
Carden Av *BRI* BN1 .... 82 E8
Carden Cl *BRI* BN1 .... 82 F7
Carden Crs *BRI* BN1 .... 82 F7
Carden Hl *BRI* BN1 .... 82 E8
Cardew Rd *LISS* GU33 .... 192 D10
Card Hl *FROW* RH18 .... 48 E8
Cardiff Rd *STLEO* TN38 .... 12 A7
Cardinal Dr *WVILLE* PO7 .... 288 C8
Cardinals Cl *BEX* TN40 .... 97 L1
Cardinal's Dr *BOGR* PO21 .... 170 F4
Carew Rd *EAST* BN21 .... 10 B3
Carey Down *PEAHV* BN10 .... 157 G4
Carfax *HORS* RH12 .... 14 C6
Carfax Cl *BRIE/ROTT* BN2 * 97 G5
Cargo Forecourt Rd *HORL* RH6 ... 27 J2
Cargo Rd *HORL* RH6 .... 27 J1
Carinus Gdns *HAV* PO9 .... 103 J3
Carisbrooke Cl *HAV* PO9 .... 103 J3
LAN/SOMP BN15 .... 118 D5
LGNY BN23 .... 164 A1
Carisbrooke Dr *SALV* BN13 ...... 116 A3
Carisbrooke Rd *BRIE/ROTT* BN2 ... 5 L2
STLEO TN38 .... 99 G6
Carleton Rd *CCH* PO19 .... 6 A1
Carlingford Ct *BOGR* PO21 .... 2 E7
Carlisle Pde *HAS* TN34 .... 13 G5
Carlisle Rd *EAST* BN21 .... 10 F9
EDEN/EASTW BN20 .... 10 F9
HOVE BN3 .... 121 L7
Carlton Av *BOGR* PO21 .... 171 L1
Carlton Cl *SEAF* BN25 .... 174 D1
Carlton Ct *HORL* RH6 * 23 G4
Carlton Crs *RTW* TN1 .... 38 B5
Carlton Hl *BRIE/ROTT* BN2 * 5 L6
Carlton Ldg *RTW* TN1 * 38 B5
Carlton Ms *WTHG* BN11 * 20 A5
Carlton Rd *BOR* GU35 .... 179 R5
LW/ROSE BN22 .... 11 J3
RTW TN1 .... 38 B5
SEAF BN25 .... 159 J8
Carlton Ter *CROW* TN6 * 210 C1
Carlton Tye *HORL* RH6 .... 23 G4
Carlyle Av *BRIE/ROTT* BN2 .... 123 J4
Carlyle St *BRIE/ROTT* BN2 .... 5 K3
Carmel Cl *BEXW* TN39 .... 136 C2
Carmelstead Cl *HWH* RH16 * 73 H2
Carmino Ter *LIPH* GU30 * 193 Q1
Carnation Cl *LHPTN* BN17 .... 148 A2
Carnegie Cl *SALV* BN13 .... 117 H8
Carnegie Gdns *SALV* BN13 .... 117 H8
Carnegie Rd *SALV* BN13 .... 117 H8
Carnforth Rd *LAN/SOMP* BN15 ... 118 F4
Carol Cl *BRI* BN1 .... 82 E7
Caroline Cl *SEAF* BN25 .... 159 J8
Caroline Ct *CRAWE* RH10 .... 44 B1
Caroline Wy *LGNY* BN23 .... 165 G4
Caron La *LAN/SOMP* BN15 .... 118 D3
Carousel Ct *MSEA/BNM* PO22 ...... 2 A1
Carpenter Dr *STLEO* TN38 .... 98 E4
Carpenters Cft *RING/NEW* BN8 ... 276 H4
Carpenters Meadow
PUL/STOR RH20 .... 265 K3
Carpenters Wy *HAIL* BN27 .... 91 M7
Carriers Rd *RTW* TN1 .... 35 G5
Carron La *MIDH* GU29 .... 226 C10
Carse Rd *CCH* PO19 .... 108 B4
Carter Rd *CRAWE* RH10 .... 44 B4
Cartersland *SALV* BN13 * 193 Q10
Carterslodge La *RHWH* RH17 ...... 58 B8
Cartersmead Cl *HORL* RH6 * 23 G5
Carters Wy *BIL* RH14 .... 231 J1
Carvel Ct *STLEO* TN38 .... 283 M10
Carvel Wy *LHPTN* BN17 .... 147 M3
Carylls Meadow *SWTR* RH13 ...... 234 C6
Casher Rd *CRAWE* RH10 .... 44 B6
Caspian Cl *RCCH* PO18 .... 107 G5
Cassells Rd *CCH* PO19 .... 107 M4
Cassidy Pl *PUL/STOR* RH20 ...... 265 Q12
Castle Av *HAV* PO9 .... 103 J3
Castle Banks *LEWES* BN7 * 16 F6
Castle Bolton *LGNY* BN23 .... 164 B1
Castle Cl *SALV* BN13 .... 150 E1
STEY/UB BN44 .... 78 D3
Castle Ditch La *LEWES* BN7 ...... 16 F6
Castledown Av *HAS* TN34 .... 13 H6
Castledown Ter *HAS* TN34 .... 13 H6
Castle Dr *HORL* RH6 .... 23 H8
PEV BN24 .... 165 H4
Castlefields *HRTF* TN7 .... 50 B5
Castle Gdns *ARUN* BN18 .... 112 F2
HAS TN34 .... 13 H7

MIDH GU29 * 227 J10
Castle Ga *LEWES* BN7 * 16 F6
Castlegate Rd *PUL/STOR* RH20 ... 265 Q6
Castleham Rd *STLEO* TN38 .... 283 N12
Castle Hl *CROW* TN6 .... 211 P4
HAS TN34 .... 13 J4
Castle Hill Pas *HAS* TN34 .... 13 H6
Castle Hill Rd *HAS* TN34 .... 13 H7
Castle Hurst *RBTBR* TN32 .... 217 J9
Castle La *STEY/UB* BN44 .... 78 D3
Castle Precincts *LEWES* BN7 ...... 16 F6
Castlereagh Gn
MSEA/BNM PO22 .... 3 M2
Castle Ri *UCK* TN22 .... 76 F3
Castle Rd *HAV* PO9 .... 288 E10
HORS RH12 .... 201 N2
PEV BN24 .... 133 N4
SALV BN13 .... 150 E1
SBGH/RUST TN4 .... 37 L6
Castleross Rd *PEV* BN24 .... 165 H1
Castle Sq *BRI* BN1 .... 4 E7
HAS TN34 .... 13 H6
Castle St *BRI* BN1 .... 4 B7
HAS TN34 .... 13 J4
RTW TN1 .... 37 M7
WSEA TN36 .... 286 E2
Castle Ter *LEWES* BN7 * 16 F6
The Castle *HORS* RH12 .... 56 D2
Castle View Gdns *PEV* BN24 ...... 133 L7
Castle View Ms *HAS* TN34 * 13 H7
Castle Wk *WADH* TN5 .... 71 K5
Castle Wy *SALV* BN13 .... 150 E1
STEY/UB BN44 .... 78 D3
UCK TN22 .... 76 F3
Castlewood Rd *SWTR* RH13 ...... 201 R11
Caterways *HORS* RH12 .... 201 K2
Cathedral Ctyd *CCH* PO19 * 6 D5
Cathedral La *CCH* PO19 * 6 D5
Cathedral Wk *HAIL* BN27 * 90 A2
Cathedral Wy *CCH* PO19 .... 107 J8
Catherine Pl *RTW* TN1 .... 38 A6
Catherine V *BRIE/ROTT* BN2 ...... 124 D5
Catherington La *HORN* PO8 ...... 256 B12
Catherington Wy *HAV* PO9 ...... 103 G5
Catkin Wy *HWH* RH16 .... 73 L5
Catsfield Cl *LGNY* BN23 .... 163 L1
STLEO TN38 .... 98 C3
Catsfield Rd *BAT* TN33 .... 281 Q6
Catslands La *HFD* BN5 .... 269 P4
Cat St *HRTF* TN7 .... 49 L3
Catt's Hl *CROW* TN6 .... 69 J8
TENT TN30 .... 221 L5
Cattswood La *HWH* RH16 .... 72 F7
Causeway Farm *HORN* PO8 ...... 288 C3
The Causeway *ARUN* BN18 .... 113 H3
BOGR PO21 .... 170 F5
BRIE/ROTT BN2 * 5 M5
EPSF GU31 .... 223 M8
FERR BN12 .... 150 C2
RCCH PO18 .... 14 C7
PSF GU32 .... 223 M7
SEAF BN25 .... 174 E3
SELS PO20 .... 140 E7
SELS PO20 .... 301 L5
Cavalier Cl *MIDH* GU29 .... 226 H10
Cavalier Wy *EGRIN* RH19 .... 47 L2
Cavalry Crs *EDN/EASTW* BN20 ... 163 G8
Cavell Av *PEAHV* BN10 .... 157 G6
Cavell Av North *PEAHV* BN10 ... 157 H5
Cavell Wy *CRAWE* RH10 .... 44 B4
Cavendish Av *LW/ROSE* BN22 ... 11 G4
STLEO TN38 .... 98 F6
Cavendish Br *EAST* BN21 .... 10 F4
Cavendish Cl *FERR* BN12 .... 150 C2
HORS RH12 .... 56 C2
PEAHV BN10 .... 157 G5
Cavendish Ct *BRIE/ROTT* BN2 ... 5 G7
CCH PO19 .... 6 B7
Cavendish Dr *RTWE/PEM* TN2 ... 38 A7
WVILLE PO7 .... 288 A10
Cavendish Ms *WTHG* BN11 * 20 E7
Cavendish Pl *BRI* BN1 .... 4 E7
EAST BN21 .... 10 F5
Cavendish Rd *BOGR* PO21 .... 2 C2
BRIE/ROTT BN2 * 5 G7
CCH PO19 .... 6 B7
Caveridge La *RING/NEW* BN8 ... 273 P1
Caves Rd *STLEO* TN38 .... 98 F5
Cawley Rd *CCH* PO19 .... 6 B6
Caxton Ct *STLEO* TN38 .... 43 J6
Caxton Wy *HWH* RH16 .... 73 H5
Cecilian Av *SALV* BN13 .... 21 G1
Cecil Pashley Wy *SHOR* BN43 ... 119 J5
Cecil Rd *LAN/SOMP* BN15 .... 152 D1
Cedar Av *SALV* BN13 .... 116 E7
Cedar Cl *ANG/EP* BN16 .... 148 F1
BOGR PO21 .... 171 J2
BURH RH15 .... 75 G4
CRAWW RH11 .... 27 H8
FERR BN12 .... 149 K4
HORS RH12 .... 14 B5
LAN/SOMP BN15 .... 152 C1
LW/ROSE BN22 .... 163 H3
SALV BN13 .... 116 E7
SWTR RH13 .... 284 A12
Cedar Cl East *BOGR* PO21 .... 171 J2
Cedar Crs *HORN* PO8 .... 288 C6
Cedar Dr *CCH* PO19 .... 6 C2
SWTR RH13 .... 201 R11
Cedar Gdns *HAV* PO9 .... 103 H3
Cedar Ldg *ANG/EP* BN16 * 148 B4
HASM GU27 .... 181 P12
Cedar Rdg *RTWE/PEM* TN2 ...... 38 C2
Cedars Cl *SWTR* RH13 .... 201 R11
Cedars Farm Cl *BIL* RH14 .... 231 R1
Cedars Gdns *BRI* BN1 .... 122 C2
The Cedars *ANG/EP* BN16 .... 148 D3
BRI BN1 .... 122 D2
BRIE/ROTT BN2 * 5 G1
HAIL BN27 .... 92 A4
HWH RH16 .... 73 H2
PEAHV BN10 * 157 H4
UCK TN22 .... 76 F4
Cedar Wy *HFD* BN5 .... 269 L5
Cedarwell Cl *NEWHV* BN9 * 158 A3
Celandine Av *HORN* PO8 .... 288 C6
Celandine Cl *CRAWW* RH11 * 42 D7
Celandine Dr *STLEO* TN38 .... 98 F4
Celia Cl *WILLE* PO7 * 288 C9
Cemetery La *EMRTH* PO10 ...... 104 D3
PETW GU28 .... 228 G8
Centenary Gdns *HAV* PO9 .... 103 J3

Central Av *ANG/EP* BN16 .... 148 B5
BOGR PO21 .... 143 M7
EDN/EASTW BN20 .... 163 G8
PEAHV BN10 .... 156 F6
POLE BN26 .... 132 A6
SALV BN13 .... 116 E2
Central Dr *BOGR* PO21 .... 143 L7
MSEA/BNM PO22 .... 145 M8
Central Pde *HORL* RH6 * 22 F7
UCK TN22 * 209 N12
Central Rd *BOGR* PO21 .... 2 C2
SELS PO20 .... 178 G3
Centrecourt Cl *SALV* BN13 .... 20 F2
Centrecourt Rd *SALV* BN13 ...... 20 F2
Centurion Ri *HAS* TN34 .... 99 M1
Centurion Rd *BRI* BN1 .... 4 D5
Ceres Pl *MSEA/BNM* PO22 .... 173 J1
Ceylon Pl *EAST* BN21 .... 11 G6
Ceylon Wk *BEXW* TN39 .... 136 D2
Chadborn Cl *BRIE/ROTT* BN2 ...... 5 M8
Chadswell Meadow *HAV* PO9 ... 102 E4
Chadwick Cl *CRAWW* RH11 .... 43 G8
Chaffer La *SELS* PO20 .... 168 C1
Chaffinch Cl *BURH* RH15 .... 74 C5
CRAWW RH11 .... 43 J1
HORS RH12 .... 56 C2
SALV BN13 .... 116 B8
Chaffinch Rd *LGNY* BN23 .... 164 B3
Chaffinch Wk *UCK* TN22 .... 76 F7
Chaffinch Wy *HORL* RH6 .... 22 D5
Chafford La *RRTW* TN3 .... 35 M4
Chailey Av *BRIE/ROTT* BN2 ...... 155 M4
Chailey Cl *CRAWW* RH11 .... 42 F6
HAS TN34 .... 284 D12
LGNY BN23 .... 164 D4
Chailey Crs *BRIE/ROTT* BN2 ...... 156 D4
Chailey Rd *RING/NEW* BN8 ...... 240 A8
Chailey Rd *BRI* BN1 .... 123 K1
Chainbridge La *SELS* PO20 .... 300 C13
Chain La *BAT* TN33 .... 282 D4
Chalcraft Cl *LIPH* GU30 .... 193 P1
Chalcraft La *BOGR* PO21 .... 143 L8
Chalder La *SELS* PO20 .... 169 L2
Chaldon Rd *CRAWW* RH11 .... 43 H8
Chalet Cl *FERR* BN12 .... 149 K5
Chalet Gdns *FERR* BN12 .... 149 L5
Chalet Hl *BOR* GU35 .... 178 H6
Chalet Rd *FERR* BN12 .... 149 K4
Chalfont Cl *MSEA/BNM* PO22 ... 145 K8
Chalfont Dr *HOVE* BN3 .... 122 B2
Chalfont Wy *SALV* BN13 .... 116 C8
Chalkdock La *SELS* PO20 .... 139 M8
Chalkers La *HPPT/KEY* BN6 ...... 271 J1
Chalket La *RTWE/PEM* TN2 ...... 39 H4
Chalk Farm Cl
EDN/EASTW BN20 .... 163 G4
Chalkland Ri *BRIE/ROTT* BN2 ... 124 D5
Chalk La *SELS* PO20 .... 169 K6
Chalk Rdg *HORN* PO8 .... 256 E10
Chalk Rd *BIL* RH14 .... 198 D2
RCCH PO18 .... 293 K5
Chalky Rd *PTSD* BN41 .... 120 E2
Challen Cl *SELS* PO20 .... 109 H6
Challoners *RHWH* RH17 .... 207 M5
Challoners Cl *BRIE/ROTT* BN2 ... 155 L3
Challoners Ms *BRIE/ROTT* BN2 ... 155 L3
Challow *HPPT/KEY* BN6 .... 271 M5
Chalmers Cl *HWH* RH16 .... 26 D3
Chaloner Cl *HWH* RH16 .... 73 L2
Chaloner Rd *HWH* RH16 .... 73 L2
Chalton Crs *HAV* PO9 .... 288 E12
Chalton La *HORN* PO8 .... 256 F7
Chalvington Cl *BRI* BN1 .... 83 K7
SEAF BN25 .... 159 L7
Chalvington Dr *SLVH* TN37 ...... 283 R11
Chalvington Rd *EAST* BN21 ...... 163 H8
Chamberlaines La
RING/NEW BN8 .... 275 L11
Chamberlain Rd *EAST* BN21 ...... 176 C1
Chambers Cl *STLEO* TN38 .... 98 E2
Chambers Rd *STLEO* TN38 .... 98 E3
Champions Rw *HOVE* BN3 * 122 C5
Champney Cl *BOR* GU35 .... 178 F8
Chancellors Pk *HPPT/KEY* BN6 ... 271 N5
Chanctonbury
PUL/STOR RH20 .... 267 K9
Chanctonbury Cl
ANG/EP BN16 .... 148 A5
PUL/STOR RH20 .... 298 H3
Chanctonbury Dr *HAS* TN34 ...... 284 D11
SHOR BN43 .... 119 K4
Chanctonbury Ring Rd
STEY/UB BN44 .... 299 N3
Chanctonbury Rd
ANG/EP BN16 .... 148 A5
BURH RH15 .... 74 F7
HOVE BN3 .... 4 A2
Chanctonbury Vw *HFD* BN5 ...... 269 J5
Chanctonbury Wk
PUL/STOR RH20 * 266 A12
Chanctonbury Wy *CRAWW* RH11 ... 8 C7
Chancton Cl *WTHG* BN11 .... 150 E2
Chancton Copse
PUL/STOR RH20 .... 266 E10
Chancton View Rd
WTHG BN11 .... 150 E2
Chandler Cl *CRAWE* RH10 .... 8 E8
Chandler Rd *BEXW* TN39 .... 96 F8
CCH PO19 .... 6 B7
Chandler's Md *RING/NEW* BN8 ... 273 R1
Chandlers Reach *SELS* PO20 * ... 139 M6
Chandlers Wy *STEY/UB* BN44 ...... 78 B3
Chandos Ct *BEX* TN40 * 137 J7
Chandos Rd *RTW* TN1 .... 38 B4
WTHG BN11 .... 21 G7
Channel Keep *LHPTN* BN17 * 147 M4
Channel Vw *BOGR* PO21 .... 170 F5
STHW BN42 * 120 D6
Channel Vw East *BEX* TN40 ...... 137 H2
Channel View Rd
BRIE/ROTT BN2 * 124 A5
LW/ROSE BN22 .... 11 L1
PEV BN24 .... 134 D8
Channel Wy West *BEX* TN40 ...... 137 H2
Channel Wy *RHAS* TN35 .... 101 K2
Channers La *RING/NEW* BN8 ...... 245 J5
Chant La *CROW* TN6 .... 69 G8
Chantlers Cl *EGRIN* RH19 .... 31 H7
Chantlers Md *EDEN* TN8 .... 33 M4
Chantrey Rd *CRAWE* RH10 .... 44 K6
Chantry Av *BEX* TN40 .... 97 L1
Chantry Cl *HFD* BN5 .... 269 K5
HORL RH6 .... 22 E5
PUL/STOR RH20 .... 298 G3
Chantryfield Rd *ANG/EP* BN16 ... 114 B12
Chantry La *BEX* TN40 .... 97 H8
PUL/STOR RH20 .... 298 A4

Chantry Rd *HORN* PO8 .... 288 C1
SALV BN13 .... 116 F7
The Chantry *EAST* BN21 * 10 B4
Chapel Barn Cl *HAIL* BN27 .... 92 A3
Chapel Cl *BURH* RH15 .... 74 E4
LHPTN BN17 .... 147 H3
PUL/STOR RH20 .... 264 B9
SEAF BN25 .... 174 A1
Chapel Fld *RYE* TN31 .... 218 D10
WADH TN5 .... 191 P10
Chapelfields *RHWH* RH17 .... 72 C1
Chapel Gdns *BOR* GU35 .... 179 J4
Chapel Gn *CROW* TN6 .... 67 G7
Chapel Hl *BAT* TN33 .... 97 J3
BAT TN33 .... 283 M1
LEWES BN7 .... 17 J5
MFD/CHID GU8 .... 184 A6
Chapel La *CRAWE* RH10 .... 29 L5
EGRIN RH19 .... 48 C3
FROW RH18 .... 48 E5
LEWES BN7 .... 273 K6
PUL/STOR RH20 .... 265 P12
RCCH PO18 .... 293 M3
RHAS TN35 .... 285 K9
RHWH RH17 .... 207 M4
SELS PO20 .... 167 L3
UCK TN22 .... 243 J6
Chapel Ms *HOVE* BN3 * 122 C8
Chapel Park Rd *SLVH* TN37 ...... 12 C5
Chapel Pl *PTSD* BN41 .... 121 G6
RTWE/PEM TN2 .... 38 M7
Chapel Rd *HORL* RH6 .... 26 C3
LEWES BN7 .... 272 H2
PTSD BN41 .... 120 F6
SWTR RH13 .... 201 J11
WTHG BN11 .... 21 H4
Chapel Rw *EGRIN* RH19 .... 62 D2
RCCH PO18 .... 293 M3
Chapel St *BOGR* PO21 .... 2 D8
BRIE/ROTT BN2 * 5 L8
CCH PO19 .... 6 D5
NEWHV BN9 .... 19 G3
PSF GU32 .... 223 N5
Chapel Ter *BRIE/ROTT* BN2 * 5 L8
Chapel Wk *BEX* TN40 .... 97 K7
Chapman Rd *CRAWE* RH10 .... 44 A7
Chapman's La *EGRIN* RH19 ...... 31 L8
Chapmans Town Rd
HTHF TN21 .... 245 L12
Chapman Wy *RTWE/PEM* TN2 ... 38 B1
Chappell Cl *LIPH* GU30 .... 193 R1
Chappell Cft *WTHG* BN11 * 20 D5
Charity Farm Wy *CROW* TN6 ...... 67 M6
Charlecote Rd *WTHG* BN11 ...... 21 H6
Charles Av *BURH* RH15 .... 74 D8
CCH PO19 .... 7 L5
Charles Cl *HOVE* BN3 .... 121 M2
SEAF BN25 .... 159 J4
Charlesfield Rd *HORL* RH6 ...... 23 J5
Charles Moore Ct *POLE* BN26 * ... 131 M6
Charles Rd *STLEO* TN38 .... 12 A7
Charles Rd West *STLEO* TN38 ...... 99 G5
Charles St *BRIE/ROTT* BN2 ...... 4 B8
PSF GU32 .... 223 N5
SBGH/RUST TN4 .... 37 M1
Charleston Ct *CRAWE* RH10 ...... 9 M9
CRAWE RH10 .... 44 A6
Charleston Rd *EAST* BN21 ...... 176 C1
Charlesworth Pk *HWH* RH16 ...... 73 M5
Charlmead *SELS* PO20 .... 167 L3
Charlock Cl *CRAWW* RH11 ...... 42 C7
Charlock Gv *HORL* RH6 .... 23 M5
Charlotte St *BRIE/ROTT* BN2 ...... 5 M8
Charlston Av *NEWHV* BN9 ...... 18 B7
Charlton Dr *EPSF* GU31 .... 223 L7
Charlton Mill Wy *RCCH* PO18 ... 293 J3
Charlton Rd *RCCH* PO18 .... 292 H2
The Charltons *BRI* BN1 .... 83 J7
Charlton St *STEY/UB* BN44 ...... 78 A6
Charlton's Wy *SBGH/RUST* TN4 ... 37 K8
Charlwood Gdns *BURH* RH15 ...... 75 H4
Charlwood La *RDKG* RH5 .... 25 M4
Charlwood Rd *BURH* RH15 ...... 75 H4
CRAWW RH11 .... 26 E7
CRAWW RH11 .... 27 F5
HORL RH6 .... 27 H1
HORL RH6 .... 27 E7
Charlwoods Pl *EGRIN* RH19 ...... 31 K6
Charlwoods Rd *EGRIN* RH19 ...... 31 K6
Charlwood St *BOGR* PO21 .... 2 D7
Charlwood Wk *CRAWW* RH11 ...... 27 G6
Charmandean La *SALV* BN13 ...... 117 J3
Charmandean Rd *SALV* BN13 ...... 117 J2
Charmans Cl *HORS* RH12 * 57 G4
Charm Cl *HORL* RH6 .... 22 D5
Charnwood Rd *MSEA/BNM* PO22 ... 2 A1
Charrington Wy *HORS* RH12 ...... 201 M2
Charter Wk *HASM* GU27 * 181 M11
Chartfield *HOVE* BN3 .... 121 M3
Chartfield Wy *HOVE* BN3 * 122 A3
Chartres *BEX* TN40 .... 97 J7
Chartres Ct *BEX* TN40 .... 97 J7
Chart Wy *HORS* RH12 .... 14 D6
Chartwell Cl *SEAF* BN25 .... 159 K7
Chartwell Dr *HAV* PO9 .... 103 J3
Chartwell Rd *LAN/SOMP* BN15 ... 118 J2
The Chase *CRAWE* RH10 .... 298 H12
SALV BN13 .... 298 H12
Chatburn Av *HORN* PO8 .... 288 A6
Chatelet Cl *HORL* RH6 .... 23 G5
Chatfield Cl *STLEO* TN38 .... 98 D1
Chatfield Crs *LW/ROSE* BN22 ... 163 H3
Chatfield Rd *RHWH* RH17 .... 72 D3
Chatfields *CRAWW* RH11 .... 8 B3
Chatham Gn *LGNY* BN23 .... 165 G3
Chatham Pl *BRI* BN1 .... 4 C5
SEAF BN25 .... 174 E5
Chatham Rd *SLVH* TN37 .... 99 G3
WTHG BN11 .... 151 M2
Chatsmore Crs *HASM* GU27 ...... 181 M9
PEAHV BN10 .... 156 F4
Chatsworth Cl *ANG/EP* BN16 ... 148 A2
PEAHV BN10 .... 156 F4
Chatsworth Ct *ANG/EP* BN16 ... 148 A2
Chatsworth Gdns
EDN/EASTW BN20 .... 176 A5
Chatsworth Pk *PEAHV* BN10 ...... 157 G4
Chatsworth Rd *BRI* BN1 .... 4 B1
CCH PO19 .... 7 L5

WTHG BN11 21 H6
Chatsworth Sq HOVE BN3 122 C6
Chaucer Av ANG/EP BN16 148 A4
EGRIN RH19 47 H1
Chaucer Dr SELS PO20 167 L5
Chaucer Rd CRAWE RH10 44 A1
WTHG BN11 20 D4
Chaucer Wy MSEA/BNM PO22 145 H7
Chaucher Av ANG/EP BN16 148 A4
Chawbrook Ms
LW/ROSE BN22 * 11 G3
Chawbrook Rd LW/ROSE BN22 11 G3
Chawkmare Coppice
BOGR PO21 171 L3
Cheal Cl SHOR BN43 119 M7
Cheam Rd ANG/EP BN16 148 C5
Cheapside BRI BN1 4 F4
Cheeleys RHWH RH17 207 M4
Cheesemans La RCCH PO18 105 K1
Chelgates BEXW TN39 136 B3
Chelsea Ar HWH RH16 * 73 G5
Chelsea Cl BEX TN40 137 J1
Chelston Av HOVE BN3 121 J6
Cheltenham Pl BRI BN1 4 F5
Chelwood Av FERR BN12 150 B4
Chelwood Cl BRI BN1 83 H7
CRAWE RH10 9 J8
Chelwood Gate Rd UCK TN22 208 E3
Chelworth Rd LW/ROSE BN22 163 J3
Chene Rd PEAHV BN10 157 L7
Chenies Cl RTWE/PEM TN2 53 M1
Chennells Brook Cottages
HORS RH12 * 56 E2
Chennells Wy HORS RH12 56 C4
Chepbourne Rd BEXW TN39 137 G1
Chepstow Cl CRAWE RH10 44 D3
Chepstow Ct BRI BN1 * 83 L8
WVILLE PO7 288 C8
Chequer Gra FROW RH18 48 D8
Chequer La RCCH PO18 106 C7
Chequer Rd EGRIN RH19 * 31 L8
Chequers Cl CROW TN6 67 M7
HORL RH6 22 F5
Chequers Ct SWTR RH13 15 G4
Chequers Dr HORL RH6 22 F5
Chequers Wy CROW TN6 67 M7
Cherington Cl HPPT/KEY BN6 271 J4
Cheriton Cl HAV PO9 288 E12
HORN PO8 288 B2
Cherrimans Orch HASM GU27 181 J11
Cherry Av ARUN BN18 145 L3
Cherry Cl BOGR PO21 171 J3
BURH RH15 74 D6
Cherry Ct SWTR RH13 14 F7
Cherry Cft LHPTN BN17 147 J2
Cherry Garden Rd
EDN/EASTW BN20 176 B2
Cherry Gdns HTHF TN21 244 E8
SALV BN13 116 D4
SELS PO20 * 301 K8
Cherrylands Cl HASM GU27 195 L8
Cherry La CRAWW RH11 27 H8
RHWH RH17 205 N4
RHWH RH17 236 D2
SELS PO20 140 E8
Cherry Orchard Rd CCH PO19 7 G7
Cherry Rw PETW GU28 * 229 L9
Cherry Side HAIL BN27 91 M6
Cherry Tree Av HASM GU27 181 J10
HORN PO8 288 C7
Cherry Tree Cl BIL RH14 199 R12
CRAWE RH10 44 C1
SALV BN13 116 C4
SLVH TN37 12 B6
Cherry Tree Dr SELS PO20 110 E5
Cherry Tree Gdns BEX TN40 97 L7
Cherry Tree Rd RTWE/PEM TN2 37 K8
Cherry Wk SALV BN13 116 D4
Chervil Cl HORN PO8 256 D12
Cherwell Cl PEV BN24 132 E8
Cherwell Rd HTHF TN21 244 D5
SALV BN13 116 B5
Cherwell Wk CRAWW RH11 42 E4
Chesham Cl FERR BN12 150 D3
Chesham Pl BRIE/ROTT BN2 5 M9
Chesham Rd BRIE/ROTT BN2 5 M9
Chesham St BRIE/ROTT BN2 5 M9
Cheshire Cl BOGR PO21 2 E5
Cheshire Crs SELS PO20 109 H4
Cheshire Wy EMRTH PO10 104 F3
Chesholt Cl HASM GU27 195 L7
Chesley Cl SALV BN13 116 B7
Chesnut Cl HAIL BN27 91 M4
Chess Brook Gn HFD BN5 269 L2
Chesswood Av
MSEA/BNM PO22 145 H7
Chesswood Cl WTHG BN11 21 M2
Chesswood Rd WTHG BN11 21 K3
Chester Av LAN/SOMP BN15 152 D1
RTWE/PEM TN2 38 C7
WTHG BN11 21 M3
Chesterfield Cl EGRIN RH19 30 B5
Chesterfield Gdns
EDN/EASTW BN20 176 E5
Chesterfield Rd
EDN/EASTW BN20 176 E5
FERR BN12 150 C2
Chesters HORL RH6 22 D4
Chester Ter BRI BN1 122 F4
Chesterton Av SEAF BN25 175 H2
Chesterton Cl EGRIN RH19 47 L2
Chesterton Ct SWTR RH13 15 L2
Chesterton Dr SEAF BN25 175 H2
Chestnut Av CCH PO19 107 L2
HAIL BN27 * 90 A2
HASM GU27 181 M10
HAV PO9 102 C2
HORN PO8 288 D4
SBGH/RUST TN4 38 A1
Chestnut Cl ANG/EP BN16 * 148 E1
BURH RH15 75 G4
EGRIN RH19 31 M8
GSHT GU26 180 E6
HAIL BN27 279 P11
LIPH GU30 194 A2
MIDH GU29 226 G12
PUL/STOR RH20 266 E11
RYE TN31 250 E8
SBGH/RUST TN4 38 A1
Chestnut Ct ANG/EP BN16 148 F4
BOR GU35 178 H7
RTWE/PEM TN2 53 M1
Chestnut Dr POLE BN26 131 M7
Chestnut End BOR GU35 179 N5
Chestnut Gdns HORS RH12 14 C1
HPPT/KEY BN6 270 G2
Chestnut Gv MSEA/BNM PO22 2 D1
Chestnut Rdg PUL/STOR RH20 265 R6
Chestnut Rd BIL RH14 232 A2
HORL RH6 22 F4
Chestnuts Cl HWH RH16 73 K2
The Chestnuts BRIE/ROTT BN2 * 5 G1
HAWK TN18 216 F1
HPPT/KEY BN6 236 E12
HWH RH16 73 J2
SELS PO20 141 M5
Chestnut Wk BEXW TN39 96 B8
CRAWW RH11 27 H8
EGRIN RH19 31 H2
PUL/STOR RH20 265 J3
SALV BN13 150 A1
SELS PO20 109 H4
Chestnut Wy HFD BN5 269 K4
NEWHV BN9 18 C4
Chesworth Cl SWTR RH13 14 D9
Chesworth Crs SWTR RH13 14 D8
Chesworth Gdns SWTR RH13 14 D8
Chesworth La SWTR RH13 14 D8
Chetwood Rd CRAWW RH11 42 C7
Cheveley Gdns BOGR PO21 171 J3
Chevening Cl CRAWW RH11 43 H8
Cheviot Cl ANG/EP BN16 148 F3
LGNY BN23 164 B2
SALV BN13 116 D5
Cheviot Rd SALV BN13 116 D5
The Cheviots HAS TN34 100 A1
Cheviot Wk CRAWW RH11 8 A3
Cheyne Wk HORL RH6 22 F7
Chichester By-Pass CCH PO19 6 A7
Chichester Cl BEXW TN39 97 G7
BRIE/ROTT BN2 * 5 M9
BRIE/ROTT BN2 * 156 B4
CRAWE RH10 43 K7
HOVE BN3 121 K1
LW/ROSE BN22 163 G3
PEAHV BN10 157 L6
Chichester Ct WTHG BN11 * 20 A7
Chichester Dr SELS PO20 109 H4
Chichester Dr East
BRIE/ROTT BN2 156 B5
Chichester Dr West
BRIE/ROTT BN2 156 B4
Chichester Ga CCH PO19 6 C7
Chichester Pl BRIE/ROTT BN2 5 M9
Chichester Rd ARUN BN18 112 B2
BOGR PO21 2 B2
BOGR PO21 143 L6
MIDH GU29 227 J12
SEAF BN25 174 E2
SELS PO20 141 J8
SELS PO20 301 M3
STLEO TN38 99 G3
Chichester Ter HORS RH12 14 E6
Chichester Wy BURH RH15 75 H4
SELS PO20 301 N5
Chick Hl RHAS TN35 286 A9
Chicks La CRBK TN17 191 M3
Chiddingfold Rd
MFD/CHID GU8 183 P6
Chiddingley Cl BRIE/ROTT BN2 123 L8
Chiddingly Cl CRAWE RH10 9 M5
Chidham Cl HAV PO9 102 F3
Chidham Dr HAV PO9 102 F3
Chidham La RCCH PO18 105 K6
Chidham Sq HAV PO9 102 F3
Chidham Wk HAV PO9 102 F3
Chiddingstone Dr RTWE/PEM TN2 38 B8
Chievely Cottages
STLEO TN38 * 99 G4
Chilbolton Ct HAV PO9 289 J11
Chilcomb BURH RH15 75 H8
Chilcombe Cl HAV PO9 103 G2
Chilcroft La HASM GU27 195 L4
Chilcroft Rd HASM GU27 181 J10
Chilcrofts Rd HASM GU27 195 K4
Childerstone Cl LIPH GU30 193 Q1
Chilgrove Cl FERR BN12 150 A2
Chilgrove Pl ARUN BN18 * 145 M3
Chilham Cl LGNY BN23 164 C3
Chillies La UCK TN22 210 B9
Chilling St EGRIN RH19 63 J5
RHWH RH17 207 L1
Chillis Wood Rd HWH RH16 72 F4
Chilmark Ct LISS GU33 192 C9
Chilsham La HAIL BN27 279 N10
Chilston Cl SBGH/RUST TN4 37 M4
Chilston Rd SBGH/RUST TN4 37 M4
Chiltern Cl ANG/EP BN16 148 F3
CRAWW RH11 8 B4
HASM GU27 181 L12
LGNY BN23 164 C2
SHOR BN43 120 B5
Chiltern Crs SALV BN13 116 D5
Chiltern Dr HAS TN34 100 A2
Chiltern Wk RTWE/PEM TN2 38 C5
Chiltington Cl BRIE/ROTT BN2 156 B3
BURH RH15 74 E4
PUL/STOR RH20 265 R7
Chiltington La LEWES BN7 273 M6
Chiltington Wy
BRIE/ROTT BN2 156 B3
Chiltlee Cl LIPH GU30 193 R1
Chiltlee Mnr LIPH GU30 193 R1
Chiltley La LIPH GU30 194 A3
Chiltley Wy LIPH GU30 193 R3
Chilton Cl CRAN GU6 184 G7
Chilworth Gdns HORN PO8 * 256 D9
The Chine LHPTN BN17 147 M5
Chippendale Rd CRAWW RH11 43 G8
Chippers Cl SALV BN13 150 E1
Chippers Rd SALV BN13 116 E8
Chippers Wk SALV BN13 * 150 E1
Chiswick Pl EAST BN21 10 F8
Chitcombe Rd RYE TN31 250 B8
Chithurst La CRAWE RH10 29 K2
LIPH GU30 225 Q3
Chorley Av BRIE/ROTT BN2 156 A3
Chownes Mead La HWH RH16 72 E5
Chown's Hl RHAS TN35 284 D11
Chrisdory Rd PTSD BN41 120 D2
Christchurch Crs BOGR PO21 171 K2
Christchurch Rd WTHG BN11 21 G4
Christie Av RING/NEW BN8 275 J11
Christie Pl MSEA/BNM PO22 2 E1
Christie Rd LEWES BN7 16 B5
Christies EGRIN RH19 47 J1
Christine Cl BEX TN40 97 M7
Christopher Rd EGRIN RH19 31 K8
Christopher Wy EMRTH PO10 104 A3
Christ's Hospital Rd
SWTR RH13 201 L7
Church Ap LHPTN BN17 147 K5
Church Av HWH RH16 73 H3
PEV BN24 133 M7
Church Cl BOGR PO21 170 D6
BRI BN1 82 E8
BURH RH15 74 F6
EDN/EASTW BN20 162 F1
HASM GU27 181 Q7
HORN PO8 256 C7
LAN/SOMP BN15 118 D5
PUL/STOR RH20 267 J9
SALV BN13 115 L4
STEY/UB BN44 78 F2
STPH/PW TN12 188 H1
SWTR RH13 203 M6
SWTR RH13 233 N9
Churchdale Pl LW/ROSE BN22 164 A7
Churchdale Rd LW/ROSE BN22 164 A7
Churcher Rd EMRTH PO10 104 C1
Church Farm Cl
BUR/ETCH TN19 215 P8
Church Farm Ct SELS PO20 * 167 M5
Church Farm La SELS PO20 167 M5
Churchfarm La SELS PO20 169 K3
Church Farm Wk
STEY/UB BN44 78 F2
Churchfield PUL/STOR RH20 264 B2
Churchfield Rd EPSF GU31 223 Q5
Church Flds BOR GU35 179 M4
Churchfields UCK TN22 208 H4
Church Gn SHOR BN43 120 B6
Church Gn Cottages
HASM GU27 * 181 M10
Church Gv PUL/STOR RH20 266 A4
Church Hl ARUN BN18 294 H12
BRI BN1 82 D7
BUR/ETCH TN19 215 N7
EGRIN RH19 62 D3
MIDH GU29 227 J9
NEWHV BN9 18 E5
POY/PYE BN45 271 K11
PUL/STOR RH20 265 J3
RING/NEW BN8 275 J11
TENT TN30 221 L6
Church Hill Av BEXW TN39 136 C1
Church House Cl STHW BN42 120 E4
Church House Ms
MSEA/BNM PO22 * 3 L4
Churchill Av BOGR PO21 171 K1
HORS RH12 14 A4
RHAS TN35 284 G12
Churchill Cl EDN/EASTW BN20 176 D2
Churchill Ct CRAWE RH10 27 L8
HORN PO8 * 288 B3
Churchill Crs BOR GU35 179 N5
Churchill Dr EMRTH PO10 104 A1
Churchill Pde ANG/EP BN16 * 148 B4
Churchill Rd HTHF TN21 244 E7
LEWES BN7 16 C2
SEAF BN25 159 J8
Churchill Sq BRI BN1 * 4 C6
Churchill Wy BURH RH15 75 H7
Church in the Wood La
STLEO TN38 98 E2
Churchland La BAT TN33 249 M10
Church La ARUN BN18 111 K5
ARUN BN18 145 L1
BAT TN33 95 H6
BAT TN33 281 N12
BAT TN33 281 R9
BOGR PO21 170 C5
BOR GU35 179 L3
BUR/ETCH TN19 215 P8
CRAWE RH10 9 K2
CRAWE RH10 28 F7
EAST BN21 * 176 D2
EGRIN RH19 31 L8
FERR BN12 149 K3
GSHT GU26 180 F6
HAIL BN27 278 D12
HASM GU27 181 M10
HAV PO9 103 J5
HFD BN5 269 K4
HORL RH6 28 D3
HORS RH12 201 N2
HPPT/KEY BN6 270 C4
HPPT/KEY BN6 270 E10
HPPT/KEY BN6 271 R6
LAN/SOMP BN15 117 M6
LEWES BN7 16 F3
LEWES BN7 85 J8
LHPTN BN17 113 H7
LHPTN BN17 146 D4
LIPH GU30 179 Q11
LISS GU33 192 A3
MFD/CHID GU8 182 B1
MIDH GU29 260 G6
MSEA/BNM PO22 2 D2
MSEA/BNM PO22 145 G2
PETW GU28 228 A7
PEV BN24 134 A7
POLE BN26 162 B6
POY/PYE BN45 271 K11
PUL/STOR RH20 264 D7
PUL/STOR RH20 267 J9
PUL/STOR RH20 296 B2
RBTBR TN32 216 D12
RCCH PO18 109 J2
RCCH PO18 290 H12
RCCH PO18 292 C4
RHAS TN35 284 B6
RHAS TN35 285 L8
RHWH RH17 75 L3
RHWH RH17 206 C1
RHWH RH17 207 M3
RHWH RH17 207 R6
RHWH RH17 236 B9
RING/NEW BN8 89 L5
RING/NEW BN8 276 D11
RRTW TN3 54 A5
RYE TN31 218 F11
RYE TN31 252 A5
RYE TN31 252 G1
SEAF BN25 174 E3
SELS PO20 109 H4
SELS PO20 110 E6
SELS PO20 140 D8
SELS PO20 141 M5
SELS PO20 169 K2
STEY/UB BN44 78 C2
STEY/UB BN44 78 F3
STEY/UB BN44 268 C4
STHW BN42 120 D6
SWTR RH13 201 N12
SWTR RH13 203 M4
SWTR RH13 234 E10
UCK TN22 210 D12
Church Marks La
RING/NEW BN8 276 G4
Church Md HPPT/KEY BN6 271 P6
STEY/UB BN44 78 C1
Churchmead Cl RCCH PO18 292 C11
Church Meadow RCCH PO18 106 A8
STPH/PW TN12 * 189 M2
Church Pk CRAWW RH11 * 42 F2
Church Pas HAS TN34 * 13 K6
Church Pth BAT TN33 * 281 N12
EMRTH PO10 104 A5
HORN PO8 288 E3
RCCH PO18 290 H5
Church Pl PUL/STOR RH20 265 J3
Church Platt RHWH RH17 72 B4
Church Rd ANG/EP BN16 114 E8
ANG/EP BN16 148 B4
ARUN BN18 145 L2
BAT TN33 281 R9
BURH RH15 74 F7
CCH PO19 7 L2
CRAWE RH10 29 G6
CRAWE RH10 44 D3
CRAWE RH10 45 L6
CRBK TN17 189 R9
CRBK TN17 191 L3
CROW TN6 67 K7
EMRTH PO10 104 C2
EMRTH PO10 104 E6
EMRTH PO10 138 E4
HAIL BN27 93 M4
HASM GU27 181 M10
HASM GU27 195 L8
HAWK TN18 217 N5
HORL RH6 22 E7
HORL RH6 27 K4
HORL RH6 28 F2
HORS RH12 57 G4
HORS RH12 201 N2
HOVE BN3 121 M7
HWH RH16 73 H5
LEWES BN7 17 G5
LHPTN BN17 113 H7
LIPH GU30 179 R11
LYDD TN29 255 R7
MFD/CHID GU8 183 R4
MIDH GU29 227 K11
POLE BN26 131 M7
PSF GU32 223 M2
PTSD BN41 121 G6
RBTBR TN32 248 C8
RHWH RH17 239 J2
RING/NEW BN8 240 D9
RING/NEW BN8 274 D7
RRTW TN3 188 G11
SALV BN13 116 F8
SBGH/RUST TN4 37 L6
SELS PO20 109 M5
SELS PO20 142 C4
SELS PO20 167 L6
SELS PO20 301 L5
SLVH TN37 12 B6
SWTR RH13 202 H4
SWTR RH13 234 E10
UCK TN22 77 K1
Church Rw LEWES BN7 * 16 F5
Churchsettle La WADH TN5 214 B2
Churchside CCH PO19 6 D2
Church Sq RYE TN31 252 H8
Church St ARUN BN18 296 E2
BEX TN40 97 J8
BRI BN1 4 D6
CRAWW RH11 8 D4
CROW TN6 211 P1
EAST BN21 176 D2
EDEN TN8 34 A4
EDN/EASTW BN20 163 G4
HFD BN5 269 K4
HORS RH12 186 B9
HORS RH12 187 Q10
HRTF TN7 50 C5
HTHF TN21 244 C8
LHPTN BN17 147 K4
LISS GU33 192 A7
PETW GU28 229 L9
PTSD BN41 121 G6
PUL/STOR RH20 266 A12
PUL/STOR RH20 266 B4
RHAS TN35 100 B2
RHWH RH17 72 B3
SEAF BN25 174 E2
SHOR BN43 119 L6
STEY/UB BN44 78 C2
UCK TN22 76 E4
WADH TN5 71 M5
Church Vale Rd BEX TN40 97 J8
Church Vw EMRTH PO10 * 104 C2
Church View Cl HORL RH6 22 E7
Church Wk CRAWE RH10 8 F4
HORL RH6 22 E7
WTHG BN11 21 M5
Church Wy BOGR PO21 170 F4
RCCH PO18 292 C2
SALV BN13 116 F8
Church Way Cl SALV BN13 116 F8
Churchwood PUL/STOR RH20 264 C2
Church Wd PUL/STOR RH20 264 C2
Churchwood Dr SELS PO20 109 J4
Church Wood Dr STLEO TN38 98 E1
Church Wood Wy STLEO TN38 98 E3
Churt Rd BOR GU35 179 Q1
RFNM GU10 180 C1
Churt Wynde GSHT GU26 180 G2
Chute Av SALV BN13 116 D4
Chute Wy SALV BN13 116 D5
Chyngton Av SEAF BN25 175 H1
Chyngton Cl LGNY BN23 163 M1
Chyngton Gdns SEAF BN25 175 H1
Chyngton La SEAF BN25 175 J2
Chyngton La North
SEAF BN25 175 J2
Chyngton Pl SEAF BN25 175 H3
Chyngton Rd SEAF BN25 175 G3
Chyngton Wy SEAF BN25 175 J3
Cider Hollow HAIL BN27 * 280 A12
Cinderford La HAIL BN27 278 H9
Cinder Hl EGRIN RH19 63 G8
RING/NEW BN8 239 Q10
Cinquefoil PEAHV BN10 157 H5
Cinque Ports St RYE TN31 252 H7
Cinque Ports Wy SEAF BN25 175 J1
STLEO TN38 98 D7
Cintra Vls HAIL BN27 * 92 B7
Circus Pde BRIE/ROTT BN2 * 4 F6
Circus St BRIE/ROTT BN2 4 F6
The Circus LGNY BN23 164 C5
Cissbury Av PEAHV BN10 157 K7
SALV BN13 116 E3
Cissbury Cl HORS RH12 56 F3
Cissbury Crs BRIE/ROTT BN2 156 D4
Cissbury Dr SALV BN13 116 E2
Cissbury Gdns SALV BN13 116 F2
Cissbury Hl CRAWW RH11 8 C7
Cissbury Rd BURH RH15 74 D5
FERR BN12 149 K2
HOVE BN3 4 A2
SALV BN13 117 H7
City Fields Wy SELS PO20 109 J3
Civic Ap UCK TN22 76 E5
Civic Centre Rd HAV PO9 103 G3
Civic Wy BURH RH15 74 F6
RTW TN1 38 A6
Clackhams La CROW TN6 211 L2
Claigmar Rd ANG/EP BN16 148 B4
Claire Gdns HORN PO8 256 D11
Clair Rd HWH RH16 73 H4
Clairville MFD/CHID GU8 * 182 F5
Clanricarde Gdns RTW TN1 37 M6
Clanricarde Rd RTW TN1 * 37 M6
Clapgate La SWTR RH13 186 F12
Clapham Cl SALV BN13 115 L4
Clapham Common SALV BN13 115 K5
Clapham La POLE BN26 160 F5
Claphatch La WADH TN5 190 F8
Clappers Ga CRAWE RH10 8 F1
Clappers La HFD BN5 270 A10
SELS PO20 168 A7
Clappers Meadow CRAN GU6 184 H7
Clappers Orch CRAN GU6 * 184 G6
The Clappers RBTBR TN32 248 C1
Clare Cl CRAWE RH10 28 B8
Clare Gdns EPSF GU31 223 R6
Clare Ldg ANG/EP BN16 * 148 A4
Claremont HAS TN34 12 F7
Claremont Gdns
RTWE/PEM TN2 38 A7
Claremont Ri UCK TN22 76 E3
Claremont Rd BEXW TN39 97 G6
NEWHV BN9 158 E4
RTW TN1 38 A7
SEAF BN25 174 D2
Claremont Wy MIDH GU29 226 H10
Clarence Av LHPTN BN17 147 H2
Clarence Ct HORL RH6 * 23 J5
Clarence Dr ANG/EP BN16 148 E3
EGRIN RH19 47 L2
Clarence Gdns BRI BN1 4 B6
Clarence Ms SEAF BN25 * 174 E2
Clarence Rd BOGR PO21 2 F7
LW/ROSE BN22 11 G3
RTW TN1 37 M6
SLVH TN37 12 A3
SWTR RH13 14 F7
Clarence Rw RTW TN1 * 37 M6
Clarence Sq BRI BN1 4 C6
Clarence Ter HFD BN5 * 269 K5
Clarence Wy HORL RH6 23 J6
Clarendon Cl SLVH TN37 99 G1
Clarendon Gdns
RTWE/PEM TN2 37 M8
Clarendon Pl BRIE/ROTT BN2 * 5 K8
PTSD BN41 121 H7
Clarendon Rd HAV PO9 102 F4
HOVE BN3 122 A6
SALV BN13 117 K7
SHOR BN43 120 B5
Clarendon Ter BRIE/ROTT BN2 5 M9
Clarendon Vls HOVE BN3 121 M6
Clarendon Wy RTWE/PEM TN2 37 L8
Clare Rd LEWES BN7 16 B4
Clarke Av HOVE BN3 121 L2
Clark Rd CRAWW RH11 42 F8
Claverham Cl BAT TN33 282 C5
Claverham Wy BAT TN33 282 C5
Clavering Wk BEXW TN39 136 A3
Claxton Cl EAST BN21 163 J8
Claxton Rd BEX TN40 97 M8
Clayfields PEAHV BN10 157 G6
Clay Hall La CRAWE RH10 29 H5
Clayhill CRBK TN17 189 Q10
Clay Hl Rd RRTW TN3 188 C12
Clay La CCH PO19 107 H6
PUL/STOR RH20 265 P12
RCCH PO18 106 C4
Claypit La RCCH PO18 108 D3
Clays Cl EGRIN RH19 47 K1
Clays Hl STEY/UB BN44 78 D3
Clayton Av HPPT/KEY BN6 271 N6
Clayton Dr BURH RH15 74 E8
Clayton Hl CRAWW RH11 8 C7
POY/PYE BN45 271 L10
Clayton La SELS PO20 168 A6
Clayton Mill Rd PEV BN24 133 G8
Clayton Rd BRIE/ROTT BN2 5 L3
HPPT/KEY BN6 271 R7
SELS PO20 301 J7
Claytons Cnr SELS PO20 140 D8
Clayton's La RRTW TN3 35 K8
Clayton Wy HOVE BN3 121 L2
Clearwater La RHWH RH17 239 K2
Clearwaters La HWH RH16 75 J1
Cleaver's La RHWH RH17 205 J7
Cleeve Av RTWE/PEM TN2 38 C7
Cleevelands EDN/EASTW BN20 163 G3
Cleeves Wy ANG/EP BN16 148 C3
Clegg St HAS TN34 13 H5
Clement Hill Rd HAS TN34 100 A2
Clementine Av SEAF BN25 159 J8
Clement La POLE BN26 131 M8
Clerks Acre HPPT/KEY BN6 271 P6
Clermont Rd BRI BN1 122 D3
Clermont Ter BRI BN1 122 D3
Cleve Cl UCK TN22 77 K7
Clevedon Rd BEXW TN39 96 E7
Cleveland RTWE/PEM TN2 38 C4
Cleveland Cl LGNY BN23 164 B2
SALV BN13 116 E5
Cleveland Gdns BURH RH15 75 G7
Cleveland Rd BRI BN1 122 F3
CCH PO19 7 H6
SALV BN13 116 E5
Clevelands HWH RH16 * 73 H3
Cleve Ter LEWES BN7 16 E8
Cleve Wy BIL RH14 232 A1
Cliff Ap BRIE/ROTT BN2 154 E1
Cliff Av PEAHV BN10 157 K8
Cliff Cl SEAF BN25 174 F4
Cliffe High St LEWES BN7 17 H6
Cliff End La RHAS TN35 286 A10
Cliff Gdns PEAHV BN10 156 E5
SEAF BN25 174 F4
Clifford Av EAST BN21 163 H7

Clifford Rd BEX TN40....137 H1
Cliff Park Cl PEAHV BN10....157 L6
Cliff Rd BRIE/ROTT BN2....154 E2
  EDN/EASTW BN20....176 B6
  SEAF BN25....174 F4
The Cliff BRIE/ROTT BN2....154 E1
Cliff Wy RHAS TN35....285 Q12
Clifton Cl SALV BN13....163 J5
  HORL RH6....23 J6

Clifton Cottages
  RTWE/PEM TN2 *....38 C1
Clifton Ct WTHG BN11 *....20 F4
Clifton Gdns WTHG BN11 *....20 F4
Clifton Hl BRI BN1....4 B4
Clifton Pl BRI BN1....4 B5
  RTW TN1....38 A7
Clifton St BRI BN1....4 B4
Clifton Ter BRI BN1....4 C5
Cliftonville Rd STLEO TN38....98 C4
Clifton Wy PEAHV BN10....156 F5
Climping Cl HWH RH16....73 L6
Climping Pk LHPTN BN17 *....146 E5
Climping Rd CRAWW RH11....43 G1
Climping St LHPTN BN17....146 D6
Clinch Green Av BEXW TN39....96 A5
Clinton Crs STLEO TN38....99 G4
Clinton La SEAF BN25....174 E2
Clinton Pl SEAF BN25....174 E2
Clinton Wy RHAS TN35....285 Q12
Clitherow Gdns CRAWE RH10....9 G6
Clive Av FERR BN12....150 C3
  RHAS TN35....100 B3
Clive Ct EAST BN21....11 G1
Clivedale Gdns STEY/UB BN44....78 C2
Clive Vls BAT TN33 *....282 F6
Clive Wy CRAWE RH10....44 B3
Clockhouse RTWE/PEM TN2 *....38 C3
Clock House La HASM GU27 *....181 M11
Clock House La UCK TN22....208 H5
Clock Pk MSEA/BNM PO22 *....144 D7
Clock Tower Ct BEXW TN39 *....137 G2
Cloisters NEWHV BN9....18 F3
The Cloisters BAT TN33....282 E2
  LHPTN BN17....147 L5
  LW/ROSE BN22....163 H3
  SLVH TN37....12 C7
Close Eight LGNY BN23....164 D2
Close Eighteen LGNY BN23....164 D3
Close Eleven LGNY BN23....164 D2
Close Fifteen LGNY BN23....164 D3
Close Five LGNY BN23....164 D2
Close Fourteen LGNY BN23....164 D3
Close Nine LGNY BN23....164 D3
Close One LGNY BN23....164 C3
Close Seven LGNY BN23....164 D3
Close Seventeen LGNY BN23....164 D3
Close Six LGNY BN23....164 D3
Close Sixteen LGNY BN23....164 D3
Close Ten LGNY BN23....164 D3
The Close ANG/EP BN16....148 C5
  BIL RH14....198 D2
  BOGR PO21....171 H4
  BRI BN1....82 C8
  BURH RH15....75 H5
  CROW TN6....67 K6
  EDN/EASTW BN20....163 G5
  EDN/EASTW BN20....302 G4
  EGRIN RH19....47 J1
  HORL RH6....23 H8
  HPPT/KEY BN6....271 N5
  LAN/SOMP BN15....152 N1
  MSEA/BNM PO22....145 M8
  NEWHV BN9....158 A3
  PSF GU32....222 C6
  PUL/STOR RH20....267 K8
  RCCH PO18....109 J2
  RCCH PO18....292 C12
  RHAS TN35....101 H1
  RRTW TN3....52 B3
  RYE TN31....252 F7
  SEAF BN25....174 F3
  SELS PO20....301 N5
  SHOR BN43....119 L5
  UCK TN22....243 J7
Close Three LGNY BN23....164 C3
Close Twelve LGNY BN23....164 D3
Close Twenty LGNY BN23....164 D3
Close Twentyfive LGNY BN23....164 C3
Close Twentyfour
  LGNY BN23....164 D3
Close Two LGNY BN23....164 C3
Closewalks MIDH GU29....227 J10
Clothalls La SWTR RH13....234 A8
Cloudesley Rd SLVH TN37....12 A5
Clovelly Av MSEA/BNM PO22....145 M8
Clovelly Dr GSHT GU26....180 F2
Clovelly Rd EMRTH PO10....103 M5
  EMRTH PO10....104 E4
  GSHT GU26....180 F3
Clover Cl BOR GU35....179 K4
Clover Ct HWH RH16 *....73 H6
Cloverlands CRAWE RH10....43 L1
Clover La FERR BN12....149 G4
Cloverlea HAS TN34....284 D12
Clovers End BRI BN1....83 G6
  HORS RH12....56 F4
Clovers Wy HORS RH12....57 J2
Clover Wy PTSD BN41....121 G3
Club Wk ANG/EP BN16....148 F5
Clun Rd LHPTN BN17....147 H2
Cluny St LEWES BN7....16 E8
Clyde Cl SALV BN13....116 B6
  MSEA/BNM PO22....3 B6
  SALV BN13....116 B6
  STLEO TN38....12 H3
Clyde Rd BRI BN1....4 E1
Clyde Ter STEY/UB BN44 *....78 D2
Coach & Horses La
  RHWH RH17....208 B3

Coach & Horses Pas
  RTWE/PEM TN2 *....37 M7
Coach House Cl SELS PO20....301 L6
Coach House Ms WTHG BN11....20 D8
Coach La RHWH RH17....208 B3
Coachmans Dr CRAWW RH11....43 G1
Coach Rd HORL RH6....28 A2
  RCCH PO18....28 A2
  SBGH/RUST TN4....37 H6
  SELS PO20....108 C5
Coastal Rd ANG/EP BN16....149 G5
Coastguard La RHAS TN35....101 H1
  SELS PO20....166 H1
Coastguard Pde BOGR PO21....171 J4
Coastguard La LHPTN BN17....147 J5
Coastguard Sq LW/ROSE BN22....11 J3
  RYE TN31....253 M10
Coast Rd PEV BN24....134 D8
Coates La PUL/STOR RH20....263 P5
Cobald Rd PEV BN24....134 D8
Cobbett Cl CRAWE RH10....44 B1
Cobbetts Md RHWH RH17....73 L6
Cobbett's Ride RTWE/PEM TN2....37 L8
Cobbles Crs CRAWE RH10....9 G2
Cobblewood EMRTH PO10....104 A3
Cobbold Av EAST BN21....163 H7
Cob Cl CRAWE RH10....46 B1
Cobden La HASM GU27....181 N10
Cobden Rd BRIE/ROTT BN2....5 J3
  MIDH GU29....226 H10
  WTHG BN11....20 F4
Cobdown La UCK TN22....241 P1
Cobham Cl ARUN BN18....145 L1
Cobhams RRTW TN3....36 F1
Cobham Wy CRAWE RH10....28 A5
Cob La RHWH RH17....62 A8
Cobnor Cl CRAWW RH11....42 E5
Cobourg Flats HAS TN34 *....13 K6
Cobourg Pl HAS TN34....13 K6
Cobton Dr HOVE BN3....121 M2
Cob Wk CRAWW RH11....42 F4
Cochrane Cl LGNY BN23....164 D6
Cockcrow Rd SLVH TN37....284 A12
Cocking Hl RCCH PO18....260 F9
Cockmount La WADH TN5....71 K3
Cockshut Rd LEWES BN7....16 E9
Cogger's La HTHF TN21....278 C3
Coggins Mill Rd MAYF TN20....212 F6
Coghurst Rd RHAS TN35....100 B3
Cohen Cl SELS PO20....110 C8
Cokeham Gdns
  LAN/SOMP BN15....118 B8
Cokeham La LAN/SOMP BN15....118 B8
Cokeham Rd LAN/SOMP BN15....118 B8
Colbourne Av BRIE/ROTT BN2....123 J3
Colbourne Rd HOVE BN3....4 A3
Colbury Gv HAV PO9....102 D1
Colchester V FROW RH18....48 D7
Colchins BURH RH15....74 E8
Coldean La BRI BN1....83 H5
Coldharbour Cl CROW TN6....67 L8
Coldharbour Farm Rd
  EMRTH PO10....104 A4
Coldharbour La
  RING/NEW BN8....239 R6
  RYE TN31....252 E1
  SALV BN13....115 J3
  HAIL BN27....91 G3
Coldharbour Rd EDEN TN8....35 J1
Coldthorn La POLE RH26....131 M2
Coldwaltham La BURH RH15....75 J8
Colebrook Cl CRAWE RH10....21 M3
Colebrooke Rd BEXW TN39....136 F2
Colebrook La PUL/STOR RH20....264 C8
Colebrook Rd BRI BN1....122 C1
  LHPTN BN17....147 H2
  SBGH/RUST TN4....38 D2
  STHW BN42....120 E6
Cole Cl CRAWW RH11....43 G1
Coleman Av HOVE BN3....121 K6
Colemans Hatch Rd
  FROW RH18....65 G4
Colemore Sq HAV PO9 *....103 G1
Coleridge Cl FERR BN12....150 A2
  HORS RH12....56 D3
Coleridge Crs CRAWE RH10....44 B1
Coleridge Gdns HORN PO8....288 A5
Coleridge Rd FERR BN12....150 A2
Coleridge St HOVE BN3....5 G1
Coles La RDKG RH5....24 A4
Colet Rd CRAWE RH10....43 J6
Colgate Cl BRIE/ROTT BN2....123 J1
  CRAWW RH11....43 G1
Colindale Rd FERR BN12....149 K3
Colindale Rd North
  FERR BN12....149 K3
Collards Ga HASM GU27....181 N11
Collards La HASM GU27....181 N11
Collard Wy LISS GU33....192 C9
College Cl BOGR PO21....171 J4
  EGRIN RH19....31 L8
  HAV PO9....289 K8
  PTSD BN41....120 C2
  RHWH RH17....59 H7
College Ct RTWE/PEM TN2....38 C5
College Gdns BRIE/ROTT BN2....5 H4
  WTHG BN11....20 B5
College Gn EAST BN21....10 B3
College Hl HASM GU27....181 N11
  STEY/UB BN44....78 C3
College Hill Ter HASM GU27....181 M11
College La CCH PO19....107 L6
  EGRIN RH19....31 L8
  HPPT/KEY BN6....271 K4
College Pl BRIE/ROTT BN2....5 H4
  HPPT/KEY BN6....271 K4
College Rd BEX TN40....137 K1
  BRIE/ROTT BN2....5 H4
  CRAWE RH10....10 D8
  EAST BN21....10 D3
  HWH RH16....73 H3
  HWH RH16....206 H3
  SEAF BN25....174 F3
  STEY/UB BN44....79 H4
  SWTR RH13....233 P1
College St BRIE/ROTT BN2....5 H4
  EPSF GU31....223 N6
College Ter BRIE/ROTT BN2....5 K6
Coller Ms CROW TN6....211 L1
Collett Cl STLEO TN38....283 P12
Collier Cl LW/ROSE BN22....164 A6
  PEV BN24....165 J1
Collier Rw CRAWE RH10....8 F3
Collingford La RHWH RH17....208 A5

Collington Av BEXW TN39....136 F2
Collington Cl
  EDN/EASTW BN20....176 E4
Collington Gv BEXW TN39....136 D1
Collington La East
  BEXW TN39....136 E1
Collington La West
  BEXW TN39....136 D2
Collington Park Crs
  BEXW TN39....136 E1
Collington Ri BEXW TN39....136 D1
Collingwood Av HTHF TN21....244 D6
Collingwood Cl EGRIN RH19....47 L2
  HORL RH6....23 G7
  LGNY BN23....164 D7
  PEAHV BN10....157 H4
Collingwood Ri HTHF TN21....244 D6
Collingwood Rd CRAWE RH10....44 C4
  FERR BN12....150 B1
  HORS RH12....14 C1
Collingwood Wy EPSF GU31....223 R5
Collins Cl SELS PO20....110 E5
Collins La EPSF GU31....224 C10
Collins Rd CRAWW RH11....42 D5
Collinstone Rd STLEO TN38....98 F6
Collinswood Dr STLEO TN38....98 F6
Collyer Av BOGR PO21....2 A3
Collyers Crs LIPH GU30....194 B1
Colmer Cl BURH RH15....74 D6
Colmer Pl BURH RH15....74 D6
Colne Cl SALV BN13....116 B7
Colonnade Rd EAST BN21....11 H6
Colonsay Rd CRAWW RH11....8 A9
Coltash Rd CRAWE RH10....9 L6
Colt's Bay BOGR PO21....171 J4
Coltsfoot Dr HORS RH12....56 B3
  WVILLE PO7....288 B12
Colts Ford Rd BOR GU35....179 K4
Coltstaple La SWTR RH13....202 B5
Coltstocks Rd
  EDN/EASTW BN20....176 D5
Colt St SELS PO20....301 L5
Columbia Dr SALV BN13....116 B7
Columbine Wy LHPTN BN17....148 A1
Columbus Dr LGNY BN23....164 E7
Colvill Av SHOR BN43....119 J5
Colwell Cl HWH RH16....73 J6
Colwell Gdns HWH RH16....73 J6
Colwell La RHWH RH17....73 J8
Colwell Rd HWH RH16....73 J7
Colwood Crs
  EDN/EASTW BN20....163 G7
Colwood La RHWH RH17....204 C11
Colwyn Cl CRAWW RH11....42 D5
Combe Dr STEY/UB BN44....78 C3
Combe End CROW TN6....210 G1
Combe La BAT TN33....281 L11
  EDN/EASTW BN20....176 D6
  MFD/CHID GU8....182 A4
Combe Rd EDN/EASTW BN20....163 G3
  LEWES BN7....17 H3
Combe Rd LISS GU33....192 E12
The Combe EDN/EASTW BN20....162 F6
Combe Vw MFD/CHID GU8....182 F5
Comfrey Cl HORN PO8....256 D12
Comley Hl HAV PO9....289 K10
Commanders Wk RHAS TN35....101 K1
Command Rd
  EDN/EASTW BN20....163 G8
Commerce Wy
  LAN/SOMP BN15....118 B8
  EAST BN21....10 E5
  RTW TN1....38 A4
Commercial Square Rbt
  HWH RH16....73 H1
Common Hl PUL/STOR RH20....265 R6
Common La HPPT/KEY BN6....272 A4
  POLE BN26....129 M4
  RING/NEW BN8....276 B9
Commonmead La BOGR PO21....170 F3
Common Rd EMRTH PO10....290 C12
  RCCH PO18....290 G12
Commonside EMRTH PO10....289 Q12
The Common MIDH GU29 *....226 G9
  PUL/STOR RH20....265 R5
  SBGH/RUST TN4....37 L6
Common Vw MIDH GU29....226 C8
  SBGH/RUST TN4....37 H6
Common Wood Ri CROW TN6....67 L5
Compass Cl LHPTN BN17....147 M3
Compass Ct PTSD BN41 *....120 E2
Compasses La HAIL BN27....94 A1
Compassion Cl CRAWW RH11....42 C2
Compass La BAT TN33....281 L9
Comper Cl CRAWW RH11....42 D5
Comphurst La HAIL BN27....94 A1
Compton Av BRI BN1....4 C4
  FERR BN12....150 A3
Compton Cl BEX TN40....137 K1
  CCH PO19....107 M2
  HAV PO9....103 G2
Compton Dr
  EDN/EASTW BN20....176 D6
  MSEA/BNM PO22....145 J7
Compton Place Rd
  EDN/EASTW BN20....176 D2
Compton Rd BRI BN1....122 D4
  HWH RH16....73 L1
Comptons Brow La SWTR RH13....15 K3
Comptons Ct SWTR RH13....15 J3
Comptons La SWTR RH13....15 J3
Compton St EAST BN21....10 E7
Compton Ter HAIL BN27....92 B7
The Compts PEAHV BN10....157 H4
Conbar Av BEXW TN39....148 B3
Concord Cl RTWE/PEM TN2....38 B5
Concorde St RTWE/PEM TN39....96 E7
  PUL/STOR RH20....266 D10
Conde Wy BOR GU35....178 H7
Condor Wy BURH RH15....74 D6
Conduit Hl RYE TN31....252 H8
Conduit Md CCH PO19....7 J1
Coneyburrow Gdns
  STLEO TN38....98 D1
Coneyburrow La BEXW TN39....95 M8
Coneyburrow Rd
  RTWE/PEM TN2....38 C4
Coney Cl CRAWW RH11....43 G1
  SELS PO20....167 L7
Coney Cft HORS RH12....57 G4
Coney Furlong PEAHV BN10....157 J4
Coneyhurst Rd BIL RH14....232 B1
Coney Rd SELS PO20....167 L7

Coney Six SELS PO20....167 L7
Conford Ct HAV PO9....288 E11
Conghurst La HAWK TN18....216 H3
Congreve Rd SALV BN13....21 J1
Conifer Cl BOR GU35....178 F8
  HAS TN34....99 G3
  HORN PO8 *....288 B7
Conifer Dr RCCH PO18....105 K3
Conifers Wy BOGR PO21....170 E3
The Conifers EAST BN21....10 D3
Conifer Wy BOGR PO21....170 E3
Conigar Rd EMRTH PO10....104 A2
Coniston Av SBGH/RUST TN4....37 K5
Coniston Cl CRAWW RH11....42 C5
  HORS RH12....57 G4
  LAN/SOMP BN15....118 B7
  MSEA/BNM PO22....145 G7
Coniston Rd BOR GU35....178 F4
  FERR BN12....150 B1
  LGNY BN23....164 B1
Coniston Wy LHPTN BN17....147 M2
Connaught Av SHOR BN43....119 K5
Connaught Cl BOR GU35....178 G7
Connaught Gdns CRAWE RH10....43 J1
Connaught Rd EAST BN21....10 D3
  HAV PO9....103 H4
  HOVE BN3....121 M7
  LHPTN BN17....147 J4
  SEAF BN25....174 D2
Connaught Ter HOVE BN3....122 A6
Connaught Wy SBGH/RUST TN4....37 L4
Connell Dr BRIE/ROTT BN2....124 D6
Connolly Wy CCH PO19....107 M4
Conqueror Ter BAT TN33 *....249 N12
Consort Wy BURH RH15....74 D7
  HORL RH6....22 F6
Consort Wy East HORL RH6....23 G7
Constable Dr SELS PO20....301 M6
Constable Rd CRAWE RH10....43 L7
  LGNY BN23....164 C4
Constable Wy BEX TN40....97 K8
Convent Gdns SALV BN13....298 H11
Convent La EMRTH PO10....104 A5
Conway Ct STLEO TN38 *....99 G7
Conway Dr BOGR PO21....170 F5
Conway Pl HOVE BN3....122 A5
Conway St HOVE BN3....122 A5
Cooden Cl BEXW TN39....136 B2
Cooden Dr BEXW TN39....136 C3
Cooden Ledge STLEO TN38....283 N10
Cooden Sea Rd BEXW TN39....136 B3
Cook Av LGNY BN23....164 D7
Cook Rd CRAWE RH10....9 H8
Cooksbridge Rd
  BRIE/ROTT BN2....123 K7
Cooks Hl HORS RH12....185 N8
Cooks La EMRTH PO10....104 F4
  RCCH PO18....290 E7
Cooks Md HORS RH12....41 J2
Cooks Meadow HORS RH12....41 J2
Cookson Gdns HAS TN34....100 B3
Cook's Pond Rd LIPH GU30....225 P1
Cookstown Cl BAT TN33....281 L11
Coolham Dr BRIE/ROTT BN2....123 J4
Coolham Rd PUL/STOR RH20....266 E3
  SWTR RH13....232 G9
Coolhurst La SWTR RH13....15 L7
Coombe Cl BIL RH14....200 A12
  CRAWW RH11....27 J8
  HAIL BN27....280 A12
Coombe Crs PUL/STOR RH20....296 B2
Coombe Dro STEY/UB BN44....78 C3
Coombe Hl BIL RH14....200 A12
Coombe Hill Rd EGRIN RH19....47 H3
Coombe Lands TENT TN30....220 C5
Coombelands La
  PUL/STOR RH20....264 D2
Coombe La ARUN BN18....297 K10
  WADH TN5....213 M2
Coombe Lea HOVE BN3 *....122 B7
Coombe Ri BRIE/ROTT BN2....156 C2
  SALV BN13....116 F3
Coombe Rd BRIE/ROTT BN2....123 J4
  EDN/EASTW BN20....176 C1
  LEWES BN7....17 H3
  STEY/UB BN44....78 B3
Coombers RHWH RH17....60 F8
Coombes La HWH RH16....73 L4
Coombe Shaw BAT TN33....283 M11
Coombes Rd LAN/SOMP BN15....78 B3
  LAN/SOMP BN15....119 H4
Coombe Ter BRIE/ROTT BN2....123 H4
Coombe V BRIE/ROTT BN2....156 C2
Coombs Cl HORN PO8....256 D12
  RYE TN31....219 M12
Coomes Wy LHPTN BN17....147 J1
Cooper Dr BEXW TN39....97 G3
Cooper Ri SLVH TN37....283 P12
Cooper Rd RYE TN31....252 F1
Cooper Rw CRAWE RH10....8 F3
Coopers Farm Cl
  MSEA/BNM PO22....2 F2
Cooper's Hl BUR/ETCH TN19....246 C1
  EDN/EASTW BN20....163 G3
Coopers La CROW TN6....67 J5
  RRTW TN3....36 B3
The Coopers SWTR RH13....200 C9
Cooper St CCH PO19....6 E5
Coopers Wy HAIL BN27....91 M7
  HFD BN5....269 L4
Coopers Wd CROW TN6....67 J5
Coos La RHWH RH17....204 B5
Cootes La MSEA/BNM PO22....145 J4
Cootes La MSEA/BNM PO22....201 R2
Copeland Rd MSEA/BNM PO22....3 M5
Copestake Dr BURH RH15....75 J6
Coplands Ri RYE TN31....218 E10
Copnall Wy HORS RH12....14 D6
Coppards La RHWH RH17....238 F9
Copped Hall Dr RYE TN31....218 F9
Copper Beech Dr SELS PO20....109 H4
Copper Hall Cl ANG/EP BN16 *....148 A5
Copper Beeches SLVH TN37....99 H1
Copperfield Pl HORS RH12....14 A2
Copperfields LYDD TN29....255 Q7
  SWTR RH13....202 B5
Copthall Hawk TN18 *....218 G3

Coppice Pl MFD/CHID GU8....182 E1
Coppice Rd HORS RH12....56 F4
The Coppice BAT TN33....282 H6
  CRAWE RH10....12 F4
  HAS TN34....12 F4
  HORN PO8....288 B3
  RHWH RH17....239 J2
  RTWE/PEM TN2....39 J2
Coppice Vw HTHF TN21....244 E7
Coppice Wk CRAWE RH10....9 M1
Coppice Wy HWH RH16....73 G6
Coppice Wd SWTR RH13....202 D12
Copse Cl CRAWE RH10....46 A1
  EGRIN RH19....1 L6
  EPSF GU31....223 R5
  HORS RH12....56 E3
  LISS GU33....192 D9
  STLEO TN38....98 C2
Copse Crs CRAWW RH11....8 C2
Copse Hl BRI BN1....82 C8
Copse La ARUN BN18....111 H4
  HORL RH6....23 J5
Copse Rd BEXW TN39....136 D1
  HASM GU27....180 G12
The Copse CCH PO19....107 M3
  HWH RH16....73 L4
  RTWE/PEM TN2....201 Q11
Copse Vw ANG/EP BN16....148 E3
Copthall HAWK TN18 *....218 G3
Copthorne Bank CRAWE RH10....29 G5
Copthorne Cl SALV BN13....116 F6
  CRAWE RH10....29 H6
Copthorne Common Rd
  CRAWE RH10....29 H6
Copthorne Hl SALV BN13....116 E6
Copthorne Rd CRAWE RH10....28 D8
  CRAWE RH10....30 A5
Copthorne Wy BOGR PO21....171 J1
  CRAWE RH10....28 E7
Copwood Av UCK TN22....76 D5
Copyhold Hl HASM GU27....195 M5
Copyhold La HWH RH16....72 C5
  RHWH RH17....72 C5
Coral Cl SELS PO20....300 H5
Coralin Gv WVILLE PO7....288 C8
Coral La SELS PO20....300 H5
Coral Reef Cl LGNY BN23....164 F4
Cora's Wk POY/PYE BN45....81 H1
Corbishley Gn
  MSEA/BNM PO22....144 B7
Corbishley Rd MSEA/BNM PO22....2 C1
Corbyn Crs SHOR BN43....119 M6
Cordal Cl ANG/EP BN16....148 A6
Cordons LEWES BN7....85 J8
Corfe Cl SALV BN13....116 A8
  SWTR RH13....201 R12
Corhampton Crs HAV PO9....102 E1
Cormorant Cl LGNY BN23....164 B3
Cormorant Wy SELS PO20....167 M7
Cornbrook Gv WVILLE PO7....288 D8
Cornelius Av NEWHV BN9....18 B7
Cornelius Dr WVILLE PO7....288 C8
Corner Garth FERR BN12....149 L4
Cornfield Cl LHPTN BN17....147 K2
  SEAF BN25....174 F2
Cornfield La EAST BN21....10 E8
Cornfield Rd EAST BN21....10 E7
  SEAF BN25....174 F2
The Cornfields SELS PO20....10 E7
Cornfield Ter EAST BN21....10 E7
  SLVH TN37....12 C8
Cornflower Cl CCH PO19....7 K1
Cornflower Wy SWTR RH13....201 R10
Cornford Cl BURH RH15....74 D4
  CROW TN6....67 M8
  PTSD BN41....121 G3
  RTWE/PEM TN2....39 G2
Cornford La RTWE/PEM TN2....38 D5
Cornford Pk RTWE/PEM TN2....39 G5
Cornish Cl LGNY BN23....164 A1
Cornmill Gdns POLE RH26....162 D1
Cornwall Av PEAHV BN10....157 K8
Cornwall Gdns BRI BN1....122 D2
  EGRIN RH19....47 L1
  LHPTN BN17....147 J3
Cornwallis Cl LGNY BN23....164 E6
Cornwallis Gdns HAS TN34....13 H7
Cornwallis St HAS TN34....13 H6
Cornwallis Ter HAS TN34....13 H6
Cornwall Rd BEXW TN39....137 G2
  BOR GU35....178 G8
  LHPTN BN17....147 J3
Cornwood Rd BIL RH14 *....198 C11
Coronation Cottages
  RBTBR TN32....216 D12
  BUR/ETCH TN19....216 A6
Coronation Gdns BAT TN33....282 G4
Coronation Rd EGRIN RH19....47 K2
Coronation St BRIE/ROTT BN2....5 J2
  LYDD TN29....255 R7
The Coronet HORL RH6....23 H8
Corry Rd GSHT GU26....180 F3
Corseley Rd RRTW TN3....51 L6
Corsica Cl SEAF BN25....174 F4
Corsica Rd SEAF BN25....174 F4
Corsletts Av HORS RH12....201 N2
Cortis Av SALV BN13....117 H8
Corunna Dr SWTR RH13....15 J5
Cory Cl CCH PO19....6 F5
Costells Edge RHWH RH17....239 J1
Cotchford Hl HRTF TN7....50 A8
Cotchford La HRTF TN7....50 A8
Cote St SALV BN13....116 B4
Cotland Rd SELS PO20....301 M7
Cot La RCCH PO18....105 J3
Cotsford Rd CRAWW RH11....59 G3
Cotswold Cl CRAWW RH11....8 A1
  HAS TN34....100 A1
  HAV PO9....288 F11
  LGNY BN23....164 B1
  SALV BN13....116 C3
Cotswold Ct SWTR RH13....15 G5
Cotswold Rd BRIE/ROTT BN2 *....123 J8
Cotswold Rd SALV BN13....116 C3
The Cotswolds STHW BN42....120 E6
Cotswold Wy ANG/EP BN16....148 F5
Cottage Cl BOGR PO21....171 G3
  HORS RH12....57 G3
  NEWHV BN9....158 C4
Cottage La BAT TN33....283 M2
  PEV BN24....132 D4
  RHAS TN35....284 B5
Cottage Pl CRAWE RH10....9 K3
Cottenham Rd WTHG BN11....21 H4
Cottingham Av HORS RH12....56 C2

Cotton Dr EMRTH PO10 103 M2
Cottrell Cl ANG/EP BN16 114 E8
The Cottrells ANG/EP BN16 114 E8
Cotwell Av HORN PO8 288 C5
Coulstock Rd BURH RH15 74 B5
Coultershaw Br PETW GU28 263 K2
Countisbury Cl BOGR PO21 171 L2
Countryman La SWTR RH13 233 L10
Countryside Farm Pk
STEY/UB BN44 * 78 F2
County Oak Av BRI BN1 83 G7
County Oak La CRAWE RH10 27 J6
County Oak Wy CRAWW RH11 27 J7
The Course LEWES BN7 16 D8
Court Barn La SELS PO20 140 D8
Court Cl BRI BN1 82 D6
EGRIN RH19 31 L8
LIPH GU30 193 Q2
Court Crs EGRIN RH19 31 M8
Courtenwell RRTW TN3 * 36 D5
Court Farm Cl NEWHV BN9 158 A3
Court Farm Rd
BRIE/ROTT BN2 155 K2
HOVE BN3 121 L3
NEWHV BN9 18 D8
Courtfields LAN/SOMP BN15 * 118 C8
Courthope Av WADH TN5 71 L5
Courthope Dr BEXW TN39 96 D8
Courthouse St HAS TN34 13 K6
Courtland Rd POLE BN26 131 M8
Courtlands HWH RH16 73 H6
UCK TN22 209 J7
Courtlands Cl FERR BN12 150 D4
Courtlands Pl CROW TN6 67 K8
Courtlands Rd LW/ROSE BN22 10 F1
Courtlands Ter HORN PO8 * 288 B5
Courtlands Wy FERR BN12 150 D4
MSEA/BNM PO22 145 H7
Court Lodge Rd HORL RH6 22 D5
RASHW TN26 221 P2
Court Meadow CROW TN6 211 Q1
Courtmead Rd RHWH RH17 72 C3
Court Ord Rd BRIE/ROTT BN2 155 K2
Court Rd LEWES BN7 17 H7
LW/ROSE BN22 163 L3
SBGH/RUST TN4 37 K5
Courts Hill Rd HASM GU27 181 L11
Courts Mount Rd HASM GU27 181 L11
The Court BOGR PO21 170 F4
EDN/EASTW BN20 * 163 G4
Courtwick La LHPTN BN17 147 H1
Courtwick Rd LHPTN BN17 147 H2
The Courtyard CRAWE RH10 * 8 F5
EGRIN RH19 32 A8
EPSF GU31 223 N6
HAS TN34 * 12 E4
HORS RH12 * 14 C5
WTHG BN11 * 20 C4
Cousins Wy PUL/STOR RH20 265 K2
Cousley Wood Rd WADH TN5 71 M3
Coventry Cl BOGR PO21 171 J1
Coventry Ct LW/ROSE BN22 * 164 C7
WTHG BN11 * 20 A6
Coventry Rd STLEO TN38 98 F2
Coventry St BRI BN1 122 D5
Coverdale Av BEXW TN39 136 B2
Cove Rd ANG/EP BN16 148 A5
The Covers SEAF BN25 174 F3
Covert Cl CRAWE RH10 9 G1
Covert Gv WVILLE PO7 288 B12
Covert Md PUL/STOR RH20 267 J8
RHWH RH17 204 C2
The Covert BEXW TN39 136 B3
The Covey CRAWE RH10 44 D1
Covington Rd EMRTH PO10 289 Q12
Cowden Cl HAWK TN18 216 F1
Cowden Hall La HTHF TN21 278 G4
Cowden La HAWK TN18 216 F2
Cowden Ms EDEN TN8 33 M4
Cowden Rd BRIE/ROTT BN2 156 C5
Cowdens Cl HOVE BN3 121 J1
Cowdown La RCCH PO18 257 R9
Cowdray Cl ANG/EP BN16 148 A2
BEXW TN39 96 C7
CRAWE RH10 44 B4
FERR BN12 150 C4
Cowdray Ct FERR BN12 * 150 A5
MIDH GU29 227 J9
Cowdray Dr ANG/EP BN16 148 A2
FERR BN12 150 C4
Cowdray Park Rd BEXW TN39 96 B7
Cowdray Rd MIDH GU29 227 K8
Cowfold Cl CRAWW RH11 42 E6
Cowfold Rd BRIE/ROTT BN2 123 K8
RHWH RH17 236 B3
SWTR RH13 234 E4
Cowhurst La BEXW TN39 97 H6
Cow La EPSF GU31 258 D2
POLE BN26 160 E5
SELS PO20 169 J6
Cowley Dr BRIE/ROTT BN2 124 E6
LAN/SOMP BN15 118 E8
Cowper Rd WTHG BN11 20 D5
Cowper St HOVE BN3 121 M6
Cowslip Cl BOR GU35 179 K5
SWTR RH13 201 R11
Coxcombe La MFD/CHID GU8 182 G5
Coxes Meadow PSF GU32 223 M4
Coxes Rd SELS PO20 301 J7
Cox Green Rd HORS RH12 185 Q7
Cox Gv BURH RH15 74 D4
Coxham La STEY/UB BN44 78 B1
Coxheath Cl STLEO TN38 283 M10
Coxswain Wy SELS PO20 301 L8
Crabbet Rd CRAWE RH10 44 A2
Crabden La HORN PO8 288 F1
Crablands SELS PO20 301 J6
Crablands Cl SELS PO20 301 K6
Crabtree Ar LAN/SOMP BN15 * 118 D7
Crabtree Av BRI BN1 82 F8
Crabtree Gdns BOR GU35 179 M4
Crabtree La BOR GU35 179 M4
LAN/SOMP BN15 118 D7
Crabtree Rd CRAWW RH11 8 D2
Crabwood Ct HAV PO9 288 E10
Cradle Hill Rd SEAF BN25 159 M7
Cradock Pl SALV BN13 116 D5
Crafts La EPSF GU31 223 P4
Craggits La HFD BN5 269 K4
Craigans CRAWW RH11 42 F3
Craig Cl BAT TN33 282 H11
Craignair Av BRI BN1 82 E6
Craigwell La BOGR PO21 171 K4
Craigwell Mnr BOGR PO21 171 J4
Cranborne Av
EDN/EASTW BN20 176 C5
Cranborne Wk CRAWE RH10 9 K8
Cranbourne Cl HORL RH6 * 23 G4
Cranbourne St BRI BN1 4 D6
Cranbrook Rd SLVH TN37 12 B4
Cranedown LEWES BN7 85 M6
Crane St CCH PO19 6 E4
Cranfield Rd BEX TN40 137 H1
Cranford Gdns BOGR PO21 2 D4
Cranford Rd PSF GU32 223 M7
Cranham Av BIL RH14 231 R3
Cranleigh Av BRIE/ROTT BN2 156 A4
Cranleigh Cl BEXW TN39 136 F1
Cranleigh Rd SALV BN13 117 G8
Cranmer Av HOVE BN3 121 L4
Cranmer Cl LEWES BN7 * 17 H3
Cranmer Rd SALV BN13 20 A3
Cranston Av BEXW TN39 136 E1
Cranston Cl BEXW TN39 136 E1
Cranston Ri BEXW TN39 136 E1
Cranston Rd EGRIN RH19 31 L7
Cranwell Rd SBGH/RUST TN4 37 H5
Cranworth Rd WTHG BN11 21 L3
Craven Pl BRIE/ROTT BN2 * 5 L6
Craven Rd BRIE/ROTT BN2 5 L6
CRAWE RH10 44 A4
The Cravens HORL RH6 23 M6
Crawford Gdns SWTR RH13 15 H2
Crawfurd Wy EGRIN RH19 31 L7
Crawley Av CRAWE RH10 28 B7
CRAWE RH10 43 K1
CRAWW RH11 8 A6
HAV PO9 288 H11
Crawley Crs LW/ROSE BN22 163 K3
Crawley Down Rd EGRIN RH19 30 D6
Crawley La CRAWE RH10 44 B2
RHWH RH17 60 D5
Crawley Rd BRI BN1 83 J7
HORS RH12 15 K2
Crawters Cl CRAWE RH10 9 J2
Crayford Rd BRIE/ROTT BN2 123 J4
Cray La PUL/STOR RH20 231 L12
Cray's La PUL/STOR RH20 266 F6
Crazy La BAT TN33 283 M2
Creasys Dr CRAWW RH11 59 G1
Crecy Cl SLVH TN37 283 N10
Crede La RCCH PO18 106 B7
Creek End CCH PO19 107 G7
Cremorne Pl PSF GU32 223 N5
Crescenta Wk BOGR PO21 171 M2
Crescent Cl BRIE/ROTT BN2 124 D5
BURH RH15 75 G6
Crescent Ct HORL RH6 * 22 F8
Crescent Dr North
BRIE/ROTT BN2 124 E5
Crescent Dr South
BRIE/ROTT BN2 124 E6
Crescent Pl BRIE/ROTT BN2 5 K9
Crescent Ri PUL/STOR RH20 266 D10
Crescent Rd BOGR PO21 2 D7
BRIE/ROTT BN2 5 G1
BURH RH15 74 F6
EGRIN RH19 31 J8
RTW TN1 38 A6
WTHG BN11 20 F6
The Crescent ANG/EP BN16 147 M5
ANG/EP BN16 * 148 F5
BOGR PO21 170 F5
BRIE/ROTT BN2 123 K3
EDN/EASTW BN20 162 F2
EDN/EASTW BN20 163 G8
EGRIN RH19 31 H1
EMRTH PO10 104 E5
HORL RH6 22 F8
HORS RH12 201 R3
HPPT/KEY BN6 271 Q6
LAN/SOMP BN15 152 D1
MSEA/BNM PO22 3 M4
NEWHV BN9 158 E4
PUL/STOR RH20 265 P12
SELS PO20 167 K6
SLVH TN37 99 H2
STEY/UB BN44 78 C3
STHW BN42 120 E5
Crescent Wy BURH RH15 74 F6
HORL RH6 22 F8
Crespin Wy BRI BN1 123 H4
Cresta Cl POLE BN26 131 M6
Cresta Rd NEWHV BN9 18 A5
Crestland Cl HORN PO8 288 B6
Crest Rd NEWHV BN9 158 E4
Crest Wy PTSD BN41 121 G2
Crestway Pde BRI BN1 * 123 H3
The Crestway BRI BN1 123 H4
Crewdson Rd HORL RH6 23 G6
Cricket Ct EGRIN RH19 31 K6
Cricket Dr HORN PO8 288 B4
Cricketers Cl PUL/STOR RH20 267 K8
Cricketers Fld RBTBR TN32 249 M4
Cricketers Pde SALV BN13 * 117 J7
Cricketfield RING/NEW BN8 240 C5
Cricket Field Rd HORS RH12 14 A8
Cricketfield Rd SEAF BN25 174 F3
Cricketing La HAIL BN27 93 H1
Cricket Lea BOR GU35 179 J4
Criers La UCK TN22 211 N10
Crimbourne La BIL RH14 230 D5
Crink Hl RING/NEW BN8 274 E6
Cripland Cl HWH RH16 73 L3
Cripplecrutch Hl
MFD/CHID GU8 182 E11
Cripplegate La SWTR RH13 233 R1
Cripps Av PEAHV BN10 157 J4
Cripps La STEY/UB BN44 78 D2
Crisp Rd LEWES BN7 16 B2
Crisspyn Cl HORN PO8 * 288 C3
Critchel's La SELS PO20 169 H4
Critchfield Rd RCCH PO18 106 A8
Critchmere Dr SELS PO20 110 E6
Critchmere Hl HASM GU27 180 H10
Critchmere La HASM GU27 180 H11
Critchmere V HASM GU27 180 G11
Crittle's Ct WADH TN5 71 L5
Crocket Cl GSHT GU26 180 G3
Crockendale Fld
RING/NEW BN8 * 275 K11
Crockers La RYE TN31 218 E9
Crockford Rd EMRTH PO10 104 C1
Crockham Cl CRAWW RH11 8 C7
Crockhurst SWTR RH13 201 R11
Crockhurst Hl SALV BN13 116 E5
Crocks Dean PEAHV BN10 157 J3
Croft Av STHW BN42 120 E6
Croft Cl POLE BN26 162 F1
Croft Ct EAST BN21 * 10 A4
EAST BN21 * 11 G5
SEAF BN25 174 E2
Croft Dr PTSD BN41 120 F2
Crofters Wd STEY/UB BN44 78 E3
Croft La HFD BN5 269 J5
SEAF BN25 174 E2
Croft Md CCH PO19 107 M3
Crofton Park Av BEXW TN39 136 D2
Croft Rd BRI BN1 122 C1
CROW TN6 67 L8
HAS TN34 13 L4
SELS PO20 301 K7
Crofts Cl MFD/CHID GU8 182 G4
Croft Ter HAS TN34 13 K5
The Croft ANG/EP BN16 148 F4
ARUN BN18 145 L1
BEXW TN39 * 136 F1
BOGR PO21 143 L8
BRI BN1 * 4 B1
CRAWW RH11 42 F3
EDN/EASTW BN20 163 G4
HAS TN34 13 K5
HPPT/KEY BN6 271 N4
MIDH GU29 260 G5
PETW GU28 228 A6
Croft Vls HFD BN5 * 269 L4
Croft Wy HORS RH12 201 R2
MSEA/BNM PO22 145 H7
SELS PO20 301 K6
Croft Works HAIL BN27 92 A6
Croham Rd CROW TN6 67 L6
Crombie Cl HORN PO8 288 A5
Cromer Wk HAS TN34 13 H3
Cromer Wy HAIL BN27 91 M4
Cromleigh Wy STHW BN42 120 D3
Crompton Flds CRAWE RH10 27 K8
Crompton Wy CRAWE RH10 43 K1
Cromwell Pl EGRIN RH19 47 L2
Cromwell Rd BURH RH15 74 E6
HOVE BN3 122 B6
RTWE/PEM TN2 38 B6
Cromwell St BRIE/ROTT BN2 5 K3
Crondall Av HAV PO9 288 F11
Crooked La SEAF BN25 174 F3
SELS PO20 140 D8
Crookham Cl HAV PO9 102 D1
Crookthorn La LHPTN BN17 146 E5
Cropthorne Dr LHPTN BN17 146 D4
Crosbie Cl CCH PO19 141 L2
Crosby Cl SALV BN13 116 C7
Croshaw Cl LAN/SOMP BN15 118 C8
Crossbill Cl HORN PO8 * 288 B2
Crossbush La ARUN BN18 113 K4
Crossbush Rd BRIE/ROTT BN2 123 K7
MSEA/BNM PO22 173 H1
Cross Colwood La RHWH RH17 203 R12
Cross Eels SELS PO20 300 H5
Crossfield HASM GU27 195 K8
Crosshaven LHPTN BN17 147 M3
Cross Keys CRAWE RH10 8 F4
Crossland Dr HAV PO9 103 H2
Cross La HORL RH6 29 H1
HORN PO8 288 B4
SALV BN13 298 H11
SWTR RH13 201 J12
WTHG BN11 20 F6
Cross Lane Gdns WADH TN5 191 J12
Cross Levels Wy EAST BN21 163 K7
Cross Oak La REDH RH1 23 H2
Crosspath CRAWE RH10 9 H2
Cross Rd ANG/EP BN16 148 D4
STHW BN42 120 C5
Crossroad Cl STHW BN42 120 C5
Cross St BRI BN1 4 E2
HOVE BN3 122 C8
POLE BN26 131 M7
SLVH TN37 12 B8
WTHG BN11 20 F3
Cross Wy HAV PO9 102 F3
LEWES BN7 16 A5
Crossways ANG/EP BN16 149 G3
CRAWE RH10 9 L1
MIDH GU29 227 K7
MSEA/BNM PO22 145 L8
PUL/STOR RH20 266 A7
RHWH RH17 236 E3
Crossways Av EGRIN RH19 31 H8
FERR BN12 149 M1
Crossways Cl CRAWE RH10 9 K2
Crossways Man BEX TN40 * 137 H2
Crossways Pk PUL/STOR RH20 266 A6
Crossways Rd GSHT GU26 180 G6
The Crossways LHPTN BN17 147 H2
PEV BN24 132 F7
The Crossway BRI BN1 123 G3
PTSD BN41 120 F3
SBGH/RUST TN4 37 J7
Crouch Cl EDN/EASTW BN20 163 G4
Crouch Cross La RCCH PO18 109 H2
Crouchfield Cl SEAF BN25 * 174 F3
Crouch Hl HFD BN5 269 L2
Crouchlands Farm RHWH RH17 72 B1
Crouch La BAT TN33 96 A1
HAWK TN18 218 A4
HORN PO8 288 B2
SEAF BN25 174 E3
Crowberry Cl CRAWW RH11 42 F7
Crowborough Dr FERR BN12 150 A3
Crowborough Hl CROW TN6 67 M8
Crowborough Ms CROW TN6 * 67 K7
Crowborough Rd
BRIE/ROTT BN2 156 C5
RHAS TN35 100 D1
UCK TN22 209 K3
Crowders La BAT TN33 281 P6
Crowhurst Cl CRAWE RH10 44 D3
LGNY BN23 163 M1
Crowhurst Crs
PUL/STOR RH20 265 R11
Crowhurst Rd BRI BN1 83 G6
STLEO TN38 97 M2
Crowmere Av BEX TN40 97 H8
Crowmere Ter BEX TN40 97 H8
Crown Buildings
LAN/SOMP BN15 * 152 B1
Crown Cl HAIL BN27 91 M6
HOVE BN3 * 122 C7
UCK TN22 76 E4
Crown Gdns BRI BN1 * 4 D5
Crown Hl SEAF BN25 159 K7
Crown La HAS TN34 13 L6
Crown Rd PTSD BN41 120 F5
SHOR BN43 120 A5
Crown St BRI BN1 4 C6
EAST BN21 176 D1
Crowsbury Cl EMRTH PO10 103 M2
Croxden Wy LW/ROSE BN22 163 K2
Croxton La HWH RH16 73 L3
Croy Cl CCH PO19 6 B9
Croydon Cottages CROW TN6 * 67 L6
The Crumbles LGNY BN23 * 164 E4
Crunden Rd EDN/EASTW BN20 176 B1
Crundens Cnr ANG/EP BN16 148 D3
Crundles EPSF GU31 223 P6
Cryals Rd STPH/PW TN12 188 C4
Crypt La MIDH GU29 260 G6
Crystal Wy WVILLE PO7 288 C9
Cubitt Ter BRIE/ROTT BN2 * 5 M9
Cubitt Wy STLEO TN38 98 D1
Cuckfield Cl BEX TN40 97 M7
CRAWW RH11 42 E6
Cuckfield Crs SALV BN13 116 E7
Cuckfield La RHWH RH17 204 C8
Cuckfield Rd HPPT/KEY BN6 270 H2
RHWH RH17 74 A1
RHWH RH17 204 G5
Cuckmere Ct POLE BN26 * 160 E2
Cuckmere Crs CRAWW RH11 42 E4
Cuckmere Dr PEV BN24 132 F8
Cuckmere Ri HTHF TN21 244 D6
Cuckmere Rd NEWHV BN9 18 B7
SEAF BN25 175 H3
Cuckmere Wk LW/ROSE BN22 163 J4
Cuckmere Wy BRI BN1 83 G8
Cuckoo Dr HTHF TN21 244 D7
Cuckoo La STPH/PW TN12 188 F7
Cuckoo Trail HAIL BN27 92 A5
HTHF TN21 244 D7
POLE BN26 131 M5
Cudlow Av ANG/EP BN16 148 B4
Cudlow Gdn ANG/EP BN16 148 B5
Cudworth Pk RDKG RH5 * 25 K1
Cuffs Hl CRAWE RH10 44 D7
Cuilfail LEWES BN7 17 K5
Culimore Cl SELS PO20 167 K6
Culimore Rd SELS PO20 167 K6
Culpepers CRBK TN17 189 R10
Culpepper BURH RH15 74 D5
Culpepper Cl BRIE/ROTT BN2 123 J3
Culross Av HWH RH16 73 G4
Culver Cl LGNY BN23 164 A1
Culverden Av SBGH/RUST TN4 37 L3
Culverden Down
SBGH/RUST TN4 37 L4
Culverden Pk SBGH/RUST TN4 37 L4
Culverden Park Rd
SBGH/RUST TN4 37 L3
Culverden Sq SBGH/RUST TN4 37 M4
Culverden St SBGH/RUST TN4 37 M5
Culver Rd LAN/SOMP BN15 118 D7
MSEA/BNM PO22 3 L5
Culvers EPSF GU31 258 E2
Cumberland Av EMRTH PO10 103 M1
FERR BN12 116 C8
Cumberland Crs ANG/EP BN16 114 E8
Cumberland Dr BRI BN1 122 D3
Cumberland Gdns
RTWE/PEM TN2 * 37 M7
STLEO TN38 99 G5
Cumberland Ms RTW TN1 37 M7
Cumberland Rd ANG/EP BN16 114 F8
BEXW TN39 97 G6
BRI BN1 122 D3
Cumberland Wk
RTWE/PEM TN2 37 M7
Cumberland Yd RTW TN1 * 37 M7
Cumbrian Cl SALV BN13 116 D6
Cunliffe Cl SELS PO20 167 H3
Cunningham Cl
SBGH/RUST TN4 38 A2
Cunningham Dr LGNY BN23 164 D6
Cunningham Gdns
MSEA/BNM PO22 145 H8
Cunningham Rd HORN PO8 288 D2
SBGH/RUST TN4 38 A2
Curbey Cl PUL/STOR RH20 266 A4
Curdridge Cl HAV PO9 288 H12
Curf Wy BURH RH15 75 H6
Curlescroft BOGR PO21 171 L3
Curlew Cl EMRTH PO10 103 M6
Curlew Ct STLEO TN38 98 D2
Curlew Gdns HORN PO8 288 A5
The Curlews SHOR BN43 119 M5
Currie Rd SBGH/RUST TN4 37 M3
Curtis Cl BOR GU35 179 M3
Curtis La BOR GU35 179 M3
The Curve HORN PO8 288 A3
Curvins Wy LAN/SOMP BN15 118 E6
Curwen Pl BRI BN1 122 D2
Curzon Av HORS RH12 14 A5
Curzon Cl SALV BN13 116 E7
Cutfield Cl CCH PO19 141 L2
Cuthbert Cl BEXW TN39 96 F6
Cuthbert Rd BRIE/ROTT BN2 5 K6
Cuttinglye La CRAWE RH10 29 M8
Cuttinglye Rd CRAWE RH10 30 B7
Cygnet Rd CHAM PO6 102 A6
The Cygnets SHOR BN43 119 L5
Cygnet Wk MSEA/BNM PO22 144 A7
The Cylinders HASM GU27 195 K8
Cypress Av SALV BN13 116 B8
Cypress Cl SHOR BN43 119 L4
STLEO TN38 98 F6
Cypress Crs HORN PO8 288 B4
Cypress Gv RTWE/PEM TN2 54 B1
Cypress Rd BOR GU35 178 D6
Cypress Wy BOGR PO21 171 H3
GSHT GU26 180 G7
Cyprus Pl RYE TN31 252 G8
Cyprus Rd BURH RH15 74 F6
Cyprus Vls LHPTN BN17 * 147 H4

D

Dacre Gdns STEY/UB BN44 79 G6
Dacre Rd EDN/EASTW BN20 176 C1
HAIL BN27 279 P11
NEWHV BN9 19 G3
Dagbrook La HFD BN5 269 K6
Dagg La RBTBR TN32 217 M12
Dagmar St WTHG BN11 21 H3
Dairyfields CRAWW RH11 42 F4
Dairy La ARUN BN18 111 J5
RCCH PO18 108 E4
The Daisycroft HFD BN5 269 L5
Daisy Md WVILLE PO7 288 B11
Dakin Cl CRAWE RH10 44 B7
The Dakins EGRIN RH19 47 K1
Dale Av BRI BN1 82 E8
HPPT/KEY BN6 271 N6
Dale Cl HORS RH12 56 E4
Dale Crs BRI BN1 82 E7
Dale Dr BRI BN1 82 F7
Dale Hl POY/PYE BN45 270 H11
Dalehurst Rd BEXW TN39 96 F6
Dale Rd FROW RH18 48 E8
LEWES BN7 16 B8
WTHG BN11 152 A1
Dales Cl HAIL BN27 280 A12
Dale St RTW TN1 38 A5
Dale Vw HASM GU27 181 J12
HOVE BN3 121 J3
Dale View Gdns HOVE BN3 121 J3
Dalewood Gdns BURH RH15 75 H7
CRAWE RH10 43 L1
Dallas La RING/NEW BN8 274 E3
Dallaway Dr PEV BN24 133 G8
Dallaway Gdns EGRIN RH19 31 K8
Dallaway Rd CCH PO19 7 H8
Dallington Cl BEX TN40 97 M7
Dallington Rd HOVE BN3 121 L5
LW/ROSE BN22 163 L4
Dalloway Rd ARUN BN18 112 D4
Dalmeny Rd BEXW TN39 96 F8
Dalmore Ct BEX TN40 * 137 H2
Dalton Cl CRAWW RH11 42 F8
Dalton Rd EDN/EASTW BN20 176 E5
Daltons Pl ARUN BN18 112 F3
Damask Gdns WVILLE PO7 288 C8
Damer's Br PETW GU28 229 L9
Damian Wy HPPT/KEY BN6 271 Q5
Damon Cl PEAHV BN10 157 H6
Dampier Wk CRAWW RH11 * 43 G8
Dana Ldg PEAHV BN10 * 156 F6
Danbury Ct EMRTH PO10 104 B3
Danebury Cl HAV PO9 288 F11
Dane Cl SEAF BN25 174 D3
Dane Court Cl BEXW TN39 97 G7
Danefield Rd SELS PO20 301 J8
Danehill La RHWH RH17 207 P4
Danehill Rd BRIE/ROTT BN2 123 L8
Danehurst Crs SWTR RH13 15 K5
Dane Rd SEAF BN25 174 D3
STLEO TN38 99 G5
Danesbrook La WVILLE PO7 288 B10
Daniel Cl LAN/SOMP BN15 118 E6
Daniel Wy RYE TN31 254 A11
Dankton Gdns
LAN/SOMP BN15 118 A6
Dankton La LAN/SOMP BN15 118 A5
Danley La HASM GU27 194 D2
Danum Cl HAIL BN27 92 B2
Danworth La HPPT/KEY BN6 74 A7
Dapper's La ANG/EP BN16 114 F7
Darby's La WADH TN5 71 M7
Darcey Dr BRI BN1 82 F7
Darent Cl PEV BN24 132 E8
Darenth Wy HORL RH6 22 E4
Daresbury Cl BEXW TN39 96 F7
Dark La BOGR PO21 171 K3
Darleydale CRAWW RH11 8 C9
Darley Rd EDN/EASTW BN20 176 E6
Darlington Cl ANG/EP BN16 114 F8
The Darlingtons ANG/EP BN16 148 D2
Dart Cl SALV BN13 116 C5
Dartmouth Cl
BRIE/ROTT BN2 123 L4
Dartmouth Crs
BRIE/ROTT BN2 123 K4
Darvel Down BAT TN33 247 N11
Darwall Dr SEAF BN25 175 G2
Darwell Cl RBTBR TN32 248 C2
STLEO TN38 98 D4
Darwell Dr PEV BN24 132 F8
Darwin Cl HORS RH12 15 K1
D'Aubigny Rd BRIE/ROTT BN2 123 G5
Daux Av BIL RH14 232 A3
Daux Hl HORS RH12 56 A3
Daux Rd BIL RH14 232 A2
Daux Wy BIL RH14 232 A3
Dauxwood Cl BIL RH14 232 A3
Davenport Rd MSEA/BNM PO22 3 M5
Davey Dr BRI BN1 123 G4
Davey's La LEWES BN7 17 J4
Davids Cl BOGR PO21 143 L8
Davigdor Rd HOVE BN3 122 C6
Davis Cl BEXW TN39 96 F6
CRAWW RH11 42 F8
Davits Dr LHPTN BN17 147 M3
Dawes Av WTHG BN11 21 M3
Dawes Cl WTHG BN11 21 M3
Dawlish Cl BRIE/ROTT BN2 123 K4
Dawn Cl STEY/UB BN44 79 G4
Dawn Crs STEY/UB BN44 79 G4
Dawson Ter BRIE/ROTT BN2 5 K5
Dawtrey Cl ANG/EP BN16 148 D3
Dawtrey Rd PETW GU28 * 229 L10
Daynes Wy BURH RH15 74 D8
Dayseys Hl REDH RH1 23 M1
Days La ARUN BN18 110 E2
Deacons Dr PTSD BN41 121 G3
Deacons Wy STEY/UB BN44 79 G3
Deacon Wy SALV BN13 117 L8
Deadmans La RYE TN31 252 H7
Deadmantree Hl
RING/NEW BN8 274 A6
Deak's La RHWH RH17 205 J11
Deal Av SEAF BN25 160 B8
The Deals RYE TN31 252 G8
Dean Cl LHPTN BN17 147 H2
PTSD BN41 121 H3
Dean Court Rd
BRIE/ROTT BN2 155 M3
Deane Ct HAV PO9 * 289 J12
Deanery Cl CCH PO19 6 D6
LEWES BN7 17 H2
Dean Gdns PTSD BN41 121 H3
Deanland Rd RHWH RH17 60 F8
Dean La HORN PO8 289 L4
PETW GU28 228 E9
Dean Rd SEAF BN25 174 F3
Deans Cl BEXW TN39 97 G6
BRIE/ROTT BN2 124 D5
Deans Dr BEXW TN39 96 F7
Deans Meadow
RING/NEW BN8 274 D4
Deans Rd POLE BN26 160 E2
Dean St BRI BN1 4 B6
Deans Yd ARUN BN18 * 110 F2
Deanway HOVE BN3 122 A2
Dean Wy PUL/STOR RH20 265 R11
Dean Wood Cl LGNY BN23 163 M1
Deborah Ter PEAHV BN10 156 F6
De Braose Wy
STEY/UB BN44 78 D3
De Cham Av SLVH TN37 12 C6
De Cham Rd SLVH TN37 12 B6
De Chardin Dr HAS TN34 284 D12

Decimus Burton Wy
  STLEO TN38 .... 12 A8
De Courcel Rd BRIE/ROTT BN2 .. 154 D2
Decoy Dr ANG/EP BN16 .... 114 C6
  LW/ROSE BN22 .... 163 K4
Decoy La ARUN BN18 .... 114 D5
Decoy Rd SALV BN13 .... 117 L8
Dedisham Cl CRAWE RH10 .... 9 M5
Deep Dene HASM GU27 .... 180 H11
Deepdene WADH TN5 .... 71 L3
Deepdene La MSEA/BNM PO22 .... 145 M8
Deepdene Gdns RHAS TN35 ...... 100 A2
Deepfields HORL RH6 .... 22 E4
Deeping Ga WVILLE PO7 .... 288 B10
Deer Cl CCH PO19 .... 141 K2
Deer Hvn HAIL BN27 * 90 B2
Deerleap BOR GU35 * 179 R5
Deer Pk HFD BN5 .... 269 K3
Deer Park Cl SELS PO20 .... 300 H5
Deer Park Dr SELS PO20 .... 300 H5
Deer Park La SELS PO20 .... 300 H5
Deers Leap HWH RH16 .... 72 F8
Deerswood Cl CRAWW RH11 .... 8 B2
  SALV BN13 .... 116 A8
Deerswood La BEXW TN39 .... 96 E8
Deerswood Rd CRAWW RH11 .... 8 B2
Deeside Av CCH PO19 .... 107 G6
The Deeside BRI BN1 .... 82 F6
Defiance Pl
  MSEA/BNM PO22 * 173 H1
De Grey Cl LEWES BN7 .... 17 H3
Delaware Dr SLVH TN37 .... 283 N11
Delaware Rd LEWES BN7 .... 16 B8
De La Warr Ct BEX TN40 * 137 J2
De La Warr Gn LEWES BN7 .... 16 C2
De La Warr Ms BEX TN40 * 137 H1
De La Warr Pde BEX TN40 ...... 137 H4
De La Warr Rd BEX TN40 .... 97 K8
  EGRIN RH19 .... 31 L8
Delfont Cl CRAWE RH10 .... 44 C5
Delius Gdns SWTR RH13 .... 57 G9
Dell Cl HASM GU27 .... 181 K10
  STLEO TN38 .... 98 F3
Dell Dr ANG/EP BN16 .... 148 L1
  RTWE/PEM TN2 .... 38 C5
Delling Cl RCCH PO18 .... 106 A7
Delling La RCCH PO18 .... 106 H1
Dell La BIL RH14 .... 232 A1
Dellney Av HWH RH16 .... 73 J9
Dell Piece East HORN PO08 .... 288 E4
Dell Piece West HORN PO08 .... 288 D4
Dell Quay Rd SELS PO20 .... 141 G3
The Dell EGRIN RH19 .... 32 M8
  HAV PO9 .... 102 C3
  HORL RH6 .... 22 B5
  HORL RH6 .... 23 G5
  HWH RH16 .... 72 F4
  MSEA/BNM PO22 .... 143 M7
Delmonden Rd HAWK TN18 .... 216 D1
Delphi Wy WVILLE PO7 .... 102 A3
Delta Dr HORL RH6 .... 22 F8
Delves Av RTWE/PEM TN2 .... 38 B8
Delves Cl RING/NEW BN8 .... 275 J11
Delves Wy RING/NEW BN8 .... 275 J11
De Moleyns Cl BEX TN40 * 137 J4
De Montfort Rd BRIE/ROTT BN2 .. 5 J2
  LEWES BN7 .... 16 C6
Dempsey Rd CCH PO19 .... 107 M3
Den Av BOGR PO21 .... 2 F6
Denbigh Rd HASM GU27 .... 181 N12
  SBGH/RUST TN4 .... 38 B2
Dencher Rd FERR BN12 .... 125 K2
Denchers Plat CRAWW RH11 ...... 27 J8
Dene Cl BOR GU35 .... 178 G7
  EDN/EASTW BN20 .... 302 H4
  HASM GU27 .... 181 M11
  HORL RH6 .... 22 D4
Dene Dr LW/ROSE BN22 .... 163 H4
Denehurst Gdns HAS TN34 ...... 284 D12
Dene Pth UCK TN22 .... 76 F3
Deneside BRI BN1 .... 82 C8
Dene Side EDN/EASTW BN20 ..... 302 H4
The Denes RING/NEW BN8 * 275 M11
The Dene EDN/EASTW BN20 ...... 162 F3
  HOVE BN3 .... 121 J2
  RHAS TN35 .... 284 D12
  SWTR RH13 .... 201 H4
Dene Tye CRAWE RH10 .... 44 B2
Dene V BRI BN1 .... 82 C8
Dene Wy RRTW TN3 .... 36 F2
The Deneway BRI BN1 .... 122 C1
  LAN/SOMP BN15 .... 118 B7
Dengemarsh Rd LYDD TN29 ...... 255 R10
Denham Cl MSEA/BNM PO22 ...... 145 K8
  STLEO TN38 .... 98 E1
Denham Rd BURH RH15 .... 74 C5
Denham Wy RYE TN31 .... 253 R11
Den HI EDN/EASTW BN20 .... 176 A1
Denmans CRAWE RH10 .... 44 C2
Denman's Cl HWH RH16 .... 73 K1
Denman's La HWH RH16 .... 73 K2
  SELS PO20 .... 110 D3
Denmark Pl HAS TN34 .... 13 H7
Denmark Rd PTSD BN41 .... 121 H6
Denmark Ter BRI BN1 .... 4 B4
Denmark Vls HOVE BN3 .... 122 A6
Denne Pde HORS RH12 .... 14 D7
Denne Rd CRAWW RH11 .... 8 B2
  HORS RH12 .... 14 C8
Dennes La LYDD TN29 .... 255 R6
Dennis Hobden Cl
  BRIE/ROTT BN2 .... 123 K4
Dennis Wy LISS GU33 .... 192 D10
Denny's Cl SELS PO20 .... 301 L6
Denshare Rd SELS PO20 .... 301 L6
Denshire Dr PUL/STOR RH20 .... 266 B11
Densihale BOGR PO21 .... 171 G2
Denton Cl FERR BN12 .... 150 A2
  RYE TN31 .... 252 F12
Denton Dr BRI BN1 .... 82 F8
  NEWHV BN9 .... 158 F4
Denton Island NEWHV BN9 .... 18 F2
Denton Ri NEWHV BN9 .... 158 D3
Denton Rd EDN/EASTW BN20 ..... 176 D5
  NEWHV BN9 .... 158 E3
The Dentons
  EDN/EASTW BN20 .... 176 A1
The Denture ARUN BN18 .... 295 N1
Denville CHAM PO06 .... 102 A4
Denvilles Cl HAV PO9 .... 103 J3
Departures Rd HORL RH6 .... 27 J4
Depot Rd CRAWW RH11 .... 27 J8
  SWTR RH13 .... 15 G5
Derby Rd HASM GU27 .... 181 L10
Derek Av HOVE BN3 .... 121 J7
Derek Rd LAN/SOMP BN15 .... 118 C5

Dern La RING/NEW BN8 .... 277 P5
De Roos Rd BN21 .... 176 D1
Derwent Cl BOR GU35 .... 178 G4
  CRAWW RH11 .... 42 E4
  HAIL BN27 .... 91 M4
  HORN PO08 .... 256 D11
  HORS RH12 .... 57 G3
  LAN/SOMP BN15 .... 118 B8
  LHPTN BN17 .... 147 M3
  SELS PO20 .... 109 H4
Derwent Dr FERR BN12 .... 116 C8
  SBGH/RUST TN4 .... 38 C1
Derwent Gv MSEA/BNM PO22 .... 145 G7
Derwent Rd EDN/EASTW BN20 .... 176 E5
  LW/ROSE BN22 .... 11 L2
Desmond Rd BRIE/ROTT BN2 .... 123 L7
Detling Rd CRAWW RH11 .... 43 H8
Devils Dyke Rd BRI BN1 .... 81 H4
Devils La LIPH GU30 .... 194 B2
Devonian Cl BRIE/ROTT BN2 * ... 5 G7
Devonport Pl WTHG BN11 .... 151 M2
Devonport Rd WTHG BN11 .... 151 M2
Devon Rd BOR GU35 .... 178 G6
Devonshire Cl RTWE/PEM TN2 .... 53 L1
Devonshire Pl BRIE/ROTT BN2 .... 5 G8
  EAST BN21 .... 10 F7
Devonshire Rd BEX TN40 .... 137 H2
  BOGR PO21 .... 2 C7
  HAS TN34 .... 13 G6
  SWTR RH13 .... 14 F6
De Walden Ms
  EDN/EASTW BN20 .... 176 E5
Dewar Cl CRAWW RH11 * 42 D4
De Warrenne Rd LEWES BN7 ...... 16 D5
Dewe Rd BRIE/ROTT BN2 .... 123 H4
Dewhurst La WADH TN5 .... 71 G1
Dewlands HI CROW TN6 .... 211 M8
Dew La RYE TN31 .... 251 R6
Dew Pond Cl SWTR RH13 .... 15 K4
The Dewpond PEAHV BN10 .... 157 H4
Dexter Dr EGRIN RH19 .... 47 K1
Dial Cl MSEA/BNM PO22 .... 111 H8
Diana Cl BEX TN40 .... 97 M7
  EMRTH PO10 .... 103 M1
Dibden Cl HAV PO9 .... 102 D1
Dickens Cl BRI BN1 .... 83 H8
Dickens Wy LGNY BN23 .... 164 D12
Dickins La EPSF GU31 .... 223 P4
Dickinson Pl MSEA/BNM PO22 ..... 2 C7
Dickins Wy SWTR RH13 .... 15 J9
The Dicklands LEWES BN7 ...... 126 C5
Dillingburgh Rd
  EDN/EASTW BN20 .... 176 C1
Dillon Wy RTWE/PEM TN2 .... 38 C7
Dingle Cl CRAWW RH11 .... 8 A2
The Dingle CRAWW RH11 .... 8 A3
Dingley Rd BRI BN1 .... 148 A4
Dinsdale Gdns ANG/EP BN16 .... 148 B3
Diplock Cl POLE BN26 .... 131 L7
Diplocks Wy HAIL BN27 .... 91 M6
Dirty La EGRIN RH19 .... 48 D3
Ditcham Crs HAV PO9 .... 102 F1
Ditchfield Cl MSEA/BNM PO22 .. 145 J7
Ditchling Bostall
  HPPT/KEY BN6 .... 272 A10
Ditchling Cl FERR BN12 .... 150 A1
  LGNY BN23 .... 163 L1
Ditchling Crs BRI BN1 .... 83 H8
Ditchling Dr RHAS TN35 .... 100 D1
Ditchling Gdns BRI BN1 .... 122 F1
Ditchling HI CRAWW RH11 .... 8 D9
Ditchling Ri BRI BN1 .... 4 E1
  BRI BN1 .... 83 H2
Ditchling Rd BRI BN1 * 91 M7
  BRI BN1 .... 83 H1
  HAIL BN27 .... 91 M7
Dittons Ms STLEO TN38 * 98 F1
Dittons Rd EAST BN21 .... 10 B6
  PEV BN24 .... 132 C7
Dixter La RYE TN31 .... 218 D10
Dixter Rd RYE TN31 .... 218 D10
Dobbins Pl CRAWW RH11 .... 42 C4
Dobson Rd CRAWW RH11 .... 27 J8
Dockenfield Cl HAV PO9 * 102 D1
The Dock RING/NEW BN8 .... 128 B2
Dodshill CROW TN6 .... 67 M8
Dodsley Gv MIDH GU29 .... 227 K7
Dodsley La MIDH GU29 .... 227 K7
Dog Kennel La UCK TN22 .... 211 M11
Dog La STEY/UB BN44 .... 78 C2
Dogs Hill Rd WSEA TN36 .... 286 G4
Dogwood Dell WVILLE PO7 ...... 288 A12
Dolby Ter HORL RH6 * 26 D3
Doleham La RHAS TN35 .... 284 D4
Dollis Cl CRAWE RH10 .... 44 B4
Dolphin Cl CCH PO19 .... 107 G7
  HASM GU27 .... 180 H11
Dolphin Ms BRI BN1 * 4 B4
  CCH PO19 .... 107 J7
  SHOR BN43 .... 119 M6
Dolphin Rd LYDD TN29 .... 255 R7
  SHOR BN43 .... 119 M6
Dolphin Wy ANG/EP BN16 .... 148 C5
  SHOR BN43 .... 119 M6
Domehouse Cl SELS PO20 .... 301 L8
Dominion Buildings
  SALV BN13 .... 21 L1
Dominion Cl SALV BN13 .... 21 K1
Dominion Rd SALV BN13 .... 117 L8
Dominion Wy ANG/EP BN16 ...... 148 L8
  SALV BN13 .... 117 L8
Dominion Wy West
  SALV BN13 .... 117 L8
Donald Hall Rd BRIE/ROTT BN2 ... 5 M7
Donaldson Cl SELS PO20 .... 301 J5
Donald Wy WSEA TN36 .... 286 F4
Doncaster Wk CRAWE RH10 .... 9 L8
Donkey La HORL RH6 .... 28 C2
Donkey Ms HOVE BN3 .... 122 C8
Donne Cl CRAWE RH10 .... 44 A1
Donnington Ct CRAWW RH11 ...... 42 E6
Donnington Pk SELS PO20 ...... 141 G2
Donnington Rd ANG/EP BN16 * .. 148 B3
Donnington Rd
  BRIE/ROTT BN2 .... 124 D7
Doomsday Gdn SWTR RH13 .... 15 L9
Doomsday La SWTR RH13 .... 15 L9
Doone End FERR BN12 .... 149 L5
Dorcas Cl WVILLE PO7 .... 288 D5
Dorchester Gdns WTHG BN11 ..... 20 A5
Dordrecht Wy HAS TN34 .... 12 E3
Dorking Rd HORS RH12 .... 40 A3
  RH KRH12 .... 187 R9
  RTW TN1 .... 38 B3
Dormans CRAWW RH11 .... 42 F4
Dorman's Cl LING RH7 .... 31 M1

Dormans High St LING RH7 ...... 31 M2
Dormans Park Rd EGRIN RH19 .... 31 J6
Dormans Station Rd LING RH7 ... 31 L2
Dornden Dr RRTW TN3 .... 36 F5
Dormere La WVILLE PO7 .... 288 B10
Dorothy Av PEAHV BN10 .... 157 H5
Dorothy Av North
  PEAHV BN10 .... 157 H5
Dorothy Rd HOVE BN3 .... 121 J5
Dorrita Av HORN PO08 .... 288 B5
Dorset Av EGRIN RH19 .... 31 H6
Dorset Cl HORN PO08 .... 288 C5
  LHPTN BN17 .... 147 K4
Dorset Gdns BRIE/ROTT BN2 * 5 G7
  EGRIN RH19 .... 31 H6
Dorset Ms BRIE/ROTT BN2 * 4 F7
Dorset Pl BRIE/ROTT BN2 * 5 G7
  HAS TN34 .... 12 F7
  SALV BN13 .... 116 F8
Dorset Rd BEX TN40 .... 137 J1
  BOGR PO21 .... 2 C7
  LEWES BN7 .... 17 G7
  RTWE/PEM TN2 .... 38 C7
Dorset Rd South BEX TN40 ..... 137 J1
Dorset St BRIE/ROTT BN2 * 4 F7
Doubledays BURH RH15 .... 75 G2
Doucegrove STLEO TN38 .... 98 F4
Douglas Av CRAWW RH11 .... 43 J1
  HORN PO08 .... 288 C5
Douglas Cl ARUN BN18 .... 146 A3
  HAIL BN27 .... 92 A1
  MSEA/BNM PO22 .... 145 L8
  WTHG BN11 .... 150 D3
Douglas Gdns HAV PO9 .... 103 H1
Douglas Martin Rd CCH PO19 * ... 7 K2
Douglas Rd CROW TN6 .... 69 J8
Dove Cl CRAWW RH11 .... 43 J1
  HORN PO08 .... 288 C5
Dove Ct MSEA/BNM PO22 .... 2 A2
  UCK TN22 .... 76 E4
Dovecote Ms LAN/SOMP BN15 ... 118 D3
Dovedale Crs CRAWW RH11 .... 8 B9
Dovedale Gdns
  LW/ROSE BN22 .... 163 L3
Dover Cl SEAF BN25 .... 160 D8
  SWTR RH13 .... 201 Q11
Dover Rd BRI BN1 .... 122 F3
  POLE BN26 .... 132 A6
  WTHG BN11 .... 20 A8
Dower Cl BRIE/ROTT BN2 .... 155 J2
Dower Wk CRAWW RH11 * 42 F4
Downash Cl BRIE/ROTT BN2 .... 123 K7
Down Av RRTW TN3 .... 190 F2
Downe Cl HORL RH6 .... 22 D4
Downey Cl SLVH TN37 .... 283 Q11
Down Farm Pl HORN PO08 * 256 D12
Downham Cl HORN PO08 .... 288 A6
Downhill Vw BRIE/ROTT BN2 .... 124 D6
Downhouse Rd HORN PO08 .... 256 D9
Downing Cl BOGR PO21 .... 171 K1
Downland Av PEAHV BN10 .... 157 K7
  STHW BN42 .... 142 A5
Downland Cl BRIE/ROTT BN2 .... 124 A5
  LGNY BN23 .... 164 B11
  SALV BN13 .... 298 H11
  STEY/UB BN44 .... 79 G3
  STHW BN42 .... 120 C4
Downland Copse UCK TN22 .... 76 E4
Downland Crs HOVE BN3 .... 121 L2
Downland Dr CRAWW RH11 .... 8 C9
  HOVE BN3 .... 121 L2
Downland Pl CRAWW RH11 .... 8 C8
Downland Rd BRIE/ROTT BN2 ... 124 A5
  STEY/UB BN44 .... 79 G3
Downlands Av BEXW TN39 .... 137 G1
  SWTR RH13 .... 234 E10
Downlands Cl BEXW TN39 .... 136 F1
  BOGR PO21 .... 170 F3
  LAN/SOMP BN15 .... 118 B6
Downlands Gdns SALV BN13 .... 117 K6
Downlands Pde SALV BN13 ..... 117 K6
Downlands Wy
  EDN/EASTW BN20 .... 302 H5
Down La RRTW TN3 .... 70 B7
Downley Point HAV PO9 * 103 J1
Downley Rd HAV PO9 .... 103 J1
Downline Cl HTHF TN21 .... 278 C2
Down Rd BEXW TN39 .... 96 F8
  HORN PO08 .... 256 D12
Downs Av EDN/EASTW BN20 ...... 163 G9
Downs Cl LAN/SOMP BN15 .... 16 A4
  LEWES BN7 .... 16 A4
  WVILLE PO7 .... 102 A2
Downscroft BURH RH15 .... 75 J4
Downside BRI BN1 .... 122 C8
  GSHT GU26 .... 180 C2
  HOVE BN3 .... 16 A7
  LEWES BN7 .... 16 A7
  SHOR BN43 .... 119 M4
Downside Av SALV BN13 .... 116 C2
Downside Cl
  EDN/EASTW BN20 .... 176 B2
  SALV BN13 .... 119 L4
  SHOR BN43 .... 119 L4
Downs Link HFD BN5 .... 269 J7
  HORS RH12 .... 185 R9
  STEY/UB BN44 .... 78 F5
  SWTR RH13 .... 200 D1
  SWTR RH13 .... 201 L5
  SWTR RH13 .... 234 D9
Downs Md LAN/SOMP BN15 * 118 B5
Downs Rd BURH RH15 .... 74 D5
  HAS TN34 .... 99 L2
  LW/ROSE BN22 .... 163 G3
  RCCH PO18 .... 291 J11
  SEAF BN25 .... 175 G2
Down St RCCH PO18 .... 106 A2
  UCK TN22 .... 208 H9
Downs Valley Rd
  BRIE/ROTT BN2 .... 124 D5
Downsvalley Rd
  EDN/EASTW BN20 .... 162 F1
Downs Vw BAT TN33 .... 281 M12
Downsview HFD BN5 .... 269 L10
  HOVE BN3 .... 121 J2
  HTHF TN21 .... 244 E5
Downs Vw PEAHV BN10 .... 157 H7
  STEY/UB BN44 * 268 C4
Downsview Av
  BRIE/ROTT BN2 .... 124 B4
  PUL/STOR RH20 .... 266 B11

Downs View Cl
  EDN/EASTW BN20 .... 303 J4
  RING/NEW BN8 .... 239 P7
Downsview Crs UCK TN22 .... 76 E5
Downsview Dr MIDH GU29 .... 226 H12
  RHWH RH17 .... 238 F9
Downs View La
  EDN/EASTW BN20 .... 303 J5
Downs View Rd
  HPPT/KEY BN6 .... 271 N6
Downsview Rd ANG/EP BN16 .... 149 J5
  BOR GU35 .... 179 R4
  EDN/EASTW BN20 .... 162 F2
  HAIL BN27 .... 90 A2
  HORS RH12 .... 57 G3
  PTSD BN41 .... 120 F5
  SEAF BN25 .... 175 G2
Downsway Wy HAIL BN27 * 92 A6
Downs Wk PEAHV BN10 .... 157 H5
Downs Wy ANG/EP BN16 .... 148 E2
Downsway BRIE/ROTT BN2 ...... 124 C5
  SHOR BN43 .... 119 L4
  STHW BN42 .... 120 E3
Down Ter BRIE/ROTT BN2 .... 5 M4
The Down HOVE BN3 .... 121 H1
Downview Av FERR BN12 .... 149 K2
Downview Cl ARUN BN18 .... 145 M2
  GSHT GU26 .... 180 G3
  RCCH PO18 .... 292 B11
  SELS PO20 .... 167 M7
Downview Rd ARUN BN18 .... 145 M2
  FERR BN12 .... 149 K2
  MSEA/BNM PO22 .... 3 J1
  MSEA/BNM PO22 .... 110 F6
  PETW GU28 .... 229 K10
  SALV BN13 .... 298 H10
Downwood Wy HORN PO08 .... 256 D12
Draffin La RYE TN31 .... 253 Q10
Dragons Green Rd SWTR RH13 .. 233 M3
Dragons La SWTR RH13 .... 233 L6
  SWTR RH13 .... 235 K6
Dragon St EPSF GU31 .... 223 N7
Drake Av FERR BN12 .... 150 C1
  LGNY BN23 .... 164 D6
Drake Cl HORS RH12 .... 56 D3
Drake Gv ARUN BN18 .... 146 A3
Drakeleys Fld LIPH GU30 ...... 193 Q11
Drake Pk MSEA/BNM PO22 .... 173 H1
Drake Rd CRAWE RH10 .... 9 H9
  HORL RH6 .... 22 D6
Drakes Cl LAN/SOMP BN15 ..... 119 G7
Drapers Wy STLEO TN38 .... 98 F3
Draxmont Wy BRI BN1 .... 122 E2
Draycliff Cl FERR BN12 .... 149 K4
Draycote Rd HORN PO08 .... 256 D10
Drayton La SELS PO20 .... 108 E7
Drayton Pk SELS PO20 * 142 F1
Drayton Ri BEXW TN39 .... 136 C1
Drewetts Cl ANG/EP BN16 ...... 148 A2
Drewitts Ms SELS PO20 .... 109 G6
Drift La RCCH PO18 .... 105 K6
  SELS PO20 .... 301 J6
Drift Rd BOGR PO21 .... 171 G5
  BOR GU35 .... 178 E9
  HORN PO08 .... 256 D9
  SELS PO20 .... 301 N5
The Drift HAV PO9 .... 289 J8
The Driftway ANG/EP BN16 .... 148 A2
  STEY/UB BN44 .... 79 G2
The Drills ANG/EP BN16 * 114 C8
The Drive ANG/EP BN16 .... 149 G5
  BIL RH14 .... 198 E3
  BOGR PO21 .... 171 G4
  BURH RH15 .... 75 C5
  CCH PO19 .... 107 M2
  CRAWE RH10 .... 29 H6
  CROW TN6 .... 67 J7
  EMRTH PO10 .... 104 E5
  HAIL BN27 .... 92 A7
  HAIL BN27 .... 278 F12
  HAV PO9 .... 103 G2
  HORL RH6 .... 23 G7
  HOVE BN3 .... 122 B7
  LAN/SOMP BN15 .... 119 G4
  LAN/SOMP BN15 .... 152 C1
  NEWHV BN9 .... 18 F8
  PETW GU28 .... 262 C7
  RCCH PO18 .... 106 A8
  RRTW TN3 .... 35 L4
  RTWE/PEM TN2 .... 37 M8
  SHOR BN43 .... 119 L4
  STHW BN42 .... 120 D4
  STLEO TN38 .... 98 E3
  UCK TN22 .... 76 F3
  UCK TN22 .... 209 M12
  WTHG BN11 .... 150 E2
The Driveway SHOR BN43 .... 119 L5
Drockmill Cl POLE BN26 .... 132 B7
Droke La RCCH PO18 .... 293 P5
Dropping Holms HFD BN5 .... 269 J7
Drove Av BRIE/ROTT BN2 .... 124 C5
Drove Crs PTSD BN41 .... 120 F3
Drove La ARUN BN18 .... 145 J3
  SELS PO20 .... 168 C2
Drove Rd BRIE/ROTT BN2 .... 123 M5
  NEWHV BN9 .... 19 H2
  PTSD BN41 .... 19 G2
Drovers RHWH RH17 .... 236 D2
Drovers Cl PTSD BN41 .... 121 H5
Drovers Wy BURH RH15 .... 75 H8
The Drove BRI BN1 .... 84 B8
  BRI BN1 .... 122 C4
  LEWES BN7 .... 273 R12
  NEWHV BN9 .... 19 K1
The Droveway HOVE BN3 .... 121 M3
  HWH RH16 .... 72 F3
Drum Md PSF GU32 .... 223 M6
Drummond Cl HWH RH16 .... 73 G5
Drummond Ct FERR BN12 * 150 C4
  HWH RH16 .... 73 G5
Drummond Rd CRAWW RH11 .... 42 D4
  FERR BN12 .... 150 D4
Drungewick La BIL RH14 .... 199 K7
Drury Cl CRAWE RH10 .... 44 C5
Drury La STLEO TN38 .... 99 J5
Dryad Wk MSEA/BNM PO22 ...... 173 J1
Dryad Wy MSEA/BNM PO22 ...... 173 J1
Dryden Vy LIPH GU30 .... 179 P12
Drygrounds La MSEA/BNM PO22 . 173 J1
Duchess Dr SEAF BN25 .... 159 K7
Ducklands BOR GU35 .... 178 H7
Duck La MIDH GU29 .... 227 J9
  SELS PO20 .... 300 F5
Duckmead La LISS GU33 .... 192 E7

Dudleston Heath Dr
  HORN PO08 .... 288 C7
Dudley Cl BOR GU35 .... 178 D9
Dudley Rd BRI BN1 .... 123 G4
  LW/ROSE BN22 .... 11 G3
  RTW TN1 .... 37 M5
Dudwell Rd BRIE/ROTT BN2 .... 124 D6
Duffield La EMRTH PO10 .... 104 C2
Duke Cl CRAWE RH10 .... 44 B7
Duke Ms SLVH TN37 * 99 G3
Duke Rd SLVH TN37 .... 99 G3
Dukes Cl ARUN BN18 .... 112 E3
  PSF GU32 .... 223 L5
  SEAF BN25 .... 159 J8
Dukes Ct CCH PO19 * 7 L6
Dukes Dr EDN/EASTW BN20 ..... 176 E6
Dukes HI BAT TN33 .... 282 E3
  PUL/STOR RH20 .... 266 D5
Dukes La BRI BN1 * 4 D7
  STEY/UB BN44 .... 78 C2
Dukes Meadow BOGR PO21 ...... 171 G2
  RCCH PO18 .... 290 H12
Duke's Mound BRIE/ROTT BN2 .... 5 J6
Dukes Rd ARUN BN18 .... 110 D1
  HWH RH16 .... 73 L1
  RDKG RH5 .... 25 H3
  RDKG RH5 .... 25 L4
  RTW TN1 .... 38 B4
Duke St BEXW TN39 .... 96 E8
  BRI BN1 * 4 D7
  LHPTN BN17 .... 147 J4
  SLVH TN37 .... 99 G3
Dukes Yd STEY/UB BN44 * 78 C2
Duke Ter HAV PO9 * 102 E1
  SLVH TN37 .... 99 G3
Dulwich Cl SEAF BN25 .... 175 H1
Dumbrells Cottages
  RHWH RH17 * 75 M4
Dumbrells Court Rd
  HPPT/KEY BN6 .... 272 A5
Dumbrills Cl BURH RH15 .... 74 F4
Dumb Woman's La RYE TN31 .... 252 C10
Dummer Ct HAV PO9 .... 288 E11
Dumpford La EPSF GU31 .... 225 J9
Dunbar Dr HAIL BN27 .... 91 M4
Duncan Rd CCH PO19 .... 7 L6
Dunclutha Rd HAS TN34 .... 99 L1
Duncton Cl HWH RH16 .... 73 G5
  MSEA/BNM PO22 .... 173 G1
Duncton High St PETW GU28 ... 262 H6
Duncton Rd ANG/EP BN16 .... 148 B3
  MSEA/BNM PO22 .... 256 E9
Dundale Rd RRTW TN5 .... 55 H1
Dunes Av RYE TN31 .... 254 A11
The Dunes BOGR PO21 .... 171 G5
Dunford Hollow MIDH GU29 .... 260 H1
Dunhurst Cl HAV PO9 .... 103 H1
Dunlop Cl HPPT/KEY BN6 .... 236 E12
Dunnings Rd EGRIN RH19 .... 47 K3
Dunnock Cl HAV PO9 .... 289 J8
Dunsbury Wy HAV PO9 .... 288 F12
Dunsfold Cl CRAWW RH11 .... 42 F4
Dunsfold Common Rd
  MFD/CHID GU8 .... 184 A12
Dunsfold Rd BIL RH14 .... 197 R2
  CRAN GU6 .... 184 F6
  MFD/CHID GU8 .... 183 P10
  UCK TN22 .... 184 C1
Dunstall Av BURH RH15 .... 74 D5
Dunstall Farm Rd BURH RH15 ... 74 E4
Dunstan Cl CCH PO19 .... 107 M2
Dunstan Gv SBGH/RUST TN4 ...... 38 A4
Dunstan Rd SBGH/RUST TN4 ...... 38 A3
Dunstans Cft MAYF TN20 .... 212 F6
Dunster Cl BRI BN1 .... 123 G4
Dunvan Cl LEWES BN7 .... 16 E1
Durban Pk MSEA/BNM PO22 .... 2 E2
Durban Rd MSEA/BNM PO22 ..... 144 B7
Durbans Rd BIL RH14 .... 199 J12
Durfold Rd RHV5 .... 56 D2
Durfold Wd BIL RH14 .... 183 P11
Durford Ct HAV PO9 .... 288 E11
Durford Rd EPSF GU31 .... 223 R6
Durham Cl BOGR PO21 .... 170 F5
  BRIE/ROTT BN2 .... 123 M4
  CRAWE RH10 .... 43 K7
Durham Gdns CCH PO19 .... 107 L4
  WVILLE PO7 .... 288 A12
Durkins Rd EGRIN RH19 .... 31 J4
Durlands Rd HORN PO08 .... 288 D1
Durley Av HORN PO08 .... 288 A6
Durlston Dr MSEA/BNM PO22 * 2 B1
Durlston Pde MSEA/BNM PO22 * .. 2 B1
Durnford Cl CCH PO19 .... 6 B3
Durrants Gdns HAV PO9 .... 289 J9
Durrants Rd HAV PO9 .... 289 J10
Durrell Cl LGNY BN23 .... 164 G3
Durrington Gdns FERR BN12 * . 150 C2
Durrington HI SALV BN13 ...... 116 C6
Durrington La SALV BN13 ...... 116 C6
Dursley Rd LW/ROSE BN22 ...... 10 F4
Dutchells Copse HORS RH12 ..... 56 D3
Dutchells La LW/ROSE BN22 ... 163 J1
Duxhurst La REIG RH2 .... 22 A2
Dyall Cl BURH RH15 .... 74 D5
Dye House La PETW GU28 .... 262 H6
Dyers La ARUN BN18 .... 294 H3
Dyke Cl HOVE BN3 .... 122 A1
Dyke Rd BRI BN1 .... 4 B2
  HOVE BN3 .... 4 B2
Dyke Road Av BRI BN1 .... 122 A1
Dyke Road Pl BRI BN1 * 4 C1
Dyke Road Pl BRI BN1 .... 122 B2
Dymchurch La POLE BN26 .... 132 B6
  SEAF BN25 .... 160 A8
Dymock Cl SEAF BN25 .... 175 J1
The Dymock's HPPT/KEY BN6 ... 272 A11
Dymoke St EMRTH PO10 .... 103 M1
Dymond Rd STLEO TN38 .... 98 F3
Dynevor Rd SBGH/RUST TN4 ...... 38 D7
Dyson Wk CRAWW RH11 * 43 G8

E

Eady Cl SWTR RH13 .... 15 J6
Eagle Cl UCK TN22 .... 77 G7
Eagle Rd RYE TN31 .... 252 H7
Eagles Cha LHPTN BN17 .... 147 H1
Earles Meadow HORS RH12 .... 57 G3
Earls Cl SEAF BN25 .... 159 H8
Earls Gdn LEWES BN7 .... 17 G5
Earl's Rd SBGH/RUST TN4 .... 37 L5
Earl St HAS TN34 .... 13 G5
Earlswood Cl SWTR RH13 .... 15 L2

Early Commons CRAWE RH10 9 K2
Earnley Manor Cl SELS PO20 168 C6
Earnley Rd HISD PO11 166 A3
Earwig La RHWH RH17 203 R11
Easebourne La MIDH GU29 227 K8
Easebourne St MIDH GU29 227 M6
PETW GU28 227 Q2
East Albany Rd SEAF BN25 174 F1
East Ascent STLEO TN38 99 G7
East Av FERR BN12 150 E4
MSEA/BNM PO22 145 L7
East Bank ARUN BN18 * 111 M8
SELS PO20 301 M6
Eastbank STHW BN42 120 E4
East Beach Rd SELS PO20 301 N6
East Beach St HAS TN34 13 K7
East Beeches Rd CROW TN6 67 M7
Eastbourne Av PEV BN24 134 C8
Eastbourne La POLE BN26 162 B6
Eastbourne Rd
BRIE/ROTT BN2 123 J4
EDN/EASTW BN20 162 F1
EGRIN RH19 30 E3
LGNY BN23 164 E1
PEV BN24 165 H1
POLE BN26 131 M8
RING/NEW BN8 276 C3
SEAF BN25 175 J2
UCK TN22 76 F7
Eastbourne Ter SEAF BN25 * 175 G2
Eastbourne Vls CROW TN6 * 210 G1
East Bracklesham Dr
SELS PO20 168 A8
Eastbridge Rd NEWHV BN9 19 J4
Eastbrook Rd PTSD BN41 121 G6
Eastbrook Wy PTSD BN41 120 F6
East Cliff RYE TN31 252 H8
East Cliff Rd SBGH/RUST TN4 37 M3
East Cl MSEA/BNM PO22 145 K8
POLE BN26 132 A7
East Ct EGRIN RH19 * 31 L7
Eastcourt Rd SALV BN13 20 F2
East Court Wy ANG/EP BN16 148 C3
Eastdale Rd BURH RH15 75 H5
Eastdean Hl RCCH PO18 293 M4
East Dean Ri SEAF BN25 159 M8
East Dean Rd
EDN/EASTW BN20 303 K5
East Dr ANG/EP BN16 148 D1
BRIE/ROTT BN2 5 J6
MSEA/BNM PO22 145 M8
Easteds La SWTR RH13 201 R11
East End La HPPT/KEY BN6 272 B7
Eastergate BEXW TN39 96 C8
Eastergate Cl FERR BN12 149 M3
Eastergate La ARUN BN18 111 G4
SELS PO20 110 E4
Eastergate Rd BRIE/ROTT BN2 123 L1
Eastern Av POLE BN26 132 A7
SHOR BN43 119 M6
Eastern Cl ANG/EP BN16 149 G3
SHOR BN43 119 M6
Eastern Pl BRIE/ROTT BN2 154 D1
Eastern Rd BOR GU35 178 G3
BRIE/ROTT BN2 5 H7
HAV PO9 103 H3
HWH RH16 73 J6
LYDD TN29 255 R7
Eastern Ter BRIE/ROTT BN2 5 L9
Eastern Terrace Ms
BRIE/ROTT BN2 5 L9
East Field Cl EMRTH PO10 104 F3
Eastfield La EPSF GU31 258 H2
East Front Rd BOGR PO21 170 F6
East Gdns HPPT/KEY BN6 272 A6
Eastgate Sq CCH PO19 * 6 F4
Eastgate St LEWES BN7 17 G5
Eastgate Whf LEWES BN7 17 H5
East Gun Copse Rd
SWTR RH13 201 N8
East Hampnett La RCCH PO18 109 K3
East Ham Rd LHPTN BN17 147 H4
East Harting St EPSF GU31 258 G2
East Highland Furlong
SEAF BN25 * 174 F1
East Hl EGRIN RH19 31 K3
East Hill Dr LISS GU33 192 D10
Easthill Dr PTSD BN41 121 G3
East Hill La CRAWE RH10 29 J3
East Hill Pas HAS TN34 13 L6
Easthill Wy PTSD BN41 121 G4
Easting Cl SALV BN13 117 L8
East Lake BOGR PO21 2 E5
Eastlake Cl EPSF GU31 223 R6
Eastland Rd CCH PO19 7 H8
Eastlands Cl SBGH/RUST TN4 53 K1
Eastlands Rd SBGH/RUST TN4 53 K1
East Leigh Rd HAV PO9 103 L1
East Lodge Pk CHAM PO6 102 A5
East Mascalls La HWH RH16 206 H10
East Md BOGR PO21 170 F5
FERR BN12 149 L4
East Meadway SHOR BN43 119 M7
East Ms HORS RH12 * 14 D6
Easton Crs BIL RH14 232 B1
Easton La SELS PO20 169 G7
East Onslow Cl FERR BN12 149 K3
Eastover Ct HAV PO9 288 E11
Eastover Wy MSEA/BNM PO22 3 K5
East Pallant CCH PO19 6 E5
East Pde HAS TN34 13 K7
East Pk CRAWE RH10 8 F5
Eastport La LEWES BN7 16 F8
East Rw CCH PO19 6 F4
Eastshaw La MIDH GU29 226 F5
East Strd SELS PO20 167 G5
East St ARUN BN18 296 F2
BIL RH14 232 A1
BRI BN1 4 E7
BRI BN1 84 B7
CCH PO19 6 E4
CRAWE RH10 46 A5
EMRTH PO10 104 C2
HAS TN34 13 K7
HAV PO9 103 G4
HORS RH12 14 D7
HORS RH12 41 K2
LAN/SOMP BN15 152 D1
LEWES BN7 17 G5
LHPTN BN17 147 K4
MAYF TN20 212 F6
PETW GU28 229 L9
PTSD BN41 121 H7
PUL/STOR RH20 266 B4
RYE TN31 252 H8
SEAF BN25 174 E2
SELS PO20 301 L6
SHOR BN43 119 L6
East Tyne SALV BN13 116 C7
East View Cl RCCH PO18 292 C10
East View Flds LEWES BN7 272 H4
East View Ter BAT TN33 249 N12
East Walls CCH PO19 6 F4
East Walls Cl CCH PO19 6 F4
Eastway BEXW TN39 136 B1
HORL RH6 28 A2
East Wy LEWES BN7 85 L3
SELS PO20 301 M6
East Wick HWH RH16 73 M2
Eastwick Cl BRI BN1 83 G6
Eastwood CRAWE RH10 9 J4
Eastwood Rd BEXW TN39 136 F1
Eatenden La BAT TN33 248 A11
Eaton Gdns HOVE BN3 122 B6
Eaton Gv HOVE BN3 122 B6
Eaton Mnr HOVE BN3 * 122 B6
Eaton Pl BRIE/ROTT BN2 5 M9
Eaton Rd HOVE BN3 122 B7
Eaton Vls HOVE BN3 122 A6
Eaton Wk BAT TN33 249 L12
Eaves Cottages CROW TN6 * 211 K2
Ebden's Hl SLVH TN37 283 Q8
Ebenezer Rd HAS TN34 13 M5
Ecmod Rd LW/ROSE BN22 164 B7
Edburton Av BRI BN1 122 E2
Edburton Dro HFD BN5 269 Q10
Edburton Gdns SHOR BN43 119 L4
Eddeys Cl BOR GU35 179 Q3
Eddeys La BOR GU35 179 Q4
Eddington Hl CRAWW RH11 42 F8
Edenbridge Rd EDEN TN8 34 C7
Eden Cl PEV BN24 132 F8
Eden Dr BEXW TN39 136 D1
Eden Rd CRAWW RH11 42 E5
RTW TN1 37 M7
Edensor Rd EDN/EASTW BN20 176 D6
Eden V EGRIN RH19 31 K5
Eden Wk RTW TN1 37 M7
Edgar Cl CRAWE RH10 44 D4
Edgar Rd RHAS TN35 100 B3
Edgefield Gv WVILLE PO7 288 D8
Edgehill Cl HTHF TN21 244 C6
SALV BN13 116 E6
Edgehill Wy PTSD BN41 120 E3
Edgell Rd EMRTH PO10 104 C1
Edinburgh Cl BOGR PO21 171 K3
SWTR RH13 201 R12
Edinburgh Rd BEX TN40 97 H8
BRIE/ROTT BN2 5 H1
SEAF BN25 174 D2
STLEO TN38 98 D6
Edinburgh Sq MIDH GU29 227 J10
Edinburgh Wy EGRIN RH19 47 L2
Edison Rd LGNY BN23 163 M4
Edith Av PEAHV BN10 157 G7
Edith Av North PEAHV BN10 157 H5
Edith Rd RHAS TN35 100 C2
Edmond Cl LGNY BN23 164 D5
Edmonton Rd BEXW TN39 97 G6
SALV BN13 116 B7
Edmund Rd RHAS TN35 100 B3
Edrich Rd CRAWW RH11 42 F8
Edward Av BRIE/ROTT BN2 156 C2
HOVE BN3 121 M2
Edward Cl HOVE BN3 121 M2
SEAF BN25 158 F7
Edward Gdns HAV PO9 102 D4
Edward Rd HWH RH16 73 H6
LW/ROSE BN22 163 M4
SLVH TN37 12 C7
Edwards Av SELS PO20 109 H3
Edwards Cl HORN PO8 288 A7
Edwards Ter
LAN/SOMP BN15 * 117 L6
Edward St BRIE/ROTT BN2 5 G7
LEWES BN7 17 G5
SBGH/RUST TN4 37 G5
Edwards Wy LHPTN BN17 147 H1
Edward Ter STLEO TN38 98 F1
Edward Wy BURH RH15 74 C7
Edwen Cl BOGR PO21 171 G2
Edwin Cl LAN/SOMP BN15 118 B7
Edwin Rd RHAS TN35 100 B3
Effingham Cl BRIE/ROTT BN2 156 B3
Effingham Dr BEXW TN39 136 C1
Effingham La CRAWE RH10 29 K4
Effingham Rd HORL RH6 29 H3
Egan Wy LHPTN BN17 147 G3
Egerton Rd BEXW TN39 137 G2
Egginton Cl BRIE/ROTT BN2 83 M8
Egginton Rd BRIE/ROTT BN2 123 L1
Eglantine Cl HORN PO8 288 C5
Eglantine Wk HORN PO8 288 C5
Egles Gv UCK TN22 76 D4
Egmont Rd HOVE BN3 121 J4
MIDH GU29 227 K7
Egremont Pl BRIE/ROTT BN2 5 H7
HAS TN34 13 L2
Egremont Rw PETW GU28 * 229 L9
Eight Acre La RHAS TN35 284 G8
Eight Acres GSHT GU26 180 F2
Eight Bells Cl UCK TN22 242 D1
Eighth Av LAN/SOMP BN15 118 D6
Eileen Av BRIE/ROTT BN2 156 A4
Eirene Av FERR BN12 150 E4
Eirene Rd FERR BN12 150 D4
Eisenhower Dr SLVH TN37 283 N11
Elaine Gdns HORN PO8 288 A4
Elbridge Crs BOGR PO21 171 H3
Elcombe Cl SELS PO20 168 A8
Elderberry Cl HORN PO8 256 E9
Elderberry Rd BOR GU35 179 Q4
Elderberry Wy HORN PO8 288 C5
Elder Cl PTSD BN41 121 G3
Elderfield Cl EMRTH PO10 104 B2
Elderfield Rd HAV PO9 288 E10
Elder Pl BRI BN1 4 E2
Elder Rd HAV PO9 103 J2
Elderwood Cl BEXW TN39 97 H6
LW/ROSE BN22 163 J3
Eldon Rd EAST BN21 163 H8
WTHG BN11 21 L4
Eldon Wy LHPTN BN17 147 G3
Eldred Av BRI BN1 82 C8
Eldridge Wy SLVH TN37 283 R11
Eleanor Cl LEWES BN7 16 D4
LIPH GU30 179 L9
SEAF BN25 159 J8
Eleanor Gdns
MSEA/BNM PO22 145 J8
Eley Crs BRIE/ROTT BN2 155 K2
Eley Dr BRIE/ROTT BN2 155 K1
Elfin Gv BOGR PO21 2 A7
Elford St HAS TN34 13 H5
Elgar Wk WVILLE PO7 102 A1
Elgar Wy LGNY BN23 164 D2
SWTR RH13 57 G5
Elger Wy CRAWE RH10 28 F5
Elgin Gdns SEAF BN25 175 J1
Elgin Rd FERR BN12 150 C3
Elim Court Gdns CROW TN6 67 K5
Elim Wk HAS TN34 13 H1
Eling Ct HAV PO9 288 E11
Eliot Dr HASM GU27 180 H11
Elizabethan Cl BAT TN33 95 L3
Elizabethan Wy CRAWE RH10 44 B4
Elizabeth Av BOGR PO21 171 H2
HOVE BN3 121 M2
Elizabeth Cl BOGR PO21 171 H2
HOVE BN3 121 M2
SEAF BN25 158 F7
Elizabeth Ct HORL RH6 * 22 F6
Elizabeth Crs EGRIN RH19 31 L6
Elizabeth Pl LAN/SOMP BN15 118 B8
Elizabeth Rd CCH PO19 7 L3
SHOR BN43 120 B5
STLEO TN38 98 F3
WTHG BN11 20 F5
WVILLE PO7 288 A11
Ella Cl SELS PO20 167 K6
Ellanore La SELS PO20 167 G3
Ellasdale Rd BOGR PO21 2 A8
Ellenslea Rd SLVH TN37 12 B7
Ellen St HOVE BN3 122 A6
PTSD BN41 121 H6
Ellenwhorne La RBTBR TN32 249 P6
Ellerslie La BEXW TN39 96 E6
Ellesmere Orch EMRTH PO10 104 C1
Elliot Cl CRAWE RH10 44 B4
Elliots Wy HTHF TN21 244 D5
Ellis Av SALV BN13 116 D5
Ellis Cl ARUN BN18 112 E3
HAS TN34 12 E7
Ellisfield Rd HAV PO9 102 F1
Ellison Cl CROW TN6 67 K5
Ellis Wy BOGR PO21 170 F5
UCK TN22 76 C5
Ellman Rd CRAWW RH11 42 D6
Ellson Cl CRAWE RH10 44 B5
Ellwood Pl CRAWW RH11 * 42 E3
Elm Av ANG/EP BN16 149 G4
HAIL BN27 * 90 A2
Elm Cl BOGR PO21 170 F4
BOR GU35 178 H6
HOVE BN3 122 B3
RING/NEW BN8 276 D10
SEAF BN25 175 J2
SELS PO20 168 A7
SHOR BN43 119 L4
Elm Ct NEWHV BN9 18 D3
Elmcroft Pl SELS PO20 110 C7
Elm Dr EGRIN RH19 31 M8
HOVE BN3 121 K4
MSEA/BNM PO22 146 A8
Elmer Cl MSEA/BNM PO22 146 A8
Elmer Ct MSEA/BNM PO22 146 B8
Elmer Rd MSEA/BNM PO22 145 L8
Elmeswelle Rd HORN PO8 288 B3
Elm Gv BOGR PO21 171 M2
BRIE/ROTT BN2 5 J3
LAN/SOMP BN15 118 C8
LW/ROSE BN22 163 L4
MSEA/BNM PO22 110 F6
SELS PO20 301 K6
SWTR RH13 15 G7
WTHG BN11 150 E2
Elm Grove La STEY/UB BN44 78 C2
Elmgrove Rd LHPTN BN17 147 L3
Elm Gv South
MSEA/BNM PO22 110 F7
Elmhurst Av RTWE/PEM TN2 39 J1
Elmhurst Cl ANG/EP BN16 114 F7
Elmhurst La SWTR RH13 200 E7
Elm La HAV PO9 103 G4
Elmleigh MIDH GU29 226 H9
Elmleigh Ct MIDH GU29 * 226 H9
Elmleigh Rd HAV PO9 103 G3
Elmore Rd BRIE/ROTT BN2 5 G5
Elm Pk FERR BN12 149 L2
RCCH PO18 106 B7
Elm Park Rd HAV PO9 103 G3
Elm Pl ANG/EP BN16 148 C4
Elm Ri SALV BN13 298 H11
Elm Rd HAV PO9 103 H5
PTSD BN41 121 G5
SELS PO20 110 D6
WTHG BN11 21 J6
Elms Av EAST BN21 11 G7
Elmsdown Pl HAIL BN27 92 B6
Elms Dr LAN/SOMP BN15 118 C7
Elmsfield SELS PO20 301 L6
Elms La RHAS TN35 285 R8
SELS PO20 167 H4
Elms Lea Av BRI BN1 122 D3
Elmsmead RYE TN31 252 G1
Elms Ride SELS PO20 167 H4
Elms Rd EAST BN21 11 G7
Elmstead Gdns SELS PO20 167 H3
Elmstead Park Rd SELS PO20 167 H3
Elmstead Rd BEX TN40 97 K8
The Elms RING/NEW BN8 274 H12
Elmstone Cl LAN/SOMP BN15 118 C7
Elms Wy SELS PO20 167 H3
Elm Ter LISS GU33 192 B8
Elm Tree Cl BOGR PO21 143 M7
HORL RH6 * 22 F5
SELS PO20 301 L5
Elm Vls SEAF BN25 * 174 E3
Elm Wy HTHF TN21 244 E8
Elmwood Av MSEA/BNM PO22 2 F3
Elmwood Cl LGNY BN23 164 B1
Elmwood Gdns LGNY BN23 164 B1
Elphick Pl CROW TN6 67 L6
Elphick Rd NEWHV BN9 18 E2
RING/NEW BN8 275 L10
Elphick's Pl RTWE/PEM TN2 54 A1
Elphinstone Av HAS TN34 13 H1
Elphinstone Gdns HAS TN34 99 L2
Elphinstone Rd HAS TN34 13 H2
Elrington Rd HOVE BN3 122 B4
Elsie Rd WTHG BN11 20 D7
Elsted Cl CRAWW RH11 43 G1
Elsted Crs BRI BN1 83 H7
Elsted Rd BEXW TN39 136 B3
MIDH GU29 225 N12
Elven Cl EDN/EASTW BN20 303 J4
Elven La EDN/EASTW BN20 303 J4
Elverlands Cl FERR BN12 149 L5
Elvetham Mt SLVH TN37 * 12 B7
Elvin Crs BRIE/ROTT BN2 155 K1
Elwood Cl BURH RH15 74 E8
Ely Cl CRAWE RH10 43 L7
SALV BN13 150 E1
SELS PO20 167 L5
Ely Ct RTW TN1 * 38 A5
Ely Gdns BOGR PO21 171 J2
Ely Rd SALV BN13 150 E1
Emberwood CRAWW RH11 * 43 J1
Embleton Rd BOR GU35 179 Q3
Emerald Cl WVILLE PO7 288 B10
Emerald Quay SHOR BN43 119 M7
Emlyn Rd HORL RH6 22 D5
Emmanuel Rd HAS TN34 13 K3
Emms La SWTR RH13 201 J11
Empire Vls REDH RH1 22 F2
Emsbrook Dr EMRTH PO10 104 A3
Emsworth Cl CRAWE RH10 * 44 B6
Emsworth Common Rd
HAV PO9 289 L12
Emsworth House Cl
EMRTH PO10 103 M4
Emsworth Rd EMRTH PO10 138 C1
HAV PO9 103 J4
End La HFD BN5 268 F4
Ends Pl HORS RH12 * 187 M10
Endwell Rd BEX TN40 137 H2
Enfield Rd CRAWW RH11 43 G7
Engalee EGRIN RH19 31 H7
Englefield HORS RH12 201 Q3
English Cl HOVE BN3 121 K5
English Pas LEWES BN7 17 H5
Enholms La RHWH RH17 207 R5
Ennerdale Cl CRAWW RH11 8 B8
HORN PO8 256 D11
Ennerdale Dr LAN/SOMP BN15 118 A8
Ennerdale Rd BOR GU35 178 G4
Ensign Ct STLEO TN38 * 98 F7
Ensign Wy LHPTN BN17 147 M3
Enterprise Ct FERR BN12 * 150 B2
Enterprise Rd HORN PO8 288 D1
Enys Rd EAST BN21 10 C5
E Plan Est NEWHV BN9 * 158 C4
Epping Wk CRAWE RH10 9 K8
Epsom Cl STLEO TN38 98 F5
Epsom Rd CRAWE RH10 9 L8
Erica Cl HORN PO8 288 C6
LGNY BN23 164 A3
Erica Wy CRAWE RH10 28 F7
HORN PO8 288 C6
HORS RH12 56 C4
Ericsson Wy BURH RH15 74 C7
Eridge Cl BEXW TN39 136 E1
CRAWE RH10 44 B3
Eridge Dr CROW TN6 67 L6
Eridge Gdns CROW TN6 67 M6
Eridge Gn LEWES BN7 16 C3
Eridge La CROW TN6 69 G7
Eridge Rd CROW TN6 67 L6
CROW TN6 68 B5
EAST BN21 163 H6
HOVE BN3 121 M3
RRTW TN3 52 C3
RTWE/PEM TN2 37 L7
Erin Wy BURH RH15 74 D6
Eriskay Ct SALV BN13 116 A8
Eriswell Rd WTHG BN11 20 F6
Erles Rd LIPH GU30 193 R1
Ernest Cl EMRTH PO10 104 A4
Ernest Rd HAV PO9 102 D1
Erringham Rd SHOR BN43 119 K5
Erroll Rd HOVE BN3 121 H7
Ersham Rd HAIL BN27 92 A8
Ersham Wy HAIL BN27 92 A7
Erskine Cl CRAWW RH11 42 D7
Erskine Park Rd
SBGH/RUST TN4 37 G5
Esher Cl BOGR PO21 171 G3
SEAF BN25 174 F1
Esher Dr LHPTN BN17 147 L4
Eshton Rd LW/ROSE BN22 11 J2
Eskbank Av BRI BN1 82 F6
Eskdale Cl HORN PO8 256 D11
LGNY BN23 164 A1
Esmond Cl EMRTH PO10 104 A5
Esmonde Cl LHPTN BN17 147 L3
Esplanade SEAF BN25 174 F4
Esplanade Ct WTHG BN11 * 21 M6
Esplanade Ms SEAF BN25 174 E3
The Esplanade BOGR PO21 2 D8
PEAHV BN10 156 F6
WTHG BN11 21 L6
Essenden Rd STLEO TN38 98 F7
Essenhigh Dr SALV BN13 116 A7
Essex Cl RTWE/PEM TN2 53 L1
Essex Ms NEWHV BN9 * 18 F3
Essex Pl BRIE/ROTT BN2 * 5 J8
NEWHV BN9 * 18 F3
Essex Rd BOGR PO21 2 C3
BOR GU35 178 G5
STLEO TN38 98 F1
Essex St BRIE/ROTT BN2 5 H7
Estate Rd NEWHV BN9 19 H3
Estcots Dr EGRIN RH19 31 M8
The Estuary LHPTN BN17 147 L5
Etchingham Rd LGNY BN23 164 D4
Ethelred Cl LGNY BN23 164 D5
Ethelred Rd SALV BN13 20 A2
Ethel St HOVE BN3 122 A6
Ethelwulf Rd SALV BN13 20 A2
Etherington Hl RRTW TN3 37 H1
Etherton Wy SEAF BN25 175 G1
Ethnam La HAWK TN18 218 B6
Eton Cl BOGR PO21 171 K1
SEAF BN25 175 G1
Eton Dr SELS PO20 167 L5
Eton Rd WTHG BN11 20 B3
Ettrick Cl CCH PO19 7 G6
Ettrick Rd CCH PO19 6 F6
Eugene Wy LGNY BN23 165 G4
Evans Cl CRAWE RH10 44 C4
Evans Pl MSEA/BNM PO22 2 E1
Eveley Cl BOR GU35 178 E9
Evelyn Av ANG/EP BN16 148 C5
NEWHV BN9 18 E3
Evelyn Rd LEWES BN7 16 C3
SALV BN13 21 H1
Evelyn Ter BRIE/ROTT BN2 5 K6
Evelyn Wk CRAWE RH10 9 G9
Everglades Av HORN PO8 288 A6
Eversfield SWTR RH13 202 A8
Eversfield Pl SLVH TN37 12 C8
Eversfield Rd EAST BN21 10 E5
SWTR RH13 15 G7
Evershed Ct PEAHV BN10 * 156 E6
Evershed Wy SHOR BN43 120 A6
Eversley Cl SLVH TN37 12 B2
Eversley Crs HAV PO9 102 E1
SLVH TN37 12 B2
Eversley Rd BEX TN40 137 H2
SLVH TN37 12 B1
Ewart St BRIE/ROTT BN2 5 H4
Ewehurst La RRTW TN3 36 E3
Ewelands HORL RH6 23 H5
Ewens Gdns MSEA/BNM PO22 110 F6
Ewhurst Cl CRAWW RH11 8 C3
HAS TN34 99 L1
HAV PO9 102 E1
Ewhurst La RYE TN31 250 C1
Ewhurst Rd BRIE/ROTT BN2 123 H5
CRAWW RH11 8 C3
Exbury Rd HAV PO9 288 H12
Excalibur Cl CRAWW RH11 42 D3
Exceat Cl BRIE/ROTT BN2 123 K7
LGNY BN23 163 M1
The Excelsior BRI BN1 * 122 C1
Exchange Rd CRAWE RH10 9 H3
Exeter Cl BOGR PO21 171 L2
CRAWE RH10 43 K7
EMRTH PO10 104 A2
LW/ROSE BN22 163 G3
Exeter Ct WTHG BN11 * 20 A7
Exeter Rd CCH PO19 107 K4
Exeter St BRI BN1 4 B1
Exmoor Cl SALV BN13 116 C6
Exmoor Crs SALV BN13 116 D6
Exmoor Dr SALV BN13 116 D5
Exmouth Pl HAS TN34 13 K6
Exton Rd CCH PO19 7 G8
HAV PO9 289 J12
Eyles Cl HORS RH12 14 A1

F

Faber Cl HAV PO9 103 H1
Fabian Cl WVILLE PO7 288 B9
Fabians Wy HFD BN5 269 J4
Factory La HAIL BN27 91 M7
Fairbanks HWH RH16 73 H5
Fairbridge Wy BURH RH15 74 E4
Faircox La HFD BN5 269 J4
Faircrouch La WADH TN5 71 H5
Fairdene STHW BN42 120 E4
Fairfax Av SLVH TN37 283 N10
Fairfield HAIL BN27 279 P11
PEAHV BN10 * 157 G6
Fairfield Av HORL RH6 22 F8
RTWE/PEM TN2 38 B4
Fairfield Cha BEXW TN39 136 E1
Fairfield Cl BURH RH15 74 E5
EMRTH PO10 104 A3
RCCH PO18 106 B8
RHWH RH17 206 D1
SHOR BN43 120 A4
Fairfield Cottages SWTR RH13 235 K3
Fairfield Crs HPPT/KEY BN6 270 H3
Fairfield Gdns PTSD BN41 121 G4
Fairfield Ms PUL/STOR RH20 * 267 J9
Fairfield Ri PETW GU28 229 L10
Fairfield Rd BURH RH15 74 E6
EDN/EASTW BN20 176 E4
EGRIN RH19 47 L1
HAV PO9 103 G4
PUL/STOR RH20 267 K9
RCCH PO18 106 A8
SLVH TN37 283 R11
Fairfields SALV BN13 116 F8
Fairfield Ter HAV PO9 * 103 G4
Fairfield Wy HWH RH16 73 G1
PUL/STOR RH20 267 K9
Fairford Cl HWH RH16 73 H4
Fairglen Rd WADH TN5 71 G6
Fairhazel UCK TN22 76 A4
Fairholme Dr ARUN BN18 145 M3
Fairholme Rd NEWHV BN9 158 E4
Fairhurst PEAHV BN10 * 156 E6
Fairisle Cl HAIL BN27 91 M3
Fair Isle Cl LGNY BN23 * 164 D5
Fairlands ANG/EP BN16 148 E4
MSEA/BNM PO22 2 A1
Fair La RBTBR TN32 248 D1
Fairlawn ANG/EP BN16 148 B3
Fairlawn Crs EGRIN RH19 31 G7
Fairlawn Dr EGRIN RH19 31 G7
SALV BN13 21 H1
Fairlawns HORL RH6 23 G7
SHOR BN43 119 M5
Fairlawns Dr HAIL BN27 279 P11
Fairlea Cl BURH RH15 74 E5
Fairlead LHPTN BN17 147 L5
Fairlea Rd EMRTH PO10 104 A2
Fairlie Gdns BRI BN1 122 D2
Fairlight Av PEAHV BN10 156 E6
RHAS TN35 100 C2
Fairlight Cl BEX TN40 97 M8
POLE BN26 131 M7
Fairlight Fld RING/NEW BN8 275 J12
Fairlight Gdns RHAS TN35 101 L1
Fairlight Pl BRIE/ROTT BN2 5 J1
Fairlight Rd LW/ROSE BN22 11 K2
RHAS TN35 100 C2
Fairman's La STPH/PW TN12 188 G3
Fairmead Cl PUL/STOR RH20 266 B2
Fair Meadow RYE TN31 252 H6
Fairmead Wk HORN PO8 288 B6
Fairmile Bottom ARUN BN18 295 M10
Fairmile Rd RTWE/PEM TN2 38 D4
Fairmount Rd BEX TN40 97 J8
Fairoak POLE BN26 132 B7
Fair Oak Cl HTHF TN21 244 D6
Fair Oak Dr HAV PO9 103 G2
Fair Pl RHWH RH17 * 238 F9
Fairplace RHWH RH17 238 F9
Fairstone Cl RHAS TN35 100 D1
Fairstone Ct HORL RH6 23 G5
Fair Vw HORS RH12 201 R2
Fairview Av FERR BN12 150 B4
Fairview La CROW TN6 67 K5
RRTW TN3 * 53 G1
Fairview Ri BRI BN1 82 C8
Fairview Rd BOR GU35 179 Q4
LAN/SOMP BN15 118 D5
Fairview Ter BOR GU35 * 179 P3
Fairway CRAWE RH10 29 G7
CRAWW RH11 42 C4
LHPTN BN17 147 L5
Fairway Cl CRAWE RH10 28 F7
EDN/EASTW BN20 176 C3
LIPH GU30 193 L2

Fairway Crs PTSD BN41....121 H3
Fairways GSHT GU26....180 E3
Fairways Cl SEAF BN25....175 J3
Fairways Rd SEAF BN25....175 J3
The Fairways SBGH/RUST TN4....37 M2
The Fairway BEXW TN39....96 E7
　BOGR PO21....171 H5
　BOR GU35....178 E8
　HAV PO9....289 K7
　LAN/SOMP BN15....118 C3
　MIDH BN22....226 H12
　NEWHV BN9....18 B5
　STLEO TN38....98 E5
Fairy Crossway HORN PO8....288 C7
Faithful Crs PUL/STOR RH20....265 Q11
Falaise Rd HAS TN34....12 D7
　NEWHV BN9....158 A4
Falconbury Dr BEXW TN39....136 C2
Falcon Cl CRAWW RH11....43 J1
　SHOR BN43....120 B7
Falconer Dr BAT TN33....282 C5
Falcon Gdns LHPTN BN17....147 H1
Falcon Rd HORN PO8....288 B2
Falcon Wy HAIL BN27....92 A3
Falkland Av LHPTN BN17....147 L1
Falklands Cl MSEA/BNM PO22....2 F7
Falklands Dr SWTR RH13....57 G6
Fallow Deer SWTR RH13....57 G6
Fallowfield Cl HOVE BN3....121 L3
Fallowfield Crs HOVE BN3....121 L3
Fallowfield Wy HORL RH6....23 G5
Falmer Av BRIE/ROTT BN2....156 D4
　FERR BN12....150 A4
Falmer Cl CRAWW RH11....8 E7
　EDN/EASTW BN20....163 G6
　FERR BN12....150 A4
Falmer Ct UCK TN22 *....76 A4
Falmer Gdns BRIE/ROTT BN2....124 C5
Falmer House Rd BRI BN1....84 A6
Falmer Rd BRIE/ROTT BN2....124 C3
Falmouth Cl LGNY BN23....164 E5
Falmouth Ms SWTR RH13 *....201 R12
Faraday Av EGRIN RH19....47 L3
Faraday Cl LW/ROSE BN22....163 L4
　SALV BN13....116 D7
Faraday Rd CRAWE RH10....27 L7
Farebrothers HORS RH12 *....187 Q9
Faresmead BOGR PO21....171 J4
Farhalls Crs HORS RH12....56 E3
Farlaine Rd EDN/EASTW BN20....163 H4
Farleigh Cl HAV PO9....288 E12
Farley Bank RHAS TN35....13 L2
Farleys Wy RYE TN31....252 A3
Farley Wy RHAS TN35....285 P12
Farlington Av HWH RH16....73 J4
Farlington Ct HWH RH16....73 H4
Farm Acre HORL RH6 *....148 E3
Farman St HOVE BN3 *....122 C7
Farm Av HORS RH12....14 A4
Farm Cl BIL RH14....198 H2
　CRAWE RH10....9 K2
　EGRIN RH19....48 A1
　HFD BN5....269 K4
　HORS RH12....187 Q10
　HPPT/KEY BN6....271 M5
　MSEA/BNM PO22....146 A8
　PTSD BN41....120 F3
　SEAF BN25....175 H4
Farmcombe Cl
　RTWE/PEM TN2 *....38 A7
Farmcombe La RTW TN1....38 A7
Farmcombe Rd
　RTWE/PEM TN2 *....38 A7
Farm Cnr MSEA/BNM PO22....145 M8
Far Meadow Wy EMRTH PO10....103 L5
Farmfield Dr HORL RH6....27 G1
Farm Gdns RYE TN31....252 B3
Farm Hl BRIE/ROTT BN2....124 B3
Farmhouse Wy HORN PO8....288 B4
Farmlands Av POLE BN26....162 E1
Farmlands Cl
　EDN/EASTW BN20....162 F1
　SLVH TN37....283 R12
Farmlands Wy POLE BN26....131 L8
Farmland Wy HAIL BN27....92 B4
Farm La HPPT/KEY BN6....272 B6
　RCCH PO18....105 G6
　RYE TN31....253 Q10
Farmleigh Cl CRAWE RH10....44 B1
Farm Ms HOVE BN3 *....122 C7
Farm Rd HOVE BN3....122 C7
　SELS PO20....168 A4
Farm Vw EMRTH PO10....104 A2
Farm View Av HORN PO8....256 C8
Farm Wy ANG/EP BN16....148 A4
　BURH RH15....75 J8
　STHW BN42....120 F6
Farmway Cl HOVE BN3....121 L3
Farncombe Cl RHWH RH17....238 C8
Farncombe Rd LEWES BN7 *....17 J6
　WTHG BN11....21 L5
Farndell Cl CCH PO19....7 J3
Farne Cl HAIL BN27....91 M3
　SELS PO20....168 C1
Farnefold Rd STEY/UB BN44....78 C1
Farne La SELS PO20....168 D1
Farnham Av HPPT/KEY BN6....271 P4
Farnham Beeches RRTW TN3....36 F3
Farnham Cl CRAWW RH11....59 H1
　RRTW TN3....36 F6
Farnham La HASM GU27....181 J8
　RRTW TN3....36 F5
Farnham Pl RRTW TN3....36 F6
Farnham Rd BOR GU35....178 D9
　LISS GU33....192 B9
　PSF GU32....223 Q1
Farnhurst La CRAN GU6....184 C5
Farnhurst Rd
　MSEA/BNM PO22....111 G7
Farningham Rd CROW TN6....211 K2
Farnlea Rd BURH RH15....75 J4
The Faroes LHPTN BN17....147 M3
Farrance Ct RTW TN1 *....38 A5
Farr Cl RHWH RH17....72 C1
Farriers Cl BIL RH14....231 R2
Farriers Pl RING/NEW BN8....275 J12
Farriers Wy UCK TN22....76 E6
　WVILLE PO7....288 D8
Farthing Cl HAV PO9....103 H1
Farthing Flds BOR GU35....179 M4
Farthing Hl WADH TN5....191 K12
Farthing La HAIL BN27....92 A5
Farthings Ct BAT TN33....282 D6
Farthings Hl HORS RH12 *....14 A7
The Farthings CROW TN6....67 M6
Farthings Wk HORS RH12....201 Q3
Fastnet Cl LGNY BN23....164 D5

Fastnet Wy LHPTN BN17....147 M4
Faulkner Cl CRAWW RH11....59 H1
Faulkners Wy BURH RH15....74 F4
Faversham Rd LGNY BN23....164 C3
Fawley Ct HAV PO9....289 J12
Fawn Ri HFD BN5....269 K3
Faygate Cl BEXW TN39....97 G5
Faygate La HORS RH12....41 K2
Faygate Rd LW/ROSE BN22....163 K3
Fayre Meadow RBTBR TN32....248 E1
Fearon Rd HAIL BN27....13 G2
Felbridge Av CRAWE RH10....44 C3
Felbridge Cl EGRIN RH19....31 H6
Felbridge Pl EGRIN RH19....30 F5
Felbridge Pl EGRIN RH19 *....30 F5
Felcot Rd EGRIN RH19....30 B6
Felcourt Rd EGRIN RH19....31 H1
The Feld EGRIN RH19....30 F6
Fellcott Wy HORS RH12....201 Q4
Fellows Rd HAS TN34....99 M3
Felpham Gdns
　MSEA/BNM PO22....145 G8
Felpham Rd MSEA/BNM PO22....3 K5
Felpham Wy MSEA/BNM PO22....3 J5
Felride HWH RH16....73 H6
Fenby Cl SWTR RH13....57 G5
Fenchurch Rd CRAWE RH10....44 A5
Fen Ct STLEO TN38....98 D4
Fenhurst Cl HORS RH12....201 Q4
Fennel Crs CRAWW RH11....43 G6
Fennell's Cl EAST BN21....10 A1
Ferbies RRTW TN3....36 F2
Ferdinand Ter RRTW TN3 *....52 B7
Fereday Cl LAN/SOMP BN15....118 D7
Fermandy La CRAWE RH10....29 M8
Fermor Rd CROW TN6....210 G2
Fermor Wy CROW TN6....210 G1
Fern Cl EPSF GU31....223 R6
　LGNY BN23....164 B2
Ferncote Rd BOR GU35....178 H6
Fern Cottages CROW TN6 *....68 A7
Ferndale RTWE/PEM TN2....38 C4
　WVILLE PO7....288 A10
Ferndale Cl RTWE/PEM TN2....38 B5
Ferndale Point
　RTWE/PEM TN2 *....38 B5
Ferndale Rd BURH RH15....75 G8
　CCH PO19....107 M3
　HOVE BN3....122 C6
Ferndale Wk ANG/EP BN16....114 F7
Fernden La HASM GU27....195 M2
Ferndown CRAWE RH10....28 C7
　HORL RH6....22 F4
Ferndown Gdns
　MSEA/BNM PO22....3 M3
Fern Dr HAV PO9....103 H3
Fern Gn HAIL BN27....92 A4
Fernhill Cl CRAWE RH10....30 A8
Fernhill Rd HORL RH6....28 C3
Fernhurst Cl BRI BN1....83 H7
　CRAWW RH11....43 G1
Fernhurst Crs BRI BN1....83 G8
Fernhurst Dr FERR BN12....149 M3
Fernhurst Gdns BOGR PO21....171 J3
Fernhurst Rd LIPH GU30....193 Q10
Fernlea BOR GU35....178 B8
Fernlea Cl RHAS TN35....284 B5
Fern Rd PUL/STOR RH20....265 R12
　STLEO TN38....98 E4
Fernside Av STLEO TN38....98 E5
The Ferns RTW TN1....38 A5
Fern Wy HORS RH12....56 C4
Fernwood Ri BRI BN1....82 C8
Feroners Cl CRAWE RH10....9 M7
Ferrers Cl CRAWW RH11....8 A1
Ferring Cl CRAWW RH11....8 A1
　FERR BN12....149 K5
　RYE TN31....252 F7
Ferring Gdns MSEA/BNM PO22....3 L3
Ferring Grange Gdns
　FERR BN12....149 K3
Ferringham La FERR BN12....149 K4
Ferringham Wy FERR BN12....149 K5
Ferring La FERR BN12....149 L2
Ferring Marine FERR BN12....149 L5
Ferring St FERR BN12....149 K3
Ferry Hl WSEA TN36....286 D1
Ferry Rd LHPTN BN17....147 G5
　RYE TN31....252 G8
　SHOR BN43....119 L2
Festival Gdns BEXW TN39....97 H4
Fetherston Rd
　LAN/SOMP BN15....118 D6
Feversham Cl SHOR BN43....120 A7
Fidler Cl SELS PO20....301 M4
Field Cl ARUN BN18....111 J4
　BURH RH15....74 D5
　LAN/SOMP BN15....118 C7
　SEAF BN25....175 H3
Fieldend HORS RH12....57 G4
Field End PUL/STOR RH20....266 B11
　UCK TN22....241 M1
Fielden La CROW TN6....67 J8
Fielden Rd CROW TN6....67 H7
Fieldfare Cl HORN PO8....256 D9
Fieldgate Cl RRTW RH13....202 H5
The Fieldings HORL RH6....23 G5
　SWTR RH13....233 G2
Field Pl LHPTN BN17....147 J4
　LIPH GU30....193 J2
Field Place Pde FERR BN12 *....150 D2
Field Rd SELS PO20....167 L6
Field Rw WTHG BN11....21 G6
Fields End Cl HWH RH16....73 J5
The Fields SELS PO20 *....110 C2
Fieldview HORL RH6....23 G5
Fieldway HASM GU27....181 M10
　HPPT/KEY BN6....272 A2
　HWH RH16....73 J1
　RYE TN31....250 E8
Field Wy STLEO TN38....98 D5
Fiennes Rd HAIL BN27....279 P11
Fifth Av HAV PO9....103 J3
　LAN/SOMP BN15....118 D3
　SALV BN13....117 H5
Figg La CROW TN6....210 G1
Filbert Crs CRAWW RH11....42 F3
Filching Cl POLE BN26....162 D2
Filching Rd EDN/EASTW BN20....163 G8
Filder Cl LW/ROSE BN22....163 M7
Filey Cl CRAWW RH11....42 G5
Filsham Dr BEX TN40....97 M7
Filsham Rd STLEO TN38....98 E6
Filsham Va STLEO TN38....98 E6
Fincham Cl ANG/EP BN16....148 E4

Finch Crs CRAWE RH10....46 B4
Finchdean Rd HAV PO9....102 E1
Finches Cl LAN/SOMP BN15....118 C8
　LHPTN BN17....147 H1
　SWTR RH13....234 F10
Finches Gdns MSEA/BNM PO22....206 D8
Finches La HWH RH16....73 K1
　PUL/STOR RH20....265 K5
Finches Park Rd HWH RH16....73 K1
The Finches BEX TN40....137 L1
　SHOR BN43....119 M5
　STLEO TN38....283 P12
Finch Gdns MSEA/BNM PO22....144 A6
Finchmead La PSF GU32....223 J5
Findon Av BRIE/ROTT BN2....156 D4
Findon By-Pass SALV BN13....298 G11
Findon Cl BEXW TN39....136 D2
　HOVE BN3....121 J2
　SEAF BN25....175 J2
Findon Dr MSEA/BNM PO22....145 J7
Findon Rd BRIE/ROTT BN2....123 L8
　CRAWW RH11....43 G1
　SALV BN13....116 E2
Findon Wy HORS RH12....201 N2
Finians La LW/SOMP BN15....118 C8
Finisterre Cl LGNY BN23....164 D5
Finisterre Wy LHPTN BN17....147 M5
Finmere Cl LW/ROSE BN22....164 B7
Finmere Rd LW/ROSE BN22....164 B7
Finsbury Cl HAV PO9....117 H7
Finsbury Rd BRIE/ROTT BN2....5 H4
Fir Cl BRIE/ROTT BN2....124 E6
　MSEA/BNM PO22....145 G8
Fircroft Av LAN/SOMP BN15....118 D2
Fircroft Cl CRAWW RH11....43 H7
Fircroft Crs ANG/EP BN16....148 C5
Fir Gv BOR GU35....178 E8
Firgrove Rd BOR GU35....178 E8
Fir Grove Rd HTHF TN21....243 Q6
Firlands HORL RH6....23 H5
Firle Bostal RING/NEW BN8....128 A3
Firle Cl CRAWE RH10....43 K1
　RHAS TN35....100 D1
　SEAF BN25....159 K8
Firle Dr SEAF BN25....159 K8
Firle Gra SEAF BN25....159 K8
Firle Rd BEXW TN39....136 C1
　BRIE/ROTT BN2....5 M3
　LAN/SOMP BN15....118 C4
　LW/ROSE BN22....11 G3
　PEAHV BN10....157 G4
　RING/NEW BN8....89 G7
　SEAF BN25....159 K8
Firs Av HORN PO8....288 A7
　MSEA/BNM PO22....145 G8
Firs Av West MSEA/BNM PO22....145 G8
Firsdown Cl SALV BN13....116 D3
Firsdown Rd SALV BN13....116 D4
First Av BEX TN40....97 L8
　EMRTH PO10....104 E5
　HAV PO9....103 J3
　HORN PO8....256 D10
　HOVE BN3....122 B8
　LAN/SOMP BN15....118 D5
　MSEA/BNM PO22....145 G7
　NEWHV BN9....18 B5
　RYE TN31....254 A11
　SALV BN13....117 H5
　SELS PO20....168 A8
The Firs LIPH GU30....193 Q2
　RHAS TN35 *....100 A4
First St RRTW TN3....36 E6
Firtoft Cl BURH RH15....75 G6
Fir Toll Rd MAYF TN20....211 R7
Fir Tree Av HASM GU27....180 C11
Fir Tree Cl BEXW TN39....136 B2
　CRAWW RH11....27 G8
　HAIL BN27....92 B6
　PUL/STOR RH20....266 A7
　SWTR RH13....203 M6
Fir Tree La PUL/STOR RH20....266 A7
Firtree Rd HAS TN34....13 K1
Fir Tree Rd SBGH/RUST TN4....37 L7
Fir Tree Wy HPPT/KEY BN6....271 P5
　MSEA/BNM PO22....144 B6
Firway GSHT GU26....180 B4
Firwood Cl HTHF TN21....244 D5
　LW/ROSE BN22....163 K4
Firwood Hl HTHF TN21....244 D5
Fishbourne Rd (East)
　CCH PO19....107 J7
Fishbourne Rd (West)
　CCH PO19....107 H7
Fisher Cl CRAWE RH10....9 G8
　LGNY BN23....164 E6
Fisher La MFD/CHID GU8....183 M10
　SELS PO20....110 C6
The Fishermans EMRTH PO10....104 B5
Fisherman's Wk BOGR PO21....171 J4
　SELS PO20....301 M7
　SHOR BN43....119 J7
Fishers Cl LHPTN BN17....147 M5
Fishers Ct HORS RH12....14 C1
Fishersgate Cl PTSD BN41....120 F6
Fishersgate Ter PTSD BN41....120 F6
Fisher St LEWES BN7....16 F6
Fish La BOGR PO21....171 L3
　SELS PO20....300 H5
Fishmarket Rd RYE TN31....252 H8
Fishponds La RHAS TN35....284 B6
Fitch Dr BRIE/ROTT BN2....123 K4
Fitchet Cl CRAWW RH11....43 G1
Fittleworth Cl FERR BN12....149 M1
Fittleworth Dr
　MSEA/BNM PO22....145 J7
Fittleworth Rd BIL RH14....230 D3
Fitzalan Rd ARUN BN18....112 F4
　LHPTN BN17....147 K5
　SWTR RH13....15 L1
Fitzgerald Av SEAF BN25....174 F5
Fitzgerald Cl
　EDN/EASTW BN20....176 F4
Fitzgerald Pk SEAF BN25....174 F5
Fitzgerald Rd LEWES BN7....17 H2
Fitzherbert Dr BRIE/ROTT BN2....5 K5
Fitzjohns Rd LEWES BN7....16 E4
Fitzmaurice Av LW/ROSE BN22....11 H1
Fitzroy Rd LEWES BN7....16 E4
Fitzwilliam Cl BOGR PO21....171 J4
Fitzwygram Crs HAV PO9....103 G2
Five Acres CRAWE RH10....43 K1

　RCCH PO18....290 H12
Five Acres Cl BOR GU35....179 J4
Five Chimneys La UCK TN22....210 H12
Five Heads Rd HORN PO8....288 B1
Five Houses WSEA TN36....286 D1
Five Oaks SWTR RH13....200 H5
Flag Sq SHOR BN43....119 L7
Flag Wk HORN PO8....288 A5
Flamsteed Hts CRAWW RH11 *....43 G8
Flamsteed Rd HAIL BN27....93 M4
Flansham La MSEA/BNM PO22....145 H6
Flansham Ms
　MSEA/BNM PO22....145 H7
Flansham Pk
　MSEA/BNM PO22....145 H7
Flatt Rd RCCH PO18....105 J5
Flaxman Av CCH PO19....107 J7
Flax Mean MSEA/BNM PO22....145 G8
Fleet Cl LHPTN BN17....147 M3
Fleetend Cl HAV PO9....288 F11
Fleet Wood Cl SLVH TN37....283 Q11
Fleming Cl LGNY BN23....164 E3
Fleming Ct BOGR PO21....170 F4
Fleming Wy CRAWE RH10....27 K7
Fletcher Av SLVH TN37....283 N10
Fletcher Cl BOGR PO21....171 G3
　CRAWE RH10....9 G8
　HAIL BN27....92 B6
Fletcher Pl SELS PO20....142 B4
Fletcher Rd SALV BN13....117 K3
Fletchers SWTR RH13....201 Q10
Fletchers Cl SWTR RH13....15 L1
Fletchers Fld LIPH GU30....193 Q2
Fletcher's La RCCH PO18....140 C4
　SELS PO20....169 J2
Fletcher Wy ANG/EP BN16....114 E7
　BOGR PO21....72 F7
　HWH RH16....72 F7
Fletching Cl BRIE/ROTT BN2....123 L5
Fletching Rd LW/ROSE BN22....163 M3
Fletching St MAYF TN20....212 E6
Flexford Gdns HAV PO9....103 H2
Flimwell Cl BRIE/ROTT BN2....123 K8
　LGNY BN23....163 M1
　STLEO TN38....98 C3
　WADH TN5....191 Q9
Flint Cl ANG/EP BN16....148 E3
　CRAWE RH10....44 A6
　PTSD BN41....120 C3
　SEAF BN25....159 K7
The Flints LEWES BN7....85 K8
Flitterbrook La HTHF TN21....245 N11
Florance La RRTW TN3....52 A3
Florence Av HOVE BN3....121 J5
Florence Cl SELS PO20....168 C1
Florence Pl BRI BN1....123 C4
Florence Rd BRI BN1....122 F5
　CCH PO19....7 K4
Florentine Wy WVILLE PO7....288 D9
The Florets STEY/UB BN44 *....79 C4
Florida Cl FERR BN12....149 L5
Florida Gdns FERR BN12....149 L5
Florida Rd FERR BN12....149 L5
Florlandia Cl LAN/SOMP BN15....118 A8
Flower Farm Cl HFD BN5....269 J4
Foamcourt Waye FERR BN12....149 K4
Folders Cl BURH RH15....75 H8
Folders Gra BURH RH15....75 H8
Folders La BURH RH15....75 H8
Folders La East BURH RH15....75 K8
Foley Cl LGNY BN23....164 D6
Folkestone Cl SEAF BN25....160 B8
Folkestone Rd SLVH TN37....253 P2
Folkington Gdns SLVH TN37....283 R12
Folkington Rd POLE BN26....131 J8
Follett Cl BOGR PO21....171 K4
Follis Gdns CCH PO19....107 G6
Folly Fld NEWHV BN9....18 F3
Folly La EPSF GU31....223 N6
　PETW GU28....263 K10
Fontana Cl CRAWE RH10....44 A4
Fonthill Rd HOVE BN3....122 A5
Fontridge La BUR/ETCH TN19....247 J2
Fontwell Av BEXW TN39....96 B8
　SELS PO20....110 B4
Fontwell Cl ANG/EP BN16....148 A5
　ARUN BN18....110 F3
　SALV BN13....116 F5
Fontwell Ms WVILLE PO7....288 B8
Fontwell Rd CRAWE RH10....9 G8
　SELS PO20....301 N5
Foords La PEV BN24....133 G6
Foot's La BUR/ETCH TN19....246 A2
Forbes Cl CRAWE RH10....44 A7
Fordbrook Hl CROW TN6....210 E7
Fordcombe Rd RRTW TN3....36 A4
Fordingbridge Site
　MSEA/BNM PO22 *....110 F6
Ford La ARUN BN18....146 D1
　STEY/UB BN44....146 D2
Ford Rd ARUN BN18....146 D2
　STLEO TN38....98 E3
Fordwater Gdns ARUN BN18....146 A2
Fordwater La CCH PO19....107 H2
Fordwater Rd CCH PO19....107 H2
Fore Br EPSF GU31....223 R6
Foredown Cl
　EDN/EASTW BN20....176 C3
　PTSD BN41....121 G3
Foredown Dr PTSD BN41....121 G4
Foredown Rd PTSD BN41....121 G3
Forest Av HORN PO8....288 A4
Forest Cl CRAWE RH10....46 A1
　HORN PO8....288 A4
　SWTR RH13....57 G5
　SWTR RH13....202 H3
Forest Dene CROW TN6....68 C8
　RTWE/PEM TN2....38 B8
Forester Rd ARUN BN18....9 G4
Forestfield CRAWE RH10....44 A5
　SWTR RH13....15 L4
Forest Fold Cottages
　CROW TN6 *....67 J4
Forest Ga CRAWW RH11....43 H7
Forest Gra HORS RH12 *....57 K5
Forest La BOR GU35....179 J3
　HTHF TN21....245 N8
Forest Lane Cl LIPH GU30....193 Q2
Forest Ms HORS RH12....57 G4
Forest Oaks SWTR RH13....15 M3
Forest Pk CROW TN6....67 J7

　SWTR RH13....203 K3
　UCK TN22....209 L12
Forest Ri HTHF TN21....243 N7
Forest Ri CROW TN6....68 C3
　LISS GU33....192 D7
Forest Rd BOR GU35....178 D8
　BRI BN1....83 K8
　FROW RH18....49 G8
　HORS RH12....57 G5
　LISS GU33....192 B4
　MIDH GU29....226 G11
　RTWE/PEM TN2....38 B3
　SALV BN13....117 J7
The Forestry Rd BIL RH14....198 C1
Forestside Av HAV PO9....288 H12
Forest Vw CRAWE RH10....9 L9
　HAIL BN27....91 M5
　UCK TN22....208 H6
Forest View Rd EGRIN RH19....47 K3
Forest Wy EGRIN RH19....48 A3
　HAIL BN27 *....90 A2
　HAS TN34....12 F4
　HRTF TN7....51 H3
　RTWE/PEM TN2....38 B8
　RTWE/PEM TN2....39 J1
Forewood La BAT TN33....282 H9
Forewood Ri BAT TN33....282 F11
Forge Cl ANG/EP BN16....148 E3
　CCH PO19....141 K2
　HORS RH12....201 P1
　PTSD BN41....121 G3
　UCK TN22....76 E6
Forge Fld WADH TN5....214 E3
Forge La CRAWE RH10....9 L1
　HORS RH12....201 N1
　RBTBR TN32....249 M4
Forge Meadow TENT TN30....221 M5
Forge Meads TENT TN30....220 D6
Forge Pl HORL RH6....22 D8
Forge Ri UCK TN22....76 E6
Forge Rd BOR GU35....178 D1
　CRAWE RH10....9 L1
　RRTW TN3....52 A6
The Forge HORL RH6 *....26 D2
　HORS RH12....187 P10
　RHWH RH17....204 D1
　SELS PO20....301 K6
　SWTR RH13....201 Q12
Forge Wy BIL RH14....231 R1
　BURH RH15....74 F5
　SLVH TN37....283 R12
Forge Wd CRAWE RH10....28 C6
Forrester Rd SWTR RH13....234 E10
Forstall RRTW TN3....36 F5
The Forstal RTWE/PEM TN2....36 F5
Forsters Yd LHPTN BN17 *....147 G4
Forsythia Cl HAV PO9....103 J1
Fort Hvn SHOR BN43....120 B7
Fort La LW/ROSE BN22....164 C7
Fort Ri NEWHV BN9....19 G5
Fort Rd LHPTN BN17....147 H5
　LW/ROSE BN22....164 C7
　NEWHV BN9....19 G5
Fortunes Wy HAV PO9....102 A4
Forty Acre La EPSF GU31....257 Q2
The Forum HORS RH12....14 B6
Forward Cl NEWHV BN9....158 D3
The Fosse LEWES BN7....16 F5
Foster Cl SEAF BN25....174 E1
Foster La PUL/STOR RH20....267 J9
Fosters Cl ANG/EP BN16....148 E3
Foundry Cl SWTR RH13....15 G2
Foundry La HASM GU27....181 K11
　LEWES BN7....17 J6
　SWTR RH13....15 J6
Foundry Rd ARUN BN18....145 L2
Foundry St BRI BN1....4 E5
Foundry Ter LEWES BN7 *....17 J6
Fountains Cl BRI BN1....123 C3
　CRAWW RH11....42 F5
　LW/ROSE BN22....163 K2
Founthill Av BRIE/ROTT BN2....156 A4
Founthill Rd BRIE/ROTT BN2....156 A4
Fourteen Acre La RHAS TN35....284 C5
Fourth Av HAV PO9....103 J3
　HOVE BN3....122 A8
　LAN/SOMP BN15....118 D4
　MSEA/BNM PO22....173 H1
　SALV BN13....117 J5
Fowey Cl SHOR BN43....120 A7
Fowler Cl CRAWE RH10....44 B5
Fowlers Cl BEXW TN39....96 D8
Fowly La UCK TN22....210 D10
Foxbridge Dr SELS PO20....142 A4
Foxbridge La BIL RH14....198 D4
Foxbury La EMRTH PO10....104 D1
Fox Cl BURH RH15....74 E8
　CCH PO19....7 G3
　CCH PO19....7 J1
　SALV BN13....43 G1
Foxcote SLVH TN37....99 J1
Foxcott Gv HAV PO9....288 G12
Fox Ct PUL/STOR RH20....265 Q12
Foxdale Dr ANG/EP BN16....148 L1
Foxdown Rd BRIE/ROTT BN2....124 E6
Foxes Cl ANG/EP BN16....148 A4
　SWTR RH13....233 G2
Foxes Cft MSEA/BNM PO22....111 H7
Foxfield Cottages SWTR RH13....233 G2
Foxglove Av HORS RH12....56 D3
Foxglove Cl BURH RH15....74 C5
　RING/NEW BN8....275 M10
Foxglove Dr BOR GU35....178 H9
Foxglove Rd LGNY BN23....164 A2
Foxglove Wk SALV BN13....150 A3
Foxglove Wy LHPTN BN17....147 M2
Foxhill BEXW TN39....96 D8
Fox Hl HWH RH16....73 H8
Foxhill PEAHV BN10....157 H4
Fox Hill Cl HWH RH16....73 H8
Foxhill Ct HWH RH16....73 H6
Fox Hill Village HWH RH16....75 L1
Foxhole La RHWH RH17....236 C3
　STPH/PW TN12....188 B1
　WADH TN5....190 A10
Foxholes HORS RH12....186 A9
Fox Hollow HAIL BN27 *....90 A2
Foxhunters Rd PTSD BN41....120 E2
Fox Lea SALV BN13....298 H12
Foxleigh Cha HORS RH12....15 J1
Foxley La SALV BN13....116 E5
Fox Rd HASM GU27....180 H11
　MIDH GU29....227 K7
Foxwarren HWH RH16....72 F4

Foxwarren Cl *SELS* PO20 .... 167 L6
Fox Wy *PTSD* BN41 .... 120 F5
Foxwells *RHWH* RH17 .... 60 F8
Foxwood *HORS* RH12 .... 40 A4
Foxwood Av *ANG/EP* BN16 .... 148 F1
Foxwood Cl *MFD/CHID* GU8 .... 182 C2
Framelle Mt *UCK* TN22 .... 77 K6
Framfield Cl *BRI* BN1 .... 83 K7
CRAWW RH11 .... 42 F1
Framfield Rd *UCK* TN22 .... 76 F2
UCK TN22 .... 77 K1
Framfield Wy *EAST* BN21 .... 163 J7
Frampton Ct *LEW* TN22 * 150 B3
Frampton Pl *SHOR* BN43 .... 119 K5
The Framptons *ANG/EP* BN16 .... 149 G4
France La *SALV* BN13 .... 115 J5
Franciscan Wy *LHPTN* BN17 .... 147 J1
Francis Edwards Wy
CRAWW RH11 .... 42 D7
Francis Rd *HORN* PO8 .... 256 D10
HWH RH16 .... 73 L1
Francis St *BRI* BN1 .... 4 F1
Frandor Rd *BOGR* PO21 .... 143 L8
Frankfield Ri *RTWE/PEM* TN2 .... 37 L3
Frankland Rd *PUL/STOR* RH20 .... 298 H3
Franklands Cl *BURH* RH15 .... 271 P3
SALV BN13 .... 116 E4
Franklands Gdns *BURH* RH15 .... 271 P1
Franklands Wy *BURH* RH15 .... 271 P1
Frankland Ter *EMRTH* PO10 .... 104 D4
Franklin Pl *CCH* PO19 .... 6 E3
Franklin Rd *BRIE/ROTT* BN2 .... 5 J1
CRAWE RH10 .... 44 B4
PTSD BN41 .... 121 H6
SALV BN13 .... 116 D6
SHOR BN43 .... 120 B5
Franklin St *BRIE/ROTT* BN2 .... 5 J2
Franklynn Rd *HWH* RH16 .... 73 H1
Frankton Av *HWH* RH16 .... 73 K6
Frant Av *BEXW* TN39 .... 96 E5
Frant Cl *BEXW* TN39 .... 96 E5
Frant Green Rd *RRTW* TN3 .... 54 A5
Frant Rd *HOVE* BN3 .... 121 M3
RRTW TN3 .... 53 M2
Frarydene *EMRTH* PO10 .... 104 E4
Fraser Av *LGNY* BN23 .... 164 G6
Fraser Cl *SELS* PO20 .... 301 M6
Fraser Gdns *EMRTH* PO10 .... 104 F3
Fraser Rd *HAV* PO9 .... 102 E3
Freckley Hollow *BAT* TN33 .... 281 N1
Frederick Gdns *BRI* BN1 * 4 F5
Frederick Pl *BRI* BN1 .... 4 F5
Frederick Rd *CCH* PO19 * 107 H7
RHAS TN35 .... 100 D3
Frederick St *BRI* BN1 .... 4 D5
Frederick Ter *BRIE/ROTT* BN1 * 4 E4
Free Heath Rd *RRTW* TN3 .... 190 B2
Freehold St *SHOR* BN43 .... 119 K6
Freehold Ter *BRIE/ROTT* BN2 .... 123 H4
Freek's La *BURH* RH15 .... 74 F3
Freeland Cl *CCH* PO19 .... 107 H7
SEAF BN25 .... 159 G7
Freeman Av *LW/ROSE* BN2 .... 163 K4
Freeman Cl *ARUN* BN18 .... 111 G4
Freeman Rd *HORS* RH12 .... 187 P9
Freemans Cl *BIL* RH14 .... 231 R1
Freemans Rd *PTSD* BN41 .... 120 F5
Freeways *SELS* PO20 .... 301 J5
Freezeland La *BEXW* TN39 .... 96 E4
Fremlin Cl *SBGH/RUST* TN4 .... 37 G5
Frenches *PUL/STOR* RH20 .... 266 A11
Frenches Farm Dr *HTHF* TN21 .... 244 D8
Frenches Md *BIL* RH14 .... 231 R1
French Gdns *HWH* RH16 .... 73 J3
Frenchgate Cl *LW/ROSE* BN22 .... 163 L3
Frenchgate Rd
LW/ROSE BN22 .... 163 L3
Frenchmans Rd *PSF* GU32 .... 225 M5
French Rd *LISS* GU33 .... 192 G2
Freshdale Rd *WVILLE* PO7 .... 288 B12
Fresham La *BOR* GU35 .... 179 K3
Freshbrook Cl
LAN/SOMP BN15 .... 118 D8
Freshbrook Rd
LAN/SOMP BN15 .... 118 C8
Freshfield Bank *FROW* RH18 .... 48 D7
Freshfield Cl *CRAWE* RH10 .... 9 M5
HAIL BN27 .... 42 A7
Freshfield La *RHWH* RH17 .... 207 M9
Freshfield Pl *BRIE/ROTT* BN2 .... 5 J7
Freshfield Rd *BRIE/ROTT* BN2 .... 5 J7
Freshfields Cl
LAN/SOMP BN15 .... 118 C7
Freshfields Dr
LAN/SOMP BN15 .... 118 C7
Freshfield St *BRIE/ROTT* BN2 .... 5 K4
Freshfield Wy *BRIE/ROTT* BN2 .... 5 J7
Freshford Cl *LGNY* BN23 .... 164 G3
Freshwater Av *HAS* TN34 .... 12 F1
Freshwater Pde *HORS* RH12 * 14 B6
Freshway *LW/ROSE* BN22 .... 163 H2
Freshwoods *HORS* RH12 .... 186 A3
Frewen Cl *RYE* TN31 .... 218 L10
Frewyn Cl *STLEO* TN38 .... 98 E1
Freya Cl *MSEA/BNM* PO22 .... 173 L1
Friar Cl *BRI* BN1 .... 122 F1
Friar Crs *BRI* BN1 .... 122 F1
Friar Rd *BRI* BN1 .... 122 F1
Friars' Av *PEAHV* BN10 .... 147 K6
Friars Bank *RHAS* TN35 .... 285 L10
Friars Cl *HPPT/KEY* BN6 .... 271 M5
Friars Hl *RHAS* TN35 .... 285 J10
Friars Hill Ter *RHAS* TN35 * 285 K10
Friars Oak Rd
HPPT/KEY BN6 .... 271 M4
Friars Rd *WSEA* TN36 .... 286 E2
Friars Rookery *CRAWE* RH10 .... 9 J3
Friars' Wk *LEWES* BN7 .... 17 H6
Friar's Wy *HAS* TN34 .... 99 L1
RTWE/PEM TN2 .... 38 C2
Friar Wk *BRI* BN1 .... 122 E1
SALV BN13 .... 150 E2
Friary Cl *MSEA/BNM* PO22 .... 145 K3
Friary La *CCH* PO19 .... 6 F5
Friary Wy *CRAWE* RH10 .... 8 E3
Friday St *HORS* RH12 .... 40 D4
HORS RH12 .... 187 P10
LGNY BN23 .... 164 B3
Friends Cl *CRAWW* RH11 .... 27 L5
Friezland Rd *SBGH/RUST* TN4 .... 37 J8
Frimley Cl *BRIE/ROTT* BN2 .... 124 A5
Friston Av *LW/ROSE* BN22 .... 163 H4
Friston Cl *BRIE/ROTT* BN2 .... 123 L1
EDN/EASTW BN20 .... 302 G4
SEAF BN25 .... 174 D1

Friston Downs
EDN/EASTW BN20 .... 302 H3
Friston Hl *EDN/EASTW* BN20 .... 302 G4
Friston Wk *CRAWW* RH11 .... 42 F2
Frith Pk *BEXW* TN39 .... 31 K6
Frith Rd *BOGR* PO21 .... 143 M8
HOVE BN3 .... 121 M5
Frobisher Cl *FERR* BN12 .... 150 C1
LGNY BN23 .... 164 D6
Frobisher Gdns *EMRTH* PO10 .... 104 A5
Frobisher Rd *BOGR* PO21 .... 171 H3
Frobisher Wy *ANG/EP* BN16 .... 148 D5
FERR BN12 .... 150 C1
Frog Hole La *MAYF* TN20 .... 211 Q12
Frogmore La *HORN* PO8 .... 288 B3
Froxfield Rd *HAV* PO9 .... 289 J12
Froyle Ct *HAV* PO9 .... 289 J12
Fruitfields *WADH* TN5 .... 191 P10
Fryatts Wy *BEXW* TN39 .... 96 E7
Fry Cl *CRAWW* RH11 .... 43 G8
Fry Crs *BURH* RH15 .... 74 D4
Fryern Cl *PUL/STOR* RH20 .... 265 R11
Fryern Rd *PUL/STOR* RH20 .... 266 A10
Fryland La *HFD* BN5 .... 235 N9
Fryman's La *RYE* TN31 .... 250 A11
Fulbeck Av *SALV* BN13 .... 116 A7
Fulflood Rd *HAV* PO9 .... 288 F12
Fulford Cl *STLEO* TN38 .... 98 F5
Fulfords Hl *SWTR* RH13 .... 201 K6
Fuller Cl *CRAWW* RH11 .... 43 G7
Fuller La *RYE* TN31 .... 218 E11
Fuller Rd *LEWES* BN7 .... 16 B1
Fullers Cl *BOR* GU35 .... 179 N4
Fullers La *RYE* TN31 .... 218 E11
Fullers V *BOR* GU35 .... 179 N4
Fullers Wk *LHPTN* BN17 .... 113 J8
Fullerton Cl *HAV* PO9 .... 289 J12
Fullwood Av *NEWHV* BN9 .... 18 D3
Fulmar Cl *CRAWW* RH11 * 42 C4
HOVE BN3 .... 122 C4
Fulmar Dr *EGRIN* RH19 .... 31 N6
Fulmar Wy *SELS* PO20 .... 109 K4
Fulmer Rd *BEX* TN40 * 137 H1
Furlong Cl *ARUN* BN18 .... 111 G2
The Furlongs *POLE* BN26 .... 160 E2
STEY/UB BN44 .... 78 C3
Furlong Wy *HORL* RH6 .... 27 L1
Furnace Av *RRTW* TN3 .... 54 A5
Furnace Dr *CRAWE* RH10 .... 9 K8
Furnace Farm Rd *CRAWE* RH10 .... 9 M8
EGRIN RH19 .... 30 B6
Furnace La *HTHF* TN21 .... 244 H11
HTHF TN21 .... 278 A1
RRTW TN3 .... 190 C1
RYE TN31 .... 250 E8
Furnace Pde *CRAWE* RH10 .... 9 M7
Furnace Pl *CRAWE* RH10 .... 9 M7
Furnace Wy *UCK* TN22 .... 77 G5
Furners La *HFD* BN5 .... 269 M4
Furners Md *HFD* BN5 .... 269 L4
Furness Cl *EAST* BN21 * 10 C8
Furness Rd *EDN/EASTW* BN20 .... 10 C8
Furnival Ct *RTWE/PEM* TN2 * 53 L1
Furnston Gv *EMRTH* PO10 .... 104 F4
Furse Feld *BOGR* PO21 .... 171 M3
Furze Common Rd
PUL/STOR RH20 .... 266 C7
Furzedown *LHPTN* BN17 .... 147 K5
Furzedown Crs *HAV* PO9 .... 288 H12
Furzefield *CRAWW* RH11 .... 8 B1
SELS PO20 .... 167 L4
Furzefield Av *RRTW* TN3 .... 36 F1
Furzefield Cha *EGRIN* RH19 .... 31 K3
Furzefield Cl *ANG/EP* BN16 .... 114 C6
Furzefield Rd *EGRIN* RH19 .... 31 J3
HORS RH12 .... 57 G4
Furze Hl *HOVE* BN3 .... 122 C7
Furze Hill Rd *BOR* GU35 .... 179 M5
Furzeholme *SALV* BN13 .... 116 C3
Furzeland Wy *HPPT/KEY* BN6 .... 270 E1
Furze La *EGRIN* RH19 .... 31 G6
Furze Meadow *EPSF* GU31 .... 224 H9
Furzen La *HORS* RH12 .... 186 D6
Furze Rd *HORS* RH12 .... 186 A9
SALV BN13 .... 116 C3
Furze Vale Rd *BOR* GU35 .... 179 Q5
Furze Vw *SWTR* RH15 .... 200 E7
Furze Wy *HORN* PO8 .... 288 C5
Furzley Ct *HAV* PO9 .... 288 D11
Fushia Cl *HAV* PO9 .... 103 K1
Fyning Pl *BEXW* TN39 .... 96 E3
Fyrsway *RHAS* TN35 .... 101 K2
Fysie La *BUR/ETCH* TN19 .... 215 Q5

G

Gableson Av *BRI* BN1 .... 122 A1
The Gables *HAS* TN34 * 99 K2
HORS RH12 .... 14 E1
PUL/STOR RH20 * 266 B12
SWTR RH13 .... 233 Q1
Gabriel Rd *CRAWE* RH10 .... 44 B7
Gage Cl *CRAWE* RH10 .... 30 B8
Gage Rdg *FROW* RH18 .... 48 D8
The Gages *HAIL* BN27 .... 92 C6
Gaggle Wd *SWTR* RH15 .... 202 H3
Gainsboro Rd *BOGR* PO21 .... 2 C7
Gainsborough Av *SALV* BN13 .... 117 K6
Gainsborough Crs *LGNY* BN23 .... 164 C4
Gainsborough Dr *SELS* PO20 .... 301 L6
Gainsborough La *POLE* BN26 .... 131 K2
Gainsborough Ldg *SALV* BN13 * 20 F1
Gainsborough Rd *BEX* TN40 .... 97 K3
CRAWE RH10 .... 43 L7
Gaisford Cl *SALV* BN13 .... 20 E2
Gaisford Rd *SALV* BN13 .... 20 D1
Galahad Rd *CRAWW* RH11 .... 42 D3
Galaxie Rd *HORN* PO8 .... 288 D3
Gales Dr *CRAWE* RH10 .... 9 J3
CRAWE RH10 .... 9 L3
Gales Pl *CRAWE* RH10 .... 9 K3
Galley Hill Vw *BEX* TN40 .... 137 L1
Galliers Cl *BRI* BN1 .... 83 G7
Gallipot Hl *HRTF* TN7 .... 50 B6
The Gallops *LEWES* BN7 .... 16 B6
Galloways Rd *LYDD* TN29 .... 255 R12
Gallows Cl *PEV* BN24 .... 133 G4
Gallows La *PEV* BN24 .... 133 G5
Galsworthy Cl *CRAWW* RH11 .... 150 A2
Galsworthy Rd *FERR* BN12 .... 150 A2
Galveston Cl *LGNY* BN23 .... 164 E6
Gamecock Ter *SELS* PO20 .... 109 J4
Gammon Cl *EPSF* GU31 .... 223 P4

Gammons Wy *BAT* TN33 .... 249 M12
Gander Cl *BURH* RH15 .... 74 F4
Gander Gn *HWH* RH16 .... 73 J2
Gander Hi *HWH* RH16 .... 73 J2
Gandersgate La *BIL* RH14 .... 230 B2
Gannon Rd *WTHG* BN11 .... 21 M4
Garbutts La *EPSF* GU31 .... 225 J6
Garden Av *SELS* PO20 .... 168 A7
Garden Cl *ANG/EP* BN16 .... 114 F6
BEX TN40 .... 137 H1
EGRIN RH19 .... 47 L3
LAN/SOMP BN15 .... 118 B7
PTSD BN41 .... 121 H5
PUL/STOR RH20 .... 266 A11
SHOR BN43 .... 120 A4
Garden Cottages *HAS* TN34 * 12 F7
HAS TN34 * 13 L5
Garden Ct *BOGR* PO21 .... 171 K3
Garden Crs *MSEA/BNM* PO22 .... 111 P9
Gardeners Gn *HORS* RH12 .... 187 P9
Gardeners Gn *HORS* RH12 .... 41 H5
Gardener St *PTSD* BN41 .... 120 F5
Garden House La *EGRIN* RH19 .... 47 L2
Garden Pl *HORS* RH12 * 14 D7
The Gardens *HAV* PO9 .... 103 J5
HAV PO9 .... 121 H5
PUL/STOR RH20 .... 264 B2
RCCH PO18 .... 106 A2
STHW BN42 .... 120 C6
Garden St *LEWES* BN7 .... 16 F7
RTW TN1 .... 38 A5
Garden Wk *CRAWW* RH11 .... 8 C4
UCK TN22 .... 14 D1
Garden Wood Cl
PUL/STOR RH20 .... 266 A7
Garden Wood Rd *EGRIN* RH19 .... 31 H8
Gardner Cl *LGNY* BN23 .... 164 D6
Gardner La *CRAWE* RH10 .... 45 M1
Gardner Rd *PTSD* BN41 .... 120 F6
Gardner's Hl *RYE* TN31 .... 220 C11
Gardner St *BRI* BN1 .... 4 E6
HAIL BN27 .... 279 Q11
Gardner Wy *STLEO* TN38 * 99 G7
Garfield Rd *HAIL* BN27 .... 92 B6
Garland Av *EMRTH* PO10 .... 104 A2
Garland Cl *EGRIN* RH19 .... 31 J8
Garland Ct *EGRIN* RH19 .... 31 J8
Garland Rd *SELS* PO20 .... 109 J3
Garland Sq *SELS* PO20 .... 109 J3
Garnet Dr *EDN/EASTW* BN20 .... 163 H6
Garnet Rd *BOR* GU35 .... 178 A7
Garrett Cl *SALV* BN13 .... 44 B5
Garrick Cl *SALV* BN13 .... 21 H1
Garrick Wk *CRAWE* RH10 .... 9 G9
The Garrones *CRAWE* RH10 * 44 D2
Garsons Rd *EMRTH* PO10 .... 104 E5
Garston Pk *BUR/ETCH* TN19 .... 214 G11
Garth Cl *BEXW* TN39 .... 96 F3
Garton Cl *CRAWW* RH11 .... 42 D4
Gaskyns Cl *HORS* RH12 .... 186 A10
Gasson Wood Rd
CRAWW RH11 .... 42 D5
Gaston Wy *PUL/STOR* RH20 .... 292 B10
Gatcombe Cl *SALV* BN13 * 116 A8
Gateford Dr *HORS* RH12 .... 56 E3
Gatehouse La *BURH* RH15 .... 74 B5
EPSF GU31 .... 225 N3
UCK TN22 .... 77 L5
Gatelands Dr *BEXW* TN39 .... 96 F7
Gates Cl *CRAWE* RH10 .... 44 B7
Gatesmead *HWH* RH16 .... 73 H1
Gatewycke Ter *STEY/UB* BN44 * 78 C2
The Gattons *BURH* RH15 .... 74 D2
Gatwick Rd *CRAWE* RH10 .... 28 A6
HORL RH6 .... 27 M5
Gatwick Wy *HORL* RH6 .... 27 L1
Gaudick Cl *EDN/EASTW* BN20 .... 176 A7
Gaudick Rd *EDN/EASTW* BN20 .... 176 A7
Gaugemaster Wy *ARUN* BN18 .... 112 D8
Gaulter Cl *HAV* PO9 .... 103 H2
Gay St *PUL/STOR* RH20 .... 231 R12
Gay Street La *PUL/STOR* RH20 .... 231 P10
Geddes Wy *EPSF* GU31 .... 223 R5
Geering Rd *PEV* BN24 .... 133 G8
Geers Wd *HTHF* TN21 .... 244 C7
Gemini Cl *CRAWW* RH11 .... 42 C5
Gemma Cl *HAIL* BN27 .... 92 C6
Geneva Rd *NEWHV* BN9 .... 19 G6
The Genistas *HPPT/KEY* BN6 * 271 M5
Genoa Cl *LHPTN* BN17 .... 147 M3
Gensing Rd *STLEO* TN38 .... 12 A1
Gentles La *LIPH* GU30 .... 179 P8
George Denyer Cl *HASM* GU27 .... 181 M10
George Hi *RBTBR* TN32 .... 248 C2
George Iv Wk *MSEA/BNM* PO22 .... 3 L2
George St *BRIE/ROTT* BN2 * 5 F7
CCH PO19 * 6 E2
HAIL BN27 .... 92 B6
HOVE BN3 .... 122 A7
PTSD BN41 .... 120 F6
WADH TN5 .... 71 L4
George V Av *LAN/SOMP* BN15 .... 119 G8
WTHG BN11 .... 150 E3
George Wood Cl *LYDD* TN29 .... 255 R7
Georgia Av *WTHG* BN11 .... 21 G1
Georgian Cl *BEX* TN40 .... 97 K8
CRAWE RH10 .... 44 C4
Georgian Gdns *ANG/EP* BN16 .... 148 D5
Georgian Wk *STLEO* TN38 .... 98 E5
Gerald Cl *BURH* RH15 .... 75 J4
Gerald Rd *SEAF* BN25 .... 174 F4
WTHG BN11 .... 150 E4
Gerard St *BRI* BN1 .... 4 E1
German St *WSEA* TN36 .... 286 D2
Ghyll Cl *SWTR* RH13 .... 201 Q12
Ghyll Crs *SWTR* RH13 .... 15 K9
Ghyll Rd *CROW* TN6 .... 36 C6
HTHF TN21 .... 244 C7
Ghyllside *BRIE/ROTT* BN2 .... 123 K4
Ghyllside Av *HAS* TN34 .... 99 H1
Ghyllside Dr *HAS* TN34 .... 99 J1
Ghyllside Wy *HAS* TN34 .... 99 H1
Gibb Cl *HAV* PO9 .... 289 L8
Gibbet La *STPH/PW* TN12 .... 189 L3
Gibbetts *RRTW* TN3 .... 36 E5
Gibbon Rd *NEWHV* BN9 .... 18 D6
Gibbons Cl *CRAWW* RH10 * 44 B6
Gibb's La *BOR* GU35 .... 178 D3
Giblets La *HORS* RH12 .... 56 D1
Giblets Wy *HORS* RH12 .... 56 D1
Gibraltar Ri *HTHF* TN21 .... 244 D6

Gibson Rd *SELS* PO20 .... 109 H3
Gibson Wy *BOGR* PO21 .... 2 E5
Giffards Cl *EGRIN* RH19 .... 31 L8
Gifford Rd *RCCH* PO18 .... 106 B6
Gilbert Rd *CCH* PO19 .... 6 A1
LW/ROSE BN22 .... 11 H3
STLEO TN38 .... 99 G5
Gilberts Dr *EDN/EASTW* BN20 .... 302 H6
The Gilberts *ANG/EP* BN16 .... 148 A8
Gilbert Wy *HAIL* BN27 .... 92 A8
Gilda Crs *POLE* BN26 .... 131 M7
Gildredge Rd *EAST* BN21 .... 10 C7
SEAF BN25 .... 174 F2
Giles Cl *ARUN* BN18 .... 145 L2
Gillam La *FROW* RH18 .... 48 D7
Gillett Ct *SWTR* RH13 .... 57 J5
Gillett Ct *SWTR* RH13 .... 57 G5
Gilham's La *HASM* GU27 .... 194 D7
Gilham Wood Rd *BEXW* TN39 .... 136 C2
The Gilligans *BURH* RH15 .... 74 E4
Gillridge Gn *CROW* TN6 .... 67 L5
Gillman's Dr *STLEO* TN38 .... 98 E4
Gillman's Hi *STLEO* TN38 .... 98 E4
Gillman's Pk *STLEO* TN38 .... 98 E4
The Gill *RTWE/PEM* TN2 .... 39 K1
Gillway *SELS* PO20 .... 301 N5
Gilmore Rd *CCH* PO19 .... 7 K4
Gilpin Cl *CCH* PO19 .... 107 G7
Gilwynes *BOGR* PO21 .... 171 L3
Gimble Wy *RTWE/PEM* TN2 .... 39 J1
Ginhams Rd *CRAWW* RH11 .... 8 B3
Gipps Cross La *RRTW* TN3 .... 36 A5
Githa Rd *RHAS* TN35 .... 100 B3
The Glades *BEX* TN40 .... 97 K7
EGRIN RH19 .... 32 A8
The Glade *BOGR* PO21 .... 170 F5
CRAWE RH10 .... 9 L7
HAIL BN27 .... 91 J7
HTHF TN21 * 244 C6
MAYF TN20 .... 212 D7
SWTR RH13 .... 15 L3
UCK TN22 .... 76 F5
WVILLE PO7 .... 288 B9
Gladonian Rd *LHPTN* BN17 .... 147 J4
Gladstone Cl *LW/ROSE* BN22 .... 11 K7
Gladstone Pl *BRIE/ROTT* BN2 .... 123 H5
Gladstone Rd *ARUN* BN18 .... 145 L3
BURH RH15 .... 75 H4
CROW TN6 .... 210 C1
HAS TN34 .... 13 K4
HORS RH12 .... 187 K6
PTSD BN41 .... 121 C6
SBGH/RUST TN4 .... 37 G5
Gladstone Ter *BRIE/ROTT* BN2 * 5 H2
HAS TN34 .... 13 K4
LHPTN BN17 .... 147 J2
Gladys Av *HORN* PO8 .... 288 B5
PEAHV BN10 .... 157 J7
Gladys Rd *HOVE* BN3 .... 121 J5
Glamis Cl *WVILLE* PO7 .... 288 B9
Glamis St *BOGR* PO21 .... 2 E6
Glamorgan Rd *HORN* PO8 .... 256 C11
Glamorgan's Yd *WADH* TN5 .... 191 M10
Glaseby La *PUL/STOR* RH20 .... 298 G5
Glassenbury Dr *BEX* TN40 .... 97 L8
Glasshouse La *BIL* RH14 .... 230 B4
Glastonbury Rd *HOVE* BN3 .... 121 J7
Glatting La *PUL/STOR* RH20 .... 263 K12
Glayshers Hi *BOR* GU35 .... 179 N3
Glaziers La *MIDH* GU29 .... 227 K7
Gleave Cl *EGRIN* RH19 .... 31 M7
Glebe Cl *BEXW* TN39 .... 136 C1
CRAWE RH10 .... 8 F1
EDN/EASTW BN20 .... 176 D2
LEWES BN7 .... 16 B3
SELS PO20 .... 110 A4
STHW BN42 .... 120 E6
Glebe Dr *SEAF* BN25 .... 174 E2
Glebe Field Rd *SELS* PO20 .... 139 M8
Glebelands *BIL* RH14 .... 198 C5
CRAWE RH10 .... 45 M1
PUL/STOR RH20 .... 265 C12
Glebelands Cl *SHOR* BN43 .... 120 A5
Glebelands Meadow
CRAN GU6 .... 184 C8
The Glebelands *CROW* TN6 .... 67 L7
Glebe Park Av *HAV* PO9 .... 102 B4
Glebe Rd *BOR* GU35 .... 179 M4
EPSF GU31 .... 223 L12
HASM GU27 .... 195 L4
RHWH RH17 .... 72 C3
SALV BN13 .... 116 F8
Glebeside Av *SALV* BN13 .... 116 F8
Glebeside Cl *SALV* BN13 .... 117 G8
The Glebe *CRAWE* RH10 .... 29 G6
EGRIN RH19 .... 30 F5
HAS TN34 .... 13 H6
HORL RH6 .... 22 E6
HPPT/KEY BN6 .... 270 H4
HWH RH16 .... 73 K1
RTWE/PEM TN2 .... 39 J1
SELS PO20 .... 109 H4
Glebe Twitten *RHWH* RH17 * 72 C3
Glebe Vw *RHWH* RH17 .... 60 F8
Glebe Ws *HOVE* BN3 .... 121 J6
Glebe Wy *BIL* RH14 .... 231 K1
LAN/SOMP BN15 .... 118 D6
Glenbarrie Wy *FERR* BN12 .... 149 K2
Glencathara Rd *BOGR* PO21 .... 2 A7
Glen Cl *GSHT* GU26 .... 180 F3
POLE BN26 .... 162 E1
Glencoe *CROW* TN6 * 67 L7
Glen Crs *SELS* PO20 .... 301 L6
Glen Dl *HAV* PO9 .... 289 L8
Glendale Av *EAST* BN21 .... 163 H7
Glendale Cl *HORS* RH12 .... 56 F7
Glendale Rd *BURH* RH15 .... 75 G7
HOVE BN3 .... 122 C6
Glendor Rd *HOVE* BN3 .... 121 K7
Glendyne Cl *EGRIN* RH19 .... 47 M1
Glendyne Wy *EGRIN* RH19 .... 47 M1
Gleneagles Cl *BEX* TN40 .... 97 K8
SEAF BN25 .... 218 E10
Gleneagles Ct *CRAWE* RH10 * 8 F7
Gleneagles Dr *HAIL* BN27 .... 91 L5
HORN PO8 .... 288 B5
STLEO TN38 .... 98 E6
WVILLE PO7 .... 288 C7
Glenelg Cl *BOGR* PO21 .... 143 L7
Glenfalls Av *BRI* BN1 .... 146 A2
Glenfergus *HWH* RH16 .... 73 H3
Glen Gdns *FERR* BN12 .... 149 L3
Glengorse *BAT* TN33 .... 282 C6
Glenlea *GSHT* GU26 .... 180 H8

Glenlea Hollow *GSHT* GU26 .... 180 H9
Glenlea Vls *CROW* TN6 * 67 L8
Glenleigh Av *BEXW* TN39 .... 96 E7
Glenleigh Pk *HAV* PO9 .... 103 J3
Glenleigh Wk *RBTBR* TN32 .... 248 B1
Glenmere Ms *EAST* BN21 .... 10 C5
Glenmore Pk *RTWE/PEM* TN2 .... 53 L1
Glenmore Rd *CROW* TN6 .... 67 H6
Glenmore Rd East *CROW* TN6 .... 67 J6
Glen Ri *BRI* BN1 .... 82 A8
Glen Rise Cl *BRI* BN1 .... 82 A8
Glen Rd *GSHT* GU26 .... 180 F3
Glenrosa Cottages
CROW TN6 * 210 H3
The Glen *SALV* BN13 .... 116 F6
SWTR RH13 .... 201 R11
UCK TN22 .... 76 F3
Glenthorn Rd *BEXW* TN39 .... 136 F1
Glenview Ct *CRAWE* RH10 .... 43 L1
RHAS TN35 .... 100 C4
Glenville Gdns *GSHT* GU26 .... 181 J5
Glenville Rd *ANG/EP* BN16 .... 148 B5
Glen Vue *EGRIN* RH19 .... 31 K8
Glenway *MSEA/BNM* PO22 2
Glenwood Av *MSEA/BNM* PO22 2
Glenwood Gdns *HORN* PO8 .... 288 A7
Glenwood Rd *EMRTH* PO10 .... 104 C4
Glessing Rd *PEV* BN24 .... 133 G8
Gieton Av *HOVE* BN3 .... 121 J3
Globe Pl *LHPTN* BN17 .... 147 J2
Gloster Dr *BOGR* PO21 .... 171 G3
Gloucester Av *BEX* TN40 .... 97 M8
PSF GU32 .... 225 J6
Gloucester Cl *LW/ROSE* BN22 .... 163 H3
Gloucester Cottages *HAS* TN34 * 13 K6
Gloucester La *LHPTN* BN17 .... 147 J4
Gloucester Ms *BRI* BN1 * 4 F5
Gloucester Pas *BRI* BN1 * 4 F5
Gloucester Pl *BRI* BN1 .... 4 F5
LHPTN BN17 .... 147 J4
Gloucester Rd *BOGR* PO21 .... 3 G7
BRI BN1 .... 4 F5
BURH RH15 .... 74 E6
CRAWE RH10 .... 43 K7
LHPTN BN17 .... 147 H4
WADH TN5 .... 71 L3
WVILLE PO7 .... 288 A11
Gloucester St *BRI* BN1 * 4 F5
Gloucester Wy *CCH* PO19 .... 107 G7
Glovers La *BEXW* TN39 .... 97 J6
Glover's Rd *HORL* RH6 .... 26 C3
Glynde Av *BRIE/ROTT* BN2 .... 156 B3
FERR BN12 .... 149 L3
LW/ROSE BN22 .... 163 K4
Glyndebourne Av
BRIE/ROTT BN2 .... 156 B4
Glyndebourne Gdns
SLVH TN37 .... 283 R12
Glynde Cl *FERR* BN12 .... 149 L3
NEWHV BN9 .... 158 C3
Glynde Ct *BEXW* TN39 * 136 B2
Glynde Crs *MSEA/BNM* PO22 .... 3 L2
Glynde Pl *HORS* RH12 * 14 C11
Glynde Rd *BRIE/ROTT* BN2 .... 5 L3
Glyne Ascent *BEX* TN40 .... 97 L8
Glyne Barn Cl *BEX* TN40 .... 97 M8
Glyne Dr *BEX* TN40 .... 97 M8
Glyne Hall *BEX* TN40 * 137 J2
Glynleigh Dr *POLE* BN26 .... 132 B7
Glynleigh Rd *PEV* BN24 .... 132 D4
Glynn House *SELS* PO20 .... 301 K6
Glynn Ri *PEAHV* BN10 .... 157 H4
Glynn Rd *PEAHV* BN10 .... 157 H4
Glynn Rd West *PEAHV* BN10 .... 157 G4
Goatham La *RYE* TN31 .... 250 A1
Goda Rd *LHPTN* BN17 .... 147 K4
Goddard Cl *CRAWE* RH10 .... 44 A6
Godden Cl *RYE* TN31 .... 218 E9
Godden Rd *RING/NEW* BN8 .... 240 G7
Godfrey Cl *LEWES* BN7 .... 16 F2
Godman Cl *BOGR* PO21 .... 171 J3
Godolphin Ct *CRAWE* RH10 * 8 F6
Godstalls La *STEY/UB* BN44 .... 78 B2
Godwin Cl *EMRTH* PO10 .... 103 M2
Godwin Crs *HORN* PO8 .... 256 D9
Godwin Rd *HOVE* BN3 .... 121 J5
RHAS TN35 .... 100 B4
Godwin Wy *RCCH* PO18 .... 106 F5
SWTR RH13 .... 15 K2
Goffs Cl *CRAWW* RH11 .... 8 B4
Goffs La *CRAWW* RH11 .... 8 B4
Goffs Park Rd *CRAWW* RH11 .... 8 C6
The Goffs *EAST* BN21 .... 10 B5
Goldbridge Rd *RING/NEW* BN8 .... 240 D6
Goldcrest Av *LHPTN* BN17 .... 147 H1
Goldcrest Cl *HORL* RH6 .... 22 C5
HORN PO8 .... 288 B2
Goldcrest Dr *UCK* TN22 .... 76 F7
Golden Acre *ANG/EP* BN16 .... 149 G5
BOGR PO21 .... 170 F5
Golden Av *ANG/EP* BN16 .... 149 G5
Golden Avenue Cl
ANG/EP BN16 .... 149 G5
Goldenfield Cl *LIPH* GU30 .... 194 A2
Golden Flds *LIPH* GU30 .... 194 A2
Golden Gate Wy *LGNY* BN23 .... 165 G4
Golden Hl *BURH* RH15 .... 75 J9
Golden Jubilee Wy
LW/ROSE BN22 .... 163 M3
Golden La *HOVE* BN3 * 122 A7
STEY/UB BN44 .... 268 C3
Golden Miller La *POLE* BN26 .... 131 K7
Goldfinch Cl *CRAWW* RH11 .... 43 J1
HORS RH12 .... 55 B2
Goldhurst Gn *WSEA* TN36 .... 285 P4
Golding Cl *CRAWE* RH10 .... 44 B4
Golding La *SWTR* RH13 .... 203 J2
Golding Rd *LGNY* BN23 .... 164 E3
Gold La *PEAHV* BN10 .... 157 H3
Goldsmid Rd *HOVE* BN3 .... 4 B3
Goldsmith Cl *LGNY* BN23 .... 164 D3
Goldsmith Rd *SALV* BN13 .... 21 J1
Goldsmiths Av *CROW* TN6 .... 67 J6
Goldstone Crs *HOVE* BN3 .... 121 J4
Goldstone La *HOVE* BN3 .... 122 A4
Goldstone Rd *HOVE* BN3 .... 122 A4
Goldstone St *HOVE* BN3 .... 122 A5
Goldstone Vls *HOVE* BN3 .... 122 A4
Goldstone Wy *HOVE* BN3 .... 121 H5
Golf Club La *PUL/STOR* RH20 .... 265 N7
Golf Dr *BRI* BN1 .... 123 G2
Golf La *BOR* GU35 .... 178 D6
Golf Links Av *GSHT* GU26 .... 180 E3
Golf Links La *SELS* PO20 .... 301 L4

Golf Links Rd
MSEA/BNM PO22 144 F7
Goodacres MSEA/BNM PO22 111 H8
Goodhew Cl ARUN BN18 145 M2
Goods Station Rd RTW TN1 37 M5
Goodtrees La EDEN TN8 34 A7
Goodwin Cl CRAWW RH11 42 D6
HAIL BN27 91 M4
Goodwins Cl EGRIN RH19 31 J6
The Goodwins RTWE/PEM TN2 37 L8
Goodwood Av MSEA/BNM PO22 3 L2
Goodwood Cl ANG/EP BN16 148 D3
CRAWE RH10 9 L9
EDN/EASTW BN20 163 G3
HORN PO8 288 C8
MIDH GU29 226 H12
Goodwood Ct EMRTH PO10 104 F5
Goodwood Gdns SELS PO20 142 D4
Goodwood Pl BOGR PO21 * 2 D8
Goodwood Rd SALV BN13 116 F6
Goodwood Wy
BRIE/ROTT BN2 123 K2
Gooseberry La RYE TN31 250 D2
Goose Green Cl HORS RH12 56 C4
Goosegreen La
PUL/STOR RH20 266 F2
Gordon Av BOGR PO21 2 E4
CCH PO19 141 K2
MSEA/BNM PO22 2 E3
SHOR BN43 119 M6
Gordon Av West
MSEA/BNM PO22 2 E3
Gordon Cl HWH RH16 73 H3
Gordon Pl RYE TN31 * 253 L10
Gordon Rd BRI BN1 122 E3
BURH RH15 75 H5
CROW TN6 67 L7
EMRTH PO10 104 C6
HAIL BN27 92 A6
HAS TN34 13 J5
HORS RH12 14 E1
HWH RH16 73 J3
LAN/SOMP BN15 118 C7
PTSD BN41 120 F6
SBGH/RUST TN4 38 B2
SHOR BN43 119 L6
UCK TN22 77 L1
WTHG BN11 21 H4
Gordon Ter LYDD TN29 * 255 R8
Gore La CRBK TN17 189 R6
Gore Park Av EAST BN21 176 D1
Gore Park Rd EAST BN21 176 D1
Goreside La RHWH RH17 72 C1
Gorham Av BRIE/ROTT BN2 155 M3
Gorham Cl BRIE/ROTT BN2 155 M3
Gorham Wy PEAHV BN10 156 D5
Goring Av HORN PO8 256 E9
Goring Cha FERR BN12 149 M1
Goring Rd FERR BN12 150 C3
STEY/UB BN44 78 C3
WTHG BN11 150 E3
Goring's Md SWTR RH13 14 E8
Goring St FERR BN12 149 M2
Goring Wy FERR BN12 149 M3
SWTR RH13 234 F9
Gorley Ct HAV PO9 288 E11
Gorling Cl CRAWW RH11 42 D4
Gorringe Cl EDN/EASTW BN20 162 F2
SHOR BN43 120 C6
Gorringe Dr EDN/EASTW BN20 162 F2
Gorringe Rd LW/ROSE BN22 10 D2
Gorringes Brook HORS RH12 56 C3
Gorringe Valley Rd
EDN/EASTW BN20 162 F2
Gorse Av ANG/EP BN16 149 J6
MSEA/BNM PO22 145 J7
SALV BN13 117 G7
Gorse Bank Cl PUL/STOR RH20 266 F10
Gorse Cl CRAWE RH10 29 G7
CRAWW RH11 59 G1
EDN/EASTW BN20 163 G8
PTSD BN41 120 E1
Gorsedown Cl BOR GU35 178 E8
Gorse Dr SEAF BN25 159 L7
Gorse End HORS RH12 56 C4
Gorse Hl HTHF TN21 244 H3
Gorselands BAT TN33 249 M12
BIL RH14 232 B1
Gorselands Cl BOR GU35 179 R5
Gorse La SALV BN13 116 D3
Gorse Rd EPSF GU31 223 R6
RTWE/PEM TN2 38 D4
The Gorses BEXW TN39 136 B3
Gorsethorn Wy RHAS TN35 101 K1
Gorse Vw ANG/EP BN16 * 149 H5
The Gorseway BEXW TN39 96 B8
Gosden Cl CRAWE RH10 9 M5
Gosden Rd LHPTN BN17 147 L3
Gosford Wy POLE BN26 131 L7
Gospond Rd MSEA/BNM PO22 110 F8
Gossamer La BOGR PO21 171 J2
Gossops Dr CRAWW RH11 42 F4
Gossops Green La
CRAWW RH11 42 F4
Gostrode La MFD/CHID GU8 182 F12
Gote La RING/NEW BN8 87 J1
Goudhurst Cl CRAWE RH10 44 D3
LGNY BN23 164 C4
Goudhurst Rd STPH/PW TN12 189 N4
Goverlands Cl BURH RH15 74 E8
Gower Rd HORL RH6 22 D6
HWH RH16 73 H5
Gowers Cl RHWH RH17 206 E1
Gows Cft LEWES BN7 85 K8
Gowscroft LEWES BN7 * 85 K8
Grace Rd CRAWW RH11 42 F8
Gradwell End RING/NEW BN8 273 M2
Graffham Cl BRIE/ROTT BN2 123 K7
CCH PO19 107 M2
CRAWW RH11 43 G1
Grafton Av MSEA/BNM PO22 145 H7
Grafton Cl ANG/EP BN16 148 B3
BOR GU35 178 H7
Grafton Dr LAN/SOMP BN15 118 B7
Grafton Gdns LAN/SOMP BN15 118 B7
Grafton Pl WTHG BN11 21 G6
Grafton Rd SELS PO20 301 L8
WTHG BN11 21 G6
Grafton St BRIE/ROTT BN2 5 H8
Graham Av BRI BN1 122 D1
PTSD BN41 120 E1
Graham Crs PTSD BN41 120 E1
Graham Rd ARUN BN18 145 L4
WTHG BN11 21 G6
Grailands Cl HASM GU27 195 M7
Grampian Cl LGNY BN23 164 B2
RTWE/PEM TN2 38 C4
Granada Cl HORN PO8 288 B6
Granary Cl HORL RH6 22 F4
Granary La SELS PO20 301 K5
Granary Wy HORS RH12 201 Q4
LHPTN BN17 147 J1
Grand Av BEX TN40 97 M7
HOVE BN3 122 B7
HPPT/KEY BN6 271 N5
LAN/SOMP BN15 118 D6
LHPTN BN17 147 H2
SEAF BN25 159 H8
WTHG BN11 20 A4
Grand Crs BRIE/ROTT BN2 155 M4
Grand Junction Rd BRI BN1 4 E8
Grand Pde BRIE/ROTT BN2 4 F5
CRAWE RH10 * 8 E4
EAST BN21 11 G8
POLE BN26 131 L7
STLEO TN38 12 A9
Grand Parade Ms
BRIE/ROTT BN2 4 F6
Grange Av HAS TN34 99 H1
Grange Cl BRI BN1 122 D4
BURH RH15 75 H4
CRAWE RH10 43 M1
CROW TN6 67 J8
FERR BN12 149 K4
HAV PO9 103 J3
HTHF TN21 278 C3
Grange Ct BOGR PO21 171 K4
FERR BN12 * 149 K3
Grange Court Dr BEXW TN39 97 G7
Grange Crs CRAWE RH10 46 A2
Grange End HORL RH6 23 M6
Grange Field Wy BOGR PO21 171 J4
Grange Gdns EDN/EASTW BN20 10 C8
SBGH/RUST TN4 37 J5
Grange La SELS PO20 301 N3
Grange Park Rd FERR BN12 149 K4
Grange Rd CRAWE RH10 45 M2
EDN/EASTW BN20 10 D8
HAS TN34 284 B12
HOVE BN3 121 K6
LEWES BN7 16 E7
MIDH GU29 227 J10
PSF GU32 223 M7
RING/NEW BN8 274 C5
SBGH/RUST TN4 37 J5
STHW BN42 120 D6
UCK TN22 76 E5
The Grange RING/NEW BN8 274 C5
Grangeway HORL RH6 23 M6
Grange Wy SWTR RH13 201 Q11
Grangeways BRI BN1 82 D8
The Grangeway ANG/EP BN16 148 B4
Grangewood Dr BOGR PO21 171 J3
Granston Wy CRAWE RH10 46 B1
Grant Cl SELS PO20 301 K6
Grantham Bank
RING/NEW BN8 274 D5
Grantham Cl RING/NEW BN8 273 P2
Grantham Rd BRI BN1 122 F4
Grantsmead LAN/SOMP BN15 118 D6
Grant St BRIE/ROTT BN2 5 H3
Granville Cl HAV PO9 103 J5
Granville Rd EDN/EASTW BN20 10 C9
HOVE BN3 4 A3
LHPTN BN17 147 K5
RTW TN1 38 A4
The Graperies BRIE/ROTT BN2 5 J7
Grasmere Av LAN/SOMP BN15 118 A7
Grasmere Cl BOR GU35 178 G4
LGNY BN23 164 A1
Grasmere Gdns HORS RH12 57 G3
Grassington Rd
EDN/EASTW BN20 10 C9
Grasslands HORL RH6 23 M6
Grassmere HORL RH6 23 G5
Grassmere Av PEAHV BN10 156 E5
Grassmere Cl LHPTN BN17 147 M2
MSEA/BNM PO22 3 K4
Grassmere Wy WVILLE PO7 288 C8
Grateley Crs HAV PO9 102 D1
Gratten La HFD BN5 235 Q10
RHWH RH17 236 B10
Grattons Dr CRAWE RH10 28 B8
The Grattons SWTR RH13 200 H2
Gratwicke Cl BIL RH14 232 A1
Gratwicke Rd WTHG BN11 20 F7
Gravel La CCH PO19 7 J7
Gravelly Crs LAN/SOMP BN15 118 E7
Gravelye Cl HWH RH16 73 L4
Gravelye La HWH RH16 73 L4
Graveney Rd CRAWE RH10 44 B4
Gravett Ct BURH RH15 74 E7
Gravetye Cl CRAWE RH10 9 M8
Gravits La BOGR PO21 143 M8
Graycoats Dr CROW TN6 67 L7
Graydon Av CCH PO19 6 B9
Graylingwell Dr CCH PO19 107 M4
Grays Cl HASM GU27 181 P9
Grayshott Laurels BOR GU35 179 K3
Grayshott Rd BOR GU35 179 R4
Graystone La RHAS TN35 100 B2
Grays Wd HORL RH6 23 H6
Grayswood Av SELS PO20 168 A7
Grayswood Ms HASM GU27 * 181 Q7
Grayswood Rd HASM GU27 181 N9
Graywood La RING/NEW BN8 277 L3
Graywood Rd RING/NEW BN8 277 K3
Grazebrook Cl BEXW TN39 136 B2
Great Brooms Rd
SBGH/RUST TN4 38 A1
Great Cliffe Rd LGNY BN23 164 D4
Great College St
BRIE/ROTT BN2 5 K8
Great Copse Dr HAV PO9 288 G12
Great Courtlands RRTW TN3 36 F6
Greater Paddock
RING/NEW BN8 275 K11
Greatfield Wy HAV PO9 289 J7
Great Footway RRTW TN3 36 E5
Great Hall Ar RTW TN1 * 37 M6
Greatham Br PUL/STOR RH20 264 F8
Greatham Rd CRAWE RH10 44 B6
SALV BN13 116 E4
Great Hanger EPSF GU31 223 Q6
Great House Ct EGRIN RH19 * 47 L1
Greatlake Ct HORL RH6 23 G5
Great Lime Kilns SWTR RH13 201 R12
Great Oak BUR/ETCH TN19 216 B6
Greatpin Cft PUL/STOR RH20 264 B2
Great Rough RING/NEW BN8 239 R7
Great Wd BAT TN33 282 H5
Grebe Cl EMRTH PO10 104 C1
Grebe Crs SWTR RH13 15 M9
Grecian Rd RTW TN1 38 A7
Greeba Ct STLEO TN38 * 99 G7
Greenacre Cl
PUL/STOR RH20 * 265 Q12
Greenacres BOR GU35 179 J5
BRI BN1 * 122 E4
CRAWE RH10 9 M6
HORS RH12 14 D1
PEAHV BN10 157 J3
PUL/STOR RH20 267 K7
RHAS TN35 284 B6
SHOR BN43 119 K5
STEY/UB BN44 78 C3
Greenacres Dr HAIL BN27 92 B5
RING/NEW BN8 87 H1
Greenacres Ring
ANG/EP BN16 114 F7
Greenacres Wy HAIL BN27 92 B5
Greenbank MSEA/BNM PO22 111 H8
Greenbank Av BRIE/ROTT BN2 156 B4
Green Bushes Cl ANG/EP BN16 148 A5
Green Cl RING/NEW BN8 275 K11
STHW BN42 120 D6
SWTR RH13 201 Q11
Green Ct STHW BN42 * 120 D6
Greencourt Dr BOGR PO21 143 M8
Greenfield PUL/STOR RH20 263 L11
Greenfield Cl BRI BN1 82 F8
LIPH GU30 179 R12
SBGH/RUST TN4 37 H4
Green Field Cl STHW BN42 120 D5
Greenfield Crs BRI BN1 82 E8
HORN PO8 288 D5
Greenfield Dr UCK TN22 76 F8
Greenfield Ri HORN PO8 288 C6
Greenfield Rd BUR/ETCH TN19 214 H10
CCH PO19 7 J2
EAST BN21 176 D2
SWTR RH13 200 G2
Greenfields EPSF GU31 224 H10
HAIL BN27 91 M4
LHPTN BN17 147 G2
LISS GU33 192 D9
MSEA/BNM PO22 145 K8
Greenfields Cl EPSF GU31 224 H9
HORL RH6 22 D4
HORS RH12 56 F3
SLVH TN37 283 Q11
Greenfields Rd HORL RH6 22 D4
HORS RH12 56 F4
Greenfields Wy HORS RH12 56 F3
Greenfield Wy
PUL/STOR RH20 266 B11
Greenfinch Wy HORS RH12 56 C2
Green Ga PEAHV BN10 157 H4
Greengates PETW GU28 196 C11
Green Gv HAIL BN27 92 A5
Greenhanger RFNM GU10 180 C1
Green Hedges Av EGRIN RH19 31 J7
Green Hedges Cl EGRIN RH19 31 J7
Greenhill Pk RHWH RH17 73 K7
Greenhill Wy PEAHV BN10 157 H3
RHWH RH17 73 K7
Greenhurst La PUL/STOR RH20 266 B8
Greening Wd GSHT GU26 * 181 J4
Greenland Cl SALV BN13 116 D6
Greenland Rd SALV BN13 116 D7
Greenlands Cl BURH RH15 271 Q1
Greenlands Dr BURH RH15 271 Q1
Green La BEXW TN39 96 C8
BRIE/ROTT BN2 124 D7
CCH PO19 7 H3
CRAN GU6 184 G5
CRAWE RH10 29 L5
CRAWE RH10 43 K1
CRAWE RH10 44 C3
CROW TN6 68 A6
HASM GU27 195 L2
HORL RH6 22 B7
HORN PO8 256 E8
HORS RH12 40 D5
HTHF TN21 244 E7
LEWES BN7 16 F7
POLE BN26 162 B5
RCCH PO18 105 M5
RCCH PO18 106 B8
RDKG RH5 25 J1
RFNM GU10 180 C1
RING/NEW BN8 239 P12
RING/NEW BN8 275 M8
SEAF BN25 174 E3
SELS PO20 141 K7
SELS PO20 142 E1
SELS PO20 142 E3
SELS PO20 169 H4
SELS PO20 301 K7
SWTR RH13 234 A4
Green Lane Cl ARUN BN18 112 E3
Greenlea Av BOGR PO21 171 G3
Greenleaf Gdns POLE BN26 131 M6
Greenleas HOVE BN3 121 J3
RTWE/PEM TN2 39 H3
Green Mdw HWH RH16 73 L1
Greenoaks LAN/SOMP BN15 118 C5
Green Pk FERR BN12 149 L2
Green Park Cnr RHWH RH17 75 M5
Green Pond Cnr HAV PO9 * 103 J4
Green Rdg BRI BN1 82 A8
Green Rd RHWH RH17 75 M4
STPH/PW TN12 189 M4
Greensand Wy GSHT GU26 181 K7
HASM GU27 181 M10
Greens La SWTR RH13 203 J2
Green Sq WADH TN5 71 L4
Greenstede Av EGRIN RH19 31 L6
Green St ALTN GU34 178 A1
EAST BN21 176 C1
The Green BAT TN33 281 M11
BAT TN33 281 R9
BAT TN33 283 M1
BOGR PO21 170 F5
BRIE/ROTT BN2 155 L3
CCH PO19 7 J2
CRAWE RH10 29 G6
CRAWW RH11 8 C2
HAIL BN27 * 92 B3
HOVE BN3 122 B3
LISS GU33 192 B8
MFD/CHID GU8 182 H6
PUL/STOR RH20 * 265 K1
PUL/STOR RH20 266 C11
RING/NEW BN8 240 C6
RRTW TN3 36 D6
RRTW TN3 54 A6
STLEO TN38 99 G4
SWTR RH13 267 P2
UCK TN22 242 H7
Greentree La SWTR RH13 234 H8
Greentrees LAN/SOMP BN15 * 118 B7
Greentrees Cl
LAN/SOMP BN15 118 B7
Greentrees Crs
LAN/SOMP BN15 118 B7
Green Wk CRAWE RH10 43 K1
HAIL BN27 92 B4
SEAF BN25 175 H3
Green Wy EDN/EASTW BN20 163 G7
Greenway HORS RH12 14 A3
Green Wy LYDD TN29 255 R8
MSEA/BNM PO22 145 L8
RTWE/PEM TN2 38 D1
Greenway La EPSF GU31 223 K11
Greenways BEXW TN39 96 E6
BOGR PO21 171 G4
BRIE/ROTT BN2 155 J2
HWH RH16 73 J3
PTSD BN41 * 121 G4
STHW BN42 120 E4
Greenways Cnr
BRIE/ROTT BN2 * 155 J1
Greenways Crs FERR BN12 149 L4
SHOR BN43 120 A4
The Green Wy FERR BN12 150 A1
Greenwell Cl SEAF BN25 175 H1
Greenwich Cl CRAWW RH11 43 H7
Greenwich Rd HAIL BN27 92 C6
Greenwich Wy PEAHV BN10 157 H6
Greenwood Av MSEA/BNM PO22 2 B1
Greenwood Cl MSEA/BNM PO22 2 B1
Greenwood Ct CRAWW RH11 * 43 G8
Greenwood Dr ANG/EP BN16 148 E2
Greenwoods La HTHF TN21 245 N7
Greet Rd LAN/SOMP BN15 118 C6
Greggs Wood Rd
RTWE/PEM TN2 38 D3
Gregory Cl CRAWE RH10 44 B7
Gregory La PEV BN24 133 L8
Gregory Wk BAT TN33 283 M1
Gregsons HORS RH12 187 P9
Grenada Cl BEXW TN39 136 C1
Grendon Cl HORL RH6 22 E4
Grenehurst Wy EPSF GU31 223 N6
Grenville Av FERR BN12 150 C2
Grenville Cl FERR BN12 150 B2
LIPH GU30 193 R1
Grenville Gdns CCH PO19 6 C9
Grenville Rd PEV BN24 165 H1
Gresham Cl EAST BN21 163 H7
Gresham Pl HFD BN5 269 J3
Gresham Wk CRAWE RH10 43 K6
Gresham Wy STLEO TN38 98 F5
Gresley Rd STLEO TN38 283 N12
Grevatt's La ARUN BN18 145 M6
Grevatt's La West ARUN BN18 145 L5
Greville Gn EMRTH PO10 103 M2
Greville Rd RHAS TN35 100 B2
Grey Alders HWH RH16 73 L3
Greyfriars HOVE BN3 122 C5
Greyfriars Cl BOGR PO21 171 L2
SALV BN13 116 F7
Greyfriars Ct LEWES BN7 * 17 H6
Greyfriars La PUL/STOR RH20 297 R1
Greyfriars Pl WSEA TN36 286 G3
Greyhound Slip CRAWE RH10 44 C2
Greynville Cl BOGR PO21 171 H3
Greys Rd EDN/EASTW BN20 176 D2
Greystoke Ms FERR BN12 149 K3
Greystoke Rd FERR BN12 149 K3
Greystone Av BOGR PO21 143 L6
SALV BN13 116 E8
Greywell Rd HAV PO9 288 F12
Gribble La SELS PO20 109 H6
Grier Cl CRAWW RH11 42 D4
Griffin Crs LHPTN BN17 147 J1
Griffith's Av LAN/SOMP BN15 118 C5
Griggs Meadow
MFD/CHID GU8 184 A2
Grinder's La SWTR RH13 267 P3
Grinstead Av LAN/SOMP BN15 118 D7
Grinstead La EGRIN RH19 63 H1
LAN/SOMP BN15 118 D7
Grinstead Mt BRIE/ROTT BN2 * 123 L8
Grisedale Cl CRAWW RH11 8 C8
Gromenfield RRTW TN3 52 B2
Groombridge Hl RRTW TN3 52 B1
Groombridge Rd RRTW TN3 51 M1
Groombridge Wy HORS RH12 201 Q4
Grooms Cl ANG/EP BN16 114 F8
Groomsland Dr BIL RH14 231 R3
The Grooms CRAWE RH10 44 C1
Grosvenor Br RTW TN1 38 A4
Grosvenor Cl HORL RH6 22 F8
POLE BN26 131 L8
Grosvenor Crs STLEO TN38 98 F7
Grosvenor Gdns BOGR PO21 171 H2
STLEO TN38 98 E7
Grosvenor Pk RTW TN1 37 M5
Grosvenor Rd CCH PO19 141 L2
EGRIN RH19 31 J8
RTW TN1 37 M5
SEAF BN25 174 E1
WTHG BN11 21 G5
Grosvenor St BRIE/ROTT BN2 5 H7
Grosvenor Wk RTW TN1 37 M5
Grosvenor Wy BOGR PO21 171 H2
Grouse Rd SWTR RH13 58 B6
SWTR RH13 203 M1
Grove Av RTW TN1 37 M7
Grove Bank BRIE/ROTT BN2 * 5 G5
Grove Crs LHPTN BN17 147 K3
Grove Hl BRIE/ROTT BN2 5 G5
HAIL BN27 278 F12
Grove Hill Gdns RTW TN1 38 A7
Grove Hill Ms RTW TN1 * 38 A6
Grove Hill Rd RTW TN1 38 A6
Grovehurst La STPH/PW TN12 189 P4
Grovelands Cottages
BURH RH15 * 74 E8
Grovelands Rd HAIL BN27 91 M4
The Grovelands
LAN/SOMP BN15 152 D1
Grove La PETW GU28 229 M11
PUL/STOR RH20 266 A7
RYE TN31 252 H1
Grovely La HTHF TN21 246 A12
Grove Pk CCH PO19 107 J7
Grover Av LAN/SOMP BN15 118 C6
Grove Rd BURH RH15 75 G7
CCH PO19 7 G6
EAST BN21 10 D7
GSHT GU26 180 F3
HAV PO9 103 G4
HORL RH6 22 D5
RHAS TN35 100 C1
SALV BN13 117 H7
SEAF BN25 174 F2
SELS PO20 301 K7
Grove St BRIE/ROTT BN2 5 H4
PETW GU28 229 L10
The Grove BAT TN33 282 G6
BEXW TN39 96 D8
CRAWW RH11 8 C3
CROW TN6 67 K8
EDN/EASTW BN20 162 E2
EDN/EASTW BN20 163 G6
EMRTH PO10 104 C2
FERR BN12 149 K3
HAIL BN27 92 A7
HORL RH6 23 G7
HWH RH16 73 L6
LIPH GU30 193 Q1
MAYF TN20 212 D7
MSEA/BNM PO22 3 M4
NEWHV BN9 158 D3
RTWE/PEM TN2 39 J1
RYE TN31 252 H7
Growers End RING/NEW BN8 240 C6
Guardswell Pl SEAF BN25 174 E2
Guernsey Cl CRAWW RH11 42 F7
Guernsey Farm La
MSEA/BNM PO22 145 H8
Guernsey Rd FERR BN12 149 L5
Guestling Rd LW/ROSE BN22 11 L2
Guilden Rd CCH PO19 7 H4
Guildford Cl EMRTH PO10 104 E4
SALV BN13 20 B3
Guildford Pl CCH PO19 107 L4
Guildford Rd ANG/EP BN16 148 D3
BIL RH14 184 G12
BRI BN1 4 D4
HORS RH12 185 N9
HORS RH12 201 R3
RTW TN1 38 A6
SALV BN13 20 B3
SWTR RH13 186 E10
Guildford St BRI BN1 4 D4
Guildhall St CCH PO19 6 E3
Guillards Oak MIDH GU29 226 H10
Guinevere Rd CRAWW RH11 42 D3
Guinness Trust Bungalows
NEWHV BN9 * 158 D3
Guldeford La RYE TN31 254 A2
Guldeford Rd RYE TN31 253 K7
Gun Back La STPH/PW TN12 189 M4
Gundreda Rd LEWES BN7 16 C4
Gun Hl HTHF TN21 277 R8
Gunlands STPH/PW TN12 189 M3
Gunning Cl CRAWW RH11 42 F6
Gunns Farm LIPH GU30 193 R3
Gun Rd UCK TN22 242 H7
Gunter's La BEXW TN39 96 F6
Gunwin Ct BOGR PO21 171 J3
Gurth Rd RHAS TN35 100 B4
Gwatkin Cl HAV PO9 102 D2
Gwyneth Gv BEX TN40 97 L6
Gwynne Gdns EGRIN RH19 31 H7
POLE BN26 * 160 E2
Gypsy La HORN PO8 288 A4

H

Habin Hl EPSF GU31 225 J5
Hackenden Cl EGRIN RH19 31 K6
Hackenden Cottages
EGRIN RH19 * 31 K6
Hackenden La EGRIN RH19 31 L5
Hacketts La HFD BN5 * 269 K4
Hackhurst La HAIL BN27 91 G1
Hackwood RBTBR TN32 247 R1
Haddington Cl HOVE BN3 122 A7
Haddington St HOVE BN3 122 A6
Hadlands BOGR PO21 170 F4
Hadley Av SALV BN13 117 J6
Hadley Cl MSEA/BNM PO22 145 K7
Hadlow Av LGNY BN23 163 M1
Hadlow Cl BRIE/ROTT BN2 5 L5
Hadlow Down Rd CROW TN6 210 G7
Hadlow Wy LAN/SOMP BN15 118 E7
Hadmans Cl HORS RH12 14 C7
Hadrian Av STHW BN42 120 E5
Hadrian Gdns SLVH TN37 283 P11
Haglands Copse
PUL/STOR RH20 266 A6
Haglands La PUL/STOR RH20 266 A6
Haig Av BRI BN1 83 J7
Haigh Cl LAN/SOMP BN15 119 G8
Hailsham Av BRIE/ROTT BN2 156 C2
Hailsham Cl ANG/EP BN16 149 G2
Hailsham Ct BEX TN40 * 137 H2
Hailsham Rd HAIL BN27 279 P12
HTHF TN21 244 D7
POLE BN26 131 L6
POLE BN26 132 E5
WTHG BN11 150 E4
Hairpin Cft PEAHV BN10 157 H4
Hale Cl SELS PO20 168 A7
Hales Fld HASM GU27 181 M11
Halewick Cl LAN/SOMP BN15 118 B5
Halewick La LAN/SOMP BN15 118 B5
Haleybridge Wk SELS PO20 109 J4
Half Mile Dro RING/NEW BN8 275 N11
Half Moon Hl HASM GU27 181 M11
Half Moon La SALV BN13 116 E6
Half Moon Pde SALV BN13 * 116 E6
Halfrey Cl RCCH PO18 106 F6
Halfrey Rd RCCH PO18 106 F6
Halifax Cl CRAWE RH10 28 D8
Halifax Dr SALV BN13 116 B7
Halifax Ri WVILLE PO7 288 A10
Halland Cl CRAWE RH10 9 L1
LW/ROSE BN22 163 J4
Halland Rd BRIE/ROTT BN2 123 L1
Hall Av SALV BN13 116 F6
Hall Cl SALV BN13 116 F6
Hallett Rd BRIE/ROTT BN2 5 L3
HAV PO9 103 J3
Halley Cl CRAWW RH11 43 G8
Halley Rd HAIL BN27 94 A4
HTHF TN21 244 H5
Halliford Dr MSEA/BNM PO22 111 H8
Halliwick Gdns
MSEA/BNM PO22 173 G1
Hall La UCK TN22 211 K12
Halls Dr HORS RH12 41 L8
Hall's Hole Rd RTWE/PEM TN2 38 C7

Hallsland CRAWE RH10....46 B1
Hallyburton Rd HOVE BN3....121 J5
Halnaker Barn La RCCH PO18....109 M1
Halnaker Gdns BOGR PO21....171 H3
Halnaker Wk CRAWW RH11 *....42 E6
Halsbury Cl WTHG BN11....21 K3
Halsbury Rd WTHG BN11....21 L3
Halsford La EGRIN RH19....31 J3
Halsford Park Rd EGRIN RH19....31 K1
Halson Cl BOGR PO21....2 C4
Halters End GSHT GU26....180 D6
Halton Crs HAS TN34....13 M2
Halton Pl HAS TN34....13 M2
Halton Rd LW/ROSE BN22....11 J4
Halton Shaws HPPT/KEY BN6....271 J12
Halton Ter HAS TN34....13 M2
Hambledon Pl BOGR PO21....2 E3
Hambledon Rd HORN PO8....256 D9
Hamble Gdns SALV BN13....116 B6
Hamble Rd LAN/SOMP BN15....118 D4
PEV BN24....132 E8
Hambleton Cl LGNY BN23....164 C4
Hambleton Hl CRAWW RH11....8 D3
Hamble Wy SALV BN13....116 B6
Hambrook BURH RH15....75 H8
Hambrook Hl (North)
RCCH PO18....105 J2
Hambrook Hl (South)
RCCH PO18....105 J3
Hamelsham Ct HAIL TN27....91 M5
Hamilton Cl ANG/EP BN16....148 A1
BOR GU35....179 J3
HAV PO9....103 G5
PTSD BN41....120 F2
SALV BN13....117 K8
Hamilton Ct FERR BN12....150 C2
Hamilton Dr ANG/EP BN16....148 A1
Hamilton Gdns BOGR PO21....171 J3
RCCH PO18....106 B5
RHAS TN35....100 C2
Hamilton Ms
LAN/SOMP BN15 *....118 B6
Hamilton Rd BRI BN1....4 C1
HORS RH12....14 B3
LAN/SOMP BN15....118 C6
LISS GU33....192 G3
LYDD TN29....255 R8
Hamilton Ter BEXW TN39....136 F1
Hamlands La LW/ROSE BN22....163 G2
Ham La BUR/ETCH TN19....214 C11
EMRTH PO10....104 E6
HORN PO8....288 A1
LEWES BN7....17 H8
RHWH RH17....238 D2
RING/NEW BN8....274 C11
SELS PO20....109 J6
Ham Manor Cl ANG/EP BN16....148 A1
Ham Manor Wy ANG/EP BN16....148 D1
RHWH RH17....204 H6
Hammer Hl HASM GU27....194 F1
Hammer La GSHT GU26....180 F9
GSHT GU26....180 F9
HASM GU27....180 D11
HTHF TN21....279 J1
MIDH GU29....226 F9
Hammerpond Rd SWTR RH13....15 L9
SWTR RH13....202 H1
SWTR RH13....203 H1
Hammerwood Copse
HASM GU27....180 G12
Hammerwood Rd EGRIN RH19....48 D1
Hammer Yd CRAWE RH10 *....8 E2
Hammingden La EGRIN RH19....62 D6
RHWH RH17....206 H2
Hammond Dr SALV BN13....116 C5
Hammond Pl
PUL/STOR RH20 *....266 A12
Hammond Rd CRAWW RH11....59 G3
Hammonds Dr LGNY BN23....164 B6
Hammonds Gdns BURH RH15....74 B8
Hammonds Rdg BURH RH15....74 D8
Hammy Cl SHOR BN43....120 A5
Hammy La SHOR BN43....120 A5
Hammy Wy SHOR BN43....120 A5
Hampden Av LW/ROSE BN22....163 G4
Hampden Cl BAT TN33....282 C5
CRAWE RH10....28 D3
MSEA/BNM PO22....145 L8
Hampden Park Dr
LW/ROSE BN22....163 G5
Hampden Rd BRIE/ROTT BN2....5 J3
Hampden Ter LW/ROSE BN22 *....11 J4
Hampers Gn PETW GU28....229 L7
Hampers La PUL/STOR RH20....298 E1
SWTR RH13....15 M5
SWTR RH13....57 H7
Hampshire Av BOGR PO21....2 A3
Hampshire Ct BRIE/ROTT BN2 *....5 H8
Hampshire Rd BOR GU35....178 C5
Hampstead Rd BRI BN1....122 C4
Hampton Cl WVILLE PO7....288 B10
Hampton Ct BOGR PO21....171 J4
Hampton Flds LPHTN BN17....147 J3
Hampton Pl BRI BN1....4 B6
Hampton St BRI BN1....4 B5
Hampton Ter EGRIN RH19....47 L2
Hampton Wy EGRIN RH19....47 L2
Ham Rd SELS PO20....169 H8
SHOR BN43....119 L6
WTHG BN11....151 M2
Hamsey Cl BRIE/ROTT BN2....123 L8
EDN/EASTW BN20....163 G7
Hamsey Crs LEWES BN7....16 A3
Hamsey Rd RING/NEW BN8....273 R10
SEAF BN25....175 J3
Hamsey Rd BRIE/ROTT BN2....156 C5
EGRIN RH19....62 F3
Ham Shaw Ct
LW/ROSE BN22 *....163 L1
Hamshire Hl RHWH RH17....204 A5
Hamsland RHWH RH17....207 M5
Hamstead Meadow
RCCH PO18....105 K6
Ham Wy WTHG BN11....151 M1
Hanbury La RHWH RH16....73 H4
Hanbury Rd CRAWW RH11....42 D4
Hancock Wy SHOR BN43....120 A7
Handcross Rd RHWH RH17....60 B7
SWTR RH13....203 N5
Handford Wy SWTR RH13....203 Q3
Hangers Wy EGRIN RH19....223 M11
EPSF GU31....257 K1
HORN PO8....256 H9
The Hanger BOR GU35....179 M2

Hanger Wy EPSF GU31....223 Q6
Hanging Birch La HTHF TN21....244 A10
Hangleton Cl HOVE BN3....121 J3
Hangleton Gdns HOVE BN3....121 H3
Hangleton Gra FERR BN12....149 K2
Hangleton La FERR BN12....149 J1
HOVE BN3....121 H3
Hangleton Manor Cl
HOVE BN3....121 J3
Hangleton Rd HOVE BN3....121 K3
Hangleton Valley Dr
HOVE BN3....121 J3
Hankham Hall Rd PEV BN24....133 G3
Hankham Rd PEV BN24....133 G2
Hankham St PEV BN24....133 G4
Hanlye La RHWH RH17....72 D1
Hannah Gdns WVILLE PO7....288 A9
Hannah Sq CCH PO19....107 J6
Hannington Pl HPPT/KEY BN6....270 F2
Hannington Rd HAV PO9....288 E10
Hanover Cl BEX TN40....97 H8
CRAWE RH10....9 J7
PUL/STOR RH20....296 B2
SEAF BN25....159 G2
SELS PO20....301 M6
Hanover Ct MIDH GU29....227 K7
Hanover Crs BRIE/ROTT BN2....5 H3
Hanover Gdns SWTR RH13....235 K3
Hanover Ms BRIE/ROTT BN2....5 H3
Hanover Pl BRIE/ROTT BN2....5 H2
Hanover Rd LW/ROSE BN22....11 J4
RTW TN1 *....37 M5
Hanover St BRIE/ROTT BN2....5 H3
Hanover Ter BRIE/ROTT BN2....5 H3
Hanover Wk PUL/STOR RH20....266 A12
Hanson Rd NEWHV BN9....18 E6
Harberton Crs CCH PO19....107 M2
Harbolets Rd BIL RH14....232 C12
Harborough Cl
PUL/STOR RH20....265 Q5
Harborough Dr
PUL/STOR RH20....265 Q5
Harborough Gorse
PUL/STOR RH20....265 Q5
Harborough Hl
PUL/STOR RH20....265 P6
Harborough Meadow
PUL/STOR RH20....265 Q5
Harbour Barn WSEA TN36....286 A1
Harbour Ct RCCH PO18....106 B8
Harbour Quay LGNY BN23....164 F4
Harbour Rd BOGR PO21....170 E7
RCCH PO18....140 A1
RYE TN31....252 H9
Harbourside HAV PO9....103 G2
Harbours Yd BAT TN33 *....282 F5
Harbour View Cl SEAF BN25 *....159 G2
Harbour View Rd BOGR PO21....170 F5
NEWHV BN9....18 D6
Harbour Wy EMRTH PO10....104 B5
RCCH PO18....140 B1
SHOR BN43....119 M7
STLEO TN38....283 M10
Harbridge Cl HAV PO9....288 E10
Harcourt Cl HORN PO8....288 B5
UCK TN22....76 E6
Harcourt Rd UCK TN22....76 E6
Harcourt Wy SELS PO20....301 M5
Hardbarrow Woods
PUL/STOR RH20....266 D7
Hardham Cl ANG/EP BN16....148 A5
CRAWW RH11....42 F1
Hardham Rd CCH PO19 *....7 G8
Harding Av LW/ROSE BN22....164 A7
Hard's Hl SWTR RH13....202 C4
The Hard MSEA/BNM PO22....146 B8
Hardwicke Rd HAS TN34....13 M2
Hardwick Rd EAST BN21....10 E8
HOVE BN3....121 K1
Hardwick Wy HOVE BN3....121 K1
Hardy Av EPSF GU31....223 P4
Hardy Cl CRAWE RH10....44 B2
HORL RH6....22 D6
HORS RH12....14 B2
MSEA/BNM PO22....145 J8
SHOR BN43....119 L7
Hardy Dr LGNY BN23....164 E7
Harebeating Cl HAIL BN27....92 A3
Harebeating Crs HAIL BN27....92 A2
Harebeating Dr HAIL BN27....92 A2
Harebeating Gdns HAIL BN27....92 A3
Harebeating La HAIL BN27....92 B3
Harebell Cl LGNY BN23....164 B2
LPHTN BN17....148 A2
Harebell Dr PTSD BN41....120 F2
Harecombe Ri CROW TN6....210 F1
Harecombe Rd CROW TN6....210 F1
Harefield Av SALV BN13....150 E1
Harefield Rd MSEA/BNM PO22....145 J4
Hare La CRAWW RH11....27 G8
SELS PO20....300 H5
Haremere Hl BUR/ETCH TN19....215 Q8
Harescroft RTWE/PEM TN2....53 L2
Haresfield Ter SELS PO20....109 J4
Haresfoot Cl RCCH PO18....290 E10
Hares La RCCH PO18....290 E10
Harestock Rd HAV PO9....102 E2
Hare Wy SLVH TN37....283 R12
Harewood Cl BEXW TN39....136 F2
CRAWE RH10....27 M8
Harfield Cl NEWHV BN9....18 E4
Hargate Cl RTWE/PEM TN2....53 L2
Hargreaves Rd LGNY BN23....164 E7
Harison Rd SEAF BN25....175 G1
Harkness Dr HAS TN34....284 E12
WVILLE PO7....288 C9
Harlands Cl HWH RH16....72 F3
Harlands Rd HWH RH16....72 F3
Harlech Cl SALV BN13....116 A8
Harlequin Gdns SLVH TN37....283 P11
Harlequin La CROW TN6....210 F1
Harlequin Pl CROW TN6....210 F1
Harley La HTHF TN21....244 D7
Harley Shute Rd STLEO TN38....98 C2
Harley Wy STLEO TN38....98 C3
Harmans Dr EGRIN RH19....32 A8
Harmans Md EGRIN RH19....31 M8
Harmers Hay Rd HAIL BN27....92 B4
Harmers Hl RING/NEW BN8....240 B6
Harmony Cl CRAWW RH11....42 D5
Harmony Dr SELS PO20....168 A3
Harmsworth Crs HOVE BN3....121 K2
Harold Cl BOGR PO21....143 L7
PEV BN24....134 E6

Harold Dr LGNY BN23....164 D5
Harold Ms STLEO TN38....12 A9
Harold Pl HAS TN34....13 G7
Harold Rd CRAWE RH10....44 D4
EMRTH PO10....104 C1
RHAS TN35....13 M4
Haroldslea HORL RH6....23 K7
Haroldslea Cl HORL RH6....23 H8
Haroldslea Dr HORL RH6....23 H8
Harper Dr CRAWE RH10....44 B7
Harpers Rd NEWHV BN9....18 E3
Harrier Cl HORN PO8....288 B3
Harrier La BAT TN33....282 C5
Harrier Wy EPSF GU31....223 R7
Harries Rd RTWE/PEM TN2....38 C2
Harrington Pl BRI BN1....123 G3
Harrington Rd BRI BN1....122 D3
Harrington Vls BRI BN1....122 E3
Harriots Cl SWTR RH13....202 F9
Harris Cl CRAWW RH11....43 G6
Harris La HORN PO8....257 L8
Harrison Cl SALV BN13....117 L8
Harrison Rd SALV BN13....117 K8
Harrisons La RING/NEW BN8....275 K12
Harris Pth CRAWW RH11....8 B9
Harrison Cl SEAF BN25....175 G1
Harrow Dr SELS PO20....167 L6
Harrow La PSF GU32....223 N3
SLVH TN37....283 Q12
Harrow Rd WTHG BN11....20 C3
Harrowsley Ct HORL RH6....23 G5
Harsfold Cl ANG/EP BN16....147 M5
Harsfold Rd ANG/EP BN16....148 A5
Hart Cl UCK TN22....76 C5
Hartfield Av BRI BN1....122 F1
Hartfield Meadow STLEO TN38....98 C2
Hartfield Rd BEXW TN39....136 C3
BRIE/ROTT BN2....156 C4
EAST BN21....10 D4
EDEN TN8....34 C6
FROW RH18....48 F7
SEAF BN25....175 J3
Harting Cl FERR BN12....150 A1
HORN PO8....256 E9
Harting Ct CRAWW RH11....42 E6
Harting Down EPSF GU31....223 Q6
Harting Rd MSEA/BNM PO22....145 J7
Hartington Pl BRIE/ROTT BN2....5 K1
EAST BN21....10 C1
Hartington Rd BRIE/ROTT BN2....5 K1
Hartington Ter BRIE/ROTT BN2....5 K1
Hartington Vls HOVE BN3....122 A5
Hartland Ct EMRTH PO10....104 E4
Hart Plain Av HORN PO8....288 A7
Harts Farm Wy HAV PO9....102 E5
Hartsgrove MFD/CHID GU8....182 G4
Hartwell Cottages HRTF TN7 *....50 B3
Harvard Cl LEWES BN7....16 F1
Harvard Rd RING/NEW BN8....275 J12
Harvest Cl HWH RH16....73 L2
PEAHV BN10....157 F5
Harvester Cl CROW TN6....7 L7
Harvesters HORS RH12....14 F1
HWH RH16....73 L2
Harvest Hl EGRIN RH19....47 K1
Harvesting La PSF GU32....222 B11
PSF GU32....256 E1
Harvest Rd CRAWE RH10....44 B5
Harvestside HORL RH6....23 H5
Harvest Wy SLVH TN37....283 R12
Harvey Cl CRAWW RH11....42 F8
STLEO TN38....98 E1
Harvey Rd FERR BN12....150 D4
Harvey's La RING/NEW BN8....275 N6
UCK TN22....276 A1
Harveys Wy LEWES BN7....17 J5
Harwarden Cl CRAWE RH10....46 B1
Harwood Av FERR BN12....150 C1
Harwood Cl LGNY BN23....164 D6
Harwood Pk REDH RH1....22 F1
Harwood Rd LPHTN BN17....147 H3
SWTR RH13....15 H3
Harwoods Cl EGRIN RH19....47 L2
Harwood's La EGRIN RH19....47 L1
Haslam Crs BEX TN40....97 L7
Hasle Dr HASM GU27....181 L12
Haslemere Gdns HISD PO11....166 A3
Haslemere Rd EMRTH PO10....104 E3
HASM GU27....195 L3
LIPH GU30....194 A1
Hasler's La RCCH PO18....292 B4
Haslett Av CRAWE RH10....9 K4
Haslett Av East CRAWE RH10....9 J4
Haslett Av West CRAWE RH10....8 F5
Hasletts Cl RTW TN1....38 A3
Haslingbourne La PETW GU28....229 K12
Hassocks Cl LGNY BN23....163 L1
Hassocks Ct CRAWW RH11....42 A5
Hassocks Rd HPPT/KEY BN6....271 J4
The Hassocks WVILLE PO7....288 B10
Haste Hl HAIL BN27....181 N12
Haste Hill Top HASM GU27 *....181 N12
Hastings Av SEAF BN25....160 B8
Hastings Cl BOGR PO21....171 L1
POLE BN26....132 A6
Hastings Rd BAT TN33....282 F6
BEX TN40....97 J8
BRIE/ROTT BN2....5 J1
CRAWE RH10....44 A3
CRBK TN17....218 F3
HAWK TN18....216 G2
RTWE/PEM TN2....39 J3
WTHG BN11....20 A8
Hatch Cl CRAN GU6....184 H6
Hatch Cl HAV PO9....288 D10
Hatch End FROW RH18....48 E7
Hatchetts Dr HASM GU27....180 F11
Hatchetts Rd HORL RH6....22 F2
Hatchgate Cl RHWH RH17....72 D3
Hatchgate La HAIL BN27....181 K12
Hatchlands HORS RH12....56 D2
Hatch La HASM GU27....195 L4
HTHF TN21....279 M3
Hatch La HASM GU27....195 L4
LISS GU33....192 F9
Hatchmans Rd SALV BN13....116 D4
Hatfield Gn BOGR PO21....143 M8
Hatherleigh Gdns BOGR PO21....143 M8
Hatherleigh Rd SLVH TN37....12 A7
Hathersham La HORL RH6....23 M5
Hathersham La HORL RH6....23 M5
Hatmill La STPH/PW TN12....188 F2

Havana Ct LGNY BN23....164 E5
Havant Farm Cl HAV PO9....103 G2
Havant Rd EMRTH PO10....103 L5
HAV PO9....102 D5
HAV PO9....103 J5
HORN PO8....288 D2
Havelock Rd BEX TN40....97 H7
BOGR PO21....2 D5
BRI BN1....122 C4
HAS TN34....13 G6
LW/ROSE BN22....11 G3
Havelock Vls CROW TN6 *....210 F1
Haven Brow SEAF BN25....175 G4
Haven Cl LW/ROSE BN22....163 G2
PEV BN24....134 D2
Haven Gdns CRAWE RH10....29 M8
Haven Rd BIL RH14....200 A2
STLEO TN38....98 C7
Havenside HOVE BN3....119 J8
Havenstoke Cl CCH PO19....107 M4
The Haven HAIL BN27....92 B7
LAN/SOMP BN15 *....152 E1
LPHTN BN17....147 M4
Haven Wy NEWHV BN9....18 C6
Havering Cl RTWE/PEM TN2....38 C7
Haversham Cl CRAWE RH10....9 K4
Haweswater Cl BOR GU35....178 C4
Hawke Cl ANG/EP BN16....148 D4
Hawkenbury Cl
RTWE/PEM TN2....38 C7
Hawkenbury Md
RTWE/PEM TN2....38 C8
Hawkenbury Rd RRTW TN3....38 C8
Hawkenbury Wy LEWES BN7....16 A6
Hawker Close. SELS PO20....109 J3
Hawkesbourne Rd HORS RH12....56 F4
Hawkesmoor Rd CRAWW RH11....42 C5
Hawkhurst Cl LGNY BN23....164 C5
Hawkhurst Pl BRI BN1 *....83 J7
Hawkhurst Rd BRI BN1....83 J7
WADH TN5....311 R11
Hawkhurst Wk CRAWE RH10....44 A5
Hawkhurst Wy BEXW TN39....136 C3
Hawkins Cl BOGR PO21....171 G3
SHOR BN43....120 C4
Hawkins Crs SHOR BN43....120 C3
Hawkins Rd CRAWE RH10....9 H8
SHOR BN43....120 C4
Hawkins Wy HAIL BN27....92 A5
Hawkley Cl HAV PO9....288 F11
Hawksbridge Cl
LW/ROSE BN22....163 H2
Hawks Farm Cl HAIL BN27....92 A3
Hawksfold La East
HASM GU27....195 K7
Hawksfold La West
HASM GU27....195 K7
Hawkshaw Cl LIPH GU30....194 A1
Hawks Pl MSEA/BNM PO22....144 E8
Hawkstown Cl HAIL BN27....92 A3
Hawkstown Gdns HAIL BN27....92 A3
Hawkstown Vw HAIL BN27....92 B3
Hawkswood Dr HAIL BN27....92 B2
Hawkswood Rd HAIL BN27....92 B2
Hawley Rd ANG/EP BN16....148 A5
Hawmead CRAWE RH10....46 B1
Haworth Rd CRAWE RH10....44 A4
Hawth Av CRAWE RH10....9 J7
Hawth Cl CRAWE RH10....9 J7
SEAF BN25....174 C1
Hawth Crs SEAF BN25....174 C1
Hawth Gv SEAF BN25....159 G8
Hawth Hl SEAF BN25....159 G8
Hawthorn RASHW TN26....221 Q1
Hawthorn Av BEXW TN39....136 C2
Hawthorn Bank
BRIE/ROTT BN2 *....123 L1
Hawthorn Cl BRIE/ROTT BN2....156 B3
BURH RH15....75 J4
CCH PO19....6 C3
CRAWW RH11....27 H8
HORS RH12....14 D1
MIDH GU29....226 G11
Hawthorn Ct EPSF GU31....223 R6
Hawthorn Crs SALV BN13....117 J7
Hawthorne Cl HTHF TN21....244 E7
The Hawthornes RYE TN31....250 D9
Hawthorn Gdns SALV BN13....117 J7
Hawthorn Ri NEWHV BN9....18 C4
Hawthorn Rd BOGR PO21....171 M2
HORN PO8....256 D12
LGNY BN23....164 B5
LPHTN BN17....147 J1
RHAS TN35....100 C3
SALV BN13....117 J7
The Hawthorns BURH RH15 *....74 F4
HAIL BN27....91 M6
PUL/STOR RH20....266 B6
Hawthorn Wk RTWE/PEM TN2....38 D1
Hawthorn Wy PTSD BN41....120 F2
PUL/STOR RH20....266 A11
Haybarn Dr HORS RH12....56 D2
Haybourne Cl BRIE/ROTT BN2....123 K6
Haybourne Rd BRIE/ROTT BN2....123 K6
Haydock Ms WVILLE PO7....288 C8
Haydon Cl BOGR PO21....171 H4
Hayes Cl PTSD BN41....121 H5
RCCH PO18....292 B10
RING/NEW BN8....275 J12
Hayes La RYE TN31....251 L8
Hayes Plat RYE TN31....218 F12
Hayes Wk HORL RH6....23 H5
Hayes Wood Rd BIL RH14....200 C8
Hayfields HWH RH16....73 L4
Hayley Rd LAN/SOMP BN15....118 E6
Hayley's Gdns HWH RH16....73 L4
Hayling Cl HWH RH16....73 L4
Hayling Rd SALV BN13....116 D4
Haymans Hl STPH/PW TN12....189 N2
Hay Rd CCH PO19....6 C4
Haystoun Cl LW/ROSE BN22....163 H3

Haystoun Pk LW/ROSE BN22....163 H3
Hayward Rd LEWES BN7....16 B1
Haywards CRAWE RH10....28 C8
Haywards Heath Rd
RHWH RH17....60 F7
Haywards Rd BRI BN1....82 F7
HWH RH16....73 H4
Haywood Wy RHAS TN35....100 B3
Hazelbank RRTW TN3....36 E6
Hazelbank Cl EPSF GU31....223 Q5
LIPH GU30....194 A1
Hazel Cl CRAWE RH10....46 B1
CRAWW RH11....27 H8
NEWHV BN9....18 D4
PTSD BN41....121 H2
SWTR RH13....201 R12
Hazeldean Dr HAV PO9....289 J8
Hazeldene SEAF BN25....175 G2
Hazeldene Meads BRI BN1....122 C2
Hazeldene Rd LIPH GU30....193 L1
Hazeledene La RING/NEW BN8....239 Q6
Hazel Gv ARUN BN18....112 D3
BEXW TN39....96 F6
BURH RH15....75 G8
EDN/EASTW BN20....162 F2
GSHT GU26....180 H8
Hazelgrove HORN PO8....256 D8
Hazelgrove Rd HWH RH16....73 H5
Hazelholt Dr HAV PO9....102 D2
Hazelhurst HORL RH6....23 H5
Hazelhurst Crs HORS RH12....201 Q4
SALV BN13....116 E2
Hazelhurst Dr CRAWE RH10....44 D3
Hazel Ldg ANG/EP BN16 *....148 B5
Hazelmead Dr ANG/EP BN16....148 F1
Hazel Rd ANG/EP BN16....148 F1
HORN PO8....256 D8
MSEA/BNM PO22....144 A7
Hazel Wy CRAWE RH10....46 A1
Hazelwick Av CRAWE RH10....43 M1
Hazelwick Mill La CRAWE RH10....43 M1
Hazelwood CRAWW RH11....42 F3
Hazelwood Av HAV PO9....102 C2
LW/ROSE BN22....163 K1
Hazelwood Cl BEXW TN39....136 A2
CRAWE RH10....45 L1
MIDH GU29....227 J6
PUL/STOR RH20....266 E11
RTWE/PEM TN2....38 C1
SALV BN13....21 M1
Hazelwood Gdns SLVH TN37....284 A12
Hazelwood Rd SWTR RH13....234 F10
Hazleton Int HORN PO8 *....288 D3
Hazleton Wy HORN PO8....288 D3
Head Down EPSF GU31....223 Q6
Headland Av SEAF BN25....175 G2
Headland Cnr SEAF BN25 *....175 G3
Headlands Cl PEAHV BN10....157 K6
Headley Cl CRAWE RH10....28 C8
Headley Hill Rd BOR GU35....179 N4
Headley La LIPH GU30....179 M7
Headley Rd BOR GU35....179 K4
GSHT GU26....180 C5
LIPH GU30....179 P11
Heansill La HAWK TN18....216 H1
Hearn Cl SELS PO20....109 H4
Hearnfield Rd LPHTN BN17....147 J1
Hearn V BOR GU35....179 P2
Heasewood HWH RH16....72 F6
Heath Cl GSHT GU26....180 F2
HORN PO8....288 C2
HORS RH12....201 P2
HPPT/KEY BN6....236 G12
HWH RH16 *....73 H5
SELS PO20....141 M5
SWTR RH13....203 J3
Heathcote Dr EGRIN RH19....31 G7
Heathcote Rd BOR GU35....178 H6
Heath Cottages GSHT GU26 *....180 F3
Heathdown Cl PEAHV BN10....157 J3
Heather Bank HWH RH16....72 F4
Heather Cl BOR GU35....178 G8
CRAWE RH10....29 G7
HORS RH12....56 C4
LGNY BN23....164 C2
RCCH PO18....106 A2
WVILLE PO7....288 A11
Heather Dr BOR GU35....179 J4
Heatherdune Rd BEXW TN39....96 F8
Heatherfield EPSF GU31....223 L12
Heatherlands HORL RH6....23 H5
PUL/STOR RH20....266 C11
Heather La PUL/STOR RH20....265 R7
SALV BN13....116 D3
Heathermead PUL/STOR RH20....265 R7
Heather Rd EPSF GU31....223 R6
The Heathers ANG/EP BN16 *....114 C7
Heatherstone Rd WTHG BN11....151 M2
Heatherton Ms EMRTH PO10....104 A2
Heatherway EGRIN RH19....30 G2
Heather Wy GSHT GU26....181 J7
PUL/STOR RH20....266 C12
RHAS TN35....101 J3
Heatherwood MIDH GU29....226 G9
Heathfield CRAWE RH10....28 C8
Heathfield Av ANG/EP BN16....148 E2
BRIE/ROTT BN2....156 C3
MIDH GU29....226 H10
SALV BN13....116 E8
Heathfield Copse
PUL/STOR RH20....265 Q6
Heathfield Crs PTSD BN41....120 E1
Heathfield Dr PTSD BN41....120 E1
Heathfield Gdns MIDH GU29....226 H10
RBTBR TN32....248 C2
Heathfield Gn MIDH GU29....226 H10
Heathfield Pk MIDH GU29....226 G10
Heathfield Rd EPSF GU31....223 R6
SEAF BN25....174 F2
Heath Hill Av BRIE/ROTT BN2....123 J4
Heathlands HORS RH12....284 D6
Heath Pl MSEA/BNM PO22....144 C6
Heath Rd EPSF GU31....223 R5
HASM GU27....180 C12
HWH RH16....73 H4
Heath Rd East EPSF GU31....223 R5
Heath Rd West EPSF GU31....223 R5
Heathside Rd GSHT GU26....180 G3
Heath Sq HWH RH16 *....73 G4
Heath Wy HORS RH12....56 C4
Heathy Brow PEAHV BN10....157 G4
Heavegate Rd CROW TN6....210 D1

Hebe Rd *SHOR* BN43......119 K6
Hechle Wd *BOGR* PO21......171 L3
Heckfield Ct *HAV* PO9......289 J12
Hectors La *EGRIN* RH19......48 B2
Hedgecourt Pl *EGRIN* RH19......30 D5
Hedge End Rd
 MSEA/BNM PO22......111 H7
Hedgehog La *HASM* GU27......181 L12
Hedgerow Gdns *EMRTH* PO10......104 A2
Hedgers Hl *ARUN* BN18......111 L4
Hedgeside *CRAWW* RH11......43 H8
Hedgeway *HORL* RH6......23 H5
Hedingham Cl *HORL* RH6......23 H5
Heene Pl *WTHG* BN11......20 D7
Heene Rd *WTHG* BN11......20 D4
Heene Ter *WTHG* BN11......20 D7
Heene Wy *WTHG* BN11......20 C6
Heghbrok Wy *BOGR* PO21......171 M3
Heighton Cl *NEWHV* BN9......136 C2
Heighton Crs *NEWHV* BN9......158 C3
Heighton Rd *NEWHV* BN9......158 D3
The Heights *BRI* BN1......82 A8
 RHAS TN55......100 D1
 SALV BN13......116 F4
Helena Cl *PTSD* BN41......121 H4
Helena Rd *BRIE/ROTT* BN2......124 B4
Helensdene Wk *SLVH* TN37 *......12 C1
Hellingly Cl *BRIE/ROTT* BN2......123 K8
Helston Dr *EMRTH* PO10......103 M2
Helvellyn Dr *LGNY* BN23......164 B1
Helyer's Gn *LHPTN* BN17......147 H3
Hempstead Gdns *UCK* TN22......76 F5
Hempstead La *HAIL* BN27......91 L4
Hempstead Ri *UCK* TN22 *......76 E5
Hempstead Rd
 BRIE/ROTT BN2......156 C3
 UCK TN22......76 E5
Hemsby Wk *CRAWE* RH10......44 A5
Hemsley Wk *HORN* PO8......288 D10
Henderson Ct *CRAWW* RH11......43 G8
Henderson Rd *HAS* TN34......99 L2
Henderson Wk *STEY/UB* BN44......78 D1
Hendon Av *ANG/EP* BN16......147 M6
Hendon Rd *BOR* GU35......178 H7
Hendon St *BRIE/ROTT* BN2......5 L6
Henfield Cl *BRIE/ROTT* BN2......154 E1
 FERR BN12......150 A1
Henfield Rd *HFD* BN5......79 K1
 HPPT/KEY BN6......235 R12
 HPPT/KEY BN6......270 D1
 LW/ROSE BN22......163 K3
 STEY/UB BN44......79 G4
Henfield Wy *HOVE* BN3......121 L2
 MSEA/BNM PO22......145 J7
Henge Wy *PTSD* BN41......121 G3
Hengist Cl *HORS* RH12......201 R4
 LGNY BN23......164 D5
Henley Cl *CRAWE* RH10......44 C6
 RTWE/PEM TN2......38 B5
 RYE TN31......252 F7
Henley Rd *BRIE/ROTT* BN2......154 E1
Henley's Hl *BAT* TN33......280 F8
Henry Av *LHPTN* BN17......147 M4
Henry Burt Wy *BURH* RH15......74 D8
Henry Cl *CCH* PO19......7 L4
Henry Fletcher Cl
 ANG/EP BN16......114 F8
Henry St *BOGR* PO21......2 E5
Henshaw Cl *CRAWW* RH11......42 E5
Hensil La *HAWK* TN18......216 F1
Henson Rd *CRAWE* RH10......44 A2
Henty Cl *ARUN* BN18......111 L5
 CRAWW RH11......42 D6
Henty Gdns *CCH* PO19......6 C4
Henty Rd *FERR* BN12......149 L5
 SALV BN13......20 E2
Henwood Down *EPSF* GU31......223 P6
Henwood Green Rd
 RTWE/PEM TN2......39 K3
Henwoods Crs *RTWE/PEM* TN2......39 J3
Henwoods Mt *RTWE/PEM* TN2......39 K3
Hepplewhite Cl *CRAWW* RH11......43 G8
Herald Dr *CCH* PO19......6 F7
Herbert Rd *BRI* BN1......122 E5
 LAN/SOMP BN15......118 A4
Herbrand Wk *PEV* BN24......135 L4
Hercules Pl *MSEA/BNM* PO22......145 J8
Hereford Cl *CCH* PO19......107 L4
 CRAWE RH10......43 K7
Hereford St *BRIE/ROTT* BN2......5 H7
Hereward Rd *LGNY* BN23......164 C5
Hereward Wy *LEWES* BN7......17 H2
Herington Rd *ARUN* BN18......112 L3
Heritage Lawn *HORL* RH6......23 H5
Herm Cl *CRAWW* RH11 *......42 F7
Hermione Cl *FERR* BN12......149 J2
Hermitage Cl *HAV* PO9......102 F1
 SELS PO20......142 C4
Hermitage La *EGRIN* RH19......47 L1
Hermitage Rd *EGRIN* RH19......31 J6
Hermits Rd *CRAWE* RH10......9 K1
Hermit Ter *SALV* BN13 *......298 H11
Hermonger La *HORS* RH12......186 C7
Herm St *FERR* BN12......149 L5
Hernbrook Dr *SWTR* RH13......15 H9
Herne Ct *ANG/EP* BN16 *......148 C3
Herne Down *CROW* TN6......210 G2
Herne Gdns *ANG/EP* BN16......148 C3
Herne La *ANG/EP* BN16......148 C3
Herne Rd *CROW* TN6......210 H1
 EPSF GU31......223 P6
Heron Cl *CRAWW* RH11......43 H1
 LGNY BN23......164 B3
 MSEA/BNM PO22......144 A6
 RCCH PO18......292 B10
 STLEO TN38......98 D5
 UCK TN22......76 F7
Herondale *HASM* GU27......180 H11
Heron La *SELS* PO20......300 H5
Heron Md *BOGR* PO21......170 E6
Heron Pl *EGRIN* RH19......47 L1
Heron Quay *EMRTH* PO10......104 B6
Heron Rdg *POLE* BN26......132 A7
Herons Cl *BIL* RH14......198 C11
 CRAWE RH10......29 M4
Heronscourt Cl *ANG/EP* BN16......148 B5
Heronsdale Rd
 BRIE/ROTT BN2......124 E5
Herons Lea *CRAWE* RH10......29 M4
The Herons *LAN/SOMP* BN15 *......152 E1
Herons Wy *HAIL* BN27 *......90 B1
 RTWE/PEM TN2......39 K1
Heronswood Ct *HORL* RH6......23 G5
Herons Wood Ct *HORL* RH6 *......23 G5
Heron Tye *HPPT/KEY* BN6 *......271 N6

Herontye Dr *EGRIN* RH19......47 L1
Heron Wy *SWTR* RH13......15 L6
Herrick Cl *CRAWE* RH10......44 B1
Herring's Rd *HTHF* TN21......246 D12
Herriott Cl *HORN* PO8......288 B4
Herschel Wk *CRAWW* RH11 *......43 G8
Hersee Wy *SELS* PO20......301 M5
Hertford Cl *BOGR* PO21......171 L2
 STLEO TN38......98 F1
Hertford Rd *BRI* BN1......123 G3
 WTHG BN11......21 G4
Heskett Pk *RTWE/PEM* TN2......39 K3
Heston Av *BRI* BN1......82 E6
Heston Gv *BOGR* PO21......171 H4
Hett Cl *RHWH* RH17......206 E1
Hever Cl *LGNY* BN23......164 C1
Hever Crs *BEXW* TN39......96 E8
Hevers Av *HORL* RH6......22 C5
Hewart's Cl *BOGR* PO21......171 J2
Hewitts *HFD* BN5......269 K5
Hewitts End *HFD* BN5......269 K5
Hewshott Gv *LIPH* GU30......180 B12
Hewshott La *LIPH* GU30......180 A12
Hexham Cl *CRAWE* RH10......44 D3
Heyshott Cl *LAN/SOMP* BN15......118 D5
Heyworth Cl *BRIE/ROTT* BN2......124 E5
Heyworth Ride *HWH* RH16......72 F6
Hibiscus Gv *BOR* GU35......178 H7
Hickling Cl *LGNY* BN23......164 A1
Hickling Wk *CRAWE* RH10......44 A5
Hickman's Cl *HWH* RH16......73 L1
Hickman's La *HWH* RH16......73 K1
Hickman Wy *HAS* TN34......99 J1
Hickstead La *RHWH* RH17......236 D8
Hide Cl *RHWH* RH17......59 J7
Hide Gdns *ANG/EP* BN16......148 A3
Hide Hollow *LGNY* BN23......164 C2
Higglers La *UCK* TN22......77 L1
Higham Gdns *RHAS* TN35......285 K9
Higham La *RYE* TN31......218 D11
Highams Hl *CRAWW* RH11......42 E4
Highbank *BRI* BN1......82 B8
High Bank *RHAS* TN35......100 B3
High Bank Cl *RHAS* TN35 *......100 B3
High Bar La *PUL/STOR* RH20......266 C7
Highbarn *SALV* BN13......298 H10
High Barn Rd *HAIL* BN27......90 E6
High Beech Cl *SLVH* TN57......283 N11
High Beeches *RTWE/PEM* TN2......38 C3
High Beeches La *RHWH* RH17......59 J7
High Beech La *HWH* RH16......73 J1
High Branches *BEXW* TN39......96 D1
Highbridge La *LEWES* BN7......273 L5
Highbrook Cl *BRIE/ROTT* BN2......123 J3
Highbrook Pl
 PUL/STOR RH20 *......266 A12
High Broom La *CROW* TN6......210 F2
High Broom Rd *CROW* TN6......210 F2
High Brooms Rd
 SBGH/RUST TN4......38 B1
Highbury Gv *HASM* GU27......181 M9
Highclere Av *HAV* PO9......102 F1
Highclere Wy *SALV* BN13......116 A8
High Cl *EDN/EASTW* BN20......303 J3
 PTSD BN41......120 F4
Highcroft Av *MSEA/BNM* PO22......3 G3
Highcroft Crs *HTHF* TN21......244 D6
 MSEA/BNM PO22......3 G2
Highcroft Dr *HORS* RH12......186 B8
Highcroft La *HORN* PO8......288 D1
Highcroft Rd *EGRIN* RH19......62 F3
Highcroft Vls *BRI* BN1......122 D4
High Cross Flds *CROW* TN6......67 L6
Highdown *STHW* BN42......120 E4
Highdown Av *SALV* BN13......116 F8
Highdown Cl *ANG/EP* BN16......114 F8
 FERR BN12......149 K2
 STHW BN42......120 E4
Highdown Ct *CRAWE* RH10......44 A6
Highdown Dr *LHPTN* BN17......147 K4
Highdown Rd *HOVE* BN3......4 A3
 LEWES BN7......16 A3
Highdown Wy *FERR* BN12......149 K2
 HORS RH12......56 E2
Highercombe Rd *HASM* GU27......181 P9
Highfield *LHPTN* BN17......147 L3
Highfield Av *WVILLE* PO7......288 B9
Highfield Cl *ANG/EP* BN16......114 F8
 MIDH GU29......227 K7
 RTWE/PEM TN2......39 J3
 WVILLE PO7......288 A8
Highfield Crs *BRI* BN1......82 F8
 GSHT GU26......180 H5
Highfield Dr *HPPT/KEY* BN6......271 J4
 STLEO TN38......98 F2
Highfield Gdns *ANG/EP* BN16......148 A5
 LISS GU33......192 E9
 MSEA/BNM PO22......2 F3
Highfield La *LIPH* GU30......194 A3
 SELS PO20......109 H7
Highfield Rd *EGRIN* RH19......31 J6
 HTHF TN21......278 C2
 MSEA/BNM PO22......2 F4
 PSF GU32......223 N5
 SALV BN13......116 F7
 SBGH/RUST TN4......38 B2
Highfields *BRI* BN1......83 K8
 BUR/ETCH TN19......214 F12
 FROW RH18......48 E7
High Fords *WSEA* TN36......285 P4
High Fords Cl *WSEA* TN36......285 P4
Highgate Dr *BOGR* PO21......143 M6
Highgate Rd *FROW* RH18......48 E8
Highground La
 MSEA/BNM PO22......145 G1
Highgrove *BAT* TN33......282 C4
Highgrove La *RTWE/PEM* TN2......53 M1
Highgrove Gdns *WTHG* BN11......20 D6
High Hatch La *HPPT/KEY* BN6......74 A5
High Hurst Cl *RING/NEW* BN8......240 C6
Highland Av *BOGR* PO21......2 F7
Highland Cl *EMRTH* PO10......103 M5
 HWH RH16 *......73 H5
Highland Rd *CCH* PO19......107 L3
 EMRTH PO10......103 M5
 HWH RH16......73 J6
Highlands Av *RHWH* RH17......72 C1
 SWTR RH13......15 G5
 UCK TN22......76 F8
Highlands Cl *BEXW* TN39......96 E6
 CROW TN6......67 K6
 HPPT/KEY BN6......271 P6
 SALV BN13......116 D4
Highlands Crs *SWTR* RH13......15 G5
Highlands Dr *BURH* RH15......74 F5

Highlands Gdns *STLEO* TN38......99 G6
Highlands Ms *STLEO* TN38 *......99 G7
Highlands Rd *PTSD* BN41......121 G4
 SEAF BN25......174 D1
 SWTR RH13......15 J5
The Highlands *BEXW* TN39......96 E5
 RHWH RH17......72 C1
High La *HASM* GU27......181 M9
High Lawn Wy *HAV* PO9......288 G12
Highlea Cl *SLVH* TN37......283 R12
Highleigh Rd *SELS* PO20......169 H3
High Loxley Rd
 MFD/CHID GU8......184 C3
High Meadow *MIDH* GU29......260 G5
 RYE TN31......218 D10
High Oaks *CRAWW* RH11......8 B7
High Pk *RYE* TN31......218 D10
High Park Av *HOVE* BN3......121 K4
High Pitfold *GSHT* GU26......180 G8
High Point *HWH* RH16......73 K6
High Rdg *CRBK* TN17......189 Q10
High Ridge Cl *ARUN* BN18......112 E4
High Rocks La *RRTW* TN3......37 H8
High Seat Gdns *BIL* RH14......200 A12
High Spinney *PUL/STOR* RH20......266 B8
High St *LEWES* BN7......17 G6
Highstanding La *MIDH* GU29......227 K11
Highstead La *PETW* GU28......227 R1
Highsted Pk *PEAHV* BN10......157 J3
High St *ANG/EP* BN16......114 E8
 ARUN BN18......113 G2
 ARUN BN18......296 F6
 BAT TN33......281 M11
 BAT TN33......282 E4
 BIL RH14......198 G2
 BIL RH14......232 A1
 BOGR PO21......2 E7
 BOR GU35......178 G6
 BOR GU35......179 M4
 BRIE/ROTT BN2......5 G7
 BRIE/ROTT BN2......155 L4
 BUR/ETCH TN19......214 F11
 BUR/ETCH TN19......215 N9
 CCH PO19 *......6 D7
 CRAWE RH10......8 F3
 CRBK TN17......189 R9
 CROW TN6......67 L6
 CROW TN6......211 Q1
 EDEN TN8......33 M4
 EGRIN RH19......47 L1
 EMRTH PO10......104 A5
 EPSF GU31......223 L12
 HAIL BN27......92 B5
 HAS TN54......13 L5
 HASM GU27......181 N10
 HFD BN5......269 L5
 HORL RH6......23 G6
 HORS RH12......41 H1
 HPPT/KEY BN6......270 H4
 HPPT/KEY BN6......272 A6
 HRTF TN7......50 C5
 HTHF TN21......244 D6
 HWH RH16......73 L1
 LEWES BN7......16 C3
 LHPTN BN17......147 J4
 LYDD TN29......255 Q8
 MAYF TN20......212 D7
 NEWHV BN9......18 F3
 PETW GU28......229 M10
 PEV BN24......133 J4
 POLE BN26......131 L8
 POLE BN26......160 E3
 PSF GU32......223 N6
 PTSD BN41......120 F4
 PUL/STOR RH20......266 A12
 RBTBR TN32......248 C1
 RCCH PO18......139 M1
 RHWH RH17......60 A5
 RHWH RH17......72 B3
 RHWH RH17......204 D1
 RHWH RH17......206 E1
 RING/NEW BN8......240 G6
 RING/NEW BN8......276 H4
 RRTW TN3......54 B5
 RRTW TN3......190 F1
 RTW TN1......37 M7
 RTWE/PEM TN2......39 H3
 RYE TN31......252 H8
 SALV BN13......116 F8
 SEAF BN25......174 E3
 SELS PO20......109 H7
 SELS PO20......301 K6
 SHOR BN43......119 K6
 STEY/UB BN44......78 C2
 STEY/UB BN44......78 F3
 STPH/PW TN12......188 D1
 SWTR RH13......234 F10
 UCK TN22......76 E6
 UCK TN22......77 L1
 UCK TN22......208 H5
 UCK TN22......241 N1
 UCK TN22......242 H7
 WADH TN5......71 K4
 WADH TN5......190 C12
 WADH TN5......191 P10
 WSEA TN36......286 D2
 WTHG BN11......21 J5
High Street Gn *MFD/CHID* GU8......183 M3
High Titten *ARUN* BN18......296 E4
High Trees *BOGR* PO21......171 L3
 HWH RH16......73 H5
 SELS PO20......141 M4
 WVILLE PO7......288 A9
Highview *LAN/SOMP* BN15......118 C4
High Vw *PSF* GU32......223 N5
 SALV BN13......116 E4
Highview Av North *BRI* BN1......82 D7
Highview Av South *BRI* BN1......82 D7
Highview Cl *HAIL* BN27......280 A12
 SLVH TN37......284 A12
High View Ct
 EDN/EASTW BN20 *......176 F4
Highview La *UCK* TN22......76 F8
Highview Rd *BRI* BN1......82 D7
 HTHF TN21......244 H4
 PEAHV BN10......156 C5
 SELS PO20......110 C6
Highview Wy *BRI* BN1......82 D7
Highwater Vw *STLEO* TN38......283 M10
Highway Cl *BRIE/ROTT* BN2......123 J3
Highways *PTSD* BN41......120 F4
The Highway *BRIE/ROTT* BN2......123 K2
 PEAHV BN10......157 L7
High Weald Landscape Trail
 CROW TN6......67 H1

 EGRIN RH19......47 J2
 EGRIN RH19......62 C4
 FROW RH18......49 J3
 HRTF TN7......51 H7
 RRTW TN3......205 Q8
High Weald Wk *RRTW* TN3......37 G2
 RRTW TN3......52 B2
 SBGH/RUST TN4......37 L7
High Wickham *RHAS* TN35......13 M4
Highwoods Av *BEXW* TN39......96 C5
Highwoods Ct *BEXW* TN39 *......96 D8
High Woods *RRTW* TN3......38 C7
Highworth *SWTR* RH13 *......15 K7
Hiham Gn *WSEA* TN36......286 D2
Hilary Cl *POLE* BN26......131 L8
Hilary Rd *CCH* PO19......6 A2
Hilbert Cl *RTW* TN1......38 B4
Hilbert Rd *RTWE/PEM* TN2......38 C4
Hilders Farm Cl *CROW* TN6......68 A3
Hildon Cl *SALV* BN13......116 C8
Hildon Pk *FERR* BN12......116 C8
Hilgrove Rd *BRIE/ROTT* BN2......156 C2
Hilland Ri *BOR* GU35......179 N5
Hillary Cl *EGRIN* RH19......31 M7
Hillbank Cl *PTSD* BN41......120 E2
Hillbank La *MIDH* GU29......260 F7
Hill Barn La *SALV* BN13......117 H6
Hillbarn Pde
 LAN/SOMP BN15 *......118 B5
Hillborough Cl *BEXW* TN39......136 C1
Hill Brow *HOVE* BN3......122 A1
Hill Brow Cl *HAV* PO9......289 J8
Hillbrow Rd *BRI* BN1......122 B1
Hill Brow Rd *LISS* GU33......192 C10
Hillbury Gdns *WADH* TN5......191 J12
Hill Cl *CROW* TN6......67 K8
Hill Cnr *RRTW* TN3......36 K4
Hillcrest *BRI* BN1......82 B8
Hillcrest *EGRIN* RH19......31 K3
Hillcrest *HASM* GU27 *......195 L8
 RHWH RH17......207 M4
 RYE TN31......252 C6
Hill Crest *SBGH/RUST* TN4......38 A1
Hillcrest Av *BEXW* TN39......96 F3
Hillcrest Cl *CRAWE* RH10......44 C1
 PUL/STOR RH20......267 K8
 RHWH RH17......239 J3
Hillcrest Dr *PUL/STOR* RH20......267 K9
Hillcrest La *RHWH* RH17......239 J2
Hillcrest Pk *PUL/STOR* RH20......265 C3
 RTWE/PEM TN2......38 C2
Hill Crest Rd *NEWHV* BN9......18 F6
Hillcrest Rd *NEWHV* BN9......18 F6
 NEWHV BN9......19 G5
Hillcroft *PTSD* BN41......120 E3
Hill Dr *HOVE* BN3......122 A2
Hill Farm Cl *HASM* GU27 *......181 J10
Hill Farm La *PUL/STOR* RH20......230 H12
Hill Farm Wy *STHW* BN42......120 C3
Hillfield Rd *CRAWE* RH10......43 G6
 SBGH/RUST TN4......37 M1
Hill House Cl *CRAWE* RH10......45 M4
Hill House Hl *LIPH* GU30......179 N10
Hillhouse La *HORS* RH12......185 M8
Hillingdale *CRAWW* RH11......43 H8
Hill La *EPSF* GU31......258 F3
 MSEA/BNM PO22......145 H1
Hillman Cl *LEWES* BN7......17 J6
Hillmead *CRAWW* RH11......42 F5
Hill Md *HORS* RH12......201 R4
 UCK TN22......208 H5
Hillmead Gdns *HAV* PO9......102 C3
Hill Pl *CRAWW* RH11......8 C6
Hillrise *CROW* TN6......68 A3
Hill Ri *NEWHV* BN9......158 C6
 SEAF BN25......159 H8
Hillrise Av *LAN/SOMP* BN15......118 B5
Hill Rd *BRIE/ROTT* BN2......156 A4
 EDN/EASTW BN20......162 F8
 GSHT GU26......180 F3
 HASM GU27......181 M11
 LEWES BN7......16 B3
 LHPTN BN17......147 K3
 NEWHV BN9......158 A4
 RHAS TN35......101 H1
Hillsboro Rd *BOGR* PO21......2 F7
Hills Farm La *HORS* RH12......201 Q4
Hill Side *NEWHV* BN9......19 G4
Hillside *BRIE/ROTT* BN2......123 K5
 CRAWE RH10......46 A1
 EDN/EASTW BN20......162 F8
 HORS RH12......201 R5
 PTSD BN41......121 H4
 STHW BN42......120 E4
Hillside Av *SALV* BN13......117 G6
 SEAF BN25......160 B8
Hillside Cl *BOR* GU35......179 P3
 CRAWW RH11......8 B7
 EGRIN RH19......31 K6
Hillside Crs *ANG/EP* BN16......114 F8
Hillside Dr *HTHF* TN21......278 C2
Hillside La *HFD* BN5......269 K12
Hillside Rd *BEX* TN40......97 G8
 HAS TN54......99 H2
 HASM GU27......195 L8
 LAN/SOMP BN15......118 B5
 PUL/STOR RH20......266 D11
Hillside Wk *HWH* RH16......72 F3
 PUL/STOR RH20......266 D11
Hillside Wy *BRI* BN1......122 D1
Hills Pl *HORS* RH12......201 R3
Hills Rd *STEY/UB* BN44......78 B3
Hill St *RTW* TN1 *......38 A4
Hill Ter *ARUN* BN18......112 E3
Hill Top *BRI* BN1......82 A8
Hill Top Cl *PTSD* BN41......120 E3
Hilltop Dr *RYE* TN31......252 C6
Hilltop Gdns *HORN* PO8......256 F10
Hilltop Rd *EGRIN* RH19......62 D3
Hill Top Wy *NEWHV* BN9......18 C6
Hillview *HORN* PO8......288 D10
Hillview Crs *ANG/EP* BN16......148 F3
Hillview Rd *BRI* BN1......82 D7
Hillview Ri *SALV* BN13......116 E4
Hillview Rd *BRIE/ROTT* BN2......123 M5
 SALV BN13......116 E3
Hill View Rd *SBGH/RUST* TN4......37 G5
Hillyarn Rd *CRAWW* RH11......26 B8
Hillyfield *LEWES* BN7......16 C3
Hillyglen Cl *HAS* TN34......12 C1
Hiltingbury Rd *HAV* PO9......288 H11
Hilton Pk *SELS* PO20......167 M5
Hinde Rd *MSEA/BNM* PO22......173 H1

Hindhead Cl *CRAWW* RH11......8 C8
Hindhead Rd *HASM* GU27......180 H9
 HASM GU27......181 J11
Hindleap La *FROW* RH18......64 D4
Hindle Cl *PUL/STOR* RH20......266 A6
Hindover Crs *SEAF* BN25......175 G1
Hindover Rd *SEAF* BN25......175 G1
Hinton Cl *BRI* BN1......123 H3
 HAV PO9......102 F1
Hinton Manor La *HORN* PO8......256 A10
Hipley Rd *HAV* PO9......103 H2
Hislop Wk *BOGR* PO21......2 F7
Hither Chantlers *RRTW* TN3......36 F6
Hither Gn *EMRTH* PO10......104 F3
Hitherwood Cl *WVILLE* PO7......288 C7
Hoadlands *EPSF* GU31......223 P5
Hoad La *HWH* RH16......206 F5
Hoadleys La *CROW* TN6......67 J4
Hoad Rd *LW/ROSE* BN22......11 H4
Hoad's Wood Rd *HAS* TN34......99 M2
Hoath Hl *RBTBR* TN32......248 D8
Hoath Meadow
 STPH/PW TN12 *......189 M3
Hobart Cl *SALV* BN13......116 B7
Hobbs Cl *RYE* TN31......219 M12
Hobbs La *RYE* TN31......219 N11
Hobbs Rd *CRAWW* RH11......42 F8
Hobbs Sq *EPSF* GU31......223 P4
Hobbs Wy *ANG/EP* BN16......148 B4
Hobdens La *RHWH* RH17......206 D2
Hoblands *HWH* RH16......73 L5
Hobney Ri *PEV* BN24......133 L8
Hobs Acre *STEY/UB* BN44......79 G4
Hocken Md *CRAWE* RH10......44 C1
Hockham Ct *HAV* PO9......288 D10
Hockington La
 EDN/EASTW BN20......163 C4
Hoddern Av *PEAHV* BN10......157 G2
Hodges Cl *HAV* PO9......103 H2
Hodgkin Ct *CRAWE* RH10......44 C1
Hodshrove Pl
 BRIE/ROTT BN2......123 K2
Hodshrove Rd *BRIE/ROTT* BN2......123 K2
Hoe Ct *LAN/SOMP* BN15......118 F4
Hoefield La *MIDH* GU29......260 F8
Hoe La *ARUN* BN18......112 B6
 MSEA/BNM PO22......144 F5
 RCCH PO18......140 B4
The Hoe *SLVH* TN37......283 Q11
Hoewood *HFD* BN5......269 K10
Hogarth Rd *CRAWE* RH10......43 L6
 HOVE BN3......121 L6
 LGNY BN23......164 C4
Hoggarth Cl *EPSF* GU31......223 P4
Hog Hole La *RRTW* TN3......190 D3
Hog La *ARUN* BN18......296 F2
Hogmoor Rd *BOR* GU35......178 E5
Hogs Edge *BRIE/ROTT* BN2......123 M3
Hogs Lodge La *HORN* PO8......256 F4
Hogtrough La *WSEA* TN36......286 D2
Hogwood Rd *BIL* RH14......198 D2
Holbein Rd *CRAWE* RH10......43 L6
Holbrook Cl *EDN/EASTW* BN20......176 E5
Holbrook School La *HORS* RH12......56 C2
Holbury Ct *HAV* PO9......289 J12
Holdenhurst Cl *HORN* PO8......256 D10
Holden Park Rd
 SBGH/RUST TN4......37 L1
The Holdens *RCCH* PO18......105 M8
Holder Rd *CRAWE* RH10......44 A6
Holders *HPPT/KEY* BN6......270 D3
Holdfast La *HASM* GU27......181 Q9
The Holdings *LEWES* BN7......85 L7
 RING/NEW BN8......274 G10
Hole Farm Cl *HAS* TN34......12 C1
Hole St *PUL/STOR* RH20......267 K10
Holford Gv *SELS* PO20......301 M5
Holland Av *BEXW* TN39......136 B3
Holland Cl *BOGR* PO21......143 L4
Holland Ms *HOVE* BN3......122 C4
Holland Rd *HOVE* BN3......122 C7
 STEY/UB BN44......78 C2
Hollands Fld *HORS* RH12......201 P1
Hollands La *HFD* BN5......268 A5
Hollands Rd *HFD* BN5......269 J4
Holland St *BRIE/ROTT* BN2......5 H5
Hollands Wy *EGRIN* RH19......31 M5
 HORS RH12......187 Q9
Hollier's Hl *BEX* TN40......97 H4
The Hollies *BOGR* PO21......143 L8
Hollin Cl *SBGH/RUST* TN4......37 L5
Hollin Ct *CRAWW* RH11......27 K8
Hollingbourne Crs
 CRAWW RH11......59 H1
Hollingbury Copse *BRI* BN1......122 F1
Hollingbury Crs *BRI* BN1......123 C4
Hollingbury Gdns *SALV* BN13......116 C2
Hollingbury Park Av *BRI* BN1......122 F3
Hollingbury Pl *BRI* BN1......123 G5
Hollingbury Ri *BRI* BN1......123 G2
Hollingbury Ri West *BRI* BN1......123 G5
Hollingbury Rd *BRI* BN1......123 G4
Hollingbury Ter *BRI* BN1......122 F5
Hollingdean La *BRI* BN1......123 G5
Hollingdean Rd
 BRIE/ROTT BN2......123 G5
Hollingdean St *BRI* BN1......123 G5
Hollingdean Ter *BRI* BN1......123 G4
Hollinghurst Cl *SLVH* TN37......283 Q12
Hollinghurst Rd *SLVH* TN37......99 C1
Hollington Ct *STLEO* TN38......98 F5
Hollington Old La *STLEO* TN38......98 F8
Hollington Park Cl *STLEO* TN38......98 F4
Hollington Park Rd *STLEO* TN38......98 F4
Hollist La *EPSF* GU31......258 C1
 MIDH GU29......226 G9
Hollow La *BOR* GU35......179 M3
 LING RH7......32 H1
 RING/NEW BN8......277 J3
 PUL/STOR RH20......242 H9
The Hollow *CRAWW* RH11......42 F4
 EGRIN RH19......62 G3
 HWH RH16......73 L4
 PUL/STOR RH20......296 H1
 PUL/STOR RH20......298 H1
Hollyacres *SALV* BN13......116 B5
Holly Bank *STPH/PW* TN12......188 G1
Holly Bank Cl *HORN* PO8......288 D4
Hollybank Gdns *STLEO* TN38......99 G6
Hollybank La *EMRTH* PO10......104 A1
Hollybrook Pk *BOR* GU35......178 H6
Hollybush Cl *CRAWE* RH10......9 K1
Hollybush Rd *CRAWE* RH10......9 H1
Holly Cl *BEXW* TN39......96 B7

BOR GU35 179 R4
BRI BN1 122 D2
CRAWE RH10 43 M1
HAIL BN27 92 A7
HORS RH12 56 F4
HTHF TN21 244 D7
PUL/STOR RH20 265 R12
PUL/STOR RH20 266 A4
SALV BN13 116 B8
Hollycombe Cl LIPH GU30 193 R3
Holly Ct CROW TN6 67 J7
MSEA/BNM PO22 144 B7
PUL/STOR RH20 265 R11
Hollydene Rd WADH TN5 71 L3
Holly Dr HTHF TN21 244 D7
LHPTN BN17 147 K1
WVILLE PO7 288 B11
Hollyhock Wy LHPTN BN17 147 M2
Holly Ms HPPT/KEY BN6 * 271 J4
Holly Pl LW/ROSE BN22 163 K2
Hollyridge HASM GU27 181 M11
Holly Rd HWH RH16 73 J6
Hollyshaw Cl RTWE/PEM TN2 38 B7
Holly Vls STPH/PW TN12 * 188 B2
Hollywater Rd LIPH GU30 179 J9
Holman Cl CRAWW RH11 59 G1
HORN PO8 288 B7
Holmans RHWH RH17 206 D1
Holmbury Cl CRAWW RH11 8 D8
Holmbush Cl HWH RH16 73 H7
SHOR BN43 120 C3
Holmbush Ct HORS RH12 * 42 A8
Holmbush La HFD BN5 269 R9
Holmbush Wy MIDH GU29 226 H12
STHW BN42 120 C4
Holmcroft CRAWE RH10 9 G6
Holmcroft Gdns SALV BN13 298 H12
Holmdale Est SELS PO20 * 110 E4
Holmdale Rd NEWHV BN9 158 E4
Holmes Av HOVE BN3 121 L4
Holmes Cl SEAF BN25 158 F7
Holmesdale Cl WADH TN5 71 K4
Holmesdale Gdns HAS TN34 12 E6
Holmesdale Rd BEXW TN39 136 F1
BURH RH15 74 E8
Holmes Foundation
ARUN BN18 * 113 G3
Holmes La ANG/EP BN16 148 A5
Holmewood Rdg RRTW TN3 36 E6
Holmewood Rd
SBGH/RUST TN4 38 B2
Holmfield Cl ANG/EP BN16 148 B3
Holmhurst Cl SBGH/RUST TN4 37 K5
Holmhurst La SLVH TN37 283 Q11
Holming End HORS RH12 57 G4
Holm Oak PUL/STOR RH20 265 R12
Holm Oak Cl BEXW TN39 136 D2
Holm Oaks SWTR RH13 235 L4
Holmsted Hl RHWH RH17 204 H7
Holst Wy WVILLE PO7 288 A12
Holt Down EPSF GU31 223 Q6
Holters Wy SEAF BN25 159 L8
Holt Gdns HAV PO9 289 J6
Holton Hl BRIE/ROTT BN2 124 D6
The Holt BURH RH15 75 H7
HAIL BN27 91 M7
PUL/STOR RH20 298 H3
SEAF BN25 159 L8
Holtview Rd BRIE/ROTT BN2 124 A5
Holtye Av EGRIN RH19 31 M6
Holtye Pl EGRIN RH19 32 A6
Holtye Rd EGRIN RH19 31 L7
Holtye Wk CRAWE RH10 9 M8
Holybourne Rd HAV PO9 103 G2
Holyhead Cl HAIL BN27 91 M4
Holyrood Cl WVILLE PO7 288 B10
Holyrood Pl CRAWW RH11 43 G7
Holywell Cl EDN/EASTW BN20 176 E6
Holywell Rd EDN/EASTW BN20 176 E6
Homebush Av BRIE/ROTT BN2 156 C4
Home Cl CRAWE RH10 44 B1
Home Farm La RTWE/PEM TN2 38 D1
Home Farm Rd BRI BN1 123 K1
Homefield Av
MSEA/BNM PO22 145 H7
Homefield Cl HORL RH6 23 G5
SEAF BN25 174 F1
Homefield Crs ARUN BN18 111 J5
Homefield Rd EMRTH PO10 104 C1
SEAF BN25 174 F1
WTHG BN11 21 K3
Homefield Wy HORN PO8 256 C7
Homelands Av ANG/EP BN16 148 F5
Homelands Cl BEXW TN39 96 F7
Homelands Copse HASM GU27 195 N10
Home Platt EGRIN RH19 62 F3
Home Rd BRI BN1 122 D3
Homestall Rd EGRIN RH19 48 D1
Homestead La BURH RH15 75 H3
The Homestead RRTW TN3 52 B2
Home Wy EPSF GU31 223 R6
Homewell HAV PO9 103 G4
Homewood SALV BN13 298 H10
Homewood Cl LW/ROSE BN22 164 A7
Homewood Rd RRTW TN3 36 E6
Homing Gdns
MSEA/BNM PO22 144 A6
Honer La SELS PO20 170 C1
Honeybridge La SWTR RH13 267 P4
Honeycrag Cl POLE BN26 131 L6
Honey Cft HOVE BN3 121 J1
Honey La ANG/EP BN16 114 F8
RING/NEW BN8 89 J6
Honeypot La LEWES BN7 273 L2
Honeysuckle Cl HAIL BN27 92 A8
HORL RH6 23 H5
LAN/SOMP BN15 118 C4
LGNY BN23 164 A2
LHPTN BN17 147 M2
SLVH TN37 284 A12
Honeysuckle Ct WVILLE PO7 288 A12
Honeysuckle Dr BOGR PO21 170 E3
Honeysuckle La BOR GU35 179 Q4
CRAWW RH11 27 H8
HAIL BN27 * 90 A2
SALV BN13 116 B1
SELS PO20 301 J5
Honeysuckle Wk HORS RH12 56 F4
Honeyway Cl POLE BN26 162 E2
Honeywick La RING/NEW BN8 277 N7
Honeywood La RDKG RH5 186 H4
Honeywood Rd SWTR RH13 15 M1
Hood Cl LGNY BN23 164 D6
The Hooe LHPTN BN17 147 M4
Hoo Gdns EDN/EASTW BN20 163 G4
Hook Hl WADH TN5 190 F7
Hookhouse Rd MFD/CHID GU8 183 R3
Hooklands La SWTR RH13 267 K2
Hook La BOGR PO21 170 F3
EGRIN RH19 62 B7
MSEA/BNM PO22 2 F4
RCCH PO18 140 E3
RHWH RH17 62 B7
SELS PO20 109 M6
Hook Lane Cl BOGR PO21 171 G2
Hook's Farm Wy HAV PO9 102 E2
Hook's La HAV PO9 102 E3
The Hooks HFD BN5 269 K5
Hookswood Cl CROW TN6 67 M6
Hoopers Cl LEWES BN7 16 F1
Hoover Cl SLVH TN37 283 N10
Hope Ct CRAWW RH11 * 43 G8
Hopehouse La HAWK TN18 218 B2
Hopeswood LISS GU33 192 C2
Hopfield Gdns UCK TN22 77 G4
Hop Gdn UCK TN22 209 P7
Hopgarden Cl HAS TN34 12 E5
Hop Garden La SELS PO20 142 C5
The Hop Gdn EPSF GU31 258 E2
The Hopgarton BOGR PO21 * 171 K2
Hophurst Cl CRAWE RH10 46 A1
Hophurst Dr CRAWE RH10 46 A1
Hophurst Hl CRAWE RH10 30 C7
Hophurst La CRAWE RH10 30 A8
Hopkins Ct CRAWW RH11 * 43 G8
Hoppers Croft La
BUR/ETCH TN19 214 G11
Hopwood Gdns
SBGH/RUST TN4 37 M3
Horam Park Cl HTHF TN21 278 C2
The Hordens SWTR RH13 201 J11
Hordle Rd HAV PO9 102 D1
Horebeech La HTHF TN21 278 C2
Horizon Cl SBGH/RUST TN4 38 A1
Horleigh Green Rd MAYF TN20 211 R8
Horley Lodge La REDH RH1 22 E1
Horley Pl BRIE/ROTT BN2 123 K7
Horley Rd HORL RH6 26 F2
Horley Rw HORL RH6 22 E5
Hormare Crs PUL/STOR RH20 265 R11
Hornbeam BUR/ETCH TN19 214 G10
Hornbeam Av BEXW TN39 96 F6
Hornbeam Cl BOGR PO21 171 L4
SWTR RH13 15 J7
Hornbeam Rd HAV PO9 103 J2
Hornbeam Wy MIDH GU29 226 G12
Hornbrook Copse SWTR RH13 202 E1
Hornbuckles Cl
RING/NEW BN8 273 P2
Hornby Pl BRIE/ROTT BN2 * 123 M4
Hornby Rd BRIE/ROTT BN2 123 L4
Horndean Cl CRAWE RH10 28 C7
Horndean Prec HORN PO8 * 288 E2
Horndean Rd EMRTH PO10 103 L1
Hornet Rd EMRTH PO10 138 B2
The Hornet CCH PO19 7 G4
Horning Cl LGNY BN23 164 A1
Horn La HFD BN5 269 N8
Hornshill La HORS RH12 185 N10
Hornshurst Rd CROW TN6 69 G6
Horns La BOGR PO21 170 E4
Horns Rd HAWK TN18 216 C1
Horntye Pk SLVH TN37 12 C6
Horntye Rd SLVH TN37 12 B4
Horse Br HAIL BN27 94 E6
Horsebridge Hl BIL RH14 230 F7
Horsebridge Rd HAV PO9 103 H1
Horsefield Rd SELS PO20 301 K6
Horsegrove Av WADH TN5 191 L12
Horsegrove La CROW TN6 211 Q1
Horse Hl HORL RH6 22 A5
Horsemere Green La
LHPTN BN17 146 D4
Horseshoe Bend GSHT GU26 180 D6
Horseshoe Cl CRAWE RH10 44 D2
STLEO TN38 99 G3
Horseshoe Crs BOR GU35 178 H6
Horseshoe La RYE TN31 251 J2
The Horse Shoe SELS PO20 301 K6
Horsewalk BAT TN33 94 F7
Horsfield Rd LEWES BN7 16 C2
Horsgate La RHWH RH17 72 D3
Horsham Av PEAHV BN10 157 H7
Horsham Av North
PEAHV BN10 157 H5
Horsham Cl BRIE/ROTT BN2 123 L7
Horsham Gates SWTR RH13 * 15 G4
Horsham Rd BIL RH14 200 D7
CRAN GU6 185 P1
CRAWW RH11 8 C6
HORS RH12 40 F5
HORS RH12 185 L8
LHPTN BN17 147 L3
PETW GU28 229 M8
RDKG RH5 24 B7
RDKG RH5 186 G3
RHWH RH17 204 B2
SALV BN13 298 G9
STEY/UB BN44 268 B10
Horsham Rd West
LHPTN BN17 147 L3
Horsmonden Rd
STPH/PW TN12 188 H2
Horsted La EGRIN RH19 63 G5
RHWH RH17 207 R5
UCK TN22 275 K2
Horsted Pond La UCK TN22 241 M10
Horsye Rd LW/ROSE BN22 164 A6
Horton Pl ANG/EP BN16 148 F1
Horton Rd BRI BN1 123 G4
Hoskins Pl EGRIN RH19 31 L5
Hosmers Fld CROW TN6 69 J8
Hospital Vls HWH RH16 73 J7
Hotham Gdns MSEA/BNM PO22 3 G4
Hotham Wy BOGR PO21 2 E4
Houghton Br ARUN BN18 296 E5
Houghton Cl HAV PO9 * 289 J11
Houghton Green La RYE TN31 253 J4
Houghton La PUL/STOR RH20 296 B2
RYE TN31 252 H2
Houghton Rd CRAWE RH10 * 44 B6
Houndean Cl LEWES BN7 16 A7
Houndean Ri LEWES BN7 85 L5
Hova Vls HOVE BN3 122 A7
Hove Park Gdns HOVE BN3 122 A5
Hove Park Rd HOVE BN3 122 B4
Hove Park Vls HOVE BN3 122 A5
Hove Park Wy HOVE BN3 122 B4
Hove Pl HOVE BN3 122 A8
Hove St HOVE BN3 121 M8
Howard Av BURH RH15 74 D5
SELS PO20 167 J6
Howard Cl HAIL BN27 92 C7
Howard Ct HOVE BN3 * 121 L3
Howard Pl BRI BN1 4 C3
LHPTN BN17 147 J4
Howard Rd ARUN BN18 112 F3
BRIE/ROTT BN2 5 J3
CRAWW RH11 42 C7
LAN/SOMP BN15 118 B4
LHPTN BN17 147 H4
SWTR RH13 15 L2
Howards Crs BEXW TN39 136 B1
Howard Sq EAST BN21 10 F9
Howard St WTHG BN11 20 E5
Howards Wy ANG/EP BN16 148 A6
Howard Ter BRI BN1 4 C3
Howbourne La UCK TN22 210 F12
Howey Cl NEWHV BN9 158 E4
Howlett Cl STLEO TN38 98 E1
Howlett Dr HAIL BN27 92 A3
Howletts Cl LW/ROSE BN22 163 L4
How's Cl RYE TN31 250 E8
Hoylake Cl CRAWW RH11 42 C4
Hoyle La MIDH GU29 261 M5
Hoyle Rd PEAHV BN10 157 H6
Hucksteps Rw RYE TN31 * 252 H8
Hudson Cl LGNY BN23 164 F6
LIPH GU30 193 R2
SALV BN13 116 C7
Hudson Dr ANG/EP BN16 148 C5
Hudson Rd CRAWE RH10 9 H7
Huggett's La LW/ROSE BN22 163 G2
Hughenden Pl HAS TN34 13 H2
Hughenden Rd HAS TN34 13 H2
Hughes Cl BOGR PO21 171 L1
Hughes Rd BRIE/ROTT BN2 123 G5
Hughes Wy UCK TN22 76 E4
Hugletts La HTHF TN21 245 K7
Hugo Platt EPSF GU31 224 H5
Hulbert Rd HAV PO9 102 D2
WVILLE PO7 288 A10
Humber Av SALV BN13 116 B6
Humber Cl LHPTN BN17 147 L5
SALV BN13 116 B6
Humboldt Ct RTWE/PEM TN2 38 C4
Humphrey's Gap SHOR BN43 119 M7
Humphrys Rd WTHG BN11 21 G6
Hundred Acre La
HPPT/KEY BN6 238 E12
Hundredhouse La RYE TN31 251 J10
Hundredsteddle La SELS PO20 168 C3
Hungershall Pk
SBGH/RUST TN4 37 K7
Hungershall Park Cl
SBGH/RUST TN4 * 37 K7
Hunloke Av LW/ROSE BN22 164 A7
Hunnisett Cl SELS PO20 301 M4
Hunstanton Cl CRAWW RH11 42 C4
Hunston Cl BRIE/ROTT BN2 124 E6
Hunter Rd CRAWE RH10 8 E9
EMRTH PO10 138 B2
Hunters Cha LIPH GU30 179 Q12
Hunters Cl BOGR PO21 171 H4
Hunters Ga SELS PO20 * 109 H4
Hunters Md HPPT/KEY BN6 * 270 E3
SWTR RH13 234 F10
Hunters Ms ARUN BN18 110 F2
Hunters Race CCH PO19 107 J2
Hunters Rd LISS GU33 192 G3
Hunters Wy CCH PO19 107 L2
RTWE/PEM TN2 37 L8
UCK TN22 76 D4
Hunting Cl BEX TN40 97 H8
Huntingdon House Dr
GSHT GU26 180 H5
Huntingdon Wy BURH RH15 75 J4
Huntingford Cl GSHT GU26 * 180 F2
Huntley Mill Rd WADH TN5 191 J10
Huntleys Pk SBGH/RUST TN4 37 L3
Huntsbottom La LISS GU33 192 E10
Hurdis Rd SEAF BN25 158 F7
Hurland La BOR GU35 179 N5
Hurlands La MFD/CHID GU8 184 A8
Hurley Rd SALV BN13 116 D7
Hurn Ct HAV PO9 289 J11
Huron Dr LIPH GU30 193 R2
Hurrell Rd HAS TN34 13 L1
Hursley Rd HAV PO9 288 E12
Hurst Av HORS RH12 14 E3
WTHG BN11 150 E3
Hurstbourne Cl HAV PO9 * 288 E11
Hurst Cl ARUN BN18 296 F2
CRAWW RH11 42 E5
LIPH GU30 179 P12
Hurst Cottages ARUN BN18 296 F2
Hurst Ct HORS RH12 14 E4
Hurst Crs PTSD BN41 121 G5
Hurst Farm Rd EGRIN RH19 47 J1
Hurstfield LAN/SOMP BN15 118 C8
Hurstfield Cl RHWH RH17 73 K7
Hurst Gdns HPPT/KEY BN6 270 G3
Hurst Green Cl HORN PO8 288 C7
Hurst Hl BRI BN1 83 H8
Hurstlands BIL RH14 231 R2
Hurstlands La BAT TN33 249 M10
EAST BN21 176 D1
HAIL BN27 280 A12
Hurstmere Cl GSHT GU26 180 G6
Hurston Cl PUL/STOR RH20 265 Q11
SALV BN13 116 F5
Hurston Gv PUL/STOR RH20 265 Q11
Hurston La PUL/STOR RH20 265 N10
Hurst Pk MIDH GU29 226 G2
Hurst Rd ANG/EP BN16 148 D3
EAST BN21 176 D1
HORL RH6 22 D5
HORS RH12 14 E3
HPPT/KEY BN6 271 L5
The Hurst RTWE/PEM TN2 38 D2
Hurstville Dr WVILLE PO7 288 A11
Hurst Wickham Cl
HPPT/KEY BN6 271 K4
Hurstwood Av EMRTH PO10 104 F4
Hurstwood Cl BEX TN40 98 A8
Hurstwood La EGRIN RH19 63 J8
RHWH RH17 73 K8
SBGH/RUST TN4 37 K6
Hurstwood Pk SBGH/RUST TN4 37 K6
Hurstwood Rd UCK TN22 210 B11
Hurtis Hl CROW TN6 210 F2
Hutchinson Cl LHPTN BN17 148 A2
Hutchins Wy HORL RH6 22 E4
Huxley Rd BRI BN1 123 G2
Hyde Cl LEWES BN7 85 K8
Hyde Dr CRAWW RH11 42 D4
Hyde Gdns EAST BN21 10 E7
Hydehurst Cl CROW TN6 67 L8
Hyde La STEY/UB BN44 79 G4
Hyde Rd EAST BN21 10 D7
Hyde Sq STEY/UB BN44 * 79 G3
Hyde St STEY/UB BN44 79 G3
The Hyde BRIE/ROTT BN2 123 L4
Hyde Tynings Cl
EDN/EASTW BN20 176 C5
Hydneye St LW/ROSE BN22 11 K2
The Hydneye LW/ROSE BN22 163 L4
Hylands Cl CRAWE RH10 9 M6
RYE TN31 218 E11
Hylden Cl BRIE/ROTT BN2 124 A5
Hylter's La RCCH PO18 259 R12
Hylton Rd PSF GU32 223 N6
Hyndman Cl CRAWW RH11 59 G1
Hyperion Av POLE BN26 131 K7
Hyperion Ct CRAWW RH11 42 D5
Hythe Av STLEO TN38 98 A8
Hythe Cl POLE BN26 132 B6
SEAF BN25 160 B8
WTHG BN11 20 A8
Hythe Crs SEAF BN25 175 J1
Hythe Rd BRI BN1 122 F3
WTHG BN11 20 A7
Hythe Vw SEAF BN25 175 J1

I

Ian Cl BEX TN40 97 L6
Ibsley Gv HAV PO9 102 E2
Icarus Pl WVILLE PO7 102 A3
Icarus Wy MSEA/BNM PO22 145 H8
Icklesham Dr STLEO TN38 98 C2
Iden Cl BRIE/ROTT BN2 123 K8
Iden Hurst HPPT/KEY BN6 270 H2
Iden Rd RYE TN31 252 G3
Iden's La HTHF TN21 244 G5
Iden St LW/ROSE BN22 163 M3
Idsworth Cl HORN PO8 288 F3
Idsworth Rd HORN PO8 288 C7
Ifield Av CRAWW RH11 8 D1
Ifield Cl BRIE/ROTT BN2 156 E3
Ifield Dr CRAWW RH11 42 F2
Ifield Gn CRAWW RH11 26 F8
Ifield Mill Cl PEV BN24 133 G8
Ifield Pk CRAWW RH11 * 42 E3
Ifield Rd CRAWW RH11 8 B2
HORL RH6 26 D4
Ifield St CRAWW RH11 42 E1
Ifield Wd CRAWW RH11 26 C8
Ifold Bridge La BIL RH14 198 D1
Ifoldhurst BIL RH14 198 D3
Iford Cl NEWHV BN9 158 C3
Iford Ct HAV PO9 289 J11
Ilex Cl ANG/EP BN16 148 A5
Ilex Ct FERR BN12 * 150 A3
Ilex Wy FERR BN12 150 A3
MSEA/BNM PO22 145 K7
Imadene Crs BOR GU35 179 J5
Imberhorne La EGRIN RH19 46 F2
Imberhorne Wy EGRIN RH19 31 G6
Impala Gdns SBGH/RUST TN4 38 A3
Imperial Ar BRI BN1 * 4 C6
Infirmary Dr SWTR RH13 201 P7
Infirmary Ter CCH PO19 6 D1
Ingham Dr BRI BN1 83 J7
Inglecroft Ct
LAN/SOMP BN15 * 118 B6
Ingledene Cl HAV PO9 102 E3
Ingle Green Cl FERR BN12 149 K5
Ingleside STLEO TN38 98 D1
Ingleside Crs LAN/SOMP BN15 118 D8
Ingleside Dr CROW TN6 67 K7
Ingleside Rd LAN/SOMP BN15 118 D8
Inglewood Dr BOGR PO21 171 G4
Inglewood Gdns STLEO TN38 98 D1
Ingram Cl ANG/EP BN16 148 A4
HORS RH12 201 R3
Ingram Crs HOVE BN3 121 K5
Ingram Crs East HOVE BN3 121 K6
Ingram Crs West HOVE BN3 121 K6
Ingram Rd STEY/UB BN44 78 B3
Ingrams Av BEXW TN39 97 H6
Ingram's Green La MIDH GU29 225 R11
MIDH GU29 259 R3
Ingrams Wy HAIL BN27 91 M8
Inham's La RCCH PO18 291 Q12
Inholmes Cl BURH RH15 75 H7
Inholmes Park Rd BURH RH15 75 H6
Inhurst Av WVILLE PO7 288 B9
Inkpen La FROW RH18 48 E8
Inlands Rd RCCH PO18 105 G4
Inmans La PSF GU32 223 Q4
Innerwyke Cl
MSEA/BNM PO22 145 G8
Innes Rd HORS RH12 15 K1
Innham's Wd CROW TN6 67 J5
Innings Dr PEV BN24 165 H1
Innovation Dr BURH RH15 74 C7
Insley Ct BEXW TN39 * 136 E2
Inval Hl HASM GU27 181 M9
Inverness Rd BRIE/ROTT BN2 5 J1
Inwood Crs BRI BN1 122 C4
Inwood Rd LISS GU33 192 D10
Iona Cl CRAWW RH11 8 B9
HAIL BN27 91 M2
Iona Wy HWH RH16 73 H5
Iping Av HAV PO9 288 E12
Iping La MIDH GU29 226 A3
Iping Rd LIPH GU30 193 Q11
MIDH GU29 226 A1
Irelands La LEWES BN7 16 D6
Irene Av LAN/SOMP BN15 118 C6
Iris Cl LHPTN BN17 148 A2
Ironlatch Av STLEO TN38 98 E4
Ironlatch Cl STLEO TN38 98 E3
Iron Latch Cottages
STLEO TN38 * 98 E3
Ironstones RRTW TN3 37 G6
Ironstone Wy UCK TN22 76 F5
Irvine Rd LHPTN BN17 147 K5
Irving Wk CRAWE RH10 43 K6
Irwin Dr HORS RH12 201 R3
Isaac's La BURH RH15 74 E3
HWH RH16 72 E6
Isabel Cl SEAF BN25 159 K8
Isabel Crs HOVE BN3 121 K5
Isfield Rd BRI BN1 123 H3
UCK TN22 275 K5
Isherwood BAT TN33 282 D4
Island La SELS PO20 300 H5
Island Loop SELS PO20 300 H5
Islingword Pl BRIE/ROTT BN2 5 J4
Islingword Rd BRIE/ROTT BN2 5 H3
Islingword St BRIE/ROTT BN2 5 H4
Itchen Cl EPSF GU31 223 M7
Itchenor Rd HISD PO11 166 A3
SELS PO20 167 M1
Itchen Rd HAV PO9 289 J11
Itchingfield Rd SWTR RH13 201 K5
Ivanhoe Cl CRAWW RH11 27 J8
Ivanhoe Pl MSEA/BNM PO22 145 H8
Iveagh Cl CRAWW RH11 43 H8
Iveagh Crs NEWHV BN9 158 C4
Ivor Rd BRIE/ROTT BN2 124 B4
Ivors La RING/NEW BN8 274 A12
Ivory Pl BRIE/ROTT BN2 5 G5
Ivory Wk CRAWW RH11 42 D6
Ivy Arch Cl SALV BN13 299 J11
Ivy Arch Rd SALV BN13 21 H3
Ivy Cl PUL/STOR RH20 267 K8
SELS PO20 110 C6
SWTR RH13 201 P12
Ivy Crs MSEA/BNM PO22 2 F2
Ivydale Rd BOGR PO21 171 M1
Ivydene Crs RCCH PO18 105 J6
Ivydene Gdns HORN PO8 288 B5
Ivy Dene La EGRIN RH19 48 C3
Ivydore Av SALV BN13 116 C5
Ivydore Cl SALV BN13 116 C6
Ivyhouse La RHAS TN35 284 E12
Ivy La MSEA/BNM PO22 2 F3
PUL/STOR RH20 267 K7
RRTW TN3 54 F4
SELS PO20 110 C6
Ivy Ms HOVE BN3 * 122 C8
Ivy Pl HOVE BN3 122 C8
WTHG BN11 20 D7
Ivy Ter EAST BN21 10 D6

J

Jaarlen Rd LYDD TN29 255 Q7
Jacaranda Rd BOR GU35 178 G7
Jackdaw Cl CRAWW RH11 43 H1
Jackdaw La HORS RH12 56 D4
The Jackdaws UCK TN22 77 G8
Jacken Cl MSEA/BNM PO22 173 H1
Jackies La RING/NEW BN8 240 A6
Jack O'Dandy Cl EAST BN21 * 163 H6
Jackrells La SWTR RH13 202 A6
Jacks Hl HRTF TN7 50 C7
Jackson Ms NEWHV BN9 18 F3
Jackson Rd CRAWW RH11 59 G1
Jacksons Pl HRTF TN7 * 49 J8
Jackson St BRIE/ROTT BN2 5 H4
Jacobean Cl CRAWE RH10 44 B4
Jacobs Acre BEX TN40 97 H8
Jacobs Cl HORN PO8 256 D8
Jamaica Wy LGNY BN23 164 E5
James Av HAIL BN27 279 P11
James Cl SALV BN13 116 E7
James Copse Rd HORN PO8 288 A4
Jameson Crs STLEO TN38 98 F2
Jameson Rd BEX TN40 137 J2
James Rd HAV PO9 102 E3
James St SELS PO20 301 L7
James Watt Wy CRAWE RH10 27 M5
Jane Murray Wy BURH RH15 74 B5
Janes Cl BURH RH15 75 H4
Janes La BURH RH15 75 J5
PETW GU28 228 D7
Jan Smuts Cl LISS GU33 192 G4
Japonica Cl SHOR BN43 120 A4
Japonica Wy HAV PO9 103 K1
Jardine Ct CROW TN6 67 L7
Jarretts Cl RYE TN31 252 H8
Jarvisbrook Cl BEXW TN39 136 C2
Jarvis La STEY/UB BN44 78 C2
Jarvis Rd ARUN BN18 112 E3
Jasmine Cl LHPTN BN17 147 M2
Jasmine Ct HORS RH12 14 C5
Jasmine Gv WVILLE PO7 288 B11
Jasmine Wy BOR GU35 178 H7
HORN PO8 256 D8
Jason Cl PEAHV BN10 157 H6
Javelin Rd EMRTH PO10 138 B2
Jay Cl HORN PO8 288 B2
LGNY BN23 164 B3
SWTR RH13 201 R11
Jay Rd PEAHV BN10 157 K7
Jays Cl LHPTN BN17 147 J3
Jay's La HASM GU27 196 A2
The Jays BURH RH15 74 D5
UCK TN22 76 F8
Jay Wk CRAWE RH10 46 B4
Jefferies RHWH RH17 207 M5
Jefferies La FERR BN12 150 B4
Jefferies Wy CROW TN6 67 L5
Jeffreys Av CCH PO19 107 M4
Jellicoe Cl LGNY BN23 164 E7
Jengers Md BIL RH14 200 A12
Jenner Rd CRAWE RH10 27 L6
Jenner's La RHAS TN35 284 H11
Jennings Wy HORL RH6 23 J6
Jephson Cl EDN/EASTW BN20 176 F5
Jeremy's La RHWH RH17 204 C11
Jerome Cl LGNY BN23 164 D3
Jerrard Rd SELS PO20 109 J3
Jersey Rd CRAWW RH11 42 F7
FERR BN12 149 L4
Jersey St BRIE/ROTT BN2 5 G4
Jervis Av ANG/EP BN16 148 C4
LGNY BN23 164 D7
Jesmond Rd HOVE BN3 121 K6
Jessica Cl WVILLE PO7 288 C8
Jessie Rd HAV PO9 102 D2
Jesters HWH RH16 75 H2
The Jetty MSEA/BNM PO22 173 M1
Jevington Cl BEXW TN39 136 C3
SALV BN13 116 A8
Jevington Dr BRIE/ROTT BN2 123 J4
SEAF BN25 174 C1
Jevington Gdns EAST BN21 176 F4
Jevington Rd POLE BN26 162 B5
Jew St BRI BN1 4 E6
Jib Cl LHPTN BN17 147 M2
Jobes RHWH RH17 60 E8
Job's La HPPT/KEY BN6 236 G8
Jobson's La HASM GU27 196 B5
Jockey Md HORS RH12 201 R4
Jodrell Cl HORN PO8 288 D2
Joe's La HAIL BN27 280 A12
John Arundel Rd CCH PO19 6 A2
John Dann Cl UCK TN22 242 H7
John Howard Cottages
BRIE/ROTT BN2 * 154 E1
John Macadam Wy SLVH TN37 283 P11

Johns Cl PEAHV BN10 ...... 157 H3
John's Cross Rd RBTBR TN32 .. 248 C2
Johnson Bank BRIE/ROTT BN2 * ... 5 J2
Johnson Dr SLVH TN37 ...... 283 N11
Johnson Dr BURH BN15 ...... 75 J4
Johnson Wy ARUN BN18 ...... 146 A3
John St BOGR PO21 ...... 2 E7
  BRIE/ROTT BN2 ...... 5 G6
  SBGH/RUST TN4 ...... 37 M4
  SHOR BN43 ...... 119 K6
Jolesfield CRAWW RH11 ...... 42 E6
  SWTR TN13 ...... 234 E9
Jolliffe Rd SELS PO20 ...... 167 J6
Jonas Dr WADH TN5 ...... 71 K4
Jonas La WADH TN5 ...... 71 K4
Jones Sq SELS PO20 ...... 301 L2
Jordans Cl CRAWW RH11 ...... 43 J1
Jordans Crs CRAWW RH11 ...... 27 J8
Jordans La East
  LW/ROSE BN22 ...... 163 J2
Jordans La West
  LW/ROSE BN22 ...... 163 J2
The Jordans EGRIN RH19 ...... 47 K1
Joyce Cl LHPTN BN17 ...... 147 H2
Joys Cft CCH PO19 ...... 7 H3
Jubilee Av ANG/EP BN16 ...... 148 B3
Jubilee Cl HWH RH16 ...... 73 K5
Jubilee Ct BRIE/ROTT BN2 * .. 123 K3
Jubilee Est SWTR TN13 ...... 15 C3
Jubilee Fld TENT TN30 ...... 220 D5
Jubilee Gdns SEAF BN25 ...... 159 M8
Jubilee Homes NEWHV BN9 * .. 18 E4
Jubilee Rd BEXW TN39 ...... 96 F6
  BURH RH15 ...... 74 D7
  CCH PO19 ...... 6 F3
  HORS RH12 ...... 186 A9
  STHW BN42 ...... 120 F5
Jubilee St BRI BN1 ...... 4 E6
Jubilee Ter CCH PO19 ...... 6 F2
Jubilee Wk CRAWE RH10 ...... 9 M3
Jubilee Wy PUL/STOR RH20 .. 266 C10
Judge's Ter EGRIN RH19 ...... 47 K1
Juggs Cl LEWES BN7 ...... 16 C8
Juggs La HPPT/KEY BN6 ...... 272 F2
Juggs Rd LEWES BN7 ...... 16 B9
The Juggs PUL/STOR RH20 .. 266 F2
Julian Rd HOVE BN3 ...... 4 B3
Juliet Ct WVILLE PO7 * 288 D7
Junction Cl ARUN BN18 ...... 146 A3
  BURH RH15 ...... 75 H5
Junction Ms BURH RH15 ...... 75 G6
Junction Rd BRI BN1 ...... 4 D4
  BURH RH15 ...... 75 G5
  EAST BN21 ...... 10 E6
  RBTBR TN32 ...... 249 L8
  SLVH TN37 ...... 283 Q10
Junction St POLE BN26 ...... 132 A7
June Cl BOGR PO21 ...... 170 E2
June La MIDH GU29 ...... 226 C9
June Mdw MIDH GU29 ...... 226 C9
Juniper Cl BOR GU35 ...... 178 D7
  MSEA/BNM PO22 * 145 K7
  PTSD BN41 ...... 121 G2
  SALV BN13 ...... 116 B6
  SEAF BN25 ...... 175 J2
  STLEO TN38 ...... 98 D2
Juniper Rd CRAWW RH11 ...... 27 H8
  HORN PO8 * 256 D12
Juniper Sq HAV PO9 ...... 103 C5
Juno Cl FERR BN12 ...... 150 B5
Jupp's La FERR BN12 ...... 150 A2
Jura Cl CRAWW RH11 ...... 43 C6
Jury La SELS PO20 ...... 141 J8
Jury's Gap Rd LYDD TN29 .... 255 M9
  RYE TN31 ...... 254 G11
Juventu Cl HAV PO9 ...... 103 H2
Juxon Cl CCH PO19 ...... 6 F6
  CRAWW RH11 ...... 42 E5

K

Kammond Av SEAF BN25 ...... 160 A8
Kassel Cl WVILLE PO7 ...... 288 C8
Katherine Wy SEAF BN25 ...... 159 J8
Kay Crs BOR GU35 ...... 179 Q3
Kearsley Dr SALV BN13 ...... 116 F4
Keats Cl HORN PO8 ...... 288 A5
  HORS RH12 ...... 56 D2
  STLEO TN38 ...... 98 E7
Keats Pl EGRIN RH19 ...... 31 J8
Keats Wk BOGR PO21 ...... 2 A7
Keble Cl BOGR PO21 ...... 171 L2
  CRAWE RH10 ...... 28 C8
Kedale Rd SEAF BN25 ...... 174 L1
Keel Gdns SBGH/RUST TN4 ...... 37 K1
Keelson Wy LHPTN BN17 ...... 147 M3
Keepers Wd CCH PO19 ...... 107 L2
Keere St LEWES BN7 ...... 16 C7
Kefford Ct HORN PO8 * 288 C5
Keld Av UCK TN22 ...... 76 F4
Keld Cl UCK TN22 ...... 76 F6
Keld Dr UCK TN22 ...... 76 F6
Kelly Rd HOVE BN3 ...... 122 C4
Kelmscott Ri CRAWW RH11 ...... 59 G3
Kelsey Av EMRTH PO10 ...... 104 F4
Kelsey Cl HORL RH6 ...... 22 E6
  LISS GU33 ...... 192 D8
Kelso Cl CRAWE RH10 ...... 44 D2
  SALV BN13 ...... 150 D1
Kelvin La CRAWE RH10 ...... 27 L7
Kelvin Wy CRAWE RH10 ...... 27 L7
Kemble Cl RTWE/PEM TN2 ...... 38 D2
Kemnal Pk HASM GU27 ...... 181 N9
Kemps HPPT/KEY BN6 ...... 270 G3
Kemps Farm Rd CROW TN6 ...... 68 A8
Kempshott Rd HORS RH12 ...... 14 B2
Kemp St BRI BN1 ...... 4 E5
Kempton Pk WVILLE PO7 ...... 288 C8
Kemptown Ms
  BRIE/ROTT BN2 * 154 D1
Kemp Town Pl BRIE/ROTT BN2 .. 5 M9
Kemshott Ct HAV PO9 ...... 288 E11
Ken Berry Ct HAV PO9 ...... 289 J11
Kendal Cl HORN PO8 ...... 288 B5
  LHPTN BN17 ...... 147 M2
Kendale Cl CRAWE RH10 ...... 44 D2
Kendal Pk SBGH/RUST TN4 ...... 37 K4
Kendal Rd HOVE BN3 ...... 121 K6
  LAN/SOMP BN15 ...... 118 B7
Kenilworth Cl BRIE/ROTT BN2 . 123 M4
  CRAWW RH11 ...... 43 J6
Kenilworth Pl BIL RH14 ...... 231 R3

Kenilworth Rd BOGR PO21 ...... 171 M1
  STLEO TN38 ...... 99 G6
Kenlegh BOGR PO21 ...... 171 L3
Kenley Rd BOR GU35 ...... 179 Q4
Kenmara Cl CRAWE RH10 ...... 28 A8
Kenmara Ct CRAWE RH10 ...... 27 M7
Kenmure Av BRI BN1 ...... 82 F6
Kennard Ct FROW RH18 * 48 D6
Kennedy Av EGRIN RH19 ...... 31 J5
Kennedy Cl HTHF TN21 ...... 244 E7
Kennedy Rd BEX TN40 ...... 137 K1
  SWTR TN13 ...... 14 F8
Kennedy Wy NEWHV BN9 ...... 18 D3
Kennel Hl RCCH PO18 ...... 292 H10
Kennet Cl BEXW TN39 ...... 136 B1
  HORL RH6 ...... 22 C7
  SWTR TN13 ...... 234 D3
Kennet Cl CRAWW RH11 ...... 42 E4
  SALV BN13 ...... 116 C6
Kennet Rd EPSF GU31 ...... 223 M7
Kennett Cl PEV BN24 ...... 132 E8
Kensington Cl
  PUL/STOR RH20 * 265 R6
  STLEO TN38 ...... 98 D2
Kensington Gdns BRI BN1 ...... 4 E5
Kensington Pl BRI BN1 ...... 4 E5
Kensington Rd CCH PO19 ...... 7 K5
  CRAWW RH11 ...... 43 G7
Kensington St BRI BN1 ...... 4 E5
Kent Cl BEX TN40 ...... 97 M8
  WSEA TN36 ...... 286 D2
Kent Flds LEWES BN7 ...... 85 K8
Kentish Gdns RTWE/PEM TN2 .. 53 L1
Kent La RBTBR TN32 ...... 247 M6
Kenton Cl BEXW TN39 ...... 96 F8
Kenton Rd HOVE BN3 ...... 121 J6
Kent Rd BOR GU35 ...... 178 D7
  CCH PO19 ...... 7 H3
  LHPTN BN17 ...... 147 J3
  SBGH/RUST TN4 ...... 37 M3
  STLEO TN38 ...... 98 E1
Kent's La EDN/EASTW BN20 *. 163 G7
Kent's Rd HWH RH16 ...... 73 J3
Kent St BAT TN33 ...... 285 N5
  SWTR TN13 ...... 235 P7
Kentstreet La SWTR TN13 ...... 235 P4
Kentwyns Dr SWTR TN13 ...... 15 G9
Kenwards BRI BN1 ...... 83 H3
Kenwood Cl HAS TN34 ...... 100 A1
Kenwood Quay
  LAN/SOMP BN15 * 118 E8
Kenya St HORL RH6 * 22 E5
Keppel Rd HAS TN34 ...... 13 G1
Kerrara Ter LW/ROSE BN22 ...... 11 H2
Kerry Gdns ANG/EP BN16 ...... 148 F3
Kerves La SWTR TN13 ...... 15 H9
Kestral Ct HAIL TN27 ...... 92 C6
Kestrel Cl BEX TN40 ...... 137 K1
  CRAWW RH11 ...... 43 H1
  HORN PO8 ...... 256 D9
  HORS RH12 ...... 56 B5
  HOVE BN3 ...... 122 C5
  SELS PO20 ...... 167 M7
Kestrel Ct BOGR PO21 ...... 170 E6
Kestrel Pl CHAM PO6 ...... 102 A6
The Kestrels STLEO TN38 ...... 283 N12
Kestrel Wk CRAWE RH10 ...... 46 B4
Kestrel Wy LHPTN BN17 ...... 147 H1
Keswick Cl CRAWW RH11 ...... 43 G7
  FERR BN12 ...... 116 C8
Ketche's La HWH RH17 ...... 207 P10
  UCK TN22 ...... 208 A11
Ketch Rd LHPTN BN17 ...... 147 M5
Kevin Gdns BRIE/ROTT BN2 .. 124 D5
Kewell's Cnr SELS PO20 ...... 140 D8
Kew Gdns BOGR PO21 ...... 143 L3
Kewhurst Av BEXW TN39 ...... 136 B2
Kew St BRI BN1 ...... 4 D4
Keydell Av HORN PO8 ...... 288 B4
Keydell Cl HORN PO8 ...... 288 B4
Keyhaven Dr HAV PO9 ...... 288 D12
Keymer Av PEAHV BN10 ...... 157 J7
Keymer Ct LGNY BN23 ...... 164 D4
  STLEO TN38 ...... 98 E7
Keymer Ct BURH RH15 ...... 75 G8
Keymer Crs FERR BN12 ...... 150 B4
Keymer End BURH RH15 ...... 75 G6
Keymer Gdns BURH RH15 ...... 75 G8
Keymer Pde BURH RH15 ...... 75 G7
Keymer Pk HPPT/KEY BN6 ...... 271 Q6
Keymer Rd BRI BN1 ...... 83 G8
  BURH RH15 ...... 75 G8
  CRAWW RH11 ...... 8 E7
  HPPT/KEY BN6 ...... 271 N6
Keymer Ter HPPT/KEY BN6 *. 271 P6
Keymer Wy FERR BN12 ...... 150 B4
Keynor La SELS PO20 ...... 169 K5
Keysford La HWH RH16 ...... 206 H6
Keystone Cl FERR BN12 ...... 150 B2
Key West LGNY BN23 ...... 164 E6
Khandala Gdns WVILLE PO7 .. 102 A1
Kibbles La SBGH/RUST TN4 ...... 37 L1
Kidborough Rd CRAWW RH11 .. 42 E5
Kidbrook HWH RH16 ...... 73 L3
Kidders La HFD BN5 ...... 269 K1
Kidd Rd CCH PO19 ...... 108 A4
Kidd's Hl HRTF TN7 ...... 65 L4
Kidmans Cl HORS RH12 ...... 56 E4
Kidworth Cl HORL RH6 ...... 22 E4
Kilburn Ter EAST BN21 * 10 E5
Kildare Cl HAS TN34 ...... 100 A1
Kildare Rd BOR GU35 ...... 178 C5
Kilda St LW/ROSE BN22 ...... 11 H3
Killinghurst La HASM GU27 .. 182 B11
Kilmore Cl SALV BN13 ...... 298 H11
Kilnbarn Rd HWH RH16 ...... 73 G7
Kilnbarn Wy HWH RH16 ...... 73 G7
Kiln Cl UCK TN22 ...... 76 F8
Kiln Dr RYE TN31 ...... 252 G5
Kiln Fld LISS GU33 ...... 192 B8
Kilnfield Rd HORS RH12 ...... 186 A9
Kiln Flds HASM GU27 ...... 181 M9
Kiln La BAT TN33 ...... 95 G6
  EPSF GU31 ...... 257 K1
  HORL RH6 ...... 22 B5
  HWH RH16 ...... 73 J4
  UCK TN22 ...... 275 K4
Kilnmead CRAWE RH10 ...... 8 F2
Kilnmead Cl CRAWE RH10 ...... 9 G2
Kiln Rd RING/NEW BN8 ...... 46 A2
  RING/NEW BN8 ...... 275 M9
The Kiln Barn HWH RH16 ...... 75 J6
Kiln Wy GSHT GU26 ...... 180 B4
Kilnwood Cl SELS PO20 ...... 301 L6

Kilnwood La HORS RH12 ...... 41 M6
  RING/NEW BN8 ...... 273 P2
Kilsham La PETW GU28 ...... 263 J1
Kilwich Cl MSEA/BNM PO22 .. 145 J7
Kimber Cl LAN/SOMP BN15 .. 118 C8
Kimberley Cl HORL RH6 ...... 22 D6
Kimberley Rd BRIE/ROTT BN2 . 123 J5
  CRAWE RH10 ...... 44 A2
  LISS GU33 ...... 192 F3
  SEAF BN25 ...... 174 C1
Kimbers PSF GU32 ...... 223 M5
Kimbridge Crs HAV PO9 ...... 288 H11
Kimbridge Rd SELS PO20 ...... 167 M7
Kimpton Ct HAV PO9 ...... 289 J11
Kindersley Rd EGRIN RH19 ...... 32 A6
Kinfauns Av LW/ROSE BN22 .. 164 A7
Kinfauns Dr SALV BN13 ...... 116 C3
King Alfred Cl STEY/UB BN44.. 78 C4
King Edward Av HAS TN34 ...... 99 H2
  SALV BN13 ...... 21 H2
King Edward Cl HAS TN34 ...... 99 H2
  SALV BN13 ...... 21 J2
  SWTR TN13 ...... 201 N7
King Edward's Pde EAST BN21.. 10 F9
  EDN/EASTW BN20 ...... 176 E6
Kingfisher Cl BOR GU35 ...... 178 D7
  CRAWE RH10 ...... 27 M8
  HAV PO9 ...... 289 J3
  SALV BN13 ...... 116 B8
  UCK TN22 ...... 77 G7
Kingfisher Dr EMRTH PO10 .. 104 C1
  LGNY BN23 ...... 164 B3
  LHPTN BN17 ...... 147 H1
Kingfisher La CRAWE RH10 ...... 46 B4
Kingfisher Ri EGRIN RH19 ...... 47 L1
Kingfisher Wy HORS RH12 ...... 56 B5
King George Av EGRIN RH19 .. 31 H6
  PSF GU32 ...... 223 N5
King George Gdns CCH PO19 .. 6 E2
King George Ms PSF GU32 ...... 223 N5
King George Rd SHOR BN43 .. 120 B5
King George V Hl RTW TN1 ...... 38 D4
King George VI Av HOVE BN3 .. 121 H1
King George VI Dr HOVE BN3 .. 121 M2
King George VI Man
  HOVE BN3 * 121 L3
King Henry's Rd LEWES BN7 .. 16 D4
King La PSF GU32 ...... 222 G1
King Offa Wy BEX TN40 ...... 97 J8
King Pl BRI BN1 ...... 4 D6
King's Arms Hl ARUN BN18 .. 113 G2
King's Av CCH PO19 ...... 6 A2
  EAST BN21 ...... 10 A2
  NEWHV BN9 ...... 158 D4
  RYE TN31 ...... 253 J7
King's Bank La RYE TN31 ...... 251 K3
Kings Barn End
  STEY/UB BN44 * 78 A2
King's Barn La STEY/UB BN44.. 78 E1
King's Barn Vls STEY/UB BN44.. 78 D2
Kingsbridge Ms LAN/SOMP BN15 . 116 D6
Kingsbury Ct HORN PO8 ...... 256 C7
Kingsbury Rd BRI BN1 ...... 4 E4
Kings Cha CROW TN6 ...... 67 J6
Kingsclere Av HAV PO9 ...... 288 E12
Kings Cl ARUN BN18 ...... 145 M2
  BEX TN40 ...... 137 H1
  EAST BN21 ...... 10 C1
  HAV PO9 ...... 288 H7
  LAN/SOMP BN15 ...... 118 E8
  PEAHV BN10 ...... 157 G4
Kings Copse EGRIN RH19 * 47 L1
Kingscote Hl CRAWW RH11 ...... 8 A7
Kingscott Cl BEXW TN39 ...... 96 F5
Kings Ct SELS PO20 ...... 301 L5
  SWTR TN13 * 15 C4
Kings Crs SHOR BN43 ...... 119 J8
Kingscroft Ct HAV PO9 ...... 102 E4
King's Croft La HAV PO9 ...... 102 D4
Kingsdale Ct BAT TN33 ...... 282 C6
  SLVH TN37 ...... 283 R11
Kings Dr BOGR PO21 ...... 171 G5
  EAST BN21 ...... 163 J6
  HPPT/KEY BN6 ...... 271 N5
  MIDH GU29 ...... 227 J2
  SHOR BN43 ...... 119 J7
King's Esp HOVE BN3 ...... 121 M8
Kingsey Av EMRTH PO10 ...... 103 M5
Kingsfernsden La PSF GU32 .. 223 P4
Kingsfield PUL/STOR RH20 .. 266 B11
Kingsfold Cl BIL RH14 ...... 232 A3
Kingsfold Ct HORS RH12 * 40 A4
Kings Gap SHOR BN43 ...... 119 J8
King's Gdns HOVE BN3 ...... 122 A8
Kingsgate CRAWE RH10 * 9 G3
Kings Ga HORS RH12 ...... 14 B5
Kingsham Av CCH PO19 ...... 7 G7
Kingsham Rd CCH PO19 ...... 6 F6
Kings Head Ms EGRIN RH19 * . 225 L2
King's Hill Rd BUR/ETCH TN19 . 246 C1
Kingsland Cl PUL/STOR RH20 . 266 B11
  SHOR BN43 ...... 120 B6
Kingsland Ct CRAWE RH10 * 9 M3
Kingsland Rd SALV BN13 ...... 117 K7
Kings La PUL/STOR RH20 ...... 264 D6
  PUL/STOR RH20 ...... 265 N4
  SWTR TN13 ...... 201 R9
  SWTR TN13 ...... 235 N5
Kingslea SWTR TN13 ...... 15 H4
Kingslea Ms BIL RH14 * 232 B2
Kingsley Cl HORL RH6 ...... 21 M1
  SALV BN13 ...... 21 H1
  SLVH TN37 ...... 283 P12
Kingsley Gdn HAIL TN27 ...... 92 A7
Kingsley Rd BRI BN1 ...... 122 C4
  CRAWW RH11 ...... 42 F6
  HORL RH6 ...... 22 E4
  LEWES BN7 ...... 17 G5
Kingsmarsh La LYDD TN29 .. 255 R1
Kingsmead LHPTN BN17 ...... 113 H9
  MSEA/BNM PO22 ...... 3 J5
  SEAF BN25 ...... 159 J8
Kingsmead Cl SEAF BN25 ...... 174 E1
  STEY/UB BN44 * 78 A2
Kings Mead La SEAF BN25 ...... 174 D1
Kingsmead Pl HORS RH12 ...... 201 M4
Kingsmead Rd HORS RH12 ...... 201 M4
  MSEA/BNM PO22 ...... 3 J5
Kingsmead Wk SEAF BN25 ...... 174 E1
Kingsmead Wy SEAF BN25 ...... 174 E1
Kings Mede HORN PO8 ...... 288 C3
Kingsmere BRI BN1 * 122 D3
Kingsmere Wy LGNY BN23 ...... 164 D3
Kings Ms HORS RH12 ...... 14 B5

  HOVE BN3 ...... 122 A7
Kingsmill Rd MSEA/BNM PO22 . 111 H7
King's Pde BOGR PO21 ...... 171 M5
  BRI BN1 * 122 A7
The Kings Peace GSHT GU26 * . 180 F6
Kingspit La PETW GU28 ...... 229 P10
Kings Platt SWTR TN13 ...... 233 M9
Kings Ride BURH RH15 ...... 75 J3
  POLE BN26 ...... 160 E3
  SEAF BN25 ...... 174 D1
King's Rd BRI BN1 ...... 4 B7
  EMRTH PO10 ...... 103 M5
  HASM GU27 ...... 181 K11
  HORL RH6 ...... 22 F6
  HORN PO8 ...... 288 A6
  HWH RH16 ...... 73 J7
  LAN/SOMP BN15 ...... 118 D8
  PSF GU32 ...... 223 L5
  SLVH TN37 ...... 4 B8
  STHW BN42 ...... 120 C5
  SWTR TN13 ...... 15 H3
Kings Road Arches BRI BN1 * . 4 C7
King's Stone Av STEY/UB BN44 . 78 E3
King's Ter EMRTH PO10 ...... 104 A5
Kingsthorpe Rd HOVE BN3 .. 121 K5
Kings Toll Rd RTWE/PEM TN2 . 39 M3
Kingston Av SEAF BN25 ...... 175 J2
Kingston Bay Rd SHOR BN43 . 120 B7
Kingston Broadway
  SHOR BN43 ...... 120 B4
  HOVE BN3 ...... 121 K3
  SEAF BN25 ...... 175 H2
  SHOR BN43 ...... 120 B5
Kingston Cl BRI BN1 ...... 83 K7
Kingston Gn SEAF BN25 ...... 175 H2
Kingston La ANG/EP BN16 ...... 149 G4
  STHW BN42 ...... 120 C6
Kingston Rdg LEWES BN7 ...... 85 J7
Kingston Rd LEWES BN7 ...... 85 M7
  LW/ROSE BN22 ...... 163 G3
Kingston Wy SEAF BN25 ...... 175 J3
  SHOR BN43 ...... 120 B4
King St ARUN BN18 ...... 112 F2
  BRI BN1 ...... 4 E6
  EGRIN RH19 ...... 31 K8
  EMRTH PO10 ...... 104 A5
  EMRTH PO10 ...... 104 C2
  SALV BN13 ...... 21 J1
Kingston's Cott CRAWW RH11 . 42 F2
Kingswood BURH RH15 ...... 75 H4
Kingswood Cl CRAWE RH10 ...... 44 B6
Kingsway BOGR PO21 ...... 171 J4
Kingsway HOVE BN3 ...... 121 L7
  SEAF BN25 ...... 174 D1
  SELS PO20 ...... 301 L5
  WTHG BN11 ...... 150 E3
Kingswood PUL/STOR RH20 .. 265 Q6
Kingswood Av BEXW TN39 ...... 96 E7
Kingswood Firs GSHT GU26 .. 180 F7
Kingswood La CSHT GU26 ...... 180 F7
Kingswood Rd RTWE/PEM TN2 . 38 B6
Kingswood St BRIE/ROTT BN2 . 4 E7
Kingsworthy Rd HAV PO9 ...... 103 G2
King Wood Hl RYE TN31 ...... 250 E10
Kinleside Wy ANG/EP BN16 .. 114 F8
Kinneil Cl EMRTH PO10 ...... 104 A6
Kinver La BEX TN40 ...... 97 M7
Kipling Av BRIE/ROTT BN2 .. 124 D5
  FERR BN12 ...... 150 A2
Kipling Cl CRAWE RH10 ...... 44 B3
Kipling Ct SWTR TN13 * 15 M2
Kipling Wy EGRIN RH19 ...... 31 H8
Kippens La SWTR TN13 * 234 A3
Kirby Dr PEAHV BN10 ...... 156 F4
Kirdford Cl ANG/EP BN16 ...... 148 A5
  BURH RH15 ...... 75 J4
  CRAWW RH11 ...... 42 F1
Kirdford Rd ARUN BN18 ...... 112 F3
  BIL RH14 ...... 198 H11
Kirkby Cl RCCH PO18 ...... 109 J2
Kirkdale Rd RTW TN1 ...... 38 A5
Kirkins Cl STPH/PW TN12 ...... 189 M3
Kirk Knoll BOR GU35 ...... 179 N4
Kirkland Cl ANG/EP BN16 ...... 148 A4
Kirkstall Cl ANG/EP BN16 ...... 148 A4
Kirkstall Cl LW/ROSE BN22 .. 163 K2
Kitchener Rd LISS GU33 ...... 192 F3
Kitchenour La RYE TN31 ...... 219 P12
Kite Cl STLEO TN38 ...... 98 D1
Kite La STPH/PW TN12 ...... 188 F3
Kites Cl CRAWW RH11 ...... 8 D3
Kithurst Cl ANG/EP BN16 ...... 148 A5
  CRAWW RH11 ...... 8 E7
  FERR BN12 ...... 150 A1
Kithurst Crs FERR BN12 ...... 150 A1
Kithurst Farm Rd
  PUL/STOR RH20 ...... 297 Q1
Kithurst La PUL/STOR RH20 .. 265 R12
Kithurst Pk PUL/STOR RH20 .. 265 Q12
Kitsmead CRAWE RH10 ...... 28 F7
Kittiwake Cl CRAWW RH11 ...... 42 C5
Kitts La RFNM GU10 ...... 180 C1
Kitwood Gn HAV PO9 * 289 J12
Knebworth Rd BEXW TN39 ...... 96 E8
Knelle Rd RBTBR TN32 ...... 248 A1
Knepp Cl BRIE/ROTT BN2 .. 123 L3
  CRAWE RH10 ...... 44 B3
Knighton Cl CRAWE RH10 ...... 28 C7
Knightons La MFD/CHID GU8 . 184 A5
Knightsbridge Cl
  SBGH/RUST TN4 ...... 37 L4
Knights Cl RTWE/PEM TN2 ...... 39 J2
Knightscroft Av ANG/EP BN16 . 148 B5
Knightscroft Pde ANG/EP BN16.. 92 A7
Knights Gdn HAIL TN27 ...... 92 A7
Knights Meadow BAT TN33 .. 282 G5
Knight's Hl RCCH PO18 ...... 292 H1
Knights Pl CRAWE RH10 * 9 J2
Knight's Rdg RTWE/PEM TN2 . 39 J2
Knights Wy RTWE/PEM TN2 .. 38 E1
Knightwood Av HAV PO9 ...... 288 H12
Knob Hl HORS RH12 ...... 187 M7
Knock Hl TENT TN30 ...... 221 M7
Knockhundred Rw
  MIDH GU29 ...... 227 J3
Knole Cl CRAWE RH10 ...... 44 D2
Knole Gv EGRIN RH19 ...... 31 H6
Knole Rd BEX TN40 ...... 137 J2
  BRIE/ROTT BN2 ...... 155 M4
Knoll Cl HOVE BN3 ...... 121 J6
Knoll Hl HWH RH16 ...... 73 L5
Knoll Ri STLEO TN38 ...... 98 D3
Knoll Rd LW/ROSE BN22 ...... 163 L3
Knowle Av RHAS TN35 ...... 101 K1
Knowle Cl CRAWE RH10 ...... 29 H6

  CROW TN6 ...... 211 K1
  RRTW TN3 ...... 36 D6
Knowle Dr CRAWE RH10 ...... 29 G6
Knowle HI MAYF TN20 ...... 212 D8
Knowle La CRAN GU6 ...... 185 L1
  HORS RH12 ...... 185 N8
Knowle Pk CROW TN6 ...... 67 J7
Knowle Rd RHAS TN35 ...... 285 P12
Knowles Meadow LISS GU33 . 192 E12
The Knowle BOR GU35 ...... 179 Q3
  RHWH RH17 ...... 72 B2
Knowsley Ter
  MFD/CHID GU8 * 182 F5
Knox Rd HAV PO9 ...... 102 E4
Knoyle Rd BRI BN1 ...... 122 D3
Kymer Gdns HPPT/KEY BN6 .. 271 P6
Kynon Gdns MSEA/BNM PO22.. 145 J7
Kyoto Ct BOGR PO21 ...... 171 M2

L

Laburnum Av HOVE BN3 ...... 121 K4
Laburnum Cl FERR BN12 ...... 149 L4
  LAN/SOMP BN15 ...... 152 C1
Laburnum Gdns BEX TN40 ...... 97 L2
  CCH PO19 ...... 6 E5
  MSEA/BNM PO22 ...... 2 C1
Laburnum Ms BOGR PO21 * 2 E6
Laburnum Wy HWH RH16 ...... 73 G7
Lackenhurst La SWTR TN13 .. 233 J3
Lacock Cl SELS PO20 ...... 168 B8
Lacys Hl RING/NEW BN8 ...... 87 K5
Ladbroke Rd HORL RH6 ...... 22 F4
Ladies Mile HRTF TN7 ...... 51 J5
Ladies Mile Cl BRI BN1 ...... 82 E7
Ladies' Mile Rd BRI BN1 ...... 82 D7
Ladycross Cl SEAF BN25 ...... 175 J4
Ladydell Rd WTHG BN11 ...... 21 L3
Ladygate Dr GSHT GU26 ...... 180 D6
Lady Margaret Rd
  CRAWW RH11 ...... 42 F2
Ladymead BURH RH15 ...... 75 H4
Ladymead Cl CRAWE RH10 ...... 44 B6
Ladymile Rd SWTR TN13 ...... 233 J3
Ladysmith Pl BOR GU35 ...... 178 F4
Ladysmith Rd BRIE/ROTT BN2 . 123 J5
Lagness Rd SELS PO20 ...... 142 C4
Lagoon Rd BOGR PO21 ...... 170 E7
Lagwood Cl HPPT/KEY BN6 .. 271 N6
Laine Cl BRI BN1 ...... 122 D2
Laines Rd STEY/UB BN44 ...... 78 B3
Lake Dr BOR GU35 ...... 178 H6
  PEAHV BN10 ...... 157 G5
Lakehurst La BAT TN33 ...... 280 E1
Lakelands LW/ROSE BN22 ...... 163 M4
Lakelands Dr BEXW TN39 ...... 136 C1
Lake La ARUN BN18 ...... 111 L8
  HORL RH6 ...... 23 H4
  MSEA/BNM PO22 ...... 111 J7
Lake Rd CCH PO19 ...... 7 K5
  SBGH/RUST TN4 ...... 37 K5
Lakes Meadow BIL RH14 ...... 232 A1
Lakeside HORS RH12 ...... 56 B4
  MIDH GU29 ...... 226 H11
  RTWE/PEM TN2 ...... 38 C3
Lakeside Av SWTR TN13 ...... 201 R12
Lakeside Gdns HAV PO9 ...... 103 H3
Lakesmere Rd HORN PO8 ...... 288 D3
Lake Vw HORN PO8 ...... 69 M8
Lake Vw Rd CROW TN6 ...... 69 M8
Lake View Rd EGRIN RH19 ...... 30 A6
  EGRIN RH19 ...... 31 L4
Laleham Cl EAST BN21 ...... 10 A4
  SLVH TN37 ...... 283 P12
Lamberhurst By-Pass
  RRTW TN3 ...... 190 H1
Lamberhurst Rd
  STPH/PW TN12 ...... 188 H8
  STPH/PW TN12 ...... 188 H3
Lamberhurst Wk CRAWE RH10.. 9 L4
Lambersart CL SBGH/RUST TN4 . 38 C1
Lambert Pl LEWES BN7 ...... 17 G1
Lambert Rd LGNY BN23 ...... 164 C2
Lambert's La MIDH GU29 ...... 227 J9
Lamberts Pl STPH/PW TN12 .. 189 N4
Lamberts Rd RTWE/PEM TN2 . 38 C1
Lambeth Cl CRAWW RH11 ...... 43 G7
Lambeth Rd RTWE/PEM TN2 .. 38 C1
Lambeth Wk CRAWW RH11 * . 43 G7
Lambleys La SALV BN13 ...... 117 L6
Lamborne Av LHPTN BN17 ...... 147 L2
Lamorna Cl EGRIN RH19 ...... 31 K6
Lambourne Cl BRI BN1 ...... 123 L3
  CRAWE RH10 ...... 28 C7
Lambourne La LIPH GU30 ...... 194 A10
Lambourn Wy RTWE/PEM TN2.. 38 C8
Lambs Crs HORS RH12 ...... 56 E3
Lambs Farm Cl HORS RH12 ...... 56 F4
Lambs Farm Rd HORS RH12 ...... 56 E4
Lambs Green Rd HORS RH12 ...... 41 M4
Lambyn Cft HORS RH12 ...... 56 F4
Lamerton Rd BOR GU35 ...... 178 H5
Lammas Cl LHPTN BN17 ...... 147 K2
Lamorna Gdns FERR BN12 ...... 149 L5
  SELS PO20 ...... 110 C2
Lamorna Gv SALV BN13 ...... 117 K7
Lampington Rw RRTW TN3 ...... 36 D6
Lanark Cl SWTR TN13 ...... 15 L5
Lancaster Cl CRAWE RH10 ...... 28 C8
Lancaster Dr EGRIN RH19 ...... 31 M6
Lancaster Pl MSEA/BNM PO22 . 2 C2
Lancaster Rd FERR BN12 ...... 150 D4
  STLEO TN38 ...... 283 N12
Lancaster St LEWES BN7 ...... 17 G5
Lancastrian Gra CCH PO19 * 6 D3
Lancelot Cl CRAWW RH11 ...... 42 D3
  HAS TN34 ...... 99 H3
Lancing Cl CRAWW RH11 ...... 42 D3
  HAS TN34 ...... 99 H3
Lancing Ct HORS RH12 ...... 15 M1
Lancing Pk LAN/SOMP BN15 .. 152 C1
Lancing Wy POLE BN26 ...... 162 E1
Landen Pk HORL RH6 ...... 22 D4
Landgate RYE TN31 ...... 252 H7
Landsdowne Wy BEX TN40 ...... 97 L3
Landsdown Rd SEAF BN25 ...... 160 B8

Landseer Dr SELS PO20 ....301 M6
Landseer Rd HOVE BN3 ....121 M5
Lands End La BOR GU35 ....178 H4
Lane End MFD/CHID GU14 ....182 G5
Lane End Dr EMRTH PO10 ....104 A5
Lane End Rd MSEA/BNM PO22 ....145 M8
Lanercost Rd CRAWW RH11 .... 8 D7
The Lane BIL RH14 ....198 D1
  CCH PO19 ....107 L3
  RRTW TN3 .... 36 A1
  SEAF BN25 ....302 A1
Lanfranc Rd SALV BN13 .... 20 C2
Langbrook Cl HAV PO9 ....103 G5
Langbury Cl FERR BN12 ....149 K2
Langbury La FERR BN12 ....149 K2
Langdale Av CCH PO19 .... 7 J9
  MSEA/BNM PO22 ....145 M8
Langdale Cl LAN/SOMP BN15 ....118 B8
  LGNY BN23 ....164 B1
Langdale Gdns HOVE BN3 ....121 L7
  HOVE BN3 ....121 L7
Langham Cl HAS TN34 .... 99 L1
  RING/NEW BN8 ....275 J12
Langham Gdns WTHG BN11 .... 20 B6
Langham Rd HAS TN34 .... 99 L1
  RBTBR TN32 ....248 A1
Langholm Rd RRTW TN3 .... 36 E4
Langhurst Cl HORS RH12 .... 40 C5
Langhurst La CRAWW RH11 .... 41 M1
Langhurstwood Rd HORS RH12 .. 40 C5
Langley Cl BEXW TN39 .... 97 G5
Langley Dr CRAWW RH11 .... 43 H1
Langley Gv BOGR PO21 ....171 H4
Langley La CRAWW RH11 .... 42 F1
Langley Pde CRAWW RH11 .... 27 H8
Langley Pl RWHH RH17 .... 27 H8
Langley Wk CRAWW RH11 .... 27 H8
Langmead Cl HORS RH12 ....146 D5
Langmeads Cl LHPTN RH17 ....146 D5
Langney Gn LGNY BN23 ....164 D5
Langney Ri LGNY BN23 ....164 C5
Langney Rd EAST BN21 .... 11 G6
Langridge Dr EGRIN RH19 .... 47 K1
  PTSD BN41 ....120 F3
Langridge La HWH RH16 .... 73 J4
Langridge Wy BURH RH15 .... 74 D4
Langrish Cl HAV PO9 ....288 H11
Langshott HORL RH6 .... 23 J5
Langshott La HORL RH6 .... 23 H5
Langstone Av HAV PO9 ....103 G6
Langstone Br HAV PO9 ....103 H4
Langstone Cl CRAWE RH10 .... 44 B6
Langstone Gdns RCCH PO18 ....105 J5
Langstone High St HAV PO9 ....103 G6
Langstone Rd HAV PO9 ....103 G6
Langton Cl BAT TN33 ....282 F5
  SELS PO20 ....301 K7
Langton Dr BOR GU35 ....179 Q2
Langton La HPPT/KEY BN6 ....270 F1
Langton Pl PUL/STOR RH20 * 266 A12
Langton Rd CCH PO19 .... 6 A3
  RRTW TN3 .... 36 A1
  RRTW TN3 .... 36 F2
  SALV BN13 .... 21 G2
  SBGH/RUST TN4 .... 37 H6
Langtye La RING/NEW BN8 .... 89 K7
Lansbury Rd CRAWW RH11 .... 43 G8
Lansdown Cl RHWH RH17 .... 57 G3
Lansdowne Cl ANG/EP BN16 ....114 C4
  WTHG BN11 .... 20 A6
Lansdowne Crs HAIL BN27 .... 91 M3
Lansdowne Dr HAIL BN27 .... 91 M3
Lansdowne Gdns HAIL BN27 .... 91 M3
Lansdowne Ms HOVE BN3 ....122 C7
Lansdowne Pl HOVE BN3 ....122 C8
  WTHG BN11 .... 20 A5
Lansdowne Rd ANG/EP BN16 ....114 C4
  HAIL BN27 .... 91 M3
  HOVE BN3 ....122 C7
  LHPTN BN17 ....147 J2
  RTW TN1 .... 38 D3
Lansdowne Sq EAST BN21 ....122 C7
  RTW TN1 .... 38 A5
Lansdowne Ter EAST BN21 * 177 C4
Lansdowne Wy ANG/EP BN16 ....114 C4
  HAIL BN27 .... 91 M2
Lansdown Pl LEWES BN7 .... 17 G7
Lantana Cl WILLE PO7 ....288 A11
Lanthorne Ms RTW TN1 .... 38 A4
Lanyards LHPTN BN17 ....147 M2
Lanyon Cl HORS RH12 .... 56 F3
Lanyon Ms HORS RH12 * 56 F3
Lapierre Rd NEWHV BN9 .... 18 C3
Lapwing Cl HORN PO8 ....288 D7
  LGNY BN23 ....164 B6
  SWTR RH13 .... 15 K3
Larch Cl ANG/EP BN16 ....148 C4
  BRIE/ROTT BN2 ....124 C4
  CCH PO19 ....107 L3
  HTHF TN21 ....244 E5
  LIPH GU30 ....193 Q2
  MSEA/BNM PO22 ....144 C3
  STLEO TN38 .... 98 F4
Larch End HORS RH12 .... 14 A3
  PUL/STOR RH20 ....266 A6
The Larches EGRIN RH19 .... 31 M5
  HORS RH12 .... 57 G3
Larches Wy CRAWE RH10 .... 46 B3
Larchfield Cl BOGR PO21 ....171 J4
Larchfield Wy HORN PO8 ....288 D7
Larch Gdns LW/ROSE BN22 ....150 F2
Larch Wy HWH RH16 .... 73 L5
Larchwood Av HAV PO9 ....102 C1
Larcombe Rd PEAV BN24 ....223 L8
Large Acres SELS PO20 ....301 K6
Larke Cl SHOR BN43 ....119 M8
Larkfield Cl LAN/SOMP BN15 ....118 C8
  STLEO TN38 .... 98 F2
Larkfield Ct HORL RH6 .... 23 M6
Larkfield Wy BRI BN1 ....122 F1
Larkhill BEX TN40 ....137 H1
Lark Hl HOVE BN3 ....121 K2
Larkins Rd HORL RH6 .... 27 J2
Lark Ri CRAWE RH10 .... 46 B3
  CRAWW RH11 .... 43 H1
  LIPH GU30 ....179 P12
Larksfield HORL RH6 .... 23 G5
Larkspur Cl LHPTN RH17 ....147 M2
Larkspur Dr LGNY BN23 ....164 A2
Larkspur Wy SWTR RH13 ....201 R10
Larks Vw BIL RH14 ....231 R1
Larnach Cl UCK TN22 .... 76 F4
Lascelles Ter EAST BN21 .... 10 F9

Lasham Gn HAV PO9 * 289 J12
Lashbrooks Rd UCK TN22 .... 76 D5
Lashmar Rd BRI BN16 ....148 H4
Lashmere CRAWE RH10 .... 29 J6
Latchmore Forest Gv
  HORN PO8 ....288 A6
Latchmore Gdns HORN PO8 ....288 A6
Latham Cl LHPTN RH17 ....147 G3
Latham Rd SELS PO20 ....301 K7
Latimer Cl CRAWW RH11 .... 27 J8
Latimer Rd LW/ROSE BN22 .... 11 J5
  WTHG BN11 ....150 F4
Laton Rd HAS TN34 .... 13 G2
Laud Dr CRAWE RH10 .... 44 C4
Lauder Cl EMRTH PO10 ....104 E3
Laughton Cl LGNY BN23 ....163 M1
Laughton Rd BRIE/ROTT BN2 ....124 E5
  HORS RH12 .... 56 F4
  RING/NEW BN8 ....275 Q11
Laundry Cl RHWH RH17 .... 64 C5
Laundry Wy RDKG RH5 .... 24 B4
Laurel Bank SBGH/RUST TN4 .... 38 A1
Laurel Cl BURH RH15 .... 75 H4
  CRAWE RH10 .... 9 M9
  SALV BN13 ....116 B8
Laurel Cottages CROW TN6 * 67 L6
  RHAS TN35 * 100 B3
Laurel Dene EGRIN RH19 .... 31 L8
Laurel Gv MSEA/BNM PO22 ....144 B7
Laurel La WSEA TN36 ....285 L6
Laurel Mt PUL/STOR RH20 ....265 K3
Laurel Rd HORN PO8 ....288 D5
  RTWE/PEM TN2 .... 38 C2
The Laurels BRIE/ROTT BN2 * 5 G1
  CRAWE RH10 * 27 M8
  HFD BN5 ....269 K4
  SWTR RH13 ....201 Q12
  UCK TN22 .... 77 G4
Laurel Wk STLEO TN38 * 98 D2
  WTHG BN11 .... 15 J7
Lauriston Rd BRI BN1 ....122 D3
Laurus Cl WVILLE PO7 ....288 B12
Lavant Cl BEXW TN39 .... 96 B7
  CRAWW RH11 .... 42 A4
  FERR BN12 ....149 M1
  HORN PO8 ....288 C8
Lavant Down Rd RCCH PO18 ....292 B10
Lavant Dr HAV PO9 ....103 G2
Lavant Rd CCH PO19 ....107 L2
Lavant St PSF GU32 ....223 M6
Lavender Cl LGNY BN23 ....164 A2
Lavender Gdns BOR GU35 ....178 A5
  WADH TN5 ....191 K12
Lavender Hl SHOR BN43 ....120 A4
Lavender St WVILLE PO7 ....288 B11
Lavender St BRIE/ROTT BN2 * 5 G1
Lavengro Ct CRAWW RH11 .... 42 E2
Lavington Rd SALV BN13 ....117 G7
Lavinia Ct FERR BN12 ....150 B2
Lavinia Wy ANG/EP BN16 ....148 A2
  NEWHV BN9 .... 18 E3
Lawns Av EAST BN21 ....176 D1
Lawns Rd HORS RH12 ....185 P6
The Lawns ANG/EP BN16 ....148 A2
  EDN/EASTW BN20 * 163 C4
  HAIL BN27 * 92 B7
  LAN/SOMP BN15 ....118 A6
  LW/ROSE BN22 * 11 J3
  STPH/PW TN12 ....188 C1
Lawnswood CI HORN PO8 ....288 A7
  STLEO TN38 .... 12 A8
Lawrence Av ANG/EP BN16 ....148 C3
Lawrence Cl LGNY BN23 ....164 C3
  SELS PO20 ....301 L2
Lawrence Rd HOVE BN3 ....121 L6
Lawrie La HWH RH16 .... 73 L4
Laws Cl CRAWW RH11 .... 42 A4
Lawyer's La HFD BN5 ....268 H4
Laylands Rd PTSD BN41 ....120 F6
The Layne MSEA/BNM PO22 ....145 M8
Lazy Acre EMRTH PO10 ....104 A4
Lea Av RYE TN31 ....252 F7
Lea Cl CRAWW RH11 .... 42 A4
Leacroft EGRIN RH19 .... 31 J7
Lea Farm La PUL/STOR RH20 ....264 D5
Leaf Gln EAST BN21 * 10 B4
Leaf Hall Rd LW/ROSE BN22 .... 11 L5
Leaf Rd EAST BN21 .... 10 F5
Leahurst Cl BRI BN1 ....122 A4
Leahurst Court Rd BRI BN1 ....122 D2
Lealands Cl RRTW TN3 .... 52 B2
Lealands Dr UCK TN22 * 76 E3
Lealands Dr UCK TN22 .... 76 E4
Leaman Cl MSEA/BNM PO22 ....145 L8
Leander Rd RCCH PO18 ....106 B4
Lea Rd PEAHV BN10 ....157 G5
Leasam La RYE TN31 ....252 F6
Leas Ct MSEA/BNM PO22 .... 2 D2
Leasingham Gdns BEXW TN39 .... 96 F5
The Leas ANG/EP BN16 ....148 D2
  BURH RH15 * 74 E5
  PEAHV BN10 ....157 L8
  STLEO TN38 * 98 F7
  WADH TN5 .... 71 M3
Leatherbottle La CCH PO19 .... 7 K4
Le Brun Rd EAST BN21 .... 10 C2
Lechford Rd HORL RH6 .... 22 E8
Leckford Rd HAV PO9 ....289 J11
Leconfield Rd
  LAN/SOMP BN15 ....118 C8
Ledbury Wy BOGR PO21 ....171 G3
Ledgers Meadow RHWH RH17 .. 72 C3
Ledra Dr BOGR PO21 ....171 G3
Ledsham Av SLVH TN37 ....283 Q12
Ledsham Cl SLVH TN37 ....283 Q12
Ledsham Pk SLVH TN37 ....283 Q12
Ledsham Wy SLVH TN37 ....283 Q12
Leechpond Hl SWTR RH13 ....203 M1
Leechpool La SWTR RH13 .... 15 M1
Leecroft BOGR PO21 ....171 K3
Leeds Av LGNY BN23 ....164 C5
Leeds Cl RHAS TN35 ....100 C2
  SALV BN13 ....116 A8
  SWTR RH13 ....201 R11
Leeds La MAYF TN20 ....211 R11
Leeds Rd LEWES BN7 .... 16 D3
Leeside HORS RH12 * 41 H3
Lee St HORL RH6 .... 22 D5
Leeves Cl HTHF TN21 ....244 C7
Leeves Wy HTHF TN21 ....244 C7
Leeward Cl SALV BN13 ....116 E8
Leeward Quay LGNY BN23 ....164 E5
Leeward Rd LHPTN BN17 ....147 L4
  SALV BN13 ....116 E8
Lee Wy NEWHV BN9 .... 18 E3

Leggs' La RRTW TN3 .... 36 D4
Legion Wy SELS PO20 ....167 M7
Legsheath La EGRIN RH19 .... 47 J8
Leicester Dr RTWE/PEM TN2 .... 53 L1
Leicester St BRIE/ROTT BN2 * 5 H7
Leicester Vls HOVE BN3 ....121 J6
Leighlands CRAWE RH10 .... 44 B1
Leigh Rd CCH PO19 .... 6 C7
  HAV PO9 ....103 G3
  SALV BN13 ....117 J7
Leighton Av SALV BN13 ....117 K7
Leighton Cl SBGH/RUST TN4 .... 37 M2
Leighton Rd HOVE BN3 ....121 M5
  HWH RH17 ....207 M4
Leinster Gdns
  MSEA/BNM PO22 ....145 L8
Leith View Rd HORS RH12 .... 56 F4
Le May Cl HORL RH6 .... 6 F2
Lemmington Wy HORS RH12 .... 56 E2
Lemon Gv BOR GU35 ....178 F8
Leneda Dr RTWE/PEM TN2 .... 53 K1
Lenham Av BRIE/ROTT BN2 ....156 A4
Lenham Rd East
  BRIE/ROTT BN2 ....156 A4
Lenham Rd West
  BRIE/ROTT BN2 ....155 M4
Lenhurst Wy SALV BN13 ....116 E8
Lennox Cl CRAWW RH10 ....163 G8
Lennox Rd SWTR RH13 .... 15 J6
Leonardslee Ct CRAWE RH10 * ... 44 A6
Leonard Wy SWTR RH13 .... 36 F8
Leonora Dr BOGR PO21 ....171 G3
Leopold Cl MSEA/BNM PO22 .... 3 M2
Leopold Flats BEXW TN39 ....137 L5
Leopold Rd BEXW TN39 ....137 L5
  BRI BN1 .... 4 C5
  CRAWW RH11 .... 8 C4
Lepeland HAIL BN27 .... 91 M4
Lesley Cl BEX TN40 .... 97 L6
Leslie St LW/ROSE BN22 .... 11 H3
Lesser Foxholes SHOR BN43 ....119 J4
Lester Av HAV PO9 ....102 D5
Letchworth Cl FERR BN12 ....149 K4
Letheren Pl EAST BN21 ....176 D2
Leveller Rd RING/NEW BN8 ....240 C6
Level Mare La SELS PO20 ....110 D3
Leveret La CRAWW RH11 .... 9 M8
Leverton Av MSEA/BNM PO22 ....173 J1
Levett Av POLE BN26 ....132 B6
Levett Cl FERR BN12 ....150 B2
Levett Rd POLE BN26 ....132 B7
Levetts La RBTBR TN32 ....217 L8
Levett Wy POLE BN26 ....132 B7
Lewes Av BEXW TN39 .... 96 F7
  BOGR PO21 ....171 L1
  BRIE/ROTT BN2 ....156 D4
  CRAWE RH10 .... 44 B3
Lewes Crs BRIE/ROTT BN2 ....154 D2
Lewes Ms BRIE/ROTT BN2 * 154 D1
Lewes Rd BRI BN1 .... 83 M7
  BRIE/ROTT BN2 .... 5 G4
  EAST BN21 .... 10 D3
  EGRIN RH19 .... 47 M1
  FROW RH18 .... 48 D6
  HPPT/KEY BN6 ....272 B7
  HWH RH16 .... 73 L2
  NEWHV BN9 .... 18 F3
  POLE BN26 ....129 K5
  POLE BN26 ....131 G7
  RHWH RH17 .... 64 C5
  RHWH RH17 .... 73 L6
  RHWH RH17 ....207 M5
  RING/NEW BN8 ....129 G2
  RING/NEW BN8 ....275 J12
  RING/NEW BN8 ....276 H11
  UCK TN22 .... 76 D7
Lewes St BRIE/ROTT BN2 .... 5 G4
Lewin Cl LAN/SOMP BN15 ....118 E6
Lewis Av LW/ROSE BN22 .... 11 H3
Lewis Cl SALV BN13 ....116 A8
Lewis La ARUN BN18 ....146 A2
Lewis Rd CCH PO19 .... 7 J5
  EMRTH PO10 ....104 B2
  LAN/SOMP BN15 ....118 C5
  SELS PO20 ....301 K6
  STLEO TN38 .... 98 F2
Lewry Cl NEWHV BN9 .... 18 C4
Lexden Ct SEAF BN25 * 175 G1
Lexden Dr SEAF BN25 ....159 L8
Lexden Rd SEAF BN25 ....159 L8
Leybourne Cl BRIE/ROTT BN2 ....123 M4
  CRAWW RH11 .... 43 H8
Leybourne Gdns SLVH TN37 .... 99 H1
Leybourne Pl EGRIN RH19 .... 30 E6
Leybourne Rd BRIE/ROTT BN2 ....123 M3
Leyland Rd PEV BN24 ....165 J1
Leylands Pk BURH RH15 .... 75 G4
Leylands Rd BURH RH15 .... 74 F5
Ley Rd MSEA/BNM PO22 ....173 C1
The Leys HASM GU27 ....195 K8
  RCCH PO18 ....292 H2
Leyton Lea RHWH RH17 .... 72 B3
Liam Cl HAV PO9 ....103 H1
Library Gdns HAV PO9 ....102 F2
Library Pl WTHG BN11 .... 21 J6
Library Wy UCK TN22 .... 76 E5
Lichfield Cl WTHG BN11 * 20 A7
Lichfield Gdns BOGR PO21 ....171 G3
Lichfield Rd HAV PO9 ....103 H1
Lidsey Rd MSEA/BNM PO22 ....144 C3
Lidwells La CRBK TN17 ....189 Q8
Lifeboat Wy SELS PO20 ....301 L4
Lilac Cl BOR GU35 ....178 G7
  HAV PO9 ....103 K2
  SALV BN13 ....116 F5
  LW/ROSE BN22 ....163 J3
  MSEA/BNM PO22 ....145 K7
  SALV BN13 ....116 A8
Lillywhite Cl BURH RH15 .... 74 E4
Limbourne La PUL/STOR RH20 ....264 C2
Limbrick Cl FERR BN12 ....150 B2
Limbrick Cnr FERR BN12 ....150 B2
Limbrick La FERR BN12 ....150 B2
Limbrick Wy FERR BN12 ....150 A1
Limden Cl WADH TN5 ....214 E3
Lime Av HORS RH12 .... 15 L1
  SELS PO20 ....110 D4

Lime Cha PUL/STOR RH20 ....266 A11
Lime Cl CCH PO19 .... 7 H2
  CRAWE RH10 .... 29 G6
  CRAWW RH11 .... 27 H4
  RRTW TN3 .... 54 A6
  STLEO TN38 .... 98 F3
  UCK TN22 .... 76 F4
Lime Hill Rd RTW TN1 .... 37 M5
Limekiln Ct CRAWE RH10 .... 68 B6
Limekiln La PSF GU32 ....222 D10
  PSF GU32 ....256 F1
Lime Kiln Rd SWTR RH13 ....202 H5
Lime Pk HAIL BN27 * 279 Q12
Limes Av HORL RH6 .... 23 G8
Limes Av SALV BN13 ....298 H10
Limes La UCK TN22 .... 77 M1
The Limes ARUN BN18 ....145 L2
  BRIE/ROTT BN2 * 5 G1
  EAST BN21 * 10 B4
  EGRIN RH19 .... 30 F7
  SALV BN13 * 298 H10
  UCK TN22 * 77 K7
Lime Tree Av ANG/EP BN16 * 148 E3
Lime Tree Av SALV BN13 ....116 E8
  UCK TN22 .... 76 F5
Lime Wy HTHF TN21 ....244 E7
Limmard Wy MSEA/BNM PO22 ....173 H1
Limmer La MSEA/BNM PO22 .... 3 L4
Limney Rd BRIE/ROTT BN2 ....123 K6
Linacre Dr CRAN GU6 ....185 R3
  HORS RH12 ....185 R3
Lincett Av HASM GU27 ....150 E2
Lincett Dr SALV BN13 ....150 E2
Linch Rd LIPH GU30 ....194 D10
Lincoln Av BOGR PO21 ....171 H1
  PEAHV BN10 ....156 H6
Lincoln Av South PEAHV BN10 ....156 H6
Lincoln Cl CRAWE RH10 .... 43 K6
  EDN/EASTW BN20 ....176 D1
  STLEO TN38 .... 98 E5
Lincoln Cottages
  BRIE/ROTT BN2 * 5 H4
Lincoln Gn CCH PO19 ....107 L4
Lincoln Ri HORN PO8 ....288 C5
Lincoln Rd PTSD BN41 ....121 H6
  SALV BN13 ....150 E1
Lincoln St BRIE/ROTT BN2 * 5 H4
Lincoln Wy CROW TN6 ....210 H1
Linda Gv HORN PO8 ....288 C5
Lindale Pl PUL/STOR RH20 * 266 A12
Lind Cl WVILLE PO7 ....288 A2
Linden Av EGRIN RH19 .... 31 K7
Linden Cha UCK TN22 .... 76 E5
Linden Cl CRAWE RH10 .... 9 M9
  HORS RH12 .... 15 H1
  LW/ROSE BN22 ....163 K2
  RTWE/PEM TN2 .... 52 L7
Linden Ct UCK TN22 .... 76 E5
Linden Dr LISS GU33 ....192 C9
Linden Gdns RTWE/PEM TN2 .... 37 L8
  HAIL BN27 * 92 B2
  HWH RH16 .... 73 K3
Linden Pk RTWE/PEM TN2 * 37 L8
Linden Park Rd RTWE/PEM TN2 .. 37 L8
Linden Rd BEX TN40 ....137 K2
  BOGR PO21 .... 2 B5
  BOR GU35 ....179 Q4
  LHPTN BN17 ....147 H4
Lindens EMRTH PO10 ....104 A2
The Lindens BRIE/ROTT BN2 * 5 G1
  CRAWE RH10 .... 29 G6
  HORN PO8 ....288 C4
Linden Wy HAV PO9 * 103 G3
Lindfield PTSD BN41 ....120 F7
Lindfield Av SEAF BN25 ....175 J3
Lindfield Cl BRIE/ROTT BN2 ....156 A3
Lindfield Dr HAIL BN27 .... 92 A6
Lindfield Rd LW/ROSE BN22 ....163 J3
  RHWH RH17 ....206 F3
Linden Gv HAIL BN27 .... 92 B2
Lindford Cha BOR GU35 ....179 L4
Lindford Rd BOR GU35 ....179 L4
Lindford Wey BOR GU35 ....179 L4
Lindgren Wk CRAWW RH11 * 43 G8
Lindon Cl EDN/EASTW BN20 ....302 H4
Lindsay Cl EDN/EASTW BN20 ....176 D3
Lindsey Ct MSEA/BNM PO22 .... 3 M1
Lindum Rd SALV BN13 ....116 A8
Lindum Wy SALV BN13 ....116 A8
Lineside Wy LHPTN BN17 ....147 M3
Linfield Copse PUL/STOR RH20 ....266 C1
The Linfields PUL/STOR RH20 * 266 C2
Linford Ct HAV PO9 ....288 E10
Ling Crs BOR GU35 ....179 Q3
Lingfield Cl SALV BN13 ....116 E3
Lingfield Dr CRAWE RH10 .... 45 J7
Lingfield Rd EGRIN RH19 .... 31 J4
Lingfield Wy SELS PO20 ....301 M6

  HORL RH6 .... 28 B2
The Linkway BRI BN1 ....123 G3
  WTHG BN11 * 20 H4
Linley Cl BEX TN40 ....137 J1
  HAS TN34 .... 99 M2
Linley Dr HAS TN34 .... 99 M2
Linnet Cl CRAWW RH11 .... 59 G5
  EPSF GU31 ....223 R7
  LGNY BN23 ....164 B3
  LHPTN BN17 ....147 H1
Linnet Gn UCK TN22 * 76 F7
Linnett Cl CRAWE RH10 * 46 B3
Linsted La BOR GU35 ....179 L2
Linthouse Cl PEAHV BN10 ....157 J3
Linton Crs HAS TN34 .... 12 E6
Linton Rd HAS TN34 .... 12 E6
  HOVE BN3 ....121 L5
Lintott Gdns SWTR RH13 .... 15 H3
Lionel Av MSEA/BNM PO22 ....145 H7
Lionel Rd BEX TN40 ....137 K2
Lion Hl PEV BN24 ....133 C8
Lion House Pk HAIL BN27 * 92 D7
Lion La CRAWE RH10 .... 45 M5
  EAST BN21 .... 11 H6
  GSHT GU26 ....181 J8
Lion Md HASM GU27 ....181 J11
Lion Rd BOGR PO21 ....170 F5
Lions Cl BRIE/ROTT BN2 * 123 K8
Lions Fld BOR GU35 ....178 A5
Lions Pl PSF GU32 ....174 F3
Lion St RYE TN31 ....252 H8
Liphook Cl BRI BN1 ....123 H4
Liphook Rd BOR GU35 ....178 F9
  BOR GU35 ....179 J4
  HASM GU27 ....180 H11
  HASM GU27 ....194 D1
Lipscombe Rd RTWE/PEM TN2 .. 38 C3
Liptraps La RTWE/PEM TN2 .... 38 C2
Lisher Rd LAN/SOMP BN15 ....118 E6
Lisle Wy EMRTH PO10 ....103 M2
Lismore Crs CRAWW RH11 .... 8 A9
Lismore Rd EAST BN21 .... 10 F7
Lister Av EGRIN RH19 .... 47 K3
Lister Rd LGNY BN23 ....163 M4
Listers RHWH RH17 ....204 A3
Lith Av HORN PO8 ....288 D1
Litcote Ct MIDH GU29 ....256 D12
Litle Hyden La HORN PO8 ....256 H6
Litlington Rd SEAF BN25 ....175 M1
Litten Ter CCH PO19 .... 6 F7
Little Ashfield MIDH GU29 ....226 H9
Little Babbsham BOGR PO21 ....171 K3
Little Barn Pl LISS GU33 ....192 E9
Little Bentswood HWH RH16 ... 73 J4
Little Black Hl HWH RH16 .... 73 L2
Little Boultons SELS PO20 ....141 L6
Little Breach CCH PO19 .... 6 B7
Little Bridges Cl SWTR RH13 ....201 Q12
Little Cl SWTR RH13 ....233 G2
Little Common Rd BEXW TN39 ... 96 D8
Little Comptons SWTR RH13 .. 15 K8
Little Copse Rd HPPT/KEY BN6 ....271 M5
Littlecote PETW GU28 ....229 L10
Little Court Cl MIDH GU29 ....226 G9
Little Crabtree CRAWW RH11 ..... 8 D2
Little Crs BRIE/ROTT BN2 ....155 M4
Little Dipper's PUL/STOR RH20 ....265 K3
Little Dr FERR BN12 ....149 K4
Little Dro STEY/UB WN44 .... 78 C4
Little East St BIL RH14 ....200 A12
  BRI BN1 * 4 E4
  LEWES BN7 .... 17 G5
Littlefield Cl SELS PO20 ....301 L6
Littlefield Rd CCH PO19 .... 7 H6
Little Finches SWTR RH13 ....234 F10
Little Footway RRTW TN3 .... 36 C6
Little Gables SALV BN13 ....116 E7
Little Grebe HORS RH12 .... 56 B4
Littlegreen Av HAV PO9 ....103 J1
Littlehampton Rd FERR BN12 ....149 H2
  SALV BN13 ....116 E7
Little Hatch HORS RH12 .... 56 E4
Little Haven La HORS RH12 .... 15 K1
Littleheath Rd ARUN BN18 ....110 D2
Little High St BOGR PO21 * 2 B9
  SHOR BN43 ....119 K6
  WTHG BN11 .... 21 H4
Little Hl PUL/STOR RH20 ....265 J3
Little Hyden La HORN PO8 ....256 C6
Little King St EGRIN RH19 .... 31 K8
Little Ledgers RHWH RH17 .... 72 C3
Little London CCH PO19 .... 6 F7
Little London Rd HTHF TN21 ....278 C1
Little Mallett RRTW TN3 .... 36 D5
Little Md FERR BN12 * 150 B3
  RING/NEW BN8 ....273 R10
Little Mount Sion RTW TN1 .... 37 M7
Little Paddock CROW TN6 .... 67 K8
  RING/NEW BN8 ....275 K11
Little Paddocks Wy
  FERR BN12 ....149 L2
Little Pk WADH TN5 .... 71 K4
Littlepark Av HAV PO9 ....102 C2
Little Pembrokes WTHG BN11 .. 20 B8
Little Preston St BRI BN1 * 4 B7
Little Ridge Av SLVH TN37 ....283 Q11
Littlestone Rd SALV BN13 ....116 D7
Little Sunnyside CROW TN6 .... 67 L6
Littleton Gv HAV PO9 ....103 G1
Little Trogers La MAYF TN20 ....212 B1
Little Twitten BEXW TN39 ....136 B2
Little Western St BRI BN1 ....122 C8
Littlewood La CCH PO19 ....242 D11
Littleworth Cl BRIE/ROTT BN2 ....124 D4
Littleworth Cottages
  RRTW TN3 * 37 G1
Littleworth La SWTR RH13 ....234 F5
Liverpool Gdns WTHG BN11 .... 21 H5
Liverpool Rd WTHG BN11 .... 21 H5
Liverpool Ter WTHG BN11 .... 21 H4
Livesay Crs SALV BN13 ....21 H1
Livingstone Rd BURH RH15 .... 74 E6
  CRAWE RH10 ....43 G8
  HOVE BN3 ....122 A5
  SWTR RH13 ....15 L1
Livingstone St BRIE/ROTT BN2 * 5 G4
Lizard Head CRAWW RH11 ....147 M3
Lloyd Cl HOVE BN3 ....122 B5
Lloyd Goring Cl ANG/EP BN16 ....114 E7
Lloyd Rd HOVE BN3 ....122 C5
Lloyds Bank Chambers
  SEAF BN25 * 174 E2
Lloyds Ct CRAWE RH10 * 27 K8
Lloyds Gn TENT TN30 ....220 C5

Loats La *BOGR* PO21 .... 143 L6
Lobster La *SELS* PO20 .... 300 H5
Lobs Wood La
  PUL/STOR RH20 .... 266 A11
Lockerley Rd *HAV* PO9 .... 103 H2
Locke Rd *LIPH* GU30 .... 194 A1
Lockgate Rd *SELS* PO20 .... 169 K2
Lockitt Wy *LEWES* BN7 .... 85 K8
Lock La *SELS* PO20 .... 140 E7
Locksash Cl *SELS* PO20 .... 167 G3
Locksash La *RCCH* PO18 .... 290 B1
Locks Crs *PTSD* BN41 .... 121 G5
Locksheath Cl *HAV* PO9 .... 288 E11
Locks Hl *PTSD* BN41 .... 121 G4
Lockwood Cl *BRIE/ROTT* BN2 .... 124 D6
  HORS RH12 .... 56 F4
Lockwood Ct *CRAWE* RH10 * 43 L1
Lockwood Crs
  BRIE/ROTT BN2 .... 124 D6
Loddon Cl *SALV* BN13 .... 116 D5
Loder Gdns *SALV* BN13 .... 117 H8
Loder Pl *BRI* BN1 .... 122 E3
Loder Rd *BRI* BN1 .... 122 E3
Lodge Av *LW/ROSE* BN22 .... 163 H3
Lodgebury Cl *EMRTH* PO10 .... 104 F5
Lodge Cl *CRAWW* RH11 .... 8 C4
  EGRIN RH19 .... 31 H5
  LEWES BN7 .... 16 B7
  MSEA/BNM PO22 .... 145 M8
  PTSD BN41 .... 120 E3
  SHOR BN43 .... 119 K4
Lodge Gn *PETW* GU28 * 263 K5
Lodge Hill La *HPPT/KEY* BN6 . ... 271 G8
Lodgelands *RHWH* RH17 .... 206 D3
Lodge La *HAV* PO9 .... 290 A3
  HPPT/KEY BN6 .... 271 Q8
  RHWH RH17 .... 236 C6
Lodge Rd *HAV* PO9 .... 102 C4
  RHAS TN35 .... 100 B8
Lodsworth *BRIE/ROTT* BN2 .... 123 L6
  HORN PO8 .... 256 E9
Lodsworth Rd *BOGR* PO21 .... 171 G2
Lomas La *HAWK* TN18 .... 218 D4
Lombard St *PETW* GU28 .... 229 L9
Lombardy Ri *WVILLE* PO7 .... 288 A12
Lomond Av *BRI* BN1 .... 82 F6
London La *RHWH* RH17 .... 72 C3
London Rd *ARUN* BN18 .... 110 F2
  ARUN BN18 .... 112 F2
  ARUN BN18 .... 295 R11
  BAT TN33 .... 248 D11
  BEX TN40 .... 97 G8
  BOGR PO21 .... 2 E7
  BRI BN1 .... 4 F2
  BRI BN1 .... 82 D6
  BUR/ETCH TN19 .... 216 D6
  BURH RH15 .... 74 E6
  CRAWE RH10 .... 8 F1
  CRAWE RH10 .... 27 K6
  CROW TN6 .... 67 K5
  EGRIN RH19 .... 31 K8
  EPSF GU31 .... 223 M4
  FROW RH18 .... 48 D5
  HAIL BN27 .... 91 M4
  HFD BN5 .... 269 K2
  HORL RH6 .... 27 M1
  HORN PO8 .... 256 E11
  HORN PO8 .... 288 B1
  HORS RH12 .... 14 C5
  HPPT/KEY BN6 .... 271 J4
  LIPH GU30 .... 193 R1
  PUL/STOR RH20 .... 264 C8
  PUL/STOR RH20 .... 265 J3
  PUL/STOR RH20 .... 298 H2
  RBTBR TN32 .... 248 E7
  RHWH RH17 .... 72 E7
  RHWH RH17 .... 207 R5
  RING/NEW BN8 .... 276 H4
  RTW TN1 .... 37 M6
  SLVH TN37 .... 12 A4
  UCK TN22 .... 76 E1
  WADH TN5 .... 191 Q10
London St *WTHG* BN11 * 20 E4
London Ter *BRI* BN1 * 4 F3
Long Acre *CRAWE* RH10 .... 45 M1
Long Acre Cl *EAST* BN21 .... 163 J8
Longacre Cl *LISS* GU33 .... 192 D9
  SLVH TN37 .... 283 R11
Longacre Crs *RHWH* RH17 .... 72 C11
Longacre La *SELS* PO20 .... 301 K7
Long Av *BEX* TN40 .... 97 M7
Long Beach Ms *LGNY* BN23 .... 164 F4
Long Beach Vw *LGNY* BN23 .... 165 G4
Longbridge Rd *HORL* RH6 .... 22 E8
Longbridge Wk *HORL* RH6 .... 22 E8
Longbridge Wy *HORL* RH6 .... 22 E8
Longbrook *MSEA/BNM* PO22 .... 3 J6
Longbury *UCK* TN22 .... 76 E7
Longchamp Cl *HORL* RH6 .... 23 H6
Long Copse La *EMRTH* PO10 .... 104 B1
Long Cross Hl *BOR* GU35 .... 179 M4
Longdene Rd *HASM* GU27 .... 181 J11
Long Down *EPSF* GU31 .... 223 N5
Longfellow Rd *WTHG* BN11 .... 20 D4
Longfield *EMRTH* PO10 .... 103 M1
  HORS RH12 .... 201 H5
  RTWE/PEM TN2 .... 38 D1
Longford Rd *BOGR* PO21 .... 2 D6
Long Furlong *SALV* BN13 .... 115 K1
Longfurlong La *SALV* BN13 .... 115 K1
Long Hl *SWTR* RH13 .... 203 L9
Longhill Cl *BRIE/ROTT* BN2 .... 155 L2
Longhill Rd *BRIE/ROTT* BN2 .... 155 L2
Longhurst *BURH* RH15 .... 75 J7
Longhurst La *CRAWW* RH11 .... 42 F8
Longland Av *PUL/STOR* RH20 .... 265 R11
Longland Rd
  EDN/EASTW BN20 .... 176 C1
Longlands *SALV* BN13 .... 117 J5
Longlands Gld *SALV* BN13 .... 117 J5
Longlands Rd *EMRTH* PO10 .... 104 E5
Longlands *SELS* PO20 .... 167 L7
Longlands Spinney
  SALV BN13 .... 117 J6
Long La *ARUN* BN18 .... 295 P12
  BAT TN33 .... 249 M12
  RCCH PO18 .... 258 H10
Long Md *ARUN* BN18 .... 111 J4
Longmead *LISS* GU33 .... 192 C10
Long Meadow *SALV* BN13 .... 116 C1
Longmead Gdns *HAV* PO9 .... 103 G6
Longmeadow Vls *HORL* RH6 *.. .... 26 D4

Long Meads *RRTW* TN3 .... 37 G6
Longmere Rd *CRAWE* RH10 .... 43 J1
Longmoor Dr *LIPH* GU30 .... 193 L1
Longmoor Rd *LIPH* GU30 .... 193 K1
  LISS GU33 .... 192 D3
Long Park Cnr *HPPT/KEY* BN6 .... 272 A7
Longport *BNM* PO22
  MSEA/BNM PO22 .... 173 G1
Longridge Av *BRIE/ROTT* BN2 .... 156 B5
Long Rd *PSF* GU32 .... 223 P4
Longships *LHPTN* BN17 .... 147 M3
Long Slip *RRTW* TN3 .... 36 F6
Longstock Rd *HAV* PO9 .... 289 J11
Longstone Rd *EAST* BN21 .... 10 F6
Longview *HTHF* TN21 .... 244 D8
Longview Wy *RTWE/PEM* TN2 .... 38 C1
Longwood Av *HORN* PO8 .... 288 A6
Longwood Vw *CRAWE* RH10 .... 9 L9
Lonsdale Gdns *RTW* TN1 * 37 H6
The Lookout *PEAHV* BN10 .... 157 H2
The Loop *MSEA/BNM* PO22 .... 173 H1
Loose La *LAN/SOMP* BN15 .... 117 M8
Loppets Rd *CRAWE* RH10 .... 9 J8
Lordine La *RBTBR* TN32 .... 249 Q1
Lordings La *PUL/STOR* RH20 .... 266 A6
Lordings Rd *BIL* RH14 .... 231 N4
Lordslaine Cl
  EDN/EASTW BN20 .... 176 C5
Lords La *RHAS* TN35 .... 100 C3
The Lords *SEAF* BN25 .... 159 K7
Lordswell La *CROW* TN6 .... 210 F1
Loriners *CRAWE* RH10 .... 8 E3
Lorna Rd *HOVE* BN3 .... 122 C6
Lorne Rd *BRI* BN1 .... 4 F1
Lorraine Rd *NEWHV* BN9 .... 19 G4
Lossenham La *HAWK* TN18 .... 218 G3
Lottbridge Dro
  LW/ROSE BN22 .... 163 L4
Lotts La *LAN/SOMP* BN15 .... 118 B7
Loudoun Rd *LHPTN* BN17 .... 147 H4
Louisburg Rd *BOR* GU35 .... 178 G3
Lovage Wy *HORN* PO8 .... 256 D12
Lovat Md *STLEO* TN38 .... 98 D7
Lovedean La *HORN* PO8 .... 256 B11
  HORN PO8 .... 288 B4
Love La *EPSF* GU31 .... 223 N6
  MAYF TN20 .... 212 C12
  RYE TN31 .... 252 C7
Love Lane Ter *MAYF* TN20 * 212 C6
Loveletts *CRAWW* RH11 .... 42 F4
Lovells Cl *BOGR* PO21 .... 171 G3
Lovers La *CRBK* TN17 .... 189 F3
Lover's Wk *BRI* BN1 .... 122 E5
Lovers Walk Cottages
  BRI BN1 * 122 D5
Lovett Ct *FERR* BN12 * 150 B1
Loveys Rd *ARUN* BN18 .... 145 L3
Lowdells Cl *EGRIN* RH19 .... 31 H5
Lowdells Dr *EGRIN* RH19 .... 31 J5
Lowdells La *EGRIN* RH19 .... 31 H6
Lowe Cl *CRAWW* RH11 .... 59 G1
Lower Barn Cl *HORS* RH12 .... 56 F4
Lower Beach Rd
  SHOR BN43 .... 119 L7
Lower Bere Wd *WVILLE* PO7 .... 288 A10
Lower Bevendean Av
  BRIE/ROTT BN2 .... 123 K4
Lower Bognor Rd *BOGR* PO21 .... 171 K1
  SELS PO20 .... 143 G7
Lower Chalvington Pl
  BRIE/ROTT BN2 .... 123 K8
Lower Church Rd *BURH* RH15 .... 74 F6
Lower Dene *EGRIN* RH19 .... 31 M8
Lower Dr *SEAF* BN25 .... 159 L8
  STHW BN42 .... 120 D4
Lower Faircox *HFD* BN5 .... 269 J4
Lower Forecourt *HORL* RH6 .... 28 A2
Lower Glen Rd *SLVH* TN37 .... 99 G1
Lower Green Rd *RRTW* TN3 .... 37 H3
  RTWE/PEM TN2 .... 39 J3
Lower Grove Rd *HAV* PO9 .... 103 H5
Lower Hanger *HASM* GU27 .... 180 F11
Lower Hazelhurst *WADH* TN5 .... 190 F9
Lower Heyshott *EPSF* GU31 .... 223 P5
Lower High St *WADH* TN5 .... 71 M6
Lower Hone La *RCCH* PO18 .... 139 M4
Lower Lake *BAT* TN33 .... 282 F5
Lower Market St *HOVE* BN3 .... 122 C8
Lower Md *EPSF* GU31 .... 223 Q6
  LISS GU33 .... 192 C5
Lower Mere *EGRIN* RH19 .... 31 L7
Lower Park Rd *HAS* TN34 .... 12 E3
Lower Platts *WADH* TN5 .... 191 K12
Lower Rd *EAST* BN21 .... 176 D1
  HAIL BN27 .... 93 J2
  HASM GU27 .... 181 Q7
  HAV PO9 .... 102 D4
  PTSD BN41 .... 121 G2
  TENT TN30 .... 221 J4
Lower Rock Gdns
  BRIE/ROTT BN2 .... 5 L8
Lower Saxonbury *CROW* TN6 .... 67 L7
Lower South Rd *SLVH* TN37 .... 12 A4
Lower Station Rd *BIL* RH14 .... 232 A3
  HFD BN5 .... 269 J5
  RING/NEW BN8 .... 239 P7
Lower Stoneham
  RING/NEW BN8 .... 86 D1
Lower St *BAT* TN33 .... 96 A1
  EDN/EASTW BN20 .... 302 H5
  HASM GU27 .... 181 M11
  PUL/STOR RH20 .... 264 A4
  PUL/STOR RH20 .... 265 J3
Lower Tanbridge Wy
  HORS RH12 .... 14 B6
Lower Village *HWH* RH16 .... 72 W4
Lower Waites La *RHAS* TN35 .... 101 L1
Lower Wardown *EPSF* GU31 .... 223 Q5
Lower Wick St *POLE* BN26 .... 89 M8
Loweswater Gdns *BOR* GU35 .... 178 G4
Lowfield Heath Rd *HORL* RH6 .... 26 B3
Lowfield Wy *HORL* RH6 .... 27 K4
  SWTR RH13 .... 200 D3
Lowlands Rd *BURH* RH15 .... 75 J4
The Lowlands *HAIL* BN27 .... 91 M4
Lowther Cl *LGNY* BN23 .... 164 C2
Lowther Rd *BRI* BN1 .... 122 F3
  SALV BN13 .... 116 E6
Loxfield Cl *MAYF* TN20 .... 212 D7
Loxley Gdns *SALV* BN13 * 20 E2
Loxwood *ANG/EP* BN16 .... 149 G2
Loxwood Av *SALV* BN13 .... 117 G8
Loxwood Cl *BEXW* TN39 .... 96 B8
  LW/ROSE BN22 .... 163 H5

Loxwood Farm Pl *BIL* RH14 .... 198 G1
Loxwood Rd *BIL* RH14 .... 184 G10
  BIL RH14 .... 198 B3
  BIL RH14 .... 199 J1
  CRAN GU6 .... 184 C5
  HORN PO8 .... 288 A3
Loxwood Wk *CRAWW* RH11 .... 42 N2
Luard Ct *HAV* PO9 .... 103 J4
Lucas Cl *EGRIN* RH19 * 31 L8
Lucas Fld *HASM* GU27 .... 180 H11
Lucas Gra *HWH* RH16 .... 73 G4
Lucas Rd *HORS* RH12 .... 187 P9
Lucas Shadwell Wy
  RYE TN31 .... 253 L11
Lucastes Av *HWH* RH16 .... 72 F3
Lucastes La *HWH* RH16 .... 72 F4
Lucastes Rd *HWH* RH16 .... 72 F4
Lucastes Rd *HWH* RH16 .... 72 F4
Lucerne Cl *PTSD* BN41 .... 121 G4
Lucerne Ct *BOGR* PO21 .... 171 K3
Lucerne Dr *CRAWE* RH10 .... 44 C5
Lucinda Wy *SEAF* BN25 .... 159 L8
Lucking La *MSEA/BNM* PO22 .... 145 L8
Lucksfield Wy *ANG/EP* BN16 .... 114 F8
Lucraft Rd *BRIE/ROTT* BN2 .... 83 L8
Ludley Hl *RYE* TN31 .... 251 K7
Ludlow Cl *BOGR* PO21 .... 171 K3
Ludlow Ri *BRIE/ROTT* BN2 .... 123 M4
Ludpit La *BUR/ETCH* TN19 .... 215 P11
Ludshott Gv *BOR* GU35 .... 179 Q4
Luffs Meadow *PETW* GU28 .... 196 F6
Luggs *BIL* RH14 .... 232 A1
Lulham Cl *PEAHV* BN10 .... 157 G3
Lucking La *MSEA/BNM* PO22 .... 145 L8
Lullington Av *HOVE* BN3 .... 121 L5
Lullington Cl *BEX* TN40 .... 97 M7
  EAST BN21 .... 163 H6
  SEAF BN25 .... 175 H3
Lullington Gdns *SLVH* TN37 .... 283 R12
Lullington Rd *POLE* BN26 .... 160 F2
Lulworth Cl *CRAWW* RH11 .... 8 A9
Lumley Rd *EMRTH* PO10 .... 104 A8
  HORL RH6 .... 22 F6
Lunce's Hl *HWH* RH16 .... 75 L1
Lundy Cl *LHPTN* BN17 .... 147 M5
Lundy Wk *HAIL* BN27 .... 91 L3
Lupin Cl *LHPTN* BN17 .... 147 M2
Lurgashall *BURH* RH15 .... 75 H8
Lurkins Ri *CRBK* TN17 .... 189 Q10
Lushington Cl *EAST* BN21 .... 10 E7
Lushington La *EAST* BN21 .... 10 E7
Lushington Rd *EAST* BN21 .... 10 E7
Lustrells Cl *BRIE/ROTT* BN2 .... 156 A3
Lustrells Crs *BRIE/ROTT* BN2 .... 156 A3
Lustrells Rd *BRIE/ROTT* BN2 .... 155 M3
Lustrells V *BRIE/ROTT* BN2 .... 156 A3
Lutener Rd *MIDH* GU29 .... 227 J8
Luther St *BRIE/ROTT* BN2 * 5 J8
The Luth *BIL* RH14 .... 199 J12
  BIL RH14 .... 230 H1
Lutman St *EMRTH* PO10 .... 103 M1
Luton Cl *EAST* BN21 .... 163 H7
Lutyens Cl *CRAWW* RH11 .... 42 D5
Luxford Cl *HWH* RH16 .... 56 E4
Luxford La *CROW* TN6 .... 210 H1
Luxford Rd *CROW* TN6 .... 68 A8
  HWH RH16 .... 73 L2
  RYE TN31 .... 252 C2
Luxfords La *EGRIN* RH19 .... 48 A4
Lybburn Cl *HAV* PO9 .... 103 H4
Lychgate Dr *HORN* PO8 .... 288 C2
Lychgates Cl *BEX* TN40 .... 97 J8
The Lychgates *ARUN* BN18 .... 145 L1
Lydd Cl *LGNY* BN23 .... 164 C3
Lydd Rd *RYE* TN31 .... 253 R11
Lye La *RCCH* PO18 .... 106 E1
Lymbourn Rd *HAV* PO9 .... 103 H4
Lymden La *WADH* TN5 .... 214 F2
Lyminster Av *BRI* BN1 .... 82 F8
Lyminster Rd *ARUN* BN18 .... 113 J4
  LHPTN BN17 .... 113 J8
Lynchborough Rd
  LIPH GU30 .... 179 L9
Lynch Down *RCCH* PO18 .... 290 H11
Lynchet Cl *BRI* BN1 .... 123 H3
Lynchet Down *BRI* BN1 .... 123 H3
Lynchets Crs *HOVE* BN3 .... 121 J2
The Lynchets *LEWES* BN7 .... 17 J2
The Lynchette *SHOR* BN43 .... 119 L4
Lynchet Wk *BRI* BN1 .... 123 H3
Lynchmere Av
  LAN/SOMP BN15 .... 118 C5
Lyndhurst Av *HAS* TN34 .... 99 M1
Lyndhurst Cl *CRAWW* RH11 .... 8 B6
Lyndhurst Cnr *HOVE* BN3 * 122 C6
Lyndhurst Cottages
  CROW TN6 * 210 G1
Lyndhurst Farm Cl
  EGRIN RH19 .... 30 C5
Lyndhurst Rd *CCH* PO19 .... 7 G6
  HOVE BN3 .... 122 C6
  WTHG BN11 .... 21 J5
Lyndum Cl *PSF* GU32 .... 223 N6
Lyndum Pl *BOR* GU35 .... 179 J4
Lyne Pl *HORN* PO8 .... 288 C3
Lynholm Rd *POLE* BN26 .... 132 A7
Lyn Rd *SALV* BN13 .... 116 B7
Lynton Cl *EGRIN* RH19 .... 31 M7
  HPPT/KEY BN6 .... 271 J4
Lynton Park Av *EGRIN* RH19 .... 31 L7
Lynton Rd *BOR* GU35 .... 178 G6
  PSF GU32 .... 223 M5
Lyntons *PUL/STOR* RH20 .... 264 H3
Lynton St *BRIE/ROTT* BN2 * 5 K3
Lynwick St *HORS* RH12 .... 186 A8
Lynwood Cl *BOR* GU35 .... 179 K4
Lynwood Rd *BRIE/ROTT* BN2 .... 156 B5
  SLVH TN37 .... 284 A12
Lynwood St *HORS* RH12 .... 14 C3
Lyon Cl *CRAWE* RH10 .... 122 C6
  HOVE BN3 .... 122 C6
Lyons Cl *SWTR* RH13 .... 200 H2
Lyon St *BOGR* PO21 .... 2 D6
Lyon St West *BOGR* PO21 .... 2 D6
Lyons Wy *SALV* BN13 .... 117 K5
Lyoth La *HWH* RH16 .... 73 J4
Lysander Wy *SELS* PO20 .... 109 L4
  WVILLE PO7 .... 288 B9
Lyss Ct *LISS* GU33 .... 192 C5
Lytham Cl *STLEO* TN38 .... 98 E3
Lythe La *PSF* GU32 .... 222 H4
Lytton Dr *CRAWE* RH10 .... 44 C2

M

Maberley Rd *BEXW* TN39 .... 97 H7
Mackerelclose *SELS* PO20 .... 300 H5
Mackerel Rd *RYE* TN31 .... 219 Q12
Mackerel's Rocks
  RING/NEW BN8 .... 240 E10
Mackie Av *BRI* BN1 .... 82 E7
  HPPT/KEY BN6 .... 271 J7
Macklin Rd *MSEA/BNM* PO22 .... 3 G4
Macleod Rd *SWTR* RH13 .... 15 J7
Macmichaels Wy
  BUR/ETCH TN19 .... 216 B6
Macmillan Dr *EAST* BN21 .... 163 H8
Macquarie Quay *LGNY* BN23 .... 164 F5
Maddox Dr *CRAWE* RH10 .... 44 C3
Madehurst Cl *ANG/EP* BN16 .... 148 A3
  BRIE/ROTT BN2 .... 5 M7
Madehurst Ct *CRAWW* RH11 .... 42 E4
Madehurst Wy *LHPTN* BN17 .... 147 J3
Madeira Av *HORS* RH12 .... 14 D5
  MSEA/BNM PO22 .... 3 G4
  WTHG BN11 .... 21 K5
Madeira Dr *BRIE/ROTT* BN2 .... 4 F8
  HAS TN34 .... 99 L6
Madeira Pde *MSEA/BNM* PO22 * 3 G3
Madeira Pk *RTWE/PEM* TN2 .... 37 H7
Madeira Wy *LGNY* BN23 .... 164 G4
Madeline Rd *EPSF* GU31 .... 223 N5
Madgwick La *RCCH* PO18 .... 108 C4
Madgdalen Cl *LGNY* BN23 .... 164 B2
Magdalene Ct *CRAWE* RH10 .... 28 B8
Magdalen Rd *BRIE/ROTT* BN2 .... 123 K8
  SLVH TN37 .... 12 C7
Magdalen Rw *PSF* GU32 .... 223 M6
Magellan Ter *CRAWE* RH10 * 27 K7
Magellan Wy *LGNY* BN23 .... 164 F7
Magnolia Cl *HTHF* TN21 .... 244 E8
  SALV BN13 .... 116 A8
Magnolia Ct *HORL* RH6 * 22 F6
Magnolia Dr *LW/ROSE* BN22 .... 163 J3
Magnolia Wy *HORN* PO8 .... 288 A5
Magpie Cl *BEXW* TN39 .... 96 B7
  BOR GU35 .... 178 H7
  STLEO TN38 .... 98 D5
Magpie La *SELS* PO20 .... 301 L11
  SWTR RH13 .... 202 E3
Magpie Rd *HORN* PO8 .... 289 K4
  LGNY BN23 .... 164 B2
Magreed La *HTHF* TN21 .... 244 H5
Maidenbower Dr *CRAWE* RH10 .... 44 C5
Maidenbower La *CRAWE* RH10 .... 44 C5
Maidenbower Pl *CRAWE* RH10 .... 44 C6
Maiden La *CRAWW* RH11 .... 43 H1
Maidment Cl *HFD* BN5 .... 269 L3
Maidstone Rd *RTWE/PEM* TN2 .... 39 J1
Main Dr *MSEA/BNM* PO22 .... 145 L8
Main Rd *ARUN* BN18 .... 145 L2
  EMRTH PO10 .... 104 D5
  RCCH PO18 .... 105 G6
  RCCH PO18 .... 293 M5
  RHAS TN35 .... 100 D1
  SELS PO20 .... 168 D1
  WSEA TN36 .... 285 M4
Mainstone Rd *HOVE* BN3 .... 121 L6
  RYE TN31 .... 252 A5
Main St *RYE* TN31 .... 252 C2
Maisemore Gdns *EMRTH* PO10 .... 103 L4
Maitland Cl *HAS* TN34 .... 284 B11
Maizecroft *HORL* RH6 .... 23 H5
Major Cl *LGNY* BN23 .... 164 C3
Major's Rd *CRAWE* RH10 .... 45 J5
Major's Yd
  SBCH/RUST TN4 .... 37 L6
Malcolm Cl *FERR* BN12 .... 149 K4
Malcolm Gdns *HORL* RH6 .... 22 E7
  POLE BN26 .... 131 M6
Malcolm Rd *SELS* PO20 .... 109 H4
Maldon Rd *BRI* BN1 .... 122 C3
Malham Cl *CRAWE* RH10 .... 44 B6
Malines Av *PEAHV* BN10 .... 157 G6
Malines Av South *PEAHV* BN10 .... 156 F6
Malin Rd *LHPTN* BN17 .... 147 H5
Mallard Cl *HASM* GU27 .... 180 H11
  HORL RH6 .... 22 F4
  HORS RH12 .... 56 F4
  LW/ROSE BN22 .... 163 L4
Mallard Crs *BOGR* PO21 .... 170 E6
Mallard Dr *UCK* TN22 .... 76 F7
Mallard Pl *EGRIN* RH19 .... 47 L1
Mallard Rd *HAV* PO9 .... 289 J8
Mallards La *SELS* PO20 .... 300 H4
The Mallards *HAV* PO9 .... 103 G6
Mallard Wy *EMRTH* PO10 .... 104 D1
  HFD BN5 .... 269 K3
Mallett Cl *SEAF* BN25 .... 174 E3
Malling Cl *LEWES* BN7 .... 17 H2
Malling Down *LEWES* BN7 .... 17 J2
Malling Hl *LEWES* BN7 .... 17 J2
The Mallings *LEWES* BN7 .... 17 J2
Malling St *LEWES* BN7 .... 17 J5
Mallion's La *RHWH* RH17 .... 204 F1
Mallon Dene *ANG/EP* BN16 .... 148 B5
Mallory Rd *HOVE* BN3 .... 122 B3
Mallow Cl *BOR* GU35 .... 179 K4
  HORS RH12 .... 56 D3
  WVILLE PO7 .... 288 A11
Malmsbury Cl *BOR* GU35 .... 178 G4
Malthouse Cl *ARUN* BN18 .... 112 F3
  LAN/SOMP BN15 .... 118 A4
Malthouse La *BRIE/ROTT* BN2 * 5 G4
  BURH RH15 .... 74 B6
  HPPT/KEY BN6 .... 271 J4
  RCCH PO18 .... 106 A2
  RYE TN31 .... 252 A3
Malthouse Mdw *LIPH* GU30 .... 193 R1
Malthouse Pas *LHPTN* BN17 .... 147 J3
Malthouse Rd *CRAWE* RH10 .... 8 C1
  SELS PO20 .... 301 L6
The Malthouse *LEWES* BN7 * 16 E1
Malthouse Wy *LEWES* BN7 * 273 R11
The Maltings *BIL* RH14 * 200 A12
  BURH RH15 .... 74 C5
  CCH PO19 .... 6 C1
  EPSF GU31 .... 223 N6
  LIPH GU30 .... 194 A1
Malton Wy *RTWE/PEM* TN2 .... 38 D2
Maltravers Dr *LHPTN* BN17 .... 147 K5
Maltravers St *ARUN* BN18 .... 113 G2
Malvern Cl *WTHG* BN11 .... 152 M1
Malvern Ms *EMRTH* PO10 .... 104 A4

Malvern Rd *CRAWW* RH11 .... 8 D7
  LISS GU33 .... 192 E11
Malvern St *HOVE* BN3 .... 122 A6
Malvern Wy *BOGR* PO21 .... 171 G3
  HAS TN34 .... 100 A2
Malwood Cl *HAV* PO9 .... 288 H11
Manaton Cl *HAV* PO9 .... 73 J5
Manchester Rd *BAT* TN33 .... 281 M11
Manchester St *BRIE/ROTT* BN2 .... 4 F8
Manet Sq *MSEA/BNM* PO22 .... 144 E4
Manhood La *SELS* PO20 .... 169 L5
Manica Cl *BOR* GU35 .... 178 G6
Manifold Rd *LW/ROSE* BN22 .... 11 G4
Manitoba Wy *SALV* BN13 .... 116 B7
Manley's Hl *PUL/STOR* RH20 .... 266 A12
Mann Cl *CRAWW* RH11 .... 59 J5
Manning Cl *EGRIN* RH19 .... 31 J7
Manning Rd *LHPTN* BN17 .... 147 H3
Mannings Cl *CRAWE* RH10 .... 28 C8
Mann St *HAS* TN34 .... 13 G6
Manor Av *HPPT/KEY* BN6 .... 271 P4
Manor Cl *ANG/EP* BN16 .... 148 E4
  BRIE/ROTT BN2 .... 123 K8
  BURH RH15 .... 75 J5
  CCH PO19 .... 141 L2
  EDN/EASTW BN20 .... 162 F3
  HASM GU27 .... 180 H11
  HAV PO9 .... 103 G4
  HFD BN5 .... 269 L4
  HORL RH6 .... 22 E6
  HTHF TN21 .... 278 C1
  LAN/SOMP BN15 .... 118 E6
  LAN/SOMP BN15 .... 119 C7
  MSEA/BNM PO22 .... 3 L4
  PUL/STOR RH20 .... 266 A12
  RING/NEW BN8 .... 275 L10
  SBGH/RUST TN4 .... 37 K5
  SEAF BN25 .... 175 H2
  STHW BN42 .... 120 F5
  UCK TN22 .... 76 E4
  WSEA TN36 .... 285 Q4
  WTHG BN11 .... 20 C6
Manor Ct *ANG/EP* BN16 * 148 A3
  BEX TN40 * 97 J8
  BURH RH15 * 75 H4
  HORS RH12 * 15 L1
  HTHF TN21 * 278 C2
  LAN/SOMP BN15 * 118 C5
  PUL/STOR RH20 * 266 A12
  SEAF BN25 * 175 H2
  STHW BN42 * 120 F6
Manor Crs *BRIE/ROTT* BN2 .... 123 K8
  HASM GU27 .... 180 H11
Manor Dr *HORL* RH6 .... 22 E6
  PEAHV BN10 .... 157 G4
  RHWH RH17 .... 72 B2
Manor End *UCK* TN22 .... 76 E4
Manor Farm Cl *SELS* PO20 .... 301 L5
Manor Farm Ct *SELS* PO20 .... 301 L5
Manor Field Ct *SALV* BN13 * 117 J8
Manorfields *CRAWW* RH11 .... 42 C7
Manor Flds *LIPH* GU30 .... 194 A1
  SWTR RH13 .... 15 M2
Manor Gdns *BRIE/ROTT* BN2 .... 123 K8
  EMRTH PO10 .... 104 E4
  HPPT/KEY BN6 .... 270 C3
Manor Gn *BRIE/ROTT* BN2 .... 123 K8
Manor Hall Rd *STHW* BN42 .... 120 F5
Manor Hl *BRIE/ROTT* BN2 .... 123 K7
Manor La *SELS* PO20 .... 142 C7
  SELS PO20 .... 301 M5
  SWTR RH13 .... 202 C1
Manor Lea *WTHG* BN11 * 20 D7
Manor Lodge Rd *HAV* PO9 .... 288 H8
Manor Paddock
  BRIE/ROTT BN2 .... 154 C1
Manor Pde *SALV* BN13 * 116 C6
Manor Pk *BOGR* PO21 .... 170 F4
  SBGH/RUST TN4 .... 37 K6
Manor Park Rd *HAIL* BN27 .... 91 M3
Manor Pl *BOGR* PO21 .... 2 D8
  BRIE/ROTT BN2 .... 154 D1
Manor Rd *ANG/EP* BN16 .... 148 B3
  ANG/EP BN16 .... 148 E5
  BEX TN40 .... 137 J1
  BRIE/ROTT BN2 .... 154 C1
  BURH RH15 .... 75 H5
  EGRIN RH19 .... 31 H7
  EMRTH PO10 .... 104 E4
  HAS TN34 .... 13 J3
  HORS RH12 .... 56 F4
  HPPT/KEY BN6 .... 270 C3
  HTHF TN21 .... 278 C1
  LAN/SOMP BN15 .... 118 C5
  LW/ROSE BN22 .... 163 M3
  LYDD TN29 .... 255 R8
  PTSD BN41 .... 121 G4
  SBGH/RUST TN4 .... 37 H5
  SELS PO20 .... 301 M5
  STEY/UB BN44 .... 79 H3
  WTHG BN11 .... 20 C6
Manor Rd North *SEAF* BN25 .... 175 H2
Manor Royal *CRAWE* RH10 .... 27 K8
Manor Ter *LEWES* BN7 * 16 E8
The Manor *WTHG* BN11 * 20 D7
Manor View Ct *SALV* BN13 .... 117 J8
Manor Vls *RCCH* PO18 .... 106 E3
Manor Wy *BOGR* PO21 .... 171 H4
  BRIE/ROTT BN2 .... 123 K8
  CROW TN6 .... 210 F1
  EDN/EASTW BN20 .... 163 G5
  EMRTH PO10 .... 104 E4
  HFD BN5 .... 269 J4
  LAN/SOMP BN15 .... 118 C6
  MSEA/BNM PO22 .... 146 A8
  POLE BN26 .... 131 M7
  UCK TN22 .... 76 E4
Mansbergh Rd *CCH* PO19 .... 108 A4
Mansell Cl *BEXW* TN39 .... 136 B5
Mansell Rd *SHOR* BN43 .... 120 B5
Manser Rd *ARUN* BN18 .... 111 L4
Mansers La *HAIL* BN27 .... 91 H2
Mansfield Cl *WTHG* BN11 .... 151 M1
Mansfield Rd *HOVE* BN3 .... 121 K6
  MSEA/BNM PO22 .... 2 A4
  WTHG BN11 .... 151 M2
Mansion Cl *BURH* RH15 .... 75 J5
Manston Wy *HAS* TN34 .... 12 E2
Mant Cl *LHPTN* BN17 .... 146 C2
  PUL/STOR RH20 .... 266 A12
Mantell Cl *LEWES* BN7 .... 86 B1
Mantling Rd *LHPTN* BN17 .... 147 J3
Manton Cl *SELS* PO20 .... 168 B8
Manton Rd *BRIE/ROTT* BN2 .... 123 K4
Mant Rd *PETW* GU28 .... 229 L10
Manvers Rd *EDN/EASTW* BN20 .. .. 176 B2

The Manwarings
  STPH/PW TN12 .... 189 M3
Maple Av BEXW TN39 .... 136 B2
Maple Cl BEXW TN39 .... 136 B2
  BIL RH14 .... 199 R12
  BRIE/ROTT BN2 ..... 124 D6
  BURH RH15 .... 75 G4
  CRAWW RH11 .... 27 H8
  EMRTH PO10 .... 104 A3
  HORS RH12 .... 56 F4
  HWH RH16 .... 73 L6
  MSEA/BNM PO22 .... 145 K7
  SALV BN13 .... 116 D4
  UCK TN22 .... 241 M1
Maple Ct HAIL BN27 .... 91 M5
Maple Crs HORN PO8 .... 256 D7
Mapledown Cl SWTR TN13 201 Q11
Maple Dr BURH RH15 .... 74 F1
  EGRIN RH19 .... 31 M8
Maple Gdns HOVE BN3 ... 121 K4
  MSEA/BNM PO22 .... 144 B6
Maple Hts SLVH TN37 ... 283 Q10
Maplehurst Cl SLVH TN37 283 Q10
Maplehurst Dr SLVH TN37 283 R9
Maplehurst Ri SLVH TN37 283 Q10
Maplehurst Rd CCH PO19 107 M2
  LW/ROSE BN22 ..... 163 J3
  PTSD BN41 .... 120 F2
  SWTR TN13 .... 234 E1
Maple Leaf PUL/STOR RH20 264 D7
Maple Leaf Cl NEWHV BN9 18 C3
Maple Leaf Dr BOR GU35 178 C5
Mapleleaf Gdns POLE BN26 131 M5
Maple Ldg HASM GU27 ... 195 P1
Maple Pde ARUN BN18 ... 111 K5
  BIL RH14 .... 232 C4
  LGNY BN23 .... 164 C6
The Maples FERR BN12 .. 149 L5
Mapletree Av HORN PO8 . 288 D5
Maple Wk BEXW TN39 ... 136 B2
  LAN/SOMP BN15 .... 118 A2
Maple Wy BOR GU35 .... 179 Q3
Maple Wd HAV PO9 ..... 102 C4
Mapsons La SELS PO20 ... 168 F2
Marama Gdns ANG/EP BN16 148 A6
Marbles Rd RING/NEW BN8 240 C6
Marchants STPH/PW TN12 188 C1
Marchants Cl HPPT/KEY BN6 270 H1
Marchants Dr RYE TN31 . 253 R11
Marchants Rd HPPT/KEY BN6 270 H3
Marches Rd HORS RH12 . 187 N5
The Marches HASM GU27 195 L8
  HORS RH12 .... 40 A4
Marchwood CCH PO19 ... 107 M2
Marchwood Ga CCH PO19 107 M2
Marchwood Rd HAV PO9 . 288 F11
Marcia Cl EDN/EASTW BN20 162 F5
Marcus Gdns SLVH TN37 . 283 P12
Mardale Rd SALV BN13 .. 116 E7
Marden Av CCH PO19 ... 141 K2
Marden's Hl CROW TN6 .. 67 G3
The Mardens CRAWW RH11 8 A1
Marden Wy EPSF GU31 .. 223 P6
Mardyke SHOR BN43 .... 119 J7
Mare Bay Cl STLEO TN38 283 M10
Mare Hill Rd PUL/STOR RH20 265 N4
Maresfield Dr PEV BN24 . 134 D7
Maresfield Rd BRIE/ROTT BN2 123 K4
Margaret Cl BOGR PO21 . 171 K2
Margaret St BRIE/ROTT BN2 5 D8
Margery Rd HOVE BN3 .. 121 J5
Marianne Pk RHAS TN35 . 13 M3
Marian Wy BOGR PO21 .. 3 C6
Marigolds Ldg
  ANG/EP BN16 .... 148 A5
The Marigolds
  MSEA/BNM PO22 * .. 144 A4
Marina BEX TN40 ...... 137 K2
Marina Cl EMRTH PO10 . 104 B5
Marina Court Av BEX TN40 137 K2
Marina Wk LGNY BN23 .. 164 D5
Marina Wy BRIE/ROTT BN2 154 E2
Marine Av HOVE BN3 ... 121 J7
Marine Cl BRIE/ROTT BN2 156 A4
  PEV BN24 .... 134 E7
  SELS PO20 .... 167 K7
  WTHG BN11 .... 20 A8
Marine Ct PEAHV BN10 * 156 E6
  PEV BN24 .... 134 C8
  STLEO TN38 .... 12 A4
Marine Crs FERR BN12 .. 150 C4
  SEAF BN25 .... 174 E3
Marine Dr BRIE/ROTT BN2 154 E2
  BRIE/ROTT BN2 ..... 155 C2
  FERR BN12 .... 149 M5
  SELS PO20 .... 158 F7
  SELS PO20 .... 167 K6
  SELS PO20 .... 301 M6
Marine Dr West BOGR PO21 171 M3
  SELS PO20 .... 167 J6
Marine Gdns BRIE/ROTT BN2 5 H8
  EAST BN21 * 11 G7
  SELS PO20 .... 301 K8
Marine Pde BOGR PO21 .. 2 B9
  BRIE/ROTT BN2 ..... 5 G8
  EAST BN21 .... 11 H7
  HAS TN34 .... 13 J7
  SEAF BN25 .... 174 B1
  WTHG BN11 .... 20 E8
Marine Parade Rd EAST BN21 11 H6
Marine Pl WTHG BN11 .. 21 J7
Marine Rd LW/ROSE BN22 11 H6
  PEV BN24 .... 134 C4
Mariners Cl SHOR BN43 . 119 J4
The Mariners
  LAN/SOMP BN15 * .. 152 C2
Mariners Wk ANG/EP BN16 148 C6
Marineside SELS PO20 ... 168 A4
Marine Sq BRIE/ROTT BN2 5 K9
Marine Terrace Ms
  BRIE/ROTT BN2 ..... 5 J8
Marine Vw BRIE/ROTT BN2 5 J8
  NEWHV BN9 .... 18 C5
Marion Rd CRAWE RH10 . 44 A6
Marisfield Pl SELS PO20 . 301 M5
Marjoram Crs HORN PO8 . 288 C6
Marjoram Pl SHOR BN43 . 120 A4
Mark Cl SEAF BN25 .... 175 J3
Market Av CCH PO19 ... 6 E6
Market Cl MSEA/BNM PO22 111 G4
Market Fld STEY/UB BN44 78 C2
Market La LEWES BN7 .. 17 G6
Market Pde HAV PO9 ... 103 G4

Market Pl BURH RH15 * .. 74 F7
  HAIL BN27 .... 92 B6
  HWH RH16 .... 73 G4
Market Rd BAT TN33 .... 282 D4
  CCH PO19 .... 6 F5
  RYE TN31 .... 252 G8
Market Sq HORS RH12 * . 14 C7
  MIDH GU29 .... 227 J10
  PETW GU28 .... 229 L9
  RTW TN1 * 38 A5
Market St BOGR PO21 ... 2 D8
  BRI BN1 .... 4 E7
  HAIL BN27 .... 92 B6
  LEWES BN7 .... 17 G6
  RTWE/PEM TN2 ..... 37 M7
  RYE TN31 .... 252 H8
  STLEO TN38 .... 12 A3
  WTHG BN11 .... 21 H6
Market Ter STLEO TN38 * 12 A3
Markfield MSEA/BNM PO22 144 A7
Markham Rd RDKG RH5 .. 24 B4
Markland Wy UCK TN22 . 76 C5
Markle La EAST BN21 ... 10 E7
Marklye La HTHF TN21 .. 244 E4
  HTHF TN21 .... 245 M10
Markstakes Cnr
  RING/NEW BN8 ..... 239 P12
Markstakes La RING/NEW BN8 239 P12
Markway Cl EMRTH PO10 103 L4
Markwick Ms WTHG BN11 21 J4
Markwick Ter STLEO TN38 99 G5
Marlborough Ct CCH PO19 7 L5
  CRAWW RH11 .... 43 H7
  HORS RH12 .... 56 F4
  LGNY BN23 .... 164 C2
  SBGH/RUST TN4 .... 37 K5
  STLEO TN38 .... 98 F4
Marlborough Ct BOGR PO21 143 L8
Marlborough Dr BURH RH15 75 H6
Marlborough Ms BRI BN1 4 C6
Marlborough Pk HAV PO9 103 J2
Marlborough Pl BRI BN1 . 4 F6
Marlborough Rd FERR BN12 150 C3
  LAN/SOMP BN15 .... 152 B1
Marlborough St BRI BN1 . 4 E6
Marlborough Wy FERR BN12 * 150 C3
Marldell Cl HAV PO9 .... 288 H12
Marle Av BURH RH15 ... 74 F5
Marle Place Rd
  STPH/PW TN12 ..... 188 H5
Marles La BIL RH14 .... 199 R4
Marley Cl BAT TN33 .... 282 C5
Marley Combe Rd HASM GU27 181 J12
Marley Gdns BAT TN33 .. 282 C5
Marley Hanger HASM GU27 195 K2
Marley La BAT TN33 .... 282 H4
  HASM GU27 .... 180 H12
Marley Ri BAT TN33 .... 282 G5
Marley Rd RYE TN31 .... 252 F7
Marley Wy PUL/STOR RH20 266 B11
Marline Av STLEO TN38 . 98 F2
Marline Cl STLEO TN38 .. 98 F1
The Marlinspike SHOR BN43 119 M7
Marlow Av LW/ROSE BN22 164 A7
Marlow Ct CRAWE RH10 . 8 F1
  SLVH TN37 .... 283 Q12
Marlowe Cl MSEA/BNM PO22 145 K7
Marlowes Rd SALV BN13 . 117 K8
The Marlowes BEX TN40 * 97 J8
Marlow Rd BRIE/ROTT BN2 154 E1
Marlpit Cl EGRIN RH19 .. 31 K6
Marlpit La EMRTH PO10 . 105 H1
  SELS PO20 .... 109 G7
Marlpits Cl EGRIN RH19 . 62 F3
Marlpits La BAT TN33 ... 281 M10
The Marlpit WADH TN5 .. 71 K4
Marlpost Rd SWTR TN13 . 201 M12
Marmion Rd CRAWE RH10 121 L6
Marples Wy HAV PO9 ... 102 A4
Marquis Wy BOGR PO21 . 171 K4
Marringdean Rd BIL RH14 232 A4
Marsden Rd LGNY BN23 . 164 D4
Marshall Av BOGR PO21 . 2 B6
  SALV BN13 .... 116 E2
Marshall Cl MSEA/BNM PO22 111 G8
Marshall La NEWHV BN9 . 18 F3
Marshall Rd CRAWE RH10 44 B5
  LW/ROSE BN22 ..... 163 M5
Marshalls Rw BRI BN1 * . 4 F3
Marshall Wy HAIL BN27 . 121 L4
Marsh Barns SELS PO20 . 142 E3
Marsh Cl BOR GU35 .... 179 J6
Marshfoot La HAIL BN27 . 92 B5
Marshlands La HTHF TN21 244 D5
Marsh La RCCH PO18 .... 109 M3
  RCCH PO18 .... 139 J1
  RCCH PO18 .... 292 C10
  SELS PO20 .... 142 E4
Marsh Quarter La HAWK TN18 217 R5
Marshwood Av WVILLE PO7 288 B10
Marston Rd SALV BN13 .. 21 J1
Martello Cl RYE TN31 ... 252 G9
Martello Ms SEAF BN25 * 174 E3
Martello Rd LW/ROSE BN22 164 C7
  SEAF BN25 .... 174 E3
Martha Gunn Rd
  BRIE/ROTT BN2 ..... 123 J4
Martin Cl CRAWW RH11 .. 43 J1
Martindale Pl MFD/CHID GU8 * 182 F5
Martineau Cl BOGR PO21 171 K4
Martineau La RHAS TN35 285 J12
Martingale Cl SLVH TN37 283 R12
Martinique Wy LGNY BN23 164 C5
Martin Rd HAV PO9 ..... 103 H1
  HOVE BN3 .... 121 J4
Martins La SELS PO20 ... 140 E8
The Martins CRAWE RH10 46 B1
  PEAHV BN10 .... 157 C4
Martlet Cl CCH PO19 .... 6 F7
Martlet Rd PETW GU28 .. 229 K10
Martlets BEX TN40 ..... 97 K8
  PUL/STOR RH20 ..... 265 R5
Martlets Cl HORS RH12 .. 56 F4
The Martlets ANG/EP BN16 147 N6
  CRAWE RH10 .... 9 G4
  CROW TN6 .... 67 L8
  HAS TN34 * 12 F4
  LAN/SOMP BN15 .... 118 D7
  LEWES BN7 .... 17 H2
  RING/NEW BN8 ..... 273 N2
  RYE TN31 .... 250 E5
  SHOR BN43 .... 119 L5
Martlets Wy FERR BN12 * 150 B3
The Martlet HOVE BN3 .. 122 C5
Martletts LW/ROSE BN22 * 163 G2

Martletts Cnr HORS RH12 * 186 A10
The Martletts RING/NEW BN8 275 K11
Martlet Wy BOGR PO21 .. 170 G6
The Marts HORS RH12 ... 186 A10
Martyn Cl HFD BN5 ..... 269 K4
Martyn's Cl BRIE/ROTT BN2 155 K1
Martyns Pl EGRIN RH19 . 47 M1
Martyns Av BEX TN40 ... 97 M8
Martyrs Wy CRAWW RH11 27 H8
Marvell Cl CRAWE RH10 . 44 B1
Marvic Ct HAV PO9 ..... 288 F11
Mary Day's CRBK TN17 .. 189 R10
Mary Stamford Gn RYE TN31 253 M10
Maryland Rd RTWE/PEM TN2 38 C4
Marylands HWH RH16 ... 73 L3
Marylands Crs MSEA/BNM PO22 * 3 H3
Masefield Crs HORN PO8 . 288 C6
Masefield Rd CRAWW RH11 42 C6
Maskelyne Rd HAIL BN27 93 M5
Mason Cl EGRIN RH19 ... 31 K7
  RYE TN31 .... 252 F8
  SEAF BN25 .... 174 F1
Masons Fld SWTR TN13 .. 202 H3
Masons Wy PUL/STOR RH20 231 K12
Massetts Rd HORL RH6 .. 22 E7
Matlock Rd BRI BN1 .... 122 C4
  EDN/EASTW BN20 ... 176 D5
Matthews Cl HAV PO9 ... 102 D3
Matthews Dr CRAWE RH10 44 B7
Matthey Pl CRAWE RH10 . 28 C8
Maudlin La STEY/UB BN44 78 C4
Maudlin Pk STEY/UB BN44 78 C4
Maudlyn Pk STEY/UB BN44 78 C4
Maudlyn Pkwy STEY/UB BN44 78 C4
Mauldmare Cl BOGR PO21 171 L3
Maunsell Pk CRAWE RH10 44 A3
Maunsell Rd STLEO TN38 283 N12
Maurice Rd SEAF BN25 .. 174 F4
Mavis Crs HAV PO9 ..... 103 G3
Maxfield Cl EDN/EASTW BN20 163 G8
Maxfield La RHAS TN35 .. 284 C7
Maxton Wk CRAWW RH11 * 43 G7
Maxwell Rd ARUN BN18 . 112 C4
  LHPTN BN17 .... 147 H4
Maxwell Wy CRAWE RH10 27 M8
Maybridge Crs FERR BN12 150 B2
Maybridge Sq FERR BN12 150 B3
Maybush Dr RCCH PO18 . 105 J6
May Cl BOR GU35 ...... 179 M5
  FERR BN12 .... 150 B2
  LHPTN BN17 .... 146 C4
  MSEA/BNM PO22 .... 2 F2
  SELS PO20 .... 169 L5
May Cottages
  BRIE/ROTT BN2 * ... 123 H5
Maydwell Av SWTR TN13 200 E3
Mayes Cl CRAWE RH10 .. 44 B5
Mayes La HORS RH12 ... 187 P8
Mayfair Cl POLE BN26 ... 162 E1
Mayfield ANG/EP BN16 .. 148 F2
  CRAWE RH10 .... 44 C3
Mayfield Av PEAHV BN10 157 J7
Mayfield Cl BOGR PO21 . 171 J3
  BRI BN1 .... 82 F8
  MAYF TN20 .... 212 C7
  SALV BN13 .... 116 F5
Mayfield Crs BRI BN1 ... 82 E8
Mayfield Flat HTHF TN21 243 P5
Mayfield La STLEO TN38 . 98 D5
  WADH TN5 .... 71 H5
Mayfield Pk WADH TN5 . 71 J4
Mayfield Pl LW/ROSE BN22 10 E4
Mayfield Rd BOGR PO21 . 171 M1
  CROW TN6 .... 211 Q2
  SBGH/RUST TN4 .... 37 H5
Mayfields RHWH RH17 .. 236 D1
Mayfield Wy BEX TN40 .. 97 K8
Mayflower Cl CRAWE RH10 44 C4
Mayflower Ct HWH RH16 73 J5
Mayflower Rd BOR GU35 178 C5
  HWH RH16 .... 73 J5
Mayflower Sq BRI BN1 .. 4 E8
Mayhew Cl LEWES BN7 . 17 G3
Mayhouse Rd BURH RH15 74 E8
Maylands Rd HAV PO9 .. 102 C3
Maynard Cl CRAWE RH10 29 H5
Maynard Pl HORN PO8 .. 288 C2
Mayne Waye HAS TN34 . 99 M1
Mayo La BRIE/ROTT BN2 . 123 K4
Mayo Ri BEXW TN39 .... 96 F5
Mayo Rd BRIE/ROTT BN2 123 K4
Maypole Cottages UCK TN22 210 C9
Maypole La ARUN BN18 . 111 L8
  CRBK TN17 .... 189 R9
Maypole Rd EGRIN RH19 . 31 J7
  EGRIN RH19 .... 48 D3
Maypolegate SELS PO20 . 300 H5
May Rd BRIE/ROTT BN2 .. 5 M2
Maytham Rd CRBK TN17 . 219 M2
May Tree Av SALV BN13 . 116 E2
Maytree Cl ANG/EP BN16 148 C1
  LAN/SOMP BN15 .... 118 A7
May Tree Gdns BEX TN40 97 L7
Maytree Wk HOVE BN3 .. 121 K4
Maywood Av LW/ROSE BN22 163 K3
Maze Hi STLEO TN38 .... 99 G5
Maze Hill Ter STLEO TN38 * 99 G6
McIndoe Rd EGRIN RH19 31 J6
McIver Cl EGRIN RH19 ... 30 J6
McKerchar Cl LAN/SOMP BN15 118 E6
McWilliam Rd BRIE/ROTT BN2 124 B4
Meadend Cl HAV PO9 ... 289 J12
Mead Hawks LISS GU33 . 192 B8
Mead La BOGR PO21 .... 3 G5
  MSEA/BNM PO22 .... 2 F4
  PUL/STOR RH20 ..... 266 B11

WTHG BN11 .... 151 M2
Meadowcroft Cl CRAWW RH11 42 E4
  EGRIN RH19 .... 31 H7
Meadow Croft La HORL RH6 28 B1
Meadow Dr HWH RH16 .. 73 L3
Meadow Farm La HORS RH12 56 E2
Meadowfield Dr CCH PO19 7 N2
Meadowland SELS PO20 . 301 K1
Meadowlands CRAWW RH11 8 C3
Meadowlands Av
  LW/ROSE BN22 ..... 163 J3
  BURH RH15 .... 74 E8
  HWH RH16 .... 73 L3
  LAN/SOMP BN15 .... 118 D8
  SELS PO20 .... 167 J3
Meadow Pde BRIE/ROTT BN2 155 L2
Meadow Pk CRAWW RH11 8 A2
Meadow Ri HORN PO8 ... 288 C6
Meadow Rd HAIL BN27 .. 91 M7
  RRTW TN3 .... 52 A2
  SBGH/RUST TN4 .... 37 H5
  WTHG BN11 .... 151 M2
Meadows HPPT/KEY BN6 271 M4
  HORL RH6 .... 23 G5
  PUL/STOR RH20 ..... 266 A12
Meadowside ANG/EP BN16 114 F7
  SELS PO20 .... 167 J3
The Meadows ARUN BN18 111 J4
  CCH PO19 .... 141 K2
  CROW TN6 .... 67 J7
  HAIL BN27 * 90 A2
  HOVE BN3 .... 121 H2
  LEWES BN7 .... 17 J1
  SLVH TN37 .... 283 P12
  TENT TN30 .... 220 C5
Meadowsweet HORN PO8 288 C8
Meadowsweet Cl SALV BN13 115 M8
Meadowsweet Cl STLEO TN38 98 D4
Meadow Ter RHWH RH17 * 60 F7
The Meadow CRAWE RH10 28 F6
  RTWE/PEM TN2 ..... 39 J1
Meadow V SELS PO20 * . 181 K11
Meadow Vw BAT TN33 * . 281 N12
  BOR GU35 .... 178 H6
  CROW TN6 .... 211 P2
Meadowview Rd
  LAN/SOMP BN15 .... 118 C5
  MSEA/BNM PO22 .... 145 M8
Meadow Wy BOGR PO21 . 171 G6
  FERR BN12 .... 149 K3
  HTHF TN21 .... 244 D8
  LHPTN BN17 .... 147 L4
  LIPH GU30 .... 179 R12
  MSEA/BNM PO22 .... 143 M7
  PETW GU28 .... 229 K10
  RHAS TN35 .... 101 K1
  SEAF BN25 .... 175 H2
  SELS PO20 .... 109 H4
  SELS PO20 .... 110 C7
Mead Rd CRAWE RH10 ... 9 J2
  GSHT GU26 .... 181 J5
Meads Av BEXW TN39 ... 136 B1
  HOVE BN3 .... 121 H2
Meads Brow
  EDN/EASTW BN20 ... 176 D3
Meads Cl HOVE BN3 .... 121 H2
Meads Rd BEXW TN39 ... 136 B1
  EDN/EASTW BN20 ... 176 D5
  SEAF BN25 .... 174 F4
Meads St EDN/EASTW BN20 176 D5
The Meads BRI BN1 .... 83 H7
  EGRIN RH19 .... 47 K2
  HASM GU27 .... 181 J11
  RTWE/PEM TN2 ..... 38 B7
Mead Sway ARUN BN18 . 111 J4
The Mead BEXW TN39 .. 136 C1
  LIPH GU30 .... 179 Q12
  LISS GU33 .... 192 C9
  PSF GU32 .... 223 K7
Meadvale HORS RH12 ... 201 Q3
Meadway ANG/EP BN16 . 148 C6
  HASM GU27 .... 181 J11
Meadway WVILLE PO7 ... 288 B9
Meadway Ct SALV BN13 * 150 D1
  STHW BN42 .... 120 C5
Meadway Crs HOVE BN3 . 121 L3
The Meadway BRIE/ROTT BN2 123 L8
  HORL RH6 .... 23 G5
  SHOR BN43 .... 119 L7
Mealla Cl LEWES BN7 ... 16 F1
Measham Cl FERR BN12 . 149 L4
Meath Green Av HORL RH6 22 E4
Meath Green La HORL RH6 22 C1
Medina Dr PEV BN24 .... 133 P4
Medina Rd HOVE BN3 ... 122 A4
Medina Ter HOVE BN3 ... 122 A8
  STLEO TN38 * 98 F7
Medina Vls HOVE BN3 .. 122 A8
Medlar Cl CRAWW RH11 . 27 H8
Medmerry Cl SELS PO20 . 300 F5
Medmerry Hi SELS PO20 . 123 K3
Medstead Rd HAV PO9 .. 103 G3
Medway CRAWE RH10 ... 45 M4
  CROW TN6 .... 68 B8
  HAIL BN27 .... 91 M8
Medway Cl SALV BN13 .. 116 C6
Medway Dr EGRIN RH19 . 47 J3
  FROW RH18 .... 48 D7
Medway La PEV BN24 ... 132 F8
Medway Rd CRAWW RH11 42 E6
  RTW TN1 .... 38 A4
Medwin Wy HORS RH12 . 14 C5
Meeching Pl NEWHV BN9 18 F3
Meeching Ri NEWHV BN9 18 F3
Meeching Rd NEWHV BN9 19 G4
Meeds Rd BURH RH15 ... 74 E6
Meeting House La BRI BN1 4 E6
Megrims Hl HAWK TN18 . 217 P3
Meiros Wy PUL/STOR RH20 267 J3
Melbourne Av FERR BN12 150 B3
Melbourne Rd CCH PO19 7 G3
  FERR BN12 .... 150 B3
  LW/ROSE BN22 ..... 11 G5
Melbourne St BRIE/ROTT BN2 5 J1
Melbourne Vls CROW TN6 210 H1
Melbourne Wy HORS RH12 * 56 E4

Melfort Rd CROW TN6 ... 67 J3
Melksham Cl SWTR TN13 15 G7
Melrose Av PTSD BN41 . 120 F4
  SALV BN13 .... 150 D1
Melrose Cl BOR GU35 ... 178 C7
  BRI BN1 .... 123 H3
  HAIL BN27 .... 91 M5
  SALV BN13 .... 150 D1
Melrose Pl PUL/STOR RH20 266 F10
Melton Av PUL/STOR RH20 266 A10
Melton Cl PUL/STOR RH20 266 B10
Melton Dr PUL/STOR RH20 266 A10
Melville Rd HOVE BN3 ... 4 B3
Melville Wy FERR BN12 .. 150 B1
Mendip Av LGNY BN23 .. 164 B2
Mendip Cl EDN/EASTW BN20 163 G5
Mendip Crs SALV BN13 .. 116 D6
Mendip Gdns HAS TN34 . 100 A3
Mendip Rd SALV BN13 .. 116 D6
Mendip Wk CRAWW RH11 42 B6
  RTWE/PEM TN2 ..... 38 C4
Menzies Rd STLEO TN38 . 99 G3
Meon Cl HORN PO8 .... 256 D9
  PEV BN24 .... 132 F8
  PSF GU32 .... 223 M5
Mercatoria STLEO TN38 . 12 A3
Mercer Cl CRAWE RH10 . 44 B6
Mercer Rd HORS RH12 .. 36 F6
Mercers RRTW TN3 .... 51 R6
Mercers Md SWTR TN13 . 235 K4
Mercer St RTW TN1 .... 38 A4
Merchant St BOGR PO21 7 F6
Merchistoun Rd HORN PO8 288 D2
Mercia Ct BEX TN40 * ... 97 L8
Mercread Rd SEAF BN25 . 174 F2
Mercury Cl BOR GU35 ... 178 H6
  CRAWW RH11 .... 42 D6
Mere Cl SELS PO20 ..... 168 A3
Meredith Rd SALV BN13 . 21 L2
Meres La HTHF TN21 .... 243 Q2
Merevale BRI BN1 ...... 123 G3
Mereworth Dr CRAWE RH10 44 C1
Mereworth Rd SBGH/RUST TN4 38 C4
Meridian Cl CRAWW RH11 42 E6
Meridian Gv HORL RH6 .. 23 H5
Meridian Rd LEWES BN7 16 C3
Meridian Wy EGRIN RH19 31 L6
  PEAHV BN10 .... 157 H6
Merle Wy HORS RH12 ... 195 K7
Merlin Cl CRAWW RH11 . 42 D3
  HOVE BN3 .... 122 C5
Merlin Wy EGRIN RH19 .. 31 M6
  MSEA/BNM PO22 .... 145 J7
Mermaid St RYE TN31 ... 252 G8
Merrimede Cl STLEO TN38 98 F5
Merriments La
  BUR/ETCH TN19 .... 216 B5
Merrion Av MSEA/BNM PO22 2 B2
Merrion Cl SBGH/RUST TN4 38 A2
Merrion Wy SBGH/RUST TN4 38 A2
Merry End MSEA/BNM PO22 145 J4
Merryfield Av HAV PO9 .. 288 E12
Merryfield Crs ANG/EP BN16 114 F7
Merryfield Dr HORS RH12 201 R2
Merryfield Rd EPSF GU31 223 Q5
  PUL/STOR RH20 ..... 266 A11
Merryfield Wy
  PUL/STOR RH20 ..... 266 A11
Merryhills La BIL RH14 .. 184 H12
Merryweather Rd RCCH PO18 106 A8
Merrywood La
  PUL/STOR RH20 ..... 266 C9
Mersey Cl SALV BN13 ... 116 B6
Mersey Rd SALV BN13 .. 116 B6
Mersham Gdns FERR BN12 150 B3
Merston Cl BRIE/ROTT BN2 124 C3
Merton Av ANG/EP BN16 148 B5
Merton Cl BOGR PO21 .. 171 K1
Merton Dr LHPTN BN17 . 147 J3
Merton Rd CRAWW RH11 59 C5
  WTHG BN11 .... 21 L6
Metcalfe Av NEWHV BN9 18 C3
Metcalf Wy CRAWW RH11 27 J7
Meteor Rd EGRIN RH19 .. 47 J3
Methuen Rd LISS GU33 .. 192 F2
Mews Ct EGRIN RH19 ... 47 L3
Mews Rd STLEO TN38 * . 99 G3
The Mews ARUN BN18 .. 113 G3
  BOGR PO21 * 2 D6
  EPSF GU31 .... 223 P5
  HAV PO9 .... 102 F1
  HORS RH12 * 201 N1
  MFD/CHID GU8 ..... 184 A4
  MSEA/BNM PO22 .... 3 G5
  PUL/STOR RH20 ..... 265 L3
  PUL/STOR RH20 ..... 267 K9
  RING/NEW BN8 ..... 276 H4
  RTWE/PEM TN2 ..... 39 J1
  WTHG BN11 .... 20 E5
Mey Cl WVILLE PO7 .... 288 A10
Meyers Wd SWTR TN13 . 234 E12
Meyners Cl HOVE BN3 .. 121 H2
Meyrick Rd HAV PO9 .... 102 E4
Michael Crs HORL RH6 .. 22 F8
Michael Crook Cl HAV PO9 102 D2
Michael Flds FROW RH18 48 D7
Michelbourne Cl BURH RH15 74 D8
Michel Cl EDN/EASTW BN20 302 H4
Michel Dene Cl
  EDN/EASTW BN20 ... 303 J4
Michel Dene Rd
  EDN/EASTW BN20 ... 303 J4
Michele Cl STLEO TN38 .. 99 G4
Michell Cl HORL RH6 ... 22 D8
  EAST BN21 .... 10 A4
Micheham Cl LGNY BN23 163 M1
Micheham Rd UCK TN22 77 G3
Michell Cl HORS RH12 ... 201 R3
Michelson Cl STLEO TN38 98 E1
Micklam Cl BOGR PO21 . 171 H3
Micklefield Wy SEAF BN25 175 L1
Midas Cl BAT TN33 ..... 247 N11
Middle Dr UCK TN22 .... 209 M11
Middlefield HORL RH6 ... 23 H5
Middle Fld RTWE/PEM TN2 39 K1
Middle Furlong SEAF BN25 174 F2
Middleham Cl RING/NEW BN8 87 H1
Middleham Wy LGNY BN23 164 B1
Middle La HTHF TN21 ... 245 P10

Middle Md STEY/UB BN44 .... 78 C1
Middle Meadow LISS GU33 .... 192 D9
Middle Onslow Cl FERR BN12 * 149 K2
Middle Park Wy HAV PO9 .... 288 E12
Middle Rd BRI BN1 .... 122 D4
 LAN/SOMP BN15 .... 118 C8
 RHAS TN35 .... 100 C2
 RRTW TN3 .... 54 F4
 SHOR BN43 .... 120 A6
 SWTR RH13 .... 234 F10
Middlesex Rd BEX TN40 .... 137 J2
Middle St BRI BN1 .... 4 D8
 BRI BN1 .... 84 B7
 HAS TN34 .... 13 G6
 HORS RH12 .... 14 C6
 PETW GU28 .... 229 L9
 PTSD BN41 .... 121 H7
 SHOR BN43 .... 119 L6
Middleton Cl SELS PO20 .... 168 A7
Middleton Dr LGNY BN23 .... 164 D6
Middleton Gdns SELS PO20 .... 109 J3
Middleton Ri BRI BN1 .... 83 K8
 HORN PO8 .... 256 E9
Middleton Rd HORS RH12 .... 201 R3
 MSEA/BNM PO22 .... 145 H8
Middleton Wy CRAWW RH11 .... 42 D4
Middle Tyne SALV BN13 .... 116 C8
Middle View Ga UCK TN22 * 275 K5
Middle Wk ANG/EP BN16 .... 149 J5
 BURH 74 F6
 LEWES BN7 .... 16 A5
Middleway HAIL BN27 .... 280 A12
Midfields Cl BURH RH15 .... 75 G6
Midfields Dr BURH RH15 .... 75 G6
Midfields Wk BURH RH15 .... 75 G5
Midgley Rd CRAWE RH10 .... 43 H4
Midhurst Cl CRAWW RH11 * 42 F7
 FERR BN12 .... 149 L3
Midhurst Dr FERR BN12 .... 149 L3
Midhurst Ri BRI BN1 .... 83 G7
Midhurst Rd HASM GU27 .... 181 L12
 HASM GU27 .... 195 L11
 LIPH GU30 .... 193 R2
 LW/ROSE BN22 .... 163 L3
 RCCH PO18 .... 292 B10
Midhurst Wk HOVE BN3 .... 121 H5
Midway Rd BRIE/ROTT BN2 .... 124 B5
The Midway MSEA/BNM PO22 .... 3 M4
 SBGH/RUST TN4 .... 37 L7
Mighell St BRIE/ROTT BN2 .... 5 G6
Milbeck Cl HORN PO8 .... 288 D6
Milborne Rd CRAWE 44 B7
Milbury Cl FERR BN12 .... 149 L5
Milcote Av HOVE BN3 .... 121 L6
Mildenhall Dr SLVH TN37 .... 99 G1
Mildmay Cl RING/NEW BN8 .... 275 J11
Mildmay Rd LEWES BN7 .... 16 B5
Mile End La SELS PO20 .... 141 J3
Mile Oak Crs STHW BN42 .... 120 E4
Mile Oak Gdns PTSD BN41 .... 120 D4
Mile Oak Rd STHW BN42 .... 120 E4
Miles Cl ARUN BN18 .... 146 A3
Milfoil Dr LGNY BN23 .... 164 B2
Milford Rd HAV PO9 .... 102 E2
Military Rd RYE TN31 .... 221 L12
 TENT TN30 .... 221 N7
Millais SWTR RH13 .... 15 L4
Millais Cl CRAWW RH11 .... 42 E7
Millais Ct SWTR RH13 .... 15 L2
Milland Cl BEX TN40 .... 97 K7
Milland La LIPH GU30 .... 193 P8
Milland Ms HAIL BN27 * 92 A4
Milland Rd HAIL BN27 .... 92 A4
Mill Av SHOR BN43 * 119 L4
Millbank BURH RH15 .... 75 G5
The Millbank CRAWW RH11 .... 42 E4
Mill Bay La HORS RH12 .... 14 B7
Millberg Rd SEAF BN25 .... 175 L4
Millbrook Cl HTHF TN21 .... 278 D2
 LISS GU33 .... 192 D9
Millbrook Dr HAV PO9 .... 288 H11
Millbrook Gdns
 EDN/EASTW BN20 .... 163 G2
Millbrook Rd CROW TN6 .... 67 M7
Mill Brooks RING/NEW BN8 .... 273 N2
Mill Chase Rd BOR GU35 .... 178 H6
Mill Cl ANG/EP BN16 .... 148 C3
 CCH PO19 .... 107 G4
 EDN/EASTW BN20 .... 302 C4
 EGRIN RH19 .... 47 K2
 HASM GU27 .... 180 H11
 HORL RH6 .... 22 D5
 HTHF TN21 .... 244 C6
 POLE BN26 .... 162 E1
 POY/PYE BN45 .... 270 D12
 PTSD BN41 .... 121 H4
 RBTBR TN32 .... 249 M3
 RHAS TN35 .... 100 D1
 RHAS TN35 .... 284 B4
 SWTR RH13 .... 203 M10
Mill Copse Rd HASM GU27 .... 195 L11
Mill Cottages EGRIN RH19 * 47 K2
 HORS RH12 * 186 A12
 LYDD TN29 .... 255 P12
Mill Crs CROW TN6 .... 67 L6
Millcroft BRI BN1 .... 82 B8
Millcroft Av STHW BN42 .... 120 D4
Millcroft Gdns STHW BN42 .... 120 D4
Millcross Rd PTSD BN41 .... 121 G4
Milldown Rd SEAF BN25 .... 174 F1
Mill Dr CROW TN6 .... 67 L6
 HFD BN5 .... 269 L5
 HOVE BN3 .... 121 M4
 SEAF BN25 .... 175 G2
Mill Dro UCK TN22 .... 76 E6
Mill End EMRTH PO10 .... 104 C5
 HFD BN5 .... 269 K5
 PUL/STOR RH20 .... 265 R6
Millennium Cl
 LAN/SOMP BN15 .... 119 G7
Miller Rd BRI BN1 .... 122 D4
Millers Cl ANG/EP BN16 .... 148 C3
Millers Ga HORS RH12 .... 56 C3
Miller's Hill Cottage La
 RHAS TN35 .... 284 B3
Millers Hl HAIL BN27 .... 91 M7
Miller's Rd BRI BN1 .... 122 D4
The Millers ARUN BN18 .... 145 L3
Millers Wy BURH RH15 .... 74 F5
Millfarm Dr PTSD BN41 .... 170 F3
Millfield BAT TN33 .... 281 M11
 LAN/SOMP BN15 .... 118 B6

 STEY/UB BN44 * 78 F3
 SWTR RH13 .... 233 R1
Millfield Cl ANG/EP BN16 .... 148 A6
 CCH PO19 .... 108 B5
 RING/NEW BN8 .... 240 B6
 SEAF BN25 .... 175 G1
Millfield Cottages
 BRIE/ROTT BN2 .... 5 L9
Millfield Ri BEX TN40 .... 137 H1
Mill Gap Rd EAST BN21 .... 10 C4
Mill Gdns HTHF TN21 .... 244 D8
 RING/NEW BN8 .... 275 J12
 SELS PO20 .... 167 L6
Mill Green Rd HWH RH16 .... 73 H3
Millham Cl BEXW TN39 .... 96 C6
Mill Hl SHOR BN43 .... 79 K7
Mill Hill Cl HWH RH16 .... 73 H2
 SHOR BN43 .... 119 K4
Mill Hill Dr SHOR BN43 .... 119 K4
Mill Hill Gdns SHOR BN43 .... 119 K4
Mill House Gdns WTHG BN11 .... 20 B5
Millington Dr SELS PO20 .... 301 L4
Mill La ANG/EP BN16 .... 148 C3
 ARUN BN18 .... 111 J4
 ARUN BN18 .... 113 G2
 ARUN BN18 .... 294 H11
 ARUN BN18 .... 296 F3
 BAT TN33 .... 95 L3
 BOR GU35 .... 179 L4
 CCH PO19 .... 107 G2
 CRAWE RH10 .... 29 K6
 CRAWW RH11 .... 42 F1
 CROW TN6 .... 67 K7
 EGRIN RH19 .... 30 C4
 EMRTH PO10 .... 104 C3
 EPSF GU31 .... 225 N9
 EPSF GU31 .... 258 E2
 HAIL BN27 .... 278 D12
 HAV PO9 .... 102 D4
 HAV PO9 .... 102 F7
 HORL RH6 .... 236 F11
 HPPT/KEY BN6 .... 271 M10
 LEWES BN7 .... 126 B6
 LHPTN BN17 .... 113 J8
 LING RH7 .... 31 L1
 MFD/CHID GU8 .... 182 F6
 MFD/CHID GU8 .... 183 R5
 MIDH GU29 .... 226 D7
 MIDH GU29 .... 260 G5
 MIDH GU29 .... 261 J3
 POY/PYE BN45 .... 270 D12
 PSF GU32 .... 223 M1
 PSF GU32 .... 223 Q3
 PTSD BN41 .... 121 H4
 PUL/STOR RH20 .... 265 K3
 PUL/STOR RH20 .... 266 A11
 PUL/STOR RH20 .... 267 J10
 RHAS TN35 .... 284 B4
 RHAS TN35 .... 284 H12
 RHWH RH17 .... 61 H3
 RING/NEW BN8 .... 273 L1
 RING/NEW BN8 .... 274 C7
 RING/NEW BN8 .... 276 H4
 RYE TN31 .... 251 Q2
 SALV BN13 .... 116 C3
 SELS PO20 .... 169 L6
 SELS PO20 .... 300 H6
 SHOR BN43 .... 119 K5
 SWTR RH13 .... 203 M10
 SWTR RH13 .... 234 E8
 UCK TN22 .... 76 E6
Mill Md PUL/STOR RH20 .... 267 K9
Mill Pond La RCCH PO18 .... 105 R5
Mill Pond Wy ANG/EP BN16 .... 148 E3
Mill Quay EMRTH PO10 .... 104 B6
Mill Race HPPT/KEY BN6 .... 271 M1
The Millrace POLE BN26 .... 162 L1
Mill Ri BRI BN1 .... 82 B8
 HTHF TN21 .... 244 D5
 RBTBR TN32 .... 248 B2
Mill Rd ANG/EP BN16 .... 114 E8
 ARUN BN18 .... 111 J2
 ARUN BN18 .... 113 G2
 BRI BN1 .... 82 B7
 BURH RH15 .... 75 G5
 CRAWE RH10 .... 44 A4
 EAST BN21 .... 163 J8
 EAST BN21 .... 176 D1
 EMRTH PO10 .... 104 C1
 HAIL BN27 .... 92 A4
 HAIL BN27 .... 244 C6
 LAN/SOMP BN15 .... 118 D5
 LEWES BN7 .... 17 J2
 LISS GU33 .... 192 D8
 LISS GU33 .... 121 G6
 PUL/STOR RH20 .... 265 R5
 RCCH PO18 .... 105 M2
 RING/NEW BN8 .... 275 J12
 RYE TN31 .... 252 H6
 STEY/UB BN44 .... 78 D3
 WSEA TN36 .... 286 D1
 WTHG BN11 .... 20 B5
Mill Road ANG/EP BN16 .... 114 E8
Mill Rw BRI BN1 * 4 C4
Mill Straight SWTR RH13 .... 233 Q1
Millstream Cl RRTW TN3 .... 35 J7
Millstream Gdns POLE BN26 .... 162 L1
Mill Stream Meadow
 HWH RH16 .... 73 G2
The Millstream HASM GU27 .... 180 H12
Mill St BRI BN1 .... 84 B6
Millthorpe Rd HORS RH12 .... 15 J1
Mill Vale Mdw LIPH GU30 .... 193 Q10
Mill Vw RING/NEW BN8 .... 87 L1
Millview Cl BOGR PO21 .... 170 F3
Mill View Ct PEV BN24 .... 133 J7
Mill View Rd ARUN BN18 .... 145 L3
 BEXW TN39 .... 97 G3
Millward Rd PEV BN24 .... 165 H2
Mill Wy BIL RH14 .... 199 R12
 EGRIN RH19 .... 30 C4
 POLE BN26 .... 162 D1
Mill Wd BURH RH15 .... 75 G6
Millwood CRAWE RH10 .... 46 D6
Millwood Cl UCK TN22 .... 241 Q1
Millwood La UCK TN22 .... 241 P1
Millwood Rd BEXW TN39 .... 96 F5
Millyard Crs BRIE/ROTT BN2 .... 124 C6
Milne Cl CRAWW RH11 .... 42 D6
Milner Rd BRIE/ROTT BN2 .... 123 H4
Milnthorpe Gdns
 EDN/EASTW BN20 * 176 E5

Milnthorpe Rd
 EDN/EASTW BN20 .... 176 E5
 HOVE BN3 .... 121 L5
Milton Av ANG/EP BN16 .... 148 A5
Milton Cl ANG/EP BN16 .... 148 A4
 EGRIN RH19 .... 31 H8
Milton Dr RTWE/PEM TN2 .... 38 C2
 STHW BN42 .... 120 E5
Milton Mount Av CRAWE RH10 .... 44 B1
Milton Rd BRIE/ROTT BN2 .... 5 H3
 CRAWE RH10 .... 44 B2
 EAST BN21 .... 176 C1
 HORS RH12 .... 14 C3
 HWH RH16 .... 73 G4
 SBGH/RUST TN4 .... 38 A2
 WTHG BN11 .... 20 E7
Milton St PEV BN24 .... 132 F7
 WTHG BN11 .... 20 E7
Milward Crs HAS TN34 .... 13 J5
Milward Rd HAS TN34 .... 13 J6
Mimmack Cl STEY/UB BN44 .... 78 C1
Mimosa Cl BOR GU35 .... 179 K4
 POLE BN26 .... 131 M5
Mimram Rd PEV BN24 .... 132 F8
Mindleheim Av EGRIN RH19 .... 32 A7
Minley Ct HAV PO9 .... 289 J12
The Minnels HPPT/KEY BN6 .... 271 P6
Minsted Rd MIDH GU29 .... 226 B12
Minsted Sq BEXW TN39 .... 136 B3
Minster Ct POLE BN26 .... 131 M6
Minster Ct LHPTN BN17 * 147 H1
Minton Rd MSEA/BNM PO22 .... 3 M5
Mint Rd LISS GU33 .... 192 E7
The Mint RYE TN31 .... 252 G8
Misbrooks Green Rd RDKG RH5 .... 24 D7
Mistley Cl BEX TN40 .... 97 M7
Mistley Gdns HORL RH6 .... 22 C7
Mitchelldean PEAHV BN10 .... 157 G4
Mitchell Gdns SWTR RH13 .... 200 H2
Mitchell Cl HAV PO9 .... 102 H2
Mitchells Rd CRAWE RH10 .... 9 J3
Mitten Rd BEX TN40 .... 137 H1
Mixon Cl SELS PO20 .... 301 L7
Moat Croft Rd EAST BN21 .... 10 A5
Moat Farm BRIE/ROTT BN2 .... 53 N2
Moatfield La SWTR RH13 .... 235 M5
Moat La BAT TN33 .... 283 Q7
 EDEN TN8 .... 34 C2
 HTHF TN21 .... 243 L12
 PUL/STOR RH20 .... 265 K3
Modena Rd HOVE BN3 .... 121 L6
Moggs Md EPSF GU31 .... 223 P6
Mole Cl CRAWW RH11 .... 43 G1
 PEV BN24 .... 132 F8
Molecomb Broadwalk
 RCCH PO18 .... 293 K8
Mole Hl WVILLE PO7 .... 288 A12
Molesworth St HOVE BN3 .... 121 L5
The Mole LHPTN BN17 .... 147 M4
Molyneux Park Gdns
 SBGH/RUST TN4 .... 37 L5
Molyneux Park Rd
 SBGH/RUST TN4 .... 37 L5
Monarch Cl CRAWW RH11 .... 42 F6
 WVILLE PO7 .... 288 B10
Monarch Gdns LGNY BN23 .... 164 D4
 SEAF BN25 * 159 M8
 SLVH TN37 .... 283 P12
Monarch's Wy ARUN BN18 .... 296 C6
 BRI BN1 .... 81 J7
 HAV PO9 .... 289 Q7
 HORN PO8 .... 288 E4
 HOVE BN3 .... 122 A4
 PTSD BN41 .... 120 D2
 PUL/STOR RH20 .... 266 A4
 RCCH PO18 .... 290 G5
 RCCH PO18 .... 291 L5
 RCCH PO18 .... 293 L5
 SALV BN13 .... 298 A11
 SHOR BN43 .... 79 M6
 STEY/UB BN44 .... 78 D3
 STEY/UB BN44 .... 299 M9
Mona Rd LW/ROSE BN22 .... 11 H3
Monastery Gdns CROW TN6 .... 211 Q1
Monastery La PUL/STOR RH20 .... 265 R12
Monceux Rd
 EDN/EASTW BN20 .... 176 C1
 HAIL BN27 .... 279 P11
Monckton Wy LEWES BN7 .... 85 K8
Monger's Md RING/NEW BN8 .... 274 D9
Monk Cl BRI BN1 .... 83 K7
Monkmead Copse
 PUL/STOR RH20 .... 265 R7
Monkmead La PUL/STOR RH20 .... 265 Q6
Monks Av LAN/SOMP BN15 .... 118 D5
Monks Cl LAN/SOMP BN15 .... 118 D7
Monksfield CRAWE RH10 .... 9 J3
Monk's Hl EMRTH PO10 .... 289 P11
Monks La LEWES BN7 .... 16 E8
 RDKG RH5 .... 187 J4
 WADH TN5 .... 190 A6
Monks Orch PSF GU32 .... 223 N4
Monks Wk STEY/UB BN44 .... 79 G3
 WSEA TN36 .... 286 D3
Monks Wy LEWES BN7 .... 16 E1
 RYE TN31 .... 218 G9
Monks Wd PSF GU32 .... 223 N4
Monkwood Cl CCH PO19 .... 107 G5
Monmouth St HOVE BN3 .... 122 A6
Mons Av BOGR PO21 .... 2 A7
Monson Rd RTW TN1 .... 37 M5
Monson Wy RTW TN1 * 38 A1
Montacute Gdns
 RTWE/PEM TN2 .... 37 L7
Montacute Rd LEWES BN7 .... 16 A8
 RTWE/PEM TN2 .... 37 M8
Montacute Wy UCK TN22 .... 76 D7
Montague Cl SHOR BN43 .... 120 C6
Montague Gdns EPSF GU31 .... 223 R6
Montague Pl BRIE/ROTT BN2 * 5 K7
 WTHG BN11 .... 21 H7
Montague St BRIE/ROTT BN2 .... 5 J8
 WTHG BN11 .... 20 D7
Montague Wy PEV BN24 .... 133 L8
Montalan Crs SELS PO20 .... 300 H5
Montargis Wy CROW TN6 .... 67 L8
Montefiore Rd HOVE BN3 .... 4 A3

Monteith Cl RRTW TN3 .... 36 F6
Monterey Dr HAV PO9 .... 103 H1
Monterey Gdns BEXW TN39 .... 136 C2
 BOGR PO21 .... 171 M1
Monterey Pines
 MSEA/BNM PO22 .... 3 M4
Montes Hl HWH RH16 .... 207 L9
Monteswood La HWH RH16 .... 207 L9
Montford Cl SHOR BN43 .... 120 C5
Montfort Cl PEV BN24 .... 133 L7
Montfort Rd PEV BN24 .... 133 L7
Montgomeri Dr ANG/EP BN16 .... 148 A2
Montgomery Dr
 MSEA/BNM PO22 .... 145 J7
Montgomery Rd HAV PO9 .... 103 H4
 RHAS TN35 .... 284 G12
 SBGH/RUST TN4 .... 38 A2
Montgomery St HOVE BN3 .... 121 M6
Montier Ter PETW GU28 * 229 L9
Montpelier Crs BRI BN1 .... 4 B4
Montpelier Gdns
 PUL/STOR RH20 .... 298 H1
Montpelier Pl BRI BN1 .... 4 A5
Montpelier Rd ANG/EP BN16 .... 148 A5
 BRI BN1 .... 4 A5
Montpelier St BRI BN1 .... 4 B5
Montpelier Ter BRI BN1 .... 4 B5
Montpelier Vls BRI BN1 .... 4 B5
Montreal Rd BRIE/ROTT BN2 .... 5 H3
Montreal Wy SALV BN13 .... 116 B7
Montrose Cl BOR GU35 .... 178 G8
 FERR BN12 .... 150 B2
Monument Cha BOR GU35 .... 178 H8
Monument La RCCH PO18 .... 290 C10
Monument Vw BRIE/ROTT BN2 .... 5 M1
Moonrise Wy HAIL BN27 * 90 A2
Moons Hl BAT TN33 .... 281 N11
Moon's La LING RH7 .... 32 C2
 SWTR RH13 .... 14 F8
Moons Yd CROW TN6 * 211 Q1
Moor Cl BOR GU35 .... 178 G6
Moor Cl SALV BN13 .... 116 A7
Moore Pl BOGR PO21 * 2 C5
Moore's La RYE TN31 .... 250 H6
Moorfield HASM GU27 .... 181 J12
Moorfoot Rd SALV BN13 .... 116 G6
Moorgreen Rd HAV PO9 .... 288 H12
Moor Hall Dr BAT TN33 .... 281 L11
Moorhead Rd HORS RH12 .... 57 G4
Moorhen Cl STLEO TN38 .... 98 D5
Moorhen Wy
 MSEA/BNM PO22 .... 144 A7
Moor Hi HAWK TN18 .... 216 G1
Moorhouse La MIDH GU29 .... 225 R3
Moorhurst Rd STLEO TN38 .... 283 N12
The Moorings
 EDN/EASTW BN20 * 176 E5
 EGRIN RH19 .... 30 F6
 GSHT GU26 .... 180 H5
 LAN/SOMP BN15 .... 118 C5
 LEWES BN7 * 17 K6
 SHOR BN43 .... 120 B7
Moorland Rd CRAWE RH10 .... 44 B6
Moorlands Cl GSHT GU26 .... 180 H5
Moor La RHAS TN35 .... 284 G12
 RING/NEW BN8 .... 87 M2
Moor Pk HORL RH6 * 23 G7
Moor Park Crs CRAWW RH11 .... 42 C4
Moor Pl EGRIN RH19 .... 31 K7
Moor Rd HASM GU27 .... 180 F12
 LISS GU33 .... 192 E4
The Moor HAWK TN18 .... 216 G1
Morants Cl CROW TN6 .... 7 K2
Moraunt Dr MSEA/BNM PO22 .... 145 J7
Morecambe Cl CRAWW RH11 .... 42 E5
Morecambe Rd BRI BN1 .... 82 F7
Morestead PEAHV BN10 .... 157 J4
Moreton Rd RCCH PO18 .... 106 A8
Morgan Cl BRI BN1 .... 99 C5
Morgay Wood La RHAS TN35 .... 284 H11
Morlais Pl WSEA TN36 .... 286 C3
Morlais Rdg WSEA TN36 .... 286 C3
Morland Av SALV BN13 .... 117 K6
Morland Dr RRTW TN3 .... 188 G12
Morlands Cl BAT TN33 .... 281 N11
Morley Cl LEWES BN7 .... 16 D9
Morley Crs HORN PO8 .... 288 B6
Morley Dr STPH/PW TN2 .... 189 L3
Morleys PUL/STOR RH20 .... 267 K9
Morley St BRIE/ROTT BN2 .... 5 J5
Morningside Cl SEAF BN25 .... 174 F1
Mornington Crs HOVE BN3 .... 121 M6
 MSEA/BNM PO22 .... 3 M2
Mornington Man BRIE/ROTT BN3 * 121 L5
Mornington Rd BOR GU35 .... 178 D7
Morrell Av HORS RH12 .... 56 F4
Morris Dr BIL RH14 .... 231 K2
Morris Rd LEWES BN7 .... 17 K2
Morris Wy PUL/STOR RH20 .... 265 R6
Mortain Rd PEV BN24 .... 133 L7
Mortimer Gdns POLE BN26 .... 131 M5
Mortimer Rd LW/ROSE BN22 .... 163 M7
 RDKG RH5 .... 24 C3
Morton Cl CRAWW RH11 .... 59 G1
Morton Rd EGRIN RH19 .... 47 K2
Moscow Rd RHAS TN35 .... 100 B2
Mosdell Rd EMRTH PO10 .... 104 A5
Mosford Cl HORL RH6 .... 22 C7
Moss Cl LISS GU33 .... 192 D9
Moss Dell HAIL BN27 * 90 A2
Mosse Gdns CCH PO19 .... 107 G6
Motcombe La EAST BN21 .... 176 D1
Motcombe Rd EAST BN21 .... 176 D1
Motte Fld HRTF TN7 .... 50 D5
Mottins Hl CROW TN6 .... 211 Q1
Moulsecoomb Pl
 BRIE/ROTT BN2 * 123 J3
Moulsecoomb Wy
 BRIE/ROTT BN2 .... 123 K2
Mountain Ash Cl HAIL BN27 .... 91 M7
Mountbatten Cl CRAWW RH11 * 43 H7
 RHAS TN35 .... 284 G12
Mountbatten Ct
 LHPTN BN17 * 147 H1
Mountbatten Dr LGNY BN23 .... 164 D6
Mount Caburn Crs
 PEAHV BN10 .... 157 H5
Mount Cl BRIE/ROTT BN2 .... 44 B2
 NEWHV BN9 .... 19 L1
Mount Edgcumbe Rd
 SBGH/RUST TN4 .... 37 M6
Mount Ephraim RTW TN1 .... 37 M5

Mount Ephraim Rd RTW TN1 .... 37 M5
Mountfield Gdns RTW TN1 .... 38 A6
Mountfield La RBTBR TN32 .... 247 N6
Mountfield Rd LEWES BN7 .... 16 A6
 RTW TN1 .... 38 A6
Mountfields BRI BN1 .... 123 H6
Mount Harry Rd LEWES BN7 .... 16 A4
Mount Heath UCK TN22 .... 76 E4
Mount Idol Vw BEXW TN39 .... 96 F5
Mount Joy BAT TN33 .... 282 D4
Mount La CCH PO19 .... 6 C3
 CRAWE RH10 .... 45 G5
Mountney Dr PEV BN24 .... 134 E7
Mountney Rd EAST BN21 .... 176 C1
Mount Noddy RHWH RH17 .... 237 K2
Mount Pl LEWES BN7 .... 16 F6
Mount Pleasant ARUN BN18 .... 112 F2
 BRIE/ROTT BN2 .... 5 H7
 CROW TN6 .... 211 K2
 PETW GU28 * 229 L9
 RHAS TN35 .... 284 B5
 RING/NEW BN8 * 274 D3
 STLEO TN38 .... 12 A9
 UCK TN22 .... 76 B6
 UCK TN22 .... 242 H7
 WADH TN5 .... 71 K4
Mount Pleasant Av RTW TN1 .... 37 M6
Mount Pleasant La RRTW TN3 .... 188 E11
Mount Pleasant Rd BOR GU35 .... 179 J4
 HAS TN34 .... 13 J2
 RTW TN1 .... 37 M6
Mountreed MAYF TN20 .... 211 Q10
Mount Rd EDN/EASTW BN20 .... 176 E5
 NEWHV BN9 .... 19 L1
 RHAS TN35 .... 100 B3
Mount Sion RTW TN1 .... 37 M7
Mount St BAT TN33 .... 282 E4
 LEWES BN7 .... 16 F8
The Mount BOR GU35 .... 179 P3
 CRAWW RH11 .... 26 A8
 EDN/EASTW BN20 * 176 A4
 HAIL BN27 .... 92 B7
 HASM GU27 .... 181 Q7
 STLEO TN38 .... 99 G6
 UCK TN22 .... 76 E4
Mountview Rd
 LAN/SOMP BN15 .... 118 B5
Mount View Ter HAIL BN27 .... 92 B7
Mountway LGNY BN23 * 155 H8
Mountwood Rd EMRTH PO10 .... 104 E4
 SELS PO20 .... 301 M5
Mount Zion Pl BRI BN1 .... 4 D5
Mouse La STEY/UB BN44 .... 78 A9
 STEY/UB BN44 .... 299 M9
Mouthey's La RCCH PO18 .... 106 D3
Mowbray Dr CRAWW RH11 .... 42 F5
Moy Av LW/ROSE BN22 .... 11 G2
Moyne Cl HOVE BN3 .... 121 K4
Moyne Rd CRAWW RH11 .... 43 H7
Muccleshell Cl HAV PO9 .... 103 H1
Mudberry La RCCH PO18 .... 105 M5
Muggeridge's Hl RDKG RH5 .... 40 D1
Muirfield Cl CRAWW RH11 .... 42 C4
 SALV BN13 .... 116 D7
Muirfield Ri STLEO TN38 .... 98 C6
Muirfield Rd SALV BN13 .... 116 C7
Mulberry Cl BEXW TN39 .... 136 B1
 BRI BN1 .... 122 E2
 FERR BN12 .... 150 B2
 HORS RH12 .... 56 B4
 LAN/SOMP BN15 .... 118 D7
 LW/ROSE BN22 .... 163 K2
 SHOR BN43 .... 120 C6
Mulberry Ct FERR BN12 * 150 B2
Mulberry Gdns FERR BN12 .... 150 B3
Mulberry La FERR BN12 .... 150 B3
 HPPT/KEY BN6 .... 272 A6
Mulberry Ldg ANG/EP BN16 * 148 B4
Mulberry Pk UCK TN22 .... 209 N12
Mulberry Rd CRAWW RH11 .... 27 G8
Mulberry Wk SLVH TN37 .... 284 A12
Mulberry Wy HTHF TN21 .... 244 E8
Mumford Pl CCH PO19 * 7 H8
Mundays Rw HORN PO8 .... 256 D12
Munmere Wy ANG/EP BN16 .... 148 D3
Munnion Rd RHWH RH17 .... 206 E2
Munns Dr BURH RH15 .... 75 G5
Munster Gn RING/NEW BN8 .... 274 D5
Muntham Dr SWTR RH13 .... 200 H10
Murina Av BOGR PO21 .... 2 C3
Murray Av NEWHV BN9 .... 18 E3
Murray Cl SWTR RH13 .... 57 G5
Murray Rd HORN PO8 .... 288 D3
 SELS PO20 .... 301 J7
Murrey Ct SWTR RH13 * 57 G5
Muscliffe Ct HAV PO9 .... 289 J12
Museum Hl HASM GU27 .... 181 N11
Musgrave Av EGRIN RH19 .... 47 K2
Mushroom Fld LEWES BN7 .... 85 K8
Mustang Cl ARUN BN18 .... 146 A2
Muster Gn HWH RH16 .... 73 G5
Muster Gn South HWH RH16 .... 73 G5
Mutton Hall Hl HTHF TN21 .... 244 D5
Mutton Hall La HTHF TN21 .... 244 D5
Mutton Hl LING RH7 .... 31 M7
Mutton's La PUL/STOR RH20 .... 266 C10
Myrtle Cottages CROW TN6 * 67 L6
Myrtle Gv LAN/SOMP BN15 .... 118 D8
Myrtle Gv ANG/EP BN16 .... 148 D4
Myrtle La BIL RH14 .... 232 A2
Myrtle Rd CROW TN6 .... 67 L8
 LAN/SOMP BN15 .... 118 C8
 LW/ROSE BN22 .... 164 C7
Myrtle Ter HFD BN5 * 269 K5
Myrtle Vls CROW TN6 * 67 L6
Mytten Bank RHWH RH17 .... 72 C3
Mytten Cl RHWH RH17 .... 72 C3

N

Nab Tower La SELS PO20 .... 300 H5
Nab Wk SELS PO20 .... 167 L7
Nagels Cl SELS PO20 .... 167 M7
Naiad Gdns MSEA/BNM PO22 .... 173 J1
Naish Ct HAV PO9 .... 288 D10
Naldrett Cl HORS RH12 .... 15 J1
Naldretts La HORS RH12 .... 185 N13
Namrik Ms HOVE BN3 .... 121 M7
Nanson Rd BRI BN1 .... 83 J7
Nan Tucks La UCK TN22 .... 77 L1
Napier Rd HORN PO8 .... 288 D3
 RTWE/PEM TN2 .... 38 C7
 STLEO TN38 .... 283 N12
Napier Wy CRAWE RH10 .... 27 L8

Nappers Wd HASM GU27 195 K7
Nash La RHWH RH17 239 L1
Nash Rd CRAWE RH10 43 K6
Nash Wy ARUN BN18 111 J4
Natal Rd BRIE/ROTT BN2 123 J4
Natts La BIL RH14 231 R2
Navarino Rd WTHG BN11 151 M2
Neale Cl EGRIN RH19 31 G6
Neaves La RING/NEW BN8 275 M12
Needlemakers CCH PO19 * 7 G4
Needles Cl HORS RH12 14 A8
Need's Hl SWTR RH13 234 D7
Neill's Cl NEWHV BN9 18 F4
Neills Rd RRTW TN3 190 C3
Nell Ball BIL RH14 197 R3
Nellington Rd SBGH/RUST TN4 37 G5
Nelson Cl CRAWE RH10 44 B4
LAN/SOMP BN15 118 C5
SELS PO20 109 J4
Nelson Crs HORN PO8 * 288 D2
Nelson Dr LGNY BN23 164 D7
Nelson Rd BOGR PO21 171 M2
FERR BN12 150 C1
HAS TN34 13 J4
HORS RH12 14 B3
RTWE/PEM TN2 38 C7
Nelson Rw ARUN BN18 146 D2
BRIE/ROTT BN2 5 G6
Nepcote SALV BN13 298 H12
Nepfield Cl SALV BN13 298 H12
Nep Town Rd HFD BN5 269 K5
Neptune Cl CRAWW RH11 42 D5
Neptune Ct MSEA/BNM PO22 173 J1
Neptune Rd BOR GU35 178 H7
Neptune Wy LHPTN BN17 147 M5
Nerissa Cl WVILLE PO7 288 C9
Nesbitt Rd BRIE/ROTT BN2 123 J4
Ness Rd LYDD TN29 255 R7
Netherfield Av LGNY BN23 164 E3
Netherfield Cl HAV PO9 103 H5
Netherfield Gn
BRIE/ROTT BN2 124 E5
Netherfield Hl BAT TN33 282 C2
Netherfield Rd BAT TN33 247 R12
Netherfield Wy BAT TN33 247 R11
Nether La UCK TN22 208 H6
Netherton Cl SELS PO20 301 L6
SWTR RH13 201 Q9
Netherwood CRAWW RH11 8 A8
Netherwood Cl HAS TN34 284 B12
Netley Cl CRAWW RH11 59 H1
Nettleton Av SELS PO20 109 H3
Nevile Cl CRAWW RH11 42 F6
Nevill Av HOVE BN3 121 L4
LW/ROSE BN22 163 K4
Nevill Cl CROW TN6 * 210 D1
HOVE BN3 121 M3
Nevill Ct SBGH/RUST TN4 37 J7
Nevill Crs LEWES BN7 16 B4
Neville Gdns EMRTH PO10 103 M2
Neville Rd CCH PO19 107 J6
LW/ROSE BN22 11 G3
MSEA/BNM PO22 2 F4
PEAHV BN10 157 J7
Nevill Gdns HOVE BN3 121 M3
Nevill Ga RTWE/PEM TN2 38 A8
Nevill Pk SBGH/RUST TN4 37 K6
Nevill Pl HOVE BN3 121 M3
Nevill Rdg SBGH/RUST TN4 37 J6
Nevill Rd BRIE/ROTT BN2 155 L4
CROW TN6 67 L6
HOVE BN3 121 M3
LEWES BN7 16 B4
UCK TN22 76 F3
Nevill St RTWE/PEM TN2 37 M7
Nevill Ter CROW TN6 * 67 L6
LEWES BN7 16 C6
RTWE/PEM TN2 37 L7
Nevill Wy HOVE BN3 121 M3
Newark Pl BRIE/ROTT BN2 5 G4
Newark Rd CRAWE RH10 43 L1
New Barn BIL RH14 198 B11
New Barn Cl HAIL BN27 92 B7
PTSD BN41 121 G3
SHOR BN43 * 120 A4
New Barn Hl RCCH PO18 108 F1
RCCH PO18 293 K12
New Barn La PUL/STOR RH20 265 Q5
UCK TN22 76 E7
Newbarn La BOGR PO21 143 L6
HFD BN5 269 L8
MSEA/BNM PO22 145 G8
RCCH PO18 290 C9
New Barn Rd ARUN BN18 296 E4
BRIE/ROTT BN2 155 K2
SHOR BN43 120 A4
Newbarn Rd EPSF GU31 257 K2
HAV PO9 102 D2
New Br BIL RH14 231 N1
Newbridge Cl HORS RH12 201 M2
Newbridge Rd BIL RH14 231 Q1
New Brighton Rd
EMRTH PO10 104 A3
New Broadway WTHG BN11 * 20 B3
Newbury La RHWH RH17 72 B4
WADH TN5 190 B5
Newbury Rd CRAWE RH10 44 C3
New Church Rd HOVE BN3 121 J6
New Coastguard Cottages
RHAS TN35 * 286 B9
SEAF BN25 * 174 C1
Newcomen Rd SBGH/RUST TN4 37 M4
New Cottages CROW TN6 * 211 K1
RRTW TN3 * 54 B3
New Courtwick La
LHPTN BN17 147 H1
New Cut ARUN BN18 113 G2
RBTBR TN32 248 D8
RHAS TN35 284 B5
Newdigate Rd HORS RH12 41 J1
New Dorset St BRI BN1 4 D5
Newells Cl BRIE/ROTT BN2 124 D4
Newells La RCCH PO18 105 M3
SWTR RH13 203 J7
New England La BAT TN33 283 N3
New England Ri PTSD BN41 120 F1
New England Rd BRI BN1 4 D2
HWH RH16 73 H5
SBGH/RUST TN4 37 M2
New England St BRI BN1 4 E3
New Farthingdale LING RH7 31 M1
Newfield La NEWHV BN9 18 F3
Newfield Rd LISS GU33 192 D7
NEWHV BN9 18 E3
SELS PO20 301 N5
New Gdns LAN/SOMP BN15 * 117 L6
Newgate Rd SLVH TN37 12 A4
Newhall Cl BOGR PO21 171 M2
New Hall La HFD BN5 269 J10
Newham Cl STEY/UB BN44 78 B2
Newham La STEY/UB BN44 78 A3
Newhaven Fort NEWHV BN9 * 19 H8
Newhaven Hts NEWHV BN9 * 18 E8
Newhaven Rd SEAF BN25 158 F8
Newhaven Sq NEWHV BN9 19 G3
Newhaven St BRIE/ROTT BN2 5 G4
Newhouse La PUL/STOR RH20 266 F10
RCCH PO18 293 N2
Newick Cl SEAF BN25 175 J3
Newick Dr RING/NEW BN8 240 B6
Newick Hl RING/NEW BN8 240 B5
Newick La MAYF TN20 212 D9
Newick Rd BRI BN1 123 K1
EDN/EASTW BN20 163 H7
Newland Rd STEY/UB BN44 79 G3
WTHG BN11 21 H3
Newlands RHWH RH17 60 E8
RRTW TN3 36 F5
Newlands Av BEXW TN39 96 F8
Newlands Cl HAS TN34 284 B12
HORL RH6 22 E4
HPPT/KEY BN6 271 P6
Newlands Crs EGRIN RH19 31 J7
Newlands La CCH PO19 107 J5
Newlands Pk CRAWE RH10 29 K6
Newlands Park Wy
RING/NEW BN8 240 B6
Newlands Pl FROW RH18 * 48 E6
Newlands Ri SBGH/RUST TN4 37 M3
Newlands Rd BRIE/ROTT BN2 155 M4
CRAWW RH11 8 D5
HORS RH12 14 C2
SBGH/RUST TN4 38 A3
Newland St WTHG BN11 21 H3
Newlands Wy SBGH/RUST TN4 37 M2
New La EPSF GU31 258 E3
HAV PO9 103 H3
LYDD TN29 255 R7
New Langney Ct LGNY BN23 * 164 D4
Newlease Rd WVILLE PO7 288 A12
Newling Wy SALV BN13 116 D4
New Lydd Rd RYE TN31 253 R11
Newman Cl CRAWE RH10 44 B4
Newman's Gdns
LAN/SOMP BN15 118 A6
Newmans Wy RHAS TN35 100 C1
Newmarket Rd
BRIE/ROTT BN2 123 H5
CRAWE RH10 9 L9
Newmarket Ter
BRIE/ROTT BN2 123 H5
Newmer Ct HAV PO9 288 D11
New Moorhead Dr HORS RH12 57 H3
New Moorsite RHAS TN35 284 C6
Newnham Ct HAV PO9 * 289 J12
Newnham Rd HTHF TN21 244 D7
Newnham Wy HTHF TN21 244 D6
New Pde SELS PO20 * 301 K6
WTHG BN11 21 L6
New Park Av BEX TN40 137 H1
New Park Rd CCH PO19 6 F3
New Pl EAST BN21 176 D2
UCK TN22 76 E7
New Place Rd PUL/STOR RH20 265 K2
New Pond Hl HTHF TN21 244 A7
Newport Dr CCH PO19 107 G6
Newport Ms WTHG BN11 152 A2
Newport Rd BURH RH15 74 E6
Newport St BRIE/ROTT BN2 5 H2
Newpound BIL RH14 199 M10
Newpound La BIL RH14 199 L11
New Rd ANG/EP BN16 148 C2
BIL RH14 200 B11
BOR GU35 178 F8
BRI BN1 4 E6
CROW TN6 67 L6
CROW TN6 69 H8
EMRTH PO10 104 C2
EMRTH PO10 104 F5
HAIL BN27 92 B1
HASM GU27 181 J12
HAV PO9 102 E3
HORN PO8 256 D8
HPPT/KEY BN6 271 N8
LEWES BN7 16 F6
LHPTN BN17 147 J5
LW/ROSE BN22 11 G5
MFD/CHID GU8 182 F1
MIDH GU29 226 H11
MIDH GU29 261 P2
NEWHV BN9 19 J1
PETW GU28 228 F8
POLE BN26 132 A7
RCCH PO18 108 F1
RCCH PO18 261 Q12
RHAS TN35 100 C3
RHAS TN35 101 J1
RING/NEW BN8 87 J2
RYE TN31 250 D2
RYE TN31 253 J7
SALV BN13 116 B6
SHOR BN43 119 L6
STEY/UB BN44 79 G4
SWTR RH13 201 Q9
UCK TN22 241 Q10
New Salts Farm Rd
SHOR BN43 119 H7
Newstead Hall HORL RH6 23 J7
New Steine BRIE/ROTT BN2 5 G8
New Steine Ms BRIE/ROTT BN2 5 G8
New St CRAWE RH10 9 M2
LYDD TN29 255 R7
SWTR RH13 14 F7
WTHG BN11 21 G7
Newtimber Av FERR BN12 150 A2
Newtimber Dr PTSD BN41 120 F4
Newtimber Gdns SHOR BN43 119 L4
Newton Av EGRIN RH19 47 L3
Newton Cl HWH RH16 73 L2
Newton Pk HAIL BN27 92 C6
Newton Rd CRAWE RH10 27 L7
HWH RH16 73 L2
LEWES BN7 16 D4
PEAHV BN10 157 H6
RTW TN1 38 A5
Newton Willows RRTW TN3 52 B2
New Town CCH PO19 6 F5
CRAWE RH10 29 G6
Newtown Av BOGR PO21 143 M7
Newtown Rd HOVE BN3 122 A5
LIPH GU30 193 R2
New Town Rd PUL/STOR RH20 265 Q12
New Upperton Rd EAST BN21 10 A4
New Vls POLE BN26 * 132 A7
New Way La HPPT/KEY BN6 271 J7
New Winchelsea Rd RYE TN31 252 G11
Nicholsfield BIL RH14 198 C1
Nicholson Wy HAV PO9 102 F2
Nickleby Rd HORN PO8 256 C7
Nicolson Cl SELS PO20 109 H3
Nicolson Dr SHOR BN43 119 L5
Nightingale Cl CRAWW RH11 43 H1
EGRIN RH19 47 J2
HAV PO9 288 H8
LGNY BN23 164 B3
PUL/STOR RH20 266 B12
Nightingale Ct EMRTH PO10 104 C1
Nightingale La BURH RH15 271 N1
CRAWE RH10 46 B4
PUL/STOR RH20 266 B12
RCCH PO18 105 H2
Nightingale Pk HAV PO9 103 J4
PUL/STOR RH20 266 B12
Nightingale Ri UCK TN22 76 F8
Nightingale Rd BOR GU35 178 H7
HORS RH12 14 F4
PSF GU32 223 L7
Nightingales PUL/STOR RH20 266 A6
SALV BN13 298 H10
Nightingales Cl SWTR RH13 15 J6
Nightingale Wk BIL RH14 232 A1
Nightjar Cl HORN PO8 288 B3
Nile St BRI BN1 4 E7
EMRTH PO10 104 A5
Nimbus Cl LHPTN BN17 147 M3
Ninfield Pl BRIE/ROTT BN2 123 K6
Ninfield Rd BEXW TN39 96 D4
Niven Cl CRAWE RH10 44 C4
Nizells Av HOVE BN3 122 C6
Noahs Ark La HWH RH16 73 M2
Noahs Ct CRAWE RH10 * 45 M5
Nodes La HAIL BN27 92 E1
Noel Gn BURH RH15 75 G5
Noel Ri BURH RH15 75 G5
Nolan Rd BRIE/ROTT BN2 124 D6
Nonnington La PETW GU28 262 A4
Nook Cl RHAS TN35 100 C2
The Nookery ANG/EP BN16 148 F4
The Nook BAT TN33 * 282 F6
UCK TN22 76 F8
Nor'Bren Av BOGR PO21 143 M8
Norbury Cl CROW TN6 67 K5
LAN/SOMP BN15 118 E5
Norbury Dr LAN/SOMP BN15 118 D5
Nore Crs EMRTH PO10 103 L4
Nore Down Wy RCCH PO18 290 B1
Nore Farm Av EMRTH PO10 103 L4
Nore Rd NEWHV BN9 18 C5
Noreuil Rd PSF GU32 223 L6
Nore Wood La ARUN BN18 294 H11
Norfolk Buildings BRI BN1 4 A6
Norfolk Cl BEXW TN39 97 G6
BOGR PO21 2 B8
CRAWW RH11 42 D7
HORL RH6 22 F7
Norfolk Ct WTHG BN11 * 20 E4
Norfolk Dr STLEO TN38 98 E1
Norfolk Gdns LHPTN BN17 147 L5
Norfolk Ms BRI BN1 4 A6
LHPTN BN17 * 147 L5
Norfolk Pl LHPTN BN17 147 L5
Norfolk Rd BRI BN1 4 A6
HORS RH12 14 E6
LHPTN BN17 147 L5
RTW TN1 38 A7
Norfolk Sq BOGR PO21 2 B8
BRI BN1 4 A6
Norfolk St BOGR PO21 2 D8
BRI BN1 4 A7
WTHG BN11 20 E4
Norfolk Ter BRI BN1 4 A5
HORS RH12 14 E6
Norfolk Wy MSEA/BNM PO22 145 M8
Norley Cl HAV PO9 288 F12
Norlington Ct RING/NEW BN8 275 J11
Norlington Flds
RING/NEW BN8 274 H11
Norlington La RING/NEW BN8 275 K9
Norman Cl BAT TN33 282 G5
BIL RH14 200 B12
BOR GU35 178 H6
LHPTN BN17 147 L4
SEAF BN25 159 G7
Norman Ct HAS TN34 * 12 E8
Norman Crs SHOR BN43 119 L5
Normandale BEXW TN39 136 E2
Normandy HORS RH12 14 C8
Normandy Cl CRAWE RH10 44 A5
EGRIN RH19 * 47 L1
Normandy Dr ANG/EP BN16 148 F5
Normandy Gdns HORS RH12 14 C8
Normandy La ANG/EP BN16 148 F5
Normandy Rd SALV BN13 20 F1
SLVH TN37 99 H2
Normanhurst Cl ANG/EP BN16 148 B5
CRAWE RH10 9 K4
Norman Rd BURH RH15 74 E6
HOVE BN3 121 K7
NEWHV BN9 18 F4
PEV BN24 165 J1
RTW TN1 38 A4
SLVH TN37 12 B9
Normansal Cl SEAF BN25 159 M7
Normansal Park Av
SEAF BN25 159 M7
Normans Ct SHOR BN43 * 119 L4
Norman's Dr
MSEA/BNM PO22 145 G7
Normansland UCK TN22 209 N7
The Normans BEXW TN39 * 136 E1
Normanton Av BOGR PO21 2 A6
Normanton St BRIE/ROTT BN2 5 J2
Norman Wy HAV PO9 102 D3
MSEA/BNM PO22 145 L8
STEY/UB BN44 78 C1
Norris Cl BOR GU35 178 E8
Norris Gdns HAV PO9 103 H5
Norstead Gdns SBGH/RUST TN4 38 A2
Northampton Wy STLEO TN38 98 E1
North Av EDN/EASTW BN20 163 G8
FERR BN12 150 D4
MSEA/BNM PO22 145 L8
North Av South
MSEA/BNM PO22 145 M8
North Bank HPPT/KEY BN6 271 M5
North Barnes La LEWES BN7 273 J4
North Bay EMRTH PO10 138 B2
North Beeches Rd CROW TN6 67 M7
North Bersted St
MSEA/BNM PO22 143 M6
Northbourne Cl SHOR BN43 119 L5
Northbourne Rd
LW/ROSE BN22 164 A6
Northbridge St RBTBR TN32 216 C12
Northbrook Cl SALV BN13 117 K7
Northbrook Rd SALV BN13 117 K7
North Camp La SEAF BN25 159 L8
Northcliffe Cl SEAF BN25 174 F1
Northcliffe Rd MSEA/BNM PO22 3 G4
North Cl CCH PO19 * 6 E3
CRAWE RH10 9 J1
HAV PO9 103 H5
POLE BN26 132 A6
PTSD BN41 120 F4
North Common Rd
RHWH RH17 238 C8
Northcote Gdns EMRTH PO10 104 F5
Northcote La PEAHV BN10 156 F4
Northcote Rd BOGR PO21 171 M1
North Ct HPPT/KEY BN6 271 M5
LEWES BN7 17 J5
Northcourt Cl ANG/EP BN16 148 C3
Northcourt Rd SALV BN13 20 F2
Northcroft HFD BN5 269 J4
Northdown Cl HORS RH12 15 J1
NEWHV BN9 18 E5
Northdown Rd NEWHV BN9 18 D5
Northdown Ter EGRIN RH19 * 31 J6
North Dr ANG/EP BN16 148 E1
BRIE/ROTT BN2 5 J5
Northease Cl HOVE BN3 121 J3
Northease Dr HOVE BN3 121 K2
Northease Gdns HOVE BN3 121 K2
North End EGRIN RH19 * 31 G6
HPPT/KEY BN6 272 A5
North End Cl PETW GU28 229 L8
Northend La HPPT/KEY BN6 236 G10
North End Rd ARUN BN18 145 L2
Northern Av POLE BN26 132 A6
Northern Crs SELS PO20 167 K6
North Farm La RTWE/PEM TN2 38 C1
North Farm Rd
LAN/SOMP BN15 118 E7
SBGH/RUST TN4 38 B2
Northfield POLE BN26 131 L8
SELS PO20 301 M6
Northfield Cl HORN PO8 256 D11
SEAF BN25 159 L8
Northfield Ri BRIE/ROTT BN2 155 M3
HOVE BN3 121 J1
Northfield Rd SALV BN13 116 F7
Northfields RRTW TN3 36 F1
Northfields La SELS PO20 110 C5
Northfield Wy BRI BN1 122 F1
North Gdns BRI BN1 4 D5
Northgate CCH PO19 6 E3
Northgate Av CRAWE RH10 9 J2
Northgate Cl BRIE/ROTT BN2 155 L3
LAN/SOMP BN15 118 A7
Northgate Pl CRAWE RH10 9 H1
Northgate Rd CRAWE RH10 8 F3
HORL RH6 22 E8
North Ham Rd LHPTN BN17 147 J4
North Heath Cl HAIL BN27 * 92 B3
HORS RH12 56 C4
North Heath La HORS RH12 56 C4
North Holmes Cl HORS RH12 57 G4
Northiam Ri STLEO TN38 98 C3
Northiam Rd
EDN/EASTW BN20 176 C1
RYE TN31 250 D6
Northlands Av HWH RH16 73 K6
Northlands La PUL/STOR RH20 266 B9
Northlands Rd HORS RH12 56 D2
HORS RH12 187 N8
North La ANG/EP BN16 148 A3
ANG/EP BN16 149 G3
EGRIN RH19 62 D4
EPSF GU31 223 M12
EPSF GU31 258 E1
HORN PO8 256 C7
NEWHV BN9 18 F3
PTSD BN41 120 F3
RCCH PO18 261 K12
RHAS TN35 284 H4
STEY/UB BN44 267 M11
North Md CRAWE RH10 43 K1
HFD BN5 269 K3
Northney Rd HISD PO11 103 H8
North Pallant CCH PO19 6 E5
North Pde BOR GU35 178 F3
HORS RH12 14 C1
North Pl BRI BN1 4 F6
LHPTN BN17 147 K5
North Pound ARUN BN18 111 J4
North Quay Rd NEWHV BN9 158 C4
Northridge RYE TN31 218 D11
North Rd BEXW TN39 97 H6
BRI BN1 4 E5
CRAWE RH10 9 L1
CRBK TN17 189 R8
HAIL BN27 280 B7
HORN PO8 256 D11
HWH RH16 73 K5
LAN/SOMP BN15 118 D7
PEV BN24 165 J1
POLE BN26 160 D2
PSF GU32 223 N5
PTSD BN41 120 F3
RCCH PO18 106 B6
RING/NEW BN8 275 J11
SELS PO20 301 L6
SLVH TN37 12 A4
North Rw UCK TN22 76 E4
North Salts RYE TN31 252 H7
North St BRI BN1 4 D6
CCH PO19 6 E4
CRAWE RH10 45 M5
CROW TN6 211 Q1
EAST BN21 11 G7
EDEN TN8 33 M3
EMRTH PO10 104 A4
EMRTH PO10 104 C1
HAIL BN27 91 L1
HAIL BN27 92 A6
HAV PO9 102 E3
HAV PO9 103 G4
HORS RH12 14 F4
HTHF TN21 243 N8
HTHF TN21 245 N8
LEWES BN7 17 G5
LHPTN BN17 147 J2
MAYF TN20 212 E6
MIDH GU29 227 J9
PETW GU28 229 L8
POLE BN26 160 F2
PUL/STOR RH20 266 A12
RTWE/PEM TN2 38 B6
SHOR BN43 119 K6
STLEO TN38 12 A8
WSEA TN36 286 D1
WTHG BN11 21 H4
North Street Ar HAV PO9 * 103 G4
North Street Qd BRI BN1 * 4 D6
North Stroud La PSF GU32 222 F7
North Ter HAS TN34 13 M2
North Trade Rd BAT TN33 282 C5
Northumberland Rd
BOR GU35 178 G8
North Vw RRTW TN3 * 36 F1
Northview Ter SALV BN13 * 298 H11
North Walls CCH PO19 6 D4
North Wy HAV PO9 102 F4
LEWES BN7 16 A4
MSEA/BNM PO22 3 J4
NEWHV BN9 19 G3
PETW GU28 229 K10
SEAF BN25 159 L8
Northway BURH RH15 75 H5
HORL RH6 27 L1
Northway Rd LHPTN BN17 147 J1
Northwood Av
BRIE/ROTT BN2 156 D4
Northwood Pk CRAWE RH10 * 27 M7
Northwyke Cl
MSEA/BNM PO22 145 H8
Northwyke Rd
MSEA/BNM PO22 145 H8
Norton Cl HOVE BN3 122 A7
Norton Dr BRIE/ROTT BN2 124 E5
Norton La SELS PO20 110 A4
Norton Rd HOVE BN3 122 A7
LAN/SOMP BN15 118 C8
NEWHV BN9 19 J4
Norton Ter NEWHV BN9 19 J4
Norway La LHPTN BN17 147 L2
Norway Rd LW/ROSE BN22 164 C7
Norway St PTSD BN41 121 H6
Norwich Cl BRIE/ROTT BN2 123 M3
Norwich Ct WTHG BN11 * 20 A7
Norwich Dr BRIE/ROTT BN2 123 M3
Norwich Rd CCH PO19 107 L5
Norwood La PETW GU28 262 D5
Norwood La South
PETW GU28 262 D8
Nottidge Rd SBGH/RUST TN4 37 J8
Novington La LEWES BN7 273 K8
Nowhurst La HORS RH12 187 K12
Nuffield Cl BOGR PO21 171 K2
Nugent Cl MFD/CHID GU8 184 A3
Nunnery La RTON TN11 35 L1
Nunnery Stable LEWES BN7 * 16 D6
Nunns Fld RDKG RH5 * 24 B3
The Nurseries BOGR PO21 171 H2
RHWH RH17 60 F8
Nursery Cl ANG/EP BN16 148 F5
EMRTH PO10 104 A2
HAIL BN27 92 B5
HPPT/KEY BN6 270 G2
HWH RH16 73 G4
LAN/SOMP BN15 118 C5
MSEA/BNM PO22 111 G7
POLE BN26 132 A7
PTSD BN41 120 D1
RDKG RH5 24 B4
SHOR BN43 120 A5
WADH TN5 191 N10
Nursery Fld LISS GU33 192 B10
UCK TN22 242 C1
Nursery Gdns HORN PO8 288 B4
LHPTN BN17 147 J2
Nurserylands CRAWW RH11 42 F3
Nursery La CCH PO19 107 G6
HAIL BN27 280 A12
HORL RH6 22 C7
RHWH RH17 * 238 G8
UCK TN22 76 F8
UCK TN22 208 H5
UCK TN22 209 N12
UCK TN22 209 N8
UCK TN22 243 M4
WTHG BN11 20 E7
Nursery Rd ANG/EP BN16 148 F1
HAV PO9 102 D3
SBGH/RUST TN4 38 A1
The Nursery BURH RH15 75 H5
Nursery Wy HTHF TN21 244 B6
Nursling Crs HAV PO9 288 H12
Nutbourne La PUL/STOR RH20 231 P11
Nutbourne Rd
PUL/STOR RH20 265 P4
SALV BN13 20 C1
Nutcombe La GSHT GU26 180 H8
Nutcroft PUL/STOR RH20 265 K2
Nutham La SWTR RH13 201 R12
Nuthatch Cl HAV PO9 289 J8
Nuthatch Rd LGNY BN23 164 B2
Nuthatch Wy CRAWE RH10 46 B4
Nuthurst Cl BRIE/ROTT BN2 123 L8
CRAWW RH11 42 F2
Nuthurst Pl BRIE/ROTT BN2 123 L8
Nuthurst Rd SWTR RH13 202 E12
Nuthurst St SWTR RH13 202 F9
Nutley Av BRIE/ROTT BN2 156 C5
FERR BN12 150 B4
Nutley Cl BOR GU35 178 G7
FERR BN12 150 B4
HOVE BN3 121 L2
RYE TN31 252 F7
Nutley Crs FERR BN12 150 B4
Nutley Dr FERR BN12 150 B4
Nutley Mill Rd PEV BN24 133 G8
Nutley Rd HAV PO9 288 E12
Nutwick Rd HAV PO9 103 J2
Nye Cl CROW TN6 67 L8
Nye La HPPT/KEY BN6 272 A9
Nye Rd BURH RH15 75 G6
Nyes Cl HFD BN5 269 L4
Nyes La SWTR RH13 201 Q10
Nyetimber Copse
PUL/STOR RH20 265 R7
Nyetimber Crs BOGR PO21 171 G3
Nyetimber Hl BRIE/ROTT BN2 123 K3
Nyetimber La BOGR PO21 170 F3
PUL/STOR RH20 265 Q6
Nyetimber Ml BOGR PO21 170 F3
The Nyetimbers BOGR PO21 170 F3
Nyewood Gdns BOGR PO21 * 2 B6
Nyewood La BOGR PO21 2 A5
Nyewood Pl BOGR PO21 2 A8

Nymans Cl HORS RH12 56 F2
Nymans Ct CRAWE RH10 * 44 A6
Nyton Rd RCCH PO18 109 M3
SELS PO20 110 B5

O

Oakapple Cl CRAWW RH11 43 G8
SWTR RH13 235 K4
Oakapple Rd STHW BN42 120 C4
Oak Av CCH PO19 6 B2
HAIL BN27 * 90 A2
PUL/STOR RH20 266 E10
Oak Bank HWH RH16 73 J2
Oak Bungalows LYDD TN29 * 255 R7
Oak Cl BRI BN1 122 D2
CCH PO19 6 B2
CRAWE RH10 28 E6
MFD/CHID GU8 182 F5
MSEA/BNM PO22 144 B7
PUL/STOR RH20 266 C11
SALV BN13 116 D4
SWTR RH13 233 Q2
Oak Cottages CROW TN6 * 210 C2
HASM GU27 * 180 H11
Oak Ct CRAWE RH10 * 27 J7
Oak Cft EGRIN RH19 47 M1
Oakcroft Gdns LHPTN BN17 147 L2
Oakdale Rd HWH RH16 73 J6
SBGH/RUST TN4 37 L5
Oak Dell CRAWE RH10 44 B2
Oakdene Av PTSD BN41 120 D2
Oakdene Cl PTSD BN41 120 D2
Oakdene Crs PTSD BN41 120 D2
Oakdene Gdns PTSD BN41 120 D2
Oakdene Ri PTSD BN41 120 D1
Oakdene Wy PTSD BN41 120 D2
Oak End ARUN BN18 112 D3
PUL/STOR RH20 266 A6
Oakenfield BURH RH15 74 E4
Oakfield BIL RH14 197 R2
Oakfield Av SELS PO20 167 L6
Oakfield Cl HWH RH16 73 K2
Oakfield Ct HAV PO9 * 289 J12
Oakfield Court Rd
RTWE/PEM TN2 38 B6
Oakfield Rd RHAS TN35 100 B2
SELS PO20 167 L6
STPH/PW TN12 188 C1
SWTR RH13 235 K4
Oakfields CRAWE RH10 44 C2
RDKG RH5 186 H1
The Oak Fld RHAS TN35 285 Q9
The Oakfield RYE TN31 252 G5
Oakfield Wy BEXW TN39 96 B7
EGRIN RH19 31 L6
Oak Gv BIL RH14 198 H1
MSEA/BNM PO22 144 B7
Oak Hall Pk BURH RH15 75 G8
Oakhanger Rd BOR GU35 178 D4
Oakhaven CRAWE RH10 * 8 E7
Oakhill Dr RYE TN31 250 E8
Oakhill Rd BOR GU35 179 Q4
SWTR RH13 14 F5
Oakhurst GSHT GU26 180 G6
HFD BN5 269 K3
HPPT/KEY BN6 236 E12
MIDH GU29 226 G9
Oakhurst Cl HAS TN34 284 B12
Oakhurst Dr CROW TN6 67 M6
WVILLE PO7 288 B9
Oakhurst Gdns ANG/EP BN16 148 D3
EGRIN RH19 31 H7
Oakhurst La BIL RH14 184 F11
HWH RH16 73 G2
Oakhurst Ms SWTR RH13 * 15 M1
Oakhurst Rd BAT TN33 282 F3
Oakland Dr RBTBR TN32 247 Q1
Oaklands BIL RH14 232 A2
HASM GU27 181 M10
HORL RH6 23 H6
PEV BN24 133 J7
RHWH RH17 206 E1
SWTR RH13 15 G6
Oaklands Av BRIE/ROTT BN2 156 B4
Oaklands Cl POLE BN26 132 A7
SWTR RH13 202 D1
Oaklands La MIDH GU29 261 J1
Oaklands Rd HAV PO9 103 H4
HWH RH16 73 G4
PSF GU32 223 M5
RRTW TN3 52 A3
Oaklands Wy CCH PO19 6 E2
Oak La HORS RH12 201 P2
LYDD TN29 255 Q7
Oaklea Cl SLVH TN37 99 H1
Oakleaf Dr POLE BN26 131 M6
Oaklea Wy UCK TN22 76 D5
Oak Lees HWH RH16 * 73 L1
Oakleigh Cl WTHG BN11 151 M1
Oakleigh Ct STPH/PW TN12 189 L3
Oakleigh Dr HTHF TN21 244 E7
Oakleigh Rd BEXW TN39 136 B1
HORS RH12 15 K1
WTHG BN11 151 M1
Oakley Cl EGRIN RH19 48 A2
Oakley Gdns ANG/EP BN16 148 F5
Oakley Rd BOR GU35 178 G4
HAV PO9 288 E12
Oak Little SWTR RH13 234 E10
Oak Ldg HASM GU27 * 195 P1
Oak Meadow SELS PO20 140 D8
Oakmeadow Cl EMRTH PO10 104 B2
Oakmead Rd BURH RH15 74 E8
Oakmede Wy RING/NEW BN8 274 H12
Oakmont Dr HORN PO8 288 A7
Oak Park Dr HAV PO9 103 H2
Oak Rd CRAWW RH11 8 D5
HORN PO8 256 D8
RTWE/PEM TN2 38 C2
SWTR RH13 201 P12
Oakroyd Cl BURH RH15 75 H4
Oaks Cl BUR/ETCH TN19 215 N8
HORS RH12 57 G3
SELS PO20 110 C7
Oaks Coppice HORN PO8 288 B3
Oaks Forstal HAWK TN18 217 R4
Oakshott Dr HAV PO9 288 H12
Oakside Ct HORL RH6 23 H5
Oakside La HORL RH6 23 H5
The Oaks ANG/EP BN16 148 D4
BOGR PO21 171 K2
BURH RH15 74 B5
EGRIN RH19 47 M1
HFD BN5 * 269 L11
HTHF TN21 244 E7
HWH RH16 73 K4
HWH RH16 73 M5
MFD/CHID GU8 * 182 G5
SLVH TN37 284 A12
Oak Ter STLEO TN38 * 99 G4
Oaktree RING/NEW BN8 274 D5
Oaktree Cl BOGR PO21 170 E3
Oak Tree Cl BOR GU35 179 N5
EGRIN RH19 * 31 H6
LGNY BN23 164 B1
RTWE/PEM TN2 37 M8
Oak Tree Ct UCK TN22 76 F4
Oak Tree Dr EMRTH PO10 103 M1
EMRTH PO10 104 A1
LISS GU33 192 D9
Oak Tree Farm RCCH PO18 105 J4
Oak Tree La HASM GU27 180 G11
LGNY BN23 164 B1
MFD/CHID GU8 184 A4
SELS PO20 110 C8
Oak Tree Rd BOR GU35 178 F8
Oak Tree Wy HAIL BN27 92 B3
SWTR RH13 15 K2
Oakvale PUL/STOR RH20 265 R6
Oak Wk HORS RH12 41 L7
Oak Wy CRAWE RH10 43 K1
Oakway SWTR RH13 202 H2
Oakwood SWTR RH13 234 F10
Oakwood Av BEXW TN39 97 G6
HAV PO9 102 C2
Oakwood Cl BURH RH15 75 G7
HAS TN34 99 L2
MIDH GU29 226 G10
SELS PO20 109 J3
Oakwood Dr ANG/EP BN16 148 F1
UCK TN22 77 G4
Oakwood Flats HWH RH16 * 73 G5
Oakwood Gdns BOGR PO21 2 C4
Oakwood Pk UCK TN22 208 H4
Oakwood Ri RTWE/PEM TN2 38 D2
Oakwood Rd BURH RH15 75 G7
HORL RH6 22 F5
HWH RH16 73 G5
Oast Cl RTWE/PEM TN2 38 C2
Oasthouse Cl SLVH TN37 284 A12
Oast House Dr RYE TN31 252 E9
Oast House Fld WSEA TN36 285 Q3
Oast House Rd WSEA TN36 285 Q4
Oast Vw STPH/PW TN12 189 M4
Oates Wk CRAWE RH10 9 J9
Oathall Av HWH RH16 73 J3
Oathall Rd HWH RH16 73 H4
Oatlands CRAWW RH11 42 F4
HORL RH6 23 G5
Oban Rd SLVH TN37 99 G2
Oberon Cl WVILLE PO7 288 B9
Oberon Wy CRAWW RH11 42 D6
Observatory Vw HAIL BN27 92 C7
Ocean Cl FERR BN12 149 K5
Ocean Dr FERR BN12 149 K5
Ocean Pde FERR BN12 149 K4
Ochiltree Cl HAS TN34 99 M1
Ochiltree Rd HAS TN34 99 M1
Ockenden La RHWH RH17 72 B3
Ockenden Wy HPPT/KEY BN6 271 M6
Ockley Ct BOGR PO21 2 D7
Ockley Hl HPPT/KEY BN6 271 Q3
Ockley La HPPT/KEY BN6 271 P5
Ockley Rd BOGR PO21 2 C7
Ockley Wy HPPT/KEY BN6 271 P5
Ocklynge Av EAST BN21 * 176 D1
Ocklynge Cl BEXW TN39 96 C8
Ocklynge Rd EAST BN21 176 D1
Ockman La RYE TN31 * 252 H8
Octavius Ct WVILLE PO7 288 C8
Offa Ct BEX TN40 * 137 H1
Offa Rd RHAS TN35 100 C2
Offham Cl LGNY BN23 163 L1
SEAF BN25 159 L8
Offham Rd LEWES BN7 16 C3
Offham Ter LEWES BN7 * 16 F5
The Office Village UCK TN22 * 76 E5
Offington Av SALV BN13 117 G6
Offington Ct SALV BN13 117 H7
Offington Dr SALV BN13 117 G6
Offington Gdns SALV BN13 116 F6
Offington La SALV BN13 116 F7
Okehurst La BIL RH14 199 R9
Okehurst Rd BIL RH14 199 P7
EDN/EASTW BN20 176 C2
Oldaker Rd RING/NEW BN8 240 C6
Old Arundel Rd RCCH PO18 108 E3
Old Bakery Gdns CCH PO19 7 H6
Old Barn Cl BOGR PO21 170 F3
EDN/EASTW BN20 163 G4
Old Barn Dr RDKG RH5 24 C3
Old Barn Wy STHW BN42 120 F6
Old Boat Wk BRI BN1 83 G6
Old Br PUL/STOR RH20 265 J3
Old Bridge Rd RCCH PO18 106 B6
Old Brighton Rd (North)
CRAWW RH11 59 H2
Old Brighton Rd (South)
CRAWW RH11 59 G4
Old Brighton Rd South
HORL RH6 27 K5
Old Broyle Rd CCH PO19 107 H3
Old Buddington La
MIDH GU29 226 H7
Oldbury Cl HORS RH12 56 F2
Old Camp Rd
EDN/EASTW BN20 176 C3
Old Church Rd STLEO TN38 98 F1
Old Coastguards
MSEA/BNM PO22 3 K5
Old Convent EGRIN RH19 * 31 K7
Old Copse Rd HAV PO9 103 H3
Old Cottage Cl SELS PO20 109 H4
Old Court Cl BRI BN1 122 E1
Old Crawley Rd HORS RH12 57 H3
Old Denne Gdns HORS RH12 14 C8
Old Dr POLE BN26 131 L7
Old Dro LGNY BN23 164 B2
Olde Place Ms BRIE/ROTT BN2 155 L4
Older Wy ANG/EP BN16 114 E7
Old Farm Cl BOGR PO21 171 J3
RHWH RH17 73 K7
Old Farm Dr SELS PO20 110 C6
Old Farm La EMRTH PO10 104 D2
Old Farm Rd BEXW TN39 97 G7
BRI BN1 82 E8
SELS PO20 301 J5
Old Farm Wy CHAM PO6 102 A6
Oldfield Av EDN/EASTW BN20 162 F1
Oldfield Crs HAIL BN27 92 A4
STHW BN42 120 C6
Oldfield Rd EDN/EASTW BN20 162 F1
HORL RH6 22 E8
The Old Flour Ml
EMRTH PO10 * 104 B5
Old Forest La CROW TN6 211 M1
Old Forewood La BAT TN33 282 G11
Old Forge Cl HORS RH12 41 L8
Old Forge La UCK TN22 209 L9
Old Fort Rd SHOR BN43 119 M7
Old Gardens Cl RTWE/PEM TN2 54 A1
Old Ghyll Rd HTHF TN21 244 D8
Old Glebe HASM GU27 195 L7
The Old Granary RCCH PO18 * 109 J1
Old Guildford Rd HORS RH12 201 N1
Old Harrow Rd SLVH TN37 99 G1
Old Haslemere Rd HASM GU27 181 M12
Old Heath Cl RING/NEW BN8 276 D3
Old Holbrook HORS RH12 56 D1
Old Hollow CRAWE RH10 44 E1
The Old Hop Gdn RYE TN31 252 B3
Old Horsham Rd CRAWW RH11 8 B7
Old House Gdns HAS TN34 99 L1
Old House La RRTW TN3 36 C4
SWTR RH13 233 L3
UCK TN22 77 G8
Oldhouse La HAV PO9 290 A3
PUL/STOR RH20 232 D10
SELS PO20 169 G6
SWTR RH13 232 E6
Old House Ms HORS RH12 * 14 C5
Old Humphrey Av HAS TN34 13 M5
Oldlands Av HPPT/KEY BN6 271 P5
RHWH RH17 60 E8
Oldlands Hl UCK TN22 209 P7
Oldlands Wy MSEA/BNM PO22 144 D6
Old La CROW TN6 67 J6
CROW TN6 68 A8
MAYF TN20 212 C7
Old London Rd BRI BN1 82 D8
HAS TN34 100 B1
PUL/STOR RH20 264 E7
PUL/STOR RH20 298 H1
RHAS TN35 13 M3
Old Lydd Rd RYE TN31 253 R11
Old Malling Wy LEWES BN7 16 F2
Old Manor Cl BEX TN40 137 J1
CRAWW RH11 42 F1
Old Manor Farm HAV PO9 * 102 C4
Old Manor House Gdns
MSEA/BNM PO22 145 G8
Old Manor Rd ANG/EP BN16 148 A4
Old Mansion Cl
EDN/EASTW BN20 162 F5
Old Market Av CCH PO19 6 E5
Old Market Sq STEY/UB BN44 * 78 D2
Old Martyrs CRAWW RH11 27 J8
Old Mead Rd LHPTN BN17 113 H8
Old Mill Cl BRI BN1 82 D8
HAIL BN27 * 91 M2
Old Mill Dr PUL/STOR RH20 266 A12
Old Mill La EPSF GU31 223 Q4
POLE BN26 162 E1
Old Millmeads HORS RH12 56 B4
Old Mill Pk BEXW TN39 96 F7
Old Mill Pl HASM GU27 181 J10
PUL/STOR RH20 265 L4
The Old Ml ARUN BN18 * 113 G2
Old Motcombe Ms EAST BN21 176 D1
Old Nursery Cl SEAF BN25 160 A8
Old Orch HAWK TN18 217 Q4
Old Orchard Pl HAIL BN27 92 A6
Old Orchard Rd EAST BN21 10 C7
Old Orchards CRAWE RH10 44 D3
Old Palace STPH/PW TN12 * 188 G1
Old Parish La BRIE/ROTT BN2 124 C5
Old Park Cl RHWH RH17 72 D3
Old Park La RCCH PO18 140 B3
Old Pl BOGR PO21 171 K3
Old Point MSEA/BNM PO22 173 K1
Old Printing House Sq
ARUN BN18 * 113 G2
The Old Quarry HASM GU27 195 J1
Old Rectory Cl EMRTH PO10 104 C2
Old Rectory Ct
MSEA/BNM PO22 * 3 L4
Old Rectory Dr SELS PO20 110 D6
Old Rectory Gdns
MSEA/BNM PO22 3 L4
STHW BN42 120 C6
Old Rectory Rd CHAM PO6 102 A5
The Old Rectory
MSEA/BNM PO22 3 L5
Old River Wy WSEA TN36 286 G2
Old Rd EGRIN RH19 47 L1
HAIL BN27 92 E1
Old Roar Rd SLVH TN37 283 R12
Old Salts Farm Rd
LAN/SOMP BN15 118 F8
Old School Cl POLE BN26 131 L6
RING/NEW BN8 * 275 K11
SELS PO20 168 C1
Old School Ct HWH RH16 73 G5
Old School Flds UCK TN22 76 E7
Old School La POLE BN26 * 131 M6
Old School Ms
MSEA/BNM PO22 3 L3
Old School Pl BURH RH15 74 E7
Old School Rd LISS GU33 192 C9
The Old School CRBK TN17 189 R9
PUL/STOR RH20 * 264 B3
Old Shoreham Rd BRI BN1 4 B2
LAN/SOMP BN15 119 H4
SHOR BN43 119 J5
STHW BN42 120 E5
The Old Stables
MSEA/BNM PO22 * 3 K4
Old Station Cl CRAWE RH10 45 M2
Old Station Rd WADH TN5 71 K3
Old Station Wy BOR GU35 178 D4
Old Steine BRI BN1 4 F7
Old Stocks SALV BN13 * 298 H11
Old Swan La HAIL BN27 92 C8
The Old Theatre CCH PO19 * 6 E4
Old Timbers La UCK TN22 76 E6
Old Top Rd RHAS TN35 100 C1
Old Tree Pde SEAF BN25 * 174 E3
Old Wardsdown WADH TN5 191 N10
Old Wy RASHW TN26 221 Q2
Old Wickham La HWH RH16 73 G2
Old Wickhurst La HORS RH12 201 N4
Oldwick Mdw RCCH PO18 292 C12
Old Willingdon Rd
EDN/EASTW BN20 302 H3
Old Wish Rd EAST BN21 10 D9
Old Worthing Rd
ANG/EP BN16 149 G3
Old Yard Cl SWTR RH13 234 F10
Oliver Cl CROW TN6 67 M8
HAS TN34 12 E7
Olive Rd HOVE BN3 121 K5
Oliver Rd HORS RH12 201 R4
Olivers Meadow SELS PO20 110 C6
Oliver Whitby Rd CCH PO19 6 A2
Olives Meadow UCK TN22 76 F5
Olives Yd UCK TN22 * 76 E5
Olivia Cl WVILLE PO7 288 B8
Olivier Cl BRIE/ROTT BN2 5 K6
Olivier Rd CRAWE RH10 44 C4
Onslow Dr FERR BN12 149 K3
Onslow Rd HOVE BN3 122 B4
Ontario Cl HORL RH6 23 M7
SALV BN13 116 B7
Ontario Gdns SALV BN13 116 B7
Ontario Wy LIPH GU30 193 R2
Openfields BOR GU35 179 M3
Ophir Rd WTHG BN11 151 M2
Orange Rw EMRTH PO10 104 A5
Orchard Av CCH PO19 6 D2
HOVE BN3 121 M4
LAN/SOMP BN15 118 D6
SALV BN13 116 F8
SELS PO20 301 L7
Orchard Cl BEX TN40 * 97 J8
BOGR PO21 2 B7
EPSF GU31 258 H1
FERR BN12 149 K2
HAS TN34 99 L2
HFD BN5 269 L11
HORL RH6 22 E5
HORN PO8 288 D3
HWH RH16 73 G1
MIDH GU29 259 L1
PETW GU28 229 L10
RHWH RH17 239 J2
RTWE/PEM TN2 38 C2
SALV BN13 117 G8
SHOR BN43 119 K5
STHW BN42 120 E5
STPH/PW TN12 189 L3
Orchard Cnr HWH RH16 73 L4
Orchard Crs ARUN BN18 110 F2
STPH/PW TN12 189 M3
Orchard Dell PUL/STOR RH20 266 B3
Orchard Gdns ANG/EP BN16 148 C3
CCH PO19 6 D3
HOVE BN3 122 A4
SELS PO20 110 C8
Orchard Gra HAIL BN27 91 H2
Orchard Gv HORN PO8 288 A6
Orchard Hl HORS RH12 185 R10
Orchard La EMRTH PO10 104 B5
HPPT/KEY BN6 271 N5
SELS PO20 139 M6
Orchard Ms NEWHV BN9 158 D3
Orchard Pl ARUN BN18 113 G2
Orchard Ri RRTW TN3 52 A2
Orchard Rd ANG/EP BN16 148 F5
BEX TN40 97 H7
BURH RH15 74 D7
HAV PO9 103 G5
HOVE BN3 121 M4
LEWES BN7 17 J3
SWTR RH13 15 H7
Orchard Side SELS PO20 141 L5
The Orchards CRAWW RH11 42 C4
Orchard St CCH PO19 6 D3
CRAWW RH11 8 E3
Orchard Ter RYE TN31 * 218 E11
The Orchard BOGR PO21 171 H4
BUR/ETCH TN19 215 P8
EDN/EASTW BN20 * 163 G4
HASM GU27 181 J12
HORL RH6 * 22 F6
RYE TN31 250 E9
SWTR RH13 57 G5
UCK TN22 208 H5
Orchard Wy ARUN BN18 110 F2
BAT TN33 249 M12
BURH RH15 74 E6
EGRIN RH19 31 K8
HPPT/KEY BN6 270 G3
HWH RH16 73 G1
LAN/SOMP BN15 118 D6
MIDH GU29 227 J9
MSEA/BNM PO22 2 D2
MSEA/BNM PO22 111 G7
PUL/STOR RH20 265 K2
RHWH RH17 204 E9
RYE TN31 252 B4
STPH/PW TN12 189 M4
Orchid Cl LGNY BN23 164 A2
Orchidhurst RTWE/PEM TN2 38 C2
Orchid Pk HWH RH16 73 M5
Orchid Vw BRI BN1 83 H7
Orde Cl CRAWE RH10 28 C8
Ore Pl HAS TN34 284 D12
Oriel Cl CRAWE RH10 28 B8
MSEA/BNM PO22 111 G7
Oriental Pl BRI BN1 4 A7
Orient Rd LAN/SOMP BN15 119 H8
Orion Ct HAIL BN27 92 C6
Orkney Ct SALV BN13 116 A8
Orltons La HORS RH12 25 L7
Orme Rd WTHG BN11 20 E3
Ormerod Av STLEO TN38 98 F1
Ormesby Crs MSEA/BNM PO22 3 K1
Ormesby Wk CRAWE RH10 44 A5
Ormonde Av CCH PO19 7 H5
Ormonde Wy SHOR BN43 119 J7
Orpen Pl SELS PO20 301 M6
Orpen Rd HOVE BN3 122 C4
Orwell Rd EPSF GU31 223 M7
Osbern Cl BEXW TN39 136 B2
Osborn Crs CCH PO19 107 M4
Osborne Cl HAS TN34 12 F1
LAN/SOMP BN15 118 B7
WVILLE PO7 288 B10
Osborne Crs CCH PO19 7 L5
Osborne Dr LAN/SOMP BN15 118 B7
Osborne Hl CROW TN6 211 K1
Osborne Rd BRI BN1 122 E3
CROW TN6 68 B8
EDN/EASTW BN20 176 B1
PSF GU32 223 N5
Osborne Vls HOVE BN3 122 A8
Osmers Hl WADH TN5 71 L2
Osmonde Cl SALV BN13 20 F2
Osmond Rd HOVE BN3 4 A3
Osmunda Bank EGRIN RH19 31 K3
Osmund Cl CRAWE RH10 44 D3
Osney Cl CRAWW RH11 8 D6
Osprey Dr UCK TN22 77 G7
Osprey Gdns MSEA/BNM PO22 144 B6
Osprey Quay EMRTH PO10 104 C6
Ospringe Pl RTWE/PEM TN2 38 E8
Ostlers Vw BIL RH14 231 R2
Oswald Ct BEX TN40 * 137 H1
Otard Cl SELS PO20 301 L6
Otford Cl CRAWW RH11 59 H1
Otham Court La POLE BN26 131 M5
Otham Rd LW/ROSE BN22 163 M3
Othello Dr WVILLE PO7 288 B9
Ottawa Dr LIPH GU30 193 R2
Otteham Cl POLE BN26 132 A7
Otterbourne Crs HAV PO9 288 E12
Otterbourne Pl EGRIN RH19 * 31 G8
Otter Cl CCH PO19 107 K5
Otway Cl CRAWW RH11 42 E5
Otway Rd CCH PO19 107 L4
Oulton Cl LGNY BN23 164 A2
Oulton Wk CRAWE RH10 44 A5
Ousedale Cl LEWES BN7 16 D6
Outerwyke Av MSEA/BNM PO22 3 M1
Outerwyke Gdns
MSEA/BNM PO22 3 M1
Outerwyke Rd
MSEA/BNM PO22 3 L1
Outlook Av PEAHV BN10 157 L7
The Outlook
EDN/EASTW BN20 302 G4
Outram Rd MSEA/BNM PO22 3 K6
Outram Wy SELS PO20 141 M4
Oval Cl PEAHV BN10 157 H3
Oval La SELS PO20 301 L8
The Oval LISS GU33 192 C9
SALV BN13 116 E8
SALV BN13 298 H10
Oval Waye FERR BN12 149 K5
Overdale Pl BOR GU35 * 178 G8
Overdale Wk BOR GU35 178 G8
Overdene Dr CRAWW RH11 42 F3
Overdown Ri PTSD BN41 120 E1
Overdown Rd
MSEA/BNM PO22 145 G8
Overhill STHW BN42 120 D4
Overhill Dr BRI BN1 82 D8
Overhill Gdns BRI BN1 82 D8
Overhill Wy BRI BN1 82 D7
Overmead SHOR BN43 119 K5
Overstrand Av ANG/EP BN16 148 B6
Over St BRI BN1 4 E4
Overton Crs HAV PO9 288 E12
Overton Shaw EGRIN RH19 31 K6
Ovingdean Cl BRIE/ROTT BN2 124 C8
Ovingdean Rd BRIE/ROTT BN2 155 J1
Oving Rd CCH PO19 7 J4
SELS PO20 109 G6
Oving Ter CCH PO19 * 7 K4
Owen Cl BURH RH15 74 E8
Owers Cl SWTR RH13 15 H5
Owers Wy SELS PO20 167 K6
Owlbeech Wy SWTR RH13 57 G5
Owletts CRAWE RH10 44 C2
Owlscastle Cl HORS RH12 56 C4
Owslebury Gv HAV PO9 288 G12
Oxbottom Cl RING/NEW BN8 240 A7
Oxen Av SHOR BN43 119 L5
Oxenbridge La
BUR/ETCH TN19 215 N9
Oxendean Gdns
LW/ROSE BN22 163 G1
Oxford Cl SELS PO20 167 L6
Oxford Ct BRI BN1 4 F3
Oxford Dr BOGR PO21 171 K2
Oxford Ms HOVE BN3 122 B6
Oxford Pl BRI BN1 4 F3
Oxford Rd CRAWE RH10 43 L7
LW/ROSE BN22 11 H4
STLEO TN38 98 F2
SWTR RH13 14 F6
WTHG BN11 21 G4
Oxford St BOGR PO21 2 A8
BRI BN1 4 F3
Oxford Ter HAS TN34 13 L6
STEY/UB BN44 * 78 C2
Ox Lea RRTW TN3 36 F6
Oyster Creek RYE TN31 253 L10

P

Pacific Dr LGNY BN23 164 F5
Pacific Wy SELS PO20 301 L8
Packham Wy BURH RH15 74 E5
Paddock Cl HASM GU27 195 K8
LYDD TN29 255 Q7
RRTW TN3 36 A4
SALV BN13 * 20 C1
Paddock Fld BRI BN1 * 84 A8
Paddock Gdns EGRIN RH19 47 K2
POLE BN26 162 E1
Paddock Gn ANG/EP BN16 148 D3
Paddockhall Rd HWH RH16 73 G4
Paddockhurst La RHWH RH17 61 J5
Paddockhurst Rd CRAWE RH10 45 H7
CRAWW RH11 42 F4
Paddock La LEWES BN7 16 E6
SELS PO20 301 K6
Paddock Rd LEWES BN7 16 E6
Paddocks MSEA/BNM PO22 111 G7
The Paddocks EDEN TN8 34 A2
HAIL BN27 91 M3
HWH RH16 72 F6
LAN/SOMP BN15 118 E8
LEWES BN7 126 C5
LEWES BN7 272 H4
STEY/UB BN44 79 G2
The Paddock BOR GU35 179 M4
CRAWE RH10 44 C2
GSHT GU26 180 D5
HASM GU27 181 K9
HOVE BN3 122 B4
LHPTN BN17 113 H7
LW/ROSE BN22 163 L3
MSEA/BNM PO22 2 D2
RRTW TN3 35 L4
RTWE/PEM TN2 39 H3
RYE TN31 218 E10
SHOR BN43 119 J4
UCK TN22 241 M1
Paddock Wy HASM GU27 181 R7
LIPH GU30 179 Q12
PSF GU32 223 L7
SALV BN13 298 H11
Padgham La HTHF TN21 280 C1

Padnell Av HORN PO8 ... 288 C7
Padnell Rd HORN PO8 ... 288 C6
Padwick Rd SWTR RH13 ... 15 L5
Padwicks Fld PUL/STOR RH20 ... 264 B2
Pages Av BEXW TN39 ... 136 E2
Pages Cl HTHF TN21 ... 244 B6
Pages Hl HTHF TN21 ... 244 B6
Pages La BEXW TN39 ... 136 D2
Paget Cl SWTR RH13 ... 151 M7
The Pagets RING/NEW BN8 ... 240 C6
Pagewood Cl CRAWE RH10 ... 44 C5
Pagham Cl EMRTH PO10 ... 104 B5
  LGNY BN23 ... 164 A1
Pagham Gdns HISD PO11 ... 166 A3
Pagham Rd BOGR PO21 ... 170 F5
  SELS PO20 ... 142 F8
Paine Av LYDD TN29 ... 255 R7
Paines Cottages RYE TN31 * ... 253 M10
Pain's Flat RHWH RH17 ... 74 C1
Palace Pl BRI BN1 * ... 4 F3
Palatine Rd FERR BN12 ... 150 B1
Palesgate Rd CROW TN6 ... 68 G3
Palesgate Wy
  EDN/EASTW BN20 ... 163 C8
Palings Wy HASM GU27 ... 195 K8
Palk Rd HAV PO9 ... 102 E5
The Pallant FERR BN12 ... 150 A4
  HAV PO9 ... 103 G4
Pallingham Dr CRAWE RH10 ... 44 B6
Pallingham La BIL RH14 ... 230 C7
Palliser Cl LGNY BN23 ... 164 D7
Palma Cl POLE BN26 ... 131 M6
Palma Ct WTHG BN11 * ... 20 C6
Palm Ct SALV BN13 ... 116 D6
Palmeira Av HOVE BN3 ... 122 B7
Palmeira Sq HOVE BN3 ... 122 B8
Palmer Cl HORL RH6 ... 22 E4
  PUL/STOR RH20 ... 266 C11
Palmer Pl SELS PO20 ... 142 C4
Palmer Rd ANG/EP BN16 ... 114 D7
  CRAWE RH10 ... 44 B6
Palmers Field Av CCH PO19 ... 108 A5
Palmers Green La
  STPH/PW TN12 ... 189 J1
Palmer's Rd EMRTH PO10 ... 104 A4
Palmerston Av FERR BN12 ... 150 B3
Palmerston Rd NEWHV BN9 ... 158 F4
Palmers Wy SALV BN13 ... 116 C4
Pangdean La HPPT/KEY BN6 ... 74 B6
Pangdean Cl BURH RH15 ... 74 D8
Pankhurst Av BRIE/ROTT BN2 ... 5 L9
Pankhurst Cl BEXW TN39 ... 96 F5
Pankhurst Ri BEXW TN39 ... 96 F5
Pannel La RHAS TN35 ... 285 Q7
Pannell Cl EGRIN RH19 ... 31 J8
Pannells Ash BIL RH14 ... 198 D2
Pannett BURH RH15 ... 74 D5
Pantiles BOR GU35 ... 179 Q4
  RTWE/PEM TN2 * ... 37 M7
The Pantiles FERR BN12 * ... 149 K4
  RTWE/PEM TN2 * ... 37 M7
Panton Cl EMRTH PO10 * ... 103 M2
Parade Man ANG/EP BN16 ... 148 F5
The Parade ANG/EP BN16 * ... 148 F5
  BOGR PO21 * ... 2 A2
  BOGR PO21 * ... 170 F6
  BRI BN1 * ... 122 A1
  CRAWE RH10 * ... 9 H1
  EGRIN RH19 * ... 31 G6
  HORS RH12 * ... 201 R2
  HOVE BN3 * ... 121 K3
  PEV BN24 ... 134 D8
Paradise Cl EDN/EASTW BN20 ... 176 D3
Paradise Dr EDN/EASTW BN20 ... 176 D4
Paradise Rd EMRTH PO10 ... 104 C1
The Paragon
  EDN/EASTW BN20 ... 162 E2
Parchment St CCH PO19 ... 6 D2
The Parchment HAV PO9 ... 103 G4
Parham Cl ANG/EP BN16 ... 148 A5
  BRIE/ROTT BN2 ... 5 L6
  LHPTN BN17 ... 147 J3
  SALV BN13 ... 116 A4
Parham Rd CRAWW RH11 ... 42 E5
  SALV BN13 ... 116 A4
Parish La CRAWE RH10 ... 59 L3
Park Av BEXW TN39 ... 137 G2
  EAST BN21 ... 163 H6
  HAS TN34 ... 99 J2
  HOVE BN3 ... 121 K6
  HPPT/KEY BN6 ... 271 P7
  PEAHV BN10 ... 156 F5
  SELS PO20 ... 301 M6
  SHOR BN43 ... 119 M5
  WTHG BN11 ... 21 K3
Park Cl BRI BN1 ... 83 K8
  BURH RH15 ... 74 E6
  EDN/EASTW BN20 ... 176 D2
  HAIL BN27 ... 92 A7
  HAS TN34 ... 99 J3
  HASM GU27 ... 181 Q8
  HOVE BN3 ... 121 C4
  PTSD BN41 ... 121 G4
  SALV BN13 ... 116 F6
  SBGH/RUST TN4 * ... 37 K7
Park Copse SELS PO20 ... 301 P4
Park Crs BRIE/ROTT BN2 * ... 5 G2
  BRIE/ROTT BN2 ... 155 L4
  CROW TN6 * ... 67 G6
  EMRTH PO10 ... 103 J4
  FROW RH18 ... 48 F7
  HAS TN34 ... 12 D1
  MIDH GU29 ... 226 H9
  PTSD BN41 ... 120 C6
  SELS PO20 ... 301 N5
  WTHG BN11 ... 20 C5
Park Crescent Pl
  BRIE/ROTT BN2 * ... 5 H1
Park Crescent Rd
  BRIE/ROTT BN2 ... 5 G2
Park Crescent Ter
  BRIE/ROTT BN2 ... 5 H2
Park Cft POLE BN26 ... 162 F1
Park Dr ANG/EP BN16 ... 148 C4
  ARUN BN18 ... 145 M3
  FERR BN12 ... 149 L3
  HAS TN34 ... 12 D1
  MSEA/BNM PO22 ... 145 J8
Park Drive NEWHV BN9 ... 158 F4
Park East HWH RH16 * ... 73 J7
Parker Cl CRAWE RH10 ... 44 C4
  EAST BN21 ... 10 A1
Parker Ct PTSD BN41 ... 121 G3
Parker Rd HAS TN34 ... 13 J1
Park Farm Cl BUR/ETCH TN19 ... 215 N9

HORS RH12 ... 56 C2
  HORS RH12 ... 14 D3
  LW/ROSE BN22 ... 163 K4
Parkfield HORS RH12 ... 14 D3
Parkfield Av BOGR PO21 ... 171 J2
  LW/ROSE BN22 ... 163 K4
Parkfield Cl CRAWW RH11 ... 42 E3
  SALV BN13 ... 20 A2
Parkfield Ct SALV BN13 * ... 20 A2
Parkfield Wy HWH RH16 ... 72 E6
Park Ga HAIL BN27 ... 92 C2
Park Hl BRIE/ROTT BN2 ... 128 A2
Park House Farm Wy HAV PO9 ... 288 D12
Parkhurst Gv HORL RH6 ... 22 D5
  HORL RH6 ... 22 D5
Parkhurst Rd BEX TN40 ... 137 H2
Parklands SHOR BN43 ... 120 B5
  UCK TN22 ... 209 M12
Parklands Av BOGR PO21 ... 2 B5
  FERR BN12 ... 150 C4
  HORN PO8 ... 288 B4
Parklands Rd CCH PO19 ... 6 C3
  HPPT/KEY BN6 ... 271 N6
Park La ARUN BN18 ... 111 H1
  BAT TN33 ... 248 H8
  BAT TN33 ... 282 E5
  BEXW TN39 ... 96 F7
  EAST BN21 ... 163 H5
  EMRTH PO10 ... 289 Q9
  HASM GU27 ... 195 L7
  HAV PO9 ... 102 D2
  HORN PO8 ... 288 B1
  HWH RH16 ... 206 D7
  MFD/CHID GU8 ... 181 P7
  PUL/STOR RH20 ... 266 C8
  RCCH PO18 ... 293 N12
  RING/NEW BN8 ... 276 F11
  SELS PO20 ... 110 A7
  SELS PO20 ... 301 M4
  STHW BN42 ... 120 C6
  SWTR RH13 ... 202 F11
  SWTR RH13 ... 234 D5
  WILLE PO7 ... 288 D9
Parklawn Av HORL RH6 ... 22 E4
Park Lodge Cl STLEO TN38 * ... 99 G6
Park Mnr BRI BN1 * ... 122 C2
Parkmore Ter BRI BN1 ... 4 D1
Park Pde HAV PO9 ... 102 F1
  HWH RH16 * ... 73 H5
Park Pl ARUN BN18 ... 112 F2
  HORS RH12 ... 14 D7
Park Ri HORS RH12 ... 14 A2
  HOVE BN3 ... 121 K2
  PETW GU28 ... 229 K10
Park Rd ARUN BN18 ... 145 M2
  BEXW TN39 ... 137 G2
  BOGR PO21 ... 2 B9
  BRI BN1 ... 83 K8
  BRIE/ROTT BN2 ... 155 L4
  BURH RH15 ... 74 E6
  CROW TN6 ... 67 L6
  EGRIN RH19 ... 31 J8
  EGRIN RH19 ... 31 K3
  EMRTH PO10 ... 104 B3
  FROW RH18 ... 48 F7
  HAIL BN27 ... 92 A2
  HASM GU27 ... 181 M11
  HFD BN5 ... 269 K5
  HORS RH12 ... 41 L8
  HTHF TN21 ... 244 E7
  HWH RH16 ... 73 C5
  LEWES BN7 ... 16 E5
  MSEA/BNM PO22 ... 111 J7
  PEAHV BN10 ... 157 L8
  PETW GU28 ... 229 L9
  PSF GU32 ... 223 N6
  RCCH PO18 ... 293 K11
  RHWH RH17 ... 204 C2
  SBGH/RUST TN4 ... 38 A4
  SEAF BN25 ... 174 D2
  SELS PO20 ... 301 N5
  SHOR BN43 ... 119 M5
  SWTR RH13 ... 200 C2
  WTHG BN11 ... 21 J3
Park Rd North HAV PO9 ... 102 F3
Park Rd South HAV PO9 ... 103 C4
Park Road Ter BRIE/ROTT BN2 ... 5 H6
Park Shaw BAT TN33 ... 249 M12
Parkside BOGR PO21 ... 2 F4
  CRAWE RH10 ... 9 G4
  EGRIN RH19 ... 31 H8
  HAV PO9 ... 102 D3
  HPPT/KEY BN6 ... 271 P6
  HTHF TN21 ... 244 E7
  SHOR BN43 ... 119 M4
  WTHG BN11 ... 21 J1
Parkside Av LHPTN BN17 ... 147 L4
Parkside Ms HORS RH12 ... 14 E5
Parkside Rd SEAF BN25 ... 174 F1
Park Sq BRIE/ROTT BN2 ... 154 E2
The Parks PTSD BN41 ... 121 G2
Parkstone Rd HAS TN34 ... 99 J1
Park St BOR GU35 ... 178 C6
  BRI BN1 ... 84 B7
  BRIE/ROTT BN2 ... 5 H7
  HORS RH12 ... 14 E6
  LYDD TN29 ... 255 Q7
  RTWE/PEM TN2 ... 38 B6
  SWTR RH13 ... 200 F2
Park Ter BOGR PO21 ... 2 B9
Park Ter East SWTR RH13 ... 14 E7
Park Ter West SWTR RH13 ... 14 E7
The Park BRIE/ROTT BN2 ... 155 M4
  CROW TN6 ... 67 L2
  CROW TN6 ... 210 C2
Park Vw CRAWW RH11 ... 8 C5
  HAIL BN27 ... 279 P12
  HAS TN34 ... 99 J2
  HORL RH6 ... 22 F6
  HWH RH16 ... 73 H3
  LGNY BN23 ... 164 B5
  RYE TN31 ... 218 D11
  RYE TN31 ... 252 A3
  UCK TN22 ... 242 D1
Park View Cl PEAHV BN10 ... 156 F4
Park View Ct ANG/EP BN16 * ... 148 B3
Park View Gdns EGRIN RH19 * ... 31 J6
Park View Rd HOVE BN3 ... 122 A4
  HWH RH16 ... 156 F5
  RHAS TN35 ... 284 B5
Parkview UCK TN22 ... 76 F3
Park View Ter BRI BN1 * ... 122 D5
  RHAS TN35 ... 284 B5
Park Vis HTHF TN21 * ... 244 E7
Park Wy CRAWE RH10 ... 44 B1
  HAS TN34 ... 99 J2

HAV PO9 ... 102 F4
  HORS RH12 ... 14 D6
  MIDH GU29 ... 227 L7
  STHW BN42 ... 120 B5
Parkway BOGR PO21 ... 171 M2
  EDN/EASTW BN20 ... 163 M2
Park Way Cl STHW BN42 ... 120 C6
Park West HWH RH16 * ... 73 J7
Parkwood RYE TN31 ... 252 D1
Parkwood Cl RTWE/PEM TN2 ... 38 B3
Park Wood Rd HAS TN34 ... 284 C11
Parnell Cl CRAWE RH10 ... 44 C2
Parochial Ms BRIE/ROTT BN2 * ... 4 F7
Parochial Ter BRIE/ROTT BN2 * ... 4 F7
Parrock Cl HRTF TN7 ... 49 J7
Parry Cl LGNY BN23 ... 164 D2
  SWTR RH13 ... 57 H5
Parry Dr ANG/EP BN16 ... 148 A4
Parsonage Cl PSF GU32 ... 223 Q4
  SBGH/RUST TN4 ... 37 G4
Parsonage Est EPSF GU31 ... 224 H5
Parsonage La RHAS TN35 ... 283 R5
  RRTW TN3 ... 188 G11
  WSEA TN36 ... 285 Q3
Parsonage Rd EAST BN21 ... 176 D1
  HFD BN5 ... 269 K4
  HORS RH12 ... 14 F1
  SBGH/RUST TN4 ... 37 G4
Parsonage Wy HORS RH12 ... 15 G1
Parsons Cl ANG/EP BN16 ... 148 F1
  HASM GU27 ... 181 M9
  HORL RH6 ... 22 D5
  STLEO TN38 ... 98 E1
Parsons Hl ARUN BN18 ... 113 G2
Parsons La CSHT GU26 ... 180 F3
Parsons Wk ARUN BN18 ... 111 K5
Parthings La HASM GU27 ... 201 Q5
Partridge Green Rd
  SWTR RH13 ... 234 H10
Partridge La HORS RH12 ... 25 K7
  RDKG RH5 ... 25 K7
Partridge Pl CRAWE RH10 ... 46 B3
Partridges La WADH TN5 ... 70 D2
Pashley Rd EDN/EASTW BN20 ... 176 B3
Passfield Cl LIPH GU30 ... 179 M9
Passfield Wk HAV PO9 ... 289 J12
Passingham Wk HORN PO8 ... 288 B5
Paston Pl BRIE/ROTT BN2 ... 5 L9
Pasture Hill Rd HWH RH16 ... 73 G3
The Pasture CRAWE RH10 ... 44 B3
Patcham By-Pass BRI BN1 ... 82 D7
Patcham Gra BRI BN1 ... 82 D8
Patcham Mill Rd PEV BN24 ... 133 G8
Patchdean BRI BN1 ... 82 E8
Patching Cl CRAWW RH11 ... 42 E2
  FERR BN12 ... 150 A1
Patchings SWTR RH13 ... 15 J4
Paterson Rd CROW TN6 ... 67 L6
Paterson Wilson Rd
  LHPTN BN17 ... 147 K4
Pathfield MFD/CHID GU8 ... 182 G5
Pathfield Cl HORS RH12 ... 186 A10
Pathfield Rd HASM GU27 ... 186 A10
Pathfields Cl HASM GU27 ... 181 N10
Path Link CRAWE RH10 ... 9 H2
Paton Rd BEXW TN39 ... 96 E5
Patricia Av FERR BN12 ... 150 C4
Patricia Cl FERR BN12 ... 150 C4
Patrick's Cl LISS GU33 ... 192 D9
Patrington Cl CRAWW RH11 ... 42 F6
Patterdale Cl CRAWW RH11 ... 8 B9
Paul Cl HAIL BN27 ... 91 M2
Pavilion Buildings BRI BN1 ... 4 E7
Pavilion Cl HPPT/KEY BN6 ... 271 M4
Pavilion Pde BRIE/ROTT BN2 ... 4 F6
Pavilion Rd SALV BN13 ... 20 D3
The Pavilions CRAWW RH11 ... 59 H3
Pavilion St BRIE/ROTT BN2 ... 4 F7
Pavilion Wy EGRIN RH19 ... 47 K1
Pax Cl CRAWW RH11 ... 42 D5
Paxhill Cl STLEO TN38 ... 98 D1
Paxmead Crs SALV BN13 ... 117 L7
Paygate Rd BAT TN33 ... 283 M2
Payne Av HOVE BN3 ... 121 L5
Payne Cl BOGR PO21 ... 170 F5
  CRAWE RH10 ... 44 C1
Paynesfield RHWH RH17 ... 236 D2
Paynsbridge Wy HTHF TN21 ... 278 C2
Paynters Wy
  RING/NEW BN8 ... 240 B6
Paynton Rd SLVH TN37 ... 99 G2
Paythorne Cl STHW BN42 ... 120 C4
Paythorne Dro HFD BN5 ... 269 Q12
Payton Dr BURH RH15 ... 74 E7
Peace Cl BRI BN1 ... 123 H4
Peacemaker Cl CRAWW RH11 ... 42 D5
Peace Rd MIDH GU29 ... 261 K3
The Peacheries CCH PO19 ... 7 K6
Peachey Rd SELS PO20 ... 301 N7
Peacock Cl CCH PO19 ... 108 B5
Peacock La BRI BN1 ... 122 D1
Peacock's Hl SWTR RH13 ... 202 H11
Peacocks La PUL/STOR RH20 ... 266 F3
Peakdean Cl
  EDN/EASTW BN20 ... 302 H3
Peakdean La
  EDN/EASTW BN20 ... 302 H3
Peak La ANG/EP BN16 ... 149 H5
Peak Rd HORN PO8 ... 256 B8
The Peak HAV PO9 ... 289 K7
Pear Tree Cl BOR GU35 ... 179 J5
Peartree Cl BURH RH15 ... 74 D6
Pear Tree Hl REDH RH1 ... 22 F1
Peartree Hl WADH TN5 ... 214 C6
Peartree La BEXW TN39 ... 96 C4
Pear Tree Rd BOR GU35 ... 179 J4
Peary Cl HORS RH12 ... 56 C3
Pease Cft EPSF GU31 ... 258 G2
Peasley La CRBK TN17 ... 189 Q11
Pebble Rd PEV BN24 ... 134 D8
Pebble Wk LHPTN BN17 ... 147 M2
Pebsham Dr BEX TN40 ... 97 M7
Pebsham La BEX TN40 ... 97 L5
Peckham Cl LEWES BN7 ... 16 F2

Peckhams Copse La
  SELS PO20 ... 142 C2
Peeks Brook La HORL RH6 ... 23 L1
Peel Cl LHPTN BN17 ... 147 H3
Peelings La PEV BN24 ... 133 G7
Peel Rd BRIE/ROTT BN2 ... 154 E1
Peerley Cl SELS PO20 ... 167 M7
Peerley Rd SELS PO20 ... 167 M7
Pegasus Cl HASM GU27 ... 180 G12
Pegasus Wy EGRIN RH19 ... 31 K6
Pegler Wy CRAWW RH11 ... 8 C4
Pegwell Cl CRAWW RH11 ... 42 E5
  HAS TN34 ... 12 E2
Pelham Ar HAS TN34 ... 13 J7
Pelham Cl BOR GU35 ... 178 C8
  PEAHV BN10 ... 157 J4
  PEV BN24 ... 133 L8
Pelham Ct CRAWW RH11 ... 43 F5
  HORS RH12 * ... 14 A6
Pelham Crs HAIL BN27 ... 92 B2
  HAS TN34 ... 13 H7
Pelham Dr CRAWW RH11 ... 42 E5
Pelham Pl CRAWW RH11 ... 43 G7
  HAS TN34 ... 13 J7
Pelham Ri PEAHV BN10 ... 157 H4
Pelham Rd HWH RH16 ... 73 K3
  SALV BN13 ... 116 E8
  SEAF BN25 ... 174 C3
Pelham Sq BRI BN1 ... 4 F5
  BRI BN1 ... 4 F5
  HAS TN34 ... 13 H7
Pelham Ter EMRTH PO10 ... 104 B5
  LEWES BN7 ... 16 F5
Pelham Yd SEAF BN25 ... 174 C3
Pellbrook Rd LEWES BN7 ... 16 B2
Pell Cl WADH TN5 ... 71 M3
Pelleys La SELS PO20 ... 141 L4
Pellings Farm Cl CROW TN6 ... 68 A7
Pellings Ri CROW TN6 ... 68 A6
Pelwood Rd RYE TN31 ... 254 B11
Pemberton Cl
  LAN/SOMP BN15 ... 118 D6
Pembley Gn CRAWE RH10 ... 29 K6
Pembroke Av FERR BN12 ... 150 E3
  HOVE BN3 ... 121 M7
Pembroke Cl HAIL BN27 ... 92 B2
  HOVE BN3 ... 121 M7
Pembroke Gdns HOVE BN3 ... 121 M7
Pembroke Rd CRAWE RH10 ... 28 D3
Pembroke Wy BOGR PO21 ... 171 K2
Pembury Cl HWH RH16 ... 73 J3
  RTWE/PEM TN2 * ... 39 J2
  SALV BN13 ... 21 G2
Pembury Gra RTWE/PEM TN2 ... 38 F3
Pembury Gv BEXW TN39 ... 96 F5
Pembury Rd HAV PO9 ... 103 H5
  LGNY BN23 ... 164 D5
  RTWE/PEM TN2 ... 38 B6
  RTWE/PEM TN2 ... 38 F3
Penarth Gdns LHPTN BN17 ... 113 H8
Pendean BURH RH15 ... 75 H8
Pende Cl LAN/SOMP BN15 ... 118 C5
Pendine Av WTHG BN11 ... 151 M7
Pendragon Ct HOVE BN3 * ... 121 M5
Penfold La ANG/EP BN16 ... 148 B2
Penfold Rd CRAWE RH10 ... 44 D4
  SALV BN13 ... 117 K8
Penfolds Pl ARUN BN18 ... 112 F3
Penfold Wy STEY/UB BN44 ... 78 D3
Penhale Rd LW/ROSE BN22 ... 11 L2
Penhill Rd LAN/SOMP BN15 ... 118 D8
Penhurst Dr BEX TN40 ... 97 L7
Penhurst La BAT TN33 ... 281 K4
Penhurst Pl BRIE/ROTT BN2 ... 155 L4
Penhurst Rd HAV PO9 ... 102 F4
Penk Rdg HAV PO9 ... 102 A5
Penland Cl HWH RH16 ... 73 G2
Penland Rd BEX TN40 ... 97 K8
  HWH RH16 ... 73 G3
Penland's Cl STEY/UB BN44 ... 78 B3
Penlands Ri STEY/UB BN44 ... 78 B3
Penlands V STEY/UB BN44 ... 78 B3
Penlands Wy STEY/UB BN44 ... 78 B3
Penleigh Ct LAN/SOMP BN15 ... 118 D8
Pennant Hills HAV PO9 ... 102 C3
Penn Cl CRAWW RH11 ... 27 J5
  MSEA/BNM PO22 ... 145 K8
Penn Ct CRAWW RH11 ... 42 F5
Penn Crs HWH RH16 ... 73 K4
  RING/NEW BN8 ... 275 J12
Pennells Cl LIPH GU30 ... 193 Q11
Pennerly Ct HAV PO9 ... 288 E10
Penner Rd HAV PO9 ... 102 F6
Pennine Cl CRAWW RH11 ... 8 A3
Pennine Ri HAS TN34 ... 100 A1
Pennine Wy RTWE/PEM TN2 ... 38 C4
Penns Ct STEY/UB BN44 ... 78 B1
Penns Pl EPSF GU31 ... 224 A6
Penns Yd PSF GU32 ... 223 M5
Penns Yd RTWE/PEM TN2 * ... 39 J5
Pennybridge La MAYF TN20 ... 212 C4
Pennycord Cl SELS PO20 ... 301 L8
Pennycress Av SALV BN13 ... 115 M8
Pennyfields MSEA/BNM PO22 ... 145 K8
Penny La BEX TN40 ... 97 M8
  EMRTH PO10 ... 104 C5
Penrith Wy LGNY BN23 ... 164 B1
Penryn Dr BOR GU35 ... 179 K4
Pensfold La HORS RH12 ... 186 D3
Pensford Dr LGNY BN23 ... 164 C1
Penshurst Cl CRAWE RH10 ... 44 C2
Penstone Pk LAN/SOMP BN15 ... 118 C7
Pentere Rd HORN PO8 ... 288 B3
Pentland Cl LGNY BN23 ... 164 C2
  SLVH TN37 ... 283 R12
Pentland Rd SALV BN13 ... 116 D6
Penton Ct HAV PO9 ... 289 J11
Penwarden Wy RCCH PO18 ... 106 B6
Penwith Dr HASM GU27 ... 180 F10
Penwood Gn HAV PO9 ... 289 J12
Peperham Rd HASM GU27 ... 181 M9
Peper Harow HORN PO8 ... 288 C3
Peppard Rd CRAWE RH10 ... 44 C5
Peppercombe Rd
  EDN/EASTW BN20 ... 176 B3
Pepper Dr BURH RH15 ... 74 E8
Peppering La ARUN BN18 ... 296 H9
Pepperscoombe La
  STEY/UB BN44 ... 78 F2
Peppersgate SWTR RH13 ... 203 M10
Pepper's La STEY/UB BN44 ... 268 B4
Peppers Yd HORS RH12 * ... 14 F4
Perche Ct MIDH GU29 * ... 226 G11

Perching Dro HFD BN5 ... 269 R12
Perch La RRTW TN3 ... 188 C8
Percival Crs LW/ROSE BN22 ... 163 L2
Percival Rd LW/ROSE BN22 ... 163 L2
Percival Ter BRIE/ROTT BN2 ... 5 L7
Percy Av HORS RH12 ... 14 B3
  RHAS TN35 ... 100 B3
Percy Ter PETW GU28 ... 229 L9
  SBGH/RUST TN4 * ... 37 M3
Peregrine Rd LHPTN BN17 ... 147 L3
Perimeter Rd East HORL RH6 ... 22 D8
Perimeter Rd North HORL RH6 ... 22 D8
Perimeter Rd South HORL RH6 ... 27 L4
Periwinkle Cl BOR GU35 ... 179 K4
Perrots La STEY/UB BN44 ... 78 B3
Perry Av EGRIN RH19 ... 31 K6
Perryfield La SWTR RH13 ... 203 P11
Perryfield Rd CRAWW RH11 ... 8 E6
Perrylands BURH RH15 ... 74 B7
Perry Hl BRIE/ROTT BN2 ... 156 B3
Perryhill La HRTF TN7 ... 50 D1
Perrylands HORL RH6 ... 26 C3
Perrylands La HORL RH6 ... 23 L7
Perrymans La UCK TN22 ... 208 C6
Perrymount Rd HWH RH16 ... 73 H4
Perry Wy BOR GU35 ... 179 N5
Perseus Pl WVILLE PO7 ... 102 A2
Perth Cl CRAWW RH11 ... 27 J8
  SEAF BN25 ... 175 J2
Perth Rd SLVH TN37 ... 99 G2
Perth Wy HORS RH12 ... 15 K1
Pescott's Cl SELS PO20 ... 140 D8
Peskett Cl SWTR RH13 ... 201 J10
Peterborough Rd CRAWE RH10 ... 43 G7
Peterhouse Cl BOGR PO21 ... 171 L1
Peter James Cl RYE TN31 ... 253 P11
Peter James La RHAS TN35 ... 285 M10
Peter Rd LAN/SOMP BN15 ... 152 D1
Petersfield Cl HWH RH16 ... 73 F8
  EPSF GU31 ... 223 L12
  HAV PO9 ... 103 G2
  LISS GU33 ... 178 E12
  LISS GU33 ... 192 G4
  MIDH GU29 ... 226 G9
Peter's La SELS PO20 ... 300 G5
Peter's Pl SELS PO20 ... 300 G5
Peter Weston Pl CCH PO19 ... 7 G5
Petlands Gdns HWH RH16 ... 73 J6
Petlands Rd HWH RH16 ... 73 H6
Pett Cl BRIE/ROTT BN2 ... 123 L7
Pett La WSEA TN36 ... 286 A5
Pett Level Rd RHAS TN35 ... 285 Q11
  WSEA TN36 ... 286 E6
Pett Rd RHAS TN35 ... 285 L10
Petts Cl SELS PO20 ... 301 L4
Petworth Av FERR BN12 ... 150 B5
Petworth Ct CRAWW RH11 ... 42 E6
  MSEA/BNM PO22 ... 3 L4
Petworth Dr BURH RH15 ... 74 F5
  HORS RH12 ... 56 E2
Petworth Rd LW/ROSE BN22 ... 163 K3
Petworth Rd BIL RH14 ... 231 J1
  BRI BN1 ... 83 G7
  HASM GU27 ... 181 N12
  MFD/CHID GU8 ... 182 H5
Pevensey Bay Rd LGNY BN23 ... 164 D5
Pevensey Cl CRAWE RH10 ... 44 B4
  SEAF BN25 ... 175 H1
Pevensey Gdn WTHG BN11 ... 20 A7
Pevensey Park Rd PEV BN24 ... 133 L2
Pevensey Rd BOGR PO21 ... 171 L1
  BRIE/ROTT BN2 ... 5 J3
  EAST BN21 ... 11 G6
  NEWHV BN9 ... 18 B7
  POLE BN26 ... 132 B7
  STLEO TN38 ... 99 G5
  SWTR RH13 ... 201 Q12
  WTHG BN11 ... 150 A7
The Peverells SEAF BN25 ... 159 M8
Peverel Rd CRAWW RH11 ... 42 D4
  SALV BN13 ... 20 A2
The Peverels SEAF BN25 ... 159 M8
Peveril Cl LAN/SOMP BN15 ... 117 M7
Peveril Dr LAN/SOMP BN15 ... 117 M7
Peyton Cl LGNY BN23 ... 164 E6
Philip Cole Cl HAS TN34 * ... 13 J7
Philip Rd WVILLE PO7 ... 288 A12
Philips Crs BOR GU35 ... 179 N4
Phillips Cl BOR GU35 ... 179 N4
  CRAWE RH10 ... 44 A8
Philliswood La RCCH PO18 ... 259 H11
Phoenix Cswy LEWES BN7 ... 17 H5
Phoenix Cl CCH PO19 ... 6 F7
  HAIL BN27 ... 92 C6
  LHPTN BN17 ... 147 G2
Phoenix Crs STHW BN42 ... 120 C5
Phoenix Dr LGNY BN23 ... 164 F5
Phoenix La EGRIN RH19 ... 48 B3
Phoenix Pl BRIE/ROTT BN2 ... 5 G4
  LEWES BN7 ... 17 G5
Phoenix Ri BRIE/ROTT BN2 ... 5 G4
Phoenix Wy STHW BN42 ... 120 C5
Phrosso Rd WTHG BN11 ... 150 A4
Phyllis Av PEAHV BN10 ... 157 G7
Picardy Cl BAT TN33 ... 282 F5
Piccadilly La MAYF TN20 ... 212 G4
Pickers Gn HWH RH16 ... 73 K1
Picketts La REDH RH1 ... 23 H1
  UCK TN22 ... 209 J10
Pickforde La WADH TN5 ... 191 K12
Pickhurst La PUL/STOR RH20 ... 231 J10
Pickhurst Rd MFD/CHID GU8 ... 182 H3
Pickwell La RHWH RH17 ... 236 C1
Picton St BRIE/ROTT BN2 ... 5 J2
Picts La SWTR RH13 ... 203 L12
Piddinghoe Av PEAHV BN10 ... 157 J7
Piddinghoe Cl PEAHV BN10 ... 157 J6
Piddinghoe Md NEWHV BN9 ... 18 C1
Pierces La RHWH RH17 ... 72 F7
Pier Rd LHPTN BN17 ... 147 J5
Piers Secombe Cl
  PUL/STOR RH20 ... 264 E8
Pigeonhouse La ANG/EP BN16 ... 148 C5
Pigeon Pass CRAWE RH10 ... 46 B4
Piggery Hall La SELS PO20 ... 167 L6
The Pike PUL/STOR RH20 ... 298 H3
Pilgrims Cl SALV BN13 ... 20 B1
Pilgrims Ter SALV BN13 * ... 20 A3
Pilgrims Wk SALV BN13 ... 20 A3
Pilgrims Wy BOGR PO21 ... 171 C4
  BOR GU35 ... 179 M4

HAS TN34 .... 99 L1
Pilmer Rd CROW TN6 .... 67 L6
Pilot Rd HAS TN34 .... 99 M1
Piltdown Cl BEXW TN39 ...... 137 G1
  HAS TN34 .... 12 F5
Piltdown Ri UCK TN22 .... 76 F4
Piltdown Rd BRIE/ROTT BN2 .. 123 L2
Piltdown Wy LGNY BN23 ...... 163 M1
Pinckards MFD/CHID GU8 ..... 182 F4
Pinders Rd RHAS TN35 .... 100 C3
Pine Av HAS TN34 .... 100 A2
Pine Bank GSHT GU26 .... 180 H5
Pine Cl BIL RH14 .... 199 R12
  CRAWW RH11 .... 27 H8
  MIDH GU29 .... 227 J12
  PUL/STOR RH20 .... 266 E10
Pine Gv CCH PO19 .... 107 H4
  CROW TN6 .... 67 K7
  EGRIN RH19 .... 31 G6
  HAV PO9 .... 102 C3
Pineham Copse HWH RH16 ...... 73 J5
Pinehill Rd BOR GU35 .... 178 H7
Pinehurst BURH RH15 .... 74 F8
  HORS RH12 .... 14 D2
Pinehurst Cl WVILLE PO7 .... 288 D7
Pinehurst Pk BOR GU35 ...... 171 G1
Pinehurst Wk HAS TN34 ...... 100 A2
Pines Av SALV BN13 .... 117 G6
Pines Rd LIPH GU30 .... 193 M1
The Pines ANG/EP BN16 ...... 148 A5
  ARUN BN18 .... 145 L2
  BRIE/ROTT BN2 * 5 G2
  HORS RH12 .... 57 H4
  HPPT/KEY BN6 * 270 C2
  HWH RH16 .... 73 L5
Pinetops HORS RH12 * 57 H5
Pine Tree HPPT/KEY BN6 ..... 271 J4
Pine Tree Gdns HORN PO8 .... 288 C8
Pine Tree Rd HPPT/KEY BN6 .. 244 D8
Pine Trees HPPT/KEY BN6 .... 271 J5
Pine Trees Cl ANG/EP BN16 .. 114 G6
Pinetrees Cl CRAWE RH10 ..... 29 G6
Pine Vw BOR GU35 .... 179 Q3
Pine View Cl HASM GU27 ..... 181 M9
Pine Wk BOGR PO21 .... 171 J1
  LISS GU33 .... 192 D7
  UCK TN22 .... 76 F4
Pine Wy HAIL BN27 .... 91 M6
Pine Way Cl EGRIN RH19 ...... 47 K2
Pinewood Av HAV PO9 .... 102 C3
Pinewood Cha CROW TN6 .... 67 J6
Pinewood Cl ANG/EP BN16 .... 148 F3
  HORS RH12 .... 201 N2
  LW/ROSE BN22 .... 163 J3
  SEAF BN25 .... 174 F1
Pinewood Ct MIDH GU29 ...... 227 J4
Pinewood Gdns BOGR PO21 .... 171 M2
Pinewood Rd RTWE/PEM TN2 .... 38 C4
Pinewoods BEXW TN39 .... 136 D1
Pinewood Wy HWH RH16 .... 73 J5
  MIDH GU29 .... 226 H12
  STLEO TN38 .... 98 D2
Pinfold Cl BRIE/ROTT BN2 ... 124 D7
Pinkhurst La SWTR RH13 ..... 201 K3
Pinks La SELS PO20 .... 168 C2
Pinland Rd SWTR RH13 .... 234 E12
Pinton Hl WADH TN5 .... 190 C10
Pinwell Rd LEWES BN7 .... 17 G7
Pipe Pas LEWES BN7 * 16 E6
Pipers Cl BEX TN40 .... 97 H8
  HOVE BN3 .... 121 H2
  WADH TN5 .... 71 M5
Pipers End SWTR RH13 .... 200 H2
Piper's Ga UCK TN22 .... 76 F8
Pipers La PETW GU28 .... 196 G6
  PETW GU28 .... 197 M6
Pipers Md HORN PO8 .... 256 B8
  SELS PO20 .... 168 C2
Pipit Meadow UCK TN22 .... 76 F7
Pippin Cl HAIL BN27 * 280 X12
Pitcairn Av LGNY BN23 ...... 165 G3
Pitcroft La EPSF GU31 ...... 223 N12
The Pitcroft CCH PO19 ...... 108 B5
Pitfold Av HAIL BN27 .... 180 G11
Pitfold Cl HASM GU27 .... 180 H11
Pitreavie Dr HAIL BN27 ...... 91 M5
Pit Rd HPPT/KEY BN6 .... 270 H4
Pitsham La MIDH GU29 .... 226 C12
Pitsham Wd MIDH GU29 .... 226 C11
Pitt Dr SEAF BN25 .... 159 M8
Pitt Gdns BRIE/ROTT BN2 .... 124 C5
Place Crs WVILLE PO7 .... 288 A12
Place La SEAF BN25 .... 174 E2
Plainfields Av BRI BN1 ...... 82 F6
Plainwood Cl CCH PO19 ...... 107 L3
Plaistow Cl BRIE/ROTT BN2 .. 123 L7
Plaistow Rd BIL RH14 .... 198 B10
  BIL RH14 .... 198 C5
  MFD/CHID GU8 .... 183 L3
Plaitford Gv HAV PO9 .... 102 D1
Plantain Crs CRAWW RH11 ..... 42 F7
Plantation Cl SALV BN13 .... 116 C6
Plantation Ri SALV BN13 .... 116 C6
Plantation Rd LISS GU33 .... 192 E11
The Plantation ANG/EP BN16 . 148 F4
  PUL/STOR RH20 .... 265 Q12
  SALV BN13 .... 116 E6
Plantation Wy BOR GU35 ..... 178 D9
  PUL/STOR RH20 .... 265 Q12
  SALV BN13 .... 116 C6
The Plat HORS RH12 .... 201 R3
  RYE TN31 .... 218 E11
Platts Meadow BIL RH14 ..... 231 M5
The Platt HWH RH16 .... 73 L4
  LING RH7 .... 31 M1
Plaw Hatch La EGRIN RH19 .... 63 K4
Playden Cl BRIE/ROTT BN2 ... 154 D1
Playden Gdns HAS TN34 ...... 100 A1
Playden La RYE TN31 .... 252 H12
Plaza Pde WTHG BN11 * 20 F7
Pleasant La EMRTH PO10 ..... 138 C4
Pleasant View CROW TN6 ...... 67 K5
Plemont Gdns BEXW TN39 ...... 96 F4
Pleyden Rd LEWES BN7 .... 95 L8
Plough Cl CRAWW RH11 .... 42 F1
Plough La RHAS TN35 .... 56 D4
  SLVH TN37 .... 283 Q12
Plover Cl CRAWW RH11 .... 43 H1
  LGNY BN23 .... 164 B3
  MSEA/BNM PO22 .... 144 A6
  SELS PO20 .... 167 M7
Plover Ct STLEO TN38 .... 98 D2
Plovers Pl HORN PO8 .... 288 B3

SWTR RH13 .... 15 K3
Plumer Rd LISS GU33 .... 192 F2
Plumey Feathers CROW TN6 * .. 51 K6
Plummerden La HWH RH16 ..... 206 H7
Plumpton Bostall LEWES BN7 . 272 G11
Plumpton Cl BEX TN40 .... 97 H7
  LGNY BN23 .... 163 M1
Plumpton Gv WVILLE PO7 ..... 288 C8
Plumpton La LEWES BN7 ...... 272 H9
Plumpton La BRIE/ROTT BN2 ... 5 L4
Plumtree Cross La SWTR RH13 201 J9
Plymouth Av BRIE/ROTT BN2 .. 123 L4
Plymouth Cl LGNY BN23 ...... 164 E5
Plynlimmon Rd HAS TN34 ...... 13 J5
Pockford Rd MFD/CHID GU8 ... 183 J5
Pocock's Rd EAST BN21 ...... 163 J8
Polecat La SWTR RH13 .... 202 B8
Polegate By-Pass POLE BN26 . 131 L6
Polesden Rd RTWE/PEM TN2 .... 38 C7
Poles La CRAWW RH11 .... 27 H6
Polestub La RHWH RH17 .... 72 C2
Poling Cl FERR BN12 .... 150 A1
Poling St ARUN BN18 .... 113 M1
Pollards CRAWW RH11 .... 42 F4
Pollards Dr SWTR RH13 .... 15 J5
Pollard's Hl SWTR RH13 ..... 233 H3
Polley Cl RTWE/PEM TN2 ...... 39 J2
Pollington Pl CROW TN6 ...... 67 L7
Polperro Cl FERR BN12 ...... 149 K4
Pomper La HPPT/KEY BN6 ..... 236 H11
Pond Cl BIL RH14 .... 198 G1
  BIL RH14 .... 231 H1
  RYE TN31 .... 250 E8
Pond Copse La BIL RH14 ..... 184 G12
Pondcroft Rd HWH RH16 .... 73 L2
Pondfield Rd HORS RH12 ..... 186 A9
Pond La HORN PO8 .... 256 C7
  SALV BN13 .... 116 C6
Ponds Md SALV BN13 * 116 C7
Pond Ri PUL/STOR RH20 ...... 266 C6
Pond Rd BOR GU35 .... 179 P5
  SELS PO20 .... 168 A3
  SHOR BN43 .... 119 L6
Pondside HWH RH16 .... 72 F6
Pondtail Cl HORS RH12 .... 56 C3
Pondtail Copse HORS RH12 .... 56 C3
Pondtail Dr HORS RH12 .... 56 C2
Pondtail Pk HORS RH12 .... 56 C3
Pondtail Rd HORS RH12 .... 56 B4
Pond Wy EGRIN RH19 .... 32 A8
Pond Wood Rd CRAWE RH10 ..... 43 M1
Ponswood Rd STLEO TN38 ...... 99 G3
Pont Cl HTHF TN21 .... 245 M7
Pony Farm SALV BN13 .... 299 J11
Pookbourne La
  HPPT/KEY BN6 .... 236 F8
Pook Hl MFD/CHID GU8 .... 182 D6
Pook La HAV PO9 .... 103 J5
Pook Reed La HTHF TN21 ..... 244 A4
Pool Va BRI BN1 .... 4 D6
Poona Rd RTW TN1 .... 38 A7
Popes Md HASM GU27 .... 181 M10
Popham Ct HAV PO9 .... 288 D11
Poplar Av HOVE BN3 .... 121 K2
  BRI BN1 .... 122 C4
  CRAWW RH11 .... 27 H8
  HOVE BN3 .... 121 K2
Poplar Rd SALV BN13 .... 116 B8
  TENT TN30 .... 220 C6
The Poplars ARUN BN18 ...... 145 M1
  BRIE/ROTT BN2 * 5 G1
  SLVH TN37 * 99 H1
  SWTR RH13 .... 15 G4
Poplar Wy MIDH GU29 .... 226 H12
The Poplers HPPT/KEY BN6 ... 271 P6
Poppinghole La RBTBR TN32 .. 248 E3
Popps La BEXW TN39 .... 136 B2
Poppy Cl LHPTN BN17 .... 147 M2
  SWTR RH13 .... 201 R11
Porchester Cl SWTR RH13 .... 201 R11
Porters Cl STPH/PW TN12 .... 188 E3
Porters Wy POLE BN26 .... 131 M7
Porters Wd STPH/PW TN12 * .. 188 D3
Portfield Av BRI BN1 .... 82 F7
Portfield Cl BEX TN40 .... 97 J8
Portland Av HOVE BN3 .... 120 G11
Portland Cl CCH PO19 .... 7 L1
Port Hall Av BRI BN1 .... 122 D5
Port Hall Ms BRI BN1 .... 4 A3
Port Hall Pl BRI BN1 .... 122 D5
Port Hall Rd BRI BN1 * 4 B1
Port Hall St BRI BN1 .... 122 D5
Portland Av HAIL BN27 .... 91 M4
  LHPTN BN17 .... 147 M3
Portland Ms BRIE/ROTT BN2 * 5 K9
Portland Pl BRIE/ROTT BN2 ... 5 K9
  HAS TN34 .... 13 H6
Portland Rd BURH RH15 .... 74 E6
  EGRIN RH19 .... 47 K1
  HOVE BN3 .... 121 G6
  WTHG BN11 .... 21 G6
Portland's Cl PSF GU32 ..... 223 Q4
Portland Sq LISS GU33 ...... 192 C9
  WTHG BN11 * 21 G6
The Portlands LGNY BN23 .... 164 C6
Portland St BRI BN1 .... 4 D6
Portland Ter HAS TN34 * 13 H6
Portland Vls HAS TN34 * 13 H6
  HOVE BN3 .... 121 G6
Port Offices NEWHV BN9 * 19 G6
Port Rd LW/ROSE BN22 .... 163 M4
Portsdown Rd
  EDN/EASTW BN20 .... 163 G3
Portsmouth La HWH RH16 ...... 73 J2
Portsmouth Rd GSHT GU26 .... 181 K5
  HORN PO8 .... 288 D5
  LIPH GU30 .... 193 M4
Portsmouth Wood Cl
  HWH RH16 .... 73 J1
Portswood Rd HAV PO9 .... 288 D11
Port Vw NEWHV BN9 .... 158 D3
Portway STEY/UB BN44 .... 78 B3
Possingworth Cl HTHF TN21 .. 243 N5
Post Horn La FROW RH18 ...... 48 B1
Posthorses PUL/STOR RH20 ... 267 K9
Post Office Ca SELS PO20 ... 142 C4
Post Office Pas HAS TN34 * .. 13 K6
Post Vw PUL/STOR RH20 ...... 298 B1
Posth Ter HAV PO9 .... 102 F4
Potato La RING/NEW BN8 ..... 275 K12
Potman's La BEXW TN39 .... 96 D3
Potten Mill La HTHF TN21 ... 245 J11
The Potteries HPPT/KEY BN6 * 75 M8

UCK TN22 .... 76 F8
Potters Cft SWTR RH13 .... 15 H6
Potters Fld LISS GU33 ...... 192 D9
Potters Gn SWTR RH13 .... 235 M3
Potters La BURH RH15 .... 74 E8
  BEX TN40 .... 16 E8
Potters Md LHPTN BN17 ...... 147 H2
Potters Pl HORS RH12 .... 14 C5
Pottery La RYE TN31 .... 250 C11
Pottery La RCCH PO18 .... 105 J2
  RYE TN31 .... 250 C11
Pottingfield Rd RYE TN31 ... 252 F7
Pouchlands Dr RING/NEW BN8 . 273 M3
Poulner Cl MSEA/BNM PO22 .... 3 L3
Poulner Ct HAV PO9 .... 288 D11
Poulter's La SWTR RH13 ..... 117 G7
Pound Cl BIL RH14 .... 184 G12
  BOR GU35 .... 179 N4
  LGNY BN23 .... 164 E2
  PETW GU28 .... 229 L10
Pound Farm Rd CCH PO19 ...... 7 J4
Poundfield La BIL RH14 ..... 198 C2
Poundfield Rd CROW TN6 ...... 68 A7
  HAWK TN18 .... 217 Q4
Pound Hill Pl CRAWE RH10 .... 44 B3
Pound La RING/NEW BN8 ...... 276 D10
  STEY/UB BN44 .... 79 G3
  SWTR RH13 .... 202 H3
  SWTR RH13 .... 233 N9
  UCK TN22 .... 77 M6
Pound Pl PETW GU28 * 229 L9
Pound Rd ARUN BN18 .... 111 J4
  SELS PO20 .... 167 G4
The Pound BURH RH15 .... 74 E5
Pound Wy ANG/EP BN16 .... 114 F8
Povey Cross Rd HORL RH6 ..... 22 D8
Poveys Cl BURH RH15 .... 74 C6
Powdermill Cl SBGH/RUST TN4 38 B1
Powdermill La BAT TN33 ..... 281 R9
  RYE TN31 .... 250 A10
Powder Mill La SBGH/RUST TN4 38 A2
Powell Cl HORL RH6 .... 22 D5
Powell Gdns NEWHV BN9 ...... 158 C4
Powell Rd RING/NEW BN8 ..... 240 C6
Powis Gv BRI BN1 .... 4 B5
Powis Rd BRI BN1 .... 4 B5
Powis Sq BRI BN1 .... 4 B4
Powis Vls BRI BN1 .... 4 B5
Poynes Rd HOVE BN3 .... 22 D4
Poynings Cl SEAF BN25 ...... 175 J3
Poynings Dr HOVE BN3 .... 121 L2
Poynings Rd CRAWW RH11 ...... 42 C4
Poynter Rd HOVE BN3 .... 121 M5
Poyntz Cl CCH PO19 .... 141 L2
Pratton Av LAN/SOMP BN15 ... 118 C6
Pratt's Folly La CROW TN6 ... 67 K8
Prawn Cl SELS PO20 .... 301 J5
Preegmans La UCK TN22 ...... 209 R7
Premier Pde HORL RH6 * 23 G6
Prescott Gdns BURH RH15 * ... 74 F6
Preston Av HOVE BN3 .... 121 K2
Preston Circ BRI BN1 * 4 E2
Preston Dro BRI BN1 .... 122 E3
Preston Gra BRI BN1 * 122 D4
Preston Hall Ms
  ANG/EP BN16 * 148 E3
Preston Paddock
  ANG/EP BN16 .... 148 D4
Preston Park Av BRI BN1 .... 122 E4
Preston Rd BEXW TN39 .... 97 H6
  BRI BN1 .... 4 B7
Preston St BRI BN1 .... 4 B7
Preston Village Ms BRI BN1 * 122 D4
Prestonville Rd BRI BN1 ..... 4 C3
Prestwick Cl CRAWW RH11 ..... 42 C4
Prestwick La HASM GU27 ..... 181 R7
  MFD/CHID GU8 .... 181 R7
Prestwood Cl CRAWW RH11 ..... 27 G8
Prestwood La CRAWW RH11 ..... 26 B7
Pretoria Av MIDH GU29 ...... 226 H10
Pretoria La LISS GU33 ...... 192 H10
Price Wy RHWH RH17 .... 226 H10
Prideaux Rd EAST BN21 ...... 10 A2
Pride Vw PEV BN24 .... 133 G8
Priest Croft Cl CRAWW RH11 . 42 F5
Priestlands Cl HORL RH6 .... 22 C4
Priestley Wy CRAWE RH10 * ... 27 M7
  MSEA/BNM PO22 .... 145 J3
Prime Cl ARUN BN18 .... 111 K5
Primrose Acre HAIL BN27 * ... 90 A2
Primrose Av HORL RH6 .... 23 G8
Primrose Cl BURH RH15 .... 74 C5
  CRAWW RH11 .... 43 G6
  LGNY BN23 .... 164 A3
Primrose Copse HORS RH12 .... 56 C2
Primrose Hl BEXW TN39 .... 96 E2
  RHAS TN35 .... 285 Q12
Primrose La FROW RH18 .... 48 A3
  LISS GU33 .... 192 H9
Primrose Wy HAIL BN27 * 90 A2
Primula Rd BOR GU35 .... 178 N6
Prince Albert St BRI BN1 .... 4 D7
Prince Av LAN/SOMP BN15 .... 119 C9
Prince Charles Cl STHW BN42 120 E4
Prince Charles Rd LEWES BN7 17 J2
Prince Edward's Rd LEWES BN7 16 C5
Prince George's St HAV PO9 . 103 G4
Prince of Wales Cl
  WVILLE PO7 * 288 B10
Prince Regent's Cl
  BRIE/ROTT BN2 * 154 D1
Princes Av HOVE BN3 .... 121 M7
Princes Cl BOR GU35 .... 178 D3
  SEAF BN25 .... 159 K8
  UCK TN22 .... 76 C5
Prince's Crs BRI BN1 * 5 G1
  HOVE BN3 .... 121 M7
Princes Cft BOGR PO21 ...... 170 F4
Prince's Dr RCCH PO18 ...... 292 H7
  WVILLE PO7 .... 288 B8
Prince's Pl BRI BN1 .... 4 E7
Prince's Rd BRI BN1 .... 123 G6
  LGNY BN23 .... 164 D6
  PSF GU32 .... 223 L5
  SLVH TN37 .... 12 C7
Princess Anne Rd HORS RH12 . 186 A11
Princess Av BOGR PO21 ...... 171 M3
  SALV BN13 .... 150 E2
Princess Ct HWH RH16 .... 73 J1
Princess Dr SEAF BN25 ...... 159 J8

Princess Gdns HORN PO8 ..... 288 C2
Princess Margaret Rd
  HORS RH12 .... 186 A10
Princes Sq HOVE BN3 .... 121 M7
Princess Rd CRAWW RH11 ...... 8 C4
Prince's St BRI BN1 .... 4 F7
  RTWE/PEM TN2 .... 38 B6
Prince's Ter BRIE/ROTT BN2 . 154 D1
Prince William Cl SALV BN13 116 F5
Prince William Pde
  LGNY BN23 .... 164 E7
Prings La SWTR RH13 .... 203 J9
Prinkle La HAIL BN27 .... 280 B8
Prinsep Rd HOVE BN3 .... 121 M5
Prinsted La EMRTH PO10 ..... 104 E6
Priors Acre RCCH PO18 ...... 109 J2
Priors Cl EMRTH PO10 .... 104 F4
Priorsdean Crs HAV PO9 ..... 102 E1
Priors Leaze La RCCH PO18 .. 105 H4
Priors Wk CRAWE RH10 .... 9 J4
Prior's Wy EDN TN8 * 33 M3
Priors Waye BOGR PO21 ...... 170 F3
Priors Wd HASM GU27 .... 181 J11
Priory Av HAS TN34 .... 12 F4
Priory Cl BOGR PO21 .... 171 G5
  HAS TN34 .... 12 F4
  HORL RH6 .... 22 E5
  LAN/SOMP BN15 .... 118 A6
  PEV BN24 .... 134 C3
  RCCH PO18 .... 109 J2
  SALV BN13 .... 20 A1
Priory Crs LEWES BN7 .... 16 F8
Priory Fld STEY/UB BN44 ..... 78 F3
Priory Hts EDN/EASTW BN20 .. 162 F8
  EDN/EASTW BN20 .... 163 G8
Priory La CCH PO19 .... 6 D3
  LGNY BN23 .... 164 D2
Priory Meadow HAS TN34 * 13 J6
Priory Orch SALV BN13 ...... 164 D5
Priory Rd ANG/EP BN16 ...... 148 A3
  ARUN BN18 .... 112 F3
  BURH RH15 .... 74 F8
  CCH PO19 .... 6 E3
  FROW RH18 .... 63 M3
  HAS TN34 .... 13 K5
  HPPT/KEY BN6 .... 271 M4
  LGNY BN23 .... 164 D2
Priory St HAS TN34 .... 13 J6
  LEWES BN7 .... 16 F8
Priory Ter LEWES BN7 * 17 G8
The Priory BRI BN1 * 82 D8
Priory Wy HWH RH16 .... 73 J5
Privet Rd BOR GU35 .... 179 K4
Prochurch Rd HORN PO8 ...... 288 D5
Proctor Cl CRAWE RH10 .... 44 B5
Promenade PEAHV BN10 .... 156 F7
  PEAHV BN10 .... 157 H7
The Promenade EMRTH PO10 ... 104 A6
  PEV BN24 .... 165 J1
Prospect Gdns EAST BN21 .... 176 D1
Prospect La HAV PO9 .... 289 J12
Prospect Pl CRAWW RH11 ...... 8 D4
  HAS TN34 .... 12 F7
  HAV PO9 .... 102 F4
  WTHG BN11 .... 21 G7
Prospect Rd HTHF TN21 ...... 244 D1
  RTWE/PEM TN2 .... 38 A6
Providence Pl BRI BN1 .... 4 E3
Providence Ter CRAWE RH10 * 45 M5
  CCH PO19 * 6 C3
The Providence CCH PO19 ..... 6 D3
  WTHG BN11 .... 21 D7
Prowting Md BEXW TN39 ...... 136 B1
Pruetts La LISS GU33 .... 192 C12
Pryors La BOGR PO21 .... 171 H4
Puckshott Wy HASM GU27 ..... 181 M9
Pudding Cake La UCK TN22 .... 76 E5
Pudding La HORL RH6 .... 26 D1
Puffin Hl CRAWE RH10 .... 46 B4
Puffin Rd CRAWW RH11 * 42 C4
Pulborough Av
  LW/ROSE BN22 .... 163 K4
Pulborough Cl BRIE/ROTT BN2 123 L6
Pulborough Rd
  PUL/STOR RH20 .... 265 Q11
  MSEA/BNM PO22 .... 145 J7
Pulens Crs EPSF GU31 .... 223 R5
Pulens La EPSF GU31 .... 223 Q5
Pump La HORN PO8 .... 288 B4
  UCK TN22 .... 77 M6
Punch Copse Rd CRAWE RH10 ... 9 K2
Punches La SELS PO20 .... 142 C4
Purbeck Cl LGNY BN23 .... 164 B2
Purbeck Pl LHPTN BN17 ...... 147 M3
Purbrook Wy WVILLE PO7 ..... 102 A1
Purcell Rd CRAWW RH11 ...... 42 A4
Purley Cl CRAWE RH10 .... 44 D5
The Purrocks PSF GU32 ...... 223 L4
Purton Rd HORS RH12 .... 14 B2
Putmans La EPSF GU31 .... 224 C11
Puttick Cl PUL/STOR RH20 ... 266 B11
Puttocks Cl HASM GU27 ...... 180 C12
Pyecombe Cl CRAWW RH11 ...... 42 E6
Pyecombe St POY/PYE BN45 ... 270 H11
Pyle Cl HORN PO8 .... 288 B5
Pyrford Cl BOGR PO21 .... 171 G3

Quarry Ri EGRIN RH19 .... 31 M6
Quarry Rd HAS TN34 .... 13 H3
  NEWHV BN9 .... 19 G6
  RTW TN1 .... 38 A7
Quarry Wy SWTR RH13 .... 201 Q12
Quarterbrass Farm Rd
  SALV BN13 .... 56 C2
The Quashetts SALV BN13 .... 21 H2
Quayside LHPTN BN17 .... 147 G4
Quebec Cl BEXW TN39 .... 96 F8
  HORL RH6 .... 23 M6
  LGNY BN23 .... 164 E6
  LIPH GU30 .... 193 R2
Quebec Rd STLEO TN38 .... 98 F1
Quebec St BRIE/ROTT BN2 ..... 5 H5
Queen Alexandra Av
  HOVE BN3 .... 121 M2
Queen Anne's Cl LEWES BN7 * 16 E5
Queen Anne's Dr HAV PO9 .... 102 D3
Queen Caroline Cl HOVE BN3 . 121 M2
Queen Elizabeth Av
  BURH RH15 .... 74 E7
Queen Elizabeth Rd
  HORS RH12 .... 186 A10
Queen Mary Av HOVE BN3 ..... 121 M2
Queen's Ap UCK TN22 .... 76 F4
Queen's Av CCH PO19 .... 6 C9
  HAS TN34 .... 13 G7
Queensbury Ms BRI BN1 * 4 B7
Queen's Colonnade Gdns
  EAST BN21 .... 11 H6
Queens Cottages WADH TN5 ... 71 K4
Queens Crs BURH RH15 .... 74 F7
  HORN PO8 .... 288 D2
  LGNY BN23 .... 164 C6
Queensdown School Rd
  BRI BN1 .... 123 H2
Queens Dr HPPT/KEY BN6 ..... 271 N5
  UCK TN22 .... 241 L1
Queens Flds East BOGR PO21 . 171 L1
Queens Flds West BOGR PO21 . 171 L1
Queen's Gdns BRI BN1 .... 4 E5
  CCH PO19 .... 6 C9
  EAST BN21 .... 11 G6
  HOVE BN3 .... 122 B8
  SBGH/RUST TN4 .... 38 A3
Queens Ga HORL RH6 .... 27 M1
Queens La ARUN BN18 .... 113 G3
Queensmead BOGR PO21 .... 170 E5
Queen's Md MFD/CHID GU8 .... 182 G5
Queensmount MAYF TN20 ...... 211 Q10
Queens Pde
  LAN/SOMP BN15 * 118 D7
  SWTR RH13 * 14 E7
Queens Park Gdns SEAF BN25 . 174 E1
Queen's Park Ri BRIE/ROTT BN2 5 H6
Queen's Park Rd BRIE/ROTT BN2 5 H6
Queen's Park Ter
  BRIE/ROTT BN2 .... 5 K5
Queen's Pl BRI BN1 .... 4 F3
  HOVE BN3 .... 122 B7
  SHOR BN43 .... 119 L6
Queen Sq BRI BN1 .... 4 D6
Queen's Rd BRI BN1 .... 4 D5
  CROW TN6 .... 67 L8
  EGRIN RH19 .... 31 K8
  HAIL BN27 .... 279 P12
  HAS TN34 .... 13 H6
  HORL RH6 .... 22 F6
  HWH RH16 .... 73 H3
  LAN/SOMP BN15 .... 152 E1
  LEWES BN7 .... 17 H2
  LGNY BN23 .... 164 C6
  LIPH GU30 .... 193 K2
  LYDD TN29 .... 255 R7
  PSF GU32 .... 223 L5
  SBGH/RUST TN4 .... 38 A3
  STHW BN42 .... 120 D4
  WTHG BN11 .... 20 E7
Queens Sq BOGR PO21 * 2 E4
  CRAWE RH10 .... 8 F4
  HAS TN34 .... 13 G6
Queens St MIDH GU29 .... 226 D7
Queen St ARUN BN18 .... 113 H3
  EMRTH PO10 .... 104 A3
  HAWK TN18 .... 217 R4
  LHPTN BN17 .... 147 J4
  SALV BN13 .... 20 F1
  SWTR RH13 .... 14 C7
Queensway BOGR PO21 .... 2 D7
  BRIE/ROTT BN2 .... 5 L5
  CRAWE RH10 .... 9 G4
  EGRIN RH19 .... 31 K8
  LAN/SOMP BN15 .... 118 D7
  LYDD TN29 .... 255 R7
  SEAF BN25 .... 159 M8
  STLEO TN38 .... 283 M12
  SWTR RH13 .... 14 C8
Queen Victoria Av HOVE BN3 . 121 M2
Querneby Cl SHOR BN43 ...... 120 C6
Quest Cl CCH PO19 .... 7 H5
Quickbourne Cottages
  RYE TN31 .... 218 G9
Quickbourne La RYE TN31 .... 218 F10
Quinnell Dr HAIL BN27 ...... 92 A3
Quintin Cl HAIL BN27 .... 91 M8
The Quintins HAIL BN27 * 92 B5

Q

The Quadrangle SALV BN13 ... 298 H12
The Quadrant EAST BN21 ...... 10 A3
  FERR BN12 .... 150 B2
  HPPT/KEY BN6 .... 271 P5
Quail Cl HORS RH12 .... 56 C2
Quail Wy HORN PO8 .... 288 B5
Quakers La HWH RH16 .... 73 K4
Quantock Cl CRAWW RH11 ...... 8 C4
  LGNY BN23 .... 164 C2
  RTWE/PEM TN2 .... 38 C4
  SALV BN13 .... 116 C5
Quantock Gdns HAS TN34 ..... 100 A3
Quantock Rd SALV BN13 ...... 116 C5
The Quantocks LHPTN BN17 * . 147 J3
Quarely Rd HAV PO9 .... 288 D11
The Quarries SWTR RH13 ..... 203 J3
Quarry Bank Rd BRI BN1 ..... 123 G4
Quarry Cl BURH RH15 .... 75 J6
  HORS RH12 .... 56 E3
Quarry Crs HAS TN34 .... 13 H3
Quarry Hl HWH RH16 .... 72 F3
  STLEO TN38 .... 99 G8
Quarry La CCH PO19 .... 7 H5
  SEAF BN25 .... 159 M8

R

Racecourse Wy HORL RH6 ...... 27 L2
Rackfield HASM GU27 .... 180 G10
Rackham Cl CRAWW RH11 .... 8 C4
  SALV BN13 .... 116 B8
Rackham Rd ANG/EP BN16 * ... 148 A5
  ARUN BN18 .... 296 G2
  SALV BN13 .... 116 C6
Rackham St ARUN BN18 .... 296 G2
  PUL/STOR RH20 .... 297 K1
Racton Rd EMRTH PO10 .... 104 A2
Radbone Rd SALV BN13 .... 117 K7
Radcliffe Cl HAS TN34 .... 99 H2
Radford Rd BOGR PO21 .... 2 B2
  HORS RH12 .... 28 B5
Radinden Dr HOVE BN3 .... 122 C4
Radinden Manor Rd
  HOVE BN3 .... 122 B5
Radnor Cl SALV BN13 * 150 E1
Radnor Ms STLEO TN38 * 98 D3
Radnor Rd SALV BN13 .... 150 E1
Rafati Wy BEX TN40 .... 97 J2
Ragged Dog La HTHF TN21 .... 243 Q10
Raglan Av SALV BN13 .... 116 D8
Railey Rd CRAWE RH10 .... 9 H3

Railway Ap EGRIN RH19.............31 J8
NEWHV BN9.............19 H3
WTHG BN11.............20 F3
Railway La LEWES BN7.............17 H5
Railway Rd LISS GU33.............192 G2
NEWHV BN9.............19 H3
Railway St BRI BN1.............4 D4
Rainbow Wy PUL/STOR RH20..266 C10
Rake Rd LIPH GU30.............193 N11
LISS GU33.............192 E9
Rakers Rdg HORS RH12.............56 C4
Raleigh Cl LGNY BN23.............164 D7
SHOR BN43.............119 K7
Raleigh Ct CRAWE RH10 *.............27 M6
Raleigh Crs FERR BN12.............150 C2
Raleigh Dr RHR6.............23 M6
Raleigh Rd BOGR PO21.............171 H2
Raleigh Wk CRAWE RH10.............1 H9
Raleigh Wy HORS RH12.............150 B1
Rambledown La
PUL/STOR RH20.............265 R7
Ramblers Wy CRAWW RH11.....43 G8
WVILLE PO7.............288 C4
Ramillies Gdns
MSEA/BNM PO22.............145 H8
Ramsay Wy LGNY BN23.............164 D6
Ramsdale Av HAV PO9.............288 D12
Ramsdean Rd PSF GU32.............222 E8
Ramsey Cl HORL RH6.............22 F6
HORS RH12.............56 C4
Ramshill EPSF GU31.............223 P5
Rams La MFD/CHID GU8.............184 B7
Ramslye Rd SBGH/RUST TN4...37 J3
Randolph La RTW TN31.............252 F2
Ranelagh Rd HAV PO9.............102 E4
Ranelagh Vls HORS RH12.............122 A5
Rangemore Dr EAST BN21.............163 J6
Rankine Rd RTWE/PEM TN2.....38 C2
Ranmore Cl CRAWW RH11.............59 H1
HAS TN34.............284 B12
Rannoch Rd CROW TN6.............67 J7
Rannoch Rd West CROW TN6..67 J7
Ranscombe Hl RING/NEW BN8..86 F1
Ranscombe La RING/NEW BN8...87 G7
Ransome Cl CRAWW RH11.............42 C5
Ranters La CRBK TN17.............191 M1
Ranville Cl LGNY BN23.............164 A1
MSEA/BNM PO22.............3 K2
Raphael Rd HOVE BN3.............121 L4
Rapley Av PUL/STOR RH20.....265 Q11
Rapson's Rd EDN/EASTW BN20..162 E2
Rascals Cl SWTR RH13.............233 Q2
Rastrick Cl BURH RH15.............74 E8
Ratham La RCCH PO18.............106 B4
Rathbone Ct PUL/STOR RH20 *..265 K3
Rathlin Rd CRAWW RH11.............43 G4
Rattle Rd PEV BN24.............133 G8
Ratton Dr EDN/EASTW BN20...163 G6
Ratton Rd EAST BN21.............10 A3
Raughmere Dr RCCH PO18.....107 L1
Raven Cl CRAWE RH10.............46 B4
Raven Ct BAT TN33.............282 G5
STLEO TN38.............98 D2
Raven La CRAWW RH11.............43 H1
Ravensbourne Av SHOR BN43...119 L4
Ravensbourne Cl SHOR BN43..119 L4
Ravens Cl BEXW TN39.............136 B2
Ravenscroft ANG/EP BN16.....148 B5
Ravens Cft EDN/EASTW BN20..176 F5
Ravenscroft PUL/STOR RH20..298 A1
Ravenscroft Ct HORS RH12 *....14 C3
Raven's Rd SHOR BN43.............119 L6
Ravens Wy MSEA/BNM PO22..144 A1
Ravenswood Av
RTWE/PEM TN2.............38 B3
Ravenswood Dr
BRIE/ROTT BN2.............124 E7
Ravenswood Rd BURH RH15....75 G6
Ravine Cl HAS TN34.............99 M2
Raworth Cl CRAWE RH10 *......44 B5
Rawson Vls ANG/EP BN16 *....148 B3
Raycroft Cl BOGR PO21.............171 J5
Rayden Cl LHPTN BN17.............147 K4
Rayford Cl PEAHV BN10.............157 H6
Raymer Wk HORL RH6.............23 H5
Raymond Cl SEAF BN25.............159 M8
Readers La RYE TN31.............220 E12
Reading Rd BRIE/ROTT BN2....154 F1
Readon Cl EPSF GU31.............223 P5
Reapers Cl HORL RH6.............56 C4
The Rear RTWE/PEM TN2 *.....37 M7
Record Rd EMRTH PO10.............103 M4
Rectory Av CHAM PO6.............102 A4
Rectory Cl BUR/ETCH TN19...214 G11
EDN/EASTW BN20.............176 D2
HOVE BN3 *.............121 H4
NEWHV BN9.............18 F5
PUL/STOR RH20.............265 K3
PUL/STOR RH20.............266 A12
PUL/STOR RH20.............267 K8
RING/NEW BN8.............276 H4
SHOR BN43.............120 C6
STLEO TN38.............99 G4
Rectory Farm Rd
LAN/SOMP BN15.............118 A6
Rectory Fld HRTF TN7.............50 D1
Rectory Gdns SALV BN13.............117 H8
Rectory La ANG/EP BN16.............114 E1
CRAWW RH11.............42 E1
HORL RH6.............26 C2
LIPH GU30.............180 A10
PUL/STOR RH20.............265 K3
PUL/STOR RH20.............266 C7
RYE TN31.............219 J12
RYE TN31.............252 G5
SELS PO20.............301 M3
WSEA TN36.............286 D3
Rectory Park Rd
STPH/PW TN12.............189 M7
Rectory Pl PUL/STOR RH20....267 J8
Rectory Rd HAV PO9.............103 G5
NEWHV BN9.............158 D3
PUL/STOR RH20.............266 A12
SALV BN13.............20 B1
SHOR BN43.............120 B6
Rectory Wk LAN/SOMP BN15..118 A6
PUL/STOR RH20.............266 A12
Rectory Wy BEX TN40.............97 J7
Red Admiral St HORS RH12......56 C4
Redbridge Cottages
RHWH RH17 *.............60 D7
Redbridge Gv HAV PO9.............102 E2
Redbridge La CROW TN6.............210 E4
RHWH RH17.............60 A6

Redbrook La UCK TN22.............242 E1
Redcross St BRI BN1.............4 F4
Red Deer Cl SWTR RH13.............57 G6
Redditch Cl CRAWW RH11.............42 D7
Redford Av HORS RH12.............14 A2
Redford Cl EGRIN RH19.............31 G6
Redgarth Ct EGRIN RH19 *......31 H4
Redgeland Ri STLEO TN38.............98 D3
Redgill La RING/NEW BN8.....240 A4
Redgrave Cl CRAWE RH10.............44 C4
Redhill BRI BN1.............82 B8
Redhill Dr BRI BN1.............122 B1
Red House Ct EPSF GU31.....225 J5
Redhill Rd HAV PO9.............289 J9
Redkiln Cl SWTR RH13.............15 J3
Redkiln Wy SWTR RH13.............15 J3
Red Lake Ter RHAS TN35.....100 C1
Redlands La EMRTH PO10.....104 A1
SWTR RH13.............167 L2
Red La BOR GU35.............179 Q2
SWTR RH13.............233 N8
Redleaf Cl RTWE/PEM TN2......38 C3
Red Lion St MIDH GU29.....227 J10
Redlynch Cl HAV PO9 *.............103 J1
Redmayne Dr HAS TN34.............12 E2
Red Oak HAWK TN18.............216 F1
Redoubt Rd LW/ROSE BN22....11 J3
Red River Ct HORS RH12 *......56 A4
Redshank Rd HORN PO8.....288 C3
Redvers Rd BRIE/ROTT BN2..123 J4
Redwell Av BEXW TN39.............97 G5
Redwing Cl LHPTN BN17.............147 H1
SWTR RH13.............15 K4
Redwing Rd HORN PO8.....256 D9
Redwood Cl CRAWE RH10.............43 K1
SALV BN13.............116 B8
Redwood Gv HAV PO9.............103 H1
Redwood Rd BRI WH16.............73 G2
Reed Cl PUL/STOR RH20.....265 R12
Reed Ct LGNY BN23.............164 A1
Reedings CRAWW RH11.............42 C5
Reedmace Cl WVILLE PO7 *...288 B11
Reed Pond Wk HWH RH16......73 K5
Reed's La HPPT/KEY BN6.....270 C1
LISS GU33.............192 H7
SWTR RH13.............202 A6
Reedswood Rd RYE TN31.....250 E9
STLEO TN38.............98 D5
Reef Cl LHPTN BN17.............147 H5
Reeves Hl BRI BN1.............83 J8
Reeves Ter WADH TN5.............191 K12
Regal Dr EGRIN RH19.............47 L1
Regency Cl UCK TN22.............76 B7
Regency Gdns STLEO TN38.....98 F5
Regency Ms BRI BN1 *.............4 B6
EDN/EASTW BN20.............176 F4
Regency Rd BRI BN1.............4 C7
Regency Sq BRI BN1.............4 B6
Regency Ter UCK TN22 *.............76 B7
Regent Ar BRI BN1.............4 C6
Regent Cl LAN/SOMP BN15..119 G7
Regent Pl HTHF TN21.............244 D5
RTWE/PEM TN2 *.............38 C2
SLVH TN37.............283 N10
Regent Rw BRI BN1.............4 C6
Regents Cl CRAWW RH11.............43 H7
Regents Ct HAV PO9.............103 G5
Regents Ms HORL RH6.............22 F6
Regents Pl EAST BN21.............163 J5
Regents Wy BOGR PO21.....171 L1
Reginald Rd BEXW TN39.....137 G1
Regis Av BOGR PO21.............171 G4
Regnum Cl LW/ROSE BN22....163 K1
Reigate Cl CRAWE RH10.............28 C8
Reigate Rd BRI BN1.............122 C4
HORL RH6.............22 C7
REIG RH2.............22 B7
WTHG BN11.............150 E3
Renfields HWH RH16.............72 F6
Renn Gdns PUL/STOR RH20..266 H8
Renoir Cl MSEA/BNM PO22....143 H7
Renoir Ms BOGR PO21.............143 M7
Renown Cl BEX TN40.............97 J7
Renown Gdns HORN PO8.....288 A4
Renton Cl BIL RH14.............232 A1
Reservoir La PSF GU32.............223 N4
The Residence LW/ROSE BN22 *..11 H5
Resting Oak Hl RING/NEW BN8..273 Q5
Rew La CCH PO19.............107 L2
Reynard Cl HORS RH12.............57 G4
Reynolds Dr BEX TN40.............97 K8
Reynolds La ARUN BN18.....111 J1
SBGH/RUST TN4.............37 L3
Reynolds Rd CRAWW RH11.......8 C2
HOVE BN3.............121 H5
LGNY BN23.............164 C4
Reynoldstown La POLE BN26..131 J2
Rhee Wall RASHW TN26.............221 Q2
Rhinefield Cl HAV PO9 *.............102 D1
Rhodes Wy CRAWE RH10.............9 K3
Riccards La BAT TN33.............248 H11
Rice Br RHWH RH17.............236 D6
Rices Hl EGRIN RH19.............31 K8
Richardson Rd HOVE BN3.....121 L7
SBGH/RUST TN4.............37 M3
Richborough Cl HAS TN34.......99 J1
Richborough Ct CRAWW RH11...8 A3
Richington Wy SEAF BN25.....160 A8
Richland Cl RHAS TN35.............100 D1
Richmead Gdns MAYF TN20..212 E7
Richmond Av BEXW TN39.....136 D6
BOGR PO21.............171 M2
CCH PO19.............107 M3
Richmond Av West
BOGR PO21.............171 M3
Richmond Cl ANG/EP BN16...148 D3
BEXW TN39.............136 F2
BOR GU35.............178 G8
Richmond Ct CRAWE RH10.......9 G6
WTHG BN11.............20 D5
Richmond Gv BEXW TN39.....136 F5
Richmond Pde BRIE/ROTT BN2..4 F4
Richmond Pl BRIE/ROTT BN2...4 F4
EAST BN21.............10 C5
RTWE/PEM TN2.............54 C1
Richmond Rd BEXW TN39.....136 E2
BOGR PO21.............2 D6
HORS RH12.............56 D6
RCCH PO18.............108 D2
SEAF BN25.............174 D2
WTHG BN11.............20 D6

Richmond Rd North BOGR PO21...2 E5
Richmond St BRIE/ROTT BN2....5 H5
HAS TN34.............100 B3
Richmond Ter BRI BN1.............5 G3
SEAF BN25.............174 D2
Richmond Wy EGRIN RH19......47 L1
Rickfield CRAWW RH11.............42 F4
Rickman's La BIL RH14.............198 A3
Rickwood Rd HAV PO9.............23 C5
Riddens Cl LEWES BN7.............272 H4
Riddens La LEWES BN7.............272 H4
The Riddens LEWES BN7 *.....272 H4
Riddlesdale Av SBGH/RUST TN4..37 H3
Riders Bolt BEXW TN39.............96 D8
Riders La HAV PO9.............102 F1
The Ride BIL RH14.............198 D3
Ridge Cl HORN PO8.............256 D9
PTSD BN41.............120 F1
UCK TN22.............208 H4
Ridge Common La PSF GU32..223 K3
Ridgehurst Dr HORS RH12.....201 Q4
Ridge Lands Cl
EDN/EASTW BN20.............176 C2
Ridge Moor Cl GSHT GU26...180 H4
Ridge Rd BRI BN1.............84 B5
Ridgeside CRAWE RH10.............9 K3
Ridgeside Av BRI BN1.............82 D8
The Ridge HAS TN34.............100 A1
HORS RH12.............186 B9
RRTW TN3.............51 M3
SLVH TN37.............283 R11
WSEA TN36.............286 D2
Ridge Top La PSF GU32.............222 E3
Ridge Vw BRI BN1.............83 K8
Ridge Wy RHWH RH17.............73 L7
Ridgeway BUR/ETCH TN19.....216 A6
EGRIN RH19.............47 K2
LGNY BN23.............164 B3
LHPTN BN17.............147 H1
SWTR RH13.............201 R11
Ridgeway Gdns
BRIE/ROTT BN2.............124 C6
The Ridgeway BURH RH15......75 C5
CCH PO19.............6 A2
HAIL BN27.............279 P11
HASM GU27.............195 L7
HORL RH6.............22 F8
HORS RH12.............14 A2
SEAF BN25.............174 F1
The Ridge West SLVH TN37..283 P10
Ridgewood Av
BRIE/ROTT BN2.............156 B2
Ridgewood Cl UCK TN22.............76 F8
Ridgewood Gdns BEX TN40..137 L1
HAS TN34.............284 B12
Ridgley Rd BRIE/ROTT BN2..124 C5
Ridgway HAV PO9.............102 E4
Ridgway Cl BRIE/ROTT BN2..124 C5
Ridgway Paddock BRIE/ROTT BN2...85 J7
The Ridgway BRIE/ROTT BN2..124 C5
MSEA/BNM PO22.............3 M5
The Ridings ANG/EP BN16.....148 A4
ARUN BN18.............110 F3
BEXW TN39.............96 E6
BOGR PO21.............171 H4
BRIE/ROTT BN2.............155 J1
BURH RH15.............75 H8
CRAWE RH10.............44 D3
LISS GU33.............192 E9
PEAHV BN10.............157 G4
RING/NEW BN8.............240 B6
RTWE/PEM TN2.............38 E3
SEAF BN25.............159 L8
SLVH TN37.............283 R12
STEY/UB BN44.............78 C4
Ridleys EGRIN RH19.............62 D3
Rifeside Gdns FERR BN12.....149 K2
Rife Wy FERR BN12.............149 K3
MSEA/BNM PO22.............3 J4
Rigden Rd HOVE BN3.............122 B5
Riley Rd BRIE/ROTT BN2.....123 H4
Rillside CRAWE RH10.............43 M6
Rill Wk EGRIN RH19.............32 A8
Rimmer Cl CRAWW RH11.............59 G1
Ringley Av HORL RH6.............22 F6
Ringley Oak HORS RH12.............15 J2
Ringley Rd HORS RH12.............15 H2
Ringmer Cl BRI BN1.............123 K1
Ringmer Rd NEWHV BN9.............18 C6
SALV BN13.............116 D8
SEAF BN25.............174 E3
Ringmer Wy LGNY BN23 *....163 M1
Ring Rd LAN/SOMP BN15.....118 D4
Ring Rd North HORL RH6.............28 D3
Ring Rd South HORL RH6.............28 B2
Ringwood Cl CRAWE RH10.......9 H7
LW/ROSE BN22.............11 G1
Ringwood Ct LW/ROSE BN22 *..11 G1
Ringwood Rd BEXW TN39.....97 H6
LW/ROSE BN22.............10 F1
Ripe La RING/NEW BN8.............89 L2
Ripley Cha EAST BN21 *.............10 B5
Ripley Rd WTHG BN11.............150 E2
Ripon Ct WTHG BN11 *.............20 A6
Ripon Gdns BOGR PO21.....171 K2
WVILLE PO7.............288 C5
Risden La HAWK TN18.............217 K2
Riseden Rd WADH TN5.............213 M1
Rise Park Gdns LGNY BN23....163 D3
The Rise CRAWE RH10.............44 B3
EGRIN RH19.............47 L1
HTHF TN21 *.............278 C2
HWH RH16.............73 L4
PTSD BN41.............120 D6
SWTR RH13.............234 F10
The Rising LGNY BN23.............164 D3
Ritchie Cl CRAWE RH10.............44 B7
Rival Moor Rd EPSF GU31.....223 Q7
River Cl SHOR BN43.............119 K7
Riverdale LEWES BN7.............16 F3
Riverhall Av WVILLE PO7.....288 B10
Riverhall Hl WADH TN5.............70 E1
Riverhill La RTWE/PEM TN2..229 Q11
River La PETW GU28.............228 D3
RYE TN31.............252 H7
River Md CRAWW RH11.............26 F8
Rivermead PUL/STOR RH20..265 L4
Rivermede BOR GU35.............178 H5
River Rd ARUN BN18.............113 G3
LHPTN BN17.............147 H4
Riverside CCH PO19.............7 H3
FROW RH18.............48 D1

HORL RH6.............22 F8
HORS RH12.............201 R3
PUL/STOR RH20.............266 A11
SHOR BN43.............119 L7
STEY/UB BN44.............78 F3
STHW BN42.............120 D7
UCK TN22.............243 J4
Riverside Cl LISS GU33.............192 C9
Riverside Gdns CRAWW RH11....9 K3
Riverside North NEWHV BN9...19 H6
Riverside Rd SHOR BN43.....119 L7
Riverside South NEWHV BN9..19 H6
River St EMRTH PO10.............104 C1
UCK TN22.............76 E5
Rixons Cl RHWH RH17.............207 M4
Rixons Orch RHWH RH17.....207 M4
Roadean Cl SEAF BN25.............175 G1
Roads Hl HORN PO8.............256 A12
Robell Wy PUL/STOR RH20..266 B10
Roberts Cl SWTR RH13.............201 Q3
Robert's Hl WSEA TN36.............286 D2
Robertson Pas HAS TN34.............12 F7
Robertson Hl RHAS TN35.............13 M2
Robertson St HAS TN34.............13 G7
Robertson Ter HAS TN34.............13 G7
Roberts Rd LAN/SOMP BN15..152 D1
LISS GU33.............192 F3
Robert St BRI BN1.............4 E4
Robert Tressell Cl HAS TN34....12 E4
Robian Cl UCK TN22.............241 M1
Robina Cl WVILLE PO7.............288 B10
Robin Cl CRAWW RH11.............43 H1
EGRIN RH19.............31 K7
LGNY BN23.............164 B3
LHPTN BN17.............147 H1
SWTR RH13.............201 R11
Robin Davis Cl BRIE/ROTT BN2..123 K5
Robin Dene BRIE/ROTT BN2..154 D1
Robin Hood La HORS RH12..187 P12
LYDD TN29.............255 T9
Robin La LYDD TN29.............255 R7
Robin Ms SLVH TN37 *.............12 E4
Robin Post La POLE BN26.....131 H3
Robin Rw BURH RH15.............74 D7
Robin Rw CRAWE RH10.............56 B8
Robins Cl SELS PO20.............301 L6
Robins Dr BOGR PO21.............171 J2
Robins La MIDH GU29.............226 A2
Robinson Cl LAN/SOMP BN15..118 D7
SELS PO20.............301 L4
Robinson Rd NEWHV BN9.............18 F2
Robinson Wy BOR GU35.....178 G9
Robins Reach HORS RH12 *....90 A2
Robinswood Ct HORS RH12 *...15 J1
Roborough Cl EAST BN21.............10 A4
Robsack Av STLEO TN38.............98 D3
Robson Cl SWTR RH13 *.............56 B2
Robson Rd FERR BN12.............150 D3
Rochdale Rd RTW TN1.............38 D3
Rochester Cl CCH PO19.............107 L4
EDN/EASTW BN20.............176 C1
HOVE BN3 *.............122 C7
SALV BN13 *.............116 A6
Rochester Ct WTHG BN11 *....20 A6
Rochester Gdns HOVE BN3..122 C7
Rochester St SLVH TN37.............99 G3
Rochester St BRIE/ROTT BN2....5 L6
Rochester Wy BOGR PO21..171 G4
CROW TN6.............68 B8
Rochford Wy CROW TN6.....210 H1
Rochmans Wy CROW TN6....210 H1
Rockall Av LGNY BN23.............164 E5
Rockall Cl LHPTN BN17.............147 M2
Rockall Dr HAIL BN27.............91 M3
Rock-a-Nore Pde HAS TN34....13 H6
Rock-a-Nore Rd HAS TN34.....13 L7
Rockbourne Cl HAV PO9.............102 D1
Rock Channel RYE TN31.....252 H8
Rock Cl RHAS TN35.............100 C1
Rockdale Dr GSHT GU26.....180 G6
Rock Gdns BOGR PO21.............2 C7
Rock Gv BRIE/ROTT BN2.............5 M9
Rockhurst Dr
EDN/EASTW BN20.............163 G7
Rockingham Cl SALV BN13..116 D7
Rockingham Ct SALV BN13..116 D7
Rockington Wy CROW TN6..211 J1
Rocklands La RHAS TN35.....100 B4
Rock La PUL/STOR RH20.....266 H12
RHAS TN35.............284 C9
Rockmead Rd RHAS TN35.....101 L1
Rock Pl BRIE/ROTT BN2.............5 H8
Rock Rd PUL/STOR RH20.....266 D10
Rocks Hl RBTBR TN32.............216 F11
Rocks La RHWH RH17.............60 E8
UCK TN22.............209 R11
Rocks Park Rd UCK TN22.............76 D5
The Rocks EGRIN RH19.............48 B3
Rock Slip BRIE/ROTT BN2..154 D1
Rock Villa Rd RTW TN1.............37 M5
Rockwood Pk EGRIN RH19 *....47 H4
Rocky La HWH RH16.............72 F7
Roderick Av PEAHV BN10.....157 G7
Rodgate La HASM GU27.....182 D12
Rodmell Av BRIE/ROTT BN2..156 C4
Rodmell Pl BRI BN1 *.............82 F7
Rodmell Rd RTWE/PEM TN2...37 M8
SALV BN13.............116 D8
SEAF BN25.............175 H3
Rodmill Dr EAST BN21.............163 J8
Rodmill Rd EAST BN21.............163 J8
Rodney Cl BOGR PO21.............171 H2
LGNY BN23.............164 D6
Rodney Crs ARUN BN18.....146 D2
Rodney Wy HORN PO8.............288 C3
Rodwell CROW TN6.............68 B8
Roebuck St HAS TN34.............13 L6
Roedale Rd BRI BN1.............123 G4
Roedean Cl BEXW TN39.............96 F8
Roedean Crs BRIE/ROTT BN2..154 F1
Roedean Hts BRIE/ROTT BN2..154 F1
Roedean Pth BRIE/ROTT BN2..154 F1
Roedean Rd BRIE/ROTT BN2..154 F2
RTWE/PEM TN2.............37 M8
SALV BN13.............116 D7
Roedean V BRIE/ROTT BN2..155 G2
Roedean Wy BRIE/ROTT BN2..154 F2
Roedeer Copse HASM GU27..180 H11
Roffey Cl HORL RH6.............22 E6

Roffey Pk HORS RH12 *.............57 K3
Roffeys RRTW TN3 *.............52 D5
Roffey's Cl CRAWE RH10.............28 F5
Roffrey Av LW/ROSE BN22..163 J4
Roffye Ct HORS RH12.............15 L1
Rogate Cl LAN/SOMP BN15..118 A6
Rogate Rd SALV BN13.............116 F7
Roger's La SALV BN13.............116 D1
Rogers Rough Rd CRBK TN17..191 M3
Rogerstown EDEN TN8 *.............33 L5
Roland Cl HORN PO8.............288 C3
Rolfe Dr BURH RH15.............75 J6
Rollaston Pk ARUN BN18.....146 A3
Romaine Cl BURH RH15.............75 J4
Roman Acre LHPTN BN17.....147 H3
Roman Av ANG/EP BN16.....148 F1
Roman Cl SEAF BN25.............159 G7
Roman Crs STHW BN42.....120 D5
Roman Cft EAST BN21.............10 A4
Roman Flds BOGR PO21.....171 M1
Roman La SALV BN13.............116 B7
Roman Landing SELS PO20..166 D3
Roman Rd HOVE BN3.............121 J7
STEY/UB BN44.............78 D3
STHW BN42.............120 D5
Romans Wy PEV BN24.............133 K7
Roman Wy LAN/SOMP BN15..118 A6
CCH PO19.............107 G7
HAV PO9.............102 D3
STHW BN42.............120 D5
UCK TN22.............77 G5
Romany Cl PTSD BN41.............121 G5
Romany Rd SALV BN13.............116 B7
Romford Rd RTWE/PEM TN2...39 K2
Romney Broadwalk
MSEA/BNM PO22.............143 M7
Romney Cl SEAF BN25.............175 J1
Romney Garth SELS PO20..301 M6
Romney Rd BRIE/ROTT BN2..155 M4
POLE BN26.............132 B7
WTHG BN11.............150 E4
Romney St LW/ROSE BN22..11 K1
Romney Vw BRI BN1.............123 G3
Romsey Rd HORN PO8.............256 D11
Rona Cl CRAWW RH11.............8 A9
Rookcross La SWTR RH13.....267 K1
Rookery Cl BRI BN1.............122 D4
NEWHV BN9.............158 D3
Rookery La HTHF TN21.............245 N12
SELS PO20.............169 L5
WSEA TN36.............286 E3
The Rookery EMRTH PO10.....104 B4
Rookery Wy HWH RH16.............73 M5
NEWHV BN9.............158 E3
SEAF BN25.............159 G8
Rookes Cl HORN PO8.............288 C3
Rookhurst Rd BEX TN40.............97 L5
Rookley Cl RTWE/PEM TN2....38 C7
Rooksbury Cft HAV PO9.....288 H12
Rook Wy HORS RH12.............56 D3
Rookwood Cl UCK TN22.............77 G4
Rookwood La SELS PO20.....167 J1
Rookwood Pk HORS RH12..201 R2
Rookwood Rd SELS PO20.....167 J3
Roopers RRTW TN3 *.............36 F3
Ropeland Wy HORS RH12......56 D2
Ropers Ga SBGH/RUST TN4...37 M3
Ropes La HASM GU27.............195 M8
Ropetackle SHOR BN43.............119 K6
Rope Wk HAIL BN27.............92 A5
LHPTN BN17.............147 H4
RYE TN31.............252 H7
SHOR BN43.............119 K6
The Rope Wk HAWK TN18.....217 Q4
Ropley Rd HAV PO9.............289 J3
Rosamund Rd CRAWE RH10...44 A5
Rose Av MSEA/BNM PO22.....145 J4
Rosebarn Cl BURH RH15.............75 H8
Rosebay Ct WVILLE PO7.....288 B10
Rosebery Av BRIE/ROTT BN2..124 B5
FERR BN12.............150 D3
LW/ROSE BN22.............163 K4
Rose Cottage La RHWH RH17..204 H5
Rosecroft Cl LAN/SOMP BN15..118 D3
Rosecroft Pk RRTW TN3 *.....36 F5
Rosedale Cl CRAWW RH11.......42 F5
Rosedale Pl LW/ROSE BN22..163 J2
Rosedene Cl BRIE/ROTT BN2..124 D7
Rose Green Rd BOGR PO21..171 H2
Rose Gv HAIL BN27 *.............90 A2
Rosehill BIL RH14.............200 A12
Rose Hl BRI BN1.............5 G2
HORN PO8.............288 B6
TENT TN30.............220 C4
Rose Hill Cl BRI BN1.............4 F2
Rose Hill Ter BRI BN1.............4 F2
Rosehill Wk RTW TN1 *.............37 M6
Rosehurst Vls
SBGH/RUST TN4 *.............38 B2
Roselands BEXW TN39.............96 E7
HORN PO8.............288 B6
Roselands Av LW/ROSE BN22..164 A7
MAYF TN20.............212 C8
Roselands Cl LGNY BN23.............11 J1
Roselands Ct LW/ROSE BN22 *..11 J1
Rose Lea CROW TN6.............67 L6
Roseleigh Gdns RHWH RH17..239 J2
Rosemary Av STEY/UB BN44...78 D2
Rosemary Cl BOGR PO21.....171 H2
HWH RH16.............73 E3
PEAHV BN10.............157 H5
PUL/STOR RH20.............266 A12
STEY/UB BN44.............78 D2
Rosemary Ct HORL RH6 *.............22 D5
Rosemary Dr SHOR BN43.....120 A4
Rosemary Gdns
BUR/ETCH TN19.............214 G10
Rosemary La CRAN GU6.....184 F9
HORL RH6.............23 G7
HORL RH6.............26 D2
PETW GU28.............229 J9
RHAS TN35.............285 P11
WADH TN5.............191 M8
Rosemary Wy HORN PO8.....288 C3
Rosemead LHPTN BN17.............147 K4
Rosemount RING/NEW BN8..277 N10
Rosemount Cl SEAF BN25.....159 M8
Roseneath Gv MFD/CHID GU8..182 G5
Rose Pl LHPTN BN17.............148 A2
Rosetti Rd PEV BN24.............165 H1
Roseveare Rd
LW/ROSE BN22.............164 A7
Rose Wk CRAWW RH11 *.............8 D7
FERR BN12.............150 D3
SEAF BN25.............159 F1

Rose Walk Cl NEWHV BN9...18 E4
The Rose Wk NEWHV BN9...18 E4
Rosewood Gdns HORN PO8...256 D8
Rosewood La BOR GU35...179 K4
Rosier Wy BIL RH14...232 B3
Rosina Cl WVILLE PO7...288 C9
Rossalyn Cl BOGR PO21...171 G2
Ross Cl BOGR PO21...171 G3
  CRAWE RH10...9 J9
Rossdale RTWE/PEM TN2...38 B4
Rossington Cl EAST BN21...10 A1
Rossiter Rd LAN/SOMP BN15...118 D5
Rosslyn Av SHOR BN43...119 M6
Rosslyn Ct SHOR BN43...119 L6
Rosslyn Rd SHOR BN43...119 L6
Rossmore Cl CRAWE RH10...28 C3
Rothbury Rd HOVE BN3...121 J6
Rother Av PEV BN24...132 E8
Rotherbank Farm La
  LISS GU33...192 C7
Rotherbridge La PETW GU28...229 J12
  CROW TN6...210 H2
  EPSF GU31...223 R5
  PUL/STOR PO20...266 C10
Rothercombe La PSF GU32...222 H5
Rother Crs CRAWW RH11...42 E4
Rotherfield Av BEX TN40...137 J1
  HAS TN34...13 M3
  LGNY BN23...163 M1
Rotherfield Cl BRI BN1...83 C7
Rotherfield Crs BRI BN1...83 C6
Rotherfield La MAYF TN20...212 D6
Rotherfield Rd CROW TN6...211 M1
Rotherhill Rd CROW TN6...210 H1
Rotherhurst La CROW TN6...211 M3
Rother La EPSF GU31...225 P8
Rothermead MAYF TN20...212 C8
  PETW GU28...229 K10
Rother Rd SEAF BN25...175 G3
Rothervale HORL RH6...22 E4
Rother Vw BUR/ETCH TN19...214 G10
Rotherview RBTBR TN32...216 D12
Rothesay Cl SALV BN13...150 D1
Rothley Cha HWH RH16...73 J5
Rothwell Cl NEWHV BN9...18 B4
Rotten Rw LEWES BN7...16 D7
  SELS PO20...169 J2
Rottingdean Pl
  BRIE/ROTT BN2 *...155 L1
Rotunda Rd LGNY BN23...164 C13
The Rotyngs BRIE/ROTT BN2...155 L3
Rough Brow SEAF BN25...175 G1
Rough Fld EGRIN RH19...31 J5
The Rough RING/NEW BN8...240 B6
Rough Wy HORS RH12...56 E4
Roundabout Copse
  PUL/STOR PO20...266 A8
Roundabout La
  PUL/STOR PO20...266 A8
The Roundabouts LISS GU33...192 C10
Roundacres Wy BEX TN40...97 K7
Roundals La MFD/CHID GU8...183 K2
The Roundel SLVH TN37...284 A12
Roundhay Av PEAHV BN10 *...157 K7
Roundhill Crs BRIE/ROTT BN2...5 H1
Round Hill Rd BRI BN1...5 G1
Roundhill Rd RTWE/PEM TN2...38 C8
Roundhouse Meadow
  EMRTH PO10...104 B6
Roundle Av MSEA/BNM PO22...145 G7
Roundle Rd MSEA/BNM PO22...145 H7
Roundle Square Rd
  MSEA/BNM PO22...145 G8
Round Piece La SELS PO20...301 J5
Round Piece SELS PO20...300 L5
Round Robin Ldg
  STEY/UB BN44 *...299 H7
Roundstone By-Pass Rd
  ANG/EP BN16...148 E2
Roundstone Crs ANG/EP BN16...148 F3
Roundstone Dr ANG/EP BN16...148 F3
Roundstone La ANG/EP BN16...148 F2
Roundstone Wy SELS PO20...301 N5
Roundway BRI BN1...83 K8
  WVILLE PO7...288 B10
The Roundway ANG/EP BN16...148 C5
Roundwood La HWH RH16...73 J1
Roundwood Rd SLVH TN37...283 Q12
Rowan Av HORN PO8...288 C7
  HOVE BN3...121 K4
  LW/ROSE BN22...163 J2
Rowan Cl CRAWE RH10...9 J4
  HORS RH12...57 G4
  HTHF TN21...244 D8
  HWH RH16...73 L5
  PTSD BN41...120 D2
  SEAF BN25...175 J2
  SLVH TN37...284 A11
Rowan Dr BIL RH14...199 R12
Rowan Gdns BEX TN40...97 L7
Rowan Rd HAV PO9...103 J2
Rowans Ct LEWES BN7...16 E5
Rowanside Cl BOR GU35...179 R5
The Rowans GSHT GU26...180 G7
  RTWE/PEM TN2 *...39 K3
  WTHG BN11...20 B6
Rowan Tree Rd RTWE/PEM TN2...37 K8
Rowan Wy ANG/EP BN16...148 F1
  BRIE/ROTT BN2...155 G2
  HORS RH12...57 H4
  MSEA/BNM PO22...144 B6
Rowbarns BAT TN33...282 D5
Rowbury Rd HAV PO9...288 E11
Rowe Av PEAHV BN10...157 G6
Rowfant Cl CRAWE RH10...44 D5
Rowhill La RHWH RH17...205 M2
Rowhook Rd HORS RH12...187 J8
Rowland Cl CRAWE RH10...29 K4
Rowlands Castle Rd
  HORN PO8...288 F3
Rowlands Rd HORS RH12...56 F3
  WTHG BN11...20 D7
Rownhams Rd HAV PO9...288 E12
Rowplatt La EGRIN RH19...30 D6
Rowsley Rd EDN/EASTW BN20...176 D6
Roxburgh Cl SALV BN13...116 C4
Roxburghe Cl SLVH TN37...178 C7
Royal Buildings
  LAN/SOMP BN15 *...152 C1
Royal Cha SBGH/RUST TN4...37 L5
Royal Cl CCH PO19...7 J5
Royal Crs BRIE/ROTT BN2...5 J8
Royal Crescent Ms
  BRIE/ROTT BN2 *...5 J8

Royal Dr SEAF BN25...159 K7
Royal Gdns HAV PO9...288 H8
Royal George Pde SHOR BN43...120 B5
Royal George Rd BURH RH15...74 D7
Royal Ms STLEO TN38 *...F7
Royal Military Canal Pth
  TENT TN30...221 M9
Royal Military Rd WSEA TN36...286 F1
Royal Oak La UCK TN22...210 C8
Royal Pde BOGR PO21 *...143 M7
  LGNY BN23...11 J5
Royal Sovereign Vw
  LGNY BN23...164 C13
Royal Sussex Crs
  EDN/EASTW BN20...163 G8
Royal Ter SLVH TN37 *...12 C8
Royal Victoria Pl RTW TN1 *...38 A5
Royal Wy WVILLE PO7...288 B10
Royce Cl SELS PO20...167 H4
Royce Rd CRAWE RH10...27 M6
Royce Wy SELS PO20...167 H4
Royles Cl BRIE/ROTT BN2...155 M3
Royston Cl CRAWE RH10...27 M7
  EDN/EASTW BN20...302 G4
Royston Gdns BEX TN40...97 L8
The Roystons ANG/EP BN16...148 E5
Rozeldene GSHT GU26...180 H6
Ruck La STPH/PW TN12...189 K6
Ruckmans La MAYF TN20...189 A5
Rucrofts Cl BOGR PO21...171 J2
Rudgwick Av FERR BN12...149 M3
Rudgwick Cl ANG/EP BN16...148 A5
Rudgwick Rd CRAWW RH11...42 C2
  EDN/EASTW BN20...302 C4
Rudwick's Cl MSEA/BNM PO22...173 H1
Rudwick Wy MSEA/BNM PO22...173 J1
Rudyard Cl BRIE/ROTT BN2...124 D5
Rudyard Rd BRIE/ROTT BN2...124 D5
Rue De Bayeux BAT TN33...282 E4
Rufus Cl LEWES BN7...16 E5
Rufwood CRAWE RH10...45 M1
Rugby Cl SEAF BN25...175 H1
Rugby Pl BRIE/ROTT BN2...154 D1
Rugby Rd BRI BN1...122 F4
Ruislip Gdns BOGR PO21...171 H3
Rumbolds Cl CRAWW RH11...7 J8
Rumbolds Hl MIDH GU29...227 J10
Rumbolds La HWH RH16...73 G7
The Rummers CCH PO19...107 L3
Runcorn Cl CRAWW RH11...42 D7
Runcton La SELS PO20...142 D7
Runnymede Ct BOGR PO21...143 L8
Rusbridge Cl BOGR PO21...171 J1
Rusbridge La LEWES BN7...17 J6
Rushams Rd HORS RH12...14 A5
Rushes Farm PSF GU32...223 M5
Rushes Rd PSF GU32...223 M5
The Rushes HWH RH16...73 M5
Rushetts Pl CRAWW RH11...27 H8
Rushetts Rd CRAWW RH11...27 G8
Rushey Cl RING/NEW BN8...275 K12
Rushfield Rd LISS GU33...192 C10
Rushlake Cl BRI BN1...83 K8
Rushlake Crs EAST BN21...163 K7
Rushlake Rd BRI BN1...83 K7
Rushlye Cl RRTW TN3...54 E4
Rushmere Ri STLEO TN38...98 D4
Rushmere Rd HWH RH16...73 L5
Rushwood Cl HWH RH16...73 L5
Ruskin Cl CRAWE RH10...28 B8
  SELS PO20...301 M6
Ruskin Rd EDN/EASTW BN20...163 G4
  HOVE BN3...121 L5
  SALV BN13...21 L1
Ruskin Wy HORN PO8...288 A5
Rusper Rd BRI BN1...83 J7
  CRAWW RH11...41 M2
  CRAWW RH11...42 E1
  EDN/EASTW BN20...163 G2
  HORS RH12...15 J1
  HORS RH12...25 J8
  HORS RH12...56 E2
  RDKG RH5...24 C6
  RDKG RH5...25 D1
  SALV BN13...116 E8
Rusper Rd South SALV BN13...116 E8
Ruspers BURH RH15...75 J7
Ruspers Keep CRAWW RH11...42 E2
Russell Cl SALV BN13...117 K8
Russell Crs BRI BN1...4 C3
Russell Ms BRI BN1...4 B6
Russell Pl BRI BN1...4 C3
Russell Rd BRI BN1...4 C3
  HAV PO9...103 G3
  SELS PO20...167 K6
Russell Rw LEWES BN7...16 F1
Russell's Cl ANG/EP BN16...149 G3
Russells Crs HORL RH6...22 F7
Russells Dr LAN/SOMP BN15...118 C8
Russell Sq CCH PO19...7 J4
  HAS TN34...13 H1
Russell Wy CRAWE RH10...9 H1
  EPSF GU31...223 P7
Russet Cl HORL RH6...23 H6
  POLE BN26...132 C4
Russet Gdns EMRTH PO10...104 C5
Russ Hl HORL RH6...25 M5
Russ Hill Rd HORL RH6...26 C3
Rusthall Gra SBGH/RUST TN4...37 H3
Rusthall High St
  SBGH/RUST TN4...37 G5
Rusthall Pk SBGH/RUST TN4...37 J6
Rusthall Pl SBGH/RUST TN4 *...37 J6
Rusthall Rd SBGH/RUST TN4...37 J6
Rustic Cl PEAHV BN10...157 G4
Rustic Rd PEAHV BN10...157 G4
Rustington Rd BRI BN1...82 F8
Rustlings Cl HWH RH16...73 L4
Ruston Av ANG/EP BN16...148 C6
Ruston Cl CRAWE RH10...46 B6
Ruston Pk ANG/EP BN16...148 D6
Rutherford Wy CRAWE RH10...27 M6
Rutherwick Cl HORL RH6...22 E6
Rutland Cl EAST BN21...163 J7
Rutland Gdns HOVE BN3...121 L6
Rutland Rd HOVE BN3...121 L6
  PTSD BN41...120 C5
Rutton Hill Rd MFD/CHID GU8...181 P1
Ryecroft Cl LEWES BN7...150 C4
Rydal Cl BOR GU35...178 G4
  CRAWW RH11...7 K8
  LHPTN BN17 *...147 M3
Rydal Dr SBGH/RUST TN4...37 K4
Rydal Wy LGNY BN23...164 A1

Ryde Rd BRIE/ROTT BN2...5 L2
Ryders RRTW TN3...36 F6
Ryders Wy HORS RH12...56 E2
Rye Ash CRAWE RH10...9 M1
Rye Cl BRIE/ROTT BN2...156 D3
  POLE BN26...132 B6
  SEAF BN25...175 J1
  WTHG BN11...20 A8
Ryecroft HAV PO9...103 J4
  HWH RH16...73 G6
Ryecroft Gdns FERR BN12...150 B4
Ryecroft La PUL/STOR RH20...266 A12
Ryecroft Meadow
  SWTR RH13...202 H3
Ryecroft Rd RHWH RH17...236 D2
Rye Farm La SWTR RH13...201 K11
Ryefield Cl EAST BN21...163 H6
Ryefield GU31...223 R6
Ryelands CRAWW RH11...42 F4
  HORL RH6...23 H5
Ryelands Dr BRIE/ROTT BN2...123 J2
Rye Rd HAWK TN18...217 L1
  RHAS TN55...100 C1
  RYE TN31...252 E3
  TENT TN31...220 F8
Ryersh La RDKG RH5...24 B2
Rye St LW/ROSE BN22...164 B7
Rylstone Rd LW/ROSE BN22...11 J4
Rymers Cl RTWE/PEM TN2...38 C7
Rymill Rd STLEO TN38...98 F2
Rype Cl LYDD TN29...255 R8
Ryst Wood Rd FROW RH18...49 G7

S

Sabre Rd EMRTH PO10...138 B2
Sachel Court Rd CRAN GU6...184 E6
Sack La MSEA/BNM PO22...144 E4
  LEWES BN7 *...16 E5
Sackville Ct EGRIN RH19...47 L1
Sackville Crs SALV BN13...21 K1
Sackville Gdns HOVE BN3...121 L7
Sackville La EGRIN RH19...31 G6
Sackville Ms BEX TN40 *...137 J2
Sackville Rd BEXW TN39...137 G2
  HAIL BN27...92 B7
  HOVE BN3...121 M7
  LW/ROSE BN22...163 L3
  SWTR RH13...234 E10
  WTHG BN11...21 L4
The Sackville BEX TN40 *...137 J2
Saddler Rw CRAWE RH10...8 F7
Saddlers Cl BURH RH15...75 J8
Saddlers Scarp GSHT GU26...180 D5
Saddlescombe Rd
  POY/PYE BN45...81 J1
The Sadlers RCCH PO18...108 C4
Sadler St BOGR PO21...2 B8
Sadlers Wk EMRTH PO10...104 B5
Sadlers Wy RING/NEW BN8...87 J1
Sadler Wy BRIE/ROTT BN2...123 L7
Saffron Cl CRAWW RH11...42 F6
  SHOR BN43...119 L6
Saffron Gdns POLE BN26...160 E2
Saffrons Pk EDN/EASTW BN20...10 B9
Saffrons Rd EAST BN21...10 C6
The Saffrons EDN/EASTW BN21...74 D4
Sage Cl WVILLE PO7...288 B11
St Agnes Pl CCH PO19...7 G4
St Agnes Rd EGRIN RH19...31 K7
St Alban's Rd HAV PO9...103 H1
St Andrew Cl HORN PO8...256 D11
St Andrews HORL RH6 *...23 K3
St Andrew's Cl FERR BN12...149 K3
  HAIL BN27...91 M4
  SELS PO20...109 H7
St Andrews Ct CCH PO19 *...6 E4
St Andrew Dr SEAF BN25...158 F7
St Andrews Gdns SALV BN13 *...20 A1
St Andrew's La LEWES BN7...17 G6
St Andrew's Rd BEX TN40...97 H8
  BOR GU35...178 E7
  BRI BN1...4 B5
  BURH RH15...75 H5
  CHAM PO6...102 A5
  CRAWW RH11...42 C4
  PTSD BN41...121 G7
  SALV BN13...150 E1
St Andrew's Sq HAS TN34...13 J4
St Andrews Vls HAS TN34 *...13 J4
St Anne's Cl BEX TN40...97 J8
St Anne's Crs LEWES BN7...16 C7
St Annes HI MIDH GU29...227 J10
St Annes Rd CRAWE RH10...28 B7
  EAST BN21...10 B3
  EDN/EASTW BN20...163 G2
St Annes Ter LEWES BN7 *...16 C7
St Ann's HI MIDH GU29...227 J10
St Ann's Rd HORN PO8...288 D2
St Anselm's Rd SALV BN13...20 C2
St Anthonys Av LGNY BN23...164 C6
St Anthony's Av BOGR PO21...171 J2
St Anthony's Wy
  ANG/EP BN16...148 C3
St Aubin Cl CRAWW RH11 *...42 E7
St Aubins Rd FERR BN12...149 L5
St Aubyns HOVE BN3...121 M7
St Aubyn's Crs PTSD BN41...121 G7
St Aubyn's Md BRIE/ROTT BN2...155 K4
St Aubyn's Rd LW/ROSE BN22...11 H5
  PTSD BN41...120 F7
St Aubyns South HOVE BN3...121 M8
St Augustine Rd RHWH RH17...239 J2
St Augustine's Rd LHPTN BN17...147 K5
St Augustine's Cl BEXW TN39...136 E7
St Austins GSHT GU26 *...180 G6
St Barnabas' Cl RTW TN1...38 A4
St Bartholomews Cl CCH PO19 *...6 C3
St Bernards Ct
  LAN/SOMP BN15...118 D8
St Blaises Rd RCCH PO18...109 H1
St Boswells Cl HAIL BN27...91 L5
St Botolph's Rd WTHG BN11...20 C5
St Brelades EAST BN21 *...11 G8
St Brelades Pk CRAWW RH11...42 E7
St Brelades Rd CRAWW RH11...42 E7
St Catherines Cl SLVH TN37...12 C6
St Catherines Rd CRAWE RH10...28 B7
  LHPTN BN17...147 J7
St Christopher's Cl CCH PO19...107 H2
St Christopher's Rd
  HASM GU27 *...181 K11

  HORS RH12...14 D2
St Christopher's Rd
  HASM GU27...181 K11
  HAV PO9...102 D2
St Clares Av HAV PO9...288 E10
St Clare's Cl BOGR PO21...143 M7
St Clement Rd CRAWW RH11...42 E7
St Clements Pl STLEO TN38 *...12 C8
St Crispians SEAF BN25...174 D2
St Cuthmans Cl
  BRIE/ROTT BN2...123 K7
St Cuthman's Rd
  STEY/UB BN44...268 C12
St Cyriacs CCH PO19...6 D3
St David's Cl LW/ROSE BN22...163 H8
St Davids Rd HORN PO8...256 D8
  SBGH/RUST TN4...38 A3
St Dominic Cl STLEO TN38...98 H6
St Dunstan's Rd SALV BN13...20 A3
St Edmunds Cl CRAWW RH11...27 J8
St Edmund's Rd HWH RH16...73 J6
St Edward's Cl EGRIN RH19...31 H8
St Elmo Rd SALV BN13...20 D2
St Flora's Cl LHPTN BN17...147 L4
St Flora's Wy LHPTN BN17...147 L4
St Francis Cha BEXW TN39...96 F8
St Francis Cl HWH RH16...73 H7
St Francis Gdns CRAWE RH10...29 H5
St Francis Pl HAV PO9...102 F2
St Gabriels Rd BIL RH14...232 A1
St Georges Av HAV PO9...103 J4
St Georges Cl HORL RH6...23 G7
  SELS PO20...301 M5
St George's Ct CRAWE RH10...8 F1
St George's Dr CCH PO19...141 L2
St George's Gdns HORS RH12...15 H2
  WTHG BN11 *...21 L5
St George's La HPPT/KEY BN6...271 J4
St George's Ms BRI BN1 *...4 F5
St George's Pk RTWE/PEM TN2...53 L1
St George's Pl BRI BN1...4 F4
  HPPT/KEY BN6...271 J4
St George's Rd BEX TN40...97 H8
  BRIE/ROTT BN2...5 K3
  HAS TN34...13 K3
  LW/ROSE BN22...11 H4
  SWTR RH13...234 E10
  WTHG BN11...21 L4
St George's Ter BRIE/ROTT BN2...5 J8
St Georges Wk SELS PO20...110 G6
St Giles Cl SHOR BN43...120 B5
  WSEA TN36...286 D2
St Giles Wy HORN PO8...256 D11
St Gregory Cl
  EDN/EASTW BN20...176 E5
St Helen's Av HAS TN34...99 K2
St Helen's Ct HAS TN34...12 F1
St Helen's Crs HAS TN34...12 F2
  HOVE BN3...121 J7
St Helen's Down HAS TN34...99 K2
  HAS TN34...100 A1
St Helen's Dr HOVE BN3...121 J2
St Helen's Park Rd HAS TN34...12 F1
  HAS TN34...99 L2
St Helen's Rd BRIE/ROTT BN2...5 L2
  HAS TN34...99 K2
St Helens Wood Rd
  HAS TN34...284 B12
St Helier Cl CRAWW RH11...42 F6
St Helier Rd FERR BN12...149 L5
St Heliers Av HOVE BN3...121 K6
St Hilda Av HORN PO8...256 D11
St Hilda's Cl CRAWE RH10 *...28 B8
  HORL RH6...23 G6
Saint Hill Rd EGRIN RH19...47 G3
St Hubert Rd HORN PO8...256 D11
St Hugh's Cl CRAWE RH10...28 B8
St Itha Cl SELS PO20...301 L1
St Itha Rd SELS PO20...301 L1
St Ives CRAWE RH10 *...44 B2
St James' Av BEX TN40...97 J8
  LAN/SOMP BN15...118 D5
St James' Cl HORN PO8...256 D9
St James' Crs BEX TN40...97 J6
St James' Pk RTW TN1...38 C6
St James' Rd BEX TN40...97 H7
  CCH PO19...7 J3
  EGRIN RH19...31 J8
  EMRTH PO10...104 D4
  LW/ROSE BN22...11 J4
  RTW TN1...38 C6
St James' Sq CCH PO19...7 J3
St James' St BRI BN1...4 F7
  BRIE/ROTT BN2...5 G7
St James's Street Ms
  BRIE/ROTT BN2...5 G7
St James St LEWES BN7...16 F7
St Joan Cl CRAWW RH11...27 J4
St John Bank RING/NEW BN8...273 N1
St John Cl SWTR RH13...15 G7
St John's Av BURH RH15...74 E6
St John's Cl BOGR PO21...171 J1
  CROW TN6...67 K6
  FERR BN12...150 B4
  MIDH GU29...226 H10
  SELS PO20...110 C7
St John's Crs HORS RH12...201 P2
St John's Dr PEV BN24...133 K7
St John's HI LEWES BN7...16 F5
St Johns Ms BRIE/ROTT BN2 *...5 L8
St John's Pk SBGH/RUST TN4...37 M1
St John's Pl BRIE/ROTT BN2...5 L8
  HOVE BN3...122 B7
St John's Rd BEX TN40...97 H7
  BURH RH15...74 D7
  CRAWW RH11...44 A1
  CROW TN6...67 K6
  EDN/EASTW BN20...176 E5
  EGRIN RH19...31 K7
  EMRTH PO10...104 D4
  HAV PO9...102 D1
  HOVE BN3...122 B8
  HWH RH16...73 G6
  POLE BN26...131 M7
  SBGH/RUST TN4...37 M2
  SEAF BN25...174 C2
  SLVH TN37...12 D1
St John's St CCH PO19...6 E4

St John's Ter LEWES BN7...16 F5
St John St LEWES BN7...17 G5
St Joseph's Cl HOVE BN3...121 M5
St Josephs Wy HWH RH16...73 H5
St Julians Cl SHOR BN43...120 B6
St Julian's La SHOR BN43...120 B6
St Keyna Av HOVE BN3...121 J7
St Kitts BEXW TN39 *...136 F3
St Kitts Dr LGNY BN23...164 F6
St Laurence Cl PEAHV BN10 *...156 F4
St Lawrence Cl LAN/SOMP BN15...118 C1
St Lawrence Rd BEXW TN39...97 G6
St Lawrence Wy
  HPPT/KEY BN6...270 H2
  LGNY BN23...164 F4
St Leodegar's Wy SELS PO20...141 M4
St Leonard's Av HORN PO8...256 D8
St Leonards Cl NEWHV BN9...158 C8
St Leonards Dr CRAWE RH10...9 M8
St Leonard's La
  HOVE BN3...121 J7
St Leonard's Pl
  EDN/EASTW BN20...176 C2
St Leonards Rd BEX TN40...137 H2
  BRIE/ROTT BN2 *...5 H1
  EAST BN21...10 E5
  HOVE BN3...121 H7
  NEWHV BN9...158 E3
  SWTR RH13...15 H9
St Leonards Ter POLE BN26...131 L6
St Louie Cl STHW BN42...120 F5
St Lucia BEXW TN39 *...136 F3
St Luke's Cl LAN/SOMP BN15...152 A1
St Luke's Rd BRIE/ROTT BN2...5 K4
  SBGH/RUST TN4...38 A3
St Luke's Ter BRIE/ROTT BN2...5 K4
St Malo Cl FERR BN12...149 L5
St Margarets BRIE/ROTT BN2 *...155 M4
  STPH/PW TN12...189 M3
St Margaret's Av EGRIN RH19...31 K3
St Margaret's Pl BRI BN1 *...4 B7
St Margaret's Ri SEAF BN25...158 F7
St Margaret's Rd EGRIN RH19...31 L6
  SLVH TN37...12 C8
St Margarets Ter MIDH GU29 *...227 K8
  RYE TN31...252 C8
  SLVH TN37...12 C8
St Marks Cl BEXW TN39...136 C1
St Mark's Crs LAN/SOMP BN15...152 A1
St Marks Fld UCK TN22...211 J12
St Mark's La HORS RH12...56 D3
St Mark's Rd RTWE/PEM TN2...53 L2
St Mark's St BRIE/ROTT BN2...154 D1
St Martin's Cl RHWH RH17...204 C2
St Martins Crs NEWHV BN9...158 C4
St Martin's La LEWES BN7...16 F7
  LHPTN BN17...147 J4
St Martin's Pl BRIE/ROTT BN2...5 J4
St Martins Rd LHPTN BN17...147 J4
  LW/ROSE BN22...163 J2
St Martin's Sq BRIE/ROTT BN2...5 J4
St Martin's St BRIE/ROTT BN2...5 H1
  CCH PO19...6 D4
St Mary-in-the-Fields
  MAYF TN20...212 E7
St Mary Magdalene St
  BRIE/ROTT BN2...5 H1
St Marys Av HAIL BN27...92 C5
St Mary's Cl BIL RH14...232 A1
  LAN/SOMP BN15...117 M6
  LHPTN BN17...147 L4
  LW/ROSE BN22...163 L4
  MSEA/BNM PO22...2 E2
  PUL/STOR PO20...265 K3
  RCCH PO18...292 B10
  RYE TN31...250 D11
  SEAF BN25...174 C1
  SHOR BN43...119 L6
  WADH TN5...191 J12
St Mary's Cottages
  EDN/EASTW BN20 *...176 D2
St Marys Ct SLVH TN37 *...12 D1
St Mary's Dr ANG/EP BN16...148 E4
  CRAWE RH10...44 A1
St Marys Gdn CCH PO19...6 E4
St Marys Gdns BAT TN33...282 D7
  HORS RH12...14 C8
  LHPTN BN17...147 L4
Saint Marys Garth UCK TN22...242 D1
St Marys Gate Ms
  ARUN BN18 *...112 F2
St Mary's La BEXW TN39...96 F3
  RRTW TN3...36 F1
  WADH TN5...191 J12
St Marys Meadow ARUN BN18...145 L2
St Mary's Pl BRIE/ROTT BN2...5 H8
St Mary's Rd EAST BN21...176 D1
  HAS TN34...13 J3
  LISS GU33...192 C9
  RCCH PO18...109 H1
  SHOR BN43...119 L6
St Mary's Rd West BURH RH15...74 D5
St Mary's Sq BRIE/ROTT BN2...5 M9
St Mary's Ter HAS TN34...13 J3
St Mary's Wy LHPTN BN17...147 L4
St Matthew's Gdns STLEO TN38...99 G4
St Matthew's Rd STLEO TN38...99 G4
  WTHG BN11...20 B6
St Maur's Rd FERR BN12...149 K3
St Mellion Cl HAIL BN27...91 M4
St Michaels Cl CROW TN6...211 J1
  PETW GU28...196 F6
  PEV BN24...132 F7
St Michael's Ct WTHG BN11...20 C6
St Michael's Pl BRI BN1...4 B5
  HAS TN34...12 F1
St Michaels Rd EGRIN RH19...31 K7
  HAV PO9...102 D2
  PTSD BN41...121 G6
  SBGH/RUST TN4...38 A2
  WTHG BN11...20 D6
St Michael's Ter LEWES BN7...17 G2
St Michaels Wy HORN PO8...256 D11
  SWTR RH13...234 E10
St Nicholas La LEWES BN7...17 G6
  MSEA/BNM PO22...145 L8
St Nicholas Rd BRI BN1...4 C5
  HAV PO9...102 D2
  PTSD BN41...121 G6
  RCCH PO18...292 B10
St Nicolas Cl BRI BN1...134 A7
St Nicolas La SHOR BN43...119 J5
St Olive's Cl HTHF TN21...243 R6
St Osmund Rd FERR BN12...149 L3
St Pancras CCH PO19...7 H1
St Pancras Gdns LEWES BN7...16 D8

St Pancras Gn LEWES BN7 85 J8
St Pancras Rd LEWES BN7 16 D7
St Patrick's Crs BEX TN40 97 H8
St Patrick's La LISS GU33 192 F8
St Patrick's Rd HOVE BN3 121 M6
St Paul's Av LAN/SOMP BN15 152 A1
St Paul's Cl HWH RH16 73 J4
LW/ROSE BN22 163 J2
St Paul's Gdns CCH PO19 6 D2
St Paul's Pl SLVH TN37 12 C6
St Paul's Rd CCH PO19 6 D2
SLVH TN37 12 B4
St Paul's St BRIE/ROTT BN2 5 H1
SBGH/RUST TN4 37 H5
St Peter's CCH PO19 6 E3
St Peter's Av PEAHV BN10 156 F5
St Peters Cl BOGR PO21 171 K1
SEAF BN25 159 K8
SWTR RH13 235 K4
St Peters Ct BEX TN40 * 97 J8
St Peter's Crs BEX TN40 97 J8
SELS PO20 301 L5
St Peters Market CCH PO19 * 6 D4
St Peter's Pl BRI BN1 4 F4
LAN/SOMP BN15 * 152 B1
LEWES BN7 16 E6
St Peters Rd BURH RH15 74 F6
CRAWW RH11 8 D4
PSF GU32 223 N6
PTSD BN41 121 G6
SEAF BN25 159 K8
SLVH TN37 12 A4
St Peters Rw RRTW TN3 36 A4
St Peter's Sq EMRTH PO10 104 A5
St Peter's St BRI BN1 4 F3
RTWE/PEM TN2 38 B6
St Philip's Av LW/ROSE BN22 11 G2
St Philips Ms HOVE BN3 121 L6
St Raphael's Rd WTHG BN11 150 E3
St Richards Cl FERR BN12 150 B2
St Richard's Dr BOGR PO21 171 J2
St Richards Ms CRAWE RH10 * 9 K3
St Richards Rd CROW TN6 210 H2
PTSD BN41 121 G6
SELS PO20 110 D6
St Richard's Wy BOGR PO21 171 J2
St Roche's Cl RCCH PO18 292 C10
St Sampson Rd CRAWW RH11 42 E7
St Saviours UCK TN22 * 76 F6
St Saviour's Rd STLEO TN38 98 D7
Saints Hl RTON TN11 35 M1
St Stephens Cl HASM GU27 181 M10
St Stephens Cottages
RTW TN1 * 38 A4
St Stephens Ct RTW TN1 * 38 A4
St Stephons Ct RTW TN1 * 38 A4
St Swithun's Cl EGRIN RH19 * 31 L8
St Swithun's La LEWES BN7 * 16 F7
St Swithun's Ter LEWES BN7 16 F7
St Theresas Cl HAV PO9 102 D2
St Thomas BEXW TN39 * 136 F2
St Thomas Dr BOGR PO21 170 E5
St Thomas's Rd HAS TN34 13 K3
St Thomas's St WSEA TN36 286 E2
St Valerie Rd WTHG BN11 20 B7
St Vincent Cl CRAWE RH10 44 C4
St Vincent Crs HORN PO8 288 C3
St Vincents SLVH TN37 * 99 G1
St Vincents Pl
EDN/EASTW BN20 176 E4
St Vincents Rd STLEO TN38 98 E6
St Wilfreds Cl SELS PO20 301 N5
St Wilfred's Pl SEAF BN25 175 H3
St Wilfreds Rd BURH RH15 75 G5
SALV BN13 21 H1
St Wilfreds Vw SELS PO20 * 301 J7
St Wilfrid Rd CCH PO19 107 J6
St Wilfrids Cl BURH RH15 75 G5
St Wilfrid's Gn HAIL BN27 92 A5
St Wilfrid's Wy HWH RH16 73 H5
St Winefride's Rd LHPTN BN17 147 K5
St Winifred's Cl BOGR PO21 2 B8
Sake Ride La HFD BN5 235 P12
Salcey Cl STLEO TN38 98 D3
Salehurst Gdns STLEO TN38 98 C3
Salehurst Rd CRAWE RH10 44 D3
EAST BN21 176 C2
Salet Wy WVILLE PO7 288 C8
Salisbury Cl LW/ROSE BN22 163 H3
Salisbury Rd BEX TN40 97 G8
CRAWE RH10 43 L7
EDN/EASTW BN20 176 C5
HOVE BN3 122 B7
RRTW TN3 36 E6
SBGH/RUST TN4 38 B1
SEAF BN25 174 E2
SLVH TN37 12 B4
WTHG BN11 21 G5
Salisbury Ter HTHF TN21 * 243 Q5
Salisbury Wy CCH PO19 107 L4
Salt Box Cl SWTR RH13 201 J11
Saltcote St RYE TN31 252 H5
Saltdean Cl BEXW TN39 136 D2
CRAWE RH10 8 E9
Saltdean Dr BRIE/ROTT BN2 156 A4
Saltdean Park Rd
BRIE/ROTT BN2 156 B4
Saltdean V BRIE/ROTT BN2 156 C2
Saltdean Wy BEXW TN39 136 C2
Salterns Rd CRAWE RH10 44 B6
Saltham La SELS PO20 142 D4
Salthill La CCH PO19 107 H5
Salthill Rd CCH PO19 107 G6
The Saltings HAV PO9 103 G7
LAN/SOMP BN15 118 E8
LHPTN BN17 147 M3
SELS PO20 168 D1
SHOR BN43 119 J7
Saltings Wy STEY/UB BN44 78 F3
Salt Marsh La HAIL BN27 132 C1
Saltwood Rd SEAF BN25 175 J1
Salvador Cl LGNY BN23 164 E6
Salvia Cl WVILLE PO7 288 B11
Salvington Cl SALV BN13 116 D6
Salvington Crs BEXW TN39 136 E1
Salvington Gdns SALV BN13 116 E7
Salvington Hl SALV BN13 116 D4
Salvington Rd CRAWW RH11 42 E6
SALV BN13 116 D6
Samaritan Cl CRAWW RH11 42 D5
Samoa Wy LGNY BN23 165 G3
Samphire Cl CRAWW RH11 42 F6
Samphire Dr SALV BN13 115 M8
Sampsons Dr SELS PO20 109 H6
Sancroft Rd
EDN/EASTW BN20 176 B2
Sanctuary Ct
PUL/STOR RH20 * 265 M7
Sanctuary La PUL/STOR RH20 266 F12
The Sanctuary
EDN/EASTW BN20 176 B1
Sandbanks Cl HAIL BN27 91 M8
Sandbanks Gdns HAIL BN27 91 M8
Sandbanks Gv HAIL BN27 92 A7
Sandbanks Rd HAIL BN27 91 M7
Sandbanks Wy HAIL BN27 91 M7
Sandeman Wy SWTR RH13 15 H9
Sandfield Av LHPTN BN17 147 J1
Sandfield Rd RTON TN11 35 L2
Sandgate Cl SEAF BN25 160 B8
Sandgate La PUL/STOR RH20 266 D11
Sandgate Rd BRI BN1 122 F3
Sandhawes Hl EGRIN RH19 31 M5
Sandheath Rd GSHT GU26 180 F2
Sand Hill La RING/NEW BN8 276 B3
UCK TN22 242 D12
Sandhill La CRAWE RH10 46 B3
HAIL BN27 279 R4
PUL/STOR RH20 298 H2
RRTW TN3 68 D2
Sandhills Rd SWTR RH13 201 J10
Sandhurst Av BRIE/ROTT BN2 124 C4
RTWE/PEM TN2 39 L4
Sandhurst Cl RTWE/PEM TN2 38 B2
Sandhurst Gdns HAS TN34 284 C11
Sandhurst La BEXW TN39 135 M1
Sandhurst Pk RTWE/PEM TN2 38 C3
Sandhurst Rd RTWE/PEM TN2 38 C2
Sandleford Rd HAV PO9 288 E10
Sandlewood Cl HORN PO8 256 D8
Sandore Cl SEAF BN25 175 G1
Sandore Rd SEAF BN25 175 G1
Sandown Av FERR BN12 150 B5
Sandown Cl FERR BN12 150 B4
LGNY BN23 164 A1
RTWE/PEM TN2 38 E3
Sandown Gv RTWE/PEM TN2 38 E3
Sandown Pk RTWE/PEM TN2 38 E4
Sandown Rd BRIE/ROTT BN2 5 L2
RHAS TN35 100 B2
STHW BN42 120 C5
Sandown Wy BEX TN40 97 K7
Sandpiper Cl CRAWW RH11 42 C5
HORN PO8 288 B2
Sandridge CROW TN6 67 L8
Sandridge La HWH RH16 206 C8
Sandringham Cl HOVE BN3 121 M2
SEAF BN25 159 M7
SELS PO20 168 A8
Sandringham Ct BEX TN40 * 137 J2
LAN/SOMP BN15 * 118 E8
Sandringham Dr HOVE BN3 121 M2
Sandringham Hts STLEO TN38 98 C2
Sandringham Ms SALV BN13 116 C6
SALV BN13 * 117 J7
Sandringham Rd CCH PO19 7 K5
CRAWW RH11 43 G7
PSF GU32 223 N5
Sandringham Wy BOGR PO21 2 A4
Sand Rd RRTW TN3 190 F1
Sandrock HASM GU27 181 M11
MIDH GU29 226 G9
Sandrock Hl BAT TN33 97 M1
Sandrock Pk HAS TN34 284 C12
Sandrock Rd RTWE/PEM TN2 38 B5
Sandrocks Wy HWH RH16 73 H7
Sandsbury La PSF GU32 223 J4
Sands La HFD BN5 269 K11
The Sands BOR GU35 178 D7
PUL/STOR RH20 267 J8
Sandwich Dr STLEO TN38 98 E6
Sandwich Rd WTHG BN11 150 E4
Sandwich St LW/ROSE BN22 164 B7
Sandy Cl EPSF GU31 223 R6
SLVH TN37 283 Q12
Sandy Cross La HTHF TN21 244 E8
Sandygate La SWTR RH13 203 L6
Sandy La CRAWE RH10 45 M1
EGRIN RH19 31 K8
EGRIN RH19 62 D3
GSHT GU26 181 J7
HASM GU27 180 F10
HASM GU27 181 P8
HFD BN5 269 J5
HRTF TN7 26 D8
HTHF TN21 244 B12
LISS GU33 192 H10
PUL/STOR RH20 264 B3
PUL/STOR RH20 264 B8
PUL/STOR RH20 266 E12
RCCH PO18 106 C1
RHWH RH17 208 B1
UCK TN22 77 H5
Sandymount Av
MSEA/BNM PO22 2 B2
Sandymount Cl
MSEA/BNM PO22 2 C1
Sandy Point Cl SELS PO20 300 H5
Sandy Point La SELS PO20 300 H5
Sandy Rd BOGR PO21 170 F6
Sandy V HWH RH16 73 G7
San Feliu Ct EGRIN RH19 32 A7
Sangers Dr HORL RH6 22 E7
San Jose Cl RHAS TN35 100 B3
Santa Cruz Dr LGNY BN23 164 E6
Santos Whf LGNY BN23 164 E5
Sanyhils Av BRI BN1 82 E6
Sapphire Cl WVILLE PO7 * 288 B10
Sapphire Rdg WVILLE PO7 288 B10
Sarel Wy HORL RH6 23 G4
Sargent Cl CRAWE RH10 43 L7
Sarisbury Cl MSEA/BNM PO22 3 M3
Sark Cl CRAWW RH11 42 F7
Sark Gdns FERR BN12 149 L4
Satinwood Cl
MSEA/BNM PO22 145 K7
Saturn Cl CRAWW RH11 42 D5
Saucelands La SWTR RH13 232 G9
Saunders Cl CRAWE RH10 44 A3
HAS TN34 13 J3
UCK TN22 76 C4
Saunders Hl BRI BN1 83 J6
Saunders Park Ri
BRIE/ROTT BN2 123 H4
Saunders Park Vw
BRIE/ROTT BN2 123 H4
Saunders Rd SBGH/RUST TN4 53 K1
Saunders Wy RYE TN31 254 B11
Savernake Wk CRAWE RH10 9 K9
Savile Crs BOR GU35 178 H6
Saville Gdns BIL RH14 232 A2
Savill Rd HWH RH16 73 K1
Sawyers Cl BURH RH15 75 J8
Saxby Cl LGNY BN23 164 D4
MSEA/BNM PO22 111 G8
Saxby Rd BEXW TN39 96 F8
BURH RH15 74 C5
Saxifrage Wy SALV BN13 115 M8
Saxley HORL RH6 23 H5
Saxley Ct HAV PO9 288 E11
Saxonbury Cl CROW TN6 67 L7
Saxon Cl ANG/EP BN16 149 G2
BIL RH14 200 A12
BOGR PO21 170 E5
BRIE/ROTT BN2 156 B3
EAST BN21 163 H7
HORN PO8 256 D9
Saxon Crs HORS RH12 14 A1
Saxon Gnd EAST BN21 10 B4
Saxon La SEAF BN25 174 E3
Saxon Ri BEX TN40 137 K1
Saxon Rd CRAWE RH10 44 D4
HOVE BN3 121 J7
NEWHV BN9 18 F4
RHAS TN35 100 C2
STEY/UB BN44 78 E2
Saxons SHOR BN43 119 L4
Saxon Shore Wy HAS TN34 13 M6
RASHW TN26 221 P2
RHAS TN35 100 D4
RHAS TN35 286 A11
RYE TN31 253 K5
TENT TN30 221 L7
WSEA TN36 286 C6
The Saxons BEXW TN39 * 136 E2
Saxon St SLVH TN37 12 B9
Saxonwood Rd BAT TN33 282 D4
Saxony Rd SALV BN13 20 E1
Sayerland La POLE BN26 131 M5
Sayerland Rd POLE BN26 131 L6
Sayers Cl SWTR RH13 15 H5
The Sayers EGRIN RH19 31 H8
Scallows Cl CRAWE RH10 9 L2
Scallows Rd CRAWE RH10 9 L2
Scamps Hl HWH RH16 73 M3
Scanlon Cl EDN/EASTW BN20 162 F2
Scant Rd RCCH PO18 105 L2
Scant Rd (East) RCCH PO18 105 K3
Scant Rd (West) RCCH PO18 105 J3
Scarborough Rd BRI BN1 122 C4
Scarletts Cl UCK TN22 76 D5
Schofield Wy LGNY BN23 164 E6
School Cl BURH RH15 74 E7
HORS RH12 56 F3
PUL/STOR RH20 264 B3
STHW BN42 120 D6
School Dell RCCH PO18 105 M2
School Fld RING/NEW BN8 274 D5
School Gdns RING/NEW BN8 274 C5
School Hl ARUN BN18 294 H12
HORS RH12 187 Q9
PUL/STOR RH20 266 A12
RING/NEW BN8 274 D5
RRTW TN3 188 G11
SALV BN13 298 H11
WSEA TN36 286 D1
School House La
STPH/PW TN12 189 R2
School La ARUN BN18 112 F3
BIL RH14 232 B1
BRIE/ROTT BN2 156 B3
CROW TN6 67 H5
EGRIN RH19 48 C3
EMRTH PO10 104 A5
EMRTH PO10 104 C1
EMRTH PO10 289 Q12
FROW RH18 48 E7
LISS GU33 192 C9
MFD/CHID GU8 182 G5
MIDH GU29 226 G8
PETW GU28 229 L12
POLE BN26 131 M6
POY/PYE BN45 271 K11
PSF GU32 223 P3
PUL/STOR RH20 263 L9
PUL/STOR RH20 264 B3
PUL/STOR RH20 297 R1
PUL/STOR RH20 298 H3
RCCH PO18 105 G6
RCCH PO18 106 B8
RCCH PO18 258 C11
RHWH RH17 207 R5
RYE TN31 251 R4
RYE TN31 252 H4
SELS PO20 110 E6
SELS PO20 142 G5
SELS PO20 301 K5
STEY/UB BN44 78 C2
STEY/UB BN44 268 C4
SWTR RH13 233 M8
UCK TN22 208 H4
UCK TN22 211 J12
UCK TN22 242 H7
School Pl BEX TN40 97 M8
School Ri BRIE/ROTT BN2 123 K7
RTWE/PEM TN2 37 L8
School Rd ARUN BN18 296 F2
BIL RH14 199 K12
BOR GU35 178 G5
GSHT GU26 180 E6
HASM GU27 181 J12
HAV PO9 102 F4
HOVE BN3 121 L6
RHAS TN35 100 B2
STEY/UB BN44 78 F3
Schwerte Wy HAS TN34 12 E8
Scory Cl CRAWW RH11 42 F6
Scotland La HASM GU27 181 M12
Scotlands Cl HASM GU27 181 L12
Scotlands Dr HASM GU27 181 L12
Scotland St BRIE/ROTT BN2 5 H5
Scotney Cl SALV BN13 116 A8
Scotney Ct HAV PO9 289 J11
Scotsford Hl MAYF TN20 212 H7
Scotsford Rd HTHF TN21 245 J4
Scott Rd CRAWE RH10 9 J9
HOVE BN3 121 L6
Scotts Acre RYE TN31 253 R11
Scott St BOGR PO21 2 C8
Scotts Wy RTWE/PEM TN2 53 K1
Scraper's Hl RING/NEW BN8 277 N9
Scratchface La HAV PO9 102 D3
WVILLE PO7 102 A1
Scratchings La PETW GU28 197 M8
Scutes Cl HAS TN34 99 L2
Sea Av ANG/EP BN16 148 C5
Seabeach La LW/ROSE BN22 11 K2
Seabourne Rd BEX TN40 97 L7
Seabrook Cl BOGR PO21 171 J2
Seacliffe PEAHV BN10 * 156 E6
Sea Cl FERR BN12 150 D3
MSEA/BNM PO22 173 K1
Seacourt Cl BOGR PO21 171 J4
Seadown Pde
LAN/SOMP BN15 * 118 A8
Sea Dr FERR BN12 149 L5
MSEA/BNM PO22 173 J1
Seafield Av FERR BN12 150 C5
Seafield Cl SEAF BN25 160 A8
SELS PO20 167 L7
Seafield Rd ANG/EP BN16 148 B6
ANG/EP BN16 148 E5
HOVE BN3 122 A8
Seafields EMRTH PO10 103 M5
SELS PO20 300 A1
Seafield Wy SELS PO20 167 M7
Seaford Rd CRAWW RH11 42 F8
EDN/EASTW BN20 302 E4
HOVE BN3 121 H7
LW/ROSE BN22 11 K1
NEWHV BN9 19 L2
Seagrave Cl SEAF BN25 * 158 F7
Sea Gv SELS PO20 301 J7
Seagrove Wy SEAF BN25 159 L8
Seagull Cl SELS PO20 300 H4
Seagull La EMRTH PO10 104 A4
Seahaven Gdns SHOR BN43 119 H8
Sea La ANG/EP BN16 148 E5
ANG/EP BN16 149 J5
BOGR PO21 170 E5
FERR BN12 149 L3
FERR BN12 150 B4
MSEA/BNM PO22 145 K8
Sea Lane Cl ANG/EP BN16 148 E4
FERR BN12 149 L3
Sea Lane Gdns FERR BN12 149 L4
Seal Rd SELS PO20 301 K8
Seal Sq SELS PO20 301 K8
Seaman's Gn RDKG RH5 24 C1
Seamill Park Av WTHG BN11 152 B2
Seamill Park Crs WTHG BN11 152 A2
Seamill Wy WTHG BN11 152 A2
Sea Pl FERR BN12 150 D5
Searle Av PEAHV BN10 157 K7
Searle's Vw HORS RH12 56 E4
Sea Rd ANG/EP BN16 147 L6
ANG/EP BN16 148 F5
BEX TN40 137 J2
MSEA/BNM PO22 3 K7
PEV BN24 134 C8
RHAS TN35 285 R12
RYE TN31 254 A11
STLEO TN38 98 F7
WSEA TN36 286 F2
Sea-saw Wy BRIE/ROTT BN2 123 L6
Seaside LGNY BN23 164 C6
LW/ROSE BN22 11 J2
Seaside Av LAN/SOMP BN15 118 E8
Seaside Cl LAN/SOMP BN15 118 E8
Seaside Rd EAST BN21 11 G7
LAN/SOMP BN15 118 E8
STLEO TN38 98 E7
Seaside Wy STLEO TN38 98 E7
Seaton Cl LHPTN BN17 147 J1
Seaton La LHPTN BN17 147 J1
Seaton Pk LHPTN BN17 147 J1
Seaton Rd LHPTN BN17 147 J1
Seattle Dr LGNY BN23 164 F4
Seaview Av ANG/EP BN16 148 F5
PEAHV BN10 157 K8
Seaview Ct LAN/SOMP BN15 152 C1
Seaview Rd ANG/EP BN16 148 E5
BRIE/ROTT BN2 124 A5
NEWHV BN9 158 E4
PEAHV BN10 157 K8
Sea View Rd WTHG BN11 20 C8
Seaview Ter RYE TN31 * 252 H8
Sea View Wy BRIE/ROTT BN2 124 C4
Seaville Dr LGNY BN23 164 C5
PEV BN24 134 C8
Seaward Dr SELS PO20 167 H4
Seawaves Cl ANG/EP BN16 148 F4
Sea Wy BOGR PO21 170 E5
MSEA/BNM PO22 146 A8
MSEA/BNM PO22 173 J1
Sebastian Gv WVILLE PO7 288 B9
Sebastopol Rd MFD/CHID GU8 182 C1
Second Av BEX TN40 97 L8
EMRTH PO10 104 E5
HAV PO9 103 J3
HOVE BN3 122 B8
LAN/SOMP BN15 118 D7
MSEA/BNM PO22 173 G1
NEWHV BN9 18 E4
RYE TN31 254 A11
SALV BN13 117 J6
SELS PO20 168 A8
SELS PO20 168 E4
Second Rd PEAHV BN10 156 F6
Sedbury Rd LAN/SOMP BN15 118 B5
Seddon Cl CCH PO19 7 J1
Sedgebrook Gdns HAS TN34 12 E2
Sedgefield Cl CRAWE RH10 44 D2
The Sedges STLEO TN38 98 D4
Sedgewick Cl CRAWE RH10 44 B3
Sedgewick Rd BEX TN40 97 H7
Sedgwick La SWTR RH13 202 D5
Sedlescombe Gdns STLEO TN38 99 G3
Sedlescombe Rd North
SLVH TN37 12 A1
Sedlescombe Rd South
STLEO TN38 99 G4
Sefter Rd BOGR PO21 171 G1
Sefton Av BOGR PO21 171 J2
Sefton Cha CROW TN6 67 M6
Sefton Cl SALV BN13 116 C7
Sefton Rd PTSD BN41 120 E2
Sefton Wy CROW TN6 67 M6
Segrave Cl LEWES BN7 16 C4
Selangor Av EMRTH PO10 103 L4
Selba Dr BRIE/ROTT BN2 123 K3
Selborne Av HAV PO9 288 E12
Selborne Cl PSF GU32 223 P4
Selborne Pl HOVE BN3 122 B6
LHPTN BN17 * 147 K5
Selborne Rd HOVE BN3 122 B7
LHPTN BN17 147 K5
WTHG BN11 21 L3
Selborne Wy ANG/EP BN16 148 E4
BOR GU35 178 D7
Selbourne Cl CRAWE RH10 28 C7
Selbourne Rd HAV PO9 102 F4
Selby Ct HWH RH16 73 H6
Selby Gdns UCK TN22 76 F7
Selby Ri UCK TN22 76 F7
Selby Rd EAST BN21 163 J8
UCK TN22 76 F6
Selden La SALV BN13 115 G4
WTHG BN11 21 L5
Selden Pde SALV BN13 * 116 E6
Selden Rd WTHG BN11 21 L4
Selden's Ms SALV BN13 116 E7
Selden's Wy SALV BN13 116 E7
Selham Cl BRI BN1 83 J7
CCH PO19 107 M2
CRAWW RH11 42 F2
Selham Dr BRI BN1 83 J7
Selham Pl BRI BN1 * 83 J7
Selham Rd MIDH GU29 227 J10
Selhurst Cl ANG/EP BN16 148 D4
Selhurstpark Rd RCCH PO18 293 N5
Selhurst Rd BRIE/ROTT BN2 124 D7
Selkirk Cl SALV BN13 150 D1
Sellbourne Pk RRTW TN3 54 B5
Selmeston Cl HAS TN34 12 D4
Selmeston Pl BRIE/ROTT BN2 123 L7
Selmeston Rd EAST BN21 163 H6
Selsey Av BOGR PO21 171 M3
Selsey Cl BRI BN1 83 K7
HISD PO11 166 A3
SALV BN13 116 E8
Selsey Rd CCH PO19 141 K2
CRAWW RH11 42 F7
SELS PO20 141 J6
SELS PO20 169 K3
Selsfield Cl EAST BN21 163 J7
Selsfield Dr BRIE/ROTT BN2 123 J2
Selsfield Rd CRAWE RH10 45 M7
EGRIN RH19 62 B2
RHWH RH17 62 A8
Selway La LHPTN BN17 147 L3
Selwyn Av LHPTN BN17 147 J2
Selwyn Cl BOGR PO21 171 L1
CRAWE RH10 28 B8
Selwyn Dr EAST BN21 10 A3
Selwyn Rd EAST BN21 10 A3
Semley Rd BRI BN1 122 F4
HPPT/KEY BN6 271 M5
Sempstead La RBTBR TN32 249 Q4
Senlac Gdns BAT TN33 282 F5
Senlac Pl RRTW TN3 * 52 B2
Senlac Rd NEWHV BN9 19 G3
Senlac Wy SLVH TN37 283 R12
Sentinel Cl WVILLE PO7 288 C8
Sequoia Pk CRAWW RH11 8 E7
Sergison Cl HWH RH16 72 F4
Sergison Rd HWH RH16 73 G4
Serrin Wy HORS RH12 56 D4
Service Rd HORL RH6 27 M2
Servite Cl BOGR PO21 2 A5
Setfords Fld RING/NEW BN8 239 P12
Sevelands Cl BRIE/ROTT BN2 123 L6
Seven Acre Cl SLVH TN37 283 P12
Sevenfields BURH RH15 74 B5
Sevenoaks Rd LGNY BN23 164 C4
Seven Sisters Rd
LW/ROSE BN22 163 H2
Seventh Av LAN/SOMP BN15 118 D5
Severals Rd MIDH GU29 226 E9
Severn Rd CRAWE RH10 44 B4
Seville St BRIE/ROTT BN2 5 J2
Sewell Av BEX TN40 97 H8
Sewill Cl HORL RH6 26 E2
Seymour Rd BOR GU35 179 R5
CRAWW RH11 42 F7
Seymour St BRIE/ROTT BN2 5 L9
Shackleton Rd CRAWE RH10 9 H9
Shadwells Cl LAN/SOMP BN15 118 E6
Shadwells Rd LAN/SOMP BN15 118 E6
Shaftesbury Av FERR BN12 150 D2
Shaftesbury Pl BRI BN1 122 F5
Shaftesbury Rd ANG/EP BN16 148 B5
BRI BN1 4 F1
CRAWE RH10 44 C5
SBGH/RUST TN4 37 M3
Shakespeare Rd WTHG BN11 20 D4
Shakespeare St HOVE BN3 121 M5
Shalbourne Crs SELS PO20 168 B8
Shaldon Rd HAV PO9 289 J11
Shalesbrook La FROW RH18 48 F8
Shalfleet Cl LGNY BN23 164 A2
Shamrock Cl CCH PO19 7 H1
RCCH PO18 106 B8
Shandon Cl RTWE/PEM TN2 38 B5
Shandon Gdns SALV BN13 117 J7
Shandon Rd SALV BN13 117 J7
Shandon Wy SALV BN13 117 J7
Shandys Cl HORS RH12 201 R4
Shanklin Cl LGNY BN23 164 A1
Shanklin Rd BRIE/ROTT BN2 5 K1
Shannon Cl LHPTN BN17 147 M5
PEAHV BN10 157 G4
Shannon Wy LGNY BN23 164 E5
Shardeloes Rd ANG/EP BN16 114 E7
Sharon Cl CRAWE RH10 9 M9
Sharps Rd HAV PO9 289 J12
Sharpthorne Cl CRAWW RH11 42 E3
Sharpthorne Crs PTSD BN41 121 H4
Shaves Wood La
HPPT/KEY BN6 270 B7
Shaves Wood Rd
HPPT/KEY BN6 270 B8
Shaw Cl MSEA/BNM PO22 145 M8
Shawfield CROW TN6 68 A7
Shawfield Rd HAV PO9 103 H5
Shawford Gv HAV PO9 288 D12
Shaw's La SWTR RH13 233 N1
Shaws Rd CRAWE RH10 9 J1
The Shaw RTWE/PEM TN2 38 B7
Shear Hl EPSF GU31 223 Q4
Shearwater Dr CHAM PO6 102 A6
MSEA/BNM PO22 144 B7
Sheddington Cl BURH RH15 74 F5
Sheen Rd LW/ROSE BN22 11 H4
Sheepbell Cl PTSD BN41 121 G2
Sheepcote La HAIL BN27 90 C3
Sheepdown Cl PETW GU28 229 M10
Sheepdown Dr PETW GU28 229 L10
Sheepfair LEWES BN7 16 A3
Sheep Fold Av ANG/EP BN16 148 D3
Sheep La MIDH GU29 227 J9
Sheep Pen La SEAF BN25 175 G2
STEY/UB BN44 78 C2
Sheep Pln CROW TN6 210 E2
Sheepsetting La HTHF TN21 244 B6
Sheep St PSF GU32 223 N6
Sheepstreet La
BUR/ETCH TN19 215 K5
WADH TN5 214 G3
Sheep Wk BRIE/ROTT BN2 155 L4

Sheepwash La RCCH PO18 ...... 292 C12
  SELS PO20 .... 167 J2
  UCK TN22 .... 243 K5
Sheerwater Crs HAS TN54 ...... 99 J1
Sheffield Br UCK TN22 .... 240 A1
Sheffield CI CRAWE RH10 .... 44 A5
Sheffield Mill La UCK TN22 .... 208 B9
Sheffield Park Wy LGNY BN23 .. 163 M1
Sheiling Rd CROW TN6 .... 67 K6
Shelby Rd SALV BN13 .... 116 B7
Sheldon CI CRAWE RH10 .... 44 C4
Sheldon Ct WTHG BN11 * 20 C7
Shellbridge Rd ARUN BN18 ..... 111 K1
Shelldale Av PTSD BN41 .... 121 C6
Shelldale Crs PTSD BN41 ...... 121 C6
Shelldale Rd PTSD BN41 .... 121 C5
Shelley CI CRAWE RH10 .... 44 B1
  LEWES BN7 .... 16 D6
Shelley Ldg LPHTN BN17 * 147 L5
Shelley Rd BOGR PO21 .... 171 K2
  EGRIN RH19 .... 31 J8
  HORS RH12 .... 14 B3
  HOVE BN3 .... 121 L6
  RING/NEW BN8 .... 275 J12
  WTHG BN11 .... 20 E6
Shelleys CI SWTR RH13 * 15 M3
Shelley Vls UCK TN22 * 209 N12
Shell La RHWH RH17 .... 61 H8
Shellys Ct SWTR RH13 * 15 M3
Shenfield Wy BRI BN1 .... 123 C3
Shenstone RH WHRH RH16 .... 73 L1
Shepham Av BRIE/ROTT BN2 ..... 156 B4
Shepham La POLE BN26 .... 132 B6
Shepherd CI CRAWE RH10 .... 8 F9
Shepherd's CI BEXW TN39 ...... 136 B1
  LW/ROSE BN22 .... 163 L2
  NEWHV BN9 .... 158 A3
  RING/NEW BN8 .... 275 K12
Shepherds Cot PEAHV BN10 *... 157 J5
Shepherds Cft BRI BN1 .... 122 C1
Shepherdsgrove La
  EGRIN RH19 .... 32 E4
  HRTF TN7 .... 49 J8
Shepherds La PETW GU28 .... 228 A6
Shepherds Md BURH RH15 .... 74 C5
  SALV BN13 .... 116 F2
Shepherd St STLEO TN38 .... 12 A9
Shepherds Wk CROW TN6 .... 68 B8
  HPPT/KEY BN6 .... 271 M1
  RTWE/PEM TN2 .... 38 C5
Shepherds Wy HORS RH12 .... 56 F4
  LIPH GU30 .... 194 A2
  RHAS TN35 .... 101 L1
  RING/NEW BN8 .... 273 M2
  RING/NEW BN8 .... 275 L12
  UCK TN22 .... 76 E7
Sheppard CI HORN PO8 .... 288 B3
Sheppard PI BAT TN33 * 282 E4
Sheppard Wy PTSD BN41 .... 120 F2
Sheppey CI CRAWW RH11 .... 43 G6
Sheppeys HWH RH16 .... 73 G7
Sheppey Wk HAIL BN27 .... 91 M2
Shepway Pde SEAF BN25 * 174 E2
The Shepway SEAF BN25 .... 175 H1
Sheraton CI EAST BN21 .... 10 E8
Sheraton Wk CRAWW RH11 * 43 G8
Sherborne CI RTWE/PEM TN2 .... 38 C7
Sherborne Rd CCH PO19 .... 6 A3
Sherbourne CI HOVE BN3 .... 121 J2
Sherbourne La SELS PO20 ...... 300 H5
Sherbourne Rd HOVE BN3 .... 121 J2
Sherbourne Wy HOVE BN3 .... 121 J2
Sherbrooke CI SALV BN13 ...... 116 C7
Sherfield Av HAV PO9 .... 288 H12
Sheridan CI EGRIN RH19 .... 31 H8
Sheridan Rd SALV BN13 .... 117 J8
Sheridan Ter HOVE BN3 .... 121 M5
Sheriff's La CROW TN6 .... 211 H3
Sheringham CI RBTBR TN32 ..... 249 M3
Sherlock Av CCH PO19 .... 6 A2
Sherman Br POLE BN26 .... 130 B6
Shermanbury Dr
  PUL/STOR RH20 .... 265 R11
Shermanbury Gra
  SWTR RH13 * 234 H11
Shermanbury Rd SALV BN13 ..... 20 D2
  SWTR RH13 .... 234 F10
Sherrington Rd
  BRIE/ROTT BN2 .... 124 E5
  LISS GU33 .... 192 D6
  MSEA/BNM PO22 .... 2 A1
Sherwood Br HWH RH16 .... 72 F4
Sherwood Gn HAIL BN27 .... 92 A7
Sherwood Pk RTWE/PEM TN2 * ... 38 D6
Sherwood PI RRTW TN3 .... 36 D6
Sherwood Ri RRTW TN3 .... 36 D6
Sherwood Rd MSEA/BNM PO22 .... 2 A1
  RTWE/PEM TN2 .... 38 D6
  SEAF BN25 .... 174 F1
Sherwood Wk CRAWE RH10 .... 9 K9
Sherwood Wy SELS PO20 .... 167 K7
Shetland CI CRAWE RH10 .... 44 D2
Shetland Ct SALV BN13 .... 116 A8
Shillinglee Rd MFD/CHID GU8 .. 182 G12
Shinewater La LGNY BN23 ...... 164 A2
Shingle Ct STLEO TN38 .... 283 M10
Shingle Rd SHOR BN43 .... 119 M7
Shingle Wk SELS PO20 .... 167 L7
Shinwell Wk CRAWW RH11 * 43 G7
Shipfield BOGR PO21 .... 171 L3
Shipleybridge La HORL RH6 .... 28 E4
Shipley CI LIPH GU30 .... 193 Q2
Shipley La BEXW TN39 .... 136 C5
Shipley Mill CI PEV BN24 ..... 135 H8
Shipley Paygate SWTR RH13 .... 233 N8
Shipley Rd BRIE/ROTT BN2 ..... 124 D6
  CRAWW RH11 .... 42 F5
  SWTR RH13 .... 233 P5
Ship St BRI BN1 .... 4 C1
  EGRIN RH19 .... 47 K1
  NEWHV BN9 .... 158 A6
  SHOR BN43 .... 119 K6
Ship Street Gdns BRI BN1 * ... 4 D7
Shipton Green La SELS PO20 ... 168 A2
Shire Pde CRAWE RH10 * 44 C2
Shire CI WVILLE PO7 .... 288 C8
Shire PI CRAWE RH10 * 44 C2
Shirlea Wy BAT TN33 .... 282 F5
Shirley Av HOVE BN3 .... 122 A3
Shirley CI ANG/EP BN16 .... 148 C5
  BOGR PO21 .... 170 F5
  SALV BN13 .... 117 G6
  SHOR BN43 .... 120 B5

Shirley Cottages
  SBGH/RUST TN4 * 37 M4
Shirley Dr HOVE BN3 .... 122 B4
  MSEA/BNM PO22 .... 144 F7
  SALV BN13 .... 117 G6
  SLVH TN37 .... 99 G1
Shirley Gdns SBGH/RUST TN4 ... 37 H5
Shirley Gv SBGH/RUST TN4 ..... 37 J4
Shirley Rd HOVE BN3 .... 122 B5
Shirleys HPPT/KEY BN6 .... 272 B7
Shirleys Gdn MSEA/BNM PO22 ... 3 M2
Shirley St HOVE BN3 .... 122 A6
Sholing Ct HAV PO9 .... 288 E11
Shooting Fld STEY/UB BN44 .... 78 C1
Shopfield CI ANG/EP BN16 ..... 148 B3
Shopham Br PETW GU28 .... 263 M3
Shop La RCCH PO18 .... 292 D12
Shopsdam Rd
  LAN/SOMP BN15 .... 152 E1
Shopwhyke Rd SELS PO20 .... 108 D6
Shorecroft BOGR PO21 .... 171 L4
Shoreham By-Pass PTSD BN41... 120 F1
  SHOR BN43 .... 119 L3
Shoreham Rd CRAWE RH10 .... 44 B6
  HFD BN5 .... 269 K10
  STEY/UB BN44 .... 79 J5
Shore Rd RCCH PO18 .... 139 M2
  SELS PO20 .... 167 K7
Shoreside Wk SELS PO20 .... 167 K7
Short Brow SEAF BN25 .... 175 G1
Short Brow CI
  LW/ROSE BN22 * 163 G2
Short CI CRAWW RH11 .... 43 J1
Shortdean PI EAST BN21 .... 176 D1
Short Furlong LPHTN BN17 * ... 147 L4
Short Gallop CRAWE RH10 * 44 C2
Shortgate La RING/NEW BN8.... 276 B7
Shortgate Rd BRIE/ROTT BN2 .. 123 L1
Shortlands CI LW/ROSE BN22 .. 163 H4
Shorts CI HWH RH16 .... 73 H6
Shortsfield CI HORS RH12 ..... 56 C2
Shotterfield Ter LISS GU33 .. 192 C9
Shottermill HORS RH12 .... 56 E1
Shottermill Pk HASM GU27 * .. 180 H10
Shotters BURH RH15 .... 74 D8
Shovelstrode La EGRIN RH19 .. 32 D7
Showfields Rd RTWE/PEM TN2 .. 37 L8
Shripney La MSEA/BNM PO22 ... 144 A5
Shripney Rd MSEA/BNM PO22 ... 2 B2
Shrubbs Dr MSEA/BNM PO22 .... 145 L9
Shrublands Cottages
  CROW TN6 * 67 J5
Shrublands Ct
  RTWE/PEM TN2 * 38 B5
The Shrublands BEXW TN39 .... 136 D2
Shrub La BUR/ETCH TN19 ...... 214 H4
Sicklehatch La HTHF TN21 .... 244 D11
Sickle Rd HASM GU27 .... 181 J12
Sidcup CI LGNY BN23 .... 164 C3
Sidehill Dr PTSD BN41 .... 120 E3
Sidehills RING/NEW BN8 .... 274 C5
Sideways La HORL RH6 .... 22 B8
Sidlaw Ter BOGR PO21 * 2 C7
Sidlesham CI HISD PO11 .... 166 A3
Sidlesham La SELS PO20 .... 140 E8
Sidley Gn BEXW TN39 .... 97 H6
Sidley Rd LW/ROSE BN22 .... 11 K3
Sidley St BEXW TN39 .... 97 H6
Sidney CI RTWE/PEM TN2 .... 53 K1
Silchester Dr CRAWW RH11 .... 8 A8
Silchester Rd STLEO TN38 .... 12 E8
Silkin Wk CRAWW RH11 * 43 C8
Silkstead Av HAV PO9 .... 288 G11
Sillwood PI BRI BN1 .... 4 A6
Sillwood Rd BRI BN1 .... 4 A6
Sillwood St BRI BN1 .... 4 A6
Sillwood Ter BRI BN1 .... 4 A6
Silva CI BEX TN40 .... 97 M7
Silvan Rd STLEO TN38 .... 98 D2
Silver Birch CI LISS GU33 ... 192 D9
Silver Birch Dr
  MSEA/BNM PO22 .... 145 K7
  SALV BN13 .... 116 B8
Silver Birches HFD BN5 .... 269 L10
  HWH RH16 .... 73 K5
  SBGH/RUST TN4 * 38 A1
Silverdale Av HOVE BN3 .... 122 C6
Silverdale CI BOGR PO21 ...... 170 F5
Silverdale Dr LAN/SOMP BN15.. 118 B9
Silverdale La HAWK TN18 ...... 217 N5
  SBGH/RUST TN4 .... 38 A3
Silverdale Rd BURH RH15 ...... 75 G7
  EDN/EASTW BN20 .... 176 F4
  HOVE BN3 .... 122 C6
  SBGH/RUST TN4 * 38 A3
Silver Gld PUL/STOR RH20 .... 266 B7
Silverhill Av SLVH TN37 ...... 99 H1
Silverlands Rd SLVH TN37 ..... 99 G3
Silver La BIL RH14 .... 232 A2
Silverlea Gdns HORL RH6 ...... 23 H7
Silverlock CI CCH PO19 .... 7 J1
Silverlock PI EMRTH PO10 .... 289 Q12
Silverston Av BOGR PO21 ...... 171 M3
Silvertrees EMRTH PO10 .... 104 A3
Silver Wy SELS PO20 .... 168 B8
Silverwood CRAWE RH10 * 29 L6
  PUL/STOR RH20 .... 265 Q6
Silverwood Copse
  PUL/STOR RH20 .... 265 Q6
Silverwood Rd ANG/EP BN16 * . 148 B4
Silvester Rd BEX TN40 .... 97 H8
Simons CI CROW TN6 .... 67 M8
Sinclair CI CRAWE RH10 .... 44 B5
Sincox La SWTR RH13 .... 232 H11
Singleton CI BOGR PO21 .... 171 G4
  FERR BN12 .... 149 L2
Singleton Crs FERR BN12 ...... 149 L2
Singleton Gdns HORN PO8 ...... 256 E9
Singleton Mill Rd PEV BN24 .. 133 H8
Singleton Rd BRI BN1 .... 82 F7
  HORS RH12 .... 201 N2
Singleton Wk BEX TN40 .... 97 M7
Singleton Wy BGH RH15........ 266 B4
Sinnocks PUL/STOR BN8 .... 276 B6
Sinnock Sq HAS TN34 .... 13 K6
Sion Houses RTW TN1 * 37 M1
Sion Wk RTW TN1 * 37 M1
Sir George's PI STEY/UB BN44 . 78 B2
Siskin Av CRAWE RH10 .... 46 B4
Siskin CI HORS RH12 .... 56 D5
Sissinghurst CI CRAWE RH10... 44 B5
Six Acres SWTR RH13 .... 200 E3

Six Acres CI SWTR RH13 .... 201 J11
Six Bells Ms RYE TN31 .... 218 F12
Skeyne Dr PUL/STOR RH20 * ... 265 K3
Skiff La BIL RH14 .... 198 G10
Skinner Rd LYDD TN29 .... 255 R8
Skinner's La BAT TN33 .... 281 P10
  MFD/CHID GU8 .... 183 J4
Skipton Wy HORL RH6 .... 23 G4
Skylarks BIL RH14 .... 231 R2
Skylark Vw HORS RH12 .... 56 C2
Skyline Vw PEAHV BN10 .... 157 J4
Slade La EPSF GU31 .... 224 F5
The Slade RRTW TN3 .... 190 F2
Slate Ter MAYF TN20 * 212 E7
Slattsfield CI SELS PO20 .... 301 M6
Slaugham Ct CRAWW RH11 ...... 42 E6
Slaugham La RHWH RH17 .... 204 B5
Sleepers Stile Rd WADH TN5 .. 190 C4
Sleets Rd HORS RH12 .... 201 P2
Slider's La UCK TN22 .... 207 Q11
The Slides STLEO TN38 .... 98 C2
Slimbridge Rd BURH RH15 ..... 74 B5
Slindon Av PEAHV BN10 .... 157 J7
Slindon Bottom Rd
  ARUN BN18 .... 110 F1
Slindon CI HORN PO8 .... 256 E8
Slindon CI LGNY BN23 .... 164 D4
Slindon Gdns HAV PO9 .... 103 G5
Slindon Rd SALV BN13 .... 117 J7
Slinfold Wk CRAWW RH11 ...... 42 F7
Slinford CI BRIE/ROTT BN2 ... 5 M7
The Slipe ARUN BN18 .... 112 F3
Slipper MI EMRTH PO10 * 104 B6
Slipper Rd EMRTH PO10 .... 104 B6
Sliverick's La BAT TN33 ...... 280 E2
Sloe CI CCH PO19 .... 7 J2
Sloe La POLE BN26 .... 160 F2
Slonk Hill Rd SHOR BN43 ..... 119 M4
Sloop La RHWH RH17 .... 207 M12
Sloughbrook CI HORS RH12 .... 56 E3
Sloughgreen La RHWH RH17 .... 204 G8
Slugwash La RHWH RH17 .... 238 C4
Small Acre HAIL BN27 * 90 A2
Small Bridge Rd
  STPH/PW TN12 .... 189 N7
Smallcroft CI LPHTN BN17 .... 147 H4
Smallcutts Av EGRIN RH19 .... 47 H4
Smallfield Rd HORL RH6 .... 23 G6
Smallmead HORL RH6 .... 23 G6
Smalls Md CRAWW RH11 .... 8 C3
Smeatons La WSEA TN36 .... 286 G4
Smeeds CI EGRIN RH19 .... 31 M6
Smee La BRIE/ROTT BN2 .... 108 C4
Smithbarn SWTR RH13 .... 15 L4
Smithbarn CI HORL RH6 .... 23 C5
Smith CI BAT TN33 .... 281 N12
  CRAWE RH10 .... 8 F9
Smithers Hill La SWTR RH13 .. 233 L9
Smithlands La RING/NEW BN8... 277 P6
Smith La EMRTH PO10 .... 138 C4
Smithy's CI SLVH TN37 .... 283 K12
The Smithy SWTR RH13 .... 235 K4
  UCK TN22 .... 76 D6
  WADH TN5 .... 70 F6
Smock Aly BRIE/ROTT BN2 ..... 5 J7
Smokyhouse La PETW GU28 ..... 228 A12
Smolletts EGRIN RH19 .... 47 H1
Smugglers CI POLE BN26 ...... 160 E2
Smugglers End RHWH RH17 ..... 204 D1
Smugglers La CROW TN6 .... 67 J4
  RCCH PO18 .... 139 M4
  RDKG RH5 .... 187 P2
  STEY/UB BN44 .... 79 G3
  SWTR RH13 .... 200 G10
Smugglers Wk FERR BN12 ...... 150 D4
Smugglers Wy RHAS TN35 ...... 101 L1
  SWTR RH13 .... 201 J11
Snape La WADH TN5 .... 71 K8
Snapes Rd PUL/STOR BN20 ..... 266 C10
Snape Vw WADH TN5 .... 71 L5
Snatt's Rd UCK TN22 .... 76 E3
Snednore LEWES BN7 .... 85 L8
Snell Hatch CRAWW RH11 ...... 8 A3
Snipe CI RTWE/PEM TN2 .... 39 K1
Snipe La HASM GU27 .... 195 K4
Snowberry Crs HAV PO9 .... 103 J2
Snowdon CI LGNY BN23 .... 164 C2
Snowdrop CI CRAWW RH11 ..... 42 F7
  LPHTN BN17 .... 148 A2
Snowdrop La HWH RH16 .... 73 M5
Snowflakes La HWH RH16 ...... 206 G11
Snow HI CRAWE RH10 .... 29 L4
Snowhill La CRAWE RH10 ...... 29 L4
Soane CI CRAWW RH11 .... 42 D5
Soberton Rd HAV PO9 .... 102 D2
Soldridge CI HAV PO9 .... 289 J11
Solent CI LPHTN BN17 .... 147 M2
Solent Rd HAV PO9 .... 102 F4
  SELS PO20 .... 167 L7
Solent Wy EMRTH PO10 .... 104 A6
  HAV PO9 .... 103 H6
  HAV PO9 .... 103 K6
  SELS PO20 .... 301 K8
Solomons CI LGNY BN23 .... 165 G3
Solomon's La RBTBR TN32 ..... 248 D9
Solway HAIL BN27 .... 91 M3
Solway Av BRI BN1 .... 82 E6
Solway CI LPHTN BN17 .... 147 M4
Somborne Dr HAV PO9 .... 288 G12
Somergate HORS RH12 .... 201 Q3
Somerhill Av HOVE BN3 .... 122 C6
Somerhill Rd HOVE BN3 .... 122 C6
Somerley La SELS PO20 .... 168 C4
Somerset Av BOR GU35 .... 178 C6
Somerset CI SALV BN13 .... 116 F8
Somerset Gdns BOGR PO21 ..... 2 D3
Somerset Rd ANG/EP BN16 ..... 149 G3
  FERR BN12 .... 149 L5
  SBGH/RUST TN4 .... 37 M3
Somerset St BRIE/ROTT BN2 ... 5 J7
Somerset Vls RRTW TN3 * 52 B2
Somerstown CCH PO19 .... 6 D4
Somerton Gn MSEA/BNM PO22 .. 3 K2
Somerville CI LGNY BN23 ..... 164 D6
Somerville Dr CRAWE RH10 ... 28 C3
Somerville Gdns
  SBGH/RUST TN4 .... 37 L5
Sompting Av ANG/EP BN16 ..... 117 J8
Sompting By-Pass SALV BN13 .. 117 K6
Sompting CI BRIE/ROTT BN2 ... 123 L4
Sompting Rd SALV BN13 .... 117 K7

Sopley Ct HAV PO9 .... 289 J11
Sorrel CI CRAWW RH11 .... 42 F7
  LGNY BN23 .... 164 B2
  WVILLE PO7 .... 288 B11
Sorrel Dr LGNY BN23 .... 164 B2
Sorrel Rd HORS RH12 .... 56 D4
South Acre CI SELS PO20 ..... 258 C2
South Acre EPSF GU31 .... 257 L1
Southall Av BRIE/ROTT BN2 ... 123 J4
Southampton CI LGNY BN23 ... 164 C5
Southampton St BRIE/ROTT BN2. 5 J4
South Ash STEY/UB BN44 ...... 78 C1
South Av BOGR PO21 .... 171 K2
  BRIE/ROTT BN2 .... 5 J6
  EDN/EASTW BN20 .... 163 G8
  HAIL BN27 .... 150 D4
  HPPT/KEY BN6 .... 270 H4
South Bank CCH PO19 .... 6 D8
South Bay EMRTH PO10 .... 138 B2
South Beach SHOR BN43 * 119 L7
Southbourne Rd
  LW/ROSE BN22 .... 164 B5
Southbrook CRAWW RH11 ...... 43 H8
Southbrook CI HAV PO9 .... 103 G5
Southbrook Rd HAV PO9 .... 103 G6
  RCCH PO18 .... 105 M2
South Cliff BEXW TN39 .... 136 C5
  EDN/EASTW BN20 .... 176 D5
South Cliff Av BEXW TN39 .... 136 C6
  EDN/EASTW BN20 .... 176 F4
South Cliffe LEWES BN7 ...... 17 J6
South CI BURH RH15 .... 74 D6
  CRAWE RH10 .... 9 J1
  HAIL BN27 .... 92 A7
  HAV PO9 .... 103 H5
  PEV BN24 .... 134 E7
South Coast Rd
  BRIE/ROTT BN2 .... 156 C5
  PEAHV BN10 .... 18 A5
Southcote Av SELS PO20 ...... 167 K6
Southcourt Av BEXW TN39 .... 136 C6
Southcourt CI ANG/EP BN16 .. 148 D3
Southcourt Rd ANG/EP BN16 .. 20 D3
Southdean CI
  MSEA/BNM PO22 .... 145 L8
Southdean Dr
  MSEA/BNM PO22 .... 145 L8
Southdown Av BRI BN1 .... 122 F4
  EDN/EASTW BN20 .... 162 F2
  HAS TN34 .... 100 A2
  LEWES BN7 .... 16 A7
  PEAHV BN10 .... 157 K7
  PTSD BN41 .... 121 H5
Southdown CI CCH PO19 .... 7 J1
  HORS RH12 .... 56 F4
  HWH RH16 .... 73 G7
  MIDH GU29 .... 226 G11
  NEWHV BN9 .... 18 C6
Southdown Cnr SEAF BN25 * .. 175 C3
Southdown Ms BRIE/ROTT BN2. 5 J7
Southdown PI BRI BN1 .... 122 F4
Southdown Rd BOGR PO21 ..... 2 C7
  BRI BN1 .... 122 F4
  EDN/EASTW BN20 .... 163 H6
  HORN PO8 .... 256 D10
  NEWHV BN9 .... 18 D6
  SEAF BN25 .... 174 F2
  SHOR BN43 .... 119 L6
Southdown Ter STEY/UB BN44 .. 78 D2
Southdown View CI
  SALV BN13 .... 117 L8
Southdown View Rd
  SALV BN13 .... 117 L8
Southdown View Wy
  SALV BN13 .... 117 K7
Southdown Wy
  PUL/STOR RH20 .... 266 C10
South Dr ANG/EP BN16 .... 148 C2
  BURH RH15 .... 74 D6
  FERR BN12 .... 149 K5
  MSEA/BNM PO22 .... 145 H8
Southerden CI HAIL BN27 ..... 92 B7
Southern Av POLE BN26 .... 132 A7
Southern Ga CCH PO19 .... 6 C6
Southern Rd BOR GU35 .... 178 C4
  LW/ROSE BN22 .... 163 G3
  SELS PO20 .... 301 L7
Southey Rd WTHG BN11 .... 20 E7
South Farm La SALV BN13 .... 117 G10
Southfield POLE BN26 .... 131 L8
Southfield Rd SALV BN13 ..... 117 J8
  SBGH/RUST TN4 .... 37 M3
Southfields RRTW TN3 .... 36 F2
  WADH TN5 .... 71 L3
Southfields CI CCH PO19 ..... 141 L2
Southfields Rd EAST BN21 .... 10 C7
  LPHTN BN17 .... 147 L4
Southfields Wy
  SBGH/RUST TN4 .... 38 A1
Southgate CCH PO19 .... 6 C6
Southgate Av CRAWE RH10 .... 9 H5
Southgate Dr CRAWE RH10 .... 8 F7
Southgate Pde CRAWE RH10 ... 8 F6
Southgate Rd CRAWE RH10 .... 8 F6

Southlands La PUL/STOR RH20. 266 B6
Southlands Pk MIDH GU29 ..... 226 H12
Southlands Rd BEXW TN39 .... 96 F6
South La ARUN BN18 .... 296 C6
  EMRTH PO10 .... 104 F2
  EPSF GU31 .... 257 L1
  HTHF TN21 .... 246 D11
  NEWHV BN9 .... 19 G3
  PETW GU28 .... 228 G10
Southleigh Rd EMRTH PO10 ... 104 A2
  HAV PO9 .... 103 J4
Southleys LEWES BN7 * 195 K8
South Ldg LAN/SOMP BN15 * .. 118 B6
South Lodge CI BURH RH15 ... 74 B5
South Lynn Dr EAST BN21 .... 10 C3
Southmead CI MAYF TN20 ..... 212 G6
Southmoor La HAV PO9 .... 102 G6
Southmount BRIE/ROTT BN2 ... 123 G4
Southon CI PTSD BN41 .... 121 G5
Southover High St LEWES BN7.. 16 D8
Southover PI BRIE/ROTT BN2 .. 5 J5
Southover Rd BOGR PO21 ...... 2 C7
  LEWES BN7 .... 16 F7
Southover St BRIE/ROTT BN2 .. 5 H5
Southover Wy SELS PO20 ...... 141 M5
South Pallant CCH PO19 ...... 6 C6
South Pde HORL RH6 * 22 E5
South Pier Rd HORL RH6 ...... 147 M2
Southridge Ri CROW TN6 ...... 67 K8
Southridge Rd CROW TN6 ..... 210 F1
South Rd BRI BN1 .... 122 F4
  HAIL BN27 .... 91 M7
  HORN PO8 .... 256 D12
  HWH RH16 .... 73 H5
  LIPH GU30 .... 193 R4
  MSEA/BNM PO22 .... 3 K3
  NEWHV BN9 .... 19 G3
  RHWH RH17 .... 238 F9
South Road Ms BRI BN1 .... 122 G4
South Rough RING/NEW BN8 ... 240 B7
Southsea Av FERR BN12 .... 150 D3
Southside PUL/STOR RH20 .... 265 F5
South Strd ANG/EP BN16 ..... 148 F5
South St BRI 4 D7
  BRI BN1 .... 84 D7
  CCH PO19 .... 6 E6
  CROW TN6 .... 67 J6
  EAST BN21 .... 10 E7
  EMRTH PO10 .... 104 A4
  HAV PO9 .... 103 G4
  HORS RH12 .... 14 C6
  HPPT/KEY BN6 .... 272 A6
  LAN/SOMP BN15 .... 152 D1
  LEWES BN7 .... 17 J6
  LYDD TN29 .... 255 R7
  MAYF TN20 .... 212 E7
  MIDH GU29 .... 227 J10
  PTSD BN41 .... 120 F4
  RHWH RH17 .... 72 B4
  RING/NEW BN8 .... 276 C5
  SALV BN13 .... 20 B2
  SEAF BN25 .... 174 E3
  SLVH TN37 .... 12 B8
  SWTR RH13 .... 234 F10
  WTHG BN11 .... 13 G5
South Ter HAS TN34 .... 13 G5
  LPHTN BN17 .... 147 J5
South Undercliff RYE TN31 .. 252 H8
South Vw ANG/EP BN16 .... 149 G5
  HPPT/KEY BN6 .... 272 A4
Southview HFD BN5 * 269 L11
  CRAWE RH10 .... 29 K6
South View CI BUR/ETCH TN19. 216 A6
Southview CI CROW TN6 .... 67 K8
  SHOR BN43 .... 120 B6
  STHW BN42 .... 120 D5
Southview Dr UCK TN22 .... 76 E4
  WTHG BN11 .... 20 A6
Southview Gdns WTHG BN11 ... 150 E3
  WTHG BN11 .... 20 A6
South View Rd CROW TN6 ..... 67 K8
  SBGH/RUST TN4 .... 38 A1
  WADH TN5 .... 71 L3
Southview Rd BOR GU35 .... 179 G4
  MSEA/BNM PO22 .... 173 G3
  PEAHV BN10 .... 157 K5
  STHW BN42 .... 120 D5
South View Ter HAS TN34 .... 13 G5
Southview Ter NEWHV BN9 .... 158 D4
South Wk MSEA/BNM PO22 ..... 145 L9
Southwark CI CRAWW RH11 .... 43 G7
Southwark Wk BOGR PO21 ..... 171 K2
Southwater CI BRIE/ROTT BN2. 5 L5
  CRAWW RH11 .... 42 F3
  FERR BN12 .... 150 A4
Southwater Rd SLVH TN37 .... 12 A4
Southwater St SWTR RH13 .... 201 R10
South Wy BOGR PO21 .... 143 M8
  LEWES BN7 .... 16 A5
  NEWHV BN9 .... 19 G4
  SEAF BN25 .... 175 J4
Southway BURH RH15 .... 147 L5
  LPHTN BN17 .... 147 L5
Southways Av SALV BN13 ..... 117 K7
Southways Pk CRAWE RH10 * .. 27 J3
Southwick CI EGRIN RH19 .... 31 J7
Southwick Sq STHW BN42 ..... 120 D5
Southwick St STHW BN42 ..... 120 D5
Southwold CI SALV BN13 ..... 116 C4
Southwood Av SBGH/RUST TN4. 37 M3
Southwood Dr STLEO TN38 .... 99 G4
South Woodlands BRI BN1 .... 122 D1
Southwood Rd
  SBGH/RUST TN4 .... 37 G4
Sovereign CI HAS TN34 .... 99 M1
  SEAF BN25 .... 159 M8
The Spain PSF GU32 .... 223 M6
The Spaldings STLEO TN38 ... 98 D2
Sparks Ct LPHTN BN17 .... 147 J4
Spark's La RHWH RH17 .... 205 M7
Sparrow CI HORN PO8 .... 288 A5
The Sparrows PEAHV BN10 .... 157 J4
Sparrow Wy BURH RH15 .... 74 C6
Sparsholt CI HAV PO9 .... 288 D12
Sparsholt Rd SELS PO20 ..... 301 L8
Spartan CI EMRTH PO10 ...... 138 B2
Spatham La HPPT/KEY BN6 .... 272 C5
Spats La BOR GU35 .... 179 N1
Spear HI PUL/STOR RH20 ..... 267 K6
Speckled Wd RHAS TN35 ...... 100 B2
Speedwell CI SALV BN13 ..... 115 M8
Speedwell Wy HORS RH12 ..... 56 D4
Speldhurst HI RRTW TN3 ..... 37 G1
Speldhurst Rd RRTW TN3 ..... 36 D1

SBGH/RUST TN4 .... 37 L1
Spelmonden Rd
STPH/PW TN12 ... 189 L5
Spencer Av HOVE BN3 .... 121 J2
Spencer Ms RTW TN1 * 37 M7
Spencer Rd EAST BN21 .... 10 E3
EMRTH PO10 .... 103 M1
LAN/SOMP BN15 .... 118 C3
Spencers Pl HORS RH12 .... 14 A1
HORS RH12 .... 14 B4
Spencer St BOGR PO21 .... 2 E5
Spences Fld LEWES BN7 .... 17 J3
Spences La LEWES BN7 .... 17 J3
Spey Cl SALV BN13 .... 116 D5
Spicers Cl BURH RH15 .... 74 E4
Spierbridge Rd
PUL/STOR RH20 .... 265 R11
Spiers Wy HORL RH6 .... 23 G8
Spindle Cl BEXW TN39 .... 96 D8
Spindle Warren HAV PO9 .... 103 K2
Spindle Wy CRAWE RH10 .... 9 J4
Spindlewood Dr BEXW TN39 .... 136 B3
Spinnaker Cl LPHTN BN17 .... 147 M4
Spinnaker Vw HAV PO9 .... 102 B4
Spinnals Gv STHW BN42 .... 120 C6
Spinney Cl CRAWE RH10 .... 46 B1
HORS RH12 .... 57 G3
HPPT/KEY BN6 .... 271 N4
SELS PO20 .... 301 K5
Spinney La PUL/STOR RH20 .... 265 K8
SELS PO20 .... 139 M7
Spinney North
PUL/STOR RH20 .... 265 L3
The Spinneys HTHF TN21 .... 244 E7
LEWES BN7 .... 17 J3
The Spinney ANG/EP BN16 .... 148 F5
BAT TN33 .... 282 C6
BEXW TN39 .... 136 C2
BOGR PO21 .... 171 K2
CRAWW RH11 .... 8 B7
GSHT GU26 .... 180 D5
HAIL BN27 * 90 A2
HAS TN34 .... 12 E4
HASM GU27 .... 180 C12
HASM GU27 .... 181 M9
HORL RH6 .... 22 F4
HORN BN3 .... 288 B3
HOVE BN3 .... 122 B2
HPPT/KEY BN6 .... 271 N4
HWH RH16 .... 73 G2
PUL/STOR RH20 .... 265 L3
RBTBR TN32 .... 248 A2
SELS PO20 .... 139 L8
Spinney Wk MSEA/BNM PO22 .... 111 G2
Spion Kop CROW TN6 * 210 C1
Spitalfield La CCH PO19 * 7 H2
Spital Rd LEWES BN7 .... 16 C5
Spithandle La STEY/UB BN44 .... 267 N12
Spithurst Rd RING/NEW BN8 .... 274 C2
Spode La EDEN TN8 .... 33 N1
Sponden La HAWK TN18 .... 217 N1
Spooners Rd HORS RH12 .... 15 L1
Spotted Cow La UCK TN22 .... 210 F12
Spout Hi CROW TN6 .... 69 J8
Spout La STPH/PW TN12 .... 188 G4
Spray Hi RRTW TN3 .... 190 O1
Springate La STHW BN42 .... 120 E5
Springbank CCH PO19 .... 107 L4
Spring Cl CRAWW RH11 .... 8 E5
EDN/EASTW BN20 .... 163 O4
Springfield Av PEAHV BN10 .... 157 K3
Springfield Cl ANG/EP BN16 .... 148 A7
CROW TN6 .... 68 A7
HAV PO9 .... 133 L7
PEV BN24 .... 180 E7
RCCH PO18 .... 292 C10
RHWH RH17 .... 236 D1
SELS PO20 .... 140 E8
Springfield Crs HORS RH12 .... 14 B5
Springfield La HORS RH12 .... 58 A5
Springfield Pk HORS RH12 * 14 C4
Springfield Park Rd HORS RH12 .... 14 B5
Springfield Pl RRTW TN3 * 52 B2
Springfield Rd BEX TN40 .... 97 H7
BRI BN1 .... 122 F5
CRAWW RH11 .... 8 D5
HORS RH12 .... 14 C5
LW/ROSE BN22 .... 11 H4
RRTW TN3 .... 52 B2
STLEO TN38 .... 99 G4
Springfields WADH TN5 * 191 K12
Springfields Vale Rd STLEO TN38 .... 99 G4
Springfield Va STLEO TN38 .... 99 G4
Spring Gdns BRI BN1 .... 4 D6
CRAWE RH10 .... 29 H6
EMRTH PO10 .... 104 A5
LEWES BN7 .... 17 G5
PUL/STOR RH20 .... 266 H11
SBGH/RUST TN4 * 37 G6
Springhead RTWE/PEM TN2 .... 38 C4
Springhead Wy CROW TN6 .... 210 F1
Spring Hi RRTW TN3 .... 35 M3
RYE TN31 .... 218 E10
Spring La BEXW TN39 .... 96 B5
BUR/ETCH TN19 .... 214 B9
HPPT/KEY BN6 .... 271 M9
HWH RH16 .... 206 E8
SWTR RH13 .... 200 F2
UCK TN22 .... 211 N12
Spring Lodge Cl LGNY BN23 .... 164 C1
Spring Meadow FROW RH18 .... 48 E8
MIDH GU29 .... 226 H11
Springpark HTHF TN21 * 244 D5
Spring Plat CRAWE RH10 .... 44 B3
Spring Plat Ct CRAWE RH10 * 44 B3
Springside Wk STLEO TN38 .... 98 E4
Spring St BRI BN1 .... 4 B6
SLVH TN37 .... 12 A4
Spring V HORN PO8 .... 288 C5
Spring Wy EGRIN RH19 .... 31 M5
Springwell HAV PO9 .... 103 H3
Springwood Av WVILLE PO7 .... 288 A11
Springwood Rd HTHF TN21 .... 244 D5
Spronkett's La RHWH RH17 .... 235 R1
Sproule Cl ARUN BN18 .... 146 A3
Sproutes La SWTR RH13 .... 232 F4
Spruce Av GU35 .... 178 G6
WVILLE PO7 .... 288 B10
Spruce Cl LW/ROSE BN22 .... 163 J3

Spurgeon Cl CRAWW RH11 .... 8 D2
Spur Rd CCH PO19 .... 7 L6
POLE BN26 .... 132 A8
Spurway Pk POLE BN26 .... 132 A8
Spy La BIL RH14 .... 198 H1
Squab La HAIL BN27 .... 92 F1
Squadron Dr BRI BN13 .... 116 A7
Square Dr HASM GU27 .... 195 L8
The Square CRAWE RH10 * 8 A4
EMRTH PO10 .... 104 C2
EPSF GU31 .... 258 E1
LIPH GU30 .... 193 Q1
MSEA/BNM PO22 .... 111 G7
PEV BN24 .... 134 E7
PSF GU32 .... 223 N6
SALV BN13 * 117 J8
Squires Cl EAST BN21 .... 45 M1
Squirrel Cl BEXW TN39 .... 96 D8
CRAWW RH11 .... 27 G8
Squirrel Rdg CRAWE RH10 * 46 A2
Squirrels Copse
PUL/STOR RH20 .... 266 F10
Squirrel Wk HAIL BN27 * 90 A2
Squirrels La CRAWE RH10 .... 44 C6
Stable Cl CRAWE RH10 .... 44 C6
Stabledene Wy RTWE/PEM TN2 .... 39 J3
Stable Fld MSEA/BNM PO22 .... 146 A8
Stablefield RHAS TN35 .... 284 B5
Stablefields RHAS TN35 * 284 B5
Stable La SALV BN13 .... 298 H11
Stable Ms SLVH TN37 * 283 F12
Stable Rd BOR GU35 .... 178 F3
Stables La EAST BN21 .... 10 A6
Stacey Ct HAV PO9 .... 288 E10
Stackfield Rd CRAWW RH11 .... 42 D4
CRAWW RH11 .... 26 F8
PSF GU32 .... 223 N4
RTWE/PEM TN2 .... 38 D5
SEAF BN25 .... 174 F2
Stag Cl HFD BN5 .... 269 K3
Stagelands CRAWW RH11 .... 43 G1
Stagshorn Rd HORN PO8 .... 288 B3
Stainsby St SLVH TN37 .... 12 B7
Stairbridge La RHWH RH17 .... 236 F5
Stakers La SWTR RH13 .... 233 R1
Stakes Hill Rd WVILLE PO7 .... 102 A1
Stalham Wy MSEA/BNM PO22 * 3 L1
Stalkers La RING/NEW BN8 .... 277 L3
Stallard Ct EMRTH PO10 .... 103 M4
Stall House La PUL/STOR RH20 .... 231 P10
Stammers Hi HFD BN5 .... 80 E2
Stanam Rd RTWE/PEM TN2 .... 39 K4
Stanbridge Cl CRAWW RH11 .... 42 D4
Stanbridge Rd HAV PO9 .... 103 J2
Stanbridge Wy RHWH RH17 .... 206 D2
Stanbrok Cl BOGR PO21 .... 171 K2
Stanbury Cl RCCH PO18 .... 106 A6
Standard Hill Cl BAT TN33 .... 281 L11
Standean Cl BRI BN1 .... 83 J7
Standen Cl EGRIN RH19 .... 30 F6
Standen Ms UCK TN22 .... 211 K12
Standen Pl HORS RH12 .... 56 F7
Standen St CRBK TN17 .... 218 B1
SBGH/RUST TN4 .... 37 M4
Standford Hi BOR GU35 .... 179 K8
Standford La BOR GU35 .... 179 K6
Standgrove Pl RHWH RH17 .... 206 D3
Standinghall La CRAWE RH10 .... 44 F5
Stane St BIL RH14 .... 200 A12
BIL RH14 .... 231 R3
PUL/STOR RH20 .... 265 K11
RCCH PO18 .... 108 D4
RCCH PO18 .... 109 G2
SWTR RH13 .... 200 E4
Stane Street Cl
PUL/STOR RH20 .... 265 K1
Stanford Av BRI BN1 .... 122 F3
HPPT/KEY BN6 .... 271 M5
Stanford Cl HOVE BN3 .... 122 B4
HPPT/KEY BN6 .... 271 M5
MSEA/BNM PO22 .... 3 L1
Stanford Cottages
SWTR RH13 * 202 D5
Stanford Ct HAV PO9 .... 289 J12
Stanford Orch HORS RH12 .... 187 Q10
Stanford Rd BRI BN1 .... 122 D5
Stanford Sq WTHG BN11 .... 21 J6
Stanford Ter HPPT/KEY BN6 * 271 M5
Stanford Wy HORS RH12 .... 201 N2
Stan Hi HORL RH6 .... 26 B1
Stanhope Pl STLEO TN38 .... 12 A9
Stanhope Rd LPHTN BN17 .... 147 K3
RTW TN1 .... 38 B4
WTHG BN11 .... 21 G4
Stanier Cl CRAWE RH10 .... 44 A4
Stanier Rd STLEO TN38 .... 283 N12
Stanley Av PTSD BN41 .... 120 E2
Stanley Cl BOGR PO21 .... 2 E5
CRAWE RH10 .... 9 H8
Stanley Rd BRI BN1 .... 4 F2
EMRTH PO10 .... 104 B5
HAS TN34 .... 12 F5
LHPTN BN17 .... 147 J2
LW/ROSE BN22 .... 11 H3
PEAHV BN10 .... 157 G4
PTSD BN41 .... 120 F5
RTW TN1 .... 38 A4
WTHG BN11 .... 21 H3
Stanley St BRIE/ROTT BN2 .... 5 H6
Stanley Wk SWTR RH13 .... 14 E6
Stanley Wy SWTR RH13 .... 14 E6
Stanmer Av BRIE/ROTT BN2 .... 156 C2
Stanmer Dr LW/ROSE BN22 .... 163 J4
Stanmer Park Rd BRI BN1 .... 122 F3
Stanmer St BRI BN1 .... 123 G3
Stanmer Vis BRI BN1 .... 123 G2
Stanmore Gdns BOGR PO21 .... 171 K3
Stanover La MIDH GU29 .... 144 F6
Stansfield Ct ANG/EP BN16 * 148 C3
Stansfield Rd LEWES BN7 .... 16 D4
Stanstead Cl HAV PO9 .... 289 K7
Stanstead Crs BRIE/ROTT BN2 .... 124 E7
Stansted Crs BRIE/ROTT BN2 .... 289 J11
Stansted Rd LW/ROSE BN22 .... 10 F3
Stanswood Rd HAV PO9 .... 288 E11
Stanton Dr CCH PO19 .... 107 L2
Stanton Rd PSF GU32 .... 223 P6
Stanwater La MIDH GU29 .... 226 B5
Staple Ash La PSF GU32 .... 222 D2
Staplecross Ct CRAWW RH11 .... 42 E7
Staplefield Dr BRIE/ROTT BN2 .... 123 L2
Staplefield Rd RHWH RH17 .... 204 F5

RHWH RH17 .... 205 K9
Staple La RCCH PO18 .... 292 C9
Staples Barn HFD BN5 .... 269 J4
Staples Barn La HFD BN5 .... 269 J4
Stapleton Ct BOGR PO21 .... 171 J2
Stapley Rd HOVE BN13 .... 121 J5
Star Cl SWTR RH13 .... 15 L2
Starfield CROW TN6 .... 67 K8
Star La MAYF TN20 .... 212 E7
Starina Gdns WVILLE PO7 .... 288 C9
Starling Cl BURH RH15 .... 74 C6
Star Ms MAYF TN20 * 212 E7
Star Rd EAST BN21 .... 10 A4
SWTR RH13 .... 234 F11
Starrs Cottages HAS TN34 * 13 L6
Starr's Green La BAT TN33 .... 282 G6
Starrs Md BAT TN33 .... 282 H5
Starvecrow La RYE TN31 .... 251 L7
Starwell Cl HAS TN34 .... 99 J1
Station Ap BAT TN33 .... 282 F6
BOGR PO21 * 2 D6
BRI BN1 .... 84 A7
BUR/ETCH TN19 .... 215 P8
CROW TN6 * 69 J6
EMRTH PO10 * 104 A4
HAS TN34 .... 12 F6
HORL RH6 .... 23 G6
HORS RH12 .... 41 L8
HPPT/KEY BN6 .... 271 M5
HTHF TN21 .... 244 D6
LW/ROSE BN22 .... 163 L4
MAYF TN20 .... 212 C7
MFD/CHID GU8 .... 182 E1
PUL/STOR RH20 .... 264 H3
RDKG RH5 .... 24 A4
RHWH RH17 .... 207 K2
RTW TN1 .... 37 M6
RYE TN31 .... 252 C7
SEAF BN25 .... 174 E2
SWTR RH13 * 12 B7
Station Approach Rd
HORL RH6 .... 28 A1
Station Cl CROW TN6 .... 69 H8
LEWES BN7 .... 272 H4
SWTR RH13 .... 14 C5
Station La MFD/CHID GU8 .... 182 D1
Station Pde ANG/EP BN16 * 148 D5
EAST BN21 .... 10 D6
LAN/SOMP BN15 * 118 D8
WTHG BN11 * 20 B3
Station Rd ANG/EP BN16 .... 148 C3
ARUN BN18 .... 113 J4
BAT TN33 .... 282 H11
BEX TN40 .... 137 H1
BIL RH14 .... 198 G2
BIL RH14 .... 232 A1
BOGR PO21 .... 2 D6
BOR GU35 .... 178 F4
BRI BN1 .... 122 C2
BUR/ETCH TN19 .... 216 A6
BURH RH15 .... 74 F7
CRAWE RH10 .... 8 F5
CRAWE RH10 .... 46 A1
CRBK TN17 .... 189 P10
CROW TN6 .... 69 H8
EGRIN RH19 .... 31 J8
EGRIN RH19 .... 62 F3
EPSF GU31 .... 223 N5
FROW RH18 .... 48 E6
HAIL BN27 .... 92 A4
HAIL BN27 .... 278 D12
HFD BN5 .... 269 J4
HORL RH6 .... 23 G6
HORL RH6 .... 56 A1
HORS RH12 .... 185 Q7
HORS RH12 .... 186 A10
HRTF TN7 .... 51 C4
HTHF TN21 .... 244 D6
LEWES BN7 .... 17 G8
LEWES BN7 .... 272 H3
LIPH GU30 .... 193 G3
LISS GU33 .... 192 C9
MAYF TN20 .... 212 C7
MIDH GU29 .... 226 G10
NEWH BN9 .... 158 E4
PETW GU28 .... 229 K11
POLE BN26 .... 130 A1
POLE BN26 .... 131 M7
PSF GU32 .... 223 N5
PUL/STOR RH20 .... 264 H3
RBTBR TN32 .... 248 B2
RCCH PO18 .... 106 B6
RHWH RH17 .... 207 H4
RING/NEW BN8 .... 239 P6
RRTW TN3 .... 52 B2
RYE TN31 .... 218 F8
SEAF BN25 .... 159 G8
STEY/UB BN44 .... 78 D2
STHW BN42 .... 120 D6
SWTR RH13 .... 14 C5
SWTR RH13 .... 201 N6
SWTR RH13 .... 234 F3
SWTR RH13 .... 235 K3
UCK TN22 .... 275 J1
WADH TN5 .... 71 H3
WADH TN5 .... 214 D4
WSEA TN36 .... 252 D12
WTHG BN11 .... 21 H3
Station St BRI BN1 .... 4 D6
EAST BN21 .... 10 D6
LEWES BN7 .... 17 G6
Staunton Av HAV PO9 .... 102 F4
Staunton Rd HAV PO9 .... 102 F4
Staunton Wy EPSF GU31 .... 257 K4
HAV PO9 .... 102 D5
HAV PO9 .... 102 D5
HORN PO8 .... 256 H5
Staveley Md
LAN/SOMP BN15 .... 118 B5
Staveley Rd EDN/EASTW BN20 .... 176 E5
Stavely Gdns CCH PO19 .... 107 L2
Stean Furlong LHPTN BN17 .... 147 N2
Stedham La MIDH GU29 .... 226 D6
Stedton Cl PUL/STOR RH20 .... 266 B4
Steellands Rd WADH TN5 .... 191 K12
Steels La RCCH PO18 .... 105 K4
Steep Cl SALV BN13 .... 298 H12
Steepdown Rd
LAN/SOMP BN15 .... 118 B5
Steep Hi RYE TN31 .... 250 B11
Steep La SALV BN13 .... 298 H12
Steeple Vw SALV BN13 .... 116 F8

Steep Rd CROW TN6 .... 211 K3
Steepways GSHT GU26 .... 180 E3
Steeres Hi RTW TN1 .... 41 G7
Steers La CRAWE RH10 .... 28 B5
Steine Gdns BRIE/ROTT BN2 .... 4 E7
Steine St BRIE/ROTT BN2 .... 4 E7
Stein Rd EMRTH PO10 .... 104 E3
Stemp Dr BIL RH14 .... 231 R1
Stempswood Wy
MSEA/BNM PO22 .... 111 G2
The Stennings EGRIN RH19 .... 31 H6
Stephen Cl CRAWW RH11 .... 27 J8
HORN PO8 .... 288 C7
Stephens Cl RING/NEW BN8 .... 275 J12
Stephenson Dr EGRIN RH19 .... 47 L3
Stephenson Pl CRAWE RH10 .... 44 A3
Stephenson Wy CRAWE RH10 .... 9 M4
Stephens Rd BRI BN1 .... 123 G3
SBGH/RUST TN4 .... 37 M3
Stepney Cl CRAWE RH10 .... 44 B5
Sterling Buildings HORS RH12 * 14 C3
Sterling Pde ANG/EP BN16 * 148 A3
Sterling Pk CRAWE RH10 * 28 A6
Sternway LHPTN BN17 .... 147 M4
Stevenage Rd CRAWW RH11 .... 42 D7
Stevens Cl BEXW TN39 .... 97 H6
Stevenson Cl LGNY BN23 .... 164 D2
Stevenson Rd BRIE/ROTT BN2 .... 5 K7
SLVH TN37 .... 99 G2
Stewards Inn La LEWES BN7 .... 16 F7
Stewards Ri ARUN BN18 .... 112 A4
Stewart Rd SBGH/RUST TN4 .... 38 B2
Steyne Cl SEAF BN25 .... 174 E3
Steyne Gdns WTHG BN11 .... 21 J6
Steyne Rd SEAF BN25 .... 174 E3
Steyne St BOGR PO21 .... 2 D8
The Steyne BOGR PO21 * 2 D8
SEAF BN25 * 174 E3
WTHG BN11 .... 21 J6
Steyning Av HOVE BN3 .... 121 L2
PEAHV BN10 .... 157 H7
Steyning By-Pass
STEY/UB BN44 .... 78 E4
FERR BN12 .... 150 A2
LAN/SOMP BN15 .... 118 C5
SEAF BN25 .... 175 J3
Steyning Crs PUL/STOR RH20 .... 265 R11
Steyning Rd BRIE/ROTT BN2 .... 155 L4
SEAF BN25 .... 175 J3
SHOR BN43 .... 79 H8
Steyning Ter HAV PO9 * 103 G3
Steyning Wy MSEA/BNM PO22 .... 144 A6
Stile Gdns HASM GU27 .... 181 J11
The Stiles HAIL BN27 .... 92 B6
Stillers MFD/CHID GU8 * 182 G5
Stipenhoke HFD BN5 * 269 L5
Stirling Av SEAF BN25 .... 175 J1
Stirling Cl BURH RH15 .... 75 H5
CRAWE RH10 .... 44 A4
SEAF BN25 .... 175 J2
Stirling Court Rd BURH RH15 * 75 H4
Stirling Pl HOVE BN3 .... 121 M7
Stirling Rd CCH PO19 .... 6 E7
STLEO TN38 .... 283 N12
Stirling Wy BOGR PO21 .... 171 K3
EGRIN RH19 .... 32 A6
EPSF GU31 .... 223 R7
SWTR RH13 .... 15 H5
Stirrup Wy CRAWE RH10 .... 44 C2
Stoatley Hollow HASM GU27 .... 181 K9
Stoatley Ri HASM GU27 .... 181 J9
Stoatley River HASM GU27 .... 181 K9
Stockbridge Cl HAV PO9 .... 289 J12
Stockbridge Gdns CCH PO19 .... 6 B9
Stockbridge Pl CCH PO19 * 6 B9
Stockcroft Rd RHWH RH17 .... 60 F8
Stock Dl RHAS TN35 .... 101 L1
Stocker Rd BOGR PO21 .... 2 A9
Stockfield HORL RH6 * 23 G5
Stockheath La HAV PO9 .... 102 F2
Stockheath Rd HAV PO9 .... 102 F1
Stockheath Wy HAV PO9 .... 103 G2
Stockland Green Rd
RRTW TN3 .... 37 H1
Stockland Cl UCK TN22 .... 211 J11
Stocklands Cl RHWH RH17 .... 72 C1
Stockleigh Rd STLEO TN38 .... 12 A7
Stocks Cl HORL RH6 .... 23 G7
Stocks Flds STEY/UB BN44 * 267 N12
Stocks La RCCH PO18 .... 108 A1
SELS PO20 .... 167 M7
Stocks Md PUL/STOR RH20 .... 298 H3
Stocks Meadow BAT TN35 .... 281 N12
Stocks Rd TENT TN30 .... 220 D6
Stockwell Rd EGRIN RH19 .... 47 K3
Stoddards La RYE TN31 .... 218 H12
Stodham La LISS GU33 .... 192 B11
Stoke Abbott Rd WTHG BN11 .... 21 G5
Stoke Cl SEAF BN25 .... 175 H2
Stoke Manor Cl SEAF BN25 .... 175 H2
Stoke Rd ARUN BN18 .... 296 D7
Stokes Cl CRAWE RH10 .... 44 B6
Stoneage Cl MSEA/BNM PO22 .... 144 B2
Stonebeach Ri STLEO TN38 .... 283 N10
Stone Br TENT TN30 .... 221 N7
Stonebridge Ct HORS RH12 * 201 R3
Stonebridge La UCK TN22 .... 242 G8
Stonechat Cl EPSF GU31 .... 223 R7
Stonechat Rd HORN PO8 .... 288 B3
Stone Cl SALV BN13 .... 116 E7
Stonecott Cl CROW TN6 .... 210 C1
Stone Court La RTWE/PEM TN2 .... 39 K1
Stonecroft Cl HOVE BN3 .... 121 K1
Stonecrop Cl HWH RH16 .... 42 G6
Stonecross Rd
BRIE/ROTT BN2 .... 123 L1
Stone Cross Rd CROW TN6 .... 210 C3
WADH TN5 .... 71 M6
Stonedene Cl BOR GU35 .... 179 K1
FROW RH18 .... 48 E8
Stonefield Cl CRAWE RH10 .... 8 F6
Stonefield Pl HAS TN34 .... 13 H6
Stonefield Rd HAS TN34 .... 13 H6
Stonefield Wy BURH RH15 .... 74 E4
Stonegate Cl LGNY BN23 .... 163 M1
Stonegate Rd WADH TN5 .... 190 B12
Stonegate Wy HTHF TN21 .... 244 E5
Stonehall La RHWH RH17 .... 205 Q2

PSF GU32 .... 223 L5
Stoneham Pk PSF GU32 .... 223 L5
Stoneham Rd HOVE BN3 .... 121 L6
Stone Hatch CRAN GU6 .... 184 H6
Stonehill HTHF TN21 .... 277 R5
Stonehill Crs BOGR PO21 .... 171 G2
Stonehill Pk BOR GU35 .... 179 G5
Stonehill Rd BOR GU35 .... 179 G5
Stonehouse Dr SLVH TN37 .... 283 N8
STLEO TN38 .... 98 F3
Stonehouse La SWTR RH13 .... 234 G5
Stonehouse Rd LIPH GU30 .... 194 A1
Stonehurst Ct BRIE/ROTT BN2 .... 5 L4
UCK TN22 .... 211 K11
Stonehurst La MAYF TN20 .... 211 P9
UCK TN22 .... 211 K11
Stonehurst Rd SALV BN13 .... 116 E8
Stone La SALV BN13 .... 116 E8
Stoneleigh Av BRI BN1 .... 82 E7
Stoneleigh Cl BRI BN1 .... 82 E7
EGRIN RH19 .... 31 L7
Stonelink Cl SLVH TN37 .... 283 N10
Stonepark Dr FROW RH18 .... 48 F7
Stone Pit La HAWK TN18 .... 218 B4
Stonepit La HFD BN5 .... 268 G4
Stonepound Rd
HPPT/KEY BN6 .... 271 M5
Stone Quarry Rd
RHWH RH17 .... 208 C2
Stone Rw RRTW TN3 * 36 A4
Stoners Cl HORL RH6 .... 27 J1
Stonery Cl PTSD BN41 .... 120 F3
Stonery Rd PTSD BN41 .... 120 F3
Stone Sq HAV PO9 .... 103 G1
Stonestile La RHAS TN35 .... 284 B6
Stone St BRI BN1 .... 4 B6
HAS TN34 .... 13 H6
RTW TN1 .... 38 A3
Stonewall Park Rd RRTW TN3 .... 36 B1
Stonewood Cl
SBGH/RUST TN4 * 37 M1
SEAF BN25 .... 175 J2
Stoneworks Cottages
RYE TN31 * 253 L10
Stoney Bottom GSHT GU26 .... 180 E3
Stoneybrook HORS RH12 .... 201 Q4
Stoney Hi PETW GU28 .... 229 K12
Stoney La RHWH RH17 .... 60 F4
SELS PO20 .... 300 C1
SHOR BN43 .... 120 B5
Stoney Stile Cl BOGR PO21 .... 171 H4
Stoney Stile La BOGR PO21 .... 171 H4
Stopham Cl SALV BN13 .... 116 F3
Stopham Rd CRAWE RH10 .... 44 B6
PUL/STOR RH20 .... 264 F2
Stor Meadow
PUL/STOR RH20 .... 266 A11
Storrington Cl HOVE BN3 .... 121 K3
RCCH PO18 .... 107 G6
Storrington Rd SALV BN13 .... 116 E1
Storrington Rd HORN PO8 .... 256 F9
PUL/STOR RH20 .... 298 E1
Story Rd CCH PO19 .... 7 J2
Stour Cl EPSF GU31 .... 223 N7
SALV BN13 .... 116 B5
Stour Rd SALV BN13 .... 116 B5
Stovolds Hi CRAN GU6 .... 184 D1
Straight Half Mile UCK TN22 .... 209 M10
Strand RYE TN31 .... 252 C8
Strand Cl CRAWE RH10 .... 44 C4
Strand Hi WSEA TN36 .... 286 E2
Strand Meadow
BUR/ETCH TN19 .... 214 G10
Strand Pde FERR BN12 .... 150 D1
The Strand BRIE/ROTT BN2 .... 154 F2
FERR BN12 .... 149 K5
Strand Wy MSEA/BNM PO22 .... 173 G2
Strange Gdn BOGR PO21 .... 171 K4
Stratford Pl BOGR PO21 * 2 C4
Stratford Rd WVILLE PO7 .... 288 B9
Stratford St RTW TN1 .... 38 B4
Strathfield Cl HWH RH16 .... 73 J5
Strathmoor Gdns MIDH GU29 .... 227 J4
Strathmore Cl SALV BN13 .... 150 D1
Strathmore Ct BEX TN40 * 137 K2
Strathmore Rd CRAWW RH11 .... 26 F8
SALV BN13 .... 150 D1
Stratton Cl MSEA/BNM PO22 .... 3 H3
Strawberry Cl RTWE/PEM TN2 .... 53 K1
Strawberry Flds RYE TN31 .... 218 D10
Strawberry La
PUL/STOR RH20 .... 266 E9
Strawson Ct HORL RH6 .... 22 E5
Stream Cl RCCH PO18 * 106 A8
Stream La BAT TN33 .... 249 J11
HAWK TN18 .... 216 G2
PUL/STOR RH20 .... 265 Q4
RHAS TN35 .... 285 F12
Stream Pk EGRIN RH19 .... 30 F6
Stream Pit La HAWK TN18 .... 217 Q4
Streamside Cl HAS TN34 .... 99 K2
Streat Bostall HPPT/KEY BN6 .... 272 F10
Streatfield Gdns HTHF TN21 .... 244 C5
Streatfield Rd HTHF TN21 .... 244 C5
UCK TN22 .... 76 D5
Streat La HPPT/KEY BN6 .... 272 F1
Streele La UCK TN22 .... 77 M3
Streele Vw UCK TN22 .... 76 F4
Street End La HTHF TN21 .... 244 C5
SELS PO20 .... 169 K2
Street End Rd SELS PO20 .... 169 K2
Streetfield Rd SWTR RH13 .... 200 C2
Street Hi CRAWE RH10 .... 44 F1
Streetlands BAT TN33 .... 249 M12
Street La HPPT/KEY BN6 .... 272 F1
RHWH RH17 .... 206 D1
The Street ANG/EP BN16 .... 148 B4
ARUN BN18 .... 111 K5
BAT TN33 .... 283 M1
BIL RH14 .... 197 R3
EPSF GU31 .... 258 D2
HORL RH6 .... 26 D2
HPPT/KEY BN6 .... 270 D3
HPPT/KEY BN6 .... 271 R1
LAN/SOMP BN15 .... 118 D5
LEWES BN7 .... 85 K8
MIDH GU29 .... 226 G7
POLE BN26 .... 89 J8
POLE BN26 .... 130 D2
POLE BN26 .... 160 F4
PUL/STOR RH20 .... 265 P3
PUL/STOR RH20 .... 266 G6
PUL/STOR RH20 .... 296 B2
PUL/STOR RH20 .... 298 G3
RASHW TN26 .... 221 H1
RCCH PO18 .... 109 J2

RDKG RH5 .... 24 C3
RHWH RH17 .... 236 D3
RING/NEW BN8 .... 128 A1
SALV BN13 .... 115 K4
SELS PO20 .... 139 L6
SHOR BN43 .... 119 J4
STEY/UB BN44 .... 78 E3
SWTR RH13 .... 200 G1
SWTR RH13 .... 235 K3
TENT TN30 .... 220 L2
TENT TN30 .... 221 L5
UCK TN22 .... 77 K7
Stretch HI PUL/STOR RH20 .... 230 B12
Stretham La HFD BN5 .... 269 K9
Strettington La RCCH PO18 .... 108 F2
Strettons Copse LIPH GU30 .... 193 Q10
Strickland CI CRAWE RH11 .... 42 D4
Stride CI CCH PO19 .... 7 J4
Stringer Rd RH17 .... 122 E2
The Stringwalk HAIL BN27 .... 92 B7
Stroma Gdns HAIL BN27 .... 91 L3
Strongs Pas HAS TN34 .... 13 L6
Strood Ga RHWH RH17 .... 238 F8
Strood La HORS RH12 .... 187 M10
Strood Rd HAS TN34 .... 12 A2
Strouden Ct HAV PO9 .... 288 E10
Stroud End PSF GU32 .... 223 J5
Stroudley CI CRAWE RH11 .... 44 A4
Stroudwood Rd HAV PO9 .... 103 H2
Strudgate CI CRAWE RH10 .... 45 A5
Stuart Av EAST BN21 .... 163 H7
Stuart CI CRAWE RH10 .... 44 B4
RTWE/PEM TN2 .... 53 L1
WTHG BN11 .... 21 M2
Stuart Wy EGRIN RH19 .... 47 L2
Stubbington Av BOR GU35 .... 178 F8
Stubb La RYE TN31 .... 250 E12
Stubcroft La SELS PO20 .... 168 A6
Stubfield HORS RH12 .... 201 R2
Stubpond La LING RH7 .... 30 C2
Studdens La HAIL BN27 .... 279 N8
Stumblemead RHWH RH17 .... 60 F8
Stumblets CRAWE RH10 .... 44 B2
Stumps La RCCH PO18 .... 140 B1
Sturdee CI LGNY BN23 .... 164 E6
Sturdee PI HAS TN34 * 13 J7
Sturges Rd BOGR PO21 .... 2 C6
Sturt Av HASM GU27 .... 181 J12
Sudbury CI BOGR PO21 .... 171 H4
Sudeley PI BRIE/ROTT BN2 .... 5 M9
Sudeley La BRIE/ROTT BN2 .... 5 L8
Sudeley Ter BRIE/ROTT BN2 .... 5 L8
Sudley Gdns BOGR PO21 .... 2 E7
Sudley Rd BOGR PO21 .... 2 E6
Suffolk CI HORL RH6 .... 22 F7
Suffolk Rd BEXW TN39 .... 97 H6
Suffolk St HOVE BN3 .... 121 L5
Sugar La RHWH RH17 .... 207 L4
Sugden Rd WTHG BN11 .... 21 L9
Sugworth CI HWH RH16 .... 73 G2
Sullington BRIE/ROTT BN2 .... 123 L1
Sullington Copse
PUL/STOR RH20 .... 266 B11
Sullington Gdns SALV BN13 .... 116 L1
Sullington HI CRAWW RH11 .... 8 E8
Sullington La
PUL/STOR RH20 .... 298 C1
Sullington Md HORS RH12 .... 201 P2
Sullington Wy SHOR BN43 .... 119 M5
Sullivan Dr CRAWW RH11 .... 42 D7
Sultan Rd EMRTH PO10 .... 104 A4
Sumach CI LW/ROSE BN22 .... 163 K3
Summer CI PTSD BN41 .... 120 F6
Summer Cottages
SBGH/RUST TN4 * 37 G5
Summercourt HAIL BN27 .... 92 A5
Summerdale Rd HOVE BN3 .... 121 J3
Summerdown CI
EDN/EASTW BN20 .... 176 D2
SALV BN13 .... 116 A8
Summerdown La
EDN/EASTW BN20 .... 303 J4
Summerdown Rd
EDN/EASTW BN20 .... 176 C2
Summerfield Rd SELS PO20 .... 167 H3
Summerfields SALV BN13 .... 298 H11
Summerfields Av HAIL BN27 .... 91 M5
Summerheath Rd HAIL BN27 .... 92 A5
Summer HI STLEO TN38 .... 98 F5
Summerhill CI HWH RH16 .... 73 H2
MSEA/BNM PO22 .... 145 J7
Summerhill Dr HWH RH16 .... 73 J2
MSEA/BNM PO22 .... 145 H7
Summerhill Gra HWH RH16 .... 73 J2
Summerhill La HWH RH16 .... 73 J2
Summer Hill Rd BEXW TN39 .... 96 E3
Summerhill Rd HORN PO8 .... 288 B6
Summerlands Rd
LW/ROSE BN22 .... 163 G3
Summerlands Wk HAV PO9 * 289 J12
Summer La BOGR PO21 .... 170 E4
Summerlea CI ANG/EP BN16 .... 148 A2
Summerlea Gdns
LHPTN BN17 * 147 K4
Summerley Cnr
MSEA/BNM PO22 * 173 C7
Summerley La
MSEA/BNM PO22 .... 145 G8
Summersdale Rd CCH PO19 .... 107 M4
Summersdeane STHW BN42 .... 120 L4
Summersvere CI CRAWE RH10 .... 27 M8
Summervale Rd
SBGH/RUST TN4 .... 37 J8
Sumner Rd EPSF GU31 .... 223 L12
Sumners RHWH RH17 .... 206 D2
Sun Brow HASM GU27 .... 181 J12
Sunbury CI BOR GU35 .... 178 H6
Sundale La MSEA/BNM PO22 .... 145 K8
Sunderland CI SELS PO20 .... 109 J3
Sunderland Ms
ANG/EP BN16 * 148 C4
Sunderton La HORN PO8 .... 256 D9
Sundew CI CRAWW RH11 .... 42 H1
Sunflower CI LHPTN BN17 .... 147 M1
Sunhill PI RTWE/PEM TN2 * 39 H3
Sunneymead CI SELS PO20 .... 301 L7
Sunningdale CI BEX TN40 .... 97 K8
HAIL BN27 .... 91 M4
SEAF BN25 .... 175 G3
Sunningdale Ct CRAWW RH11 * 8 E7
FERR BN12 * 150 B2
Sunningdale Dr STLEO TN38 .... 98 E6
Sunningdale Gdns
MSEA/BNM PO22 .... 144 A6

SELS PO20 * 167 J6
Sunningdale Rd SALV BN13 .... 116 C7
Sunninghill Av HOVE BN3 .... 121 K3
Sunninghill CI HOVE BN3 .... 121 K3
Sunny CI CRAWE RH10 .... 45 N1
Sunnybox La ARUN BN18 .... 111 J1
Sunnycroft CI UCK TN22 .... 76 F5
Sunny CI FERR BN12 .... 150 D4
Sunnycroft CI RHWH RH17 .... 238 H3
Sunnydale Av BRI BN1 .... 82 F7
Sunnydale CI BRI BN1 .... 82 F7
Sunnyheath HAV PO9 .... 102 F1
Sunnyhill CI CRAWE RH10 .... 45 N1
CRAWW RH11 * 8 E3
Sunnymead CI
MSEA/BNM PO22 .... 145 M8
Sunnymead Dr SELS PO20 .... 301 M7
Sunnyridge RRTW TN3 * 36 F1
Sunnyside CI ANG/EP BN16 .... 148 F1
Sunnyside Rd BOR GU35 .... 179 R5
SBGH/RUST TN4 .... 37 H5
Sunnywood Dr HWH RH16 .... 73 G6
Sunny Wy RCCH PO18 .... 106 A3
Sunnywood Dr HWH RH16 .... 73 G6
Sunset Av HAIL BN27 .... 90 A2
Sunset CI PEAHV BN10 .... 157 G4
PEV BN24 .... 134 D7
Sunstar La POLE BN26 .... 131 K7
Sun St LEWES BN7 .... 16 F5
Sunte Av HWH RH16 .... 73 J2
Sunte CI HWH RH16 .... 73 H2
Sunvale Av HASM GU27 .... 180 G11
Sunvale CI HASM GU27 .... 180 G11
Sunview Av PEAHV BN10 .... 157 J7
Sunwood Rd HAV PO9 .... 288 E10
CRAWW RH11 * 8 E3
Surrenden CI BRI BN1 .... 122 E1
Surrenden Crs BRI BN1 .... 122 E2
Surrenden Holt BRI BN1 .... 122 E2
Surrenden Pk BRI BN1 .... 122 F2
Surrenden Ri CRAWW RH11 .... 59 H1
Surrenden Rd BRI BN1 .... 122 E2
Surrey CI RTWE/PEM TN2 .... 53 L1
Surrey Rd SEAF BN25 .... 174 C1
Surrey St ARUN BN18 .... 112 F3
BRI BN1 .... 4 D4
LHPTN BN17 .... 147 J5
WTHG BN11 .... 20 F1
Surrey Whf ARUN BN18 .... 113 G3
Surry CI SHOR BN43 .... 119 L6
Susans CI RING/NEW BN8 .... 276 H4
Susan's Rd EAST BN21 .... 10 F6
Sussex Av HAIL BN27 .... 92 A5
Sussex Border Pth BRI BN1 .... 80 F4
BRI BN1 .... 82 A5
EDEN TN8 .... 33 H1
EGRIN RH19 .... 47 M4
EMRTH PO10 .... 104 B3
EMRTH PO10 .... 138 A2
EPSF GU31 .... 224 C12
HASM GU27 .... 182 E12
HASM GU27 .... 195 Q4
HAV PO9 .... 289 N9
HAWK TN18 .... 216 H3
HFD BN5 .... 80 F3
HORL RH6 .... 27 H1
HORL RH6 .... 28 D1
HORN PO8 .... 257 K9
HORN PO8 .... 289 L2
HORS RH12 .... 41 H2
HORS RH12 .... 185 K9
LIPH GU30 .... 193 R4
LISS GU33 .... 193 J7
MFD/CHID GU8 .... 183 R11
POY/PYE BN45 .... 81 L3
PTSD BN41 .... 80 D7
RDKG RH5 .... 186 N4
RHWH RH17 .... 207 N1
RRTW TN3 .... 35 J5
RYE TN31 .... 219 N11
TENT TN30 .... 220 C10
WADH TN5 .... 70 E4
WADH TN5 .... 191 M9
Sussex CI BEXW TN39 .... 96 E8
HAIL BN27 .... 92 A5
RTWE/PEM TN2 .... 38 B8
Sussex Ct BEX TN40 * 137 J1
HWH RH16 * 73 H6
Sussex Dr BOGR PO21 .... 170 F4
Sussex Gdns ANG/EP BN16 .... 148 A3
EDN/EASTW BN20 .... 302 H4
EPSF GU31 .... 223 N7
RHWH RH17 .... 73 L6
Sussex Gv SELS PO20 .... 168 B8
Sussex Hts BRI BN1 * 4 D1
Sussex Ms BRIE/ROTT BN2 .... 154 D1
RTWE/PEM TN2 .... 37 M7
Sussex PI BOGR PO21 * 2 F7
BRIE/ROTT BN2 .... 5 G5
HAIL BN27 * 279 P11
Sussex Rd EPSF GU31 .... 223 P7
HOVE BN3 .... 122 A4
HWH RH16 .... 73 H6
LAN/SOMP BN15 .... 119 H8
STLEO TN38 .... 98 F7
WTHG BN11 .... 21 H4
Sussex Sq BRIE/ROTT BN2 .... 154 D1
Sussex St BOGR PO21 .... 2 E7
BRIE/ROTT BN2 .... 5 G6
LHPTN BN17 .... 147 J3
Sussex Ter BRIE/ROTT BN2 .... 5 G5
MIDH GU29 .... 226 H10
Sussex Wy BURH RH15 .... 74 D5
PEAHV BN10 .... 156 E6
Sussex Whf SHOR BN43 * 120 A7
Sutherland Av BEXW TN39 .... 136 F2
Sutherland CI ANG/EP BN16 .... 148 A5
BEXW TN39 .... 136 F1
BOGR PO21 .... 2 C7
BOR GU35 .... 178 G8
Sutherland Rd
BRIE/ROTT BN2 .... 5 K7
RTW TN1 .... 38 A7
Sutton Av ANG/EP BN16 .... 148 B5
PEAHV BN10 .... 157 G6
SEAF BN25 .... 175 H2
Sutton Av North
PEAHV BN10 .... 157 G5
Sutton CI BRIE/ROTT BN2 .... 124 D4
MSEA/BNM PO22 .... 3 K1
Sutton Croft La SEAF BN25 .... 174 E2
Sutton Dro SEAF BN25 .... 174 E1
Sutton Fld BOR GU35 .... 178 F8
Sutton Park Rd SEAF BN25 .... 174 F1

Sutton PI BEX TN40 .... 137 K1
SEAF BN25 * 175 H1
Sutton Rd EAST BN21 .... 10 E6
SEAF BN25 .... 174 F2
The Suttons RYE TN31 .... 254 A12
STLEO TN38 .... 98 A13
Swaines Pas HAS TN34 .... 13 L6
Swaines Wy HTHF TN21 .... 244 D7
Swainham La STLEO TN38 .... 97 M2
Swainsthorpe CI HWH RH16 .... 73 J6
Swaledale CI CRAWW RH11 .... 8 E3
Swallow Bank STLEO TN38 .... 98 E3
Swallow CI HAV PO9 .... 103 J3
LGNY BN23 .... 164 A3
Swallow Ct UCK TN22 .... 76 F7
Swallow Dr BAT TN33 .... 282 G5
RTWE/PEM TN2 .... 38 E3
Swallowfield CI SWTR RH13 .... 202 H4
Swallow Fld Copse
SWTR RH13 .... 201 R10
Swallow Rd CRAWW RH11 .... 43 H1
Swallows CI
LAN/SOMP BN15 .... 119 H8
Swallows Green Dr
SALV BN13 .... 116 B8
Swallows La SWTR RH13 .... 267 Q1
The Swallows LHPTN BN17 * 147 G4
PEAHV BN10 .... 157 G4
Swallow St CRAWE RH10 .... 46 B4
PEV BN24 .... 132 F8
SALV BN13 .... 116 B6
Swallowtail Rd HORS RH12 .... 56 D3
Swamp Rd LYDD TN29 .... 255 P1
Swan Av HAS TN34 .... 13 K6
Swan Barn Rd HASM GU27 .... 181 N11
Swanborough Dr
BRIE/ROTT BN2 .... 123 L6
Swanborough Dro
LEWES BN7 .... 125 L2
Swanborough Hollow
LEWES BN7 .... 125 M1
Swanborough PI
BRIE/ROTT BN2 .... 123 L6
Swanbourne CI
LAN/SOMP BN15 .... 118 E5
Swanbourne Rd
LHPTN BN17 .... 147 J2
Swan CI EMRTH PO10 .... 104 B6
PUL/STOR RH20 .... 265 K11
RING/NEW BN8 .... 273 P2
SWTR RH13 .... 201 R11
Swan Cnr PUL/STOR RH20 .... 265 J3
Swan Cottages TENT TN30 .... 220 C6
Swan Ct PUL/STOR RH20 * 265 J3
Swandean CI SALV BN13 .... 116 D5
Swan Dene BOGR PO21 .... 170 D4
Swanfield Dr CCH PO19 .... 7 J2
Swan La CRBK TN17 .... 189 R6
HORL RH6 .... 26 E2
Swanley CI LGNY BN23 .... 164 C3
Swanmore Rd HAV PO9 .... 288 E10
Swann CI BURH RH15 .... 75 H4
Swannee CI PEAHV BN10 .... 157 J4
Swann Wy HORS RH12 .... 201 P2
Swan Rd HAIL BN27 .... 92 B7
Swansbrook La HTHF TN21 .... 278 A8
Swansea Gdns BOGR PO21 .... 2 B7
Swans Ghyll FROW RH18 .... 48 D6
Swan St PSF GU32 .... 223 M6
TENT TN30 .... 220 B4
Swan Ter HAS TN34 .... 13 K6
Swan Vw PUL/STOR RH20 .... 265 K3
Swan Wk HORS RH12 * 14 C9
Swarraton Rd HAV PO9 .... 103 H2
Sway Ct HAV PO9 .... 289 J12
Swaylands Av CROW TN6 .... 210 G2
Swaythling Rd HAV PO9 .... 288 E11
Sweeps Hill CI RTWE/PEM TN2 .... 39 J2
Sweetbriar Gdns WVILLE PO7 .... 288 A12
Sweethaws La CROW TN6 .... 210 D3
Sweetings La WADH TN5 .... 190 C4
Sweetlands HPPT/KEY BN6 .... 271 P4
Swife La HTHF TN21 .... 245 M2
Swift CI BURH RH15 .... 74 B6
CROW TN6 .... 67 J8
HORN PO8 .... 288 B2
UCK TN22 .... 76 F7
Swift La CRAWW RH11 .... 43 H1
Swift Rd EMRTH PO10 .... 138 B2
Swift Wy LHPTN BN17 .... 147 H1
Swillage La SALV BN13 .... 114 F1
Swinburne Av
LW/ROSE BN22 .... 163 G2
Swinburn Gdns HORN PO8 .... 288 A5
Swindon Rd HORS RH12 .... 14 A2
Swiss Gdns SHOR BN43 .... 119 K6
Swissland HI EGRIN RH19 .... 31 K3
Sword CI HORN PO8 .... 256 C8
Swynford Dr STLEO TN38 .... 283 N12
Sybron Wy CROW TN6 .... 211 L1
Sycamore Av CRAWW RH11 .... 57 H4
HOVE BN3 .... 122 A8
Sycamore CI ANG/EP BN16 .... 148 E1
BEXW TN39 .... 96 B8
BRIE/ROTT BN2 .... 124 D5
CRAWW RH11 .... 27 H8
HORN PO8 .... 256 D8
HTHF TN21 .... 244 C7
LW/ROSE BN22 .... 163 J2
PTSD BN41 .... 121 H2
SEAF BN25 .... 175 J2
STLEO TN38 .... 98 F4
Sycamore Ct UCK TN22 .... 76 F4
Sycamore Dr EGRIN RH19 .... 31 M8
HAIL BN27 .... 92 A8
Sycamore Rd
MSEA/BNM PO22 .... 144 B6
The Sycamores
PEAHV BN10 .... 157 J4
Sydmonton Ct HAV PO9 .... 289 J11
Sydney CI STLEO TN38 .... 99 G2
Sydney Little Rd
STLEO TN38 .... 98 C1
Sydney Rd BOR GU35 .... 178 G6
HWH RH16 .... 73 H3
LW/ROSE BN22 .... 11 G5
Sydney St BRI BN1 .... 4 E5
Syers Rd LISS GU33 .... 192 C9
Syke Cluan CI
MSEA/BNM PO22 .... 111 G7
Sylvan CI HWH RH16 .... 73 L5
Sylvan Rd CRAWE RH10 .... 9 K8
LAN/SOMP BN15 .... 118 A7
Sylvan Vw WVILLE PO7 .... 288 A12
Sylvan Wy BOGR PO21 .... 2 A7
Sylvester Wy HOVE BN3 .... 121 L4
Sylvia CI BOGR PO21 .... 170 F4
Symbister Rd PTSD BN41 .... 121 H6
Syresham Gdns HWH RH16 .... 73 H5

Tabard Ga BOGR PO21 .... 171 G4
Tack Lee Rd ARUN BN18 .... 145 L2
Tackleway HAS TN34 .... 13 L6
Taddington Rd LW/ROSE BN22 .... 11 J3
Tagdell La HORN PO8 .... 288 A4
Tainter's Brook UCK TN22 .... 77 H4
Talbot CI HAV PO9 .... 102 E3
Talbot Crs BRI BN1 .... 83 J7
Talbot La RHWH RH12 .... 14 D7
Talbot Pk RTWE/PEM TN2 .... 38 C4
Talbot Rd HAV PO9 .... 102 E2
HAWK TN18 .... 216 H3
LHPTN BN17 .... 147 H4
Talbot Ter LEWES BN7 .... 16 F5
Talland Pde SEAF BN25 * 174 E3
Tall Ash Dr SLVH 99 J1
Tallis CI CRAWW RH11 .... 42 E6
Tall Oaks HWH RH16 .... 73 L4
Tall Timbers HAIL BN27 * 90 A2
Tall Trees EGRIN RH19 * 47 L1
Talman CI CRAWW RH11 * 42 D4
Tamarack CI LW/ROSE BN22 .... 163 J3
Tamar Av SALV BN13 .... 116 B5
Tamar CI CRAWE RH10 .... 44 A3
PEV BN24 .... 132 F8
SALV BN13 .... 116 B6
Tamar Down WVILLE PO7 .... 288 B10
Tamarisk CI MSEA/BNM PO22 .... 144 B7
WVILLE PO7 .... 288 B12
Tamarisk Wk SELS PO20 .... 167 J3
Tamarisk Wy ANG/EP BN16 .... 148 D5
FERR BN12 .... 149 L3
Tamar Wy SELS PO20 .... 109 J3
Tamplin Ter BRIE/ROTT BN2 .... 5 G3
Tamworth Rd HOVE BN3 .... 121 L6
Tanbridge Pk HORS RH12 .... 14 A7
Tanbridge PI HORS RH12 .... 14 A8
Tanbridge Rd LGNY BN23 .... 164 E4
Tandridge Rd HOVE BN3 .... 121 K7
Tangier La RRTW TN3 .... 54 A3
Tangle Oak EGRIN RH19 .... 30 D5
Tanglewood Coppice
BEXW TN39 .... 136 D2
Tangley Wk HAV PO9 .... 289 J12
Tangmere CI BEXW TN39 .... 136 D2
Tangmere Gdns BOGR PO21 .... 171 J3
Tangmere Rd BRI BN1 .... 82 F7
CRAWW RH11 .... 42 B5
SELS PO20 .... 108 B5
Tanhouse La RYE TN31 .... 251 Q3
Tankerdale La LISS GU33 .... 223 R1
The Tanneries HAV PO9 * 102 F4
Tanners Brook LEWES BN7 .... 17 C7
Tanners Cross HWH RH16 .... 72 F7
Tanners Fld RHWH RH17 .... 204 F4
Tanners La HASM GU27 .... 181 M10
Tanners Md RHWH RH17 .... 204 F4
Tanners Wy CROW TN6 .... 67 M8
Tannery CI CCH PO19 * 6 A5
SWTR RH13 .... 200 F1
Tansy CI WVILLE PO7 .... 288 B11
Tansy Md PUL/STOR RH20 .... 265 Q11
Tanyard HAWK TN18 .... 217 Q4
Tanyard Av EGRIN RH19 .... 47 M1
Tanyard CI CRAWE RH10 .... 44 B6
SWTR RH13 .... 15 C3
Tanyard La RHWH RH17 .... 208 C3
STEY/UB BN44 .... 78 B2
Tanyard Wy HORL RH6 .... 23 G4
Tapsell's La WADH TN5 .... 71 H4
Tarbery Crs HORN PO8 .... 288 C5
Tarham CI HORL RH6 .... 22 D4
Tarmount La SHOR BN43 .... 119 L6
Tarner Rd BRIE/ROTT BN2 .... 5 H6
Tarn Ri HORN PO8 .... 256 D11
Tarn Rd GSHT GU26 .... 180 G6
Tarragon Wy SHOR BN43 .... 120 B4
Tarrant Gdns HAV PO9 .... 102 E2
Tarrant Sq ARUN BN18 * 113 G3
Tarrant St ARUN BN18 .... 113 G3
Tarrant Whf ARUN BN18 .... 113 G3
Tarring CI RHWH RH9 .... 158 C3
Tarring Ga SALV BN13 * 20 L3
Tarring Rd WTHG BN11 .... 20 C3
Tas Combe Wy
EDN/EASTW BN20 .... 163 G2
Tasman CI ANG/EP BN16 .... 148 C5
Tasmania Wy LGNY BN23 .... 164 F3
Tasman Wy SALV BN13 .... 116 B6
Tate Crs BURH RH15 .... 74 E4
Tates Wy HORS RH12 .... 186 A10
Taunton Rd BRIE/ROTT BN2 .... 123 L4
Taunton Wy BRIE/ROTT BN2 .... 123 M4
Tavern CI HASM GU27 .... 195 L7
Taverner PI CCH PO19 .... 7 L8
Tavistock Down BRI BN1 .... 123 H3
Tavistock Gdns HAV PO9 .... 103 J4
Tavy CI SALV BN13 .... 116 B7
Tavy Rd SALV BN13 .... 116 B7
Taw CI SALV BN13 .... 116 C6
Taylor CI STLEO TN38 .... 98 E1
Taylors CI BOR GU35 .... 179 J2
Taylors La MIDH GU29 .... 226 H11
RCCH PO18 .... 140 B1
Taylors Ri MIDH GU29 .... 226 H11
Taylor St SBGH/RUST TN4 .... 37 L1
Taylor Wk CRAWW RH11 .... 8 D3
Tea Garden La RRTW TN3 .... 37 H1
Teal CI HORN PO8 .... 288 B2
HORS RH12 .... 56 B4
Teal Ct STLEO TN38 .... 98 D2
Teal La SELS PO20 .... 301 L5
Teasel CI CRAWW RH11 .... 43 G6
Teazle CI EPSF GU31 .... 223 P8
Tedder St SBGH/RUST TN4 .... 38 A2
Teesdale CRAWW RH11 .... 8 D9
Teg CI PTSD BN41 .... 121 H3
Teise CI RTWE/PEM TN2 .... 38 D2
Telconia CI BOR GU35 .... 179 R5
Telgarth Rd FERR BN12 .... 149 K5
Telham La HAS TN34 .... 284 D12
Telham Ct CRAWW RH11 * 42 E6
Telham La BAT TN33 .... 282 F8
Telscombe Cliffs Wy
PEAHV BN10 .... 156 F5
Telscombe CI PEAHV BN10 .... 157 J3

Telscombe Pk PEAHV BN10 .... 157 H3
Telscombe Rd LGNY BN23 .... 164 E3
PEAHV BN10 .... 157 H3
Tempest Av WVILLE PO7 .... 288 B10
Templars CI MSEA/BNM PO22 .... 145 J7
The Templars SALV BN13 .... 117 K6
Temple CI CRAWE RH10 .... 44 C4
Temple Gdns HOVE BN3 4
Temple Gv BURH RH15 .... 74 C5
Temple La RDKG RH5 .... 24 C3
Temple Rd LISS GU33 .... 192 D7
Templesheen Rd
MSEA/BNM PO22 .... 146 A3
Temple St BRI BN1 .... 4 A6
Tenacre CI CCH PO19 .... 108 B5
Ten Acres WTHG BN11 .... 151 M2
Tenantry Down Rd
BRIE/ROTT BN2 .... 123 K6
Tenantry Rd BRIE/ROTT BN2 .... 123 J5
Tennis CI HAIL BN27 .... 92 A6
Tennis Rd HOVE BN3 .... 121 K7
Tennyson Av ANG/EP BN16 .... 147 M4
Tennyson CI CRAWE RH10 .... 44 A1
HORS RH12 .... 56 D3
Tennyson Ri EGRIN RH19 .... 31 H8
Tennyson Rd BOGR PO21 .... 171 M2
WTHG BN11 .... 20 F5
Tennyson's La HASM GU27 .... 195 P1
Tenterden CI LGNY BN23 .... 164 C4
Tenterden Ri HAS TN34 .... 12 D1
Tenterden Rd RASHW TN26 .... 221 P11
Terminus Av BEXW TN39 .... 136 E2
Terminus CI EGRIN RH19 * 47
Terminus MI CCH PO19 * 6 C4
Terminus PI BRI BN1 .... 4 D3
LHPTN BN17 .... 147 J4
Terminus Rd UCK TN22 .... 242 G7
BEXW TN39 .... 136 F2
BRI BN1 .... 4 D3
CCH PO19 .... 7 G5
EAST BN21 .... 10 E6
LHPTN BN17 .... 147 H4
Terminus St BRI BN1 .... 4 D3
Tern Rd CRAWW RH11 .... 42 C4
Terrace Rd SLVH TN37 .... 12 B8
The Terrace ARUN BN18 * 113 K4
FERR BN12 * 150 B3
LAN/SOMP BN15 .... 152 D1
Terringes Av SALV BN13 .... 116 D8
Terry Rd CRAWW RH11 .... 43 G8
Terwick La EPSF GU31 .... 225 P9
Test CI EPSF GU31 .... 223 M8
Testers CI SWTR RH13 .... 233 R2
Test Rd LAN/SOMP BN15 .... 118 A7
Testwood Rd HAV PO9 .... 288 B7
Teville Ga WTHG BN11 .... 21 G3
Teville PI WTHG BN11 .... 20 F5
Teville Rd WTHG BN11 .... 21 G3
Thackeray CI LGNY BN23 .... 164 D2
Thackeray Rd SALV BN13 .... 21 L1
Thakeham CI ANG/EP BN16 .... 149 G2
BEX TN40 .... 97 M7
FERR BN12 .... 149 M3
Thakeham Copse
PUL/STOR RH20 .... 266 E11
Thakeham Dr FERR BN12 .... 149 M3
Thakeham Rd PUL/STOR RH20 .... 266 C11
Thalassa Rd WTHG BN11 .... 152 A2
Thames CI BRIE/ROTT BN2 .... 5 H8
LHPTN BN17 .... 147 M5
Thames Wy SALV BN13 .... 116 C6
Thanet Wy HAS TN34 .... 12 B2
The Thatch Ct
LAN/SOMP BN15 * 118 E5
Thatcher CI CRAWE RH10 .... 8 E5
Thatchers CI BURH RH15 .... 75 J8
HORL RH6 .... 23 G4
HORS RH12 .... 15 G1
The Thatchings POLE BN26 .... 131 M8
Thatchway CI LHPTN BN17 .... 147 J3
The Thatchway ANG/EP BN16 .... 114 C5
ANG/EP BN16 .... 148 C5
Theaklen Dr STLEO TN38 .... 99 G3
Theatre La CCH PO19 .... 6 E5
Thelton Av HORS RH12 .... 201 N4
Theobalds Gn HTHF TN21 .... 244 D8
Theobalds Rd BURH RH15 .... 75 H4
Theodore CI RTWE/PEM TN2 .... 38 D2
Thesiger CI HAV PO9 .... 103 J3
Thesiger Rd WTHG BN11 .... 151 M1
Theydon CI CRAWE RH10 .... 9 J7
Thicket La RCCH PO18 .... 294 A12
Third Av BEX TN40 .... 97 K7
HAV PO9 .... 103 H3
HOVE BN3 .... 122 A8
LAN/SOMP BN15 .... 118 D6
MSEA/BNM PO22 .... 173 G1
NEWHV BN9 .... 18 E5
SALV BN13 .... 117 J4
SELS PO20 .... 168 A8
SELS PO20 .... 168 D5
Third Rd PEAHV BN10 .... 156 F6
Third St RRTW TN3 .... 36 F6
Thirlmere CI BOR GU35 .... 179 J1
Thirlmere Crs LAN/SOMP BN15 .... 118 C4
SBGH/RUST TN4 .... 37 J3
Thirlmere Wy
MSEA/BNM PO22 .... 145 G8
Thistledown HORN PO8 .... 288 C4
Thistledowne Gdns
EMRTH PO10 .... 104 C5
Thistle Wy SWTR RH13 .... 201 R10
Thistledown V BIL RH14 * 198 E1
Thomas Brassey CI SLVH TN37 .... 283 Q12
Thomas St LEWES BN7 .... 17 J4
SBGH/RUST TN4 .... 37 M4
Thomas Turner Dr
RING/NEW BN8 .... 276 H4
Thompson Rd BRI BN1 .... 123 H4
MSEA/BNM PO22 .... 145 L8
NEWHV BN9 .... 158 B3
Thomson CI EGRIN RH19 .... 31 H4
Thorgate Rd LHPTN BN17 .... 147 K5
Thornbush Crs PTSD BN41 .... 121 G2
Thorn CI EPSF GU31 .... 223 R7
Thorncroft Rd LHPTN BN17 .... 147 L5
Thorndean Dr RHWH RH17 .... 204 E10
Thorndean Rd BRIE/ROTT BN2 .... 123 J2
Thorndon CI CRBK TN17 .... 219 K1
Thorndyke CI CRAWE RH10 .... 44 C4
Thorne Crs BEXW TN39 .... 96 D4
Thorney Dr SELS PO20 .... 301 J7

Thorney Old Pk EMRTH PO10 ... 138 E4
Thorney Rd EMRTH PO10 ... 104 C8
Thornfield Gdns
  RTWE/PEM TN2 ... 38 E4
Thornham La EMRTH PO10 ... 104 C7
Thornhill Av BRI BN1 ... 82 F6
Thornhill Cl HOVE BN3 ... 121 K3
Thornhill Ri PTSD BN41 ... 120 F1
Thornhill Vw GSHT GU26 * ... 180 G6
Thornhill Wy PTSD BN41 ... 120 F1
Thornhurst BURH RH15 ... 75 H8
Thorn Rd WTHG BN11 ... 20 C7
Thornscroft STEY/UB BN44 ... 78 C1
The Thorns RHAS TN35 ... 285 K6
Thornton Cl HORL RH6 ... 22 D6
Thornton Meadow BIL RH14 ... 231 J1
Thornton Pl HORL RH6 ... 22 D6
Thorntons Shaw UCK TN22 * ... 242 C11
Thornwell Rd POLE BN26 ... 130 E6
Thornwood Cl LW/ROSE BN22 ... 163 K3
Thorny Cl HTHF TN21 ... 244 D6
Threals Copse PUL/STOR RH20 ... 266 D8
Threal's La PUL/STOR RH20 ... 266 B7
Three Acres HORS RH12 ... 201 R4
Three Bridges Rd CRAWE RH10 ... 9 J4
Three Gates La HASM GU27 ... 181 N10
Three Leg Cross Rd WADH TN5 ... 191 J10
Three Oaks La WADH TN5 ... 71 H3
Threestile Rd HORS RH12 ... 166 E2
Thresher Rd WVILLE PO7 ... 288 D8
Thrusloes BOGR PO21 ... 171 L2
Thruxton Rd HAV PO9 ... 288 D12
Thurlow Rd WTHG BN11 ... 4 E5
Thurne Wy HORS RH12 ... 186 A10
Thurrock Cl LW/ROSE BN20 ... 162 F2
Thyme Cl SHOR BN43 ... 120 B4
Thyssel La RYE TN31 ... 218 E11
Tibbs Court La STPH/PW TN12 ... 188 F3
Tibbs Mill La UCK TN22 ... 210 F8
Ticehurst Av BEXW TN39 ... 95 L8
Ticehurst Cl CRAWE RH10 ... 44 D3
  RHAS TN35 ... 100 E3
Ticehurst Rd BRIE/ROTT BN2 ... 123 L8
Tichborne St BRI BN1 ... 4 E6
Tickerage La UCK TN22 ... 242 C11
Tidebrook WADH TN5 ... 71 G8
Tidebrook Gdns LGNY BN23 ... 164 C6
Tideswell Rd EAST BN21 ... 10 F6
Tideway LHPTN BN17 ... 147 M5
Tidworth Rd HAV PO9 ... 103 C1
Tidy St BRI BN1 ... 4 E5
Tilbury Pl BRIE/ROTT BN2 ... 5 C6
Tilbury's Cl BOR GU35 ... 178 C6
Tilbury Wy BRIE/ROTT BN2 ... 5 C6
Tile Barn Cl UCK TN22 ... 275 K1
Tile Barn La SLVN BN20 ... 168 B4
Tile Barn Rd STLEO TN38 ... 98 E1
Tilehurst Dr HAIL BN27 ... 91 M5
Tile Kiln RING/NEW BN8 ... 275 J11
Tilekiln La RHAS TN35 ... 100 D1
Tilers Cl BURH RH15 ... 75 J4
Tilford Rd GSHT GU26 ... 181 J4
  HORN PO8 ... 288 A3
Tilgate BRIE/ROTT BN2 ... 5 L5
  EAST BN21 ... 163 J6
Tilgate Dr BEXW TN39 ... 136 C2
  CRAWE RH10 ... 43 K8
Tilgate Forest Ldg
  CRAWW RH11 * ... 59 H5
Tilgate Pde CRAWE RH10 ... 43 K6
Tilgate Pl CRAWE RH10 ... 43 K6
Tilgate Wy CRAWE RH10 ... 9 G2
Tilletts La HORS RH13 ... 187 P9
Tilley La HAIL BN27 ... 280 C12
Tillingham Av RYE TN31 ... 252 B4
Tillingham Cl PEV BN24 ... 132 F8
Tillingham La RYE TN31 ... 251 Q7
Tillingham Vw RYE TN31 ... 250 E8
Tillinghurst La RHWH RH17 ... 61 L7
Tillington Gdns HORN PO8 ... 256 B4
Tillington Rd PETW GU28 ... 229 K10
Tillington Ter RHAS TN35 ... 100 B3
Tillotson Rd CRAWE RH10 ... 44 C4
Tillstone Cl BRIE/ROTT BN2 ... 5 H6
Tillstone St BRIE/ROTT BN2 ... 5 H7
Tilmore Gdns PSF GU32 ... 223 N4
Tilmore Rd PSF GU32 ... 223 N4
Tilsmore Cnr HTHF TN21 ... 244 C6
Tilsmore Rd HTHF TN21 ... 244 C6
Tiltwood Dr CRAWE RH10 ... 30 B8
Timber Cl SALV BN13 ... 116 D4
Timber Ct HORS RH12 ... 14 C3
Timberham Farm Rd HORL RH6 ... 27 J1
Timberlaine Rd PEV BN24 ... 165 H2
Timberlands CRAWW RH11 ... 43 G5
  PUL/STOR RH20 ... 266 B11
Timberlea Cl PUL/STOR RH20 ... 267 K9
Timberley Gdns UCK TN22 ... 77 G8
Timberley Rd LW/ROSE BN22 ... 163 L3
Timberleys LHPTN BN17 ... 147 L2
Timber Ml SWTR RH13 ... 201 Q11
Timbermill Ct HASM GU27 ... 181 J11
Timbers Ct HAIL BN27 ... 92 B5
The Timbers SWTR RH13 ... 202 H3
Timber Yd Cottages
  LEWES BN7 ... 16 J6
Timsbury Crs HAV PO9 ... 102 F4
Tindal Cl BURH RH15 ... 75 J4
Tinghall BOGR PO21 ... 171 K2
Tinker's La UCK TN22 ... 243 M1
  WADH TN5 ... 191 J10
Tinsley Cl CRAWE RH10 ... 27 M8
Tinsley Gn CRAWE RH10 ... 28 A6
Tinsley La CRAWE RH10 ... 27 M8
Tinsley La North CRAWE RH10 ... 28 A6
Tinsley La South CRAWE RH10 ... 43 M1
Tintern Cl BRI BN1 ... 123 C4
  LW/ROSE BN22 ... 163 J2
Tintern Rd CRAWW RH11 ... 42 F5
Tinwood La PUL/STOR RH20 ... 293 P12
Tipper La EPSF GU31 ... 258 C3
Tisbury Rd HOVE BN3 ... 122 B7
Tisted Ct HAV PO9 * ... 289 J12
Titchfield Cl BURH RH15 ... 75 J4
Titch Hl LAN/SOMP BN15 ... 117 M1
Tithe Barn Cl SALV BN13 ... 116 B6
Tithe Barn Fld WSEA TN36 ... 285 Q4
Tithe Barn Wy BOGR PO21 ... 171 L4
Tithe Gn ANG/EP BN16 ... 148 A4
Tithe Orch EGRIN RH19 ... 30 D5
The Tithings WVILLE PO7 ... 288 A10
Titian Rd HOVE BN3 ... 121 L6
Titnore La CRAWE RH10 ... 43 L6
Titnore La FERR BN12 ... 115 M7
Titnore Wy SALV BN13 ... 115 M8
Titus Gdns WVILLE PO7 ... 288 B9

Tiverton Dr BEX TN40 ... 97 K8
Tivoli Crs BRI BN1 ... 122 C4
Tivoli Crs North BRI BN1 ... 122 C3
Tivoli Pl BRI BN1 ... 122 C3
Tivoli Rd BRI BN1 ... 122 C3
Toat La PUL/STOR RH20 ... 230 H10
Toddington La LHPTN BN17 ... 147 J1
Toddington Pk LHPTN BN17 ... 147 K1
Todds Cl HORL RH6 ... 22 D4
Todmore LISS GU33 ... 192 C2
Toftwood Cl CRAWE RH10 ... 44 B4
Tolhurst La WADH TN5 ... 190 F12
Tolkien Rd LGNY BN23 ... 164 E3
Tollgate PEAHV BN10 ... 157 G4
Tollgate Gdns LGNY BN23 * ... 164 C6
Tollgate Hl CRAWW RH11 ... 59 H1
Tollgate La RHWH RH17 ... 72 B1
Tollgates BAT TN33 ... 282 C5
The Tollgate RBTBR TN32 ... 249 M4
Tollhouse Cl CCH PO19 ... 6 C1
Toll La UCK TN22 ... 209 L8
Tollwood Pk CROW TN6 ... 68 A8
Tollwood Rd CROW TN6 ... 211 J1
Toll Wood Rd HTHF TN21 ... 278 C2
Tompset's Bank FROW RH18 ... 64 E1
Tomtit Crs CRAWE RH10 ... 46 B4
Tomtits La FROW RH18 ... 48 D8
Tonbridge Rd RTWE/PEM TN2 ... 38 F1
Tonbridge Wy RYE TN31 ... 253 R11
Tongdean Av HOVE BN3 ... 122 C1
Tongdean La BRI BN1 ... 122 C1
Tongdean Ri BRI BN1 ... 122 C1
Tongdean Rd HOVE BN3 ... 122 A2
Tong La STPH/PW TN12 ... 188 G6
Tong Rd STPH/PW TN12 ... 188 G4
Toomey Rd STEY/UB BN44 ... 268 C12
Topaz Gv WVILLE PO7 ... 288 C9
Top Cross Rd BEX TN40 ... 97 M6
Top Dr UCK TN22 ... 209 M11
Top Rd ARUN BN18 ... 294 H12
  EGRIN RH19 ... 62 E4
  TENT TN30 ... 221 K6
Top St RHWH RH17 ... 236 D1
Torberry Dr EPSF GU31 ... 223 Q7
Tor Cl WVILLE PO7 ... 102 A2
Torcross Cl BRIE/ROTT BN2 ... 123 K5
Torfield Cl RHAS TN34 ... 13 L5
Torfield Rd EAST BN21 ... 10 D4
Toronto Cl SALV BN13 ... 116 C7
Toronto Dr HORL RH6 ... 23 H7
Toronto Ter BRIE/ROTT BN2 ... 5 M5
  LEWES BN7 ... 16 F5
Torrance Cl HOVE BN3 ... 121 L5
Torridge Cl SALV BN13 ... 116 B7
Torrington Cl BOR GU35 * ... 179 K4
Tor Rd PEAHV BN10 ... 157 H5
Tor Rd West PEAHV BN10 ... 157 G3
Tortington Mnr ARUN BN18 * ... 112 D6
Torton Hill Rd ARUN BN18 ... 112 F3
Tor Wy EPSF GU31 ... 223 P6
Tote La MIDH GU29 ... 226 D3
Totland Rd BRIE/ROTT BN2 ... 5 L2
Tottington Dr HFD BN5 ... 269 K11
Tottington Wy SHOR BN43 ... 120 A4
Tott Yew Rd
  EDN/EASTW BN20 ... 162 F1
Tourney Rd LYDD TN29 ... 255 Q8
Tovey Cl EAST BN21 ... 10 A3
Tower Cl CCH PO19 ... 6 D3
  EGRIN RH19 ... 31 J1
  HORL RH6 ... 22 E6
  PEV BN24 ... 134 C2
Tower Ct EGRIN RH19 * ... 31 K7
Tower Gdns HAV PO9 ... 103 C3
Towergate BRI BN1 ... 122 D3
Tower Hl SWTR RH13 ... 201 R5
Tower House Cl RHWH RH17 ... 72 B2
Tower Mill Pl POLE BN26 * ... 131 M8
Tower Ride UCK TN22 ... 76 F3
Tower Rd BRIE/ROTT BN2 ... 5 J4
  GSHT GU26 ... 180 H5
  HORS RH12 ... 57 M1
  LAN/SOMP BN15 ... 117 M1
  LIPH GU30 ... 193 M12
  SLVN TN37 ... 12 A4
  WTHG BN11 ... 21 J4
Tower Rd West STLEO TN38 ... 99 G5
Towerscroft Av SLVN TN37 ... 283 N10
Towers Rd STEY/UB BN44 ... 79 C3
Tower St CCH PO19 ... 6 D3
  EMRTH PO10 ... 104 B5
  HTHF TN21 ... 244 B5
  RYE TN31 ... 252 H7
Tower Vw UCK TN22 ... 76 F3
Town Barn Rd CRAWW RH11 ... 8 B3
Town Cross Av BOGR PO21 ... 2 C5
Town Hall Rd HAV PO9 ... 103 H4
Town Hl RRTW TN3 ... 190 F1
Townlands Rd WADH TN5 ... 71 L5
Town La PSF GU32 ... 223 Q4
Town Md CRAWW RH11 ... 8 D1
Town Quay ARUN BN18 * ... 113 G2
Townsend Crs LHPTN BN17 ... 147 L3
Tozer Wy CCH PO19 ... 7 H4
Trafalgar Cl EMRTH PO10 ... 104 C5
  PEAHV BN10 ... 157 H4
  SLVN TN37 ... 283 N10
Trafalgar Ct BRI BN1 ... 4 F4
Trafalgar Ga BRIE/ROTT BN2 ... 154 C2
Trafalgar La BRI BN1 ... 4 E5
Trafalgar Pl BRI BN1 ... 4 E4
Trafalgar Ri HORN PO8 ... 256 C8
Trafalgar Rd HORS RH12 ... 14 C2
  PTSD BN41 ... 121 G5
Trafalgar St BRI BN1 ... 4 E4
Trafalgar Ter BRI BN1 * ... 4 E4
Tram Rd RYE TN31 ... 253 M11
Tramway Cl SELS PO20 ... 141 L5
Transit Rd NEWHV BN9 ... 19 H4
Travellers La RHAS TN35 ... 100 B2
Treadcroft Dr HORS RH12 ... 56 H4
Treadwheel Rd HORN PO8 ... 288 H3
Trebilco Cl RTWE/PEM TN2 ... 38 C2
Treblers Rd CROW TN6 ... 69 L3
Tredcroft Rd HOVE BN3 ... 122 A5
Tree Av HASM GU27 ... 181 J9
Treemans Rd (Lewes Rd)
  RHWH RH17 ... 207 M6
Treetops SWTR RH13 ... 233 Q2
Tree Tops Cl BRIE/ROTT BN2 ... 124 D5
Treeview CRAWW RH11 ... 43 H8
Trefoil Cl HORS RH12 ... 56 D4
  WVILLE PO7 ... 288 A10
Trefoil Crs CRAWW RH11 ... 42 F7
Tregarth Rd CCH PO19 ... 107 M3

Treharne Cl SALV BN13 ... 116 C6
Treloar Rd HISD PO11 ... 166 A4
Tremola Av BRIE/ROTT BN2 ... 156 B3
Trenches Rd CROW TN6 ... 67 L8
Trende Gn BOGR PO21 ... 171 L2
Trenear Cl SWTR RH13 ... 15 G6
Trent Cl CRAWE RH11 ... 42 E5
  LAN/SOMP BN15 ... 118 B7
Trent Rd FERR BN12 ... 150 D3
Tretawn Gdns SELS PO20 ... 301 M10
Trevanne Plat CRAWE RH10 ... 44 C2
Trevelyan Pl HWH RH16 * ... 73 H4
Treveor Cl WTHG BN11 ... 20 F5
Treyford Rd BRIE/ROTT BN2 ... 124 D4
  CRAWW RH11 ... 42 F5
Triangle Cottages
  RHWH RH17 ... 204 D3
Triangle Rd HWH RH16 ... 73 H6
The Triangle
  EDN/EASTW BN20 ... 162 F2
Triangle Wy BURH RH15 ... 74 C4
Trig St RDKG RH5 ... 24 D1
Trimmers Wd GSHT GU26 ... 180 G3
Trinity Cl CRAWE RH10 ... 44 B1
  RTWE/PEM TN2 ... 38 C5
Trinity Ms HAS TN34 * ... 12 F7
Trinity Pl EAST BN21 ... 10 F7
Trinity Rd HPPT/KEY BN6 ... 270 C1
Trinity St BRIE/ROTT BN2 ... 5 M2
  HAS TN34 ... 12 F7
Trinity Trees EAST BN21 ... 10 F7
Trinity Vls HAS TN34 ... 12 E7
Tripp Hl PUL/STOR RH20 ... 264 A6
Tristan Gdns SBGH/RUST TN4 ... 37 H5
Tristram Cl LAN/SOMP BN15 ... 117 M6
Triton Pl MSEA/BNM PO22 ... 145 H3
Trojan Wy WVILLE PO7 ... 102 A2
Troon Cl CRAWW RH11 ... 42 C4
  SEAF BN25 ... 158 F7
Trosnant Rd HAV PO9 ... 102 F3
Trossachs Cl LGNY BN23 ... 164 C2
Trotton Cl CRAWE RH10 ... 44 B4
Trotton Rd EPSF GU31 ... 225 N9
Trout La SWTR RH13 ... 233 K1
Trout Rd HASM GU27 ... 180 H11
Troy Cl CROW TN6 ... 67 M8
Troymede RHWH RH17 ... 60 F8
True Blue Prec LHPTN BN17 ... 147 J2
Truggers RHWH RH17 ... 204 C1
Truleigh Cl BRIE/ROTT BN2 ... 124 C4
Truleigh Dr PTSD BN41 ... 120 F1
Truleigh Rd STEY/UB BN44 ... 79 G3
Truleigh Wy SHOR BN43 ... 119 M4
Truman Dr SLVN TN37 ... 283 N11
Trumpet La HAIL BN27 ... 280 A7
Trundle Cl RCCH PO18 ... 292 B11
Trundle Md HORS RH12 ... 56 B4
Trundle View Cl
  MSEA/BNM PO22 ... 111 G7
Truro Cl CCH PO19 ... 107 L4
Truro Wk WTHG BN11 * ... 20 A7
Truro Crs BOGR PO21 ... 171 K2
Trusler's Hill La HPPT/KEY BN6 ... 270 A5
Tryndel Wy MSEA/BNM PO22 ... 173 G1
Tubwell La CROW TN6 ... 211 L2
  HTHF TN21 ... 244 F11
Tudor Av EMRTH PO10 ... 103 M1
  STLEO TN38 ... 98 F6
Tudor Cl BRIE/ROTT BN2 * ... 155 L3
  CCH PO19 ... 107 L3
  CRAWE RH10 ... 44 C4
  EGRIN RH19 ... 47 L2
  GSHT GU26 ... 180 G7
  HOVE BN3 ... 121 L3
  MSEA/BNM PO22 ... 145 J3
  PUL/STOR RH20 ... 265 N4
  SALV BN13 ... 298 H11
  SEAF BN25 ... 174 D1
Tudor Ct RTWE/PEM TN2 ... 37 M3
Tudor Dr SELS PO20 ... 110 C5
  STEY/UB BN44 ... 78 F2
Tudor Gdns BURH RH15 ... 74 E5
Tudor Rd BRIE/ROTT BN2 ... 123 L6
Tudor Village PUL/STOR RH20 ... 266 F10
Tudor Wk UCK TN22 ... 77 K7
Tufts Fld MIDH GU29 ... 226 C11
Tufts Meadow MIDH GU29 ... 226 H11
Tuggles Plat HORS RH12 ... 187 P10
Tugwell Rd LW/ROSE BN22 ... 163 L3
Tulip Ct HORS RH12 * ... 14 C2
Tulip Gdns HAV PO9 ... 102 D3
Tullett Rd CRAWE RH10 ... 44 A7
Tulls La BOR GU35 ... 179 L1
Tumulus Rd BRIE/ROTT BN2 ... 156 B3
Tunbridge Crs LIPH GU30 ... 179 Q12
Tunbridge Wells Rd CROW TN6 ... 69 M6
  MAYF TN20 ... 212 C4
Tunnel Rd RTW TN1 ... 38 A4
Tunnmeade CRAWW RH11 ... 42 D4
Tunsgate STEY/UB BN44 ... 78 C2
Tunworth Ct HAV PO9 ... 289 J12
Tuppenny La EMRTH PO10 ... 104 D1
Turkey La BURH RH15 ... 75 G6
Turkey Rd BEXW TN39 ... 96 F5
Turk's Br MAYF TN20 ... 213 P9
Turnberry Cl STLEO TN38 ... 98 E6
Turnberry Dr HAIL BN27 ... 91 M5
Turnbull Rd CCH PO19 ... 7 H5
Turner Cl BEX TN40 ... 97 J8
  LGNY BN23 ... 164 C4
Turner Ct EGRIN RH19 ... 31 M6
Turner Rd SALV BN13 ... 117 K7
Turners Cl SWTR RH13 ... 233 K1
Turners Green La WADH TN5 ... 71 L3
Turners Green Rd WADH TN5 ... 71 L2
Turners Hill Rd CRAWE RH10 ... 29 L7
  CRAWE RH10 ... 44 C2
  EGRIN RH19 ... 46 A4
Turners Md MFD/CHID GU8 ... 182 H6
Turners Mill Cl HWH RH16 ... 73 G2
Turners Mill Rd HWH RH16 ... 73 G2
Turner Wy BURH RH15 ... 75 J4
  SELS PO20 ... 301 M6
Turnpike Cl CCH PO19 ... 141 K2
  PEAHV BN10 ... 157 H5
Turnpike Pl CRAWW RH11 ... 43 J1
Turnpike Rd LGNY BN23 ... 296 G3
Turnpike Wy PUL/STOR RH20 ... 267 K9
Turret House Ms
  MSEA/BNM PO22 * ... 3 L7
Turtledove Av CRAWE RH10 ... 46 B4
Turton Rd BRIE/ROTT BN2 ... 5 L7

Tuscan Av MSEA/BNM PO22 ... 145 L8
Tuscan Ct PEAHV BN10 * ... 156 E6
Tuscany Gdns CRAWE RH10 ... 43 K1
Tuscany Wy WVILLE PO7 ... 288 C9
Tushmore Ct CRAWE RH10 * ... 43 K1
Tushmore Crs CRAWE RH10 ... 43 K1
Tushmore La CRAWE RH10 ... 43 K1
Tussock Cl CRAWW RH11 ... 42 E5
Tutts Barn La LW/ROSE BN22 ... 10 D2
Tuxford Cl CRAWE RH10 ... 44 B5
Tuxford Rd SBGH/RUST TN4 ... 37 H5
Tweed La CRAWW RH11 ... 42 E5
Tweedsmuir Cl LGNY BN23 ... 164 B2
Twineham Cl BRIE/ROTT BN2 ... 123 L6
Twineham La HPPT/KEY BN6 ... 236 B12
Twineham Rd EAST BN21 ... 163 J6
Twitten Cl STHW BN42 ... 120 D6
Twitten La EDN/EASTW BN20 ... 30 D5
Twittenside STEY/UB BN44 * ... 79 H1
Twittens Wy HAV PO9 ... 103 G4
The Twitten BURH RH15 ... 75 G5
  CRAWW RH11 ... 8 B3
  CROW TN6 ... 67 K8
  HPPT/KEY BN6 ... 270 D3
  STHW BN42 ... 120 D6
Twitten Wy SALV BN13 ... 20 B1
Two Barns La RCCH PO18 ... 292 A12
Two Mile Ash Rd SWTR RH13 ... 201 J10
Two Ways BIL RH14 ... 198 H1
Twyford Cl SALV BN13 ... 116 D7
Twyford Crs SLVN TN37 ... 99 H1
Twyford Gdns SALV BN13 ... 116 D7
Twyford Rd BRI BN1 ... 83 J7
  SALV BN13 ... 116 D7
Twyfords CROW TN6 ... 67 J8
Twyhurst Ct EGRIN RH19 ... 31 J6
Twyne Cl CRAWW RH11 ... 42 E5
Twyner Cl HORL RH6 ... 23 H5
Tye Cl BRIE/ROTT BN2 ... 156 C5
Tyedean Rd PEAHV BN10 ... 156 E5
Tye Hill Rd POLE BN26 ... 130 E1
Tye La ARUN BN18 ... 111 K4
Tye Vw PEAHV BN10 ... 156 E5
Tyhurst Rd UCK TN22 ... 76 E6
Tylden Wy HORS RH12 ... 56 E3
Tyler's Gn HWH RH16 ... 72 E5
Tylers La UCK TN22 ... 209 K8
Tylston Meadow LIPH GU30 ... 179 Q12
Tyndale Av BEXW TN39 ... 136 B2
Tyndalls GSHT GU26 ... 181 J5
Tyne Cl CRAWE RH10 ... 44 B4
  SALV BN13 ... 116 B6
Tyne Wy BOGR PO21 ... 171 K1
The Tynings LAN/SOMP BN15 ... 118 D8
Tythe Barn RHWH RH17 ... 236 D2
Tythe Barn Rd SELS PO20 ... 301 L7

U

Uckfield Cl BRIE/ROTT BN2 ... 123 L7
Uckfield Rd CROW TN6 ... 210 C3
  RING/NEW BN8 ... 274 G10
Uckham La BAT TN33 ... 282 F3
Udimore Rd RYE TN31 ... 250 E9
  RYE TN31 ... 252 D9
Ullswater Dr LHPTN BN17 ... 147 M2
Ullswater Gn MSEA/BNM PO22 ... 145 H3
Ullswater Rd LAN/SOMP BN15 ... 118 A4
Undercliff STLEO TN38 ... 12 A9
Undercliff Ter STLEO TN38 ... 12 A9
Underdown Rd STHW BN42 ... 120 D5
Underhill UCK TN22 ... 209 L12
Underhill La HPPT/KEY BN6 ... 271 M9
Undermill Rd STEY/UB BN44 ... 79 G3
Under Rd HAIL BN27 ... 93 G2
Underwood Cl CRAWE RH10 ... 46 A1
Underwood Rd HASM GU27 ... 181 J10
Union Cl HAIL BN27 ... 92 A3
Union Pl WTHG BN11 ... 21 H5
Union Ri LISS GU33 ... 192 G3
Union Rd BRIE/ROTT BN2 ... 5 G3
  HAV PO9 ... 103 F4
Union Sq RTWE/PEM TN2 ... 37 M7
Union St BRI BN1 ... 4 F4
  STLEO TN38 ... 12 A8
  UCK TN22 ... 76 E3
  WTHG BN11 ... 191 N10
Updown Hl HWH RH16 ... 72 E5
Upfield HORL RH6 ... 22 F8
Upfield Cl HORL RH6 ... 22 F8
Uphill Wy SELS PO20 ... 141 M5
Upland Rd EDN/EASTW BN20 ... 176 B2
Uplands Cl BEXW TN39 ... 96 E7
  HASM GU27 ... 181 N9
  UCK TN22 ... 76 E3
Uplands Av SALV BN13 ... 116 E4
Uplands Pk HTHF TN21 ... 244 H4
Uplands Rd BRI BN1 ... 123 H5
  HAV PO9 ... 289 K7
The Uplands STLEO TN38 * ... 99 G6
Uppark Gdns HORS RH12 ... 56 E3
Uppark Wy MSEA/BNM PO22 ... 145 J7
Upper Abbey Rd BRIE/ROTT BN2 ... 5 L8
Upper Av EAST BN21 ... 10 F4
Upper Bannings Rd
  BRIE/ROTT BN2 ... 156 D2
Upper Bedford St
  BRIE/ROTT BN2 ... 5 H8
Upper Belgrave Rd SEAF BN25 ... 159 L8
Upper Bere Wd WVILLE PO7 ... 288 A11
Upper Bevendean Av
  LAN/SOMP BN15 ... 118 C6
Upper Bognor Rd BOGR PO21 ... 2 F5
Upper Boundstone La
  LAN/SOMP BN15 ... 118 C6
Upper Brighton Rd
  LAN/SOMP BN15 ... 117 M6
Upper Broomgrove Rd
  HAS TN34 ... 100 A2
Upper Carlisle Rd
  EDN/EASTW BN20 ... 176 C5
Upper Chalvington Pl
  BRIE/ROTT BN2 ... 123 K8
Upper Church Rd SLVN TN37 ... 99 G1
Upper Chyngton Gdns
  SEAF BN25 ... 160 A8
Upper Cl FROW RH18 ... 48 E7
Upper Cumberland Wk
  RTWE/PEM TN2 ... 38 A8
Upper Dr ANG/EP BN16 ... 149 G5
The Upper Dr HOVE BN3 ... 122 B5

Upper Duke's Dr
  EDN/EASTW BN20 ... 176 D6
Upper Dunstan Rd
  SBGH/RUST TN4 ... 38 A3
Upperfield RH8 GU29 ... 227 J7
Upper Forecourt HORL RH6 ... 28 A5
Upper Gardner St BRI BN1 ... 4 E5
Upper Glen Rd SLVN TN37 ... 283 N10
Upper Gloucester Rd BRI BN1 ... 4 D4
Upper Greenwoods La
  HTHF TN21 ... 245 L7
Upper Grosvenor Rd RTW TN1 ... 38 A4
Upper Hamilton Rd BRI BN1 ... 4 B5
Upper Heyshott EPSF GU31 ... 223 P6
Upper High St WTHG BN11 ... 21 J3
Upper Hollingdean Rd
  BRI BN1 ... 123 G4
Upper Horsebridge Rd
  HAIL BN27 ... 91 M2
Upper King's Dr
  EDN/EASTW BN20 ... 163 H4
Upper Kingston La
  STHW BN42 ... 120 C4
Upper Lake BAT TN33 ... 282 E5
Upper Lewes Rd BRIE/ROTT BN2 ... 5 J2
Upper Market St HOVE BN3 ... 122 C8
Upper Maze Hl STLEO TN38 ... 99 C5
Upper Mt HASM GU27 ... 181 Q8
  LISS GU33 ... 192 B10
Upper Nellington RRTW TN3 ... 37 G5
Upper North St BRI BN1 ... 4 B5
Upper Park Pl BRIE/ROTT BN2 ... 5 H6
Upper Park Rd SLVN TN37 ... 12 B3
Upper Profit RRTW TN3 ... 36 F6
Upper Ratton Dr
  EDN/EASTW BN20 ... 163 G5
Upper Rock Gdns
  BRIE/ROTT BN2 ... 5 H7
Upper St James's St
  BRIE/ROTT BN2 ... 5 H8
Upper St Johns Rd BRIE/ROTT BN2 ... 74 F6
Upper School Dr HASM GU27 ... 181 J12
Upper Sea Rd BEX TN40 ... 137 J1
Upper Sherwood Rd
  SEAF BN25 ... 174 F1
Upper Shoreham Rd
  SHOR BN43 ... 119 K5
Upper South Rd SLVN TN37 ... 12 A4
Upper Station Rd HFD BN5 ... 269 J4
  HTHF TN21 ... 244 D6
Upper Stephens RRTW TN3 ... 36 F6
Upper Stoneham
  RING/NEW BN8 ... 86 E1
Upper St EDN/EASTW BN20 ... 302 H5
  PUL/STOR RH20 ... 264 A2
  SBGH/RUST TN4 ... 37 J3
Upper Sudeley St
  BRIE/ROTT BN2 ... 5 L8
Upperton Gdns EAST BN21 ... 10 D5
Upperton La EAST BN21 ... 10 C5
Upperton Rd EAST BN21 ... 10 A4
  PETW GU28 ... 228 G7
Upper Valley Rd NEWHV BN9 ... 18 C5
Upper Wardown EPSF GU31 ... 223 Q5
Upper Wellington Rd
  BRIE/ROTT BN2 ... 5 J2
Upper West Dr FERR BN12 ... 149 K4
Upper West La
  LAN/SOMP BN15 ... 118 C6
Upper Winfield Av BRI BN1 ... 82 E7
Upper Wish Hl
  EDN/EASTW BN20 ... 163 H5
Upton Av STHW BN42 ... 120 C4
Upton Cl HAV PO9 ... 288 E10
Upton Gdns SALV BN13 ... 150 E1
Upton Quarry RRTW TN3 ... 36 F6
Upton Rd CCH PO19 ... 6 C8
  SALV BN13 ... 150 E1
Upways Cl SELS PO20 ... 301 L4
Upwick Rd EDN/EASTW BN20 ... 176 C2
Ursula Av SALV PO20 ... 301 K7
Ursula Av North SELS PO20 ... 301 K7
Ursula Sq SELS PO20 ... 301 K8

V

Vachery La CRAN GU6 ... 185 N1
Vale Av BRI BN1 ... 82 D9
  RTW TN1 ... 37 M6
  SALV BN13 ... 116 E3
Valebridge Cl BURH RH15 ... 75 H3
Valebridge Dr BURH RH15 ... 75 H4
Valebridge Rd BURH RH15 ... 75 H4
Vale Cl SEAF BN25 ... 175 G4
Vale Dr HORS RH12 ... 14 A5
  SALV BN13 ... 116 E3
Vale Rd BAT TN33 ... 282 C4
  BRIE/ROTT BN2 ... 156 C2
  HWH RH16 ... 73 C7
  MAYF TN20 ... 212 E7
  PTSD BN41 ... 121 H6
  RTW TN1 ... 37 M6
  SEAF BN25 ... 159 M8
  SLVN TN37 ... 12 A1
The Vale BRIE/ROTT BN2 ... 124 D4
  HORN PO8 ... 256 D12
Valetta Pk EMRTH PO10 ... 103 M5
Valetta Rd EMRTH PO10 ... 138 E4
Vale Vw RHAS TN35 ... 284 D9
Vale View Rd HTHF TN21 ... 244 E7
Vale Wk SALV BN13 ... 116 E3
Valewood Cl SWTR RH13 ... 203 G12
Valewood La GSHT GU26 ... 180 D5
Valewood Rd SWTR RH13 ... 203 G12
Valewood Rd HASM GU27 ... 195 M11
Valiant Rd EMRTH PO10 ... 138 E4
Vallance Cl BURH RH15 ... 74 D5
Vallance Gdns HOVE BN3 ... 121 M7
Vallance Rd HOVE BN3 ... 121 M7
Valley Cl BRI BN1 ... 82 B1
  NEWHV BN9 ... 18 B1
Valley Dene NEWHV BN9 ... 18 C5
Valley Dr BRI BN1 ... 122 B1
  SEAF BN25 ... 159 M8
Valley Gdns SALV BN13 ... 116 F4

Valley Park Dr *HORN* PO08 .... 256 E10
Valley Ri *SEAF* BN25 .... 174 F1
Valley Rd *CROW* TN6 .... 67 L8
  LAN/SOMP BN15 .... 118 B5
  LEWES BN7 .... 16 B8
  NEWHV BN9 .... 18 B4
  PEAHV BN10 .... 157 H3
  PTSD BN41 .... 120 F3
  SBGH/RUST TN4 .... 37 J3
Valley Side *LIPH* GU30 .... 179 Q12
Valley Side Rd *RHAS* TN35 .... 100 B2
Valley View Cl *CROW* TN6 .... 67 L8
Val Prinseps Rd *PEV* BN24 .... 165 H1
Vanbrugh Cl *CRAWW* RH11 .... 42 D6
Vancouver Cl *SALV* BN13 .... 116 C7
Vancouver Ct *HORL* RH6 .... 23 M6
Vancouver Dr *CRAWW* RH11 .... 27 J8
Vancouver Rd *LGNY* BN23 .... 165 G3
  SALV BN13 .... 116 B9
Van Dyck Pl *MSEA/BNM* PO22 .... 143 M7
Van Gogh Pl *MSEA/BNM* PO22 .... 144 A7
Vanguard Wy *CROW* TN6 .... 210 A2
  EGRIN RH19 .... 32 E4
  HAIL BN27 .... 90 B4
  POLE BN26 .... 129 L4
  RING/NEW BN8 .... 277 N7
  SEAF BN25 .... 175 G4
  UCK TN22 .... 210 D9
  UCK TN22 .... 242 H10
Vann Bridge Cl *HASM* GU27 .... 195 K7
Vanners *CRAWE* RH10 * 9 G1
Vann Rd *HASM* GU27 .... 195 K7
Vantage Wk *STLEO* TN38 .... 99 G3
Vanzell Rd *MIDH* GU29 .... 227 K8
Varey Rd *SALV* BN13 .... 116 A7
Varna Rd *BOR* GU35 .... 178 H6
Varndean Cl *BRI* BN1 .... 122 D2
Varndean Dr *BRI* BN1 .... 122 D2
Varndean Gdns *BRI* BN1 .... 122 D2
Varndean Holt *BRI* BN1 .... 122 E2
Varndean Rd *BRI* BN1 .... 122 D2
Varsity Rd *EMRTH* PO10 .... 138 E4
Vauxhall Wy *PSF* GU32 .... 223 M6
Vega Cl *HAIL* BN27 .... 92 C6
Velyn Av *CCH* PO19 .... 7 G4
Venice Cl *WVILLE* PO7 .... 288 B9
Ventnor Cl *LGNY* BN23 .... 164 A1
Ventnor Vls *HOVE* BN3 .... 122 A7
Venture Cl *BEX* TN40 .... 137 L1
Venus La *BOGR* PO21 .... 170 D6
Veras Wk *PUL/STOR* RH20 .... 266 F12
Verbania Wy *EGRIN* RH19 .... 32 A8
Verbena Crs *FERR* BN12 .... 150 C5
Verbena Crs *FERR* PO08 .... 288 C5
Verdant Cl *HAS* TN34 .... 12 D5
Verdley Pl *HASM* GU27 .... 195 M10
Vere Rd *BRI* BN1 .... 4 F1
Vermont Cl *ANG/EP* BN16 .... 148 F4
Vermont Rd *SBGH/RUST* TN4 .... 37 H5
Vermont Wy *ANG/EP* BN16 .... 148 F4
  SLVH TN37 .... 283 N11
Verner Cl *BOR* GU35 .... 179 M5
Vernon Av *BRIE/ROTT* BN2 .... 124 C7
  PEAHV BN10 .... 157 J7
Vernon Cl *ANG/EP* BN16 .... 148 F5
  HORS RH12 .... 15 L1
  LGNY BN23 .... 164 D6
Vernon Gdns *BRI* BN1 .... 4 B5
Vernon Rd *RTW* TN1 .... 38 B3
  UCK TN22 .... 76 F6
Vernons Rd *RING/NEW* BN8 .... 240 B6
Vernon Ter *BRI* BN1 .... 4 B5
Veronica Cl *ANG/EP* BN16 .... 148 F5
Veronica Wy *BRIE/ROTT* BN2 .... 5 K3
Verralls Wk *LEWES* BN7 .... 16 E8
Verulam Pl *SLVH* TN37 .... 12 E8
Verwood Rd *HAV* PO09 .... 289 J11
Viaduct Rd *BRI* BN1 .... 4 E2
Vian Av *LGNY* BN23 .... 164 E7
Via Ravenna *CCH* PO19 .... 6 B6
Via Ravenna Rbt *CCH* PO19 .... 6 B6
Vicarage Cl *HORS* RH12 .... 58 B3
  NEWHV BN9 .... 158 D3
  RING/NEW BN8 .... 274 H12
  SEAF BN25 .... 174 F2
Vicarage Dr *EDN/EASTW* BN20 .... 176 D7
Vicarage Flds *SALV* BN13 .... 116 C6
Vicarage Flats *HAS* TN34 * 13 K3
Vicarage Gdns *GSHT* GU26 .... 180 D6
Vicarage La *ANG/EP* BN16 .... 148 E4
  BRIE/ROTT BN2 .... 155 L4
  BUR/ETCH TN19 .... 245 P2
  EAST BN21 .... 176 D2
  HAIL BN27 .... 92 B5
  HAIL BN27 .... 278 D11
  HASM GU27 .... 181 J11
  HORL RH6 .... 22 E5
  MSEA/BNM PO22 .... 3 A7
  PETW GU28 .... 228 A7
  RDKG RH5 .... 24 A7
  RHAS TN35 .... 284 A6
  RHWH RH17 .... 239 J2
  STEY/UB BN44 .... 78 C2
Vicarage Rd *BUR/ETCH* TN19 .... 245 P2
  CRAWE RH10 .... 45 M2
  EDN/EASTW BN20 .... 176 D2
  HAIL BN27 .... 92 B6
  HAS TN34 .... 13 J4
Vicarage Ter *BRIE/ROTT* BN2 .... 155 L4
Vicarage Wy *BUR/ETCH* TN19 .... 216 B6
  RING/NEW BN8 .... 275 J12
Vicars Cl *CCH* PO19 .... 6 D5
Victor Cl *SEAF* BN25 .... 159 J8
Victoria Av *BURH* RH15 .... 74 D6
  MIDH GU29 .... 227 K8
  PEAHV BN10 .... 157 H7
  RHAS TN35 .... 100 B1
Victoria Cl *BURH* RH15 .... 74 D7
  HORL RH6 .... 22 F6
  MIDH GU29 .... 226 H10
  POLE BN26 .... 131 L6
Victoria Ct *STLEO* TN38 .... 99 G3
Victoria Dr *BOGR* PO21 .... 2 B8
  EDN/EASTW BN20 .... 163 H8
Victoria Gdns *BURH* RH15 .... 74 D7
  EDN/EASTW BN20 .... 176 C1
  LHPTN BN17 * 147 G3
  SELS PO20 .... 110 C6
Victoria Gv *HOVE* BN3 .... 122 B7
Victoria Ms *BOGR* PO21 * 2 D4
  BRIE/ROTT BN2 * 155 L4
Victoria Pl *BRI* BN1 .... 4 B5
Victoria Rd *BEXW* TN39 .... 137 G1
  BOGR PO21 .... 2 B8
  BRI BN1 * 4 B5
  BURH RH15 .... 74 E7

CCH PO19 .... 7 L3
CRAWW RH11 .... 8 D4
CROW TN6 .... 211 K1
EDN/EASTW BN20 .... 163 H8
EMRTH PO10 .... 103 M4
HAIL BN27 .... 92 B6
HAIL BN27 .... 280 A12
HORL RH6 .... 22 F6
HWH RH16 .... 73 J6
MAYF TN20 .... 212 D6
POLE BN26 .... 131 L6
PTSD BN41 .... 121 G5
RHWH RH17 .... 60 F8
RTW TN1 .... 38 A5
SHOR BN43 .... 119 K6
SLVH TN37 .... 12 C6
STHW BN42 .... 120 C6
WTHG BN11 .... 20 F4
Victoria Rd South *BOGR* PO21 .... 2 B9
Victoria St *BRI* BN1 .... 4 B5
  SWTR RH13 .... 14 E6
Victoria Vls *ARUN* BN18 * 145 M2
  CROW TN6 .... 210 G1
  RTW TN1 * 38 A5
Victoria Wy *BURH* RH15 .... 74 E7
  EGRIN RH19 .... 47 L2
  LIPH GU30 .... 193 Q1
  WSEA TN36 .... 286 F4
Victor Rd *EMRTH* PO10 .... 138 E4
Victory Av *HORN* PO08 .... 288 B3
Victory Ms *BRIE/ROTT* BN2 .... 154 F2
Victory Rd *HORS* RH12 .... 14 B3
View Bank *RHAS* TN35 .... 100 C3
View Rd *PEAHV* BN10 .... 157 H5
Views Pth *HWH* RH16 * 73 L5
The View *BOGR* PO21 .... 170 F5
Viking Cl *SEAF* BN25 .... 158 F7
Viking Wy *HORN* PO08 .... 256 D10
The Village Barn *BRI* BN1 .... 82 D6
Village Cl *BEXW* TN39 .... 136 B1
  PTSD BN41 .... 121 G3
Village Ms *BEXW* TN39 .... 136 B1
Village St *PSF* GU32 .... 223 Q3
The Village *EDN/EASTW* BN20 .... 176 D5
  POLE BN26 .... 129 J5
  POLE BN26 .... 129 L6
Village Wy *BRI* BN1 .... 84 B7
Villa Rd *SLVH* TN37 .... 12 C8
Villiers Cl *BRIE/ROTT* BN2 .... 124 D5
Vinall Gdns *HORS* RH12 .... 201 N1
Vincent Cl *LAN/SOMP* BN15 .... 118 C2
  LGNY BN23 .... 164 E6
  SWTR RH13 .... 15 J6
Vincent Rd *SELS* PO20 .... 301 J7
Vinehall Cl *HAS* TN34 .... 284 D12
Vinehall Rd *RBTBR* TN32 .... 248 F7
Vine Lands *LYDD* TN29 .... 255 Q2
Vine Pl *BRI* BN1 .... 4 C5
Vineries Cl *SALV* BN13 .... 116 F7
The Vineries *BURH* RH15 .... 75 J6
  LGNY BN23 .... 164 C3
Vines Cross Rd
  BRIE/ROTT BN2 .... 123 L6
  HTHF TN21 .... 278 D12
Vine Sq *LW/ROSE* BN22 .... 164 C7
Vine St *BRI* BN1 .... 4 E5
Vineyard La *BOGR* PO21 .... 190 G11
Viney Cl *PUL/STOR* RH20 .... 267 J8
Vinnetrow Rd *CCH* PO19 * 7 M8
  SELS PO20 .... 142 D2
Vinson Rd *LISS* GU33 .... 192 D9
The Vintry *EAST* BN21 * 163 H6
Virgin's Cft *BAT* TN33 .... 282 E3
Virgin's La *BAT* TN33 .... 282 E3
Viscount Dr *BOGR* PO21 .... 171 G5
Vivienne La *CRAWW* RH11 .... 27 J8
Vowels La *EGRIN* RH19 .... 46 C7
Vulcan Cl *CRAWW* RH11 .... 43 H7
Vulcan Rd *EMRTH* PO10 .... 138 E4

W

Waddington Cl *CRAWW* RH11 .... 42 F6
Wade Cl *LGNY* BN23 .... 164 E6
Wade Court Rd *HAV* PO09 .... 103 H5
Wade End *SELS* PO20 .... 301 J5
Wade La *HAV* PO09 .... 103 H6
The Wadeway *SELS* PO20 .... 301 J5
The Wadeys *BIL* RH14 .... 231 R1
Wadham Cl *CRAWE* RH10 .... 28 B8
Wadhurst Cl *BOGR* PO21 .... 2 A4
  LW/ROSE BN22 .... 163 L3
  SLVH TN37 .... 283 Q12
Wadhurst Dr *FERR* BN12 .... 150 A5
Wadhurst La *BAT* TN33 .... 281 R4
Wadhurst Ri *BRIE/ROTT* BN2 .... 123 L8
Wadhurst Rd *CROW* TN6 .... 70 E6
  RRTW TN3 .... 54 B3
Wadlands Brook Rd
  EGRIN RH19 .... 31 J4
The Wad *SELS* PO20 .... 167 G4
Wagg Cl *EGRIN* RH19 .... 31 M8
Waggoners Wy *GSHT* GU26 .... 180 D6
Waggoners Wells Rd
  GSHT GU26 .... 180 D7
Waghorns La *UCK* TN22 .... 211 K12
Wagtail Cl *HORS* RH12 .... 56 B2
Wagtail Wy *HORN* PO08 .... 288 B3
Wain End *HORS* RH12 .... 56 C4
Wainwright Cl *STLEO* TN38 .... 98 C2
Wainwright Rd *BEXW* TN39 .... 137 G1
Wainwrights *CRAWE* RH10 .... 8 E9
Waite Cl *LEWES* BN7 .... 17 H5
Waites La *RHAS* TN35 .... 285 P12
Wakefield Rd *BRIE/ROTT* BN2 .... 5 J4
Wakefield Wy *BOGR* PO21 .... 171 K1
Wakefords Wy *HAV* PO09 .... 289 J11
Wakehams *BEXW* TN39 .... 97 H6
Wakehams Green Dr
  CRAWE RH10 .... 28 C8
Wakehurst Cl *CRAWE* RH10 .... 8 F9
Wakehurst La *RHWH* RH17 .... 206 D1
Wakehurst Ms *HORS* RH12 .... 201 Q4
Wakehurst Pl *ANG/EP* BN16 .... 148 B4
Wakestone La *PUL/STOR* RH20 .... 230 B8
Walburton Wy *HORN* PO08 .... 256 E9
Waldegrave Rd *BRI* BN1 .... 122 E3
Waldegrave St *HAS* TN34 .... 13 H6
Waldene Cl *HAS* TN34 .... 13 H1
Walden Gdns *HORN* PO08 .... 288 C2
Walden Ter *BAT* TN33 * 282 F5
Walders Rd *ANG/EP* BN16 .... 147 M3
Waldron Av *BRI* BN1 .... 83 J7

Waldron Cl *LW/ROSE* BN22 .... 163 J5
Waldron Ct *HTHF* TN21 * 244 E5
Waldron Pl *BRI* BN1 * 83 J7
Waldron Rd *RING/NEW* BN8 .... 276 H4
Waldron Thorns *HTHF* TN21 .... 244 D7
Waldshut Rd *LEWES* BN7 .... 16 B2
Walesbeech *CRAWE* RH10 * 9 M6
Walesbeech Rd
  BRIE/ROTT BN2 .... 156 C5
Walhatch Cl *FROW* RH18 .... 48 E3
Walk Cl *LGNY* BN23 .... 164 E6
Walker Rd *CRAWE* RH10 .... 44 A5
The Walkway *RING/NEW* BN8 * 148 F1
Wallace Av *WTHG* BN11 .... 150 A5
Wallace Cl *RTWE/PEM* TN2 .... 53 M1
Wallace Ms *WTHG* BN11 * 150 A5
Wallace Pde *FERR* BN12 * 150 E3
Wallace Rd *ANG/EP* BN16 .... 148 B3
Wallands Crs *LEWES* BN7 .... 16 E4
Walldown Rd *BOR* GU35 .... 178 H8
The Walled Gdns *UCK* TN22 .... 241 Q1
The Walled Gdn *BIL* RH14 .... 184 G10
Wallers *RRTW* TN3 .... 36 F1
Wallfield Rd *BOGR* PO21 .... 171 L4
Wallis Cl *CROW* TN6 .... 67 M8
Wallis Ct *SEAF* BN25 * 27 L7
Wallis Fld *RRTW* TN3 * 52 A3
Wallis Pl *LGNY* BN23 .... 164 D6
Wallis Wy *BURH* RH15 .... 74 D5
Walmsleys Wy *ANG/EP* BN16 .... 148 A4
  CCH PO19 .... 6 B1
Walnut Cl *BRI* BN1 .... 122 D2
  HTHF TN21 .... 244 F7
Walnut La *CRAWW* RH11 .... 27 C8
Walnut Ldg *SALV* BN13 * 20 E2
Walnut Pk *HWH* RH16 .... 73 L5
The Walnuts *HORS* RH12 * 14 C2
Walnut Tree Dr *EMRTH* PO10 .... 104 F2
Walnut Tree Wk
  EDN/EASTW BN20 .... 163 G5
Walnut Tree Wy *SALV* BN13 .... 116 B9
Walnut Wy *POLE* BN26 .... 131 M7
Walpole Av *FERR* BN12 .... 150 C3
Walpole Rd *BRIE/ROTT* BN2 * 5 L7
Walpole Ter *BRIE/ROTT* BN2 * 5 L7
Walsham Cl *MSEA/BNM* PO22 .... 3 K1
Walshes Cottages
  CROW TN6 * 210 F2
Walshes Rd *CROW* TN6 .... 210 F2
Walsingham Cl *LW/ROSE* BN22 .... 163 J2
Walsingham Rd *HOVE* BN3 .... 121 L7
Walters Gn *LHPTN* BN17 * 113 J8
Walters Green Rd *RTON* TN11 .... 35 K3
Waltham Park Rd
  PUL/STOR RH20 .... 264 C7
Walton Av *BOGR* PO21 * 3 G7
Walton Bank *BRI* BN1 .... 83 K8
Walton Dr *BEXW* TN39 .... 136 E1
  SLVH TN37 .... 283 R12
Walton Dr *SWTR* RH13 .... 57 H5
Walton Heath *CRAWE* RH10 .... 44 A5
Walton La *RCCH* PO18 .... 106 B8
Walton Ldg *SALV* BN13 .... 116 A7
Walton Pk *BEXW* TN39 .... 136 E1
Walton Rd *BOGR* PO21 .... 2 A7
Walwyn Cl *SELS* PO20 .... 168 D1
Wanderdown Cl
  BRIE/ROTT BN2 .... 155 K1
Wanderdown Dr
  BRIE/ROTT BN2 .... 155 K1
Wanderdown Rd
  BRIE/ROTT BN2 .... 155 J1
Wanderdown Wy
  BRIE/ROTT BN2 .... 155 K1
Wandle Cl *CRAWE* RH10 .... 44 B4
Wandleys Cl *SELS* PO20 .... 110 F3
Wandleys Dr *SELS* PO20 .... 110 F3
Wandleys La *SELS* PO20 .... 110 F4
Wannock Av
  EDN/EASTW BN20 .... 162 E2
Wannock Cl *BEX* TN40 .... 97 M7
Wannock Dr *POLE* BN26 .... 131 L8
Wannock Gdns *POLE* BN26 .... 162 E2
Wannock La
  EDN/EASTW BN20 .... 162 E2
Wannock Rd *LW/ROSE* BN22 .... 11 L2
  POLE BN26 .... 131 L8
Wansford Wy
  MSEA/BNM PO22 .... 173 H1
Wantage Cl *CRAWE* RH10 .... 44 B6
Wantley Hill Est *HFD* BN5 .... 269 L3
Wantley La *PUL/STOR* RH20 .... 266 B11
Wantley Rd *SALV* BN13 .... 116 F4
Wappingthorn Farm La
  STEY/UB BN44 * 268 D7
Warberry Park Gdns
  SBGH/RUST TN4 .... 37 K5
Warble Heath Cl *RCCH* PO18 .... 292 C11
Warbler Cl *HORN* PO08 .... 288 B3
Warblers Wy *MSEA/BNM* PO22 .... 144 A6
Warbleton Cl *BRIE/ROTT* BN2 .... 123 K8
Warblington Av *HAV* PO09 .... 103 J4
Warblington Rd *EMRTH* PO10 .... 103 M6
Warbrook Ct *HAV* PO09 .... 289 J12
Warburton Cl *EAST* BN21 .... 163 H5
  EGRIN RH19 .... 31 M8
  UCK TN22 .... 76 D7
Ward Cl *WADH* TN5 .... 71 K4
Ward Crs *EMRTH* PO10 .... 104 D4
Warden Ct *RHWH* RH17 .... 72 C7
Wardsbrook Rd *WADH* TN5 .... 215 J2
Ward's La *WADH* TN5 .... 190 D10
Ward Wy *BEXW* TN39 .... 96 F7
Warelands *BURH* RH15 .... 74 A5
Warenne Rd *HOVE* BN3 .... 121 H2
Wares Fld *UCK* TN22 .... 76 F8
Wares Rd *UCK* TN22 .... 76 F8
Warleigh Rd *BRI* BN1 .... 4 F1
Warltersville Wy *HORL* RH6 .... 23 H8
Warmdene Av *BRI* BN1 .... 82 E7
Warmdene Cl *BRI* BN1 .... 82 E7
Warmdene Rd *BRI* BN1 .... 82 E7
Warminghurst Cl
  PUL/STOR RH20 .... 267 J8
Warminster Rd *PEV* BN24 .... 134 C8

Warner Cl *CRAWE* RH10 .... 44 B7
Warner Rd *SALV* BN13 .... 21 L1
  SELS PO20 .... 301 J7
Warner's La *SELS* PO20 .... 300 H5
Warnford Crs *HAV* PO09 .... 288 E12
Warnham Cl *FERR* BN12 .... 150 C4
Warnham Court Ms
  HORS RH12 * 186 H5
Warnham Gdns *BEXW* TN39 .... 136 C3
Warnham Ms *FERR* BN12 * 150 D4
Warnham Ri *BRI* BN1 .... 82 F8
Warnham Rd *CRAWE* RH10 * 9 M8
  FERR BN12 .... 150 C3
  HORS RH12 .... 56 A4
  HORS RH12 .... 201 N1
Warninglid La *SWTR* RH13 .... 203 P5
Warren Av *BRIE/ROTT* BN2 .... 124 B4
  BRIE/ROTT BN2 .... 124 A5
  CROW TN6 .... 67 J7
  EDN/EASTW BN20 .... 176 C5
  EDN/EASTW BN20 .... 302 H4
  EGRIN RH19 .... 30 D6
  HTHF TN21 .... 243 N7
  LEWES BN7 .... 16 C7
  SALV BN13 .... 117 G6
  STLEO TN38 .... 98 D5
Warren Crs *ANG/EP* BN16 .... 148 E3
Warren Cft *PUL/STOR* RH20 .... 265 Q12
Warren Dr *CRAWW* RH11 .... 42 F7
  LEWES BN7 .... 16 C7
  SWTR RH13 .... 201 R10
Warren Farm Cl *CCH* PO19 .... 107 L3
  RRTW TN3 .... 52 B5
Warren Farm Pl *SALV* BN13 .... 116 F5
Warren Gdn *CROW* TN6 .... 67 J7
Warren Gdns *SALV* BN13 .... 117 G6
Warren Hl *EDN/EASTW* BN20 .... 176 A4
Warren La *EDN/EASTW* BN20 .... 302 H4
  HTHF TN21 .... 243 P5
  RING/NEW BN8 .... 239 P5
Warren Rdg *CROW* TN6 .... 67 J7
  RRTW TN3 .... 54 B6
Warren Ri *BRIE/ROTT* BN2 .... 124 B6
Warren Rd *BRIE/ROTT* BN2 .... 123 K6
  CROW TN6 .... 67 H8
  LISS GU33 .... 192 D6
  RHAS TN35 .... 101 H1
  SALV BN13 .... 117 G6
Warren Side *EPSF* GU31 .... 258 E2
The Warren *BURH* RH15 .... 75 H8
  FERR BN12 .... 149 L5
  MAYF TN20 .... 212 F7
  WADH TN5 .... 191 K12
Warren Wy *BRIE/ROTT* BN2 .... 124 C5
  MSEA/BNM PO22 .... 111 G7
  PEAHV BN10 .... 156 F4
  RING/NEW BN8 .... 239 Q5
Warrenwood *RING/NEW* BN8 .... 239 R5
Warr Gn *LEWES* BN7 .... 16 C7
Warrington Ct *CRAWW* RH11 .... 42 D7
Warrior Cl *PTSD* BN41 .... 121 G5
Warrior Gdns *SLVH* TN37 .... 12 B7
Warrior Sq *LW/ROSE* BN22 .... 11 J4
  SLVH TN37 .... 12 B8
Warrs Hill La *RING/NEW* BN8 .... 239 P4
Warsash Cl *HAV* PO09 .... 288 F11
Wartling Cl *STLEO* TN38 .... 98 E12
Wartling Dr *BEXW* TN39 .... 95 L8
Wartling Rd *HAIL* BN27 .... 94 B3
  LW/ROSE BN22 .... 11 K1
Warwick Cl *HAIL* BN27 .... 92 K1
Warwick Gdns *WTHG* BN11 .... 21 J6
Warwick La *RTWE/PEM* TN2 * 53 M3
Warwick Mt *BRIE/ROTT* BN2 * 5 L8
Warwick Pk *RTWE/PEM* TN2 .... 38 A8
Warwick Pl *MSEA/BNM* PO22 .... 145 J8
  WTHG BN11 .... 21 K5
Warwick St *BEXW* TN39 .... 96 E8
  RTW TN1 .... 37 M7
  SEAF BN25 * 174 E2
  WTHG BN11 .... 21 K6
Warwick St *WTHG* BN11 .... 21 J6
Wasdale Cl *HORN* PO08 .... 256 D11
Washford La *BOR* GU35 .... 179 J5
Washington Av *SLVH* TN37 .... 283 N11
Washington Bostal
  PUL/STOR RH20 .... 298 H4
Washington Rd *CRAWW* RH11 .... 42 D7
  EMRTH PO10 .... 104 D4
  HWH RH16 .... 73 J4
  PUL/STOR RH20 .... 298 D1
  STEY/UB BN44 .... 299 N2
Washington St *BRIE/ROTT* BN2 .... 5 J4
  CCH PO19 .... 6 D2
Washwell La *WADH* TN5 .... 71 L6
Wassall La *CRBK* TN17 .... 218 H2
Wassand Cl *CRAWE* RH10 .... 9 M3
Watchbell La *RYE* TN31 .... 252 H8
Watchbell St *RYE* TN31 .... 252 H8
Waterbury Hl *RHWH* RH17 .... 207 L3
Waterdown Rd
  SBGH/RUST TN4 .... 37 J8
Waterdyke Av *STHW* BN42 .... 120 D6
Waterfield *RTWE/PEM* TN2 .... 53 M2
Waterfield Cl *SWTR* RH13 .... 15 J7
Waterfield Gdns *CRAWW* RH11 .... 42 D5
Waterford Cl *PEAHV* BN10 .... 157 H3
Waterford Gdns *LHPTN* BN17 .... 146 D4
Watergate *BEXW* TN39 .... 97 G5
Watergate La *LEWES* BN7 .... 16 F6
Waterhall Rd *BRI* BN1 .... 82 B7
Waterlands La *HORS* RH12 .... 186 H9
Water La *ANG/EP* BN16 .... 115 H6
  LHPTN BN17 .... 147 J3
  PUL/STOR RH20 .... 266 C11
  STEY/UB BN44 .... 267 M12
Water Lea *CRAWE* RH10 .... 9 M6
Waterloo Cl *SLVH* TN37 .... 283 N10
Waterloo Pl *LEWES* BN7 * 17 G5
Waterloo Rd *HAV* PO09 .... 103 L4
  MSEA/BNM PO22 .... 3 L4
Waterloo Sq *BOGR* PO21 * 2 D8
  POLE BN26 .... 160 F2
Waterloo St *HOVE* BN3 .... 122 C8
Waterman Cl *BOR* GU35 .... 179 J7
Watermen's Cl *HAS* TN34 .... 99 K2
Watermill Cl *BEXW* TN39 .... 97 G5
  POLE BN26 .... 131 M8
Watermill Dr *STLEO* TN38 .... 98 C2
Watermill La *BEXW* TN39 .... 96 F1
  RHAS TN35 .... 285 M8
  RYE TN31 .... 250 G3
Water Mint Cl *STLEO* TN38 .... 98 D4
The Waterplat *CCH* PO19 .... 188 B5
Waters Cottages *WADH* TN5 .... 71 M5

Waters Edge *BOGR* PO21 .... 171 K4
  PUL/STOR RH20 .... 264 H4
Waters Edge Gdns
  EMRTH PO10 .... 104 A5
Watersedge Gdns *SELS* PO20 .... 167 K7
Watersfield Rd *SALV* BN13 .... 117 G8
Waterside *EGRIN* RH19 .... 32 A8
  HORL RH6 .... 22 F4
Waterside Cl *BOR* GU35 .... 178 H5
  CRAWW RH11 .... 42 D5
  HAS TN34 .... 100 A2
Waterside Dr *CCH* PO19 .... 141 L2
The Waterside *LHPTN* BN17 * 147 H4
Waterstone Cl *SELS* PO20 .... 139 M6
Waterworks Cl *FROW* RH18 .... 48 E5
Waterworks Cottages
  HAS TN34 * 13 H5
  LW/ROSE BN22 .... 11 G5
Waterworks Rd *HAS* TN34 .... 13 H5
  PSF GU32 .... 223 P3
Watery La *CCH* PO19 .... 6 F9
  RCCH PO19 .... 290 H12
Watling Cl *STHW* BN42 .... 120 D6
Watling Rd *STHW* BN42 .... 120 D6
Watson Cl *CRAWE* RH10 .... 44 A5
Watson Wy *SELS* PO20 .... 110 C6
Wattle's Wish *BAT* TN33 .... 282 D3
Watts Cl *WADH* TN5 .... 71 L4
Watts La *EAST* BN21 .... 10 A4
Watts' Palace La *RYE* TN31 .... 250 F11
Waveney Wk *CRAWE* RH10 .... 44 A5
Waverley Ct *HORS* RH12 * 14 C2
  SLVH TN37 * 12 E8
Waverley Crs *BRI* BN1 .... 123 G4
Waverley Dr *RTWE/PEM* TN2 .... 38 E3
Waverley Gdns *PEV* BN24 .... 134 C8
Waverley Rd *ANG/EP* BN16 .... 148 B4
  BOGR PO21 .... 171 K4
Wavertree Rd *FERR* BN12 .... 150 C2
Wawmans Ms *PEV* BN24 * 134 C8
Wayfarer's Wk *EMRTH* PO10 .... 103 M6
  HAV PO09 .... 102 H4
Wayfaring Down *POLE* BN26 .... 162 C2
Wayfield Av *HOVE* BN3 .... 121 K4
Wayfield Cl *HOVE* BN3 .... 121 K4
Wayford Cl *LGNY* BN23 .... 164 C3
Waykeham Wy *BURH* RH15 .... 75 H7
Wayland Av *BRI* BN1 .... 122 B1
Wayland Hts *BRI* BN1 * 122 B1
Wayside *BRI* BN1 .... 82 C7
  CRAWW RH11 .... 42 D5
  EDN/EASTW BN20 .... 302 H5
  LAN/SOMP BN15 * 118 B8
  RDKG RH5 .... 24 C3
  SLVH TN37 .... 99 G3
Wayside Av *SALV* BN13 .... 116 C5
Wayside Cottages *SWTR* RH13 .... 203 J6
Wayside Wk *HTHF* TN21 .... 244 C7
The Way *ANG/EP* BN16 .... 148 F5
Weald Av *HOVE* BN3 .... 121 L4
Weald Cl *HPPT/KEY* BN6 .... 270 G3
  LEWES BN7 .... 16 E4
  RING/NEW BN8 .... 15 C9
  SWTR RH13 .... 15 G9
Weald Dr *CRAWE* RH10 .... 9 J4
Weald Drive Rbt *CRAWE* RH10 * 9 K5
Weald Dyke *SHOR* BN43 .... 119 L7
Wealden *BUR/ETCH* TN19 .... 214 G10
Wealden Cl *CROW* TN6 .... 67 L6
Wealden Pk *LW/ROSE* BN22 .... 163 H3
Wealden Wy *BEXW* TN39 .... 96 B7
  HWH RH16 .... 73 G5
Wealdon Cl *SWTR* RH13 .... 233 Q1
Weald Ri *HWH* RH16 .... 73 H6
Weald Rd *BURH* RH15 .... 74 D6
The Weald *EGRIN* RH19 .... 31 L6
Weald Vw *RBTBR* TN32 .... 249 M4
  RING/NEW BN8 .... 274 D5
  WADH TN5 .... 71 L3
Wealdview Rd *HTHF* TN21 .... 244 D6
Wealdway *CROW* TN6 .... 66 B7
  EDN/EASTW BN20 .... 176 D2
  HAIL BN27 .... 278 C10
  HRTF TN7 .... 50 J7
  POLE BN26 .... 130 C4
  POLE BN26 .... 162 A3
  RING/NEW BN8 .... 277 J10
  RRTW TN3 .... 36 D3
  UCK TN22 .... 209 Q11
  UCK TN22 .... 211 R1
  UCK TN22 .... 242 G8
  UCK TN22 .... 259 H1
Wear Cl *SALV* BN13 .... 116 B6
Weare Rd *SBGH/RUST* TN4 .... 38 B1
Weare St *RDKG* RH5 .... 187 M6
Wear Rd *SALV* BN13 .... 116 B6
Weatherby Cl *EAST* BN21 .... 163 H5
Weatherhill Cl *HORL* RH6 .... 23 M6
Weatherhill Rd *HORL* RH6 .... 23 M6
Weaver Cl *CRAWW* RH11 * 42 D4
Weavers Cl *BURH* RH15 .... 75 J4
  MIDH GU29 .... 227 J7
Weavers Down *LIPH* GU30 * 193 J2
Weavers Gn *HAV* PO09 .... 103 K2
Weavers Hl *ANG/EP* BN16 .... 114 F7
Weavers La *POLE* BN26 .... 160 E2
Weavers Ring *ANG/EP* BN16 .... 114 F8
Weavers Rock La *HTHF* TN21 .... 244 F5
Webb Cl *BOGR* PO21 .... 170 F6
  CRAWW RH11 .... 43 G8
Weddell Rd *CRAWE* RH10 * 9 J9
Wedderburn Rd
  EDN/EASTW BN20 .... 163 G5
The Wedges *SWTR* RH13 .... 200 G8
Wedgwood Rd
  MSEA/BNM PO22 * 3 M5
Week La *RING/NEW* BN8 .... 87 J3
Weirbrook *CRAWE* RH10 .... 9 L9
Welbeck Av *HOVE* BN3 .... 121 K7
  SBGH/RUST TN4 .... 38 B1
  STLEO TN38 .... 98 F6
Welbeck Cl *BURH* RH15 .... 75 J5
  LW/ROSE BN22 .... 163 J2
Welchwood Cl *HORN* PO08 .... 288 A3
Welesmere Rd *BRIE/ROTT* BN2 .... 155 M2
The Welkin *HWH* RH16 .... 73 L1
Welland Cl *SALV* BN13 .... 116 C5
Welland Rd *SALV* BN13 .... 116 C5
Wellcombe Crs
  EDN/EASTW BN20 .... 176 D6
Well Copse Cl *HORN* PO08 .... 256 D12

Wellcroft Cottages
HPPT/KEY BN6 270 D4
Weller Cl CRAWE RH10 44 C4
Weller Rd SBGH/RUST TN4 37 H5
Wellesley Av FERR BN12 150 C3
Wellesley Cl BEXW TN39 136 C2
CROW TN6 67 J8
Wellesley Ct HAS TN34 13 L6
Wellesley Rd EAST BN21 10 F5
Wellfield EGRIN RH19 48 B2
Wellgreen La LEWES BN7 85 L8
Wellhouse La BURH RH15 271 Q2
Well House Pl LEWES BN7 16 E6
Well House Rd
PUL/STOR RH20 * 267 K8
Wellingham La
RING/NEW BN8 274 F10
SALV BN13 116 D4
Wellingham Wy HORS RH12 42 B7
Wellington Av BOR GU35 178 G7
Wellington Cl CRAWE RH10 28 D8
HORN PO8 288 E3
Wellington Ct LW/ROSE BN22 * 11 J1
Wellington Gdns SELS PO20 301 L5
Wellington Ms HAS TN34 13 H5
Wellington Pk SEAF BN25 175 G2
Wellington Pl HAS TN34 13 G7
Wellington Rd BOGR PO21 2 B7
BRIE/ROTT BN2 5 H2
CCH PO19 107 M4
HAS TN34 13 J6
HORS RH12 14 E6
NEWHV BN9 158 D3
PEAHV BN10 157 K7
PTSD BN41 121 G7
Wellington Sq HAS TN34 13 H7
Wellington St BRIE/ROTT BN2 5 J3
LEWES BN7 17 G5
Wellington Ter HAS TN34 * 13 H6
Wellington Town Rd
EGRIN RH19 31 J6
Wellington Wy HORL RH6 22 E4
Wellis Gdns STLEO TN38 98 F5
Well La HASM GU27 181 N11
MFD/CHID GU8 * 182 C1
MIDH GU29 260 H1
Well Meadow HAV PO9 288 F11
Wellow Cl HAV PO9 102 E2
Well Rd BOGR PO21 170 E6
Wellsbourne Rd PEV BN24 132 F8
Wells Cl EDN/EASTW BN20 176 C5
HORS RH12 201 Q3
LEWES BN7 272 H3
RTW TN1 * 37 M6
Wells Ct WTHG BN11 * 20 A7
Wells Crs BOGR PO21 171 J2
CCH PO19 107 L4
Wellsfield SELS PO20 167 H4
Wells Lea EGRIN RH19 31 J6
Wells Meadow EGRIN RH19 31 J6
Wells Rd CRAWE RH10 * 43 K7
Wellswood Gdns HAV PO9 289 K6
Wellsworth La HAV PO9 289 K6
Wellwood Cl SWTR RH13 57 G5
Welton Ri SLVH TN37 283 Q11
Welwyn Cl CRAWW RH11 42 D6
Wembley Av LAN/SOMP BN15 118 C7
Wembley Gdns
LAN/SOMP BN15 118 C7
Wembury Pk LING RH7 30 D1
Wenban Rd WTHG BN11 21 G4
Wenceling Cottages
LAN/SOMP BN15 119 H8
Wendale Dr PEAHV BN10 157 J3
Wendover Rd HAV PO9 102 F3
Wendy Rdg ANG/EP BN16 148 A3
Wenham Gdns RING/NEW BN8 276 D4
Wenlock Cl CRAWW RH11 42 F5
Wensleydale CRAWW RH11 43 H6
Wensley Gdns EMRTH PO10 104 A3
Wenthill Cl EDN/EASTW BN20 302 H4
Went Hill Gdns LW/ROSE BN22 163 G2
Went Hill Pk SEAF BN25 175 G2
Went La EDN/EASTW BN20 303 J4
Went Wy EDN/EASTW BN20 302 H5
Wentworth Cl BEX TN40 97 L8
HAIL BN27 91 L4
MSEA/BNM PO22 111 G6
SALV BN13 116 E5
Wentworth Ct ANG/EP BN16 * 148 F4
Wentworth Dr CRAWE RH10 44 C2
HORN PO8 288 C2
Wentworth St BRIE/ROTT BN2 5 G8
Wentworth Wy STLEO TN38 98 E5
Wesermarsch Rd HORN PO8 288 B5
Wesley Cl CRAWW RH11 42 D6
HORL RH6 22 F4
Wesley Ms CROW TN6 * 67 L7
Wesley Pl LW/ROSE BN22 * 11 J2
Wessex Av BOGR PO21 2 A9
SELS PO20 167 M6
Wessex Rd HORN PO8 256 E10
West Ascent STLEO TN38 99 G7
West Ashling Rd RCCH PO18 105 K2
West Av BOGR PO21 171 L2
CRAWE RH10 43 L1
LAN/SOMP BN15 118 F8
MSEA/BNM PO22 145 L7
WTHG BN11 20 A5
Westaway Dr BEXW TN39 136 F1
West Bank ARUN BN18 * 111 M8
West Beach Pk South
LHPTN BN17 * 147 H5
West Beach Rd SHOR BN43 119 J8
West Beeches Rd CROW TN6 67 M7
Westbourne Av EMRTH PO10 104 B3
SALV BN13 21 G2
Westbourne Cl EMRTH PO10 104 B3
Westbourne Gdns HOVE BN3 121 M7
Westbourne Pl HOVE BN3 121 M7
Westbourne Rd EMRTH PO10 104 B2
Westbourne St HOVE BN3 121 M6
Westbourne Vls HOVE BN3 121 L7
West Bracklesham Dr
SELS PO20 167 M8
Westbrook BRIE/ROTT BN2 * 156 B3
FROW RH18 * 48 D6
West Brook Cl RCCH PO18 105 M8
Westbrooke WTHG BN11 21 G5
Westbrooke Cl HORN PO8 288 B3
Westbrook Fld RCCH PO18 105 M8
Westbrook La RHAS TN35 284 B4
Westbrook Ter RTWE/PEM TN2 38 C8
Westbrook Wy STHW BN42 120 E6
West Broyle Dr CCH PO19 107 H3
West Buildings WTHG BN11 21 G7
West Burton La
PUL/STOR RH20 263 R12
West Chiltington La BIL RH14 232 C7
SWTR RH13 200 H7
West Chiltington Rd
PUL/STOR RH20 265 N5
PUL/STOR RH20 266 A9
PUL/STOR RH20 266 D4
West Cl HASM GU27 195 L7
MSEA/BNM PO22 145 J8
MSEA/BNM PO22 173 G1
POLE BN26 132 A6
POLE BN26 160 E2
West Common HWH RH16 73 J2
West Common Dr HWH RH16 73 K2
Westcott Cl CRAWW RH11 59 H1
Westcourt Dr BEXW TN39 136 E2
Westcourt Pl SALV BN13 20 F2
Westcourt Rd SALV BN13 20 F3
Westcroft SELS PO20 * 301 J7
Westdean Av NEWHV BN9 18 B7
West Dean Ri SEAF BN25 175 G1
Westdean Rd SALV BN13 117 G8
Westdene Cl SLVH TN37 283 R11
Westdene Dr BRI BN1 82 B8
Westdown La BUR/ETCH TN19 245 R2
Westdown Pk
BUR/ETCH TN19 245 R2
West Down Rd BEXW TN39 96 F8
Westdown Rd SEAF BN25 174 D1
West Dr ANG/EP BN16 148 C1
BOGR PO21 171 H4
BRIE/ROTT BN2 5 H6
FERR BN12 149 K5
MSEA/BNM PO22 145 M8
West End HAIL BN27 279 P11
West End La HASM GU27 182 C9
HFD BN5 268 F6
West End Wy LAN/SOMP BN15 152 C1
Westergate Cl FERR BN12 149 L3
Westergate Ms SELS PO20 110 C6
Westergate Rd
BRIE/ROTT BN2 123 K1
Westergate St SELS PO20 110 C7
Westerham Rd LGNY BN23 164 C4
Westerleigh Cl STLEO TN38 98 F5
Western Av EMRTH PO10 103 M5
POLE BN26 132 A7
Western Cl LAN/SOMP BN15 152 B1
Western Esp PTSD BN41 121 J7
Western Gdns CROW TN6 211 L2
Western Ldg
LAN/SOMP BN15 * 118 B6
Western Pde EMRTH PO10 103 M6
Western Pl WTHG BN11 20 F7
Western Rd BEX TN40 137 H2
BOR GU35 178 F3
BURH RH15 74 E6
CROW TN6 211 K2
HAIL BN27 91 M5
HAV PO9 102 F3
HPPT/KEY BN6 270 G3
HWH RH16 73 J6
LAN/SOMP BN15 152 B1
LEWES BN7 16 C6
LHPTN BN17 147 K5
LISS GU33 192 C9
LW/ROSE BN22 11 G3
NEWHV BN9 18 E5
RING/NEW BN8 240 B6
RTW TN1 38 B4
SELS PO20 301 L7
SHOR BN43 119 K6
SLVH TN37 12 B7
WADH TN5 71 L3
Western Rd North
LAN/SOMP BN15 118 B7
Western Rw WTHG BN11 20 F7
Western St BRI BN1 122 C8
Western Ter BRI BN1 4 B6
LAN/SOMP BN15 * 117 L6
Westfield MSEA/BNM PO22 144 A6
Westfield Av ANG/EP BN16 148 F5
BRIE/ROTT BN2 156 C2
Westfield Av North
BRIE/ROTT BN2 156 D2
Westfield Av South
BRIE/ROTT BN2 156 C2
Westfield Cl BRI BN1 122 F1
MAYF TN20 211 Q11
POLE BN26 131 M6
Westfield Ct POLE BN26 131 M7
Westfield Crs BRI BN1 82 F8
Westfield La SLVH TN37 283 R9
Westfield Ri BRIE/ROTT BN2 156 C2
Westfield Rd CRAWW RH11 8 B4
EAST BN21 163 J7
West Front Rd BOGR PO21 170 E7
West Furlong La
HPPT/KEY BN6 270 H4
Westgate CCH PO19 6 B4
West Ga LEWES BN7 272 H3
Westgate St LEWES BN7 16 E6
West Green Dr CRAWW RH11 8 C3
West Gun Copse Rd
SWTR RH13 201 N8
Westham Cl BEXW TN39 136 D2
Westham Dr PEV BN24 134 F7
Westhampnett Rd CCH PO19 7 K2
West Head LHPTN BN17 147 L5
West Hl EGRIN RH19 31 K3
EGRIN RH19 47 J1
RHWH RH17 206 B1
SALV BN13 116 D3
West Hill Cl SALV BN13 * 116 D3
Westhill Dr BURH RH15 74 D6
West Hill Pl BRI BN1 4 D4
West Hill Rd BRI BN1 4 C4
STLEO TN38 98 F7
West Hill St BRI BN1 4 D3
West Hoathly Rd EGRIN RH19 47 H6
Westingway BOGR PO21 171 M2
Westlake Cl SALV BN13 116 E8
Westland Av SALV BN13 20 B2
Westlands ANG/EP BN16 147 M3
FERR BN12 149 J4
Westland's Copse La
PETW GU28 228 E5
Westlands La SELS PO20 140 C8
Westlands Rd HWH RH16 73 L4
SELS PO20 141 M5
West La EGRIN RH19 47 J1
LAN/SOMP BN15 118 D7
Westleas HORL RH6 22 D4
West Leigh EGRIN RH19 47 L2
Westloats Gdns BOGR PO21 2 A3
BOGR PO21 * 143 M8
Westloats La BOGR PO21 2 A3
Westlords EDN/EASTW BN20 * 163 H6
West Mare La PUL/STOR RH20 265 N4
West Md ANG/EP BN16 148 D5
West Meade LIPH GU30 193 Q11
Westmead Rd CCH PO19 107 H7
West Meads HORL RH6 23 H6
West Meads Dr BOGR PO21 143 L8
BOGR PO21 171 L1
Westmeston Av
BRIE/ROTT BN2 156 A3
Westminster Cl
LW/ROSE BN22 163 J2
Westminster Crs HAS TN34 99 M1
Westminster Dr BOGR PO21 171 J2
Westminster Rd CRAWE RH10 44 B4
Westmoreland Cl STLEO TN38 98 E2
Westmorland Dr
MSEA/BNM PO22 145 G7
Westmount Cl STHW BN42 120 C5
Weston La PSF GU32 223 J9
RCCH PO18 290 G12
Weston Rd EPSF GU31 223 P6
Westons Hl SWTR RH13 201 L8
West Onslow Cl FERR BN12 * 149 K2
West Pallant CCH PO19 6 E5
West Pde BEXW TN39 136 F3
HORS RH12 14 C2
WTHG BN11 20 A8
West Park Crs BURH RH15 74 C5
Westpark La FERR BN12 150 D3
West Park Rd CRAWE RH10 29 L6
LING RH7 30 B1
RHWH RH17 204 C2
Westpoint RING/NEW BN8 240 B6
West Preston Ms
ANG/EP BN16 * 148 D4
West Quay NEWHV BN9 19 G3
West Ridings ANG/EP BN16 148 D5
West Rd CRBK TN17 189 R9
CRBK TN17 191 L2
EMRTH PO10 103 M5
POY/PYE BN45 270 E11
PTSD BN41 120 F6
West Sands La SELS PO20 300 H5
West Stoke Rd CCH PO19 107 J3
West Strd SELS PO20 166 F5
West St BIL RH14 231 R1
BOGR PO21 2 D8
BRI BN1 4 D7
BRIE/ROTT BN2 155 L4
BURH RH15 74 D5
CCH PO19 6 C4
CRAWW RH11 8 E5
EAST BN21 10 D7
EGRIN RH19 47 K1
EMRTH PO10 104 A5
HAS TN34 13 K7
HASM GU27 181 M11
HAV PO9 102 F4
HORS RH12 14 B6
HPPT/KEY BN6 271 R6
LAN/SOMP BN15 117 M6
LEWES BN7 17 G5
MAYF TN20 212 D8
MIDH GU29 227 J10
POLE BN26 160 E1
PTSD BN41 121 H6
PUL/STOR RH20 265 R12
RYE TN31 252 H8
SEAF BN25 174 E3
SELS PO20 301 J7
SHOR BN43 119 K6
WTHG BN11 20 F7
West Street La HTHF TN21 244 C11
West Street Ms EAST BN21 * 10 D7
West Ter EAST BN21 10 D7
HAIL BN27 279 P11
West Tyne SALV BN13 116 C8
West Undercliff RYE TN31 252 F8
Westup Rd RHWH RH17 60 D7
West Vw BOR GU35 * 178 E8
HAS TN34 13 M2
HOVE BN3 * 122 B5
HWH RH16 73 L3
SEAF BN25 174 E3
West View Ct SEAF BN25 * 174 E3
West View Dr ARUN BN18 145 L3
West View Gdns EGRIN RH19 47 K1
West View Rd BOR GU35 179 R5
Westview Ter SALV BN13 298 H11
Westville Rd BEXW TN39 136 F1
West Walberton La
ARUN BN18 111 H3
Westward Cl RCCH PO18 106 B8
Westward La PUL/STOR RH20 265 R7
West Wy CCH PO19 107 H4
CRAWE RH10 9 L2
Westway CRAWE RH10 28 F6
HORL RH6 28 A2
West Wy HOVE BN3 121 J3
LAN/SOMP BN15 118 F8
Westway LHPTN BN17 147 H2
MSEA/BNM PO22 2 F3
RTWE/PEM TN2 39 J2
West Wy SALV BN13 116 C4
SWTR RH13 200 G2
Westway Cl PTSD BN41 120 D1
Westway Gdns PTSD BN41 120 D1
Westways HAV PO9 102 A5
Westwood Cl EMRTH PO10 104 B2
Westwood Rd
SBGH/RUST TN4 37 G4
Wetherdown EPSF GU31 223 P6
Weycombe Rd HASM GU27 181 M9
Weydown Rd HASM GU27 181 L10
Wey Hl HASM GU27 181 K11
Weyhill Cl HAV PO9 288 E12
Weyland Cl LIPH GU30 179 R12
Wey Lodge Cl LIPH GU30 * 194 A1
Wey South Pth CRAN GU6 184 D7
PUL/STOR RH20 230 E9
PUL/STOR RH20 264 F7
Weysprings HASM GU27 181 J10
Whaddon Ct HAV PO9 288 D11
Wharf Rd EAST BN21 10 D6
HOVE BN3 121 J7
LHPTN BN17 147 H4
The Wharf MIDH GU29 227 J10
Whatlington Rd BAT TN33 282 F3
Whatlington Wy STLEO TN38 98 C3
Wheatcroft LHPTN BN17 147 H2
Wheatear Dr EPSF GU31 223 R7
Wheatfield Ct SLVH TN37 283 R12
Wheatfield Rd SELS PO20 301 M5
Wheatfield Wy
BRIE/ROTT BN2 123 L2
HORL RH6 23 G5
Wheatland Cl PEAHV BN10 157 G3
Wheatsheaf Cl BURH RH15 74 D4
HORS RH12 56 D4
Wheatsheaf Gdns LEWES BN7 17 K4
Wheatsheaf La RHWH RH17 72 D3
Wheatsheaf Rd HFD BN5 269 M1
Wheatstone Cl CRAWE RH10 28 A6
Wheelbarrow Castle
MIDH GU29 227 K7
Wheeler Ct HWH RH16 * 73 J7
Wheeler Rd CRAWE RH10 44 A5
Wheelers La HORL RH6 23 M7
UCK TN22 211 L11
Wheelers Wy EGRIN RH19 30 D6
Wheel La RHAS TN35 284 A6
Wheelwright Cl
LW/ROSE BN22 163 J1
Wheelwright La BURH RH15 75 J8
Wheelwrights HASM GU27 195 L7
PUL/STOR RH20 266 B4
Wheelwrights La GSHT GU26 180 D5
Wherwell Ct HAV PO9 289 J12
Whichelo Pl BRIE/ROTT BN2 5 J4
Whichers Cl HAV PO9 289 J9
Whichers Gate Rd HAV PO9 289 J9
Whin Croft Pk CROW TN6 210 E1
Whippingham Rd
BRIE/ROTT BN2 5 K1
Whippingham St
BRIE/ROTT BN2 5 K1
Whistler Av CCH PO19 107 M4
Whistler Cl CRAWE RH10 43 L6
Whitbread Cl LGNY BN23 164 A1
White Av LISS GU33 192 F3
Whitebeam Cl HORN PO8 288 D4
White Beam Ri HORN PO8 256 D8
Whitebeam Rd SALV BN13 116 B8
Whitebeam Wy
MSEA/BNM PO22 145 K7
SELS PO20 109 J4
White Bear Pas RTW TN1 * 37 M7
Whitebread La RYE TN31 219 L11
Whitechimney Rw
EMRTH PO10 104 C2
White City MIDH GU29 226 H10
Whitecroft ANG/EP BN16 * 148 B4
Whitecross St BRI BN1 4 F4
White Dirt La HORN PO8 256 D10
Whitefield Rd SBGH/RUST TN4 37 M3
Whitefriars Rd HAS TN34 13 K3
Whitegate Cl SBGH/RUST TN4 37 L1
Whitegates Cl RING/NEW BN8 273 N2
Whitegates La WADH TN5 71 H1
Whitehall Dr CRAWW RH11 42 D3
Whitehall Pde EGRIN RH19 * 31 K8
White Hart Ct HORS RH12 14 C2
Whitehaven HORN PO8 288 E3
Whitehawk Cl BRIE/ROTT BN2 123 K7
Whitehawk Crs
BRIE/ROTT BN2 123 K8
Whitehawk Hill Rd
BRIE/ROTT BN2 5 M7
Whitehawk Rd
BRIE/ROTT BN2 123 K7
Whitehawk Wy
BRIE/ROTT BN2 123 L7
White Hl LEWES BN7 16 F5
White Hill Av BEXW TN39 136 D1
Whitehill Cl CROW TN6 67 L8
EDN/EASTW BN20 163 G8
White Hill Dr BEXW TN39 136 D1
Whitehill Rd BOR GU35 179 K8
CROW TN6 67 L8
Whitehorse Rd HORS RH12 57 G3
White Horses Wy LHPTN BN17 147 M4
Whitehouse Av BEXW TN39 97 G6
Whitehouse Gdns PSF GU32 223 M4
Whitehouse La HTHF TN21 243 P10
White House Pl SALV BN13 116 D5
The Whitehouse CROW TN6 * 67 K6
White Ladies Cl HAV PO9 103 H4
Whitelands HWH RH16 * 73 J6
MSEA/BNM PO22 3 M1
Whitelea Rd LHPTN BN17 147 J3
Whitelot Cl STHW BN42 120 D4
Whitelot Wy STHW BN42 120 D3
Whitely Hl CRAWE RH10 44 E8
Whiteman's Cl RHWH RH17 72 B1
Whitemans Gn RHWH RH17 72 A1
White Rock HAS TN34 12 F8
White Rock Gdns HAS TN34 12 F7
Whiterock Pl STHW BN42 120 E6
White Rock Rd HAS TN34 12 E8
White's Cl HPPT/KEY BN6 270 H2
Whites Cottages SWTR RH13 * 202 D6
Whiteside Cl CCH PO19 7 G2
Whites La HASM GU27 194 H10
Whitesmith La RING/NEW BN8 277 J8
White St BRIE/ROTT BN2 5 G7
White Styles Rd
LAN/SOMP BN15 118 A7
Whitethorn Dr BRI BN1 122 A1
Whitethroat La RHWH RH17 205 K3
White Wy LEWES BN7 126 A4
POLE BN26 160 E4
Whiteway Cl SEAF BN25 159 K7
Whiteway La BRIE/ROTT BN2 155 M3
Whiteways MSEA/BNM PO22 143 M7
Whiteways Cl LHPTN BN17 147 J3
MSEA/BNM PO22 143 M7
Whitfeld La RING/NEW BN8 274 B11
Whitfield Cl HASM GU27 181 M8
MSEA/BNM PO22 3 G2
Whitfield Rd HASM GU27 181 M9
Whitley Cl EMRTH PO10 289 Q12
Whitley Rd HORN PO8 288 A3
LW/ROSE BN22 11 G3
Whitmoor Vale Rd GSHT GU26 180 C2
Whitmore V GSHT GU26 180 C3
Whitmore Vale Rd GSHT GU26 180 E5
Whitmore Wy HORL RH6 22 C5
Whitsbury Rd HAV PO9 288 H12
Whittingehame Gdns BRI BN1 122 E2
Whittington College
EGRIN RH19 * 30 F5
Whittington Ct EMRTH PO10 104 A5
Whittington Rd CRAWE RH10 43 J6
Whittington's Wy HAS TN34 100 A1
Whittle Dr LGNY BN23 163 M4
Whittle Wy CRAWE RH10 27 M5
Whittlewood Cl STLEO TN38 98 D3
Whitworth Rd CRAWW RH11 27 J6
SLVH TN37 283 Q10
Whybourne Crest
RTWE/PEM TN2 38 C8
Whydown Cottages
BEXW TN39 * 96 B6
Whydown Hl BAT TN33 283 M3
Whydown Rd BEXW TN39 96 A5
Whyke Cl CCH PO19 7 H8
Whyke La CCH PO19 7 G5
Whyke Rd CCH PO19 7 H4
Whylands Av SALV BN13 116 C5
Whylands Cl SALV BN13 116 C5
Whylands Crs SALV BN13 116 C5
Whytings SWTR RH13 202 H3
Wick Cl MSEA/BNM PO22 145 G8
The Wickets BURH RH15 74 E4
Wick Farm Rd LHPTN BN17 147 H3
Wickham Av BEXW TN39 137 G2
Wickham Cl HORL RH6 22 E5
HWH RH16 73 H2
Wickham Dr HPPT/KEY BN6 271 J4
Wickham Gdns SBGH/RUST TN4 37 J4
Wickham Hl HPPT/KEY BN6 271 K5
Wickham La LEWES BN7 273 P7
Wickham Rock La WSEA TN36 286 C4
Wickham Wy HWH RH16 73 H2
Wickhurst Cl PTSD BN41 120 E3
Wickhurst La HORS RH12 201 P3
Wickhurst Ri PTSD BN41 120 E2
Wickhurst Rd PTSD BN41 120 E3
Wicklands Av BRIE/ROTT BN2 156 C4
Wick La MIDH GU29 227 L5
MSEA/BNM PO22 145 G8
Wickor Cl EMRTH PO10 104 B3
Wickor Wy EMRTH PO10 104 A2
Wick Sreet POLE BN26 90 B8
Wicks Rd BIL RH14 231 R1
Wick St LHPTN BN17 147 J2
POLE BN26 90 D7
RING/NEW BN8 88 B8
Widbury RRTW TN3 * 36 E6
Widbury Cl RRTW TN3 36 E6
Widdicombe Wy
BRIE/ROTT BN2 123 K3
Widewater Cl
LAN/SOMP BN15 119 H8
Widewater Ct SHOR BN43 * 119 J8
Widgeon La SELS PO20 300 H5
Widgeon Wy HORS RH12 56 B4
Wield Cl HAV PO9 102 D1
Wigan Crs HAV PO9 102 C3
Wight Wy SELS PO20 301 L8
Wigmore Cl BRI BN1 123 G4
Wigmore Rd SALV BN13 117 J7
Wilberforce Cl CRAWW RH11 59 H1
Wilberforce Wy SWTR RH13 201 R9
Wilbury Av HOVE BN3 122 B5
Wilbury Crs HOVE BN3 122 C6
Wilbury Gdns HOVE BN3 122 B5
Wilbury Gv HOVE BN3 122 B7
Wilbury Rd HOVE BN3 122 B7
Wilbury Vls HOVE BN3 122 B6
Wilby Av STHW BN42 120 D4
Wildacre Cl BIL RH14 198 E2
Wildbrooks Cl PUL/STOR RH20 265 L3
Wilderness Gdns RYE TN31 218 D10
Wilderness La UCK TN22 243 J4
Wilderness Pk CROW TN6 67 K7
Wilderness Ri EGRIN RH19 31 M4
Wilderness Rd HPPT/KEY BN6 270 H3
The Wilderness HWH RH16 73 L1
Wilderwick Rd EGRIN RH19 31 M2
Wildgoose Dr HORS RH12 201 Q2
Wild Orchid Wy SWTR RH13 201 R10
Wild Park Cl BRIE/ROTT BN2 123 K2
Wildwood LGNY BN23 * 164 B1
Wildwood La CRAN GU6 184 H4
Wilfrid Rd HOVE BN3 121 J5
Wilkins Cl HORN PO8 256 C7
Wilkinson Cl ANG/EP BN16 148 F1
BRIE/ROTT BN2 155 L2
Wilkinson Wy SEAF BN25 174 E1
Wilkins Wy BEX TN40 97 L7
Willard Cl LW/ROSE BN22 163 M7
Willard Wy PUL/STOR RH20 267 J8
Willett Cl PETW GU28 262 G6
Willetts Fld RING/NEW BN8 277 M9
Willetts La RRTW TN3 35 H5
Willetts Wy BIL RH14 198 G2
William Allen La HWH RH16 73 L4
William Morris Wy
CRAWW RH11 59 G1
William Olders Rd
ANG/EP BN16 148 F1
William Rd CCH PO19 7 L4
STLEO TN38 98 D6
Williamson Cl HASM GU27 181 Q8
Williams Rd RCCH PO18 106 B6
SHOR BN43 120 A5
William St BOGR PO21 2 E6
BRIE/ROTT BN2 4 F6
PTSD BN41 121 G6
SBGH/RUST TN4 37 M4
Williams Wy CRAWE RH10 44 A3
Willicombe Pk
RTWE/PEM TN2 38 C5
Willingdon Av BEXW TN39 136 F1
STLEO TN38 283 P12
Willingdon Cl
EDN/EASTW BN20 163 G4
SLVH TN37 283 P12
Willingdon Ct
EDN/EASTW BN20 162 F2
Willingdon Dro LGNY BN23 163 M4
Willingdon La POLE BN26 162 B6
Willingdon Park Dr
LW/ROSE BN22 163 J5
Willingdon Rd BRIE/ROTT BN2 123 K4
EAST BN21 163 H7
Willingdon Wy LW/ROSE BN22 163 G3
STLEO TN38 283 P12
Willingford La
BUR/ETCH TN19 246 B3
Willoughby Crs
LW/ROSE BN22 164 B7
Willow Av ANG/EP BN16 148 D4
HAIL BN27 92 A4
Willow Bank RBTBR TN32 248 C2
Willowbed Av CCH PO19 7 J8
Willowbed Dr CCH PO19 7 J8
Willowbed Wk HAS TN34 99 K1
Willow Brean HORL RH6 22 D5
Willow Brook LHPTN BN17 147 H2
MSEA/BNM PO22 145 M8
Willowbrook Rd SALV BN13 21 M1
Willowbrook Wy
HPPT/KEY BN6 271 P6

Willow Cl BOR GU35 ....178 H6
  BRIE/ROTT BN2.......124 D5
  BUR/ETCH TN19 ....215 N9
  CRAWE RH10 ....43 K1
  EGRIN RH19 ....31 J6
  HAV PO9.......103 H4
  HPPT/KEY BN6.......270 G2
  HTHF TN21 ....244 H6
  LAN/SOMP BN15 ....119 H8
  LIPH GU30 ....194 A4
  PUL/STOR RH20 ....266 A1
  STEY/UB BN44 ....78 D1
Willow Cnr HORL RH6 * 26 E2
Willow Ct HORL RH6 * 23 H7
  WTHG BN11 ....20 A4
Willow Crs SALV BN13 ....116 B8
Willowdale Cl PSF GU32 ....222 G5
Willowdene Cl HAV PO9 ....102 C1
Willow Dr BEXW TN39 ....96 B8
  BIL RH14 ....232 A1
  POLE BN26 ....131 M8
  SEAF BN25 ....175 J2
Willow End HAS TN34 ....99 L1
The Willow Est NEWHV BN9 * 19 J1
Willowfield Rd LW/ROSE BN22 ....11 H5
Willowfield Sq LW/ROSE BN22 ....11 H4
Willow Gdns EMRTH PO10 ....104 C1
  HPPT/KEY BN6 ....270 H2
  LIPH GU30 ....194 A2
Willowhale Av BOGR PO21 ....171 J3
Willowhayne Av ANG/EP BN16 ....148 F5
Willowhayne Cl ANG/EP BN16 ....148 F5
Willowhayne Crs
  ANG/EP BN16 ....148 F5
Willow La WSEA TN36 ....286 G3
Willowmead CROW TN6 ....210 F4
Willow Md EGRIN RH19 ....47 L1
Willow Ms RBTBR TN32 ....248 C1
Willow Pk HWH RH16 ....73 L5
Willow Rdg CRAWE RH10 ....45 M6
Willow Rd HORS RH12 ....57 G4
  LISS GU33 ....192 C9
Willows Ri UCK TN22 ....77 K7
The Willows ANG/EP BN16 ....148 F5
  ARUN BN18 * 112 D8
  BIL RH14 ....231 R2
  BRIE/ROTT BN2 * 5 G1
  BURH RH15 ....75 G4
  LAN/SOMP BN15 * 118 D8
  MFD/CHID GU8 ....182 F5
  PUL/STOR RH20 ....264 H4
  PUL/STOR RH20 * 265 R12
  RING/NEW BN8 ....274 D4
  SALV BN13 * 298 H11
  SEAF BN25 * 174 E2
  SELS PO20 ....301 L5
  SLVH TN37 ....283 P12
Willow Stream Cl RHAS TN35 ....284 H6
Willow Tree Av HORN PO8 ....288 C7
Willow Tree Rd RTWE/PEM TN2.. 37 K8
Willow Wk NEWHV BN9 ....18 S2
  RTWE/PEM TN2 ....38 D1
Willow Wy BOGR PO21 ....171 G4
  HPPT/KEY BN6 ....270 H1
  PUL/STOR RH20 ....267 J9
Wills Cl ARUN BN18 ....146 A3
Wilman Gdns BOGR PO21 ....171 J3
Wilman Rd SBGH/RUST TN4 ....37 M2
Wilmington Cl BRI BN1 ....82 F1
  CRAWW RH11 ....59 G3
  HPPT/KEY BN6 ....271 N6
Wilmington Pde BRI BN1 ....82 E8
Wilmington Rd HAS TN34 ....99 M2
  NEWHV BN9 ....18 C6
  SEAF BN25 ....174 D1
Wilmington Sq EAST BN21 ....10 E5
Wilmington Wy BRI BN1 ....82 E8
  HWH RH16 ....73 K4
Wilmot Rd SHOR BN43 ....120 B5
Wilson Av BRIE/ROTT BN2 ....154 E1
Wilson Cl CCH PO19 ....107 J4
  CRAWE RH10 ....44 C6
Wilson Ct ARUN BN18 ....146 A3
Wilson Gv UCK TN22 ....76 C5
Wilsons Rd BOR GU35 ....179 Q4
Wilton Av LW/ROSE BN22 ....163 L2
Wilton Cl ANG/EP BN16 ....148 A2
  SELS PO20 ....168 A5
  SWTR RH13 ....234 F10
Wilton Court Man BEX TN40 * 137 L2
Wilton Dr ANG/EP BN16 ....148 A2
  HORN PO8 ....288 B4
Wilton Rd BEX TN40 ....137 L2
Wiltshire Wy RTWE/PEM TN2 ....38 C2
Wilverley Av HAV PO9 ....103 H1
Wimblehurst Rd HORS RH12 ....14 C1
Wimland HI HORS RH12 ....41 J7
Wimland Rd HORS RH12 ....41 H5
Wimlands La HORS RH12 ....41 J6
Wincanton Cl CRAWE RH10 ....44 C3
Wincanton Wy WVILLE PO7 ....288 C4
Winceby Cl BEXW TN39 ....136 D3
Winchcombe Rd
  LW/ROSE BN22 ....10 F4
Winchelsea Cl SEAF BN25 ....160 A4
Winchelsea Gdns WTHG BN11 ....20 A8
Winchelsea La RHAS TN35 ....284 H12
  RYE TN31 ....251 Q11
Winchelsea Rd LW/ROSE BN22 ....164 C1
  RHAS TN35 ....100 C1
  RYE TN31 ....252 G8
Winchester Dr CCH PO19 ....107 L5
Winchester Rd ANG/EP BN16 ....148 C3
  CRAWE RH10 ....43 K7
  PSF GU32 ....222 C3
  PSF GU32 ....223 H5
  WTHG BN11 ....20 D6
Winchester St BRI BN1 ....4 E1
Winchester Wy
  LW/ROSE BN22 ....163 G3
The Winches SWTR RH13 * 58 B3
Winchfield Crs HAV PO9 ....102 C1
Wincombe Rd BRI BN1 ....122 C4
Winden Av CCH PO19 ....7 H5
Windermere Ct FERR BN12 * 150 A3
Windermere Crs FERR BN12 ....116 C8
  LW/ROSE BN22 ....11 J1
Windermere Rd BOR GU35 ....178 G8
  HWH RH16 ....73 L6
Winding St HAS TN34 ....13 K6
Windlesham Cl PTSD BN41 ....120 A7
Windlesham Gdns
  ANG/EP BN16 ....148 F1
  BRI BN1 ....4 B8
  SHOR BN43 ....119 L3

Windlesham Rd BRI BN1 ....4 B4
  SHOR BN43 ....119 L5
Windmill SELS PO20 ....109 J4
Windmill Av HPPT/KEY BN6 ....271 N6
Windmill Cl ANG/EP BN16 ....148 F1
  BOGR PO21 ....171 G4
  EAST BN21 ....163 H7
  HORL RH6 ....23 C8
  HORN PO8 ....256 D8
  HOVE BN3 ....121 L3
  HTHF TN21 ....244 E5
  PUL/STOR RH20 ....267 K8
  STEY/UB BN44 ....79 G3
  SWTR RH13 ....15 L3
Windmill Copse
  PUL/STOR RH20 ....266 A11
Windmill Ct CRAWE RH10 ....43 J1
  SELS PO20 ....167 L6
Windmill Dr ANG/EP BN16 ....148 C3
  BEXW TN39 ....97 G7
  BOR GU35 ....179 Q3
  BRI BN1 ....82 B7
  HOVE BN3 * 74 F5
Windmill Fld RCCH PO18 ....105 M8
Windmill Gn PEV BN24 ....133 G8
Windmill La EDN/EASTW BN20 .....302 G4
  EGRIN RH19 ....31 J6
  EGRIN RH19 ....48 B2
  HFD BN5 ....269 J6
  WADH TN5 ....71 J5
  WADH TN5 ....190 B5
Windmill Pl POLE BN26 ....162 F1
Windmill Platt RHWH RH17 ....204 D1
Windmill Rd LHPTN BN17 ....147 J6
  POLE BN26 ....131 M8
  STHW BN42 ....120 D4
  STLEO TN38 ....99 G3
Windmill St BRIE/ROTT BN2 ....5 H6
  RTWE/PEM TN2 * 38 B1
Windmill Ter BRIE/ROTT BN2 ....5 H5
  WADH TN5 ....82 F7
Windover Crs LEWES BN7 ....16 A4
Windover Wy LW/ROSE BN22 ....163 G2
Windrush Cl CRAWW RH11 ....42 E5
  SALV BN13 ....116 B5
Windsor Cl ANG/EP BN16 ....148 A2
  BOGR PO21 ....171 K1
  CRAWW RH11 ....43 H7
  HOVE BN3 ....121 M2
  HWH RH16 ....73 K4
  SEAF BN25 ....159 G7
  SWTR RH13 ....201 R12
Windsor Ct CROW TN6 ....211 K1
Windsor Dr ANG/EP BN16 ....148 K1
  SELS PO20 ....167 K6
Windsor Pl CROW TN6 ....211 K1
  EGRIN RH19 ....47 M1
Windsor Rd BEXW TN39 ....137 G1
  BOR GU35 ....179 J4
  CCH PO19 ....7 K5
  CROW TN6 ....211 K1
  HAIL BN27 ....92 A7
  PSF GU32 ....223 N6
  SELS PO20 ....301 L7
  SLVH TN37 ....99 G2
  WTHG BN11 ....21 M4
Windsor St BRI BN1 ....4 D6
Windsor Wk BOR GU35 ....179 J4
Windsor Wy LAN/SOMP BN15 ....119 L7
  POLE BN26 ....131 M6
  WSEA TN36 ....286 F5
Windward Cl LHPTN BN17 ....147 M4
Windward Quay SALV BN13 ....164 E5
Windways MFD/CHID GU8 ....184 A4
Windyacre RING/NEW BN8 * 240 B6
Windyridge CRAWW RH11 ....42 F4
Wineham Wy HFD BN5 ....235 Q10
Winfield Av BRI BN1 ....82 E7
Winfield Cl BRI BN1 ....82 E8
  PTSD BN41 ....120 F2
Winfield Wy EMRTH PO10 ....104 A1
Wingate Cl STLEO TN38 ....98 F14
Wingle Tye Rd BURH RH15 ....271 P1
Winguard Wy CCH PO19 ....6 E2
Winkfield Rw HORN PO8 ....288 B4
Winkhurst Wy BURH RH15 ....75 J8
Winkney Rd LW/ROSE BN22 ....163 L2
Winkton Cl HAV PO9 ....102 E2
Winnet Wy SWTR RH13 ....201 R11
Winnipeg Cl LIPH GU30 ....193 R2
Winscombe Av HORN PO8 ....288 B7
Winscote Cl CROW TN6 ....67 J8
Winslade Rd HAV PO9 ....288 E12
Winston Cl BOGR PO21 ....143 L7
Winston Crs BOGR PO21 ....143 L7
  LGNY BN23 ....164 C6
Winston Dr BEXW TN39 ....136 D1
Winstone Scott Av RRTW TN3 ....36 D5
Winterbourne Cl HAS TN34 ....12 E5
  LEWES BN7 ....16 B8
  SALV BN13 ....116 A8
Winterbourne Hollow
  LEWES BN7 ....16 C7
Winterbourne La LEWES BN7 ....16 C8
Winterbourne Ms LEWES BN7 ....16 C8
Winterbourne Rd CCH PO19 ....107 M3
Winterbourne SALV BN13 ....116 A8
Winterfold CRAWE RH10 ....9 L2
Winter Gdns CRAWW RH11 ....8 D6
The Winter Knoll LHPTN BN17 ....147 L4
Winterpit Cl SWTR RH13 ....203 J3
Winterpit La SWTR RH13 ....203 J3
Winters La MIDH GU29 ....227 K6
Winterslow Dr HAV PO9 ....288 F11
Winterton Cl SWTR RH13 ....14 F6
Winterton Ldg LHPTN BN17 * 147 K4
Winterton Wy SHOR BN43 ....120 M3
Winton Av BRIE/ROTT BN2 ....156 B3
Winton Pl WTHG BN11 ....21 G5
Winton Rd PSF GU32 ....223 N6
Winton St POLE BN26 ....160 D4
Wire Mill La LING RH7 ....30 D1
Wisborough Cl CRAWW RH11 ....42 E6
Wisborough Gdns BIL RH14 ....231 L1
Wisborough La
  PUL/STOR RH20 ....266 B12
Wisden Av BURH RH15 ....74 D4
Wiseacre RRTW TN3 ....190 F2
Wish HI EDN/EASTW BN20 ....163 G1
Wishing Tree La STLEO TN38 ....98 E3

Wishing Tree Rd STLEO TN38 ....98 E3
Wishing Tree Rd North
  STLEO TN38 ....98 E3
Wish Rd EAST BN21 ....10 E7
  HOVE BN3 ....121 K7
Wish Ward RYE TN31 ....252 G8
Wisteria Dr BOR GU35 ....178 G2
Wisteria Gdns HAV PO9 ....103 J1
Wiston Av CCH PO19 ....6 D3
Wiston Cl SALV BN13 ....117 G8
Wiston Ct CRAWW RH11 ....42 E6
Wiston Rd BRIE/ROTT BN2 ....123 L6
Wiston Wy BRIE/ROTT BN2 ....123 L6
Witchampton Cl HAV PO9 * 288 H12
Withdean Av BRI BN1 ....122 C3
  FERR BN12 ....150 A5
Withdean Cl BRI BN1 ....122 C2
Withdean Court Av BRI BN1 ....122 C2
Withdean Crs BRI BN1 ....122 D2
Withdean Ri BRI BN1 ....122 C2
Withdean Rd BRI BN1 ....122 C3
Wither Dl HORL RH6 ....22 E8
Witherenden Rd MAYF TN20 ....212 H8
Witherslack Cl BOR GU35 ....179 Q5
Withey Brook HORL RH6 ....22 B3
Withey Mdw HORL RH6 ....22 B3
Withy Bush BURH RH15 ....74 D5
Withyham Av BRIE/ROTT BN2 ....156 B5
Withyham Cl LW/ROSE BN22 ....163 L4
Withyham Rd BEXW TN39 ....136 B3
  RRTW TN3 ....51 M3
Withypitts CRAWE RH10 ....45 M6
Withypitts East CRAWE RH10 ....45 M6
Wittcomb Ter BOR GU35 * 178 F8
Wittering Rd HISD PO11 ....166 A3
Wittersham La RYE TN31 ....220 C12
Wittersham Ri STLEO TN38 ....98 D3
Wittersham Rd CRBK TN17 ....219 N5
  RYE TN31 ....220 C6
  TENT TN30 ....220 G6
Wivelsfield Rd BRIE/ROTT BN2 ....156 B2
  HWH RH16 ....73 H7
Woburn Cl HAIL BN27 ....91 M4
Woburn Pl BRI BN1 ....83 L8
Woburn Rd CRAWW RH11 ....42 F5
Woburn Wy LW/ROSE BN22 ....163 J2
Wode Cl HORN PO8 ....256 D10
Wode Rd BAT TN33 ....95 M2
Woelfs Cl PUL/STOR RH20 * 267 K8
Wold Cl CRAWW RH11 ....42 E5
Woldhurstlea Cl CRAWW RH11 * 42 E5
Wolfe Cl UCK TN22 ....210 H1
Wolmere Rd HORL RH6 ....22 E8
Wolmere La LISS GU33 ....192 D3
Wolseley Rd BRI BN1 ....83 J7
  CROW TN6 ....210 G1
  HTHF TN21 ....244 E7
  RHAS TN35 ....285 P12
  SWTR RH13 ....15 M3
Wolsey Cl BOGR PO21 ....171 G4
Wolstonbury Rd ANG/EP BN16 ....148 B2
Wolstonbury Rd CRAWW RH11 ....8 D7
Wolstonbury Wy BURH RH15 ....75 G7
Wolverstone Dr BRI BN1 ....123 H5
Wolverton Cl HORL RH6 ....22 E8
Wolverton Gdns HORL RH6 ....22 E7
Wolverton Rd HAV PO9 ....288 F12
Wolves HI RDKG RH5 ....24 B5
Wonston Ct HAV PO9 ....289 K11
Woodard Rd LAN/SOMP BN15 ....118 E6
Woodards Vw SHOR BN43 ....119 L6
Woodberry Cl MFD/CHID GU8 ....182 F4
Woodberry La HAV PO9 ....289 L8
Woodborough Cl SELS PO20 ....168 B7
Woodbourne Av BRI BN1 ....122 C1
Woodbourne Cl HAV PO9 ....192 D9
Woodbridge Ct HORS RH12 * 56 F4
Woodbridge Pk ANG/EP BN16 ....148 F4
Woodbrook Rd HAS TN34 ....99 J1
Woodbury Av EGRIN RH19 ....48 A1
  HAV PO9 ....103 G5
  PSF GU32 ....223 M4
Woodbury Cl EGRIN RH19 ....48 A1
  SBGH/RUST TN4 ....38 A4
Woodbury Gv HORN PO8 ....288 A4
Woodbury Park Gdns
  SBGH/RUST TN4 ....38 A4
Woodbury Park Rd
  SBGH/RUST TN4 ....37 M4
Wood Cl REDH RH1 ....22 F1
Woodcock HI EGRIN RH19 ....30 F3
Woodcombe HAS TN34 ....99 L1
Woodcot Crs HAV PO9 ....288 H11
Woodcote HORL RH6 ....23 L6
Woodcote La LHPTN BN17 ....113 J7
  PUL/STOR RH20 ....230 E12
Woodcote Rd FROW RH18 ....48 D7
Woodcourt CRAWW RH11 ....43 G4
Woodcrest Rd BURH RH15 ....74 E8
Woodcroft HORL RH6 ....74 E4
Woodcroft Dr EAST BN21 ....163 H6
Woodcroft La HORN PO8 ....288 A4
Woodcroft Rd CRAWW RH11 ....42 E5
Woodcutters RHWH RH17 ....239 J2
Wooddale La BIL RH14 ....200 D12
Woodend BOGR PO21 ....171 M1
Woodend HORS RH12 ....57 H4
Woodend RCCH PO18 ....291 K12
Woodend CRAWE RH10 ....43 M1
Woodfield SWTR RH13 ....201 P12
Woodfield Park Rd
  EMRTH PO10 ....104 C5
Woodfield Rd CRAWE RH10 * 9 H1
  HORS RH12 ....186 A10
Woodgate Cl SELS PO20 ....110 C8
Woodgate Meadow
  LEWES BN7 ....272 H2
Woodgate Pk SELS PO20 ....110 C8
Woodgate Rd LW/ROSE BN22 ....11 H1
  SELS PO20 ....110 C8
Woodgates Cl SWTR RH13 ....15 H4
Woodgreen Av HAV PO9 ....102 C3
Woodhall Cl RHWH RH17 ....72 C2
Woodhams Cl BAT TN33 ....282 F5
Woodhatch SWTR RH13 ....201 Q11
Woodhayes HORL RH6 ....23 M6
Woodhill Pk RTWE/PEM TN2 ....39 H3
Woodhouse Cl HOVE BN3 ....121 K6
Woodhouse La HAV PO9 ....289 H5
  HORN PO8 ....288 H3
Woodhouse Rd HORN PO8 ....288 G2
  HOVE BN3 ....121 K6
Wooding Gv CRAWW RH11 ....43 G8

Woodington Cl HAV PO9 ....288 H11
  HOVE BN3 ....121 M2
  LW/ROSE BN22 ....163 M3
  SALV BN13 ....116 E4
Woodland Av BURH RH15 ....75 H5
  HOVE BN3 ....121 H5
  HOVE BN3 ....122 A3
  SBGH/RUST TN4 ....38 A2
  SWTR RH13 ....57 G5
Woodland Cl BIL RH14 ....200 B7
  BURH RH15 ....75 H5
  HOVE BN3 ....122 A3
Woodland Dr CRAWE RH10 ....46 A1
  HOVE BN3 ....122 A3
Woodland La SWTR RH13 ....58 A6
Woodland Ms HTHF TN21 ....244 E7
Woodland Ri BEX TN40 ....137 K1
Woodland Rd SBGH/RUST TN4 ....38 D8
  SELS PO20 ....301 M5
Woodlands CRAWE RH10 ....44 A1
  HOVE BN3 ....122 B3
  RTWE/PEM TN2 ....39 J4
Woodlands Av ANG/EP BN16 ....148 B4
  EMRTH PO10 ....103 M2
Woodlands Cl ANG/EP BN16 ....114 F6
  BIL RH14 * 200 B7
  CRAWE RH10 ....46 A2
  HAIL BN27 ....92 B3
  HPPT/KEY BN6 ....271 M5
  HTHF TN21 ....244 E8
  PEAHV BN10 ....157 G4
  RYE TN31 ....252 B3
  SALV BN13 ....115 L4
  UCK TN22 ....76 F7
Woodlands La CCH PO19 ....6 C1
  HASM GU27 ....181 J10
  LISS GU33 ....192 E11
  RCCH PO18 ....290 C7
Woodlands Pk ARUN BN18 ....145 L2
  HWH RH16 ....73 J5
  LHPTN BN17 ....147 K5
  MSEA/BNM PO22 ....144 A7
The Woodlands BOR GU35 ....178 D8
  BRI BN1 ....82 D8
  HAS TN34 ....284 B11
Woodlands Wk SWTR RH13 ....202 H4
Woodlands Wy BIL RH14 ....232 B3
  HAS TN34 ....284 B11
  HAV PO9 ....103 M3
  SWTR RH13 ....233 P1
Woodland V POLE BN26 * 131 L4
Woodland Vale Rd SLVH TN37 ....12 A5
Woodland Vw HORN PO8 ....288 A3
  TENT TN30 ....220 D5
Woodland Wk BRIE/ROTT BN2 ....155 J1
Woodland Wy BAT TN33 ....97 L1
  BRI BN1 ....122 C1
  CROW TN6 ....210 G1
  HTHF TN21 ....244 E7
  RHAS TN35 ....285 P12
  SWTR RH13 ....15 M3
Wood La HAIL BN27 ....94 D2
  HFD BN5 ....269 L11
Woodlark Gdns EPSF GU31 ....223 R6
Woodlea Rd SALV BN13 ....20 A4
Woodleigh Cl HAV PO9 ....103 K2
Woodleigh Rd BURH RH15 ....75 H5
Woodmancote La
  EMRTH PO10 ....104 F1
Woodmancote Rd SALV BN13 ....20 C1
Woodmans HI CRAWW RH11 ....43 H8
Woodpecker Cl BOR GU35 ....178 G7
  HAV PO9 ....103 J4
Woodpecker Crs BURH RH15 ....74 C7
Woodpecker Dr HAIL BN27 ....91 M6
Woodpecker La PUL/STOR RH20 * 90 A2
  PUL/STOR RH20 ....266 B12
  PETW GU28 ....229 L10
Woodpecker Wy CRAWE RH10 ....46 B3
  HAIL BN27 * 90 A2
  SALV BN13 ....116 B8
  UCK TN22 ....76 F7
Wood Ride HWH RH16 ....73 C6
Woodridge Cl HWH RH16 ....73 K6
Wood Rd GSHT GU26 ....180 G3
Woodroyd Av HORL RH6 ....22 E6
Woodroyd Gdns HORL RH6 ....22 E7
Woodruff Av HOVE BN3 ....122 B3
Woodsedge WVILLE PO7 ....288 B12
Woodsgate Pk BEXW TN39 ....97 H7
Woodsgate Wy RTWE/PEM TN2... 39 G5
Woods Hill Cl EGRIN RH19 ....48 C3
Woods Hill La EGRIN RH19 ....48 C3
Woodside CROW TN6 ....67 K7
  MSEA/BNM PO22 ....111 J2
  SWTR RH13 ....57 G5
Woodside Av BRI BN1 ....122 C3
Woodside Cl BOR GU35 ....178 G6
  PUL/STOR RH20 ....266 B11
  RTWE/PEM TN2 ....39 K3
  SWTR RH13 ....235 J9
Woodside Crs BOR GU35 ....178 G6
  HORL RH6 ....23 M6
Woodside Pk BOR GU35 ....178 G6
Woodside Rd CRAWE RH10 ....43 J7
  MFD/CHID GU8 ....182 F5
  RTWE/PEM TN2 ....39 K3
  SALV BN13 ....20 D2
  SBGH/RUST TN4 ....37 M3
Woodside Wy HAIL BN27 ....131 M1
Woodsland Cl HPPT/KEY BN6 ....271 M5
Woodsland Rd HPPT/KEY BN6 ....271 N5
Woodslands HORL RH6 ....23 M6
Woods Pas HAS TN34 ....13 M6
Woodspring Cl SLVH TN37 ....283 Q12
Woodstock Av HORN PO8 ....288 B4
Woodstock Cl HORS RH12 ....56 C4
Woodstock Gdns
  BOGR PO21 ....171 J2
Woodstock Rd BEXW TN39 ....96 B7
  HAV PO9 ....102 D3
Wood St BOGR PO21 ....2 A8
  EGRIN RH19 ....31 J8
Woods Wy FERR BN12 ....150 B2
Wood Vw ARUN BN18 ....112 F4
Woodview SHOR BN43 ....119 L4
Woodview Ct SHOR BN43 * 119 L4
Woodville Rd BEXW TN39 ....137 G2
  HAV PO9 ....102 D3
Woodward Cl LGNY BN23 ....164 D6
Woodwards CRAWW RH11 ....43 G4
Woodyard La BURH RH15 ....75 G8
Woolbeding La MIDH GU29 ....226 E6

Woolborough Cl CRAWE RH10 ....9 G1
Woolborough La CRAWE RH10 ....27 L8
  CRAWE RH10 * 43 M1
  REDH RH1. ....23 L1
Woolborough Rd CRAWE RH10 ....8 F2
Wooldridge Wk LHPTN BN17 ....146 A3
Wool La MIDH GU29 ....227 J10
Woolmer Ct HAV PO9 ....289 J11
Woolmer Hill Rd HASM GU27 ....180 F10
Woolmer La LIPH GU30 ....179 R9
Woolmer Rd LISS GU33 ....192 G2
Woolmer St EMRTH PO10 ....103 M1
Woolmer Wy BOR GU35 ....178 F7
Woolner Av PSF GU32 ....223 N5
The Woolstaplers CCH PO19 ....6 D4
Woolston Rd HAV PO9 ....288 D11
Woolven Cl BURH RH15 ....74 D8
Woolvens Rw HFD BN5 * 269 L4
Wophams La SELS PO20 ....141 H6
Worcester Ct WTHG BN11 * 20 A7
  CRAWE RH10 ....43 K7
Worcester Rd CCH PO19 ....107 L4
  CRAWE RH10 ....43 K7
Worcester Vls HOVE BN3 ....121 H6
Wordsworth Cl CRAWE RH10 ....44 A1
Wordsworth Dr LGNY BN23 ....164 D3
Wordsworth Gdns
  MSEA/BNM PO22 ....145 J7
Wordsworth Pl HORS RH12 ....56 D7
Wordsworth Ri EGRIN RH19 ....31 H8
Wordsworth St HOVE BN3 ....121 M6
Workhouse La RHAS TN35 ....284 B5
  HAS TN36 ....285 Q4
Worms La MSEA/BNM PO22 ....145 H6
Worsham La BEX TN40 ....97 L6
Worsted La EGRIN RH19 ....48 A2
Worth Rd ANG/EP BN16 ....148 B2
  LHPTN BN17 ....147 K2
  SWTR RH13 ....14 A9
  SWTR RH13 ....201 Q11
  SWTR RH13 ....267 P2
Worthing Road Picts HI
  SWTR RH13 ....202 A1
Worth Park Av CRAWE RH10 ....44 B2
Worth Rd CRAWE RH10 ....44 B3
Worth Wy CRAWE RH10 ....44 C3
Worthy Ct HAV PO9 ....289 J12
Wray Cl EGRIN RH19 ....48 C3
Wraysbury Park Dr
  EMRTH PO10 ....104 A1
Wren Cl HORS RH12 ....56 C2
  HTHF TN21 ....244 D6
  PUL/STOR RH20 * 265 J3
Wren Crs MSEA/BNM PO22 ....144 A7
Wrenfield Pl BOGR PO21 * 2 D3
Wren St CRAWE RH10 ....46 B4
Wrestwood Av
  LW/ROSE BN22 ....163 H4
Wrestwood Cl BEX TN40 ....97 J7
Wrestwood Rd BEX TN40 ....97 J7
Wrexham Gv HORN PO8 ....256 C10
Wright Cl CRAWE RH10 * 44 A7
Wrotham Cl HAS TN34 ....284 B12
  LGNY BN23 ....164 C4
Wroxham Rd LGNY BN23 ....164 A1
Wroxham Wk CRAWE RH10 ....44 A5
Wroxham Wy
  MSEA/BNM PO22 ....3 K1
Wyatt Cl BIL RH14 ....231 J1
Wyatts La RHWH RH17 ....207 N4
Wyberlee Rd BURH RH15 ....74 F5
Wychperry Rd HWH RH16 ....73 G4
Wychurst Gdns BEX TN40 ....97 J7
Wychwood BIL RH14 ....198 E2
Wychwood Cl BOGR PO21 ....171 K4
Wychwood Gdns WTHG BN11 ....152 A2
Wychwood Wk BOGR PO21 ....171 K4
Wyde Feld BOGR PO21 ....171 L3
Wye Cl CRAWW RH11 ....59 H1
Wyeford Cl HAV PO9 ....289 J11
Wyke Av WTHG BN11 ....21 J4
Wykeham Cl STEY/UB BN44 ....78 C2
Wykeham Rd HAS TN34 ....12 E4
  LHPTN BN17 ....20 E5
Wykeham Ter BRI BN1 * 4 C6
Wykeham Wy BURH RH15 ....75 H7
Wyke La North
  MSEA/BNM PO22 ....145 H8
Wykwood LIPH GU30 ....194 A1
Wylde Green La LISS GU33 ....192 D8
Wylds La PSF GU32 ....223 K9
Wyncombe Cl
  PUL/STOR RH20 ....264 B2
Wyndham Cl HORN PO8 ....288 C5
Wyndham Lea
  PUL/STOR RH20 ....265 R7
Wyndham Rd PETW GU28 ....229 L10
Wyndham St BRIE/ROTT BN2 ....5 J8
Wynlea Cl CRAWE RH10 ....45 M1
Wynnes Ms HOVE BN3 ....121 M6
Wynnstay BURH RH15 * 75 G7
Wysemead HORL RH6 ....23 H5
The Wyshe POY/PYE BN45 ....271 K11
Wythering Cl BOGR PO21 ....170 E6
Wythwood HWH RH16 ....73 H4
Wyvern Cl SELS PO20 ....109 K4
Wyvern Wy BURH RH15 ....75 H6

Y

Yaldhurst Ct HAV PO9 ....289 J11
Yapton La ARUN BN18 ....111 L5
Yapton Rd MSEA/BNM PO22 ....111 J8
  MSEA/BNM PO22 ....289 J8
Yardley Cl HAV PO9 ....289 J8
Yardley St BRI BN1 ....4 F1
Yarmouth Cl CRAWE RH10 ....9 M7
Yarrow Cl HORS RH12 ....56 D4
Yarrow Rd LEWES BN7 ....16 D4
  HAV PO9 ....288 D12
Yateley Cl HAV PO9 ....288 D12
Yates Cl RYE TN31 ....254 B11
Yattendon Rd HORL RH6 ....23 G6
Yeoman Rd SALV BN13 ....116 A9
Yeomans RING/NEW BN8 ....275 M10
Yeomans Acre BOGR PO21 ....171 J2
Yeomans Fld RCCH PO18 ....105 J4
Yeomans La LIPH GU30 ....193 P1
Yeomans Pl BOR GU35 ....179 M4
Yeoman Wy SALV BN13 ....150 A1

Yewens *MFD/CHID* GU8 .... 182 G4
Yew La *EGRIN* RH19 .... 31 G6
The Yews *HORN* PO8 .... 288 C2
Yew Tree CI *HAS* TN34 .... 284 B11
  HORL RH6 .... 22 F4
  HTHF TN21 * 244 D7
  MSEA/BNM PO22 .... 2 B1
  RING/NEW BN8 .... 275 L10
Yewtree CI *SWTR* RH13 .... 235 K3
Yewtree La *CROW* TN6 .... 212 A1
Yew Tree PI *LISS* GU33 .... 192 D9

Yew Tree Rd *HORL* RH6 .... 26 D2
  SBGH/RUST TN4 .... 37 M1
Yielding's CI *EAST* BN21 .... 163 J8
Yoells Crs *HORN* PO8 .... 288 A3
Yoells La *HORN* PO8 .... 288 A3
York Av *EGRIN* RH19 .... 47 M1
  HOVE BN3 .... 4 A4
York Buildings *HAS* TN34 * 13 F4
York Cha *CCH* PO19 .... 107 L3
York CI *BOR* GU35 .... 178 D7
  PSF GU32 .... 223 L6

  SWTR RH13 .... 15 K3
  SWTR RH13 .... 201 R12
York Gdns *HAS* TN34 .... 13 C7
  LHPTN BN17 .... 147 J4
York Gv *BRI* BN1 .... 4 C2
York HI *BRI* BN1 .... 4 E3
Yorkhurst HI *RCCH* PO18 .... 261 J12
York PI *BRI* BN1 .... 4 F4
York Rd *BEX* TN40 .... 97 M8
  BOGR PO21 .... 2 E7
  BURH RH15 .... 74 C7

  CCH PO19 .... 7 J6
  CRAWE RH10 .... 43 K7
  EAST BN21 .... 10 D7
  HOVE BN3 .... 4 A6
  LHPTN BN17 .... 147 J4
  PEAHV BN10 .... 157 K7
  RTW TN1 .... 37 M5
  SELS PO20 .... 301 L8
  SLVH TN37 .... 12 A2
  WTHG BN11 .... 21 J6
York VIs *BRI* BN1 .... 4 C2

Yorkwood *LISS* GU33 .... 192 C9
Youngsmere CI *BRI* BN1 .... 83 G7

Z

Zeus La *WVILLE* PO7 .... 102 A2
Zion Gdns *BRI* BN1 .... 4 D6

Index - featured places

36 On the Quay Hotel
  EMRTH PO10 .... 104 A5
1066 Battle of Hastings Abbey
  & Battlefield
  BAT TN33 .... 282 E5
1066 Story in Hastings Castle
  HAS TN34 .... 13 J6
Abbotsford Special School
  BURH RH15 .... 74 E3
ACE Primary Department
  BRI BN1 .... 122 D3
Adult Education Centre
  HAS TN34 .... 13 K4
Afton Hotel
  EAST BN21 .... 11 G7
Aids Positive Underground
  Theatre
  BRIE/ROTT BN2 .... 5 J8
Albany Lions Hotel
  EAST BN21 .... 10 F8
Albourne CE Primary School
  HPPT/KEY BN6 .... 270 D3
Aldingbourne Primary School
  SELS PO20 .... 110 C7
Aldrington House Hospital
  HOVE BN3 .... 121 L7
Alexander House Hotel
  CRAWE RH10 .... 46 B4
Alexandra Hotel
  EAST BN21 .... 10 F9
Alfriston Clergy House (NT)
  POLE BN26 .... 160 F3
Alfriston School
  POLE BN26 .... 160 E2
Alias Hotel Seattle
  BRIE/ROTT BN2 .... 154 E2
All England Jumping Course
  RHWH RH17 .... 236 E9
Allman Business Park
  SELS PO20 .... 141 G7
All Saints CE Junior School
  RHAS TN35 .... 100 B4
All Saints CE Primary School
  BEXW TN39 .... 97 G6
  HORS RH12 .... 56 E3
All Saints Hospital
  EDN/EASTW BN20 .... 176 E6
All Saints & St Richards CE
  Primary School
  HTHF TN21 .... 244 G7
Amberley CE First School
  ARUN BN18 .... 296 F2
Amberley Railway
  ARUN BN18 .... 296 E4
Amberley School
  BEX TN40 .... 137 H1
Amberley Working Museum
  ARUN BN18 .... 296 E5
Amberstone Hospital
  HAIL BN27 .... 92 D1
Amesbury School
  GSHT GU26 .... 180 H8
Amey Industrial Estate
  PSF GU32 .... 223 M6
AMF Bowling
  CRAWW RH11 .... 8 E3
  WTHG BN11 .... 21 G7
Amusement Centre
  BEX TN40 .... 137 H3
The Angel Hotel
  MIDH GU29 .... 227 J9
Annecy RC Primary School
  SEAF BN25 .... 175 G3
Anne of Cleves House
  LEWES BN7 .... 16 E8
Aquarena Swimming Pool
  WTHG BN11 .... 21 K6
Archery Youth Centre
  LW/ROSE BN22 .... 164 B7
Archway Theatre
  HORL RH6 .... 22 F7
The Arden Foot &
  Health Clinic
  BRIE/ROTT BN2 .... 4 F7
Ardingly College & Ardingly
  College Junior &
  Pre-Preparatory School
  RHWH RH17 .... 206 C3
Ardington Hotel
  WTHG BN11 .... 21 J6
Ardmore School
  WTHG BN11 .... 21 G5
Arlington Stadium
  HAIL BN27 .... 91 J7
Arndale Shopping Centre
  EAST BN21 .... 10 E6
Arthur Blackman Clinic
  SLVH TN37 .... 99 Q1
Arthur Griffiths Clinic
  BOGR PO21 .... 170 F6
Arts Centre
  HAV PO9 .... 103 G4
Arun Business Park
  MSEA/BNM PO22 .... 3 G2
Arundale Preparatory School
  PUL/STOR RH20 .... 265 L3
Arundel Castle
  ARUN BN18 .... 113 G2
Arundel CE Primary School
  ARUN BN18 .... 112 D3
Arundel & District Hospital
  ARUN BN18 .... 112 F2
Arundel FC
  ARUN BN18 .... 113 H2
Arun Fitzalan Swimming Pool
  ARUN BN18 .... 113 H3

Arun House
  HORS RH12 .... 14 E4
Arun Indoor Bowling Club
  BOGR PO21 .... 171 M2
Arun Leisure Centre
  MSEA/BNM PO22 .... 3 J3
Arun Retail Park
  MSEA/BNM PO22 .... 144 D7
Arunside Primary School
  HORS RH12 .... 201 R3
Arun Vale Infant School
  LHPTN BN17 .... 147 J3
Arun Yacht Club
  LHPTN BN17 .... 147 J5
Ashdown Forest Golf Club
  FROW RH18 .... 48 E8
Ashdown Forest
  Health Centre
  FROW RH18 .... 48 D6
Ashdown Forest Llama Park
  FROW RH18 .... 64 D6
The Ashdown Hospital
  HWH RH16 .... 73 G3
Ashdown House School
  FROW RH18 .... 49 J5
Ashdown Park Hotel &
  Country Club
  FROW RH18 .... 64 F4
Ash Grove Industrial Park
  MSEA/BNM PO22 .... 144 C6
Ashington CE Primary School
  PUL/STOR RH20 .... 267 J8
Ashley Grange Hotel
  EAST BN21 .... 10 E3
Ashton Park School
  ANG/EP BN16 .... 148 E4
  PUL/STOR RH20 .... 231 P8
Ashurst CE Primary School
  STEY/UB BN44 .... 268 C4
Ashurst Wood Primary
  School
  EGRIN RH19 .... 48 D3
Ashwyn Business Centre
  BURH RH15 .... 74 F4
Assembly Hall
  WTHG BN11 .... 21 G5
Assembly Hall Theatre
  RTW TN1 .... 38 A6
Astra Business Centre
  REDH RH1 .... 22 F2
Atlas Medical Centre
  HORL RH6 .... 27 M2
The Atman Clinic
  SBGH/RUST TN4 .... 37 M3
The Audrey Wickens
  School of Music
  EAST BN21 .... 10 A5
Avalon Health Centre
  ANG/EP BN16 .... 148 C3
The Avenue Surgery
  BURH RH15 .... 74 E7
Aviation Trading Estate
  HPPT/KEY BN6 .... 270 D6
Avisford Park Golf Club
  ARUN BN18 .... 111 K4
Avocet Industrial Estate
  BURH RH15 .... 74 D7
Avocet Trading Estate
  BURH RH15 .... 74 D7
Balcombe CE Primary School
  RHWH RH17 .... 60 E7
Baldwins Hill Primary School
  EGRIN RH19 .... 31 H6
Balfour J & I School
  BRI BN1 .... 122 E2
Baliffscourt Hotel &
  Health Spa
  LHPTN BN17 .... 146 D7
Barclays Business Centre
  HTHF TN21 .... 244 D5
Barcombe CE Primary
  School
  RING/NEW BN8 .... 274 C4
Barkham Manor Vineyard
  UCK TN22 .... 240 G6
Barncroft Infant School
  HAV PO9 .... 102 E1
Barncroft Junior School
  HAV PO9 .... 102 D1
Barnham Medical Centre
  MSEA/BNM PO22 .... 111 G6
Barnham Primary School
  MSEA/BNM PO22 .... 111 G7
Barn Theatre
  SEAF BN25 .... 174 E5
The Barry Clinic
  SBGH/RUST TN4 .... 37 M3
Bartons Infant School
  MSEA/BNM PO22 .... 144 A7
Bateman's (NT)
  BUR/ETCH TN19 .... 246 E1
Battle Abbey Preparatory
  School
  BEX TN40 .... 97 K8
Battle Abbey School
  BAT TN33 .... 282 E5
Battle & Langton CE
  Primary School
  BAT TN33 .... 282 D5
Battle Museum of
  Local History
  BAT TN33 .... 282 E5
Bayham Abbey
  RRTW TN3 .... 55 M3
Bay View Park
  LGNY BN23 .... 165 G3

Beachcroft Hotel
  MSEA/BNM PO22 .... 3 K6
Beach Hotel
  WTHG BN11 .... 20 E8
Beachy Head Countryside
  Centre (Visitor Centre)
  EDN/EASTW BN20 .... 303 P9
Beachy Head Lighthouse
  EDN/EASTW BN20 .... 303 N10
Beacon Business Park
  CROW TN6 .... 211 K1
Beacon Community College
  CROW TN6 .... 67 M7
Beacon Community College
  (Lower)
  CROW TN6 .... 67 M7
Beacon Hill CP School
  GSHT GU26 .... 180 F3
Beauport Park Hotel
  SLVH TN37 .... 283 N9
Beaver Industrial Estate
  LIPH GU30 .... 193 R3
Beckley CE Primary School
  RYE TN31 .... 251 K1
Bedales School
  PSF GU32 .... 223 M2
Bedgebury Junior School
  CRBK TN17 .... 191 R4
Beeching Park Industrial
  Estate
  BEXW TN39 .... 137 G1
Beechwood Sacred Heart
  School
  RTWE/PEM TN2 .... 38 D5
Bellbrook Industrial Estate
  UCK TN22 .... 76 D5
Bellerbys College
  HOVE BN3 .... 122 B6
Bellerbys College Mayfield
  WADH TN5 .... 71 H5
Bell Tower Industrial Estate
  BRIE/ROTT BN2 .... 154 E1
Benfield Junior School
  PTSD BN41 .... 121 H5
Bennett Memorial Diocesan
  CE School
  SBGH/RUST TN4 .... 37 K3
Bentley Wildfowl &
  Motor Museum
  RING/NEW BN8 .... 276 A1
Ben Turner Industrial Estate
  CCH PO19 .... 7 M4
Berkeley Hotel
  WTHG BN11 .... 20 F7
Best Western Roundabout
  Hotel
  PUL/STOR RH20 .... 265 R7
Bevendean Primary School
  BRIE/ROTT BN2 .... 123 L3
Bewbush Community
  Primary School
  CRAWW RH11 .... 42 D6
Bewbush Leisure Centre
  CRAWW RH11 .... 42 E7
Bewbush Medical Centre
  CRAWW RH11 .... 42 D6
Bewhurst County First School
  CRAWW RH11 .... 42 M4
Bexhill Amateur Athletic Club
  BEXW TN39 .... 137 G1
Bexhill Cemetery
  BEXW TN39 .... 96 D5
Bexhill College
  BEXW TN39 .... 96 F6
Bexhill High School
  Technology College
  BEXW TN39 .... 97 G8
Bexhill Hospital
  BEX TN40 .... 97 H7
Bexhill Leisure Centre
  BEXW TN39 .... 97 G8
Bexhill Sailing Club
  BEX TN40 .... 137 J2
Bexhill Squash Rackets Club
  BEX TN40 .... 137 K1
Bidbury J & I School
  HAV PO9 .... 102 E3
Bignor Roman Villa &
  Museum
  PUL/STOR RH20 .... 263 N11
Billingshurst Junior School
  BIL RH14 .... 232 A2
  SALV BN13 .... 115 J5
Binswood View
  Business Centre
  BOR GU35 .... 178 A5
Birches Industrial Estate
  EGRIN RH19 .... 30 F6
The Birch Hotel
  RHWH RH17 .... 73 K6
Birch Industrial Estate
  LGNY BN23 .... 164 C6
Birchwood Grove Primary
  School
  BURH RH15 .... 75 H8
Birdham Primary School
  SELS PO20 .... 140 D8
The Bishop Bell CE School
  LGNY BN23 .... 164 D4
Bishop Luffa School
  CCH PO19 .... 107 J6
Bishops Down Primary
  School
  SBGH/RUST TN4 .... 37 J4
Bishops Palace
  CCH PO19 .... 6 C4

Bishop Tufnell CE J & I School
  MSEA/BNM PO22 .... 145 H7
Blackboys CE Primary School
  UCK TN22 .... 242 H7
Black Down (NT)
  HASM GU27 .... 196 A3
Blackmoor Golf Club
  BOR GU35 .... 178 D8
Blackthorns Primary School
  HWH RH16 .... 73 K3
Blackwell Primary School
  EGRIN RH19 .... 31 K6
Blatchington Mill School
  HOVE BN3 .... 121 M3
Blatchington Mill School &
  Sixth Form College
  HOVE BN3 .... 121 M4
Blatchington Road Industrial
  Estate
  SEAF BN25 .... 174 E2
Bleach's Yard Industrial
  Estate
  LIPH GU30 .... 193 R3
Bluebell Railway
  EGRIN RH19 .... 62 E5
  RHWH RH17 .... 207 K6
  UCK TN22 .... 207 Q11
Bodiam Castle (NT)
  RBTBR TN32 .... 217 N9
Bodiam CE Primary School
  RBTBR TN32 .... 217 L9
Bodiam Manor School
  RBTBR TN32 .... 217 M8
Bognor Lawn Tennis Club
  BOGR PO21 .... 171 M1
Bognor Regis Community
  College
  BOGR PO21 .... 143 M8
Bognor Regis Golf Club
  MSEA/BNM PO22 .... 144 F7
Bognor Regis Museum
  BOGR PO21 .... 2 D8
The Bognor Regis Retail
  Park
  MSEA/BNM PO22 .... 144 C6
Bognor Regis Town FC
  BOGR PO21 .... 171 M2
Bognor Regis Yacht Club
  BOGR PO21 .... 2 B9
Bognor RFC
  BOGR PO21 .... 2 B3
Bohunt Manor
  LIPH GU30 .... 193 Q2
Bohunt School
  LIPH GU30 .... 193 Q1
Bolney CE Primary School
  RHWH RH17 .... 236 D3
Bolney Grange Industrial
  Park
  RHWH RH17 .... 236 G7
Boltons Clinic
  MAYF TN20 .... 211 Q11
  STLEO TN38 .... 99 G4
Bonners CE Primary School
  UCK TN22 .... 241 N1
Bookers Vineyard
  RHWH RH17 .... 236 C2
Booth Museum of
  Natural History
  HOVE BN3 .... 122 C5
Borde Hill Garden
  HWH RH16 .... 205 R7
Bordon Infant School
  BOR GU35 .... 178 F5
Bordon Trading Estate
  BOR GU35 .... 178 D4
Borers Business Park
  CRAWE RH10 .... 29 H6
Borough Cemetery
  RTWE/PEM TN2 .... 54 B1
Bosham Abbey
  RCCH PO18 .... 139 M1
Bosham CP School
  RCCH PO18 .... 106 B8
Bosham FC
  RCCH PO18 .... 106 B8
Bosham Sailing Club
  RCCH PO18 .... 139 M1
Boship Farm Hotel
  HAIL BN27 .... 91 K2
Bosmere Junior School
  HAV PO9 .... 103 G4
Bourne Community College
  EMRTH PO10 .... 104 D4
Bourne CP School
  LW/ROSE BN22 .... 11 H5
Bowden House School
  SEAF BN25 .... 174 E1
Bowles Outdoor Centre &
  Dry Ski Slope
  RRTW TN3 .... 68 D2
Bowling Alley
  BRIE/ROTT BN2 .... 154 E2
Bowls Club
  BEX TN40 .... 137 J2
Boxgrove CE Primary
  School
  RCCH PO18 .... 109 J1
Brakes Coppice Park
  BAT TN33 .... 282 H10
Bramber Castle
  STEY/UB BN44 .... 78 E3
Bramber Road First School
  SALV BN13 .... 117 K7
Brambletye School
  EGRIN RH19 .... 48 B4

Brampton Road Trading
  Estate
  LW/ROSE BN22 .... 163 L5
Brantridge School
  RHWH RH17 .... 204 F4
Braybon Business Park
  BURH RH15 .... 74 D7
Breaky Bottom Vineyard
  LEWES BN7 .... 125 M6
Brede CP School
  RYE TN31 .... 250 E9
Brenchley & Matfield CE
  Primary School
  STPH/PW TN12 .... 188 F1
Bricklehurst Manor
  Preparatory School
  WADH TN5 .... 214 D2
Brickwall Hotel
  BAT TN33 .... 249 M12
Bridge Industrial Estate
  HORL RH6 .... 23 C6
  NEWHV BN9 .... 19 H1
Bridge Medical Centre
  CRAWE RH10 .... 9 M3
Bridge Road Business Park
  HWH RH16 .... 73 H2
Brighton Business Centre
  BRI BN1 .... 4 F2
The Brighton Centre
  BRI BN1 .... 4 C7
Brighton College of Technology
  BRI BN1 .... 4 D1
  BRIE/ROTT BN2 .... 5 G3
Brighton County Court
  BRIE/ROTT BN2 .... 4 F6
Brighton Fishing Museum
  BRI BN1 .... 4 D8
Brighton General Hospital
  BRIE/ROTT BN2 .... 5 M3
Brighton & Hove Albion FC
  (Withdean Stadium)
  BRI BN1 .... 122 C2
Brighton & Hove Golf Club
  BRI BN1 .... 81 J6
Brighton & Hove
  Greyhound Stadium
  HOVE BN3 .... 121 M4
Brighton & Hove High School
  HOVE BN3 .... 122 B5
Brighton & Hove High School
  GDST
  BRI BN1 .... 4 A5
Brighton Hove & Sussex
  VI Form College
  HOVE BN3 .... 4 A1
Brighton Media Centre
  BRI BN1 .... 4 D7
Brighton Museum & Art
  Gallery
  BRI BN1 .... 4 F6
Brighton Pier
  BRIE/ROTT BN2 .... 4 F9
Brighton Racecourse
  BRIE/ROTT BN2 .... 123 K6
Brighton RFC
  BRI BN1 .... 82 A7
Brighton University
  LEWES BN7 .... 16 C2
Brighton Youth Centre
  BRIE/ROTT BN2 .... 5 H7
Brightwell Industrial Estate
  NEWHV BN9 .... 19 J4
British Engineerium - Museum
  of Steam & Mechanical
  Antiquities
  HOVE BN3 .... 122 A3
Broadbridge Business Centre
  RCCH PO18 .... 106 A6
Broadbridge Heath Retail
  Park
  HORS RH12 .... 201 P2
Broadbridge Heath Stadium
  HORS RH12 .... 201 P3
Broadfield East First School
  CRAWW RH11 .... 43 H7
Broadfield Health Centre
  CRAWW RH11 .... 43 G7
Broadlands Business Campus
  HORS RH12 .... 40 B5
  HORS RH12 .... 58 A1
Broadmarsh Business &
  Innovation Centre
  HAV PO9 .... 102 C9
Broad Oak Primary School
  HTHF TN21 .... 244 H3
Broadwater CE F&M School
  SALV BN13 .... 117 H8
Broadwater Down Primary
  School
  RTWE/PEM TN2 .... 37 L8
Broadwater Industrial Estate
  SALV BN13 .... 117 L7
Broadwater Manor School
  SALV BN13 .... 117 J8
Broadwater & Worthing
  Cemetery
  SALV BN13 .... 117 H8
Brookers Road Industrial
  Estate
  BIL RH14 .... 232 B2
Brookfield Hotel
  EMRTH PO10 .... 103 L4
Brookham School
  LIPH GU30 .... 194 B3
The Brook Health Centre
  CROW TN6 .... 68 B8

Brooklands Trading Estate
SALV BN13 .... 20 D3
The Brook School
CRAWE RH10 .... 44 B6
Brookside Industrial Estate
ANG/EP BN16 .... 148 B2
Broomhill Bank School
RRTW TN3 .... 37 H3
Bross Estate
NEWHV BN9 .... 19 H1
Broxhead Trading Estate
BOR GU35 .... 179 J3
Buchanan Hospital
STLEO TN38 .... 99 G4
Buchan Country Park
CRAWW RH11 .... 42 D8
Buckingham Middle School
SHOR BN43 .... 119 L5
Buckswood School
RHAS TN35 .... 285 K6
Burfield Park Industrial
Estate
HAIL BN27 .... 91 M6
Burgess Hill Clinic
BURH RH15 .... 74 F7
Burgess Hill Golf Club
BURH RH15 .... 74 D3
Burgess Hill School for Girls
BURH RH15 .... 75 G7
Burgess Hill Town FC
BURH RH15 .... 75 G4
Buriton Business Park
EPSF GU31 .... 223 K10
Buriton Primary School
EPSF GU31 .... 223 L12
Burleigh Infant School
CRAWE RH10 .... 46 A1
Burrswood Medical Centre
RRTW TN3 .... 51 M1
Burstow Lodge Business
Centre
HORL RH6 .... 23 G8
Burstow Primary School
HORL RH6 .... 23 M6
Burwash CE Primary School
BUR/ETCH TN19 .... 214 C11
Bury CE First School
PUL/STOR RH20 .... 296 A2
Butser Ancient Farm
HORN PO8 .... 256 H8
Butter Market
CCH PO19 .... 6 E4
Buxted CE Primary School
UCK TN22 .... 77 H1
Buxted Park Country House
Hotel
UCK TN22 .... 77 H2
Camber Castle
WSEA TN36 .... 252 H11
Camber Sands Holiday Park
RYE TN31 .... 254 A11
Cambridge Gardens College
HAS TN34 .... 12 F7
Camelsdale County First
School
HASM GU27 .... 181 J12
Cardinal Newman School
HOVE BN3 .... 122 C5
Carlton Hill Primary School
BRIE/ROTT BN2 .... 5 G6
Carrier Business Park
CRAWE RH10 .... 44 A2
Castledean School
BRI BN1 .... 123 H3
Castledown CPN School
HAS TN34 .... 13 K3
Catherine Corbett Clinic
HAV PO9 .... 103 G3
Catherington CE Controlled
Infant School
HORN PO8 .... 256 C12
Catsfield CE Primary School
BAT TN33 .... 282 A9
Cattle Market
HAIL BN27 .... 92 B6
Causeway Secondary School
LGNY BN23 .... 163 M2
Cavendish Hotel
WTHG BN11 .... 20 F8
The Cavendish School
EAST BN21 .... 163 H8
Centenary Industrial Estate
BRI BN1 .... 123 G4
Central CE Junior School
CCH PO19 .... 6 C3
Central Industrial Estate
HAV PO9 .... 102 F4
Central Library
EAST BN21 .... 10 D7
Central Sussex College
CRAWE RH10 .... 9 H4
Central Sussex College
(East Grinstead Campus)
EGRIN RH19 .... 31 K8
Centre of Arts
CCH PO19 .... 6 E4
Chailey Heritage School
RING/NEW BN8 .... 239 M6
Chailey School
RING/NEW BN8 .... 273 N2
Chalklin Business Park
RTWE/PEM TN2 .... 38 D1
Chanctonbury Leisure Centre
PUL/STOR RH20 .... 265 Q11
Chanctonbury Ring
STEY/UB BN44 .... 299 L4
Chantry Industrial Estate
PUL/STOR RH20 .... 298 B1
Chapel Royal
BRI BN1 .... 4 E6
Charleston Farmhouse
RING/NEW BN8 .... 128 E3
Charlwood Place
HORL RH6 .... 26 D1
Charlwoods Industrial
Estate
EGRIN RH19 .... 31 K6
Charlwood Village Infant
School
HORL RH6 .... 26 E2
Charter Medical Centre
HOVE BN3 .... 122 C6
Charters Ancaster College
BEXW TN39 .... 96 F7
Charters Ancaster School
BEX TN40 .... 97 L8

Chartham Park Golf Club
EGRIN RH19 .... 31 H3
Chase Community Hospital
BOR GU35 .... 178 G7
Chatsworth Hotel
HAS TN34 .... 12 F8
Chaucer Industrial Estate
POLE BN26 .... 132 C7
Chesswood Middle School
WTHG BN11 .... 21 K2
Chesworth Junior School
SWTR RH13 .... 15 H1
Chichester Airfield
RCCH PO18 .... 108 B1
Chichester Cathedral
CCH PO19 .... 6 D5
Chichester College
ANG/EP BN16 .... 148 E4
CCH PO19 .... 6 B5
PUL/STOR RH20 .... 231 N8
Chichester College of Arts,
Science & Technology
BOGR PO21 .... 2 E7
CCH PO19 .... 6 E4
Chichester College of
Technology
CCH PO19 .... 6 B4
Chichester Crematorium
CCH PO19 .... 7 K1
Chichester District Museum
CCH PO19 .... 6 F4
Chichester Festival Theatre
CCH PO19 .... 6 E1
Chichester Golf Club
SELS PO20 .... 141 M8
Chichester High School
for Boys
CCH PO19 .... 6 D8
Chichester High School
for Girls
CCH PO19 .... 6 C8
CCH PO19 .... 6 E7
Chichester Lawn Tennis &
Squash Club
CCH PO19 .... 6 F2
Chichester Nuffield Hospital
CCH PO19 .... 107 L4
Chichester Priory Park
Cricket & Hockey Club
CCH PO19 .... 6 F3
Chichester RFC
CCH PO19 .... 107 M5
Chichester Yacht Club
SELS PO20 .... 140 E6
Chiddingfold Golf Club
MFD/CHID GU8 .... 182 G8
Chiddingly CC
RING/NEW BN8 .... 277 M8
Chiddingly CP School
RING/NEW BN8 .... 277 M9
Chidham Parochial Primary
School
RCCH PO18 .... 105 K7
Child Clinic
BRIE/ROTT BN2 .... 4 F6
Christchurch Medical Centre
HAV PO9 .... 103 K2
Christ's Hospital Infirmary
SWTR RH13 .... 201 P7
Christ's Hospital School
SWTR RH13 .... 201 N8
The Christ's Hospital Sports
Centre
SWTR RH13 .... 201 N7
Churchers College
EPSF GU31 .... 223 P5
Churchers College Junior
Department
PSF GU32 .... 223 M6
Churchfields Industrial
Estate
STLEO TN38 .... 98 C1
Churchill Square Shopping
Centre
BRI BN1 .... 4 C7
Churchwood Primary School
STLEO TN38 .... 98 E2
Circe Health & Beauty Clinic
UCK TN22 .... 76 E5
Cissbury Ring
SALV BN13 .... 299 L12
Cisswood House Hotel
SWTR RH13 .... 203 K6
City Business Centre
CCH PO19 .... 6 E7
SWTR RH13 .... 14 E7
The City Business Centre
CRAWW RH11 .... 27 J7
City College of Brighton
& Hove
BRI BN1 .... 4 F4
City Fields Business Park
SELS PO20 .... 109 J3
Clair Hall Cinema
HWH RH16 .... 73 H4
Clanfield Junior School
HORN PO8 .... 256 C6
Clanricarde Medical Centre
RTW TN1 .... 37 M6
Clapham & Patching CE
Primary School
SALV BN13 .... 115 K4
Claremont Primary School
RTWE/PEM TN2 .... 38 A7
Claremont School
SLVH TN37 .... 283 Q8
Clarence Road School
SWTR RH13 .... 14 F7
Clarks Industrial Estate
HOVE BN3 .... 122 A5
Claverham Community
College
BAT TN33 .... 282 B5
Clayton Tunnel
POY/PYE BN45 .... 271 K10
Clayton Windmills
HPPT/KEY BN6 .... 271 M10
Cliffe Business Centre
LEWES BN7 .... 17 J6
Cliffe Industrial Estate
RING/NEW BN8 .... 17 L8
The Clockhouse Business
Centre
MIDH GU29 .... 227 P7
Cloudesley Shovell House
HAS TN34 .... 13 L6

Coldean Primary School
BRI BN1 .... 83 J6
Colgate Primary School
SWTR RH13 .... 58 B3
Colhook Industrial Park
PETW GU28 .... 197 J12
The College of Richard
Collyer
HORS RH12 .... 14 E2
The College of St Barnabas
LING RH7 .... 31 L1
Comfort Inn
LHPTN BN17 .... 113 J5
Community & Adult Education
Centre
HORL RH6 .... 22 D6
Community Mental Health
Centre
BRIE/ROTT BN2 .... 74 F5
Compton & Up Marden CE
School
RCCH PO18 .... 258 C11
The Congress Theatre
EAST BN21 .... 10 E9
Conifers School
MIDH GU29 .... 227 K8
Connaught Theatre & Cinema
WTHG BN11 .... 21 H5
Conqueror Industrial Estate
STLEO TN38 .... 283 N11
Conquest Hospital
SLVH TN37 .... 284 A11
Conway Court Clinic
HOVE BN3 .... 122 A5
Cooden Beach Golf Club
BEXW TN39 .... 136 A3
Coombe Road Primary School
BRIE/ROTT BN2 .... 123 J4
The Copthorne Business
Centre
CRAWE RH10 .... 29 G6
Copthorne CE Junior School
CRAWE RH10 .... 29 G6
Copthorne Fairway Infant
School
CRAWE RH10 .... 29 G6
Copthorne Golf Club
CRAWE RH10 .... 29 H6
Copthorne Hotel
CRAWE RH10 .... 28 F7
Copthorne Hotel & Resort
Effingham Park
CRAWE RH10 .... 29 L5
Copthorne Junior School
CRAWE RH10 .... 29 G6
Copthorne Preparatory School
CRAWE RH10 .... 29 K6
Copthorne Squash Club
CRAWE RH10 .... 28 F7
Corn Exchange Theatre
BRI BN1 .... 4 E6
Cornfield School
BRIE/ROTT BN2 .... 147 K2
Corsica Hall Education
Training Centre
SEAF BN25 .... 174 F3
Cosmic Cycle
HORS RH12 .... 14 B6
Cottesmore Golf &
Country Club
CRAWW RH11 .... 58 D2
Cottesmore St Marys RC
Primary School
HOVE BN3 .... 122 C5
Cottesmore School
CRAWW RH11 .... 58 E1
County Mall Shopping Centre
CRAWE RH10 .... 9 G4
County Oak Retail Park
CRAWW RH11 .... 27 J7
County Record Office
CCH PO19 .... 6 C4
Courtlands Hotel
EAST BN21 .... 10 E9
The Courtlands Hotel
HOVE BN3 .... 122 B7
Courtlands Road Industrial
Estate
LW/ROSE BN22 .... 10 F1
Court Meadow Special School
RHWH RH17 .... 72 D1
Cowdray Park Golf Club
MIDH GU29 .... 227 L8
Cradle Hill Community
Primary School
SEAF BN25 .... 159 L8
Cradle Hill Industrial Estate
SEAF BN25 .... 160 A8
Crawley College Annexe
CRAWW RH11 .... 8 D2
Crawley Down CE School
CRAWE RH10 .... 46 A1
Crawley Down Health Centre
CRAWE RH10 .... 45 M1
Crawley Health Clinic
CRAWE RH10 .... 9 G3
Crawley Hospital
CRAWW RH11 .... 8 C3
The Crawley Lawn Tennis Club
CRAWE RH10 .... 44 A1
Crawley Leisure Centre &
Athletics Arena
CRAWE RH10 .... 9 K5
Crawley Museum
(Goffs Park House)
CRAWW RH11 .... 8 B6
Crawley RFC
CRAWW RH11 .... 26 F7
Crawley Town FC
CRAWW RH11 .... 43 H7
The Crookhorn Community
School
WVILLE PO7 .... 102 A1
Cross In Hand CE Primary
School
HTHF TN21 .... 244 C6
Crosspost Industrial Estate
RHWH RH17 .... 236 C4
Crossways Hotel
POLE BN26 .... 130 D7
Crouchers Country Hotel &
Restaurant
SELS PO20 .... 141 H5
Crowborough Beacon
Golf Club
CROW TN6 .... 210 E1

Crowborough War Memorial
Hospital
CROW TN6 .... 67 K8
Crowhurst CE Primary School
BAT TN33 .... 282 G12
Cumnor House School
RHWH RH17 .... 208 A4
Curzon Cinema
EAST BN21 .... 10 F6
Curzon Picture Playhouse
Cinema
BEXW TN39 .... 137 H1
Cyril Richings Business Centre
SHOR BN43 .... 120 A6
Dale Hill Hotel & Golf Club
WADH TN5 .... 191 L12
Dallington CE Primary
School
HTHF TN21 .... 246 C10
Danehill CE Primary School
RHWH RH17 .... 208 A5
David Lloyd Health &
Fitness Centre
BRIE/ROTT BN2 .... 154 D2
David Lloyd Leisure Centre
LW/ROSE BN22 .... 163 K5
David Salomon's House
RRTW TN3 .... 37 J1
Davigdor Infant School
HOVE BN3 .... 122 C7
Davison CE High School
for Girls
WTHG BN11 .... 21 M3
D-Day Museum
SHOR BN43 .... 119 J6
Deacon Trading Estate
SALV BN13 .... 117 L8
Dean Farm Golf Club
BOR GU35 .... 178 E1
Deans Place Hotel
POLE BN26 .... 160 E3
Deepdene School
HOVE BN3 .... 121 J6
De La Warr Pavilion
BEXW TN39 .... 137 H2
Dell Quay Sailing Club
SELS PO20 .... 140 F3
De Luxe Leisure Centre
HAS TN34 .... 13 J7
Denmans Garden
ARUN BN18 .... 110 D2
Denton Community School
NEWHV BN9 .... 158 D4
Denvale Trade Park
CRAWE RH10 .... 9 H5
Desmond Anderson Primary
School
CRAWE RH10 .... 43 J7
The De Vere Grand Hotel
BRI BN1 .... 4 B7
Devil's Dyke
BRI BN1 .... 81 H2
Devonshire Park Theatre
EAST BN21 .... 10 F9
Dewlands Manor Golf Club
CROW TN6 .... 211 P2
Dharma School
BRI BN1 .... 82 F7
Ditcham Park School
EPSF GU31 .... 257 N5
Ditchling St Margarets CEP
School
HPPT/KEY BN6 .... 272 A6
Ditton Place School
RHWH RH17 .... 204 H1
Dittons Park Industrial
Estate
POLE BN26 .... 132 D7
Doll House Museum
PETW GU28 .... 229 L10
Dolphin House Clinic
for Adults
BRI BN1 .... 4 E6
Dolphin Industrial Estate
SHOR BN43 .... 120 B6
Dolphin Leisure Centre
HWH RH16 .... 73 G3
Dome Cinema
WTHG BN11 .... 21 J7
Dorset House School
PUL/STOR RH20 .... 296 C2
Downland Medical Centre
POLE BN26 .... 131 M7
Downlands Business Park
SALV BN13 .... 117 K5
Downlands School
HPPT/KEY BN6 .... 271 N6
Downsbrook Middle School
SALV BN13 .... 117 K8
Downsbrook Trading Estate
SALV BN13 .... 117 K7
Downs Crematorium
BRIE/ROTT BN2 .... 123 J5
Downs Infant School
BRI BN1 .... 122 F5
Downs Junior School
BRI BN1 .... 122 F4
Downs Leisure Centre
SEAF BN25 .... 175 G1
Downs Park School
PTSD BN41 .... 121 G3
Downview CP School
MSEA/BNM PO22 .... 3 K1
Drayton House
SELS PO20 .... 108 D8
Driving Test Centre
CRAWW RH11 .... 8 D4
LW/ROSE BN22 .... 164 C1
The Dr Jan De Winter Clinic for
Cancer Prevention Advice
BRI BN1 .... 4 E7
Drusillas Park
POLE BN26 .... 130 A7
Dudley Infant School
RHAS TN35 .... 100 B4
Duke of York's Premier
Picture House Cinema
BRI BN1 .... 4 E2
Dunannie School
PSF GU32 .... 223 M3
Duncton CE First School
PETW GU28 .... 262 G6
Dunhurst School
PSF GU32 .... 223 M3
Dunnings Squash Club
EGRIN RH19 .... 47 K3

Dunsfold Aerodrome
CRAN GU6 .... 184 E4
Durgates Industrial Estate
WADH TN5 .... 71 K4
Durrington First School
SALV BN13 .... 116 D6
Durrington Health Centre
SALV BN13 .... 116 C7
Durrington High School
SALV BN13 .... 116 D8
Eagle Industrial Estate
BIL RH14 .... 232 A2
Easebourne CE Primary
School
MIDH GU29 .... 227 L7
Eastbourne Arts Centre
EAST BN21 .... 10 C6
Eastbourne Bowling Club
EAST BN21 .... 10 C7
The Eastbourne Clinic
EDN/EASTW BN20 ...... 10 C8
Eastbourne College
EAST BN21 .... 10 D8
EDN/EASTW BN20 ...... 10 C8
Eastbourne County Court
EAST BN21 .... 10 C5
Eastbourne Crematorium
LGNY BN23 .... 164 C2
Eastbourne District General
Hospital
EAST BN21 .... 163 K6
Eastbourne Downs Golf Club
EDN/EASTW BN20 ...... 176 A3
Eastbourne & Hailsham
Magistrates Court
EAST BN21 .... 10 B7
Eastbourne Heritage Centre
EAST BN21 .... 10 F9
Eastbourne Pier
EAST BN21 .... 11 H7
Eastbourne RFC
LW/ROSE BN22 .... 163 J5
Eastbourne Saffrons
Sports Club
EAST BN21 .... 10 B7
Eastbourne School of English
EAST BN21 .... 10 F7
Eastbourne Sovereign
Sailing Club
LW/ROSE BN22 .... 11 L3
Eastbourne Sports Park
Track
EAST BN21 .... 163 K6
Eastbourne Technology
College
LW/ROSE BN22 .... 163 J3
Eastbourne United
Football Club
LW/ROSE BN22 .... 11 L1
East Brighton Golf Club
BRIE/ROTT BN2 .... 154 E1
East Court
EGRIN RH19 .... 31 L7
Eastergate CE Primary School
SELS PO20 .... 110 D6
East Grinstead Health Clinic
EGRIN RH19 .... 31 K7
East Grinstead Sports Club
EGRIN RH19 .... 47 H4
East Hill Cliff Lift
HAS TN34 .... 13 L6
East Hoathly CE Primary
School
RING/NEW BN8 .... 276 G4
Eastmead Industrial Estate
RCCH PO18 .... 292 B10
East Preston CP School
ANG/EP BN16 .... 148 F3
East Street Medical Centre
LHPTN BN17 .... 147 J4
East Sussex County Music
School
LEWES BN7 .... 17 G7
East Sussex National
Golf Club
UCK TN22 .... 275 Q1
East Wittering Business
Centre
SELS PO20 .... 167 M5
East Wittering CP School
SELS PO20 .... 167 L6
East Worthing Industrial
Estate
SALV BN13 .... 117 L10
Eaton Place Surgery
BRIE/ROTT BN2 .... 5 M9
Ebernoe Common National
Nature Reserve
PETW GU28 .... 197 L10
The Edge Sports Centre
HASM GU27 .... 180 G9
Edward Bryant CP School
BOGR PO21 .... 2 E6
Effingham Park Golf Club
CRAWE RH10 .... 29 L5
EF International School
of English
SLVH TN37 .... 12 B7
The Elizabeth Johnson
Organisation
LIPH GU30 .... 179 L9
Ellscott Park
SELS PO20 .... 168 E1
Elm Grove County First
School
WTHG BN11 .... 150 E2
Elm Grove Primary School
BRIE/ROTT BN2 .... 5 K2
Elphinstone Community
School
HAS TN34 .... 13 J1
Emerson College
FROW RH18 .... 49 G6
Emsworth Museum
EMRTH PO10 .... 104 A5
Emsworth Primary School
EMRTH PO10 .... 103 M4
English Bowling Association
WTHG BN11 .... 21 K5
English Martyr Catholic
Primary School
FERR BN12 .... 116 C8
Enterprise Industrial Estate
HORN PO8 .... 288 D1
Enterprise Shopping Centre
EAST BN21 .... 10 D6

Environment Agency
 WTHC BN11 .... 21 H6
Esperance Private Hospital
 EAST BN21 .... 10 F8
Estcots CP School
 EGRIN RH19 .... 31 M8
Etchingham CE Primary
 School
 BUR/ETCH TN19 .... 215 Q7
Euro Business Park
 NEWHV BN9 .... 158 C4
Eversfield Hospital
 STLEO TN38 .... 98 F7
Evolution Health Centre
 BRI BN1 .... 4 B5
Fairfield Infant School
 HAV PO9 .... 103 H3
Fairfield Medical Centre
 PETW GU28 .... 229 L10
Fairlight Primary School
 BRIE/ROTT BN2 .... 5 J1
Fairway Trading Estate
 BRIE/ROTT BN2 .... 123 K1
Falaise Hall
 HAS TN34 .... 12 E7
Falmer High School
 BRI BN1 .... 83 M8
Farlington School
 HORS RH12 .... 187 L11
Farney Close School
 RHWH RH17 .... 236 E3
Faygate Business Centre
 HORS RH12 .... 41 L8
Felbridge Primary School
 EGRIN RH19 .... 30 E5
Felpham Community College
 MSEA/BNM PO22 .... 3 K2
Felpham & Middleton
 Health Centre
 MSEA/BNM PO22 .... 145 J1
Felpham Sailing Club
 MSEA/BNM PO22 .... 3 L1
Fernbank Shopping Centre
 CROW TN6 .... 67 L6
Fernhurst Primary School
 HASM GU27 .... 195 L7
Ferring CE Primary School
 FERR BN12 .... 149 L3
Ferring FC
 FERR BN12 .... 149 K3
Ferryfield Industrial Estate
 NEWHV BN9 .... 19 J4
Field Place First School
 FERR BN12 .... 150 C1
Filching Manor
 POLE BN26 .... 162 C3
Filsham Valley School
 STLEO TN38 .... 98 D6
Finchcocks
 CRBK TN17 .... 189 M12
Findon Manor Hotel
 SALV BN13 .... 298 H11
Finmere Road Industrial
 Estate
 LW/ROSE BN22 .... 164 B7
Firle CE Primary School
 RING/NEW BN8 .... 128 A1
Firle Place
 RING/NEW BN8 .... 128 B2
Firsland Park Estate
 HPPT/KEY BN6 .... 236 A12
Fishbourne CE Primary School
 CCH PO19 .... 107 G7
Fishbourne Roman Palace
 CCH PO19 .... 107 G7
Fisheries Museum
 HAS TN34 .... 13 L7
Fishermen's Club
 LW/ROSE BN22 .... 11 L3
Fishers Farm Park
 BIL RH14 .... 199 L11
Fishersgate First School
 PTSD BN41 .... 120 F6
Fishing Club House
 FROW RH18 .... 48 A6
Fittleworth CE First School
 PUL/STOR RH20 .... 264 B2
Five Ashes CE Primary School
 MAYF TN20 .... 211 Q11
Five Lord's Burgh
 SEAF BN25 .... 159 K1
Flackley Ash Hotel
 RYE TN31 .... 251 R2
Flansham Business Centre
 MSEA/BNM PO22 .... 145 G6
Fletching CE Primary School
 UCK TN22 .... 240 E2
Flora McDonald Junior School
 LHPTN BN17 .... 147 H3
Flower Makers Museum
 HAS TN34 .... 13 J6
The Fold School
 HOVE BN3 .... 121 J6
Fonthill Lodge School
 EGRIN RH19 .... 47 H3
Fontigarry Farm Business Park
 REIG RH2 .... 22 B1
Fontwell Medical Centre
 ARUN BN18 .... 110 F2
Fontwell Park Racecourse
 ARUN BN18 .... 110 E3
Ford Airfield Industrial Estate
 ARUN BN18 .... 146 A2
Fordcombe CE Primary School
 RRTW TN3 .... 36 A4
Ford Lane Business Park
 ARUN BN18 .... 146 C1
Fordwater Special School
 CCH PO19 .... 107 M4
Forest Row Business Park
 FROW RH18 .... 48 E6
Forest Row CE Infant School
 FROW RH18 .... 48 E7
Forest Row CE Primary School
 FROW RH18 .... 48 E7
The Forest School
 SWTR RH13 .... 15 K8
The Forest Shopping Centre
 BOR GU35 .... 178 H6
Forge Wood Industrial Estate
 CRAWE RH10 .... 28 A7
Fort Fun & Rocky's Adventure
 Land
 LW/ROSE BN22 .... 164 D8
Forum House Business Centre
 CCH PO19 .... 6 F5

Fowlers Business Centre
 SWTR RH13 .... 235 K4
Foxbridge Golf Club
 BIL RH14 .... 198 D4
Framfield CE Primary School
 UCK TN22 .... 77 M6
Frant CE Primary School
 RRTW TN3 .... 54 A5
The Freda Gardham
 Community School
 RYE TN31 .... 253 J7
French Business
 Communications
 PUL/STOR RH20 .... 266 D11
Freshbrook County
 First School
 LAN/SOMP BN15 .... 118 D7
Freshfield Industrial
 Estate
 BRIE/ROTT BN2 .... 5 K6
Frewen College
 RYE TN31 .... 218 F12
Friary Hall
 CRAWE RH10 .... 8 F5
Friends of Arundel Castle CC
 ARUN BN18 .... 112 F1
Front Lawn Junior School
 HAV PO9 .... 288 G12
Funpark
 LHPTN BN17 .... 147 J6
Funtington CP School
 RCCH PO18 .... 106 A2
Garcia Trading Estate
 SALV BN13 .... 150 E2
Gardner Arts Centre Cinema
 BRI BN1 .... 83 M6
The Gattons Infant School
 BURH RH15 .... 74 D6
Gatwick Gate Industrial
 Estate
 HORL RH6 .... 27 K4
Gatwick Industrial Estate
 HORL RH6 .... 26 E3
Gatwick Manor Golf Club
 CRAWE RH10 .... 27 K6
Gatwick Medical Centre
 HORL RH6 .... 28 A2
Gatwick Moat House Hotel
 HORL RH6 .... 22 D8
Gatwick Park Hospital
 HORL RH6 .... 22 D7
Gatwick Worth Hotel
 CRAWE RH10 .... 44 E2
Gemini Business Centre
 HOVE BN3 .... 121 M5
Genesis Business Centre
 SWTR RH13 .... 15 J3
George Gale & Co Brewery
 HORN PO8 .... 288 E2
George II Statue
 BRI BN1 .... 4 E6
Georgian Gardens CP School
 ANG/EP BN16 .... 148 C3
Georgian House Business
 Centre
 BRIE/ROTT BN2 .... 4 F7
Georgian House Hotel
 HASM GU27 .... 181 N10
Gerald Daniel Sailing Club
 RCCH PO18 .... 139 K3
Gerrard House Business
 Centre
 ANG/EP BN16 .... 148 E3
Gerston Business Park
 PUL/STOR RH20 .... 297 R1
Ghyll House Farm Estate
 SWTR RH13 .... 202 C8
Ghyll Industrial Estate
 HTHF TN21 .... 244 D8
Gilmans Industrial Estate
 BIL RH14 .... 232 A3
The Glade Infant School
 BOGR PO21 .... 143 M8
Glebe Middle School
 STHW BN42 .... 120 C6
Glenhurst School
 HAV PO9 .... 103 H4
Glennys Estate
 LW/ROSE BN22 .... 11 J2
Glenwood School
 EMRTH PO10 .... 103 M4
Glyndebourne Opera House
 RING/NEW BN8 .... 87 K3
Glynde Place
 RING/NEW BN8 .... 87 L6
Glyne Gap Special School
 BEX TN40 .... 97 M8
Goldsmith Leisure Centre
 CROW TN6 .... 67 L5
Goldstone Primary School
 HOVE BN3 .... 121 K4
Goldstone Retail Park
 HOVE BN3 .... 122 A5
Goodwood Country Park
 RCCH PO18 .... 293 L5
Goodwood Motor Circuit
 RCCH PO18 .... 108 C2
Goodwood Racecourse
 RCCH PO18 .... 293 J6
Gordon Centre
 BOGR PO21 .... 2 C7
Goring CE First School
 FERR BN12 .... 150 B3
Goring CC
 FERR BN12 .... 149 M3
Gossops Green Clinic
 CRAWW RH11 .... 42 E5
Gossops Green Community
 Primary School
 CRAWW RH11 .... 42 F4
Graffham First School
 PETW GU28 .... 262 A7
Granary Business Centre
 HAIL BN27 .... 278 C11
The Grand Hotel
 EAST BN21 .... 177 G4
The Grange Leisure Centre
 MIDH GU29 .... 226 H10
Granville Hotel
 BRI BN1 .... 4 B7
Gravetye Manor Hotel
 EGRIN RH19 .... 62 D1
Graylingwell Hospital
 CCH PO19 .... 107 H2
Grayshott CE Primary School
 GSHT GU26 .... 180 E6

Grayshott Clinic
 GSHT GU26 .... 180 E5
Grays School
 NEWHV BN9 .... 19 G5
Grayswood CE Aided Infant
 School
 HASM GU27 .... 181 Q7
Great Ballard School
 RCCH PO18 .... 294 C10
Great Dixter House & Gardens
 RYE TN31 .... 218 D10
Great Hall Arcade
 RTW TN1 .... 37 M6
Greatham Primary School
 LISS GU33 .... 192 C3
Great Walstead School
 HWH RH16 .... 207 J11
Green Field Effective
 Education
 EGRIN RH19 .... 31 J8
Greenfields School
 FROW RH18 .... 48 B8
Green Street Clinic
 EAST BN21 .... 176 C1
Greenviews Caravan Park
 HTHF TN21 .... 244 F4
Greenway School
 HORS RH12 .... 14 A3
Greywell Shopping Centre
 HAV PO9 .... 288 G12
Groombridge Place Gardens &
 Enchanted Forest
 RRTW TN3 .... 52 B1
Groombridge St Thomas CE
 Aided Primary School
 RRTW TN3 .... 52 B1
Grosvenor Medical Centre
 RTW TN1 .... 38 A5
Grove Bowls Club
 RTW TN1 .... 38 A6
Grovelands Comm Primary
 School
 HAIL BN27 .... 91 M4
Grove Park Special School
 CROW TN6 .... 67 K8
The Grove School
 STLEO TN38 .... 98 E4
Guestling Bradshaw CE
 Primary School
 RHAS TN35 .... 285 K9
Guildbourne Shopping Centre
 WTHG BN11 .... 21 J6
The Guildhall
 CCH PO19 .... 6 F3
Hackhurst Lane Industrial
 Estate
 HAIL BN27 .... 91 G1
Hailsham Cemetery
 HAIL BN27 .... 92 A8
Hailsham Community College
 HAIL BN27 .... 92 A5
Hailsham Institute
 HAIL BN27 .... 92 A6
Hailsham Town FC
 HAIL BN27 .... 92 A6
Halsford Park Primary School
 EGRIN RH19 .... 31 G7
Ham Bridge Trading Estate
 SALV BN13 .... 151 M1
Hambrook Business Centre
 RCCH PO18 .... 105 J1
Ham Business Centre
 SHOR BN43 .... 119 M6
Hamilton Lodge School
 BRIE/ROTT BN2 .... 5 L7
Ham Manor Golf Club
 ANG/EP BN16 .... 148 C1
Hammerwood Park
 EGRIN RH19 .... 33 H7
Hampden Park Infant School
 LW/ROSE BN22 .... 163 K3
Hampden Park Sports Centre
 LW/ROSE BN22 .... 163 J3
Hampers Common Industrial
 Estate
 PETW GU28 .... 229 L7
Hamsey Primary School
 RING/NEW BN8 .... 273 R9
Handcross Park School
 RHWH RH17 .... 59 J7
Handcross Primary School
 RHWH RH17 .... 59 H8
Hangdown Mead Business
 Park
 EGRIN RH19 .... 62 F4
Hangleton County J & I
 School
 HOVE BN3 .... 121 K3
Hankham Primary School
 PEV BN24 .... 133 G5
Hapstead Business Centre
 RHWH RH17 .... 206 E1
Harbour Park
 LHPTN BN17 .... 147 J6
Harlands CP School
 UCK TN22 .... 76 F7
Harlands Primary School
 HWH RH16 .... 73 G2
Harveys Brewery
 LEWES BN7 .... 17 H5
Harvington Business Park
 LW/ROSE BN22 .... 163 L5
Haslemere Hall
 HASM GU27 .... 181 M10
Haslemere Hospital & Health
 Centre
 HASM GU27 .... 181 N10
Haslemere Museum
 HASM GU27 .... 181 N10
Hassocks Golf Club
 HPPT/KEY BN6 .... 271 M4
Hassocks Infant School
 HPPT/KEY BN6 .... 271 N5
Hasting Medical Centre
 HAS TN34 .... 13 G6
Hastings Cemetery
 HAS TN34 .... 284 E12
Hastings College of Arts &
 Technology
 STLEO TN38 .... 99 G7
Hastings Country Park
 RHAS TN35 .... 101 G2
Hastings Crematorium
 HAS TN34 .... 284 D12
Hastings Education College
 STLEO TN38 .... 98 E6

Hastings Indoor Market
 HAS TN34 .... 13 H7
Hastings Museum & Art Gallery
 HAS TN34 .... 12 E6
Hastings Pier
 HAS TN34 .... 12 E9
Hastings & St Leonards
 Sailing Club
 STLEO TN38 .... 12 A9
Hastings Town FC
 HAS TN34 .... 99 M2
Havant Business Centre
 HAV PO9 .... 102 E5
Havant Leisure Centre
 HAV PO9 .... 103 G3
Havant Museum
 HAV PO9 .... 103 H4
Havant Retail Park
 HAV PO9 .... 102 C4
Havant Rugby Football Club
 HAV PO9 .... 102 E3
Havant Sixth Form College
 HAV PO9 .... 102 F2
Havant War Memorial Hospital
 HAV PO9 .... 102 F3
Havant & Waterlooville FC
 HAV PO9 .... 288 H12
The Haven Vace Methodist
 Primary School
 LGNY BN23 .... 164 E5
Hawkes Farm CP School
 HAIL BN27 .... 92 A3
The Hawthorns First School
 SALV BN13 .... 116 B8
The Hawth Theatre, Cinema &
 Conference Complex
 CRAWE RH10 .... 9 J5
Hayward Business Centre
 HAV PO9 .... 103 J2
Haywards Heath College
 HWH RH16 .... 73 G3
Haywards Heath FC
 HWH RH16 .... 73 K5
Haywards Heath Golf Club
 HWH RH16 .... 206 C8
Haywards Heath Hospital
 HWH RH16 .... 72 F4
Haywards Heath RFC
 RHWH RH17 .... 72 A1
Hazel Cottage Clinic
 BRIE/ROTT BN2 .... 124 B5
Hazel Court School
 LGNY BN23 .... 164 A2
Hazel Court School FE
 Department
 EAST BN21 .... 163 J6
Hazel Court Secondary
 Special School
 LGNY BN23 .... 164 A1
Hazelwick School
 CRAWE RH10 .... 43 M1
Hazelwood Trading Estate
 SALV BN13 .... 21 L1
The Health Centre
 BIL RH14 .... 199 J12
Heath Business Centre
 REDH RH1 .... 23 G2
Heathfield Community
 College
 HTHF TN21 .... 244 H6
Heaven Farm
 RHWH RH17 .... 208 A7
Heaven Farm (Museum)
 UCK TN22 .... 208 A8
Heene CE First School
 WTHG BN11 .... 20 E4
Heene Community Centre
 WTHG BN11 .... 20 D6
Helensmead Upper School
 HAS TN34 .... 99 M1
Hellingly Cemetery
 HAIL BN27 .... 91 L1
Hellingly CP School
 HAIL BN27 .... 278 C12
The Henfield Business Park
 HFD BN5 .... 269 M8
Henfield & District Leisure
 Centre
 HFD BN5 .... 269 K3
Henry VIII Experience
 HRTF TN7 .... 50 B1
Herbert Hone Clinic
 BRIE/ROTT BN2 .... 5 G2
Herbert Shiner School
 PETW GU28 .... 229 L10
Heritage Centre &
 Town Model
 RYE TN31 .... 252 G8
The Herne Farm Leisure
 Centre
 EPSF GU31 .... 223 P5
Herne Junior School
 CROW TN6 .... 210 G1
The Herne Junior School
 EPSF GU31 .... 223 P5
Herons Dale School
 SHOR BN43 .... 120 C4
The Herons Swimming &
 Fitness Centre
 HASM GU27 .... 181 J11
Heron Way Primary School
 SWTR RH13 .... 15 L7
Herstmonceux CE Primary
 School
 HAIL BN27 .... 279 P12
Hertford Junior School
 BRI BN1 .... 123 H2
Heyworth Primary School
 HWH RH16 .... 73 H4
The Hickstead Hotel
 RHWH RH17 .... 236 F8
Hickstead International
 Arena
 RHWH RH17 .... 236 E9
High Beech Hotel
 SLVH BN37 .... 283 N11
Highcroft Industrial Estate
 HORN PO8 .... 288 D1
Highdown Hill
 FERR BN12 .... 115 K8
Highfield Business Park
 STLEO TN38 .... 98 C1
Highfield Industrial Estate
 LGNY BN23 .... 163 M4
Highfield Junior School
 LW/ROSE BN22 .... 163 L4

Highfield School
 LIPH GU30 .... 194 B3
High Hurstwood CE Primary
 School
 UCK TN22 .... 210 B8
Highwoods Golf Club
 BEXW TN39 .... 96 D6
Hill Barn Golf Club
 SALV BN13 .... 117 H5
Hillcrest School
 RHAS TN35 .... 284 H12
Hill's Cemetery
 HORS RH12 .... 201 Q3
Hillside Industrial Estate
 HORN PO8 .... 288 D1
Hillside Special School
 PTSD BN41 .... 120 F3
Hilltop Primary
 CRAWW RH11 .... 8 D8
Hilton Park Hotel
 RHWH RH17 .... 72 D5
The Hindhead Golf Club
 GSHT GU26 .... 180 E3
Hindleap Warren Outdoor
 Education Centre
 FROW RH18 .... 64 C4
HM Prison
 LEWES BN7 .... 16 B6
Hobbs Industrial Estate
 LING RH7 .... 30 C2
Hoddern County Junior
 School
 PEAHV BN10 .... 157 G5
Holbrook Primary School
 HORS RH12 .... 56 C2
Holbrook Recreation Centre
 HORS RH12 .... 56 D2
Holiday Village
 BOGR PO21 .... 3 H6
 RYE TN31 .... 253 R10
Hollingbury Castle
 BRI BN1 .... 123 H1
Hollingbury Industrial Estate
 BRI BN1 .... 83 G6
Hollingbury Park Golf Club
 BRI BN1 .... 123 G1
Hollybush Business Centre
 HORL RH6 .... 28 E5
Hollycombe Primary School
 LIPH GU30 .... 193 R9
Hollycombe Steam Collection
 LIPH GU30 .... 194 B7
Hollywood Bowl
 CRAWE RH10 .... 8 L1
Holmbush First School
 SHOR BN43 .... 120 C4
Holmbush Industrial Estate
 MIDH GU29 .... 226 H11
The Holme Primary School
 BOR GU35 .... 179 L3
Holmewood House School
 RRTW TN3 .... 36 F7
Holtye Golf Club
 EDEN TN8 .... 33 L6
Holy Cross CE Primary School
 UCK TN22 .... 76 D1
Holy Cross Hospital
 HASM GU27 .... 181 J10
Holy Gate Cactus Gardens
 PUL/STOR RH20 .... 267 K6
Holy Trinity CE (A) Primary
 School
 RHWH RH17 .... 72 C2
Holy Trinity CE Primary School
 SWTR RH13 .... 203 M1
The Holy Trinity CE School
 CRAWW RH11 .... 42 F5
Homecare Business Centre
 LEWES BN7 .... 17 J6
Home Farm Business Centre
 BRI BN1 .... 123 J2
Homeopathic Hospital
 RTW TN1 .... 37 M6
Honeybridge Park
 SWTR RH13 .... 267 P4
The Hope Anchor Hotel
 RYE TN31 .... 252 G8
Horam Manor Touring Park
 HTHF TN21 .... 278 B2
Horam Park Golf Course
 HTHF TN21 .... 278 A4
Horley Anderson Centre
 HORL RH6 .... 22 D6
Horley Health Centre
 HORL RH6 .... 22 F6
Horley Infant School
 HORL RH6 .... 22 F6
Horndean CE Junior School
 HORN PO8 .... 288 D2
Horndean FC
 HORN PO8 .... 288 D2
Horndean Health Centre
 HORN PO8 .... 288 D2
Horndean Infant School
 HORN PO8 .... 288 D2
Horndean Technology
 College
 HORN PO8 .... 288 C2
Horselunges Industrial Estate
 HAIL BN27 .... 278 E12
Horsham Arts Centre
 HORS RH12 .... 14 E5
Horsham Cricket & Sports Club
 HORS RH12 .... 14 B8
Horsham FC
 SWTR RH13 .... 14 E8
Horsham Golf & Fitness Club
 SWTR RH13 .... 201 R7
Horsham Hospital
 HORS RH12 .... 14 D3
Horsham Museum
 HORS RH12 .... 14 C7
Horsham Trading Estate
 SWTR RH13 .... 15 G3
Horsham YMCA FC
 SWTR RH13 .... 14 E8
Horsmonden Primary School
 STPH/PW TN12 .... 189 M3
Horsted Keynes Industrial
 Estate
 RHWH RH17 .... 207 L2
Horsted Place Hotel
 UCK TN22 .... 241 N11
Hotel du Vin
 BRI BN1 .... 4 D7

Hotel du Vin & Bistro
 RTW TN1 .... **38** A6
Hotel Ibis
 CRAWE RH10 .... **27** K6
Hove Business Centre
 HOVE BN3 .... **122** A5
Hove General Hospital
 HOVE BN3 .... **121** M6
Hove Medical Centre
 HOVE BN3 .... **121** K3
Hove Museum & Art Gallery
 HOVE BN3 .... **121** M6
Hove Park School
 HOVE BN3 .... **121** M4
Hove Polyclinic
 HOVE BN3 .... **121** L4
Hove RFC
 HOVE BN3 .... **122** A4
'How We Lived Then' Museum
 of Shops & Social History
 EAST BN21 .... **10** A7
Hubbard School
 EGRIN RH19 .... **31** H4
Huffwood Trading Estate
 BIL RH14 .... **232** A2
 SWTR RH13 .... **234** F10
Hulbert Junior School
 WVILLE PO7 .... **288** A11
Hunter's Burgh
 POLE BN26 .... **161** L1
Hurst Green CE Primary
 School
 BUR/ETCH TN19 .... **216** B6
Hurstpierpoint College
 HPPT/KEY BN6 .... **271** J1
Hurstpierpoint Preparatory
 School
 HPPT/KEY BN6 .... **271** J1
Hurstwood Park Hospital
 RHWH RH17 .... **73** K7
The Hyde Business Park
 BRIE/ROTT BN2 .... **123** L4
Hydro Hotel
 EDN/EASTW BN20 .... **176** F5
Icklesham Primary School
 WSEA TN36 .... **285** P3
Ifield Community College
 CRAWW RH11 .... **42** F2
Ifield Golf & Country Club
 CRAWW RH11 .... **42** C3
Iford & Kingston CE Primary
 School
 LEWES BN7 .... **85** L8
Imberhorne Business Centre
 EGRIN RH19 .... **31** G6
Imberhorne School
 EGRIN RH19 .... **31** G7
The Imber Sports Centre
 EGRIN RH19 .... **31** J6
Imperial Hotel
 HOVE BN3 .... **122** B8
Independent Business Park
 EGRIN RH19 .... **30** F6
Ingfield Manor School
 BIL RH14 .... **200** F3
The Inglenook Hotel
 BOGR PO21 .... **170** F3
Innkeeper's Lodge
 BRI BN1 .... **82** D7
 HAV PO9 .... **289** J9
 LW/ROSE BN22 .... **163** M4
Intensive School of English
 BRI BN1 .... **4** D6
International Lawn Tennis
 Centre
 EAST BN21 .... **10** E8
Itchenor Sailing Club
 SELS PO20 .... **139** M6
Itchingfield Primary School
 SWTR RH13 .... **201** K7
Ivydene Industrial Estate
 EGRIN RH19 .... **48** C2
James Searle Industrial Estate
 HORS RH12 .... **15** H1
Jarvis Brook CP School
 CROW TN6 .... **211** K2
J D English Tuition
 NEWHV BN9 .... **158** E4
Jempsons Trading Estate
 RYE TN31 .... **252** C8
Jessie Younghusband
 Primary School
 CCH PO19 .... **107** L5
Jikack Industrial Estate
 HPPT/KEY BN6 .... **74** A5
Jolesfild CE Primary
 School
 SWTR RH13 .... **234** F9
Jubilee Hall Clinic
 CRAWE RH10 .... **9** M3
K-Bis Theatre School
 BRI BN1 .... **122** D3
Kelvin Business Centre
 CRAWE RH10 .... **27** L8
Kemptown Brewery
 BRIE/ROTT BN2 .... **5** J8
Kent & East Sussex Railway
 CRBK TN17 .... **219** L5
 RBTBR TN32 .... **217** N10
 RYE TN31 .... **218** E8
Kent & Sussex Crematorium
 RTWE/PEM TN2 .... **54** A1
Kent & Sussex Hospital
 SBGH/RUST TN4 .... **37** M5
Kenwood Business Park
 HAV PO9 .... **103** H2
King Alfred Leisure Centre
 HOVE BN3 .... **121** M8
King Business Centre
 HPPT/KEY BN6 .... **236** D12
King Edward VII Hospital
 MIDH GU29 .... **226** G3
Kingley Vale National
 Nature Reserve
 RCCH PO18 .... **291** M8
King Offa Primary School
 BEXW TN39 .... **96** F8
Kings Court School
 HORN PO8 .... **256** B12
Kingsham Primary School
 CCH PO19 .... **6** B7
The Kings Hotel
 BRI BN1 .... **4** A7
Kingsmanor Community
 College
 SHOR BN43 .... **120** B5

Kings Road Industrial Estate
 HASM GU27 .... **181** K11
Kingston Buci First School
 SHOR BN43 .... **120** A5
Kingsway Hotel
 WTHG BN11 .... **20** E7
King's Windmill
 SWTR RH13 .... **233** M9
The Knoll Business Centre
 HOVE BN3 .... **121** J5
Komedia
 BRI BN1 .... **4** E5
Laburnum Grove Junior
 School
 MSEA/BNM PO22 .... **2** C1
Lady Bee Marina Industrial
 Estate
 PTSD BN41 .... **120** D7
Ladycross Business Park
 LING RH7 .... **32** B2
Lagoon Leisure Centre
 HAIL BN27 .... **92** B5
Lamberhurst CE Primary
 School
 RRTW TN3 .... **188** G11
Lamberhurst Golf Club
 RRTW TN3 .... **188** G11
Lamb House (NT)
 RYE TN31 .... **252** H8
Lancastrian Infant School
 CCH PO19 .... **6** C2
Lancing Business Centre
 LAN/SOMP BN15 .... **118** B8
Lancing College
 LAN/SOMP BN15 .... **118** F3
Lancing College Chapel
 LAN/SOMP BN15 .... **119** G3
Lancing Health Centre
 LAN/SOMP BN15 .... **118** D7
Landerry Industrial Estate
 SELS PO20 .... **301** K5
Landgate Arch
 RYE TN31 .... **252** H7
The Lanes
 BRI BN1 .... **4** E7
Langham Hotel
 LW/ROSE BN22 .... **11** J4
Langley Green Primary School
 CRAWW RH11 .... **43** H1
Langney Cemetery
 LGNY BN23 .... **164** C2
Langney Primary School
 LGNY BN23 .... **164** D4
Langney Shopping Centre
 LGNY BN23 .... **164** B2
Langney Sports Club
 LGNY BN23 .... **164** E2
Langrish House Hotel
 PSF GU32 .... **222** D6
Langrish Primary School
 PSF GU32 .... **222** H6
Langshott County Infant
 School
 HORL RH6 .... **23** H6
Langshott Manor Hotel
 HORL RH6 .... **23** J4
Langton Green CP School
 RRTW TN3 .... **36** D5
Lansdowne Hotel
 EAST BN21 .... **177** G4
Lansdowne Road Clinic
 RTW TN1 .... **38** A5
The Lansdowne Place Hotel
 HOVE BN3 .... **122** C8
Laughton Primary School
 RING/NEW BN8 .... **276** D11
The Laurels County First
 School
 SALV BN13 .... **116** A7
Lavant CE Primary School
 RCCH PO18 .... **292** B11
Lavant House Rosemead
 RCCH PO18 .... **292** B12
Lavender Line
 UCK TN22 .... **275** K1
The Lavinia Norfolk Centre
 ANG/EP BN16 .... **148** E2
Lawn Tennis Club
 EAST BN21 .... **10** E8
 HORL RH6 .... **22** E6
Lawson Hunt Industrial Park
 HORS RH12 .... **201** N1
Leap Cross Small Business
 Centre
 HAIL BN27 .... **91** M3
Leechpool Lane Primary
 School
 SWTR RH13 .... **15** M2
Leonardslee Lakes & Gardens
 SWTR RH13 .... **203** M9
Lewes Athletics Track
 LEWES BN7 .... **17** J8
Lewes Business Centre
 LEWES BN7 .... **16** F4
Lewes Castle & Barbican House
 Museum
 LEWES BN7 .... **16** F6
Lewes College
 LEWES BN7 .... **17** H8
Lewes FC
 LEWES BN7 .... **17** G8
Lewes Golf Club
 LEWES BN7 .... **17** L7
Lewes Grammar School
 LEWES BN7 .... **16** F6
Lewes Leisure Centre
 LEWES BN7 .... **17** J8
Lewes Little Theatre
 LEWES BN7 .... **17** G5
Lewes Magistrates Court
 LEWES BN7 .... **17** H6
Lewes Natural Health Centre
 LEWES BN7 .... **17** J5
Lewes New School
 LEWES BN7 .... **16** F4
Lewes Sports Club
 LEWES BN7 .... **86** A6
Lewes Victoria Hospital
 LEWES BN7 .... **16** B5
Lexden Lodge Industrial
 Estate
 CROW TN6 .... **211** L4
Library & Council Building
 CRAWE RH10 .... **9** H3
Lifeboat Museum
 EAST BN21 .... **10** F9

Lillies Caravan Park
 MSEA/BNM PO22 .... **111** H8
Limeburners
 BIL RH14 .... **231** P1
Limeburners (Camping)
 ANG/EP BN16 .... **114** F5
Limes Business Centre
 HORL RH6 .... **26** E3
Lindfield Junior School
 HWH RH16 .... **73** L2
Lindfield Medical Centre
 HWH RH16 .... **73** L1
Lindfield Primary School
 HWH RH16 .... **73** K2
The Lindfield Special School
 LW/ROSE BN22 .... **163** J3
Lineside Industrial Estate
 LHPTN BN17 .... **147** G3
Liongate Clinic
 SBGH/RUST TN4 .... **37** M4
Liphook CE Junior School
 LIPH GU30 .... **193** P1
Liphook Golf Club
 LIPH GU30 .... **193** P6
Liphook Infant School
 LIPH GU30 .... **193** P1
Liss Business Centre
 LISS GU33 .... **192** B8
Liss J & I School
 LISS GU33 .... **192** D10
Little Common Primary School
 BEXW TN39 .... **136** C1
Littlegreen School
 RCCH PO18 .... **258** B9
Littlehampton Community
 School
 LHPTN BN17 .... **147** K3
Littlehampton Golf Club
 LHPTN BN17 .... **147** H5
Littlehampton Health Centre
 LHPTN BN17 .... **147** K5
Littlehampton Hospital
 LHPTN BN17 .... **147** K4
Littlehampton Museum
 LHPTN BN17 .... **147** K4
Littlehampton Swimming
 Centre
 LHPTN BN17 .... **147** L6
Littlehampton Town FC
 LHPTN BN17 .... **147** L4
Littlehampton Tutorial Unit
 LHPTN BN17 .... **147** K3
Littlehaven Infant School
 HORS RH12 .... **56** E4
Little Horsted CE Primary
 School
 UCK TN22 .... **241** P12
Littlemead School
 SELS PO20 .... **108** F6
Little Ridge CP School
 SLVH TN37 .... **283** R12
Little Ridge Surgery
 SLVH TN37 .... **283** R12
Little Theatre
 SEAF BN25 .... **174** E3
The Living World
 SEAF BN25 .... **175** M1
Local Education Office
 HAV PO9 .... **103** G2
London-Gatwick Airport
 HORL RH6 .... **27** L2
London Meed CP School
 BURH RH15 .... **74** F8
Long Burgh
 POLE BN26 .... **160** D2
Longhill High School
 BRIE/ROTT BN2 .... **155** K1
Longley Industrial Estate
 BRI BN1 .... **4** E2
Longley Trading Estate
 CRAWE RH10 .... **9** G5
The Long Man of Wilmington
 POLE BN26 .... **161** K2
Look & Sea! Visitor Centre
 LHPTN BN17 .... **147** H5
Lord's Burghs
 RING/NEW BN8 .... **128** C6
Lowfield Heath Industrial
 Estate
 HORL RH6 .... **27** K4
Loxwood Primary School
 BIL RH14 .... **198** H1
Ludshott Common (NT)
 GSHT GU26 .... **180** B6
Lullington Heath Nature
 Reserve
 POLE BN26 .... **161** K5
Lurgashall Vineyard
 PETW GU28 .... **196** A9
Lydd Camp
 LYDD TN29 .... **255** Q8
Lydd Primary School
 LYDD TN29 .... **255** R7
Lydd Ranges
 LYDD TN29 .... **255** L12
Lydd Town Museum
 LYDD TN29 .... **255** Q7
Lyminster County Infant
 School
 LHPTN BN17 .... **147** J2
Lyndhurst First School
 WTHG BN11 .... **21** M3
Lyons Farm Estate
 SWTR RH13 .... **201** K3
Lythe Hill Hotel & Spa
 HASM GU27 .... **182** A12
Mackley Industrial Estate
 HFD BN5 .... **269** L11
Maidenbower First & Middle
 School
 CRAWE RH10 .... **44** C5
Maidenbower Junior School
 CRAWE RH10 .... **44** C5
Mainline Business Centre
 LISS GU33 .... **192** C9
Males Burgh
 RING/NEW BN8 .... **127** M5
Malling Industrial Estate
 LEWES BN7 .... **17** H3
Malthouse Business Park
 RYE TN31 .... **252** B3
Malt House Trading Estate
 SHOR BN43 .... **120** A6
Manhood Community
 College
 SELS PO20 .... **301** K5

Mannings Heath Golf Club
 SWTR RH13 .... **203** K2
Manor CP School
 UCK TN22 .... **76** K2
Manor Farm Business Centre
 POY/PYE BN45 .... **270** E12
Manor Field Primary School
 BURH RH15 .... **75** H5
Manorfield Primary School
 HORL RH6 .... **22** E6
Manor Green College
 CRAWW RH11 .... **42** F1
Manor Green Primary School
 CRAWW RH11 .... **27** J7
Manor Hall County Middle
 School
 STHW BN42 .... **120** D5
Manor Hall First School
 STHW BN42 .... **120** E6
Manor House Hospital
 HOVE BN3 .... **121** M6
Manor Park Medical Centre
 POLE BN26 .... **131** L7
Manor Sports Ground Pavilion
 SALV BN13 .... **117** J8
Mansion Lions Hotel
 EAST BN21 .... **10** F8
March CE Primary School
 RCCH PO18 .... **108** D4
Marchwell Industrial Estate
 CCH PO19 .... **108** A4
Maresfield Leisure Centre
 UCK TN22 .... **241** M1
Marine Clinic
 BRIE/ROTT BN2 .... **155** M4
Mark Cross CE Primary School
 CROW TN6 .... **69** M6
Market Cross
 CCH PO19 .... **6** C4
Marlborough Business Centre
 LAN/SOMP BN15 .... **152** B1
Marle Place
 STPH/PW TN12 .... **188** C4
Marlipins Museum
 SHOR BN43 .... **119** K7
Marriott Goodwood Park
 Hotel & Country Club
 RCCH PO18 .... **293** J11
Marshlands CP School
 HAIL BN27 .... **92** C5
Martello Tower & Seaford
 Museum
 SEAF BN25 .... **174** E4
Martlets Trading Estate
 FERR BN12 .... **150** B2
Matform Business Centre
 CCH PO19 .... **6** A6
 CCH PO19 .... **107** J8
Mayfield CE Primary School
 MAYF TN20 .... **212** E6
Maynards Green CP School
 HTHF TN21 .... **244** D11
Meadowbrook Industrial
 Centre
 CRAWE RH10 .... **27** M8
Meadow Road Industrial
 Estate
 WTHG BN11 .... **152** A1
The Meadow School
 BOR GU35 .... **179** K5
The Mead School
 RTWE/PEM TN2 .... **37** M8
The Meads Primary School
 EGRIN RH19 .... **47** K2
Meath Green Infant School
 HORL RH6 .... **22** E4
Meath Green Junior School
 HORL RH6 .... **22** E4
Mechanical Music &
 Doll Collection
 CCH PO19 .... **7** L2
The Medmerry Primary School
 SELS PO20 .... **301** L2
Meeching Valley CP School
 NEWHV BN9 .... **18** C3
Megabowl
 BEX TN40 .... **137** M1
Mercateria Business Centre
 STLEO TN38 .... **12** A9
The Meridian Industrial
 Estate
 PEAHV BN10 .... **157** H6
Meridian Leisure Centre
 PEAHV BN10 .... **157** H5
Meridian Primary School
 PEAHV BN10 .... **157** H4
Meridian Shopping Centre
 HAV PO9 .... **103** G4
Mermaid Inn Hotel
 RYE TN31 .... **252** C8
The Mews Business Centre
 BEX TN40 .... **137** H1
The Mews Clinic
 EAST BN21 .... **10** A4
Michael Ayres Junior School
 BOGR PO21 .... **143** M8
Michael Hall School
 FROW RH18 .... **48** C8
Michelham Priory
 HAIL BN27 .... **91** G6
Middle Park Medical Centre
 HAV PO9 .... **102** D1
Middle Street Primary School
 BRI BN1 .... **4** D7
Middleton Business Park
 MSEA/BNM PO22 .... **145** K7
Middleton Medical Centre
 MSEA/BNM PO22 .... **145** L8
Midhurst CE Primary School
 MIDH GU29 .... **226** G10
Midhurst Grammar School
 MIDH GU29 .... **226** H9
Midhurst Intermediate School
 MIDH GU29 .... **227** K7
Mid Sussex Golf Club
 HPPT/KEY BN6 .... **272** C4
Mile Oak Clinic
 PTSD BN41 .... **120** E2
Mile Oak Primary School
 PTSD BN41 .... **120** E2
Millais School
 SWTR RH13 .... **15** J6
Millbrook Business Park
 CROW TN6 .... **211** L1
Mill Chase Community School
 BOR GU35 .... **179** J6

Mill Green Industrial Estate
 HWH RH16 .... **73** H3
The Mill Primary School
 CRAWW RH11 .... **42** F3
Mill Road Industrial Estate
 PTSD BN41 .... **121** G6
The Millstream Hotel &
 Restaurant
 RCCH PO18 .... **105** M8
Mill View Hospital
 HOVE BN3 .... **121** K4
Milton Mount Primary School
 CRAWE RH10 .... **44** A1
Minerva Studio Theatre Cinema
 CCH PO19 .... **6** E1
Minerva Theatre
 CCH PO19 .... **6** E1
Mobility Centre
 EAST BN21 .... **10** F5
Modern Mould Business
 Centre
 LHPTN BN17 .... **147** G3
Modern Moulds Business
 Centre
 LAN/SOMP BN15 .... **152** B1
Moira House Girls School
 EDN/EASTW BN20 .... **176** D4
Monk's House (NT)
 LEWES BN7 .... **126** D4
Montague Shopping Centre
 WTHG BN11 .... **21** H6
Montessori House for
 Children
 BRI BN1 .... **122** F4
Morley Street Health Centre
 BRIE/ROTT BN2 .... **5** G5
Motcombe Community
 Infant School
 EAST BN21 .... **163** H8
Moulscoomb Clinic
 BRIE/ROTT BN2 .... **123** K2
Moulsecoomb Health Clinic
 BRIE/ROTT BN2 .... **123** K2
Moulsecoomb Primary School
 BRIE/ROTT BN2 .... **123** K2
Mount Caburn
 RING/NEW BN8 .... **87** H7
The Mount Camphill
 Community School
 WADH TN5 .... **71** G3
Mountfield & Whatlington CE
 Primary School
 RBTBR TN32 .... **248** E6
Mountney Bridge Business
 Park
 PEV BN24 .... **164** E1
Mount Pleasant Hospital
 SLVH TN37 .... **98** F1
Mowden School
 HOVE BN3 .... **122** C4
Museum of Costumes &
 Bygones
 BEX TN40 .... **137** J1
National Pinetum & Garden
 CRBK TN17 .... **191** Q5
Natural Health Centre
 CCH PO19 .... **6** D7
Nest Business Park
 HAV PO9 .... **103** J1
Netherfield CE Primary School
 BAT TN33 .... **247** P11
Net Shops
 HAS TN34 .... **13** L7
Nevill Golf Club
 RTWE/PEM TN2 .... **54** C2
Newhaven Ferry Terminal
 NEWHV BN9 .... **19** H3
Newhaven Flea Market
 NEWHV BN9 .... **18** F4
Newhaven Health Centre
 NEWHV BN9 .... **19** G3
New Horizons School
 STLEO TN38 .... **98** F1
 STLEO TN38 .... **283** N12
Newhouse Farm Business
 Centre
 HORS RH12 .... **57** H2
Newick CE Primary School
 RING/NEW BN8 .... **240** B7
Newick Health Centre
 RING/NEW BN8 .... **240** C6
Newick House School
 BURH RH15 .... **75** H8
Newick House Special School
 BURH RH15 .... **75** G8
Newick Park Hotel &
 Country Estate
 RING/NEW BN8 .... **240** D10
Newlands Health Clinic
 HWH RH16 .... **73** H5
Newlands Manor School
 SEAF BN25 .... **175** G1
Newlands Preparatory School
 SEAF BN25 .... **175** H1
New Life School
 EGRIN RH19 .... **31** J7
New Park Film Centre Cinema
 CCH PO19 .... **6** F3
New Venture Theatre
 BRI BN1 .... **4** A6
New Wilmington Hotel
 EAST BN21 .... **10** E9
Nightingale Industrial Estate
 HORS RH12 .... **14** F3
Ninfield CE Primary School
 BAT TN33 .... **281** N12
The Noble Clinic
 STPH/PW TN12 .... **188** G1
Nore Down
 NEWHV BN9 .... **157** M4
Norfolk Arms Hotel
 ARUN BN18 .... **113** G2
Northbourne Medical Centre
 SHOR BN43 .... **119** M5
Northbrook College Sussex
 FERR BN12 .... **150** A1
 HWH RH16 .... **73** G5
 SALV BN13 .... **117** J8
 WTHG BN11 .... **21** H5
Northbrook Trading Estate
 SALV BN13 .... **117** K7
Northchapel Primary School
 PETW GU28 .... **196** F6
North Crescent Industrial
 Estate
 HAIL BN27 .... **91** M6

Northease Manor School
LEWES BN7 .... 126 B4
Northfield Business Park
HAIL BN27 .... 90 F1
Northgate Primary School
CRAWE RH10 .... 43 K1
North Heath Lane Industrial
Estate
HORS RH12 .... 56 C3
North Heath Primary School
HORS RH12 .... 56 C4
Northiam CE Primary School
RYE TN31 .... 218 E12
North Lancing First & Middle
School
LAN/SOMP BN15 .... 118 D5
Northlands Business Park
HORS RH12 .... 187 M5
Northlands Wood Primary
School
HWH RH16 .... 73 L6
North Lodge Industrial Park
LIPH GU30 .... 194 A5
North Mundham Primary
School
SELS PO20 .... 142 A1
Northolmes Junior School
HORS RH12 .... 56 H5
North Terminal
HORL RH6 .... 27 K1
Nutley CE Primary School
UCK TN22 .... 208 H5
Nyewood CE Junior & Infant
School
BOGR PO21 .... 171 M1
Nymans Garden (NT)
RHWH RH17 .... 204 E2
Oakendene Industrial Estate
SWTR RH13 .... 235 N4
Oakfield Middle School
LAN/SOMP BN15 .... 118 C6
Oakgrove College
SALV BN13 .... 116 D8
Oakhurst Business Park
SWTR RH13 .... 201 Q11
Oaklands Business Centre
WTHG BN11 .... 150 E2
Oaklands Catholic School
WVILLE PO7 .... 288 A12
Oakley School
RTWE/PEM TN2 .... 38 F4
Oakmeeds Community College
BURH RH15 .... 74 F7
The Oaks Primary School
CRAWE RH10 .... 9 K9
Oakwood Industrial Park
CRAWE RH10 .... 27 M8
Oakwood School
HORL RH6 .... 23 G6
LW/ROSE BN22 .... 163 J2
RCCH PO18 .... 106 E3
Oakwood Sports Centre
HORL RH6 .... 23 H6
Oathall Community College
HWH RH16 .... 73 J3
Oban Hotel
EAST BN21 .... 10 F9
The Observatory
Science Centre
HAIL BN27 .... 94 A4
Ockenden Manor Hotel
RHWH RH17 .... 72 B3
Ocklynge Cemetery
EAST BN21 .... 163 J8
Ocklynge Junior School
EDN/EASTW BN20 .... 163 H7
Odeon Cinema
BOGR PO21 .... 3 J6
BRI BN1 .... 4 C7
HAS TN34 .... 13 G6
RTWE/PEM TN2 .... 38 E1
Old Barn Theatre
CRAWW RH11 .... 42 E1
Old Darlington Mushroom
Farm Industrial Estate
ANG/EP BN16 .... 114 F8
The Olde Forge Hotel
& Restaurant
HAIL BN27 .... 92 E2
Old Grammar School (Juniors)
LEWES BN7 .... 16 D5
Old Grammar School
(Seniors & Sixth Form)
LEWES BN7 .... 16 D6
The Old Museum
RYE TN31 .... 251 J3
Old Salehurst School
RBTBR TN32 .... 216 C12
Old Ship Hotel
BRI BN1 .... 4 D8
Old Thorns Hotel, Golf &
Country Club
LIPH GU30 .... 193 L2
The Old Tollgate Restaurant
& Hotel
STEY/UB BN44 .... 78 J2
Old Town Hall
HORS RH12 .... 14 C7
Old Town Hall Museum of
Local History
HAS TN34 .... 13 K6
Open University
EGRIN RH19 .... 31 K8
Orchard Business Centre
REDH RH1 .... 22 F1
SBGH/RUST TN4 .... 38 C1
The Orchards Community
Middle School
FERR BN12 .... 150 C1
The Orchards Shopping
Centre
HWH RH16 .... 73 H5
Ore Business Park
RHAS TN35 .... 13 M1
Oriel High School
CRAWE RH10 .... 8 F3
Orion Cinema
BURH RH15 .... 74 F6
Our Lady of Lourdes RC
Primary School
BRIE/ROTT BN2 .... 155 L3
Our Lady of Sion Junior
School
WTHG BN11 .... 21 G5
Our Lady of Sion School
WTHG BN11 .... 20 F6

Our Lady Queen of Heaven
CP School
CRAWW RH11 .... 43 G1
Ouse Valley Viaduct
RHWH RH17 .... 205 R5
Ovingdean Hall School
BRIE/ROTT BN2 .... 155 J1
Owl House
RTW TN3 .... 188 D10
Padnell Infant School
HORN PO8 .... 288 B6
Padnell Junior School
HORN PO8 .... 288 C6
Pagham CC
BOGR PO21 .... 170 F4
Pagham FC
BOGR PO21 .... 170 F4
Pagham Harbour
(Nature Reserve)
BOGR PO21 .... 170 B7
Pagham Yacht Club
BOGR PO21 .... 170 F6
Palatine School
FERR BN12 .... 116 C8
Pallant House & Art Gallery
CCH PO19 .... 6 E5
Palmers Road Industrial
Estate
EMRTH PO10 .... 104 B4
The Pantiles Shopping Arcade
RTWE/PEM TN2 .... 37 M7
Paradise Park & Gardens
NEWHV BN9 .... 158 C4
Parham House & Gardens
PUL/STOR RH20 .... 265 L12
Park College
EAST BN21 .... 163 J6
Park Community School
HAV PO9 .... 288 D12
Park House Primary School
HAV PO9 .... 288 D12
Parkland Business Centre
LAN/SOMP BN15 .... 152 C1
Parkland Junior School
LW/ROSE BN22 .... 163 J4
Parklands Community School
CCH PO19 .... 6 A3
Park Mead Primary School
HAIL BN27 .... 90 F5
Park Recreation Centre
HORS RH12 .... 14 D5
Parkside Community Primary
School
HTHF TN21 .... 244 F8
Park View Leisure Centre
HOVE BN3 .... 121 K6
Parsonage Business Centre
HORS RH12 .... 15 G1
Pashley Down County Infant
School
EDN/EASTW BN20 .... 176 B1
Pashley Manor & Gardens
WADH TN5 .... 215 N2
Passfield Mill Business Park
LIPH GU30 .... 179 L8
Patcham High School
BRI BN1 .... 82 E7
Patcham House Special School
BRI BN1 .... 82 D7
Patcham Infant School
BRI BN1 .... 82 D7
Patcham Junior School
BRI BN1 .... 82 E7
Pavilion Cinema
HAIL BN27 .... 92 A6
The Pavilion Clinic
BRI BN1 .... 4 B6
Pavilion Retail Park
BRIE/ROTT BN2 .... 123 H3
Pavilions in the Park
HORS RH12 .... 14 D4
Pavilion Theatre
BRI BN1 .... 4 E6
WTHG BN11 .... 21 H7
Paxhill Park Golf Club
HWH RH16 .... 206 H9
Paxton Business Centre
HOVE BN3 .... 121 J5
Peacehaven Community
School
PEAHV BN10 .... 157 H5
Peacehaven Golf Club
NEWHV BN9 .... 18 B5
Peacehaven Infant School
PEAHV BN10 .... 157 G6
Peacehaven Sports Centre
PEAHV BN10 .... 157 H5
Peacock Industrial Estate
HOVE BN3 .... 122 C6
Peasmarsh CE Primary
School
RYE TN31 .... 252 A4
Pebsham Community
Primary School
BEX TN40 .... 97 M8
Pelham Court Business
Centre
CRAWW RH11 .... 43 G7
Pells CE Primary School
LEWES BN7 .... 16 D4
Pembury Hospital
RTWE/PEM TN2 .... 38 F1
Pembury Primary School
RTWE/PEM TN2 .... 39 J1
Pennthorpe School
HORS RH12 .... 185 R10
The Peter Gladwin Primary
School
PTSD BN41 .... 121 G3
Petersfield Business Park
PSF GU32 .... 223 L6
Petersfield Community
Hospital
PSF GU32 .... 223 M6
Petersfield Golf Club
(new course)
LISS GU33 .... 223 R1
Petersfield Golf Club
(old course)
EPSF GU31 .... 223 P8
Petersfield Infant School
PSF GU32 .... 223 N6
Petersfield Rugby FC
EPSF GU31 .... 224 A5
The Petersfield School
PSF GU32 .... 223 M7

Petersfield Swimming Pool
EPSF GU31 .... 223 P6
Petersfield Town FC
EPSF GU31 .... 223 P5
Petersgate Infant School
HORN PO8 .... 256 D9
Petworth CE Primary School
PETW GU28 .... 229 L10
Petworth Cottage Museum
PETW GU28 .... 229 L9
Petworth House & Park (NT)
PETW GU28 .... 229 L9
Petworth Industrial Estate
PETW GU28 .... 229 L7
Pevensey Bay Sailing Club
PEV BN24 .... 165 H3
Pevensey Castle
PEV BN24 .... 134 A7
Pevensey & Westham CE
Primary School
PEV BN24 .... 133 M7
Philpots Manor School
EGRIN RH19 .... 62 B4
Phoenix Industrial Estate
LEWES BN7 .... 17 G4
Picturedome Cinema
BOGR PO21 .... 2 C6
The Picture House Cinema
UCK TN22 .... 76 E5
Piggott's Business Park
WTHG BN11 .... 20 F4
The Piltdown Golf Club
UCK TN22 .... 76 A2
Piries Place
HORS RH12 .... 14 D6
Plaistow & Kirdford Primary
School
BIL RH14 .... 198 A2
Plumpton College
LEWES BN7 .... 272 G9
Plumpton Primary School
LEWES BN7 .... 273 J4
Plumpton Racecourse
LEWES BN7 .... 272 H5
Polegate CP School
POLE BN26 .... 131 M6
Polegate Windmill
POLE BN26 .... 162 F1
Pool Valley Coach Station
BRI BN1 .... 4 F8
Portfield Community School
CCH PO19 .... 7 J3
Portfield FC
CCH PO19 .... 7 K2
Portfield Retail Park
CCH PO19 .... 7 L2
Portland Business Park
HOVE BN3 .... 121 K6
Portland Road Trading Estate
HOVE BN3 .... 121 J5
Portslade Community
College
PTSD BN41 .... 120 F2
STHW BN42 .... 120 E3
Portslade Health Centre
PTSD BN41 .... 121 G6
Portslade Sixth Form Centre
PTSD BN41 .... 120 F4
Potts Marsh Industrial Estate
PEV BN24 .... 164 E1
Pound Hill Infant School
CRAWE RH10 .... 44 B2
Pound Hill Junior School
CRAWE RH10 .... 44 B2
Powder Mills Hotel
BAT TN33 .... 282 D7
Prebendal School
CCH PO19 .... 6 C4
Premier Travel Inn
ARUN BN18 .... 113 J4
BRI BN1 .... 4 D7
CCH PO19 .... 6 C7
CRAWE RH10 .... 27 K6
CRAWE RH10 .... 28 C5
CRAWW RH11 .... 8 A6
CRAWW RH11 .... 8 C7
EGRIN RH19 .... 30 F5
HAV PO9 .... 102 C4
HORL RH6 .... 22 E8
HORS RH12 .... 14 F4
LGNY BN23 .... 164 B2
MSEA/BNM PO22 .... 144 C4
POLE BN26 .... 131 L5
SLVH TN37 .... 283 P11
The Prependal School
CCH PO19 .... 6 E3
Preston Manor
BRI BN1 .... 122 D4
Preston Park Clinic
BRI BN1 .... 122 F4
Preston Park Hotel
BRI BN1 .... 122 D3
Priests House
EGRIN RH19 .... 62 D3
Prince Regent Swimming
Complex
BRI BN1 .... 4 E6
Princes Marine Hotel
HOVE BN3 .... 121 M7
Princess Alice Hospital
EAST BN21 .... 10 E4
The Princess Royal Hospital
HWH RH16 .... 73 J7
The Priory Arts Centre
HWH RH16 .... 73 J6
Priory Lane Arcade
CCH PO19 .... 6 E2
Priory Meadow Shopping
Centre
HAS TN34 .... 13 G6
Priory Ruins
LEWES BN7 .... 16 F8
Priory (ruins)
RCCH PO18 .... 109 J1
Priory School
LEWES BN7 .... 17 J8
Pulborough Brooks RSPB
Nature Reserve
PUL/STOR RH20 .... 265 M6
Punnett's Town Primary
School
HTHF TN21 .... 245 L7
Pyecombe Golf Club
POY/PYE BN45 .... 271 L11
Quality Hotel
BRI BN1 .... 4 C7

Quarry Lane Industrial Estate
CCH PO19 .... 7 K7
Queen Alexandra Hospital
Home
WTHG BN11 .... 20 D6
Queen Elizabeth Country
Park
HORN PO8 .... 256 H2
Queen Elizabeth II
Silver Jubilee School
SWTR RH13 .... 15 K7
Queensdown School
BRI BN1 .... 123 H2
Queens Hotel
EAST BN21 .... 11 H7
Queens Inclosure Primary
School
WVILLE PO7 .... 288 B8
Queen Victoria Hospital
EGRIN RH19 .... 31 L6
Queen Victoria Statue
HOVE BN3 .... 122 B8
Quell Farm Industrial Estate
PUL/STOR RH20 .... 264 F9
Quintin Medical Centre
HAIL BN27 .... 92 B2
The Quintins Shopping
Centre
HAIL BN27 .... 92 B5
Rake Business Park
LISS GU33 .... 192 H9
Rake CE First School
LISS GU33 .... 193 H7
Ramada Hotel
CRAWE RH10 .... 43 M1
RTWE/PEM TN2 .... 39 G2
Ranalah Estate
NEWHV BN9 .... 19 H1
Ratton School
EAST BN21 .... 163 H6
Ravenside Retail &
Leisure Park
BEX TN40 .... 137 M1
Raystede Centre for
Animal Welfare
RING/NEW BN8 .... 275 R8
Recycling Centre
LW/ROSE BN22 .... 164 B7
Red Lake CP School
RHAS TN35 .... 100 C1
Regent Business Centre
BURH RH15 .... 74 D7
Regis Centre & Alexandra
Theatre
BOGR PO21 .... 2 E8
Rich Industrial Estate
NEWHV BN9 .... 158 D4
Riders J & I School
HAV PO9 .... 288 E12
Ridgewood Industrial Estate
UCK TN22 .... 77 G8
Rikkyo School in England
HORS RH12 .... 185 L9
Ringmer Business Centre
RING/NEW BN8 .... 275 L11
Ringmer Community College
RING/NEW BN8 .... 275 L11
Ringmer CP School
RING/NEW BN8 .... 275 K12
Ringmer FC
RING/NEW BN8 .... 275 J12
Ritz Cinema
HORS RH12 .... 14 E5
Riverbank Business Centre
SHOR BN43 .... 119 J6
Riverside Business Centre
SHOR BN43 .... 119 L6
Riverside Industrial Estate
LEWES BN7 .... 17 G4
LHPTN BN17 .... 147 G4
Riverside School
WVILLE PO7 .... 102 A2
RNIB
HOVE BN3 .... 122 C7
Robertsbridge Community
College
RBTBR TN32 .... 248 A1
Roborough Day Hospital
EAST BN21 .... 10 E4
Robsack Wood Community
School
STLEO TN38 .... 98 D3
Rock & Bowl Bowling Alley
EGRIN RH19 .... 31 K8
Rocks Park CP School
UCK TN22 .... 76 D4
Rockys Leisure Centre
HAS TN34 .... 12 F8
Rodmell CE Primary School
LEWES BN7 .... 126 D4
Roedean School
BRIE/ROTT BN2 .... 155 G2
Roffey Park Institute
HORS RH12 .... 57 L3
Roffey Social & Sports Club
HORS RH12 .... 56 F4
Rogate CE Primary School
EPSF GU31 .... 225 J5
Rope Walk Shopping Centre
RYE TN31 .... 252 G7
Rose Green County Infant
School
BOGR PO21 .... 171 H3
Rose Green County Junior
School
BOGR PO21 .... 171 G2
Rose Hill School
SBGH/RUST TN4 .... 37 K4
Roselands Infant School
LW/ROSE BN22 .... 11 H1
Rotherfield CP School
CROW TN6 .... 211 Q1
The Rotherfield Sports
Ground
MIDH GU29 .... 227 J7
Rottingdean FC
BRIE/ROTT BN2 .... 155 L2
Roussillon Barracks
CCH PO19 .... 107 M4
Rowfant Business Centre
CRAWE RH10 .... 45 K3
Rowland's Castle Golf Club
HAV PO9 .... 289 J7
Royal Ashdown Forest
Golf Club
FROW RH18 .... 48 F8

Royal Eastbourne Golf Club
EDN/EASTW BN20 .... 10 A7
Royal George Clinic
BURH RH15 .... 74 D6
Royal Hippodrome Theatre
EAST BN21 .... 11 G6
The Royal Hotel
BOGR PO21 .... 2 D8
The Royal Junior School
CSHT GU26 .... 180 G8
Royal Pavilion
BRI BN1 .... 4 E7
The Royal Pavilion Townhouse
Hotel
BRI BN1 .... 4 A7
The Royal School
HASM GU27 .... 181 L7
Royal & Sun Alliance Sports
Club
HORS RH12 .... 56 D3
Royal Sussex County Hospital
BRIE/ROTT BN2 .... 5 L8
Royal Victoria Hotel
STLEO TN38 .... 99 G7
Royal Victoria Place Shopping
Centre
RTW TN1 .... 38 A5
RSPCA HQ
HORS RH12 .... 14 C7
Rudford Industrial Estate
ARUN BN18 .... 146 C3
Rudgwick Medical Centre
HORS RH12 .... 185 R10
Rudgwick Primary School
HORS RH12 .... 186 A10
Rudyard Kipling CP School
BRIE/ROTT BN2 .... 124 D6
Rumboldswhyke CE Infant
School
CCH PO19 .... 7 J6
Rusper Golf Club
RDKG RH5 .... 25 H5
Rusper Primary School
HORS RH12 .... 41 H2
Russell Hotel
SBGH/RUST TN4 .... 37 M5
Rusthall Medical Centre
SBGH/RUST TN4 .... 37 G5
Rustington Community
Primary School
ANG/EP BN16 .... 148 A3
Rustington Retail Park
ANG/EP BN16 .... 148 C2
Rustington Trading Estate
ANG/EP BN16 .... 148 B2
Rutherfords Business Park
BAT TN33 .... 283 J7
Rutherford Way Industrial
Estate
CRAWE RH10 .... 27 M6
The Rydon Community School
PUL/STOR RH20 .... 266 C11
Rye Bay Club House
WSEA TN36 .... 286 F4
Rye Castle Museum
RYE TN31 .... 252 H8
Rye Community Clinic
RYE TN31 .... 252 G7
Rye Football & CC
RYE TN31 .... 252 H7
Rye Golf Club
RYE TN31 .... 253 N10
Rye Harbour Sailing Club
RYE TN31 .... 253 M10
Rye Industrial Estate
RYE TN31 .... 253 J9
Rye Lodge Hotel
RYE TN31 .... 252 H8
Rye Sports Centre
RYE TN31 .... 252 G7
Sackville Community College
EGRIN RH19 .... 31 M8
Sackville Trading Estate
HOVE BN3 .... 121 M5
Sacred Heart RC Primary
School
WADH TN5 .... 71 J4
Saddlers Walk Shopping Centre
CCH PO19 .... 6 F4
St Albans CE Primary School
HAV PO9 .... 103 J7
St Andrews CE First & Middle
School
CRAWE RH10 .... 9 M7
St Andrews CE High School
for Boys
SALV BN13 .... 21 J1
St Andrews CE Infants School
LW/ROSE BN22 .... 164 B7
St Andrews CE Primary School
HOVE BN3 .... 122 A7
SWTR RH13 .... 202 F8
St Andrews Market
HAS TN34 .... 13 H6
St Andrews School
EDN/EASTW BN20 .... 176 D6
St Annes School
LEWES BN7 .... 16 D7
St Anthonys School
CCH PO19 .... 107 L5
St Aubyns School
BRIE/ROTT BN2 .... 155 M4
St Augustines CE Primary
School
RHWH RH17 .... 239 J2
St Augustines RC Primary
School
SBGH/RUST TN4 .... 37 M2
St Barnabas CE Primary School
RTW TN1 .... 38 A4
St Bartholomews CE Primary
School
BRI BN1 .... 4 E3
St Bartholomews Primary
School
HASM GU27 .... 181 M9
St Bartholomews Tutorial
College
BRI BN1 .... 4 E4
St Bedes Preparatory School
EDN/EASTW BN20 .... 176 E6
St Bedes School
HAIL BN27 .... 90 E5
St Bernadettes RC Primary
School
BRI BN1 .... 122 D3

St Catherine's Hospice
CRAWE RH10 .... 8 F7
St Catherines RC School
LHPTN BN17 .... 147 J3
St Christophers School
HOVE BN3 .... 121 L7
St Edmunds School
GSHT GU26 .... 180 G6
St Faith Clinic
BRIE/ROTT BN2 .... 154 D1
St Francis of Assisi Primary
School
CRAWE RH10 .... 9 C6
St Georges Hall
CCH PO19 .... 7 H6
St Giles CE Primary School
RHWH RH17 .... 207 M3
St Giles College
EAST BN21 .... 176 F4
St Gregorys Catholic
Comprehensive School
SBGH/RUST TN4 .... 37 L2
St Hill Manor
EGRIN RH19 .... 47 H5
St Hugh's Monastery
SWTR RH13 .... 235 J7
St Ives School
HASM GU27 .... 181 P9
St James CE Primary School
EMRTH PO10 .... 104 A3
PUL/STOR RH20 .... 264 D7
St James Industrial Estate
CCH PO19 .... 7 K2
St James Medical Centre
RTW TN1 .... 38 B5
St James's J & I School
RTWE/PEM TN2 .... 38 B5
St Johns Catholic Primary
School
HORS RH12 .... 201 R4
St Johns CE Primary School
CROW TN6 .... 67 H5
SBGH/RUST TN4 .... 38 A2
St Johns Infant School
SBGH/RUST TN4 .... 37 M4
St John's Meads CE Primary
School
EDN/EASTW BN20 .... 176 C6
St Johns Primary School
Rowlands Castle
HAV PO9 .... 289 J9
St Johns School & College
SEAF BN25 .... 159 K8
St John the Baptist Primary
School
SALV BN13 .... 298 G11
St John the Baptist RC
Primary School
BRIE/ROTT BN2 .... 5 L6
St Josephs Business Park
HOVE BN3 .... 121 M5
St Josephs RC Primary School
BRI BN1 .... 123 G4
HWH RH16 .... 73 H5
St Josephs RC School
LW/ROSE BN22 .... 11 J2
St Josephs Trading Estate
HOVE BN3 .... 121 L5
St Lawrence CE Primary
School
HPPT/KEY BN6 .... 270 H3
St Leonards CE Primary School
STLEO TN38 .... 98 F6
St Leonards Community
Infant School
SWTR RH13 .... 14 F6
St Leonards FC
HAS TN34 .... 99 M1
St Lukes CE Infant School
SBGH/RUST TN4 .... 38 B2
St Lukes Swimming Pool
BRIE/ROTT BN2 .... 5 K4
St Lukes Terrace Junior School
BRIE/ROTT BN2 .... 5 K5
St Margarets CE Primary School
CRAWW RH11 .... 8 A1
St Margarets Convent of
Mercy Junior School
MIDH GU29 .... 226 H9
St Margarets Primary School
ANG/EP BN16 .... 114 E6
St Marks CE Primary School
BRIE/ROTT BN2 .... 154 D1
RHWH RH17 .... 204 G4
SBGH/RUST TN4 .... 37 J8
UCK TN22 .... 211 K12
St Martins CE Primary School
BRIE/ROTT BN2 .... 5 J1
St Mary Magdalen Primary
School
BEX TN40 .... 97 L7
BRI BN1 .... 4 B5
St Marys CE First School
PUL/STOR RH20 .... 298 G3
St Marys CE Primary School
EGRIN RH19 .... 31 J7
HORS RH12 .... 14 C6
LHPTN BN17 .... 146 D5
MFD/CHID GU8 .... 182 G6
PUL/STOR RH20 .... 265 K2
St Marys Hospital
(Almhouses)
CCH PO19 .... 6 E4
St Marys RC Primary School
BOGR PO21 .... 2 F7
PTSD BN41 .... 121 G6
WTHG BN11 .... 20 E5
St Marys School
BEX TN40 .... 97 K7
St Mary's Slindon CE Primary
School
ARUN BN18 .... 111 J1
St Marys Special School
HTHF TN21 .... 244 D12
St Mary Star of the Sea RC
Primary School
SLVH TN37 .... 12 C6
St Mary the Virgin CE Primary
School
HRTF TN7 .... 50 C5
St Matthews Primary School
SBGH/RUST TN4 .... 38 A1
St Michaels CE Primary School
RYE TN31 .... 252 H3
St Michaels Primary School
HRTF TN7 .... 51 G4

St Nicholas & St Mary CE
First & Middle School
SHOR BN43 .... 119 M5
St Pancras RC Primary School
LEWES BN7 .... 16 C6
St Pauls Catholic College
HWH RH16 .... 73 J4
St Pauls CE Infant School
RRTW TN3 .... 37 G5
St Pauls CE Primary School
BRI BN1 .... 4 C5
SLVH TN37 .... 12 C4
St Pauls CE Junior School
RRTW TN3 .... 37 G5
St Peter & St Paul CE Primary
School
BEX TN40 .... 137 H1
St Peters Catholic Primary
School
EGRIN RH19 .... 31 H7
SHOR BN43 .... 119 M5
WVILLE PO7 .... 288 A12
St Peters CE Infants School
SBGH/RUST TN4 .... 37 L1
St Peters CE Primary School
HFD BN5 .... 269 J3
RHWH RH17 .... 206 D1
RING/NEW BN8 .... 239 P9
RTWE/PEM TN2 .... 38 B6
SWTR RH13 .... 235 J3
St Peters Infant School
PTSD BN41 .... 121 G6
St Peters Medical Centre
BRI BN1 .... 4 F3
St Philip Howard Catholic
High School
MSEA/BNM PO22 .... 110 F7
St Philips Catholic Primary
School
ARUN BN18 .... 112 F2
St Phillips RC Primary School
UCK TN22 .... 76 E7
St Richards Catholic College
BEX TN40 .... 137 K1
St Richards Hospital
CCH PO19 .... 7 G1
St Richards RC Primary School
CCH PO19 .... 6 E6
St Robert Southwell Primary
School
HORS RH12 .... 56 F3
St Thomas A Becket RC Junior
School
LW/ROSE BN22 .... 10 D2
St Thomas A Beckett Infant
School
LW/ROSE BN22 .... 10 D2
St Thomas Mores RC Primary
School
HAV PO9 .... 102 E2
St Vincent School
STLEO TN38 .... 98 E7
St Wilfrids Catholic Primary
School
BURH RH15 .... 74 E6
St Wilfrids CE Primary School
HWH RH16 .... 73 K6
St Wilfrids RC Primary
School
ANG/EP BN16 .... 114 E7
St Wilfrids RC School
CRAWW RH11 .... 8 B6
Salehurst CE Primary School
RBTBR TN32 .... 248 C2
Salfords Industrial Estate
REDH RH1 .... 22 F1
Saltdean Primary School
BRIE/ROTT BN2 .... 156 B3
Sandhurst CP School
HAWK TN18 .... 217 R4
Sandhurst School
WTHG BN11 .... 21 L5
Sandown Primary School
HAS TN34 .... 100 B1
Satellite Business Village
CRAWE RH10 .... 27 K7
Saxon Mount Special School
STLEO TN38 .... 98 E6
Scotney Castle Garden (NT)
RRTW TN3 .... 191 J2
Scott Broadwood CE Infant
School
RDKG RH5 .... 24 C3
The Seaford Business
Centre
SEAF BN25 .... 174 E2
Seaford College
PETW GU28 .... 262 D8
Seaford Day Hospital
SEAF BN25 .... 174 F2
Seaford Golf Club
SEAF BN25 .... 159 L7
Seaford Head Community
College
SEAF BN25 .... 174 F3
Seaford Head Golf Club
SEAF BN25 .... 175 G4
Seaford Head Lower School
SEAF BN25 .... 174 F3
Seaford Health Centre
SEAF BN25 .... 174 E2
Seaford Primary School
SEAF BN25 .... 174 E1
Seaford RFC
SEAF BN25 .... 174 D2
Seaford Sports & Leisure
Centre
SEAF BN25 .... 174 E2
Seal CP School
SELS PO20 .... 301 L6
Sealife Aquarium
HAS TN34 .... 13 M7
Sea Life Centre
BRIE/ROTT BN2 .... 4 F8
Sea Road Surgery
BEX TN40 .... 137 J2
Seaside Medical Centre
LW/ROSE BN22 .... 11 H4
Sedlescombe CE Primary
School
BAT TN33 .... 249 M12
Sedlescombe Golf Club
BAT TN33 .... 283 M4
Selsey Business Centre
SELS PO20 .... 301 K6
Selsey Country Club
SELS PO20 .... 301 K3

Selsey CC
SELS PO20 .... 301 K6
Selsey Golf Club
SELS PO20 .... 301 K3
Selsey Health Centre
SELS PO20 .... 301 K5
Selsey Indoor Market
SELS PO20 .... 301 K6
The Seven Dials Medical
Centre
BRI BN1 .... 4 C5
Seven Sisters Country Park
SEAF BN25 .... 302 A3
Seymour First & Middle School
CRAWW RH11 .... 43 D7
Sharps Copse Primary School
HAV PO9 .... 289 J12
Sharpthorne Tunnel
EGRIN RH19 .... 62 F4
Shearbarn Holiday Park
RHAS TN35 .... 100 C3
Sheddingdean Business Centre
BURH RH15 .... 74 E4
Sheddingdean Primary School
BURH RH15 .... 74 F4
Sheet CP School
PSF GU32 .... 223 Q3
Sheffield Park Garden (NT)
UCK TN22 .... 208 C12
Shelley Primary School
HORS RH12 .... 201 N2
Shelleys Hotel
LEWES BN7 .... 16 E7
Sherwood Park Infant School
RTWE/PEM TN2 .... 38 C3
Sherwood Park Primary School
RTWE/PEM TN2 .... 38 C3
Shinewater Primary School
LGNY BN23 .... 164 A1
Ship & Anchor Marina
ARUN BN18 .... 112 D8
The Ship Hotel
CCH PO19 .... 6 E3
Shipley CE Primary School
SWTR RH13 .... 233 L8
Shipwreck Heritage Centre
HAS TN34 .... 13 M7
Shopwhyke Industrial Centre
CCH PO19 .... 7 M3
Shoreham Airport
SHOR BN43 .... 119 H6
Shoreham Beach First School
SHOR BN43 .... 119 M7
Shoreham College
SHOR BN43 .... 120 C6
Shoreham FC
PTSD BN41 .... 121 G6
Shoreham First School
SHOR BN43 .... 119 K5
Shoreham Health Centre
SHOR BN43 .... 119 L6
Shottermill Infant School
HASM GU27 .... 181 J10
Sidlesham CP School
SELS PO20 .... 169 J5
Sidlesham FC
SELS PO20 .... 169 L5
Sidley Primary School
BEXW TN39 .... 97 H7
Sidley Sports Club
BEXW TN39 .... 97 H6
Silverdale Primary School
SLVH TN37 .... 99 G2
Simpsons Industrial Estate
RYE TN31 .... 253 K10
Singing Hills Golf Course
HPPT/KEY BN6 .... 270 C7
Singleton CE Primary School
RBTBR TN32 .... 249 L3
Sir Henry Fermor Primary
School
CROW TN6 .... 67 M7
The Skinners Company School
SBGH/RUST TN4 .... 37 M3
Skippers Hill Manor
MAYF TN20 .... 211 Q9
SLC Eastbourne - Swiss Hotel
Management School
EDN/EASTW BN20 .... 176 F2
Slindon College
ARUN BN18 .... 294 G12
Slindon Common (NT)
ARUN BN18 .... 111 J2
Slindon Wood (NT)
ARUN BN18 .... 110 F2
Slinfold CE Primary School
SWTR RH13 .... 200 G1
Slinfold Park Golf &
Country Club
SWTR RH13 .... 200 E3
Smugglers Adventure
HAS TN34 .... 13 K5
Snowhill Business Centre
CRAWE RH10 .... 29 M5
Sofitel
HORL RH6 .... 27 L1
Somerhill Junior School
HOVE BN3 .... 122 C7
Somerset Hospital
PETW GU28 .... 229 L9
Sompting Abbots School
LAN/SOMP BN15 .... 117 M5
South Bersted CE Primary
School
MSEA/BNM PO22 .... 2 D1
South Bersted Industrial
Estate
MSEA/BNM PO22 .... 2 E1
Southbourne CE Primary
School
SBGH/RUST TN4 .... 37 L1
Southbourne County J & I
School
EMRTH PO10 .... 104 F5
Southdown Junior School
NEWHV BN9 .... 18 F3
South Downs Business Park
LEWES BN7 .... 17 J3
South Downs College
WVILLE PO7 .... 102 B2
The South Downs
Comprehensive Special
School
EDN/EASTW BN20 .... 176 B1
Southdowns Country Hotel
EPSF GU31 .... 225 M9

South Downs Health Clinic
BRI BN1 .... 4 D4
Southfields Industrial Estate
RCCH PO18 .... 106 A5
Southgate Magistrates Court
CCH PO19 .... 6 C6
Southgate Primary School
CRAWE RH10 .... 8 F8
South Lodge Hotel
SWTR RH13 .... 203 L10
South Malling CE Primary
School
LEWES BN7 .... 17 H2
South of England
Showground
RHWH RH17 .... 61 M8
Southover CE Primary School
LEWES BN7 .... 16 D7
South Terminal
HORL RH6 .... 27 M2
Southwater Business Centre
SWTR RH13 .... 201 Q12
Southwater Country Club
SWTR RH13 .... 233 Q1
Southwater Junior School
SWTR RH13 .... 201 Q11
Southwick Business Centre
STHW BN42 .... 120 D6
Sovereign Business Park
BURH RH15 .... 74 D7
Sovereign Leisure Centre
LW/ROSE BN22 .... 164 D2
The Spa Hotel
SBGH/RUST TN4 .... 37 K6
Spa Industrial Park
RTWE/PEM TN2 .... 38 D1
Spa Valley Railway
RRTW TN3 .... 52 D1
Special Support Facility
CCH PO19 .... 7 J3
Speldhurst CE Primary School
RRTW TN3 .... 36 F1
Spinney School
HTHF TN21 .... 244 A10
The Spread Eagle Hotel &
Health Spa
MIDH GU29 .... 227 J10
Spring Copse Business Park
SWTR RH13 .... 200 E2
Springfield First School
SALV BN13 .... 21 K1
Springfield Industrial Estate
RHWH RH17 .... 75 L4
Squires Farm Industrial Estate
UCK TN22 .... 242 F12
The Stables Theatre
HAS TN34 .... 13 L5
Stafford County Junior School
LW/ROSE BN22 .... 163 M4
Stakes Hill Infant School
WVILLE PO7 .... 288 A11
Stammerham Business Centre
HORS RH12 .... 40 D2
Standen (NT)
EGRIN RH19 .... 47 J5
Stanford Infant School
BRI BN1 .... 122 D5
Stanford Road Junior School
BRI BN1 .... 4 C1
Stanley Deason Leisure
Centre
BRIE/ROTT BN2 .... 123 L8
Stansted House
HAV PO9 .... 289 R8
Staple Cross MCP Primary
School
RBTBR TN32 .... 249 L3
The Star Inn Hotel
POLE BN26 .... 160 F2
Star Road Industrial Estate
SWTR RH13 .... 234 E11
Star Road Trading Estate
SWTR RH13 .... 234 F10
Station Approach Industrial
Estate
PUL/STOR RH20 .... 264 H3
Station Road Industrial
Estate
HAIL BN27 .... 92 B7
SWTR RH13 .... 201 Q12
Staunton Country Park
HAV PO9 .... 288 F7
Staunton Park Community
School
HAV PO9 .... 289 J10
Stedham CP School
MIDH GU29 .... 226 C8
Steep School
PSF GU32 .... 223 M2
The Stepping Stone School
GSHT GU26 .... 181 J6
Steyning Athletic Club
STEY/UB BN44 .... 78 B2
Steyning Grammar Upper
School
STEY/UB BN44 .... 78 C1
Steyning Health Centre
STEY/UB BN44 .... 78 C2
Steyning St Andrews CE
Primary School
STEY/UB BN44 .... 78 C1
Steyning Sports Centre
STEY/UB BN44 .... 78 B1
Steyning Town FC
STEY/UB BN44 .... 78 C1
Stone Cross CP School
PEV BN24 .... 132 F8
Stonegate CE Primary School
WADH TN5 .... 214 E4
Stonelands School
HOVE BN3 .... 122 A7
Storrington First School
PUL/STOR RH20 .... 265 R11
Storrington Lawn Tennis
Club
PUL/STOR RH20 .... 265 R12
Suffolk House Hotel &
Restaurant
CCH PO19 .... 6 F4
Summerfield Leisure Centre
HAS TN34 .... 12 E6
Summerfields Business
Centre
HAS TN34 .... 12 C5
Summerheath Hall
HAIL BN27 .... 92 A5

Summerlea Community
Primary School
LHPTN BN17 .... 148 A2
Sumners Ponds Fishery &
Campsite
SWTR RH13 .... 200 H11
Sundridge School
HORN PO8 .... 288 A7
The Surgery
BRI BN1 .... 4 F5
The Surrey & Sussex
Crematorium
CRAWE RH10 .... 28 C6
Sussex County CC
HOVE BN3 .... 122 B6
Sussex Downs College
HAIL BN27 .... 92 B6
LEWES BN7 .... 17 H7
NEWHV BN9 .... 19 G2
Sussex English Language
School
WTHG BN11 .... 21 G6
Sussex Eye Hospital
BRIE/ROTT BN2 .... 5 L8
Sussex House Business Park
HOVE BN3 .... 121 L5
Sussex Manor Business Park
CRAWE RH10 .... 27 M7
Sussex Nuffield Hospital
BRIE/ROTT BN2 .... 124 B5
HOVE BN3 .... 121 L7
Sussex Police & Register
Office
SALV BN13 .... 116 C8
Sussex Private Clinic
STLEO TN38 .... 99 G5
The Sussex Toy &
Model Museum
BRI BN1 .... 4 E4
Sussex University
LEWES BN7 .... 17 J4
Sutton Industrial Park
WSEA TN36 .... 286 F2
Swan Barn Business Centre
HAIL BN27 .... 92 C7
Swan Business Centre
HAIL BN27 .... 92 B7
Swandean Hospital
SALV BN13 .... 116 C5
Swandean School of English
WTHG BN11 .... 20 F5
The Swan Inn Hotel
MFD/CHID GU8 .... 182 H6
Swan Walk Shopping Centre
HORS RH12 .... 14 C6
Swedish Folk High School
PTSD BN41 .... 121 G5
Swedish School
CRAWE RH10 .... 9 K8
Sweetwoods Park Golf Club
EDEN TN8 .... 33 M5
Swimming Pool
CRAWE RH10 .... 9 J5
Sydney West Sports Centre
BURH RH15 .... 74 E5
TA Centre
CRAWE RH10 .... 9 G2
HORS RH12 .... 14 D7
LW/ROSE BN22 .... 11 H4
Tanbridge House School
HORS RH12 .... 201 Q3
Tanbridge Retail Park
HORS RH12 .... 14 A6
Tangmere Military Aviation
Museum Trust
SELS PO20 .... 109 J4
Tangmere Primary School
SELS PO20 .... 109 J3
The Tanneries Industrial
Estate
HAV PO9 .... 102 F4
Taro Leisure Centre
EPSF GU31 .... 224 A6
Tavistock & Summerhill School
HWH RH16 .... 73 J2
Telephone Exchange
HORL RH6 .... 22 F7
Telscombe Cliffs Primary
School
PEAHV BN10 .... 156 F5
Templars County Infants
School
LAN/SOMP BN15 .... 118 A7
Temple Bar Business Park
RCCH PO18 .... 108 F2
TEN66 Golf Club
SLVH TN37 .... 283 N9
Terminus Road Industrial
Estate
CCH PO19 .... 6 A7
Thakeham First School
PUL/STOR RH20 .... 266 E6
Theatre Royal
BRI BN1 .... 4 E6
Thistle Hotel
BRI BN1 .... 4 E8
HORL RH6 .... 22 F4
Thomas A Becket First School
SALV BN13 .... 116 F8
Thomas A Becket Middle
School
SALV BN13 .... 117 G8
Thomas Bennett Community
College
CRAWE RH10 .... 43 J6
Thomas Peacocke
Community College
RYE TN31 .... 252 G7
Thornberry Middle School
LAN/SOMP BN15 .... 118 E8
Thorney Island Airfield
EMRTH PO10 .... 138 D3
Thorney Island Primary
School
EMRTH PO10 .... 138 B2
Three Bridges Community
Centre
CRAWE RH10 .... 9 L2
Three Bridges CC
CRAWE RH10 .... 9 L4
Three Bridges FC
CRAWE RH10 .... 9 M4
Three Bridges First School
CRAWE RH10 .... 9 L2
Three Bridges Junior School
CRAWE RH10 .... 9 K3

Ticehurst CE Primary School
WADH TN5 .... 215 J1
Ticehurst Clinic
HOVE BN3 .... 121 M7
Tideway School
NEWHV BN9 .... 18 D6
Tilgate Forest Business Centre
CRAWW RH11 .... 43 J8
Tilgate Forest Golf Centre
CRAWE RH10 .... 43 M7
Tilgate Park
CRAWE RH10 .... 43 L8
Tilling Green Infant School
RYE TN31 .... 252 F8
Timberlaine Industrial Estate
CCH PO19 .... 7 J6
Timberlaine Trading Estate
SALV BN13 .... 117 L8
Toat Monument
PUL/STOR RH20 .... 231 J9
Tobias School of Art
EGRIN RH19 .... 47 J3
Tollgate Junior School
LGNY BN23 .... 164 C6
Torah Academy
HOVE BN3 .... 121 M7
Torfield Special School
HAS TN34 .... 13 L4
Touch for Health Centre
BOGR PO21 .... 2 B6
The Towers Convent School
STEY/UB BN44 .... 79 H4
Towner Art Gallery & Local
History Museum
EAST BN21 .... 176 D2
Town Hall Museum &
Art Gallery
WTHG BN11 .... 21 H5
Toyhorse International
Stud Farm
BIL RH14 .... 199 R1
Toy & Model Museum
RRTW TN5 .... 188 H10
Trafalgar County Infant
School
HORS RH12 .... 14 B2
Travelodge
ARUN BN18 .... 110 F2
BIL RH14 .... 200 B9
BRI BN1 .... 122 E5
EMRTH PO10 .... 103 M3
HAS TN34 .... 12 C6
HORL RH6 .... 27 K4
LHPTN BN17 .... 147 L2
LIPH GU30 .... 179 N12
RHWH RH17 .... 236 F8
Treasure Island Play Centre
LW/ROSE BN22 .... 11 K3
The Triangle
BURH RH15 .... 74 C5
Trinity Theatre & Arts
Association
RTW TN1 .... 37 M5
Tristar Business Centre
SWTR RH13 .... 234 F11
Trosnant Primary & Infant
School
HAV PO9 .... 102 F2
The Truggery
HAIL BN27 .... 93 H1
Tunbridge Wells Borderers
Sports Club
RTWE/PEM TN2 .... 53 M2
Tunbridge Wells Girls
Grammar School
SBGH/RUST TN4 .... 37 L3
Tunbridge Wells Golf Club
SBGH/RUST TN4 .... 37 K6
Tunbridge Wells Grammar
School
SBGH/RUST TN4 .... 37 M1
Tunbridge Wells High School
RTWE/PEM TN2 .... 38 D4
Tunbridge Wells Hockey Club
RTWE/PEM TN2 .... 38 A8
Tunbridge Wells Independent
Hospital
RRTW TN3 .... 36 A6
Tunbridge Wells Museum &
Art Gallery
RTW TN1 .... 38 A5
Tunbridge Wells Nuffield
Hospital
RTWE/PEM TN2 .... 38 C6
Tunbridge Wells Sports Centre
SBGH/RUST TN4 .... 37 L2
Turners Hill CE Primary School
CRAWE RH10 .... 45 M6
Twineham CE Primary School
RHWH RH17 .... 236 B9

Tyes Cross
EGRIN RH19 .... 63 H3
Uckfield Community Hospital
UCK TN22 .... 76 F6
Uckfield Community Tech Coll
UCK TN22 .... 76 F4
Uckfield RFC
UCK TN22 .... 77 G2
UGC Cinema
BRIE/ROTT BN2 .... 154 E2
CRAWE RH10 .... 8 F1
LGNY BN23 .... 164 E4
Unicorn Trading Estate
HASM GU27 .... 181 L10
University College Chichester
CCH PO19 .... 6 F1
University of Brighton
BRI BN1 .... 83 M8
BRI BN1 .... 123 H3
BRIE/ROTT BN2 .... 4 F6
EAST BN21 .... 10 C4
EDN/EASTW BN20 .... 10 A9
EDN/EASTW BN20 .... 176 D4
EDN/EASTW BN20 .... 176 D6
University of Chichester
(Bognor Regis Campus)
MSEA/BNM PO22 .... 3 G1
University of Sussex
BRI BN1 .... 84 A6
University of Sussex Sports
Centre
BRI BN1 .... 83 M7
Uplands Community College
WADH TN5 .... 71 M5
Uplands Special School
BRI BN1 .... 123 H3
Uppark (NT)
EPSF GU31 .... 258 C5
Upper Beeding Primary
School
STEY/UB BN44 .... 78 F3
Utopia Leisure Centre
UCK TN22 .... 76 F5
Vale First & Middle School
SALV BN13 .... 116 E3
Valley Farm Business Park
HPPT/KEY BN6 .... 236 C12
Varndean College
BRI BN1 .... 122 E2
Varndean School
BRI BN1 .... 122 F2
Venture Industrial Park
STLEO TN38 .... 98 F3
Vicarage Fields Shopping
Centre
HAIL BN27 .... 92 B5
Vicarage Lane Clinic
HASM GU27 .... 181 J11
Victoria Cottage Hospital
EMRTH PO10 .... 104 A4
Victoria Industrial Estate
BURH RH15 .... 74 C7
Victoria Road Trading Estate
PTSD BN41 .... 121 H5
Vinalls Business Centre
HFD BN5 .... 269 K5
Vinehall School
RBTBR TN32 .... 248 F7
Vinnetrow Farm Business
Centre
SELS PO20 .... 142 D2
Volks Electric Railway
BRIE/ROTT BN2 .... 5 H9
Wadhurst Business Park
WADH TN5 .... 71 G2
Wadhurst CE Primary School
WADH TN5 .... 71 L4
Wakehurst Place & Millennium
Seed Bank (NT)
RHWH RH17 .... 61 L6
Walberton & Binsted CE
Primary School
ARUN BN18 .... 111 K4
Wallands Primary School
LEWES BN7 .... 16 B3
Walstead Cemetery
HWH RH16 .... 206 G11
Warblington Secondary
School
HAV PO9 .... 103 J4
Warden Park School
RHWH RH17 .... 72 D4
War Memorial Hospital
MSEA/BNM PO22 .... 2 D3
Warner Farm Touring Park
SELS PO20 .... 301 J4
Warnham CE Primary
School
HORS RH12 .... 187 Q9
Warninglid Primary School
RHWH RH17 .... 204 B7

Warren Park Primary School
HAV PO9 .... 288 E10
Waterfield First School
CRAWW RH11 .... 42 D5
Waterhall Golf Club
BRI BN1 .... 81 M7
Water Lane Industrial Estate
PUL/STOR RH20 .... 266 C10
Waterlooville Golf Club
HORN PO8 .... 288 C7
Watersmead Business Park
LHPTN BN17 .... 147 H1
Waterworks Cottages
HOVE BN3 .... 121 M3
Wattlehurst Farm
HORS RH12 .... 187 R2
Waytefield Clinic
BRI BN1 .... 122 E3
Weald & Downland
Open Air Museum
RCCH PO18 .... 292 F3
Wealden College
CROW TN6 .... 210 G1
Wealden Industrial Estate
CROW TN6 .... 211 K1
The Weald School
BIL RH14 .... 232 A2
Wedglen Industrial Estate
MIDH GU29 .... 226 G10
Welfare Clinic
HOVE BN3 .... 121 K3
Wellington Square Medical
Centre
HAS TN34 .... 13 H7
Wellshurst Golf &
Country Club
HAIL BN27 .... 278 D7
Wessex Superbowl
HAV PO9 .... 102 C4
West Bank Fort
LHPTN BN17 .... 147 J6
West Blatchington Junior
School
HOVE BN3 .... 121 L1
Westbourne CP School
EMRTH PO10 .... 104 C1
Westbourne House School
SELS PO20 .... 108 E6
West Chiltington Community
School
PUL/STOR RH20 .... 266 B4
West Chiltington Golf Club
PUL/STOR RH20 .... 266 A3
West Dean CE Primary
School
RCCH PO18 .... 292 B4
West Dean College
RCCH PO18 .... 292 D3
West Dean Gardens
RCCH PO18 .... 292 D3
Westdene Primary School
BRI BN1 .... 82 B8
Westergate Community
School
SELS PO20 .... 110 D6
Westerleigh St Leonards
School
STLEO TN38 .... 98 F4
Westerleigh School
STLEO TN38 .... 98 F5
Western Road Community
School
LEWES BN7 .... 16 E7
Western Road Primary
School
LEWES BN7 .... 16 C6
Westfield Industrial Estate
HORN PO8 .... 288 E2
Westfield Primary School
RHAS TN35 .... 284 B5
Westgate Leisure Centre
CCH PO19 .... 6 C5
West Green First School
CRAWW RH11 .... 8 C2
Westham Medical Centre
PEV BN24 .... 133 M8
West Hill Cliff Lift
HAS TN34 .... 13 J7
West Hill Community Centre
HAS TN34 .... 13 L4
West Hill Community Hall
BRI BN1 .... 4 D3
West Hoathly CE Primary
School
EGRIN RH19 .... 62 D3
Westholme Clinic
FERR BN12 .... 150 C3
WTHG BN11 .... 20 E6
West Hove Golf Club
HOVE BN3 .... 81 H8
HOVE BN3 .... 121 H3

West Hove Junior School
HOVE BN3 .... 121 L6
West Lavington CE First
School
MIDH GU29 .... 227 K11
West Park CE Controlled
School
FERR BN12 .... 150 C3
West Pier (Derelict)
BRI BN1 .... 4 B8
West Rise Junior School
LGNY BN23 .... 164 B3
West Rocks Hotel
EAST BN21 .... 10 F8
West St Leonards CP School
STLEO TN38 .... 98 E5
West Sands Leisure Centre
SELS PO20 .... 300 H6
West Sussex College of Design
WTHG BN11 .... 21 H5
West Sussex Golf Club
PUL/STOR RH20 .... 265 P7
West Sussex School
of English
STEY/UB BN44 .... 78 C2
West Terrace Clinic
EAST BN21 .... 10 D7
West Wittering Parochial
Primary School
SELS PO20 .... 167 G4
Weydown Industrial Estate
HASM GU27 .... 181 M10
Weyford Infant School
BOR GU35 .... 179 J5
Weyford Junior School
BOR GU35 .... 179 J5
Wheel Park Farm Industrial
Estate
RHAS TN35 .... 284 A5
Whitehawk Clinic
BRIE/ROTT BN2 .... 123 L8
The Whitehawk College
EAST BN21 .... 10 E6
Whitehawk Primary School
BRIE/ROTT BN2 .... 123 K7
Whitehill Cemetery
BOR GU35 .... 179 K6
Whitehill Infant School
CROW TN6 .... 67 M8
White Horse
SEAF BN25 .... 160 D7
White House Primary School
HAS TN34 .... 92 A5
White Rock Theatre
HAS TN34 .... 12 E8
White Rose Touring Park
LHPTN BN17 .... 113 J8
Whitestyles Middle School
LAN/SOMP BN15 .... 118 A7
Whytemead First School
LHPTN BN17 .... 147 H3
Wick FC
LHPTN BN17 .... 147 J1
Wigmore AFC
SALV BN13 .... 117 J6
Wigmore Trading Estate
SALV BN13 .... 117 L8
Wildfowl Reserve
LEWES BN7 .... 125 G2
The Wildwood Golf Club
CRAN GU6 .... 184 H7
William Parker Community
Athletics Arena
HAS TN34 .... 99 J2
William Parker School
HAS TN34 .... 99 J1
William Penn Primary School
SWTR RH13 .... 232 H7
Willingdon Cemetery
EDN/EASTW BN20 .... 162 F3
Willingdon Community
School
POLE BN26 .... 162 E1
Willingdon Golf Club
EDN/EASTW BN20 .... 163 G6
Willingdon Primary School
EDN/EASTW BN20 .... 162 F2
The Willows First School
LAN/SOMP BN15 .... 118 D6
Wilmington Priory
POLE BN26 .... 130 D8
Winchelsea Court Hall
Museum
WSEA TN36 .... 286 D2
Winchelsea St Thomas CE
Primary School
WSEA TN36 .... 286 D2
Windlesham House School
PUL/STOR RH20 .... 298 F6

Windmills Junior School
HPPT/KEY BN6 .... 271 P6
Windmill Theatre & Cinema
LHPTN BN17 .... 147 J6
Windsor Hotel
WTHG BN11 .... 151 M3
Winifred Lee Health Centre
LW/ROSE BN22 .... 11 K1
Winston Business Centre
LAN/SOMP BN15 .... 118 B8
Winter Garden
EAST BN21 .... 10 E9
Winterpick Business Park
HFD BN5 .... 235 Q12
Wisborough Green Primary
School
BIL RH14 .... 199 K10
Wish Tower
EAST BN21 .... 177 G4
Wish Tower Puppet Museum
EAST BN21 .... 177 G4
Wispers School
HASM GU27 .... 181 M8
Wiston Business Park
PUL/STOR RH20 .... 266 H11
Witterings Health Centre
SELS PO20 .... 167 K6
Wittersham CE Primary
School
TENT TN30 .... 220 C7
Wivelsfield Primary School
RHWH RH17 .... 75 L3
Woodingdean Primary School
BRIE/ROTT BN2 .... 124 B5
Woodlea Primary School
BOR GU35 .... 178 G8
Woodruff Business Centre
CCH PO19 .... 6 A6
Woods Mill Nature Reserve
HFD BN5 .... 269 L9
Woodvale Brighton
Crematorium
BRIE/ROTT BN2 .... 5 M1
Woolmer Hill Athletics Track
HASM GU27 .... 180 G9
Woolmer Hill Technology
College
HASM GU27 .... 180 G10
Worthing Athletics Track
FERR BN12 .... 150 D2
Worthing College
SALV BN13 .... 150 D2
Worthing Crematorium
SALV BN13 .... 298 F9
Worthing & District
Magistrates Court
WTHG BN11 .... 20 F5
Worthing FC
SALV BN13 .... 20 D2
Worthing Golf Club
SALV BN13 .... 117 G4
Worthing High School
SALV BN13 .... 20 E1
Worthing Hospital
WTHG BN11 .... 21 J3
Worthing Pavilion Bowling
Club
SALV BN13 .... 20 D3
Worthing Pier
WTHG BN11 .... 21 J7
Worthing Priority Care
ANG/EP BN16 .... 148 C4
Worthing RFC
ANG/EP BN16 .... 149 G1
Worthing & Southlands
Hospital
SHOR BN43 .... 120 A5
Worth School
CRAWE RH10 .... 45 G8
WWT Arundel
ARUN BN18 .... 113 H1
Wych Cross Place
RHWH RH17 .... 64 B5
Wyndham Business Park
MIDH GU29 .... 226 G10
Yapton CE Primary School
MSEA/BNM PO22 .... 145 L1
Yattendon School
HORL RH6 .... 22 F5
Yeowart Business Centre
UCK TN22 .... 76 D6
Yesterday's World
BAT TN33 .... 282 E5
York House Hotel
LW/ROSE BN22 .... 11 J5
Ypres Tower
RYE TN31 .... 252 H8

Acknowledgements

Schools address data provided by Education Direct.

Petrol station information supplied by Johnsons

One-way street data provided by © Tele Atlas N.V. Tele Atlas

Garden centre information provided by

Garden Centre Association Britains best garden centres

Wyevale Garden Centres

The statement on the front cover of this atlas is sourced, selected and quoted
from a reader comment and feedback form received in 2004